CASES AND MATERIALS ON
FEDERAL COURTS

Third Edition

■ ■ ■

by

Michael L. Wells
Professor of Law
University of Georgia School of Law

William P. Marshall
Professor of Law
University of North Carolina School of Law

Gene R. Nichol
Professor of Law
University of North Carolina School of Law

AMERICAN CASEBOOK SERIES®

Mat #41618473

American Casebook Series is a trademark registered in the U.S. Patent and Trademark Office.

© West, a Thomson business, 2007
© 2011 Thomson Reuters
© 2015 LEG, Inc. d/b/a West Academic
    444 Cedar Street, Suite 700
    St. Paul, MN 55101
    1-877-888-1330

West, West Academic Publishing, and West Academic are trademarks of West Publishing Corporation, used under license.

Printed in the United States of America

ISBN: 978-1-62810-034-1

To Glenn, to Jeanette, to Kara,
to the memory of John D. Butzner, Jr.,
U.S. Circuit Judge, and to the memory of
Professor David Currie, University of
Chicago Law School

ACKNOWLEDGMENTS

The authors would like to thank John Albers, Elizabeth Ferril, Catherine Henson, William Kaleva, Keith Kollmeyer, Shawn Lanphere, Teresa Gallego O'Rourke, and Stefanie B. Weigmann for their valuable assistance.

Summary of Contents

TABLE OF CONTENTS

TABLE OF CASES

The principal cases are in bold type.

CASES AND MATERIALS ON
FEDERAL COURTS

Third Edition

INTRODUCTION

. . .

MARBURY V. MADISON

5 U.S. (1 Cranch) 137 (1803).

CHIEF JUSTICE MARSHALL delivered the opinion of the Court.

At the last term, on the affidavits then read and filed with the clerk, a rule was granted in this case requiring the Secretary of State to show cause why a mandamus should not issue directing him to deliver to William Marbury his commission as a justice of the peace for the county of Washington, in the District of Columbia. No cause has been shown, and the present motion is for a mandamus. The peculiar delicacy of this case, the novelty of some of its circumstances, and the real difficulty attending the points which occur in it require a complete exposition of the principles on which the opinion to be given by the Court is founded.

These principles have been, on the side of the applicant, very ably argued at the bar. In rendering the opinion of the Court, there will be some departure in form, though not in substance, from the points stated in that argument. In the order in which the Court has viewed this subject, the following questions have been considered and decided.

1. Has the applicant a right to the commission he demands?
2. If he has a right, and that right has been violated, do the laws of his country afford him a remedy?
3. If they do afford him a remedy, is it a mandamus issuing from this court?

The first object of inquiry is:

1. Has the applicant a right to the commission he demands?

His right originates in an act of Congress passed in February, 1801, concerning the District of Columbia. After dividing the district into two counties, the eleventh section of this law enacts, that there shall be appointed in and for each of the said counties such number of discreet persons to be justices of the peace as the President of the United States shall, from time to time, think expedient, to continue in office for five years.

It appears from the affidavits that, in compliance with this law, a commission for William Marbury as a justice of peace for the County of Washington was signed by John Adams, then President of the United States, after which the seal of the United States was affixed to it, but the commission has never reached the person for whom it was made out.

In order to determine whether he is entitled to this commission, it becomes necessary to inquire whether he has been appointed to the office. For if he has been appointed, the law continues him in office for five years, and he is entitled to the possession of those evidences of office, which, being completed, became his property. * * *

It is . . . decidedly the opinion of the Court that, when a commission has been signed by the President, the appointment is made, and that the commission is complete when the seal of the United States has been affixed to it by the Secretary of State. Where an officer is removable at the will of the Executive, the circumstance which completes his appointment is of no concern, because the act is at any time revocable, and the commission may be arrested if still in the office. But when the officer is not removable at the will of the Executive, the appointment is not revocable, and cannot be annulled. It has conferred legal rights which cannot be resumed.

The discretion of the Executive is to be exercised until the appointment has been made. But having once made the appointment, his power over the office is terminated in all cases, where by law the officer is not removable by him. The right to the office is then in the person appointed, and he has the absolute, unconditional power of accepting or rejecting it.

Mr. Marbury, then, since his commission was signed by the President and sealed by the Secretary of State, was appointed, and as the law creating the office gave the officer a right to hold for five years independent of the Executive, the appointment was not revocable, but vested in the officer legal rights which are protected by the laws of his country. To withhold the commission, therefore, is an act deemed by the Court not warranted by law, but violative of a vested legal right.

This brings us to the second inquiry, which is:

2.   *If he has a right, and that right has been violated, do the laws of his country afford him a remedy?*

The very essence of civil liberty certainly consists in the right of every individual to claim the protection of the laws whenever he receives an injury. One of the first duties of government is to afford that protection. * * * The Government of the United States has been emphatically termed a government of laws, and not of men. It will certainly cease to deserve this high appellation if the laws furnish no remedy for the violation of a vested legal right . . . It behooves us, then, to inquire whether there be in its composition any ingredient which shall exempt from legal investigation or exclude the injured party from legal redress.

Is it in the nature of the transaction? Is the act of delivering or withholding a commission to be considered as a mere political act belonging to the Executive department alone, for the performance of which entire confidence is placed by our Constitution in the Supreme Executive, and for any misconduct respecting which the injured individual has no remedy? That there may be such cases is not to be questioned. But that every act of duty to be performed in any of the great departments of government constitutes such a case is not to be admitted.

By the Constitution of the United States, the President is invested with certain important political powers, in the exercise of which he is to use his own discretion, and is accountable only to his country in his political character and to his own conscience. To aid him in the performance of these duties, he is authorized to appoint certain officers, who act by his authority and in conformity with his orders. In such cases, their acts are his acts; and whatever opinion may be entertained of the manner in which executive discretion may be used, still there exists, and can exist, no power to control that discretion. The subjects are political. They respect the nation, not individual rights, and, being entrusted to the Executive, the decision of the Executive is conclusive. The application of this remark will be perceived by adverting to the act of Congress for establishing the Department of Foreign Affairs. This officer, as his duties were prescribed by that act, is to conform precisely to the will of the President. He is the mere organ by whom that will is communicated. The acts of such an officer, as an officer, can never be examinable by the Courts.

But when the Legislature proceeds to impose on that officer other duties; when he is directed peremptorily to perform certain acts; when the rights of individuals are dependent on the performance of those acts; he is so far the officer of the law, is amenable to the laws for his conduct, and cannot at his discretion, sport away the vested rights of others.

The conclusion from this reasoning is that, where the heads of departments are the political or confidential agents of the Executive, merely to execute the will of the President, or rather to act in cases in which the Executive possesses a constitutional or legal discretion, nothing can be more perfectly clear than that their acts are only politically examinable. But where a specific duty is assigned by law, and individual rights depend upon the performance of that duty, it seems equally clear that the individual who considers himself injured has a right to resort to the laws of his country for a remedy.

The question whether a right has vested or not is, in its nature, judicial, and must be tried by the judicial authority. That question has been discussed, and the opinion is that the latest point of time which can be taken as that at which the appointment was complete and evidenced was when, after the signature of the President, the seal of the United States was affixed to the commission.

It is then the opinion of the Court . . . [that Marbury has] a legal right to the office . . . for which the laws of his country afford him a remedy.

It remains to be inquired whether,

3. *He is entitled to the remedy for which he applies.*

This depends on the nature of the writ applied for, and the power of this court.

The nature of the writ.

This writ, if awarded, would be directed to an officer of government, and its mandate to him would be, to use the words of Blackstone, to do a particular thing therein specified, which appertains to his office and duty and which the Court has previously determined or at least supposes to be consonant to right and justice. Or, in the words of Lord Mansfield, the applicant, in this case, has a right to execute an office of public concern, and is kept out of possession of that right. These circumstances certainly concur in this case. Still, to render the mandamus a proper remedy, the officer to whom it is to be directed must be one to whom, on legal principles, such writ may be directed, and the person applying for it must be without any other specific and legal remedy.

The intimate political relation, subsisting between the President of the United States and the heads of departments, necessarily renders any legal investigation of the acts of one of those high officers peculiarly irksome, as well as delicate, and excites some hesitation with respect to the propriety of entering into such investigation. Impressions are often received without much reflection or examination, and it is not wonderful that, in such a case as this, the assertion by an individual of his legal claims in a court of justice, to which claims it is the duty of that court to attend, should, at first view, be considered by some as an attempt to intrude into the cabinet and to intermeddle with the prerogatives of the Executive. It is scarcely necessary for the Court to disclaim all pretensions to such a jurisdiction. An extravagance so absurd and excessive could not have been entertained for a moment. The province of the Court is solely to decide on the rights of individuals, not to inquire how the Executive or Executive officers perform duties in which they have a discretion. Questions, in their nature political or which are, by the

Constitution and laws, submitted to the Executive, can never be made in this Court.

But where [an Executive officer] is directed by law to do a certain act affecting the absolute rights of individuals, in the performance of which he is not placed under the particular direction of the President, and the performance of which the President cannot lawfully forbid, and therefore is never presumed to have forbidden—as for example, to record a commission, or a patent for land, which has received all the legal solemnities; or to give a copy of such record—in such cases, it is not perceived on what ground the courts of the country are further excused from the duty of giving judgment that right to be done to an injured individual than if the same services were to be performed by a person not the head of a department.

This, then, is a plain case of a mandamus, either to deliver the commission or a copy of it from the record, and it only remains to be inquired:

Whether it can issue from this Court.

The act to establish the judicial courts of the United States authorizes the Supreme Court to issue writs of mandamus, in cases warranted by the principles and usages of law, to any courts appointed, or persons holding office, under the authority of the United States.

The Secretary of State, being a person, holding an office under the authority of the United States, is precisely within the letter of the description, and if this Court is not authorized to issue a writ of mandamus to such an officer, it must be because the law is unconstitutional, and therefore absolutely incapable of conferring the authority and assigning the duties which its words purport to confer and assign.

The Constitution vests the whole judicial power of the United States in one Supreme Court, and such inferior courts as Congress shall, from time to time, ordain and establish. This power is expressly extended to all cases arising under the laws of the United States; and consequently, in some form, may be exercised over the present case, because the right claimed is given by a law of the United States. In the distribution of this power it is declared that "The Supreme Court shall have original jurisdiction in all cases affecting ambassadors, other public ministers and consuls, and those in which a State shall be a party. In all other cases, the Supreme Court shall have appellate jurisdiction."

It has been insisted at the bar, that, as the original grant of jurisdiction to the Supreme and inferior courts is general, and the clause assigning original jurisdiction to the Supreme Court contains no negative or restrictive words, the power remains to the Legislature to assign original jurisdiction to that Court in other cases than those specified in the article which has been recited, provided those cases belong to the judicial power of the United States. If it had been intended to leave it in the discretion of the Legislature to apportion the judicial power between the Supreme and inferior courts according to the will of that body, it would certainly have been useless to have proceeded further than to have defined the judicial power and the tribunals in which it should be vested. The subsequent part of the section is mere surplusage—is entirely without meaning—if such is to be the construction. If Congress remains at liberty to give this Court appellate jurisdiction where the Constitution has declared their jurisdiction shall be original, and original jurisdiction where the Constitution has declared it shall be appellate, the distribution of jurisdiction made in the Constitution, is form without substance. Affirmative words are often, in their operation, negative of other objects than those affirmed, and, in this case, a negative or exclusive sense must be given to them or they have no operation at all.

It cannot be presumed that any clause in the Constitution is intended to be without effect, and therefore such construction is inadmissible unless the words require it.

To enable this Court then to issue a mandamus, it must be shown to be an exercise of appellate jurisdiction, or to be necessary to enable them to exercise appellate jurisdiction. It has been stated at the bar that the appellate jurisdiction may be exercised in a variety of forms, and that, if it be the will of the Legislature that a mandamus should be used for that purpose, that will must be obeyed. This is true; yet the jurisdiction must be appellate, not original. It is the essential criterion of appellate jurisdiction that it revises and corrects the proceedings in a cause already instituted, and does not create that case. Although, therefore, a mandamus may be directed to courts, yet to issue such a writ to an officer for the delivery of a paper is, in effect, the same as to sustain an original action for that paper, and therefore seems not to belong to appellate, but to original jurisdiction. Neither is it necessary in such a case as this to enable the Court to exercise its appellate jurisdiction.

The authority, therefore, given to the Supreme Court by the act establishing the judicial courts of the United States to issue writs of mandamus to public officers appears not to be warranted by the Constitution, and it becomes necessary to inquire whether a jurisdiction so conferred can be exercised.

The question whether an act repugnant to the Constitution can become the law of the land is a question deeply interesting to the United States, but, happily, not of an intricacy proportioned to its interest. It seems only necessary to recognize certain principles, supposed to have been long and well established, to decide it. That the people have an original right to establish for their future government such principles as, in their opinion, shall most conduce to their own happiness is the basis on which the whole American fabric has been erected. The exercise of this original right is a very great exertion; nor can it nor ought it to be frequently repeated. The principles, therefore, so established are deemed fundamental. And as the authority from which they proceed, is supreme, and can seldom act, they are designed to be permanent. This original and supreme will organizes the government and assigns to different departments their respective powers. It may either stop here or establish certain limits not to be transcended by those departments.

The Government of the United States is of the latter description. The powers of the Legislature are defined and limited; and that those limits may not be mistaken or forgotten, the Constitution is written. To what purpose are powers limited, and to what purpose is that limitation committed to writing, if these limits may at any time be passed by those intended to be restrained? The distinction between a government with limited and unlimited powers is abolished if those limits do not confine the persons on whom they are imposed, and if acts prohibited and acts allowed are of equal obligation. It is a proposition too plain to be contested that the Constitution controls any legislative act repugnant to it, or that the Legislature may alter the Constitution by an ordinary act. Between these alternatives there is no middle ground. The Constitution is either a superior, paramount law, unchangeable by ordinary means, or it is on a level with ordinary legislative acts, and, like other acts, is alterable when the legislature shall please to alter it.

If the former part of the alternative be true, then a legislative act contrary to the Constitution is not law; if the latter part be true, then written Constitutions are absurd attempts on the part of the people to limit a power in its own nature illimitable. Certainly all those who have framed written Constitutions contemplate them as forming the fundamental and paramount law of the nation, and consequently the theory of every such government must be that an act of the Legislature repugnant to the Constitution is void.

This theory is essentially attached to a written Constitution, and is consequently to be considered by this Court as one of the fundamental principles of our society. It is not, therefore, to be lost sight of in the further consideration of this subject. If an act of the Legislature repugnant to the Constitution is void, does it, notwithstanding its invalidity, bind the Courts and oblige them to give it effect? Or, in other words, though it be not law, does it constitute a rule as operative as if it was a law? This would be to overthrow in fact what was established in theory, and would seem, at first view, an absurdity too gross to be insisted on. It shall, however, receive a more attentive consideration.

It is emphatically the province and duty of the Judicial Department to say what the law is. Those who apply the rule to particular cases must, of necessity, expound and interpret that rule. If two laws conflict with each other, the courts must decide on the operation of each. So, if a law be in opposition to the Constitution, if both the law and the Constitution apply to a particular case, so that the court must either decide that case conformably to the law, disregarding the Constitution, or conformably to the Constitution, disregarding the law, the Court must determine which of these conflicting rules governs the case. This is of the very essence of judicial duty.

If, then, the courts are to regard the Constitution, and the Constitution is superior to any ordinary act of the Legislature, the Constitution, and not such ordinary act, must govern the case to which they both apply. Those, then, who controvert the principle that the Constitution is to be considered in court as a paramount law are reduced to the necessity of maintaining that courts must close their eyes on the Constitution, and see only the law. This doctrine would subvert the very foundation of all written Constitutions. It would declare that an act which, according to the principles and theory of our government, is entirely void; is yet, in practice, completely obligatory. It would declare that, if the Legislature shall do what is expressly forbidden, such act, notwithstanding the express prohibition, is in reality effectual. It would be giving to the Legislature a practical and real omnipotence with the same breath which professes to restrict their powers within narrow limits. It is prescribing limits, and declaring that those limits may be passed at pleasure. That it thus reduces to nothing what we have deemed the greatest improvement on political institutions—a written Constitution—would of itself be sufficient in America, where written Constitutions have been viewed with so much reverence, for rejecting the construction. But the peculiar expressions of the Constitution of the United States furnish additional arguments in favor of its rejection.

The judicial power of the United States is extended to all cases arising under the Constitution. Could it be the intention of those who gave this power to say that, in using it, the Constitution should not be looked into? That a case arising under the Constitution should be decided without examining the instrument under which it arises?

This is too extravagant to be maintained.

In some cases then, the Constitution must be looked into by the judges. And if they can open it at all, what part of it are they forbidden to read or to obey? There are many other parts of the Constitution which serve to illustrate this subject. It is declared that "no tax or duty shall be laid on articles exported from any State." Suppose a duty on the export of cotton, of tobacco, or of flour, and a suit instituted to recover it. Ought judgment to be rendered in such a case? Ought the judges to close their eyes on the Constitution, and only see the law? The Constitution declares that "no bill of attainder or *ex post facto* law shall be passed." If, however, such a bill should be passed and a person should be prosecuted under it, must the court condemn to death those victims whom the Constitution endeavours to preserve? "No person," says the Constitution, "shall be convicted of treason unless on the testimony of two witnesses to the same overt act, or on confession in open court."

Here the language of the Constitution is addressed especially to the courts. It prescribes, directly for them, a rule of evidence not to be departed from. If the Legislature should change that rule, and declare one witness, or a confession out of court, sufficient for conviction, must the constitutional principle yield to the legislative act? From these and many other selections which might be made, it is apparent that the framers of the Constitution contemplated that instrument as a rule for the government of courts, as well as of the Legislature.

Why otherwise does it direct the judges to take an oath to support it? This oath certainly applies in an especial manner to their conduct in their official character. How immoral to impose it on them if they were to be used as the instruments, and the knowing instruments, for violating what they swear to support!

The oath of office, too, imposed by the Legislature, is completely demonstrative of the legislative opinion on this subject. It is in these words: "I do solemnly swear that I will administer justice without respect to persons, and do equal right to the poor and to the rich; and that I will faithfully and impartially discharge all the duties incumbent on me as according to the best of my abilities and understanding, agreeably to the Constitution and laws of the United States."

Why does a judge swear to discharge his duties agreeably to the Constitution of the United States if that Constitution forms no rule for his government? If it is closed upon him and cannot be inspected by him? If such be the real state of things, this is worse than solemn mockery. To prescribe or to take this oath becomes equally a crime. It is also not entirely unworthy of observation that, in declaring what shall be the supreme law of the land, the Constitution itself is first mentioned, and not the laws of the United States generally, but those only which shall be made in pursuance of the Constitution, have that rank. Thus, the particular phraseology of the Constitution of the United States confirms and strengthens the principle, supposed to be essential to all written Constitutions, that a law repugnant to the Constitution is void, and that courts, as well as other departments, are bound by that instrument.

The rule must be discharged.

NOTES ON MARBURY

1. ***Marbury* and the Law of Federal Courts.** *Marbury v. Madison* is often presented as the first case in constitutional law textbooks because it establishes the authority of the federal courts to engage in judicial review. It therefore both introduces concepts of separation of powers and sets the stage for later discussions of other constitutional law issues. For slightly different reasons, *Marbury* is also commonly the first case excerpted in federal courts textbooks. First, its conclusion that federal courts have the prerogative of judicial review explains why the stakes that inhere in the subject of the federal courts are so enormous. After all, it is only because federal courts have the power of judicial review that they have been able to craft the substantive rules of constitutional law. Second, because *Marbury* is itself a case about federal jurisdiction, it also forcefully illustrates the importance of federal jurisdictional rules. It may be, in Chief Justice Marshall's words, that it is "emphatically the province and duty of the Judicial Department to say what the law is," but that does not mean that the federal courts are unconstrained in exercising that power. The federal courts can only "say what the law is" when they have appropriate jurisdiction to do so.

2. **Historical Background.** *Marbury* grew out of an intensely partisan conflict between the Federalists, led by the out-going President John Adams, and the Democratic-Republicans Party, headed by the newly elected Thomas Jefferson. At the close of the Adams Administration, the Federalists, in their bid to retain influence over the federal judiciary, passed the Circuit Court Act of 1801, creating sixteen new federal judgeships (the so-called midnight judges) and, in a separate measure, authorized the appointment of forty-two justices of the peace for the District of Columbia. William Marbury was one of those appointed to the justice of the peace position. His commission, however, although signed by President Adams and then-Secretary of State John Marshall, was never delivered.

By the time Marbury brought suit, the Democratic-Republicans firmly controlled both the White House and the Congress and undoing the Federalist attempts to continue to control the judiciary became a major part of their agenda. Accordingly, within the first two years of Jefferson's Presidency, they repealed the Circuit Act of 1801, abolished two terms of the United States Supreme Court, and successfully impeached a Federalist District Court Judge, John Pickering. James Madison, meanwhile, had succeeded John Marshall as Secretary of State and therefore became the defendant to Marbury's action while his predecessor John Marshall, was now sitting as the Chief Justice of the United States Supreme Court.

3. **Judicial Review.** What are the reasons that Chief Justice Marshall offers in support of the proposition that courts are empowered to hold laws unconstitutional? Are you persuaded by his reasoning? Would denying courts the right of judicial review "subvert the very foundation of all written Constitutions," as Marshall suggests? And even if you agree that all laws should comport with constitutional requirements, why should the

federal judiciary have the last word on this issue? Don't legislators also take an oath to uphold the Constitution? Indeed, isn't it inconsistent with democratic principles to have non-elected officers (judges) decide some of the most important political issues of the day? Are there any reasons why judges should be in a better position than legislators to determine when statutes and the Constitution conflict?

4. *Marbury*, **the Supreme Court, and the Separation of Powers.** An important theme in federal courts law is the role of courts, and federal courts in particular, and especially the Supreme Court, in our system of government. Chief Justice Marshall said that "the province of the Court is, solely, to decide on the rights of individuals." Much of the reasoning in *Marbury* suggests that the justification for judicial review is that the Court is obliged to apply all of the law to the cases before it, and that the Constitution is part of the relevant law. Arguably, however, if this is the sole rationale for judicial intervention, then [a] federal jurisdiction should be limited to traditional common law cases; [b] Congress and the President may avoid judicial interference in their activities simply by imposing statutory limits on federal jurisdiction; and [c] the Court should avoid ruling on broad constitutional questions whenever possible. In this conception of the separation of powers, the Supreme Court takes a back seat to the other branches.

On the other hand, Chief Justice Marshall also declared: "It is emphatically the province and duty of the Judicial Department to say what the law is." And, in fact, the Court has often viewed its role more broadly than that of resolving the cases before it. It has laid down general norms for regulating other institutions of government and has resisted efforts by Congress to relegate it to a subordinate role. The tensions between the narrow and broad conceptions of the judicial role bear on the resolution of many of the issues addressed in these materials, including the scope of federal common law (Chapter 2), justiciability and standing (Chapter 4), sovereign immunity (Chapter 5), Supreme Court review of state judgments (Chapter 8), and Congress's powers over federal jurisdiction (Chapter 10).

5. Binding the Executive. *Marbury* is important not only in establishing the power of the federal courts to strike down legislation but also as authority for the power of the federal courts to review the legality of executive branch action. But subjecting the President to the control of a non-elected and insulated judiciary can create its own set of concerns. Should the federal courts, for example, have the power to oversee the actions of the President in the war on terror? What are the advantages of such an approach? What are its disadvantages?

6. Political Questions. Marshall's statement that "[q]uestions, in their nature political or which are, by the Constitution and laws, submitted to the Executive, can never be made in this court" has often been cited as authority for the proposition that the Court should not decide certain kinds of issues. But what exactly is a political question? School prayer, abortion, affirmative action, and political redistricting, for example, are intensely political issues. Does Marshall's opinion mean that the federal courts should not judge the constitutionality of provisions regulating these matters? Or does "political question" mean something else? See Chapter 4 (discussing the political question doctrine).

   7.   Rights and Remedies. *Marbury* has also been commonly noted for the proposition that if an individual has a right, she must also have a remedy. Early in the opinion, Chief Justice Marshall sets forth the key principle: "The very essence of civil liberty certainly consists in the right of every individual to claim the protection of the laws whenever he receives an injury. One of the first duties of government is to afford that protection." As the opinion states, "it seems equally clear that the individual who considers himself injured has a right to resort to the laws of his country for a remedy." Chapter 1, (part of) Chapter 2, and Chapter 9 describe the main remedies available to litigants seeking to recover for violations of federal law. Chapter 3 takes up the more general issues bearing on access to federal court under federal question and diversity jurisdiction.

   Should remedies be available in all circumstances? Should an individual always be able to collect damages from the state for violations of her constitutional rights? Or should other concerns, such as limiting the types of disputes federal courts may hear, or the protection of state treasuries and the defense of state sovereignty, or respect for the role of state courts in our system, prevail over individual interests in certain circumstances? These matters are taken up in Chapter 4 (on justiciability issues), Chapter 5 (addressing issues of state sovereign immunity), and Chapter 6 (on doctrines aimed at minimizing friction between federal and state courts).

   8.   The Limits of Article III and *Marbury*'s Ruling on the Judiciary Act. One of the more important aspects of the *Marbury* decision is the Court's conclusion that Congress cannot expand the powers of the federal courts beyond that provided in Article III. But why, if Congress chooses otherwise, should Article III be construed as a ceiling for federal judicial authority? Conversely, should Article III also be considered a floor for federal judicial power or should Congress have the power to restrict federal jurisdiction below Article III thresholds? See Chapter 10 (discussing congressional power to expand or limit federal court jurisdiction).

   9.   *Marbury* and the Political Skills of John Marshall. As noted above, *Marbury* was decided at a time when Jefferson and his Democratic-Republican allies in Congress were overtly hostile to the federal judiciary and when there existed a real question as to whether a judicial decision adverse to the President and the Congress would be enforced. The political brilliance of Chief Justice Marshall's opinion was that he reached a result favorable to Jefferson (and therefore did not have to risk the possibility that his decision would not be enforced) even as he simultaneously established principles of federal judicial power that Jefferson and his allies opposed. Indeed, many surmise that Marshall decided the case as he did expressly for this purpose.

If this indeed was Marshall's stratagem, did he act improperly? To what extent should courts be guided by political realities as well as legal principles in reaching their decisions? And speaking of ethics, should Marshall have recused himself from the case, since, after all, he was the Secretary of State charged with delivering the commission to Marbury in the first place?

10. Federalism. *Marbury* is a good vehicle for introducing many of the topics treated in this book, but not all of them. Federal courts law is concerned not only with the separation of powers issues raised by *Marbury* but also with judicial federalism—the relations between the federal courts and state governments. Chapter 1 describes federal court remedies available against state officials and local governments for violations of federal law. An important theme in Chapter 2 is the law bearing on whether a state or a federal common law rule should govern a particular substantive issue. Federalism issues also arise in connection with the constitutional (Chapter 10) and statutory (Chapters 3 and 7) provisions that deal with the division of jurisdiction between federal and state courts. State sovereign immunity from suit is the topic of Chapter 5. A variety of statutory and judge-made doctrines devised to deal with friction between federal and state courts are described in chapter 6. Litigation of federal causes of action in state court is one of the matters taken up in Chapter 7. Chapter 8 deals with Supreme Court review of state judgments. Chapter 9 examines federal habeas corpus for state prisoners, a procedure by which federal district courts may review the constitutional validity of state criminal convictions.

CHAPTER 1

CONSTITUTIONAL REMEDIES: SECTION 1983 AND RELATED DOCTRINES

■ ■ ■

Constitutional litigation to enforce federal rights against state officers and local governments is mainly undertaken in lawsuits brought under 42 U.S.C. § 1983, which, in its current form, provides:

> Every person who, under color of any statute, ordinance, regulation, custom or usage, of any State or Territory or the District of Columbia, subjects, or causes to be subjected, any citizen of the United States or other person within the jurisdiction thereof to the deprivation of any rights, privileges, or immunities secured by the Constitution and laws, shall be liable to the party injured in an action at law, suit in equity, or other proper proceeding for [redress].

Despite its sweeping language, § 1983 did not figure prominently in the federal docket before *Monroe v. Pape*, below. A cursory examination of the federal reporters will show that in the fifty years since *Monroe* litigation under § 1983 has become a major part of the work of the federal courts. Besides constitutional claims, many of the principles explored in this chapter (such as the official immunity doctrines) are applicable to litigation brought to enforce federal statutory rights as well.

I. BASIC FEATURES OF THE LAW OF CONSTITUTIONAL REMEDIES

MONROE V. PAPE
365 U.S. 167 (1961).

MR. JUSTICE DOUGLAS delivered the opinion of the Court.

This case presents important questions concerning the construction of 42 U.S.C. § 1983. [The] complaint alleges that 13 Chicago police officers broke into petitioners' home in the early morning, routed them from bed, made them stand naked in the living room, and ransacked every room, emptying drawers and ripping mattress covers. It further alleges that Mr. Monroe was then taken to the police station and detained on "open" charges for 10 hours, while he was interrogated about a two-day-old murder, that he was not taken before a magistrate, though one was accessible, that he was not permitted to call his family or attorney, that he was subsequently released without criminal charges being preferred against him. It is alleged that the officers had no search warrant and no arrest [warrant].

I.

Petitioners claim that the invasion of their home and the subsequent search without a warrant and the arrest and detention of Mr. Monroe without a warrant and without arraignment constituted a deprivation of their "rights, privileges, or immunities secured by the Constitution" within the meaning of § 1983. Section 1983 came onto the books as § 1 of the Ku Klux Act of April 20, 1871. It was one of the means whereby Congress exercised the power vested in it by § 5 of the Fourteenth Amendment to enforce the provisions of that Amendment. Its purpose is plain from the title of the legislation, "An Act to enforce the Provisions of the Fourteenth Amendment to the Constitution of the United States, and for other Purposes." Allegation of facts constituting a deprivation under color of state authority of a right guaranteed by the Fourteenth Amendment satisfies to that extent the requirement of [§ 1983]. So far petitioners are on solid ground. For the guarantee against unreasonable searches and seizures contained in the Fourth Amendment has been made applicable to the States by reason of the Due Process Clause of the Fourteenth Amendment.

II.

There can be no doubt at least since *Ex parte Virginia*, 100 U.S. 339, 346–347, that Congress has the power to enforce provisions of the Fourteenth Amendment against those who carry a badge of authority of a State and represent it in some capacity, whether they act in accordance with their authority or misuse it. See *Home Tel. & Tel. Co. v. City of Los Angeles*, 227 U.S. 278, 287–296 [(1913)]. The question with which we now deal is the narrower one of whether Congress, in enacting § 1983, meant to give a remedy to parties deprived of constitutional rights, privileges and immunities by an official's abuse of his position. We conclude that it did so intend. It is argued that "under color of" enumerated state authority excludes acts of an official or policeman who can show no authority under state law, state custom, or state usage to do what he did. In this case it is said that these policemen, in breaking into petitioners' apartment, violated the Constitution and laws of Illinois. It is pointed out that under Illinois law a simple remedy is offered for that violation and that, so far as it appears, the courts of Illinois are available to give petitioners that full redress which the common law affords for violence done to a person; and it is earnestly argued that no "statute, ordinance, regulation, custom or usage" of Illinois bars that redress.

The Ku Klux Act grew out of a message sent to Congress by President Grant on March 23, 1871, reading:

A condition of affairs now exists in some States of the Union rendering life and property insecure and the carrying of the mails and the collection of the revenue dangerous. The proof that such a condition of affairs exists in some localities is now before the Senate. That the power to correct these evils is beyond the control of State authorities I do not doubt; that the power of the Executive of the United States, acting within the limits of existing laws, is sufficient for present emergencies is not clear. Therefore, I urgently recommend such legislation as in the judgment of Congress shall effectually secure life, liberty, and property, and the enforcement of law in all parts of the United States.

The legislation—in particular the section with which we are now concerned—had several purposes. There are threads of many thoughts running through the debates. One who reads them in their entirety sees that the present section had three main aims.

First, it might, of course, override certain kinds of state laws. Mr. Sloss of Alabama, in opposition, spoke of that object and emphasized that it was irrelevant because there were no such laws:

The first section of this bill prohibits any invidious legislation by States against the rights or privileges of citizens of the United States. The object of this section is not very clear, as it is not pretended by its advocates on this floor that any State has passed any laws endangering the rights or privileges of the colored people.

Second, it provided a remedy where state law was inadequate. That aspect of the legislation was summed up as follows by Senator Sherman thus:

It is said the reason is that any offense may be committed upon a negro by a white man, and a negro cannot testify in any case against a white man, so that the only way by which any conviction can be had in Kentucky in those cases is in the United States courts, because the United States courts enforce the United States laws by which negroes may testify.

But the purposes were much broader. The third aim was to provide a federal remedy where the state remedy, though adequate in theory, was not available in [practice]. The Act of April 20, 1871, sometimes called "the third force bill," was passed by a Congress that had the Klan "particularly in mind." The debates are replete with references to the lawless conditions existing in the South in 1871. There was available to the Congress during these debates a report, nearly 600 pages in length, dealing with the activities of the Klan and the inability of the state governments to cope with it. This report was drawn on by many of the speakers. It was not the unavailability of state remedies but the failure of certain States to enforce the laws with an equal hand that furnished the powerful momentum behind this "force bill." While one main scourge of the evil—perhaps the leading one—was the Ku Klux Klan, the remedy created was not a remedy against it or its members but against those who representing a State in some capacity were unable or unwilling to enforce a state law. There was, it was said, no quarrel with the state laws on the books. It was their lack of enforcement that was the nub of the difficulty.

It was precisely that breadth of the remedy which the opposition emphasized. [The Court cited passages from the legislative history, including the objection voiced by Senator Thurman of Ohio, who noted that:]

> It authorizes any person who is deprived of any right, privilege, or immunity secured to him by the Constitution of the United States, to bring an action against the wrongdoer in the Federal courts, and that without any limit whatsoever as to the amount in controversy. The deprivation may be of the slightest conceivable character, the damages in the estimation of any sensible man may not be five dollars or even five cents; of any be what lawyers call merely nominal damages; and you may section jurisdiction of that civil action is given to the this courts instead of its being prosecuted as now in the court of States.

The debates were long and extensive. It is abundantly clear reason the legislation was passed was to afford a federal right in courts because, by reason of prejudice, passion, neglect, intolerance otherwise, state laws might not be enforced and the claims of citizens the enjoyment of rights, privileges, and immunities guaranteed by Fourteenth Amendment might be denied by the state [agencies Although the legislation was enacted because of the conditions th existed in the South at that time, it is cast in general language and is as applicable to Illinois as it is to the States whose names were mentioned over and again in the debates. It is no answer that the State has a law which if enforced would give relief. The federal remedy is supplementary to the state remedy, and the latter need not be first sought and refused before the federal one is invoked. Hence the fact that Illinois by its constitution and laws outlaws unreasonable searches and seizures is no barrier to the present suit in the federal court.

We had before us in *United States v. Classic*, 18 U.S.C. § 242, which provides a criminal punishment for anyone who "under color of any law, statute, ordinance, regulation, or custom" subjects any inhabitant of a State to the deprivation of "any rights, privileges, or immunities secured or protected by the Constitution or laws of the United States." The right involved in the *Classic* case was the right of voters in a primary to have their votes counted. The laws of Louisiana required the defendants "to count the ballots, to record the result of the count, and to certify the result of the election." But according to the indictment they did not perform their duty. In an opinion written by Mr. Justice (later Chief Justice) Stone, in which Mr. Justice Roberts, Mr. Justice Reed, and Mr. Justice Frankfurter joined, the Court ruled, "Misuse of power, possessed by virtue of state law and made possible only because the wrongdoer is clothed with the authority of state law, is action taken 'under color of' state law." There was a dissenting opinion; but the ruling as to the meaning of "under color of" state law was not questioned. [The Court discussed other cases, including *Screws v. United States*, 325 U.S. 91 (1945), in which it construed "under color of" in the same way.]

The *Classic* case was not the product of hasty action or inadvertence. It was not out of line with the cases which preceded. It was designed to fashion the governing rule of law in this important field. We are not dealing with constitutional interpretations which throughout the history of the Court have wisely remained flexible and subject to frequent re-examination. The meaning which the *Classic* case gave to the phrase "under color of any law" involved only a construction of the statute. Hence if it states a rule undesirable in its consequences, Congress can change it.

We conclude that the meaning given "under color of" law in the *Classic* case [and later cases] was the correct one; and we adhere to [it].

[The plaintiffs also sued the City of Chicago. In the remainder of the opinion, the Court dismissed that part of the case, holding that the term "person" at the beginning of the statute did not include municipal governments. That ruling was overturned in *Monell v. Department of Social Services*, below.]

MR. JUSTICE HARLAN, with whom MR. JUSTICE STEWART joins, concurring.

Were this case here as one of first impression, I would find the "under color of any statute" issue very close indeed. However, in *Classic* and *Screws* this Court considered a substantially identical statutory phrase to have a meaning which, unless we now retreat from it, requires that issue to go for the petitioners here.

From my point of view, the policy of *stare decisis*, as it should be applied in matters of statutory construction and, to a lesser extent, the indications of congressional acceptance of this Court's earlier interpretation, require that it appear beyond doubt from the legislative history of the 1871 statute that *Classic* and *Screws* misapprehended the meaning of the controlling provision, before a departure from what was decided in those cases would be justified. Since I can find no such justifying indication in that legislative history, I join the opinion of the Court. However, what has been written on both sides of the matter makes some additional observations [appropriate].

Besides the inconclusiveness I find in the legislative history, it seems to me by no means evident that a position favoring departure from

Classic and *Screws* fits better that with which the enacting Congress was concerned than does the position the Court adopted 20 years ago. There are apparent incongruities in the view of the dissent which may be more easily reconciled in terms of the earlier holding in *Classic*.

The dissent considers that the "under color of" provision of § 1983 distinguishes between unconstitutional actions taken without state authority, which only the State should remedy, and unconstitutional actions authorized by the State, which the Federal Act was to reach. If so, then the controlling difference for the enacting legislature must have been either that the state remedy was more adequate for unauthorized actions than for authorized ones or that there was, in some sense, greater harm from unconstitutional actions authorized by the full panoply of state power and approval than from unconstitutional actions not so authorized or acquiesced in by the State. I find less than compelling the evidence that either distinction was important to that Congress.

I.

If the state remedy was considered adequate when the official's unconstitutional act was unauthorized, why should it not be thought equally adequate when the unconstitutional act was authorized? For if one thing is very clear in the legislative history, it is that the Congress of 1871 was well aware that no action requiring state judicial enforcement could be taken in violation of the Fourteenth Amendment without that enforcement being declared void by this Court on direct review from the state courts. And presumably it must also have been understood that there would be Supreme Court review of the denial of a state damage remedy against an official on grounds of state authorization of the unconstitutional action. It therefore seems to me that the same state remedies would, with ultimate aid of Supreme Court review, furnish identical relief in the two situations. This is the point Senator Blair made when, having stated that the object of the Fourteenth Amendment was to prevent any discrimination by the law of any State, he argued that:

> This being forbidden by the Constitution of the United States, and all the judges, State and national, being sworn to support the Constitution of the United States, and the Supreme Court of the United States having power to supervise and correct the action of the State courts when they violated the Constitution of the United States, there could be no danger of the violation of the right of citizens under color of the laws of the States. Cong. Globe, 42d Cong., 1st Sess., at App. 231.

Since the suggested narrow construction of § 1983 presupposes that state measures were adequate to remedy unauthorized deprivations of constitutional rights and since the identical state relief could be obtained for state-authorized acts with the aid of Supreme Court review, this narrow construction would reduce the statute to having merely a jurisdictional function, shifting the load of federal supervision from the

Supreme Court to the lower courts and providing a federal tribunal for fact findings in cases involving authorized action. Such a function could be justified on various grounds. It could, for example, be argued that the state courts would be less willing to find a constitutional violation in cases involving "authorized action" and that therefore the victim of such action would bear a greater burden in that he would more likely have to carry his case to this Court, and once here, might be bound by unfavorable state court findings. But the legislative debates do not disclose congressional concern about the burdens of litigation placed upon the victims of "authorized" constitutional violations contrasted to the victims of unauthorized violations. Neither did Congress indicate an interest in relieving the burden placed on this Court in reviewing such cases.

The statute becomes more than a jurisdictional provision only if one attributes to the enacting legislature the view that a deprivation of a constitutional right is significantly different from and more serious than a violation of a state right and therefore deserves a different remedy even though the same act may constitute both a state tort and the deprivation of a constitutional right. This view, by no means unrealistic as a common-sense matter,[5] is, I believe, more consistent with the flavor of the legislative history than is a view that the primary purpose of the statute was to grant a lower court forum for fact [findings].

In my view, these considerations put in serious doubt the conclusion that § 1983 was limited to state-authorized unconstitutional acts, on the premise that state remedies respecting them were considered less adequate than those available for unauthorized acts.

II.

I think this limited interpretation of § 1983 fares no better when viewed from the other possible premise for it, namely that state-approved constitutional deprivations were considered more offensive than those not so approved. For one thing, the enacting Congress was not unaware of the fact that there was a substantial overlap between the protections granted by state constitutional provisions and those granted by the Fourteenth Amendment. Indeed one opponent of the bill, Senator Trumbull, went so far as to state in a debate with Senators Carpenter and Edmunds that his research indicated a complete overlap in every State, at least as to the

---

[5] There will be many cases in which the relief provided by the state to the victim of a use of state power which the state either did not or could not constitutionally authorize will be far less than what Congress may have thought would be fair reimbursement for deprivation of a constitutional right. I will venture only a few examples. There may be no damage remedy for the loss of voting rights or for the harm from psychological coercion leading to a confession. And what is the dollar value of the right to go to unsegregated schools? Even the remedy for such an unauthorized search and seizure as Monroe was allegedly subjected to may be only the nominal amount of damages to physical property allowable in an action for trespass to land. It would indeed be the purest coincidence if the state remedies for violations of common-law rights by private citizens were fully appropriate to redress those injuries which only a state official can cause and against which the Constitution provides protection.

protections of the Due Process Clause. Thus, in one very significant sense, there was no ultimate state approval of a large portion of otherwise authorized actions depriving a person of due-process rights. I hesitate to assume that the proponents of the present statute, who regarded it as necessary even though they knew that the provisions of the Fourteenth Amendment were self-executing, would have thought the remedies unnecessary whenever there were self-executing provisions of state constitutions also forbidding what the Fourteenth Amendment forbids. The only alternative is to disregard the possibility that a state court would find the action unauthorized on grounds of the state constitution. But if the defendant official is denied the right to defend in the federal court upon the ground that a state court would find his action unauthorized in the light of the state constitution, it is difficult to contend that it is the added harmfulness of state approval that justifies a different remedy for authorized than for unauthorized actions of state officers. Moreover, if indeed the legislature meant to distinguish between authorized and unauthorized acts and yet did not mean the statute to be inapplicable whenever there was a state constitutional provision which, reasonably interpreted, gave protection similar to that of a provision of the Fourteenth Amendment, would there not have been some explanation of this exception to the general rule? The fact that there is none in the legislative history at least makes more difficult a contention that these legislators were in fact making a distinction between use and misuse of state [power].

These difficulties in explaining the basis of a distinction between authorized and unauthorized deprivations of constitutional rights fortify my view that the legislative history does not bear the burden which *stare decisis* casts upon it. For this reason and for those stated in the opinion of the Court, I agree that we should not now depart from the holdings of the *Classic* and *Screws* cases.

MR. JUSTICE FRANKFURTER, [dissenting].

The issue in the present case concerns directly a basic problem of American federalism: the relation of the Nation to the States in the critically important sphere of municipal law administration. In this aspect, it has significance approximating constitutional dimension. Necessarily, the construction of the Civil Rights Acts raises issues fundamental to our institutions. This imposes on this Court a corresponding obligation to exercise its power within the fair limits of its judicial [discretion]. Now, while invoking the prior decisions which have given "under color of (law)" a content that ignores the meaning fairly comported by the words of the text and confirmed by the legislative history, the Court undertakes a fresh examination of that legislative history. The decision in this case, therefore, does not rest on *stare decisis*, and the true construction of the statute may be thought to be as free from the restraints of that doctrine as though the matter were before us for the first [time].

This case squarely presents the question whether the intrusion of a city policeman for which that policeman can show no such authority at state law as could be successfully interposed in defense to a state-law action against him, is nonetheless to be regarded as "under color" of state authority within the meaning of [§ 1983]. Respondents, in breaking into the Monroe apartment, violated the laws of the State of Illinois. Illinois law appears to offer a civil remedy for unlawful searches; petitioners do not claim that none is available. Rather they assert that they have been deprived of due process of law and of equal protection of the laws under color of state law, although from all that appears the courts of Illinois are available to give them the fullest redress which the common law affords for the violence done them, nor does any "statute, ordinance, regulation, custom, or usage" of the State of Illinois bar that redress.

Did the enactment by Congress of § 1 of the Ku Klux Act of 1871 encompass such a situation? [Justice Frankfurter's extensive analysis of the legislative history is omitted. He concluded that] all the evidence converges to the conclusion that Congress by § 1983 created a civil liability enforceable in the federal courts only in instances of injury for which redress was barred in the state courts because some "statute, ordinance, regulation, custom, or usage" sanctioned the grievance complained of. This purpose, manifested even by the so-called "Radical" Reconstruction Congress in 1871, accords with the presuppositions of our federal system. The jurisdiction which Article III of the Constitution conferred on the national judiciary reflected the assumption that the state courts, not the federal courts, would remain the primary guardians of that fundamental security of person and property which the long evolution of the common law had secured to one individual as against other individuals. The Fourteenth Amendment did not alter this basic aspect of our federalism. Its commands were addressed to the States. Only when the States, through their responsible organs for the formulation and administration of local policy, sought to deny or impede access by the individual to the central government in connection with those enumerated functions assigned to it, or to deprive the individual of a certain minimal fairness in the exercise of the coercive forces of the State, or without reasonable justification to treat him differently than other persons subject to their jurisdiction, was an overriding federal sanction imposed. As between individuals, no corpus of substantive rights was guaranteed by the Fourteenth Amendment, but only "due process of law" in the ascertainment and enforcement of rights and equality in the enjoyment of rights and safeguards that the States afford. This was the base of the distinction between federal citizenship and state citizenship drawn by the *Slaughter-House Cases*. This conception begot the "State action" principle on which, from the time of the *Civil Rights Cases*, this Court has relied in its application of Fourteenth Amendment guarantees. As between individuals, that body of mutual rights and duties which constitute the civil personality of a man remains essentially the creature of the legal institutions of the States.

But, of course, in the present case petitioners argue that the wrongs done them were committed not by individuals but by the police as state officials. There are two senses in which this might be true. It might be true if petitioners alleged that the redress which state courts offer them against the respondents is different than that which those courts would offer against other individuals, guilty of the same conduct, who were not the police. This is not alleged. It might also be true merely because the respondents are the police—because they are clothed with an appearance of official authority which is in itself a factor of significance in dealings between individuals. Certainly the night-time intrusion of the man with a star and a police revolver is a different phenomenon than the night-time intrusion of a burglar. The aura of power which a show of authority carries with it has been created by state government. For this reason the national legislature, exercising its power to implement the Fourteenth Amendment, might well attribute responsibility for the intrusion to the State and legislate to protect against such intrusion. The pretense of authority alone might seem to Congress sufficient basis for creating an exception to the ordinary rule that it is to the state tribunals that individuals within a State must look for redress against other individuals within that State. The same pretense of authority might suffice to sustain congressional legislation creating the exception. But until Congress has declared its purpose to shift the ordinary distribution of judicial power for the determination of causes between co-citizens of a State, this Court should not make the shift. Congress has not in § 1983 manifested that [intention].

Relevant also are the effects upon the institution of federal constitutional adjudication of sustaining under § 1983 damage actions for relief against conduct allegedly violative of federal constitutional rights, but plainly violative of state law. Permitting such actions necessitates the immediate decision of federal constitutional issues despite the admitted availability of state-law remedies which would avoid those issues. This would make inroads, throughout a large area, upon the principle of federal judicial self-limitation which has become a significant instrument in the efficient functioning of the national judiciary. See *Railroad Commission of Texas v. Pullman Co.*, 312 U.S. 496, and cases following. Self-limitation is not a matter of technical nicety, nor judicial timidity. It reflects the recognition that to no small degree the effectiveness of the legal order depends upon the infrequency with which it solves its problems by resorting to determinations of ultimate power. Especially is this true where the circumstances under which those ultimate determinations must be made are not conducive to the most mature deliberation and decision. If § 1983 is made a vehicle of constitutional litigation in cases where state officers have acted lawlessly at state law, difficult questions of the federal constitutionality of certain official practices—lawful perhaps in some States, unlawful in others—may be litigated between private parties without the participation of responsible state authorities which is obviously desirable to protect legitimate state interests, but also to better guide adjudication by competent record-making and argument.

Of course, these last considerations would be irrelevant to our duty if Congress had demonstrably meant to reach by § 1983 activities like those of respondents in this case. But where it appears that Congress plainly did not have that understanding, respect for principles which this Court has long regarded as critical to the most effective functioning of our federalism should avoid extension of a statute beyond its manifest area of operation into applications which invite conflict with the administration of local policies. Such an extension makes the extreme limits of federal constitutional power a law to regulate the quotidian business of every traffic policeman, every registrar of elections, every city inspector or investigator, every clerk in every municipal licensing bureau in this country. The text of the statute, reinforced by its history, precludes such a reading.

In concluding that police intrusion in violation of state law is not a wrong remediable under § 1983, the pressures which urge an opposite result are duly felt. The difficulties which confront private citizens who seek to vindicate in traditional common-law actions their state-created rights against lawless invasion of their privacy by local policemen are obvious, and obvious is the need for more effective modes of redress. The answer to these urgings must be regard for our federal system which presupposes a wide range of regional autonomy in the kinds of protection local residents receive. If various common-law concepts make it possible for a policeman—but no more possible for a policeman than for any individual hoodlum intruder—to escape without liability when he has vandalized a home, that is an evil. But, surely, its remedy devolves, in the first instance, on the States. Of course, if the States afford less protection against the police, as police, than against the hoodlum—if under authority of state "statute, ordinance, regulation, custom, or usage" the police are specially shielded—§ 1983 provides a remedy which dismissal of petitioners' complaint in the present case does not impair. Otherwise, the protection of the people from local delinquencies and shortcomings depends, as in general it must, upon the active consciences of state executives, legislators and judges. Federal intervention, which must at best be limited to securing those minimal guarantees afforded by the evolving concepts of due process and equal protection, may in the long run do the individual a disservice by deflecting responsibility from the state lawmakers, who hold the power of providing a far more comprehensive scope of protection. Local society, also, may well be the loser, by relaxing its sense of responsibility and, indeed, perhaps resenting what may appear to it to be outside interference where local authority is ample and more appropriate to supply needed remedies.

This is not to say that there may not exist today, as in 1871, needs which call for congressional legislation to protect the civil rights of individuals in the States. Strong contemporary assertions of these needs have been expressed. Report of the President's Committee on Civil Rights, To Secure These Rights (1947); Chafee, *Safeguarding Fundamental Human Rights: The Tasks of States and Nation*, 27 Geo.Wash. L. Rev. 519 (1959). But both the insistence of the needs and the delicacy of the issues involved in finding appropriate means for their satisfaction demonstrate that their demand is for legislative, not judicial, response. We cannot expect to create an effective means of protection for human liberties by torturing an 1871 statute to meet the problems of [1960].

NOTES ON ENFORCING FEDERAL RIGHTS IN THE FEDERAL COURTS

Besides opening the door of the federal courthouse to a larger group of litigants seeking damages for constitutional violations, *Monroe v. Pape* draws attention to broader issues regarding the role of the federal courts in implementing federal constitutional and statutory rights.

1. Defensive and Offensive Constitutional Remedies. Throughout this course it will be useful to distinguish between two kinds of constitutional remedies. Someone may assert a constitutional right as a defense to a criminal prosecution or civil liability. For example, a woman charged with the crime of procuring an abortion may assert the substantive due process right recognized in *Roe v. Wade*, 410 U.S. 113 (1973), and a newspaper sued for libel may raise a free speech defense under *New York Times v. Sullivan*, 376 U.S. 254 (1964). By contrast, the cause of action for damages, authorized by § 1983 and accorded a broad scope in *Monroe*, puts the constitutional claimant in the role of plaintiff. Rather than using the Constitution as a shield against the imposition of some sanction, the putative right holder wields the Constitution as a sword, seeking some relief for past, present, or threatened harm.

The Constitution itself contains few remedial provisions. With the ratification of the Fourteenth Amendment in 1868, States were subject to significant new constitutional constraints and pressure grew to construct a body of remedial law. One way of responding to persons seeking to pursue offensive remedies in the federal courts would be to refuse to create any such remedies, directing these plaintiffs to seek whatever relief they may obtain under state remedial law and allowing them access to federal court only when their state law causes of action happened to satisfy the jurisdictional requirements for federal question or diversity jurisdiction. For example, a litigant who claimed that the state had reneged on its contractual promise to him might sue for restitution or conversion.

Long before *Monroe*, the Supreme Court had rejected this "state law cause of action" alternative. See Ann Woolhandler, *The Common Law Origins of Constitutionally Compelled Remedies*, 107 YALE L.J. 77 (1997); Henry M. Hart, Jr., *The Relations Between State and Federal Law*, 54 COLUM. L. REV. 489, 523–24 & n. 124 (1954). The key case is *Ex parte Young*, 209 U.S. 123

(1908) (set out in Chapter 5). In that case, and later decisions that built upon the foundation it had laid, the Court made available a federal offensive remedy for persons seeking to stop present or future unconstitutional acts by state officers. *Young*, however, applied only to suits for *injunctive* relief, i.e., those seeking a judicial order telling officials what they may or may not do in the present or the future, on pain of being held in contempt of court and fined or imprisoned if they disobey. Specifically, the Court allowed a railroad to bring such a suit in federal court against the Minnesota attorney general. In this case, which arose during the era of "economic substantive due process," the railroad objected to setting freight rates at levels the railroad considered so low as to amount to deprivation of its property without due process of law. It sued in federal court and its request for injunctive relief against enforcement of the rates did not rely on any state law cause of action. Yet the Court, without making a point of this aspect of the case, allowed it to proceed. *Young* then became a template for litigation challenging state laws on constitutional grounds and requesting injunctive relief. Though the Court never discussed the "*Ex parte Young* cause of action," as such, the practical impact of allowing this type of litigation to proceed in the federal courts was to create such a cause of action as a matter of federal common law. Later the Court extended the *Young* cause of action to embrace suits for declaratory judgments, as well as suits seeking injunctive or declaratory relief for violations of federal statutes.

Young did not rely at all on § 1983. For ninety years, from its enactment in 1871 until *Monroe*, that statute had lain largely dormant. Despite its sweeping language, it was used mainly in cases alleging denial of voting rights to blacks. One reason for its neglect is that the availability of *Ex parte Young* lessened the need for it. Furthermore, lower courts before *Monroe* had often read the statutory "under color of" language in the way favored by Justice Frankfurter in his *Monroe* dissent. Under that reading, many constitutional wrongs committed by state officers could not be vindicated in a § 1983 suit because state remedies were available. Some courts erected another barrier, by applying a stringent "official immunity" defense to damages actions. (The modern scope of "official immunity" is examined in Section II of this chapter.)

The revival of § 1983 is largely attributable to the Warren Court's activism, not only in its interpretation of "under color of" in *Monroe*, but also in recognizing constitutional claims that the Court had earlier rejected, and in its large-scale incorporation of the bill of rights into the Fourteenth Amendment. In a sense, *Monroe* was the remedial analogue of the Warren Court's substantive agenda. As the content of individual rights grew richer, the Court no doubt felt the need to augment *Ex parte Young* by adding a revitalized damages remedy as well. For further discussion of the points summarized in this paragraph, see Louise Weinberg, *The* Monroe *Mystery Solved: Beyond the "Unhappy History" Theory of Civil Rights Litigation*, 1991 B.Y.U. L. REV. 737.

Ex parte Young and *Monroe v. Pape* signaled the rise of offensive remedies in the federal courts, and with them came a new chapter in the evolution of substantive constitutional rights. So long as only defensive remedies are available for constitutional violations, the universe of constitutional rights is limited to objections that may be raised against civil or criminal "enforcement actions," such as criminal prosecutions or suits for civil damages. In such a world the person who complains about the acts of government officers outside the judicial process has no federal recourse, and must resort to whatever remedies state law may provide. It would be virtually impossible to bring a federal court challenge to school segregation, malapportioned legislative districts, state prison conditions, the dismissal of state employees, the behavior of the police toward persons who are never prosecuted, or any other aspect of the State's conduct of its affairs beyond the realm of law enforcement. Much of modern constitutional law is, in this sense, a product of the growth of constitutional remedies.

2.   Competing Conceptions of the Role of the Federal Courts: A "Private Law" Model and a "Public Law" Model. The growth of offensive remedies contributed significantly to another development in federal courts law over the past half century. It may overstate the point to assert that the role of the federal courts in society has undergone a radical shift. Nonetheless, it is generally agreed that they have taken on tasks that they once shunned, and that the scope of their power has become a topic of public policy debates.

In the past, the federal courts conceived of their role, even in constitutional cases, primarily as that of resolving disputes between the parties. Under this "dispute resolution" or "private rights" model, unnecessary constitutional decisions should be avoided. The range of disputes courts would consider was limited to matters that resembled traditional common law tort, contract, and property claims, with plaintiffs who complained of discrete injuries that were plainly caused by the defendant's conduct. In these bipolar disputes, the relief available was defined by the plaintiff's injury, and consisted of eliminating or making up for the wrongful conduct.

The expansion of offensive remedies presented opportunities for litigants to pursue innovative claims for relief. Coupled with the proliferation of newly recognized constitutional rights and the general growth of government, the new remedial scheme gave rise to a new form of litigation in constitutional and other public law disputes. Rather than the bipolar model, the lawsuit may include numerous parties on either side, and the parties on either side may have a variety of disparate interests. The interests asserted may not be claims of discrete injury to specific persons, but include diffuse harms to interests held in common by large numbers of persons. The relief requested may not be a simple correction of the wrong, but consist primarily of ongoing judicial oversight over legislative apportionment, or over some government institution like a prison or a school system. More broadly, the role of the federal courts under this model is not to avoid constitutional issues, but to face them squarely as they confront systemic social problems. See Abram Chayes, *The Role of the Judge in Public Law Litigation*, 89 HARV. L. REV. 1281 (1976). For a more recent overview of the topic, see R. FALLON ET AL., HART & WECHSLER'S THE FEDERAL COURTS AND THE FEDERAL SYSTEM 72–75 (6th ed. 2009).

The "public law"/"private law" dichotomy bears not only on remedies, but also illuminates other issues in federal courts law, including, among others, the kinds of disputes that may be litigated in federal court, under the doctrines of standing, mootness and ripeness discussed in Chapter 4, the scope of Supreme Court review of state judgments, discussed in Chapter 8, and the question of Congress's power over the jurisdiction of the federal courts, discussed in Chapter 10.

MONELL V. DEPARTMENT OF SOCIAL SERVICES
436 U.S. 658 (1978).

MR. JUSTICE BRENNAN delivered the opinion of the Court.

[Female] employees of the Department of Social Services and of the Board of Education of the city of New York, commenced this action under 42 U.S.C. § 1983. [The] gravamen of the complaint was that the Board and the Department had as a matter of official policy compelled pregnant employees to take unpaid leaves of absence before such leaves were required for medical reasons. The suit sought injunctive relief and backpay for periods of unlawful forced [leave]. Plaintiffs' prayers for backpay were denied because any such damages would come ultimately from the City of New York and, therefore, to hold otherwise would be to "circumven[t]" the immunity conferred on municipalities by *Monroe v. Pape*, 365 U.S. 167 (1961). [We] now overrule *Monroe*, insofar as it holds that local governments are wholly immune from suit under § 1983.

In *Monroe* we held that "Congress did not undertake to bring municipal corporations within the ambit of [§ 1983]." The sole basis for this conclusion was an inference drawn from Congress' rejection of the "Sherman amendment" to the bill which became the Civil Rights Act of 1871, the precursor of § 1983. The Amendment would have held a municipal corporation liable for damage done to the person or property of its inhabitants by private persons "riotously and tumultuously assembled." Cong. Globe, 42d Cong., 1st Sess., 749 (1871) (hereinafter Globe). Although the Sherman amendment did not seek to amend § 1 of the Act, which is now § 1983, and although the nature of the obligation created by that amendment was vastly different from that created by § 1, the Court nonetheless concluded in *Monroe* that Congress must have meant to exclude municipal corporations from the coverage of § 1 because " 'the House [in voting against the Sherman amendment] had solemnly decided that in their judgment Congress had no constitutional power to impose any *obligation* upon county and town organizations, the mere instrumentality for the administration of state law.' " [Statement of

Representative Poland.] This statement, we thought, showed that Congress doubted its "constitutional power to impose civil liability on municipalities," and that such doubt would have extended to any type of civil liability.

A fresh analysis of the debate on the Civil Rights Act of 1871, and particularly of the case law which each side mustered in its support, shows, however, that *Monroe* incorrectly equated the "obligation" of which Representative Poland spoke with "civil liability."

[The Court discussed the legislative history, giving particular attention to the Sherman Amendment and the reasons for its rejection.] House opponents, within whose ranks were some who had supported § 1, thought the Federal Government could not, consistent with the Constitution, obligate municipal corporations to keep the peace if those corporations were neither so obligated nor so authorized by their state charters. And, because of this constitutional objection, opponents of the Sherman amendment were unwilling to impose damages liability for nonperformance of a duty which Congress could not require municipalities to perform. This position is reflected in Representative Poland's statement that is quoted in *Monroe*.

[The] meaning of the legislative history sketched above can most readily be developed by first considering the debate on the report of the first conference committee. This debate shows conclusively that the constitutional objections raised against the Sherman amendment—on which our holding in *Monroe* was based,—would not have prohibited congressional creation of a civil remedy against state municipal corporations that infringed federal rights. Because § 1 of the Civil Rights Act does not state expressly that municipal corporations come within its ambit, it is finally necessary to interpret § 1 to confirm that such corporations were indeed intended to be included within the "persons" to whom that section [applies].

Representative Shellabarger was the first to explain the function of § 1: "[Section 1] not only provides a civil remedy for persons whose former condition may have been that of slaves, but also to all people where, under color of State law, they or any of them may be deprived of rights to which they are entitled under the Constitution by reason and virtue of their national citizenship." Globe App. 68.

By extending a remedy to all people, including whites, § 1 went beyond the mischief to which the remaining sections of the 1871 Act were [addressed]. Representative Shellabarger then went on to describe how the courts would and should interpret § 1: "This act is remedial, and in aid of the preservation of human liberty and human rights. All statutes and constitutional provisions authorizing such statutes are liberally and beneficently construed. It would be most strange and, in civilized law, monstrous were this not the rule of interpretation. As has been again and again decided by your own Supreme Court of the United States, and everywhere else where there is wise judicial interpretation, the largest latitude consistent with the words employed is uniformly given in construing such statutes and constitutional provisions as are meant to protect and defend and give remedies for their wrongs to all the [people]."

[The Court also cited the widespread use of the term "person" in 1871 to include corporations, including municipal corporations.]

Our analysis of the legislative history of the Civil Rights Act of 1871 compels the conclusion that Congress did intend municipalities and other local government units to be included among those persons to whom § 1983 applies. Local governing bodies, therefore, can be sued directly under § 1983 for monetary, declaratory, or injunctive relief where, as here, the action that is alleged to be unconstitutional implements or executes a policy statement, ordinance, regulation, or decision officially adopted and promulgated by that body's officers. Moreover, although the touchstone of the § 1983 action against a government body is an allegation that official policy is responsible for a deprivation of rights protected by the Constitution, local governments, like every other § 1983 "person," by the very terms of the statute, may be sued for constitutional deprivations visited pursuant to governmental "custom" even though such a custom has not received formal approval through the body's official decisionmaking channels. As Mr. Justice Harlan, writing for the Court, said in *Adickes v. S. H. Kress & Co.*, 398 U.S. 144, 167–168 (1970): "Congress included customs and usages [in § 1983] because of the persistent and widespread discriminatory practices of state officials . . . Although not authorized by written law, such practices of state officials could well be so permanent and well settled as to constitute a 'custom or usage' with the force of law."

On the other hand, the language of § 1983, read against the background of the same legislative history, compels the conclusion that Congress did not intend municipalities to be held liable unless action pursuant to official municipal policy of some nature caused a constitutional tort. In particular, we conclude that a municipality cannot be held liable solely because it employs a tortfeasor—or, in other words, a municipality cannot be held liable under § 1983 on a *respondeat superior* theory.

We begin with the language of § 1983 as originally passed:

[A]ny person who, under color of any law, statute, ordinance, regulation, custom, or usage of any State, *shall subject, or cause to be subjected*, any person . . . to the deprivation of any rights, privileges, or immunities secured by the Constitution of the United States, shall, any such law, statute, ordinance, regulation, custom, or usage of the State to the contrary notwithstanding, be liable to the party injured in any action at law, suit in equity, or other proper proceeding for redress. . . ." 17 Stat. 13 (emphasis added).

The italicized language plainly imposes liability on a government that, under color of some official policy, "causes" an employee to violate another's constitutional rights. At the same time, that language cannot be easily read to impose liability vicariously on governing bodies solely on the basis of the existence of an employer-employee relationship with a tortfeasor. Indeed, the fact that Congress did specifically provide that A's tort became B's liability if B "caused" A to subject another to a tort suggests that Congress did not intend § 1983 liability to attach where such causation was absent.

Equally important, creation of a federal law of *respondeat superior* would have raised all the constitutional problems associated with the obligation to keep the peace, an obligation Congress chose not to impose because it thought imposition of such an obligation unconstitutional. To this day, there is disagreement about the basis for imposing liability on an employer for the torts of an employee when the sole nexus between the employer and the tort is the fact of the employer-employee relationship. See W. Prosser, Law of Torts § 69, p. 459 (4th ed. 1971). Nonetheless, two justifications tend to stand out. First is the common-sense notion that no matter how blameless an employer appears to be in an individual case, accidents might nonetheless be reduced if employers had to bear the cost of accidents. See, e. g., *ibid.*; 2 F. Harper & F. James, Law of Torts, § 26.3, pp. 1368–1369 (1956). Second is the argument that the cost of accidents should be spread to the community as a whole on an insurance theory. See, e. g., *id.*, § 26.5; Prosser, supra, at 459.

The first justification is of the same sort that was offered for statutes like the Sherman amendment: "The obligation to make compensation for injury resulting from riot is, by arbitrary enactment of statutes, affirmatory law, and the reason of passing the statute is to secure a more perfect police regulation." Globe 777 (Sen. Frelinghuysen). This justification was obviously insufficient to sustain the amendment against perceived constitutional difficulties and there is no reason to suppose that a more general liability imposed for a similar reason would have been thought less constitutionally objectionable. The second justification was similarly put forward as a justification for the Sherman amendment: "we do not look upon [the Sherman amendment] as a punishment. . . . It is a mutual insurance." *Id.*, at 792 (Rep. Butler). Again, this justification was insufficient to sustain the amendment.

We conclude, therefore, that a local government may not be sued under § 1983 for an injury inflicted solely by its employees or agents. Instead, it is when execution of a government's policy or custom, whether made by its lawmakers or by those whose edicts or acts may fairly be said to represent official policy, inflicts the injury that the government as an entity is responsible under § 1983. Since this case unquestionably involves official policy as the moving force of the constitutional violation found by the District Court, we must reverse the judgment below. In so doing, we have no occasion to address, and do not address, what the full contours of municipal liability under § 1983 may be. We have attempted only to sketch so much of the § 1983 cause of action against a local government as is apparent from the history of the 1871 Act and our prior cases, and we expressly leave further development of this action to another [day].

[The concurring opinions of JUSTICES POWELL and STEVENS and the dissenting opinion of JUSTICE REHNQUIST, joined by CHIEF JUSTICE BURGER, are omitted.]

NOTES ON MONROE, MONELL, AND THE § 1983 CAUSE OF ACTION

1. **"Under Color of" State Law.** In *Monroe* the Court construed § 1983's "under color of" requirement. The issue was whether a § 1983 suit could be brought for conduct that is illegal under state law. For many years lower courts had ruled that the "under color of" rule was not met in such circumstances. *Monroe* rejected that view of "under color of" in favor of broader access to federal court. One effect of the holding was to allow plaintiffs to bring § 1983 cases without first exhausting remedies available in the state courts. Later, following the logic of *Monroe*, the Court rejected the notion that the plaintiff should be made to exhaust state *administrative* remedies. *Patsy v. Board of Regents*, 457 U.S. 496 (1982). However, in the Prison Litigation Reform Act of 1995, 42 U.S.C. § 1997e(a) Congress carved out an exception for suits brought by prisoners challenging the conditions of their confinement, requiring them to exhaust administrative remedies. See *Porter v. Nussle*, 534 U.S. 516 (2002) (ruling that the exhaustion requirement "applies to all prisoners seeking redress for prison circumstances or occurrences").

Given that the "under color of" language does not generally require exhaustion, the next question is what it *does* oblige the plaintiff to establish. The Court has said that "conduct satisfying the state-action requirement of the Fourteenth Amendment satisfies the statutory requirement of action under color of state law." *Lugar v. Edmondson Oil Co.*, 457 U.S. 922 n.18 (1982). With regard to the police, their activity while *on* duty is generally deemed to be state action and "under color of" state law, even if they violate state law. Sometimes, however, when the motive for the act is strictly personal, courts rule that the state action/under color requirements have not been met. See, e.g., *Butler v. Sheriff of Palm Beach County,* 685 F.3d 1261 (11th Cir. 2012) (corrections officer does not act under state law when, upon returning home from work, she finds her daughter's boyfriend naked in the closet, handcuffs him, threatens him, and holds him at gunpoint for a prolonged period, using official handcuffs and gun); *Honaker v. Smith*, 256 F.3d 477 (7th Cir. 2001) (fire chief did not act under color of state law when he set a fire for personal reasons).

The state action and "under color of" requirements are not identical. When state officers are enforcing federal law, they are deemed to be acting under color of federal law and cannot be sued under § 1983. See *Rosas v. Brock*, 826 F.2d 1004, 1007 (11th Cir. 1987) (Florida disaster relief workers acted under color of federal law when, applying federal guidelines to a federal program, they denied a claim for compensation.) Conversely, federal officers ordinarily cannot be sued under § 1983. Prospective relief is available against them under the *Young* principle, a federal common law cause of action for damages may be possible, see Chapter 2, or some other federal statute may afford a remedy. There is, however, no federal officer analogue to § 1983 that would authorize a broad retrospective remedy against federal officers.

Occasionally, federal officers do act under color of state law, as when they collaborate with state officers in enforcement of state law. In such a case a § 1983 suit is available. E.g., *Strickland v. Shalala*, 123 F.3d 863 (6th Cir. 1997).

2. State Remedies and the Due Process Clause. Justice Frankfurter argued in vain that the statutory "under color of" language should be construed as authorizing federal jurisdiction only where an adequate state remedy is not available. The statutory argument he favored in *Monroe* echoes a constitutional issue the Court had addressed forty-eight years earlier, in *Home Telephone & Telegraph Co. v. City of Los Angeles*, 227 U.S. 278 (1913). Home Telephone challenged a city ordinance that capped its rates, charging that the ordinance deprived it of property without due process of law in violation of the Fourteenth Amendment. The city defended on the ground that, by its terms, the Fourteenth Amendment can only be violated by the State, and that the State has not acted until the state courts have upheld the decisions of officials or local governments. As Home Telephone had not challenged the ordinance in the state courts, no constitutional violation had yet occurred. The Court rejected the city's theory:

> To the contrary, the provisions of the Amendment . . . are generic in their terms, are addressed, of course, to the States, but also to every person, whether natural or juridical, who is the repository of state power. By this construction the reach of the Amendment is shown to be coextensive with any exercise by a State of power, in whatever form exerted.

In effect *Home Telephone* had rejected the constitutional analogue of the statutory thesis advanced by Justice Frankfurter in *Monroe*. Did Justice Frankfurter simply seek reconsideration of the *Home Telephone* ruling, by dressing his argument in statutory rather than constitutional garb, or are there good reasons to distinguish between the statutory and constitutional versions of the issue raised by these cases?

Whether the issue is framed in statutory or constitutional terms, it boils down to whether constitutional challenges to the acts of state officers and governments should ordinarily be conducted in state or federal courts. Are there good reasons to believe that the choice of forum influences outcomes in cases of this kind? For an argument that federal courts, protected by life tenure, staffed by more talented judges, and influenced by a tradition of vindicating federal rights, will likely be more sympathetic to the plaintiff's claims, see Burt Neuborne, *The Myth of Parity*, 90 HARV. L. REV. 1105 (1977). Plaintiffs raising federal constitutional claims have a choice between federal and state court, see Chapter 7. Most vote with their feet in favor of the federal forum.

Home Telephone is the general rule, but it is not without exceptions. One is the rule that a "takings" claim charging inverse condemnation may not be ripe for adjudication by a federal court where the plaintiff has not pursued a state remedy, *Williamson County Regional Planning Commission v. Hamilton Bank*, 473 U.S. 172 (1985), unless the pursuit of that remedy would be futile. *Palazzolo v. Rhode Island*, 533 U.S. 606, 620 (2001). Another is the procedural due process doctrine that, in certain circumstances, a state can satisfy the Fourteenth Amendment by providing *post*-deprivation process. See *Zinermon v. Burch,* 494 U.S. 113 (1990). An illustrative case is *Camuglia v. Albuquerque*, 448 F.3d 1214, 1220 (10th Cir. 2006). A city restaurant inspector temporarily summarily closed Camuglia's restaurant without affording him pre-deprivation due process. Camuglia sued under § 1983, charging, among other things, a deprivation of property without procedural due process. Rejecting his claim, the 10th Circuit cited longstanding Supreme Court precedent for the proposition that when "matters of public safety" are at stake, "the government must act quickly. Quick action may turn out to be wrongful action, but due process requires only a post-deprivation opportunity to establish the error."

3. Statutory Interpretation, the Common Law, and § 1983. Both Justice Douglas's majority opinion and Justice Frankfurter's dissent in *Monroe* begin from the premise that determining the content of "under color of" is a matter of statutory interpretation, and each relies heavily on statements drawn from the legislative history. On both sides the emphasis on determining legislative intent may have been altogether sincere. At the same time, Justice Frankfurter makes it clear that his interpretation of the statute is influenced by his understanding of the proper allocation of responsibility between federal and state courts for enforcing constitutional rights, and the majority could hardly have ignored the substantive implications of its holding. In any event, it would be a mistake to think that most issues in § 1983 litigation are resolved by the traditional tools of statutory interpretation. The broad language and lack of specificity of the statute has made it necessary for the Court to engage in a significant amount of law making in addressing issues that arise under it. Later developments have taken § 1983 doctrine far afield from any plausible account of the "intent of the framers." In particular, the Court (even after *Monroe*) has recognized "official immunity" defenses that do not appear in either the text or the legislative history of the statute. Early on, the Court justified these defenses by noting that the framers of the statute acted against a background of nineteenth-century tort law, which recognized such defenses. Current doctrine gives content to those defenses mainly by reference to modern tort policy considerations, with little regard for history. See Section II below.

The notion that tort law is relevant to § 1983 issues stems from a passage in Justice Douglas's opinion, stating that the statute "should be read against the background of tort liability that makes a man responsible for the natural consequences of his acts." This reference to tort was made in the context of distinguishing the state of mind needed for civil liability under § 1983 from the criminal context, where proof of "a specific intent to deprive a person of a federal right" is required for liability. Be that as it may, "the background of tort liability" is a premise for importing a number of tort concepts into § 1983 law. Besides official immunity, these include compensatory and punitive damages, causation in fact, and proximate cause. As with modern immunity law, the Court typically borrows from modern tort doctrine in addressing these matters, see, e.g., *Carey v. Piphus*, 435 U.S. 247 (1978) (on compensatory damages). Occasionally the Justices do debate the contents of nineteenth century tort law. See *Smith v. Wade*, 461 U.S. 30 (1983) (where the issue was the proper standard for punitive damages). Contract law may also be relevant, e.g., in connection with the validity of agreements to release officials from liability for constitutional violations in exchange for dismissal of criminal charges. See *Newton v. Rumery*, 480 U.S. 386 (1987).

For a detailed treatment of the substantive and remedial issues that arise in constitutional tort litigation, see SHELDON NAHMOD ET AL., CONSTITUTIONAL TORTS (3rd ed. 2010).

4.   State Court Suits. The plaintiffs in *Ex parte Young* and *Monroe* sought and obtained access to *federal* court for their constitutional claims. These suits may also be brought in *state* court. On the day it decided *Young*, the Court ruled that the state courts must also hear requests for prospective relief. *General Oil Co. v. Crain*, 209 U.S. 211 (1908). In *Haywood v. Drown*, 556 U.S. 729 (2009), and *Howlett v. Rose*, 496 U.S. 356 (1990), the Court held that state courts generally may not decline to hear § 1983 cases. For discussion of the doctrinal framework that includes *Haywood* and *Howlett*, see Chapter 7. The general point of *General Oil*, *Haywood*, and *Howlett* is that offensive constitutional remedies may be pursued in either state or federal court. Keep in mind, however, that the federal question removal statute, 28 U.S.C. § 1441, permits the defendant to remove a case (like a § 1983 case) that could have been brought in federal court originally. For this reason, plaintiffs who for whatever reason prefer to litigate in state court may nonetheless find themselves thwarted.

5.   Suing Governments. *Monell* expands § 1983 liability by authorizing suits against municipal government. At the same time, that case rejects respondeat superior liability, holding that local government liability depends on "official policy" or "custom." The doctrine is examined in Section III of this chapter. *State* governments, and such "arms of the State" as state universities and state agencies, may not be sued under § 1983. *Quern v. Jordan*, 440 U.S. 332 (1979) held that the State is not a "person" within the meaning of that term as it is used in the statute. The Court explained that an especially clear statement of congressional intent to subject States to suit was required in order to override the States' sovereign immunity. On the general topic of sovereign immunity, see Chapter 5. As for the "arm of the State" doctrine, *Northern Insurance Co. v. Chatham County, Georgia*, 547 U.S. 189 (2006), reiterated the longstanding rule that political subdivisions are not "arms of the State" even when they exercise state power, and rejected Chatham County's argument that it nonetheless enjoys "residual immunity" from suit.

6. Suing Federal Officers: The *Bivens* Doctrine. The unavailability of § 1983 for suits against federal officers does not necessarily mean that there is no redress for victims of constitutional wrongs by federal officers. Sometimes a suit can be brought against the United States under the Federal Tort Claims Act, 28 U.S.C. § 2674 or other federal statutes. Without statutory authorization, federal officers can sometimes be sued directly for constitutional violations under the doctrine stemming from *Bivens v. Six Unknown Named Agents*, 403 U.S. 388 (1971). The *Bivens* doctrine is discussed in Chapter 2.

7. Attorney's Fees. The Civil Rights Attorney's Fees Award Act of 1976, 42 U.S.C. § 1988(b), provides that, in cases brought to enforce § 1983 and other civil rights statutes, "the court, in its discretion, may allow the prevailing party, other than the United States, a reasonable attorney's fee as part of the costs." Though this language does not distinguish between successful plaintiffs and successful defendants, the Supreme Court has ruled that defendants should receive fees only when the suit was "vexatious, frivolous, or brought to harass or embarrass the defendant." *Hensley v. Eckerhart*, 461 U.S. 424, 429 n.2 (1983). For this reason, nearly all of the litigation focuses on identifying the circumstances in which the plaintiff is a "prevailing party" and on what is a "reasonable" attorney's fee.

While these issues cannot be fully developed here, a few basic points should be noted. One is that the plaintiff must have won a judgment in order to count as a prevailing party. A defendant's change of behavior, by itself, is not sufficient, even if the litigation was a "catalyst" in bringing about the change. *Buckhannon Board & Care Home v. West Virginia Department of Health & Human Resources*, 532 U.S. 598 (2001). A plaintiff who is awarded nominal damages is a prevailing party, yet the fee award should reflect the relative lack of success that such an award may manifest. *Farrar v. Hobby*, 506 U.S. 103 (1992). A plaintiff who obtains a preliminary injunction but then loses on the merits is not a prevailing party. *Sole v. Wyner*, 551 U.S. 74 (2007).

A "reasonable" fee is calculated by first determining a plausible hourly fee for lawyers similar to those involved in the suit in the locality, and then multiplying that fee by the number of hours reasonably spent on the case. This figure, called the "lodestar," may then be augmented to reflect the difficulty or importance of the case, or reduced to reflect time spent on unsuccessful claims. See *Hensley*, supra. For an illustration, see *Atlanta Journal and Constitution v. City of Atlanta Department of Aviation*, 442 F.3d

1283 (11th Cir. 2006) (newspapers challenged the city's regulation of newspaper racks at the municipal airport, prevailing on some issues and losing on others; the 11th Circuit approved a 20% reduction from the lodestar). The Prison Litigation Reform Act, 42 U.S.C. § 1997e(d), limits defendants' liability for attorney's fees to 150% of the money judgment when the suit deals with prison conditions. See, e.g., *Robbins v. Chronister*, 402 F.3d 1047 (10th Cir. 2005) (declining to apply this limitation to a pre-incarceration claim brought by someone who *subsequently* became a prisoner and brought the case while in prison).

II.   OFFICIAL IMMUNITY

Long before the revitalization of § 1983, aggrieved persons sued officials for common law torts and violations of statutes. Even where the plaintiff proves a violation, courts have long recognized a defense based on the notion that the officer was carrying out his official duties. The Court has construed § 1983 against this common law background. Though the statute says nothing about an "immunity" defense for officials who have violated the plaintiff's constitutional rights, the Supreme Court has always granted them one. Some officials enjoy "absolute" immunity, while others are only entitled to a "qualified" immunity. As will be seen, in the former case the officer cannot be sued even for knowing violations of constitutional rights. In the latter, the immunity is more circumscribed, yet it remains a formidable defense.

A.   ABSOLUTE IMMUNITY

FORRESTER V. WHITE
484 U.S. 219 (1988).

JUSTICE O'CONNOR delivered the opinion of the Court.

This case requires us to decide whether a state-court judge has absolute immunity from a suit for damages under 42 U.S.C. § 1983 for his decision to dismiss a subordinate court employee. The employee, who had been a probation officer, alleged that she was demoted and discharged on account of her sex, in violation of the Equal Protection Clause of the Fourteenth Amendment. We conclude that the judge's decisions were not judicial acts for which he should be held absolutely immune.

Respondent Howard Lee White served as Circuit Judge of the Seventh Judicial Circuit of the State of Illinois and Presiding Judge of the Circuit Court in Jersey County. Under Illinois law, Judge White had the authority to hire adult probation officers, who were removable in his discretion. In addition, as designee of the Chief Judge of the Seventh Judicial Circuit, Judge White had the authority to appoint juvenile probation officers to serve at his pleasure.

In April 1977, Judge White hired petitioner Cynthia A. Forrester as an adult and juvenile probation officer. Forrester prepared presentence reports for Judge White in adult offender cases, and recommendations for disposition and placement in juvenile cases. She also supervised persons on probation and recommended revocation when necessary. In July 1979, Judge White appointed Forrester as Project Supervisor of the Jersey County Juvenile Court Intake and Referral Services Project, a position that carried increased supervisory responsibilities. Judge White demoted Forrester to a nonsupervisory position in the summer of 1980. He discharged her on October 1, 1980.

Forrester filed this lawsuit in the United States District Court for the Southern District of Illinois in July 1982. She alleged violations of Title VII of the Civil Rights Act of 1964 and 42 U.S.C. § 1983. A jury found that Judge White had discriminated against Forrester on account of her sex, in violation of the Equal Protection Clause of the Fourteenth Amendment. The jury awarded her $81,818.80 in compensatory damages under § 1983. Forrester's other claims were dismissed in the course of the lawsuit.

[The trial judge then overrode the verdict, by granting White summary judgment on the ground that he was entitled to judicial immunity from a civil damages suit. The Seventh Circuit affirmed.]

II

Suits for monetary damages are meant to compensate the victims of wrongful actions and to discourage conduct that may result in liability. Special problems arise, however, when government officials are exposed to liability for damages. To the extent that the threat of liability encourages these officials to carry out their duties in a lawful and appropriate manner, and to pay their victims when they do not, it accomplishes exactly what it should. By its nature, however, the threat of liability can create perverse incentives that operate to inhibit officials in the proper performance of their duties. In many contexts, government officials are expected to make decisions that are impartial or imaginative, and that above all are informed by considerations other than the personal interests of the decision maker. Because government officials are engaged by definition in governing, their decisions will often have adverse effects on other persons. When officials are threatened with personal liability for acts taken pursuant to their official duties, they may well be induced to act with an excess of caution or otherwise to skew their decisions in ways that result in less than full fidelity to the objective and independent criteria that ought to guide their conduct. In this way, exposing government officials to the same legal hazards faced by other citizens may detract from the rule of law instead of contributing to it.

Such considerations have led to the creation of various forms of immunity from suit for certain government officials. Aware of the salutary effects that the threat of liability can have, however, as well as the undeniable tension between official immunities and the ideal of the rule of law, this Court has been cautious in recognizing claims that government officials should be free of the obligation to answer for their acts in court. Running through our cases, with fair consistency, is a "functional" approach to immunity questions other than those that have been decided by express constitutional or statutory enactment. Under that approach, we examine the nature of the functions with which a particular official or class of officials has been lawfully entrusted, and we seek to evaluate the effect that exposure to particular forms of liability would likely have on the appropriate exercise of those functions. Officials who seek exemption from personal liability have the burden of showing that such an exemption is justified by overriding considerations of public policy, and the Court has recognized a category of "qualified" immunity that avoids unnecessarily extending the scope of the traditional concept of absolute immunity. See [*Harlow v. Fitzgerald*, below].

This Court has generally been quite sparing in its recognition of claims to absolute official immunity. One species of such legal protection is beyond challenge: the legislative immunity created by the Speech or Debate Clause, U.S. Const., Art. I, § 6, cl. 1. Even here, however, the Court has been careful not to extend the scope of the protection further than its purposes require. Furthermore, on facts analogous to those in the case before us, the Court indicated that a United States Congressman would not be entitled to absolute immunity, in a sex-discrimination suit filed by a personal aide whom he had fired, unless such immunity was afforded by the Speech or Debate Clause. *Davis v. Passman*, 442 U.S. 228, 246 (1979).

[Among] executive officials, the President of the United States is absolutely immune from damages liability arising from official acts. *Nixon v. Fitzgerald*. This immunity, however, is based on the President's "unique position in the constitutional scheme," and it does not extend indiscriminately to the President's personal aides, see *Harlow*, or to Cabinet level officers. Nor are the highest executive officials in the States protected by absolute immunity under federal law.

III

As a class, judges have long enjoyed a comparatively sweeping form of immunity, though one not perfectly well-defined. Judicial immunity apparently originated, in medieval times, as a device for discouraging collateral attacks and thereby helping to establish appellate procedures as the standard system for correcting judicial error. More recently, this Court found that judicial immunity was "the settled doctrine of the English courts for many centuries, and has never been denied, that we are aware of, in the courts of this country." *Bradley v. Fisher*, 13 Wall. 335, 347 (1872). Besides protecting the finality of judgments or discouraging inappropriate collateral attacks, the *Bradley* Court concluded, judicial immunity also protected judicial independence by insulating judges from vexatious actions prosecuted by disgruntled litigants.

In the years since *Bradley* was decided, this Court has not been quick to find that federal legislation was meant to diminish the traditional common-law protections extended to the judicial process. On the contrary, these protections have been held to extend to Executive Branch officials who perform quasi-judicial functions, or who perform prosecutorial functions that are "intimately associated with the judicial phase of the criminal process," *Imbler v. Pachtman*, 424 U.S. 409, 430 (1976). The common law's rationale for these decisions—freeing the judicial process of harassment or intimidation—has been thought to require absolute immunity even for advocates and witnesses. See *Briscoe v. LaHue*, 460 U.S. 325 (1983).

One can reasonably wonder whether judges, who have been primarily responsible for developing the law of official immunities, are not inevitably more sensitive to the ill effects that vexatious lawsuits can have on the judicial function than they are to similar dangers in other contexts. Although Congress has not undertaken to cut back the judicial immunities recognized by this Court, we should be at least as cautious in extending those immunities as we have been when dealing with officials whose peculiar problems we know less well than our own. At the same time, we cannot pretend that we are writing on a clean slate or that we should ignore compelling reasons that may well justify broader protections for judges than for some other officials.

The purposes served by judicial immunity from liability in damages have been variously described. In *Bradley v. Fisher*, [the] Court emphasized that the nature of the adjudicative function requires a judge frequently to disappoint some of the most intense and ungovernable desires that people can have. As Judge Posner pointed out in his dissenting opinion below, this is the principal characteristic that adjudication has in common with legislation and with criminal prosecution, which are the two other areas in which absolute immunity has most generously been provided. If judges were personally liable for erroneous decisions, the resulting avalanche of suits, most of them frivolous but vexatious, would provide powerful incentives for judges to avoid rendering decisions likely to provoke such suits. The resulting timidity would be hard to detect or control, and it would manifestly detract from independent and impartial adjudication. Nor are suits against judges the only available means through which litigants can protect themselves from the consequences of judicial error. Most judicial mistakes or wrongs are open to correction through ordinary mechanisms of review, which are largely free of the harmful side-effects inevitably associated with exposing judges to personal liability.

When applied to the paradigmatic judicial acts involved in resolving disputes between parties who have invoked the jurisdiction of a court, the doctrine of absolute judicial immunity has not been particularly controversial. Difficulties have arisen primarily in attempting to draw the line between truly judicial acts, for which immunity is appropriate, and acts that simply happen to have been done by judges. Here, as in other contexts, immunity is justified and defined by the functions it protects and serves, not by the person to whom it attaches.

This Court has never undertaken to articulate a precise and general definition of the class of acts entitled to immunity. The decided cases, however, suggest an intelligible distinction between judicial acts and the administrative, legislative, or executive functions that judges may on occasion be assigned by law to perform. Thus, for example, the informal and ex parte nature of a proceeding has not been thought to imply that an act otherwise within a judge's lawful jurisdiction was deprived of its judicial character. See *Stump v. Sparkman*, 435 U.S. 349, 363, n. 12 (1978) [holding that judicial immunity bars a § 1983 action for damages against a judge who, in an ex parte proceeding, granted a petition by the parents of a 15 year old girl to have her sterilized without her knowledge.] Similarly, acting to disbar an attorney as a sanction for contempt of court, by invoking a power "possessed by all courts which have authority to admit attorneys to practice," does not become less judicial by virtue of an allegation of malice or corruption of motive. *Bradley v. Fisher*, 13 Wall., at 354. As the *Bradley* Court noted: "Against the consequences of [judges'] erroneous or irregular action, from whatever motives proceeding, the law has provided for private parties numerous remedies, and to those remedies they must, in such cases, resort." *Ibid*.

Administrative decisions, even though they may be essential to the very functioning of the courts, have not similarly been regarded as judicial acts. In *Ex parte Virginia*, 100 U.S. (10 Otto) 339 (1880), for example, this Court declined to extend immunity to a county judge who had been charged in a criminal indictment with discriminating on the basis of race in selecting trial jurors for the county's courts. The Court reasoned: "Whether the act done by him was judicial or not is to be determined by its character, and not by the character of the agent. Whether he was a county judge or not is of no importance. The duty of selecting jurors might as well have been committed to a private person as to one holding the office of a judge. . . . That the jurors are selected for a court makes no difference. So are court-criers, tipstaves, sheriffs, & c. Is their election or their appointment a judicial act?" Although this case involved a criminal charge against a judge, the reach of the Court's analysis was not in any obvious way confined by that circumstance.

Likewise, judicial immunity has not been extended to judges acting to promulgate a code of conduct for attorneys. *Supreme Court of Virginia v. Consumers Union of United States, Inc.*, 446 U.S. 719 (1980). In explaining why legislative, rather than judicial, immunity furnished the appropriate standard, we said: "Although it is clear that under Virginia law the issuance of the Bar Code was a proper function of the Virginia

Court, propounding the Code was not an act of adjudication but one of rulemaking." Similarly, in the same case, we held that judges acting to enforce the Bar Code would be treated like prosecutors, and thus would be amenable to suit for injunctive and declaratory relief. Once again, it was the nature of the function performed, not the identity of the actor who performed it, that informed our immunity analysis.

IV

In the case before us, we think it clear that Judge White was acting in an administrative capacity when he demoted and discharged Forrester. Those acts—like many others involved in supervising court employees and overseeing the efficient operation of a court—may have been quite important in providing the necessary conditions of a sound adjudicative system. The decisions at issue, however, were not themselves judicial or adjudicative. As Judge Posner pointed out below, a judge who hires or fires a probation officer cannot meaningfully be distinguished from a district attorney who hires and fires assistant district attorneys, or indeed from any other Executive Branch official who is responsible for making such employment decisions. Such decisions, like personnel decisions made by judges, are often crucial to the efficient operation of public institutions (some of which are at least as important as the courts), yet no one suggests that they give rise to absolute immunity from liability in damages under § 1983. The majority below thought that the threat of vexatious lawsuits by disgruntled ex-employees could interfere with the quality of a judge's decisions:

> "The evil to be avoided is the following: A judge loses confidence in his probation officer, but hesitates to fire him because of the threat of litigation. He then retains the officer, in which case the parties appearing before the court are the victims, because the quality of the judge's decision-making will decline."

There is considerable force in this analysis, but it in no way serves to distinguish judges from other public officials who hire and fire subordinates. Indeed, to the extent that a judge is less free than most Executive Branch officials to delegate decision making authority to subordinates, there may be somewhat less reason to cloak judges with absolute immunity from such suits than there would be to protect such other officials. This does not imply that qualified immunity, like that available to Executive Branch officials who make similar discretionary decisions, is unavailable to judges for their employment decisions. Absolute immunity, however, is "strong medicine, justified only when the danger of [officials' being] deflect[ed from the effective performance of their duties] is very great." 792 F.2d, at 660 (Posner, J., dissenting). The danger here is not great enough. Nor do we think it significant that, under Illinois law, only a judge can hire or fire probation officers. To conclude that, because a judge acts within the scope of his authority, such employment decisions are brought within the court's "jurisdiction," or converted into "judicial acts," would lift form above substance. Under Virginia law, only that State's judges could promulgate and enforce a Bar Code, but we nonetheless concluded that neither function was judicial in nature. See *Supreme Court of Virginia v. Consumers Union*, supra.

We conclude that Judge White was not entitled to absolute immunity for his decisions to demote and discharge Forrester. [The] judgment of the Court of Appeals is reversed, and the case is remanded for further proceedings consistent with this opinion.

NOTES ON ABSOLUTE IMMUNITY

1. Judicial Immunity and the "Functional" Approach. Under the functional approach illustrated by *Forrester*, judges are immune from liability for damages, no matter how badly they behave, so long as the act complained of is "judicial." *Mireles v. Waco*, 502 U.S. 9 (1991), involved a judge who, eager to get started on a trial despite the absence of one of the lawyers, told police officers to find the lawyer and bring him into the courtroom. The lawyer brought a § 1983 suit against the judge and the officers, charging that the judge ordered the officers "to seize and with excessive force bring plaintiff into his courtroom," that the officers had in fact used excessive force in carrying out this order, and that the judge "knowingly and deliberately approved and ratified" the officers' conduct. The Court dismissed the suit against the judge:

> Like other forms of official immunity, judicial immunity is an immunity from suit, not just from ultimate assessment of damages. Accordingly, judicial immunity is not overcome by allegations of bad faith or malice, the existence of which ordinarily cannot be resolved without engaging in discovery and eventual trial. Rather, our cases make clear that the immunity is overcome in only two sets of circumstances. First, a judge is not immune from liability for nonjudicial actions, i.e., actions not taken in the judge's judicial capacity. *Forrester*. Second, a judge is not immune for actions, though judicial in nature, taken in the complete absence of all jurisdiction. *Bradley*.

> We conclude that the Court of Appeals erred in ruling that Judge Mireles' alleged actions were not taken in his judicial capacity. This Court in *Stump* made clear that "whether an act by a judge is a 'judicial' one relate[s] to the nature of the act itself, i.e., whether it is a function normally performed by a judge, and to the expectations of the parties, i.e., whether they dealt with the judge in his judicial capacity." A judge's direction to court officers to bring a person who is in the courthouse before him is a function normally performed by a judge. Waco, who was called into the courtroom for purposes of a pending case, was dealing with Judge Mireles in the judge's judicial capacity.

Of course, a judge's direction to police officers to carry out a judicial order with excessive force is not a "function normally performed by a judge." But if only the particular act in question were to be scrutinized, then any mistake of a judge in excess of his authority would become a "nonjudicial" act, because an improper or erroneous act cannot be said to be normally performed by a judge. If judicial immunity means anything, it means that a judge "will not be deprived of immunity because the action he took was in error . . . or was in excess of his authority." [*Stump.*] Accordingly, as the language in *Stump* indicates, the relevant inquiry is the "nature" and "function" of the act, not the "act itself." In other words, we look to the particular act's relation to a general function normally performed by a judge, in this case the function of directing police officers to bring counsel in a pending case before the court.

Nor does the fact that Judge Mireles' order was carried out by police officers somehow transform his action from "judicial" to "executive" in character. As *Forrester* instructs, it is "the nature of the function performed, not the identity of the actor who performed it, that inform[s] our immunity analysis." A judge's direction to an executive officer to bring counsel before the court is no more executive in character than a judge's issuance of a warrant for an executive officer to search a home.

Because the Court of Appeals concluded that Judge Mireles did not act in his judicial capacity, the court did not reach the second part of the immunity inquiry: whether Judge Mireles' actions were taken in the complete absence of all jurisdiction. We have little trouble concluding that they were not. If Judge Mireles authorized and ratified the police officers' use of excessive force, he acted in excess of his authority. But such an action—taken in the very aid of the judge's jurisdiction over a matter before him—cannot be said to have been taken in the absence of jurisdiction.

2. Prosecutorial Immunity. A prosecutor is absolutely immune from liability for damages for constitutional violations "when he acts within the scope of his prosecutorial duties." *Imbler v. Pachtman*, 424 U.S. 409 (1976). Imbler had been the prosecuting attorney in a criminal case against Pachtman. Pachtman then sued Imbler under § 1983, claiming that Imbler had knowingly used perjured testimony against him. The Court ruled that absolute prosecutorial immunity applied, as the examination of witnesses in the course of a criminal trial is a prosecutorial function:

To be sure, this immunity does leave the genuinely wronged defendant without civil redress against a prosecutor whose malicious or dishonest action deprives him of liberty. But the alternative of qualifying a prosecutor's immunity would disserve the broader public interest. It would prevent the vigorous and fearless performance of the prosecutor's duty that is essential to the proper functioning of the criminal justice system. Moreover, it often would prejudice defendants in criminal cases by skewing post-conviction judicial decisions that should be made with the sole purpose of insuring justice. [We] emphasize that the immunity of prosecutors from suits under § 1983 does not leave the public powerless to deter misconduct or to punish that which occurs. This Court has never suggested that the policy considerations which compel civil immunity for certain governmental officials also place them beyond the reach of the criminal law. Even judges, cloaked with absolute civil immunity for centuries, could be punished criminally. [The] prosecutor would fare no better for his wilful acts. Moreover, a prosecutor stands perhaps unique, among officials whose acts could deprive persons of constitutional rights, in his amenability to professional discipline by an association of his peers. These checks undermine the argument that the imposition of civil liability is the only way to insure that prosecutors are mindful of the constitutional rights of persons accused of crime.

Are you persuaded that the benefits of prosecutorial immunity are worth the costs?

In a number of cases the Court has addressed the problem of distinguishing between "prosecutorial functions," for which absolute immunity is the rule, and other aspects of a prosecutor's job, for which he is entitled to only qualified immunity. In *Van de Kamp v. Goldstein*, 555 U.S. 335 (2009), for example, a unanimous Court ruled that prosecutors are absolutely immune from liability for failure to properly supervise and train subordinates, even where the failure leads to a violation of the plaintiff's constitutional rights. Most of the Supreme Court cases concern drawing the line between prosecuting and investigating crime. When prosecutors collaborate with the police in initiating or conducting investigations, they receive only the qualified immunity that is available to the police. Prosecutorial functions include initiating a prosecution, conducting a trial, and applying for a search warrant. On the other hand, *testifying* in support of a warrant, as by sworn statements in an affidavit, is not a prosecutorial function. *Kalina v. Fletcher*, 522 U.S. 118 (1997). Providing legal advice to the police is not a prosecutorial function, *Burns v. Reed*, 500 U.S. 478 (1991) (distinguishing between advocative and investigative conduct). Nor is absolute immunity available where the charge is that the prosecutor fabricated evidence in order to establish probable cause for an arrest. *Buckley v. Fitzsimmons*, 509 U.S. 259 (1993). *Buckley* also rejected absolute immunity for comments made by prosecutors to the media.

3. Absolute Legislative Immunity. In *Tenney v. Brandhove*, 341 U.S. 367 (1951), the Court relied on the history of legislative immunity in holding that state legislators may not be sued for damages under § 1983. The Court extended the immunity to *local* legislators in *Bogan v. Scott-Harris*, 523 U.S. 44 (1998). Writing for the Court, Justice Thomas recounted the history of legislative immunity, and then turned to policy considerations:

Absolute immunity for local legislators under § 1983 finds support not only in history, but also in [reason]. The rationales for according absolute immunity to federal, state, and regional legislators apply with equal force to local legislators. Regardless of the level of government, the exercise of legislative discretion should not be inhibited by judicial interference or distorted by the fear of personal [liability]. Furthermore, the time and energy required to defend against a lawsuit are of particular concern at the local level, where the part-time citizen-legislator remains [commonplace]. And the threat of liability may significantly deter service in local government, where prestige and pecuniary rewards may pale in comparison to the threat of civil liability. Moreover, certain deterrents to legislative abuse may be greater at the local level than at other levels of government. Municipalities themselves can be held liable for constitutional violations, whereas States and the Federal Government are often protected by sovereign immunity. And, of course, the ultimate check on legislative abuse—the electoral process—applies with equal force at the local level, where legislators are often more closely responsible to the [electorate]. Any argument that the rationale for absolute immunity does not extend to local legislators is implicitly foreclosed by our opinion in [*Lake Country Estates v. Tahoe Regional Planning Agency*]. There, we held that members of an interstate regional planning agency were entitled to absolute legislative immunity. Bereft of any historical antecedent to the regional agency, we relied almost exclusively on Tenney's description of the purposes of legislative immunity and the importance of such immunity in advancing the "public good." Although we expressly noted that local legislators were not at issue in that case, we considered the regional legislators at issue to be the functional equivalents of local legislators, noting that the regional agency was "comparable to a county or municipality" and that the function of the regional agency, regulation of land use, was "traditionally a function performed by local governments." Thus, we now make explicit what was implicit in our precedents: Local legislators are entitled to absolute immunity from § 1983 liability for their legislative activities.

Bogan then addressed the issue of what counts as a "legislative activity":

Respondent Janet Scott-Harris was administrator of the Department of Health and Human Services (DHHS) for the city of Fall River, Massachusetts, from 1987 to 1991. In 1990, respondent received a complaint that Dorothy Biltcliffe, an employee serving temporarily under her supervision, had made repeated racial and ethnic slurs about her colleagues. After respondent prepared termination charges against Biltcliffe, Biltcliffe used her political connections to press her case with several state and local officials, including petitioner Marilyn Roderick, the vice president of the Fall

River City Council. The city council held a hearing on the charges against Biltcliffe and ultimately accepted a settlement proposal under which Biltcliffe would be suspended without pay for 60 days. Petitioner Daniel Bogan, the mayor of Fall River, thereafter substantially reduced the punishment. While the charges against Biltcliffe were pending, Mayor Bogan prepared his budget proposal for the 1992 fiscal year. Anticipating a 5 to 10 percent reduction in state aid, Bogan proposed freezing the salaries of all municipal employees and eliminating 135 city positions. As part of this package, Bogan called for the elimination of DHHS, of which respondent was the sole employee. The city council ordinance committee, which was chaired by Roderick, approved an ordinance eliminating DHHS. The city council thereafter adopted the ordinance by a vote of 6 to 2, with petitioner Roderick among those voting in favor. Bogan signed the ordinance into law. Respondent then filed suit under [§ 1983] against the city, Bogan, Roderick, and several other city officials. She alleged that the elimination of her position was motivated by racial animus and a desire to retaliate against her for exercising her First Amendment rights in filing the complaint against [Biltcliffe]. The jury [found] the city, Bogan, and Roderick liable on respondent's First Amendment claim, concluding that respondent's constitutionally protected speech was a substantial or motivating factor in the elimination of her position.

Reversing the lower court, the Supreme Court held that the suit against the officials should have been dismissed under the legislative immunity rule:

Absolute legislative immunity attaches to all actions taken "in the sphere of legitimate legislative activity." *Tenney*. The Court of Appeals held that petitioners' conduct in this case was not legislative because their actions were specifically targeted at respondent. Relying on the jury's finding that respondent's constitutionally protected speech was a substantial or motivating factor behind petitioners' conduct, the court concluded that petitioners necessarily "relied on facts relating to a particular individual" and "devised an ordinance that targeted [respondent] and treated her differently from other managers employed by the City." Although the Court of Appeals did not suggest that intent or motive can overcome an immunity defense for activities that are, in fact, legislative, the court erroneously relied on petitioners' subjective intent in resolving the logically prior question of whether their acts were legislative. Whether an act is legislative turns on the nature of the act, rather than on the motive or intent of the official performing it. The privilege of absolute immunity "would be of little value if [legislators] could be subjected to the cost and inconvenience and distractions of a trial upon a conclusion of the pleader, or to the hazard of a judgment against them based upon a jury's speculation as to motives." [*Tenney*.] Furthermore, it simply is "not consonant with our scheme of government for a court to inquire into the motives of legislators." We therefore held that the defendant in *Tenney* had acted in a legislative capacity even though he allegedly singled out the plaintiff for investigation in order "to intimidate and silence plaintiff and deter and prevent him from effectively exercising his constitutional rights." This leaves us with the question whether, stripped of all considerations of intent and motive, petitioners' actions were legislative. We have little trouble concluding that they were. Most evidently, petitioner Roderick's acts of voting for an ordinance were, in form, quintessentially legislative. Petitioner Bogan's introduction of a budget and signing into law an ordinance also were formally legislative, even though he was an executive official. We have recognized that officials outside the legislative branch are entitled to legislative immunity when they perform legislative functions, see *Supreme Court of Va. v. Consumers Union of United States, Inc.*, 446 U.S. 719 (1980); Bogan's actions were legislative because they were integral steps in the legislative [process]. Respondent, however, asks us to look beyond petitioners' formal actions to consider whether the ordinance was legislative in substance. We need not determine whether the formally legislative character of petitioners' actions is alone sufficient to entitle petitioners to legislative immunity, because here the ordinance, in substance, bore all the hallmarks of traditional legislation. The ordinance reflected a discretionary, policymaking decision implicating the budgetary priorities of the city and the services the city provides to its constituents. Moreover, it involved the termination of a position, which, unlike the hiring or firing of a particular employee, may have prospective implications that reach well beyond the particular occupant of the office. And the city council, in eliminating DHHS, certainly governed "in a field where legislators traditionally have power to act." *Tenney*. Thus, petitioners' activities were undoubtedly legislative.

Compare *Kaahumanu v. Maui County*, 315 F.3d 1215 (9th Cir. 2003). Here the issue was whether absolute legislative immunity applied to a county council's decision (embodied in an ordinance) to deny a conditional use permit for conducting a commercial wedding business on beach-front residential property. The court held that this was an administrative rather than a legislative act and thus denied absolute immunity:

> We determine whether an action is legislative by considering four factors: (1) whether the act involves ad hoc decision making, or the formulation of policy; (2) whether the act applies to a few individuals or to the public at large; (3) whether the act is formally legislative in character; and (4) whether it bears all the hallmarks of traditional legislation.

Applying these factors, the court found that (1) the decision whether to grant a permit was ad hoc, because "it was taken based on the circumstances of the particular case and did not effectuate policy or create a binding rule of conduct;" (2) "the very limited impact of the conditional use permit at issue here weighs against absolute immunity;" (3) while "the formally legislative character of" the decision "weighs in favor of legislative immunity, it does not in itself decide the issue;" (4) "in denying a single application for a CUP, the Council did not change Maui's comprehensive zoning ordinance or the policies underlying it, nor did it affect the County's budgetary priorities or the services the County provides to residents." The Court addressed *Bogan* in its analysis of this last factor, by quoting from the last four sentences in the excerpt above, and drawing a contrast between the two cases. Did *Kaahumanu* convincingly distinguish *Bogan*?

4.   Implications of the Functional Approach for Officers Other than Judges, Prosecutors, and Legislators. *Forrester*, *Burns*, and *Buckley* illustrate that, under the functional approach to absolute immunity, the defendant's job title does not automatically entitle him to absolute immunity. Conversely, persons who are not ordinarily considered to be judges, legislators, or prosecutors are covered by absolute immunity when they carry out judicial, legislative, or prosecutorial functions. Recall the discussion in *Forrester* of *Supreme Court of Virginia v. Consumers Union*, in which the Court held that the Justices of the Virginia Supreme Court exercised a legislative function when they enacted a bar ethics code. See also *Holloway v. Ohio*, 179 F.3d 431, 441 (6th Cir. 1999) (noting that courts generally afford social workers "absolute immunity for the functions that they perform which are prosecutorial, judicial, or otherwise intimately related to the judicial process"); *Mayorga v. Missouri*, 442 F.3d 1128, 1131 (8th Cir. 2006) ("Parole board members are entitled to absolute immunity when considering and deciding parole questions, as this function is comparable to that of judges".).

Is the police officer who carried out Judge Mireles' order entitled to absolute immunity? Compare *Martin v. Hendren*, 127 F.3d 720 (8th Cir. 1997) (police officer is entitled to absolute quasi-judicial immunity for carrying out judge's order to handcuff plaintiff and remove her from the courtroom) with *Richman v. Sheahan*, 270 F.3d 430 (7th Cir. 2001) (police officer gets only qualified immunity). See generally Sheldon H. Nahmod, *From the Courtroom to the Street: Court Orders and Section 1983*, 29 HASTINGS CONST. L.Q. 613 (2002).

5.   Is Function the Sole Factor? In *Cleavinger v. Saxner*, 474 U.S. 193 (1985) the defendants were prison officials who served on the prison's Institution Discipline Committee (IDC). The plaintiffs were prisoners who had been charged with inciting other prisoners not to work, and with other offenses. After a hearing, the IDC found against the prisoners, who as a result spent time in "administrative detention." The prisoners then sued the IDC members, claiming violations of their First, Fourth, Fifth, Sixth, and Eighth Amendment rights. The issue before the Supreme Court was whether the officials were entitled to absolute judicial immunity from liability for damages. The Court held that they were not. After reiterating the functional approach to absolute immunity, the Court denied them absolute immunity, and held that they enjoyed only qualified immunity:

> We do not perceive the disciplinary committee's function as a 'classic' adjudicatory one. [Surely,] the members of the committee, unlike a federal or state judge, are not 'independent'; to say that they are is to ignore reality. They are not professional hearing officers, as are administrative law judges. They are, instead, prison officials, albeit no longer of the rank and file, temporarily diverted from their usual duties. They are employees of the Bureau of Prisons and they are the direct subordinates of the warden who reviews their decisions. They work with the fellow employee who lodges the charge against the inmate upon whom they sit in judgment. The credibility judgment they make often is one between a co-worker and an inmate. They thus are under obvious pressure to resolve a disciplinary dispute in favor of the institution and their fellow employee. It is the old situational problem of the relationship between the keeper and the kept, a relationship that hardly is conducive to a truly adjudicatory performance.

In *Cleavinger* the Court insists that it is applying the functional approach. Does the difference (whatever it may be) between the function exercised by a judge in a criminal case and the function exercised by the *Cleavinger* defendants fully explain the Court's ruling? In this regard, consider the following hypothetical case:

> Under state law, the municipal governing body, composed of elected commissioners, chooses the municipal court judge. The commission has dismissed a judge for laxity in meting out sentences for violations of local ordinances and has appointed a new judge—call her *K*—for a probationary period, with the understanding that *K* will then be considered for longer term employment based on a review of her performance. Suppose that *K* rules against a local resident for violating a noise ordinance and imposes a fine. The resident sues *K*, charging constitutional violations and seeking damages. Is *K* entitled to absolute judicial immunity? If so, how would you distinguish *Cleavinger*? If not, why not? Is the reason for denying immunity adequately described by the assertion that K was not exercising a judicial function?

6. Prospective Relief. Legislators are absolutely immune not only from liability for damages but from suits for injunctive relief as well. By contrast, the immunity of prosecutors extends only to protection against suits for damages. Though there may be other obstacles in the plaintiff's way (some are discussed in Chapters 4 and 6) prosecutors have no immunity against suits for prospective relief. For example, in *Supreme Court of Virginia v. Consumers Union*, 446 U.S. 719 (1980), the Court ruled that the Justices could not be sued at all for the legislative function of promulgating a bar ethics code, but could be sued for prospective relief for enforcing the code, as this was a prosecutorial rather than a legislative function. When judges exercise judicial functions, the situation is more complicated. In *Pulliam v. Allen*, 466 U.S. 522 (1984), the Court ruled that judges may be sued for prospective relief. The two forms of prospective relief are injunctions (which order the officer to act or not to act in some way) and declaratory judgments (which simply state the rights and duties of the parties). After *Pulliam*, Congress amended § 1983 to forbid injunctive relief against a judge "unless a declaratory decree was violated or declaratory relief was unavailable." See, e.g., *Tesmer v. Granholm*, 333 F.3d 683 (6th Cir. 2003) (holding that, even where injunctive relief is appropriate against judges who were parties to the original suit, it may not extend to non-party judges who have failed to abide by the declaratory decree).

Given that prospective relief may be obtained against prosecutors (and, in modified form, against judges), does its unavailability against legislators make any practical difference? Suppose the plaintiff in *Bogan* has a good case on the merits: Does she have any recourse in view of absolute legislative immunity?

B. QUALIFIED IMMUNITY

While some officials are entitled to absolute immunity from liability for damages, no matter how egregious their conduct, others enjoy "qualified" immunity, which they may lose in the event they violate "clearly established law." The level of immunity available to an official depends on the function he performed in taking the action that gave rise to the litigation. In *Forrester*, the Court ruled that an employment decision is the exercise of an "administrative" rather than a "judicial" function, so that the judge was entitled to no more than qualified immunity. *Harlow v. Fitzgerald* is the leading case on the scope of qualified immunity doctrine in constitutional cases.

HARLOW V. FITZGERALD
457 U.S. 800 (1982).

JUSTICE POWELL delivered the opinion of the Court.

The issue in this case is the scope of the immunity available to the senior aides and advisers of the President of the United States in a suit for damages based upon their official acts.

I

In this suit for civil damages petitioners Bryce Harlow and Alexander Butterfield are alleged to have participated in a conspiracy to violate the constitutional and statutory rights of the respondent A. Ernest Fitzgerald. Respondent avers that petitioners entered the conspiracy in their capacities as senior White House aides to former President Richard M. Nixon. [Fitzgerald, as a federal employee, had publicly charged his superiors with misconduct, and had been fired. In this lawsuit, he claimed that President Nixon and his aides conspired to have him dismissed, and that their actions violated his constitutional rights.]

Respondent claims that Harlow joined the conspiracy in his role as the Presidential aide principally responsible for congressional relations. [As] evidence of Harlow's conspiratorial activity respondent relies heavily on a series of conversations in which Harlow discussed Fitzgerald's dismissal with Air Force Secretary Robert Seamans. The other evidence most supportive of Fitzgerald's claims consists of a recorded conversation in which the President later voiced a tentative recollection that Harlow was "all for canning" Fitzgerald. Petitioner Butterfield also is alleged to have entered the conspiracy not later than May [1969].

Together with their codefendant Richard Nixon, petitioners Harlow and Butterfield moved for summary judgment on February 12, 1980. In denying the motion the District Court upheld the legal sufficiency of Fitzgerald's *Bivens* (*Bivens v. Six Unknown Fed. Narcotics Agents*, 403 U.S. 388 (1971)) claim under the First Amendment and his "inferred" statutory causes of [action]. It also ruled that petitioners were not entitled to absolute immunity. [In *Nixon v. Fitzgerald*, 457 U.S. 731 (1982), the Supreme Court held that the President is absolutely immune from damage awards for official misconduct.] Independently of former President Nixon, petitioners [appealed] the denial of their immunity defense to the Court of Appeals for the District of Columbia Circuit. The Court of Appeals dismissed the appeal without opinion. Never having determined the immunity available to the senior aides and advisers of the President of the United States, we granted certiorari.

II

[Our] decisions consistently have held that government officials are entitled to some form of immunity from suits for damages. As recognized at common law, public officers require this protection to shield them from undue interference with their duties and from potentially disabling threats of liability. Our decisions have recognized immunity defenses of two kinds. For officials whose special functions or constitutional status requires complete protection from suit, we have recognized the defense of "absolute immunity." The absolute immunity of legislators, in their legislative functions, and of judges, in their judicial functions, now is well settled. Our decisions also have extended absolute immunity to certain officials of the Executive Branch. These include prosecutors and similar officials, executive officers engaged in adjudicative functions, and the President of the United States.

For executive officials in general, however, our cases make plain that qualified immunity represents the norm. In *Scheuer v. Rhodes* we acknowledged that high officials require greater protection than those with less complex discretionary responsibilities. Nonetheless, we held that a governor and his aides could receive the requisite protection from qualified or good-faith immunity. In *Butz v. Economou*, we extended the approach of *Scheuer* to high federal officials of the Executive Branch. Discussing in detail the considerations that also had underlain our decision in *Scheuer*, we explained that the recognition of a qualified immunity defense for high executives reflected an attempt to balance competing values: not only the importance of a damages remedy to protect the rights of citizens, but also "the need to protect officials who are required to exercise their discretion and the related public interest in encouraging the vigorous exercise of official authority." Without discounting the adverse consequences of denying high officials an absolute immunity from private lawsuits alleging constitutional violations—consequences found sufficient in *Spalding v. Vilas*, and *Barr v. Matteo*, to warrant extension to such officials of absolute immunity from suits at common law—we emphasized our expectation that insubstantial suits need not proceed to trial:

> "Insubstantial lawsuits can be quickly terminated by federal courts alert to the possibilities of artful pleading. Unless the complaint states a compensable claim for relief . . . , it should not survive a motion to dismiss. Moreover, [damages] suits concerning constitutional violations need not proceed to trial, but can be terminated on a properly supported motion for summary judgment based on the defense of immunity. . . . In responding to such a motion, plaintiffs may not play dog in the manger; and firm application of the Federal Rules of Civil Procedure will ensure that federal officials are not harassed by frivolous lawsuits."

Butz continued to acknowledge that the special functions of some officials might require absolute immunity. But the Court held that "federal officials who seek absolute exemption from personal liability for unconstitutional conduct must bear the burden of showing that public policy requires an exemption of that scope." This we reaffirmed today in *Nixon v. Fitzgerald*, [which held that the President has absolute immunity].

III

Petitioners argue that they are entitled to a blanket protection of absolute immunity as an incident of their offices as Presidential aides. In deciding this claim we do not write on an empty page. In *Butz v. Economou*, the Secretary of Agriculture—a Cabinet official directly accountable to the President—asserted a defense of absolute official immunity from suit for civil damages. We rejected his claim. In so doing we did not question the power or the importance of the Secretary's office. Nor did we doubt the importance to the President of loyal and efficient subordinates in executing his duties of office. Yet we found these factors, alone, to be insufficient to justify absolute immunity. "[T]he greater power of [high] officials," we reasoned, "affords a greater potential for a regime of lawless conduct." Damages actions against high officials were therefore "an important means of vindicating constitutional guarantees." Moreover, we concluded that it would be "untenable to draw a distinction for purposes of immunity law between suits brought against state officials under [42 U.S.C.] § 1983 and suits brought directly under the Constitution against federal officials."

Having decided in *Butz* that Members of the Cabinet ordinarily enjoy only qualified immunity from suit, we conclude today that it would be equally untenable to hold absolute immunity an incident of the office of every Presidential subordinate based in the White House. Members of the Cabinet are direct subordinates of the President, frequently with greater responsibilities, both to the President and to the Nation, than White House staff. The considerations that supported our decision in *Butz* apply with equal force to this case. It is no disparagement of the offices held by petitioners to hold that Presidential aides, like Members of the Cabinet, generally are entitled only to a qualified immunity.

Petitioners also assert an entitlement to immunity based on the "special functions" of White House [aides]. For aides entrusted with discretionary authority in such sensitive areas as national security or foreign policy, absolute immunity might well be justified to protect the unhesitating performance of functions vital to the national interest. But a "special functions" rationale does not warrant a blanket recognition of absolute immunity for all Presidential aides in the performance of all their duties. This conclusion too follows from our decision in *Butz*, which establishes that an executive official's claim to absolute immunity must be justified by reference to the public interest in the special functions of his office, not the mere fact of high station. In order to establish entitlement to absolute immunity a Presidential aide first must show that the responsibilities of his office embraced a function so sensitive as to require a total shield from liability. He then must demonstrate that he was discharging the protected function when performing the act for which liability is asserted.

Applying these standards to the claims advanced by petitioners Harlow and Butterfield, we cannot conclude on the record before us that either has shown that "public policy requires [for any of the functions of his office] an exemption of [absolute] scope." *Butz.* Nor, assuming that petitioners did have functions for which absolute immunity would be warranted, could we now conclude that the acts charged in this lawsuit— if taken at all—would lie within the protected area. We do not, however, foreclose the possibility that petitioners, on remand, could satisfy the standards properly applicable to their claims.

IV

Even if they cannot establish that their official functions require absolute immunity, petitioners assert that public policy at least mandates an application of the qualified immunity standard that would permit the defeat of insubstantial claims without resort to trial. We agree.

A

The resolution of immunity questions inherently requires a balance between the evils inevitable in any available alternative. In situations of abuse of office, an action for damages may offer the only realistic avenue for vindication of constitutional guarantees. It is this recognition that has required the denial of absolute immunity to most public officers. At the same time, however, it cannot be disputed seriously that claims frequently run against the innocent as well as the guilty—at a cost not only to the defendant officials, but to society as a whole. These social costs include the expenses of litigation, the diversion of official energy from pressing public issues, and the deterrence of able citizens from acceptance of public office. Finally, there is the danger that fear of being sued will "dampen the ardor of all but the most resolute, or the most irresponsible [public officials], in the unflinching discharge of their duties." *Gregoire v. Biddle*, 177 F.2d 579, 581 (CA2 1949).

In identifying qualified immunity as the best attainable accommodation of competing values, in *Butz*, supra, we relied on the assumption that this standard would permit "[i]nsubstantial lawsuits [to] be quickly terminated." Yet petitioners advance persuasive arguments that the dismissal of insubstantial lawsuits without trial—a factor presupposed in the balance of competing interests struck by our prior cases—requires an adjustment of the "good faith" standard established by our decisions.

B

Qualified or "good faith" immunity is an affirmative defense that must be pleaded by a defendant official. Decisions of this Court have established that the "good faith" defense has both an "objective" and a "subjective" aspect. The objective element involves a presumptive knowledge of and respect for "basic, unquestioned constitutional rights." *Wood v. Strickland*, 420 U.S. 308, 322 (1975). The subjective component refers to "permissible intentions." *Ibid.* Characteristically the Court has defined these elements by identifying the circumstances in which qualified immunity would not be available. Referring both to the objective and subjective elements, we have held that qualified immunity would be defeated if an official *"knew or reasonably should have known* that the action he took within his sphere of official responsibility would violate the constitutional rights of the [plaintiff], *or* if he took the action *with the malicious intention* to cause a deprivation of constitutional rights or other injury. . . ." Ibid. (emphasis added).

The subjective element of the good-faith defense frequently has proved incompatible with our admonition in *Butz* that insubstantial claims should not proceed to trial. Rule 56 of the Federal Rules of Civil Procedure provides that disputed questions of fact ordinarily may not be decided on motions for summary judgment. And an official's subjective good faith has been considered to be a question of fact that some courts have regarded as inherently requiring resolution by a jury.

In the context of *Butz'* attempted balancing of competing values, it now is clear that substantial costs attend the litigation of the subjective good faith of government officials. Not only are there the general costs of subjecting officials to the risks of trial—distraction of officials from their governmental duties, inhibition of discretionary action, and deterrence of able people from public service. There are special costs to "subjective" inquiries of this kind. Immunity generally is available only to officials performing discretionary functions. In contrast with the thought processes accompanying "ministerial" tasks, the judgments surrounding discretionary action almost inevitably are influenced by the decision maker's experiences, values, and emotions. These variables explain in part why questions of subjective intent so rarely can be decided by summary judgment. Yet they also frame a background in which there often is no clear end to the relevant evidence. Judicial inquiry into subjective motivation therefore may entail broad-ranging discovery and the deposing of numerous persons, including an official's professional colleagues. Inquiries of this kind can be peculiarly disruptive of effective government.

Consistently with the balance at which we aimed in *Butz*, we conclude today that bare allegations of malice should not suffice to subject government officials either to the costs of trial or to the burdens of broad-reaching discovery. We therefore hold that government officials performing discretionary functions generally are shielded from liability for civil damages insofar as their conduct does not violate clearly established statutory or constitutional rights of which a reasonable person would have known.[30]

Reliance on the objective reasonableness of an official's conduct, as measured by reference to clearly established law, should avoid excessive disruption of government and permit the resolution of many insubstantial claims on summary judgment. On summary judgment, the judge appropriately may determine, not only the currently applicable law, but whether that law was clearly established at the time an action occurred. If the law at that time was not clearly established, an official could not reasonably be expected to anticipate subsequent legal developments, nor could he fairly be said to "know" that the law forbade conduct not previously identified as unlawful. Until this threshold immunity question is resolved, discovery should not be allowed. If the law was clearly

---

[30] This case involves no issue concerning the elements of the immunity available to state officials sued for constitutional violations under 42 U.S.C. § 1983. We have found previously, however, that it would be "untenable to draw a distinction for purposes of immunity law between suits brought against state officials under § 1983 and suits brought directly under the Constitution against federal officials." *Butz v. Economou*, 438 U.S., at 504.

Our decision in no way diminishes the absolute immunity currently available to officials whose functions have been held to require a protection of this scope.

established, the immunity defense ordinarily should fail, since a reasonably competent public official should know the law governing his conduct. Nevertheless, if the official pleading the defense claims extraordinary circumstances and can prove that he neither knew nor should have known of the relevant legal standard, the defense should be sustained. But again, the defense would turn primarily on objective factors.

By defining the limits of qualified immunity essentially in objective terms, we provide no license to lawless conduct. The public interest in deterrence of unlawful conduct and in compensation of victims remains protected by a test that focuses on the objective legal reasonableness of an official's acts. Where an official could be expected to know that certain conduct would violate statutory or constitutional rights, he should be made to hesitate; and a person who suffers injury caused by such conduct may have a cause of action. But where an official's duties legitimately require action in which clearly established rights are not implicated, the public interest may be better served by action taken "with independence and without fear of consequences."[34]

C

In this case petitioners have asked us to hold that the respondent's pretrial showings were insufficient to survive their motion for summary judgment.[35] We think it appropriate, however, to remand the case to the District Court for its reconsideration of this issue in light of this opinion. The trial court is more familiar with the record so far developed and also is better situated to make any such further findings as may be [necessary].

JUSTICE BRENNAN, with whom JUSTICE MARSHALL, and JUSTICE BLACKMUN join, concurring.

I agree with the substantive standard announced by the Court today, imposing liability when a public-official defendant "knew or should have known" of the constitutionally violative effect of his actions. This standard would not allow the official who actually knows that he was violating the law to escape liability for his actions, even if he could not "reasonably have been expected" to know what he actually did know. Thus the clever and unusually well-informed violator of constitutional rights will not evade just punishment for his crimes. I also agree that this standard applies "across the board," to all "government officials performing discretionary functions." I write separately only to note that given this standard, it seems inescapable to me that some measure of discovery may sometimes be required to determine exactly what a public-

---

[34] We emphasize that our decision applies only to suits for civil damages arising from actions within the scope of an official's duties and in "objective" good faith. We express no view as to the conditions in which injunctive or declaratory relief might be available.

[35] In *Butz*, we admonished that "insubstantial" suits against high public officials should not be allowed to proceed to trial. We reiterate this [admonition].

official defendant did "know" at the time of his actions. In this respect the issue before us is very similar to that addressed in *Herbert v. Lando*, in which the Court observed that "[to] erect an impenetrable barrier to the plaintiff's use of such evidence on his side of the case is a matter of some substance, particularly when defendants themselves are prone to assert their [good faith]". Of course, as the Court has already noted, summary judgment will be readily available to public-official defendants whenever the state of the law was so ambiguous at the time of the alleged violation that it could not have been "known" then, and thus liability could not [ensue].

[Other concurring statements are omitted.]

CHIEF JUSTICE BURGER, dissenting.

[The Chief Justice contended that presidential aides should receive absolute immunity.] Precisely the same public policy considerations on which the Court now relies in *Nixon v. Fitzgerald*, [are] fully applicable to senior Presidential aides. The Court's opinion in *Nixon v. Fitzgerald* correctly points out that if a President were subject to suit, awareness of personal vulnerability to suit "frequently could distract a President from his public duties, to the detriment of not only the President and his office but also the Nation that the Presidency was designed to serve." This same negative incentive will permeate the inner workings of the Office of the President if the Chief Executive's "alter egos" are not protected derivatively from the immunity of the President. In addition, exposure to civil liability for official acts will result in constant judicial questioning, through judicial proceedings and pretrial discovery, into the inner workings of the Presidential Office beyond that necessary to maintain the traditional checks and balances of our constitutional [structure].

We—judges collectively—have held that the common law provides us with absolute immunity for ourselves with respect to judicial acts, however erroneous or ill-advised. Are the lowest ranking of 27,000 or more judges, thousands of prosecutors, and thousands of congressional aides—an aggregate of not less than 75,000 in all—entitled to greater protection than two senior aides of a President?

Butz v. Economou, 438 U.S. 478 (1978), does not dictate that senior Presidential aides be given only qualified immunity. *Butz* held only that a Cabinet officer exercising discretion was not entitled to absolute immunity; we need not abandon that holding. A senior Presidential aide works more intimately with the President on a daily basis than does a Cabinet officer, directly implementing Presidential decisions literally from hour to [hour].

NOTES ON QUALIFIED IMMUNITY

1. *Harlow* **and § 1983.** *Harlow* was not a § 1983 suit. The defendants were federal officers, acting under color of federal law. The plaintiff brought a

"*Bivens*" suit, named after the case in which the Court recognized the cause of action, as a matter of federal common law. See Chapter 2. In resolving the issues, the Court relied not on legislative history, but on policy considerations. Yet the holding applies to § 1983 suits. See, e.g., the Court's n.30. Does this way of dealing with immunity cast light on the role of nineteenth-century tort law and legislative intent in resolving issues that arise in § 1983 litigation? In some cases, the Court nonetheless resorts to a historical analysis or excavates the legislative history. See, e.g., the Court's reliance on history in *Forrester*.

2. "Special Functions": May Executive Officers Ever Assert Absolute Immunity? In *Harlow* the Court rejected the defendants' argument that they should enjoy absolute immunity, but left the door open for some executive officials (besides the President) to successfully assert such a claim. But, in the years since *Harlow*, the Court has not yet identified any executive official who may fall into the "special functions" category that it identified. Nor has it repudiated the notion that such a category may exist.

3. The "Discretionary"/"Ministerial" Distinction. The *Harlow* Court limits immunity—even of the "qualified" variety—to persons exercising "discretionary" functions, distinguishing "ministerial" ones. Discretionary functions are those that require the exercise of judgment, while ministerial ones, "such as bagging and delivering prisoner mail," *Procunier v. Navarette*, 434 U.S. 555, 569 (Stevens, J., dissenting), do not. The rationale for the distinction is that only the exercise of judgment deserves protection against constitutional tort liability. See also *Davis v. Scherer*, 468 U.S. 183, 196 (1984). Cf. *Westfall v. Erwin*, 484 U.S. 292 (1988). Here the plaintiff sued federal officers under state tort law. The Court ruled that the immunity of federal officers extends only to their discretionary, but not their ministerial, actions. The Court explained:

> The central purpose of official immunity, promoting effective government, would not be furthered by shielding an official from state law tort liability without regard to whether the alleged tortious conduct is discretionary in nature. When an official's conduct is not the product of independent judgment, the threat of liability cannot detrimentally inhibit that conduct. *Id.* at 296–97.

After *Westfall* Congress amended the Federal Tort Claims Act to eliminate such suits against federal officers, by providing that a suit against the United States would be the exclusive remedy, see *United States v. Smith*, 499 U.S. 160, 163 (1991). Does that development undercut the Court's discussion of the discretionary/ministerial distinction?

4. Injunctive Relief. In its footnote 34, the Court takes care to distinguish the issue at hand—liability for damages—from injunctive and declaratory relief. Though the Court purports to leave the latter issue open, it has in fact always declined to accord executive officers *any* immunity from prospective relief. See *Supreme Court of Virginia v. Consumers Union*, 446 U.S. 719 (1980). There is, however, no clear holding as to whether the

President may be enjoined. What arguments may be advanced on either side of that question?

5.   The Defendant's Motivation After *Harlow*. In *Anderson v. Creighton*, 483 U.S. 635 (1987), the issue was whether officers who conducted a warrantless search, unsupported by probable cause or exigent circumstances, could nonetheless assert qualified immunity on the ground that a reasonable officer could have believed there was probable cause. The Court sustained the viability of this argument, and added:

> It follows from what we have said that the determination whether it was objectively legally reasonable to conclude that a given search was supported by probable cause or exigent circumstances will often require examination of the information possessed by the searching officials. But contrary to the Creightons' assertion, this does not reintroduce into qualified immunity analysis the inquiry into officials' subjective intent that *Harlow* sought to minimize. The relevant question in this case, for example, is the objective (albeit fact-specific) question whether a reasonable officer could have believed Anderson's warrantless search to be lawful, in light of clearly established law and the information the searching officers possessed. Anderson's subjective beliefs about the search are irrelevant.

Recall Justice Brennan's understanding of *Harlow,* that "the clever and unusually well-informed violator of constitutional rights will not evade just punishment for his crimes." Does *Anderson* repudiate Justice Brennan's view?

6.   Interlocutory Appeals of Denials of Official Immunity. The standard practice in litigation in the federal courts is that one may appeal only a "final judgment." On some issues, however, the loser is allowed to bring an "interlocutory" appeal without waiting for the case to be resolved by the lower court. In *Mitchell v. Forsyth*, 472 U.S. 511 (1985), the Court held that such an interlocutory appeal is available to an officer who has asserted and lost a qualified immunity claim. The Court reasoned that qualified immunity is not a mere defense, but is "an entitlement not to stand trial or face the other burdens of litigation," which "is effectively lost if a case is erroneously permitted to go to trial." Though *Mitchell* is a qualified immunity case, the Court made it clear that the same doctrine applied to absolute immunity.

Later the Court held that its rule on interlocutory appeals only applied to suits in *federal* court. When the case is litigated in a state court, state law on the availability of interlocutory appeals will govern. *Johnson v. Fankell*, 520 U.S. 911 (1997). The Court distinguished *Mitchell* on the ground that the "locus" of the right to an immediate appeal in the federal courts is 28 U.S.C. § 1291, which does not apply to the state courts.

7. The "Order of Battle" Problem. Qualified immunity cases present two questions: [a] whether the defendant committed a constitutional violation, and [b] whether, in the event he did, the right he violated was "clearly established" at the time. Questions arise as to whether a court may avoid the first question by stipulating a violation for the sake of argument and then ruling that, even if this is so, the right was not clearly established. Justice Breyer calls the question of the order in which these issues should be addressed the "order of battle." For a time, the rule was that a court should first resolve the constitutional issue and only then move to the qualified immunity question. In *Pearson v. Callahan*, 555 U.S. 223 (2009), the Court ruled that lower courts generally have discretion to take the qualified immunity issue up first.

Harlow directs that the outcome of qualified immunity cases should generally turn on whether the defendant violated "clearly established" law. The opinion does leave room for exceptions to the rule, where "the official pleading the defense claims extraordinary circumstances and can prove that he neither knew nor should have known of the relevant legal standard." For example, in *Roska ex rel. Roska v. Sneddon,* 437 F.3d 964, 971 (10th Cir. 2006), the court said that "[r]eliance on a state statute is one extraordinary circumstance which may [but does not necessarily] render an official's conduct objectively reasonable."

Nonetheless, determining the content of "clearly established law" is the key issue in most qualified immunity litigation. *Hope v. Pelzer*, and the notes that follow, address the content of that term.

HOPE V. PELZER
536 U.S. 730 (2002).

JUSTICE STEVENS delivered the opinion of the Court.

The Court of Appeals for the Eleventh Circuit concluded that petitioner Larry Hope, a former prison inmate at the Limestone Prison in Alabama, was subjected to cruel and unusual punishment when prison guards twice handcuffed him to a hitching post to sanction him for disruptive conduct. Because that conclusion was not supported by earlier cases with "materially similar" facts, the court held that the respondents were entitled to qualified immunity, and therefore affirmed summary judgment in their favor. We granted certiorari to determine whether the Court of Appeals' qualified immunity holding comports with our decision in *United States v. Lanier*, 520 U.S. 259 (1997).

I

In 1995, Alabama was the only State that followed the practice of chaining inmates to one another in work squads. It was also the only State that handcuffed prisoners to "hitching posts" if they either refused to work or otherwise disrupted work squads. [A hitching post is a sturdy horizontal bar placed 47–57 inches above the ground.] Hope was handcuffed to a hitching post on two occasions. On May 11, 1995, while Hope was working in a chain gang near an interstate highway, he got into an argument with another inmate. Both men were taken back to the Limestone prison and handcuffed to a hitching post. Hope was released two hours later, after the guard captain determined that the altercation had been caused by the other inmate. During his two hours on the post, Hope was offered drinking water and a bathroom break every 15 minutes, and his responses to these offers were recorded on an activity log. Because he was only slightly taller than the hitching post, his arms were above shoulder height and grew tired from being handcuffed so high. Whenever he tried moving his arms to improve his circulation, the handcuffs cut into his wrists, causing pain and discomfort.

On June 7, 1995, Hope was punished more severely. He took a nap during the morning bus ride to the chain gang's worksite, and when it arrived he was less than prompt in responding to an order to get off the bus. An exchange of vulgar remarks led to a wrestling match with a guard. Four other guards intervened, subdued Hope, handcuffed him, placed him in leg irons and transported him back to the prison where he was put on the hitching post. The guards made him take off his shirt, and he remained shirtless all day while the sun burned his skin. He remained attached to the post for approximately seven hours. During this 7-hour period, he was given water only once or twice and was given no bathroom breaks. At one point, a guard taunted Hope about his thirst. According to Hope's affidavit: "[The guard] first gave water to some dogs, then brought the water cooler closer to me, removed its lid, and kicked the cooler over, spilling the water onto the ground." Hope filed suit under 42 U.S.C. § 1983 [against] three guards involved in the May incident, one of whom also handcuffed him to the hitching post in June. [The 11th circuit concluded that the use of the hitching post for punitive purposes violated the Eighth Amendment.] Nevertheless, applying Circuit precedent concerning qualified immunity, the court stated that "the federal law by which the government official's conduct should be evaluated must be preexisting, obvious and mandatory," "and established, not by 'abstractions,'" but by cases that are "materially similar" "to the facts in the case in front of us." The court then concluded that the facts in the two precedents on which Hope primarily relied—*Ort v. White*, 813 F.2d 318 (C.A.11 1987), and *Gates v. Collier*, 501 F.2d 1291 (C.A.5 1974)— "[t]hough analogous," were not "materially similar to Hope's situation." 240 F.3d, at 981. We granted certiorari to review the Eleventh Circuit's qualified immunity holding.

II

The threshold inquiry a court must undertake in a qualified immunity analysis is whether plaintiff's allegations, if true, establish a constitutional violation. *Saucier v. Katz*, 533 U.S. 194, 201 (2001). [We] agree with the Court of Appeals that the attachment of Hope to the hitching post under the circumstances alleged in this case violated the Eighth Amendment. [The Court's discussion of the 8th amendment issue is omitted.]

III

Despite their participation in this constitutionally impermissible conduct, respondents may nevertheless be shielded from liability for civil damages if their actions did not violate "clearly established statutory or constitutional rights of which a reasonable person would have known." [*Harlow*.] In assessing whether the Eighth Amendment violation here met the *Harlow* test, the Court of Appeals required that the facts of previous cases be " 'materially similar' to Hope's situation." This rigid gloss on the qualified immunity standard, though supported by Circuit precedent, is not consistent with our cases. As we have explained, qualified immunity operates "to ensure that before they are subjected to suit, officers are on notice their conduct is unlawful." *Saucier v. Katz.* For a constitutional right to be clearly established, its contours "must be sufficiently clear that a reasonable official would understand that what he is doing violates that right. This is not to say that an official action is protected by qualified immunity unless the very action in question has previously been held unlawful, but it is to say that in the light of pre-existing law the unlawfulness must be apparent." Officers sued in a civil action for damages under 42 U.S.C. § 1983 have the same right to fair notice as do defendants charged with the criminal offense defined in 18 U.S.C. § 242. Section 242 makes it a crime for a state official to act "willfully" and under color of law to deprive a person of rights protected by the Constitution. In *United States v. Lanier*, 520 U.S. 259 (1997), we held that the defendant was entitled to "fair warning" that his conduct deprived his victim of a constitutional right, and that the standard for determining the adequacy of that warning was the same as the standard for determining whether a constitutional right was "clearly established" in civil litigation under § 1983.

[The defendant in *Lanier* was a state judge who sexually assaulted several litigants and court employees in his chambers.] In *Lanier*, the Court of Appeals had held that the indictment did not charge an offense under § 242 because the constitutional right allegedly violated had not been identified in any earlier case involving a factual situation " 'fundamentally similar' " to the one in [issue]. We [reversed]. We pointed out that we had "upheld convictions under § 241 or § 242 despite notable factual distinctions between the precedents relied on and the cases then before the Court, so long as the prior decisions gave reasonable warning that the conduct then at issue violated constitutional rights." We explained:

> This is not to say, of course, that the single warning standard points to a single level of specificity sufficient in every instance.

In some circumstances, as when an earlier case expressly leaves open whether a general rule applies to the particular type of conduct at issue, a very high degree of prior factual particularity may be necessary. But general statements of the law are not inherently incapable of giving fair and clear warning, and in other instances a general constitutional rule already identified in the decisional law may apply with obvious clarity to the specific conduct in question, even though 'the very action in question has [not] previously been held unlawful.'

Our opinion in *Lanier* thus makes clear that officials can still be on notice that their conduct violates established law even in novel factual circumstances. Indeed, in *Lanier*, we expressly rejected a requirement that previous cases be "fundamentally similar." Although earlier cases involving "fundamentally similar" facts can provide especially strong support for a conclusion that the law is clearly established, they are not necessary to such a finding. The same is true of cases with "materially similar" facts. Accordingly, pursuant to *Lanier*, the salient question that the Court of Appeals ought to have asked is whether the state of the law in 1995 gave respondents fair warning that their alleged treatment of Hope was unconstitutional. It is to this question that we now turn.

IV

The use of the hitching post as alleged by Hope "unnecessar[ily] and wanton[ly] inflicted pain," and thus was a clear violation of the Eighth Amendment. See Part II, supra. Arguably, the violation was so obvious that our own Eighth Amendment cases gave respondents fair warning that their conduct violated the Constitution. Regardless, in light of binding Eleventh Circuit precedent, an Alabama Department of Corrections (ADOC) regulation, and a DOJ report informing the ADOC of the constitutional infirmity in its use of the hitching post, we readily conclude that the respondents' conduct violated "clearly established statutory or constitutional rights of which a reasonable person would have known." [*Harlow*].

Cases decided by the Court of Appeals for the Fifth Circuit before 1981 are binding precedent in the Eleventh Circuit today. In one of those cases, decided in 1974, [*Gates v. Collier*, 501 F.2d 730 (5h Cir. 1974)] the Court of Appeals [squarely] held that several of those "forms of corporal punishment run afoul of the Eighth Amendment [and] offend contemporary concepts of decency, human dignity, and precepts of civilization which we profess to possess." Among those forms of punishment were "handcuffing inmates to the fence and to cells for long periods of time, . . . and forcing inmates to stand, sit or lie on crates, stumps, or otherwise maintain awkward positions for prolonged periods." [For] the purpose of providing fair notice to reasonable officers administering punishment for past misconduct, [there is no] reason to draw a constitutional distinction between a practice of handcuffing an inmate to a fence for prolonged periods and handcuffing him to a hitching post for seven hours. The Court of Appeals' conclusion to the contrary exposes the danger of a rigid overreliance on factual [similarity].

The reasoning, though not the holding, in a case decided by the Eleventh Circuit in 1987 sent the same message to reasonable officers in that Circuit. In *Ort v. White*, 813 F.2d 318, the Court of Appeals held that an officer's temporary denials of drinking water to an inmate who repeatedly refused to do his share of the work assigned to a farm squad "should not be viewed as punishment in the strict sense, but instead as necessary coercive measures undertaken to obtain compliance with a reasonable prison rule, i.e., the requirement that all inmates perform their assigned farm squad duties." [The] court cautioned, however, that a constitutional violation might have been present "if later, once back at the prison, officials had decided to deny [Ort] water as punishment for his refusal to work." So too would a violation have occurred if the method of coercion reached a point of severity such that the recalcitrant prisoner's health was at risk. Although the facts of the case are not identical, *Ort*'s premise is that "physical abuse directed at [a] prisoner after he terminate[s] his resistance to authority would constitute an actionable eighth amendment violation." This premise has clear applicability in this case. Hope was not restrained at the worksite until he was willing to return to work. Rather, he was removed back to the prison and placed under conditions that threatened his health. *Ort* therefore gave fair warning to respondents that their conduct crossed the line of what is constitutionally permissible. Relevant to the question whether *Ort* provided fair warning to respondents that their conduct violated the Constitution is a regulation promulgated by ADOC in 1993. The regulation authorizes the use of the hitching post when an inmate refuses to work or is otherwise disruptive to a work squad. It provides that an activity log should be completed for each such inmate, detailing his responses to offers of water and bathroom breaks every 15 minutes. Such a log was completed and maintained for petitioner's shackling in May, but the record contains no such log for the 7-hour shackling in June and the record indicates that the periodic offers contemplated by the regulation were not made. The regulation also states that an inmate "will be allowed to join his assigned squad" whenever he tells an officer "that he is ready to go to work." [This] important provision of the regulation was frequently ignored by corrections officers. If regularly observed, a requirement that would effectively give the inmate the keys to the handcuffs that attached him to the hitching post would have made this case more analogous to the practice upheld in *Ort*, rather than the kind of punishment *Ort* described as impermissible. A course of conduct that tends to prove that the requirement was merely a sham, or that respondents could ignore it with impunity, provides equally strong support for the conclusion that they were fully aware of the wrongful character of their conduct. Respondents violated clearly established law. Our conclusion [is] buttressed by the fact that the DOJ specifically advised the ADOC of the unconstitutionality of its practices before the incidents in this case took place. The DOJ had conducted a study in 1994 of Alabama's use of the hitching post. Among other findings, the DOJ report noted that ADOC's officers consistently failed to comply with the policy of immediately releasing any inmate from the hitching post who agrees to return to work. The DOJ concluded that the systematic use of the restraining bar in Alabama constituted improper corporal punishment. Accordingly, the DOJ advised the ADOC to cease use of the hitching post in order to meet constitutional [standards]. Although there is nothing in the record indicating that the DOJ's views were communicated to respondents, this exchange lends support to the view that reasonable officials in the ADOC should have realized that the use of the hitching post under the circumstances alleged by Hope violated the Eighth Amendment prohibition against cruel and unusual [punishment].

The judgment of the Court of Appeals is [reversed].

JUSTICE THOMAS, with whom THE CHIEF JUSTICE and JUSTICE SCALIA join, dissenting.

[The dissenters agreed that "certain actions so obviously run afoul of the law that an assertion of qualified immunity may be overcome even though court decisions have yet to address 'materially similar' conduct." But they took issue with the Court's conclusion that qualified immunity should not be available in this case. Among other things, Justice Thomas distinguished the Fifth and Eleventh Circuit cases relied on by the majority on their facts, and pointed out that Alabama district court decisions, decided after those cases came down, had approved the use of the hitching post and similar measures. He continued:]

If the application of this Court's general Eighth Amendment jurisprudence to the use of a restraining bar was as "obvious" as the Court claims, one wonders how Federal District Courts in Alabama could have repeatedly arrived at the opposite conclusion, and how respondents, in turn, were to realize that these courts had failed to grasp the "obvious."

NOTES ON "CLEARLY ESTABLISHED LAW"

1. **Sources of Clearly Established Law.** In order to determine whether a right is "clearly established" for purposes of the qualified immunity inquiry, one must examine the legal materials extant at the time the official acted. The opinion in *Hope* relies on a variety of sources, including a state administrative regulation and a Department of Justice Report. But the two most important sources of legal materials bearing on "clearly established law" are Supreme Court decisions and decisions of the Circuit Court in which the constitutional violation took place. In *Wilson v. Layne*, 526 U.S. 603 (1999), the Court indicated that decisions in other jurisdictions may be relevant as well, stating that a right is not clearly established where there is neither controlling authority in the jurisdiction where the violation

occurred nor a "consensus of cases of persuasive authority such that a reasonable officer could not have believed that his actions were lawful." What result if there is no Supreme Court case, five circuits have held that the plaintiff's constitutional right is violated on facts identical to those in the case at hand, and two have ruled that it is not? Can law be clearly established by district court decisions, standing alone? For one view, see *Anderson v. Romero*, 72 F.3d 518, 525 (7th Cir. 1995) (no, "because, while they bind the parties by virtue of the doctrine of res judicata, they are not authoritative as precedent and therefore do not establish the duties of non-parties.") Can law be "clearly established" in a case where the relevant authority is so obscure that the plaintiff's lawyer has failed to find it? See *Elder v. Holloway*, 510 U.S. 510 (1994) (yes). The circuit courts do not publish all of their opinions, and declare that unpublished opinions cannot be cited as precedent. Do unpublished opinions count as sources of clearly established law? Compare *Prison Legal News v. Cook*, 238 F.3d 1145, 1152 (9th Cir. 2001) (yes) with *Panagoulakis v. Yazzie*, 741 F.3d 1126, 1129–30 (10th Cir. 2013) ("an unpublished opinion provides little support for the notion that the law is clearly established on given point").

    2.   Keeping *Hope* Alive? In *Lane v. Franks*, 573 U.S. ___, 134 S.Ct. 2369 (2014), the substantive issue involved the free speech rights of public employees. The basic doctrine is that a government employee may not be fired for speech that is of public concern unless the disruption the speech causes outweighs its value. *Connick v. Myers*, 461 U.S. 138 (1983); *Pickering v. Bd. of Education*, 391 U.S. 563 (1968). In *Garcetti v. Ceballos*, 547 U.S. 410 (2006), however, the Court ruled that "when public employees make statements pursuant to their official duties, the employees are not speaking as citizens for first amendment purposes," and thus may be fired or otherwise disadvantaged on account of the speech. Lane, a community college administrator, sued Franks, his superior, alleging that Franks fired him for having testified truthfully, and under subpoena, at the criminal trial of a former coworker. An 11th Circuit panel granted summary judgment to Franks, on the ground that *Garcetti* controlled this case. The Supreme Court ruled that *Garcetti* did not apply and reversed on the First Amendment merits:

> [*Garcetti*] said nothing about speech that simply relates to public employment or concerns information learned in the course of public employment. [The] content of Lane's testimony—corruption in a public program and misuse of state funds—obviously involves a matter of significant public concern. [Here,] the employer's side of the *Pickering* scale is entirely empty. Respondents do not assert, and cannot demonstrate, any government interest that tips the balance in their favor. There is no evidence, for example, that Lane's testimony [was] false or that Lane unnecessarily disclosed any sensitive, confidential, or privileged information while testifying.

The Court nonetheless ruled that Lane could not recover damages from Franks, on account of qualified immunity:

Eleventh Circuit precedent did not preclude Franks from reasonably holding [the] belief [that] a government employer could fire an employee on account of testimony the employee gave, under oath and outside the scope of his ordinary job responsibilities. [The] Eleventh Circuit, in [*Morris v. Crow*, 142 F.3d 1379 (11th Cir. 1998)] concluded that [a deputy sheriff's] deposition testimony [regarding his investigation of a fatal car crash] was unprotected.

Although other cases, both in the Eleventh Circuit and elsewhere, were in tension with *Morris*, "[a]t the time of Lane's termination, Eleventh Circuit precedent did not provide clear notice that subpoenaed testimony concerning information acquired through public employment is speech of a citizen entitled to First Amendment protection."

According to *Hope*, what is required is "fair notice." Does the *Lane* Court's use of the term "clear notice" signal a shift in the criteria for obtaining immunity? Granting that the circuit precedent favored the qualified immunity ruling, could the Court's holding on that issue be questioned on the ground that the Supreme Court precedents provided fair (or even "clear") notice that Lane's testimony was protected? In this regard, note that in addressing the substantive constitutional issue, the Court states that "it is clear that Lane's sworn testimony is speech as a citizen," and that "the employer's side of the *Pickering* scale is entirely empty."

The Court in *Lane* did not cite *Hope*, even once. It did, however, cite *Ashcroft v. al-Kidd*, discussed below.

3.   Qualified Immunity for Federal Officers. *Ashcroft v. al-Kidd*, 563 U.S. ___, 131 S.Ct. 2074 (2011), involved federal, not state officers, sued under the *Bivens* doctrine (see note 1 after *Harlow*, above.) Federal officers may perform their functions in many jurisdictions, and questions arise as to whether their immunity depends on the "law of the circuit" in which a given act takes place. Much of the Court's reasoning is applicable to § 1983 suits as well as *Bivens* litigation. Justice Scalia wrote for the majority:

The federal material-witness statute authorizes judges to "order the arrest of [a] person" whose testimony "is material in a criminal proceeding . . . if it is shown that it may become impracticable to secure the presence of the person by subpoena."

Because this case arises from a motion to dismiss, we accept as true the factual allegations in Abdullah al-Kidd's complaint. The complaint alleges that, in the aftermath of the September 11th terrorist attacks, then-Attorney General John Ashcroft authorized federal prosecutors and law enforcement officials to use the material-witness statute to detain individuals with suspected ties to terrorist organizations. It is alleged that federal officials had no intention of calling most of these individuals as witnesses, and that they were detained, at Ashcroft's direction, because federal officials suspected them of supporting terrorism but lacked sufficient evidence to charge them with a crime.

It is alleged that this pretextual detention policy led to the material-witness arrest of al-Kidd, a native-born United States citizen. FBI agents apprehended him [as] he checked in for a flight to Saudi Arabia. Two days earlier, federal officials had informed a Magistrate Judge that, if al-Kidd boarded his flight, they believed information "crucial" to the prosecution of Sami Omar al-Hussayen would be [lost.] Al-Kidd remained in federal custody for 16 days and on supervised release until al-Hussayen's trial concluded 14 months later. Prosecutors never called him as a witness. Al-Kidd filed this *Bivens* action to challenge the constitutionality of Ashcroft's alleged [policy.]

At the time of al-Kidd's arrest, not a single judicial opinion had held that pretext could render an objectively reasonable arrest pursuant to a material-witness warrant unconstitutional. A district-court opinion had suggested, in a footnoted dictum devoid of supporting citation, that using such a warrant for preventive detention of suspects "is an illegitimate use of the statute"—implying (we accept for the sake of argument) that the detention would therefore be unconstitutional. [The] Court of Appeals thought nothing could "have given John Ashcroft fair[er] warning" that his conduct violated the Fourth Amendment, because the footnoted dictum "*call[ed] out Ashcroft by name*"*!* (emphasis added by the Court) We will indulge the assumption (though it does not seem to us realistic) that Justice Department lawyers bring to the Attorney General's personal attention all district judges' footnoted speculations that boldly "call him out by name." On that assumption, would it prove that for him (and for him only?) it became clearly established that pretextual use of the material-witness statute rendered the arrest unconstitutional? An extraordinary proposition. Even a district judge's *ipse dixit* of a holding is not "controlling authority" in any jurisdiction, much less in the entire United States; and his *ipse dixit* of a footnoted dictum falls far short of what is necessary absent controlling authority: a robust "consensus of cases of persuasive authority."

[The] Court of Appeals also found clearly established law lurking in the broad "history and purposes of the Fourth Amendment." [We] have repeatedly told courts—and the Ninth Circuit in particular, [not] to define clearly established law at a high level of generality.

[The] same is true of the Court of Appeals' broad historical assertions. The Fourth Amendment was a response to the English Crown's use of general warrants, which often allowed royal officials to search and seize whatever and whomever they pleased while investigating crimes or affronts to the Crown. [According] to the

Court of Appeals, Ashcroft should have seen that a pretextual warrant similarly "gut[s] the substantive protections of the Fourth Amendmen[t]" and allows the State "to arrest upon the executive's mere suspicion." [Ashcroft] must be forgiven for missing the parallel, which escapes us as [well.]

Qualified immunity gives government officials breathing room to make reasonable but mistaken judgments about open legal questions. When properly applied, it protects "all but the plainly incompetent or those who knowingly violate the law." [Ashcroft] deserves neither label, not least because eight Court of Appeals judges agreed with his judgment in a case of first impression. [He] deserves qualified immunity even assuming—contrafactually—that his alleged detention policy violated the Fourth Amendment.

In a concurring opinion, Justice Kennedy said this:

Some federal officers perform their functions in a single jurisdiction, say within the confines of one State or one federal judicial district. They "reasonably can anticipate when their conduct may give rise to liability for damages" and so are expected to adjust their behavior in accordance with local precedent. [In] contrast the Attorney General occupies a national office and so sets policies implemented in many jurisdictions throughout the country. The official with responsibilities in many jurisdictions may face ambiguous and sometimes inconsistent sources of decisional law. While it may be clear that one Court of Appeals has approved a certain course of conduct, other Courts of Appeals may have disapproved it, or at least reserved the [issue.]

A national officeholder intent on retaining qualified immunity need not abide by the most stringent standard adopted anywhere in the United States. And the national officeholder need not guess at when a relatively small set of appellate precedents have established a binding legal rule. If national officeholders were subject to personal liability whenever they confronted disagreement among appellate courts, those officers would be deterred from full use of their legal authority. The consequences of that deterrence must counsel caution by the Judicial Branch, particularly in the area of national [security.] Furthermore, too expansive a view of "clearly established law" would risk giving local judicial determinations the effect of rules with *de facto* national significance, contrary to the normal process of ordered appellate review.

III.   GOVERNMENTAL LIABILITY

Section 1983 authorizes suit against "every person" who violates constitutional rights under color of state law. Relying on the legislative history of the statute, *Monell v. Department of Social Services*, 436 U.S. 658 (1978), held that a municipal government is a "person" subject to

§ 1983 liability. *Monell* also held that governments may *not* be held liable on a respondeat superior basis for constitutional violations committed by their employees in the course of their duties. Rather, they are responsible only for constitutional violations that are caused by their official "policies" or "customs." A later case, *Owen v. City of Independence*, 445 U.S. 622 (1980), ruled that local governments enjoy *no* immunity defense. The Court's policy rationale for rejecting immunity was that the official immunity values (fairness to officials and encouraging them to act boldly) were "less compelling, if not wholly inapplicable, when the liability of the municipal entity is at issue." Given the weakness of these concerns, the goals served by imposing liability (vindicating rights and deterring constitutional violations) carry the day.

The lack of respondeat superior liability combined with the rejection of immunity mean that the stakes are high in litigation over governmental liability: The government cannot be held liable unless "policy" or "custom" is established; but once the plaintiff wins on that issue there is no "immunity" obstacle standing in the way of the recovery of damages. And juries tend to show far less sympathy for local governments than for, say, police officers. Virtually every plaintiff looks for a way to show policy or custom, and there is considerable litigation over the meaning of these terms. Some cases are easy. In *Monell*, the New York City Department of Social Services had issued a regulation obliging pregnant employees to take leave of absence after the fifth month of pregnancy. The Court had no difficulty concluding that the regulation was a municipal policy. (And, since the policy violated the equal protection clause, the city was liable for damages.) Similarly, when a city governing body enacts an ordinance that governs the conduct of persons subject to it, courts invariably hold that the ordinance is the municipality's policy. If the ordinance is unconstitutional as applied to the plaintiff, the city must pay damages.[1] In such cases two factors come together to compel a finding that the rule is the city's "policy": (a) the policymaking officers of the city government have formally acted, and (b) they have announced a rule of general applicability. When one or both of these factors is missing, courts must address more difficult issues. The hard cases bearing on "policy" or "custom" fall into three basic fact patterns.

---

[1]   Notice that insofar as the plaintiff seeks only prospective relief, that can be obtained by a suit against the officers whose official conduct the plaintiff objects to. The municipal liability doctrine is unnecessary in such a case, except as a means of obtaining attorney's fees. In the event a plaintiff does wish to sue the officers, but not the city, he should take care to bring suit against them in their "individual" capacities. (One is permitted to sue the officer in his "individual" capacity for constitutional violations committed in the course of his official duties.)

A suit brought against officers in their "official" capacities is treated as a suit against the municipality, so that the plaintiff can only win if he can establish "policy" or "custom." *Hafer v. Melo*, 502 U.S. 21 (1991). Of course, the plaintiff can always sue the officer in both his "official" and "individual" capacities, or sue the officer in his "individual" capacity and name the municipality as a defendant as well. The crucial point to keep in mind here is that the plaintiff *must* sue the official in his individual capacity if he is to obtain damages from the officer.

A. IDENTIFYING THE "FINAL" POLICYMAKER

Besides rules of general applicability like the one in *Monell*, the Court has held that the single act of a "final" policymaker for a government on a given issue can be the government's "policy." *Pembaur v. Cincinnati*, 475 U.S. 469 (1986) illustrates the theme. Pembaur, a doctor, was indicted for fraud. Deputy sheriffs went to his office in order to serve some of his employees with court orders. When they arrived Pembaur locked an interior door, barring their entry. Other officers arrived, and they eventually called the County Prosecutor, who instructed them to "go in and get [the witnesses]." The police then chopped down the door with an axe. Pembaur sued the local government under § 1983, asserting that the officers violated his Fourth Amendment rights (because they had no warrant) and that, because the prosecutor was the city's final decision maker on questions of whether the police should use force to enter, they did so pursuant to the government's official policy. The Court endorsed this understanding of policy:

> [It] is plain that municipal liability may be imposed for a single decision by municipal policymakers under appropriate circumstances. [The] power to establish policy is [not] the exclusive province of the legislature. [A] government frequently chooses a course of action tailored to a particular situation and not intended to control decisions in later situations. If the decision to adopt that particular course of action is properly made by that government's authorized decisionmakers, it surely represents an act of official government "policy" as that term is commonly understood. More importantly, where action is directed by those who establish governmental policy, the municipality is equally responsible whether that action is to be taken only once or to be taken repeatedly.

There was no majority opinion in *Pembaur* on the question of how one determines who is a final policymaker. Later cases indicate that the issue turns on both the formal allocation of authority under state law and "longstanding practice or custom which constitutes the 'standard operating procedure' of the local governmental entity." *Jett v. Dallas Independent School District*, 491 U.S. 701 (1989). In the years since *Jett*, the Supreme Court has offered little further guidance, yet the lower courts have faced the problem time and again. Here is an illustrative case:

WEBB V. SLOAN
330 F.3d 1158 (9th Cir. 2003).

GRABER, CIRCUIT JUDGE.

Plaintiff David Q. Webb obtained an $80,000 jury verdict in this civil rights action against Carson City, Nevada, after he was prosecuted without probable cause for obstruction of justice. [In] this opinion, we resolve [Carson] City's appeal from the adverse verdict. [We] hold that deputy district attorneys are final policymakers in Nevada for purposes of establishing municipal liability under 42 U.S.C. § 1983. As a result of our holding, we affirm the jury's [verdict].

On June 27, 1997, Deputy Darrin Sloan chased a car into the parking lot of the Carson City Inn. At the time of the pursuit, radio traffic identified the owner of the car as Freddy Little. The driver, who was African American, got out of the car, and Deputy Sloan continued the chase on foot. After leaping over several fences in pursuit, Deputy Sloan lost track of the suspect. He then returned to the abandoned car and began an inventory. During the next 20 minutes or so, the police received several reports that an African American man was running through areas near the Inn. Sloan's supervisor, Sergeant Moltz, saw an African American man suddenly jump from some bushes and run through the parking lot of the Nevada Appeal newspaper's offices. Shortly thereafter, another officer, Deputy Guimont, found Plaintiff David Q. Webb, an African American man, lying on the ground behind a vehicle parked in an adjoining parking lot. Deputy Guimont detained Plaintiff at gunpoint and waited for Deputy Sloan's arrival. Deputy Sloan arrived at the location where Deputy Guimont had detained Plaintiff. He noticed that Plaintiff's clothing did not match that of the man whom he had been chasing, but that Plaintiff did have a similar black bag. Sloan asked Plaintiff, "Why were you driving Freddy Little's car?" Plaintiff responded that he did not know who Freddy Little was. The deputies arrested Plaintiff for various traffic offenses and for obstructing police officers. On July 3, 1997, another police officer told Sloan that Freddy Little had been bragging that he had outrun the cops on June 27, 1997. Either the next day or the next business day, Sloan informed District Attorney Melanie Bruketta that he no longer believed that Plaintiff was the person whom he had been chasing on June 27. In a supplemental report, Sloan likewise wrote that he no longer believed that Plaintiff was the person who was driving the car that he had been chasing.

Despite Sloan's timely advisement, Plaintiff was not released from jail until July 16. Nor did the district attorney's office drop any of the charges. On August 15, 1997, Plaintiff met with a deputy district attorney, Ray Oster. Oster told Plaintiff that, if he pleaded guilty to the obstruction charge, Oster would drop the traffic charges. Plaintiff refused. A week later, the district attorney's office dropped the traffic charges anyhow but proceeded with the obstruction charge. Chief Deputy District Attorney Anne Langer took over prosecution of the obstruction charge. On September 3, 1997, Langer offered to drop the obstruction charge if Plaintiff signed a waiver of civil liability. Plaintiff again refused. In a later chance meeting, Langer assured Plaintiff that she would prosecute him to conviction on the obstruction charge. Plaintiff later testified that

Langer had told his lawyer that she was prosecuting him because he refused to sign the waiver.

In October of 1997, Plaintiff went to trial on the obstruction charge. At the trial, Deputy Sloan testified that Plaintiff had done nothing to delay him in performing his duties. Deputy Guimont similarly testified that Plaintiff had not obstructed the police. Plaintiff was acquitted.

Shortly after his acquittal, Plaintiff [filed suit under § 1983, as well as state law]. The jury found [in] favor of Plaintiff as against Carson City. In special interrogatories, the jury found that Defendant Carson City had a custom, policy, or practice that violated Plaintiff's federal constitutional right not to be prosecuted without probable cause, and that Carson City has a "custom, policy, or practice to falsely imprison individuals." The jury found that Deputy Sloan did not falsely arrest Plaintiff but that Carson City falsely imprisoned, maliciously prosecuted, and committed abuse of process against Plaintiff under state law. The jury awarded Plaintiff $80,000 without apportionment among the separate [claims]. Carson City timely appeals the decision that municipal liability may attach for the actions of deputy district [attorneys].

Municipal liability under § 1983 is proper in this case because the deputy district attorneys were acting as final policymakers for Carson City in deciding whether to prosecute [Plaintiff]. In Nevada, the legislature confers final policymaking authority on principal prosecutors and confers that same authority directly on deputies. [Nevada Revised Statute] § 252.070(1) provides: "All district attorneys are authorized to appoint deputies, who may transact all official business relating to the offices to the same extent as their principals." By its plain text, that statute confers authority on deputy district attorneys that is coextensive with the authority enjoyed by principal district attorneys. Thus, if principal district attorneys are final policymakers, then so are their deputies.

Whether the principal prosecutor has final policymaking authority is easily resolved. The Nevada Constitution does not create the office of the district attorney. Rather, the state's constitution confers the power to do so on the legislature. Nev. Const. art. 4, § 32. Pursuant to that power, the legislature statutorily created the office and prescribed its duties. The Nevada Supreme Court has noted that "[t]he matter of the prosecution of any criminal case is within the *entire control* of the district attorney." (emphasis added). Thus, in Nevada, principal district attorneys "are final policymakers for the local government in a particular area, or on a particular issue." *McMillian v. Monroe County*, 520 U.S. 781, 785 (1997). Specifically, Nevada district attorneys are final policymakers in the particular area or particular issue relevant here: the decision to continue to imprison and to prosecute.

The state attorney general exercises *supervisory* power over county district attorneys, but this does not remove final policymaking authority even from principal district [attorneys]. Both this court and the Nevada Supreme Court, however, have emphasized the discretionary and permissive nature of that authority. "The power to 'supervise' a district attorney which is granted to the attorney general by NRS 228.120(2), means supervision and cannot sensibly be read as a grant of power to usurp the function of the district attorney." *Ryan v. Eighth Judicial Dist. Court*, 88 Nev. 638, 503 P.2d 842, 844 (1972). "'The tenor of these statutory provisions is that with respect to the general run of prosecutions in the various counties of Nevada the attorney general of Nevada has no duties and responsibilities. His authority concerning supervision of district attorneys is permissive and discretionary.'" *Houston v. Bryan*, 725 F.2d 516, 519 (9th Cir.1984). [In] the light of these authorities, and in the absence of any evidence in the record that the attorney general in fact ever exercises that supervisory power, we hold that principal district attorneys are final policymakers for the municipality with respect to the conduct of criminal prosecutions.

As previously stated, the Nevada legislature confers the same final policymaking authority on deputy district attorneys. Nev.Rev.Stat. § 252.070(1). The principal does not delegate constrained discretion to a deputy upon appointment. Rather, the legislature states that, upon appointment, deputies may transact all official duties to the same extent as their principals. We are mindful that the Nevada statutory text is permissive, not mandatory: Deputies may transact official business to the same extent as their principals. Conceivably, the principal prosecutor could constrain that authority. That possibility does not change our analysis, because Carson City presented no evidence that its principal district attorney actually has constrained the deputies' authority. In fact, Carson City presented evidence to the [contrary].

NOTES ON THE "FINAL" POLICYMAKER

1. **Variations from State to State.** Of course, it does not follow from *Webb* that deputy prosecutors are always final policymakers. State law and practice is decisive. In *Webb* itself, the opinion goes on to distinguish an earlier case, in which it had held that under Hawaii law deputy prosecutors are not final policymakers. Thus, "the Hawaii charter gave principal prosecutors the authority to appoint deputies, but did not describe the authority that those deputies would enjoy to make decisions or to choose among alternatives. [Here,] however, the legislature directly delegates coextensive authority to the principal prosecutor and the deputies." In Hawaii, "[i]f [the deputy prosecutor] disagreed with [the principal prosecutor's] decision to prosecute Plaintiffs, she had to contact [the principal prosecutor]; she could not decide unilaterally to drop the case." Here, "any deputy in the office could have made the decision to dismiss the charges against Plaintiff without consulting with any supervisor."

2. **Delegation and Ratification.** Municipal governments are often organized in hierarchical fashion, with several layers of authority. Sometimes

policymakers delegate decision making to lower level employees. For example, in *Gschwind v. Heiden*, 692 F.3d 844 (7th Cir. 2012), the plaintiff, a former teacher, asserted that the school principal and assistant principal had forced him to resign as retaliation for protected speech. He sued these individuals as well as the school district. In reversing the district court's grant of summary judgment to the school district, Judge Posner said:

> When Gschwind complained to the superintendent about the decision of the principal and assistant to force him to resign, the superintendent replied that "it was the policy of the school district and the Board of Education to allow principals and assistant principals to make evaluation and employment decisions as they see fit with respect to the teachers they supervise and for the school district and the Board of Education to follow these decisions and recommendations." This was evidence of a policy of the school district of condoning unconstitutional terminations, since principals and assistant principals might "see fit" to fire teachers on unconstitutional grounds.

On other occasions a decision taken at one level will be implemented only if it is approved at a higher level. In such cases, the initial decision maker may not be the final policymaker. When he acts for unconstitutional reasons, e.g., in recommending that the plaintiff be fired for protected speech, the local government may not be held liable simply because higher levels adopted his recommendation. See *St. Louis v. Praprotnik*, 485 U.S. 112 (1988). If, however, policymakers endorse the unconstitutional reason behind the decision, they are deemed to have "ratified" it, and the plaintiff can sue not only the intermediate official but the city as well. Suppose the policymaker does not go so far as to affirmatively adopt the decision and the impermissible reasons, but passively allows the decision to stand. In the Second Circuit, "another method of implicating a policy making official through subordinates' conduct is to show that the policymaker was aware of a subordinate's unconstitutional actions, and consciously chose to ignore them, effectively ratifying the actions." *Amnesty America v. Town of West Hartford*, 361 F.3d 113 (2d Cir. 2004). Suppose the policymaker *should* know that the action is unconstitutional, but negligently fails to appreciate that the underling has committed a constitutional violation?

3. State or County Policymaker? State governments cannot be sued under § 1983. See *Quern v. Jordan*, 440 U.S. 332 (1979). In *McMillian v. Monroe Co., Alabama*, 520 U.S. 781 (1997), the issue was whether a sheriff was a policymaker for the State or for the county. The Court began from the premise that "our understanding of the actual function of a governmental official, in a particular area, will necessarily be dependent on the definition of the official's functions under relevant state law." Examining Alabama law, the Court ruled that the sheriff was a state policymaker. Compare *Streit v. Los Angeles County*, 236 F.3d 552 (9th Cir. 2001) (holding that, under California law, the Los Angeles sheriff is a county policymaker "when implementing its policy of conducting prisoner release records checks"). Is the ultimate issue in these cases one of federal or state law? See *Jackson v. Barnes*, 749 F.3d 755,764 (9th Cir. 2014) ("State law aids but does not dictate our determination of whether an official [is] a state or county actor for purposes of § 1983.")

Is municipal liability appropriate when a city policymaker, e.g., the police chief, enforces a *state* statute (as opposed to a municipal ordinance)? For an affirmative answer to that question, at least where the city had adopted the substance of the statute by enacting an ordinance to the same effect, see *Cooper v. Dillon*, 403 F.3d 1208, 1222–23 (11th Cir. 2005). Sound? What result if there were no ordinance?

B. INADEQUATE TRAINING AND HIRING

CITY OF CANTON V. HARRIS
489 U.S. 378 (1989).

JUSTICE WHITE delivered the opinion of the Court.

In this case, we are asked to determine if a municipality can ever be liable under 42 U.S.C. § 1983 for constitutional violations resulting from its failure to train municipal employees. We hold that, under certain circumstances, such liability is permitted by the statute.

In April 1978, respondent Geraldine Harris was arrested by officers of the Canton Police Department. Mrs. Harris was brought to the police station in a patrol wagon. When she arrived at the station, Mrs. Harris was found sitting on the floor of the wagon. She was asked if she needed medical attention, and responded with an incoherent remark. After she was brought inside the station for processing, Mrs. Harris slumped to the floor on two occasions. Eventually, the police officers left Mrs. Harris lying on the floor to prevent her from falling again. No medical attention was ever summoned for Mrs. Harris. After about an hour, Mrs. Harris was released from custody, and taken by an ambulance (provided by her family) to a nearby hospital. There, Mrs. Harris was diagnosed as suffering from several emotional ailments; she was hospitalized for one week and received subsequent outpatient treatment for an additional year.

Some time later, Mrs. Harris commenced this action alleging many state-law and constitutional claims against the city of Canton and its officials. Among these claims was one seeking to hold the city liable under 42 U.S.C. § 1983 for its violation of Mrs. Harris' right, under the Due Process Clause of the Fourteenth Amendment, to receive necessary medical attention while in police custody. A jury trial was held on Mrs. Harris' claims. Evidence was presented that indicated that, pursuant to a municipal regulation, shift commanders were authorized to determine, in their sole discretion, whether a detainee required medical care. In addition, testimony also suggested that Canton shift commanders were not provided with any special training (beyond first-aid training) to make a determination as to when to summon medical care for an injured detainee.

At the close of the evidence, the District Court submitted the case to the jury, which rejected all of Mrs. Harris' claims except one: her § 1983 claim against the city resulting from its failure to provide her with medical treatment while in custody. In rejecting the city's subsequent motion for judgment notwithstanding the verdict, the District Court explained the theory of liability as follows:

> "The evidence construed in a manner most favorable to Mrs. Harris could be found by a jury to demonstrate that the City of Canton had a custom or policy of vesting complete authority with the police supervisor of when medical treatment would be administered to prisoners. Further, the jury could find from the evidence that the vesting of such carte blanche authority with the police supervisor without adequate training to recognize when medical treatment is needed was grossly negligent or so reckless that future police misconduct was almost inevitable or substantially certain to result."

On appeal, the Sixth Circuit affirmed this aspect of the District Court's analysis. The city petitioned for certiorari, arguing that the Sixth Circuit's holding represented an impermissible broadening of municipal liability under § 1983. [We] granted the [petition]. In [*Monell*] we decided that a municipality can be found liable under § 1983 only where the municipality itself causes the constitutional violation at issue. Respondeat superior or vicarious liability will not attach under § 1983. "It is only when the 'execution of the government's policy or custom . . . inflicts the injury' that the municipality may be held liable under § 1983." Thus, our first inquiry in any case alleging municipal liability under § 1983 is the question whether there is a direct causal link between a municipal policy or custom and the alleged constitutional deprivation. The inquiry is a difficult one; one that has left this Court deeply divided in a series of cases that have followed [*Monell*]. Based on the difficulty that this Court has had defining the contours of municipal liability in these circumstances, petitioner urges us to adopt the rule that a municipality can be found liable under § 1983 only where "the policy in question [is] itself unconstitutional." [Under] such an approach, the outcome here would be rather clear: we would have to reverse and remand the case with instructions that judgment be entered for petitioner. There can be little doubt that on its face the city's policy regarding medical treatment for detainees is constitutional. The policy states that the city jailer "shall . . . have [a person needing medical care] taken to a hospital for medical treatment, with permission of his supervisor. . . ." It is difficult to see what constitutional guarantees are violated by such a policy.

Nor, without more, would a city automatically be liable [if] one of its employees happened to apply the policy in an unconstitutional manner, for liability would then rest on respondeat superior. The claim in this case, however, is that if a concededly valid policy is unconstitutionally applied by a municipal employee, the city is liable if the employee has not been adequately trained and the constitutional wrong has been caused by that failure to train. For reasons explained below, we conclude, as have all the Courts of Appeals that have addressed this issue, that there are limited circumstances in which an allegation of a "failure to train" can be the basis for liability under § 1983. Thus, we reject petitioner's contention that only unconstitutional policies are actionable under the statute.

Though we agree with the court below that a city can be liable under § 1983 for inadequate training of its employees, we cannot agree that the District Court's jury instructions on this issue were [proper]. We hold today that the inadequacy of police training may serve as the basis for § 1983 liability only where the failure to train amounts to deliberate indifference to the rights of persons with whom the police come into contact. This rule is most consistent with our admonition in *Monell* that a municipality can be liable under § 1983 only where its policies are the "moving force [behind] the constitutional violation." Only where a municipality's failure to train its employees in a relevant respect evidences a "deliberate indifference" to the rights of its inhabitants can such a shortcoming be properly thought of as a city "policy or custom" that is actionable under § 1983. [Only] where a failure to train reflects a "deliberate" or "conscious" choice by a municipality—a "policy" as defined by our prior cases—can a city be liable for such a failure under § 1983.

Monell's rule that a city is not liable under § 1983 unless a municipal policy causes a constitutional deprivation will not be satisfied by merely alleging that the existing training program for a class of employees, such as police officers, represents a policy for which the city is responsible. That much may be true. The issue in a case like this one, however, is whether that training program is adequate; and if it is not, the question becomes whether such inadequate training can justifiably be said to represent "city policy." It may seem contrary to common sense to assert that a municipality will actually have a policy of not taking reasonable steps to train its employees. But it may happen that in light of the duties assigned to specific officers or employees the need for more or different training is so obvious, and the inadequacy so likely to result in the violation of constitutional rights, that the policymakers of the city can reasonably be said to have been deliberately indifferent to the need. In that event, the failure to provide proper training may fairly be said to represent a policy for which the city is responsible, and for which the city may be held liable if it actually causes injury.

In resolving the issue of a city's liability, the focus must be on adequacy of the training program in relation to the tasks the particular officers must perform. That a particular officer may be unsatisfactorily trained will not alone suffice to fasten liability on the city, for the officer's shortcomings may have resulted from factors other than a faulty training program. It may be, for example, that an otherwise sound program has occasionally been negligently administered. Neither will it suffice to prove that an injury or accident could have been avoided if an officer had had better or more training, sufficient to equip him to avoid the particular injury-causing conduct. Such a claim could be made about almost any encounter resulting in injury, yet not condemn the adequacy of the program to enable officers to respond properly to the usual and recurring situations with which they must deal. And plainly, adequately trained officers occasionally make mistakes; the fact that they do says little about the training program or the legal basis for holding the city liable.

Moreover, for liability to attach in this circumstance the identified deficiency in a city's training program must be closely related to the ultimate injury. Thus in the case at hand, respondent must still prove that the deficiency in training actually caused the police officers' indifference to her medical needs. Would the injury have been avoided had the employee been trained under a program that was not deficient in the identified respect? Predicting how a hypothetically well-trained officer would have acted under the circumstances may not be an easy task for the factfinder, particularly since matters of judgment may be involved, and since officers who are well trained are not free from error and perhaps might react very much like the untrained officer in similar circumstances. But judge and jury, doing their respective jobs, will be adequate to the task.

To adopt lesser standards of fault and causation would open municipalities to unprecedented liability under § 1983. In virtually every instance where a person has had his or her constitutional rights violated by a city employee, a § 1983 plaintiff will be able to point to something the city "could have done" to prevent the unfortunate incident. Thus, permitting cases against cities for their "failure to train" employees to go forward under § 1983 on a lesser standard of fault would result in de facto respondeat superior liability on municipalities—a result we rejected in *Monell*. It would also engage the federal courts in an endless exercise of second-guessing municipal employee-training programs. This is an exercise we believe the federal courts are ill suited to undertake, as well as one that would implicate serious questions of federalism. Cf. *Rizzo v. Goode*, 423 U.S. 362, 378–80 (1976).

Consequently, while claims such as respondent's—alleging that the city's failure to provide training to municipal employees resulted in the constitutional deprivation she suffered—are cognizable under § 1983, they can only yield liability against a municipality where that city's failure to train reflects deliberate indifference to the constitutional rights of its inhabitants.

The final question here is whether this case should be remanded for a new trial, or whether, as petitioner suggests, we should conclude that there are no possible grounds on which respondent can prevail. It is true that the evidence in the record now does not meet the standard of § 1983 liability we have set forth above. But, the standard of proof the District Court ultimately imposed on respondent (which was consistent with Sixth Circuit precedent) was a lesser one than the one we adopt today. Whether respondent should have an opportunity to prove her case under the "deliberate indifference" rule we have adopted is a matter for the Court of Appeals to deal with on [remand].

It is so ordered.

NOTES ON INADEQUATE TRAINING, HIRING, AND SUPERVISION

1.   Hiring,   Supervision,   and   Discipline. *Bryan   County Commissioners v. Brown*, 520 U.S. 397 (1997), held that a local government could be liable for a bad hiring decision. Lower court cases also authorize recovery based on theories of inadequate supervision and discipline of employees. See, e.g., *DiRico v. City of Quincy*, 404 F.3d 464, 468 (1st Cir. 2005). To what extent should the *Canton* framework apply to these suits?

2.   Deliberate Indifference. Notice that the Court rejected the Sixth Circuit's "gross negligence" test for municipal liability (illustrated by the quotation from the district court explaining the theory of liability) in favor of a "deliberate indifference" standard. Why? Does the opinion indicate that the Court thought "deliberate indifference" was an easier test for the plaintiff to meet, thereby better serving the deterrent and vindicatory goals of § 1983? Or does the Court's reasoning suggest that it deemed "deliberate indifference" better suited to upholding federalism values and avoiding a slide into "respondeat superior liability" than "gross negligence"? Before settling on answers to these questions, consider the relevance of *Farmer v. Brennan*, 511 U.S. 825 (1994). There the Court ruled that prison guards could be liable on an Eighth Amendment theory for failing to protect an inmate from assaults, if the plaintiff can establish their "deliberate indifference" to his need for safety. In *Farmer* the Court held that, in the Eighth Amendment context, "deliberate indifference" is a subjective test, calling it "a state of mind more blameworthy than negligence," and declaring that "acting or failing to act with deliberate indifference to a substantial risk of serious harm to a prisoner is the equivalent of recklessly disregarding the risk." *Farmer* distinguished *Canton*'s "deliberate indifference" test for municipal liability: "It would be hard to describe the *Canton* understanding of deliberate indifference, permitting liability to be premised on obviousness or constructive notice, as anything but objective."

On the other hand, in *Bryan County Commissioners* the Court ruled that deliberate indifference cannot be met by a "showing of simple or even heightened negligence." 520 U.S. at 407. *Bryan County* differs from *Canton* in that the plaintiff complained about a hiring decision, not inadequate training. The Court ruled that a single inadequately vetted hiring decision could result in liability. But in the hiring context the plaintiff faces a heavy burden: "Only where adequate scrutiny of an applicant's background would lead a reasonable policymaker to conclude that the plainly obvious consequence of the decision to hire the applicant would be the deprivation of a third party's federally protected right can the official's failure to adequately scrutinize the applicant's background constitute 'deliberate indifference.' "

Does "deliberate indifference" mean one thing in hiring cases and another thing in training cases? Lower courts are routinely called upon to apply *Canton*'s "deliberate indifference" test. At least in training cases, some of them ignore *Bryan County*. One recent case declares that "[i]t is much harder for a *Monell* plaintiff to succeed on a hiring claim than a failure to train claim." *Young v. City of Providence ex rel. Napolitano*, 404 F.3d 4, 30 (1st Cir. 2005). Here is a typical formulation of the test for training cases:

> Deliberate indifference may be shown in one of two ways. First, a municipality shows deliberate indifference when it fails to train its employees to handle a recurring situation that presents an obvious potential for a constitutional violation and this failure to train results in a constitutional violation. Second, a municipality shows deliberate indifference if it fails to provide further training after learning of a pattern of constitutional violations by the police.

Dunn v. City of Elgin, 347 F.3d 641, 646 (7th Cir. 2003). Suppose that constitutional violations are rare, but the severity of the injury that they produce is high. Can severity give rise to a duty to take special care in training? See *Young*, above, 404 F.3d at 29. Here the issue was whether the city could be held liable for failure to train in connection with the "friendly fire shooting of an officer while off duty and in plain clothes." The court held, among other things, that "[a] jury could conclude that the severity of the consequences of a friendly fire shooting forced the department to take notice of the high risk despite the rarity of such an incident."

3.   A Pattern of Violations. In *Connick v.* Thompson, 563 U.S. ___, 131 S.Ct. 1350 (2011), the plaintiff had been wrongfully convicted due to the prosecuting attorneys' constitutional violations. (They had failed to disclose evidence that should have been turned over to the defense under *Brady v. Maryland*, 373 U.S. 83 (1963). He sued the municipal employer (New Orleans) claiming that the district attorney had been deliberately indifferent to his constitutional rights in failing to train deputy district attorneys to follow the constitution in prosecuting cases. Noting that "[a] municipality's culpability for a deprivation of rights is at its most tenuous where a claim turns on a failure to train," the Court rejected the plaintiff's theory. Summarizing the doctrine, the Court said that in order to win a *City of Canton* suit, the plaintiff has to show training that is so inadequate as to show "deliberate indifference" to the constitutional rights of persons subject to official action. It described "deliberate indifference" as "a stringent standard of fault, requiring proof that a municipal actor disregarded a known or obvious consequence of his action. [A] pattern of similar constitutional violations by untrained employees is 'ordinarily necessary' to demonstrate deliberate indifference for purposes of failure to train." Four reversals of convictions over the past decade for the type of violation at issue in this case, but in contexts that could be factually distinguished from this one, were not sufficient to prove deliberate indifference. 131 S.Ct. at 1360.

4.   Elements of the "Inadequate Training, Supervision, Hiring" Cause of Action. There are three. The plaintiff failed in *Connick* for failure to meet the first: that the training, etc., is so bad that it is deliberately indifferent to citizens' constitutional rights.

Second, the plaintiff must also show that the training is the "moving force" behind the constitutional violation. *Connick, supra,* at 1358 n. 5 (not reaching this issue).When the training is deliberately indifferent, but there is an insufficiently close connection between the training and the officer's violation, the plaintiff loses. *Canton* states that the "moving force" requirement is not met by satisfying the "but for" test of tort law for cause in fact. Rather, "the identified deficiency in a city's training program must be closely related to the ultimate injury." Should it be sufficient for the plaintiff to meet the common law "proximate cause" requirement?

Third (though not at issue in *Connick*, a case in which the defendant conceded the point) the plaintiff does not win merely by showing that the training was deliberately indifferent to his rights, and that the inadequate training was the moving force behind the harm he suffered. He nonetheless loses in a case where the officer who injured him has not committed a constitutional violation. *Los Angeles v. Heller*, 475 U.S. 796 (1986).

C.   CUSTOM

Before *Connick* lower courts adjudicating cases brought under the "inadequate training or hiring" theory often took the view that proof of a single constitutional violation—the one on which suit is being brought—may give rise to municipal liability. The plaintiff would, of course, bolster his case by showing a string of incidents, but he was not necessarily obliged to do so. See, e.g., *Long v. County of Los Angeles*, 442 F.3d 1178, 1186 (9th Cir. 2006). After *Connick* they have become less willing allow the plaintiff to get past summary judgment without showing a pattern of violations. Since it seems practically necessary to show a pattern of violations in any event, one consequence of *Connick* has been greater emphasis on a third basis for municipal liability: a pattern of unconstitutional acts by underlings, coupled with some degree of knowledge of the practice by policymakers. While there is little Supreme Court authority on the "custom" prong of municipal liability doctrine, the issue arises with increasing frequency in the lower courts, as one can win a "custom" suit without showing inadequate training. The following case illustrates the "custom" theory.

BARON v. SUFFOLK CO. SHERIFF'S DEPT.

402 F.3d 225 (1st Cir. 2005).

LIPEZ, CIRCUIT JUDGE.

Plaintiff Bruce Baron, a former corrections officer at the Suffolk County House of Correction, was allegedly harassed and forced to quit his job after he broke a code of silence by reporting a fellow officer's misconduct. He sued corrections officer Daniel Hickey, the Suffolk County Sheriff's Department ("Department"), and Suffolk County Sheriff Richard Rouse for civil rights violations stemming from that harassment. The district court awarded summary judgment for Rouse on the grounds of qualified immunity but denied summary judgment for the Department. Following a four-day trial, the jury returned a verdict against the Department and awarded Baron $500,000 in damages. [We] affirm.

[The court ruled in the plaintiff's favor on his First Amendment claim that officers retaliated against him for the exercise of his free speech rights. It then turned to the question whether the Sheriff's Department, a part of the municipal government, could be found liable for the acts of its employees. The plaintiff did not claim that there was a formal policy of harassment, a decision by a final policymaker to harass him, or inadequate training. Instead, he asserted the existence of a custom.]

Unlike a "policy," which comes into existence because of the top-down affirmative decision of a policymaker, a custom develops from the bottom-up. In a § 1983 suit premised on custom, then, we must first determine whether the custom is fairly attributable to the municipality. This standard is met when a custom is "so well settled and widespread that the policymaking officials of the municipality can be said to have either actual or constructive knowledge of it yet did nothing to end the practice." If a custom is attributable to the municipality, we must also inquire whether it was "the cause of and the moving force behind the deprivation of constitutional rights." The Department [insists] that Baron presented insufficient evidence to establish that the ongoing harassment he suffered was the result of a custom or policy of which a policymaker had actual or constructive knowledge. We [disagree].

The Department disputes the district court's post-trial explanation that there was sufficient evidence to establish a custom of "condoning the use of harassment to enforce the code of silence against 'rats.' " It points out that Baron testified only to his own experience. Unlike other cases involving similar claims, there was no evidence here that other House of Correction officers had suffered such retaliation or that other complaints had not been adequately investigated. Absent such evidence, the Department contends, a jury could not reasonably have concluded that Baron's harassment was attributable to a municipal custom.

As Baron points out, however, the Department's position unduly minimizes Feeney's testimony. Feeney was the deputy superintendent, fourth-in-command in the Department, in January 1997 when the harassment of Baron began. He was promoted to superintendent, third-in-command and in charge of day-to-day operations at the House of Correction, in October 1997 while the harassment was ongoing. Feeney testified at trial that "there are some officers that are reluctant to report things, and when they do, they're evasive and vague in their reports." Baron's attorney then asked Feeney to read from his earlier deposition, in which the following exchange took place:

Q: Are you aware of any code of silence between fellow officers reporting violations on each other?

A: Yes.

Q: What is it, the code of silence?

A: Lack of reporting to protect each other.

Q: When Officer Baron reported Sergeant Curtis, did he violate that?

A: Yes.

Feeney was then asked if there would be consequences if an officer were to report another officer. He answered, "There could be." Feeney also testified that Baron had complained to him about the harassment. That other Department employees denied at trial the existence of a code of silence would not preclude a reasonable trier of fact from crediting Feeney's statements as evidence of a custom. The jury could have found that Feeney's statements, together with Baron's testimony that the harassment began almost immediately after he reported Curtis, demonstrated a custom of retaliation to enforce a code of silence. Indeed, as the district court recognized, "the jury could reasonably have inferred from the failure of numerous defense witnesses (like corrections officers) to corroborate Baron's testimony that such a custom would make it extremely difficult to substantiate any allegations against it."

As an example, the court cited testimony by corrections officer Hubert Holtzclaw, regarding the cafeteria confrontation between Hickey and Baron, that "Hickey didn't slam cheese on the table in front of Baron, but instead placed a handful of napkins on the table as a gesture of good will." The court noted that "[t]he jury could reasonably have inferred that this testimony was incredible (even Hickey conceded that he bore no good will toward Baron), and was prompted by a desire not to testify against a fellow officer." In light of such difficulties in corroborating a code of silence, Baron's testimony takes on additional weight and Feeney's admission regarding his knowledge of the code is all the more significant. The Department also challenges Baron's claim of a custom by invoking the rule that a single unconstitutional incident is insufficient to impose municipal liability under § 1983. [In] considering this issue, the district court stressed that the "single incident" rule "is not immutable." It pointed to decisions recognizing that "serial misconduct" directed at a single victim may be sufficient to establish municipal liability, and concluded that this was such a case. The Department asserts that these serial misconduct cases are inapposite because this case involved only "one current employee complaining to one investigator about his work conditions."

This description of the case is not consistent with the [record]. Baron reported multiple incidents of harassment, including physical threats and property destruction, to his superior officer, to SID investigator Arthur, and to Feeney. Baron also met with union president Michael Powers and Deputy Superintendent Marie Lockhart in January 1998 to report the ongoing harassment. This is not a case, then, of attributing liability to the municipality based on a single incident of isolated employee conduct. Rather, the record demonstrates a pattern of ongoing harassment that the jury could have found high-ranking Department officials were aware of and did not stop. Compare *Kibbe v. City of Springfield*, 777 F.2d 801, 805–06 (1st Cir.1985) (actions of multiple police officers in connection with the pursuit and arrest of a single suspect were adequate basis for municipal liability because "the widespread activity here is more likely to reflect the operating procedures of the police department than would a single incidence such as occurred in *Tuttle*") with [*Oklahoma City v. Tuttle*, 471 U.S. 808, 811, 823–24 (1985)] (one shooting by a single police officer was insufficient to establish municipal liability for inadequate officer training). The Department was therefore not entitled to judgment as a matter of law or a new trial on the basis of insufficient evidence of the code of silence.

NOTES ON "CUSTOM"

1.   **Proving a Custom.** In *Palmer v. Marion Co.*, 327 F.3d 588, 595–96 (7th Cir. 2003), the plaintiff, a pretrial detainee, claimed that he was beaten by other inmates and sued the county, the city, and the sheriff, charging a custom of allowing inmates to fight. Here, the proof fell short:

> Palmer was incarcerated in the Marion County Jail for about one year, yet has personal knowledge, according to his affidavit, of only two incidents of inmate-on-inmate violence in which correctional officers failed to timely intervene. When a plaintiff chooses to challenge a municipality's unconstitutional policy by establishing a widespread practice, proof of isolated acts of misconduct will not suffice; a series of violations must be presented to lay the premise of deliberate indifference. [Essentially,] Palmer fails to avoid summary judgment on his claim that the defendants were deliberately indifferent to his safety because the record is devoid of evidence that the Jail's staff had a widespread practice of allowing violence to occur in any cell block, let alone specific gladiator cell blocks.

Does a large number of complaints about excessive force by the police, standing alone, establish the pattern necessary to show that the city condones excessive force? For a negative answer, see *Thomas v. City of Chattanooga*, 398 F.3d 426, 432 (6th Cir. 2005).

2. State of Mind. The plaintiff in a "custom" case must do more than establish the existence of a widespread practice or "serial misconduct" toward the plaintiff. *Baron* identified another requirement:

> To establish municipal liability, a plaintiff must demonstrate not only that a custom caused a deprivation of his rights, but also that the challenged practices were "so widespread or flagrant that in the proper exercise of [their] official responsibilities the [municipal policymakers] should have known of them."

The phrase "should have known" suggests that *Baron* adopts a negligence standard. Is this consistent with the adoption of "deliberate indifference" as the test in *Canton*? In this regard, recall that the Court's municipal liability definition of "deliberate indifference" may make that term a synonym for "negligence." In any event, the Supreme Court has not addressed the issue of just how much knowledge is required on the part of policymakers in a "custom" case, and the lower courts are divided, at least on terminology. For example, the quotation from *Palmer* in the preceding note suggests that the 7th Circuit requires a showing that policymakers are "deliberately indifferent."

IV. ENFORCING FEDERAL "LAWS"

Section 1983 authorizes suit against a person who deprives the plaintiff of rights under federal "laws" as well as the Constitution. In what circumstances may a litigant employ § 1983 as a means of enforcing a federal statute? The Court addressed this issue in *Maine v. Thiboutot*, 448 U.S. 1 (1980). The Court said:

> The question before us is whether the phrase "and laws," as used in section 1983, means what it says, or whether it should be limited to some subset of laws. Given that Congress attached no modifiers to the phrase, the plain language of the statute undoubtedly embraces respondents' claim that petitioners violated the Social Security Act.

It does not follow that § 1983 can be used as a general cause of action for enforcing all federal statutes. The "plain language" reasoning of *Thiboutot* is somewhat misleading. Shortly after that case, in *Middlesex County Sewerage Authority v. National Sea Clammers Association*, 453 U.S. 1 (1981), the Court imposed two constraints on use of § 1983 to redress statutory violations. The remedy would not be available if [a] "the statute at issue was [not] the kind that created enforceable 'rights' under section 1983," or [b] if "Congress had foreclosed private enforcement" of the statute.

On the latter of these two restrictions, the basic issue is whether statutory language, legislative history, and the existence of other remedial mechanisms justify an inference that Congress intended to foreclose § 1983 suits. Rulings in favor of foreclosure have been few. In *Wright v. Roanoke Redevelopment and Housing Authority*, 479 U.S. 418 (1987), for example, federal housing laws gave directions to local authorities as to how the rent should be calculated, and authorized the Department of Housing and Urban Development to enforce the benefits to which tenants were entitled. The issue was whether low income housing tenants could sue under § 1983 to enforce federal housing laws bearing on the calculation of the rent. The Housing Authority argued that private lawsuits were foreclosed. The Court disagreed:

> Not only are the [statute] and its legislative history devoid of any express indication that exclusive enforcement authority was vested in HUD, but there have also been both congressional and agency actions indicting that enforcement authority is not centralized and that private actions were anticipated. Neither, in our view, are the remedial mechanisms provided sufficiently comprehensive and effective to raise a clear inference that Congress intended to foreclose a section 1983 cause of action for the enforcement of tenants' rights secured by federal law.

Compare *City of Rancho Palos Verdes v. Abrams*, 544 U.S. 113 (2005). The Telecommunications Act, 47 U.S.C. § 332(c)(7), provided a remedy to persons seeking to enforce the Act's limits on local zoning authority over antenna towers for wireless communications. The plaintiff sought to sue under § 1983 because it provided a more expansive remedy (including, for example, the possibility of obtaining attorney's fees). Declaring that "the existence of a more restrictive private remedy for statutory violations has been the dividing line between those cases in which we have held that an action would lie under § 1983 and those in which we have held that it would not," the Court held that § 1983 was not available to this plaintiff.

Notwithstanding *City of Rancho Palos Verdes*, [b] has not often been an unsurmountable obstacle to § 1983 litigation raising statutory rights. The Court's most recent ruling on this issue came in *Fitzgerald v. Barnstable School Committee*, 555 U.S. 246 (2009). Plaintiffs sought to sue under § 1983 for peer-on-peer sexual harassment in the public schools. The issue was whether Title IX of the Education Amendments of 1972 (which, among other things, forbids gender discrimination in the public schools) precluded a § 1983 suit. A unanimous Court ruled that Title IX did not foreclose recovery under § 1983. The remedies available to enforce Title IX included withdrawal of federal funding and an implied cause of action (on the latter of these, see Chapter 2). The Court distinguished *City of Rancho Palos Verdes* and other cases finding statutory preclusion as cases in which the relevant statutory remedies were "unusually elaborate," "carefully tailored," and "restrictive." Here the § 1983 suit and the implied private right of action available under Title IX would largely follow the same track, so that "parallel and concurrent § 1983 claims [would] neither circumvent required procedures, nor allow access to new remedies." Implied rights of action to enforce federal law are discussed in detail in Chapter 2.

The juxtaposition of *Rancho Palos Verdes* and *Fitzgerald* may suggest a principle that only general regulatory statutes like the Telecommunications Act, but not civil rights statutes, are read as foreclosing § 1983 suits. But the cases do not seem to support such a general principle. Every statute receives individual assessment. Thus, several circuit courts have put the Individuals with Disabilities in Education Act on the *Rancho Palos Verdes* side of the line, ruling that "IDEA's comprehensive enforcement scheme provides the sole remedy for statutory violations." *K.A. v. Fulton County School District*, 741 F.3d 1195, 1210 (11th Cir. 2013) (joining the First, Third, Fourth, Ninth, and Tenth Circuits).

The bigger problem for plaintiffs seeking to enforce federal statutes by § 1983 suits has been [a].

GONZAGA UNIVERSITY V. DOE
536 U.S. 273 (2002).

CHIEF JUSTICE REHNQUIST delivered the opinion of the Court

The question presented is whether a student may sue [for] damages under § 1983, to enforce provisions of the Family Educational Rights and Privacy Act of 1974 (FERPA or Act), 20 U.S.C. § 1232g, which prohibit the federal funding of educational institutions that have a policy or practice of releasing education records to unauthorized persons. We hold such an action foreclosed because the relevant provisions of FERPA create no personal rights to enforce under § 1983.

[Doe] is a former undergraduate in the School of Education at Gonzaga University, a private university in Spokane, Washington. He planned to graduate and teach at a Washington public elementary school. Washington at the time required all of its new teachers to obtain an affidavit of good moral character from a dean of their graduating college or university. In October 1993, Roberta League, Gonzaga's "teacher certification specialist," overheard one student tell another that respondent engaged in acts of sexual misconduct against Jane Doe, a female undergraduate. League launched an investigation and contacted the state agency responsible for teacher certification, identifying respondent by name and discussing the allegations against him. Respondent did not learn of the investigation, or that information about him had been disclosed, until March 1994, when he was told by League and others that he would not receive the affidavit required for certification as a Washington schoolteacher.

[Doe] then sued Gonzaga and League [alleging state law claims as well as a] violation of § 1983 for the release of personal information to an "unauthorized person" in violation of FERPA. A jury found for [Doe] on all counts, awarding him $1,155,000, including $150,000 in compensatory damages and $300,000 in punitive damages on the FERPA claim. The Washington Court of Appeals reversed in relevant part, concluding that FERPA does not create individual rights and thus cannot be enforced under § 1983. The Washington Supreme Court reversed that decision, and ordered the FERPA damages reinstated. The court acknowledged that "FERPA itself does not give rise to a private cause of action," but reasoned that FERPA's nondisclosure provision "gives rise to a federal right enforceable under section 1983." Like the Washington Supreme Court and the state court of appeals below, other state and federal courts have divided on the question of FERPA's enforceability under § 1983. The fact that all of these courts have relied on the same set of opinions from this Court suggests that our opinions in this area may not be models of clarity. We therefore granted certiorari, to resolve the conflict among the lower courts and in the process resolve any ambiguity in our own opinions.

Congress enacted FERPA under its spending power to condition the receipt of federal funds on certain requirements relating to the access and disclosure of student educational records. The Act directs the Secretary of Education to withhold federal funds from any public or private "educational agency or institution" that fails to comply with these conditions. As relevant here, the Act provides:

> "No funds shall be made available under any applicable program to any educational agency or institution which has a policy or practice of permitting the release of education records (or personally identifiable information contained therein . . .) of students without the written consent of their parents to any individual, agency, or organization." 20 U.S.C. § 1232g(b)(1).

The Act directs the Secretary of Education to enforce this and other of the Act's spending conditions. The Secretary is required to establish an office and review board within the Department of Education for "investigating, processing, reviewing, and adjudicating violations of [the Act]." Funds may be terminated only if the Secretary determines that a recipient institution "is failing to comply substantially with any requirement of [the Act]" and that such compliance "cannot be secured by voluntary means."

Respondent contends that this statutory regime confers upon any student enrolled at a covered school or institution a federal right, enforceable in suits for damages under § 1983, not to have "education records" disclosed to unauthorized persons without the student's express written consent. But we have never before held, and decline to do so here, that spending legislation drafted in terms resembling those of FERPA can confer enforceable rights.

In *Maine v. Thiboutot*, six years after Congress enacted FERPA, we recognized for the first time that § 1983 actions may be brought against state actors to enforce rights created by federal statutes as well as by the

Constitution. There we held that plaintiffs could recover payments wrongfully withheld by a state agency in violation of the Social Security Act. A year later, in *Pennhurst State School and Hospital v. Halderman*, 451 U.S. 1 (1981), we rejected a claim that the Developmentally Disabled Assistance and Bill of Rights Act of 1975 conferred enforceable rights, saying:

> "In legislation enacted pursuant to the spending power, the typical remedy for state noncompliance with federally imposed conditions is not a private cause of action for noncompliance but rather action by the Federal Government to terminate funds to the State."

We made clear that unless Congress "speaks with a clear voice," and manifests an "unambiguous" intent to confer individual rights, federal funding provisions provide no basis for private enforcement by § 1983.

Since *Pennhurst*, only twice have we found spending legislation to give rise to enforceable rights. In *Wright v. Roanoke Redevelopment and Housing Authority*, we allowed a § 1983 suit by tenants to recover past overcharges under a rent-ceiling provision of the Public Housing Act, on the ground that the provision unambiguously conferred "a mandatory [benefit] focusing on the individual family and its income." The key to our inquiry was that Congress spoke in terms that "could not be clearer," and conferred entitlements "sufficiently specific and definite to qualify as enforceable rights under *Pennhurst*." Also significant was that the federal agency charged with administering the Public Housing Act "had never provided a procedure by which tenants could complain to it about the alleged failures [of state welfare agencies] to abide by [the Act's rent-ceiling provision]."

Three years later, in *Wilder v. Virginia Hospital Ass'n.*, 496 U.S. 498 (1990), we allowed a § 1983 suit brought by health care providers to enforce a reimbursement provision of the Medicaid Act, on the ground that the provision, much like the rent-ceiling provision in *Wright*, explicitly conferred specific monetary entitlements upon the plaintiffs. Congress left no doubt of its intent for private enforcement, we said, because the provision required States to pay an "objective" monetary entitlement to individual health care providers, with no sufficient administrative means of enforcing the requirement against States that failed to comply.

Our more recent decisions, however, have rejected attempts to infer enforceable rights from Spending Clause statutes. In *Suter v. Artist M.*, 503 U.S. 347 (1992), the Adoption Assistance and Child Welfare Act of 1980 required States receiving funds for adoption assistance to have a "plan" to make "reasonable efforts" to keep children out of foster homes. A class of parents and children sought to enforce this requirement against state officials under § 1983, claiming that no such efforts had been made. We [found] no basis for the suit, saying:

"Careful examination of the language ... does not unambiguously confer an enforceable right upon the Act's beneficiaries. The term 'reasonable efforts' in this context is at least as plausibly read to impose only a rather generalized duty on the State, to be enforced not by private individuals, but by the Secretary in the manner [of reducing or eliminating payments]."

Since the Act conferred no specific, individually enforceable rights, there was no basis for private enforcement, even by a class of the statute's principal beneficiaries. Similarly, in *Blessing v. Freestone*, 520 U.S. 329 (1997), Title IV-D of the Social Security Act required States receiving federal child-welfare funds to "substantially comply" with requirements designed to ensure timely payment of child support. Five Arizona mothers invoked § 1983 against state officials on grounds that state child-welfare agencies consistently failed to meet these requirements. We found no basis for the suit, saying,

"Far from creating an *individual* entitlement to services, the standard is simply a yardstick for the Secretary to measure the *systemwide* performance of a State's Title IV-D program. Thus, the Secretary must look to the aggregate services provided by the State, not to whether the needs of any particular person have been satisfied." (emphases in original).

Because the provision focused on "the aggregate services provided by the State," rather than "the needs of any particular person," it conferred no individual rights and thus could not be enforced by § 1983. We emphasized: "To seek redress through § 1983, . . . a plaintiff must assert the violation of a federal *right*, not merely a violation of federal *law*." (emphases in original).

[Doe] reads this line of cases to establish a relatively loose standard for finding rights enforceable by § 1983. He claims that a federal statute confers such rights so long as Congress intended that the statute "benefit" putative plaintiffs. He further contends that a more "rigorous" inquiry would conflate the standard for inferring a private right of action under § 1983 with the standard for inferring a private right of action directly from the statute itself, which he admits would not exist under FERPA. As authority, respondent points to *Blessing* and *Wilder*, which, he says, used the term "benefit" to define the sort of statutory interest enforceable by § 1983.

[Some] language in our opinions might be read to suggest that something less than an unambiguously conferred right is enforceable by § 1983. *Blessing,* for example, set forth three "factors" to guide judicial inquiry into whether or not a statute confers a right: "Congress must have intended that the provision in question benefit the plaintiff," "the plaintiff must demonstrate that the right assertedly protected by the statute is not so 'vague and amorphous' that its enforcement would strain judicial resources," and "the provision giving rise to the asserted right must be couched in mandatory, rather than precatory, terms." In the same paragraph, however, *Blessing* emphasizes that it is only violations of *rights*, not *laws*, which give rise to § 1983 actions. This confusion has led some courts to interpret *Blessing* as allowing plaintiffs to enforce a statute under § 1983 so long as the plaintiff falls within the general zone of interest that the statute is intended to protect; something less than what is required for a statute to create rights enforceable directly from the statute itself under an implied private right of action. Fueling this uncertainty is the notion that our implied private right of action cases have no bearing on the standards for discerning whether a statute creates rights enforceable by § 1983.

[We] now reject the notion that our cases permit anything short of an unambiguously conferred right to support a cause of action brought under § 1983. Section 1983 provides a remedy only for the deprivation of "rights, privileges, or immunities secured by the Constitution and laws" of the United States. Accordingly, it is *rights*, not the broader or vaguer "benefits" or "interests," that may be enforced under the authority of that section. This being so, we further reject the notion that our implied right of action cases are separate and distinct from our § 1983 cases. To the contrary, our implied right of action cases should guide the determination of whether a statute confers rights enforceable under § 1983.

We have recognized that whether a statutory violation may be enforced through § 1983 "is a different inquiry than that involved in determining whether a private right of action can be implied from a particular statute." But the inquiries overlap in one meaningful respect— in either case we must first determine whether Congress *intended to create a federal right.* Thus we have held that "the question whether Congress . . . intended to create a private right of action [is] definitively answered in the negative" where "a statute by its terms grants no private rights to any identifiable class." For a statute to create such private rights, its text must be "phrased in terms of the persons benefited." We have recognized, for example, that Title VI of the Civil Rights Act of 1964 and Title IX of the Education Amendments of 1972 create individual rights because those statutes are phrased "with an *unmistakable focus* on the benefited class." (emphasis added). But even where a statute is phrased in such explicit rights-creating terms, a plaintiff suing under an implied right of action still must show that the statute manifests an intent "to create not just a private *right* but also a private *remedy*." *Alexander v. Sandoval*, 532 U.S. 275, 286 (2001) (emphases added).

Plaintiffs suing under § 1983 do not have the burden of showing an intent to create a private remedy because § 1983 generally supplies a remedy for the vindication of rights secured by federal statutes. Once a plaintiff demonstrates that a statute confers an individual right, the right is presumptively enforceable by § 1983. But the initial inquiry— determining whether a statute confers any right at all—is no different from the initial inquiry in an implied right of action case, the express purpose of which is to determine whether or not a statute "confers rights on a particular class of persons." This makes obvious sense, since § 1983 merely provides a mechanism for enforcing individual rights "secured" elsewhere, *i.e.*, rights independently "secured by the Constitution and laws" of the United States. "One cannot go into court and claim a 'violation of § 1983'—for § 1983 by itself does not protect anyone against anything."

A court's role in discerning whether personal rights exist in the § 1983 context should therefore not differ from its role in discerning whether personal rights exist in the implied right of action context. [Both] inquiries simply require a determination as to whether or not Congress intended to confer individual rights upon a class of beneficiaries. [Accordingly,] where the text and structure of a statute provide no indication that Congress intends to create new individual rights, there is no basis for a private suit, whether under § 1983 or under an implied right of action.

Justice Stevens disagrees with this conclusion principally because separation-of-powers concerns are, in his view, more pronounced in the implied right of action context as opposed to the § 1983 context. But we fail to see how relations between the branches are served by having courts apply a multi-factor balancing test to pick and choose which federal requirements may be enforced by § 1983 and which may not. Nor are separation-of-powers concerns within the Federal Government the only guideposts in this sort of analysis. See *Will v. Michigan Dept. of State Police*, 491 U.S. 58, 65 (1989) ("If Congress intends to alter the 'usual constitutional balance between the States and the Federal Government,' it must make its intention to do so 'unmistakably clear in the language of the statute' ".)

With this principle in mind, there is no question that FERPA's nondisclosure provisions fail to confer enforceable rights. To begin with, the provisions entirely lack the sort of "rights-creating" language critical to showing the requisite congressional intent to create new rights. Unlike the individually focused terminology of Titles VI and IX ("no person shall be subjected to discrimination"), FERPA's provisions speak only to the Secretary of Education, directing that "no funds shall be made available" to any "educational agency or institution" which has a prohibited "policy or practice." This focus is two steps removed from the interests of individual students and parents and clearly does not confer the sort of "*individual* entitlement" that is enforceable under § 1983. [FERPA's] nondisclosure provisions further speak only in terms of institutional policy and practice, not individual instances of disclosure. See 1232g(b)(1)–(2) (prohibiting the funding of "any educational agency or institution which has a *policy or practice* of permitting the release of education records" (emphasis added)). Therefore, [they] have an "aggregate" focus, they are not concerned with "whether the needs of any particular person have been satisfied," and they cannot "give rise to individual rights." Recipient institutions can further avoid termination of funding so long as they "comply substantially" with the Act's [requirements].

Our conclusion that FERPA's nondisclosure provisions fail to confer enforceable rights is buttressed by the mechanism that Congress chose to provide for enforcing those provisions. Congress expressly authorized the Secretary of Education to "*deal with violations*" of the Act, (emphasis added), and required the Secretary to "establish or designate [a] review board" for investigating and adjudicating such violations. Pursuant to these provisions, the Secretary created the Family Policy Compliance Office (FPCO) "to act as the Review Board required under the Act and to enforce the Act with respect to all applicable programs." The FPCO permits students and parents who suspect a violation of the Act to file individual written complaints. If a complaint is timely and contains required information, the FPCO will initiate an investigation, notify the educational institution of the charge, and request a written response. If a violation is found, the FPCO distributes a notice of factual findings and a "statement of the specific steps that the agency or institution must take to comply" with FERPA. These administrative procedures squarely distinguish this case from *Wright* and *Wilder*, where an aggrieved individual lacked any federal review mechanism, and further counsel against our finding a congressional intent to create individually enforceable private rights.

Congress finally provided that "except for the conduct of hearings, none of the functions of the Secretary under this section shall be carried out in any of the regional offices" of the Department of Education. This centralized review provision was added just four months after FERPA's enactment due to "concern that regionalizing the enforcement of [FERPA] may lead to multiple interpretations of it, and possibly work a hardship on parents, students, and institutions." [It] is implausible to presume that the same Congress nonetheless intended private suits to be brought before thousands of federal-and state-court judges, which could only result in the sort of "multiple interpretations" the Act explicitly sought to avoid.

In sum, if Congress wishes to create new rights enforceable under § 1983, it must do so in clear and unambiguous terms—no less and no more than what is required for Congress to create new rights enforceable under an implied private right of action. FERPA's nondisclosure provisions contain no rights-creating language, they have an aggregate, not individual, focus, and they serve primarily to direct the Secretary of Education's distribution of public funds to educational institutions. They therefore create no rights enforceable under § 1983. Accordingly, the judgment of the Supreme Court of Washington is reversed, and the case is remanded for further proceedings not inconsistent with this opinion.

JUSTICE BREYER, with whom JUSTICE SOUTER joins, concurring in the judgment.

The ultimate question, in respect to whether private individuals may bring a lawsuit to enforce a federal statute, through 42 U.S.C. § 1983 or otherwise, is a question of congressional intent. In my view, the factors set forth in this Court's § 1983 cases are helpful indications of that intent. But the statute books are too many, the laws too diverse, and their purposes too complex, for any single legal formula to offer more than general guidance. I would not, in effect, pre-determine an outcome through the use of a presumption—such as the majority's presumption that a right is conferred only if set forth "unambiguously" in the statute's "text and structure."

At the same time, I do not believe that Congress intended private judicial enforcement of this statute's "school record privacy" provisions. [Besides the considerations mentioned by the Court] I would add one further reason. Much of the statute's key language is broad and nonspecific. The statute, for example, defines its key term, "education records," as (with certain enumerated exceptions) "those records, files, documents, and other materials which (i) contain information directly related to a student; and (ii) are maintained by an educational . . . institution." This kind of language leaves schools uncertain as to just when they can, or cannot, reveal various kinds of information. It has led, or could lead, to legal claims that would limit, or forbid, such practices as peer grading, teacher evaluations, school "honor society" recommendations, or even roll call responses and "bad conduct" marks written down in class. And it is open to interpretations that invariably favor confidentiality almost irrespective of conflicting educational needs or the importance, or common sense, of limited disclosures in certain circumstances, say, where individuals are being considered for work with young children or other positions of trust.

Under these circumstances, Congress may well have wanted to make the agency remedy that it provided exclusive—both to achieve the expertise, uniformity, wide-spread consultation, and resulting administrative guidance that can accompany agency decisionmaking and to avoid the comparative risk of inconsistent interpretations and misincentives that can arise out of an occasional inappropriate application of the statute in a private action for damages. This factor, together with the others to which the majority refers, convinces me that Congress did not intend private judicial enforcement actions here.

JUSTICE STEVENS, with whom JUSTICE GINSBURG joins, dissenting.

[It] is clear that, in substance, § 1232g(b) formulates an individual right: in respondent's words, the "right of parents to withhold consent and prevent the unauthorized release of education record information by an educational institution . . . that has a policy or practice of releasing such information." This provision plainly meets the standards we articulated in *Blessing* for establishing a federal right: It is directed to the benefit of individual students and parents; the provision is binding on States, as it is "couched in mandatory, rather than precatory, terms"; and the right is far from " 'vague and [amorphous.' "]

The Court claims that § 1232g(b), because it references a "policy or practice," has an aggregate focus and thus cannot qualify as an individual right. But § 1232g(b) does not simply ban an institution from having a policy or practice—which would be a more systemic requirement. Rather, it permits a policy or practice of releasing information, *so long as* "there is written consent from the student's parents specifying records to be released, the reasons for such release, and to whom, and with a copy of the records to be released to the student's parents and the student if desired by the parents." The provision speaks of the individual "student," not students generally. In light of FERPA's stated purpose to "protect such individuals' rights to privacy by limiting the transferability of their records without their consent," the individual focus of § 1232g(b) is [manifest].

Although § 1232g(b) alone provides strong evidence that an individual federal right has been created, this conclusion is bolstered by viewing the provision in the overall context of FERPA. Not once in its opinion does the Court acknowledge the substantial number of references to "rights" in the FERPA provisions surrounding § 1232g(b), even though our past § 1983 cases have made clear that a given statutory provision's meaning is to be discerned "in light of the entire legislative enactment." Rather, ignoring these provisions, the Court asserts that FERPA—not just § 1232g(b)—"entirely lacks" rights-creating language. The Court also claims that "we have never before held . . . that spending legislation drafted in terms resembling those of FERPA can confer enforceable rights." In making this claim, the Court contrasts FERPA's "no funds shall be made available" language with "individually focused terminology" characteristic of federal antidiscrimination statutes, such as "no person shall be subjected to discrimination." But the sort of rights-creating language idealized by the Court has *never* been present in our § 1983 cases; rather, such language ordinarily gives rise to an implied cause of action. None of our four most recent cases involving whether a Spending Clause statute created rights enforceable under § 1983—*Wright*, *Wilder*, *Suter*, and *Blessing*—involved the sort of "no person shall" rights-creating language envisioned by the Court. And in two of those cases—*Wright* and *Wilder*—we concluded that individual rights enforceable under § 1983 existed.

Although a "presumptively enforceable" right has been created by § 1232g(b), one final question remains. As our cases recognize, Congress can rebut the presumption of enforcement under § 1983 either "expressly, by forbidding recourse to § 1983 in the statute itself, or impliedly, by creating a comprehensive enforcement scheme that is incompatible with individual enforcement [actions]." FERPA has not explicitly foreclosed enforcement under § 1983. The only question, then, is whether the administrative enforcement mechanisms provided by the statute are "comprehensive" and "incompatible" with § 1983 actions. As the Court explains, FERPA authorizes the establishment of an administrative enforcement framework, and the Secretary of Education has created the Family Policy Compliance Office (FPCO) to "deal with violations" of the Act. FPCO accepts complaints from the public concerning alleged FERPA violations and, if it so chooses, may follow up on such a complaint by informing institutions of the steps they must take to comply with FERPA, and, in exceptional cases, by administrative adjudication against noncomplying institutions. These administrative avenues fall far short of what is necessary to overcome the presumption of enforceability. [In] contrast [to cases in which the Court has found a comprehensive administrative scheme precluding enforceability under § 1983,] FERPA provides no guaranteed access to a formal administrative proceeding or to federal judicial review; rather, it leaves to administrative discretion the decision whether to follow up on individual complaints. Perhaps more pernicious than its disturbing of the settled status of FERPA rights, though, is the Court's novel use of our implied right of action cases in determining whether a federal right exists for § 1983 purposes.

In my analysis of whether § 1232g(b) creates a right for § 1983 purposes, I have assumed the Court's forthrightness in stating that the question presented is "whether Congress *intended to create a federal right*," and that "plaintiffs suing under § 1983 do not have the burden of showing an intent to create a private remedy." Rather than proceeding with a straightforward analysis under these principles, however, the Court has undermined both of these assertions by needlessly borrowing from cases involving implied rights of action—cases which place a more exacting standard on plaintiffs. By using these cases, the Court now appears to require a heightened showing from § 1983 plaintiffs: "If Congress wishes to create new rights enforceable under § 1983, it must do so in clear and unambiguous terms—no less and no more than what is required for Congress to create new rights enforceable under an implied private right of action."

A requirement that Congress intend a "right to support a cause of action," as opposed to simply the creation of an individual federal right, makes sense in the implied right of action context. As we have explained, our implied right of action cases "reflect a concern, grounded in separation of powers, that Congress rather than the courts controls the availability of remedies for violations of statutes." However, imposing the implied right of action framework upon the § 1983 inquiry is not necessary: The separation-of-powers concerns present in the implied right of action context "are not present in a § 1983 case," because Congress expressly authorized private suits in § 1983 itself. Nor is it consistent with our precedent, which has always treated the implied right of action and § 1983 inquiries as [separate].

NOTES ON SECTION 1983 AND THE ENFORCEMENT
OF FEDERAL "LAWS"

1. "Laws" Litigation After *Gonzaga University*. After surveying earlier cases in which "some language in [the Court's] opinions might be read to suggest" a more liberal approach to enforcing federal spending statutes by means of § 1983 suits, the Court "reject[s] the notion that [the Court's] cases permit anything short of an unambiguously conferred right to support a cause of action brought under § 1983." What is the scope of the § 1983 "laws" action after *Gonzaga?* For one view, see Bradford C. Mank, *Suing Under § 1983: The Future After* Gonzaga University v. Doe, 39 HOUSTON L. REV. 1417, 1419–20 (2003) ("the *Gonzaga* decision places a heavy and unnecessary burden of proof on plaintiffs by requiring unambiguous and explicit evidence that Congress intended to create an individual right benefitting a class including the plaintiff").

In the wake of *Gonzaga*, some lower courts have indeed taken a restrictive view of the availability of § 1983 to enforce federal statutes. See, e.g., *31 Foster Children v. Bush*, 329 F.3d 1255 (11th Cir. 2003). A federal statute, the Adoption Assistance and Child Welfare Act, provides states with federal funds for dealing with foster children and adoptions, and conditions receipt of the money on state compliance with federal regulations. The issue was whether children for whose benefit the statute was enacted could sue under § 1983 to enforce it. Even though the statute did not provide for other means of enforcement by the children it was meant to benefit, the court held that § 1983 was not available. The statute lacked "the kind of focused-on-the-individual, rights-creating language required by *Gonzaga*."

Nonetheless, other plaintiffs succeed despite *Gonzaga*. In *Schwier v. Cox*, 340 F.3d 1284 (11th Cir. 2003), the statute was the Privacy Act, which shields certain private information from disclosure. The state of Georgia had demanded that the plaintiffs provide their social security numbers in order to vote. Claiming a violation of the Privacy Act, the plaintiffs brought a § 1983 suit against the Georgia secretary of state, seeking damages. The court focused on section 7 of the Privacy Act, which declares that "it shall be unlawful for any Federal, State or local government agency to deny to any individual any right, benefit, or privilege provided by law because of such individual's refusal to disclose his social security number." It held that this language "clearly confers a *legal right* on *individuals.*" 340 F.3d at 1292. Some plaintiffs win even when the statute was enacted under the spending clause. E.g., *Romano v. Greenstein*, 721 F.3d 373 (5th Cir. 2013) (Medicaid Act provision that eligible individuals be given an opportunity to apply, relying on *Blessing* and *Wilder*); *Center for Special Needs Trust Administration v. Olson*, 676 F.3d 676 (8th Cir. 2012) (applying the *Blessing* test, and holding that a provision in the Medicaid statute, which specified how a state treats an individual's trust assets for deciding Medicaid eligibility, created enforceable rights); *S.D. ex rel. Dickson v. Hood*, 391 F.3d 581, 603 (5th Cir. 2004) (holding that the Medicaid Act, in providing that "a

State Plan must provide for making medical assistance available" to eligible persons, is "precisely the sort of 'rights-creating' language identified in *Gonzaga* as critical to demonstrating a congressional intent to establish a new right."); *Price v. City of Stockton*, 390 F.3d 1105 (9th Cir. 2004) (statutory language directing that local governments receiving funds "shall" provide benefits to dislocated persons is sufficient to create rights enforceable by way of § 1983 under the Housing and Community Development Act).

2.   **Is *Gonzaga University* Limited to Spending Statutes?** Some of the Court's reasoning suggests that the restrictive approach may be limited to statutes enacted under Congress's spending power. Both *Gonzaga* and *31 Foster Children* involved statutes in which Congress provided funds to the states, but conditioned receipt of the funds in some way. In *Gonzaga* the Court said that "unless Congress speaks with a clear voice, and manifests an unambiguous intent to confer individual rights, federal funding provisions provide no basis for private enforcement." In this regard it may be helpful to compare spending statutes with statutes that displace state substantive regulation. In *Golden State Transit Corp. v. City of Los Angeles*, 493 U.S. 103 (1989), the plaintiff had already won on its substantive claim that federal labor law had preempted state law. The issue before the Court at this point in the litigation was whether one could sue under § 1983 to obtain damages for the violation of federal labor law. The Court ruled that the § 1983 suit was proper. But in *Boston & Maine Corp. v. Town of Ayer*, 330 F.3d 12, 18–19 (1st Cir. 2003) the court applied *Gonzaga University* to a preemption case, without asking whether *Gonzaga* is limited to spending cases. What arguments can be advanced on either side of limiting the scope of *Gonzaga*? Is there something about spending statutes that is especially hard to square with the notion that a statute creates rights?

3.   **Implied Causes of Action Under Federal Statutes.** The Court in *Gonzaga University* relies on *Alexander v. Sandoval*, a case in which the issue was whether courts should create a common law cause of action to enforce a federal statute. In *Gonzaga University*, the issue was how to *interpret* a federal statute. Is it appropriate to draw an analogy between the two contexts? Compare Justice Stevens's view with that of the Court. Who has the better of the argument? *Alexander v. Sandoval* is discussed in Chapter 2.

CHAPTER 2

FEDERAL COMMON LAW

■ ■ ■

Exercising their common law powers, American judges routinely make law, notably in a whole range of private law fields like contracts and torts. No one questions the authority of state court judges to make common law. State courts are (unless state law provides otherwise) courts of general jurisdiction, modeled on, and inheriting their authority from, the English courts that made law for centuries before the Americans declared their independence. The newly independent states adopted "reception" statutes that (with suitable modifications) adopted the common law as their own. Federal courts, on the other hand, are courts of limited jurisdiction, deriving their authority from Article III of the Constitution. A glance at Article III shows that there are limits on the range of disputes they may adjudicate, and that (at least as a general rule, see Chapter 10) they possess only the jurisdiction granted them by Congress. Starting from this premise, the Supreme Court held long ago that federal courts lack "a common law jurisdiction in criminal cases." *United States v. Hudson & Goodwin*, 11 U.S. (7 Cranch) 32 (1812).

Hudson & Goodwin did not resolve the broader question whether federal courts possess the power to make law outside the criminal context. The answer is a qualified "yes." Their lawmaking power extends only so far as there is a sufficiently strong "federal" interest in a given issue to warrant displacing state law with judge-made federal law. The law they make is called "federal common law" to distinguish it from the vast body of common law for which the state courts are responsible.

This chapter is divided into two parts. Part I deals with the scope and exercise of federal judicial power to make substantive rules of law. Part II focuses on the authority to create remedies for violations of federal law. In connection with remedies, we make a further distinction (because the Supreme Court has historically made one) between remedies for statutory rights (Section A) and constitutional rights (Section B).

Keep in mind throughout the chapter that many cases concern situations in which a federal statute bears heavily on the outcome, but does not speak directly to the issue at hand. Often the Court's reasoning may be described either as "statutory interpretation" or "federal common lawmaking." The former shades into the latter as the link between the statutory directive and the issue at hand grows more attenuated.

I.   SUBSTANTIVE RIGHTS AND DUTIES

Before 1938, federal courts applied common law rules of their own choosing in many kinds of cases, without deferring to the law of the state in which they sat. *Erie v. Tompkins*, 304 U.S. 64 (1938), overturned this regime. The Court held that

> Except in matters governed by the Federal Constitution or by acts of Congress, the law to be applied in any case is the law of the state. And whether the law of the state shall be declared by its Legislature in a statute or by its highest court in a decision is not a matter of federal concern. There is no federal general common law.

In *Erie*, for example, the substantive issue was whether an undiscovered trespasser could recover in tort. State common law provided that he could not, while the common law rule in the federal courts was that he could. The effect of the Court's holding was that federal courts must abandon their rule and apply state law instead.

Quoting Justice Holmes, *Erie* also declared:

> Law in the sense in which courts speak of it today does not exist without some definite authority behind it. The common law so far as it is enforced in a State, whether it is called common law or not, is not the common law generally but the law of that State existing by the authority of that State without regard to what it may have been in England or anywhere else. [The] authority and only authority is the State, and if that be so, the voice adopted by the State as its own [whether it be of its Legislature or its Supreme Court] should be the last word.

Notice that the proposition advanced in the second quotation does not necessarily imply that *all* common law rules rest on the authority of the States. It remains possible that some of them derive from *federal* authority. While there is no federal *general* common law, the reasoning of *Erie* clears the way for *particularized* federal common law.

A few years after *Erie*, in *D'Oench, Duhme & Co. v. FDIC,* 315 U.S. 447 (1942), Justice Jackson laid the foundations for a new federal common law. The case involved a suit by the Federal Deposit Insurance Corporation, a federal agency, against D'Oench, Duhme to recover the value of a note issued by D'Oench to the Belleville Bank and Trust Co., an Illinois bank. The FDIC insured Belleville and later acquired the note. D'Oench, Duhme resisted the FDIC's request for payment on the ground that the note was in fact an empty promise, and the FDIC sued. The outcome of the case turned on what law governed D'Oench, Duhme's obligations to the FDIC. The Court ruled that federal law should apply, "because of the federal policy evidenced in [federal law] to protect [the

FDIC,] a federal corporation, from misrepresentations made to induce or influence the action of [the FDIC,] including misstatements as to the genuineness or integrity of securities in the portfolios of banks which it insures or to which it makes loans." But the Court did not focus on the problem of squaring its holding with *Erie*.

In a concurring opinion, Justice Jackson said:

I think we should attempt a more explicit answer to the question whether federal or state law governs our decision in this sort of case than is found [in] the opinion of the [Court]. That question, as old as the federal judiciary, is met inescapably at the threshold of this case. It is the one which moved us to grant certiorari, and we could not resort to the rule announced without at least a tacit answer to it. The petitioner asserts that the decisions in *Erie R. Co. v. Tompkins,* and *Klaxon Co. v. Stentor Electric Mfg. Co.* [which held that choice of law issues under *Erie* should be resolved by applying the conflicts of laws rules of the state in which the federal court sits] govern this case. If they do, we would not be free to disregard the law of Missouri and Illinois and to apply a doctrine of estoppel actually—but not avowedly— drawn from common-law sources to effectuate the policy we think implicit in federal statutes.

Although by congressional command this case is to be deemed one arising under the laws of the United States, no federal statute purports to define the Corporation's rights as a holder of the note in suit or the liability of the maker thereof. There arises, therefore, the question whether in deciding the case we are bound to apply the law of some particular state or whether, to put it bluntly, we may make our own law from materials found in common-law sources.

This issue has a long historical background of legal and political controversy as to the place of the common law in federal jurisprudence. As the matter now stands, it seems settled that the federal courts may not resort to the common law to punish crimes not made punishable by Act of Congress; and that, apart from special statutory or constitutional provision, they are not bound in other fields by English precedents existing at any particular date. The federal courts have no *general* common law, as in a sense they have no general or comprehensive jurisprudence of any kind, because many subjects of private law which bulk large in the traditional common law are ordinarily within the province of the states and not of the federal government. But this is not to say that wherever we have occasion to decide a federal question which cannot be answered from federal statutes alone we may not resort to all of the source materials of the common law or that when we have fashioned an answer it does not become a part of the federal non-statutory or common law.

I do not understand Justice Brandeis's statement in *Erie R. Co. v. Tompkins*, that "there is no federal general common law," to deny that the common law may in proper cases be an aid to or the basis of decision of federal questions. In its context it means to me only that federal courts may not apply their own notions of the common law at variance with applicable state decisions except "where the Constitution, treaties, or statutes of the United States (so) require or provide." Indeed, in a case decided on the same day as *Erie R. Co. v. Tompkins*, Justice Brandeis said that "whether the water of an interstate stream must be apportioned between the two States is a question of 'federal common law' upon which neither the statutes nor the decisions of either State can be conclusive." *Hinderlider v. La Plata Co.*, 304 U.S. 92, 110.

Were we bereft of the common law, our federal system would be impotent. This follows from the recognized futility of attempting all-complete statutory codes, and is apparent from the terms of the Constitution [itself].

A federal court sitting in a non-diversity case such as this does not sit as a local tribunal. In some cases it may see fit for special reasons to give the law of a particular state highly persuasive or even controlling effect, but in the last analysis its decision turns upon the law of the United States, not that of any state. Federal law is no juridical chameleon, changing complexion to match that of each state wherein lawsuits happen to be commenced because of the accidents of service of process and of the application of the venue statutes. It is found in the federal Constitution, statutes, or common law. Federal common law implements the federal Constitution and statutes, and is conditioned by them. Within these limits, federal courts are free to apply the traditional common-law technique of decision and to draw upon all the sources of the common law in cases such as the present.

The law which we apply to this case consists of principles of established credit in jurisprudence selected by us because they are appropriate to effectuate the policy of the governing Act. The Corporation was created and financed in part by the United States to bolster the entire banking and credit [structure]. Under the Act the Corporation has a dual relation of creditor or potential creditor and of supervising authority toward insured banks. The immunity of such a corporation from schemes concocted by the cooperative deceit of bank officers and customers is not a question to be answered from considerations of geography. That a particular state happened to have the greatest connection in the conflict of laws sense with the making of the note involved or that the subsequent conduct happened to be chiefly centered there is not enough to make us subservient to the legislative policy or the judicial views of that state. I concur in the Court's holding because I think that the defense asserted is nowhere admissible against the Corporation and that we need not go to the law of any particular state as our authority for so [holding].

Some critics of federal common law maintain that the doctrine should be strictly cabined, because recognizing federal common law in effect grants unconstrained discretion to federal judges to make law as they see fit. Does Justice Jackson's opinion suggest a response to that objection?

A. RIGHTS AND OBLIGATIONS OF THE UNITED STATES

Shortly thereafter the Court decided *Clearfield Trust*, another commercial law case involving the interests of the United States.

CLEARFIELD TRUST CO. v. UNITED STATES
318 U.S. 363 (1943).

MR. JUSTICE DOUGLAS delivered the opinion of the Court.

On April 28, 1936, a check was drawn on the Treasurer of the United States through the Federal Reserve Bank of Philadelphia to the order of Clair A. Barner in the amount of $24.20. It was dated at Harrisburg, Pennsylvania, and was drawn for services rendered by Barner to the Works Progress Administration. The check was placed in the mail addressed to Barner at his address in Mackeyville, Pa. Barner never received the check. Some unknown person obtained it in a mysterious manner and presented it to the J. C. Penney Co. store in Clearfield, Pa., representing that he was the payee and identifying himself to the satisfaction of the employees of J. C. Penney Co. He endorsed the check in the name of Barner and transferred it to J. C. Penney Co. in exchange for cash and merchandise. Barner never authorized the endorsement nor participated in the proceeds of the check. J. C. Penney Co. endorsed the check over to the Clearfield Trust Co. which accepted it as agent for the purpose of collection and endorsed it as follows: "Pay to the order of Federal Reserve Bank of Philadelphia, Prior Endorsements Guaranteed." Clearfield Trust Co. collected the check from the United States through the Federal Reserve Bank of Philadelphia and paid the full amount thereof to J. C. Penney Co. Neither the Clearfield Trust Co. nor J. C. Penney Co. had any knowledge or suspicion of the forgery. Each acted in good faith. On or before May 10, 1936, Barner advised the timekeeper and the foreman of the W. P. A. project on which he was employed that he had not received the check in question. This information was duly communicated to other agents of the United States and on November 30, 1936, Barner executed an affidavit alleging that the endorsement of his name on the check was a forgery. No notice was given the Clearfield Trust Co. or J. C. Penney Co. of the forgery until January 12, 1937, at which time the Clearfield Trust Co. was notified. The first notice received by Clearfield Trust Co. that the United States was asking reimbursement was on August 31, 1937.

This suit was instituted in 1939 by the United States against the Clearfield Trust Co. [The] cause of action was based on the express guaranty of prior endorsements made by the Clearfield Trust Co. J. C. Penney Co. intervened as a defendant. [The] District Court held that the rights of the parties were to be determined by the law of Pennsylvania and that since the United States unreasonably delayed in giving notice of the forgery to the Clearfield Trust Co., it was barred from [recovery.] On appeal the Circuit Court of Appeals [reversed].

We agree with the Circuit Court of Appeals that the rule of *Erie R. Co.* v. *Tompkins* does not apply to this action. The rights and duties of the United States on commercial paper which it issues are governed by federal rather than local law. When the United States disburses its funds or pays its debts, it is exercising a constitutional function or power. This check was issued for services performed under the Federal Emergency Relief Act of 1935. The authority to issue the check had its origin in the Constitution and the statutes of the United States and was in no way dependent on the laws of Pennsylvania or of any other state. The duties imposed upon the United States and the rights acquired by it as a result of the issuance find their roots in the same federal sources. In absence of an applicable Act of Congress it is for the federal courts to fashion the governing rule of law according to their own [standards].

In our choice of the applicable federal rule we have occasionally selected state law. But reasons which may make state law at times the appropriate federal rule are singularly inappropriate here. The issuance of commercial paper by the United States is on a vast scale and transactions in that paper from issuance to payment will commonly occur in several states. The application of state law, even without the conflict of laws rules of the forum, would subject the rights and duties of the United States to exceptional uncertainty. It would lead to great diversity in results by making identical transactions subject to the vagaries of the laws of the several states. The desirability of a uniform rule is plain. And while the federal law merchant, developed for about a century under the regime of *Swift v. Tyson* represented general commercial law rather than a choice of a federal rule designed to protect a federal right, it nevertheless stands as a convenient source of reference for fashioning federal rules applicable to these federal questions.

United States v. National Exchange Bank, 214 U.S. 302, falls in that category. The Court held that the United States could recover as drawee from one who presented for payment a pension check on which the name of the payee had been forged, in spite of a protracted delay on the part of the United States in giving notice of the [forgery].

The *National Exchange Bank* case went no further than to hold that prompt notice of the discovery of the forgery was not a condition precedent to suit. It did not reach the question whether lack of prompt notice might be a defense. We think it may. If it is shown that the drawee on learning of the forgery did not give prompt notice of it and that damage resulted, recovery by the drawee is barred. The fact that the drawee is the United States and the laches those of its employees are not material. The United States as drawee of commercial paper stands in no different light than any other [drawee.] But the damage occasioned by the delay must be established and not left to conjecture. [One] who accepts a forged signature of a payee [should] be allowed to shift that loss to the drawee only on a clear showing that the drawee's delay in notifying him of the forgery caused him damage. No such damage has been shown by Clearfield Trust Co. who so far as appears can still recover from J. C. Penney Co. The only showing on the part of the latter is contained in the stipulation to the effect that if a check cashed for a customer is returned unpaid or for reclamation a short time after the date on which it is cashed, the employees can often locate the person who cashed it. It is further stipulated that when J. C. Penney Co. was notified of the forgery in the present case none of its employees was able to remember anything about the transaction or check in question. The inference is that the more prompt the notice the more likely the detection of the forger. But that falls short of a showing that the delay caused a manifest loss. It is but another way of saying that mere delay is enough.

Affirmed.

NOTES ON THE ORIGINS AND SCOPE OF FEDERAL COMMON LAW

1. Introduction to Federal Common Law. A useful starting point for studying federal common law is the widely accepted proposition that every legal rule has a pedigree. That is, every legal rule is the product of lawmaking by some authoritative source of law. See H.L.A. HART, THE CONCEPT OF LAW 95 (2nd ed. 1994). (For the genealogy of this proposition, see note 2, below.) Authoritative sources of law include, among others, the U.S.

Constitution, federal statutes, state constitutions, and state statutes. For centuries, courts have been authoritative sources of a body of law we call "common law." Most of this common law is state law made by state judges, including much of the law of contracts, property, and torts. One issue raised by the concept of "federal common law" is whether federal courts also have the power to make common law. As *Clearfield Trust* indicates, the answer to this question is plainly yes. The harder task, and the main topic of this chapter, is to identify the scope of this power: In what circumstances is it appropriate for the federal courts to make federal common law?

Most, but not all, federal common law is made in the federal courts. Though the focus of our attention is the federal courts, state courts are obliged by the Supremacy Clause to follow federal law, including federal common law, in the event of a conflict between federal and state law. In a given case, this obligation may entail making federal common law, just as they make state common law, by drawing on the existing body of federal common law precedents and principles. In the event a state court does this, of course, its decision is subject to review by the U.S. Supreme Court, like any other state court ruling on federal law. Supreme Court review of state judgments is the topic of Chapter 8.

2. Historical Origins of the Federal Common Law. The notion that every legal rule has a pedigree has not always attracted the broad support it enjoys today. In *Swift v. Tyson*, 41 U.S. (16 Pet.) 1 (1842), the Supreme Court ruled that in commercial law matters the federal courts could follow rules of their own choosing, whatever the state law governing a given issue. Later cases extended that holding to other contract, tort, and property issues. Under the regime of *Swift*, courts often did not pay much attention to the "pedigree" of a legal rule. A given case might be resolved differently depending on whether it was adjudicated in federal or state court, simply because the federal courts applied one rule and the state courts another.

For example, in *Black & White Taxicab & Transfer Co. v. Brown & Yellow Taxicab & Transfer Co.*, 276 U.S. 518 (1928), the substantive dispute concerned the right to solicit passengers at a railroad station. The city of Bowling Green, Kentucky, sought to grant exclusive solicitation rights to Black & White. Brown & Yellow objected to its exclusion. Before the litigation, Black & White and Brown & Yellow were both Kentucky corporations. Black & White would have had difficulty winning the case in state court, because Kentucky state court decisions refused to enforce exclusive solicitation agreements. Under the federal court decisions, however, such an agreement would be enforceable. In order to litigate the case in federal court, Black & White, a corporation, dissolved and reincorporated in Tennessee, thereby creating diversity of citizenship between itself and Brown & Yellow. Black & White's strategy worked. The federal courts upheld the exclusive solicitation agreement and the Supreme Court affirmed.

The unfairness of this outcome, highlighted by the stark jurisdictional manipulation that produced it, undermined support for *Swift*. In addition, many jurists questioned *Swift*'s casual attitude toward the pedigree of legal rules. They held the view, called "positivism" in the jargon of legal philosophy, that every legal rule was "posited" by some authoritative source, i.e., that every legal rule has a pedigree. This view remains the dominant one among legal philosophers today, and it is hardly compatible with the regime of *Swift*, under which the substantive law that governs a case may depend on whether it is adjudicated by a federal or a state court.

In *Erie* the Supreme Court overruled *Swift*. The case is best known for its holding that there is "no federal general common law." Henceforth, federal courts were to apply state substantive law unless the case was governed by a federal statute or constitutional rule. But *Erie* did not merely repudiate the authority of the "federal common law" developed under *Swift*. Paradoxically, *Erie* also sowed the seeds for the growth of a new body of "federal common law" that would owe its pedigree to federal law, apply in the state as well as the federal courts, and supplant state law in the event of a conflict between the federal rule and the state rule. The key principle driving its development, articulated by Justice Jackson in his *D'Oench, Duhme* concurrence, supra, was that there are circumstances in which the federal interest in a case is strong enough to justify making a federal rule on a given issue, even if no federal statute or constitutional provision directly controls the case. Courts must pay close attention to the substantive issues raised by the case at hand, however technical they may be, in order to decide whether federal common law should govern a particular point.

The new federal common law began to emerge a few years after *Erie*, notably in *Clearfield Trust Co.* The key holding is that *Erie* did "not apply to this action. The rights and duties of the United States on commercial paper which it issues are governed by federal rather than local law." Though no federal statute addressed the issue, "[i]n the absence of an applicable Act of Congress it is for the federal courts to fashion the governing rule of law according to their own standards."

3.   The Scope of *Clearfield Trust*. A few years after *Clearfield Trust*, in *United States v. Standard Oil Co.*, 332 U.S. 301 (1947), the Court again addressed the scope of federal common law. A soldier named Etzel had been hit by a Standard Oil truck. Etzel had settled his case against Standard Oil. The question before the Supreme Court was whether the United States was "entitled to recover from [Standard Oil] the amounts expended for hospitalization and soldier's pay, as for loss of Etzel's services." One aspect of this issue was whether it should be governed by federal or state law, with the United States arguing for the former and Standard Oil for the latter. The Court relied on *Clearfield Trust* for the proposition that the Government's rights and obligations are governed by federal law, and it explicitly rejected the notion that *Clearfield* should be limited to commercial cases: "Although the *Clearfield* case applied these principles to a situation involving contractual relations of the Government, they are equally applicable in the facts of this case where the relations affected are noncontractual or tortious in nature."

Later in the opinion, the Court explained that the case was not "within the spirit and purpose of the *Erie* decision, for 'the object and effect [of *Erie*] were [to] bring federal judicial power under subjection to state authority in matters essentially of local interest and state control. Conversely, there was no purpose or effect for broadening state power over matters essentially of federal character or for determining whether issues are of that nature.' " *Erie* does not apply "to matters exclusively federal, because made so by constitutional or valid statutory command, or others so vitally affecting interests, powers and relations of the Federal Government as to require uniform national disposition rather than diversified state rulings."

But the Government's victory on the "power-to-make-federal-common-law" issue was a hollow one, for the Court went on to make a federal common law rule that thwarted the Government's ultimate aim. It ruled that the United States may not sue for this type of loss unless Congress authorizes the suit.

> The issue comes down in final consequence to a question of federal fiscal policy. [Whatever] the merits of the policy, its conversion into law is a proper subject for congressional action, not for any creative power of ours. Congress, not this Court or the other federal courts, is the custodian of the national purse. By the same token it is the primary and most often the exclusive arbiter of federal fiscal affairs. And these comprehend [securing] the treasury or the government against financial losses however inflicted, including requiring reimbursement for injuries creating them, as well as filling the treasury itself. [Exercise] of judicial power to establish the new liability not only would be intruding within a field properly within Congress' control and as to a matter concerning which it has seen fit to take no action. To accept the challenge, making the liability effective in this case, also would involve a possible element of surprise, in view of the settled contrary practice, which action by Congress would avoid.

Does this "federal fiscal policy" reasoning convincingly distinguish *Standard Oil* from *Clearfield Trust*?

UNITED STATES v. KIMBELL FOODS, INC.
440 U.S. 715 (1979).

MR. JUSTICE MARSHALL delivered the opinion of the Court.

We granted certiorari [to] determine whether contractual liens arising from certain federal loan programs take precedence over private liens, in the absence of a federal statute setting priorities. To resolve this question, we must decide <u>first</u> whether federal or state law governs the controversies; and <u>second,</u> if federal law applies, whether this Court should fashion a uniform priority rule or incorporate state commercial law. We conclude that the source of law is federal, but that a national rule is unnecessary to protect the federal interests underlying the loan programs. Accordingly, we adopt state law as the appropriate federal rule for establishing the relative priority of these competing federal and private liens.

[This case] involves two contractual security interests in the personal property of O. K. Super Markets, Inc. Both interests were perfected pursuant to Texas' Uniform Commercial Code (UCC). The United States' lien secures a loan guaranteed by the Small Business Administration (SBA). The private lien, which arises from security agreements that preceded the federal guarantee, secures advances respondent made after the federal guarantee.

In 1968, O. K. Super Markets borrowed $27,000 from Kimbell Foods, Inc. a grocery wholesaler. Two security agreements identified the supermarket's equipment and merchandise as collateral. The agreements also contained a standard "dragnet" clause providing that this collateral would secure future advances from Kimbell to O. K. Super Markets. Kimbell properly perfected its security interests by filing financing statements with the Texas Secretary of State according to Texas law. In February 1969, O. K. Super Markets obtained a $300,000 loan from Republic National Bank of Dallas (Republic). The bank accepted as security the same property specified in Kimbell's 1968 agreements, and filed a financing statement with the Texas Secretary of State to perfect its security interest. The SBA guaranteed 90% of this [loan].

[When O. K. Super Markets declared bankruptcy, Kimbell sued] to foreclose on its lien, claiming that its security interest [was] superior to the SBA's. The District Court held for the Government. On determining that federal law controlled the controversy, the court applied principles developed by the United States Supreme Court to afford federal statutory tax liens special priority over state and private liens where the governing statute does not specify [priorities]. [A companion case raised similar issues in connection with an FHA loan.]

II

This Court has consistently held that federal law governs questions involving the rights of the United States arising under nationwide federal programs. As the Court explained in *Clearfield Trust Co.*:

> When the United States disburses its funds or pays its debts, it is exercising a constitutional function or power.... The authority [to do so] had its origin in the Constitution and the statutes of the United States and was in no way dependent on the laws [of any State]. The duties imposed upon the United States and the rights acquired by it ... find their roots in the same federal sources. In absence of an applicable Act of Congress

it is for the federal courts to fashion the governing rule of law according to their own standards.

Guided by these principles, we think it clear that the priority of liens stemming from federal lending programs must be determined with reference to federal law. The SBA unquestionably [performs] federal functions within the meaning of *Clearfield*. [When] Government activities [arise] from and [bear] heavily upon a federal [program], the Constitution and Acts of Congress require otherwise than that state law govern of its own force. In such contexts, federal interests are sufficiently implicated to warrant the protection of federal law.

That the statutes authorizing these federal lending programs do not specify the appropriate rule of decision in no way limits the reach of federal law. It is precisely when Congress has not spoken in an area comprising issues substantially related to an established program of government operation that *Clearfield* directs federal courts to fill the interstices of federal legislation "according to their own standards." *Clearfield Trust.*

Federal law therefore controls the Government's priority rights. The more difficult task, to which we turn, is giving content to this federal rule.

III

Controversies directly affecting the operations of federal programs, although governed by federal law, do not inevitably require resort to uniform federal rules. See *Clearfield Trust Co.* Whether to adopt state law or to fashion a nationwide federal rule is a matter of judicial policy dependent upon a variety of considerations always relevant to the nature of the specific governmental interests and to the effects upon them of applying state law. Undoubtedly, federal programs that by their nature are and must be uniform in character throughout the Nation necessitate formulation of controlling federal rules. Conversely, when there is little need for a nationally uniform body of law, state law may be incorporated as the federal rule of decision. Apart from considerations of uniformity, we must also determine whether application of state law would frustrate specific objectives of the federal programs. If so, we must fashion special rules solicitous of those federal interests. Finally, our choice-of-law inquiry must consider the extent to which application of a federal rule would disrupt commercial relationships predicated on state law.

[We] are unpersuaded that, in the circumstances presented here, nationwide standards favoring claims of the United States are necessary to ease program administration or to safeguard the Federal Treasury from defaulting debtors. Because the state commercial codes furnish convenient solutions in no way inconsistent with adequate protection of the federal [interests], we decline to override intricate state laws of general applicability on which private creditors base their daily commercial transactions.

A

Incorporating state law to determine the rights of the United States as against private creditors would in no way hinder administration of the SBA [loan program]. In *United States v. Yazell* this Court rejected the argument, similar to the Government's here, that a need for uniformity precluded application of state coverture rules to an SBA loan contract. Because SBA operations were "specifically and in great detail adapted to state law," the federal interest in supplanting "important and carefully evolved state arrangements designed to serve multiple purposes" was minimal. Our conclusion that compliance with state law would produce no hardship on the agency was also based on the SBA's practice of "individually [negotiating] in painfully particularized detail" each loan transaction. These observations apply with equal force here and compel us again to reject generalized pleas for uniformity as substitutes for concrete evidence that adopting state law would adversely affect administration of the federal programs.

Although the SBA Financial Assistance Manual on which this Court relied in *Yazell* is no longer "replete with admonitions to follow state law carefully," SBA employees are still instructed to, and indeed do, follow state law. In fact, a fair reading of the SBA Financial Assistance Manual indicates that the agency assumes its security interests are controlled to a large extent by the commercial law of each State.

[Nevertheless], the Government maintains that requiring the [SBA] to assess security arrangements under local law would dictate close scrutiny of each transaction and thereby impede expeditious processing of loans. We disagree. Choosing responsible debtors necessarily requires individualized selection procedures, which the agencies have already implemented in considerable detail. Each applicant's financial condition is evaluated under rigorous standards in a lengthy process. Agency employees negotiate personally with borrowers, investigate property offered as collateral for encumbrances, and obtain local legal advice on the adequacy of proposed security arrangements. In addition, they adapt the terms of every loan to the parties' needs and capabilities. Because each application currently receives individual scrutiny, the agencies can readily adjust loan transactions to reflect state priority rules, just as they consider other factual and legal matters before disbursing Government funds. As we noted in *Yazell,* these lending programs are distinguishable from "nationwide [acts] of the Federal Government, emanating in a single form from a single source." Since there is no indication that variant state priority schemes would burden current methods of loan processing, we conclude that considerations of administrative convenience do not warrant adoption of a uniform federal law.

B

The Government argues that applying state law [here] would undermine its ability to recover funds disbursed and therefore would conflict with program objectives. In the Government's view, it is difficult "to identify a material distinction between a dollar received from the collection of taxes and a dollar returned to the Treasury on repayment of a federal loan." Therefore, [just] as "the purpose of the federal tax lien statute to insure prompt and certain collection of taxes" justified our imposition of the [special priority] doctrines in the tax lien context, the federal interest in recovering on loans compels similar legal protection of the agencies' consensual liens. However, we believe significant differences between federal tax liens and consensual liens counsel against unreflective extension of rules that immunize the United States from the commercial law governing all other voluntary secured creditors. These differences persuade us that deference to customary commercial practices would not frustrate the objectives of the lending programs.

That collection of taxes is vital to the functioning, indeed existence, of government cannot be denied. Congress recognized as much over 100 years ago when it authorized creation of federal tax liens. The importance of securing adequate revenues to discharge national obligations justifies the extraordinary priority accorded federal tax liens. [By] contrast, when the United States operates as a money lending institution under carefully circumscribed programs, its interest in recouping the limited sums advanced is of a different order. Thus, there is less need here than in the tax lien area to invoke protective measures against defaulting debtors in a manner disruptive of existing credit markets.

To equate tax liens with these consensual liens also misperceives the principal congressional concerns underlying the respective statutes. The overriding purpose of the tax lien statute obviously is to ensure prompt revenue collection. The same cannot be said of the SBA and FHA lending programs. They are a form of social welfare legislation, primarily designed to assist farmers and businesses that cannot obtain funds from private lenders on reasonable terms. We believe that had Congress intended the private commercial sector, rather than taxpayers in general, to bear the risks of default entailed by these public welfare programs, it would have established a priority scheme displacing state law. Far from doing so, both Congress and the agencies have expressly recognized the priority of certain private liens over the agencies' security interests, thereby indicating that the extraordinary safeguards applied in the tax lien area are unnecessary to maintain the lending programs.

The Government's ability to safeguard its interests in commercial dealings further reveals that the rules developed in the tax lien area are unnecessary here, and that state priority rules would not conflict with federal lending objectives. The United States is an involuntary creditor of delinquent taxpayers, unable to control the factors that make tax collection likely. In contrast, when the United States acts as a lender or guarantor, it does so voluntarily, with detailed knowledge of the borrower's financial status. The agencies evaluate the risks associated with each loan, examine the interests of other creditors, choose the security believed necessary to assure repayment, and set the terms of every agreement. By carefully selecting loan recipients and tailoring each transaction with state law in mind, the agencies are fully capable of establishing terms that will secure repayment.

The Government nonetheless argues that its opportunity to evaluate the credit worthiness of loan applicants provides minimal safety. Because the SBA [makes] loans only when private lenders will not, the United States believes that its security interests demand greater protection than ordinary commercial arrangements. We find this argument unconvincing. The [SBA does] not indiscriminately distribute public funds and hope that reimbursement will follow. SBA loans must be "of such sound value or so secured as reasonably to assure repayment." 15 U.S.C. § 636 (a)(7); see 13 CFR § 120.2 (c)(1) (1978). [The SBA has] promulgated exhaustive instructions to ensure that loan recipients are financially reliable and to prevent improvident loans. The Government therefore is in substantially the same position as private lenders, and the special status it seeks is unnecessary to safeguard the public fisc. Moreover, Congress' admonitions to extend loans judiciously supports the view that it did not intend to confer special privileges on agencies that enter the commercial [field].

C

In structuring financial transactions, businessmen depend on state commercial law to provide the stability essential for reliable evaluation of the risks involved. However, subjecting federal contractual liens to the doctrines developed in the tax lien area could undermine that stability. Creditors who justifiably rely on state law to obtain superior liens would have their expectations thwarted whenever a federal contractual security interest suddenly appeared and took precedence.

Because the ultimate consequences of altering settled commercial practices are so difficult to foresee, we hesitate to create new uncertainties in the absence of careful legislative deliberation. Of course, formulating special rules to govern the priority of the federal consensual liens in issue here would be justified if necessary to vindicate important national interests. But neither the Government nor the Court of Appeals advanced any concrete reasons for rejecting well-established commercial rules which have proven workable over time. Thus, the prudent course is to adopt the readymade body of state law as the federal rule of decision until Congress strikes a different [accommodation].

NOTES ON KIMBELL FOODS AND BORROWING STATE LAW

1. **From *Clearfield Trust* to *Kimbell Foods*.** Distinguish between two issues decided by *Clearfield Trust*. One is whether, despite *Erie*, it is appropriate to make a federal common law rule for issues that in one way or another transcend the interests of a particular state. Today no one questions that holding. It is settled that, with regard to the rights and duties of the United States, *Erie* never requires the use of state law. But another aspect of *Clearfield Trust* has had a checkered career. Given the Court's affirmative answer to the first question, the other issue addressed in the case was whether the Court should "borrow" state law as the federal rule. The Court in *Clearfield Trust* justified making a federal rule requiring a showing of prejudice by stressing "the desirability of a uniform rule" for government obligations. To follow state law would "subject the rights and duties of the United States to exceptional uncertainty."

In light of this "uniformity" rationale, is *Kimbell Foods* consistent with *Clearfield Trust*? If uniformity is a compelling argument in the earlier case, why not in the later one as well? Is the "intrastate" interest in uniformity greater with regard to lien priority than it is with regard to the effect of delay in notifying an endorser of a forgery? In any event, *Kimbell Foods* suggests that the "uniformity" argument is not necessarily so strong today as it was for the Court in *Clearfield Trust*.

2. **Federal Common Law in U.S. Government Litigation: State Rules that Unfairly Prejudice the Government's Interests.** In *United States v. Little Lake Misere Land Co.*, 412 U.S. 580 (1973), the substantive issue was whether Little Lake Misere had a right to drill for oil, gas, and other minerals on two parcels of land in Louisiana owned by the United States. The government had obtained the two parcels in the 1930s, one by condemnation and the other by purchase. Under the terms of the condemnation and the purchase, Little Lake Misere retained drilling rights indefinitely, so long as it engaged in operations during a 10 year period after the government took title. But "no drilling, reworking, or other operations were conducted and no minerals were obtained for a period of more than 10 years following the act of sale and judgment of condemnation." Little Lake Misere nonetheless insisted that it still had the drilling rights, basing its claim on a state statute, Louisiana Act 315 of 1940. The statute provided that "[w]hen land is acquired [by] the United States of America, [and] oil, gas, or other minerals or royalties are reserved, [the] rights so reserved [shall] be imprescriptible." Little Lake Misere argued "that the 1940 enactment rendered inoperative the conditions set forth in 1937 and 1939 for the extinguishment of the [reservations.]" But the Court disagreed, reasoning

that this "rule of retroactive imprescriptibility [was] plainly hostile to the interests of the United States. As applied to a consummated land transaction under a contract which specifically defined conditions for prolonging the vendor's mineral reservation, retroactive application of Act 315 to the United States deprives it of bargained—for contractual interests." What would be the result if the U.S. had obtained the land in 1941? Given the vagaries of "federal common law," can you think of a way for the United States to bypass this body of doctrine and assure that it will not be ensnared in Louisiana Act 315?

Little Lake Misere seems to be an easy case. In any event, there were no dissents. Compare *United States v. 93.970 Acres of Land*, 360 U.S. 328 (1959). The United States had leased an airfield to Illinois Aircraft Services and Sales Co. Under the terms of the lease, it was revocable at will by the Government "in event of a national emergency and a decision by the Secretary of the Navy that such revocation is essential." Some years later the Army wanted to use the land for a missile site and the U.S. sought to revoke the lease. (Both the Secretary of the Navy and the Secretary of the Army signed the revocation notification.) Illinois Aircraft resisted the revocation, arguing that under the terms of the lease it could be revoked only for naval aviation activities. "In order to obtain possession and use of the land as soon as possible—and without waiting to try out the validity of the prior revocation in a separate action or actions—the Government filed a complaint to condemn whatever possessory interest [Illinois Aircraft] might be adjudicated to have." In the ensuing litigation the Government asserted both a condemnation claim (which would require it to pay for the property interest) and revocation of the lease (which, if valid, would not require it to pay anything). The lower courts ruled that Illinois Aircraft was right on the scope of the revocation-at-will clause; and that, in any event, under Illinois law, the Government had, by initiating the condemnation case, made an "election of remedies" in favor of condemnation, foregoing any claim it may have for enforcement of the revocation-at-will provision of the lease. The Supreme Court reversed. After first ruling that the Government had the right to revoke the lease, the Court said:

> It follows necessarily from this that application of the doctrine of "election of remedies" would put the Government in an impossible situation. For under the doctrine, the Government must choose either to abandon its power to revoke the lease or to give up its right to immediate possession under condemnation law. [Such] a strict rule against combining different causes of action would certainly be out of harmony with modern legislation and rules designed to make trials as efficient, expeditious and inexpensive as fairness will permit. Respondents argue, however, that election of remedies is part of the law of Illinois, and that Illinois Law applies here. We cannot agree with this view. Condemnation involves essential governmental functions. We have often held that where essential functions of the Federal Government are concerned, federal rules

apply unless Congress chooses to make state laws applicable. It is apparent that no such choice has been made here.

Note the Court's stance on "borrowing." Would this case come out the same way after *Kimbell Foods*? Can the cases be reconciled on the ground that the activity of the Small Business Administration was more "proprietary" in nature, while *93.970 Acres* involved a quintessentially governmental function?

3. **Borrowing and Its Consequences.** Deciding to borrow does not mean that state law will *always* govern an issue. When a case is controlled by the *Erie* doctrine, state law applies no matter what the *content* of state law may be. But the situation is different when there is a sufficient federal interest to justify making federal common law, yet a court decides to borrow state law as the federal rule under the doctrine illustrated by *Kimbell Foods*. In cases of this type, the court may pick and choose depending on the content of the state law, borrowing some state rules and rejecting others. In *Reconstruction Finance Corp. v. Beaver County*, 328 U.S. 204 (1946), a federal statute allowed state and local taxation of the real property of the RFC, a federal agency, but barred taxation of the RFC's personal property. Beaver County sought to tax heavy machines, reasoning that under state law the machines were real, not personal, property. Relying on *Clearfield*'s "uniformity" reasoning, the RFC argued for a federal rule to the contrary. But the Court held that nationwide uniformity could not be achieved in any event, as under the federal statute localities across the country could in any case choose to tax at different rates. In effect, the Court opted for borrowing the state's law on whether a given piece of Government property was "real" or "personal," with the proviso that state law would be followed only "so long as it is plain, as it is here, that the state rules do not effect a discrimination against the government, or patently run counter to the terms of the Act." Suppose that, after *Beaver County*, a state legislature enacts a statute providing that *all* RFC property is "real" property and a county attempts to tax the RFC's cash. Would the courts borrow state law in such a case?

4. **Congressional Directives to Borrow State Law.** Sometimes Congress commands the courts to follow state law in resolving issues that may otherwise be governed by federal common law. The Federal Tort Claims Act, 28 U.S.C. § 1346(b), provides that (subject to certain exceptions) the United States may be sued in federal court for torts committed by "any employee of the Government while acting within the scope of his office or employment under circumstances where the United States, if a private person, would be liable to the claimant in accordance with the law of the place where the act or omission occurred." Is it fair to characterize this provision as a directive that courts should borrow state law in resolving these tort cases? See also Fed. R. Evid. 501, which provides, in part, that "in civil actions and proceedings, with respect to an element of a claim or defense as to which State law supplies the rule of decision, the privilege of a witness, person, government, State, or political subdivision thereof shall be determined in accordance with State law."

5.   A Third Issue in Federal Common Law Litigation. *Clearfield Trust* and *Kimbell Foods* divide the federal common law inquiry into two questions: whether the circumstances justify reference to federal common law, and whether, in the event the answer to the first question is yes, the court should nonetheless borrow state law as the federal rule. Both cases answer the first question in the affirmative, only to diverge on the borrowing issue. Notice that in the event a court chooses to make a federal rule, a third question arises, though *Clearfield Trust* does not call attention to it. This is the question of just what the content of the federal rule should be. For example, one might decide to make federal common law, and then choose a rule that any delay of more than two months is presumptively prejudicial. As it happens (and as both *Clearfield Trust* and *Boyle*, below, illustrate) when the Supreme Court decides to make a federal rule in a case involving the interests of the United States, it generally picks a rule favoring the government. But there is no logical connection between the two issues. Whether a federal rule is appropriate and whether the content of that rule should favor the government's side of the case are separate questions. For example, in the *Standard Oil* case, supra, the Court declined to borrow state law, but then (by declining to recognize the cause of action the United States sought to assert) made a federal rule that was not to the government's liking.

B. FEDERAL COMMON LAW IN LITIGATION BETWEEN PRIVATE PARTIES

The foregoing materials mainly concern the rights and obligations of the United States. Should federal common law apply in suits between private parties as well?

BOYLE V. UNITED TECHNOLOGIES CORP.
487 U.S. 500 (1988).

JUSTICE SCALIA delivered the opinion of the Court.

This case requires us to decide when a contractor providing military equipment to the Federal Government can be held liable under state tort law for injury caused by a design defect.

On April 27, 1983, David A. Boyle, a United States Marine helicopter copilot, was killed when the CH–53D helicopter in which he was flying crashed off the coast of Virginia Beach, Virginia, during a training exercise. Although Boyle survived the impact of the crash, he was unable to escape from the helicopter and drowned. Boyle's father, petitioner here, brought this diversity action in Federal District Court against the Sikorsky Division of United Technologies Corporation (Sikorsky), which built the helicopter for the United States. At trial, petitioner presented two theories of liability under Virginia tort law that were submitted to the jury. First, petitioner alleged that Sikorsky had defectively repaired a device called the servo in the helicopter's automatic flight control system, which allegedly malfunctioned and caused the crash. Second, petitioner alleged that Sikorsky had defectively designed the copilot's emergency escape system: the escape hatch opened out instead of in (and was therefore ineffective in a submerged craft because of water pressure), and access to the escape hatch handle was obstructed by other equipment. The jury returned a general verdict in favor of petitioner and awarded him $725,000. The District Court denied Sikorsky's motion for judgment notwithstanding the verdict.

The Court of Appeals reversed and remanded with directions that judgment be entered for Sikorsky. It found, as a matter of Virginia law, that Boyle had failed to meet his burden of demonstrating that the repair work performed by Sikorsky, as opposed to work that had been done by the Navy, was responsible for the alleged malfunction of the flight control system. It also found, as a matter of federal law, that Sikorsky could not be held liable for the allegedly defective design of the escape hatch because, on the evidence presented, it satisfied the requirements of the "military contractor defense," which the court had recognized the same day in *Tozer v. LTV Corp.*, 792 F.2d 403 (CA4 1986).

II

[Petitioner's] broadest contention is that, in the absence of legislation specifically immunizing Government contractors from liability for design defects, there is no basis for judicial recognition of such a defense. We disagree. In most fields of activity, to be sure, this Court has refused to find federal pre-emption of state law in the absence of either a clear statutory prescription or a direct conflict between federal and state law. But we have held that a few areas, involving uniquely federal interests, are so committed by the Constitution and laws of the United States to federal control that state law is pre-empted and replaced, where necessary, by federal law of a content prescribed (absent explicit statutory directive) by the courts—so-called "federal common law." See, *e.g., Kimbell Foods, Clearfield Trust Co.*

The dispute in the present case borders upon two areas that we have found to involve such "uniquely federal interests." We have held that obligations to and rights of the United States under its contracts are governed exclusively by federal law. See, *e.g., Little Lake Misere Land Co.; Clearfield Trust.* The present case does not involve an obligation to the United States under its contract, but rather liability to third persons. That liability may be styled one in tort, but it arises out of performance of the contract—and traditionally has been regarded as sufficiently related to the contract that until 1962 Virginia would generally allow design defect suits only by the purchaser and those in privity with the seller.

Another area that we have found to be of peculiarly federal concern, warranting the displacement of state law, is the civil liability of federal officials for actions taken in the course of their duty. We have held in many contexts that the scope of that liability is controlled by federal law. The present case involves an independent contractor performing its obligation under a procurement contract, rather than an official performing his duty as a federal employee, but there is obviously implicated the same interest in getting the Government's work done.

We think the reasons for considering these closely related areas to be of "uniquely federal" interest apply as well to the civil liabilities arising out of the performance of federal procurement contracts. We have come close to holding as much. In *Yearsley v. W. A. Ross Construction Co.*, 309 U.S. 18 (1940), we rejected an attempt by a landowner to hold a construction contractor liable under state law for the erosion of 95 acres caused by the contractor's work in constructing dikes for the Government. We said that "if [the] authority to carry out the project was validly conferred, that is, if what was done was within the constitutional power of Congress, there is no liability on the part of the contractor for executing its will." The federal interest justifying this holding surely exists as much in procurement contracts as in performance contracts; we see no basis for a distinction.

Moreover, it is plain that the Federal Government's interest in the procurement of equipment is implicated by suits such as the present one—even though the dispute is one between private parties. It is true that where litigation is purely between private parties and does not touch the rights and duties of the United States, federal law does not govern. Thus, for example, in *Miree v. DeKalb County*, 433 U.S. 25, 30 (1977), which involved the question whether certain private parties could sue as third party beneficiaries to an agreement between a municipality and the Federal Aviation Administration, we found that state law was not displaced because "the operations of the United States in connection with FAA grants such as these . . . would [not] be burdened" by allowing state law to determine whether third-party beneficiaries could sue, and because "any federal interest in the outcome of the [dispute] before us [was] far too speculative, far too remote a possibility to justify the application of federal law to transactions essentially of local concern." But the same is not true here. The imposition of liability on Government contractors will directly affect the terms of Government contracts: either the contractor will decline to manufacture the design specified by the Government, or it will raise its price. Either way, the interests of the United States will be directly affected.

That the procurement of equipment by the United States is an area of uniquely federal interest does not, however, end the inquiry. That merely establishes a necessary, not a sufficient, condition for the displacement of state law.[3] Displacement will occur only where, as we have variously described, a "significant conflict" exists between an identifiable "federal policy or interest and the [operation] of state law," or the application of state law would "frustrate specific objectives" of federal legislation. The conflict with federal policy need not be as sharp as that which must exist for ordinary pre-emption when Congress legislates in a field which the States have traditionally occupied. Or to put the point differently, the fact that the area in question *is* one of unique federal concern changes what would otherwise be a conflict that cannot produce pre-emption into one that can. But conflict there must be. In some cases, for example where the federal interest requires a uniform rule, the entire body of state law applicable to the area conflicts and is replaced by federal rules. See, *e.g., Clearfield Trust* (rights and obligations of United States with respect to commercial paper must be governed by uniform federal rule). In others, the conflict is more narrow, and only particular elements of state law are superseded. See, e.g., *Little Lake Misere Land Co.* (even assuming state law should generally govern federal land acquisitions, particular state law at issue may not).

In *Miree,* supra, the suit was not seeking to impose upon the person contracting with the Government a duty contrary to the duty imposed by the Government contract. Rather, it was the contractual duty *itself* that the private plaintiff (as third-party beneficiary) sought to enforce. Between *Miree* and the present case, it is easy to conceive of an intermediate situation, in which the duty sought to be imposed on the contractor is not identical to one assumed under the contract, but is also not contrary to any assumed. If, for example, the United States contracts for the purchase and installation of an air-conditioning unit, specifying the cooling capacity but not the precise manner of construction, a state law imposing upon the manufacturer of such units a duty of care to include a certain safety feature would not be a duty identical to anything promised the Government, but neither would it be contrary. The contractor could comply with both its contractual obligations and the state-prescribed duty of care. No one suggests that state law would generally be pre-empted in this context.

The present case, however, is at the opposite extreme from *Miree.* Here the state-imposed duty of care that is the asserted basis of the

---

[3]   We refer here to the displacement of state law, although it is possible to analyze it as the displacement of federal-law reference to state law for the rule of decision. Some of our cases appear to regard the area in which a uniquely federal interest exists as being entirely governed by federal law, with federal law deigning to "borro[w]," *United States v. Little Lake Misere Land Co.,* 412 U.S. 580, 594 (1973), or "incorporat[e]" or "adopt", *United States v. Kimbell Foods, Inc.,* 440 U.S. 715, 728, 729, 730 (1979), state law except where a significant conflict with federal policy exists. We see nothing to be gained by expanding the theoretical scope of the federal pre-emption beyond its practical effect, and so adopt the more modest terminology. If the distinction between displacement of state law and displacement of federal law's incorporation of state law ever makes a practical difference, it at least does not do so in the present case.

contractor's liability (specifically, the duty to equip helicopters with the sort of escape-hatch mechanism petitioner claims was necessary) is precisely contrary to the duty imposed by the Government contract (the duty to manufacture and deliver helicopters with the sort of escape-hatch mechanism shown by the specifications). Even in this sort of situation, it would be unreasonable to say that there is always a "significant conflict" between the state law and a federal policy or interest. If, for example, a federal procurement officer orders, by model number, a quantity of stock helicopters that happen to be equipped with escape hatches opening outward, it is impossible to say that the Government has a significant interest in that particular feature. That would be scarcely more reasonable than saying that a private individual who orders such a craft by model number cannot sue for the manufacturer's negligence because he got precisely what he ordered.

In its search for the limiting principle to identify those situations in which a "significant conflict" with federal policy or interests does arise, the Court of Appeals, in the lead case upon which its opinion here relied, identified as the source of the conflict the *Feres* doctrine, under which the Federal Tort Claims Act (FTCA) does not cover injuries to Armed Services personnel in the course of military service. See *Feres v. United States*, 340 U.S. 135 (1950). Military contractor liability would conflict with this doctrine, the Fourth Circuit reasoned, since the increased cost of the contractor's tort liability would be added to the price of the contract, and "[s]uch pass-through costs would . . . defeat the purpose of the immunity for military accidents conferred upon the government itself." [We] do not adopt this analysis because it seems to us that the *Feres* doctrine, in its application to the present problem, logically produces results that are in some respects too broad and in some respects too narrow. Too broad, because if the Government contractor defense is to prohibit suit against the manufacturer whenever *Feres* would prevent suit against the Government, then even injuries caused to military personnel by a helicopter purchased from stock (in our example above), or by any standard equipment purchased by the Government, would be covered. Since *Feres* prohibits all service-related tort claims against the Government, a contractor defense that rests upon it should prohibit all service-related tort claims against the manufacturer—making inexplicable the three limiting criteria for contractor immunity (which we will discuss presently) that the Court of Appeals adopted. On the other hand, reliance on *Feres* produces (or logically should produce) results that are in another respect too narrow. Since that doctrine covers only service-related injuries, and not injuries caused by the military to civilians, it could not be invoked to prevent, for example, a civilian's suit against the manufacturer of fighter planes, based on a state tort theory, claiming harm from what is alleged to be needlessly high levels of noise produced by the jet engines. Yet we think that the character of the jet engines the

Government orders for its fighter planes cannot be regulated by state tort law, no more in suits by civilians than in suits by members of the Armed Services.

There is, however, a statutory provision that demonstrates the potential for, and suggests the outlines of, "significant conflict" between federal interests and state law in the context of Government procurement. In the FTCA, Congress authorized damages to be recovered against the United States for harm caused by the negligent or wrongful conduct of Government employees, to the extent that a private person would be liable under the law of the place where the conduct occurred. 28 U.S.C. § 1346(b). It excepted from this consent to suit, however, "[a]ny claim . . . based upon the exercise or performance or the failure to exercise or perform a discretionary function or duty on the part of a federal agency or an employee of the Government, whether or not the discretion involved be abused." 28 U.S.C. § 2680(a).

We think that the selection of the appropriate design for military equipment to be used by our Armed Forces is assuredly a discretionary function within the meaning of this provision. It often involves not merely engineering analysis but judgment as to the balancing of many technical, military, and even social considerations, including specifically the trade-off between greater safety and greater combat effectiveness. And we are further of the view that permitting "second-guessing" of these judgments through state tort suits against contractors would produce the same effect sought to be avoided by the FTCA exemption. The financial burden of judgments against the contractors would ultimately be passed through, substantially if not totally, to the United States itself, since defense contractors will predictably raise their prices to cover, or to insure against, contingent liability for the Government-ordered designs. To put the point differently: It makes little sense to insulate the Government against financial liability for the judgment that a particular feature of military equipment is necessary when the Government produces the equipment itself, but not when it contracts for the production. In sum, we are of the view that state law which holds Government contractors liable for design defects in military equipment does in some circumstances present a "significant conflict" with federal policy and must be displaced.

We agree with the scope of displacement adopted by the Fourth Circuit [here]. Liability for design defects in military equipment cannot be imposed, pursuant to state law, when (1) the United States approved reasonably precise specifications; (2) the equipment conformed to those specifications; and (3) the supplier warned the United States about the dangers in the use of the equipment that were known to the supplier but not to the United States. The first two of these conditions assure that the suit is within the area where the policy of the "discretionary function" would be frustrated—*i.e.*, they assure that the design feature in question was considered by a Government officer, and not merely by the contractor itself. The third condition is necessary because, in its absence, the displacement of state tort law would create some incentive for the manufacturer to withhold knowledge of risks, since conveying that knowledge might disrupt the contract but withholding it would produce no liability. We adopt this provision lest our effort to protect discretionary functions perversely impede them by cutting off information highly relevant to the discretionary decision.

We have considered the alternative formulation of the Government contractor defense, urged upon us by [petitioner]. That would preclude suit only if (1) the contractor did not participate, or participated only minimally, in the design of the defective equipment; *or* (2) the contractor timely warned the Government of the risks of the design and notified it of alternative designs reasonably known by it, *and* the Government, although forewarned, clearly authorized the contractor to proceed with the dangerous design. While this formulation may represent a perfectly reasonable tort rule, it is not a rule designed to protect the federal interest embodied in the "discretionary function" exemption. The design ultimately selected may well reflect a significant policy judgment by Government officials whether or not the contractor rather than those officials developed the design. In addition, it does not seem to us sound policy to penalize, and thus deter, active contractor participation in the design process, placing the contractor at risk unless it identifies all design defects.

III

[The Fourth Circuit, applying the "government contractor defense," had ruled for the manufacturer. But its opinion was somewhat ambiguous, leaving open the possibility that a reasonable jury could find for the plaintiff. Accordingly, the Court remanded the case for further consideration and clarification].

JUSTICE BRENNAN, with whom JUSTICE MARSHALL and JUSTICE BLACKMUN join, dissenting.

Lieutenant David A. Boyle died when the CH–53D helicopter he was copiloting spun out of control and plunged into the ocean. We may assume, for purposes of this case, that Lt. Boyle was trapped under water and drowned because respondent United Technologies negligently designed the helicopter's escape hatch. We may further assume that any competent engineer would have discovered and cured the defects, but that they inexplicably escaped respondent's notice. Had respondent designed such a death trap for a commercial firm, Lt. Boyle's family could sue under Virginia tort law and be compensated for his tragic and unnecessary death. But respondent designed the helicopter for the Federal Government, and that, the Court tells us today, makes all the difference: Respondent is immune from liability so long as it obtained approval of "reasonably precise specifications"—perhaps no more than a rubber stamp from a federal procurement officer who might or might not have noticed or cared about the defects, or even had the expertise to discover them.

If respondent's immunity "bore the legitimacy of having been prescribed by the people's elected representatives," we would be duty bound to implement their will, whether or not we approved. Congress, however, has remained silent—and conspicuously so, having resisted a sustained campaign by Government contractors to legislate for them some defense.[1] The Court—unelected and unaccountable to the people— has unabashedly stepped into the breach to legislate a rule denying Lt. Boyle's family the compensation that state law assures them. This time the injustice is of this Court's own making.

Worse yet, the injustice will extend far beyond the facts of this case, for the Court's newly discovered Government contractor defense is breathtakingly sweeping. It applies not only to military equipment like the CH–53D helicopter, but (so far as I can tell) to any made-to-order gadget that the Federal Government might purchase after previewing plans—from NASA's Challenger space shuttle to the Postal Service's old mail cars. The contractor may invoke the defense in suits brought not only by military personnel like Lt. Boyle, or Government employees, but by anyone injured by a Government contractor's negligent design, including, for example, the children who might have died had respondent's helicopter crashed on the beach. It applies even if the Government has not intentionally sacrificed safety for other interests like speed or efficiency, and, indeed, even if the equipment is not of a type that is typically considered dangerous; thus, the contractor who designs a Government building can invoke the defense when the elevator cable snaps or the walls collapse. And the defense is invocable regardless of how blatant or easily remedied the defect, so long as the contractor missed it and the specifications approved by the Government, however unreasonably dangerous, were "reasonably precise."

In my view, this Court lacks both authority and expertise to fashion such a rule, whether to protect the Treasury of the United States or the coffers of industry. Because I would leave that exercise of legislative power to Congress, where our Constitution places it, I would reverse the Court of Appeals and reinstate petitioner's jury award. Before our decision in *Erie R. Co. v. Tompkins*, federal courts sitting in diversity

---

[1] See, *e.g.*, H. R. 4765, 99th Cong., 2d Sess. (1986) (limitations on civil liability of Government contractors); S. 2441, 99th Cong., 2d Sess. (1986) (same). See also H. R. 2378, 100th Cong., 1st Sess. (1987) (indemnification of civil liability for Government contractors); H. R. 5883, 98th Cong., 2d Sess. (1984) (same); H. R. 1504, 97th Cong., 1st Sess. (1981) (same); H. R. 5351, 96th Cong., 1st Sess. (1979) (same).

were generally free, in the absence of a controlling state statute, to fashion rules of "general" federal common law. See, e. g., *Swift v. Tyson.* *Erie* renounced the prevailing scheme: "Except in matters governed by the Federal Constitution or by Acts of Congress, the law to be applied in any case is the law of the State." The Court explained that the expansive power that federal courts had theretofore exercised was an unconstitutional "invasion of the authority of the State and, to that extent, a denial of its independence." Thus, *Erie* was deeply rooted in notions of federalism, and is most seriously implicated when, as here, federal judges displace the state law that would ordinarily govern with their own rules of federal common law.[2]

[Absent] some congressional authorization to formulate substantive rules of decision, federal common law exists only in such narrow areas as those concerned with the rights and obligations of the United States, interstate and international disputes implicating conflicting rights of States or our relations with foreign nations, and admiralty cases. The enactment of a federal rule in an area of national concern, and the decision whether to displace state law in doing so, is generally made not by the federal judiciary, purposefully insulated from democratic pressures, but by the people through their elected representatives in Congress. State laws should be overridden by the federal courts only where clear and substantial interests of the National Government, which cannot be served consistently with respect for such state interests, will suffer major damage if the state law is applied.

II

Congress has not decided to supersede state law here (if anything, it has decided not to, see n. 1, *supra*) and the Court does not pretend that its newly manufactured "Government contractor defense" fits within any of the handful of narrow areas, of uniquely federal interests in which we have heretofore done so. Rather, the Court creates a new category of "uniquely federal interests" out of a synthesis of two whose origins predate *Erie* itself: the interest in administering the "obligations to and rights of the United States under its contracts," and the interest in regulating the "civil liability of federal officials for actions taken in the course of their duty." This case is, however, simply a suit between two private parties. We have steadfastly declined to impose federal contract law on relationships that are collateral to a federal contract, or to extend the federal employee's immunity beyond federal employees. And the

---

[2] Not all exercises of our power to fashion federal common law displace state law in the same way. For example, our recognition of federal causes of action based upon either the Constitution, see, *e. g., Bivens v. Six Unknown Fed. Narcotics Agents,* 403 U.S. 388 (1971), or a federal statute, see *Cort v. Ash,* 422 U.S. 66 (1975), supplements whatever rights state law might provide, and therefore does not implicate federalism concerns in the same way as does preemption of a state-law rule of decision or cause of action. Throughout this opinion I use the word "displace" in the latter sense.

Court's ability to list 2, or 10, inapplicable areas of uniquely federal interest does not support its conclusion that the liability of Government contractors is so clear and substantial an interest that this Court must step in lest state law does major damage.

The proposition that federal common law continues to govern the "obligations to and rights of the United States under its contracts" is nearly as old as *Erie* itself. Federal law typically controls when the Federal Government is a party to a suit involving its rights or obligations under a contract, whether the contract entails procurement, a loan, see *United States v. Kimbell Foods,* a conveyance of property, see *Little Lake Misere,* or a commercial instrument issued by the Government, see *Clearfield Trust Co.* or assigned to it. Any such transaction necessarily "radiate[s] interests in transactions between private parties." *Bank of America Nat. Trust & Sav. Assn. v. Parnell,* 352 U.S. 29, 33 (1956). But it is by now established that our power to create federal common law controlling the *Federal Government's* contractual rights and obligations does not translate into a power to prescribe rules that cover all transactions or contractual relationships collateral to Government contracts.

In *Miree v. DeKalb County,* for example, the county was contractually obligated under a grant agreement with the Federal Aviation Administration (FAA) to "'restrict the use of land adjacent to ... the Airport to activities and purposes compatible with normal airport operations including landing and takeoff of aircraft.'" At issue was whether the county breached its contractual obligation by operating a garbage dump adjacent to the airport, which allegedly attracted the swarm of birds that caused a plane crash. Federal common law would undoubtedly have controlled in any suit by the Federal Government to enforce the provision against the county or to collect damages for its violation. The diversity suit, however, was brought not by the Government, but by assorted private parties injured in some way by the accident. We observed that "the operations of the United States in connection with FAA grants such as these are undoubtedly of considerable magnitude," and that "the United States has a substantial interest in regulating aircraft travel and promoting air travel safety." Nevertheless, we held that state law should govern the claim because "only the rights of private litigants are at issue here," and the claim against the county "will have *no direct effect upon the United States or its Treasury.*" (emphasis added).

Miree relied heavily on *Parnell, supra,* and *Wallis v. Pan American Petroleum Corp.,* the former involving commercial paper issued by the United States and the latter involving property rights in federal land. In the former case, Parnell cashed certain bonds guaranteed by the Government that had been stolen from their owner, a bank. It is beyond dispute that federal law would have governed the United States' duty to pay the value [of the] bonds upon presentation; we held as much in *Clearfield Trust*. But the central issue in *Parnell*, a diversity suit, was whether the victim of the theft could recover the money paid to Parnell. That issue, we held, was governed by state law, because the "litigation [was] purely between private parties and [did] *not touch the rights and duties of the United States*."(emphasis added).

The same was true in *Wallis*, which also involved a Government contract—a lease issued by the United States to a private party under the Mineral Leasing Act of 1920, governed entirely by federal law. Again, the relationship at issue in this diversity case was collateral to the Government contract: It involved the validity of contractual arrangements between the lessee and other private parties, not between the lessee and the Federal Government. Even though a federal statute authorized certain assignments of lease rights, and imposed certain conditions on their validity, we held that state law, not federal common law, governed their validity because application of state law would present "no significant threat to any identifiable federal policy or interest."

Here, as in *Miree, Parnell*, and *Wallis*, a Government contract governed by federal common law looms in the background. But here, too, the United States is not a party to the suit and the suit neither "touch[es] the rights and duties of the United States," *Parnell*, nor has a "direct effect upon the United States or its Treasury." *Miree*. The relationship at issue is at best collateral to the Government contract. We have no greater power to displace state law governing the collateral relationship in the Government procurement realm than we had to dictate federal rules governing equally collateral relationships in the areas of aviation, Government-issued commercial paper, or federal lands.

That the Government might have to pay higher prices for what it orders if delivery in accordance with the contract exposes the seller to potential liability, does not distinguish this case. Each of the cases just discussed declined to extend the reach of federal common law despite the assertion of comparable interests that would have affected the terms of the Government contract—whether its price or its substance—just as "directly" (or indirectly). Third-party beneficiaries can sue under a county's contract with the FAA, for example, even though—as the Court's focus on the absence of "*direct* effect on the United States or its Treasury," (emphasis added), suggests—counties will likely pass on the costs to the Government in future contract negotiations. Similarly, we held that state law may govern the circumstances under which stolen federal bonds can be recovered, notwithstanding Parnell's argument that "the value of bonds to the first purchaser and hence their salability by the Government would be materially affected." Brief for Respondent Parnell in *Bank of America Nat'l Trust & Sav. Assn.* v. *Parnell.* As in each of the cases declining to extend the traditional reach of federal law of contracts beyond the rights and duties of the *Federal Government,* "any federal interest in the outcome of the question before us 'is far too speculative, far too remote a possibility to justify the application of federal law to transactions essentially of local concern.' " [*Miree.*]

IV

At bottom, the Court's analysis is premised on the proposition that any tort liability indirectly absorbed by the Government so burdens governmental functions as to compel us to act when Congress has not. That proposition is by no means uncontroversial. The tort system is premised on the assumption that the imposition of liability encourages actors to prevent any injury whose expected cost exceeds the cost of prevention. If the system is working as it should, Government contractors will design equipment to avoid certain injuries (like the deaths of soldiers or Government employees), which would be certain to burden the Government. The Court therefore has no basis for its assumption that tort liability will result in a net burden on the Government (let alone a clearly excessive net burden) rather than a net gain.

Perhaps tort liability is an inefficient means of ensuring the quality of design efforts, but "[w]hatever the merits of the policy" the Court wishes to implement, "its conversion into law is a proper subject for congressional action, not for any creative power of ours." *Standard Oil,* 332 U.S., at 314–315. It is, after all, "Congress, not this Court or the other federal courts, [that] is the custodian of the national purse. By the same token [Congress] is the primary and most often the exclusive arbiter of federal fiscal affairs. And these comprehend, as we have said, securing the treasury or the Government against financial losses *however inflicted. . . .*" *Ibid.* (emphasis added). If Congress shared the Court's assumptions and conclusion it could readily enact "A BILL [t]o place limitations on the civil liability of government contractors to ensure that such liability does not impede the ability of the United States to procure necessary goods and services," H. R. 4765, 99th Cong., 2d Sess. (1986); see also S. 2441, 99th Cong., 2d Sess. (1986). It has not.

Were I a legislator, I would probably vote against any law absolving multibillion dollar private enterprises from answering for their tragic mistakes, at least if that law were justified by no more than the unsupported speculation that their liability might ultimately burden the United States Treasury. Some of my colleagues here would evidently vote otherwise (as they have here), but that should not matter here. We are judges not legislators, and the vote is not ours to cast.

I respectfully dissent.

JUSTICE STEVENS, dissenting.

When judges are asked to embark on a lawmaking venture, I believe they should carefully consider whether they, or a legislative body, are better equipped to perform the task at hand. There are instances of so-called interstitial lawmaking that inevitably become part of the judicial process. But when we are asked to create an entirely new doctrine—to answer "questions of policy on which Congress has not spoken," *United States v. Gilman*, 347 U.S. 507, 511 (1954)—we have a special duty to identify the proper decisionmaker before trying to make the proper decision.

When the novel question of policy involves a balancing of the conflicting interests in the efficient operation of a massive governmental program and the protection of the rights of the individual—whether in the social welfare context, the civil service context, or the military procurement context—I feel very deeply that we should defer to the expertise of the Congress. [In] this case, as in *United States v. Gilman, supra:* "The selection of that policy which is most advantageous to the whole involves a host of considerations that must be weighed and appraised. That function is more appropriately for those who write the laws, rather than for those who interpret them."

NOTES ON BOYLE AND FEDERAL COMMON LAW IN NON-U.S. GOVERNMENT LITIGATION

1.   The Rationale and Implications of *Boyle*. Both the majority and Justice Brennan's dissenting opinion rely on *Miree v. DeKalb County*. In *Miree* one private litigant sued under state law to enforce against another private litigant a duty the latter owed, by contract, to the United States. The Court ruled that state law governed the case. Which aspects of *Miree* support the *Boyle* majority, and which support the dissent? Does Justice Brennan mean to argue that *Miree* was controlled by the *Erie* doctrine? If not, and the issue is therefore one of "borrowing," a further question arises: Is the case for borrowing state law as strong here as it was in *Kimbell Foods*, where "intra-state uniformity" carried the day? The *Boyle* majority reasons that "[t]he present case is at the opposite extreme from *Miree*," because "[h]ere the state-imposed duty . . . is precisely contrary to the duty imposed by the Government contract." Is the state law duty to pay tort damages for drowning "precisely contrary" to the contractual duty to deliver a helicopter with a door that opens outward? Can't the manufacturer take the risk of tort liability into account in calculating the price (as, indeed, the Court suggests it would do)?

Boyle applies the black letter rule that in the event of a "significant conflict [between] an identifiable federal policy or interest and the operation of state law," the state law will be displaced. But "significant conflict" is an elastic test. Its application involves the exercise of judgment as to where to draw lines. Suppose that, after *Boyle*, a civilian government employee is injured by a piece of equipment bought by the government under terms similar to those in *Boyle*. He sues the contractor who then seeks to raise the government contractor defense. Does the fact that this is not a *military* contract tip the scales away from finding a "significant conflict"? What if the contract is not a "procurement" contract, as in *Boyle*, but a "performance" contract, calling for the private party to perform some task? See, e.g., *Bennett v. MIS Corp.*, 607 F.3d 1076 (6th Cir. 2010) (ruling that under *Boyle* a government contractor defense may be available for a performance contract outside the military context, as where the U.S. contracts with a private mold removal firm and the firm is later sued for personal injuries by individuals harmed by its alleged failure to perform).

But it would be a mistake to infer from *Boyle* that every issue related to a federal contract is governed by federal common law. Consider *Empire Healthchoice Assurance, Inc. v. McVeigh*, 547 U.S. 677 (2006). A federal employee was covered by Empire's health insurance, under a contract between the U.S. and Empire. The employee was hospitalized (and later died) after an accident caused by a negligent third party and Empire paid medical bills. The employee sued the tortfeasor and recovered damages. Empire then sued the employee, seeking to recover the medical bills it had paid and citing a subrogation clause in the health insurance contract. The issue before the Supreme Court was whether the subrogation claim was governed by state law or by federal common law (as Empire wanted, presumably because it would fare better under a federal rule). The Court ruled, 5–4, against federal common law here. Empire had not demonstrated a "significant conflict . . . between an identifiable federal policy or interest and the operation of state law." On the other hand, it could be argued that there was indeed a significant conflict between federal policy and state law, as the easier access to subrogation sought by Empire under the federal rule it proposed would make the health insurance less expensive for the U.S. and its employers.

2.   A Methodology, Not a Rule. The opinions in *Kimbell Foods* and *Boyle* illustrate better than any other cases the Supreme Court's methodology when faced with the question of whether to make a federal common law rule. But the outcomes (favoring federal common law in *Boyle,* a suit between private parties, while borrowing state law in *Kimbell Foods* to govern the rights of a government agency) show that an arguably close case may go either way. *Empire* drives that point home. There is no rule that federal common law governs all cases in which national interests are implicated, nor is there a strong presumption against federal common lawmaking. Lawyers need to be familiar with the arguments that can be made on either side of the issue.

For another illustration of the Supreme Court's practice, see *O'Melveny & Myers v. FDIC*, 512 U.S. 79 (1994), in which the Federal Deposit Insurance Corporation had taken over failed banks and sued to recover money arguably owed those banks. The defendants argued that under state law the banks would be estopped (for reasons that do not concern us). The FDIC argued that the estoppel issue should be governed by a federal common law rule. Writing for the Court, Justice Scalia (the author of *Boyle*) found no major federal interest at stake, because the FDIC was merely asserting interests of the failed banks. Accordingly, there was no "significant conflict" and state law should govern. Bear in mind, however, that (as usual in cases of this type) there is a counterargument: The funds that would have been recovered by application of the federal common law rule advocated by the FDIC would have gone to the U.S. and could have been used to provide more protection to bank depositors, who are the beneficiaries of the federal policy underlying the FDIC insurance program.

3. "Significant Conflict" and Divergent Obligations. The general problem of determining what counts as a "significant conflict" may be illustrated by *Farmers Educ. & Co-op. Union v. WDAY, Inc.*, 360 U.S. 525 (1959). Section 315 of the Federal Communications Act of 1934 obliged broadcasters who ran political ads to give "equal opportunities" to opponents. Broadcasters, however, had "no power of censorship over the material broadcast." Over the years, several attempts had been made to amend the statute to provide an express immunity from liability for defamation for such broadcasts, but all had failed. WDAY allowed a U.S. Senate candidate named Townley to speak, uncensored, in reply to other candidates. Townley accused his opponents of seeking to establish a "Communist Farmers Union Soviet right here in North Dakota." The union then sued WDAY for defamation. The lower courts ruled that, as a result of the federal statute, "the state libel laws could not apply to WDAY." By a 5–4 vote the Court affirmed. Justice Black's majority opinion said that ruling otherwise would produce one or the other of two unacceptable consequences:

> [U]nless a licensee refuses to permit any candidate to talk at all, [§ 315] would sanction the unconscionable result of permitting civil and perhaps criminal liability to be imposed for the very conduct the statute demands of the licensee. [While] denying all candidates use of stations would protect broadcasters from liability, it would also effectively withdraw political discussion from the air. Instead, the thrust of § 315 is to facilitate political debate over radio and television.

Neither the majority nor dissenting Justices in *Boyle* cited *WDAY*. Is this case "closely on point in *Boyle*" because both cases involved "immunity from tort liability arising from the defendant's adherence to federal rules"? RICHARD FALLON, ET AL., HART & WECHSLER'S THE FEDERAL COURTS AND THE FEDERAL SYSTEM 643 (6th ed. 2009). Or could the *Boyle* dissenters have distinguished it on the grounds that [a] there was more unfairness to the radio station in allowing the state tort action, because it could not pass the costs on to the government; and [b] a likely consequence of denying immunity would be to frustrate the federal policy of encouraging "political debate over radio and television," while the contractor's ability to pass costs on to the government would not frustrate government procurement policy had *Boyle* come out the other way?

4. Ranging "Conflicts" Along a Spectrum. In his *WDAY* dissent Justice Frankfurter argued that:

> States should not be held to have been ousted from power traditionally held in the absence of either a clear declaration by Congress that it intends to forbid the continued functioning of the state law or an obvious and unavoidable conflict between the federal and state directives. The first does not exist here. [Whether] denying to WDAY the power to eliminate defamatory matter from broadcasts made under compulsion of § 315 while at the same time refusing to [recognize an immunity from liability for defamation] is or is not fair, is not the question with which this Court must [begin]. We are dealing with political power, not ethical imperatives. [We] are in the domain of government and practical affairs, and this Court has not stifled state action unless what the State has required, in the light of what Congress has ordered, would truly entail contradictory duties or make actual, not argumentative, inroads on what Congress has commanded or forbidden. [There] may be a burden, even unfairness to the stations. But there may be unfairness, too, after all, in depriving a defamed individual of recovery against the agency by which the defamatory communication was magnified in its deleterious effect on his ability to earn a livelihood. Adjustment of what is fair to all should be done by a congressional change in the federal law, or in the absence of such enactment, by state law, through legislation or common-law rulings that the stations are partially or totally immune.

Justice Frankfurter's dissent calls attention to a central policy issue in defining the scope of federal common law. "Conflicts" between federal policy and state law can be ranged along a spectrum, from trivial differences at one end to square contradictions on the other. Most would agree that at the "trivial difference" end of the spectrum the case for displacing state law is weak, while that case is compelling by the time one arrives at the "flatly contradicts federal law" end. The hard task is drawing a line somewhere between the two easy cases. Justice Frankfurter, a champion of state autonomy, would require an especially strong conflict before agreeing to displacement. By contrast, a proponent of strong national authority would draw the line somewhere closer to the other end of the spectrum. Near the middle of the spectrum there will be good arguments on either side and we should not expect the cases to line up neatly.

Diverse attitudes about the value of federalism do not account for all of the disagreements among the justices. In some federal common law cases, the judges may be principally concerned with the underlying substantive issues, like the tort issues raised in *Boyle* and *WDAY*, the commercial paper concern in *Clearfield Trust*, and the secured transactions matters in *Kimbell Foods*. The outcome of the "choice of federal or state law" dispute may depend on how the judges wish to resolve the substantive claim. Does this factor help explain *Boyle*? Why do you suppose Justice Scalia, a professed champion of federalism, endorsed displacement in *Boyle*? Why did Justice Brennan, who often took the side of the national government against the states, dissent in *Boyle*?

5. Grounds for Making Federal Common Law. The Supreme Court has never wavered from *Erie*'s holding that "[t]here is no federal *general* common law" (emphasis added). In *O'Melveny & Myers*, supra, Justice Scalia said that "cases in which judicial creation of a federal rule would be justified" are "few" and "extraordinary." 512 U.S. at 87. Making federal common law requires some special justification. But adjectives like "few" and "extraordinary" need to be understood in context: the regulatory role of the United States government is hardly a small one. What is required is that, in one way or another, the substantive dispute has a sufficiently strong federal dimension, transcending the interests of any one state. *Clearfield* established that litigation involving the federal government meets this threshold requirement. *Boyle* and *WDAY* illustrate the principle that a "significant conflict" between state law and federal interests or policy will meet it as well. In addition, Congress and the Supreme Court have identified a number of specific areas in which a federal interest justifies the making of common law.

a. Article III authorizes federal jurisdiction over admiralty cases—which include not only disputes arising out of activity on the high seas but also those matters related to navigable waters inside the United States. The Supreme Court has ruled that this jurisdictional grant justifies the creation of a body of federal common law in admiralty cases. See, e.g., *Moragne v. States Marine Lines, Inc.*, 398 U.S. 375 (1970); *Southern Pacific Co. v. Jensen*, 244 U.S. 205 (1917).

b. On the day the Court decided *Erie*, it also ruled in *Hinderlider v. La Plata River & Cherry Creek Ditch Co.*, 304 U.S. 92, 110 (1938), that "whether the water of an interstate stream must be apportioned between the two States is a question of 'federal common law' upon which neither the statutes nor the decisions of either State can be conclusive." The Court has created federal common law in other kinds of interstate disputes, including suits between states over the right to take intangible personal property abandoned by its owner, see *Texas v. New Jersey*, 379 U.S. 674 (1965), and disputes about interstate water pollution, see *Illinois v. Milwaukee*, 406 U.S. 91 (1972). However, the latter has since been supplanted by federal legislation. See *Milwaukee v. Illinois*, 451 U.S. 304 (1981). Compare *Klaxon Co. v. Stentor Electric Mfg. Co.*, 313 U.S. 487 (1941). *Klaxon* held that a federal court adjudicating state law issues in a diversity case should apply the choice of law rules of the state in which it sits. Is this ruling consistent in principle with *Hinderlider*? If the competing interests of two or more states in water from an interstate stream trigger federal common law making, why is not the same true of competing state interests in choice of law?

c. *Banco Nacional de Cuba v. Sabbatino*, 376 U.S. 398 (1964), explored whether certain actions by foreign nations (here, determining the scope of the "act of state" doctrine) should be governed by federal or state law. The Court ruled that "an issue concerned with a basic choice regarding the competence and function of the Judiciary and the National Executive in ordering our relationships with other members of the international community must be treated exclusively as an aspect of federal law. It seems fair to assume that the Court did not have rules like the act of state doctrine in mind when it decided *Erie R. Co. v. Tompkins.*"

d. Congress sometimes directs courts to make federal common law on particular topics. See Fed. R. Evid. 501, which provides that in the federal courts evidentiary privileges "shall be governed by the principles of the common law as they may be interpreted by the courts of the United States in the light of reason and experience." Recall, from the notes following *Kimbell Foods*, that there is an exception for "elements of a claim or defense as to which State law supplies the rule of decision." Suppose a federal claim arises in a state court. Is the state court required to follow federal common law in resolving issues related to evidentiary privileges?

e. Section 301(a) of the Labor Management Relations Act of 1947 (commonly called the Taft-Hartley Act) authorizes federal jurisdiction over suits charging violation of a collective bargaining agreement between a union and an employer. See 29 U.S.C. § 185. Unlike the Federal Rules of Evidence, supra, the statute contains no explicit directive that the courts should make federal common law. Nonetheless, in *Textile Workers Union v. Lincoln Mills*, 353 U.S. 448, 451 (1957), the Court construed this provision as an authorization for "federal courts to fashion a body of federal law for the enforcement of these collective bargaining agreements." This body of law should be "fashion[ed] from the policy of our national labor laws. [The] range of judicial inventiveness will be determined by the nature of the problem. [But] state law, if compatible with the purpose of § 301, may be resorted to in order to find the rule that will best effectuate federal policy." *Id.* at 456–57.

f. Distinguish the wholesale authorization found in *Lincoln Mills* from a more routine lawmaking problem. Statutes often contain gaps. For example, statutory terms are not always defined and the extent to which the statute is meant to be interpreted in harmony with or as a replacement for existing law is not always clear. When these "gap" issues are litigated, and the gap is a small one, we ordinarily characterize what courts do in adjudicating the issue as "statutory interpretation." When the gap is comparatively large, so that there is little guidance in the statute or its history for resolving the issue, the activity of a court is more often, and more accurately, described as making common law. For example, the Sherman Antitrust Act forbids "combinations in restraint of trade," without defining this term. The vast body of federal antitrust law under the Sherman Act is a kind of statutorily authorized federal common law. See *National Society of Professional Engineers v. United States*, 435 U.S. 679, 688 (1978).

g. Federal common law cannot be captured by a list. It applies to a wide array of disparate issues, which have in common only that there is some federal interest in their resolution. A litigator should always be on the lookout for situations in which the presence of a federal interest in a case may induce a court to adopt a federal common law rule. See, e.g., *Barr v. Matteo*, 360 U.S. 564 (1959) (federal common law provides an absolute defense to federal officers sued for defamation for statements made in the course of their duties); *Enos v. Union Stone, Inc.*, 732 F.3d 45, 48 (1st Cir. 2013) ("Where, as here, the underlying action is brought pursuant to a federal statute, whether a settlement agreement is enforceable is a question of federal law"); *Tampa Bay Water v. HDR Engineering, Inc.*, 731 F.3d 1171,1179 (11th Cir. 2013) ("federal preclusion principles apply to prior federal decisions, whether previously decided in diversity or federal question jurisdiction"); *Bower v. Egyptair Airlines Co.*, 731 F.3d 85, 91 (1st Cir. 2013) ("We rely on federal common law when determining a litigant's domicile for diversity purposes.")

    6.   Federal Common Law in Section 1983 Litigation. Recall, from Chapter 1, the broad terms of 42 U.S.C. § 1983. As with the Sherman Act, the Court has created a considerable body of federal common law in adjudicating remedial, immunity, and other issues arising in § 1983 cases. Consider, for example, *Harlow v. Fitzgerald*, 457 U.S. 800, 818 & n.30 (1982), the leading case on qualified immunity. The opinion is an extended exercise in judicial lawmaking in which the Court made no pretense of grounding its holding in statutory language or legislative history. Similarly, in *Carey v. Piphus*, 435 U.S. 247, 255 (1978), the Court adopted, as federal law, the common law "compensation principle" for deciding damages issues in § 1983 cases, linking this choice to the statute only by observing that "the principle that damages are designed to compensate persons for injuries caused by the deprivation of rights hardly could have been foreign to the many lawyers in Congress in 1871."

    Suppose a § 1983 plaintiff sues two defendants, A and B, recovering a judgment against both. The plaintiff collects the whole judgment from A, who then seeks contribution from B. Should A's claimed right to contribution be governed by federal or state law? Compare *Texas Industries, Inc. v. Radcliff Materials, Inc.*, 451 U.S. 630 (1981) (holding that federal courts lack authority to impose contribution in the Sherman Act context, for lack of a sufficiently strong federal interest to justify making federal common law) with *Musick, Peeler & Garrett v. Employers Ins. of Wausau*, 508 U.S. 286 (1993) (recognizing a federal common law right of contribution in the implied cause of action the Supreme Court had recognized under the Securities Exchange Act and SEC Rule 10b–5 [a cause of action that is discussed in Section II A, below].) Should the § 1983 context be governed by *Texas Industries* or *Musick*? Does it matter that the Court itself created the cause of action in *Musick*, while the antitrust and § 1983 causes of action have a direct congressional pedigree?

    A fair characterization of the Court's practice in § 1983 litigation is that it "borrows" common law principles. But one must distinguish between two kinds of borrowing. Looking at the common law of torts for solutions to problems is different from resorting to state law. The Court does not ordinarily borrow *state* law in this context. With one exception, it does not even consider the possibility that state law should be borrowed as the federal rule. The exception relates to situations in which tort issues are customarily governed by statute rather than by common law principles. For example, there is an old common law rule that tort actions do not survive the death of the victim. Every state has enacted "survival" statutes that allow many suits to go forward after the victim's death, but there is no federal survival statute applicable to § 1983. The Supreme Court held in *Robertson v. Wegmann*, 436 U.S. 584 (1978), that federal courts should borrow the state survival statute, so long as its operation does not undermine the aims of § 1983. In *Robertson*, it applied the state's statute even though, in the case at hand, the claim would not survive the death. For similar reasons, federal courts borrow state statutes of limitations for § 1983 litigation. See *Wilson v. Garcia*, 471 U.S. 261 (1985).

Some of the issues raised in this note can be clarified by thinking about the following problem: In the traditional common law of torts, the plaintiff is entitled to one full recovery, but any of two or more joint tortfeasors may be obliged to pay the full amount, and the plaintiff may collect the judgment from among them as he pleases. Thus, if tortfeasor A is rich and tortfeasor B is poor, the plaintiff may proceed against A for the full amount. This is the rule of "joint" liability. Some states have altered this rule in recent years, allowing the plaintiff to recover from any one defendant a share of the damages that reflects that defendant's share of responsibility for the loss (thus, liability is only "several" rather than "joint"). Under this regime, in the event the jury deemed A to be 50% responsible for the loss, plaintiff could recover only 50% of the damages from A. Suppose *Texas Industries* controls the contribution issue in the § 1983 context. Would it also control whether the liability of A and B to the plaintiff should be "joint" or merely "several"? For an argument that courts should not simply follow standard common law rules, but should make a body of constitutional common law for dealing with the distinctive issues of constitutional principle and policy that arise in the law of constitutional remedies, see Michael Wells, *Constitutional Remedies, Section 1983 and the Common Law*, 68 MISS. L.J. 157 (1998).

II.   REMEDIES

Suppose an actor violates the federal statutory or constitutional rights of another, yet no federal statute provides a (satisfactory) remedy. May courts, in the exercise of their federal common law powers, "imply" one from the statute or constitutional provision that grants the right? In answering this question, the Supreme Court has distinguished between remedies for statutory violations and for constitutional rights.

In studying these materials, keep in mind that *state* law may provide a remedy for violations of federal rights. The scope of state judicial power, and any federal limits upon it, are not addressed here. The general topic of enforcing federal rights in the state courts is examined in Chapter 7. In this chapter, we are solely concerned with whether federal common law affords a remedy. If it does, the suit may (absent some objection that is peculiar to the case at hand) be brought in either federal or state court.

A. STATUTORY REMEDIES

Federal statutes, and administrative regulations made pursuant to them, sometimes impose obligations (and create rights) without authorizing a private cause of action to vindicate those rights. Often, the statute will provide only for administrative enforcement of one kind or another. Persons who think their rights have been violated would prefer to sue for damages or other relief. They argue that the federal courts ought to use their common law powers to recognize a cause of action despite Congress's failure to enact one.

Some attention to the history of the problem is indispensable to understanding the current doctrine and the issues it raises. The first modern case was *J. I. Case Co. v. Borak*, 377 U.S. 426 (1964), which concerned enforcement of § 14(a) of the Securities Exchange Act of 1934. That section, and the regulations enacted by the Securities and Exchange Commission pursuant to it, prohibited fraud in the solicitation of proxy materials. But the Act left enforcement up to the Commission. Neither the Act nor any other federal statute authorized a person injured by the fraud to bring suit for damages or any other remedy. In *Borak*, the plaintiff, a shareholder in J. I. Case, charged fraud in violation of § 14 (a), and sued under state law for breach of fiduciary duty. In addition, he sought to bring a federal cause of action for the violation. A unanimous Court recognized the federal cause of action. Noting the limited resources available to the SEC and the large number of proxy statements filed with it annually, the Court reasoned that "[p]rivate enforcement of the proxy rules provides a necessary supplement to Commission action." As a practical matter, the most important type of litigation pursued under *Borak* concerned suits under § 10(b)(5) of the Securities and Exchange Act. See, e.g., *Musick, Peeler & Garrett v. Employers Ins. of Wausau*, 508 U.S. 286 (1993).

In the decade after *Borak*, a number of important statutes were enacted, with indications in their legislative histories that this broad "necessary supplement" rationale would govern the resolution of the implied cause of action issue. Some of these are discussed in *Alexander v. Sandoval*, below. Then, in the mid-1970s, the Court reconsidered the *Borak* rule. Notably, *Cort v. Ash*, 422 U.S. 66, 78 (1975), declared that:

> In determining whether a private remedy is implicit in a statute not expressly providing one, several factors are relevant. First, is the plaintiff one of the class for whose *especial* benefit the

statute was enacted—that is, does the statute create a federal right in favor of the plaintiff? Second, is there any indication of legislative intent, explicit or implicit, either to create such a remedy or to deny one? Third, is it consistent with the underlying purposes of the legislative scheme to imply such a remedy for the plaintiff? And finally, is the cause of action one traditionally relegated to state law, in an area basically the concern of the States, so that it would be inappropriate to infer a cause of action based solely on federal law?

A later case, *Cannon v. University of Chicago*, 441 U.S. 677 (1979), applied the *Cort* factors in recognizing a private cause of action to sue for damages for sex discrimination in violation of Title IX of the Education Amendments of 1972. But a majority of the Justices signaled that henceforth they would pay closer attention to whether Congress *intended* to create a remedy. The point is made in this passage from Justice Rehnquist's concurring opinion:

> The question of the existence of a private right of action is basically one of statutory construction. [We] do not write on an entirely clean slate, however, and the Court's opinion demonstrates that Congress, at least during the period of the enactment of the several Titles of the Civil Rights Act, tended to rely to a large extent on the courts to *decide* whether there should be a private right of action, rather than determining that question for itself. Cases such as *J. I. Case Co. v. Borak* [gave] Congress good reason to think that the federal judiciary would undertake this task. I fully agree with the Court's statement that "[w]hen Congress intends private litigants to have a cause of action to support their statutory rights, the far better course is for it to specify as much when it creates those rights." It seems to me that the factors to which I have briefly adverted apprise the lawmaking branch of the Federal Government that the ball, so to speak, may well now be in its court. Not only is it "far better" for Congress to so specify when it intends private litigants to have a cause of action, but for this very reason this Court in the future should be extremely reluctant to imply a cause of action absent such specificity on the part of the Legislative Branch.

441 U.S. at 717–18.

After *Cannon*, the Court has generally focused on congressional intent. See, e.g., *Touche Ross & Co. v. Redington*, 442 U.S. 560, 578 (1979). But the "window" between *Borak* and *Cort* retained some importance. See *Merrill Lynch, Pierce, Fenner & Smith, Inc. v. Curran*, 456 U.S. 353, 381–82 (1982), where, by a 5–4 vote, the Court recognized an implied cause of action to enforce the Commodity Exchange Act, a statute that had been extensively revised by Congress in 1974. The Court explained:

> In view of the absence of any dispute about the proposition prior to the decision of *Cort v. Ash* in 1975, it is abundantly clear that an implied cause of action under the CEA was a part of the "contemporary legal context" in which Congress legislated in 1974. Cf. *Cannon.* In that context, the fact that a comprehensive reexamination and significant amendment of the CEA left intact the statutory provisions under which the federal courts had implied a cause of action is itself evidence that Congress affirmatively intended to preserve that remedy. A review of the legislative history of the statute persuasively indicates that preservation of the remedy was indeed what Congress actually intended.

In view of *Alexander v. Sandoval,* does *Merrill, Lynch v. Curran* remain viable?

ALEXANDER V. SANDOVAL
532 U.S. 275 (2001).

JUSTICE SCALIA delivered the opinion of the Court.

This case presents the question whether private individuals may sue to enforce disparate-impact regulations promulgated under Title VI of the Civil Rights Act of 1964.

I

The Alabama Department of Public Safety (Department), of which petitioner James Alexander is the Director, accepted grants of financial assistance from the United States Department of Justice (DOJ) and Department of Transportation (DOT) and so subjected itself to the restrictions of Title VI of the Civil Rights Act of 1964. Section 601 of that Title provides that no person shall, "on the ground of race, color, or national origin, be excluded from participation in, be denied the benefits of, or be subjected to discrimination under any program or activity" covered by Title VI. Section 602 authorizes federal agencies "to effectuate the provisions of [§ 601] . . . by issuing rules, regulations, or orders of general applicability," and the DOJ in an exercise of this authority promulgated a regulation forbidding funding recipients to "utilize criteria or methods of administration which have the effect of subjecting individuals to discrimination because of their race, color, or national origin. . . ." 28 CFR § 42.104(b)(2) (1999).

The State of Alabama amended its Constitution in 1990 to declare English "the official language of the state of Alabama." Pursuant to this provision and, petitioners have argued, to advance public safety, the

Department decided to administer state driver's license examinations only in English. Respondent Sandoval, as representative of a class, brought suit in the United States District Court for the Middle District of Alabama to enjoin the English-only policy, arguing that it violated the DOJ regulation because it had the effect of subjecting non-English speakers to discrimination based on their national origin. The District Court agreed. It enjoined the policy and ordered the Department to accommodate non-English speakers. Petitioners appealed to the Court of Appeals for the Eleventh Circuit, which affirmed. Both courts rejected petitioners' argument that Title VI did not provide respondents a cause of action to enforce the regulation.

We do not inquire here whether the DOJ regulation was authorized by § 602, or whether the courts below were correct to hold that the English-only policy had the effect of discriminating on the basis of national origin. The petition for writ of certiorari raised, and we agreed to review, only the question posed in the first paragraph of this opinion: whether there is a private cause of action to enforce the regulation.

II

[Three] aspects of Title VI must be taken as given. First, private individuals may sue to enforce § 601 of Title VI and obtain both injunctive relief and damages. In *Cannon v. University of Chicago*, 441 U.S. 677 (1979), the Court held that a private right of action existed to enforce Title IX of the Education Amendments of 1972. The reasoning of that decision embraced the existence of a private right to enforce Title VI as well. "Title IX," the Court noted, "was patterned after Title VI of the Civil Rights Act of 1964." And, "in 1972 when Title IX was enacted, the [parallel] language in Title VI had already been construed as creating a private remedy." That meant, the Court reasoned, that Congress had intended Title IX, like Title VI, to provide a private cause of action. Congress has since ratified *Cannon*'s holding. Section 1003 of the Rehabilitation Act Amendments of 1986 expressly abrogated States' sovereign immunity against suits brought in federal court to enforce Title VI and provided that in a suit against a State "remedies (including remedies both at law and in equity) are available . . . to the same extent as such remedies are available . . . in the suit against any public or private entity other than a State," § 2000d–7(a)(2). We recognized in *Franklin v. Gwinnett County Public Schools*, 503 U.S. 60 (1992), that § 2000d–7 "cannot be read except as a validation of *Cannon*'s holding." It is thus beyond dispute that private individuals may sue to enforce § 601.

Second, it is similarly beyond dispute—and no party disagrees—that § 601 prohibits only intentional [discrimination].

Third, we must assume for purposes of deciding this case that regulations promulgated under § 602 of Title VI may validly proscribe activities that have a disparate impact on racial groups, even though such activities are permissible under § 601. Though [the law is unclear on this point], petitioners have not challenged the regulations here. We therefore assume for the purposes of deciding this case that the DOJ and DOT regulations proscribing activities that have a disparate impact on the basis of race are [valid].

[T]he three points we have taken as given [do not establish] that Congress must have intended a private right of action to enforce disparate-impact regulations. We do not doubt that regulations applying § 601's ban on intentional discrimination are covered by the cause of action to enforce that section. Such regulations, if valid and reasonable, authoritatively construe the statute itself, see *Chevron U.S.A., Inc. v. Natural Resources Defense Council, Inc.*, 467 U.S. 837, 843–44 (1984), and it is therefore meaningless to talk about a separate cause of action to enforce the regulations apart from the statute. A Congress that intends the statute to be enforced through a private cause of action intends the authoritative interpretation of the statute to be so enforced as well. The many cases that respondents say have "assumed" that a cause of action to enforce a statute includes one to enforce its regulations illustrate [only] this point; each involved regulations of the type we have just [described]. Our decision in *Lau v. Nichols*, 414 U.S. 563 (1974), falls within the same category. The Title VI regulations at issue in *Lau*, similar to the ones at issue here, forbade funding recipients to take actions which had the effect of discriminating on the basis of race, color, or national origin. Unlike our later cases, however, the Court in *Lau* interpreted § 601 itself to proscribe disparate-impact [discrimination].

We must face now the question avoided by *Lau*, because we have since rejected *Lau*'s interpretation of § 601 as reaching beyond intentional discrimination. It is clear now that the disparate-impact regulations do not simply apply § 601—since they indeed forbid conduct that § 601 permits—and therefore clear that the private right of action to enforce § 601 does not include a private right to enforce these regulations. That right must come, if at all, from the independent force of § 602. As stated earlier, we assume for purposes of this decision that § 602 confers the authority to promulgate disparate-impact regulations; the question remains whether it confers a private right of action to enforce them. If not, we must conclude that a failure to comply with regulations promulgated under § 602 that is not also a failure to comply with § 601 is not actionable.

Implicit in our discussion thus far has been a particular understanding of the genesis of private causes of action. Like substantive federal law itself, private rights of action to enforce federal law must be created by Congress. *Touche Ross & Co. v. Redington*, 442 U.S. 560, 578 (1979) (remedies available are those "that Congress enacted into law").

The judicial task is to interpret the statute Congress has passed to determine whether it displays an intent to create not just a private right but also a private remedy. Statutory intent on this latter point is determinative. Without it, a cause of action does not exist and courts may not create one, no matter how desirable that might be as a policy matter, or how compatible with the statute. Raising up causes of action where a statute has not created them may be a proper function for common-law courts, but not for federal tribunals.

Respondents would have us revert in this case to the understanding of private causes of action that held sway 40 years ago when Title VI was enacted. That understanding is captured by the Court's statement in *J. I. Case Co. v. Borak*, 377 U.S. 426, 433 (1964), that "it is the duty of the courts to be alert to provide such remedies as are necessary to make effective the congressional purpose" expressed by a statute. We abandoned that understanding in *Cort v. Ash*, 422 U.S. 66, 78 (1975)—which itself interpreted a statute enacted under the *ancien regime*—and have not returned to it since. [Having] sworn off the habit of venturing beyond Congress's intent, we will not accept respondents' invitation to have one last drink.

Nor do we agree with the Government that our cases interpreting statutes enacted prior to *Cort* v. *Ash* have given "dispositive weight" to the "expectations" that the enacting Congress had formed "in light of the 'contemporary legal context.' " Brief for United States 14. Only three of [our] implied-right-of-action cases have found this sort of "contemporary legal context" relevant, and two of those [including *Cannon*] involved Congress's enactment (or reenactment) of the verbatim statutory text that courts had previously interpreted to create a private right of action. In the third case, this sort of "contemporary legal context" simply buttressed a conclusion independently supported by the text of the statute. See *Thompson v. Thompson*, 484 U.S. 174 (1988). We have never accorded dispositive weight to context shorn of text. In determining whether statutes create private rights of action, as in interpreting statutes generally, legal context matters only to the extent it clarifies text.

We therefore begin (and find that we can end) our search for Congress's intent with the text and structure of Title VI. Section 602 authorizes federal agencies "to effectuate the provisions of [§ 601] . . . by issuing rules, regulations, or orders of general applicability." It is immediately clear that the "rights-creating" language so critical to the Court's analysis in *Cannon* of § 601 is completely absent from § 602. Whereas § 601 decrees that "no person . . . shall . . . be subjected to discrimination," the text of § 602 provides that "each Federal department and agency . . . is authorized and directed to effectuate the provisions of [§ 601]". Far from displaying congressional intent to create new rights,

§ 602 limits agencies to "effectuating" rights already created by § 601. And the focus of § 602 is twice removed from the individuals who will ultimately benefit from Title VI's protection. Statutes that focus on the person regulated rather than the individuals protected create no implication of an intent to confer rights on a particular class of persons. Section 602 is yet a step further removed: it focuses neither on the individuals protected nor even on the funding recipients being regulated, but on the agencies that will do the regulating. Like the statute found not to create a right of action in *Universities Research Assn., Inc. v. Coutu*, 450 U.S. 754 (1981), § 602 is "phrased as a directive to federal agencies engaged in the distribution of public funds," *id.*, at 772. When this is true, "there [is] far less reason to infer a private remedy in favor of individual persons," *Cannon, supra,* at 690–691. So far as we can tell, this authorizing portion of § 602 reveals no congressional intent to create a private right of action.

Nor do the methods that § 602 goes on to provide for enforcing its authorized regulations manifest an intent to create a private remedy; if anything, they suggest the opposite. Section 602 empowers agencies to enforce their regulations either by terminating funding to the "particular program, or part thereof," that has violated the regulation or "by any other means authorized by law." No enforcement action may be taken, however, "until the department or agency concerned has advised the appropriate person or persons of the failure to comply with the requirement and has determined that compliance cannot be secured by voluntary means." And every agency enforcement action is subject to judicial review. If an agency attempts to terminate program funding, still more restrictions apply. The agency head must "file with the committees of the House and Senate having legislative jurisdiction over the program or activity involved a full written report of the circumstances and the grounds for such action." § 2000d–1. And the termination of funding does not "become effective until thirty days have elapsed after the filing of such report." Whatever these elaborate restrictions on agency enforcement may imply for the private enforcement of rights created *outside* of § 602, compare *Cannon*, they tend to contradict a congressional intent to create privately enforceable rights through § 602 itself. The express provision of one method of enforcing a substantive rule suggests that Congress intended to preclude [others].

Both the Government and respondents argue that the *regulations* contain rights-creating language and so must be privately enforceable, but that argument skips an analytical step. Language in a regulation may invoke a private right of action that Congress through statutory text created, but it may not create a right that Congress has not. Thus, when a statute has provided a general authorization for private enforcement of regulations, it may perhaps be correct that the intent displayed in each regulation can determine whether or not it is privately enforceable. But it is most certainly incorrect to say that language in a regulation can conjure up a private cause of action that has not been authorized by Congress. Agencies may play the sorcerer's apprentice but not the sorcerer himself.

[The Court next rejected an argument that amendments to Title VI "ratified" earlier "decisions finding an implied right of action to enforce the disparate-impact regulations." Along with other arguments, the Court declared that "none of our decisions establishes (or even assumes) the private right of action at issue here."]

Neither as originally enacted nor as later amended does Title VI display an intent to create a freestanding private right of action to enforce regulations promulgated under § 602. We therefore hold that no such right of action [exists].

JUSTICE STEVENS, with whom JUSTICES SOUTER, GINSBURG, and BREYER join, dissenting.

[Among other disagreements with the majority, Justice Stevens took issue with its approach to implying a cause of action to enforce a federal statute.]

[As] the majority narrates our implied right of action jurisprudence, the Court's shift to a more skeptical approach represents the rejection of a common-law judicial activism in favor of a principled recognition of the limited role of a contemporary "federal tribunal." According to its analysis, the recognition of an implied right of action when the text and structure of the statute do not absolutely compel such a conclusion is an act of judicial self-indulgence. As much as we would like to help those disadvantaged by discrimination, we must resist the temptation to pour ourselves "one last drink." To do otherwise would be to "venture beyond Congress's intent."

Overwrought imagery aside, it is the majority's approach that blinds itself to congressional intent. While it remains true that, if Congress intends a private right of action to support statutory rights, "the far better course is for it to specify as much when it creates those rights," *Cannon,* its failure to do so does not absolve us of the responsibility to endeavor to discern its intent. In a series of cases since *Cort v. Ash,* we have laid out rules and developed strategies for this task.

The very existence of these rules and strategies assumes that we will sometimes find manifestations of an implicit intent to create such a right. Our decision in *Cannon* represents one such occasion. As the *Cannon* opinion iterated and reiterated, the question whether the plaintiff had a right of action that could be asserted in federal court was a "question of statutory construction," not a question of policy for the Court to decide.

Applying the *Cort v. Ash* factors, we examined the nature of the rights at issue, the text and structure of the statute, and the relevant legislative history.[21] Our conclusion was that Congress unmistakably intended a private right of action to enforce both Title IX and Title VI. Our reasoning—[and] our holding—was equally applicable to intentional discrimination and disparate impact [claims.]

[The] Court today adopts a methodology that blinds itself to important evidence of congressional intent. It is one thing for the Court to ignore the import of our holding in *Cannon*, as the breadth of that precedent is a matter upon which reasonable jurists may differ. It is entirely another thing for the majority to ignore the reasoning of that opinion and the evidence contained therein, as those arguments and that evidence speak directly to the question at issue today. As I stated [above,] *Cannon* carefully explained that both Title VI and Title IX were intended to benefit a particular class of individuals, that the purposes of the statutes would be furthered rather than frustrated by the implication of a private right of action, and that the legislative histories of the statutes support the conclusion that Congress intended such a right. Those conclusions and the evidence supporting them continue to have force today.

Similarly, if the majority is genuinely committed to deciphering congressional intent, its unwillingness to even consider evidence as to the context in which Congress legislated is perplexing. Congress does not legislate in a vacuum. [The] objective manifestations of congressional intent to create a private right of action must be measured in light of the enacting Congress' expectations as to how the judiciary might evaluate the question.

At the time Congress was considering Title VI, it was normal practice for the courts to infer that Congress intended a private right of action whenever it passed a statute designed to protect a particular class that did not contain enforcement mechanisms which would be thwarted by a private remedy. See *Merrill Lynch*, 456 U.S. at 374–375 (discussing this history). Indeed, the very year Congress adopted Title VI, this Court specifically stated that "it is the duty of the courts to be alert to provide such remedies as are necessary to make effective the congressional purpose." *J. I. Case Co. v. Borak*, 377 U.S. 426, 433 (1964). Assuming, as we must, that Congress was fully informed as to the state of the law, the

---

[21] The text of the statute contained "an unmistakable focus on the benefited class," its legislative history "rather plainly indicates that Congress intended to create such a remedy," the legislators' repeated references to private enforcement of Title VI reflected "their intent with respect to Title IX," and the absence of legislative action to change the prevailing view with respect to Title VI left us with "no doubt that Congress intended to create Title IX remedies comparable to those available under Title VI and that it understood Title VI as authorizing an implied private cause of action for victims of prohibited discrimination."

contemporary context presents important evidence as to Congress' intent—evidence the majority declines to consider.

Ultimately, respect for Congress' prerogatives is measured in deeds, not words. Today, the Court coins a new rule, holding that a private cause of action to enforce a statute does not encompass a substantive regulation issued to effectuate that statute unless the regulation does nothing more than "authoritatively construe the statute itself." This rule might be proper if we were the kind of "common-law court" the majority decries, inventing private rights of action never intended by Congress. For if we are not construing a statute, we certainly may refuse to create a remedy for violations of federal regulations. But if we are faithful to the commitment to discerning congressional intent that all Members of this Court profess, the distinction is untenable. There is simply no reason to assume that Congress contemplated, desired, or adopted a distinction between regulations that merely parrot statutory text and broader regulations that are authorized by statutory [text].

I respectfully dissent.

NOTE ON IMPLIED REMEDIES FOR STATUTORY VIOLATIONS

Besides stressing that legislative intent is the central issue in deciding whether to recognize a cause of action for a statutory violation, the *Sandoval* Court asserts that "[i]n determining whether statutes create private rights of action, as in interpreting statutes generally, legal context matters only to the extent it clarifies text." Will anything short of explicit statutory text suffice to establish a private cause of action? Whatever the *Sandoval* majority may have intended, that case is not the last word. In a later case the Court may have revived "contemporary legal context" in holding that a male teacher could sue for retaliation if he was fired for protesting sex discrimination in athletics at the school, even though the statute does not explicitly provide for such a cause of action. *Jackson v. Birmingham Bd. of Education*, 544 U.S. 167 (2005). Justice O'Connor, who had joined the 5–4 majority in *Alexander*, wrote the opinion (for a 5–4 majority) in *Jackson*.

Recall from Chapter 1 that § 1983 grants a cause of action not only for constitutional violations but also for violations of some federal statutes. In *Gonzaga University*, p. 90 supra, the Court relied on *Alexander v. Sandoval* in delineating the scope of § [1983] "laws" litigation. Is *Alexander v. Sandoval* an appropriate source of authority for interpreting § 1983? Consider Justice Stevens's dissenting view in *Gonzaga University*:

Perhaps more pernicious than its disturbing of the settled status of FERPA rights, though, is the Court's novel use of our implied right of action cases in determining whether a federal right exists for § 1983 purposes. In my analysis of whether § 1232g(b) creates a right for § 1983 purposes, I have assumed the Court's forthrightness in stating that the question presented is "whether Congress

intended to create a federal right," and that "plaintiffs suing under
§ 1983 do not have the burden of showing an intent to create a
private remedy." Rather than proceeding with a straightforward
analysis under these principles, however, the Court has undermined
both of these assertions by needlessly borrowing from cases
involving implied rights of action—cases which place a more
exacting standard on plaintiffs. By using these cases, the Court now
appears to require a heightened showing from § 1983 plaintiffs: "If
Congress wishes to create new rights enforceable under § 1983, it
must do so in clear and unambiguous terms—no less and no more
than what is required for Congress to create new rights enforceable
under an implied private right of action."

A requirement that Congress intend a "right to support a cause of
action," as opposed to simply the creation of an individual federal
right, makes sense in the implied right of action context. As we have
explained, our implied right of action cases "reflect a concern,
grounded in separation of powers, that Congress rather than the
courts controls the availability of remedies for violations of
statutes." However, imposing the implied right of action framework
upon the § 1983 inquiry is not necessary: The separation-of-powers
concerns present in the implied right of action context "are not
present in a § 1983 case," because Congress expressly authorized
private suits in § 1983 itself. Nor is it consistent with our precedent,
which has always treated the implied right of action and § 1983
inquiries as [separate].

Note that *Alexander v. Sandoval*, like *Gonzaga University*, could have
been litigated under a § 1983 "laws" theory. Does this similarity between the
two cases undermine Justice Stevens's reasoning?

B. CONSTITUTIONAL REMEDIES

1. A Common Law Analogue to Section 1983

Section 1983 grants a cause of action to redress constitutional
violations committed under color of *state* law. There are, as we have seen
in Chapter 1, exceptions to its availability. Nonetheless, its coverage
extends across the whole range of constitutional claims against state and
local officers and local governments. By contrast, there is no comparable
statute generally applicable to constitutional violations committed by
federal officers. Though a number of administrative and statutory
remedies are available for particular contexts, gaps remain and aggrieved
persons may find these remedies unsatisfactory for one reason or another.
The lack of a statutory analogue to § 1983 gave rise to the issue addressed
in the *Bivens* case: whether the Supreme Court should use its federal
common law powers to "imply" a remedy for constitutional violations.

BIVENS V. SIX UNKNOWN NAMED
FEDERAL NARCOTICS AGENTS

403 U.S. 388 (1971).

MR. JUSTICE BRENNAN delivered the opinion of the Court.

The Fourth Amendment provides that:

"The right of the people to be secure in their persons, houses, papers, and effects, against unreasonable searches and seizures, shall not be violated. . . ."

In *Bell v. Hood*, 327 U.S. 678 (1946), we reserved the question whether violation of that command by a federal agent acting under color of his authority gives rise to a cause of action for damages consequent upon his unconstitutional conduct. Today we hold that it does.

This case has its origin in an arrest and search carried out on the morning of November 26, 1965. Petitioner's complaint alleged that on that day respondents, agents of the Federal Bureau of Narcotics acting under claim of federal authority, entered his apartment and arrested him for alleged narcotics violations. The agents manacled petitioner in front of his wife and children, and threatened to arrest the entire family. They searched the apartment from stem to stern. Thereafter, petitioner was taken to the federal courthouse in Brooklyn, where he was interrogated, booked, and subjected to a visual strip search.

On July 7, 1967, petitioner brought suit in Federal District Court. In addition to the allegations above, his complaint asserted that the arrest and search were effected without a warrant, and that unreasonable force was employed in making the arrest; fairly read, it alleges as well that the arrest was made without probable cause. Petitioner claimed to have suffered great humiliation, embarrassment, and mental suffering as a result of the agents' unlawful conduct, and sought $15,000 damages from each of them. The District Court [dismissed] the complaint on the ground [that] it failed to state a cause of action. The Court of Appeals [affirmed] on that basis. We reverse.

Respondents do not argue that petitioner should be entirely without remedy for an unconstitutional invasion of his rights by federal agents. In respondents' view, however, the rights that petitioner asserts—primarily rights of privacy—are creations of state and not of federal law. Accordingly, they argue, petitioner may obtain money damages to redress invasion of these rights only by an action in tort, under state law, in the state courts. In this scheme the Fourth Amendment would serve merely to limit the extent to which the agents could defend the state law tort suit by asserting that their actions were a valid exercise of federal power: if the agents were shown to have violated the Fourth Amendment, such a defense would be lost to them and they would stand before the state law merely as private individuals. Candidly admitting that it is the policy of the Department of Justice to remove all such suits from the state to the federal courts for decision,[4] respondents nevertheless urge that we uphold dismissal of petitioner's complaint in federal court, and remit him to filing an action in the state courts in order that the case may properly be removed to the federal court for decision on the basis of state law.

We think that respondents' thesis rests upon an unduly restrictive view of the Fourth Amendment's protection against unreasonable searches and seizures by federal agents, a view that has consistently been rejected by this Court. Respondents seek to treat the relationship between a citizen and a federal agent unconstitutionally exercising his authority as no different from the relationship between two private citizens. In so doing, they ignore the fact that power, once granted, does not disappear like a magic gift when it is wrongfully used. An agent acting—albeit unconstitutionally—in the name of the United States possesses a far greater capacity for harm than an individual trespasser exercising no authority other than his own. Accordingly, as our cases make clear, the Fourth Amendment operates as a limitation upon the exercise of federal power regardless of whether the State in whose jurisdiction that power is exercised would prohibit or penalize the identical act if engaged in by a private citizen. It guarantees to citizens of the United States the absolute right to be free from unreasonable searches and seizures carried out by virtue of federal authority. And "where federally protected rights have been invaded, it has been the rule from the beginning that courts will be alert to adjust their remedies so as to grant the necessary relief." *Bell v. Hood*, 327 U.S. at 684.

First. Our cases have long since rejected the notion that the Fourth Amendment proscribes only such conduct as would, if engaged in by private persons, be condemned by state law. [For example] our recent decisions regarding electronic surveillance have made it clear beyond peradventure that the Fourth Amendment is not tied to the niceties of local trespass laws. *Katz v. United States*, 389 U.S. 347 (1967). In light of these cases, respondents' argument that the Fourth Amendment serves only as a limitation on federal defenses to a state law claim, and not as an

---

[4]   "Since it is the present policy of the Department of Justice to remove to the federal courts all suits in state courts against federal officers for trespass or false imprisonment, a claim for relief, whether based on state common law or directly on the Fourth Amendment, will ultimately be heard in a federal court." Brief for Respondents 13 (citations omitted); see 28 U.S.C. § 1442 (a). In light of this, it is difficult to understand our Brother BLACKMUN's complaint that our holding today "opens the door for another avalanche of new federal cases." In estimating the magnitude of any such "avalanche," it is worth noting that a survey of comparable actions against state officers under 42 U.S.C. § 1983 found only 53 reported cases in 17 years (1951–1967) that survived a motion to dismiss. Increasing this figure by 900% to allow for increases in rate and unreported cases, every federal district judge could expect to try one such case every 13 years.

independent limitation upon the exercise of federal power, must be rejected.

Second. The interests protected by state laws regulating trespass and the invasion of privacy, and those protected by the Fourth Amendment's guarantee against unreasonable searches and seizures, may be inconsistent or even hostile. Thus, we may bar the door against an unwelcome private intruder, or call the police if he persists in seeking entrance. The availability of such alternative means for the protection of privacy may lead the State to restrict imposition of liability for any consequent trespass. A private citizen, asserting no authority other than his own, will not normally be liable in trespass if he demands, and is granted, admission to another's house. But one who demands admission under a claim of federal authority stands in a far different position. The mere invocation of federal power by a federal law enforcement official will normally render futile any attempt to resist an unlawful entry or arrest by resort to the local police; and a claim of authority to enter is likely to unlock the door as well. "In such cases there is no safety for the citizen, except in the protection of the judicial tribunals, for rights which have been invaded by the officers of the government, professing to act in its name. There remains to him but the alternative of resistance, which may amount to crime." *United States v. Lee*, 106 U.S. 196, 219 (1882). Nor is it adequate to answer that state law may take into account the different status of one clothed with the authority of the Federal Government. For just as state law may not authorize federal agents to violate the Fourth Amendment, neither may state law undertake to limit the extent to which federal authority can be exercised. The inevitable consequence of this dual limitation on state power is that the federal question becomes not merely a possible defense to the state law action, but an independent claim both necessary and sufficient to make out the plaintiff's cause of action.

Third. That damages may be obtained for injuries consequent upon a violation of the Fourth Amendment by federal officials should hardly seem a surprising proposition. Historically, damages have been regarded as the ordinary remedy for an invasion of personal interests in liberty. Of course, the Fourth Amendment does not in so many words provide for its enforcement by an award of money damages for the consequences of its violation. But "it is . . . well settled that where legal rights have been invaded, and a federal statute provides for a general right to sue for such invasion, federal courts may use any available remedy to make good the wrong done." *Bell v. Hood*, 327 U.S., at 684. The present case involves no special factors counseling hesitation in the absence of affirmative action by Congress. We are not dealing with a question of "federal fiscal policy," as in *United States v. Standard Oil Co.*, 332 U.S. 301, 311 (1947). In that case we refused to infer from the Government-soldier relationship that the United States could recover damages from one who negligently injured a soldier and thereby caused the Government to pay his medical expenses and lose his services during the course of his hospitalization. Noting that Congress was normally quite solicitous where the federal purse was involved, we pointed out that "the United States [was] the party plaintiff to the suit. And the United States has power at any time to create the liability." Nor are we asked in this case to impose liability upon a congressional employee for actions contrary to no constitutional prohibition, but merely said to be in excess of the authority delegated to him by the Congress. *Wheeldin v. Wheeler*, 373 U.S. 647 (1963). Finally, we cannot accept respondents' formulation of the question as whether the availability of money damages is necessary to enforce the Fourth Amendment. For we have here no explicit congressional declaration that persons injured by a federal officer's violation of the Fourth Amendment may not recover money damages from the agents, but must instead be remitted to another remedy, equally effective in the view of Congress. The question is merely whether petitioner, if he can demonstrate an injury consequent upon the violation by federal agents of his Fourth Amendment rights, is entitled to redress his injury through a particular remedial mechanism normally available in the federal courts. Cf. *J. I. Case Co. v. Borak*, 377 U.S. 426, 433 (1964). "The very essence of civil liberty certainly consists in the right of every individual to claim the protection of the laws, whenever he receives an injury." *Marbury v. Madison*, 1 Cranch 137, 163 (1803). Having concluded that petitioner's complaint states a cause of action under the Fourth Amendment, we hold that petitioner is entitled to recover money damages for any injuries he has suffered as a result of the agents' violation of the [Amendment].

MR. JUSTICE HARLAN concurring in the judgment.

My initial view of this case was that the Court of Appeals was correct in dismissing the complaint, but for reasons stated in this opinion I am now persuaded to the contrary. Accordingly, I join in the judgment of reversal.

[The Court of Appeals] reasoned, in essence, that: (1) the framers of the Fourth Amendment did not appear to contemplate a "wholly new federal cause of action founded directly on the Fourth Amendment," and (2) while the federal courts had power under a general grant of jurisdiction to imply a federal remedy for the enforcement of a constitutional right, they should do so only when the absence of alternative remedies renders the constitutional command a "mere 'form of words.'" The Government takes essentially the same position here. And two members of the Court add the contention that we lack the constitutional power to accord Bivens a remedy for damages in the absence of congressional action creating "a federal cause of action for damages for an unreasonable search in violation of the Fourth

Amendment." Opinion of MR. JUSTICE BLACK; see also opinion of THE CHIEF JUSTICE.

For the reasons set forth below, I am of the opinion that federal courts do have the power to award damages for violation of "constitutionally protected interests" and I agree with the Court that a traditional judicial remedy such as damages is appropriate to the vindication of the personal interests protected by the Fourth Amendment.

I turn first to the contention that the constitutional power of federal courts to accord Bivens damages for his claim depends on the passage of a statute creating a "federal cause of action." Although the point is not entirely free of ambiguity, I do not understand either the Government or my dissenting Brothers to maintain that Bivens' contention that he is entitled to be free from the type of official conduct prohibited by the Fourth Amendment depends on a decision by the State in which he resides to accord him a remedy. Such a position would be incompatible with the presumed availability of federal equitable relief, if a proper showing can be made in terms of the ordinary principles governing equitable remedies. However broad a federal court's discretion concerning equitable remedies, it is absolutely clear—at least after *Erie R. Co. v. Tompkins*—that in a nondiversity suit a federal court's power to grant even equitable relief depends on the presence of a substantive right derived from federal law.

Thus the interest which Bivens claims—to be free from official conduct in contravention of the Fourth Amendment—is a federally protected interest. Therefore, the question of judicial *power* to grant Bivens damages is not a problem of the "source" of the "right"; instead, the question is whether the power to authorize damages as a judicial remedy for the vindication of a federal constitutional right is placed by the Constitution itself exclusively in Congress' hands.

II

The contention that the federal courts are powerless to accord a litigant damages for a claimed invasion of his federal constitutional rights until Congress explicitly authorizes the remedy cannot rest on the notion that the decision to grant compensatory relief involves a resolution of policy considerations not susceptible of judicial discernment. Thus, in suits for damages based on violations of federal statutes lacking any express authorization of a damage remedy, this Court has authorized such relief where, in its view, damages are necessary to effectuate the congressional policy underpinning the substantive provisions of the statute. *J. I. Case Co. v. Borak*, 377 U.S. 426 (1964).[4]

---

[4] The *Borak* case is an especially clear example of the exercise of federal judicial power to accord damages as an appropriate remedy in the absence of any express statutory authorization of a federal cause of action. There we "implied"—from what can only be characterized as an

If it is not the nature of the remedy which is thought to render a judgment as to the appropriateness of damages inherently "legislative," then it must be the nature of the legal interest offered as an occasion for invoking otherwise appropriate judicial relief. But I do not think that the fact that the interest is protected by the Constitution rather than statute or common law justifies the assertion that federal courts are powerless to grant damages in the absence of explicit congressional action authorizing the remedy. Initially, I note that it would be at least anomalous to conclude that the federal judiciary—while competent to choose among the range of traditional judicial remedies to implement statutory and common law policies, and even to generate substantive rules governing primary behavior in furtherance of broadly formulated policies articulated by statute or Constitution, see *Textile Workers v. Lincoln Mills*; *United States v. Standard Oil Co.*; *Clearfield Trust Co.* v. *United States*—is powerless to accord a damages remedy to vindicate social policies which, by virtue of their inclusion in the Constitution, are aimed predominantly at restraining the Government as an instrument of the popular will.

More importantly, the presumed availability of federal equitable relief against threatened invasions of constitutional interests appears entirely to negate the contention that the status of an interest as constitutionally protected divests federal courts of the power to grant damages absent express congressional [authorization]. If explicit congressional authorization is an absolute prerequisite to the power of a federal court to accord compensatory relief regardless of the necessity or appropriateness of damages as a remedy simply because of the status of a legal interest as constitutionally protected, then it seems to me that explicit congressional authorization is similarly prerequisite to the exercise of equitable remedial discretion in favor of constitutionally protected interests. Conversely, if a general grant of jurisdiction to the federal courts by Congress is thought adequate to empower a federal court to grant equitable relief for all areas of subject-matter jurisdiction enumerated therein, see 28 U.S.C. § 1331 (a), then it seems to me that the same statute is sufficient to empower a federal court to grant a traditional remedy at law. Of course, the special historical traditions governing the federal equity system might still bear on the comparative appropriateness of granting equitable relief as opposed to money damages. That possibility, however, relates, not to whether the federal

---

"exclusively procedural provision" affording access to a federal forum—a private cause of action for damages for violation of § 14 (a) of the Securities Exchange Act of 1934. We did so in an area where federal regulation has been singularly comprehensive and elaborate administrative enforcement machinery had been provided. The exercise of judicial power involved in *Borak* simply cannot be justified in terms of statutory construction, nor did the *Borak* Court purport to do so. The notion of "implying" a remedy, therefore, as applied to cases like *Borak*, can only refer to a process whereby the federal judiciary exercises a choice among *traditionally available* judicial remedies according to reasons related to the substantive social policy embodied in an act of positive law.

courts have the power to afford one type of remedy as opposed to the other, but rather to the criteria which should govern the exercise of our power. To that question, I now pass.

III

The major thrust of the Government's position is that, where Congress has not expressly authorized a particular remedy, a federal court should exercise its power to accord a traditional form of judicial relief at the behest of a litigant, who claims a constitutionally protected interest has been invaded, only where the remedy is "essential," or "indispensable for vindicating constitutional rights." Brief for Respondents 19, 24. While this "essentiality" test is most clearly articulated with respect to damages remedies, apparently the Government believes the same test explains the exercise of equitable remedial powers. It is argued that historically the Court has rarely exercised the power to accord such relief in the absence of an express congressional authorization and that "if Congress had thought that federal officers should be subject to a law different than state law, it would have had no difficulty in saying so, as it did with respect to state officers. . . ." Id., at 20–21; see 42 U.S.C. § 1983. Although conceding that the standard of determining whether a damage remedy should be utilized to effectuate statutory policies is one of "necessity" or "appropriateness," see *J. I. Case Co.* v. *Borak, United States v. Standard Oil Co.*, the Government contends that questions concerning congressional discretion to modify judicial remedies relating to constitutionally protected interests warrant a more stringent constraint on the exercise of judicial power with respect to this class of legally protected interests.

These arguments for a more stringent test to govern the grant of damages in constitutional cases[7] seem to be adequately answered by the point that the judiciary has a particular responsibility to assure the vindication of constitutional interests such as those embraced by the Fourth Amendment. To be sure, "it must be remembered that legislatures are ultimate guardians of the liberties and welfare of the people in quite as great a degree as the courts." *Missouri, Kansas & Texas R. Co. v. May*, 194 U.S. 267, 270 (1904). But it must also be recognized that the Bill of Rights is particularly intended to vindicate the interests of the individual in the face of the popular will as expressed in legislative majorities; at the very least, it strikes me as no more appropriate to await express congressional authorization of traditional judicial relief with regard to these legal interests than with respect to interests protected by federal statutes.

---

[7] I express no view on the Government's suggestion that congressional authority to simply discard the remedy the Court today authorizes might be in doubt; nor do I understand the Court's opinion today to express any view on that particular question.

The question then, is, as I see it, whether compensatory relief is "necessary" or "appropriate" to the vindication of the interest asserted. Cf. *J. I. Case Co. v. Borak*, supra, at 432; *United States v. Standard Oil Co.*, supra, at 307. In resolving that question, it seems to me that the range of policy considerations we may take into account is at least as broad as the range of those a legislature would consider with respect to an express statutory authorization of a traditional remedy. In this regard I agree with the Court that the appropriateness of according Bivens compensatory relief does not turn simply on the deterrent effect liability will have on federal official conduct.[8] Damages as a traditional form of compensation for invasion of a legally protected interest may be entirely appropriate even if no substantial deterrent effects on future official lawlessness might be thought to result. Bivens, after all, has invoked judicial processes claiming entitlement to compensation for injuries resulting from allegedly lawless official behavior, if those injuries are properly compensable in money damages. I do not think a court of law— vested with the power to accord a remedy—should deny him his relief simply because he cannot show that future lawless conduct will thereby be deterred.

And I think it is clear that Bivens advances a claim of the sort that, if proved, would be properly compensable in damages. The personal interests protected by the Fourth Amendment are those we attempt to capture by the notion of "privacy"; while the Court today properly points out that the type of harm which officials can inflict when they invade protected zones of an individual's life are different from the types of harm private citizens inflict on one another, the experience of judges in dealing with private trespass and false imprisonment claims supports the conclusion that courts of law are capable of making the types of judgment concerning causation and magnitude of injury necessary to accord meaningful compensation for invasion of Fourth Amendment rights.

On the other hand, the limitations on state remedies for violation of common-law rights by private citizens argue in favor of a federal damages remedy. The injuries inflicted by officials acting under color of law, while no less compensable in damages than those inflicted by private parties, are substantially different in kind, as the Court's opinion today discusses

---

8 And I think it follows from this point that today's decision has little, if indeed any, bearing on the question whether a federal court may properly devise remedies—other than traditionally available forms of judicial relief—for the purpose of enforcing substantive social policies embodied in constitutional or statutory policies. Compare today's decision with *Mapp v. Ohio*, 367 U.S. 643 (1961), and Weeks v. United States, 232 U.S. 383 (1914). The Court today simply recognizes what has long been implicit in our decisions concerning equitable relief and remedies implied from statutory schemes; *i. e.*, that a court of law vested with jurisdiction over the subject matter of a suit has the power—and therefore the duty—to make principled choices among traditional judicial remedies. Whether special prophylactic measures—which at least arguably the exclusionary rule exemplifies—are supportable on grounds other than a court's competence to select among traditional judicial remedies to make good the wrong done, is a separate question.

in detail. See *Monroe v. Pape,* 365 U.S. 167, 195 (1961) (HARLAN, J., concurring). It seems to me entirely proper that these injuries be compensable according to uniform rules of federal law, especially in light of the very large element of federal law which must in any event control the scope of official defenses to liability. Certainly, there is very little to be gained from the standpoint of federalism by preserving different rules of liability for federal officers dependent on the State where the injury occurs. Cf. *United States v. Standard Oil Co.,* 332 U.S. 301, 305–311 (1947).

Putting aside the desirability of leaving the problem of federal official liability to the vagaries of common-law actions, it is apparent that some form of damages is the only possible remedy for someone in Bivens' alleged position. It will be a rare case indeed in which an individual in Bivens' position will be able to obviate the harm by securing injunctive relief from any court. However desirable a direct remedy against the Government might be as a substitute for individual official liability, the sovereign still remains immune to suit. Finally, assuming Bivens' innocence of the crime charged, the "exclusionary rule" is simply irrelevant. For people in Bivens' shoes, it is damages or nothing.

The only substantial policy consideration advanced against recognition of a federal cause of action for violation of Fourth Amendment rights by federal officials is the incremental expenditure of judicial resources that will be necessitated by this class of litigation. There is, however, something ultimately self-defeating about this argument. For if, as the Government contends, damages will rarely be realized by plaintiffs in these cases because of jury hostility, the limited resources of the official concerned, etc., then I am not ready to assume that there will be a significant increase in the expenditure of judicial resources on these claims. Few responsible lawyers and plaintiffs are likely to choose the course of litigation if the statistical chances of success are truly *de minimis.* And I simply cannot agree with my Brother BLACK that the possibility of "frivolous" claims—if defined simply as claims with no legal merit—warrants closing the courthouse doors to people in Bivens' situation. There are other ways, short of that, of coping with frivolous lawsuits.

On the other hand, if—as I believe is the case with respect, at least, to the most flagrant abuses of official power—damages to some degree will be available when the option of litigation is chosen, then the question appears to be how Fourth Amendment interests rank on a scale of social values compared with, for example, the interests of stockholders defrauded by misleading proxies. See *J. I. Case Co.* v. *Borak, supra.* Judicial resources, I am well aware, are increasingly scarce these days. Nonetheless, when we automatically close the courthouse door solely on this basis, we implicitly express a value judgment on the comparative importance of classes of legally protected interests. And current limitations upon the effective functioning of the courts arising from budgetary inadequacies should not be permitted to stand in the way of the recognition of otherwise sound constitutional principles.

Of course, for a variety of reasons, the remedy may not often be sought. And the countervailing interests in efficient law enforcement of course argue for a protective zone with respect to many types of Fourth Amendment violations. But, while I express no view on the immunity defense offered in the instant case, I deem it proper to venture the thought that at the very least such a remedy would be available for the most flagrant and patently unjustified sorts of police conduct. Although litigants may not often choose to seek relief, it is important, in a civilized society, that the judicial branch of the Nation's government stand ready to afford a remedy in these circumstances. It goes without saying that I intimate no view on the merits of petitioner's underlying claim.

For these reasons, I concur in the judgment of the Court.

MR. CHIEF JUSTICE BURGER, dissenting.

I dissent from today's holding which judicially creates a damage remedy not provided for by the Constitution and not enacted by Congress. We would more surely preserve the important values of the doctrine of separation of powers—and perhaps get a better result—by recommending a solution to the Congress as the branch of government in which the Constitution has vested the legislative power. Legislation is the business of the Congress, and it has the facilities and competence for that task—as we do [not.]

[The bulk of CHIEF JUSTICE BURGER's opinion consisted of a critical discussion of the Fourth Amendment exclusionary rule.]

I conclude, therefore, that an entirely different remedy is necessary but it is one that in my view is as much beyond judicial power as the step the Court takes today. Congress should develop an administrative or quasi-judicial remedy against the government itself to afford compensation and restitution for persons whose Fourth Amendment rights have been violated. The venerable doctrine of *respondeat superior* in our tort law provides an entirely appropriate conceptual basis for this remedy. If, for example, a security guard privately employed by a department store commits an assault or other tort on a customer such as an improper search, the victim has a simple and obvious remedy—an action for money damages against the guard's employer, the department store. Such a statutory scheme would have the added advantage of providing some remedy to the completely innocent persons who are sometimes the victims of illegal police conduct—something that the suppression doctrine, of course, can never [accomplish].

MR. JUSTICE BLACK, dissenting.

[There] can be no doubt that Congress could create a federal cause of action for damages for an unreasonable search in violation of the Fourth Amendment. Although Congress has created such a federal cause of action against *state* officials acting under color of state law, it has never created such a cause of action against federal officials. If it wanted to do so, Congress could, of course, create a remedy against federal officials who violate the Fourth Amendment in the performance of their duties. But the point of this case and the fatal weakness in the Court's judgment is that neither Congress nor the State of New York has enacted legislation creating such a right of action. For us to do so is, in my judgment, an exercise of power that the Constitution does not give us.

Even if we had the legislative power to create a remedy, there are many reasons why we should decline to create a cause of action where none has existed since the formation of our Government. The courts of the United States as well as those of the States are choked with lawsuits. The number of cases on the docket of this Court have reached an unprecedented volume in recent years. A majority of these cases are brought by citizens with substantial complaints—persons who are physically or economically injured by torts or frauds or governmental infringement of their rights; persons who have been unjustly deprived of their liberty or their property; and persons who have not yet received the equal opportunity in education, employment, and pursuit of happiness that was the dream of our forefathers. Unfortunately, there have also been a growing number of frivolous lawsuits, particularly actions for damages against law enforcement officers whose conduct has been judicially sanctioned by state trial and appellate courts and in many instances even by this Court. My fellow Justices on this Court and our brethren throughout the federal judiciary know only too well the time-consuming task of conscientiously poring over hundreds of thousands of pages of factual allegations of misconduct by police, judicial, and corrections officials. Of course, there are instances of legitimate grievances, but legislators might well desire to devote judicial resources to other problems of a more serious nature. [There] is also a real danger that such suits might deter officials from the *proper* and honest performance of their duties.

All of these considerations make imperative careful study and weighing of the arguments both for and against the creation of such a remedy under the Fourth Amendment. I would have great difficulty for myself in resolving the competing policies, goals, and priorities in the use of resources, if I thought it were my job to resolve those questions. But that is not my task. The task of evaluating the pros and cons of creating judicial remedies for particular wrongs is a matter for Congress and the legislatures of the States. Congress has not provided that any federal court can entertain a suit against a federal officer for violations of Fourth Amendment rights occurring in the performance of his duties. A strong inference can be drawn from creation of such actions against state officials that Congress does not desire to permit such suits against federal officials. Should the time come when Congress desires such lawsuits, it has before it a model of valid legislation, 42 U.S.C. § 1983, to create a damage remedy against federal officers. Cases could be cited to support the legal proposition which I assert, but it seems to me to be a matter of common understanding that the business of the judiciary is to interpret the laws and not to make them.

I dissent.

[MR. JUSTICE BLACKMUN'S dissent is omitted.]

NOTES ON FEDERAL COMMON LAW REMEDIES FOR CONSTITUTIONAL VIOLATIONS

1. **Does *Bivens* Survive the Demise of *Borak*?** Both the Court and Justice Harlan rely upon *J. I. Case Co. v. Borak*, a 1964 decision that is discussed in the preceding section in connection with implied remedies for statutory violations. Recall that *Borak* took an expansive view of those remedies. Beginning with *Cort v. Ash* the Court has abandoned that approach in favor of closer attention to legislative intent. After *Alexander v. Sandoval*, implied remedies for statutory violations may be rare indeed, for that case suggests that the text of the statute will control the issue, so long as the text is unambiguous. Does the principle that judges may imply remedies for constitutional violations rest on the same rationale as *Borak*, so that the repudiation of *Borak* casts doubt on the continued viability of *Bivens*? In this regard, consider the grounds for and implications of Justice Harlan's statement that "arguments for a more stringent test to govern the grant of damages in constitutional cases seem to be adequately answered by the point that the judiciary has a particular responsibility to assure the vindication of constitutional interests such as those embraced by the Fourth Amendment." See also, Gene Nichol, Bivens, Chilicky, *and Constitutional Damage Claims*, 75 VA.L.REV. 1117 (1989) (arguing that Bivens cases represent constitutional interpretation, not common law decision making).

2. **Judicial Authority to Create Remedies.** For the sake of analytical clarity, it is useful to distinguish between two issues raised by *Bivens*. One is the scope of judicial *power* to create remedies for constitutional violations; the other is whether the Court ought, as a matter of *policy*, to imply a damages remedy for Fourth Amendment violations. With regard to the first of these issues, Justice Harlan's concurring opinion pays more explicit attention to it than does the Court's opinion. In defending judicial authority, Justice Harlan depends in part on the general principle, discussed throughout this chapter, that federal courts have the power to make federal common law to deal with matters of distinctively federal concern. Surely, remedies for federal constitutional violations meet this test. The Fourth

Amendment context furnishes an example, namely, the Court's rule that illegally obtained evidence cannot be introduced at the criminal trial of the person whose rights were violated. The Court has stressed that this rule is not itself a constitutional right but a judge-made remedy aimed at deterring constitutional violations. See, e.g., *Stone v. Powell*, 428 U.S. 465 (1976).

More specifically, Justice Harlan cites "the presumed availability of federal equitable relief" for constitutional violations. For many years before *Bivens* the federal courts had routinely awarded injunctions to forbid constitutional violations, without relying on any federal statute for the authority to do so. The practice originated in suits against *state* officers, see *Ex parte Young*, 209 U.S. 123 (1908); see also *General Oil Co. v. Crain*, 209 U.S. 211 (1908) (ruling that *state* courts must grant injunctive relief against an unconstitutional act of a state officer, notwithstanding state law to the contrary). The Court made clear in *Bell v. Hood*, 327 U.S. 678, 684 (1946) (in an opinion authored by Justice Black) that the principle applied to suits against *federal* officers as well. In effect, when courts granted injunctions they implicitly recognized a federal cause of action for forward-looking relief. The difference between this practice and *Bivens* is just that the *Bivens* plaintiff sought a *backward*-looking remedy (damages for a past violation of his rights) instead of a forward-looking one. Justice Harlan's point is that this difference has no bearing on the power to create remedies. Power to create a cause of action for the injunctive remedy necessarily entails power to create a cause of action for damages.

Justice Black's dissent rests on his objection to "judicial legislation." Yet he does not appear to question (here or elsewhere) *Bell v. Hood* or *Ex parte Young*. As a matter of judicial *power*, can these earlier cases be distinguished from *Bivens*?

3. The Pros and Cons of Implying a Remedy. Given judicial power to create a damages remedy (or "imply" one from the Fourth Amendment), the second issue is whether the benefits of doing so outweigh the costs.

a. One consideration is the allocation of scarce judicial resources. Does Justice Harlan convincingly answer the dissenters' concerns that allowing this kind of suit will overburden the federal courts? (In fact, the dissenters' "resources" objection seems to have been misplaced, as few *Bivens* suits are litigated.)

b. Both the Fourth Amendment right against unreasonable searches and the common law tort right against trespass protect against unjustified and unapproved entry onto the plaintiff's property. The Government argued in *Bivens* that there was no pressing need to create a damages remedy for the Fourth Amendment violation, as the plaintiff could pursue a state tort law suit for trespass to land. How do the Court and Justice Harlan rebut this contention? For the sake of argument, suppose we agree with the Government that the state remedy will suffice. Does it follow that no implied cause of action should be recognized for, say, First Amendment rights?

c. One justification for a damages remedy is that the threat of paying damages will deter constitutional violations. But suppose it could be shown that, given the exclusionary rule, the increase in deterrence from allowing suits for damages is minimal. Are there any other grounds for allowing plaintiffs to sue? Justice Harlan wrote:

> Bivens [has] invoked judicial processes claiming entitlement to compensation for injuries resulting from allegedly lawless official behavior, if those injuries are properly compensable in money damages. I do not think a court of law—vested with the power to accord a remedy—should deny him his relief simply because he cannot show that future lawless conduct will thereby be deterred.

What rationale did he have in mind? Is "corrective justice" an adequate justification for imposing constitutional tort liability? For an affirmative answer to this question, see Bernard Dauenhauer & Michael Wells, *Corrective Justice and Constitutional Torts*, 35 GA. L. REV. 903 (2001).

d. Justice Black worries about the "real danger that such suits might deter officials from the *proper* and honest performance of their duties." Is this concern better raised as a ground for rejecting a cause of action altogether or in connection with the determining the appropriate scope of official immunity from liability? The official immunity issue was not before the Court in *Bivens*. The basic rules are discussed in Chapter 1. They do not differ much depending on whether the defendant is a state or federal officer, except that under *Nixon v. Fitzgerald* the United States President is accorded an absolute immunity from suit. Note that *Harlow v. Fitzgerald*, the Court's principal ruling on qualified immunity, is itself a *Bivens* case.

4. "Special Factors Counseling Hesitation." The Court in *Bivens* did not rule that a damages remedy would routinely be implied for constitutional violations by federal officers. It acknowledged the common law pedigree of its rule by recognizing Congress's power to foreclose judicial creation of the remedy. And it said that "[t]he present case involves no special factors counseling hesitation in the absence of affirmative action by Congress." Though the *Bivens* Court left this term undefined, much later litigation centered on determining whether a given circumstance would qualify as a special factor counseling hesitation.

The early cases suggested that the defendant would have to meet a demanding standard. In *Davis v. Passman*, 442 U.S. 228 (1979), the defendant was a U.S. Congressman, and the plaintiff was a woman he had fired on account of her gender. She sued for damages, charging an equal protection violation. The Court implied a cause of action on her behalf, even though Congress had deliberately exempted its members from the coverage of federal sex discrimination laws—a move that might have been deemed a decision by Congress to forbid the cause of action. In *Carlson v. Green*, 446 U.S. 14 (1980), the mother of a deceased federal prisoner sued prison officials, asserting several constitutional objections to his treatment. She could have sued the United States under the Federal Tort Claims Act. Though that alternative might have been deemed a special factor counseling hesitation, she was allowed to maintain the *Bivens* suit.

A few years later the Court began taking a harder line. In *Bush v. Lucas*, 462 U.S. 367 (1983), the plaintiff was a civil service employee who complained that he was punished by supervisors on account of protected speech. The Court denied a *Bivens* remedy, reasoning that the existence of civil service remedies was a special factor counseling hesitation. *Schweiker v. Chilicky*, 487 U.S. 412 (1988), took a similar tack in denying a remedy to social security recipients who claimed constitutional violations in connection with benefit cut-offs. As in *Bush*, administrative remedies were available. In two cases involving suits by military personnel, the Court refused to imply a cause of action, finding that the military setting was a special factor counseling hesitation. See *Chappell v. Wallace*, 462 U.S. 296 (1983); *United States v. Stanley*, 483 U.S. 669 (1987). In all of the foregoing cases the defendants were officers of the United States. *Federal Deposit Insurance Corp. v. Meyer*, 510 U.S. 471 (1994), presented the question whether *Bivens* actions may be brought against federal *agencies*. The Court held that agencies may not be sued under a *Bivens* theory.

The *Bivens* doctrine has continued its downward spiral in recent Supreme Court terms. In *Wilkie v. Robbins*, 551 U.S. 537 (2007), the Court rejected a landowner's constitutional damages claim, rooted in alleged harassment and intimidation, against various officials of the federal Bureau of Land Management. Justice Souter's opinion rehearsed, in some detail a litany of "offensive and sometimes illegal actions" by the Bureau's officers— apparently designed to force the landowner to surrender various property rights. Still, the majority refused to recognize a distinct damages claim based directly on the constitution:

> The proposal [to] create a new *Bivens* remedy to redress such injuries collectively on a theory of retaliation for exercising his property rights [raises] a serious difficulty of devising a workable cause of action. A judicial standard to identify illegitimate pressure going beyond legitimately hard bargaining would be endlessly knotty to work out, and a general provision for tortlike liability when government employees are unduly zealous in pressing a governmental interest affecting property would invite an onslaught of *Bivens* actions.

> We think accordingly that any damages remedy for actions by government employees who push too hard for the government's benefit may come better, if at all, through legislation. "Congress is in a far better position than a court to evaluate the impact of a new species of litigation against those who act on the public's behalf." *Bush*, 462 U.S., at 389. And Congress may tailor any remedy to the problem perceived, thus lessening the risk of raising a tide of suits threatening legitimate initiative on the part of government employees.

These and other cases are discussed in *Minneci*.

MINNECI V. POLLARD

565 U.S. ___, 132 S.Ct. 617 (2012).

JUSTICE BREYER delivered the opinion of the Court.

The question is whether we can imply the existence of an Eighth Amendment-based damages action (a *Bivens* action) against employees of a privately operated federal prison. See generally *Bivens v. Six Unknown Fed. Narcotics Agents,* 403 U.S. 388, 389 (1971) ("[V]iolation of [the Fourth Amendment] by a federal agent . . . gives rise to a cause of action for damages" against a Federal Government employee). Because we believe that in the circumstances present here state tort law authorizes adequate alternative damages actions—actions that provide both significant deterrence and compensation—we cannot do so. See *Wilkie v. Robbins,* 551 U.S. 537, 550 (2007) (no *Bivens* action where "alternative, existing" processes provide adequate protection).

I.

Richard Lee Pollard was a prisoner at a federal facility operated by a private company, the Wackenhut Corrections Corporation. In 2002 he filed a *pro se* complaint in federal court against several Wackenhut employees, who (now) include a security officer, a food-services supervisor, and several members of the medical staff. As the Federal Magistrate Judge interpreted Pollard's complaint, he claimed that these employees had deprived him of adequate medical care, had thereby violated the Eighth Amendment's prohibition against "cruel and unusual" punishment, and had caused him injury. He sought damages.

Pollard said that a year earlier he had slipped on a cart left in the doorway of the prison's butcher shop. The prison medical staff took x rays, thought he might have fractured both elbows, brought him to an outside clinic for further orthopedic evaluation, and subsequently arranged for surgery. In particular, Pollard claimed:

(1) Despite his having told a prison guard that he could not extend his arm, the guard forced him to put on a jumpsuit (to travel to the outside clinic), causing him "the most excruciating pain,"

(2) During several visits to the outside clinic, prison guards made Pollard wear arm restraints that were connected in a way that caused him continued pain;

(3) Prison medical (and other) personnel failed to follow the outside clinic's instructions to put Pollard's left elbow in a posterior splint, failed to provide necessary physical therapy, and failed to conduct necessary studies, including nerve conduction studies;

(4) At times when Pollard's arms were in casts or similarly disabled, prison officials failed to make alternative arrangements for him to receive

meals, with the result that (to avoid "being humiliated" in the general food service area) Pollard had to auction off personal items to obtain funds to buy food at the commissary;

(5) Prison officials deprived him of basic hygienic care to the point where he could not bathe for two weeks;

(6) Prison medical staff provided him with insufficient medicine, to the point where he was in pain and could not sleep; and

(7) Prison officials forced him to return to work before his injuries had healed.

After concluding that the Eighth Amendment did not provide for a *Bivens* action against a privately managed prison's personnel, the Magistrate Judge recommended that the District Court dismiss Pollard's complaint. The District Court did so. But on appeal the Ninth Circuit found that the Eighth Amendment provided Pollard with a *Bivens* action, and it reversed the District Court.

The defendants sought certiorari. And, in light of a split among the Courts of Appeals, we granted the petition.

II.

Recently, in *Wilkie v. Robbins, supra,* we rejected a claim that the Fifth Amendment impliedly authorized a *Bivens* action that would permit landowners to obtain damages from government officials who unconstitutionally interfere with their exercise of property rights. After reviewing the Court's earlier *Bivens* cases, the Court stated:

> "[T]he decision whether to recognize a *Bivens* remedy may require two steps. In the first place, there is the question whether any alternative, existing process for protecting the [constitutionally recognized] interest amounts to a convincing reason for the Judicial Branch to refrain from providing a new and freestanding remedy in damages. . . . But even in the absence of an alternative, a *Bivens* remedy is a subject of judgment: 'the federal courts must make the kind of remedial determination that is appropriate for a common-law tribunal, paying particular heed, however, to any special factors counselling hesitation before authorizing a new kind of federal litigation.'" 551 U.S., at 550, (quoting *Bush v. Lucas,* 462 U.S. 367, 378 (1983)).

These standards seek to reflect and to reconcile the Court's reasoning set forth in earlier cases. In *Bivens* itself the Court held that the Fourth Amendment implicitly authorized a court to order federal agents to pay damages to a person injured by the agents' violation of the Amendment's constitutional strictures. The Court noted that "'where federally protected rights have been invaded,' " courts can " 'adjust their remedies so as to grant the necessary relief.' " (quoting *Bell v. Hood,* 327 U.S. 678, 684 (1946)). See also *Correctional Services Corp. v. Malesko,* 534 U.S. 61, 66 (2001) ("authority to imply a new constitutional tort" anchored within general " 'arising under' " jurisdiction). It pointed out that the Fourth Amendment prohibited, among other things, conduct that state law might permit (such as the conduct at issue in that very case). It added that the interests protected on the one hand by state "trespass" and "invasion of privacy" laws and on the other hand by the Fourth Amendment's guarantees "may be inconsistent or even hostile." It stated that "[h]istorically, damages have been regarded as the ordinary remedy for an invasion of personal interests in liberty." And it found "no special factors counselling hesitation in the absence of affirmative action by Congress."

In *Davis v. Passman,* 442 U.S. 228 (1979), the Court considered a former congressional employee's claim for damages suffered as a result of her employer's unconstitutional discrimination based on gender. The Court found a damages action implicit in the Fifth Amendment's Due Process Clause. In doing so, the Court emphasized the unavailability of "other alternative forms of judicial relief." And the Court noted that there was "no evidence" that Congress (or the Constitution) intended to foreclose such a remedy.

In *Carlson v. Green,* 446 U.S. 14 (1980), the Court considered a claim for damages brought by the estate of a federal prisoner who (the estate said) had died as the result of government officials' "deliberat[e] indifferen[ce]" to his medical needs—indifference that violated the Eighth Amendment. The Court implied an action for damages from the Eighth Amendment. It noted that state law offered the particular plaintiff no meaningful damages remedy. Although the estate might have brought a damages claim under the Federal Tort Claims Act, the defendant in any such lawsuit was the employer, namely the United States, not the individual officers who had committed the violation. A damages remedy against an individual officer, the Court added, would prove a more effective deterrent. And, rather than leave compensation to the "vagaries" of state tort law, a federal *Bivens* action would provide "uniform rules."

Since *Carlson,* the Court has had to decide in several different instances whether to imply a *Bivens* action. And in each instance it has decided against the existence of such an action. These instances include:

(1) A federal employee's claim that his federal employer dismissed him in violation of the First Amendment, *Bush, supra,* (congressionally created federal civil service procedures provide meaningful redress);

(2) A claim by military personnel that military superiors violated various constitutional provisions, *Chappell v. Wallace,* 462 U.S. 296, 298–300 (1983) (special factors related to the military counsel against

implying a *Bivens* action), see also *United States v. Stanley,* 483 U.S. 669, 683–684 (1987) (similar);

(3) A claim by recipients of Social Security disability benefits that benefits had been denied in violation of the Fifth Amendment, *Schweiker v. Chilicky,* 487 U.S. 412, 414, 425 (1988) (elaborate administrative scheme provides meaningful alternative remedy);

(4) A former bank employee's suit against a federal banking agency, claiming that he lost his job due to agency action that violated the Fifth Amendment's Due Process Clause, *FDIC v. Meyer,* 510 U.S. 471, 484–486 (1994) (no *Bivens* actions against government agencies rather than particular individuals who act unconstitutionally);

(5) A prisoner's Eighth Amendment-based suit against a private corporation that managed a federal prison, *Malesko,* 534 U.S., at 70–73 (to permit suit against the employer-corporation would risk skewing relevant incentives; at the same time, the ability of a prisoner to bring state tort law damages action against *private* individual defendants means that the prisoner does not "lack effective remedies."

Although the Court, in reaching its decisions, has not always similarly emphasized the same aspects of the cases, *Wilkie* fairly summarizes the basic considerations that underlie those decisions. We consequently apply its approach here. And we conclude that Pollard cannot assert a *Bivens* claim.

That is primarily because Pollard's Eighth Amendment claim focuses upon a kind of conduct that typically falls within the scope of traditional state tort law. And in the case of a privately employed defendant, state tort law provides an "alternative, existing process" capable of protecting the constitutional interests at stake. The existence of that alternative here constitutes a "convincing reason for the Judicial Branch to refrain from providing a new and freestanding remedy in damages." Our reasoning is best understood if we set forth and explain why we reject Pollard's arguments to the contrary.

III.

Pollard (together with supporting *amici*) asks us to imply a *Bivens* action for four basic reasons—none of which we find convincing. First, Pollard argues that this Court has already decided in *Carlson* that a federal prisoner may bring an Eighth Amendment-based *Bivens* action against prison personnel; and we need do no more than simply apply *Carlson's* holding here. *Carlson,* however, was a case in which a federal prisoner sought damages from personnel employed by the *government,* not personnel employed by a *private* firm. And for present purposes that fact—of employment status—makes a critical difference.

For one thing, the potential existence of an adequate "alternative, existing process" differs dramatically in the two sets of cases. Prisoners ordinarily *cannot* bring state-law tort actions against employees of the Federal Government. See 28 U.S.C. §§ 2671, 2679(b)(1) (Westfall Act) (substituting United States as defendant in tort action against federal employee); *Osborn v. Haley,* 549 U.S. 225, 238, 241 (2007) (Westfall Act immunizes federal employee through removal and substitution of United States as defendant). But prisoners ordinarily *can* bring state-law tort actions against employees of a private firm.

For another thing, the Court specifically rejected Justice Stevens' somewhat similar suggestion in his dissenting opinion in *Malesko,* namely that a prisoner's suit against a private prison-management firm should fall within *Carlson's* earlier holding because such a firm, like a federal employee, is a "federal agent." In rejecting the dissent's suggestion, the Court explained that the context in *Malesko* was "fundamentally different" from the contexts at issue in earlier cases, including *Carlson.* That difference, the Court said, reflected in part the nature of the defendant, *i.e.,* a corporate employer rather than an individual employee, and in part reflected the existence of alternative "effective" state tort remedies. This last-mentioned factor makes it difficult to square Pollard's argument with *Malesko*'s reasoning.

Second, Pollard argues that, because of the "vagaries" of state tort law we should consider only whether *federal* law provides adequate alternative remedies. This argument flounders, however, on the fact that the Court rejected it in *Malesko.* State tort law, after all, can help to deter constitutional violations as well as to provide compensation to a violation's victim. And it is consequently unsurprising that several cases have considered the adequacy or inadequacy of state-law remedies when determining whether to imply a *Bivens* remedy. See, *e.g., Bivens,* 403 U.S., at 394 (state tort law "inconsistent or even hostile" to Fourth Amendment); *Davis,* 442 U.S., at 245, n. 23 (noting no state-law remedy available); cf. *Malesko, supra,* at 70 (noting that the Court has implied *Bivens* action only where any alternative remedy against individual officers was "nonexistent" or where plaintiff "lacked *any alternative remedy*" at all).

Third, Pollard argues that state tort law does not provide remedies *adequate* to protect the constitutional interests at issue here. Pollard's claim, however, is a claim for physical or related emotional harm suffered as a result of aggravated instances of the kind of conduct that state tort law typically forbids. That claim arose in California, where state tort law provides for ordinary negligence actions, for actions based upon "want of ordinary care or skill," for actions for "negligent failure to diagnose or treat," and for actions based upon the failure of one with a custodial duty to care for another to protect that other from " 'unreasonable risk of physical harm.' " See Cal. Civ.Code Ann. §§ 1714(a), 1714.8(a) (West 2009 and Supp.2012); *Giraldo v. California Dept. of Corrections and Rehabilitation,* 168 Cal.App.4th 231, 248, 85 Cal.Rptr.3d 371, 384 (2008) (quoting *Haworth v. State,* 60 Haw. 557, 562, 592 P.2d 820, 824 (1979)). California courts have specifically applied this law to jailers, including private operators of prisons. *Giraldo, supra,* at 252, 85 Cal.Rptr.3d, at 387 ("[J]ailers owe prisoners a duty of care to protect them from foreseeable harm"); see also *Lawson v. Superior Ct.,* 180 Cal.App.4th 1372, 1389–1390, 1397, 103 Cal.Rptr.3d 834, 849–850, 855 (2010) (same).

Moreover, California's tort law basically reflects general principles of tort law present, as far as we can tell, in the law of every State. See Restatement (Second) of Torts §§ 314A(4), 320 (1963–1964). We have found specific authority indicating that state law imposes general tort duties of reasonable care (including medical care) on prison employees in every one of the eight States where privately managed secure federal facilities are currently located. See Dept. of Justice, Federal Bureau of Prisons, Weekly Population Report (Dec. 22, 2011), http://www.bop.gov/locations/weekly_report.jsp (listing States) (as visited Dec. 29, 2011, and available in Clerk of Court's case file); *Thomas v. Williams,* 105 Ga.App. 321, 326, 124 S.E.2d 409, 412–413 (1962) (In Georgia, " 'sheriff owes to a prisoner placed in his custody a duty to keep the prisoner safely and free from harm, to render him medical aid when necessary, and to treat him humanely and refrain from oppressing him' "); *Giraldo, supra,* at 248, 85 Cal.Rptr.3d, at 384 (California, same); *Farmer v. State ex rel. Russell,* 224 Miss. 96, 105, 79 So.2d 528, 531 (1955) (Mississippi, same); *Doe v. Albuquerque,* 96 N.M. 433, 438, 631 P.2d 728, 733 (App.1981) (New Mexico, same); *Multiple Claimants v. North Carolina Dept. of Health and Human Servs.,* 176 N.C.App. 278, 280, 626 S.E.2d 666, 668 (2006) (North Carolina, same); *Clemets v. Heston,* 20 Ohio App.3d 132, 135–136, 485 N.E.2d 287, 291 (1985) (Ohio, same); *Williams v. Syed,* 782 A.2d 1090, 1093–1094 (Pa.Commw.2001) (Pennsylvania, same); *Salazar v. Collins,* 255 S.W.3d 191, 198–200 (Tex.App.2008) (Texas, same); see also Schellenger, 14 A.L.R.2d 353, § 2[a] (Later Case Service and Supp.2011) (same). But cf. Miss.Code. Ann. § 11–46–9(1)(m) (Supp.2011) (statute forbidding such actions against *State*—though not private—employees); N.Y. Correc. Law Ann. §§ 24 (West 2003), 121 (2011 Cum.Supp.) (similar).

We note, as Pollard points out, that state tort law may sometimes prove less generous than would a *Bivens* action, say, by capping damages, see Cal. Civ. Code Ann. § 3333.2(b) (West 1997), or by forbidding recovery for emotional suffering unconnected with physical harm, or by imposing procedural obstacles, say, initially requiring the use of expert administrative panels in medical malpractice cases, see, *e.g.,* Me.Rev.Stat. Ann., Tit. 24, § 2853, (Supp.2010); Mass. Gen. Laws, ch.

231, § 60B (West 2010). But we cannot find in this fact sufficient basis to determine state law inadequate.

State-law remedies and a potential *Bivens* remedy need not be perfectly congruent. See *Bush, supra,* at 388 (administrative remedies adequate even though they "do not provide complete relief"). Indeed, federal law as well as state law contains limitations. Prisoners bringing federal lawsuits, for example, ordinarily may not seek damages for mental or emotional injury unconnected with physical injury. See 42 U.S.C. § 1997e(e). And *Bivens* actions, even if more generous to plaintiffs in some respects, may be less generous in others. For example, to show an Eighth Amendment violation a prisoner must typically show that a defendant acted, not just negligently, but with "deliberate indifference." *Farmer v. Brennan,* 511 U.S. 825, 834 (1994). And a *Bivens* plaintiff, unlike a state tort law plaintiff, normally could not apply principles of *respondeat superior* and thereby obtain recovery from a defendant's potentially deep-pocketed employer. See *Ashcroft v. Iqbal,* 556 U.S. 662, 676 (2009).

Rather, in principle, the question is whether, in general, state tort law remedies provide roughly similar incentives for potential defendants to comply with the Eighth Amendment while also providing roughly similar compensation to victims of violations. The features of the two kinds of actions just mentioned suggest that, in practice, the answer to this question is "yes." And we have found nothing here to convince us to the contrary.

Fourth, Pollard argues that there "may" be similar kinds of Eighth Amendment claims that state tort law does not cover. But Pollard does not convincingly show that there are such cases. Compare Brief for Respondent Pollard 32 (questioning the availability of state tort remedies for "prisoners [who] suffer attacks by other inmates, preventable suicides, or the denial of heat, ventilation or movement"), with *Giraldo, supra,* at 248–249, 85 Cal.Rptr.3d, at 384–385 (courts have long held that prison officials must protect, *e.g.,* transgender inmate from foreseeable harm by other inmates), and Restatement (Second) of Torts §§ 314A(4), 320.

Regardless, we concede that we cannot prove a negative or be totally certain that the features of state tort law relevant here will universally prove to be, or remain, as we have described them. Nonetheless, we are certain enough about the shape of present law as applied to the kind of case before us to leave different cases and different state laws to another day. That is to say, we can decide whether to imply a *Bivens* action in a case where an Eighth Amendment claim or state law differs significantly from those at issue here when and if such a case arises. The possibility of such a different future case does not provide sufficient grounds for reaching a different conclusion here.

For these reasons, where, as here, a federal prisoner seeks damages from privately employed personnel working at a privately operated federal prison, where the conduct allegedly amounts to a violation of the Eighth Amendment, and where that conduct is of a kind that typically falls within the scope of traditional state tort law (such as the conduct involving improper medical care at issue here), the prisoner must seek a remedy under state tort law. We cannot imply a *Bivens* remedy in such a case.

The judgment of the Ninth Circuit is reversed.

So ordered.

JUSTICE SCALIA, with whom JUSTICE THOMAS joins, concurring.

I join the opinion of the Court because I agree that a narrow interpretation of the rationale of *Bivens v. Six Unknown Fed. Narcotics Agents,* 403 U.S. 388 (1971), would not cause the holding of that case to apply to the circumstances of this case. Even if the narrowest rationale of *Bivens* did apply here, however, I would decline to extend its holding. *Bivens* is "a relic of the heady days in which this Court assumed common-law powers to create causes of action" by constitutional implication. We have abandoned that power in the statutory field, see *Alexander v. Sandoval,* 532 U.S. 275, 287 (2001), and we should do the same in the constitutional field, where (presumably) an imagined "implication" cannot even be repudiated by Congress. As I have previously stated, see *Malesko, supra,* at 75, I would limit *Bivens* and its two follow-on cases (*Davis v. Passman* and *Carlson v. Green*) to the precise circumstances that they involved.

JUSTICE GINSBURG, dissenting.

Were Pollard incarcerated in a federal- or state-operated facility, he would have a federal remedy for the Eighth Amendment violations he [alleges.] I would not deny the same character of relief to Pollard, a prisoner placed by federal contract in a privately operated prison. Pollard may have suffered "aggravated instances" of conduct state tort law forbids, but that same aggravated conduct, when it is engaged in by official actors, also offends the Federal Constitution. Rather than remitting Pollard to the "vagaries" of state tort law, *Carlson,* 446 U.S., at 23, I would hold his injuries, sustained while serving a federal sentence, "compensable according to uniform rules of federal law," *Bivens v. Six Unknown Fed. Narcotics Agents,* 403 U.S. 388, 409 (1971) (Harlan, J., concurring in judgment).

Indeed, there is stronger cause for providing a federal remedy in this case than there was in *Malesko.* There, the question presented was whether a *Bivens* action lies against a private corporation that manages a facility housing federal prisoners. Suing a corporate employer, the majority observed in *Malesko,* would not serve to deter individual officers from conduct transgressing constitutional limitations on their authority. Individual deterrence, the Court reminded, was the consideration central to the *Bivens* decision. Noting the availability of state tort remedies, the majority in *Malesko* declined to "exten[d] *Bivens* beyond [that decision's] core premise," *i.e.,* deterring individual officers. Pollard's case, in contrast, involves *Bivens'* core concern: His suit seeking damages directly from individual officers would have precisely the deterrent effect the Court found absent in *Malesko.*

For the reasons stated, I would hold that relief potentially available under state tort law does not block Pollard's recourse to a federal remedy for the affront to the Constitution he suffered. Accordingly, I would affirm the Ninth Circuits judgment.

NOTES ON MINNECI

1. What Is Left of *Bivens*? It is significant in *Minneci* that the defendant worked for a private prison, because this fact had a bearing on the state law remedies available to the plaintiff. But much of the Court's reasoning suggests that the factor that does most of the work of deciding the case is the "rough" adequacy of those remedies, not the fact that the defendant worked for a private prison. Would the result be any different if the defendant were a government employee, and the state remedies available to the plaintiff were identical to those in *Minneci*? If not, is the whole *Bivens* doctrine now limited to situations in which state remedies are so weak that they fail to meet the *Minneci* standard (which is as yet largely undefined, but evidently is to be developed in later cases)? In this regard, note that *federal* remedies have precluded *Bivens* claims ever since *Bush.* See, e.g., *M.E.S. Inc. v. Snell,* 712 F.3d 666 (2nd Cir. 2013) (a government contractor, charging that U.S. officers retaliated against him for protected speech, may not bring a *Bivens* suit, because the federal Contract Disputes Act provides a comprehensive scheme for reviewing claims related to federal contracts.)

2. National Security. *Vance v. Rumsfeld,* 701 F.3d 193 (7th Cir. 2012) (en banc) raised "the question whether the federal judiciary should create a right of action for damages against soldiers (and others in the chain of command) who abusively interrogate or mistreat military prisoners, or fail to prevent improper detention and interrogation." Citing *Chappell* and *Stanley* (two cases denying a *Bivens* remedy to military personnel, both of which are briefly discussed in *Minneci*) the Court rejected the *Bivens* remedy. Chief Judge Easterbrook said that in those cases "[t]he Supreme Court's principal point was that civilian courts should not interfere with the military chain of command—that is, not without statutory authority." That proposition governed even though the statutory remedies available to these plaintiffs were "not full substitutes for a *Bivens* remedy." Judge Easterbrook noted other problems with allowing a *Bivens* remedy in this context, including "diverting Cabinet officers' time from management of public affairs to the defense of their bank accounts," and "problems with . . . disclosure of secret information." Other circuits have also denied a *Bivens* remedy in national security cases. See, e.g., *Lebron v. Rumsfeld*, 670 F.3d 540 (4th Cir. 2012); *Doe v. Rumsfeld,* 683 F.3d 390 (D.C.Cir. 2012); *Arar v. Ashcroft*, 585 F.3d 559 (2nd Cir. 2009) (en banc). These cases do not distinguish between plaintiffs who are U.S. citizens and those who are not. Compare *Hernandez v. United States*, 757 F.3d 249 (5th Cir. 2014) (allowing a *Bivens* suit on behalf of a boy shot and killed by a U.S. Border Patrol Agent, since tort claims against the U.S. were barred by the FTCA's foreign country exception).

2.   Are There Any Constitutionally Compelled Remedies?

Whatever the precise scope of *Bivens*, after *Minneci* the remedy is certainly not generally available to persons complaining of unconstitutional treatment by federal officers (or contractors, or their employees.) Though *Bivens* is a remedy for constitutional violations, the doctrine does not support the notion that the remedy itself is constitutionally *compelled*. In certain contexts, however, judge-made remedies may be constitutionally required in the absence of other effective means of redress.

This issue has arisen most often in connection with federal constitutional challenges to state and local taxation. For example, in *Ward v. Love County*, 253 U.S. 17 (1920), a local government collected unconstitutional taxes by coercive methods. When the taxpayers sued in state court for a refund, the county defended on the ground that no statute authorized a refund. The Court responded that "the law, independent of any statute, will compel restitution or compensation." See also *General Oil Co. v. Crain*, supra (holding that states must provide an injunctive remedy for unconstitutional acts by state officers, regardless of state law).

Reich v. Collins, the next principal case, also involved a challenge to state taxation. In order to understand the reasoning and implications of *Reich*, it will be useful to begin with some features of the "tax challenge" context. Most constitutional challenges to the acts of state and local governments and their officers can be raised in § 1983 suits seeking injunctive relief or damages (though, as noted in Chapter 1, under *Quern v. Jordan* a state government cannot be sued directly for damages). The tax context presents special problems. A federal statute called the Tax Injunction Act, 28 U.S.C. § 1341, provides that "[t]he district courts shall not enjoin, suspend or restrain the assessment, levy, or collection of any tax under State law where a plain, speedy and efficient remedy may be had in the courts of such State." Since every state claims to provide a "plain, speedy, and efficient remedy," the practical effect of this statute is to channel constitutional challenges involving state taxes to the state courts, and the focus of Supreme Court cases in the area has been the efficacy of state remedies.

Reich was preceded by *McKesson Corp. v. Division of Alcoholic Beverages and Tobacco*, 496 U.S. 18 (1990). That case concerned a Florida excise tax on alcoholic beverages that discriminated in favor of in-state over out-of-state products in violation of the commerce clause. State law allowed taxpayers to bring a post-payment challenge to the legality of a tax, but required payment of the tax without an opportunity for a pre-payment challenge. McKesson, a distributor of out-of-state products sought a refund of taxes illegally collected. The Florida courts enjoined further preferential treatment but denied McKesson the retrospective relief it sought on account of "the equitable considerations present in this case." (The "equitable considerations" it specified were that the tax had been collected "in good faith reliance on a presumptively valid statute," and that McKesson would get a windfall if it received refund, as it would have passed the tax on to its customers already.) The Supreme Court reversed, ruling that "if a state places a taxpayer under duress promptly to pay a tax when due and relegates him to a postpayment refund action in which he can challenge the tax's legality, the Due Process Clause of the 14th Amendment obligates the state to provide meaningful backward-looking relief to rectify any unconstitutional deprivation." But in the circumstances, the 14th Amendment's command would not necessarily require a refund:

> In this case, Florida may satisfy this obligation through any form of relief, ranging from a refund of the excess taxes paid by petitioner to an offsetting charge to previously favored distributors, that will cure any unconstitutional discrimination against interstate commerce during the contested tax period.

REICH V. COLLINS
513 U.S. 106 (1994).

JUSTICE O'CONNOR delivered the opinion of the Court.

In a long line of cases, this Court has established that due process requires a "clear and certain" remedy for taxes collected in violation of federal law. A State has the flexibility to provide that remedy before the disputed taxes are paid (predeprivation), after they are paid (postdeprivation), or both. But what it may not do, and what Georgia did here, is hold out what plainly appears to be a "clear and certain" postdeprivation remedy and then declare, only after the disputed taxes have been paid, that no such remedy exists.

I

For many years, numerous States, including Georgia, exempted from state personal income tax retirement benefits paid by the State, but not retirement benefits paid by the Federal Government (or any other employer). In March 1989, this Court held that such a tax scheme violates the constitutional intergovernmental tax immunity doctrine, which dates back to *McCulloch v. Maryland*, 17 U.S. 316, 4 Wheat. 316 (1819), and has been generally codified at 4 U.S.C. § 111. See *Davis v. Michigan Dept. of Treasury*, 489 U.S. 803 (1989).

In the aftermath of *Davis*, most of these States, Georgia included, repealed their special tax exemptions for state retirees, but few offered federal retirees any refunds for the unconstitutional taxes they had paid in the years before *Davis* was decided. Not surprisingly, a great deal of litigation ensued in an effort to force States to provide refunds. The instant suit is part of that litigation.

In April 1990, Reich, a retired federal military officer, sued Georgia in Georgia state court, seeking a refund for the tax years 1980 and after. The principal legal basis for Reich's lawsuit was Georgia's tax refund statute, which provides: "A taxpayer shall be refunded any and all taxes or fees which are determined to have been erroneously or illegally assessed and collected from him under the laws of this state, whether paid voluntarily or involuntarily. . . ." Ga. Code Ann. § 48–2–35(a) (Supp. 1994).

The Georgia trial court first decided that, because of § 48–2–35's statute of limitations, Reich's refund request was limited to the tax years 1985 and after. Even as to these later tax years, however, the trial court refused to grant a refund, and the Georgia Supreme Court affirmed. The Georgia high court explained that it was construing the refund statute not to apply to "the situation where the law under which the taxes are assessed and collected is itself subsequently declared to be unconstitutional or otherwise invalid." (*Reich I*).

Reich then petitioned the Georgia Supreme Court for reconsideration of its decision on the grounds that even if the Georgia tax refund statute does not require a refund, federal due process does—due process, that is, as interpreted by *McKesson Corp. v. Division of Alcoholic Beverages and Tobacco, Fla. Dept. of Business Regulation*, 496 U.S. 18 (1990), and the long line of cases upon which *McKesson* depends. [These] cases stand for the proposition that a denial by a state court of a recovery of taxes exacted in violation of the laws or Constitution of the United States by compulsion is itself in contravention of the Fourteenth Amendment, the sovereign immunity States traditionally enjoy in their own courts notwithstanding. (We should note that the sovereign immunity States enjoy in *federal* court, under the Eleventh Amendment, does generally bar tax refund claims from being brought in that forum. See *Ford Motor Co. v. Department of Treasury of Ind.*, 323 U.S. 459 (1945).)

Reich's petition for reconsideration in light of *McKesson* was denied. He then petitioned for certiorari. While the petition was pending, we decided *Harper v. Virginia Dept. of Taxation*, 509 U.S. 86 (1993), which relied on *McKesson* in circumstances similar to this case. Accordingly, we remanded Reich's case to the Georgia Supreme Court for further consideration in light of *Harper*.

On remand, the Georgia Supreme Court focused on the portion of *Harper* explaining that, under *McKesson*, a State is free to provide its "clear and certain" remedy in an exclusively predeprivation manner. "[A] meaningful opportunity for taxpayers to withhold contested tax assessments and to challenge their validity in a predeprivation hearing," we said, is " 'a procedural safeguard [against unlawful deprivations] sufficient by itself to satisfy the Due Process Clause.' " See *Harper,* supra, at 101, quoting *McKesson,* supra, at 38, n. 21. The court then reviewed Georgia's predeprivation procedures, found them "ample," and denied Reich's refund claim. (*Reich II*).

Reich again petitioned for certiorari, and we granted the writ to consider whether it was proper for the Georgia Supreme Court to deny Reich relief on the basis of Georgia's predeprivation remedies.

II

The Georgia Supreme Court is no doubt right that, under *McKesson*, Georgia has the flexibility to maintain an exclusively predeprivation remedial scheme, so long as that scheme is "clear and certain." Due process, we should add, also allows the State to maintain an exclusively post deprivation regime, or a hybrid regime. A State is free as well to reconfigure its remedial scheme over time, to fit its changing needs. Such choices are generally a matter only of state law.

But what a State may *not* do, and what Georgia did here, is to reconfigure its scheme, unfairly, in *mid-course*—to "bait and switch," as some have described it. Specifically, in the mid-1980's, Georgia held out what plainly appeared to be a "clear and certain" postdeprivation remedy, in the form of its tax refund statute, and then declared, only after Reich and others had paid the disputed taxes, that no such remedy exists. In this regard, the Georgia Supreme Court's reliance on Georgia's predeprivation procedures was entirely beside the point (and thus error), because even assuming the constitutional adequacy of these procedures—an issue on which we express no view—no reasonable taxpayer would have thought that they represented, in light of the apparent applicability of the refund statute, the *exclusive* remedy for unlawful taxes.

Nor can there be any question that, during the 1980's, prior to *Reich I*, Georgia did appear to hold out a "clear and certain" postdeprivation remedy. To recall, the Georgia refund statute says that the State "*shall*" refund "*any and all* taxes or fees which are determined to have been erroneously or *illegally assessed* and collected from [a taxpayer] under the laws of this state, whether paid voluntarily or involuntarily. . . ." Ga. Code Ann. § 48–2–35(a) (Supp. 1994) (emphasis added). In our view, the average taxpayer reading this language would think it obvious that state taxes assessed in violation of federal law are "illegally assessed" taxes. Certainly the United States Court of Appeals for the Eleventh Circuit thought this conclusion was obvious when, in a 1986 case, it denied federal court relief to taxpayers raising claims similar to Reich's, in part because it thought Georgia's refund statute applied to the claims.

Respondents, moreover, do not point to any Georgia Supreme Court cases prior to Reich I that put any limiting construction on the statute's sweeping language; indeed, the cases we have found are all entirely consistent with that language's apparent breadth. . . . Even apart from the statute and the cases, we find it significant that, for obvious reasons, States ordinarily *prefer* that taxpayers pursue only postdeprivation remedies, *i. e.*, that taxpayers "pay first, litigate later." This preference is significant in that it would seem especially unfair to penalize taxpayers who may have ignored the possibility of pursuing predeprivation remedies out of respect for that preference.

In many ways, then, this case bears a remarkable resemblance to *NAACP v. Alabama ex rel. Patterson*, 357 U.S. 449 (1958) (Harlan, J.). There, an Alabama trial court held the National Association for the Advancement of Colored People in contempt for failing to comply with a discovery order to produce its membership lists, and the Alabama Supreme Court denied review of the constitutionality of the contempt judgment on the grounds that the organization failed earlier to pursue a mandamus action to quash the underlying discovery order. The Court found that the Alabama high court's refusal to review the contempt judgment was in error. Prior Alabama law, the Court said, showed "unambiguously" that judicial review of contempt judgments had consistently been available, the existence of mandamus notwithstanding. For good measure, the Court also looked at prior Alabama law on mandamus and found nothing "suggesting that mandamus is the *exclusive* remedy" in this situation. (emphasis in original). Justice Harlan thus concluded: "Novelty in procedural requirements cannot be permitted to thwart review in this Court applied for by those who, in justified reliance upon prior decisions, seek vindication in state courts of their federal constitutional rights." *Brinkerhoff-Faris Trust & Sav. Co. v. Hill*, 281 U.S. 673 (1930) (due process violated when state court denied injunction against collection of unlawful taxes on the basis of taxpayer's failure to pursue administrative remedies, where State's prior "settled" law made clear that no such administrative remedies existed).

Finally, Georgia contends that Reich had no idea (before *Davis*) that the taxes he was paying throughout the 1980's might be unconstitutional. Even assuming Reich had no idea, however, we are not sure we understand the argument. If the argument is that Reich would not have taken advantage of the State's predeprivation remedies no matter how adequate they were (and thus has no standing to complain of those remedies), the argument is beside the point for the same reason that we said that the Georgia Supreme Court's reliance on those remedies was beside the point: Reich was entitled to pursue what appeared to be a "clear and certain" postdeprivation remedy, regardless of the State's predeprivation remedies. Alternatively, if the argument is that Reich needed to have known of the unconstitutionality of his taxes in order to pursue the State's postdeprivation remedy, the argument is wrong. It is wrong because Georgia's refund statute has a relatively lengthy statute of limitations period, and, at least until this case, see *Reich I*, contained no contemporaneous protest requirement. Under such a regime, taxpayers need not have taken any steps to learn of the possible unconstitutionality of their taxes at the time they paid them. Accordingly, they may not now be put in any worse position for having failed to take such steps.

For the reasons stated, the judgment is reversed and the case is remanded for the provision of meaningful backward-looking relief, consistent with due process and our *McKesson* line of cases.

NOTE ON CONSTITUTIONALLY COMPELLED REMEDIES

No one challenges the proposition that persons who are charged with crimes or civil violations may raise their constitutional rights defensively, as a "shield" against liability. The constitutional pedigree of offensive remedies is more problematic, though not without some support in Supreme Court cases. In addition to *Reich*, *McKesson*, *Ward*, and *Crain*, the principle that some offensive remedies are constitutionally compelled draws support from *First English Evangelical Lutheran Church v. County of Los Angeles*, 482 U.S. 304, 316 & n. 9 (1987), where the Court said that "in the event of a taking, the compensation remedy is required by the Constitution," and cited several cases in support of that principle. The accompanying footnote rebuffed the notion that "principles of sovereign immunity" may override this principle. Besides these cases, recall the dictum from *Marbury v. Madison*, cited in *Bivens*, which states that "[t]he very essence of civil liberty certainly consists in the right of every individual to claim the protection of the laws whenever he receives an injury."

But these cases cannot fairly be read as establishing a strong rule that courts must provide retrospective remedies for all constitutional violations. Taken as whole, the Court's doctrine on constitutional remedies simply does not support the existence of such a rule. Comments in later cases suggest that *Reich* should be read solely as a rule against "bait and switch" and that sovereign immunity may limit the reach of *First Evangelical* after all. See Richard A. Fallon, *Jurisdiction-Stripping Reconsidered,* 96 VA. L. REV. 1043, 1109–10 (2010). The ever-narrowing scope of the *Bivens* doctrine, official immunity, the "policy or custom" threshold for municipal liability—all discussed either in this chapter or Chapter 1—as well as the sovereign immunity of the state and national governments (see Chapter 5) stand in the way of plaintiffs seeking to vindicate constitutional rights.

Here is a useful starting point for understanding why some constitutional remedies seem to be "compelled" while others are not:

> Distinguish [a] litigants who seek to raise the constitution as a shield against criminal or civil enforcement actions, on the one hand, from [b] those who want to wield it as a sword, taking the role of plaintiff and suing either to stop some present or threatened wrongdoing by the state (by obtaining injunctive or declaratory relief) or to obtain damages or other backward-looking relief. With respect to [a], there is authority for the proposition that the state may place some limits on the timing of and the forum in which one may raise constitutional defenses. See *Yakus v. United States*, 321 U.S. 414 (1944) (upholding provisions of the World War II price control statute). But it may not foreclose those defenses. The state is constitutionally compelled to allow litigants to raise them.

> As for [b], we need to distinguish between (i) injunctive and declaratory relief and (ii) backward-looking relief like damages. Except for a few statutory barriers (of which the tax injunction act is the most important) injunctive relief against constitutional violations is generally available in the federal courts under the principle of *Ex parte Young*. The materials in this chapter, in chapter 5 (on sovereign immunity), and in chapter 1 show that damages are more problematic. As we have seen, there are many specific reasons for restrictions on backward-looking relief. The overarching reason for these limits is that requests for retrospective remedies present a conflict between important goals. On the one hand, the vindication of constitutional rights and deterrence of constitutional violations call for a remedy. At the same time, government needs flexibility to carry out its functions effectively. Broadly speaking, retrospective remedies interfere with that need more often than instructions to government to change its practices in the future. The foregoing framework suggests that the availability of "sword-like" constitutional remedies, especially damages, is best characterized not as a rule but as a "principle" that may be overridden by competing values.

For further discussion of this model of the law of constitutional remedies, see Richard Fallon & Daniel Meltzer, *New Law, Non-Retroactivity, and Constitutional Remedies*, 104 HARV. L. REV. 1731, esp. pp. 1778–79 (1991).

CHAPTER 3

THE JURISDICTION OF THE FEDERAL DISTRICT COURTS

■ ■ ■

The two main avenues for gaining access to federal court are the "federal question" jurisdiction and the "diversity" jurisdiction. Section 1983, discussed in Chapter 1, illustrates the former. This chapter takes a broader perspective. Looking at jurisdictional issues in general terms, we examine the statutes and the case law bearing on these two grounds for federal jurisdiction.

I. FEDERAL QUESTION JURISDICTION

Article III authorizes federal jurisdiction over cases "arising under this Constitution, the Laws of the United States, and Treaties made [under] their Authority." Congress has enacted several jurisdictional provisions bearing on these "federal questions." The general statute, 28 U.S.C. § 1331, very nearly tracks the constitutional provision, declaring that "[t]he district courts shall have original jurisdiction of all civil actions arising under the Constitution, laws, or treaties of the United States." Other jurisdictional statutes deal with narrower categories of cases, yet they typically employ the same "arising under" formulation. For example, 28 U.S.C. § 1338 provides that "[t]he district courts shall have original jurisdiction of any civil action arising under any Act of Congress relating to patents, plant variety protection, copyrights and trademarks." Most of the case law concerns the construction of "arising under" in § 1331. The same principles apply to § 1338 and other similarly worded jurisdictional statutes. See, e g., *Dutcher v. Matheson*, 733 F.3d 980, 985 n.4 (10th Cir. 2013) (28 U.S.C. § 1337 "provides no additional grant of jurisdiction beyond that provided in 28 U.S.C. § 1331").

When a plaintiff initially takes a case to state court, the defendant may seek to "remove" it to federal court because it falls within the federal question jurisdiction. We deal with removal in detail in Section E below. For now, the main point to keep in mind is that a case can be removed to federal court whenever it could have been brought in federal court in the first place. The "arising under" doctrine developed in construing § 1331 and other jurisdictional statutes governs federal question removal jurisdiction as well.

There are two main differences between § 1331 and some of the narrower statutes: [1] One relates to "jurisdictional amount" requirements. For example, 28 U.S.C. § 1337 grants district court "jurisdiction of any civil action or proceeding arising under any Act of Congress regulating commerce or protecting trade and commerce against restraints and monopolies" but goes on to allow jurisdiction over some matters within this category "only if the matter in controversy [exceeds] $10,000 exclusive of interest and costs." [2] It is up to Congress to decide whether to allow litigants to proceed in state court as well as federal court. The general rule is that federal jurisdiction is *concurrent* with that of the state courts, but Congress may choose to make federal jurisdiction *exclusive*. For example, § 1338 directs that federal jurisdiction "shall be exclusive of the courts of the states in patent, plant variety protection and copyright cases."

We focus on the general principles the Court has developed for deciding whether a case "arises under" federal law within the meaning of § 1331 and similarly worded jurisdictional statutes. We bring in other "arising under" issues for the purpose of comparison and contrast, so as to better define and understand the general theme of "arising under" jurisdiction.

A. THE BASIC PRINCIPLE: A CASE ARISES UNDER THE LAW THAT CREATES THE CAUSE OF ACTION

AMERICAN WELL WORKS CO. V. LAYNE & BOWLER CO.
241 U.S. 257 (1916).

MR. JUSTICE HOLMES delivered the opinion of the Court:

[The issue before the Supreme Court was whether the case arose under the federal patent laws.]

Of course the question depends upon the plaintiff's declaration. That may be summed up in a few words. The plaintiff alleges that it owns, manufactures, and sells a certain pump, has or has applied for a patent for it, and that the pump is known as the best in the market. It then alleges that the defendants have falsely and maliciously libeled and slandered the plaintiff's title to the pump by stating that the pump and certain parts thereof are infringements upon the defendant's pump and certain parts thereof, and that without probable cause they have brought suits against some parties who are using the plaintiff's pump, and that they are threatening suits against all who use it. The allegation of the defendants' libel or slander is repeated in slightly varying form, but it all comes to statements to various people that the plaintiff was infringing the defendants' patent, and that the defendant would sue both seller and buyer if the plaintiff's pump was used. Actual damage to the plaintiff in its business is alleged to the extent of $50,000, and punitive damages to the same amount are asked.

It is evident that the claim for damages is based upon conduct; or, more specifically, language, tending to persuade the public to withdraw its custom from the plaintiff, and having that effect to its damage. Such conduct, having such effect, is equally actionable whether it produces the result by persuasion, by threats, or by falsehood, and it is enough to allege and prove the conduct and effect, leaving the defendant to justify if he can. If the conduct complained of is persuasion, it may be justified by the fact that the defendant is a competitor, or by good faith and reasonable grounds. If it is a statement of fact, it may be justified, absolutely or with qualifications, by proof that the statement is true. But all such justifications are defenses, and raise issues that are no part of the plaintiff's case. In the present instance it is part of the plaintiff's case that it had a business to be damaged; whether built up by patents or without them does not matter. It is no part of it to prove anything concerning the defendants' patent, or that the plaintiff did not infringe the same—still less to prove anything concerning any patent of its own. The material statement complained of is that the plaintiff infringes,— which may be true notwithstanding the plaintiff's patent. That is merely a piece of evidence. Furthermore, the damage alleged presumably is rather the consequence of the threat to sue than of the statement that the plaintiff's pump infringed the defendants' rights.

A suit for damages to business caused by a threat to sue under the patent law is not itself a suit under the patent law. And the same is true when the damage is caused by a statement of fact—that the defendant has a patent which is infringed. What makes the defendants' act a wrong is its manifest tendency to injure the plaintiff's business; and the wrong is the same whatever the means by which it is accomplished. But whether it is a wrong or not depends upon the law of the State where the act is done, not upon the patent law, and therefore the suit arises under the law of the State. A suit arises under the law that creates the cause of action. The fact that the justification may involve the validity and infringement of a patent is no more material to the question under what law the suit is brought than it would be in an action of contract. If the State adopted for civil proceedings the saying of the old criminal law: the greater the truth, the greater the libel, the validity of the patent would not come in question at all. In Massachusetts the truth would not be a defense if the statement was made from disinterested malevolence. The State is master of the whole matter, and if it saw fit to do away with actions of this type altogether, no one, we imagine, would suppose that they still could be maintained under the patent laws of the United States.

Judgment reversed.

MR. JUSTICE MCKENNA dissents, being of opinion that the case involves a direct and substantial controversy under the patent laws.

NOTES ON THE "LAW THAT CREATES THE CAUSE OF ACTION" TEST

1. A General Principle for Determining Federal Question Jurisdiction. The question of whether a given case may be litigated in federal court can generally be resolved by applying Holmes's maxim that "[a] suit arises under the law that creates the cause of action." There are, to be sure, exceptions to this general principle, and we will address them in the materials that follow. But it is important to keep the exceptions in perspective. Some of them are utterly lacking in clarity. As a result, someone who neglects the general principle of *American Well Works* can easily fall into the mistake of thinking that the scope of federal question jurisdiction is clouded in uncertainty. In fact, the bulk of the cases are governed by Holmes's straightforward rule: When someone sues under a cause of action granted by Congress, or one recognized by courts as part of federal common law, the suit may be brought in federal court. When the suit is brought under a state law cause of action, such as the cause of action for defamation, it ordinarily must be litigated in state court. Only in a few exceptional cases is the jurisdictional issue in doubt. The Court puts the point this way:

> There is no single, precise definition of [federal question jurisdiction]; rather, the phrase "arising under" masks a welter of issues regarding the interrelation of federal and state authority and the proper management of the federal judicial system. This much, however, is clear. The vast majority of cases that come within this grant of jurisdiction are covered by Justice Holmes' statement that a suit arises under the law that creates the cause of action. Thus, the vast majority of cases brought under the general federal-question jurisdiction of the federal courts are those in which federal law creates the cause of action.

Merrell Dow Pharmaceuticals v. Thompson, 478 U.S. 804, 808 (1986) (internal quotation marks and citations omitted).

The federal law that "creates the cause of action" will ordinarily be a federal statute. But federal common law causes of action, such as those "implied" from statutes or constitutional provisions, also qualify. Sometimes the Court recognizes the existence of a general body of federal common law, as it did with regard to interstate water pollution in *Illinois v. Milwaukee*, 406 U.S. 91 (1972). In that case the Court ruled that suits to enforce the federal common law rules in the area would "arise under" federal law.

The "law that creates the cause of action" test is not a mere formality. The principle that a case arises under federal law if federal law creates the cause of action rests on the premise that the plaintiff has a substantial claim. For any number of reasons, some litigants prefer federal court. Yet one does not gain access to federal court merely by asserting federal claims that, upon examination, have utterly no foundation. The point here is not that the existence of federal jurisdiction depends on the merits:

> Jurisdiction [is] not [defeated] by the possibility that the averments might fail to state a cause of action on which [plaintiffs] could actually recover. [Nonetheless,] a suit may sometimes be dismissed for want of jurisdiction where the alleged claim under the Constitution or federal statutes clearly appears to be immaterial and made solely for the purpose of obtaining jurisdiction or where such a claim is wholly insubstantial and frivolous.

Bell v. Hood, 327 U.S. 678, 682 (1946). See also *Hagans v. Lavine*, 415 U.S. 528, 543 (1974).

2.   A Presumption that State and Federal Jurisdiction Are Concurrent. Congress may choose to make federal jurisdiction exclusive. See, e.g., 28 U.S.C. § 1338 ("No State court shall have jurisdiction over any claim for relief arising under any Act of Congress relating to patents, plant variety protection, or copyrights.") Congress may also channel litigation to state courts, excluding the federal courts. See Chapter 10. But the Supreme Court generally presumes that state and federal jurisdiction are concurrent, absent express language or other strong reasons to the contrary. Usually the issue of whether state and federal jurisdiction are concurrent comes up in the context of whether a state court may adjudicate a federal cause of action. See Chapter 7 for discussion of that topic. An interesting variation on the problem was addressed in *Mims v. Arrow Financial Services, LLC*, 565 U.S. ___, 132 S.Ct. 740 (2012). The issue was whether Congress had authorized *federal* jurisdiction over cases brought by consumers for harassing phone calls under the Telephone Consumer Protection Act of 1991, 47 U.S.C. § 227. The statute explicitly authorizes state court jurisdiction over these suits, seems to contemplate that they will be litigated in state court, and does not explicitly provide for federal jurisdiction over them. Nonetheless, the Supreme Court ruled unanimously that "there is no convincing reason to read into the TCPA's permissive grant of jurisdiction to state courts any barrier to the U.S. district courts' exercise of the general federal-question jurisdiction they have possessed since 1875."

3.   Constitutional and Statutory Issues. This chapter focuses on the *statutory* issues related to federal district court jurisdiction. The *constitutional* issues concerning the scope of Congress's power to expand or contract federal jurisdiction are examined in Chapter 10. Yet it is unwise to try to wholly separate statutory from constitutional issues, as the relation between the two is more complicated than it may appear.

Article III, Section 2, provides that the federal judicial power extends "to all Cases, in Law and Equity, arising under this Constitution, the Laws of the United States, and Treaties made [under] their authority." Section 1331, along with most other jurisdictional statutes, adopts the constitutional language, authorizing federal jurisdiction over "all civil actions arising under the Constitution, laws, or treaties of the United States." Though the language is similar, the Supreme Court has given the statute a considerably narrower reading than the constitutional provision. Compare the statutory ruling in *American Well Works* with the Court's leading decision on the Article III issue. *Osborn v. Bank of the United States*, 22 U.S. 738 (1824), held that Congress may grant federal jurisdiction over any case that contains a federal "ingredient," whether or not any federal issue is actually litigated.

A modern illustration of the scope of the constitutional grant is *American National Red Cross v. S.G.*, 505 U.S. 247 (1992). Having contracted AIDS from a blood transfusion, S.G. brought a state tort suit against the Red Cross for providing contaminated blood. S.G. sued in state court, but the Red Cross sought removal to federal court, on the ground that the case arose under federal law, and the Supreme Court agreed. The relevant statute was not § 1331, but the statute chartering the Red Cross, 36 U.S.C. § 2, which authorizes the organization "to sue and be sued in courts of law and equity, State or Federal, within the jurisdiction of the United States." The Court ruled that this "sue and be sued" provision "confers original jurisdiction on federal courts over all cases to which the Red Cross is a party." According to the Court, this reading of the statute left "the jurisdiction of the federal courts well within Article III's limits. As long ago as *Osborn*, this Court held that Article III's 'arising under' jurisdiction is broad enough to authorize Congress to confer federal-court jurisdiction over actions involving federally chartered corporations." *Id.* at 264. This principle has been applied not only to the Red Cross but also to other federally chartered corporations. See *Wilson v. Dantas*, 746 F.3d 530 (2nd Cir. 2014) (jurisdiction under the Edge Act, 12 U.S.C. § 632, which deals with the international or foreign banking operations of federally chartered corporations).

B. EXCEPTIONS TO AMERICAN WELL WORKS

GRABLE & SONS METAL PRODUCTS, INC. V. DARUE ENGINEERING & MANUFACTURING
545 U.S. 308 (2005).

JUSTICE SOUTER delivered the opinion of the Court.

The question is whether want of a federal cause of action to try claims of title to land obtained at a federal tax sale precludes removal to federal court of a state action with non-diverse parties raising a disputed issue of federal title law. We answer no, and hold that the national interest in providing a federal forum for federal tax litigation is sufficiently substantial to support the exercise of federal question jurisdiction over the disputed issue on removal, which would not distort any division of labor between the state and federal courts, provided or assumed by Congress.

In 1994, the Internal Revenue Service seized Michigan real property belonging to petitioner Grable & Sons Metal Products, Inc., to satisfy Grable's federal tax delinquency. Title 26 U.S.C. § 6335 required the IRS to give notice of the seizure, and there is no dispute that Grable received actual notice by certified mail before the IRS sold the property to respondent Darue Engineering & Manufacturing. Although Grable also received notice of the sale itself, it did not exercise its statutory right to redeem the property within 180 days of the sale, § 6337(b)(1), and after that period had passed, the Government gave Darue a quitclaim deed. § 6339.

Five years later, Grable brought a quiet title action in state court, claiming that Darue's record title was invalid because the IRS had failed to notify Grable of its seizure of the property in the exact manner required by § 6335(a), which provides that written notice must be "given by the Secretary to the owner of the property [or] left at his usual place of abode or business." Grable said that the statute required personal service, not service by certified mail.

Darue removed the case to Federal District Court as presenting a federal question, because the claim of title depended on the interpretation of the notice statute in the federal tax law. The District Court declined to remand the case at Grable's behest after finding that the "claim does pose a significant question of federal law," and ruling that Grable's lack of a federal right of action to enforce its claim against Darue did not bar the exercise of federal jurisdiction. On the merits, the court granted summary judgment to Darue, holding that although § 6335 by its terms required personal service, substantial compliance with the statute was enough.

The Court of Appeals for the Sixth Circuit affirmed. On the jurisdictional question, the panel thought it sufficed that the title claim raised an issue of federal law that had to be resolved, and implicated a substantial federal interest (in construing federal tax law). The court went on to affirm the District Court's judgment on the merits. We granted certiorari on the jurisdictional question alone, to resolve a split within the Courts of Appeals on whether *Merrell Dow Pharmaceuticals Inc. v. Thompson*, 478 U.S. 804 (1986), always requires a federal cause of action as a condition for exercising federal-question jurisdiction. We now affirm.

II

Darue was entitled to remove the quiet title action if Grable could have brought it in federal district court originally, 28 U.S.C. § 1441(a), as a civil action "arising under the Constitution, laws, or treaties of the United States," § 1331. This provision for federal-question jurisdiction is invoked by and large by plaintiffs pleading a cause of action created by federal law (e.g., claims under 42 U.S.C. § 1983). There is, however, another longstanding, if less frequently encountered, variety of federal "arising under" jurisdiction, this Court having recognized for nearly 100 years that in certain cases federal question jurisdiction will lie over state-law claims that implicate significant federal issues. The doctrine captures the commonsense notion that a federal court ought to be able to hear claims recognized under state law that nonetheless turn on substantial questions of federal law, and thus justify resort to the experience, solicitude, and hope of uniformity that a federal forum offers on federal issues, see ALI, Study of the Division of Jurisdiction Between State and Federal Courts 164–166 (1968).

The classic example is *Smith v. Kansas City Title & Trust Co.*, 255 U.S. 180 (1921), a suit by a shareholder claiming that the defendant corporation could not lawfully buy certain bonds of the National Government because their issuance was unconstitutional. Although Missouri law provided the cause of action, the Court recognized federal-question jurisdiction because the principal issue in the case was the federal constitutionality of the bond issue. *Smith* thus held, in a somewhat generous statement of the scope of the doctrine, that a state-law claim could give rise to federal-question jurisdiction so long as it "appears from the [complaint] that the right to relief depends upon the construction or application of [federal law]." *Id.*, at 199.

The *Smith* statement has been subject to some trimming to fit earlier and later cases recognizing the vitality of the basic doctrine, but shying away from the expansive view that mere need to apply federal law in a state-law claim will suffice to open the "arising under" door. As early as 1912, this Court had confined federal-question jurisdiction over state-law claims to those that "really and substantially involv[e] a dispute or controversy respecting the validity, construction or effect of [federal] law." *Shulthis v. McDougal*, 225 U.S. 561, 569 (1912). This limitation was the ancestor of Justice Cardozo's later explanation that a request to exercise federal-question jurisdiction over a state action calls for a "common-sense accommodation of judgment to [the] kaleidoscopic situations" that present a federal issue, in "a selective process which picks the substantial causes out of the web and lays the other ones aside." *Gully v. First Nat. Bank in Meridian*, 299 U.S. 109, 117–118 (1936). It has in fact become a constant refrain in such cases that federal jurisdiction demands not only a contested federal issue, but a substantial one, indicating a serious federal interest in claiming the advantages thought to be inherent in a federal forum. E.g., *Chicago v. International College of Surgeons*, 522 U.S. 156, 164 (1997); *Merrell Dow*, supra, at 814, and n. 12; *Franchise Tax Bd. of Cal. v. Construction Laborers Vacation Trust for Southern Cal.*, 463 U.S. 1, 28 (1983).

But even when the state action discloses a contested and substantial federal question, the exercise of federal jurisdiction is subject to a possible veto. For the federal issue will ultimately qualify for a federal forum only if federal jurisdiction is consistent with congressional judgment about the sound division of labor between state and federal courts governing the application of § 1331. Thus, *Franchise Tax Bd.* explained that the appropriateness of a federal forum to hear an embedded issue could be evaluated only after considering the "welter of issues regarding the interrelation of federal and state authority and the proper management of the federal judicial system." Because arising-under jurisdiction to hear a state-law claim always raises the possibility of upsetting the state-federal line drawn (or at least assumed) by Congress, the presence of a disputed federal issue and the ostensible importance of a federal forum are never necessarily dispositive; there must always be an assessment of any disruptive portent in exercising federal jurisdiction. See also *Merrell Dow*, supra, at 810.

These considerations have kept us from stating a "single, precise, all-embracing" test for jurisdiction over federal issues embedded in state-law claims between nondiverse parties. We have not kept them out simply because they appeared in state raiment, as Justice Holmes would have done, see *Smith*, *supra*, at 214 (dissenting opinion), but neither have we treated "federal issue" as a password opening federal courts to any state action embracing a point of federal law. Instead, the question is, does a state-law claim necessarily raise a stated federal issue, actually disputed and substantial, which a federal forum may entertain without disturbing any congressionally approved balance of federal and state judicial responsibilities.

III

A

This case warrants federal jurisdiction. Grable's state complaint must specify "the facts establishing the superiority of [its] claim," Mich. Ct. Rule 3.411(B)(2)(c) (West 2005), and Grable has premised its superior title claim on a failure by the IRS to give it adequate notice, as defined by federal law. Whether Grable was given notice within the meaning of the federal statute is thus an essential element of its quiet title claim, and the meaning of the federal statute is actually in dispute; it appears to be the only legal or factual issue contested in the case. The meaning of the federal tax provision is an important issue of federal law that sensibly belongs in a federal court. The Government has a strong interest in the "prompt and certain collection of delinquent taxes," *United States v. Rodgers*, 461 U.S. 677, 709 (1983), and the ability of the IRS to satisfy its claims from the property of delinquents requires clear terms of notice to allow buyers like Darue to satisfy themselves that the Service has touched the bases necessary for good title. The Government thus has a direct interest in the availability of a federal forum to vindicate its own administrative action, and buyers (as well as tax delinquents) may find it valuable to come before judges used to federal tax matters. Finally, because it will be the rare state title case that raises a contested matter of federal law, federal jurisdiction to resolve genuine disagreement over federal tax title provisions will portend only a microscopic effect on the federal-state division of labor. See n. 3, infra.

This conclusion puts us in venerable company, quiet title actions having been the subject of some of the earliest exercises of federal-question jurisdiction over state-law claims. In *Hopkins*, 244 U.S., at 490–491, the question was federal jurisdiction over a quiet title action based on the plaintiffs' allegation that federal mining law gave them the superior claim. Just as in this case, "the facts showing the plaintiffs' title and the existence and invalidity of the instrument or record sought to be eliminated as a cloud upon the title are essential parts of the plaintiffs' cause of action."[3] As in this case again, "it is plain that a controversy respecting the construction and effect of the [federal] laws is involved and is sufficiently real and substantial." This Court therefore upheld federal jurisdiction in *Hopkins*, as well as in the similar quiet title matters of *Northern Pacific R. Co. v. Soderberg*, 188 U.S. 526, 528 (1903), and *Wilson Cypress Co. v. Del Pozo Y Marcos*, 236 U.S. 635, 643–644 (1915). Consistent with those cases, the recognition of federal jurisdiction is in order here.

B

Merrell Dow Pharmaceuticals Inc. v. Thompson, on which Grable rests its position, is not to the contrary. *Merrell Dow* considered a state tort claim resting in part on the allegation that the defendant drug company had violated a federal misbranding prohibition, and was thus presumptively negligent under Ohio law. The Court assumed that federal law would have to be applied to resolve the claim, but after closely examining the strength of the federal interest at stake and the implications of opening the federal forum, held federal jurisdiction unavailable. Congress had not provided a private federal cause of action for violation of the federal branding requirement, and the Court found "it would . . . flout, or at least undermine, congressional intent to conclude that federal courts might nevertheless exercise federal-question jurisdiction and provide remedies for violations of that federal statute solely because the violation . . . is said to be a . . . 'proximate cause' under state law."

Because federal law provides for no quiet title action that could be brought against Darue, Grable argues that there can be no federal jurisdiction here, stressing some broad language in *Merrell Dow* (including the passage just quoted) that on its face supports Grable's [position]. But an opinion is to be read as a whole, and *Merrell Dow*

---

[3]   The quiet title cases also show the limiting effect of the federal issue in a state-law claim must actually be in dispute to justify federal-question jurisdiction. In *Shulthis v. McDougal*, 225 U.S. 561 (1912), this Court found that there was no federal question jurisdiction to hear a plaintiff's quiet title claim in part because the federal statutes on which title depended were not subject to "any controversy respecting their validity, construction, or effect." As the Court put it, the requirement of an actual dispute about federal law was "especially" important in "suit[s] involving rights to land acquired under a law of the United States," because otherwise "every suit to establish title to land in the central and western states would so arise [under federal law], as all titles in those States are traceable back to those laws."

cannot be read whole as overturning decades of precedent, as it would have done by effectively adopting the Holmes dissent in *Smith*, and converting a federal cause of action from a sufficient condition for federal-question jurisdiction[5] into a necessary one.

In the first place, *Merrell Dow* disclaimed the adoption of any bright-line rule, as when the Court reiterated that "in exploring the outer reaches of § 1331, determinations about federal jurisdiction require sensitive judgments about congressional intent, judicial power, and the federal system." The opinion included a lengthy footnote explaining that questions of jurisdiction over state-law claims require "careful judgments," about the "nature of the federal interest at stake," (emphasis deleted). And as a final indication that it did not mean to make a federal right of action mandatory, it expressly approved the exercise of jurisdiction sustained in *Smith*, despite the want of any federal cause of action available to *Smith*'s shareholder plaintiff. *Merrell Dow* then, did not toss out, but specifically retained the contextual enquiry that had been *Smith*'s hallmark for over 60 years. At the end of *Merrell Dow*, Justice Holmes was still dissenting.

Accordingly, *Merrell Dow* should be read in its entirety as treating the absence of a federal private right of action as evidence relevant to, but not dispositive of, the "sensitive judgments about congressional intent" that § 1331 requires. The absence of any federal cause of action affected *Merrell Dow*'s result two ways. The Court saw the fact as worth some consideration in the assessment of substantiality. But its primary importance emerged when the Court treated the combination of no federal cause of action and no preemption of state remedies for misbranding as an important clue to Congress's conception of the scope of jurisdiction to be exercised under § 1331. The Court saw the missing cause of action not as a missing federal door key, always required, but as a missing welcome mat, required in the circumstances, when exercising federal jurisdiction over a state misbranding action would have attracted a horde of original filings and removal cases raising other state claims with embedded federal issues. For if the federal labeling standard without a federal cause of action could get a state claim into federal court, so could any other federal standard without a federal cause of action. And that would have meant a tremendous number of cases.

One only needed to consider the treatment of federal violations generally in garden variety state tort law. "The violation of federal statutes and regulations is commonly given negligence per se effect in state tort proceedings."[6] Restatement (Third) of Torts (Proposed Final

---

[5] For an extremely rare exception to the sufficiency of a federal right of action, see *Shoshone Mining Co. v. Rutter*, 177 U.S. 505, 507 (1900).

[6] Other jurisdictions treat a violation of a federal statute as evidence of negligence or, like Ohio itself in *Merrell Dow* as creating a rebuttable presumption of negligence. Restatement

Draft) § 14. a. See also W. Keeton, D. Dobbs, R. Keeton, & D. Owen, Prosser and Keeton on Torts § 36, 221, n. 9 (5th ed. 1984) ("[T]he breach of a federal statute may support a negligence per se claim as a matter of state law" (collecting authority)). A general rule of exercising federal jurisdiction over state claims resting on federal mislabeling and other statutory violations would thus have heralded a potentially enormous shift of traditionally state cases into federal courts. Expressing concern over the "increased volume of federal litigation," and noting the importance of adhering to "legislative intent," *Merrell Dow* thought it improbable that the Congress, having made no provision for a federal cause of action, would have meant to welcome any state-law tort case implicating federal law "solely because the violation of the federal statute is said to [create] a rebuttable presumption [of negligence] . . . under state law." In this situation, no welcome mat meant keep out. *Merrell Dow*'s analysis thus fits within the framework of examining the importance of having a federal forum for the issue, and the consistency of such a forum with Congress's intended division of labor between state and federal courts.

As already indicated, however, a comparable analysis yields a different jurisdictional conclusion in this case. Although Congress also indicated ambivalence in this case by providing no private right of action to Grable, it is the rare state quiet title action that involves contested issues of federal law, see n. 3, supra. Consequently, jurisdiction over actions like Grable's would not materially affect, or threaten to affect, the normal currents of litigation. Given the absence of threatening structural consequences and the clear interest the Government, its buyers, and its delinquents have in the availability of a federal forum, there is no good reason to shirk from federal jurisdiction over the dispositive and contested federal issue at the heart of the state-law title claim.[7]

The judgment of the Court of Appeals, upholding federal jurisdiction over Grable's quiet title action, is affirmed.

JUSTICE THOMAS, concurring.

The Court faithfully applies our precedents interpreting 28 U.S.C. § 1331 to authorize federal-court jurisdiction over some cases in which state law creates the cause of action but requires determination of an issue of federal law. In this case, no one has asked us to overrule those

---

(Third) of Torts (Proposed Final Draft) § 14, Comment c. Either approach could still implicate issues of federal law.

[7] At oral argument Grable's counsel espoused the position that after *Merrell Dow*, federal-question jurisdiction over state-law claims absent a federal right of action, could be recognized only where a constitutional issue was at stake. There is, however, no reason in text or otherwise to draw such a rough line. As *Merrell Dow* itself suggested, constitutional questions may be the more likely ones to reach the level of substantiality that can justify federal jurisdiction. 478 U.S., at 814, n. 12. But a flat ban on statutory questions would mechanically exclude significant questions of federal law like the one this case presents.

precedents and adopt the rule Justice Holmes set forth in *American Well Works* limiting § 1331 jurisdiction to cases in which federal law creates the cause of action pleaded on the face of the plaintiff's complaint. In an appropriate case, and perhaps with the benefit of better evidence as to the original meaning of § 1331's text, I would be willing to consider that course.*

Jurisdictional rules should be clear. Whatever the virtues of the *Smith* standard, it is anything but clear (the standard "calls for a 'common-sense accommodation of judgment to [the] kaleidoscopic situations' that present a federal issue, in 'a selective process which picks the substantial causes out of the web and lays the other ones aside' "; ("[T]he question is, does a state-law claim necessarily raise a stated federal issue, actually disputed and substantial, which a federal forum may entertain without disturbing any congressionally approved balance of federal and state judicial responsibilities"); (" '[D]eterminations about federal jurisdiction require sensitive judgments about congressional intent, judicial power, and the federal system' "; "the absence of a federal private right of action [is] evidence relevant to, but not dispositive of, the 'sensitive judgments about congressional intent' that § 1331 requires."))

Whatever the vices of the *American Well Works* rule, it is clear. Moreover, it accounts for the " 'vast majority' " of cases that come within § 1331 under our current case law—further indication that trying to sort out which cases fall within the smaller *Smith* category may not be worth the effort it entails. Accordingly, I would be willing in appropriate circumstances to reconsider our interpretation of § 1331.

GUNN V. MINTON

568 U.S. ___, 133 S.Ct. 1059 (2013).

ROBERTS, C.J., delivered the opinion for a unanimous Court.

Federal courts have exclusive jurisdiction over cases "arising under any Act of Congress relating to patents." 28 U.S.C. § 1338(a). The question presented is whether a state law claim alleging legal malpractice in the handling of a patent case must be brought in federal court.

---

* This Court has long construed the scope of the statutory grant of federal-question jurisdiction more narrowly than the scope of the constitutional grant of such jurisdiction. I assume for present purposes that this distinction is proper—that is, that the language of § 1331, "[t]he district courts shall have original jurisdiction of all *civil actions arising under* the Constitution, laws, or treaties of the United States" (emphasis added), is narrower than the language of Art. III, § 2, cl. 1, of the Constitution, "[t]he judicial Power shall extend to all *Cases*, in Law and Equity, *arising under* this Constitution, the Laws of the United States, and Treaties made, or which shall be made, under their Authority . . ." (emphases added).

I

In the early 1990s, respondent Vernon Minton developed a computer program and telecommunications network designed to facilitate securities trading. In March 1995, he leased the system—known as the Texas Computer Exchange Network, or TEXCEN—to R.M. Stark & Co., a securities brokerage. A little over a year later, he applied for a patent for an interactive securities trading system that was based substantially on TEXCEN. The U.S. Patent and Trademark Office issued the patent in January 2000.

Patent in hand, Minton filed a patent infringement suit in Federal District Court against the National Association of Securities Dealers, Inc. (NASD) and the NASDAQ Stock Market, Inc. [Minton lost, arguably because his lawyers failed to raise a doctrine called "experimental use" in a timely manner.]

Minton, convinced that his attorneys' failure to raise the experimental-use argument earlier had cost him the lawsuit and led to invalidation of his patent, brought this malpractice action in Texas state court. His former lawyers defended on the ground that the lease to Stark was not, in fact, for an experimental use, and that therefore Minton's patent infringement claims would have failed even if the experimental-use argument had been timely raised. The trial court agreed, holding that Minton had put forward "less than a scintilla of proof" that the lease had been for an experimental purpose. App. 213. It accordingly granted summary judgment to Gunn and the other lawyer defendants.

On appeal, Minton raised a new argument: Because his legal malpractice claim was based on an alleged error in a patent case, it "aris[es] under" federal patent law for purposes of 28 U.S.C. § 1338(a). And because, under § 1338(a), "[n]o State court shall have jurisdiction over any claim for relief arising under any Act of Congress relating to patents," the Texas court—where Minton had originally brought his malpractice claim—lacked subject matter jurisdiction to decide the case. Accordingly, Minton argued, the trial court's order should be vacated and the case dismissed, leaving Minton free to start over in the Federal District [Court.]

The Supreme Court of Texas [agreed.]

We granted certiorari.

II

[For] statutory purposes, a case can "aris[e] under" federal law in two ways. Most directly, a case arises under federal law when federal law creates the cause of action asserted. See *American Well Works Co.* As a rule of inclusion, this "creation" test admits of only extremely rare exceptions, see, *e.g., Shoshone Mining Co. v. Rutter,* 177 U.S. 505 (1900), and accounts for the vast bulk of suits that arise under federal law. Minton's original patent infringement suit against NASD and NASDAQ, for example, arose under federal law in this manner because it was authorized by 35 U.S.C. §§ 271, 281.

But even where a claim finds its origins in state rather than federal law—as Mintons legal malpractice claim indisputably does—we have identified a "special and small category" of cases in which arising under jurisdiction still lies. In outlining the contours of this slim category, we do not paint on a blank canvas. Unfortunately, the canvas looks like one that Jackson Pollock got to first. See 13D C. Wright, A. Miller, E. Cooper, & R. Freer, Federal Practice and Procedure § 3562, pp. 175–176 (3d ed. 2008) (reviewing general confusion on question).

In an effort to bring some order to this unruly doctrine several Terms ago, we condensed our prior cases into the following inquiry: Does the "state-law claim necessarily raise a stated federal issue, actually disputed and substantial, which a federal forum may entertain without disturbing any congressionally approved balance of federal and state judicial responsibilities"? *Grable,* 545 U.S., at 314. That is, federal jurisdiction over a state law claim will lie if a federal issue is: (1) necessarily raised, (2) actually disputed, (3) substantial, and (4) capable of resolution in federal court without disrupting the federal-state balance approved by Congress. Where all four of these requirements are met, we held, jurisdiction is proper because there is a "serious federal interest in claiming the advantages thought to be inherent in a federal forum," which can be vindicated without disrupting Congress's intended division of labor between state and federal courts.

III

Applying *Grable*'s inquiry here, it is clear that Minton's legal malpractice claim does not arise under federal patent law. Indeed, for the reasons we discuss, we are comfortable concluding that state legal malpractice claims based on underlying patent matters will rarely, if ever, arise under federal patent law for purposes of § 1338(a). Although such cases may necessarily raise disputed questions of patent law, those cases are by their nature unlikely to have the sort of significance for the federal system necessary to establish jurisdiction.

A

To begin, we acknowledge that resolution of a federal patent question is "necessary" to Minton's case. Under Texas law, a plaintiff alleging legal malpractice must establish four elements: (1) that the defendant attorney owed the plaintiff a duty; (2) that the attorney breached that duty; (3) that the breach was the proximate cause of the plaintiff's injury; and (4) that damages occurred. In cases like this one, in which the attorney's alleged error came in failing to make a particular argument, the causation element requires a "case within a case" analysis of whether, had the argument been made, the outcome of the earlier litigation would have been different. To prevail on his legal malpractice claim, therefore, Minton must show that he would have prevailed in his federal patent infringement case if only petitioners had timely made an experimental-use argument on his behalf. That will necessarily require application of patent law to the facts of Minton's case.

B

The federal issue is also "actually disputed" here—indeed, on the merits, it is the central point of dispute. Minton argues that the experimental-use exception properly applied to his lease to Stark, saving his patent from the on-sale bar; petitioners argue that it did not. This is just the sort of " 'dispute . . . respecting the . . . effect of [federal] law' " that *Grable* envisioned.

C

Minton's argument founders on *Grable*'s next requirement, however, for the federal issue in this case is not substantial in the relevant sense. In reaching the opposite conclusion, the Supreme Court of Texas focused on the importance of the issue to the plaintiff's case and to the parties before it. [As] our past cases show, however, it is not enough that the federal issue be significant to the particular parties in the immediate suit; that will *always* be true when the state claim "necessarily raise[s]" a disputed federal issue, as *Grable* separately requires. The substantiality inquiry under *Grable* looks instead to the importance of the issue to the federal system as a whole.

In *Grable* itself, for example, the Internal Revenue Service had seized property from the plaintiff and sold it to satisfy the plaintiff's federal tax delinquency. Five years later, the plaintiff filed a state law quiet title action against the third party that had purchased the property, alleging that the IRS had failed to comply with certain federally imposed notice requirements, so that the seizure and sale were invalid. In holding that the case arose under federal law, we primarily focused not on the interests of the litigants themselves, but rather on the broader significance of the notice question for the Federal Government. We emphasized the Government's "strong interest" in being able to recover delinquent taxes through seizure and sale of property, which in turn "require[d] clear terms of notice to allow buyers . . . to satisfy themselves that the Service has touched the bases necessary for good title." The Government's "direct interest in the availability of a federal forum to vindicate its own administrative action" made the question "an important issue of federal law that sensibly belong[ed] in a federal court."

A second illustration of the sort of substantiality we require comes from *Smith v. Kansas City Title & Trust Co.,* 255 U.S. 180 (1921), which

Grable described as "[t]he classic example" of a state claim arising under federal law. In *Smith,* the plaintiff argued that the defendant bank could not purchase certain bonds issued by the Federal Government because the Government had acted unconstitutionally in issuing them. We held that the case arose under federal law, because the "decision depends upon the determination" of "the constitutional validity of an act of Congress which is directly drawn in question." Again, the relevant point was not the importance of the question to the parties alone but rather the importance more generally of a determination that the Government "securities were issued under an unconstitutional law, and hence of no validity."

Here, the federal issue carries no such significance. Because of the backward-looking nature of a legal malpractice claim, the question is posed in a merely hypothetical sense: *If* Minton's lawyers had raised a timely experimental-use argument, would the result in the patent infringement proceeding have been different? No matter how the state courts resolve that hypothetical "case within a case," it will not change the real-world result of the prior federal patent litigation. Minton's patent will remain invalid.

Nor will allowing state courts to resolve these cases undermine "the development of a uniform body of [patent] law." Congress ensured such uniformity by vesting exclusive jurisdiction over actual patent cases in the federal district courts and exclusive appellate jurisdiction in the Federal Circuit. In resolving the nonhypothetical patent questions those cases present, the federal courts are of course not bound by state court case-within-a-case patent rulings. See *Tafflin v. Levitt,* 493 U.S. 455, 465 (1990). In any event, the state court case-within-a-case inquiry asks what would have happened in the prior federal proceeding if a particular argument had been made. In answering that question, state courts can be expected to hew closely to the pertinent federal precedents. It is those precedents, after all, that would have applied had the argument been made.

[As] for more novel questions of patent law that may arise for the first time in a state court "case within a case," they will at some point be decided by a federal court in the context of an actual patent case, with review in the Federal Circuit. If the question arises frequently, it will soon be resolved within the federal system, laying to rest any contrary state court precedent; if it does not arise frequently, it is unlikely to implicate substantial federal interests. The present case is "poles apart from *Grable,*" in which a state court's resolution of the federal question "would be controlling in numerous other cases."

Minton also suggests that state courts' answers to hypothetical patent questions can sometimes have real-world effect on other patents through issue preclusion. Minton, for example, has filed what is known as a "continuation patent" application related to his original patent. See 35 U.S.C. § 120; 4A D. Chisum, Patents § 13.03 (2005) (describing continuation applications). He argues that, in evaluating this separate application, the patent examiner could be bound by the Texas trial court's interpretation of the scope of Minton's original patent. It is unclear whether this is true. The Patent and Trademark Office's Manual of Patent Examining Procedure provides that res judicata is a proper ground for rejecting a patent "only when the earlier decision was a decision of the Board of Appeals" or certain federal reviewing courts, giving no indication that state court decisions would have preclusive effect. In fact, Minton has not identified any case finding such preclusive effect based on a state court decision. But even assuming that a state court's case-within-a-case adjudication may be preclusive under some circumstances, the result would be limited to the parties and patents that had been before the state court. Such "fact-bound and situation-specific" effects are not sufficient to establish federal arising under jurisdiction.

Nor can we accept the suggestion that the federal courts' greater familiarity with patent law means that legal malpractice cases like this one belong in federal court. [It] is true that a similar interest was among those we considered in *Grable*. But the possibility that a state court will incorrectly resolve a state claim is not, by itself, enough to trigger the federal courts' exclusive patent jurisdiction, even if the potential error finds its root in a misunderstanding of patent law.

There is no doubt that resolution of a patent issue in the context of a state legal malpractice action can be vitally important to the particular parties in that case. But something more, demonstrating that the question is significant to the federal system as a whole, is needed. That is missing here.

D

It follows from the foregoing that *Grable*'s fourth requirement is also not met. That requirement is concerned with the appropriate "balance of federal and state judicial responsibilities." We have already explained the absence of a substantial federal issue within the meaning of *Grable*. The States, on the other hand, have "a special responsibility for maintaining standards among members of the licensed professions." *Ohralik v. Ohio State Bar Assn.*, 436 U.S. 447, 460 (1978). Their "interest . . . in regulating lawyers is especially great since lawyers are essential to the primary governmental function of administering justice, and have historically been officers of the courts." *Goldfarb v. Virginia State Bar*, 421 U.S. 773, 792 (1975). We have no reason to suppose that Congress— in establishing exclusive federal jurisdiction over patent cases—meant to bar from state courts state legal malpractice claims simply because they require resolution of a hypothetical patent issue.

* * *

As we recognized a century ago, "[t]he Federal courts have exclusive jurisdiction of all cases arising under the patent laws, but not of all questions in which a patent may be the subject-matter of the controversy." In this case, although the state courts must answer a question of patent law to resolve Minton's legal malpractice claim, their answer will have no broader effects. It will not stand as binding precedent for any future patent claim; it will not even affect the validity of Minton's patent. Accordingly, there is no "serious federal interest in claiming the advantages thought to be inherent in a federal forum. Section 1338(a) does not deprive the state courts of subject matter jurisdiction.

The judgment of the Supreme Court of Texas is reversed, and the case is remanded for further proceedings not inconsistent with this opinion.

It is so ordered.

NOTES ON EXCEPTIONS TO AMERICAN WELL WORKS

1.   **The Grable/Gunn Distinction.** In *One and Ken Valley Housing Group v. Maine State Housing Authority*, 716 F.3d 218 (1st Cir. 2013), owners of rental housing sued a state housing agency for breach of contract, a state law cause of action. Under their contracts the Maine Housing Authority promised to pay part of the cost of rental housing for poor tenants. The money came from a federal program, known informally as "Section 8," which is administered by the Department of Housing and Urban Development (HUD). The plaintiff's theory was that the federal statute and regulations setting up and implementing the Section 8 program entitled them to annual increases in the amounts they received, but that Maine State Housing had failed to make the payments. Maine State Housing read the federal law differently. Does this case fall within *Grable*? While the "breach-of-contract claims arise under the laws of the State of Maine," the court ruled that federal jurisdiction was available under *Grable*. Among other things, [a] the case involved "a nearly pure issue of law that could be settled once and for all and thereafter would govern numerous cases." [b] "The outcomes of the legal questions in these cases will dictate whether HUD and/or the public housing agencies that administer Section 8 must pay millions of dollars in additional rents to landlords, which—in turn—could require the agencies to scale back the scope of the Section 8 program." [c] "There is no discernible state interest in a state forum that would outweigh the federal interest in uniformity." Do you agree? Would it be preferable to rule that, in light of the federal interest in the case, the contracts are governed by federal common law?

2. Does a Federal Cause of Action Always Suffice? A few pre-*American Well Works* cases hold that the fact that the plaintiff sues under a federal cause of action does not necessarily mean that the case arises under federal law for purposes of federal question jurisdiction. In *Shoshone Mining Co. v. Rutter*, 177 U.S. 505 (1900), a federal statute set up a system of property rights in mining claims on federal land and authorized lawsuits between persons with conflicting claims. The statute directed that disputes of this kind were generally to be resolved by "local customs or rules of miners in the several mining districts, so far as the same are applicable and not inconsistent with the laws of the United States." Because the adjudication of many of these cases would turn on local customs and questions of fact, the Court ruled that they did not fall within the federal question jurisdiction.

C. THE WELL-PLEADED COMPLAINT RULE

It is apparent from the foregoing notes that there is a category, the contours of which remain uncertain, consisting of cases in which federal jurisdiction is appropriate even though federal law does not create the cause of action. We can, however, be sure of one rule that defines and limits the content of this category. It is the "well-pleaded complaint" rule: Under § 1331 and similar "arising under" statutes, federal jurisdiction is not available unless the federal issue necessarily appears on the face of a well-pleaded complaint. That the federal issue arises as a defense or a reply to a defense will not be sufficient, even if in fact the federal issue dominates the litigation. The following case is a classic illustration of the rule.

LOUISVILLE & NASHVILLE R. R. CO. V. MOTTLEY
211 U.S. 149 (1908).

MR. JUSTICE MOODY delivered the opinion of the Court.

[Mr. and Mrs. Mottley], being residents and citizens of Kentucky, brought this suit in equity in the Circuit Court of the United States for the Western District of Kentucky against the appellant, a railroad company and a citizen of the same state. The object of the suit was to compel the specific performance of the following contract:

Louisville, Ky., Oct. 2d, 1871.

The Louisville & Nashville Railroad Company, in consideration that E. L. Mottley and wife, Annie E. Mottley, have this day released company from all damages or claims for damages for injuries received by them on the 7th of September, 1871, in consequence of a collision of trains on the railroad of said company at Randolph's Station, Jefferson County, Kentucky, hereby agrees to issue free passes on said railroad and branches now existing or to exist, to said E. L. & Annie E. Mottley for the remainder of the present year, and thereafter to renew said passes annually during the lives of said Mottley and wife or either of them.

The bill alleged that in September, 1871, plaintiffs, while passengers upon the defendant railroad, were injured by the defendant's negligence, and released their respective claims for damages in consideration of the agreement for transportation during their lives, expressed in the contract. It is alleged that the contract was performed by the defendant up to January 1, 1907, when the defendant declined to renew the passes. The bill then alleges that the refusal to comply with the contract was based solely upon that part of the act of Congress of June 29, 1906 which forbids the giving of free passes or free transportation. The bill further alleges: First, that the act of Congress referred to does not prohibit the giving of passes under the circumstances of this case; and, second, that, if the law is to be construed as prohibiting such passes, it is in conflict with the 5th Amendment of the Constitution, because it deprives the plaintiffs of their property without due process of law. The defendant demurred to the bill. The judge of the circuit court overruled the demurrer, entered a decree for the relief prayed for, and the defendant appealed directly to this court.

Two questions of law were raised by the demurrer to the bill, were brought here by appeal, and have been argued before us. They are, first, whether that part of the act of Congress of June 29, 1906 which forbids the giving of free passes or the collection of any different compensation for transportation of passengers than that specified in the tariff filed, makes it unlawful to perform a contract for transportation of persons who, in good faith, before the passage of the act, had accepted such contract in satisfaction of a valid cause of action against the railroad; and, second, whether the statute, if it should be construed to render such a contract unlawful, is in violation of the 5th Amendment of the Constitution of the United States. We do not deem it necessary, however, to consider either of these questions, because, in our opinion, the court below was without jurisdiction of the cause. Neither party has questioned that jurisdiction, but it is the duty of this court to see to it that the jurisdiction of the circuit court, which is defined and limited by statute, is not exceeded. This duty we have frequently performed of our own motion.

There was no diversity of citizenship, and it is not and cannot be suggested that there was any ground of jurisdiction, except that the case was a 'suit . . . arising under the Constitution or laws of the United States.' [28 U.S.C. § 1331]. It is the settled interpretation of these words, as used in this statute, conferring jurisdiction, that a suit arises under the Constitution and laws of the United States only when the plaintiff's statement of his own cause of action shows that it is based upon those laws or that Constitution. It is not enough that the plaintiff alleges some anticipated defense to his cause of action, and asserts that the defense is invalidated by some provision of the Constitution of the United States. Although such allegations show that very likely, in the course of the litigation, a question under the Constitution would arise, they do not show that the suit, that is, the plaintiff's original cause of action, arises under the Constitution. In *Tennessee v. Union & Planters' Bank*, 152 U.S. 454, the plaintiff, the state of Tennessee, brought suit in the circuit court of the United States to recover from the defendant certain taxes alleged to be due under the laws of the state. The plaintiff alleged that the defendant claimed an immunity from the taxation by virtue of its charter, and that therefore the tax was void, because in violation of the provision of the Constitution of the United States, which forbids any State from passing a law impairing the obligation of contracts. The cause was held to be beyond the jurisdiction of the circuit court, the court saying, by Mr. Justice Gray: 'A suggestion of one party, that the other will or may set up a claim under the Constitution or laws of the United States, does not make the suit one arising under that Constitution or those [laws'].

The interpretation of the act which we have stated was first announced in *Metcalf v. Watertown*, 128 U.S. 586, and has since been repeated and applied in [citing 17 cases].

[Reversed] with instructions to dismiss the suit for want of jurisdiction.

NOTES ON THE WELL-PLEADED COMPLAINT RULE

1. Applying the Well-Pleaded Complaint Rule. The Court in *Mottley* stresses that the test for federal jurisdiction is not whether the federal issue appears on the face of the complaint, but whether it appears on the face of a well-pleaded complaint, i.e., a complaint that contains all the allegations necessary to support a judgment for the plaintiff absent any defenses. In *Mottley*, the plaintiff needs to assert that there is a valid contract and that the defendant breached it. The courts will have to address the federal issues of whether the statute authorizes the railroad's refusal to honor the agreement and whether, if it does, the statute is valid. Those questions will dominate the litigation. But they do not necessarily arise until the railroad asserts the federal statute as a defense.

Is the well-pleaded complaint rule consistent with the reasoning of *Grable*? Why should federal jurisdiction depend on whether the federal issue appears on the face of a well-pleaded complaint, rather than on an assessment of the importance of the federal issue in the litigation? No doubt the answer lies in the value of a quick and certain resolution of jurisdictional issues.

The federal question removal statute, 28 U.S.C. § 1441(a), as construed by the Court, allows a defendant to remove a case from state to federal court only if it could have been brought initially in federal district court. That is, the defendant may remove a case only if the plaintiff's complaint meets the well-pleaded complaint rule. Notice that one could distinguish between the two issues, though the Court chooses not to do so. By the time the defendant seeks to remove, he may have assured that a federal issue will be litigated, simply by raising a federal defense. The need for a certain and quick determination that a federal issue will be litigated has arguably been satisfied. For an argument that removal should be allowed "by the party who puts forward the federal right," see Herbert Wechsler, *Federal Jurisdiction and the Revision of the Judicial Code*, 13 LAW & CONTEMP. PROBLEMS, 216, 233–34 (1948). For an argument that Congress initially intended the removal statute to be read as allowing removal based on a federal defense, see Michael Collins, *The Unhappy History of Federal Question Removal*, 71 IOWA L. REV. 717 (1986).

On the other side of the issue, Judge Posner argues that often "the federal defense would have little merit—would indeed have been concocted purely to confer federal jurisdiction—yet this fact might be impossible to determine with any confidence without having a trial before the trial." RICHARD POSNER, THE FEDERAL COURTS: CHALLENGE AND REFORM 302 (1996).

2. The Well-Pleaded Complaint Rule and Compulsory Counterclaims. Granting that a federal defense does not give rise to federal jurisdiction, can the well-pleaded complaint rule be satisfied by assertion of a federal issue on the face of a compulsory counterclaim? The Court addressed this issue in *Holmes Group v. Vornado Air Circulation Systems*, 535 U.S. 826 (2002):

> The well-pleaded-complaint rule has long governed whether a case "arises under" federal law for purposes of § 1331. [Respondent] argues that the well-pleaded-complaint rule, properly understood, allows a counterclaim to serve as the basis for a district court's "arising under" jurisdiction. We disagree. Admittedly, our prior cases have only required us to address whether a federal defense, rather than a federal counterclaim, can establish "arising under" jurisdiction. Nevertheless, those cases were decided on the principle that federal jurisdiction generally exists only when a federal question is presented on the face of the *plaintiff's* properly pleaded complaint. [Moreover,] we have declined to adopt proposals that "the answer as well as the complaint . . . be consulted before a determination [is] made whether the case 'ar[ises] under' federal law. . . ." *Franchise Tax Bd. of Cal. v. Construction Laborers Vacation Trust for Southern Cal.*, 463 U.S. 1, 10–11, n. 9 (1983). It follows that a counterclaim—which appears as part of the defendant's answer, not as part of the plaintiff's complaint—cannot serve as the basis for "arising under" jurisdiction.

> Allowing a counterclaim to establish "arising under" jurisdiction would also contravene the longstanding policies underlying our precedents. First, since the plaintiff is "the master of the complaint," the well-pleaded-complaint rule enables him, "by

eschewing claims based on federal law, . . . to have the cause heard in state court." [*Caterpillar Inc. v. Williams*, 482 U.S. 386, 398–399 (1987)]. The rule proposed by respondent, in contrast, would leave acceptance or rejection of a state forum to the master of the counterclaim. It would allow a defendant to remove a case brought in state court under state law, thereby defeating a plaintiff's choice of forum, simply by raising a federal counterclaim. Second, conferring this power upon the defendant would radically expand the class of removable cases, contrary to the "[d]ue regard for the rightful independence of state governments" that our cases addressing removal require. See *Shamrock Oil & Gas Corp. v. Sheets*, 313 U.S. 100, 109 (1941) (internal quotation marks omitted). And finally, allowing responsive pleadings by the defendant to establish "arising under" jurisdiction would undermine the clarity and ease of administration of the well-pleaded-complaint doctrine, which serves as a "quick rule of thumb" for resolving jurisdictional conflicts. See *Franchise Tax Bd.*, supra, at 11.

3. Exclusive Federal Jurisdiction and the Well-Pleaded Complaint Rule. The default rule is that federal and state courts have "concurrent" jurisdiction over federal question cases. The plaintiff may bring his case in either forum. But Congress sometimes provides for exclusive federal jurisdiction over a class of cases. See, e.g., the statute at issue in *Gunn,* supra, 28 U.S.C. § 1338(a) (federal "jurisdiction shall be exclusive of the courts of the states in patent, plant variety protection, and copyright cases"). Nonetheless, the well-pleaded complaint rule takes priority. An issue within exclusive federal jurisdiction must be litigated in state court if it arises as a defense or a counterclaim.

The counterclaim asserted in *Holmes Group*, supra, was for patent infringement. Given *Holmes Group*, consider this hypothetical: Suppose *A* and *B* each claim a copyright in certain material. *A* makes a contract with *B*, under which *B* will pay *A* for the right to use the material free of controversy. After a period of time, *B* stops paying and *A* brings suit for breach of contract. *A* sues in state court because, under *Mottley*, no federal issue appears on the face of his well-pleaded complaint. *B* defends on the ground that *A* has no copyright and asserts a counterclaim under the federal copyright laws for amounts already paid. He seeks to remove the case to federal court. What result?

4. Limits on the Well-Pleaded Complaint Rule. In *American National Red Cross*, supra, Congress had, in the Charter of the ANRC, authorized the organization "to sue and be sued in courts of law and equity, State or Federal, within the jurisdiction of the United States." 36 U.S.C. § 2. The Court held that this statute conferred district court jurisdiction "over all cases to which the Red Cross is a party," including a state law tort suit alleging that the Red Cross provided contaminated blood. Note, however, the absence of any federal issue on the face of a well-pleaded tort complaint. The Court made "short work of [the] argument that the charter's conferral of federal jurisdiction is nevertheless subject to the requirements of the 'well-pleaded complaint' rule. [Respondents] erroneously invoke that rule outside the realm of statutory 'arising under' jurisdiction, i.e., jurisdiction based on 28 U.S.C. § 1331, to jurisdiction based on a separate and independent jurisdictional grant, in this case, the Red Cross Charter's 'sue and be sued' provision. The 'well-pleaded complaint' rule applies only to statutory 'arising under' cases; it has no application here." 505 U.S. at 258.

Another example of such a statute is 12 U.S.C. § 1819(b)(2), which authorizes federal jurisdiction over suits involving the Federal Deposit Insurance Corporation, whether or not a federal issue appears on the fact of a well-pleaded complaint. This statute "trump[s] the general rules governing federal subject matter jurisdiction. It overcomes the well-pleaded complaint rule by permitting the FDIC to assert a federal question in its answer" and thereby obtain federal jurisdiction in certain cases. *Lindley v. Federal Deposit Insurance Corporation*, 733 F.3d 1043, 1050–51 (11th Cir. 2013).

5. Rules Versus Standards in Formulating Jurisdictional Doctrine. In order to explain (and reconcile) many of the seeming inconsistencies in the foregoing cases, one might emphasize differences among the substantive contexts in which they arose. The Court has cited, with apparent approval, the view of commentators who "have suggested that our § 1331 decisions can best be understood as an evaluation of the *nature* of the federal interest at stake." *Merrell Dow*, supra, 478 U.S. at 814 n.12. The case for federal jurisdiction is strong in *Smith* because the whole point of the litigation was to challenge the constitutionality of a federal statute. In tort cases, by contrast, state law issues may dominate the litigation. In *Shoshone* the cause of action was federal, but the references to local law guaranteed that state law would govern many outcomes, and federal jurisdiction would have added significantly to the caseload burden of the federal courts. The leading article taking this view is William Cohen, *The Broken Compass; The Requirement that a Case Arise "Directly" Under Federal Law*, 115 U. PA. L. REV. 890 (1967). Cohen writes:

> What is surprising is the continuing belief that there is, or should be, a single, all-purpose, neutral analytical concept which marks out federal question jurisdiction. A frank recognition of the pragmatic nature of the decision-making process would help throw light on the factors which actually induce decision. It would, moreover, reduce the danger that a judge would be beguiled by one of the numerous analytical tests into reaching an indefensible result.

The other side of this argument, expressed in Justice Thomas's concurring opinion in *Grable*, supra, is that there is value in making jurisdictional determinations by reference to bright-line rules. Should significant resources be expended over an issue when the only thing that is at stake is the forum? Why not stick with a simple rule like *American Well Works* and then leave it up to Congress to decide whether departures are called for, either by providing a federal forum where one is necessary in order to ensure fairness or avoid errors in a given class of cases, or channeling federal cases to state courts when caseload or other considerations make this the better choice?

At the same time, the fact that people litigate over the scope of federal question jurisdiction may show that, in reality, the choice of forum really is important to lawyers, probably because they think that the forum can, in one way or another, have a bearing on the outcome. If this is so, does the bearing of forum choice on litigation outcome undercut the case for bright-line jurisdictional rules?

D. IS THE PLAINTIFF ALWAYS "THE MASTER OF THE COMPLAINT"?

In *Holmes Group*, supra, the Court declares that the plaintiff is the master of the complaint, and thereby is free to choose whether to sue under federal or state law, and whether to proceed in federal or state court. Yet, this principle, too, has its exceptions. As the following case illustrates, the choice is not always up to the plaintiff.

BENEFICIAL NATIONAL BANK V. ANDERSON
539 U.S. 1 (2003).

JUSTICE STEVENS delivered the opinion of the Court.

The question in this case is whether an action filed in a state court to recover damages from a national bank for allegedly charging excessive interest in violation of both "the common law usury doctrine" and an Alabama usury statute may be removed to a federal court because it actually arises under federal law. We hold that it may.

Respondents are 26 individual taxpayers who made pledges of their anticipated tax refunds to secure short-term loans obtained from petitioner Beneficial National Bank, a national bank chartered under the National Bank Act. Respondents brought suit in an Alabama court against the bank and the two other petitioners that arranged the loans, seeking compensatory and punitive damages on the theory, among others, that the bank's interest rates were usurious. Their complaint did not refer to any federal law.

Petitioners removed the case to the United States District Court for the Middle District of Alabama. In their notice of removal they asserted that the National Bank Act, 12 U.S.C. § 85, [which specifies how bank interest rates may be calculated] is the exclusive provision governing the rate of interest that a national bank may lawfully charge, that the rates charged to respondents complied with that provision, that § 86 provides the exclusive remedies available against a national bank charging excessive interest,[2] and that the removal statute, 28 U.S.C. § 1441, therefore applied. The District Court denied respondents' motion to remand the case to state court but certified the question whether it had jurisdiction to proceed with the case to the Court of Appeals pursuant to 28 U.S.C. § 1292(b).

A divided panel of the Eleventh Circuit reversed. The majority held that under our "well-pleaded complaint" rule, removal is generally not permitted unless the complaint expressly alleges a federal claim and that the narrow exception from that rule known as the "complete preemption doctrine" did not apply because it could "find no clear congressional intent to permit removal under §§ 85 and 86." Because this holding conflicted with an Eighth Circuit decision, we granted certiorari.

II

A civil action filed in a state court may be removed to federal court if the claim is one "arising under" federal law. § 1441(b). To determine whether the claim arises under federal law, we examine the "well pleaded" allegations of the complaint and ignore potential defenses: "a suit arises under the Constitution and laws of the United States only when the plaintiff's statement of his own cause of action shows that it is based upon those laws or that Constitution. It is not enough that the plaintiff alleges some anticipated defense to his cause of action and asserts that the defense is invalidated by some provision of the Constitution of the United States." *Louisville & Nashville R. Co. v. Mottley*, 211 U.S. 149, 152 (1908). Thus, a defense that relies on the preclusive effect of a prior federal judgment, or the pre-emptive effect of a federal statute, will not provide a basis for removal. As a general rule, absent diversity jurisdiction, a case will not be removable if the complaint does not affirmatively allege a federal claim.

Congress has, however, created certain exceptions to that rule. For example, the Price-Anderson Act contains an unusual pre-emption provision, 42 U.S.C. § 2014(hh), that not only gives federal courts jurisdiction over tort actions arising out of nuclear accidents but also expressly provides for removal of such actions brought in state court even when they assert only state-law claims.

We have also construed § 301 of the Labor Management Relations Act, 1947 (LMRA), 29 U.S.C. § 185, as not only preempting state law but

---

[2] Section 86 provides: "Usurious interest; penalty for taking; limitations" The taking, receiving, reserving, or charging a rate of interest greater than is allowed by section 85 of this title, when knowingly done, shall be deemed a forfeiture of the entire interest which the note, bill, or other evidence of debt carries with it, or which has been agreed to be paid thereon. In case the greater rate of interest has been paid, the person by whom it has been paid, or his legal representatives, may recover back, in an action in the nature of an action of debt, twice the amount of the interest thus paid from the association taking or receiving the same: *Provided,* That such action is commenced within two years from the time the usurious transaction occurred.

also authorizing removal of actions that sought relief only under state law. *Avco Corp. v. Machinists*, 390 U.S. 557 (1968). We later explained that holding as resting on the unusually "powerful" pre-emptive force of § 301:

> [The] petitioner's action 'arose under' § 301, and thus could be removed to federal court, although the petitioner had undoubtedly pleaded an adequate claim for relief under the state law of contracts and had sought a remedy available only under state law. The necessary ground of decision was that the pre-emptive force of § 301 is so powerful as to displace entirely any state cause of action 'for violation of contracts between an employer and a labor organization.' Any such suit is purely a creature of federal law, notwithstanding the fact that state law would provide a cause of action in the absence of § 301. *Avco* stands for the proposition that if a federal cause of action completely pre-empts a state cause of action any complaint that comes within the scope of the federal cause of action necessarily 'arises under' federal law.

[*Franchise Tax Board of California v. Construction Laborers Vacation Trust*, 463 U.S. 1, 23–24 (1983).]

Similarly, in *Metropolitan Life Ins. Co. v. Taylor*, 481 U.S. 58 (1987), we considered whether the "complete pre-emption" approach adopted in *Avco* also supported the removal of state common-law causes of action asserting improper processing of benefit claims under a plan regulated by the Employee Retirement Income Security Act of 1974 (ERISA). For two reasons, we held that removal was proper even though the complaint purported to raise only state-law claims. First, the statutory text in § 502(a), not only provided an express federal remedy for the plaintiffs' claims, but also in its jurisdiction subsection, § 502(f), used language similar to the statutory language construed in *Avco,* thereby indicating that the two statutes should be construed in the same way. Second, the legislative history of ERISA unambiguously described an intent to treat such actions "as arising under the laws of the United States in similar fashion to those brought under section 301 of the Labor-Management Relations Act of 1947."

Thus, a state claim may be removed to federal court in only two circumstances—when Congress expressly so provides, such as in the Price-Anderson Act, or when a federal statute wholly displaces the state-law cause of action through complete pre-emption.[3] When the federal statute completely pre-empts the state-law cause of action, a claim which

---

[3] Of course, a state claim can also be removed through the use of the supplemental jurisdiction statute, 28 U.S.C. § 1367(a), provided that another claim in the complaint is removable.

comes within the scope of that cause of action, even if pleaded in terms of state law, is in reality based on federal law. This claim is then removable under 28 U.S.C. § 1441(b), which authorizes any claim that "arises under" federal law to be removed to federal court. In the two categories of cases[4] where this Court has found complete pre-emption—certain causes of action under the LMRA and ERISA—the federal statutes at issue provided the exclusive cause of action for the claim asserted and also set forth procedures and remedies governing that cause of action. See 29 U.S.C. § 1132 (setting forth procedures and remedies for civil claims under ERISA); § 185 (describing procedures and remedies for suits under the LMRA).

III

Count IV of respondents' complaint sought relief for "usury violations" and claimed that petitioners "charged . . . excessive interest in violation of the common law usury doctrine" and violated "Alabama Code. § 8–8–1, et seq. by charging excessive interest." Respondents' complaint thus expressly charged petitioners with usury. *Metropolitan Life*, *Avco*, and *Franchise Tax Board* provide the framework for answering the dispositive question in this case: Does the National Bank Act provide the exclusive cause of action for usury claims against national banks? If so, then the cause of action necessarily arises under federal law and the case is removable. If not, then the complaint does not arise under federal law and is not removable.

Sections 85 and 86 serve distinct purposes. The former sets forth the substantive limits on the rates of interest that national banks may charge. The latter sets forth the elements of a usury claim against a national bank, provides for a 2-year statute of limitations for such a claim, and prescribes the remedies available to borrowers who are charged higher rates and the procedures governing such a claim. If, as petitioners asserted in their notice of removal, the interest that the bank charged to respondents did not violate § 85 limits, the statute unquestionably pre-empts any common-law or Alabama statutory rule that would treat those rates as usurious. The section would therefore provide the petitioners with a complete federal defense. Such a federal defense, however, would not justify removal. Only if Congress intended § 86 to provide the exclusive cause of action for usury claims against

---

[4] This Court has also held that federal courts have subject-matter jurisdiction to hear possessory land claims under state law brought by Indian tribes because of the uniquely federal "nature and source of the possessory rights of Indian tribes." *Oneida Indian Nation of N.Y. v. County of Oneida*, 414 U.S. 661, 667 (1974). Because that case turned on the special historical relationship between Indian tribes and the Federal Government, it does not assist the present analysis.

national banks would the statute be comparable to the provisions that we construed in the *Avco* and *Metropolitan Life* cases.[5]

In a series of cases decided shortly after the Act was passed, we endorsed that approach. [The Court's discussion of the early cases is omitted.]

In addition to this Court's longstanding and consistent construction of the National Bank Act as providing an exclusive federal cause of action for usury against national banks, this Court has also recognized the special nature of federally chartered banks. Uniform rules limiting the liability of national banks and prescribing exclusive remedies for their overcharges are an integral part of a banking system that needed protection from "possible unfriendly State legislation." *Tiffany v. National Bank of Mo.*, 18 Wall. 409, 412 (1874). The same federal interest that protected national banks from the state taxation that Chief Justice Marshall characterized as the "power to destroy," *McCulloch v. Maryland*, 4 Wheat. 316, 431 (1819), supports the established interpretation of §§ 85 and 86 that gives those provisions the requisite pre-emptive force to provide removal jurisdiction. In actions against national banks for usury, these provisions supersede both the substantive and the remedial provisions of state usury laws and create a federal remedy for overcharges that is exclusive, even when a state complainant, as here, relies entirely on state law. Because §§ 85 and 86 provide the exclusive cause of action for such claims, there is, in short, no such thing as a state-law claim of usury against a national bank. Even though the complaint makes no mention of federal law, it unquestionably and unambiguously claims that petitioners violated usury laws. This cause of action against national banks only arises under federal law and could, therefore, be removed under § 1441.

The judgment of the Court of Appeals is reversed.

JUSTICE SCALIA, with whom JUSTICE THOMAS joins, dissenting.

[Today's holding] represents a sharp break from our long tradition of respect for the autonomy and authority of state courts. For example, in *Healy v. Ratta*, 292 U.S. 263, 270 (1934), we explained that "[d]ue regard for the rightful independence of state governments, which should actuate federal courts, requires that they scrupulously confine their own jurisdiction to the precise limits which the statute has defined." And in *Shamrock Oil & Gas Corp. v. Sheets*, 313 U.S. 100, 108 (1941), we

---

[5] Because the proper inquiry focuses on whether Congress intended the federal cause of action to be exclusive rather than on whether Congress intended that the cause of action be removable, the fact that these sections of the National Bank Act were passed in 1864, 11 years prior to the passage of the statute authorizing removal, is irrelevant, contrary to respondents' assertions.

insisted on a "strict construction" of the federal removal statutes.[2] Today's decision ignores these venerable principles and effectuates a significant shift in decisional authority from state to federal courts.

In an effort to justify this shift, the Court explains that "[b]ecause §§ 85 and 86 [of the National Bank Act] provide the exclusive cause of action for such claims, there is . . . no such thing as a state-law claim of usury against a national bank." But the mere fact that a state-law claim is invalid no more deprives it of its character as a state-law claim which does not raise a federal question, than does the fact that a federal claim is invalid deprive it of its character as a federal claim which does raise a federal question. The proper response to the presentation of a nonexistent claim to a state court is dismissal, not the "federalize-and-remove" dance authorized by today's opinion. For even if the Court is correct that the National Bank Act obliterates entirely any state-created right to relief for usury against a national bank, that does not explain how or why the claim of such a right is transmogrified into the claim of a federal right. Congress's mere act of creating a federal right and eliminating all state-created rights in no way suggests an expansion of federal jurisdiction so as to wrest from state courts the authority to decide questions of pre-emption under the National Bank [Act.]

There may well be good reasons to favor the expansion of removal jurisdiction that petitioners urge and that the Court adopts today. As the United States explains in its amicus brief:

> "Absent removal, the state court would have only two legitimate options—to recharacterize the claim in federal-law terms or to dismiss the claim altogether. Any plaintiff who truly seeks recovery on that claim would prefer the first option, which would make the propriety of removal crystal clear. A third possibility, however, is that the state court would err and allow the claim to proceed under state law notwithstanding Congress's decision to make the federal cause of action exclusive. The complete pre-emption rule avoids that potential error." Brief for United States as Amicus Curiae 17–18.

True enough, but inadequate to render today's decision either rational or properly within the authority of this Court. Inadequate for rationality, because there is no more reason to fear state-court error with respect to federal pre-emption accompanied by creation of a federal cause of action than there is with respect to federal pre-emption unaccompanied

---

[2] Our traditional regard for the role played by state courts in interpreting and enforcing federal law has other doctrinal manifestations. We indulge, for example, a "presumption of concurrent [state and federal] jurisdiction," which can be rebutted only "by an explicit statutory directive, by unmistakable implication from legislative history, or by a clear incompatibility between state-court jurisdiction and federal interests." *Gulf Offshore Co. v. Mobil Oil Corp.*, 453 U.S. 473, 478 (1981).

by creation of a federal cause of action—or, for that matter, than there is
with respect to any federal defense to a state-law claim. The rational
response to the United States' concern is to eliminate the well-pleaded-
complaint rule entirely. And inadequate for judicial authority, because it
is up to Congress, not the federal courts, to decide when the risk of state-
court error with respect to a matter of federal law becomes so unbearable
as to justify divesting the state courts of authority to decide the federal
matter. Unless and until we receive instruction from Congress that
claims pre-empted under the National Bank Act—in contrast to almost all
other claims that are subject to federal pre-emption—"arise under"
federal law, we simply lack authority to avoi[d] . . . "potential errors," by
permitting removal.

* * *

[I] respectfully dissent.

NOTES ON THE "COMPLETE PREEMPTION" DOCTRINE

1.   **Removal and Preemption.** The federal question raised by an
assertion that federal law preempts a state law claim is ordinarily not a
sufficient ground for federal jurisdiction. Were it otherwise, the well-pleaded
complaint rule would have little force, for many of the federal issues that may
be raised as defenses amount to claims that federal law preempts state law.
Beneficial National Bank illustrates an exception to this general rule. Notice
that in practice the question it raises will come up only in the removal
context. The plaintiff always will have proceeded in state court, taking care to
keep federal matters off of the face of the complaint. It will always be the
defendant who, seeking removal under § 1441, asserts that the cause of
action is really a federal one, and therefore within the § 1331 federal question
jurisdiction.

2.   **What Are the Stakes in *Beneficial National Bank* and
Similar Cases?** Can the Court in *Beneficial National Bank* be faulted for
giving scant attention to the competing interests at play in the case? What
are those interests?

a.   On one level, the case presents yet another iteration of the
competition between federal and state judicial power. To the extent more
cases must be litigated in state court, state courts will have greater influence
on the development of the law. Conversely, federal judicial power will be
stronger to the extent federal jurisdiction is available. Justice Scalia, a
champion of the state courts, complains that the Court's holding in favor of
removal "effectuates a significant shift in decisional authority from state to
federal courts." Is his opinion in *Beneficial National Bank* consistent in
principle with his opinion for the Court in *Boyle v. United Technologies*,
Chapter 2, supra?

b. Does the debate over federal versus state judicial power obscure a less obvious struggle between the parties over the outcome of the litigation on the merits? In order to understand why anyone would care whether preemption is only strong enough to defeat a state claim or whether it is so strong as to completely wipe the state claim off the face of the earth, it may be useful to take the perspective of a lawyer plotting litigation strategy. Lawyers act in a world of uncertainty, always pursuing their clients' interests in winning the litigation and seeking every advantage to that end. At the outset of the litigation in cases like *Beneficial National Bank*, it will probably be unclear whether federal law preempts the state cause of action. Otherwise the suit would not be brought, as few litigants would invest resources in a futile lawsuit. Were we to assume that federal and state courts would decide the issue the same way, it would make no difference to anyone where the litigation took place. In the event federal law preempts the state cause of action, that proposition would determine the outcome no matter where the case is litigated. Yet we know that the choice of forum issue *does* matter to the parties, for they fight over it. Why? The reason may be that lawyers think that outcomes on uncertain issues *do* vary depending on the forum. Of course, it does not necessarily follow that the Court's rulings are based on such substantive considerations. Though two partisans of state judicial power dissented in *Beneficial National Bank*, Justices of all ideological stripes joined the majority opinion.

c. *Avco Corp. v. Machinists*, discussed at length in the *Beneficial National Bank*, is the leading case for the proposition that preemption sometimes eradicates the state cause of action so completely that the cause of action *must* arise under federal law, no matter what the complaint says. In that case, the motivations of the litigants were easy to grasp. The case arose from a labor dispute. The employer and the union had made an agreement under which the employer agreed to arbitration of disputes and the union agreed not to strike. The union went on strike and the employer sought to enforce the agreement by getting a court to enjoin the strike. Federal court was unavailable because, under federal labor law in force at that time, the federal courts were forbidden to enjoin strikes. *Only* by gaining access to state court could the employer hope to obtain relief. Here the impact of forum on outcome is manifest. See P. LOW, J. JEFFRIES & C. BRADLEY, FEDERAL COURTS AND THE LAW OF FEDERAL-STATE RELATIONS 590–91 (7th ed. 2011), (noting that "[u]nusually, the choice of forum dictated the result.")

3. The Rationale and Scope of *Beneficial National Bank*. Justice Scalia points out, and the Court does not deny, that "the opinion in *Avco* failed to clarify the analytic basis for its unprecedented act of jurisdictional alchemy. The Court neglected to explain *why* state-law claims that are preempted by § 301 of the LMRA are exempt from the strictures of the well-pleaded complaint rule, nor did it explain *how* such a state-law claim can plausibly be said to 'arise under' federal law." Justice Douglas's opinion for the Court began by noting that, under the *Lincoln Mills* case, federal labor law preempts state contract law, and then continued: "It is thus clear that the claim under this collective bargaining agreement is one arising under the 'laws of the United States' within the meaning of the removal statute."

In *Metropolitan Life Ins. Co. v. Taylor*, 481 U.S. 58 (1987), the statute was the Employment Retirement Income Security Act of 1974 (ERISA), which regulates employee insurance benefits and preempts state law. An employee was fired and sued his employer in state court on a state law breach of contract theory. The defendant sought removal, and, citing *Avco*, the Court agreed. Congressional intent was the key to the decision. The legislative history of ERISA showed, to the Court's satisfaction, that Congress intended that the statute be interpreted like the Labor Management Relations Act. Thus, "Congress has clearly manifested an intent to make causes of action within the scope of the civil enforcement provisions of § 502(a) removable to a federal court."

The doctrinal problem the Court had to solve in *Beneficial National Bank* was to reconcile two contrary propositions: [a] the principle, reflected in the well-pleaded complaint rule and a line of cases stretching back at least as far as *Mottley*, that a preemption defense does not create federal jurisdiction; and [b] the rulings in *Avco* and *Metropolitan Life v. Taylor* that sometimes preemption *does* create federal jurisdiction; that is, "that Congress may so completely preempt a particular area, that any civil complaint raising this select group of claims is necessarily federal in character." *Metropolitan Life*, supra.

One way to reconcile the two propositions is to focus on Congress's intent, as the Court did in *Taylor*. Congress may expressly override the well-pleaded complaint rule, by providing that a particular preemption claim can be brought in federal court. The Price Anderson Act, discussed in the majority opinion in *Beneficial National Bank*, is an example. *Metropolitan Life v. Taylor* illustrates that legislative history can provide sufficient evidence of Congress's intent.

The Court in *Beneficial National Bank* apparently relies on Congress's intent (see the passage around the Court's footnote 5) in order to resolve the issue of the preemptive effect of the National Bank Act.

What are the implications of *Beneficial National Bank* for other cases raising "complete preemption" claims? Given the Court's reasoning, it seems likely that the starting point for analysis will be an effort to determine Congress's intent in enacting the particular statute at issue in the case. See, e.g., *Dutcher v. Matheson*, 733 F.3d 980, 986 (10th Cir. 2013) (noting that in the 10th Circuit, the analysis of a complete preemption issue usually begins with asking "whether Congress intended to allow removal in such a case, as manifested by the provision of a federal cause of action").

Is *Dutcher* broadly consistent with the view that, under *Beneficial National Bank,* "any federal statute that both preempts state law and provides a substitute federal remedy creates an 'exclusive cause of action' that falls within the complete preemption defense." R. FALLON, ET AL., HART

& WECHSLER'S THE FEDERAL COURTS AND THE FEDERAL SYSTEM 814–15 (6th ed. 2009)?

Does the Court's "exclusive federal cause of action" reasoning in the *Beneficial National Bank* signify that the "complete preemption" doctrine will apply whenever there is exclusive federal *jurisdiction* over a particular federal cause of action that arguably preempts state law? E.g., under § 1338 there is exclusive federal jurisdiction over copyright cases. Does *Beneficial National Bank* mean that a state cause of action for breach of contract, which is arguably preempted by copyright law, may be brought in (or removed to) federal court? The answer is almost certainly no. The Court's reasoning suggests that the notion of an "exclusive federal cause of action" is a synonym for "complete preemption," but not a synonym for "exclusive federal jurisdiction." Congress may make federal jurisdiction exclusive over certain questions (like the copyright issue in the hypothetical) without completely preempting state causes of action in the area.

E. REMOVAL

Many of the cases in the foregoing sections have involved federal question removal under 28 U.S.C. § 1441(b):

> Any civil action of which the district courts have original jurisdiction founded on a claim or right arising under the Constitution, treaties or laws of the United States shall be removable without regard to the citizenship or residence of the parties. Any other such action shall be removable only if none of the parties in interest properly joined and served as defendants is a citizen of the State in which such action is brought.

Since federal question removal turns on whether the case could have been brought in federal court in the first instance, under § 1331 for example, the answer to the removal issue is always the same as the answer to the federal question jurisdiction issue. There is no separate doctrine on the propriety of removal.

1. Federal Officer Removal. Other removal provisions have significance independent of § 1331, by authorizing removal where the federal question comes up as a defense. Federal officer removal, 28 U.S.C. § 1442, provides for removal of "[a] civil action or criminal prosecution commenced in a State court against [the] United States or any agency thereof or any officer [of] the United States sued in an official or individual capacity for any act under color of such [office]." In *Mesa v. California*, 489 U.S. 121 (1989), the Court held that this statute allows removal by an officer only when the officer asserts a federal defense. Postal Service employees charged with traffic offenses in the course of their employment, but lacking any federal defense to the charges, were therefore not allowed to remove the prosecutions to federal court. What result if the federal officer is sued on a state law tort theory for injuries incurred in a traffic accident, and the officer brings a counterclaim based on federal law?

In *Mesa* the Court rejected the Government's argument that government employees needed access to federal court in order to protect them from potentially hostile state tribunals, even though they raised no federal defense: "We have, in the past, not found the need to adopt a theory of 'protective jurisdiction' to support Art. III 'arising under' jurisdiction, and we do not see the need for doing so here because we do not recognize any federal interests that are not protected by limiting removal to situations in which a federal defense is alleged. In these prosecutions, no state court hostility or interference has even been alleged by petitioners." *Id.* at 137–38.

Though *Mesa* rejected an ambitious "need to combat state court hostility to federal interests" policy in curbing the scope of § 1442, that rationale has considerably more force when the officer *does* raise a federal defense. The notion that removal is appropriate in order to safeguard federal interests from unfriendly state tribunals has been a persistent theme in removal statutes for the past 200 years. *Mesa* is discussed at greater length in Chapter 7.

2. Civil Rights Removal. Besides justifying federal officer removal, the "hostile state forum" rationale underlies civil rights removal as well. The statute is 28 U.S.C. § 1443, which provides:

> Any of the following civil actions or criminal prosecutions, commenced in a State court may be removed by the defendant to the district court of the United States for the district and division embracing the place wherein it is pending:
>
> (1) Against any person who is denied or cannot enforce in the courts of such State a right under any law providing for the equal civil rights of citizens of the United States, or of all persons within the jurisdiction thereof;
>
> (2) For any act under color of authority derived from any law providing for equal rights, or for refusing to do any act on the ground that it would be inconsistent with such law.

The original version of this statute was enacted during Reconstruction, in an effort to enforce federal rights by removing cases from hostile state courts. Over time, both Congress and the Supreme Court have restricted its scope. See Robert D. Goldstein, Blyew: *Variations on a Jurisdictional Theme*, 41 STAN. L. REV. 469, 478–81 (1989). In the 1960s, civil rights workers in the South often ran afoul of local authorities and were prosecuted in state courts. They raised federal defenses to these prosecutions, and their lawyers tried by various means to have their cases litigated in the federal courts. One strategy was to revive the civil rights removal statute. But the Supreme Court, in *Georgia v. Rachel*, 384 U.S. 780 (1966) and *City of Greenwood v. Peacock*, 384 U.S. 808 (1966), interpreted the statute narrowly, ruling that, in the case of private individuals asserting that state courts will not enforce their federal rights, [a] the statute only applied to federal laws "providing for specific civil rights stated in terms of racial equality, *Rachel*, 384 U.S. at 792, and [b] that '[r]emoval is warranted only if it can be predicted by reference to a law of general application that the defendant will be denied or cannot enforce the specified federal rights in the state courts.'" *Rachel*, 384 U.S. at 800. Thus, a free speech claim will not satisfy [a], see *Peacock*, 384 U.S. at 825, and a claim that state courts will disregard federal law will not satisfy [b], see *Rachel*, 384 U.S. at 803.

As a result of these cases, removal is rarely available to persons who are charged with crimes in state court and would prefer to litigate the federal issues in federal court. A more promising strategy, though one that is not without difficulties of its own, is to bring a federal § 1983 suit before the state criminal case is begun, challenging the validity of the criminal statute, and seeking prospective relief.

Suppose it could be shown that state courts at a particular time and place (e.g., the South in the 1960s) are systematically biased against a class of defendants, even though state laws are facially constitutional. Would such a showing justify reading § 1443 more broadly, at least for cases arising in that time and place? For an argument in favor of this approach, made before *Rachel* and *Peacock*, see Anthony Amsterdam, *Criminal Prosecutions Affecting Federally Guaranteed Civil Rights: Federal Removal and Habeas Corpus Jurisdiction to Abort State Court Trial*, 113 U. PA. L. REV. 793 (1965).

3. Policy Issues Bearing on Federal Defense Removal. We have seen that § 1441 limits federal question removal to cases that could have originally been filed in federal court and therefore meet the well-pleaded complaint rule. Furthermore, § 1443 makes only a narrow exception to that general rule for civil rights cases. The consequence is that, unless the defendant is a federal officer (and asserts a federal defense that brings the case within § 1442), removal is rarely available for federal defenses. Proposals have been made to expand the range of cases that may be removed, for example, by allowing either party to remove in certain cases where "subsequent to the initial pleading, a substantial defense arising under [federal law] is properly asserted that, if sustained, would be dispositive of the action or of all counterclaims [therein"]. American Law Institute, Study of the Division of Jurisdiction Between State and Federal Courts 25–27 (1969).

Proposals like this one are based on the general principle that the main point of federal jurisdiction is to adjudicate matters of federal law, because federal courts acquire familiarity with federal law and expertise in adjudicating federal issues, and because they will likely be more sympathetic to federal claims than the state courts are. Is there any good argument on the other side?

Consider Paul Bator's view:

Such a scheme would impose a large and unnecessary burden on the federal courts by implicating them centrally in the task of enforcing state criminal and administrative regulation, even in cases where the federal constitutional issue is but a minor and separable feature of the controversy. It would gratuitously buy us a whole new host of *Erie* problems. It would constitute a gross interference with the power of the states to design their own institutional schemes for enforcing state law and policy. It is, therefore, not only not surprising but, I submit, virtually inevitable that Congress has been historically reluctant to provide for federal defense removal and that the Supreme Court has rejected attempts to persuade it to interpret the Civil Rights Removal Act to accord defendants a virtually automatic right to abort, by removal, state court civil and criminal enforcement proceedings involving a federal constitutional defense.

Paul M. Bator, *The State Courts and Federal Constitutional Litigation*, 22 WM. & MARY L. REV. 605, 611–12 (1981).

To what extent does the force of Bator's argument depend on the premise that state courts will be as sympathetic to federal rights, and as likely to decide them correctly, as the federal courts are? Suppose the reality is that state courts, while not generally as sympathetic to federal claims as the federal courts are, nonetheless accord sufficient respect to federal claims to satisfy the requirements of due process. On that premise, should Bator's argument prevail?

4. Removing State Law Issues to Federal Court. The focus of this discussion of removal has been federal question removal. Removal is available in other contexts as well. Section 1441(d) permits removal of "[a]ny civil action brought in a State court against a foreign state." There need be no federal question at issue in such a case, for Article III authorizes federal jurisdiction over controversies "between a State, or the Citizens thereof, and foreign States, Citizens, or Subjects." Similarly, under § 1441(a), a purely state law case may be removed if the parties are citizens of different states, thereby satisfying the requirements of federal diversity jurisdiction, 28 U.S.C. § 1332.

F. DECLARATORY JUDGMENTS

Early twentieth-century law reformers found fault with traditional modes of adjudication, which typically allow persons to sue only after they have suffered an injury:

> In their view, the existing remedial structure failed in three ways. First, it failed to address the plight of a person embroiled in a dispute who, limited by traditional remedies, could not have the controversy adjudicated because the opposing party had the sole claim to traditional relief and chose not to use it. Second, the traditional system of remedies harmed parties by forcing them to wait an unnecessarily long time before seeking relief. Third, the reformers criticized the harshness of damage and injunctive awards. Even when they could be invoked, they were thought to hamper litigants who did not need or desire coercive relief.

Donald L. Doernberg & Michael B. Mushlin, *The Trojan Horse: How the Declaratory Judgment Act Created a Cause of Action and Expanded Federal Jurisdiction While the Supreme Court Wasn't Looking*, 36 UCLA L. REV. 529, 552–53 (1989).

In order to overcome these problems, state legislatures and Congress (in 1934) enacted "declaratory judgment" statutes. The Federal Declaratory Judgment Act, 28 U.S.C. §§ 2201–02, provides that

> In a case of actual controversy within its jurisdiction [any] court of the United States [may] declare the rights and other legal relations of any interested party seeking such declaration, whether or not further relief is or could be sought.

28 U.S.C. § 2201(a).

One point of the statute is to permit someone who would be a defendant in a traditional lawsuit to seek declaratory relief, by asserting, for example, that the other party holds no valid rights against him. With the parties (potentially) reversed in this way, the matters that appear on the face of a well-pleaded complaint seeking a declaratory judgment may differ from those that would appear on the face of a well-pleaded complaint seeking traditional relief. Even if the party seeking a declaratory judgment is the one who might have sought traditional relief, the face of the declaratory judgment complaint may contain different matters than those found on the face of a traditional complaint. The advent of the declaratory judgment thus gave rise to new questions about the scope of federal question jurisdiction.

For purposes of determining whether a federal district court has jurisdiction over such a case, should one look at the declaratory judgment complaint or the hypothetical complaint that would be filed in an analogous enforcement action? *Skelly Oil* is the leading case addressing that question.

SKELLY OIL CO. V. PHILLIPS PETROLEUM CO.

339 U.S. 667 (1950).

JUSTICE FRANKFURTER delivered the opinion of the Court.

In 1945, Michigan-Wisconsin Pipe Line Company sought from the Federal Power Commission a certificate of public convenience and necessity, required by § 7(c) of the Natural Gas Act, for the construction and operation of a pipe line to carry natural gas from Texas to Michigan and Wisconsin. A prerequisite for such a certificate is adequate reserves of gas. To obtain these reserves Michigan-Wisconsin entered into an agreement with Phillips Petroleum Company on December 11, 1945, whereby the latter undertook to make available gas from the Hugoton Gas Field, [which] it produced or purchased from others. Phillips had contracted with petitioners, Skelly Oil Company, Stanolind Oil and Gas Company, and Magnolia Petroleum Company, to purchase gas produced by them in the Hugoton Field for resale to Michigan-Wisconsin. Each contract provided that "in the event Michigan-Wisconsin Pipe Line Company shall fail to secure from the Federal Power Commission on or before (October 1, 1946) a certificate of public convenience and necessity for the construction and operation of its pipe line, Seller (a petitioner) shall have the right to terminate this contract by written notice to Buyer (Phillips) delivered to Buyer at any time after December 1, 1946, but before the issuance of such certificate." The legal significance of this provision is at the core of this litigation.

The Federal Power Commission, in response to the application of Michigan-Wisconsin, on November 30, 1946, ordered that "A certificate of public convenience and necessity be and it is hereby issued to applicant (Michigan-Wisconsin), upon the terms and conditions of this order," listing among the conditions that there be no transportation or sale of natural gas by means of the sanctioned facilities until all necessary authorizations were obtained from the State of Wisconsin and the communities proposed to be served, that Michigan-Wisconsin should have the approval of the Securities and Exchange Commission for its plan of financing, that the applicant should file for the approval of the Commission a schedule of reasonable rates, and that the sanctioned facilities should not be used for the transportation of gas to Detroit and Ann Arbor except with due regard for the rights and duties of Panhandle Eastern Pipe Line Company, which had intervened before the Federal Power Commission, in its established service for resale in these areas, such rights and duties to be set forth in a supplemental order. It was also provided that Michigan-Wisconsin should have fifteen days from the issue of the supplemental order to notify the Commission whether the certificate "as herein issued is acceptable to it." Finally, the Commission's order provided that for purposes of computing the time within which applications for rehearing could be filed, "the date of issuance of this order shall be deemed to be the date of issuance of the opinions, or of the supplemental order referred to herein, whichever may be later."

News of the Commission's action was released on November 30, 1946, but the actual content of the order was not made public until December 2, 1946. Petitioners severally, on December 2, 1946, gave notice to Phillips of termination of their contracts on the ground that Michigan-Wisconsin had not received a certificate of public convenience and necessity. Thereupon Michigan-Wisconsin and Phillips brought suit against petitioners in the District Court for the Northern District of Oklahoma. Alleging that a certificate of public convenience and necessity, "within the meaning of said Natural Gas Act and said contracts" had been issued prior to petitioners' attempt at termination of the contracts, they invoked the Federal Declaratory Judgment Act for a declaration that the contracts were still "in effect and binding upon the parties thereto." Motions by petitioners to have Michigan-Wisconsin dropped as a party plaintiff were sustained, but motions to dismiss the complaint for want of jurisdiction were denied. The case then went to the merits, and the District Court decreed that the contracts between Phillips and petitioners have not been "effectively terminated and that each of such contracts remain (sic) in full force and effect." The Court of Appeals for the Tenth Circuit affirmed, and we brought the case here because it raises in sharp form the question whether a suit like this "arises under the Constitution, laws or treaties of the United States," 28 U.S.C. § 1331, so as to enable District Courts to give declaratory relief under the Declaratory Judgment Act.

"[T]he operation of the Declaratory Judgment Act is procedural only." *Aetna Life Ins. Co. of Hartford, Conn. v. Haworth*, 300 U.S. 227, 240. Congress enlarged the range of remedies available in the federal courts but did not extend their jurisdiction. When concerned as we are with the power of the inferior federal courts to entertain litigation within the restricted area to which the Constitution and Acts of Congress confine them, "jurisdiction" means the kinds of issues which give right of entrance to federal courts. Jurisdiction in this sense was not altered by the Declaratory Judgment Act. Prior to that Act, a federal court would entertain a suit on a contract only if the plaintiff asked for an immediately enforceable remedy like money damages or an injunction, but such relief could only be given if the requisites of jurisdiction, in the sense of a federal right or diversity, provided foundation for resort to the federal courts. The Declaratory Judgment Act allowed relief to be given by way of recognizing the plaintiff's right even though no immediate enforcement of it was asked. But the requirements of jurisdiction—the limited subject matters which alone Congress had authorized the District Courts to adjudicate—were not impliedly repealed or modified.

If Phillips sought damages from petitioners or specific performance of their contracts, it could not bring suit in a United States District Court on the theory that it was asserting a federal right. And for the simple reason that such a suit would "arise" under the State law governing the contracts. Whatever federal claim Phillips may be able to urge would in any event be injected into the case only in anticipation of a defense to be asserted by petitioners. [Where] a suit is brought in the federal courts upon the sole ground that the determination of the suit depends upon some question of a federal nature, it must appear, at the outset, from the declaration or the bill of the party suing, that the suit is of that character. But a suggestion of one party that the other will or may set up a claim under the Constitution or laws of the United States does not make the suit one arising under that Constitution or those laws. The plaintiff's claim itself must present a federal question "unaided by anything alleged in anticipation of avoidance of defenses which it is thought the defendant may interpose." *Taylor v. Anderson*, 234 U.S. 74, 75–76; *Louisville & Nashville R. Co. v. Mottley*, 211 U.S. 149, 152.

These decisions reflect the current of jurisdictional legislation since the Act of March 3, 1875, first entrusted to the lower federal courts wide jurisdiction in cases "arising under this Constitution, the Laws of the United States, and Treaties." U.S. Const. Art. III, § 2. [With] exceptions not now relevant, Congress has narrowed the opportunities for entrance into the federal courts, and this Court has been more careful than in earlier days in enforcing these jurisdictional limitations.

To be observant of these restrictions is not to indulge in formalism or sterile technicality. It would turn into the federal courts a vast current of litigation indubitably arising under State law, in the sense that the right to be vindicated was State-created, if a suit for a declaration of rights could be brought into the federal courts merely because an anticipated defense derived from federal law. Not only would this unduly swell the volume of litigation in the District Courts but it would also embarrass those courts—and this Court on potential review—in that matters of local law may often be involved, and the District Courts may either have to decide doubtful questions of State law or hold cases pending disposition of such State issues by State courts. To sanction suits for declaratory relief as within the jurisdiction of the District Courts merely because, as in this case, artful pleading anticipates a defense based on federal law would contravene the whole trend of jurisdictional legislation by Congress, disregard the effective functioning of the federal judicial system and distort the limited procedural purpose of the Declaratory Judgment Act. Since the matter in controversy as to which Phillips asked for a declaratory judgment is not one that "arises under the * * * laws * * * of the United States" and since as to Skelly and Stanolind jurisdiction cannot be sustained on the score of diversity of citizenship, the proceedings against them should have been dismissed.

As to Magnolia, a Texas corporation, a different situation is presented. Since Phillips was a Delaware corporation, there is diversity of [citizenship]. [The Court then addressed the merits of Magnolia's claim.]

CHIEF JUSTICE VINSON, with whom MR. JUSTICE BURTON joins, dissenting in part.

I concur in that part of the Court's judgment that directs dismissal of the cause as to Skelly and Stanolind. I have real doubts as to whether there is a federal question here at all, even though interpretation of the contract between private parties requires an interpretation of a federal statute and the action of a federal regulatory body. But the Court finds it unnecessary to reach that question because it holds that the federal question, if any, is not a part of the plaintiff's claim and that jurisdiction does not, therefore, attach. While this result is not a necessary one, I am not prepared to dissent from it at this time.

But I am forced to dissent from the vacation and remand of the cause in respect to Magnolia. [Chief Justice Vinson disagreed with the Court on the merits].

NOTES ON THE SKELLY OIL RULE

1. **Applying *Skelly Oil*.** To test your understanding of *Skelly Oil*, consider the following hypothetical cases:

a. Suppose *A* claims a patent on a certain manufacturing process, claims that *B* is infringing the patent, and so informs *B*'s customers. But *A* does not bring a suit for patent infringement. May *B* sue *A* in federal court for a declaratory judgment that the patent is invalid? *Edelmann v. Triple-A Specialty*, 88 F.2d 852 (7th Cir. 1937) held that he could, and other lower cases have followed *Edelman*'s rule. Note that in *Edelman* the declaratory plaintiff raises a federal question, by claiming that the patent is invalid. Suppose that he seeks to raise a *state law* defense to the declaratory defendant's federal law claim. In that event, dicta in *Textron Lycoming Reciprocating Engine Division v. UAW*, 523 U.S. 653, 659–60 (1998), indicate that federal jurisdiction is more doubtful. See LARRY W. YACKLE, FEDERAL COURTS 295 (3d ed. 2009).

b. Suppose *A* and *B* make a contract, under which *A* will supply *B* with widgets, in exchange for which *B* will pay a certain price. *A* delivers widgets but *B* refuses to pay, claiming that the contract is invalid because the price was the product of collusion between *A* and other suppliers, in violation of the federal antitrust laws. May *A* (or *B*) bring a federal suit for a declaratory judgment as to whether the contract violates the antitrust laws?

c. A federal statute, the Price Anderson Act, sets a ceiling on the amount of damages available in a state law tort suit brought against a nuclear power company to recover for a nuclear accident. The Carolina Environmental Study Group (CESG), a potential plaintiff in such a tort suit, sued Duke Power and the federal Nuclear Regulatory Commission (NRC) before any accident had occurred, seeking a declaratory judgment that the statute deprives CESG members of property without due process of law, in violation of their Fifth Amendment rights. Is the *Skelly Oil* rule satisfied? Or does the case arise under state tort law, with the federal issues arising only as a defense and a reply to a defense (as in *Mottley*)?

In *Duke Power Co. v. Carolina Environmental Study Group*, 438 U.S. 59 (1978), Justice Rehnquist took the latter view:

> Under the law of North Carolina a right of action arises as soon as wrongful act has created any injury, however slight, to the plaintiff. This right of action provided by state, not federal, law is the property of which the appellees contend the Act deprives them without due process. Thus, the constitutionality of the Act becomes relevant only if the appellant Duke Power Co. were to invoke the Act as a defense to appellees' suit for recovery under their North Carolina cause of action.

438 U.S. at 96–97 (Rehnquist, J., concurring in the judgment).

The majority disagreed:

> We conclude that the complaint is more fairly read as stating a claim against the NRC directly under the Due Process Clause of the Fifth Amendment. On this view the "well-pleaded" complaint rule poses no bar to the assertion of jurisdiction. Appellee's claim under the Due Process Clause is an essential ingredient of a well-pleaded complaint asserting a right under the Constitution and is not simply a claim made in anticipation of a defense to be raised in an action having its origin in state law.

438 U.S. at 69–70 n.13.

Would the majority's analysis in footnote 13 hold up today, given the current doctrine on implied causes of action? Does CESG's cause of action come within the principle of *Ex parte Young*?

2. Federal Law in Private Contracts. The Court in *Skelly Oil* sets down a general rule for determining federal jurisdiction in declaratory judgment cases, a rule that federal courts have applied ever since to a broad range of cases. A distracting feature of the case is that, quite apart from the general rule, one might argue that federal jurisdiction is improper in *Skelly Oil* just because the federal issue—whether the FPC had granted a license on time—is relevant only because the parties to a contract made it so. Arguably, "where issues of federal law are relevant only because incorporated in a private contract, there will be little federal interest in providing the protective jurisdiction of a sympathetic federal forum." William Cohen, *The*

Broken Compass: The Requirement That a Case Arise "Directly" Under Federal Law, 115 U. PA. L. REV. 890, 910 (1967). Evidently for this reason, Chief Justice Vinson had "real doubts as to whether there is a federal question here at all." Be that as it may, the Court has never chosen to limit *Skelly Oil* to its context in the way Chief Justice Vinson and Professor Cohen suggest.

    3.   Was *Skelly Oil* Rightly Decided? The opinion in *Skelly Oil* is an exercise in statutory interpretation. Yet the Court does not rely on statutory language or any evidence of the specific intent of the framers of the declaratory judgment act. It starts from the premise that Congress intended only to provide a new remedy. Therefore, the Court reasons, Congress did not intend to enlarge federal jurisdiction. Therefore, federal question jurisdiction should be available for declaratory relief only if it would be available for a traditional lawsuit. Therefore, in order to determine whether federal jurisdiction is proper in a declaratory judgment case, one asks whether a hypothetical complaint that could have been filed in an analogous enforcement action would meet the well-pleaded complaint rule.

    Critics of *Skelly Oil* take issue with Justice Frankfurter's premise:

> Congress approved the declaratory judgment device precisely because it expanded the scope of federal court power and the timing of its exercise. Congress did not indicate that federal question jurisdiction was limited to cases in which a plaintiff also had a traditional, coercive federal question claim. In fact, strong, direct evidence shows that Congress explicitly intended to include at least ["mirror-image"] federal question cases [in which the party seeking the declaratory judgment would have been the defendant in a traditional federal-question coercive action but has not yet been sued]; and "federal question defense" cases, within the ambit of district court jurisdiction.

    Doernberg & Mushlin, supra, 36 UCLA REV. at 549. While the authors go on to marshal evidence in support of their assertions, they also concede that "[t]he Declaratory Judgment Act does not have a tidy history." *Id.*

    4.   State and Federal Declaratory Judgment Acts. Since the rule of *Skelly Oil* is an interpretation of the federal Declaratory Judgment Act, the holding left open the possibility that, in dealing with *state* declaratory judgment statutes, the Court would adopt a different rule. In *Franchise Tax Board of California v. Construction Laborers Vacation Trust*, 463 U.S. 1 (1983), the Court put that notion to rest:

> [W]hile *Skelly Oil* itself is limited to the federal Declaratory Judgment Act, fidelity to its spirit leads us to extend it to state declaratory judgment actions as well. If federal district courts could take jurisdiction, either originally or by removal, of state declaratory judgment claims raising questions of federal law, without regard to the doctrine of *Skelly Oil*, the federal Declaratory

Judgment Act—with the limitations *Skelly Oil* read into it—would become a dead letter. For any case in which a state declaratory judgment action was available, litigants could get into federal court for a declaratory judgment despite our interpretation of § 2201, simply by pleading an adequate state claim for a declaration of federal law.

5. Declaratory Judgments, Preemption, and Suits Brought by States. In *Franchise Tax Board*, supra, the Court addressed a variation on the typical suit for declaratory relief. The case centered on the federal Employee Retirement Income Security Act, which regulates employee benefit schemes. Construction Laborers Vacation Trust (CLVT) held funds in trust on behalf of workers in a program covered by ERISA. Franchise Tax Board, a state agency, sought to recover those funds in payment of taxes owed by the workers. As part of this effort, Franchise Tax Board brought a declaratory action in state court under California's declaratory judgment act, seeking a ruling that ERISA did not preempt state law. CLVT removed the case to federal court under § 1441, on the rationale that the suit could have been brought to federal court initially under § 1331. The issue before the Supreme Court was whether the case should have been removed. The Court ruled that removal was improper.

So far as the complaint for a declaratory judgment was concerned, the federal issue surely appeared there:

> [T]he question of federal preemption [is] a necessary element of the declaratory judgment claim. Under Cal. Civ. Proc. Code § 1060, a party with an interest in property may bring an action for a declaration of another party's legal rights and duties with respect to that property upon showing that there is an "actual controversy relating to the respective rights and duties" of the parties. The only questions in dispute between the parties in this case concern the rights and duties of CLVT and its trustees under ERISA. Not only does [Franchise Tax Board's] request for a declaratory judgment under California law clearly encompass questions governed by ERISA, but [Franchise Tax Board's] complaint identifies no other questions as a subject of controversy between the parties. Such questions must be raised in a well-pleaded complaint for a declaratory judgment.

Yet this, of course, is not sufficient to support federal jurisdiction. *Skelly Oil* requires that the court construct the hypothetical complaint in an analogous enforcement action. Here is what the Court said about the application of *Skelly Oil* to this case:

> The application of *Skelly Oil* to such a suit is somewhat unclear. Federal courts have regularly taken original jurisdiction over declaratory judgment suits in which, if the declaratory judgment defendant brought a coercive action to enforce its rights, that suit

would necessarily present a federal question.[19] Section 502(a)(3) of ERISA specifically grants trustees of ERISA-covered plans like CLVT a cause of action for injunctive relief when their rights and duties under ERISA are at issue, and that action is exclusively governed by federal law.[20] If CLVT could have sought an injunction under ERISA against application to it of state regulations that require acts inconsistent with ERISA,[21] does a declaratory judgment suit by the State "arise under" federal law?

We think not. We have always interpreted what *Skelly Oil* called "the current of jurisdictional legislation since the Act of March 3, 1875," with an eye to practicality and necessity. "What is needed is something of that common-sense accommodation of judgment to kaleidoscopic situations which characterizes the law in its treatment of causation . . . a selective process which picks the substantial causes out of the web and lays the other ones aside." *Gully v. First National Bank*, 299 U.S., at 117–118. There are good reasons why the federal courts should not entertain suits by the States to declare the validity of their regulations despite possibly conflicting federal law.

States are not significantly prejudiced by an inability to come to federal court for a declaratory judgment in advance of a possible injunctive suit by a person subject to federal regulation. They have a variety of means by which they can enforce their own laws in their own courts, and they do not suffer if the preemption questions such enforcement may raise are tested there.[22]

---

[19] For instance, federal courts have consistently adjudicated suits by alleged patent infringers to declare a patent invalid, on the theory that an infringement suit by the declaratory judgment defendant would raise a federal question over which the federal courts have exclusive [jurisdiction].

[20] Section 502(a)(3) provides: "[A civil action may be brought] by a participant, beneficiary, or fiduciary (A) to enjoin any act or practice which violates any provision of this subchapter or the terms of the plan, or (B) to obtain other appropriate equitable relief (i) to redress such violations or (ii) to enforce any provision of this subchapter. . . ." 29 U.S.C. § 1132(a)(3). [Even] if ERISA did not expressly provide jurisdiction, CLVT might have been able to obtain federal jurisdiction under the doctrine applied in some cases that a person subject to a scheme of federal regulation may sue in federal court to enjoin application to him of conflicting state regulations, and a declaratory judgment action by the same person does not necessarily run afoul of the *Skelly Oil* doctrine. See, e.g., *Lake Carriers' Assn. v. MacMullan*, 406 U.S. 498, 506–508, 92 S.Ct. 1749, 1755–1756, 32 L.Ed.2d 257 (1972).

[21] We express no opinion, however, whether a party in CLVT's position could sue under ERISA to enjoin or to declare invalid a state tax levy, despite the Tax Injunction Act, 28 U.S.C. § 1341. See *California v. Grace Brethren Church*, 457 U.S. 393, 102 S.Ct. 2498, 73 L.Ed.2d 93 (1982). To do so, it would have to show either that state law provided no "speedy and efficient remedy" or that Congress intended § 502 of ERISA to be an exception to the Tax Injunction Act.

[22] Indeed, as appellant's strategy in this case shows, they may often be willing to go to great lengths to avoid federal-court resolution of a preemption question. Realistically, there is little prospect that States will flood the federal courts with declaratory judgment actions; most questions will arise, as in this case, because a State has sought a declaration in state court and the defendant has removed the case to federal court. Accordingly, it is perhaps appropriate to note that considerations of comity make us reluctant to snatch cases which a State has brought from the courts of that State, unless some clear rule demands it.

The express grant of federal jurisdiction in ERISA is limited to suits brought by certain parties, as to whom Congress presumably determined that a right to enter federal court was necessary to further the statute's purposes.[23] It did not go so far as to provide that any suit against such parties must also be brought in federal court when they themselves did not choose to sue. The situation presented by a State's suit for a declaration of the validity of state law is sufficiently removed from the spirit of necessity and careful limitation of district court jurisdiction that informed our statutory interpretation in *Skelly Oil* and *Gully* to convince us that, until Congress informs us otherwise, such a suit is not within the original jurisdiction of the United States district courts. Accordingly, the same suit brought originally in state court is not removable either.

––––––––––

In what sense is the application of *Skelly Oil* to this case "somewhat unclear"? Given the Court's description in the first paragraph of this excerpt of the contents of the well-pleaded complaint in an analogous enforcement action, is there any doubt that *Skelly Oil*'s requirements are met? Does the Court suggest otherwise? Would it be inaccurate to characterize the case as one in which the Court, while claiming to follow *Skelly Oil*, actually makes an exception to the *Skelly Oil* rule for cases in which a state government brings the declaratory action in state court? What is the policy behind the holding? In answering this question, consider not only the body of the opinion but also the last sentence of footnote 22. And keep in mind that on the day the Court handed down *Franchise Tax Board*, it also decided *Shaw v. Delta Air Lines*, 463 U.S. 85 (1983). That case applied the principle stated in the last sentence of footnote 20. The Court upheld federal jurisdiction over a case brought by employers and employees against state officials, asserting that ERISA preempted certain provisions of state law. The Court so held even though ERISA did not expressly provide for federal jurisdiction. As for the scope of the *Shaw* principle, in *Calstar v. State Compensation Ins. Fund*, 636 F.3d 538, 543 (9th Cir. 2011), a panel ruling on an issue of first impression in the 9th Circuit said that "[i]n *Shaw*, the Supreme Court predicted its jurisdictional holding on the fact that a state official was the defendant," and went on to hold that *Shaw* does not support declaratory judgment cases against private entities on preemption grounds. In *Independent Training and Apprenticeship Program v. California*

––––––––––

[23] Cf. nn. 19 and 20, supra. Alleged patent infringers, for example, have a clear interest in swift resolution of the federal issue of patent validity—they are liable for damages if it turns out they are infringing a patent, and they frequently have a delicate network of contractual arrangements with third parties that is dependent on their right to sell or license a product. Parties subject to conflicting state and federal regulatory schemes also have a clear interest in sorting out the scope of each government's authority, especially where they face a threat of liability if the application of federal law is not quickly made clear.

Department of Industrial Relations, 730 F.3d 1024, 1031–32 (9th Cir. 2013), a 9th Circuit panel applied *Shaw* to uphold federal jurisdiction over a preemption claim brought against state officials.

G. SUPPLEMENTAL JURISDICTION

A dispute may give rise to more than one claim for relief. One cause of action may arise under federal law, while another is based wholly on state law. In what circumstances may a federal court with jurisdiction over the federal claim also assert jurisdiction over the state cause of action?

UNITED MINE WORKERS V. GIBBS
383 U.S. 715 (1966).

JUSTICE BRENNAN delivered the opinion of the Court.

Respondent Paul Gibbs was awarded compensatory and punitive damages in this action against petitioner United Mine Workers of America (UMW) for alleged violations of § 303 of the Labor Management Relations Act and of the common law of Tennessee. The case grew out of the rivalry between the United Mine Workers and the Southern Labor Union over representation of workers in the southern Appalachian coal fields. Tennessee Consolidated Coal Company, not a party here, laid off 100 miners of the UMW's Local 5881 when it closed one of its mines in southern Tennessee during the spring of 1960. Late that summer, Grundy Company, a wholly owned subsidiary of Consolidated, hired respondent as mine superintendent to attempt to open a new mine on Consolidated's property [through] use of members of the Southern Labor Union. As part of the arrangement, Grundy also gave respondent a contract to haul the mine's coal to the nearest railroad loading point.

On August 15 and 16, 1960, armed members of Local 5881 forcibly prevented the opening of the mine, threatening respondent and beating an organizer for the rival union. [After this incident, the UMW international union stepped in.] There was no further violence at the mine site; a picket line was maintained there for nine months; and no further attempts were made to open the mine during that period.

[Gibbs] lost his job as superintendent, and never entered into performance of his haulage contract. He testified that he soon began to lose other trucking contracts and mine leases he held in nearby areas. Claiming these effects to be the result of a concerted union plan against him, he sought recovery not against Local 5881 or its members, but only against petitioner, the international union. The suit was brought in the United States District Court for the Eastern District of Tennessee, and jurisdiction was premised on allegations of secondary boycotts under § 303. The state law claim, for which jurisdiction was based upon the doctrine of pendent jurisdiction, asserted "an unlawful conspiracy and an unlawful boycott aimed at him and [Grundy] to maliciously, wantonly and willfully interfere with his contract of employment and with his contract of haulage."

The trial judge refused to submit to the jury the claims of pressure intended to cause mining firms other than Grundy to cease doing business with Gibbs; he found those claims unsupported by the evidence. The jury's verdict was that the UMW had violated both § 303 and state law. Gibbs was awarded $60,000 as damages under the employment contract and $14,500 under the haulage contract; he was also awarded $100,000 punitive damages. On motion, the trial court set aside the award of damages with respect to the haulage contract on the ground that damage was unproved. It also held that union pressure on Grundy to discharge respondent as supervisor would constitute only a primary dispute with Grundy, as respondent's employer, and hence was not cognizable as a claim under § 303. Interference with the employment relationship was cognizable as a state claim, however, and a remitted award was sustained on the state law claim. The Court of Appeals for the Sixth Circuit affirmed. We reverse. A threshold question is whether the District Court properly entertained jurisdiction of the claim based on Tennessee law. [The] Court held in *Hurn v. Oursler*, 289 U.S. 238, that state law claims are appropriate for federal court determination if they form a separate but parallel ground for relief also sought in a substantial claim based on federal law. The Court distinguished permissible from non-permissible exercises of federal judicial power over state law claims by contrasting "a case where two distinct grounds in support of a single cause of action are alleged, one only of which presents a federal question, and a case where two separate and distinct causes of action are alleged, one only of which is federal in character. In the former, where the federal question averred is not plainly wanting in substance, the federal court, even though the federal ground be not established, may nevertheless retain and dispose of the case upon the nonfederal *ground*; in the latter it may not do so upon the nonfederal *cause of action*." The question is into which category the present action fell.

Hurn was decided in 1933, before the unification of law and equity by the Federal Rules of Civil Procedure. At the time, the meaning of "cause of action" was a subject of serious dispute. [The] Court in *Hurn* identified what it meant by the term by citation of *Baltimore S.S. Co. v. Phillips*, 274 U.S. 316, a case in which "cause of action" had been used to identify the operative scope of the doctrine of *res judicata*. In that case the Court had noted that "the whole tendency of our decisions is to require a plaintiff to try his whole cause of action and his whole case at one time," 274 U.S., at 320. [Had] the Court found a jurisdictional bar to reaching the state claim in *Hurn*, we assume that the doctrine of *res judicata* would not have been applicable in any subsequent state suit. But the citation of *Baltimore S.S. Co.* shows that the Court found that the weighty policies of judicial economy and fairness to parties reflected in *res judicata* doctrine were in themselves strong counsel for the adoption of a rule which would permit federal courts to dispose of the state as well as the federal claims.

With the adoption of the Federal Rules of Civil Procedure and the unified form of action, Fed.Rule Civ.Proc. 2, much of the controversy over "cause of action" abated. The phrase remained as the keystone of the *Hurn* test, however, and, as commentators have noted, has been the source of considerable confusion. Under the Rules, the impulse is toward entertaining the broadest possible scope of action consistent with fairness to the parties; joinder of claims, parties and remedies is strongly encouraged. Yet because the *Hurn* question involves issues of jurisdiction as well as convenience, there has been some tendency to limit its application to cases in which the state and federal claims are, as in *Hurn*, "little more than the equivalent of different epithets to characterize the same group of circumstances." 289 U.S., at 246.

This limited approach is unnecessarily grudging. Pendent jurisdiction, in the sense of judicial power, exists whenever there is a claim "arising under (the) Constitution, the Laws of the United States, and Treaties made, or which shall be made, under their Authority * * *," U.S. Const., Art. III, § 2, and the relationship between that claim and the state claim permits the conclusion that the entire action before the court comprises but one constitutional "case." The federal claim must have substance sufficient to confer subject matter jurisdiction on the court. *Levering & Garrigues Co. v. Morrin*, 289 U.S. 103. The state and federal claims must derive from a common nucleus of operative fact. But if, considered without regard to their federal or state character, a plaintiff's claims are such that he would ordinarily be expected to try them all in one judicial proceeding, then, assuming substantiality of the federal issues, there is power in federal courts to hear the whole.

That power need not be exercised in every case in which it is found to exist. It has consistently been recognized that pendent jurisdiction is a doctrine of discretion, not of plaintiff's right. Its justification lies in considerations of judicial economy, convenience and fairness to litigants; if these are not present a federal court should hesitate to exercise jurisdiction over state claims, even though [under *Erie*] bound to apply state law to them. Needless decisions of state law should be avoided both as a matter of comity and to promote justice between the parties, by procuring for them a surer-footed reading of applicable law. Certainly, if the federal claims are dismissed before trial, even though not insubstantial in a jurisdictional sense, the state claims should be dismissed as well. Similarly, if it appears that the state issues

substantially predominate, whether in terms of proof, of the scope of the
issues raised, or of the comprehensiveness of the remedy sought, the state
claims may be dismissed without prejudice and left for resolution to state
tribunals. There may, on the other hand, be situations in which the state
claim is so closely tied to questions of federal policy that the argument for
exercise of pendent jurisdiction is particularly strong. In the present case,
for example, the allowable scope of the state claim implicates the federal
doctrine of pre-emption; while this interrelationship does not create
statutory federal question jurisdiction, *Louisville & N.R. Co. v. Mottley*,
its existence is relevant to the exercise of discretion. Finally, there may be
reasons independent of jurisdictional considerations, such as the
likelihood of jury confusion in treating divergent legal theories of relief,
that would justify separating state and federal claims for trial, Fed. Rule
Civ. Proc. 42(b). If so, jurisdiction should ordinarily be refused.

The question of power will ordinarily be resolved on the pleadings.
But the issue whether pendent jurisdiction has been properly assumed is
one which remains open throughout the litigation. Pretrial procedures or
even the trial itself may reveal a substantial hegemony of state law
claims, or likelihood of jury confusion, which could not have been
anticipated at the pleading stage. Although it will of course be
appropriate to take account in this circumstance of the already completed
course of the litigation, dismissal of the state claim might even then be
merited. For example, it may appear that the plaintiff was well aware of
the nature of his proofs and the relative importance of his claims;
recognition of a federal court's wide latitude to decide ancillary questions
of state law does not imply that it must tolerate a litigant's effort to
impose upon it what is in effect only a state law case. Once it appears
that a state claim constitutes the real body of a case, to which the federal
claim is only an appendage, the state claim may fairly be dismissed.

We are not prepared to say that in the present case the District Court
exceeded its discretion in proceeding to judgment on the state claim. We
may assume for purposes of decision that the District Court was correct
in its holding that the claim of pressure on Grundy to terminate the
employment contract was outside the purview of § 303. Even so, the § 303
claims based on secondary pressures on Grundy relative to the haulage
contract and on other coal operators generally were substantial. Although
§ 303 limited recovery to compensatory damages based on secondary
pressures, and state law allowed both compensatory and punitive
damages, and allowed such damages as to both secondary and primary
activity, the state and federal claims arose from the same nucleus of
operative fact and reflected alternative remedies. Indeed, the verdict
sheet sent in to the jury authorized only one award of damages, so that
recovery could not be given separately on the federal and state claims.

It is true that the § 303 claims ultimately failed and that the only recovery allowed respondent was on the state claim. We cannot confidently say, however, that the federal issues were so remote or played such a minor role at the trial that in effect the state claim only was tried. Although the District Court dismissed as unproved the § 303 claims that petitioner's secondary activities included attempts to induce coal operators other than Grundy to cease doing business with respondent, the court submitted the § 303 claims relating to Grundy to the jury. The jury returned verdicts against petitioner on those § 303 claims, and it was only on petitioner's motion for a directed verdict and a judgment *n.o.v.* that the verdicts on those claims were set aside. The District Judge considered the claim as to the haulage contract proved as to liability, and held it failed only for lack of proof of damages. Although there was some risk of confusing the jury in joining the state and federal claims—especially since [differing] standards of proof of UMW involvement applied—the possibility of confusion could be lessened by employing a special verdict form, as the District Court did. Moreover, the question whether the permissible scope of the state claim was limited by the doctrine of pre-emption afforded a special reason for the exercise of pendent jurisdiction; the federal courts are particularly appropriate bodies for the application of pre-emption principles. We thus conclude that although it may be that the District Court might, in its sound discretion, have dismissed the state claim, the circumstances show no error in refusing to do so.

[The Court reversed on the merits.]

NOTES ON SUPPLEMENTAL JURISDICTION

1. **Supplemental Jurisdiction: Codifying *Gibbs*.** In *Finley v. United States*, 490 U.S. 545 (1989), the broad issue was whether the *Gibbs* principle should extend to "pendent parties." The plaintiff, having obtained federal jurisdiction over a federal tort claim against the United States, sought to sue a private defendant under state tort law for a claim arising out of the same incident. To the dismay of many, the Court rejected pendent party jurisdiction. Congress responded by overturning *Finley* and codifying the doctrine of pendent jurisdiction, (along with "ancillary" jurisdiction, as the diversity jurisdiction analogue was called) using the term "supplemental jurisdiction" as an umbrella to cover both pendent and ancillary jurisdiction. We are concerned here with the codification of pendent jurisdiction.

The statute, 28 U.S.C. § 1367(a), provides that, with certain exceptions,

[I]n any civil action of which the district courts have original jurisdiction, the district courts shall have supplemental jurisdiction over all other claims that are so related to claims in the action within such original jurisdiction that they form part of the same case or controversy under Article III. [Such] supplemental jurisdiction shall include claims that involve the joinder or intervention of additional parties.

In *City of Chicago v. International College of Surgeons*, 522 U.S. 156, 165 (1997), the Court said that Congress by this language "codified" the *Gibbs* test for deciding whether a federal court may exercise pendent jurisdiction, i.e., that the federal and state claims must "derive from a common nucleus of operative fact."

2. Factors Bearing on Discretion to Decline Supplemental Jurisdiction. Another section of the statute borrows some of the *Gibbs* factors bearing on the federal court's exercise of discretion:

(c) The district courts may decline to exercise supplemental jurisdiction over a claim under subsection (a) if—

(1) the claim raises a novel or complex issue of State law,

(2) the claim substantially predominates over the claim or claims over which the district court has original jurisdiction,

(3) the district court has dismissed all claims over which it has original jurisdiction, or

(4) in exceptional circumstances, there are other compelling reasons for declining jurisdiction.

Though the fairness and efficiency concerns mentioned in *Gibbs* are not specified in § c, the Court in *International College of Surgeons* read this section as a codification of the whole range of *Gibbs* factors bearing on the exercise of discretion. See 522 U.S. at 172–73. A district court's failure to give due attention to the factors listed in § c can result in having its judgment vacated for "abuse of discretion". See, e.g., *Carver v. Nassau County Interim Finance Authority*, 730 F.3d 150, 156 (2nd Cir. 2013) ("the district judge should have declined to reach the pendent state law claim, which required it to interpret, as matter of first impression, an important state legislative scheme").

3. Supplemental Jurisdiction and Lack of Standing. Article III limits the federal courts to the adjudication of "cases" and "controversies." *Gibbs* and § 1367 authorize supplemental jurisdiction over cases and controversies that otherwise (e.g., for lack of a federal question) would not support federal jurisdiction.

Should the supplemental jurisdiction doctrine apply to claims that do not satisfy Article III requirements? That issue was raised in *DaimlerChrysler Corp. v. Cuno*, 547 U.S. 332 (2006). The plaintiffs were Toledo, Ohio taxpayers who sought to sue the state and city governments on account of tax breaks given to DaimlerChrysler. On account of Article III, federal courts decline to hear claims brought by persons who have not suffered "injury," a term of art we elaborate in Chapter 4. These putative litigants lack "standing" to sue, and their claims are not Article III "cases" that may be adjudicated in federal court. In particular, people who complain about the state or national government's fiscal affairs and seek to sue as taxpayers, are ordinarily turned away from federal court on the ground that they have not been injured. Municipal taxpayers often have more success.

In *DaimlerChrysler* the Court first held that the taxpayers lacked standing as state taxpayers to challenge the state tax laws. The Court assumed, however, that the plaintiffs had standing to bring the case against the city. The taxpayers argued that their standing as *municipal* taxpayers sufficed for pendent jurisdiction over their challenge to the *state* tax advantages they sought to challenge. The Court rejected the argument, declaring that it had never applied "the rationale of *Gibbs* to permit a federal court to exercise supplemental jurisdiction over a claim that does not itself satisfy those elements of the Article III inquiry, such as constitutional standing, that serve to identify those disputes which are appropriately resolved through the judicial process." (citation and internal quotation marks removed).

4. **Supplemental Jurisdiction and § 1983 Litigation.** As a practical matter, supplemental jurisdiction is most useful to litigants in areas where a given event is regulated by both state and federal law. Note, for example, that many of the encounters between state officers and citizens that give rise to § 1983 suits can also produce state law tort claims. Here are two (out of many) examples:

a. In *Draper v. Reynolds*, 369 F.3d 1270 (11th Cir. 2004), a deputy sheriff used a taser to subdue an unruly motorist in the course of a routine traffic stop. The motorist sued, charging [a] that the use of the taser constituted excessive force in violation of the Fourth Amendment; and [b] that the officer was liable under state tort law. The 11th Circuit found no merit in the constitutional claim and remanded the state tort claim to state court.

b. In *Woodward v. Correctional Medical Services*, 368 F.3d 917 (7th Cir. 2004), the suit was by the estate of a pretrial detainee who had committed suicide in a county jail. The estate sued the medical provider on federal due process grounds, and under a state wrongful death statute. The 7th Circuit affirmed a jury verdict in the plaintiff's favor.

II.   DIVERSITY JURISDICTION

Besides cases arising under federal law, Article III authorizes Congress to grant the federal district courts jurisdiction based on the citizenship of the parties, including controversies "between a State and citizens of another State, between citizens of different States, [and] between a State, or the citizens thereof, and foreign States, Citizens, or Subjects." Next to federal question jurisdiction, diversity of citizenship is by far the most important avenue for gaining access to federal court. Scholars argue over the historical background of diversity jurisdiction, with some claiming that the aim was to shield out-of-state litigants from parochial state courts, while others maintain that the concern was with state legislatures that were biased against out-of-state creditors. Some modern law reformers would curtail diversity jurisdiction, on the ground that, aside from its role in resolving complex multi-state problems, it is anachronistic. They believe the federal judicial system's scarce resources would be better spent on federal question cases. Defenders of diversity jurisdiction respond that there remains a need for access to federal court for litigation that in one way or another crosses state lines. While judicial attitudes toward diversity jurisdiction may influence the way judges resolve a close case regarding its scope, most of the debate is directed at Congress, where efforts are periodically made to limit diversity.

Ordinarily the substantive issues in diversity cases are state law questions, though federal courts follow the federal rules of civil procedure. Problems arise concerning whether federal or state law should control particular procedural issues that may significantly affect the outcome. These issues are typically addressed in courses on civil procedure and are not covered here.

Our concern is with the rules governing access to federal court by way of diversity of citizenship. The main statutory provision is 28 U.S.C. § 1332, which provides for district court jurisdiction over a broad range of diversity cases. One difference between diversity and the current law on federal question jurisdiction is that § 1332 imposes a "jurisdictional amount" requirement, restricting federal jurisdiction to cases where the matter in controversy exceeds the sum of $75,000.

Besides the jurisdictional amount requirement, there is another general rule. Ever since *Strawbridge v. Curtiss*, 7 U.S. (3 Cranch) 267 (1806), the Court has, for most purposes, required "complete" diversity. That is, federal jurisdiction will be defeated if *any* plaintiff shares citizenship with *any* defendant. *Strawbridge*, however, is not a constitutional requirement. It is an interpretation of the statute. See *State Farm Fire & Casualty Co. v. Tashire*, 386 U.S. 523 (1967). Neither the complete diversity rule nor the jurisdictional amount requirement are absolute obstacles to diversity jurisdiction in all circumstances. In particular, under the doctrine of "ancillary" jurisdiction the federal courts have adjudicated matters that would otherwise be barred by these requirements. In 1990, ancillary jurisdiction was codified in 28 U.S.C. § 1367 (along with pendent jurisdiction, see Part I, Section G). That feature of diversity jurisdiction is discussed in Section C below.

A. DETERMINING CITIZENSHIP: NATURAL PERSONS, CORPORATIONS, AND UNINCORPORATED ASSOCIATIONS

1. Natural Persons

For the purpose of diversity jurisdiction, a natural person is a citizen of the state in which he is domiciled at the time the complaint is filed. The following case illustrates one of the issues that may arise in applying this rule.

GREGG V. LOUISIANA POWER & LIGHT CO.

626 F.2d 1315 (5th Cir. 1980).

Before CHARLES CLARK, TJOFLAT and GARZA, CIRCUIT JUDGES.

GARZA, CIRCUIT JUDGE:

The question before us on this appeal is whether, for purposes of diversity jurisdiction, a United States citizen, born to migratory parents, acquires the citizenship of the State of his birth and, if so, whether he loses that State citizenship without acquiring a new citizenship or domicile. This case arises from the personal injuries sustained by plaintiff-appellant, Thomas Gregg, Jr., caused by contact with a high voltage electrical transmission line maintained by defendant-appellee, Louisiana Power & Electric (LP & L). Federal jurisdiction was alleged on grounds of diversity of citizenship under 28 U.S.C. § 1332.

It is undisputed that LP & L is a citizen of Louisiana for diversity purposes. It is also undisputed that Gregg is not a citizen of Louisiana. Instead, LP & L argued in its motion to dismiss and now on appeal that, because Gregg's parents were migratory workers at the time of his birth, Gregg acquired no domicile or citizenship by birth. LP & L also argues that, because Gregg has migrated from State to State, he has never acquired a domicile by choice and, therefore, Gregg is not a citizen of any State and, because of that fact, he cannot affirmatively establish diverse citizenship.

The record shows that Gregg was born in Kentucky but, in early childhood, moved to various States with his parents. At that time, Gregg's father was a painter, whose job required him to travel from one location to the next in pursuit of employment. At one time, the Greggs moved to Michigan, where they had close family and friends, and where Gregg, Jr. attended some school and developed many personal attachments. By helping his father, Gregg learned the painting profession and, as a young adult, he began traveling from place to place in search of painter's work.

The uncontroverted affidavits of Gregg and his father, filed in response to LP & L's motion to dismiss, refer to Michigan as being their "real home." On the other hand, Gregg's father's affidavit also states that his home was Louisville, Kentucky, at the time Gregg, Jr. was born and that he, Gregg, Sr., intended to remain in Kentucky with no fixed intention to leave at that time. Gregg argues that with these facts, the District Court should have considered him a citizen of Kentucky, but if there was any question due to his subsequent travel, he should have been considered a citizen of Michigan.

In granting LP & L's motion to dismiss, the District Court found that Gregg had failed to prove that his father was domiciled in Kentucky at the time of his birth and, therefore, Gregg had failed to establish Kentucky as his domicile of birth. The District Court also found that, although Gregg may have had an intention of being domiciled in Michigan by choice, he had failed to establish the concurrent residence requirement of domicile. In effect, the District Court held that Gregg was a Stateless citizen for diversity purposes.

Gregg asks us to adopt and enlarge the rule set forth in *Kaiser v. Loomis*, 391 F.2d 1007 (6th Cir. 1968), wherein it was held that an American citizen, born in one of the States of the United States to parents who were citizens of that State, cannot lose that citizenship which he acquired at birth, without first adopting a new domicile. Gregg also asks that this rule be enlarged, so as not to penalize him because of the migratory life-style of his parents at the time of his birth. In other words, he asks that he be considered a State citizen of his birth place, even though his parents might not be considered citizens of that State.

The basic principle underlying the *Kaiser* rule is currently applied by virtually all States in their conflicts rules and domestic relations law. A person is almost universally considered to be a domiciliary of the State of his birth, unless and until a new domicile is acquired. As applied in diversity cases, the rule would create a presumption of domicile by birth in the absence of a contrary averment. The policy and purpose of the presumption is to protect an individual from an unintended loss of State citizenship. If extended and applied in a diversity case, it would also serve to prevent the automatic exclusion of a large segment of our society the migrant worker from a neutral federal forum.

We adopt the *Kaiser* rule, and we extend the rule to hold that the presumption of domicile by birth shall include children of those parents who might not easily be defined as "citizens" of the State in which their children are born. A more restrictive presumption would open the federal diversity forum for those whose parents were fortunate enough to have a fixed home, and yet would deny that forum to those citizens whose parents' financial status required them to travel in search of employment this latter group being the very citizens for whom the neutral federal forum is designed to protect.

The burden of proving diversity when challenged is upon the plaintiff, however, with application of a presumption of domicile by birth (a presumption established in this case by affidavits), the burden of proving non-diversity shifts to the defendant. LP & L will have the chance to meet this burden on remand.

2. Corporations

The diversity statute, § 1332(c)(1) provides that, except for liability insurance companies, "a corporation shall be deemed to be a citizen of any State by which it has been incorporated and of the State where it has its principal place of business." In applying this test, the recurring issue is where a corporation has is principal place of business. Congress evidently intended, and in any event courts have taken the statutory language to mean, that for the purpose of diversity jurisdiction a corporation has *one* principal place of business. For many years, the Supreme Court left the "principal place of business" question to the circuit courts. Those courts came up with a variety of answers to the question of how to identify that place, including "the place where the corporation's home office was located," "the place where day-to-day control of the business is exercised," and "the place where the corporation carried on the bulk of its activity." Charles Alan Wright & Mary Kay Kane, Law of Federal Courts 169 (7th ed. 2011) (footnotes omitted).

In *Hertz Corp. v. Friend*, the Supreme Court finally addressed the "principal place of business" issue.

HERTZ CORP. V. FRIEND
559 U.S. 77 (2010).

JUSTICE BREYER delivered the opinion of the Court.

The federal diversity jurisdiction statute provides that a corporation shall be deemed to be a citizen of any State by which it has been incorporated *and of the State where it has its principal place of business.* 28 U.S.C. § 1332(c)(1) (emphasis added). We seek here to resolve different interpretations that the Circuits have given this phrase. In doing so, we place primary weight upon the need for judicial administration of a jurisdictional statute to remain as simple as possible. And we conclude that the phrase "principal place of business" refers to the place where the corporation's high level officers direct, control, and coordinate the corporation's activities. Lower federal courts have often metaphorically called that place the corporation's "nerve center." We believe that the "nerve center" will typically be found at a corporation's headquarters.

I

In September 2007, respondents Melinda Friend and John Nhieu, two California citizens, sued petitioner, the Hertz Corporation, in a

California state court. They sought damages for what they claimed were violations of California's wage and hour laws. And they requested relief on behalf of a potential class composed of California citizens who had allegedly suffered similar harms.

Hertz filed a notice seeking removal to a federal court. 28 U.S.C. §§ 1332(d)(2), 1441(a). Hertz claimed that the plaintiffs and the defendant were citizens of different States. §§ 1332(a)(1), (c)(1). Hence, the federal court possessed diversity-of-citizenship jurisdiction. Friend and Nhieu, however, claimed that the Hertz Corporation was a California citizen, like themselves, and that, hence, diversity jurisdiction was lacking.

To support its position, Hertz submitted a declaration by an employee relations manager that sought to show that Hertz's "principal place of business" was in New Jersey, not in California. The declaration stated, among other things, that Hertz operated facilities in 44 States; and that California-which had about 12% of the Nation's population-accounted for 273 of Hertz's 1,606 car rental locations; about 2,300 of its 11,230 full-time employees; about $811 million of its $4.371 billion in annual revenue; and about 3.8 million of its approximately 21 million annual transactions, *i.e.*, rentals. The declaration also stated that the "leadership of Hertz and its domestic subsidiaries" is located at Hertz's "corporate headquarters" in Park Ridge, New Jersey; that its "core executive and administrative functions . . . are carried out" there and "to a lesser extent" in Oklahoma City, Oklahoma; and that its "major administrative operations . . . are found" at those two locations.

The District Court of the Northern District of California accepted Hertz's statement of the facts as undisputed. But it concluded that, given those facts, Hertz was a citizen of California. In reaching this conclusion, the court applied Ninth Circuit precedent, which instructs courts to identify a corporation's "principal place of business" by first determining the amount of a corporation's business activity State by State. If the amount of activity is "significantly larger" or "substantially predominates" in one State, then that State is the corporation's "principal place of business." If there is no such State, then the "principal place of business" is the corporation's " 'nerve center,' " *i.e.*, the place where " 'the majority of its executive and administrative functions are performed.' "

Applying this test, the District Court found that the "plurality of each of the relevant business activities" was in California, and that "the differential between the amount of those activities" in California and the amount in "the next closest state" was "significant." Hence, Hertz's "principal place of business" was California, and diversity jurisdiction was thus lacking. The District Court consequently remanded the case to the state courts.

Hertz appealed the District Court's remand order. The Ninth Circuit affirmed in a brief memorandum opinion. Hertz filed a petition for certiorari. And, in light of differences among the Circuits in the application of the test for corporate citizenship, we granted the writ. Compare *Tosco Corp., supra,* at 500–502, and *Capitol Indemnity Corp. v. Russellville Steel Co.,* 367 F.3d 831, 836 (C.A.8 2004) (applying "total activity" test and looking at "all corporate activities"), with *Wisconsin Knife Works, supra,* at 1282 (applying "nerve center" test).

II

[In this section of the opinion, the Court disposed of an objection to its jurisdiction to review the case.]

III

We begin our "principal place of business" discussion with a brief review of relevant history. The Constitution provides that the "judicial Power shall extend" to "Controversies . . . between Citizens of different States." Art. III, § 2. This language, however, does not automatically confer diversity jurisdiction upon the federal courts. Rather, it authorizes Congress to do so and, in doing so, to determine the scope of the federal courts' jurisdiction within constitutional limits

Congress first authorized federal courts to exercise diversity jurisdiction in 1789 when, in the First Judiciary Act, Congress granted federal courts authority to hear suits "between a citizen of the State where the suit is brought, and a citizen of another State." § 11, 1 Stat. 78. The statute said nothing about corporations. In 1809, Chief Justice Marshall, writing for a unanimous Court, described a corporation as an "invisible, intangible, and artificial being" which was "certainly not a citizen." *Bank of United States v. Deveaux,* 5 Cranch 61, 86, 3 L.Ed. 38 (1809). But the Court held that a corporation could invoke the federal courts' diversity jurisdiction based on a pleading that the corporation's shareholders were all citizens of a different State from the defendants, as "the term citizen ought to be understood as it is used in the constitution, and as it is used in other laws. That is, to describe the real persons who come into court, in this case, under their corporate name."

In *Louisville, C. & C.R. Co. v. Letson,* 2 How. 497, 11 L.Ed. 353 (1844), the Court modified this initial approach. It held that a corporation was to be deemed an artificial person of the State by which it had been created, and its citizenship for jurisdictional purposes determined accordingly. Ten years later, the Court in *Marshall v. Baltimore & Ohio R. Co.,* 16 How. 314, 14 L.Ed. 953 (1854), held that the reason a corporation was a citizen of its State of incorporation was that, for the limited purpose of determining corporate citizenship, courts could conclusively (and artificially) presume that a corporation's *shareholders* were citizens of the State of incorporation. And it reaffirmed *Letson.* 16

How., at 325–326, 14 L.Ed. 953. Whatever the rationale, the practical upshot was that, for diversity purposes, the federal courts considered a corporation to be a citizen of the State of its incorporation. 13F C. Wright, A. Miller, & E. Cooper, Federal Practice and Procedure § 3623, pp. 1–7 (3d ed. 2009) (hereinafter Wright & Miller).

In 1928 this Court made clear that the "state of incorporation" rule was virtually absolute. It held that a corporation closely identified with State A could proceed in a federal court located in that State as long as the corporation had filed its incorporation papers in State B, perhaps a State where the corporation did no business at all. See *Black and White Taxicab & Transfer Co. v. Brown and Yellow Taxicab & Transfer Co.*, 276 U.S. 518, 522–525, 48 S.Ct. 404, 72 L.Ed. 681 (refusing to question corporation's reincorporation motives and finding diversity jurisdiction). Subsequently, many in Congress and those who testified before it pointed out that this interpretation was at odds with diversity jurisdiction's basic rationale, namely, opening the federal courts' doors to those who might otherwise suffer from local prejudice against out-of-state parties. Through its choice of the State of incorporation, a corporation could manipulate federal-court jurisdiction, for example, opening the federal courts' doors in a State where it conducted nearly all its business by filing incorporation papers [elsewhere.] Although various legislative proposals to curtail the corporate use of diversity jurisdiction were made, see, *e.g.,* S. 937, S. 939, H.R. 11508, 72d Cong., 1st Sess. (1932), none of these proposals were enacted into law.

At the same time as federal dockets increased in size, many judges began to believe those dockets contained too many diversity cases. A committee of the Judicial Conference of the United States studied the matter. And on March 12, 1951, that committee, the Committee on Jurisdiction and Venue, issued a report.

Among its observations, the committee found a general need "to prevent frauds and abuses" with respect to jurisdiction. The committee recommended against eliminating diversity cases altogether. Instead it recommended, along with other proposals, a statutory amendment that would make a corporation a citizen both of the State of its incorporation and any State from which it received more than half of its gross income. If, for example, a citizen of California sued (under state law in state court) a corporation that received half or more of its gross income from California, that corporation would not be able to remove the case to federal court, even if Delaware was its State of incorporation.

During the spring and summer of 1951 committee members circulated their report and attended circuit conferences at which federal judges discussed the report's recommendations. Reflecting those criticisms, the committee filed a new report in September, in which it revised its corporate citizenship recommendation. It now proposed that " 'a corporation shall be deemed a citizen of the state of its original creation . . . [and] shall also be deemed a citizen of a state where it has its principal place of business.' " Judicial Conference of the United States, Report of the Committee on Jurisdiction and Venue 4 (Sept. 24, 1951) (hereinafter Sept. Committee Rept.)—the source of the present-day statutory language. The committee wrote that this new language would provide a "simpler and more practical formula" than the "gross income" test. It added that the language "ha[d] a precedent in the jurisdictional provisions of the Bankruptcy Act."

In mid-1957 the committee presented its reports to the House of Representatives Committee on the Judiciary. Judge Albert Maris, representing Judge John Parker (who had chaired the Judicial Conference Committee), discussed various proposals that the Judicial Conference had made to restrict the scope of diversity jurisdiction. In respect to the "principal place of business" proposal, he said that the relevant language "ha[d] been defined in the Bankruptcy Act." He added:

> "All of those problems have arisen in bankruptcy cases, and as I recall the cases-and I wouldn't want to be bound by this statement because I haven't them before me—I think the courts have generally taken the view that where a corporation's interests are rather widespread, the principal place of business is an actual rather than a theoretical or legal one. It is the actual place where its business operations are coordinated, directed, and carried out, which would ordinarily be the place where its officers carry on its day-to-day business, where its accounts are kept, where its payments are made, and not necessarily a State in which it may have a plant, if it is a big corporation, or something of that sort."

> "But that has been pretty well worked out in the bankruptcy cases, and that law would all be available, you see, to be applied here without having to go over it again from the beginning."

The House Committee reprinted the Judicial Conference Committee Reports along with other reports and relevant testimony and circulated it to the general public "for the purpose of inviting further suggestions and comments." Subsequently, in 1958, Congress both codified the courts' traditional place of incorporation test and also enacted into law a slightly modified version of the Conference Committee's proposed "principal place of business" language. A corporation was to "be deemed a citizen of any State by which it has been incorporated and of the State where it has its principal place of business." § 2, 72 Stat. 415.

IV

The phrase "principal place of business" has proved more difficult to apply than its originators likely expected. Decisions under the Bankruptcy Act did not provide the firm guidance for which Judge Maris had hoped because courts interpreting bankruptcy law did not agree about how to determine a corporation's "principal place of business." Compare *Burdick v. Dillon,* 144 F. 737, 738 (C.A.1 1906) (holding that a corporation's "principal office, rather than a factory, mill, or mine . . . constitutes the 'principal place of business'"), with *Continental Coal Corp. v. Roszelle Bros.,* 242 F. 243, 247 (C.A.6 1917) (identifying the "principal place of business" as the location of mining activities, rather than the "principal office"); see also Friedenthal, New Limitations on Federal Jurisdiction, 11 Stan. L.Rev. 213, 223 (1959) ("The cases under the Bankruptcy Act provide no rigid legal formula for the determination of the principal place of business").

After Congress' amendment, courts were similarly uncertain as to where to look to determine a corporation's "principal place of business" for diversity purposes. If a corporation's headquarters and executive offices were in the same State in which it did most of its business, the test seemed straightforward. The "principal place of business" was located in that State.

But suppose those corporate headquarters, including executive offices, are in one State, while the corporation's plants or other centers of business activity are located in other States? In 1959 a distinguished federal district judge, Edward Weinfeld, relied on the Second Circuit's interpretation of the Bankruptcy Act to answer this question in part:

> "Where a corporation is engaged in far-flung and varied activities which are carried on in different states, its principal place of business is the nerve center from which it radiates out to its constituent parts and from which its officers direct, control and coordinate all activities without regard to locale, in the furtherance of the corporate objective. The test applied by our Court of Appeals, is that place where the corporation has an 'office from which its business was directed and controlled'-the place where 'all of its business was under the supreme direction and control of its officers.'" *Scot Typewriter Co.,* 170 F.Supp., at 865.

Numerous Circuits have since followed this rule, applying the "nerve center" test for corporations with "far-flung" business activities.

Scot's analysis, however, did not go far enough. For it did not answer what courts should do when the operations of the corporation are not "far-flung" but rather limited to only a few States. When faced with this question, various courts have focused more heavily on where a corporation's actual business activities are located.

Perhaps because corporations come in many different forms, involve many different kinds of business activities, and locate offices and plants for different reasons in different ways in different regions, a general "business activities" approach has proved unusually difficult to apply. Courts must decide which factors are more important than others: for example, plant location, sales or servicing centers; transactions, payrolls, or revenue generation. See, *e.g., R.G. Barry Corp., supra,* at 656–657 (place of sales and advertisement, office, and full-time employees); *Diaz-Rodriguez, supra,* at 61–62 (place of stores and inventory, employees, income, and sales).

The number of factors grew as courts explicitly combined aspects of the "nerve center" and "business activity" tests to look to a corporation's "total activities," sometimes to try to determine what treatises have described as the corporation's "center of gravity." A major treatise confirms this growing complexity, listing Circuit by Circuit, cases that highlight different factors or emphasize similar factors differently, and reporting that the "federal courts of appeals have employed various tests"-tests which "tend to overlap" and which are sometimes described in "language" that "is imprecise." 15 Moore's § 102.54[2], at 102–112. See also *id.,* §§ 102.54[2], [13], at 102–112 to 102–122 (describing, in 14 pages, major tests as looking to the "nerve center," "locus of operations," or "center of corporate activities"). Not surprisingly, different circuits (and sometimes different courts within a single circuit) have applied these highly general multifactor tests in different ways. *Id.,* §§ 102.54[3]–[7], [11]–[13] (noting that the First Circuit "has never explained a basis for choosing between 'the center of corporate activity' test and the 'locus of operations' test"; the Second Circuit uses a "two-part test" similar to that of the Fifth, Ninth, and Eleventh Circuits involving an initial determination as to whether "a corporation's activities are centralized or decentralized" followed by an application of either the "place of operations" or "nerve center" test; the Third Circuit applies the "center of corporate activities" test searching for the "headquarters of a corporation's day-to-day activity"; the Fourth Circuit has "endorsed neither [the 'nerve center' or 'place of operations'] test to the exclusion of the other"; the Tenth Circuit directs consideration of the "total activity of the company considered as a whole"). See also 13F Wright & Miller § 3625 (describing, in 73 pages, the "nerve center," "corporate activities," and "total activity" tests as part of an effort to locate the corporation's "center of gravity," while specifying different ways in which different circuits apply these or other factors).

This complexity may reflect an unmediated judicial effort to apply the statutory phrase "principal place of business" in light of the general purpose of diversity jurisdiction, *i.e.,* an effort to find the State where a corporation is least likely to suffer out-of-state prejudice when it is sued in a local court, *Pease v. Peck,* 18 How. 595, 599, 15 L.Ed. 518 (1856). But, if so, that task seems doomed to failure. After all, the relevant purposive concern-prejudice against an out-of-state party-will often depend upon factors that courts cannot easily measure, for example, a corporation's image, its history, and its advertising, while the factors that courts can more easily measure, for example, its office or plant location, its sales, its employment, or the nature of the goods or services it supplies, will sometimes bear no more than a distant relation to the likelihood of prejudice. At the same time, this approach is at war with administrative simplicity. And it has failed to achieve a nationally uniform interpretation of federal law, an unfortunate consequence in a federal legal system.

V

A

In an effort to find a single, more uniform interpretation of the statutory phrase, we have reviewed the Courts of Appeals' divergent and increasingly complex interpretations. Having done so, we now return to, and expand, Judge Weinfeld's approach, as applied in the Seventh Circuit. See, *e.g., Scot Typewriter Co.,* 170 F.Supp., at 865; *Wisconsin Knife Works,* 781 F.2d, at 1282. We conclude that "principal place of business" is best read as referring to the place where a corporation's officers direct, control, and coordinate the corporation's activities. It is the place that Courts of Appeals have called the corporation's "nerve center." And in practice it should normally be the place where the corporation maintains its headquarters-provided that the headquarters is the actual center of direction, control, and coordination, *i.e.,* the "nerve center," and not simply an office where the corporation holds its board meetings (for example, attended by directors and officers who have traveled there for the occasion).

Three sets of considerations, taken together, convince us that this approach, while imperfect, is superior to other possibilities. First, the statute's language supports the approach. The statute's text deems a corporation a citizen of the "State where it has its principal place of business." 28 U.S.C. § 1332(c)(1). The word "place" is in the singular, not the plural. The word "principal" requires us to pick out the "main, prominent" or "pleading" place. 12 Oxford English Dictionary 495 (2d ed. 1989) (def.(A)(I)(2)). Cf. *Commissioner v. Soliman,* 506 U.S. 168, 174, 113 S.Ct. 701, 121 L.Ed.2d 634 (1993) (interpreting "principal place of business" for tax purposes to require an assessment of "whether any one business location is the 'most important, consequential, or influential' one"). And the fact that the word "place" follows the words "State where" means that the "place" is a place *within* a State. It is not the State itself.

A corporation's "nerve center," usually its main headquarters, is a single place. The public often (though not always) considers it the corporation's main place of business. And it is a place within a State. By contrast, the application of a more general business activities test has led some courts, as in the present case, to look, not at a particular place within a State, but incorrectly at the State itself, measuring the total amount of business activities that the corporation conducts there and determining whether they are "significantly larger" than in the next-ranking State.

This approach invites greater litigation and can lead to strange results, as the Ninth Circuit has since recognized. Namely, if a "corporation may be deemed a citizen of California on th[e] basis" of "activities [that] roughly reflect California's larger population . . . nearly every national retailer-no matter how far flung its operations-will be deemed a citizen of California for diversity purposes." *Davis v. HSBC Bank Nev., N. A.,* 557 F.3d 1026, 1029–1030 (2009). But why award or decline diversity jurisdiction on the basis of a State's population, whether measured directly, indirectly (say proportionately), or with modifications?

Second, administrative simplicity is a major virtue in a jurisdictional statute. *Sisson v. Ruby,* 497 U.S. 358, 375, 110 S.Ct. 2892, 111 L.Ed.2d 292 (1990) (SCALIA, J., concurring in judgment) (eschewing "the sort of vague boundary that is to be avoided in the area of subject-matter jurisdiction wherever possible"). Complex jurisdictional tests complicate a case, eating up time and money as the parties litigate, not the merits of their claims, but which court is the right court to decide those claims. Complex tests produce appeals and reversals, encourage gamesmanship, and, again, diminish the likelihood that results and settlements will reflect a claim's legal and factual merits. Judicial resources too are at stake. Courts have an independent obligation to determine whether subject-matter jurisdiction exists, even when no party challenges it. So courts benefit from straightforward rules under which they can readily assure themselves of their power to hear a case.

Simple jurisdictional rules also promote greater predictability. Predictability is valuable to corporations making business and investment decisions. Cf. *First Nat. City Bank v. Banco Para El Comercio Exterior de Cuba,* 462 U.S. 611, 621, 103 S.Ct. 2591, 77 L.Ed.2d 46 (1983) (recognizing the "need for certainty and predictability of result while generally protecting the justified expectations of parties with interests in the corporation"). Predictability also benefits plaintiffs deciding whether to file suit in a state or federal court.

A "nerve center" approach, which ordinarily equates that "center" with a corporation's headquarters, is simple to apply *comparatively speaking*. The metaphor of a corporate "brain," while not precise, suggests a single location. By contrast, a corporation's general business activities more often lack a single principal place where they take place. That is to say, the corporation may have several plants, many sales locations, and employees located in many different places. If so, it will not be as easy to determine which of these different business locales is the "principal" or most important "place."

Third, the statute's legislative history, for those who accept it, offers a simplicity-related interpretive benchmark. The Judicial Conference provided an initial version of its proposal that suggested a numerical test. A corporation would be deemed a citizen of the State that accounted for more than half of its gross income. The Conference changed its mind in light of criticism that such a test would prove too complex and impractical to apply. That history suggests that the words "principal place of business" should be interpreted to be no more complex than the initial "half of gross income" test. A "nerve center" test offers such a possibility. A general business activities test does not.

B

We recognize that there may be no perfect test that satisfies all administrative and purposive criteria. We recognize as well that, under the "nerve center" test we adopt today, there will be hard cases. For example, in this era of telecommuting, some corporations may divide their command and coordinating functions among officers who work at several different locations, perhaps communicating over the Internet. That said, our test nonetheless points courts in a single direction, towards the center of overall direction, control, and coordination. Courts do not have to try to weigh corporate functions, assets, or revenues different in kind, one from the other. Our approach provides a sensible test that is relatively easier to apply, not a test that will, in all instances, automatically generate a result.

We also recognize that the use of a "nerve center" test may in some cases produce results that seem to cut against the basic rationale for 28 U.S.C. § 1332. For example, if the bulk of a company's business activities visible to the public take place in New Jersey, while its top officers direct those activities just across the river in New York, the "principal place of business" is New York. One could argue that members of the public in New Jersey would be *less* likely to be prejudiced against the corporation than persons in New York-yet the corporation will still be entitled to remove a New Jersey state case to federal court. And note too that the same corporation would be unable to remove a New York state case to federal court, despite the New York public's presumed prejudice against the corporation.

We understand that such seeming anomalies will arise. However, in view of the necessity of having a clearer rule, we must accept them. Accepting occasionally counterintuitive results is the price the legal system must pay to avoid overly complex jurisdictional administration while producing the benefits that accompany a more uniform legal system.

The burden of persuasion for establishing diversity jurisdiction, of course, remains on the party asserting it. When challenged on allegations of jurisdictional facts, the parties must support their allegations by competent proof. And when faced with such a challenge, we reject suggestions such as, for example, the one made by petitioner that the mere filing of a form like the Securities and Exchange Commission's Form 10-K listing a corporation's "principal executive offices" would, without more, be sufficient proof to establish a corporation's "nerve center." [Such] possibilities would readily permit jurisdictional manipulation, thereby subverting a major reason for the insertion of the "principal place of business" language in the diversity statute. Indeed, if the record reveals attempts at manipulation-for example, that the alleged "nerve center" is nothing more than a mail drop box, a bare office with a computer, or the location of an annual executive retreat-the courts should instead take as the "nerve center" the place of actual direction, control, and coordination, in the absence of such manipulation.

VI

Petitioner's unchallenged declaration suggests that Hertz's center of direction, control, and coordination, its "nerve center," and its corporate headquarters are one and the same, and they are located in New Jersey, not in California. Because respondents should have a fair opportunity to litigate their case in light of our holding, however, we vacate the Ninth Circuit's judgment and remand the case for further proceedings consistent with this opinion.

NOTE ON CORPORATE CITIZENSHIP

Not every corporation falls within § 1332(c)(1). For example, there is a special rule for national banks, which are chartered by Congress and thus are not incorporated in any state. Under 28 U.S.C. § 1348 national banks "shall . . . be deemed citizens of the States in which they are respectively located." The issue in *Wachovia Bank v. Schmidt*, 546 U.S. 303 (2006) was the meaning of "located":

Does it signal, as [Wachovia] urges, that the bank's citizenship is determined by the place designated in the bank's articles of association as the location of its main office? Or does it mean, in addition, as respondents urge and the Court of Appeals held, that a national bank is a citizen of every State in which it maintains a branch?

A unanimous Court sided with Wachovia, explaining that, under the Court of Appeals' approach,

> [T]he access of a federally chartered bank to a federal forum would be drastically curtailed in comparison to the access afforded state banks and other state-incorporated entities. Congress, we are satisfied, created no such anomaly.

Justice Thomas's opinion acknowledged that the term "located" is sometimes defined differently, particularly in connection with venue. But he stressed that "located" is "a chameleon word; its meaning depends on the context in and purpose for which it is used."

3. Unincorporated Associations

UNITED STEELWORKERS V. R.H. BOULIGNY, INC.
382 U.S. 145 (1965).

JUSTICE FORTAS delivered the opinion of the Court.

Respondent, a North Carolina corporation, brought this action in a North Carolina state court. It sought $200,000 in damages for defamation alleged to have occurred during the course of the United Steelworkers' campaign to unionize respondent's employees. The Steelworkers, an unincorporated labor union whose principal place of business purportedly is Pennsylvania, removed the case to a Federal District Court. The union asserted [that] for purposes of the diversity jurisdiction it was a citizen of Pennsylvania, although some of its members were North Carolinians.

The corporation sought to have the case remanded to the state courts, contending that its complaint raised no federal questions and relying upon the generally prevailing principle that an unincorporated association's citizenship is that of each of its members. But the District Court retained jurisdiction. The District Judge noted "a trend to treat unincorporated associations in the same manner as corporations and to treat them as citizens of the state wherein the principal office is located." Divining "no common sense reason for treating an unincorporated national labor union differently from a corporation," he declined to follow what he styled "the poorer reasoned but more firmly established rule" of *Chapman v. Barney*, 129 U.S. 677.

On interlocutory appeal the Court of Appeals for the Fourth Circuit reversed and directed that the case be remanded to the state courts. Certiorari was granted so that we might decide whether an unincorporated labor union is to be treated as a citizen for purposes of federal diversity jurisdiction, without regard to the citizenship of its members. Because we believe this properly a matter for legislative consideration which cannot adequately or appropriately be dealt with by this Court, we affirm the decision of the Court of Appeals.

Article III, § 2, of the Constitution provides:

"The judicial Power shall extend * * * to Controversies * * * between Citizens of different States * * *." Congress lost no time in implementing the grant. In 1789 it provided for federal jurisdiction in suits "between a citizen of the State where the suit is brought, and a citizen of another State." There shortly arose the question as to whether a corporation—a creature of state law—is to be deemed a "citizen" for purposes of the statute. This Court, through Chief Justice Marshall, initially responded in the negative, holding that a corporation was not a "citizen" and that it might sue and be sued under the diversity statute only if none of its shareholders was a co-citizen of any opposing party. *Bank of United States v. Deveaux*, 5 Cranch 61. In 1844 the Court reversed itself and ruled that a corporation was to be treated as a citizen of the State which created it. Ten years later, the Court reached the same result by a different approach. In a compromise destined to endure for over a century, the Court indulged in the fiction that, although a corporation was not itself a citizen for diversity purposes, its shareholders would conclusively be presumed citizens of the incorporating State.

Congress re-entered the lists in 1875, significantly expanding diversity jurisdiction by deleting the requirement imposed in 1789 that one of the parties must be a citizen of the forum State. The resulting increase in the quantity of diversity litigation, however, cooled enthusiasts of the jurisdiction, and in 1887 and 1888 Congress enacted sharp curbs. It quadrupled the jurisdictional amount, confined the right of removal to nonresident defendants, reinstituted protections against jurisdiction by collusive assignment, and narrowed venue.

It was in this climate that the Court in 1889 decided *Chapman v. Barney*, supra. On its own motion the Court observed that plaintiff was a joint stock company and not a corporation or natural person. It held that although plaintiff was endowed by New York with capacity to sue, it could not be considered a "citizen" for diversity purposes.

In recent years courts and commentators have reflected dissatisfaction with the rule of *Chapman v. Barney*. The distinction between the "personality" and "citizenship" of corporations and that of labor unions and other unincorporated associations, it is increasingly argued, has become artificial and unreal. The mere fact that a corporation is endowed with a birth certificate is, they say, of no consequence. In truth and in fact, they point out, many voluntary associations and labor unions are indistinguishable from corporations in terms of the reality of function and structure, and to say that the latter are juridical persons and "citizens" and the former are not is to base a distinction upon an inadequate and irrelevant difference. They assert, with considerable merit, that it is not good judicial administration, nor is it fair, to remit a labor union or other unincorporated association to vagaries of jurisdiction determined by the citizenship of its members and to disregard the fact that unions and associations may exist and have an identity and a local habitation of their own.

The force of these arguments in relation to the diversity jurisdiction is particularized by petitioner's showing in this case. Petitioner argues that one of the purposes underlying the jurisdiction—protection of the nonresident litigant from local prejudice—is especially applicable to the modern labor union. According to the argument, when the nonresident defendant is a major union, local juries may be tempted to favor local interests at its expense. Juries may also be influenced by the fear that unionization would adversely affect the economy of the community and its customs and practices in the field of race relations. In support of these contentions, petitioner has exhibited material showing that during organizational campaigns like that involved in this case, localities have been saturated with propaganda concerning such economic and racial fears. Extending diversity jurisdiction to unions, says petitioner, would make available the advantages of federal procedure, Article III judges less exposed to local pressures than their state court counterparts, juries selected from wider geographical areas, review in appellate courts reflecting a multistate perspective, and more effective review by this Court.

We are of the view that these arguments, however appealing, are addressed to an inappropriate forum, and that pleas for extension of the diversity jurisdiction to hitherto uncovered broad categories of litigants ought to be made to the Congress and not to the [courts].

If we were to accept petitioner's urgent invitation to amend diversity jurisdiction so as to accommodate its case, we would be faced with difficulties which we could not adequately resolve. Even if the record here were adequate, we might well hesitate to assume that petitioner's situation is sufficiently representative or typical to form the predicate of a general principle. We should, for example, be obliged to fashion a test for ascertaining of which State the labor union is a citizen. Extending the jurisdiction to corporations raised no such problem, for the State of incorporation was a natural candidate, its arguable irrelevance in terms of the policies underlying the jurisdiction being outweighed by its certainty of application. But even that easy and apparent solution did not dispose of the problem; in 1958 Congress thought it necessary to enact legislation providing that corporations are citizens both of the State of incorporation and of the State in which their principal place of business is located. Further, in contemplating a rule which would accommodate petitioner's claim, we are acutely aware of the complications arising from the circumstance that petitioner, like other labor unions, has local as well as national organizations and that these, perhaps, should be reckoned with in connection with "citizenship" and its jurisdictional incidents.

Whether unincorporated labor unions ought to be assimilated to the status of corporations for diversity purposes, how such citizenship is to be determined, and what if any related rules ought to apply, are decisions which we believe suited to the legislative and not the judicial branch, regardless of our views as to the intrinsic merits of petitioner's argument—merits stoutly attested by widespread support for the recognition of labor unions as juridical personalities.

NOTE ON THE CITIZENSHIP OF UNINCORPORATED ASSOCIATIONS

Unincorporated associations take a variety of forms and *Bouligny* does not settle all the issues that may arise in relation to them. Compare two later Supreme Court cases. *Navarro Savings Association v. Lee*, 446 U.S. 458 (1980), held that the managing trustees of a Massachusetts "business trust" could obtain diversity jurisdiction based on their own citizenship without taking account of the citizenship of the ordinary shareholders of the trust. On the other hand, *Carden v. Arkoma Associates*, 494 U.S. 185 (1990), declined to extend the reasoning of *Navarro*. The case dealt with "limited partnership" arrangements under which there are "general" as well as "limited" partners. The Court held that diversity could not be procured on the basis of the citizenship of the general partners. Rather, diversity "depends on the citizenship of all the members." *Id.* at 195.

B. THWARTING EFFORTS BY LITIGANTS TO MANIPULATE THE RULES

In order to try to obtain or defeat diversity jurisdiction, the plaintiff may try to align the parties as plaintiffs or defendants in a fashion that suits his goal. But courts do not simply defer to the plaintiff's alignment. They "look beyond the pleadings and arrange the parties according to their sides in the dispute." *Dawson v. Columbia Ave. Saving Fund, Safe Deposit, Title & Trust Co.*, 197 U.S. 178, 180 (1905). For example, "[w]hen an insured tortfeasor brings an action against his insurer for a declaratory judgment as to his coverage and names the person suing him in tort as a defendant along with the insurer, the tort claimant will be realigned as a plaintiff, since the injured party and the insured have an identical interest in having it held that the insurance covers the accident in question." Wright & Kane, supra, at 177. Similarly, a plaintiff may not defeat diversity by naming as a defendant a party as to whom his claims "lack[ ] a reasonable basis in fact and law." *Murphy v. Aurora Loan Services, LLC,* 699 F.3d 1027, 1031 (8th Cir. 2012).

Another effort to manipulate the rules is illustrated by the following case.

KRAMER V. CARIBBEAN MILLS, INC.
394 U.S. 823 (1969).

JUSTICE HARLAN delivered the opinion of the Court.

The sole question presented by this case is whether the Federal District Court in which it was brought had jurisdiction over the cause, or whether that court was deprived of jurisdiction by 28 U.S.C. § 1359. That section provides:

> A district court shall not have jurisdiction of a civil action in which any party, by assignment or otherwise, has been improperly or collusively made or joined to invoke the jurisdiction of such court.

The facts were these. Respondent Caribbean Mills, Inc. (Caribbean) is a Haitian corporation. In May 1959 it entered into a contract with an individual named Kelly and the Panama and Venezuela Finance Company (Panama), a Panamanian Corporation. The agreement provided that Caribbean would purchase from Panama 125 shares of corporate stock, in return for payment of $85,000 down and an additional $165,000 in 12 annual installments.

No installment payments ever were made, despite requests for payment by Panama. In 1964, Panama assigned its entire interest in the 1959 contract to petitioner Kramer, an attorney in Wichita Falls, Texas. The stated consideration was $1. By a separate agreement dated the same day, Kramer promised to pay back to Panama 95% of any net recovery on the assigned cause of action, "solely as a Bonus."

Kramer soon thereafter brought suit against Caribbean for $165,000 in the United States District Court for the Northern District of Texas, alleging diversity of citizenship between himself and Caribbean. The District Court denied Caribbean's motion to dismiss for want of jurisdiction. The case proceeded to trial, and a jury returned a $165,000 verdict in favor of Kramer.

On appeal, the Court of Appeals for the Fifth Circuit reversed, holding that the assignment was "improperly or collusively made" within the meaning of 28 U.S.C. § 1359, and that in consequence the District Court lacked jurisdiction. [For] reasons which follow, we affirm the judgment of the Court of Appeals.

I.

The issue before us is whether Kramer was "improperly or collusively made" a party "to invoke the jurisdiction" of the District Court, within the meaning of 28 U.S.C. § 1359. We look first to the legislative background.

Section 1359 has existed in its present form only since the 1948 revision of the Judicial Code. Prior to that time, the use of devices to create diversity was regulated by two federal statutes. The first, known as the "assignee clause," provided that, with certain exceptions not here relevant:

> No district court shall have cognizance of any suit . . . to recover upon any promissory note or other chose in action in favor of any assignee . . . unless such suit might have been prosecuted in such court . . . if no assignment had been made.

The second pre-1948 statute, 28 U.S.C. § 80 (1940 ed.), stated that a district court should dismiss an action whenever:

> it shall appear to the satisfaction of the . . . court . . . that such suit does not really and substantially involve a dispute or controversy properly within the jurisdiction of (the) court, or that the parties to said suit have been improperly or collusively made or joined . . . for the purpose of creating (federal jurisdiction).

As part of the 1948 revision, § 80 was amended to produce the present § 1359. The assignee clause was simultaneously repealed. The Reviser's Note describes the amended assignee clause as a "jumble of legislative jargon," and states that "(t)he revised section changes this clause by confining its application to cases wherein the assignment is improperly or collusively made. . . . Furthermore, . . . the original purpose of (the assignee) clause is better served by substantially following section 80." That purpose was said to be 'to prevent the manufacture of Federal jurisdiction by the device of assignment.' *Ibid.*

II.

Only a small number of cases decided under § 1359 have involved diversity jurisdiction based on assignments, and this Court has not considered the matter since the 1948 revision. Because the approach of the former assignee clause was to forbid the grounding of jurisdiction upon any assignment, regardless of its circumstances or purpose, decisions under that clause are of little assistance. However, decisions of this Court under the other predecessor statute, 28 U.S.C. § 80, seem squarely in point. These decisions, together with the evident purpose of § 1359, lead us to conclude that the Court of Appeals was correct in finding that the assignment in question was "improperly or collusively made."

The most compelling precedent is *Farmington Village Corp. v. Pillsbury*, 114 U.S. 138 (1885). There Maine holders of bonds issued by a Maine village desired to test the bonds' validity in the federal courts. In an effort to accomplish this, they cut the coupons from their bonds and transferred them to a citizen of Massachusetts, who gave in return a non-negotiable two-year note for $500 and a promise to pay back 50% of the net amount recovered above $500. The jurisdictional question was certified to this Court, which held that there was no federal jurisdiction because the plaintiff had been "improperly or collusively" made a party within the meaning of the predecessor statute to 28 U.S.C. § 80. The Court pointed out that the plaintiff could easily have been released from his non-negotiable note, and found that apart from the hoped-for creation of federal jurisdiction the only real consequence of the transfer was to enable the Massachusetts plaintiff to "retain one-half of what he collects for the use of his name and his trouble in collecting." The Court concluded that "the transfer of the coupons was 'a mere contrivance, a pretense, the result of a collusive arrangement to create' federal jurisdiction." *Ibid.*

We find the case before us indistinguishable from Farmington and other decisions of like tenor. When the assignment to Kramer is considered together with his total lack of previous connection with the matter and his simultaneous reassignment of a 95% interest back to Panama, there can be little doubt that the assignment was for purposes of collection, with Kramer to retain 5% of the net proceeds "for the use of his name and his trouble in collecting."[9] If the suit had been unsuccessful, Kramer would have been out only $1, plus costs. Moreover, Kramer candidly admits that the "assignment was in substantial part motivated by a desire by (Panama's) counsel to make diversity jurisdiction available. . . ."

The conclusion that this assignment was "improperly or collusively made" within the meaning of § 1359 is supported not only by precedent but also by consideration of the statute's purpose. If federal jurisdiction could be created by assignments of this kind, which are easy to arrange and involve few disadvantages for the assignor, then a vast quantity of ordinary contract and tort litigation could be channeled into the federal

---

[9] Hence, we have no occasion to re-examine the cases in which this Court has held that where the transfer of a claim is absolute, with the transferor retaining no interest in the subject matter, then the transfer is not "improperly or collusively made," regardless of the transferor's motive. Nor is it necessary to consider whether, in cases in which suit is required to be brought by an administrator or guardian, a motive to create diversity jurisdiction renders the appointment of an out-of-state representative "improper" or "collusive." Cases involving representatives vary in several respects from those in which jurisdiction is based on assignments: (1) in the former situation, some representative must be appointed before suit can be brought, while in the latter the assignor normally is himself capable of suing in state court; (2) under state law, different kinds of guardians and administrators may possess discrete sorts of powers; and (3) all such representatives owe their appointment to the decree of a state court, rather than solely to an action of the parties. It is not necessary to decide whether these distinctions amount to a difference for purposes of § 1359.

courts at the will of one of the parties. Such "manufacture of Federal jurisdiction" was the very thing which Congress intended to prevent when it enacted § 1359 and its predecessors.

III.

Kramer nevertheless argues that the assignment to him was not "improperly or collusively made" within the meaning of § 1359, for two main reasons. First, he suggests that the undisputed legality of the assignment under Texas law necessarily rendered it valid for purposes of federal jurisdiction. [To] accept this argument would render § 1359 largely incapable of accomplishing its purpose; this very case demonstrates the ease with which a party may "manufacture" federal jurisdiction by an assignment which meets the requirements of state law.

Second, Kramer urges that this case is significantly distinguishable from earlier decisions because it involves diversity jurisdiction under 28 U.S.C. § 1332(a)(2), arising from the alienage of one of the parties, rather than the more common diversity jurisdiction based upon the parties' residence in different States. We can perceive no substance in this argument: by its terms, § 1359 applies equally to both types of diversity jurisdiction, and there is no indication that Congress intended them to be treated differently.

IV.

In short, we find that this assignment falls not only within the scope of § 1359 but within its very core. It follows that the District Court lacked jurisdiction to hear this action, and that petitioner must seek his remedy in the state courts. The judgment of the Court of Appeals is affirmed.

In 1988 Congress addressed one of the issues mentioned in footnote 9 of *Kramer*. The new provision, codified as 28 U.S.C. § 1332(c)(2), provides that "the legal representative of the estate of a decedent shall be deemed to be a citizen only of the same State as the decedent, and the legal representative of an infant or incompetent shall be deemed to be a citizen only of the same State as the infant or incompetent."

C. "ANCILLARY" JURISDICTION AND § 1367

Part I, Section G of this chapter examined "pendent jurisdiction," the doctrine under which a court with federal question jurisdiction over a given case may decide state law claims "arising out of the same nucleus of operative fact," as the Court put it in *United Mine Workers v. Gibbs*. The "supplemental jurisdiction" statute, 28 U.S.C. § 1367, codified that doctrine, with one important modification: The statute authorized "pendent party" jurisdiction, a doctrine the Supreme Courts had rejected a year earlier in *Finley v. United States*.

Historically, the diversity analogue to pendent jurisdiction was called "ancillary" jurisdiction: A court with diversity jurisdiction could, in certain circumstances, hear claims that would not meet the ordinary requirements (i.e., complete diversity and the jurisdictional amount) for diversity jurisdiction. The following case illustrates the scope and limits of ancillary jurisdiction.

OWEN EQUIPMENT & ERECTION CO. V. KROGER
437 U.S. 365 (1978).

JUSTICE STEWART delivered the opinion of the Court.

In an action in which federal jurisdiction is based on diversity of citizenship, may the plaintiff assert a claim against a third-party defendant when there is no independent basis for federal jurisdiction over that claim? The Court of Appeals for the Eighth Circuit held in this case that such a claim is within the ancillary jurisdiction of the federal courts. We granted certiorari because this decision conflicts with several recent decisions of other Courts of Appeals.

I

On January 18, 1972, James Kroger was electrocuted when the boom of a steel crane next to which he was walking came too close to a high-tension electric power line. The respondent (his widow, who is the administratrix of his estate) filed a wrongful-death action in the United States District Court for the District of Nebraska against the Omaha Public Power District (OPPD). Her complaint alleged that OPPD's negligent construction, maintenance, and operation of the power line had caused Kroger's death. Federal jurisdiction was based on diversity of citizenship, since the respondent was a citizen of Iowa and OPPD was a Nebraska corporation.

OPPD then filed a third-party complaint pursuant to Fed. Rule Civ. Proc. 14(a) against the petitioner, Owen Equipment and Erection Co. (Owen), alleging that the crane was owned and operated by Owen, and that Owen's negligence had been the proximate cause of Kroger's death. OPPD later moved for summary judgment on the respondent's complaint against it. While this motion was pending, the respondent was granted leave to file an amended complaint naming Owen as an additional defendant. Thereafter, the District Court granted OPPD's motion for summary judgment in an unreported opinion. The case thus went to trial between the respondent and the petitioner alone.

The respondent's amended complaint alleged that Owen was "a Nebraska corporation with its principal place of business in Nebraska."

Owen's answer admitted that it was "a corporation organized and existing under the laws of the State of Nebraska," and denied every other allegation of the complaint. On the third day of trial, however, it was disclosed that the petitioner's principal place of business was in Iowa, not Nebraska, and that the petitioner and the respondent were thus both citizens of Iowa.

The petitioner then moved to dismiss the complaint for lack of jurisdiction. The District Court reserved decision on the motion, and the jury thereafter returned a verdict in favor of the respondent. In an unreported opinion issued after the trial, the District Court denied the petitioner's motion to dismiss the complaint.

The judgment was affirmed on appeal. The Court of Appeals held that under this Court's decision in *Mine Workers v. Gibbs* the District Court had jurisdictional power, in its discretion, to adjudicate the respondent's claim against the petitioner because that claim arose from the "core of 'operative facts' giving rise to both [respondent's] claim against OPPD and OPPD's claim against Owen." It further held that the District Court had properly exercised its discretion in proceeding to decide the case even after summary judgment had been granted to OPPD, because the petitioner had concealed its Iowa citizenship from the respondent.

II

It is undisputed that there was no independent basis of federal jurisdiction over the respondent's state-law tort action against the petitioner, since both are citizens of Iowa. And although Fed. Rule Civ. Proc. 14(a) permits a plaintiff to assert a claim against a third-party defendant, it does not purport to say whether or not such a claim requires an independent basis of federal jurisdiction. Indeed, it could not determine that question, since it is axiomatic that the Federal Rules of Civil Procedure do not create or withdraw federal jurisdiction.

In affirming the District Court's judgment, the Court of Appeals relied upon the doctrine of ancillary jurisdiction, whose contours it believed were defined by this Court's holding in *Mine Workers v. Gibbs*, supra. The *Gibbs* case differed from this one in that it involved pendent jurisdiction, which concerns the resolution of a plaintiff's federal-and-state-law claims against a single defendant in one action. By contrast, in this case there was no claim based upon substantive federal law, but rather state-law tort claims against two different defendants. Nonetheless, the Court of Appeals was correct in perceiving that *Gibbs* and this case are two species of the same generic problem: Under what circumstances may a federal court hear and decide a state-law claim arising between citizens of the same State? But we believe that the Court of Appeals failed to understand the scope of the doctrine of the *Gibbs* case.

The plaintiff in *Gibbs* alleged that the defendant union had violated the common law of Tennessee as well as the federal prohibition of secondary boycotts. This Court held that, although the parties were not of diverse citizenship, the District Court properly entertained the state-law claim as pendent to the federal [claim].

It is apparent that *Gibbs* delineated the constitutional limits of federal judicial power. But even if it be assumed that the District Court in the present case had constitutional power to decide the respondent's lawsuit against the petitioner,[10] it does not follow that the decision of the Court of Appeals was correct. Constitutional power is merely the first hurdle that must be overcome in determining that a federal court has jurisdiction over a particular controversy. For the jurisdiction of the federal courts is limited not only by the provisions of Art. III of the Constitution, but also by Acts of Congress.

That statutory law as well as the Constitution may limit a federal court's jurisdiction over nonfederal claims is well illustrated by two recent decisions of this Court, *Aldinger v. Howard*, 427 U.S. 1 and *Zahn v. International Paper Co.*, 414 U.S. 291. In *Aldinger* the Court held that a Federal District Court lacked jurisdiction over a state-law claim against a county, even if that claim was alleged to be pendent to one against county officials under 42 U.S.C. § 1983. In *Zahn* the Court held that in a diversity class action under Fed.Rule Civ.Proc. 23(b)(3), the claim of each member of the plaintiff class must independently satisfy the minimum jurisdictional amount set by 28 U.S.C. § 1332(a), and rejected the argument that jurisdiction existed over those claims that involved $10,000 or less as ancillary to those that involved more. In each case, despite the fact that federal and nonfederal claims arose from a "common nucleus of operative fact," the Court held that the statute conferring jurisdiction over the federal claim did not allow the exercise of jurisdiction over the nonfederal claim.

The *Aldinger* and *Zahn* cases thus make clear that a finding that federal and nonfederal claims arise from a "common nucleus of operative fact," the test of *Gibbs*, does not end the inquiry into whether a federal court has power to hear the nonfederal claims along with the federal ones. Beyond this constitutional minimum, there must be an examination of the posture in which the nonfederal claim is asserted and of the specific statute that confers jurisdiction over the federal claim, in order to

---

[10] Federal jurisdiction in Gibbs was based upon the existence of a question of federal law. The Court of Appeals in the present case believed that the "common nucleus of operative fact" test also determines the outer boundaries of constitutionally permissible federal jurisdiction when that jurisdiction is based upon diversity of citizenship. We may assume without deciding that the Court of Appeals was correct in this regard.

determine whether "Congress in [that statute] has . . . expressly or by implication negated" the exercise of jurisdiction over the particular nonfederal claim.

III

The relevant statute in this case, 28 U.S.C. § 1332(a)(1), confers upon federal courts jurisdiction over "civil actions where the matter in controversy exceeds the sum or value of $10,000 . . . and is between . . . citizens of different States." This statute and its predecessors have consistently been held to require complete diversity of citizenship. That is, diversity jurisdiction does not exist unless each defendant is a citizen of a different State from each plaintiff. Over the years Congress has repeatedly re-enacted or amended the statute conferring diversity jurisdiction, leaving intact this rule of complete diversity. Whatever may have been the original purposes of diversity-of-citizenship jurisdiction, this subsequent history clearly demonstrates a congressional mandate that diversity jurisdiction is not to be available when any plaintiff is a citizen of the same State as any defendant.

Thus it is clear that the respondent could not originally have brought suit in federal court naming Owen and OPPD as codefendants, since citizens of Iowa would have been on both sides of the litigation. Yet the identical lawsuit resulted when she amended her complaint. Complete diversity was destroyed just as surely as if she had sued Owen initially. In either situation, in the plain language of the statute, the "matter in controversy" could not be "between . . . citizens of different States."

It is a fundamental precept that federal courts are courts of limited jurisdiction. The limits upon federal jurisdiction, whether imposed by the Constitution or by Congress, must be neither disregarded nor evaded. Yet under the reasoning of the Court of Appeals in this case, a plaintiff could defeat the statutory requirement of complete diversity by the simple expedient of suing only those defendants who were of diverse citizenship and waiting for them to implead nondiverse defendants.[17] If, as the Court of Appeals thought, a "common nucleus of operative fact" were the only requirement for ancillary jurisdiction in a diversity case, there would be no principled reason why the respondent in this case could not have joined her cause of action against Owen in her original complaint as ancillary to her claim against OPPD. Congress' requirement of complete diversity would thus have been evaded completely.

---

[17] This is not an unlikely hypothesis, since a defendant in a tort suit such as this one would surely try to limit his liability by impleading any joint tortfeasors for indemnity or contribution. Some commentators have suggested that the possible abuse of third-party practice could be dealt with under 28 U.S.C. § 1359, which forbids collusive attempts to create federal jurisdiction. The dissenting opinion today also expresses this view. But there is nothing necessarily collusive about a plaintiff's selectively suing only those tortfeasors of diverse citizenship, or about the named defendants' desire to implead joint tortfeasors. Nonetheless, the requirement of complete diversity would be eviscerated by such a course of events.

It is true, as the Court of Appeals noted, that the exercise of ancillary jurisdiction over nonfederal claims has often been upheld in situations involving impleader, cross-claims or counterclaims.[18] But in determining whether jurisdiction over a nonfederal claim exists, the context in which the nonfederal claim is asserted is crucial. And the claim here arises in a setting quite different from the kinds of nonfederal claims that have been viewed in other cases as falling within the ancillary jurisdiction of the federal courts.

First, the nonfederal claim in this case was simply not ancillary to the federal one in the same sense that, for example, the impleader by a defendant of a third-party defendant always is. A third-party complaint depends at least in part upon the resolution of the primary lawsuit. Its relation to the original complaint is thus not mere factual similarity but logical dependence. The respondent's claim against the petitioner, however, was entirely separate from her original claim against OPPD, since the petitioner's liability to her depended not at all upon whether or not OPPD was also liable. Far from being an ancillary and dependent claim, it was a new and independent one.

Second, the nonfederal claim here was asserted by the plaintiff, who voluntarily chose to bring suit upon a state-law claim in a federal court. By contrast, ancillary jurisdiction typically involves claims by a defending party haled into court against his will, or by another person whose rights might be irretrievably lost unless he could assert them in an ongoing action in a federal court. A plaintiff cannot complain if ancillary jurisdiction does not encompass all of his possible claims in a case such as this one, since it is he who has chosen the federal rather than the state forum and must thus accept its limitations. "[T]he efficiency plaintiff seeks so avidly is available without question in the state courts." *Kenrose Mfg. Co. v. Fred Whitaker Co.*, 512 F.2d 890, 894 (CA4).

It is not unreasonable to assume that, in generally requiring complete diversity, Congress did not intend to confine the jurisdiction of federal courts so inflexibly that they are unable to protect legal rights or effectively to resolve an entire, logically entwined lawsuit. Those practical needs are the basis of the doctrine of ancillary jurisdiction. But neither the convenience of litigants nor considerations of judicial economy can suffice to justify extension of the doctrine of ancillary jurisdiction to a plaintiff's cause of action against a citizen of the same State in a diversity case. Congress has established the basic rule that diversity jurisdiction exists under 28 U.S.C. § 1332 only when there is complete diversity of

---

[18] The ancillary jurisdiction of the federal courts derives originally from cases such as *Freeman v. Howe*, 24 How. 450, 16 L.Ed. 749, which held that when federal jurisdiction "effectively controls the property or fund under dispute, other claimants thereto should be allowed to intervene in order to protect their interests, without regard to jurisdiction." More recently, it has been said to include cases that involve multiparty practice, such as compulsory counterclaims, impleader, cross-claims, or intervention as of right.

citizenship. "The policy of the statute calls for its strict construction." To allow the requirement of complete diversity to be circumvented as it was in this case would simply flout the congressional command.[21]

Accordingly, the judgment of the Court of Appeals is reversed.

JUSTICE WHITE, with whom MR. JUSTICE BRENNAN joins, dissenting.

[The] complete-diversity requirement, of course, could be viewed as meaning that in a diversity case, a federal district court may adjudicate only those claims that are between parties of different States. Thus, in order for a defendant to implead a third-party defendant, there would have to be diversity of citizenship; the same would also be true for cross-claims between defendants and for a third-party defendant's claim against a plaintiff. Even the majority, however, refuses to read the complete-diversity requirement so broadly; it recognizes with seeming approval the exercise of ancillary jurisdiction over nonfederal claims in situations involving impleader, cross-claims, and counterclaims. Given the Court's willingness to recognize ancillary jurisdiction in these contexts, despite the requirements of § 1332(a), I see no justification for the Court's refusal to approve the District Court's exercise of ancillary jurisdiction in the present case.

It is significant that a plaintiff who asserts a claim against a third-party defendant is not seeking to add a new party to the lawsuit. In the present case, for example, Owen had already been brought into the suit by OPPD, and, that having been done, Mrs. Kroger merely sought to assert against Owen a claim arising out of the same transaction that was already before the [court].

Because in the instant case Mrs. Kroger merely sought to assert a claim against someone already a party to the suit, considerations of judicial economy, convenience, and fairness to the litigants—the factors relied upon in *Gibbs*—support the recognition of ancillary jurisdiction here. Already before the court was the whole question of the cause of Mr. Kroger's death. Mrs. Kroger initially contended that OPPD was responsible; OPPD in turn contended that Owen's negligence had been the proximate cause of Mr. Kroger's death. In spite of the fact that the question of Owen's negligence was already before the District Court, the majority requires Mrs. Kroger to bring a separate action in state court in order to assert that very claim. [Considerations] of judicial economy are certainly not served by requiring such duplicative litigation.

The majority, however, brushes aside such considerations of convenience, judicial economy, and fairness because it concludes that

---

[21] Our holding is that the District Court lacked power to entertain the respondent's lawsuit against the petitioner. Thus, the asserted inequity in the respondent's alleged concealment of its citizenship is irrelevant. Federal judicial power does not depend upon "prior action or consent of the parties."

recognizing ancillary jurisdiction over a plaintiff's claim against a third-party defendant would permit the plaintiff to circumvent the complete-diversity requirement and thereby "flout the congressional command." Since the plaintiff in such a case does not bring the third-party defendant into the suit, however, there is no occasion for deliberate circumvention of the diversity requirement, absent collusion with the defendant. In the case of such collusion, of which there is absolutely no indication here, the court can dismiss the action under the authority of 28 U.S.C. § 1359. In the absence of such collusion, there is no reason to adopt an absolute rule prohibiting the plaintiff from asserting those claims that he may properly assert against the third-party defendant pursuant to Fed. Rule Civ. Proc. 14(a). The plaintiff in such a situation brings suit against the defendant only with absolutely no assurance that the defendant will decide or be able to implead a particular third-party defendant. Since the plaintiff has no control over the defendant's decision to implead a third party, the fact that he could not have originally sued that party in federal court should be irrelevant. Moreover, the fact that a plaintiff in some cases may be able to foresee the subsequent chain of events leading to the impleader does not seem to me to be a sufficient reason to declare that a district court does not have the power to exercise ancillary jurisdiction over the plaintiff's claims against the third-party defendant.[7]

We have previously noted that "[s]ubsequent decisions of this Court indicate that *Strawbridge* is not to be given an expansive reading." *State Farm Fire & Cas. Co. v. Tashire*, 386 U.S. 523, 531 n. 6 (1967). In light of this teaching, it seems to me appropriate to view § 1332 as requiring complete diversity only between the plaintiff and those parties he actually brings into the suit. Beyond that, I would hold that in a diversity case the District Court has power, both constitutional and statutory, to entertain all claims among the parties arising from the same nucleus of operative fact as the plaintiff's original, jurisdiction-conferring claim against the defendant. Accordingly, I dissent from the Court's disposition of the present case.

The legislative history of § 1367 indicates that Congress meant to codify without alteration the judge-made ancillary jurisdiction doctrine described in *Kroger*. With that end in view, § 1367(a) broadly authorizes

---

[7] Under the *Gibbs* analysis, recognition of the district court's power to hear a plaintiff's nonfederal claim against a third-party defendant in a diversity suit would not mean that the court would be required to entertain such claims in all cases. The district court would have the discretion to dismiss the nonfederal claim if it concluded that the interests of judicial economy, convenience, and fairness would not be served by the retention of the claim in the federal lawsuit. Accordingly, the majority's concerns that lead it to conclude that ancillary jurisdiction should not be recognized in the present situation could be met on a case-by-case basis, rather than by the absolute rule it adopts.

supplemental jurisdiction in both federal question and diversity cases, but § 1367(b) then restricts the reach of the doctrine in diversity cases:

> In any civil action of which the district courts have original jurisdiction founded solely on section 1332 of this title, the district courts shall not have supplemental jurisdiction under subsection (a) over claims by plaintiffs against persons made parties under Rule 14, 19, 20, or 24 of the Federal Rules of Civil Procedure, or over parties proposed to be joined as plaintiffs under Rule 19 of such rules, or seeking to intervene as plaintiffs under Rule 24 of such rules, when exercising supplemental jurisdiction over such claims would be inconsistent with the jurisdictional requirements of section 1332.

It is not clear that the statute precisely achieves the aim of preserving the *Kroger* rule without altering it. One much mooted issue concerns diversity class actions, which are governed by Rule 23. *Kroger* seems to endorse the *Zahn* case, which had rejected the use of ancillary jurisdiction in order to allow plaintiffs to join a class action even though they could not meet the jurisdictional amount requirement. Notice, however, that § 1367's list of claims by plaintiffs excluded from supplemental jurisdiction does not include those brought under Rule 23. Does it follow that ancillary jurisdiction is available for such plaintiffs? The Court tackled that issue in *Exxon Mobil v. Allapattah Services.*

EXXON MOBIL CORP. V. ALLAPATTAH SERVICES
545 U.S. 546 (2005).

JUSTICE KENNEDY delivered the opinion of the Court.

[All] parties to this litigation and all courts to consider the question agree that § 1367 overturned the result in *Finley*. There is no warrant, however, for assuming that § 1367 did no more than to overrule *Finley* and otherwise to codify the existing state of the law of supplemental jurisdiction. We must not give jurisdictional statutes a more expansive interpretation than their text warrants, but it is just as important not to adopt an artificial construction that is narrower than what the text provides. No sound canon of interpretation requires Congress to speak with extraordinary clarity in order to modify the rules of federal jurisdiction within appropriate constitutional bounds. Ordinary principles of statutory construction apply. In order to determine the scope of supplemental jurisdiction authorized by § 1367, then, we must examine the statute's text in light of context, structure, and related statutory provisions.

Section 1367(a) is a broad grant of supplemental jurisdiction over other claims within the same case or controversy, as long as the action is one in which the district courts would have original jurisdiction. The last sentence of § 1367(a) makes it clear that the grant of supplemental jurisdiction extends to claims involving joinder or intervention of additional parties. The single question before us, therefore, is whether a diversity case in which the claims of some plaintiffs satisfy the amount-in-controversy requirement, but the claims of others plaintiffs do not, presents a "civil action of which the district courts have original jurisdiction." If the answer is yes, § 1367(a) confers supplemental jurisdiction over all claims, including those that do not independently satisfy the amount-in-controversy requirement, if the claims are part of the same Article III case or controversy. If the answer is no, § 1367(a) is inapplicable and, in light of *Clark*[2] and *Zahn* the district court has no statutory basis for exercising supplemental jurisdiction over the additional claims. We now conclude the answer must be yes. When the well-pleaded complaint contains at least one claim that satisfies the amount-in-controversy requirement, and there are no other relevant jurisdictional defects, the district court, beyond all question, has original jurisdiction over that [claim]. Once the court determines it has original jurisdiction over the civil action, it can turn to the question whether it has a constitutional and statutory basis for exercising supplemental jurisdiction over the other claims in the action.

Section 1367(a) commences with the direction that §§ 1367(b) and (c), or other relevant statutes, may provide specific exceptions, but otherwise § 1367(a) is a broad jurisdictional grant, with no distinction drawn between pendent-claim and pendent-party cases. In fact, the last sentence of § 1367(a) makes clear that the provision grants supplemental jurisdiction over claims involving joinder or intervention of additional parties. The terms of § 1367 do not acknowledge any distinction between pendent jurisdiction and the doctrine of so-called ancillary jurisdiction. Though the doctrines of pendent and ancillary jurisdiction developed separately as a historical matter, the Court has recognized that the doctrines are "two species of the same generic problem," *Kroger*. Nothing in § 1367 indicates a congressional intent to recognize, preserve, or create some meaningful, substantive distinction between the jurisdictional categories we have historically labeled pendent and ancillary.

If § 1367(a) were the sum total of the relevant statutory language, our holding would rest on that language alone. The statute, of course, instructs us to examine § 1367(b) to determine if any of its exceptions apply, so we proceed to that section. While § 1367(b) qualifies the broad rule of § 1367(a), it does not withdraw supplemental jurisdiction over the claims of the additional parties at issue here. The specific exceptions to

---

[2]   [Editor's note] The Court refers here to a case it had discussed in a section of the opinion we have omitted, *Clark v. Paul Gray, Inc.*, 306 U.S. 583 (1939), a federal question case adjudicated during the era when there was a jurisdictional amount requirement for federal question cases. *Clark* held that "every plaintiff must separately satisfy the amount-in-controversy requirement" in federal question cases.

§ 1367(a) contained in § 1367(b), moreover, provide additional support for our conclusion that § 1367(a) confers supplemental jurisdiction over these claims. Section 1367(b), which applies only to diversity cases, withholds supplemental jurisdiction over the claims of plaintiffs proposed to be joined as indispensable parties under Federal Rule of Civil Procedure 19, or who seek to intervene pursuant to Rule 24. Nothing in the text of § 1367(b), however, withholds supplemental jurisdiction over the claims of plaintiffs permissively joined under Rule 20 [or] certified as class-action members pursuant to Rule [23]. The natural, indeed the necessary, inference is that § 1367 confers supplemental jurisdiction over claims by Rule 20 and Rule 23 plaintiffs. This inference, at least with respect to Rule 20 plaintiffs, is strengthened by the fact that § 1367(b) explicitly excludes supplemental jurisdiction over claims against defendants joined under Rule 20.

We cannot accept the view, urged by some of the parties, commentators, and Courts of Appeals, that a district court lacks original jurisdiction over a civil action unless the court has original jurisdiction over every claim in the complaint. As we understand this position, it requires assuming either that all claims in the complaint must stand or fall as a single, indivisible "civil action" as a matter of definitional necessity—what we will refer to as the "indivisibility theory"—or else that the inclusion of a claim or party falling outside the district court's original jurisdiction somehow contaminates every other claim in the complaint, depriving the court of original jurisdiction over any of these claims—what we will refer to as the "contamination theory."

The indivisibility theory is easily dismissed, as it is inconsistent with the whole notion of supplemental jurisdiction. If a district court must have original jurisdiction over every claim in the complaint in order to have "original jurisdiction" over a "civil action," then in *Gibbs* there was no civil action of which the district court could assume original jurisdiction under § 1331, and so no basis for exercising supplemental jurisdiction over any of the claims. The indivisibility theory is further belied by our practice—in both federal-question and diversity cases—of allowing federal courts to cure jurisdictional defects by dismissing the offending parties rather than dismissing the entire [action]. If the presence of jurisdictionally problematic claims in the complaint meant the district court was without original jurisdiction over the single, indivisible civil action before it, then the district court would have to dismiss the whole action rather than particular parties.

We also find it unconvincing to say that the definitional indivisibility theory applies in the context of diversity cases but not in the context of federal-question cases. The broad and general language of the statute does not permit this result. The contention is premised on the notion that the phrase "original jurisdiction of all civil actions" means different things in § 1331 and § 1332. It is implausible, however, to say that the identical phrase means one thing (original jurisdiction in all actions where at least one claim in the complaint meets the following requirements) in § 1331 and something else (original jurisdiction in all actions where every claim in the complaint meets the following requirements) in § 1332.

The contamination theory, as we have noted, can make some sense in the special context of the complete diversity requirement because the presence of nondiverse parties on both sides of a lawsuit eliminates the justification for providing a federal forum. The theory, however, makes little sense with respect to the amount-in-controversy requirement, which is meant to ensure that a dispute is sufficiently important to warrant federal-court attention. The presence of a single nondiverse party may eliminate the fear of bias with respect to all claims, but the presence of a claim that falls short of the minimum amount in controversy does nothing to reduce the importance of the claims that do meet this requirement.

It is fallacious to suppose, simply from the proposition that § 1332 imposes both the diversity requirement and the amount-in-controversy requirement, that the contamination theory germane to the former is also relevant to the latter. There is no inherent logical connection between the amount-in-controversy requirement and § 1332 diversity jurisdiction. After all, federal-question jurisdiction once had an amount-in-controversy requirement as well. If such a requirement were revived under § 1331, it is clear beyond peradventure that § 1367(a) provides supplemental jurisdiction over federal-question cases where some, but not all, of the federal-law claims involve a sufficient amount in [controversy].

In addition to the theoretical difficulties with the argument that a district court has original jurisdiction over a civil action only if it has original jurisdiction over each individual claim in the complaint, we have already considered and rejected a virtually identical argument in the closely analogous context of removal jurisdiction. In *Chicago v. International College of Surgeons*, 522 U.S. 156 (1997), the plaintiff brought federal-and state-law claims in state court. The defendant removed to federal court. The plaintiff objected to removal, citing the text of the removal statute, § 1441(a). That statutory provision, which bears a striking similarity to the relevant portion of § 1367, authorizes removal of "any civil action . . . of which the district courts of the United States have original jurisdiction. . . ." The *College of Surgeons* plaintiff urged that, because its state-law claims were not within the District Court's original jurisdiction, § 1441(a) did not authorize removal. We disagreed. The federal law claims, we held, "suffice to make the actions 'civil actions' within the 'original jurisdiction' of the district courts. . . . Nothing in the jurisdictional statutes suggests that the presence of related state law claims somehow alters the fact that [the plaintiff's] complaints, by virtue of their federal claims, were 'civil actions' within the federal courts' 'original jurisdiction.' " Once the case was removed, the District Court had original jurisdiction over the federal law claims and supplemental jurisdiction under § 1367(a) over the state-law [claims].

Although *College of Surgeons* involved additional claims between the same parties, its interpretation of § 1441(a) applies equally to cases involving additional parties whose claims fall short of the jurisdictional amount. If we were to adopt the contrary view that the presence of additional parties means there is no "civil action . . . of which the district courts . . . have original jurisdiction," those cases simply would not be removable. To our knowledge, no court has issued a reasoned opinion adopting this view of the removal statute. It is settled, of course, that absent complete diversity a case is not removable because the district court would lack original jurisdiction. This, however, is altogether consistent with our view of § 1441(a). A failure of complete diversity, unlike the failure of some claims to meet the requisite amount in controversy, contaminates every claim in the [action].

Finally, we note that the Class Action Fairness Act (CAFA), Pub. L. 109–2, 119 Stat. 4, enacted this year, has no bearing on our analysis of these cases. Subject to certain limitations, the CAFA confers federal diversity jurisdiction over class actions where the aggregate amount in controversy exceeds $5 million. It abrogates the rule against aggregating claims, a rule this Court [reaffirmed] in *Zahn*. The CAFA, however, is not retroactive, and the views of the 2005 Congress are not relevant to our interpretation of a text enacted by Congress in 1990. The CAFA, moreover, does not moot the significance of our interpretation of § 1367, as many proposed exercises of supplemental jurisdiction, even in the class-action context, might not fall within the CAFA's ambit. The CAFA, then, has no impact, one way or the other, on our interpretation of § 1367.

[JUSTICE STEVENS' dissenting opinion is omitted.]

JUSTICE GINSBURG, with whom JUSTICE STEVENS, JUSTICE O'CONNOR, and JUSTICE BREYER join, dissenting.

[The] Court adopts a plausibly broad reading of § 1367, a measure that is hardly a model of the careful drafter's art. There is another plausible reading, however, one less disruptive of our jurisprudence regarding supplemental jurisdiction. If one reads § 1367(a) to instruct, as the statute's text suggests, that the district court must first have "original jurisdiction" over a "civil action" before supplemental jurisdiction can attach, then *Clark* and *Zahn* are preserved, and supplemental jurisdiction does not open the way for joinder of plaintiffs, or inclusion of class members, who do not independently meet the amount-in-controversy requirement. For the reasons that follow, I conclude that this narrower construction is the better reading of § 1367.

[Section] 1367, by its terms, operates only in civil actions "of which the district courts have original jurisdiction." The "original jurisdiction" relevant here is diversity-of-citizenship jurisdiction, conferred by § 1332. The character of that jurisdiction is the essential backdrop for comprehension of § 1367.

The Constitution broadly provides for federal-court jurisdiction in controversies "between Citizens of different States." This Court has read that provision to demand no more than "minimal diversity," i.e., so long as one party on the plaintiffs' side and one party on the defendants' side are of diverse citizenship, Congress may authorize federal courts to exercise diversity jurisdiction. Further, the Constitution includes no amount-in-controversy limitation on the exercise of federal jurisdiction. But from the start, Congress, as its measures have been construed by this Court, has limited federal court exercise of diversity jurisdiction in two principal ways. First, unless Congress specifies otherwise, diversity must be "complete," i.e., all parties on plaintiffs' side must be diverse from all parties on defendants' side. *Strawbridge.* Second, each plaintiff's stake must independently meet the amount-in-controversy specification: "When two or more plaintiffs, having separate and distinct demands, unite for convenience and economy in a single suit, it is essential that the demand of each be of the requisite jurisdictional amount." [*Troy Bank v. G. A. Whitehead & Co.*, 222 U.S. 39, 40 (1911)].

The statute today governing federal court exercise of diversity jurisdiction in the generality of cases, § 1332, like all its predecessors, incorporates both a diverse-citizenship requirement and an amount-in-controversy specification.[5] As to the latter, the statute reads: "The district courts shall have original jurisdiction [in diversity-of-citizenship cases] where the matter in controversy exceeds the sum ... of $75,000." § 1332(a). This Court has long held that, in determining whether the amount-in-controversy requirement has been satisfied, a single plaintiff may aggregate two or more claims against a single defendant, even if the claims are unrelated. But in multiparty cases, including class actions, we have unyieldingly adhered to the nonaggregation rule stated in *Troy Bank.*

---

[5] Endeavoring to preserve the "complete diversity" rule first stated in *Strawbridge*, the Court's opinion drives a wedge between the two components of 28 U.S.C. § 1332, treating the diversity-of-citizenship requirement as essential, the amount-in-controversy requirement as more readily disposable. Section 1332 itself, however, does not rank order the two requirements. What "[o]rdinary principl[e] of statutory construction" or "sound canon of interpretation," allows the Court to slice up § 1332 this way? In partial explanation, the Court asserts that amount in controversy can be analyzed claim-by-claim, but the diversity requirement cannot. It is not altogether clear why that should be so. The cure for improper joinder of a nondiverse party is the same as the cure for improper joinder of a plaintiff who does not satisfy the jurisdictional amount. In both cases, original jurisdiction can be preserved by dismissing the nonqualifying party.

[This] Court most recently addressed "[t]he meaning of [§ 1332's] 'matter in controversy' language" in [*Zahn*, in which the Court applied the nonaggregation rule to class actions even if the named plaintiffs have claims that satisfy the jurisdictional amount.] The rule that each plaintiff must independently satisfy the amount-in-controversy requirement, unless Congress expressly orders otherwise, was thus the solidly established reading of § 1332 when Congress enacted [§ 1367].

These cases present the question whether Congress abrogated the nonaggregation rule long tied to § 1332 when it enacted § 1367. In answering that question, "context [should provide] a crucial guide." *Rosario Ortega v. Star-Kist Foods, Inc.*, 370 F.3d 124, 135 (2004). The Court should assume, as it ordinarily does, that Congress legislated against a background of law already in place and the historical development of that law. Here, that background is the statutory grant of diversity jurisdiction, the amount-in-controversy condition that Congress, from the start, has tied to the grant, and the nonaggregation rule this Court has long applied to the determination of the "matter in [controversy"].

The Court is unanimous in reading § 1367(a) to permit pendent-party jurisdiction in federal-question cases, and thus, to overrule [*Finley*]. The Court divides, however, on the impact of § 1367(a) on diversity cases controlled by § 1332. Under the majority's reading, § 1367(a) permits the joinder of related claims cut loose from the nonaggregation rule that has long attended actions under § 1332. Only the claims specified in § 1367(b) would be excluded from § 1367(a)'s expansion of § 1332's grant of diversity jurisdiction. And because § 1367(b) contains no exception for joinder of plaintiffs under Rule 20 or class actions under Rule 23, the Court concludes, *Clark* and *Zahn* have been overruled.

The Court's reading is surely plausible, especially if one detaches § 1367(a) from its context and attempts no reconciliation with prior interpretations of § 1332's amount-in-controversy requirement. But § 1367(a)'s text, as the First Circuit held [in *Rosario Ortega v. Star-Kist Foods*, 370 F.3d 124 (1st Cir. 2004), one of the cases under review], can be read another way, one that would involve no rejection of *Clark* and *Zahn*.

As explained by the First Circuit in [*Ortega*,] § 1367(a) addresses "civil action[s] of which the district courts have original jurisdiction," a formulation that, in diversity cases, is sensibly read to incorporate the rules on joinder and aggregation tightly tied to § 1332 at the time of § 1367's enactment. On this reading, a complaint must first meet that "original jurisdiction" measurement. If it does not, no supplemental jurisdiction is authorized. If it does, § 1367(a) authorizes "supplemental jurisdiction" over related claims. In other words, § 1367(a) would preserve undiminished, as part and parcel of § 1332 "original jurisdiction" determinations, both the "complete diversity" rule and the decisions restricting aggregation to arrive at the amount in controversy.[9] Section 1367(b)'s office, then, would be "to prevent the erosion of the complete diversity [and amount-in-controversy] requirement[s] that might otherwise result from an expansive application of what was once termed the doctrine of ancillary jurisdiction." See Pfander, *Supplemental Jurisdiction and Section 1367: The Case for a Sympathetic Textualism*, 148 U. PA. L.REV. 109, 114 (1999) ... In contrast to the Court's construction of § 1367, which draws a sharp line between the diversity and amount-in-controversy components of § 1332, the interpretation presented here does not sever the two jurisdictional requirements.

The more restrained reading of § 1367 just outlined [would] not discard entirely, as the Court does, the judicially developed doctrines of pendent and ancillary jurisdiction as they existed when *Finley* was decided. Instead, it would recognize § 1367 essentially as a codification of those doctrines, placing them under a single heading, but largely retaining their substance, with overriding *Finley* the only basic change: Supplemental jurisdiction, once the district court has original jurisdiction, would now include "claims that involve the joinder or intervention of additional parties." [§ 1367(a).]

[While] § 1367's enigmatic text[12] defies flawless interpretation, the precedent-preservative reading, I am persuaded, better accords with the historical and legal context of Congress' enactment of the supplemental jurisdiction statute, and the established limits on pendent and ancillary jurisdiction. It does not attribute to Congress a jurisdictional enlargement broader than the one to which the legislators adverted, and it follows the sound counsel that "close questions of [statutory] construction should be resolved in favor of continuity and against change." Shapiro, Continuity and Change in Statutory Interpretation, 67 N.Y.U.L.Rev. 921, 925 [(1992).]

NOTES ON SUPPLEMENTAL JURISDICTION IN DIVERSITY CASES

1.   Permissive Joinder. Notice that the rule announced in *Exxon* applies not only to class actions but also to permissive joinder under Rule 20.

---

[9]   On this reading of § 1367(a), it is immaterial that § 1367(b) "does not withdraw supplemental jurisdiction over the claims of the additional parties at issue here." Because those claims would not come within § 1367(a) in the first place, Congress would have had no reason to list them in § 1367(b).

[12]   The Court notes the passage this year of the Class Action Fairness Act (CAFA), Pub. L. 109–2, 119 Stat. 4, only to dismiss that legislation as irrelevant. Subject to several exceptions and qualifications, CAFA provides for federal-court adjudication of state-law-based class actions in which diversity is "minimal" (one plaintiff's diversity from one defendant suffices), and the "matter in controversy" is an aggregate amount in excess of $5,000,000. Significant here, CAFA's enlargement of federal-court diversity jurisdiction was accomplished, "clearly and conspicuously," by amending § 1332.

Yet, pursuant to the terms of § 1367, persons "needed for just adjudication" (under Rule 19) may not be joined. Does this make sense?

2.   **Statutory Interpretation.** In sections of the opinion that we have largely omitted, the Court shuns resort to legislative history in favor of the "plain meaning" of § 1367. Is the statute as unambiguous as the Court seems to suppose? See Note, *The Supreme Court, 2004 Term, Leading Cases*, 119 Harv. L. Rev. 317, 323 (2005) (arguing that "[t]he *Allopattah* majority's determination that § 1367 was not ambiguous conflicts with the common understanding of 'ambiguous.'") Assuming the text is clear, is a "plain meaning" approach to statutory interpretation consistent with the Court's focus in *Wachovia Bank v. Schmidt*, 546 U.S. 303 (2006), supra, on "context and purpose"?

CHAPTER 4

STANDING AND JUSTICIABILITY

■ ■ ■

Some disputes are fit for resolution by courts and others are not. But there is no consensus as to how and where lines should be drawn between the class of disputes courts will adjudicate and those they will reject. Grounds for dismissal include a litigant's lack of standing to raise the issue, or the dispute's lack of justiciability, which in turn may be due to mootness, or lack of ripeness, or some other shortcoming. The general issue addressed by this chapter is how the Supreme Court distinguishes between the two types of dispute in setting limits on the role of the federal courts. There are many hard questions and some open issues. In one respect, however, the line between the two categories is easy to draw. Litigants suing for damages are rarely if ever turned away from federal court on the ground that the suit is not justiciable or that the plaintiff lacks standing, though of course there are plenty of other grounds on which the plaintiff may lose.

Standing and justiciability issues come up almost exclusively in suits seeking prospective relief. Prospective relief—an injunction or a declaratory judgment—operates in the future, and the future is always uncertain. There are two general problems that prompt concerns about standing and justiciability. One is a "fitness" concern. For one reason or another, federal courts may be ill-suited to deal with the issues raised in forward-looking litigation. The specific problem may be (among others) that the facts are insufficiently developed for a court to constructively address the legal issues, or that the defendant may not take the step that worries the plaintiff, or that the plaintiff cannot benefit from the relief he seeks. If a court cannot effectively address the issues, it should not get involved. The root of the argument is that "adjudication" is the distinctive activity in which courts should engage. Adjudication can take place only when the parties are sufficiently adverse, when the facts are sufficiently concrete, and when the issues are sufficiently narrow. When these conditions are satisfied, the parties can advance arguments grounded in legal materials (and not mere policy arguments) and the judge can justify the outcome by reference to those materials. Much of the basic theory (one that only appears in bits and pieces in Supreme Court opinions) can be found in Lon L. Fuller, *The Forms and Limits of Adjudication*, 92 HARV. L. REV. 353 (1978).

The second general problem (related to the first but nonetheless distinct from it) is that judicial intervention may be unnecessary. If the defendant does not pursue the course of action that concerns the plaintiff, or if question in dispute is no longer relevant to the conduct of either side, or if nothing the court does can change the plaintiff's situation, then the case for intervention is weak. In practice, the issue is not "whether" adjudication is necessary, but "how likely" is it that judicial intervention will make a difference. Meanwhile, judicial intervention always carries with it the risk of undue interference in democratic decision making by the non-majoritarian branch of government. In short, standing and justiciability rules serve to cabin the judicial role in our system of separation of powers. It is better; the argument goes, for courts to incur the cost of friction between the branches only in situations in which courts can accomplish something of value. For a Supreme Court opinion that puts a lot of weight on this argument, see *Allen v. Wright*, 468 U.S. 737 (1984).

The other side of the debate—in favor of fewer standing and justiciability constraints on the federal courts—is that articulating and implementing public values is a crucial part of the judicial role. Even when the interest of a particular litigant is small, and even when the real-world impact of the relief sought is uncertain, that judicial role is served by judicial intervention. To take (what is today) an uncontroversial example, the Equal Protection Clause guarantees equality in the way persons are treated by the state, especially with regard to such basic civil rights as voting. Before the 1960s, many states had (often for nakedly political reasons) drawn the lines of voting districts such that the votes of certain citizens counted for much less (perhaps one tenth, in extreme cases) that of others. Notice that citizens in the disfavored districts were nonetheless allowed their right to vote. Nor were they discriminated against on the basis of race or sex or age. For a long time the Supreme Court declined to adjudicate gerrymander cases, for lack of "justiciability." See *Colgrove v. Green*, 328 U.S. 549 (1946). But eventually, in *Baker v. Carr*, 369 U.S. 186 (1962), the Warren Court took a different view. The fact that the interest at stake for a given voter was rather low—consisting of nothing more than a nonmonetary interest in voting strength, in a system in which one vote does not count for much anyway—did not deter the Supreme Court from striking down the gerrymandered districts. See *Reynolds v. Sims*, 377 U.S. 533 (1964). A recurrent issue in the law of standing and justiciability is which nonmonetary interests are nonetheless strong enough to overcome the countervailing arguments based on need and fitness. *Baker* and *Reynolds* are emblematic of the rise of "public law" litigation, in which the "fitness" and "separation of powers" constraints that animate the "private law" model often give way in order to achieve the benefits of judicial intervention.

Generally speaking, the standing and justiciability doctrines govern *what* matters are susceptible to determination in federal court, *who* can invoke federal judicial power, and *when* federal court action is timely. Some of the most basic doctrines go to *what* matters are justiciable in the sense that they disclaim duties the federal courts cannot perform: Federal courts cannot issue "advisory" opinions, render judgments that are not "final" within the judicial branch, or resolve "political" questions. The doctrine of "standing" originally identified *who* may sue in an Article III court and continues to address that question today. The "ripeness" and "mootness" doctrines govern *when* issues can be considered. But generalizations about justiciability are notoriously unreliable. All the justiciability doctrines serve the same master: the Supreme Court's sense of the federal judiciary's role in relation to the other branches of the central government and the states.

This chapter devotes the lion's share of its pages to cases and questions about standing. The other justiciability doctrines are best understood against the backdrop that standing provides. Standing doctrine, in turn, is the product of a profound struggle between competing conceptions of what federal courts are and what they do and ought to do in American public life. This great battle has obvious political and ideological significance. Standing doctrine is therefore unruly, even incoherent, and by some accounts manipulable in the service of substantive goals.

Throughout this chapter, we are concerned with the role of the *federal* courts. The main constitutional provision is Article III, which limits federal courts to adjudicating "cases" and "controversies." Much, but not all, of the Supreme Court's doctrine is framed as a gloss on those constitutional terms. The justiciability and standing rules applicable to state courts depend on state law and vary from state to state. But problems arise in certain cases, for example, when state courts adjudicate disputes that do not satisfy Article III and could not be brought in federal court. May the Supreme Court review these cases? In *ASARCO Inc. v. Kadish*, 490 U.S. 605 (1989), the Court held that, at least sometimes, the answer is yes: "When a state court has issued a judgment in a case where plaintiffs in the original action had no standing under the principles governing the federal courts, we may exercise our jurisdiction if the judgment of the state court causes direct, specific, and concrete injury to the parties who petition for our review."

I.   ADVISORY OPINIONS

According to Charles Alan Wright and Mary Kay Kane, "the oldest and most consistent thread in the federal law of justiciability is that the federal courts will not give advisory opinions." C. WRIGHT & M. KANE, LAW OF FEDERAL COURTS 65–66 (7th ed. 2011). The most famous illustration of the "rule against advisory opinions," as Wright & Kane call it, *id.*, came when Thomas Jefferson (as Secretary of State acting for President Washington) sent the Justices a letter asking whether they would be available to answer certain questions concerning treaties with France. Chief Justice Jay responded in a letter addressed directly to Washington, in which he purported to speak for the other justices, but (notably?) not for the Court: "[T]he lines of separation drawn by the Constitution between the three departments of the government . . . [t]hese being in certain respects checks upon each other, and our being judges of a court of the last resort, are considerations which afford strong arguments against the propriety of our extrajudicially deciding the questions alluded to, especially as the power given by the Constitution to the President, of calling on the heads of departments for opinions, seems to have been *purposely* as well as expressly united to the *executive* department." Chief Justice Jay and Associate Justices to President Washington, Aug. 8, 1793 (emphasis in original), reprt'd in III CORRESPONDENCE AND PUBLIC PAPERS OF JOHN JAY 488–89 (H.P. Johnston ed. 1891).

Some state courts do issue formal advisory opinions, for example, at the request of the state Attorney General. In Massachusetts the practice predates the U.S. Constitution. See R. FALLON ET. AL., HART & WECHSLER'S THE FEDERAL COURTS AND THE FEDERAL SYSTEM 57–58 (6th ed. 2009). One scholarly analysis of the practice noted that advisory opinions "allow state courts to articulate constitutional principles, while effectively 'remanding' disputes back to the other branches." Helen Hershkoff, *State Courts and the "Passive Virtues": Rethinking the Judicial Function*, 114 HARV. L. REV. 1833, 1840 n. 68 (2001). In the sense that this practice is strictly forbidden by Article III, there is indeed a rule against federal courts issuing advisory opinions. That rule reflects important policy considerations, especially (a) a "fitness" concern, that courts will in general act more effectively when they are resolving a concrete dispute between adverse parties, in which the facts are developed and the stakes are real, and (b) a separation of powers" concern, that courts, lacking the policymaking legitimacy of the majoritarian branches, should not resolve constitutional questions unless it is necessary to do so in order to adjudicate such a concrete dispute. As we will see throughout this chapter, those policies weigh heavily in the law of standing and justiciability. But neither the rule against advisory opinions nor those policies have deterred the Supreme Court from activities that could fairly be labeled "giving advice." Aside from the absolute bar to issuing formal advisory opinions, the "rule" against advisory opinions is more accurately described as a policy, albeit one that is especially strong in some standing and justiciability contexts.

Thus, the Court has held that collusive suits are nonjusticiable for want of genuinely adverse parties, e.g., *United States v. Johnson*, 319 U.S. 302 (1943), and has at least questioned special arrangements erected for the purpose of obtaining answers to particular legal questions. In *Muskrat v. United States*, 219 U.S. 346 (1911), members of the Cherokee tribe of Native Americans contended that Congress had restricted their ability to dispose of certain land. Congress enacted legislation authorizing the Cherokees to file suit in federal court to obtain a judicial determination of the validity of what Congress had done. When the Cherokees did so, the Court ruled that their action was not justiciable. The suit was not a genuine effort to enforce the Cherokees' legal rights, but was instead an artificial device for obtaining a judicial opinion on an abstract question. The Federal Government was not really an adverse party, and other private citizens who had a stake in the matter were not involved.

In other contexts, however, courts may resolve issues that are not necessary to the decision of the case at hand, and are, in that sense, "advice." *Pearson v. Callahan*, 555 U.S. 223 (2009), dealt with an issue that comes up in litigation under 42 U.S.C. § 1983. In order to recover damages, the plaintiff must prevail on two issues: both a violation of his constitutional right and an absence of official immunity, which in turn can depend on whether the right was "clearly established" at the time the defendant violated the right. A strict prohibition on "advisory opinions" would lead to a general rule that courts should resolve the immunity issue first. If the court decides that, even assuming the existence of a good constitutional claim, the right was not clearly established at the time the officer acted, then it is unnecessary to decide whether the right actually exists or not. But the Court rejected that approach. Recognizing that there may be good policy reasons in favor of deciding the substantive constitutional question first (including the value of providing guidance as to the content of constitutional guarantees), and recognizing that the strength of the competing policies may vary from context to context, it held that lower courts have discretion to decide the issues in the order that seems best in a given case, all things considered. And there is an even broader practice that is at odds with the notion that there is a "rule" against advisory opinions: Whatever may be true of inferior federal courts, the Supreme Court itself routinely expounds on legal questions without any necessity to do so in order to resolve traditional disputes between adverse parties and to issue conclusive relief. Sometimes the *dicta* is the most important passage in an opinion. The Court's discretionary docket exists to allow the justices to use particular cases as vehicles for reaching questions they want to decide and even to manipulate the issues in cases in order to isolate questions of interest.

Early on, the prohibition on advisory opinions threatened to foreclose declaratory judgment actions in the federal courts. In *Willing v. Chicago Aud. Ass'n*, 277 U.S. 274 (1928), the tenant of land in Chicago wanted to raze a building located on the parcel. Some of the landlords indicated that, in their view, the tenant needed their consent. The tenant sued the landlords in state court seeking an order clearing what the tenant regarded as a cloud on its leasehold estate. Some of the defendants removed the case to federal court on the ground that the tenant might have invoked the federal court's diversity jurisdiction. Writing for the Supreme Court, Justice Brandeis explained that the landlords had created no actionable cloud on the tenant's title simply by offering their views about the lawfulness of the tenant's plans. Accordingly, Brandeis said, "[w]hat the plaintiff seeks is simply a declaratory judgment"—a form of relief "beyond the power conferred upon the federal judiciary" to grant. Since the suit was "not a case or controversy within the meaning of [Article III]," the district court could not entertain it.

When federal drafters drew up the Declaratory Judgment Act, 28 U.S.C. § 2201, *et seq.*, they specified that a federal court would have authority to issue a declaratory judgment "in a case of actual controversy." Writing for the Court in *Aetna Life Ins. v. Haworth*, 300 U.S. 227 (1937), Chief Justice Hughes seized upon that proviso to sustain the federal Act: "Where there is such a concrete case admitting of an immediate and definitive determination of the legal rights of the parties in an adversary proceeding upon the facts alleged, the judicial function may be appropriately exercised although the adjudication of the rights of the litigants may not require the award of process or the payment of damages. And as it is not essential to the exercise of the judicial power that an injunction be sought, allegations that irreparable injury is threatened are not required." According to Hughes, the Declaratory Judgment Act is "procedural only." It provides "remedies" and defines "procedure" for suits seeking declaratory relief, but it posits that those suits satisfy the constitutional requirements for federal adjudication.

In contemporary litigation, declaratory judgment actions do not commonly ring the "advisory opinion" alarm bell. To be sure, some Supreme Court opinions assert that the declaratory judgment is a "milder alternative to the injunction remedy." *Steffel v. Thompson*, 415 U.S. 452, 467 (1974). If so, the validity of declaratory judgments might be questioned on the ground that they are merely advisory opinions. But the Court's actual practice belies the "mildness thesis." See Samuel L. Bray, *The Myth of the Mild Declaratory Judgment*, 63 DUKE L. J. 1091 (2014). Professor Bray refutes the notion that the declaratory judgment is a "milder" remedy, points out that for most purposes the two remedies are "rough substitutes," but also notes two differences. Thus, the real advantage of the injunction is that it is much more effective as a means for "managing" ongoing litigation that involves judicial oversight of remedies, such as school desegregation or prison reform. According to Professor Bray, the advantage of the declaratory judgment is that it "is sometimes available at an earlier point in the lifecycle of a dispute than an injunction is."

Consider *MedImmune v. Genentech*, 549 U.S. 118 (2007). A patent holder, Genentech, sent a letter to one of its licensees, MedImmune, stating that a drug manufactured by MedImmune was covered by Genentech's patent and that Genentech expected MedImmune to pay royalties. MedImmune took the position that Genentech's patent was invalid and that no royalties were due. Nevertheless, MedImmune paid the demanded royalties under protest rather than risk running up damages that would be assessed if Genentech's claim was ultimately sustained. MedImmune then sued Genentech for a declaratory judgment of noninfringement. In the Supreme Court, Justice Scalia said this:

> [B]ut for [MedImmune's] continuing to make royalty payments, nothing about the dispute would render it unfit for judicial resolution. [T]he continuation of royalty payments makes what would otherwise be an imminent threat at least remote, if not nonexistent. [MedImmune's] own acts, in other words, eliminate the imminent threat of harm. . . . The question before us is whether this causes the dispute no longer to be a case or controversy within the meaning of Article III.

> [W]here threatened action by *government* is concerned, we do not require a plaintiff to expose himself to liability before bringing suit to challenge the basis for the threat—for example, the constitutionality of a law threatened to be enforced. The plaintiff's own action (or inaction) in failing to violate the law eliminates the imminent threat of prosecution, but nonetheless does not eliminate Article III jurisdiction. [As Chief Justice Rehnquist explained in a concurring opinion in *Steffel v. Thompson*], "the declaratory judgment procedure is an alternative to pursuit of the arguably illegal activity." The dilemma posed by . . . coercion—putting the challenger to the choice between abandoning his rights or risking prosecution—is "a dilemma that it was the very purpose of the Declaratory Judgment Act to ameliorate." . . .

> Supreme Court jurisprudence is more rare regarding application of the Declaratory Judgment Act to situations in which the plaintiff's self-avoidance of imminent injury is coerced by threatened enforcement action of *a private party* rather than the government. Lower federal courts, however (and state courts interpreting declaratory-judgment acts requiring "actual

controversy"), have long accepted jurisdiction in such cases. . . . The only Supreme Court decision in point is, fortuitously, close on its facts to the case before us. [*Altvater v. Freeman*, 319 U.S. 359 (1943)], held that a licensee's failure to cease its payment of royalties did not render nonjusticiable a dispute over the validity of [a] patent.

We hold that petitioner was not required, insofar as Article III is concerned, to break or terminate its . . . license agreement before seeking a declaratory judgment in federal court that the underlying patent is invalid, unenforceable, or not infringed.

II.   FINALITY

PLAUT V. SPENDTHRIFT FARM
514 U.S. 211 (1995).

JUSTICE SCALIA delivered the opinion of the Court.

In 1987, petitioners brought a civil action [alleging that] respondents had committed fraud and deceit in the sale of stock in violation of § 10(b) of the Securities Exchange Act . . . and Rule 10b–5 of the Securities and Exchange Commission. The case was mired in pretrial proceedings [until] June 19, 1991, when we decided *Lampf, Pleva, Lipkind, Prupis & Petigrow v. Gilbertson*, 501 U.S. 350 (1991). *Lampf* held that "[l]itigation instituted pursuant to § 10(b) and Rule 10b–5 . . . must be commenced within one year after the discovery of the facts constituting the violation and within three years after such violation." [The] effect of *Lampf* . . . was to mandate application of the 1-year/3-year limitations period to petitioners' suit. The District Court, finding that petitioners' claims were untimely under the *Lampf* rule, dismissed their action with prejudice. Petitioners filed no appeal; the judgment accordingly became final 30 days later.

On December 19, 1991, the President signed the Federal Deposit Insurance Corporation Improvement Act of 1991. Section 476 of the Act . . . [which] became § 27A of the Securities Exchange Act of 1934 [provides that an action initiated before June 19, 1991 and dismissed as time barred thereafter shall be "reinstated on motion by the plaintiff. . . ."] [P]etitioners returned to the District Court and filed a motion to reinstate the action previously dismissed with prejudice. The District Court denied the motion, agreeing with respondents that § 27A(b) is unconstitutional. The United States Court of Appeals for the Sixth Circuit affirmed. . . . We conclude that in § 27A(b) Congress has exceeded its authority by requiring the federal courts to exercise "[t]he judicial Power of the United States" . . . in a manner repugnant to the text, structure, and traditions of Article III.

Hayburn's Case, 2 Dall. 409 (1792), . . . stands for the principle that Congress cannot vest review of the decisions of Article III courts in officials of the Executive Branch. [U]nder any application of § 27A(b) only courts are involved; no officials of other departments sit in direct review of their decisions. . . . We think, however, that § 27A(b) offends a postulate of Article III just as deeply rooted in our law. . . . Article III establishes a "judicial department" with the "province and duty . . . to say what the law is" in particular cases and controversies. [*Marbury v. Madison*]. The record of history shows that the Framers crafted this charter of the judicial department with an expressed understanding that it gives the Federal Judiciary the power, not merely to rule on cases, but to decide them, subject to review only by superior courts in the Article III hierarchy. . . .

Congress can always revise the judgments of Article III courts in one sense: When a new law makes clear that it is retroactive, an appellate court must apply that law in reviewing judgments still on appeal that were rendered before the law was enacted, and must alter the outcome accordingly. . . . But a distinction between judgments from which all appeals have been forgone or completed, and judgments that remain on appeal (or subject to being appealed), is implicit in what Article III creates: not a batch of unconnected courts, but a judicial department composed of "inferior Courts" and "one supreme Court." Within that hierarchy, the decision of an inferior court is not (unless the time for appeal has expired) the final word of the department as a whole. . . . Having achieved finality, however, a judicial decision becomes the last word of the judicial department with regard to a particular case or controversy, and Congress may not declare by retroactive legislation that the law applicable to that very case was something other than what the courts said it was. Finality of a legal judgment is determined by statute, just as entitlement to a government benefit is a statutory creation; but that no more deprives the former of its constitutional significance for separation-of-powers analysis than it deprives the latter of its significance for due process purposes. . . .

To be sure, a general statute such as this one may reduce the perception that legislative interference with judicial judgments was prompted by individual favoritism; but it is legislative interference with judicial judgments nonetheless. Not favoritism, nor even corruption, but power is the object of the separation-of-powers prohibition. [H]ypothetical horribles [are said to flow] from our assertedly "rigid holding"—for example, the inability to set aside a civil judgment that has become final during a period when a natural disaster prevented the timely filing of a certiorari petition. That is horrible not because of our holding, but because the underlying statute itself enacts a "rigid" jurisdictional bar to entertaining untimely civil petitions. Congress could undoubtedly enact prospective legislation permitting, or indeed requiring, this Court to make equitable exceptions to an otherwise applicable rule of finality, just as district courts do pursuant to Rule 60(b). It is no indication whatever of the invalidity of the constitutional rule which we announce, that it produces unhappy consequences when a legislature lacks foresight, and acts belatedly to remedy a deficiency in the law. That is a routine result of constitutional rules.

NOTES ON FINALITY

1. **Finality and Advisory Opinions.** Is Justice Scalia's analysis in *Plaut* consistent with the separation of powers rationale for the prohibition on advisory opinions? Recall the correspondence between Washington and Jay and the argument, in that context, that by answering the President's questions the justices would have placed themselves in the role of the President's underlings (who might advise him, but certainly could not control him). The key was that judicial advice, however valuable, was not dispositive; the President himself had the final say. In *Plaut*, according to Justice Scalia, it was Congress that had invaded judicial territory, presuming to dislodge judgments the courts had made final. Is it self-evident that the spheres of judicial, executive, and legislative authority are so distinct—leaving no wiggle room for accommodation? If the Court insists on delineating three powers via formally sharp lines, doesn't there have to be some explanatory rationale—some persuasive *reason* for disallowing greater cooperation?

2. *Hayburn's Case.* In *Hayburn's Case*, Congress had established pensions for disabled veterans of the Revolutionary War. Applicants were required to demonstrate that they had been injured during honorable military service. Federal circuit courts were supposed to entertain applications and provide the Secretary of War with proposed dispositions. The Secretary could accept a court's recommendation of an application or reject it and forward a different proposal to Congress, where the ultimate decision either to award or to withhold benefits would be made. A circuit court in Pennsylvania balked, and the Attorney General, William Randolph, petitioned the Supreme Court for a writ of mandamus forcing the circuit court to perform its function under the Act. The Court first declined to consider the petition, apparently because Randolph had no statutory authority to enforce the Act via mandamus and because he named no individual applicant whose interests were affected. Randolph withdrew as Attorney General and returned purporting to represent William Hayburn, the applicant whose claim the circuit court had refused to consider. The Supreme Court then seemed willing to determine whether the circuit court could be forced to participate. At that point, however, Congress defused the matter by eliminating the circuit courts' role in the pension scheme. The Supreme Court never reached a judgment on whether the unamended Act was invalid as an attempt to require Article III courts to deliver opinions that were not final. Three circuit courts (staffed in part by Supreme Court

justices) sent letters to the President indicating that it would be improper for them to make recommendations that Congress could reject.

3. The *Plaut* Case. In *Plaut*, Justice Scalia cited historical instances in which Congress had purported simply to override judicial decisions. Isn't it one thing for Congress to set a *particular* judicial decision at naught and order a new trial and another for Congress to reopen a *class* of judgments when the law has changed and justice would be served? Do all final judgments have to be treated alike, or might Congress be faulted only when it acts out of favoritism?

III. POLITICAL QUESTIONS

ZIVOTOFSKY V. CLINTON
132 S.Ct. 1421 (2012).

CHIEF JUSTICE ROBERTS delivered the opinion of the Court.

Congress enacted a statute providing that Americans born in Jerusalem may elect to have "Israel" listed as the place of birth on their passports. The State Department declined to follow that law, citing its longstanding policy of not taking a position on the political status of Jerusalem. When sued by an American who invoked the statute, the Secretary of State argued that the courts lacked authority to decide the case because it presented a political question. The Court of Appeals so held.

We disagree. The courts are fully capable of determining whether this statute may be given effect, or instead must be struck down in light of authority conferred on the Executive by the Constitution.

I

A

In 2002, Congress enacted the Foreign Relations Authorization Act, Fiscal Year 2003. The first two subsections express Congress's "commitment" to relocating the United States Embassy in Israel to Jerusalem. The third bars funding for the publication of official Government documents that do not list Jerusalem as the capital of Israel. The fourth and final provision, § 214(d), is the only one at stake in this case. Entitled "Record of Place of Birth as Israel for Passport Purposes," it provides that "[f]or purposes of the registration of birth, certification of nationality, or issuance of a passport of a United States citizen born in the city of Jerusalem, the Secretary shall, upon the request of the citizen or the citizen's legal guardian, record the place of birth as Israel."

The State Department's Foreign Affairs Manual states that "[w]here the birthplace of the applicant is located in territory disputed by another country, the city or area of birth may be written in the passport." The manual specifically directs that passport officials should enter "JERUSALEM" and should "not write Israel or Jordan" when recording the birthplace of a person born in Jerusalem on a passport.

Section 214(d) sought to override this instruction by allowing citizens born in Jerusalem to have "Israel" recorded on their passports if they wish. In signing the Foreign Relations Authorization Act into law, President George W. Bush stated his belief that § 214 "impermissibly interferes with the President's constitutional authority to conduct the Nation's foreign affairs and to supervise the unitary executive branch." Statement on Signing the Foreign Relations Authorization Act, Fiscal Year 2003, Public Papers of the Presidents, George W. Bush, Vol. 2, Sept. 30, 2002, p. 1698 (2005). He added that if the section is "construed as mandatory," then it would "interfere with the President's constitutional authority to formulate the position of the United States, speak for the Nation in international affairs, and determine the terms on which recognition is given to foreign states." He concluded by emphasizing that "U.S. policy regarding Jerusalem has not changed." The President made no specific reference to the passport mandate in § 214(d).

B

Petitioner Menachem Binyamin Zivotofsky was born in Jerusalem on October 17, 2002, shortly after § 214(d) was enacted. Zivotofsky's parents were American citizens and he accordingly was as well, by virtue of congressional enactment. 8 U.S.C. § 1401(c). Zivotofsky's mother filed an application for a consular report of birth abroad and a United States passport. She requested that his place of birth be listed as "Jerusalem, Israel" on both documents. U.S. officials informed Zivotofsky's mother that State Department policy prohibits recording "Israel" as Zivotofsky's place of birth. Pursuant to that policy, Zivotofsky was issued a passport and consular report of birth abroad listing only "Jerusalem."

Zivotofsky's parents filed a complaint on his behalf against the Secretary of State. Zivotofsky sought a declaratory judgment and a permanent injunction ordering the Secretary to identify his place of birth as "Jerusalem, Israel" in the official [documents].

II

[In] general, the Judiciary has a responsibility to decide cases properly before it, even those it "would gladly avoid." *Cohens v. Virginia,* 6 Wheat. 264, 404 (1821). Our precedents have identified a narrow exception to that rule, known as the "political question" doctrine. We have explained that a controversy "involves a political question . . . where there is

> " 'a textually demonstrable constitutional commitment of the issue to a coordinate political department; or a lack of judicially

discoverable and manageable standards for resolving it.' " *Nixon v. United States,* 506 U.S. 224, 228 (1993) (quoting *Baker v. Carr,* 369 U.S. 186, 217 (1962)). In such a case, we have held that a court lacks the authority to decide the dispute before it.

The lower courts ruled that this case involves a political question because deciding Zivotofsky's claim would force the Judicial Branch to interfere with the President's exercise of constitutional power committed to him alone. The District Court understood Zivotofsky to ask the courts to "decide the political status of Jerusalem." This misunderstands the issue presented. Zivotofsky does not ask the courts to determine whether Jerusalem is the capital of Israel. He instead seeks to determine whether he may vindicate his statutory right, under § 214(d), to choose to have Israel recorded on his passport as his place of birth.

For its part, the D.C. Circuit treated the two questions as one and the same. That court concluded that "[o]nly the Executive—not Congress and not the courts—has the power to define U.S. policy regarding Israel's sovereignty over Jerusalem," and also to "decide how best to implement that policy." Because the Department's passport rule was adopted to implement the President's "exclusive and unreviewable constitutional power to keep the United States out of the debate over the status of Jerusalem," the validity of that rule was itself a "nonjusticiable political question" that "the Constitution leaves to the Executive alone." Indeed, the D.C. Circuit's opinion does not even mention § 214(d) until the fifth of its six paragraphs of analysis, and then only to dismiss it as irrelevant: "That Congress took a position on the status of Jerusalem and gave Zivotofsky a statutory cause of action . . . is of no moment to whether the judiciary has [the] authority to resolve this dispute. . . ."

The existence of a statutory right, however, is certainly relevant to the Judiciary's power to decide Zivotofsky's claim. The federal courts are not being asked to supplant a foreign policy decision of the political branches with the courts' own unmoored determination of what United States policy toward Jerusalem should be. Instead, Zivotofsky requests that the courts enforce a specific statutory right. To resolve his claim, the Judiciary must decide if Zivotofsky's interpretation of the statute is correct, and whether the statute is constitutional. This is a familiar judicial exercise.

Moreover, because the parties do not dispute the interpretation of § 214(d), the only real question for the courts is whether the statute is constitutional. In this case, determining the constitutionality of § 214(d) involves deciding whether the statute impermissibly intrudes upon Presidential powers under the Constitution. If so, the law must be invalidated and Zivotofsky's case should be dismissed for failure to state a claim. If, on the other hand, the statute does not trench on the President's powers, then the Secretary must be ordered to issue Zivotofsky a passport that complies with § 214(d). Either way, the political question doctrine is not implicated. "No policy underlying the political question doctrine suggests that Congress or the Executive . . . can decide the constitutionality of a statute; that is a decision for the courts."

The Secretary contends that "there is 'a textually demonstrable constitutional commitment'" to the President of the sole power to recognize foreign sovereigns and, as a corollary, to determine whether an American born in Jerusalem may choose to have Israel listed as his place of birth on his passport. Perhaps. But there is, of course, no exclusive commitment to the Executive of the power to determine the constitutionality of a statute. The Judicial Branch appropriately exercises that authority, including in a case such as this, where the question is whether Congress or the Executive is "aggrandizing its power at the expense of another branch."

Our precedents have also found the political question doctrine implicated when there is "'a lack of judicially discoverable and manageable standards for resolving'" the question before the court. Framing the issue as the lower courts did, in terms of whether the Judiciary may decide the political status of Jerusalem, certainly raises those concerns. They dissipate, however, when the issue is recognized to be the more focused one of the constitutionality of § 214(d). Indeed, both sides offer detailed legal arguments regarding whether § 214(d) is constitutional in light of powers committed to the Executive, and whether Congress's own powers with respect to passports must be weighed in analyzing this question.

For example, the Secretary reprises on the merits her argument on the political question issue, claiming that the Constitution gives the Executive the exclusive power to formulate recognition policy. She roots her claim in the Constitution's declaration that the President shall "receive Ambassadors and other public Ministers." U.S. Const., Art. II, § 3. According to the Secretary, "[c]enturies-long Executive Branch practice, congressional acquiescence, and decisions by this Court" confirm that the "receive Ambassadors" clause confers upon the Executive the exclusive power of recognition.

The Secretary observes that "President Washington and his cabinet unanimously decided that the President could receive the ambassador from the new government of France without first consulting Congress." [She] notes, too, that early attempts by the Legislature to affect recognition policy were regularly "rejected in Congress as inappropriate incursions into the Executive Branch's constitutional authority." And she cites precedents from this Court stating that "[p]olitical recognition is exclusively a function of the Executive." *Banco Nacional de Cuba v. Sabbatino,* 376 U.S. 398, 410 (1964).

The Secretary further contends that § 214(d) constitutes an impermissible exercise of the recognition power because "the decision as to how to describe the place of birth . . . operates as an official statement of whether the United States recognizes a state's sovereignty over a territorial area." The Secretary will not "list[ ] as a place of birth a country whose sovereignty over the relevant territory the United States does not recognize." Therefore, she claims, "listing 'Israel' as the place of birth would constitute an official decision by the United States to begin to treat Jerusalem as a city located within Israel."

For his part, Zivotofsky argues that, far from being an exercise of the recognition power, § 214(d) is instead a "legitimate and permissible" exercise of Congress's "authority to legislate on the form and content of a passport." He points the Court to Professor Louis Henkin's observation that " 'in the competition for power in foreign relations,' Congress has 'an impressive array of powers expressly enumerated in the Constitution.' " *Id.,* at 45 (quoting L. Henkin, Foreign Affairs and the United States Constitution 63 (2d ed.1996)). Zivotofsky suggests that Congress's authority to enact § 214(d) derives specifically from its powers over naturalization, U.S. Const., Art. I, § 8, cl. 4, and foreign commerce, *id.,* § 8, cl. 3. According to Zivotofsky, Congress has used these powers to pass laws regulating the content and issuance of passports since 1856.

Zivotofsky contends that § 214(d) fits squarely within this tradition. He notes that the State Department's designated representative stated in her deposition for this litigation that the "place of birth" entry is included *only* as "an element of identification." Moreover, Zivotofsky argues, the "place of birth" entry cannot be taken as a means for recognizing foreign sovereigns, because the State Department authorizes recording unrecognized territories—such as the Gaza Strip and the West Bank—as places of birth.

Further, Zivotofsky claims that even if § 214(d) does implicate the recognition power, that is not a power the Constitution commits exclusively to the Executive. Zivotofsky argues that the Secretary is overreading the authority granted to the President in the "receive Ambassadors" clause. He observes that in the Federalist Papers, Alexander Hamilton described the power conferred by this clause as "more a matter of dignity than of authority," and called it "a circumstance, which will be without consequence in the administration of the government." The Federalist No. 69, p. 468 (J. Cooke ed.1961). Zivotofsky also points to other clauses in the Constitution, such as Congress's power to declare war, that suggest some congressional role in [recognition].

Zivotofsky argues that language from this Court's precedents suggesting the recognition power belongs exclusively to the President is inapplicable to his claim, because that language appeared in cases where the Court was asked to alter recognition policy developed by the Executive in the absence of congressional opposition. Finally, Zivotofsky contends that even if the "receive Ambassadors" clause confers some exclusive recognition power on the President, simply allowing a choice as to the "place of birth" entry on a passport does not significantly intrude on that power.

Recitation of these arguments—which sound in familiar principles of constitutional interpretation—is enough to establish that this case does not "turn on standards that defy judicial application." *Baker,* 369 U.S., at 211. Resolution of Zivotofsky's claim demands careful examination of the textual, structural, and historical evidence put forward by the parties regarding the nature of the statute and of the passport and recognition powers. This is what courts do. The political question doctrine poses no bar to judicial review of this case.

III

To say that Zivotofsky's claim presents issues the Judiciary is competent to resolve is not to say that reaching a decision in this case is simple. Because the District Court and the D.C. Circuit believed that review was barred by the political question doctrine, we are without the benefit of thorough lower court opinions to guide our analysis of the merits.

[Having] determined that this case is justiciable, we leave it to the lower courts to consider the merits in the first instance.

The judgment of the Court of Appeals for the D.C. Circuit is vacated, and the case is remanded for further proceedings consistent with this opinion.

It is so ordered.

JUSTICE SOTOMAYOR, with whom JUSTICE BREYER joins as to Part I, concurring in part and concurring in the judgment.

As this case illustrates, the proper application of *Baker*'s six factors has generated substantial confusion in the lower courts. I concur in the Court's conclusion that this case does not present a political question. I write separately, however, because I understand the inquiry required by the political question doctrine to be more demanding than that suggested by the Court.

I

The political question doctrine speaks to an amalgam of circumstances in which courts properly examine whether a particular suit is justiciable—that is, whether the dispute is appropriate for resolution by courts. The doctrine is "essentially a function of the separation of powers," *Baker v. Carr,* 369 U.S. 186, 217 (1962), which recognizes the limits that Article III imposes upon courts and accords appropriate respect to the other branches' exercise of their own constitutional powers.

In *Baker,* this Court identified six circumstances in which an issue might present a political question: (1) "a textually demonstrable constitutional commitment of the issue to a coordinate political department"; (2) "a lack of judicially discoverable and manageable standards for resolving it"; (3) "the impossibility of deciding without an initial policy determination of a kind clearly for nonjudicial discretion"; (4) "the impossibility of a court's undertaking independent resolution without expressing lack of the respect due coordinate branches of government"; (5) "an unusual need for unquestioning adherence to a political decision already made"; or (6) "the potentiality of embarrassment from multifarious pronouncements by various departments on one question." *Baker* established that "[u]nless one of these formulations is inextricable from the case at bar, there should be no dismissal for nonjusticiability." But *Baker* left unanswered when the presence of one or more factors warrants dismissal, as well as the interrelationship of the six factors and the relative importance of each in determining whether a case is suitable for adjudication.

In my view, the *Baker* factors reflect three distinct justifications for withholding judgment on the merits of a dispute. When a case would require a court to decide an issue whose resolution is textually committed to a coordinate political department, as envisioned by *Baker* 's first factor, abstention is warranted because the court lacks authority to resolve that issue. See, *e.g., Nixon v. United States,* 506 U.S. 224, 229 (1993) (holding nonjusticiable the Senate's impeachment procedures in light of Article I's commitment to the Senate of the " 'sole Power to try all Impeachments' "); see also *Marbury v. Madison,* 1 Cranch 137, 165–166 (1803) ("By the constitution of the United States, the president is invested with certain important political powers, in the exercise of which he is to use his own discretion, and is accountable only to his country in his political character, and to his own conscience"). In such cases, the Constitution itself requires that another branch resolve the question presented.

The second and third *Baker* factors reflect circumstances in which a dispute calls for decisionmaking beyond courts' competence. " 'The judicial Power' created by Article III, § 1, of the Constitution is not *whatever* judges choose to do," but rather the power "to act in the manner traditional for English and American courts." *Vieth v. Jubelirer,* 541 U.S. 267, 278 (2004) (plurality opinion). That traditional role involves the application of some manageable and cognizable standard within the competence of the Judiciary to ascertain and employ to the facts of a concrete case. When a court is given no standard by which to adjudicate a dispute, or cannot resolve a dispute in the absence of a yet-unmade policy determination charged to a political branch, resolution of the suit is beyond the judicial role envisioned by Article III. See, *e.g., Gilligan v. Morgan,* 413 U.S. 1, 10 (1973) ("[I]t is difficult to conceive of an area of governmental activity in which the courts have less competence" than "[t]he complex, subtle, and professional decisions as to the composition, training, equipping, and control of a military force"); *Vieth,* 541 U.S., at 278 ("One of the most obvious limitations imposed by [Article III] is that judicial action must be governed by *standard* . . ."). This is not to say, of course, that courts are incapable of interpreting or applying somewhat ambiguous standards using familiar tools of statutory or constitutional interpretation. But where an issue leaves courts truly rudderless, there can be "no doubt of [the] validity" of a court's decision to abstain from judgment.

The final three *Baker* factors address circumstances in which prudence may counsel against a court's resolution of an issue presented. Courts should be particularly cautious before forgoing adjudication of a dispute on the basis that judicial intervention risks "embarrassment from multifarious pronouncements by various departments on one question," would express a "lack of the respect due coordinate branches of government," or because there exists an "unusual need for unquestioning adherence to a political decision already made." We have repeatedly rejected the view that these thresholds are met whenever a court is called upon to resolve the constitutionality or propriety of the act of another branch of [Government].

Rare occasions implicating *Baker*'s final factors, however, may present an " 'unusual case' " unfit for judicial disposition. 369 U.S., at 218 (quoting the argument of Daniel Webster in *Luther v. Borden,* 7 How. 1, 29 (1849)). Because of the respect due to a coequal and independent department, for instance, courts properly resist calls to question the good faith with which another branch attests to the authenticity of its internal acts. See, *e.g., Field v. Clark,* 143 U.S. 649, 672–673 (1892) (deeming "forbidden by the respect due to a coordinate branch of the government" "[j]udicial action" requiring a belief in a "deliberate conspiracy" by the Senate and House of Representatives "to defeat an expression of the popular will"); see also *Munoz-Flores,* 495 U.S., at 409–410 (SCALIA, J., concurring in judgment) ("Mutual regard between the coordinate branches, and the interest of certainty, both demand that official representations regarding . . . matters of internal process be accepted at face value"). Likewise, we have long acknowledged that courts are particularly ill suited to intervening in exigent disputes necessitating unusual need for "attributing finality to the action of the political departments," *Coleman v. Miller,* 307 U.S. 433, 454 (1939), or creating acute "risk [of] embarrassment of our government abroad, or grave disturbance at home," *Baker,* 369 U.S., at 226. See, *e.g., Luther,* 7 How., at 43 ("After the President has acted and called out the militia, is a Circuit Court of the United States authorized to inquire whether his decision was right? . . . If the judicial power extends so far, the guarantee contained in the Constitution of the United States is a guarantee of anarchy, and not of order").[1] Finally, it may be appropriate for courts to stay their hand in cases implicating delicate questions concerning the distribution of political authority between coordinate branches until a dispute is ripe, intractable, and incapable of resolution by the political process. See *Goldwater v. Carter,* 444 U.S. 996, 997 (1979) (Powell, J., concurring in judgment). Abstention merely reflects that judicial intervention in such cases is "legitimate only in the last resort," *Chicago & Grand Trunk R. Co. v. Wellman,* 143 U.S. 339, 345 and is disfavored relative to the prospect of accommodation between the political branches.

When such unusual cases arise, abstention accommodates considerations inherent in the separation of powers and the limitations envisioned by Article III, which conferred authority to federal courts against a common-law backdrop that recognized the propriety of abstention in exceptional cases. *New Orleans Public Service, Inc. v. Council of City of New Orleans,* 491 U.S. 350, 359; see generally Shapiro, Jurisdiction and Discretion, 60 N.Y.U. L.Rev. 543 (1985) (hereinafter Shapiro). The political questions envisioned by *Baker* 's final categories find common ground, therefore, with many longstanding doctrines under which considerations of justiciability or comity lead courts to abstain from deciding questions whose initial resolution is better suited to another time, see, *e.g., National Park Hospitality Assn. v. Department of Interior,* 538 U.S. 803, 808 (2003) (ripeness); *United States Parole Comm'n v. Geraghty,* 445 U.S. 388, 397 (1980) (mootness); or another forum, see, *e.g., Gulf Oil Corp. v. Gilbert,* 330 U.S. 501, 507 (1947) *(forum non conveniens); Railroad Comm'n of Tex. v. Pullman Co.,* 312 U.S. 496, 498–500 (1941); *Louisiana Power & Light Co. v. City of Thibodaux,* 360 U.S. 25, 25–30 (1959); *Burford v. Sun Oil Co.,* 319 U.S. 315, 333–334 (1943) (abstention in favor of a state forum); *United States v. Western Pacific R. Co.,* 352 U.S. 59, 63–64 (1956) (primary jurisdiction doctrine). See also *DaimlerChrysler Corp. v. Cuno,* 547 U.S. 332, 352 (2006) ("The doctrines of mootness, ripeness, and political question all originate in Article III's 'case' or 'controversy' language"); Shapiro 550–557, 580–587

---

[1]   See also *Martin v. Mott,* 12 Wheat. 19, 29–30, 6 L.Ed. 537 (1827) (Story, J.) (declining to review the President's determination that an "exigency has arisen," necessitating the "call [of] the militia into actual service," recognizing need for "[a] prompt and unhesitating obedience to orders is indispensable"); *Ware v. Hylton,* 3 Dall. 199, 260, 1 L.Ed. 568 (1796) (Iredell, J., concurring) (to declare treaty with Great Britain void would turn on "considerations of policy, considerations of extreme magnitude, [which are] certainly entirely incompetent to the examination and decision of a Court of Justice").

(describing practices of judicial abstention sounding in justiciability, comity, *forum non conveniens,* and separation of powers).

To be sure, it will be the rare case in which *Baker*'s final factors alone render a case nonjusticiable. But our long historical tradition recognizes that such exceptional cases arise, and due regard for the separation of powers and the judicial role envisioned by Article III confirms that abstention may be an appropriate response.

II

The court below held that this case presented a political question because it thought petitioner's suit asked the court to decide an issue "textually committed" to a coordinate branch—namely, "to review a policy of the State Department implementing the President's decision" to keep the United States out of the debate over the status of Jerusalem. Largely for the reasons set out by the Court, I agree that the Court of Appeals misapprehended the nature of its task. In two respects, however, my understanding of the political question doctrine might require a court to engage in further analysis beyond that relied upon by the Court.

First, the Court appropriately recognizes that petitioner's claim to a statutory right is "relevant" to the justiciability inquiry required in this case. In order to evaluate whether a case presents a political question, a court must first identify with precision the issue it is being asked to decide. Here, petitioner's suit claims that a federal statute provides him with a right to have "Israel" listed as his place of birth on his passport and other related documents. To decide that question, a court must determine whether the statute is constitutional, and therefore mandates the Secretary of State to issue petitioner's desired passport, or unconstitutional, in which case his suit is at an end. Resolution of that issue is not one "textually committed" to another branch; to the contrary, it is committed to this one. In no fashion does the question require a court to review the wisdom of the President's policy toward Jerusalem or any other decision committed to the discretion of a coordinate department. For that reason, I agree that the decision below should be reversed.

That is not to say, however, that no statute could give rise to a political question. It is not impossible to imagine a case involving the application or even the constitutionality of an enactment that would present a nonjusticiable issue. Indeed, this Court refused to determine whether an Ohio state constitutional provision offended the Republican Guarantee Clause, Art. IV, § 4, holding that "the question of whether that guarantee of the Constitution has been disregarded presents no justiciable controversy." *Ohio ex rel. Davis v. Hildebrant,* 241 U.S. 565, 569 (1916). A similar result would follow if Congress passed a statute, for instance, purporting to award financial relief to those improperly "tried" of impeachment offenses. To adjudicate claims under such a statute would require a court to resolve the very same issue we found nonjusticiable in *Nixon*. Such examples are atypical, but they suffice to show that the foreclosure altogether of political question analysis in statutory cases is unwarranted.

Second, the Court suggests that this case does not implicate the political question doctrine's concern with issues exhibiting " 'a lack of judicially discoverable and manageable standards,' " because the parties' arguments rely on textual, structural, and historical evidence of the kind that courts routinely consider. But that was equally true in *Nixon,* a case in which we found that "the use of the word 'try' in the first sentence of the Impeachment Trial Clause lacks sufficient precision to afford any judicially manageable standard of review of the Senate's actions." We reached that conclusion even though the parties' briefs focused upon the text of the Impeachment Trial Clause, "the Constitution's drafting history," "contemporaneous commentary," "the unbroken practice of the Senate for 150 years," contemporary dictionary meanings, "Hamilton's Federalist essays," and the practice in the House of Lords prior to ratification. Such evidence was no more or less unfamiliar to courts than that on which the parties rely here.

In my view, it is not whether the evidence upon which litigants rely is common to judicial consideration that determines whether a case lacks judicially discoverable and manageable standards. Rather, it is whether that evidence in fact provides a court a basis to adjudicate meaningfully the issue with which it is presented. The answer will almost always be yes, but if the parties' textual, structural, and historical evidence is inapposite or wholly unilluminating, rendering judicial decision no more than guesswork, a case relying on the ordinary kinds of arguments offered to courts might well still present justiciability concerns.

In this case, however, the Court of Appeals majority found a political question solely on the basis that this case required resolution of an issue "textually committed" to the Executive Branch. Because there was no such textual commitment, I respectfully concur in the Court's decision to reverse the Court of Appeals.

[JUSTICE ALITO's opinion concurring in the judgment is omitted.]

JUSTICE BREYER, dissenting.

I join Part I of Justice SOTOMAYOR's opinion. As she points out, *Baker v. Carr,* 369 U.S. 186 (1962), set forth several categories of legal questions that the Court had previously held to be "political questions" inappropriate for judicial [determination]. As Justice SOTOMAYOR also points out, these categories (and in my view particularly the last four) embody "circumstances in which prudence may counsel against a court's resolution of an issue [presented]."

Justice SOTOMAYOR adds that the circumstances in which these prudential considerations lead the Court not to decide a case otherwise properly before it are rare. I agree. But in my view we nonetheless have before us such a case. Four sets of prudential considerations, *taken together,* lead me to that conclusion.

First, the issue before us arises in the field of foreign affairs. (Indeed, the statutory provision before us is a subsection of a section that concerns the relation between Jerusalem and the State of Israel. See § 214 of the Foreign Relations Authorization Act, Fiscal Year 2003, 116 Stat. 1365 ("United States Policy with Respect to Jerusalem as the Capital of Israel").) The Constitution primarily delegates the foreign affairs powers "to the political departments of the government, Executive and Legislative," not to the Judiciary. And that fact is not surprising. Decisionmaking in this area typically is highly political. It is "delicate" and "complex." It often rests upon information readily available to the Executive Branch and to the intelligence committees of Congress, but not readily available to the courts. It frequently is highly dependent upon what Justice Jackson called "prophecy." And the creation of wise foreign policy typically lies well beyond the experience or professional capacity of a judge. At the same time, where foreign affairs is at issue, the practical need for the United States to speak "with one voice and ac[t] as one," is particularly important. The result is a judicial hesitancy to make decisions that have significant foreign policy implications, as reflected in the fact that many of the cases in which the Court has invoked the political-question doctrine have arisen in this [area].

Second, if the courts must answer the constitutional question before us, they may well have to evaluate the foreign policy implications of foreign policy [decisions]. Were the statutory provision undisputedly concerned only with purely administrative matters (or were its enforcement undisputedly to involve only major foreign policy matters), judicial efforts to answer the constitutional question might not involve judges in trying to answer questions of foreign policy. But in the Middle East, administrative matters can have implications that extend far beyond the purely administrative. Political reactions in that region can prove uncertain. And in that context it may well turn out that resolution of the constitutional argument will require a court to decide how far the statute, in practice, reaches beyond the purely administrative, determining not only whether but also the extent to which enforcement will interfere with the President's ability to make significant recognition-related foreign policy decisions.

Certainly the parties argue as if that were so. Zivotofsky, for example, argues that replacing "Jerusalem" on his passport with "Israel" will have no serious foreign policy significance. And in support he points to (1) a State Department official's statement that birthplace designation serves primarily as "an element of identification," while omitting mention of recognition; (2) the fact that the State Department has recorded births in unrecognized territories in the region, such as the Gaza Strip and the West Bank, apparently without adverse effect; and (3) the fact that sometimes Jerusalem does (because of what the Government calls "clerical errors") carry with it the name of "Israel" on certain official documents, again apparently without seriously adverse effect. Moreover, Zivotofsky says, it is unfair to allow the 100,000 or so Americans born in cities that the United States recognizes as under Israeli sovereignty, such as Tel Aviv or Haifa, the right to a record that mentions Israel, while denying that privilege to the 50,000 or so Americans born in Jerusalem.

At the same time, the Secretary argues that listing Israel on the passports (and consular birth reports) of Americans born in Jerusalem will have significantly adverse foreign policy effects. She says that doing so would represent " 'an official decision by the United States to begin to treat Jerusalem as a city located within Israel,' " that it "would be interpreted as an official act of recognizing Jerusalem as being under Israeli sovereignty," and that our "national security interests" consequently "would be significantly harmed." Such an action, she says, " 'would signal, symbolically or concretely, that' " the United States " 'recognizes that Jerusalem is a city that is located within the sovereign territory of Israel,' " and doing so, " 'would critically compromise the ability of the United States to work with Israelis, Palestinians and others in the region to further the peace process.' " She adds that the very enactment of this statutory provision in 2002 produced headlines in the Middle East stating the "the U.S. now recognizes Jerusalem as Israel's capital."

A judge's ability to evaluate opposing claims of this kind is minimal. At the same time, a judicial effort to do so risks inadvertently jeopardizing sound foreign policy decisionmaking by the other branches of Government. How, for example, is this Court to determine whether, or the extent to which, the continuation of the adjudication that it now orders will itself have a foreign policy effect?

Third, the countervailing interests in obtaining judicial resolution of the constitutional determination are not particularly strong ones. Zivotofsky does not assert the kind of interest, *e.g.,* an interest in property or bodily integrity, which courts have traditionally sought to protect. See, *e.g., Ingraham v. Wright,* 430 U.S. 651, 673–674 (1977) (enduring commitment to legal protection of bodily integrity). Nor, importantly, does he assert an interest in vindicating a basic right of the kind that the Constitution grants to individuals and that courts traditionally have protected from invasion by the other branches of Government. And I emphasize this fact because the need for judicial action in such cases can trump the foreign policy concerns that I have mentioned. As Professor Jaffe pointed out many years ago, "Our courts would not refuse to entertain habeas corpus to test the constitutionality of the imprisonment of an alleged Chinese agent even if it were clear that his imprisonment was closely bound up with our relations to the Chinese government."

The interest that Zivotofsky asserts, however, is akin to an ideological interest. [And] insofar as an individual suffers an injury that is purely ideological, courts have often refused to consider the matter, leaving the injured party to look to the political branches for protection. This is not to say that Zivotofsky's claim is unimportant or that the injury is not serious or even that it is purely ideological. It is to point out that those suffering somewhat similar harms have sometimes had to look to the political branches for resolution of relevant legal issues.

Fourth, insofar as the controversy reflects different foreign policy views among the political branches of Government, those branches have nonjudicial methods of working out their differences. [The] Executive and Legislative Branches frequently work out disagreements through ongoing contacts and relationships, involving, for example, budget authorizations, confirmation of personnel, committee hearings, and a host of more informal contacts, which, taken together, ensure that, in practice, Members of Congress as well as the President play an important role in the shaping of foreign policy. Indeed, both the Legislative Branch and the Executive Branch typically understand the need to work each with the other in order to create effective foreign policy. In that understanding, those related contacts, and the continuous foreign policy-related relationship lies the possibility of working out the kind of disagreement we see before us. Moreover, if application of the political-question "doctrine ultimately turns, as Learned Hand put it, on 'how importunately the occasion demands an answer,'" *Nixon,* 506 U.S., at 253, 113 S.Ct. 732 (SOUTER, J., concurring in judgment) (quoting L. Hand, The Bill of Rights 15 (1958)), the ability of the political branches to work out their differences minimizes the need for judicial intervention here.

The upshot is that this case is unusual both in its minimal need for judicial intervention and in its more serious risk that intervention will bring about "embarrassment," show lack of "respect" for the other branches, and potentially disrupt sound foreign policy decisionmaking. For these prudential reasons, I would hold that the political-question doctrine bars further judicial consideration of this case. And I would affirm the Court of Appeals' similar conclusion.

With respect, I dissent.

NOTES ON THE POLITICAL QUESTION DOCTRINE

1. ***Zivotofsky's* Aftermath and Implications.** On remand the D.C. Circuit struck down the statute on the ground that it intruded on the Executive's exclusive power over recognition of foreign governments. *Zivotofsky v. Secretary of State*, 725 F.3d 197 (D.C. Cir. 2013)(cert. granted, No. 13–628, April 21, 2014.) As for the implications of *Zivotofsky* for the political question doctrine, see Chris Michel, Comment, *There's No Such Thing as a Political Question of Statutory Interpretation*, 123 YALE L.J. 253 (2013) (so arguing). Another commentator suggests that *Zivotofsky* casts doubt on the continuing vitality of the whole political question doctrine. See Gwynne Skinner, *Misunderstood, Misconstrued, and Now Clearly Dead: The "Political Question" as a Justiciability Doctrine*, 29 J. L. & POLITICS 427 (2014).

2. ***Luther v. Borden.*** The classic "political question" decision is *Luther v. Borden*, 48 U.S. (7 How.) 1 (1849), which grew out of the unsettled affairs in Rhode Island in the wake of Dorr's Rebellion. Chief Justice Taney explained that the Constitution gave Congress the authority to decide whether to accept the credentials of individuals who claimed to be the state's elected representatives and senators. It followed that Congress equally had the authority to decide whether those officers represented the state's lawful government. Taney acknowledged that the Guarantee Clause obligated "the United States" to "guarantee to every State" a "Republican Form of Government." Article IV, § 4. But he said that a claim under the Guarantee Clause raised a political issue to the extent it asked the courts to review Congress's decision to receive representatives and senators. In some respects, Taney appeared to rest the decision in *Luther* on an interpretation of the Constitution. Yet he also noted the difficulties that would follow if rival political camps could draw the federal courts into local struggles for power.

3. ***Baker v. Carr.*** The opinions in *Zivotofsky*, and in particular Justice Sotomayor's concurring opinion, look to *Baker v. Carr* for guidance. Before *Baker,* the Court had treated the drawing of legislative districts as a non-justiciable political question. That changed in *Baker*, one of the Warren Court's most consequential rulings. Writing for the Court, Justice Brennan concluded that an equal protection attack on the apportionment of the Tennessee state legislature didn't raise a political question. Justice Brennan distinguished *Luther* on two grounds. First, while the Constitution assigns Congress the authority to decide whether representatives and senators actually represent valid state governments, the Constitution does not give Congress (or the President) the authority to decide whether state legislatures are validly apportioned. Second, the Equal Protection Clause offers "judicially manageable" standards that the Guarantee Clause does not. The *Baker* decision, in turn, freed the Court to announce the famous "one-person, one-vote" standard in *Reynolds v. Sims*, 377 U.S. 533 (1964). Justice Brennan and the other justices in the *Baker* majority plainly saw a compelling need to prescribe constitutional standards for apportionment cases, because incumbents are rarely willing to change even plainly unrepresentative

systems in fear that reforms may favor their opponents. The *Baker* decision thus illustrates the justices' willingness on occasion to decide thorny questions they might prefer to leave to politics when it appears that political bodies are paralyzed and cannot effectively respond.

IV. STANDING AND THE INJURY REQUIREMENT

EX PARTE LEVITT
302 U.S. 633 (1937).

[In 1937, President Franklin Roosevelt nominated U.S. Senator Hugo Black to the United States Supreme Court. In *Ex parte Levitt*, the Supreme Court faced a challenge to Senator Black's appointment under Art.I, section 6, cl 2 of the Constitution, the Ineligibility Clause. That clause provides:

> "No Senator or Representative shall, during the Time for which he was elected, be appointed to any civil Office under the Authority of the United States . . . the Emoluments whereof shall have been increased during such time. . . ."

"There, a petition was filed . . . seeking an order to show cause why one of the Justices should not be disqualified to serve as an Associate Justice. The petition asserted that the appointment and confirmation of the Justice in August, 1937, was unlawful because the Act of March 1, 1937, permitting Justices to retire at full salary after a period of specified service, thereby increased the emoluments of the office, and that the statute was enacted while the challenged Justice was a Senator."]

PER CURIAM.

[The] motion papers disclose no interest upon the part of the petitioner other than that of a citizen and a member of the bar of this Court. That is insufficient. It is an established principle that to entitle a private individual to invoke the judicial power to determine the validity of executive or legislative action he must show that he has sustained, or is immediately in danger of sustaining, a direct injury as the result of that action and it is not sufficient that he has merely a general interest common to all members of the public. Tyler v. Judges of the Court of Registration, 179 U.S. 405, 406; Southern Railway Company v. King, 217 U.S. 524, 534; Newman v. U.S. ex rel. Frizzell, 238 U.S. 537, 549, 550; Fairchild v. Hughes, 258 U.S. 126, 1299; Massachusetts v. Mellon, 262 U.S. 447, 488.

NOTE ON LEVITT

Levitt held that the petitioner had no standing to pursue the appointment challenge because he had "sustained no direct injury" resulting from the government action and "held merely a general interest common to all members of the public." Does *Levitt* pose a tension with *Marbury v. Madison*'s proclamation that "it is emphatically the province and duty of the judicial department to say what the law is"? Does your response change if it seems clear that if this plaintiff has no standing no other challenger will? If Justice Black's appointment violated the Constitution does it makes sense that no one can challenge it?

How is the Court's briefly explained standing theory in *Levitt* different than the political question doctrine explored earlier in this chapter?

In what sense does the holding in *Levitt* actually serve the appropriate separation of powers?

WARTH V. SELDIN
422 U.S. 490 (1975).

JUSTICE POWELL delivered the opinion of the Court.

Petitioners, various organizations and individuals resident in the Rochester, N.Y. metropolitan area, brought this action [against the town of Penfield and members of Penfield's Zoning, Planning, and Town Boards]. Petitioners claimed that the town's zoning ordinance, by its terms and as enforced by the defendant board members, respondents here, effectively excluded persons of low and moderate income from living in the town, in contravention of petitioners' First, Ninth, and Fourteenth Amendment rights. . . . The Court of Appeals [held] that none of the plaintiffs . . . had standing to prosecute the action. [W]e affirm. . . .

Petitioners Metro-Act of Rochester [and] eight individual plaintiffs, [sued] on behalf of themselves and all persons similarly situated. . . . The complaint identified Metro-Act as a not-for-profit New York corporation, the purposes of which are to alert ordinary citizens to problems of social concern, . . . to inquire into the reasons for the critical housing shortage for low and moderate income persons in the Rochester area[,] and to urge action on the part of citizens to alleviate the general housing shortage for low and moderate income persons. Vinkey, Reichert, Warth, and Harris were described as residents of the city of Rochester, all of whom owned real property in and paid property taxes to that city. . . . Broadnax, Reyes, and Sinkler [were described] as residents of Rochester and "persons fitting within the classification of low and moderate income as hereinafter defined. . . ." [T]he record shows that Broadnax, Reyes, and Sinkler are members of ethnic or racial minority groups. . . .

Petitioners' complaint alleged that Penfield's zoning ordinance . . . has the purpose and effect of excluding persons of low and moderate income from residing in the town. In particular, the ordinance allocates 98% of the town's vacant land to single-family detached housing, and allegedly [imposes] unreasonable requirements relating to lot size, setback, floor area, and habitable space. . . .

Petitioners also alleged that . . . the defendant members of Penfield's Town, Zoning, and Planning Boards had . . . delayed action on proposals for low and moderate cost housing for inordinate periods of time; denied such proposals for arbitrary and insubstantial reasons; refused to grant necessary variances and permits, or to allow tax abatements; failed to provide necessary support services for low and moderate cost housing projects; and had amended the ordinance to make approval of such projects virtually impossible. In sum, petitioners alleged that . . . the town and its officials had made practically and economically impossible the construction of . . . low and moderate income . . . housing in the Town of Penfield [and that] by precluding low and moderate cost housing, the town's zoning practices also had the effect of excluding persons of minority racial and ethnic groups, since most such persons have only low or moderate incomes.

Petitioners further alleged certain harm to themselves. The Rochester property owners and taxpayers—Vinkey, Reichert, Warth, Harris, and Ortiz—claimed that, because of Penfield's exclusionary practices, the city of Rochester had been forced to impose higher tax rates on them and others similarly situated than would otherwise have been necessary. The low and moderate income, minority plaintiffs—Ortiz, Broadnax, Reyes, and Sinkler—claimed that Penfield's zoning practices had prevented them from acquiring . . . residential property in the town. . . .

Rochester Home Builders Association, an association of firms engaged in residential construction in the Rochester metropolitan area, moved . . . to intervene as a party plaintiff, [claiming that the defendants'] practices . . . had prevented its member firms from building low and moderate cost housing in Penfield, and thereby had deprived them of potential profits. . . . Metro-Act and the other original plaintiffs moved to join petitioner Housing Council in the Monroe County Area . . . as a party plaintiff. Housing Council is a not-for-profit New York corporation, its membership comprising some 71 public and private organizations [that] were or hoped to be involved in the development of low and moderate cost housing. [O]ne of [them]—the Penfield Better Homes Corp.—[is alleged to be] "actively attempting to develop moderate income housing" in Penfield, "but [to be] stymied by its inability to secure the necessary approvals."

In essence, the question of standing is whether the litigant is entitled to have the court decide the merits of the dispute or of particular issues. This inquiry involves both constitutional limitations on federal court jurisdiction and prudential limitations on its exercise. . . . In both dimensions, it is founded in concern about the proper—and properly limited—role of the courts in a democratic society. . . . In its constitutional dimension, standing imports justiciability: whether the plaintiff has made out a "case or controversy" between himself and the defendant within the meaning of Art. III. This is the threshold question in every federal case, determining the power of the court to entertain the suit. As an aspect of justiciability, the standing question is whether the plaintiff has "alleged such a personal stake in the outcome of the controversy" as to warrant his invocation of federal court jurisdiction and to justify exercise of the court's remedial powers on his behalf. *Baker v. Carr,* 369 U.S. 186, 224 (1962). The Art. III judicial power exists only to redress or otherwise to protect against injury to the complaining party, even though the court's judgment may benefit others collaterally. A federal court's jurisdiction therefore can be invoked only when the plaintiff himself has suffered "some threatened or actual injury resulting from the putatively illegal action . . . ."[10]

Apart from this minimum constitutional mandate, this Court has recognized other limits on the class of persons who may invoke the courts' decisional and remedial powers. First, the Court has held that when the asserted harm is a "generalized grievance" shared in substantially equal measure by all or a large class of citizens, that harm alone normally does not warrant exercise of jurisdiction. *E.g., Schlesinger v. Reservists to Stop the War* [, 418 U.S. 208 (1974)]; *United States v. Richardson* [, 418 U.S. 166 (1974)]. Second, even when the plaintiff has alleged injury sufficient to meet the "case or controversy" requirement, this Court has held that the plaintiff generally must assert his own legal rights and interests, and cannot rest his claim to relief on the legal rights or interests of third parties. . . . Without such limitations—closely related to Art. III concerns but essentially matters of judicial self-governance—the courts would be called upon to decide abstract questions of wide public significance even though other governmental institutions may be more competent to address the questions and even though judicial intervention may be unnecessary to protect individual [rights]. . . .

Although standing in no way depends on the merits of the plaintiff's contention that particular conduct is illegal, . . . it often turns on the nature and source of the claim asserted. The actual or threatened injury required by Art. III may exist solely by virtue of "statutes creating legal

---

[10] The standing question thus bears close affinity to questions of ripeness—whether the harm asserted has matured sufficiently to warrant judicial intervention—and of mootness— whether the occasion for judicial intervention persists. . . . See *Anti-Fascist Committee v. McGrath,* 341 U.S. 123, 154–156 (1951) (Frankfurter, J., concurring).

rights, the invasion of which creates standing. . . ." *See Linda R. S. v. Richard D.*, [410 U.S. 614, at 617 n. 3 (1973)]. Moreover, the source of the plaintiff's claim to relief assumes critical importance with respect to the prudential rules of standing that, apart from Art. III's minimum requirements, serve to limit the role of the courts in resolving public disputes. Essentially, the standing question in such cases is whether the constitutional or statutory provision on which the claim rests properly can be understood as granting persons in the plaintiff's position a right to judicial relief.[12]

In some circumstances, countervailing considerations may outweigh the concerns underlying the usual reluctance to exert judicial power when the plaintiff's claim to relief rests on the legal rights of third parties. . . . Moreover, Congress may grant an express right of action to persons who otherwise would be barred by prudential standing rules. Of course, Art. III's requirement remains: the plaintiff still must allege a distinct and palpable injury to himself, even if it is an injury shared by a large class of other possible litigants. . . . But so long as this requirement is satisfied, persons to whom Congress has granted a right of action, either expressly or by clear implication, may have standing to seek relief on the basis of the legal rights and interests of others, and, indeed, may invoke the general public interest in support of their claim. . . . *FCC v. Sanders Radio Station*, 309 U.S. 470, 477 (1940).

One further preliminary matter requires discussion. For purposes of ruling on a motion to dismiss for want of standing, both the trial and reviewing courts must accept as true all material allegations of the complaint, and must construe the complaint in favor of the complaining party. . . . At the same time, it is within the trial court's power to allow or to require the plaintiff to supply . . . further particularized allegations of fact deemed supportive of plaintiff's standing. If, after this opportunity, the plaintiff's standing does not adequately appear from all materials of record, the complaint must be dismissed.

[W]e turn first to the claims of petitioners Ortiz, Reyes, Sinkler, and Broadnax, each of whom asserts standing as a person of low or moderate income and, coincidentally, as a member of a minority racial or ethnic group. We must assume, taking the allegations of the complaint as true, that Penfield's zoning ordinance and the pattern of enforcement by respondent officials have had the purpose and effect of excluding persons of low and moderate income, many of whom are members of racial or ethnic minority groups. We also assume, for purposes here, that such

---

[12] A similar standing issue arises when the litigant asserts the rights of third parties defensively, as a bar to judgment against him. E.g., *Barrows v. Jackson*, 346 U.S. 249 (1953). . . . In such circumstances, there is no [Article III] standing problem, but the prudential question is governed by considerations closely related to the question whether a person in the litigant's position would have a right of action on the claim. . . .

intentional exclusionary practices, if proved in a proper case, would be adjudged violative of the constitutional and statutory rights of the persons excluded. But the fact that these petitioners share attributes common to persons who may have been excluded from residence in the town is an insufficient predicate for the conclusion that petitioners themselves have been excluded, or that the respondents' assertedly illegal actions have violated their rights. Petitioners must allege and show that they personally have been injured, not that injury has been suffered by other, unidentified members of the class to which they belong and which they purport to represent. . . .

Ortiz, Reyes, Sinkler, and Broadnax alleged in conclusory terms that they are among the persons excluded by respondents' actions. None of them has ever resided in Penfield; each claims at least implicitly that he desires, or has desired, to do so. Each asserts, moreover, that he made some effort, at some time, to locate housing in Penfield that was at once within his means and adequate for his family's needs. Each claims that his efforts proved fruitless. We may assume, as petitioners allege, that respondents' actions have contributed, perhaps substantially, to the cost of housing in Penfield. But there remains the question whether petitioners' inability to locate suitable housing in Penfield reasonably can be said to have resulted, in any concretely demonstrable way, from respondents' alleged constitutional and statutory infractions. Petitioners must allege facts from which it reasonably could be inferred that, absent the respondents' restrictive zoning practices, there is a substantial probability that they would have been able to purchase or lease in Penfield, and that, if the court affords the relief requested, the asserted inability of petitioners will be removed. . . .

We find the record devoid of the necessary allegations. [N]one of these petitioners has a present interest in any Penfield property; none is himself subject to the ordinance's strictures; and none has ever been denied a variance or permit by respondent officials. Instead, petitioners claim that respondents' enforcement of the ordinance against third parties—developers, builders, and the like—has had the consequence of precluding the construction of housing suitable to their needs at prices they might be able to afford. . . . When a governmental prohibition or restriction imposed on one party causes specific harm to a third party, harm that a constitutional provision or statute was intended to prevent, the indirectness of the injury does not necessarily deprive the person harmed of standing to vindicate his rights. But it may make it substantially more difficult to meet the minimum requirement of [Article III]: to establish that, in fact, the asserted injury was the consequence of the defendants' actions, or that prospective relief will remove the harm.

Here, by their own admission, realization of petitioners' desire to live in Penfield always has depended on the efforts and willingness of third parties to build low and moderate cost housing. The record specifically refers to only two such efforts. . . . But the record is devoid of any indication that these projects, or other like projects, would have satisfied petitioners' needs at prices they could afford, or that, were the court to remove the obstructions attributable to respondents, such relief would benefit petitioners. Indeed, petitioners' descriptions of their individual financial situations and housing needs suggest precisely the contrary— that their inability to reside in Penfield is the consequence of the economics of the area housing market, rather than of respondents' assertedly illegal acts. . . . In short, the facts alleged fail to support an actionable causal relationship between Penfield's zoning practices and petitioners' asserted injury. . . .

We hold only that a plaintiff who seeks to challenge exclusionary zoning practices must allege specific, concrete facts demonstrating that the challenged practices harm him, and that he personally would benefit in a tangible way from the court's intervention.[18] Absent the necessary allegations of demonstrable, particularized injury, there can be no confidence of "a real need to exercise the power of judicial review" or that relief can be framed "no broader than required by the precise facts to which the court's ruling would be applied."

The petitioners who assert standing on the basis of their status as taxpayers of the city of Rochester present a different set of problems. . . . Their argument, in brief, is that Penfield's persistent refusal to allow or to facilitate construction of low and moderate cost housing forces the city of Rochester to provide more such housing than it otherwise would do; that, to provide such housing, Rochester must allow certain tax abatements; and that, as the amount of tax-abated property increases, Rochester taxpayers are forced to assume an increased tax burden in order to finance essential public services. "Of course, pleadings must be something more than an ingenious academic exercise in the conceivable." . . . We think the complaint of the taxpayer petitioners is little more than such an exercise. Apart from the conjectural nature of the asserted injury, the line of causation between Penfield's actions and such injury is not apparent from the complaint. Whatever may occur in Penfield, the injury complained of—increases in taxation—results only from decisions made by the appropriate Rochester authorities, who are not parties to this case.

But even if we assume that the taxpayer petitioners could establish that Penfield's zoning practices harm them, their complaint nonetheless

---

[18] This is not to say that the plaintiff who challenges a zoning ordinance or zoning practices must have a present contractual interest in a particular project. . . . But usually the initial focus should be on a particular project. . . . We also note that zoning laws and their provisions, long considered essential to effective urban planning, are peculiarly within the province of state and local legislative authorities. They are, of course, subject to judicial review in a proper case. But citizens dissatisfied with provisions of such laws need not overlook the availability of the normal democratic process.

was properly dismissed. Petitioners do not, even if they could, assert any personal right under the Constitution or any statute to be free of action by a neighboring municipality that may have some incidental adverse effect on Rochester. On the contrary, the only basis of the taxpayer petitioners' claim is that Penfield's zoning ordinance and practices violate the constitutional and statutory rights of third parties, namely, persons of low and moderate income who are said to be excluded from Penfield. In short, the claim of these petitioners falls squarely within the prudential standing rule that normally bars litigants from asserting the rights or legal interests of others in order to obtain relief from injury to themselves.

We turn next to the standing problems presented by the petitioner associations [Metro-Act, Housing Council, and Rochester Home Builders Association]. There is no question that an association may have standing in its own right to seek judicial relief from injury to itself and to vindicate whatever rights and immunities the association itself may enjoy. Moreover, in attempting to secure relief from injury to itself, the association may assert the rights of its members, at least so long as the challenged infractions adversely affect its members' associational ties. . . . With the limited exception of Metro-Act, however, none of the associational petitioners here has asserted injury to itself.

[I]n the absence of injury to itself, an association may have standing solely as the representative of its members. . . . The possibility of such representational standing, however, does not eliminate or attenuate the constitutional requirement of a case or controversy. The association must allege that its members, or any one of them, are suffering immediate or threatened injury as a result of the challenged action of the sort that would make out a justiciable case had the members themselves brought suit. . . . So long as this can be established, and so long as the nature of the claim and of the relief sought does not make the individual participation of each injured party indispensable to proper resolution of the cause, the association may be an appropriate representative of its members, entitled to invoke the court's jurisdiction.

Metro-Act's claims to standing on its own behalf as a Rochester taxpayer, and on behalf of its members who are Rochester taxpayers or persons of low or moderate income, are precluded by our holdings . . . as to the individual petitioners, and require no further discussion. Metro-Act also alleges, however, that 9% of its membership is composed of present residents of Penfield. It claims that, as a result of the persistent pattern of exclusionary zoning practiced by respondents and the consequent exclusion of persons of low and moderate income, those of its members who are Penfield residents are deprived of the benefits of living in a racially and ethnically integrated community. Referring to our decision in *Trafficante v. Metropolitan Life Ins. Co.,* 409 U.S. 205 (1972), Metro-Act argues that such deprivation is a sufficiently palpable injury to satisfy the [Article III] case or controversy requirement, and that it has standing as the representative of its members to seek redress. . . .

[In *Trafficante*,] two residents of an apartment complex alleged that the owner had discriminated against rental applicants on the basis of race, in violation of § 804 of the Civil Rights Act of 1968. . . . They claimed that, as a result of such discrimination, they had been injured in that (1) they had lost the social benefits of living in an integrated community; (2) they had missed business and professional advantages which would have accrued if they had lived with members of minority groups; (3) they had suffered embarrassment and economic damage in social, business, and professional activities from being "stigmatized" as residents of a "white ghetto." . . . In light of the clear congressional purpose in enacting the 1968 Act, and the broad definition of "person aggrieved" in § 810(a), we held that petitioners, as "person[s] who claim[ed] to have been injured by a discriminatory housing practice," had standing to litigate violations of the Act. We concluded that Congress had given residents of housing facilities covered by the statute an actionable right to be free from the adverse consequences to them of racially discriminatory practices directed at and immediately harmful to others. . . . Congress may create a statutory right or entitlement the alleged deprivation of which can confer standing to sue even where the plaintiff would have suffered no judicially cognizable injury in the absence of statute. [*Linda R. S. v. Richard D.*] No such statute is applicable here.

Even if we assume, *arguendo,* that, apart from any statutorily created right, the asserted harm to Metro-Act's Penfield members is sufficiently direct and personal to satisfy the case or controversy requirement of [Article III], prudential considerations strongly counsel against according them or Metro-Act standing to prosecute this action. We do not understand Metro-Act to argue that Penfield residents themselves have been denied any constitutional rights. . . . [T]heir complaint is that they have been harmed indirectly by the exclusion of others. This is an attempt to raise putative rights of third parties, and none of the exceptions that allow such claims is present here.

Home Builders . . . asserted standing to represent its member firms engaged in the development and construction of residential housing in the Rochester area, including Penfield. Home Builders alleged that the Penfield zoning restrictions, together with refusals by the town officials to grant variances and permits for the construction of low and moderate cost housing, had deprived some of its members of "substantial business opportunities and profits." [T]o justify any relief, the association must show that it has suffered harm, or that one or more of its members are injured. But, apart from this, whether an association has standing to invoke the court's remedial powers on behalf of its members depends in substantial measure on the nature of the relief sought. If, in a proper case, the association seeks a declaration, injunction, or some other form of prospective relief, it can reasonably be supposed that the remedy, if granted, will inure to the benefit of those members of the association actually injured. . . . The present case, however, differs significantly, as here an association seeks relief in damages for alleged injuries to its members. Home Builders alleges no monetary injury to itself, nor any assignment of the damages claims of its members. No award therefore can be made to the association as such. Moreover, in the circumstances of this case, the damages claims are not common to the entire membership, nor shared by all in equal degree. To the contrary, whatever injury may have been suffered is peculiar to the individual member concerned, and both the fact and extent of injury would require individualized proof. Thus, to obtain relief in damages, each member of Home Builders who claims injury as a result of respondents' practices must be a party to the suit, and Home Builders has no standing to claim damages on his behalf.

Home Builders' prayer for prospective relief fails for a different reason. It can have standing as the representative of its members only if it has alleged facts sufficient to make out a case or controversy had the members themselves brought suit. No such allegations were made. The complaint refers to no specific project of any of its members that is currently precluded either by the ordinance or by respondents' action in enforcing it. There is no averment that any member has applied to respondents for a building permit or a variance with respect to any current project. Indeed, there is no indication that respondents have delayed or thwarted any project currently proposed by Home Builders' members, or that any of its members has taken advantage of the remedial processes available under the ordinance. In short, insofar as the complaint seeks prospective relief, Home Builders has failed to show the existence of any injury to its members of sufficient immediacy and ripeness to warrant judicial intervention.

A like problem is presented with respect to [Housing Council]. [W]ith one exception, the complaint does not suggest that any [of the groups represented by the Council] has focused its efforts on Penfield or has any specific plan to do so. . . . The exception is the Penfield Better Homes Corp. [which] applied to respondents in late 1969 for a zoning variance to allow construction of a housing project designed for persons of moderate income. . . . It is . . . possible that, in 1969, or within a reasonable time thereafter, Better Homes itself and possibly Housing Council as its representative would have had standing to seek review of respondents' action. The complaint, however, does not allege that the Penfield Better Homes project remained viable in 1972 when this complaint was filed, or that respondents' actions continued to block a then-current construction project. In short, neither the complaint nor the record supplies any basis from which to infer that the controversy between respondents and Better Homes, however vigorous it may once have been, remained a live, concrete dispute when this complaint was filed.

JUSTICE DOUGLAS, dissenting.

Standing has become a barrier to access to the federal courts, just as "the political question" was in earlier decades. The mounting caseload of federal courts is well known. But cases such as this one reflect festering sores in our society, and the American dream teaches that, if one reaches high enough and persists, there is a forum where justice is dispensed. I would lower the technical barriers and let the courts serve that ancient need. They can, in time, be curbed by legislative or constitutional restraints if an emergency arises. . . . The zoning power is claimed to have been used here to foist an un-American community model on the people of this area. I would let the case go to trial and have all the facts brought out. Indeed, it would be better practice to decide the question of standing only when the merits have been developed. . . .

JUSTICE BRENNAN, with whom JUSTICES WHITE and MARSHALL join, dissenting.

While the Court gives lip service to the principle, oft repeated in recent years, that "standing in no way depends on the merits of the plaintiff's contention that particular conduct is illegal," . . . in fact, the opinion, which tosses out of court almost every conceivable kind of plaintiff who could be injured by the activity claimed to be unconstitutional, can be explained only by an indefensible hostility to the claim on the merits. . . .

Ortiz, Broadnax, Reyes, and Sinkler alleged that "as a result" of respondents' exclusionary practices, they were unable, despite attempts, to find the housing they desired in Penfield, and consequently have incurred high commuting expenses, received poorer municipal services, and, in some instances, have been relegated to live in substandard housing. . . . The Court does not, as it could not, suggest that the injuries, if proved, would be insufficient to give petitioners the requisite "personal stake in the outcome of the controversy as to assure the concrete adverseness which sharpens the presentation of issues." . . . Rather, it is abundantly clear that the harm alleged satisfies the "injury in fact" [requirement]. Instead, the Court insists that these petitioners' allegations are insufficient to show that the harms suffered were caused by respondents' allegedly unconstitutional practices, because their inability to reside in Penfield [may be] the consequence of the economics of the area housing market, rather than of respondents' assertedly illegal acts. [But] these petitioners have alleged precisely what our cases require—that, *because* of the exclusionary practices of respondents, they cannot live in Penfield and have suffered harm. Thus, the Court's real holding is not that these petitioners have not *alleged* an injury resulting from respondents' action, but that they are not to be allowed to prove one. . . . Certainly, this is not the sort of demonstration that can or should be required of petitioners at this preliminary stage. . . .

Two of the [organizational] petitioners, Home Builders and Housing Council, alleged that [they] have attempted to build in Penfield low and moderate income housing, but have been stymied by the zoning ordinance and refusal to grant individual relief therefrom. . . . The Court finds that these two organizations lack standing to seek prospective relief for basically the same reasons: none of their members is, as far as the allegations show, currently involved in developing a particular project. . . . Again, the Court ignores the thrust of the complaints and asks petitioners to allege the impossible. [Experience] with Penfield officials has shown any plans for low and moderate income housing to be futile, for, again according to the allegations, the respondents are engaged in a purposeful, conscious scheme to exclude such housing. Particularly with regard to a low or moderate income project, the cost of litigating, with respect to any particular project, the legality of a refusal to approve it may well be prohibitive. And the merits of the exclusion of this or that project is not at the heart of the complaint; the claim is that respondents will not approve any project which will provide residences for low and moderate income people.

NOTES ON THE ARTICLE III STANDING REQUIREMENT

1.   **Rationale.** What underlying rationales explain standing doctrine? This is to say, what values is the system supposed to derive from these limits on federal judicial power?

a.   Chief Justice Warren said in *Flast v. Cohen*, 392 U.S. 83 (1968), that a litigant has standing only if he or she has a "personal stake in the outcome" of a case, which ensures an "adversary context" for judicial action. There is something to the idea that litigants who are personally harmed have a reason to litigate vigorously—to marshal the evidence and legal arguments on their side, to probe contrary evidence and contentions for weaknesses, and thus to facilitate informed judicial decision making. Self-interest is scarcely the only incentive for aggressive advocacy. Litigants moved by ideological commitments can also be relied upon to press claims with professional zeal. Moreover, issue-oriented organizations may have financial resources and expertise that self-interested litigants can't supply. Nevertheless, you will see that litigants who assert only ideological interests lack standing for want of a sufficient "personal stake" in the outcome of litigation.

b.   Justice Scalia has argued frequently and forcefully that a bolstered injury requirement works to limit the overjudicialization of self-governance: "The law of standing roughly restricts courts to their traditional undemocratic role of protecting individuals . . . against imposition of the majority, and excludes them from the even more undemocratic role of prescribing how the other two branches should function in order to serve the interests of the majority itself." Scalia, *The Doctrine of Standing as an Essential Element of the Separation of Powers*, 17 SUFFOLK L.REV. 835 (1983).

c. Writing for the Court in *Valley Forge Christian College v. Americans United*, 454 U.S. 464 (1982), Chief Justice Rehnquist said that the requirement of "actual injury" has methodological utility inasmuch as it ensures that legal questions will be decided in a "concrete factual context conducive to a realistic appreciation of the consequences of judicial action" and that "an actual factual setting" permits a court to act "with some confidence that its decision will not pave the way for lawsuits which have some, but not all, of the facts of the case actually decided by the court." This rationale obviously reaches back to the thinking behind the prohibition on advisory opinions. The root idea appears to be that courts do their best work in the context of genuine disputes. But wasn't there something to Justice Brennan's point in *Warth* that at least some of the plaintiffs had *alleged* a factual setting for a judicial decision and thus should have been given the chance actually to *prove* their case in court?

d. In *Warth* itself, Justice Powell explained that it takes an allegation of sufficient personal interest in the resolution of a legal question to "justify exercise of the court's remedial power." Chief Justice Rehnquist added this in *Valley Forge*: "The power to declare the rights of individuals and to measure the authority of governments . . . is legitimate only in the last resort, and as a necessity in the determination of real, earnest and vital controversy." This point also relates back to the ban on advisory opinions. Here, the idea appears to be not only that federal courts do their best work in the crucible of actual disputes, but also that they can legitimately bring judicial power to bear only as a last resort—when it is necessary to resolve genuine quarrels. So the argument goes, lawmaking in a democracy is generally the province of elected officials and can be undertaken by unelected judges only on grounds of necessity. Is it clear that courts should be so sparing? What of Justice Brennan's argument in *Warth* that the Court's grudging approach to standing suggested hostility to the plaintiffs' substantive claims?

e. Chief Justice Rehnquist also said in *Valley Forge* that standing reflects "due regard for the autonomy of those persons likely to be most directly affected by a judicial order." Consider that, in some instances, there is no one else who will be affected more concretely than the would-be litigants who are turned away for want of standing. In other instances, people whose interests make them eligible to sue may have no genuine desire to do so. The Court's standing doctrine thus may create incentives that are ironic, if not perverse: Enthusiastic individuals are forced to locate and recruit less-motivated persons to lend their names to lawsuits in order that litigation can go forward. Was there anyone else who might have successfully achieved standing in *Warth*? Was it possible for some individual low-income persons to allege sufficient facts to support a claim that the Penfield ordinance and/or its administration actually harmed them personally? Two years later, in

Arlington Heights v. Metropolitan Housing Corp., 429 U.S. 252 (1977), the Court held that an individual plaintiff had standing to challenge a zoning decision that prevented the construction of a particular low-income housing development. There a low-income housing developer had contracted to purchase a tract of land within the boundaries of the Village. Its specific re-zoning request had been denied. The plaintiff alleged that if the project were built, he would qualify for an apartment in it and would "probably" move there to be near his place of employment. Justice Powell wrote the majority opinion, which distinguished *Warth* explicitly: "The complaint alleged that [the individual plaintiff] seeks and would qualify for the housing . . . and he would probably move there since it was closer to his job." Unlike the "individual plaintiffs in *Warth*, [he] has adequately averred an actionable causal relationship between Arlington Heights' zoning practices and his injury." Id at 562.

2. *Warth*'s Implications for Challenges to Racial Discrimination. Suppose that an exclusive suburb, separately incorporated, passed a statute prohibiting blacks from purchasing housing in the locale. Assume further that the suburb is composed entirely of ten-acre privately owned parcels, each valued in excess of a million dollars. The facts, as developed, indicate that no one in the suburb has present plans to sell. How would plaintiffs achieve standing in such a case? Must they not only be black, but also able to prove capacity, opportunity and willingness to buy a million dollar home? See, Gene Nichol, *Rethinking Standing*, 72 CAL.L.REV.68, 81–82 (1984).

3. Standing to Challenge Affirmative Action Plans. In *Regents of the University of California v. Bakke*, 438 U.S. 265, 280, n. 14 (1978), it appeared unlikely that the plaintiff, Alan Bakke could prove he would have been admitted to the medical school program absent the affirmative action plan he challenged. The Court skirted the standing issue by declaring that the university's decision not to permit Bakke to compete for all one hundred places in the entering class was the relevant injury. Could the plaintiffs in *Warth* have made an analogous claim? Compare the following.

NORTHEASTERN FLA. CHAPTER OF THE ASSOCIATED GENERAL CONTRACTORS OF AMERICA [AGC] V. CITY OF JACKSONVILLE

508 U.S. 656 (1993).

JUSTICE THOMAS delivered the opinion of the Court.

[R]espondent Jacksonville enacted an ordinance entitled "Minority Business Enterprise Participation," which required that 10% of the amount spent on city contracts be set aside each fiscal year for so-called "Minority Business Enterprises" (MBE's). An MBE was defined as a business whose ownership was at least 51% "minority" or female, and a "minority" was in turn defined as a person who is or considers himself to be black, Spanish-speaking, Oriental, Indian, Eskimo, Aleut, or handicapped. Petitioner, the Northeastern Florida Chapter of the Associated General Contractors of America (AGC), is an association of individuals and firms in the construction industry. Petitioner's members do business in Jacksonville, and most of them do not qualify as MBE's under the city's ordinance. [P]etitioner filed [suit] . . . against the city and its mayor (also a respondent here), [c]laiming that Jacksonville's ordinance violated the Equal Protection Clause of the Fourteenth Amendment. [P]etitioner alleged that many of its members "regularly bid on . . . construction work for the City of Jacksonville" and that they "would have [bid on] designated set aside contracts but for the restrictions imposed" by the ordinance.

[T]he District Court entered summary judgment for petitioner, concluding that the MBE ordinance was inconsistent with the equal protection criteria established by this Court in *Richmond v. J.A. Croson Co.*, 488 U.S. 469 (1989). [R]espondents appealed. Rather than addressing the merits of petitioner's equal protection claim, the Court of Appeals held that petitioner "lacks standing to challenge the ordinance establishing the set-aside program." [After this Court granted certiorari, the city amended its ordinance and on that basis moved to dismiss the contractors' claim against the old ordinance as moot.]

[The Court's treatment of the mootness issue is omitted.]

The Court of Appeals held that petitioner could not establish standing because it failed to allege that one or more of its members would have been awarded a contract but for the challenged ordinance. Under these circumstances, the Court of Appeals concluded, there is no "injury." This holding cannot be reconciled with our precedents. . . . the decision that is most closely analogous to this case . . . is *Regents of Univ. of Cal. v. Bakke*, 438 U.S. 265 (1978), where a twice-rejected white male applicant claimed that a medical school's admissions program, which reserved 16 of the 100 places in the entering class for minority applicants, was inconsistent with the Equal Protection Clause. Justice Powell concluded that the "constitutional requirements of [Article III]" had been satisfied, because the requisite "injury" was the medical school's "decision not to permit Bakke to compete for all 100 places in the class, simply because of his race." Thus, "even if Bakke had been unable to prove that he would have been admitted in the absence of the special program, it would not follow that he lacked standing."

When the government erects a barrier that makes it more difficult for members of one group to obtain a benefit than it is for members of another group, a member of the former group seeking to challenge the barrier need not allege that he would have obtained the benefit but for the barrier in order to establish standing. The "injury in fact" in an equal protection case of this variety is the denial of equal treatment resulting from the imposition of the barrier, not the ultimate inability to obtain the benefit. And in the context of a challenge to a set-aside program, the "injury in fact" is the inability to compete on an equal footing in the bidding process, not the loss of a contract. To establish standing, therefore, a party challenging a set aside program like Jacksonville's need only demonstrate that it is able and ready to bid on contracts and that a discriminatory policy prevents it from doing so on an equal basis.[5]

[R]espondents rely primarily upon [*Warth v. Seldin*]. There the plaintiffs claimed that a town's zoning ordinance, both by its terms and as enforced, violated the Fourteenth Amendment insofar as it had the effect of preventing people of low and moderate income from living in the town. [A]n association of construction firms alleged that the zoning restrictions had deprived some of its members of business opportunities and profits. We held that the association lacked standing. . . . We think *Warth* is distinguishable. Unlike the other cases that we have discussed, *Warth* did not involve an allegation that some discriminatory classification prevented the plaintiff from competing on an equal footing in its quest for a benefit. [T]here was no claim that the construction association's members could not apply for variances and building permits on the same basis as other firms; what the association objected to were the "refusals by the town officials to grant variances and permits." The firms' complaint, in other words, was not that they could not compete equally; it was that they did not win. Thus, while there is undoubtedly some tension between *Warth* and the aforementioned line of cases, this case is governed by the latter.

In any event, the tension is minimal. Even assuming that the alleged injury in *Warth* was an inability to compete for variances and permits on an equal basis, and that *Warth*, too, is analogous to this case, it is distinguishable nonetheless. Unlike petitioner, which alleged that its members regularly bid on contracts in Jacksonville and would bid on those that the city's ordinance makes unavailable to them, the construction association in *Warth* did not allege that "any member ha[d] applied . . . for a building permit or a variance with respect to any current project." Thus, unlike the association in *Warth*, petitioner has alleged an "injury . . . of sufficient immediacy . . . to warrant judicial intervention." Furthermore, we did not hold in *Warth*, as the Court of Appeals—mutatis mutandis—did here, that the association was required to allege that but for a discriminatory policy, variances or permits would have been awarded to its members. An allegation that a "specific project" was "precluded" by the existence or administration of the zoning ordinance

---

[5]   It follows from our definition of "injury in fact" that petitioner has sufficiently alleged both that the city's ordinance is the "cause" of its injury and that a judicial decree directing the city to discontinue its program would "redress" the injury.

would certainly have been sufficient to establish standing, but there is no suggestion in *Warth* that it was necessary.

[Assuming that the allegations in the complaint are true], . . . and given the legal standard we have reaffirmed today, it was inappropriate for the Court of Appeals to order that petitioner's complaint be dismissed for lack of standing.[6] . . .

NOTES ON THE INJURY REQUIREMENT

1. Generalized Grievances. Once it is posited that interests need not be legal rights to meet the first constitutional test for standing (injury in fact), the next question is what interests are sufficient. Some factual interests are not. The principal illustration is an abstract and indefinite "generalized grievance" (more about this later)—including the desire that the law be enforced. In *Allen v. Wright*, 468 U.S. 737 (1984), African American children attempted to challenge Internal Revenue Service policies that allegedly permitted segregationist academies to obtain tax benefits to which they were not entitled under applicable federal statutes and the IRS' own rules. Writing for the Court, Justice O'Connor explained that the children lacked "standing to complain simply that their Government [was] violating the law." Her rationale was that an interest in seeing the law enforced, however genuine, is "more appropriately addressed in the representative branches." Did O'Connor mean to say that if the plaintiffs in *Allen* thought public officials were violating the law, they should vote them out of office?

2. Economic Interests. Deleterious effects on economic interests always count as factual injuries for standing purposes. Witness the interests of the competing radio station in *Sanders*. Close cases occasionally arise. In *Sprint Comm. v. APCC Svc.*, 554 U.S. 269 (2008), payphone operators assigned numerous small claims they had against long-distance carriers to collection firms, which aggregated the claims to generate large enough sums to make suits against the defaulting long-distance carriers worthwhile. The aggregators received a fee for their services, which did not vary with the size of the recovery they obtained. Chief Justice Roberts (and three other justices) insisted that the aggregators lacked standing because they had "nothing to gain from their lawsuit." Writing for the Supreme Court, Justice Breyer upheld the aggregators' standing:

> The long-distance carriers argue . . . that the aggregators lack standing because it was the payphone operators (who are not plaintiffs), not the aggregators (who are plaintiffs), who were "injured in fact" and that it is the payphone operators, not the aggregators, whose injuries a legal victory will truly "redress": The

---

[6] There has been no suggestion that even if petitioner's members have standing to sue, petitioner itself does not, because one or more of the prerequisites to "associational standing" have not been satisfied. See *Hunt v. Washington State Apple Advertising Comm'n*, 432 U.S. 333, 343 (1977). Nor, given the current state of the record, do we have any basis for reaching that conclusion on our own.

aggregators, after all, will remit all litigation proceeds to the payphone operators.

We have often said that history and tradition offer a meaningful guide to the types of cases that Article III empowers federal courts to consider. . . . Consequently, we . . . have carefully examined how courts have historically treated suits by assignors and assignees. And we have discovered that history and precedent are clear on the question before us: Assignees of a claim, including assignees for collection, have long been permitted to bring suit. A clear historical answer at least demands reasons for change. We can find no such reasons here, and accordingly we conclude that the aggregators have standing.

In any event, we find that the assignees before us satisfy the Article III standing requirements articulated in more modern decisions of this Court. . . . It is, of course, true that the aggregators did not originally suffer any injury caused by the long-distance carriers; the payphone operators did. But the payphone operators assigned their claims to the aggregators lock, stock, and barrel.

[Long-distance carriers] add that, because the aggregators will not actually benefit from a victory in this case, they lack a "personal stake" in the litigation's outcome. The problem with this argument is that the general "personal stake" requirement and the more specific standing requirements (injury in fact, redressability, and causation) are flip sides of the same coin. They are simply different descriptions of the same judicial effort to assure, in every case or controversy, "that concrete adverseness which sharpens the presentation of issues upon which the court so largely depends for illumination." . . .

Finally, we note, as a practical matter, that it would be particularly unwise for us to abandon history and precedent in resolving the question before us. Were we to agree with petitioners that the aggregators lack standing, our holding could easily be overcome. For example, the [a]greement could be rewritten to give the aggregator a tiny portion of the assigned claim itself, perhaps only a dollar or two. . . . Accordingly, the far more sensible course is to abide by the history and tradition of assignee suits and find that the aggregators possess Article III standing.

3.   **Noneconomic Interests.** The Court has disclaimed any suggestion that standing depends on economic interests. Upon the whole, fairly modest noneconomic factual harms suffice, provided they are personal to the plaintiff. In *Doe v. Chao*, 540 U.S. 614 (2004), a victim of black lung disease filed a claim for health benefits under a federal workers' compensation scheme. In its wisdom, the Department of Labor used his Social Security number to identify his file, thus disclosing the number to others in violation of the Privacy Act. The individual sued, alleging that he was "torn . . . all to

pieces" and "greatly concerned and worried" about the unlawful revelation of his number. Those allegations were sufficient to establish the factual injury required for standing. Writing for the Court, Justice Souter explained, however, that the plaintiff's claim was without merit, inasmuch as he had failed to allege and prove any "physical symptoms, medical treatment, loss of income, or impact on his behavior" and thus (for want of "actual damages" as defined by the Privacy Act) was not entitled even to the statutory minimum recovery ($1,000).

4. **Environmental Cases.** The Supreme Court has typically been generous on standing issues in environmental cases. The leading opinion is *Sierra Club v. Morton*, 405 U.S. 727 (1972). Writing for the Court, Justice Stewart found the Sierra Club's general concerns for the environment insufficient to establish standing to sue federal officials for unlawfully allowing a ski resort to be created in a wilderness area. The club's ideological commitments were too close to the abstract interest in seeing that federal regulations were enforced. Stewart explained, however, that individual members of the club could establish standing if they alleged that they frequented the area in question and would be personally affected if the mountains were turned into ski slopes. Many environmental suits have proceeded on such a basis. Then again, there are exceptions, like *Defenders of Wildlife*, where individuals' allegations have been found to be conjectural. In *Summers v. Earth Island Institute*, 555 U.S. 488 (2009), environmental organizations failed to produce satisfactory affidavits from particular members, but argued that it was statistically likely that some of their hundreds of thousands of unnamed members would be personally affected. Justice Breyer embraced that argument, but in dissent. He contended that the organizations could proceed because of the "realistic likelihood" that unnamed members would imminently suffer the required injury. Writing for the Court, Justice Scalia said this:

> [The dissent's] novel approach to the law of organizational standing would make a mockery of our prior cases, which have required plaintiff-organizations to make specific allegations establishing that at least one identified member had suffered or would suffer harm. . . . This requirement of naming the affected members has never been dispensed with in light of statistical probabilities, but only where *all* the members of the organization are affected by the challenged activity.

> A major problem with the dissent's approach is that it accepts the organizations' self-descriptions of their membership. . . . But it is well established that the court has an independent obligation to assure that standing exists, regardless of whether it is challenged by any of the parties. . . . Without individual affidavits, how is the court to assure itself that the Sierra Club, for example, has "thousands of members" who "use and enjoy the Sequoia National Forest"? And, because to establish standing plaintiffs must show that they "use the area affected by the challenged activity and not

an area roughly in the vicinity of" a project site, . . . how is the court to assure itself that some of these members plan to make use of the specific sites upon which projects may take place? . . . While it is certainly possible—perhaps even likely—that one individual will meet all of these criteria, that speculation does not suffice. . . . In part because of the difficulty of verifying the facts upon which such probabilistic standing depends, the Court has required plaintiffs claiming organizational standing to identify members who have suffered the requisite harm—surely not a difficult task here, when so many thousands are alleged to have been harmed.

5. Future Climate Change. In *Massachusetts v. Environmental Protection Agency*, 549 U.S. 497 (2007), the Court held that the Commonwealth of Massachusetts had standing to challenge the EPA's inaction on climate change: "The harms associated with climate change are serious and well recognized. The Government's own objective assessment of the relevant science [and] a strong consensus among qualified experts indicate that global warming threatens, inter alia, a precipitate rise in sea levels, severe and irreversible changes to natural ecosystems, a significant reduction in winter snowpack . . . and increases in the spread of disease and the ferocity of weather events. That these changes are widely shared does not minimize Massachusetts' interest in the outcome of this litigation. According to petitioners' uncontested affidavits, global sea levels rose between 10 and 20 centimeters over the 20th century as a result of global warming . . . remediation costs could reach hundreds of millions of dollars."

6. Pre-Enforcement Challenges to Foreign Intelligence Surveillance. In *Clapper v. Amnesty International USA*, 568 U.S. ___, 133 S.Ct. 1138 (2013) the Supreme Court, in an opinion by Justice Alito, denied standing to plaintiffs "whose work, they allege, requires them to engage in sensitive international communications with individuals who they believed were likely targets of surveillance under sec. 1881a of the Foreign Intelligence Surveillance Act. Justice Alito concluded: "Respondents assert that they can establish injury in fact because there is an objectively reasonable likelihood that their communications will be acquired under § 1881a at some point in the future. But respondents' theory of future injury is too speculative to satisfy the well-established requirement that threatened injury must be "certainly impending." And even if respondents could demonstrate that the threatened injury is certainly impending, they still would not be able to establish that this injury is fairly traceable to § 1181a.

A. CAUSATION

SIMON V. EASTERN KY. WELFARE RIGHTS ORG. [EKWRO]
426 U.S. 26 (1976).

JUSTICE POWELL delivered the opinion of the Court.

The [Internal Revenue] Code . . . accords advantageous treatment to several types of nonprofit [charitable] corporations, including exemption of their income from taxation and deductibility by benefactors of the amounts of their donations. [T]he IRS in 1956 issued Revenue Ruling 56–185, [which stated *inter alia* that a hospital would be regarded as "charitable" if it was "operated to the extent of its financial ability for those not able to pay for the services rendered"]. Revenue Ruling 56–185 remained the announced policy with respect to a nonprofit hospital's "charitable" status for 13 years, until the IRS issued Revenue Ruling 69–545 on November 3, 1969, [which expressly eliminated "the requirements relating to caring for patients without charge or at rates below cost" and explained that a hospital could be regarded as "charitable" if it "operate[d] a full time emergency room and no one requiring emergency care [was] denied treatment"]. . . .

Issuance of Revenue Ruling 69–545 led to the filing of this suit . . . by a group of organizations and individuals. The plaintiff organizations described themselves as an unincorporated association and several nonprofit corporations each of which included low-income persons among its members and represented the interests of all such persons in obtaining hospital care and services. . . . Each of the individuals described an occasion on which he or a member of his family had been disadvantaged in seeking needed hospital services because of indigency. . . . According to the complaint, each of the hospitals involved in these incidents had been determined by the Secretary and the Commissioner to be a tax-exempt charitable corporation, and each received substantial private contributions. The Secretary and the Commissioner were the only defendants. The complaint alleged that by extending tax benefits to such hospitals despite their refusals fully to serve the indigent, the defendants were "encouraging" the hospitals to deny services to the individual plaintiffs and to the members and clients of the plaintiff organizations. Those persons were alleged to be suffering "injury in their opportunity and ability to receive hospital services in nonprofit hospitals which receive . . . benefits . . . as 'charitable' organizations." . . . hey also were alleged to be among the intended beneficiaries of the Code sections that grant favorable tax treatment to "charitable" organizations.

Plaintiffs [claimed *inter alia*] that in issuing Revenue Ruling 69–545 the defendants had violated the Internal Revenue Code. . . . Plaintiffs sought various forms of declaratory and injunctive relief. The Court of Appeals for the District of Columbia Circuit . . . [ruled against the plaintiffs on the merits]. . . .

[The organization plaintiffs] can establish standing only as representatives of those of their members who have been injured in fact, and thus could have brought suit in their own right.[20] The obvious interest of all respondents, to which they claim actual injury, is that of access to hospital services. In one sense, of course, they have suffered injury to that interest. The complaint alleges specific occasions on which each of the individual respondents sought but was denied hospital services solely due to his indigency, and in at least some of the cases it is clear that the needed treatment was unavailable, as a practical matter, anywhere else. The complaint also alleges that members of the respondent organizations need hospital services but live in communities in which the private hospitals do not serve indigents. We thus assume, for purpose of analysis, that some members have been denied service.

But injury at the hands of a hospital is insufficient by itself to establish a case or controversy in the context of this suit, for no hospital is a defendant. The only defendants are officials of the Department of the Treasury, and the only claims of illegal action respondents desire the courts to adjudicate are charged to those officials. [T]he "case or controversy" limitation of [Article III] still requires that a federal court act only to redress injury that fairly can be traced to the challenged action of the defendant, and not injury that results from the independent action of some third party not before the court.

The complaint here alleged only that petitioners, by the adoption of Revenue Ruling 69–545, had "encouraged" hospitals to deny services to indigents. The implicit corollary of this allegation is that a grant of respondents' requested relief, resulting in a requirement that all hospitals serve indigents as a condition to favorable tax treatment, would "discourage" hospitals from denying their services to respondents. But it does not follow from the allegation and its corollary that the denial of access to hospital services in fact results from petitioners' new Ruling, or that a court-ordered return by petitioners to their previous policy would result in these respondents' receiving the hospital services they desire. It is purely speculative whether the denials of service specified in the complaint fairly can be traced to petitioners' "encouragement" or instead result from decisions made by the hospitals without regard to the tax implications. . . .

---

[20] The individual respondents sought to maintain this suit as a class action on behalf of all persons similarly situated. That a suit may be a class action, however, adds nothing to the question of standing, for even named plaintiffs who represent a class "must allege and show that they personally have been injured, not that injury has been suffered by other, unidentified members of the class to which they belong and which they purport to represent." . . .

It is true that the individual respondents have alleged, upon information and belief, that the hospitals that denied them service receive substantial donations deductible by the donors. This allegation could support an inference that these hospitals, or some of them, are so financially dependent upon the favorable tax treatment afforded charitable organizations that they would admit respondents if a court required such admission as a condition to receipt of that treatment. But this inference is speculative at best. The Solicitor General states in his brief that, nationwide, private philanthropy accounts for only 4% of private hospital revenues. Respondents introduced in the District Court a statement to Congress by an official of a hospital association describing the importance to nonprofit hospitals of the favorable tax treatment they receive as charitable corporations. Such conflicting evidence supports the commonsense proposition that the dependence upon special tax benefits may vary from hospital to hospital. . . .

JUSTICE STEWART, concurring.

I add only that I cannot now imagine a case, at least outside the First Amendment area, where a person whose own tax liability was not affected ever could have standing to litigate the federal tax liability of someone else.

NOTES ON CAUSATION

1. **Intermediate Actors.** Justice Thomas explained in *AGC* that causation is not established if the plaintiff's injury resulted from "the independent action of some third party not before the court." The explanation for the decision in *EKWRO* was the plaintiffs' inability to allege that the parties who actually regulated (the hospitals) would respond to the Secretary's more generous definition of "charitable" institutions in a way that would cause the injury the plaintiffs predicted.

a. Recall that, in *Warth v. Seldin*, Justice Powell insisted that low-income individuals had not sufficiently connected their alleged inability to find suitable housing in Penfield with the Penfield zoning ordinance or its administration. The problem there, too, was that the causal linkage on which the plaintiffs relied depended on the behavior of third parties—in that case construction companies whose willingness and ability to build low-cost housing was not plainly contingent on the ordinance or the town's implementation of it.

b. The African American school children in *Allen v. Wright*, 468 U.S. 737 (1984) alleged that the IRS was causing injury to their interest in attending desegregated public schools. According to the complaint, the IRS had adopted loose standards for determining whether private schools were entitled to tax exemptions; those standards allowed segregated schools to get tax breaks; the tax breaks permitted segregated schools to keep their tuition low; low tuition attracted white children fleeing public schools undergoing desegregation; and the diminution in the number of white students in public schools made it more difficult for public schools to desegregate. Writing for the Court, Justice O'Connor found the causal chain "attenuated," because it depended on speculation about the behavior of segregated private schools and the parents of white students. It wasn't clear (enough) that the standards the IRS employed permitted segregated schools to obtain tax treatment to which they were not entitled or that, if the schools did get exemptions, they reduced their rates to attract more white students. Nor was it clear (enough) that parents withdrew their children from public schools when the costs of segregated private schools were diminished. See Gene Nichol, *Abusing Standing: A Comment on* Allen v. Wright, 133 U.PA.L.REV. 635 (1985).

2. **Causal Chains.** Is it fair to say that the sufficiency of a causal chain for standing purposes is not so much an exercise in logic as it is a matter of judgment? Judgment about the likely consequences of events? Judgment about the way the world works? Dissenting in *Allen v. Wright,* Justice Stevens insisted that the plaintiffs' allegations were not speculative at all, but amounted to "elementary economics"—namely, rational expectations that schools and parents responded to economic incentives. Consider in this vein the causal chain the Court found sufficient in *Duke Power Co. v. Carolina Environmental Study Group,* 438 U.S. 59 (1978) to establish standing on the part of plaintiffs who resided near the lake on which a company planned to construct a nuclear power plant. The complaint alleged that the Price-Anderson Act fortified the power company's financial position; the company's secure status would enable it to persuade contractors to build the plant; the plant would emit particles that would increase the temperature of the water in the lake; and the elevation in water temperature would diminish the plaintiffs' enjoyment of their homes and activities on the shore. Is it cynical to suggest that the Court found the causal chain attenuated in *Allen,* because the justices were unenthusiastic about reaching the merits of the plaintiffs' claim (that the IRS was effectively promoting segregationist academies in the South), and that the Court found the causal chain sufficient in *Duke Power,* because the justices *wanted* to reach the claim that the Price-Anderson Act was unconstitutional (thus to sustain that Act and, in turn, to reassure the nuclear power industry)?

3. **Causation and the Merits.** Is it also fair to say that the facts plaintiffs allege to identify a causal connection between a defendant's behavior and their injury overlap significantly with the facts plaintiffs allege in support of their legal claim that the defendant's conduct is unlawful? If so, isn't there a way in which the Court may use the "causation" element of standing not to dodge claims the justices would rather avoid, but effectively to reject claims on the merits? Recall in this vein Justice Brennan's dissent in *Warth v. Seldin.* See, also Michael Wells, *The Impact of Substantive Interests on the Law of Federal Courts,* 30 WM. & MARY L. REV. 499 (1989).

B. REDRESSABILITY

LINDA R.S. v. RICHARD D.
410 U.S. 614 (1973).

JUSTICE MARSHALL delivered the opinion of the Court.

Appellant, the mother of an illegitimate child, brought this action in United States District Court on behalf of herself, her child, and others similarly situated to enjoin the 'discriminatory application' of Art. 602 of the Texas Penal Code. A three-judge court was convened pursuant to 28 U.S.C. 2281, but that court dismissed the action for want of standing. We postponed consideration of jurisdiction until argument and now affirm the judgment below.

Article 602 provides: 'any parent who shall willfully desert, neglect or refuse to provide for the support and maintenance of his or her child or children under eighteen years of age, shall be guilty of a misdemeanor, and upon conviction, shall be punished by confinement in the County Jail for not more than two years.' The Texas courts have consistently construed this statute to apply solely to the parents of legitimate children and to impose no duty of support on the parents of illegitimate children. In her complaint, appellant alleges that one Richard D. is the father of her child, that Richard D. has refused to provide support for the child, and that although appellant made application to the local district attorney for enforcement of Art. 602 against Richard D., the district attorney refused to take action for the express reason that, in his view, the fathers of illegitimate children were not within the scope of Art. 602.

Appellant argues that this interpretation of Art. 602 discriminates between legitimate and illegitimate children without rational foundation and therefore violates the Equal Protection Clause of the Fourteenth Amendment. . . .

Before we can consider the merits of appellant's claim or the propriety of the relief requested, however, appellant must first demonstrate that she is entitled to invoke the judicial process. She must, in other words, show that the facts alleged present the court with a 'case or controversy' in the constitutional sense and that she is a proper plaintiff to raise the issues sought to be litigated. The threshold question which must be answered is whether the appellant has 'alleged such a personal stake in the outcome of the controversy as to assure that concrete adverseness which sharpens the presentation of issues upon which the court so largely depends for illumination of difficult constitutional questions.'

Recent decisions by this Court have greatly expanded the types of 'personal stake(s)' which are capable of conferring standing on a potential plaintiff. But the 'broadening the categories of injury that may be alleged in support of standing is a different matter from abandoning the requirement that the party seeking review must himself have suffered an injury.'

Applying this test to the facts of this case, we hold that, in the unique context of a challenge to a criminal statute, appellant has failed to allege a sufficient nexus between her injury and the government action which she attacks to justify judicial intervention. To be sure, appellant no doubt suffered an injury stemming from the failure of her child's father to contribute support payments. But the bare existence of an abstract injury meets only the first half of the standing requirement. . . .

Here, appellant has made no showing that her failure to secure support payments results from the nonenforcement, as to her child's father, of Art. 602. Although the Texas statute appears to create a continuing duty, it does not follow the civil contempt model whereby the defendant 'keeps the keys to the jail in his own picket' and may be released whenever he complies with his legal obligations. On the contrary, the statute creates a completed offense with a fixed penalty as soon as a parent fails to support his child. Thus, if appellant were granted the requested relief, it would result only in the jailing of the child's father. The prospect that prosecution will, at least in the future, result in payment of support can, at best, be termed only speculative. Certainly the 'direct' relationship between the alleged injury and the claim sought to be adjudicated, which previous decisions of this Court suggest is a prerequisite of standing, is absent in this case. . . .

Appellant does have an interest in the support of her child. But given the special status of criminal prosecutions in our system, we hold that appellant has made an insufficient showing of a direct nexus between the vindication of her interest and the enforcement of the State's criminal laws. The District Court was therefore correct in dismissing the action for want of standing, and its judgment must be affirmed.

Judgment affirmed.

FRIENDS OF THE EARTH V. LAIDLAW
528 U.S. 167 (2000).

JUSTICE GINSBURG delivered the opinion of the Court.

Congress authorized the federal district courts to entertain Clean Water Act suits initiated by "a person or persons having an interest which is or may be adversely affected." To impel future compliance with the Act, a district court may prescribe injunctive relief in such a suit; additionally or alternatively, the court may impose civil penalties payable to the United States Treasury. In the Clean Water Act citizen suit now before us, the District Court determined that injunctive relief was inappropriate because the defendant, after the institution of the litigation, achieved substantial compliance with the terms of its discharge permit. The court did, however, assess a civil penalty. . . .

[D]efendant-respondent Laidlaw Environmental Services . . . bought a hazardous waste incinerator facility . . . that included a waste water treatment plant. [T]he South Carolina Department of Health and Environmental Control (DHEC), acting under 33 U.S.C. § 1342(a)(1), granted Laidlaw a . . . permit authorizing the company to discharge treated water into the North Tyger River. The permit, which became effective on January 1, 1987, placed limits on Laidlaw's discharge of several pollutants into the river, including . . . mercury, an extremely toxic pollutant. The permit also regulated the flow, temperature, toxicity, and pH of the effluent from the facility, and imposed monitoring and reporting obligations. [R]epeatedly, Laidlaw's discharges exceeded the limits set by the permit. The District Court . . . found that Laidlaw had violated the mercury limits on 489 occasions between 1987 and 1995.

On April 10, 1992, plaintiff-petitioners Friends of the Earth (FOE) and Citizens Local Environmental Action Network (CLEAN) . . . took the preliminary step necessary to the institution of litigation. They sent a letter to Laidlaw notifying the company of their intention to file a citizen suit against it . . . after the expiration of the requisite 60-day notice period, i.e., on or after June 10, 1992. Laidlaw's lawyer then contacted DHEC to ask whether DHEC would consider filing a lawsuit against Laidlaw. The District Court later found that Laidlaw's reason for requesting that DHEC file a lawsuit against it was to bar FOE's proposed citizen suit through the operation of 33 U.S.C. § 1365(b)(1)(B) [which prohibits a citizen from suing if the EPA or the State has already commenced and is "diligently prosecuting" an enforcement action]. DHEC agreed to file a lawsuit against Laidlaw; the company's lawyer then drafted the complaint for DHEC and paid the filing fee. On June 9, 1992, the last day before FOE's 60-day notice period expired, DHEC and Laidlaw reached a settlement requiring Laidlaw to pay $100,000 in civil penalties and to make "every effort" to comply with its permit obligations.

On June 12, 1992, FOE filed this citizen suit against Laidlaw under § 505(a) of the Act, alleging noncompliance with the . . . permit and seeking declaratory and injunctive relief and an award of civil penalties. [T]he District Court found that Laidlaw had gained a total economic benefit of $1,092,581 as a result of its extended period of noncompliance with the mercury discharge limit in its permit. The court concluded, however, that a civil penalty of $405,800 was adequate. . . . In reaching this determination, the court "considered that Laidlaw will be required to reimburse plaintiffs for a significant amount of legal fees." The court declined to grant FOE's request for injunctive relief, stating that an injunction was inappropriate because "Laidlaw has been in substantial compliance with all parameters in its . . . permit since at least August 1992." . . .

[T]he District Court found that FOE had demonstrated sufficient injury to establish standing. For example, FOE member Kenneth Lee Curtis averred in affidavits that he lived a half-mile from Laidlaw's facility; that he occasionally drove over the North Tyger River, and that it looked and smelled polluted; and that he would like to fish, camp, swim, and picnic in and near the river between 3 and 15 miles downstream from the facility, as he did when he was a teenager, but would not do so because he was concerned that the water was polluted by Laidlaw's discharges. . . . Other members presented evidence to similar effect. . . . These sworn statements, as the District Court determined, adequately documented injury in fact.

Laidlaw argues . . . that even if FOE had standing to seek injunctive relief, it lacked standing to seek civil penalties. Here the asserted defect is not injury but redressability. Civil penalties offer no redress to private plaintiffs, Laidlaw argues, because they are paid to the Government, and therefore a citizen plaintiff can never have standing to seek them. Laidlaw is right to insist that a plaintiff must demonstrate standing separately for each form of relief sought. . . . But it is wrong to maintain that citizen plaintiffs facing ongoing violations never have standing to seek civil penalties.

We have recognized on numerous occasions that "all civil penalties have some deterrent effect." More specifically, Congress has found that civil penalties in Clean Water Act cases do more than promote immediate compliance by limiting the defendant's economic incentive to delay its attainment of permit limits; they also deter future violations. This congressional determination warrants judicial attention and respect. . . . It can scarcely be doubted that, for a plaintiff who is injured or faces the threat of future injury due to illegal conduct ongoing at the time of suit, a sanction that effectively abates that conduct and prevents its recurrence provides a form of redress. Civil penalties can fit that description. To the extent that they encourage defendants to discontinue current violations and deter them from committing future ones, they afford redress to citizen plaintiffs who are injured or threatened with injury as a consequence of ongoing unlawful conduct. . . .

Steel Co. [*v. Citizens for a Better Environment*, 523 U.S. 83 (1998),] held that private plaintiffs, unlike the Federal Government, may not sue to assess penalties for wholly past violations, but our decision in that case did not reach the issue of standing to seek penalties for violations that are ongoing at the time of the complaint and that could continue into the future if undeterred.[4]

JUSTICE SCALIA, with whom JUSTICE THOMAS joins, dissenting.

[P]etitioners allege ongoing injury consisting of diminished enjoyment of the affected waterways and decreased property values. They allege that these injuries are caused by Laidlaw's continuing permit violations. But the remedy petitioners seek is neither recompense for their injuries nor an injunction against future violations. Instead, the remedy is a statutorily specified "penalty" for past violations, payable entirely to the United States Treasury. Only last Term, we held that such penalties do not redress any injury a citizen plaintiff has suffered from past violations. *Steel Co. v. Citizens for a Better Environment.* . . .

The new standing law that the Court makes—like all expansions of standing beyond the traditional constitutional limits—has grave implications for democratic governance. . . . The Court's opinion reads as though the only purpose and effect of the redressability requirement is to assure that the plaintiff receive *some* of the benefit of the relief that a court orders. That is not so. [The] "remediation" that is the traditional business of Anglo-American courts is relief specifically tailored to the plaintiff's injury, and not any sort of relief that has some incidental benefit to the plaintiff. Just as a "generalized grievance" that affects the entire citizenry cannot satisfy the injury-in-fact requirement even though it aggrieves the plaintiff along with everyone else, so also a generalized remedy that deters all future unlawful activity against all persons cannot satisfy the remediation requirement, even though it deters (among other things) repetition of this particular unlawful activity against these particular plaintiffs.

Thus, relief against prospective harm is traditionally afforded by way of an injunction, the scope of which is limited by the scope of the threatened injury. In seeking to overturn that tradition by giving an individual plaintiff the power to invoke a public remedy, Congress has done precisely what we have said it cannot do: convert an "undifferentiated public interest" into an "individual right" vindicable in the courts. The sort of scattershot redress approved today makes nonsense of our statement in [*Reservists*], that the requirement of injury in fact "insures the framing of relief no broader than required by the precise facts." A claim of particularized future injury has today been made the vehicle for pursuing generalized penalties for past violations,

---

[4]　Certainly the Federal Executive Branch does not share the dissent's view that such suits dissipate its authority to enforce the law. In fact, the Department of Justice has endorsed this citizen suit from the outset, submitting amicus briefs in support of FOE. [T]he Federal Government retains the power to foreclose a citizen suit by undertaking its own action. And if the Executive Branch opposes a particular citizen suit, the statute allows the Administrator of the EPA to "intervene as a matter of right" and bring the Government's views to the attention of the court.

and a threshold showing of injury in fact has become a lever that will move the world.

[It] is my view that a plaintiff's desire to benefit from the deterrent effect of a public penalty for past conduct can never suffice to establish a case or controversy of the sort known to our law. Such deterrent effect is, so to speak, "speculative as a matter of law." Even if that were not so, however, the deterrent effect in the present case would surely be speculative as a matter of fact. . . . The deterrence on which the plaintiffs must rely for standing in the present case is the marginal increase in Laidlaw's fear of future penalties that will be achieved by adding federal penalties for Laidlaw's past conduct. I cannot say for certain that this marginal increase is zero; but I can say for certain that it is entirely speculative whether it will make the difference between these plaintiffs' suffering injury in the future and these plaintiffs' going [unharmed].

Article II of the Constitution commits it to the President to "take Care that the Laws be faithfully executed," Art. II, § 3, and provides specific methods by which all persons exercising significant executive power are to be appointed, Art. II, § 2. . . . Article III, no less than Article II, has consequences for the structure of our government, and it is worth noting the changes in that structure which today's decision allows. By permitting citizens to pursue civil penalties payable to the Federal Treasury, the Act does not provide a mechanism for individual relief in any traditional sense, but turns over to private citizens the function of enforcing the law. A Clean Water Act plaintiff pursuing civil penalties acts as a self-appointed mini-EPA. Where, as is often the case, the plaintiff is a national association, it has significant discretion in choosing enforcement targets. Once the association is aware of a reported violation, it need not look long for an injured member, at least under the theory of injury the Court applies today. And once the target is chosen, the suit goes forward without meaningful public control.[2] The availability of civil penalties vastly disproportionate to the individual injury gives citizen plaintiffs massive bargaining power—which is often used to achieve settlements requiring the defendant to support environmental projects of the plaintiffs' choosing. Thus is a public fine diverted to a private interest.

To be sure, the EPA may foreclose the citizen suit by itself bringing suit. This allows public authorities to avoid private enforcement only by accepting private direction as to when enforcement should be undertaken—which is no less constitutionally bizarre. Elected officials are entirely deprived of their discretion to decide that a given violation

---

[2]   The Court points out that the Government is allowed to intervene in a citizen suit . . . , but this power to "bring the Government's views to the attention of the court," is meager substitute for the power to decide whether prosecution will occur. Indeed, according to the Chief Executive of the United States the ability to intervene does no more than place him on a par with John Q. Public, who can intervene—whether the Government likes it or not—when the United States files suit. . . .

should not be the object of suit at all, or that the enforcement decision should be postponed.[3] This is the predictable and inevitable consequence of the Court's allowing the use of public remedies for private wrongs.

NOTES ON REDRESSABILITY

1. **Incentivizing Absent Fathers.** Do you think that the Texas legislators who passed the child support statute involved in *Linda R.S.* assumed that fathers would, generally speaking, meet their financial obligations rather than go to jail?

2. **Federalism or Standing?** Is *Linda R.S.* principally a federalism decision or a standing/injury determination? Do federalism concerns fit easily into the analysis of whether an injury is likely to be redressed by a favorable ruling?

3. **Redressability and Specific Relief.** Justice O'Connor explained in *Allen v. Wright* that the distinction between causation and redressability is important in cases in which "the relief requested goes well beyond the violation of law alleged." She acknowledged that the remedies the plaintiffs sought in that case (a declaratory judgment that IRS tax-exemption practices were unlawful and an injunction requiring the IRS to deny tax breaks to more private schools) "might have a substantial effect on the desegregation of public schools." But she insisted that the difficulties public schools were having with desegregation "might not be traceable to the IRS violations of law."

4. **Redressability and Parties.** In some cases, the Court has examined redressability with considerable care. Writing for a plurality (on this point) in *Defenders of Wildlife* Justice Scalia said this:

> Besides failing to show injury, respondents failed to demonstrate redressability. Instead of attacking the separate decisions to fund particular projects allegedly causing them harm, respondents chose to challenge a more generalized level of Government action (rules regarding consultation), the invalidation of which would affect all overseas projects. This programmatic approach has obvious practical advantages, but also obvious difficulties insofar as proof of causation or redressability is concerned. "[S]uits challenging, not specifically identifiable Government violations of law, but the particular programs agencies establish to carry out their legal obligations [are] rarely if ever appropriate for federal-court adjudication."

---

[3]   The Court observes that "the Federal Executive Branch does not share the dissent's view that such suits dissipate its authority to enforce the law," since it has "endorsed this citizen suit from the outset." . . . Of course, in doubtful cases a long and uninterrupted history of Presidential acquiescence and approval can shed light upon the constitutional understanding. What we have here—acquiescence and approval by a single administration—does not deserve passing mention.

The most obvious problem in the present case is redressability. Since the agencies funding the projects were not parties to the case, the District Court could accord relief only against the Secretary: He could be ordered to revise his regulation to require consultation for foreign projects. But this would not remedy respondents' alleged injury unless the funding agencies were bound by the Secretary's regulation, which is very much an open question. . . . When the Secretary promulgated the regulation at issue here, he thought it was binding on the agencies. . . . The Solicitor General, however, has repudiated that position . . . and the agencies themselves apparently deny the Secretary's authority. Respondents assert that this legal uncertainty did not affect redressability (and hence standing) because the District Court itself could resolve the issue of the Secretary's authority as a necessary part of its standing inquiry. Assuming that it is appropriate to resolve an issue of law such as this in connection with a threshold standing inquiry, resolution by the District Court would not have remedied respondents' alleged injury anyway, because it would not have been binding upon the agencies. They were not parties to the suit, and there is no reason they should be obliged to honor an incidental legal determination the suit produced. The Court of Appeals tried to finesse this problem by simply proclaiming that "[w]e are satisfied that an injunction requiring the Secretary to publish [respondents' desired regulation] would result in consultation." We do not know what would justify that confidence, particularly when the Justice Department (presumably after consultation with the agencies) has taken the position that the regulation is not binding. The short of the matter is that redress of the only injury in fact respondents complain of requires action (termination of funding until consultation) by the individual funding agencies; and any relief the District Court could have provided in this suit against the Secretary was not likely to produce that action. . . .

A further impediment to redressability is the fact that the agencies generally supply only a fraction of the funding for a foreign project. [The Agency for International Development], for example, has provided less than 10% of the funding for the Mahaweli project. Respondents have produced nothing to indicate that the projects they have named will either be suspended, or do less harm to listed species, if that fraction is eliminated. [I]t is entirely conjectural whether the nonagency activity that affects respondents will be altered or affected by the agency activity they seek to achieve. There is no standing.

5. Redressability in *Duke Power*. Compare *Duke Power Co. v. Carolina Environmental Study Group*, (above). Significant redressability challenges were almost completely ignored in a case where the majority of the Court seemed anxious to address the constitutionality of various federal subsidies for the nuclear power industry.

C. TAXPAYER STANDING

FROTHINGHAM V. MELLON
262 U.S. 447 (1923).

JUSTICE SUTHERLAND delivered the opinion of the Court.

[Harriet Frothingham] challenge[s] the constitutionality of the . . . Maternity Act, [which appropriates federal funds for maternal and infant health care]. It is asserted that . . . the [A]ct is a usurpation of power not granted to Congress by the Constitution—an attempted exercise of the power of local self-government reserved to the states by the Tenth Amendment. [The] plaintiff alleges, in addition, that she is a taxpayer of the United States; and her contention, though not clear, seems to be that the effect of the appropriations complained of will be to increase the burden of future taxation and thereby take her property without due process of law. . . . We have reached the conclusion that the case . . . must be disposed of for want of jurisdiction, without considering the merits of the constitutional questions.

[A taxpayer's] interest in the moneys of the Treasury—partly realized from taxation and partly from other sources—is shared with millions of others; is comparatively minute and indeterminable; and the effect upon future taxation, of a payment out of the funds, so remote, fluctuating and uncertain, that no basis is afforded for an appeal to the preventive powers of a court of equity. . . . The administration of any statute, likely to produce additional taxation to be imposed upon a vast number of taxpayers, the extent of whose several liability is indefinite and constantly changing, is essentially a matter of public and not of individual concern. If one taxpayer may champion and litigate such a cause, then every other taxpayer may do the same, not only in respect of the statute here under review but also in respect of every other appropriation act and statute whose administration requires the outlay of public money, and whose validity may be questioned. . . . The party who invokes [judicial] power must be able to show not only that the statute is invalid but that he has sustained or is immediately in danger of sustaining some direct injury as the result of its enforcement, and not merely that he suffers in some indefinite way in common with people generally. . . .

FLAST V. COHEN
392 U.S. 83 (1968).

CHIEF JUSTICE WARREN delivered the opinion of the Court.

Appellants filed suit . . . to enjoin the allegedly unconstitutional expenditure of federal funds under . . . the Elementary and Secondary Education Act. [I]t is clear from the complaint that the appellants were resting their standing to maintain the action solely on their status as federal taxpayers. . . . The gravamen of the appellants' complaint was that federal funds appropriated under the Act were being used to finance instruction in . . . religious schools . . . in contravention of the Establishment Clause. . . .

[I]n ruling on standing, it is both appropriate and necessary to look to the substantive issues . . . to determine whether there is a logical nexus between the status asserted and the claim sought to be adjudicated. . . . Such inquiries into the nexus between the status asserted by the litigant and the claim he presents are essential to assure that he is a proper and appropriate party to invoke federal judicial power. Thus, our point of reference in this case is the standing of individuals who assert only the status of federal taxpayers and who challenge the constitutionality of a federal spending program. Whether such individuals have standing to maintain that form of action turns on whether they can demonstrate the necessary stake as taxpayers in the outcome of the litigation to satisfy Article III requirements.

The nexus demanded of federal taxpayers has two aspects to it. First, the taxpayer must establish a logical link between that status and the type of legislative enactment attacked. Thus, a taxpayer will be a proper party to allege the unconstitutionality only of exercises of congressional power under the taxing and spending clause . . . of the Constitution. It will not be sufficient to allege an incidental expenditure of tax funds in the administration of an essentially regulatory statute. . . . Secondly, the taxpayer must establish a nexus between that status and the precise nature of the constitutional infringement alleged. Under this requirement, the taxpayer must show that the challenged enactment exceeds specific constitutional limitations imposed upon the exercise of the congressional taxing and spending power and not simply that the enactment is generally beyond the powers delegated to Congress. . . . When both nexuses are established, the litigant will have shown a taxpayer's stake in the outcome of the controversy and will be a proper and appropriate party to invoke a federal court's jurisdiction.

The taxpayer-appellants in this case have satisfied both nexuses to support their claim of standing under the test we announce today. Their constitutional challenge is made to an exercise by Congress of its power . . . to spend for the general welfare, and the challenged program involves a substantial expenditure of federal tax funds. In addition, appellants have alleged that the challenged expenditures violate the Establishment Clause. . . . Our history vividly illustrates that one of the specific evils feared by those who drafted the Establishment Clause . . . was that the taxing and spending power would be used to favor one religion over another or to support religion in general . . . The Establishment Clause . . . operates as a specific constitutional limitation upon the exercise by Congress of the taxing and spending power. . . .

The allegations of the taxpayer in *Frothingham* . . . were quite different from those made in this case, and the result in *Frothingham* is consistent with the test of taxpayer standing announced today. The taxpayer in *Frothingham* attacked a federal spending program and she, therefore, established the first nexus required. However, she lacked standing because her constitutional attack was not based on an allegation that Congress . . . had breached a specific limitation upon its taxing and spending power [but rather] that Congress . . . had exceeded the general powers delegated to it by Art. I, § 8, and . . . had thereby invaded the legislative province reserved to the States by the Tenth Amendment. To be sure, Mrs. Frothingham made the additional allegation that her tax liability would be increased as a result of the allegedly unconstitutional enactment, and she framed that allegation in terms of a deprivation of property without due process of law. However, the Due Process Clause . . . does not protect taxpayers against increases in tax liability. . . . In essence, Mrs. Frothingham was attempting to assert the States' interest in their legislative prerogatives and not a federal taxpayer's interest in being free of taxing and spending in contravention of specific constitutional limitations imposed upon Congress' taxing and spending power. . . .

Whether the Constitution contains other specific limitations can be determined only in the context of future cases. However, whenever such specific limitations are found, we believe a taxpayer will have a clear stake as a taxpayer in assuring that they are not breached by Congress. . . . The taxpayer's allegation in such cases would be that his tax money is being extracted and spent in violation of specific constitutional protections against such abuses of legislative power. . . . Under such circumstances, we feel confident that the questions will be framed with the necessary specificity, that the issues will be contested with the necessary adverseness and that the litigation will be pursued with the necessary vigor to assure that the constitutional challenge will be made in a form traditionally thought to be capable of judicial resolution. We lack that confidence in cases such as *Frothingham* where a taxpayer seeks to employ a federal court as a forum in which to air his generalized grievances about the conduct of government or the allocation of power in the Federal System.

JUSTICE STEWART, concurring.

Because [the Establishment Clause] plainly prohibits taxing and spending in aid of religion, every taxpayer can claim a personal constitutional right not to be taxed for the support of a religious institution. The present case is thus readily distinguishable from *Frothingham*, where the taxpayer did not rely on an explicit constitutional prohibition but instead questioned the scope of the powers delegated to the national legislature by Article I of the Constitution.

JUSTICE HARLAN, dissenting.

It could hardly be disputed that federal taxpayers may, as taxpayers, contest the constitutionality of tax obligations imposed severally upon them by federal statute. . . . The lawsuits here and in *Frothingham* . . . present the question whether federal taxpayers qua taxpayers may, in suits in which they do not contest the validity of their previous or existing tax obligations, challenge the constitutionality of the uses for which Congress has authorized the expenditure of public funds. . . . An action brought to contest the validity of tax liabilities assessed to the plaintiff is designed to vindicate interests that are personal and proprietary. [This] suit cannot result in an adjudication either of the plaintiff's tax liabilities or of the propriety of any particular level of taxation. The relief available . . . consists entirely of the vindication of rights held in common by all citizens.

Nor are taxpayers' interests in the expenditure of public funds differentiated from those of the general public by any special rights retained by them in their tax payments. [T]he United States holds its general funds, not as stakeholder or trustee for those who have paid its imposts, but as surrogate for the population at large. Any rights of a taxpayer with respect to the purposes for which those funds are expended are thus subsumed in, and extinguished by, the common rights of all citizens. . . . To characterize taxpayers' interests in such expenditures as proprietary or even personal either deprives those terms of all meaning or postulates for taxpayers a Scintilla juris in funds that no longer are theirs.

Surely it is plain that the rights and interests of taxpayers who contest the constitutionality of public expenditures are markedly different from those of "Hohfeldian" plaintiffs, including those taxpayer-plaintiffs who challenge the validity of their own tax liabilities. We must recognize that these non-Hohfeldian plaintiffs complain, just as the petitioner in *Frothingham* sought to complain, not as taxpayers, but as "private attorneys-general." The interests they represent, and the rights they espouse, are bereft of any personal or proprietary coloration. They are, as litigants, indistinguishable from any group selected at random from among the general population, taxpayers and nontaxpayers alike. These are and must be . . . "public actions" brought to vindicate public rights.

It does not, however, follow that suits brought by non-Hohfeldian plaintiffs are excluded by the "case or controversy" clause of Article III of the Constitution from the jurisdiction of the federal courts. This and other federal courts have repeatedly held that individual litigants, acting as private attorneys-general, may have standing as "representatives of the public interest." *Scripps-Howard Radio v. FCC*, 316 U.S. 4, 14 (1942). See also *FCC v. Sanders Bros. Radio Station*, 309 U.S. 470, 477 (1940). . . . The problem ultimately presented by this case is, in my view, therefore to determine in what circumstances, consonant with the character and proper functioning of the federal courts, such suits should be permitted.[8] With this preface, I shall examine the position adopted by the Court.

[T]he Court's standard for the determination of standing and its criteria for the satisfaction of that standard are entirely unrelated. [I]t surely cannot matter to a taxpayer qua taxpayer whether an unconstitutional expenditure is used to hire the services of regulatory personnel or is distributed among private and local governmental agencies as grants-in-aid. His interest as taxpayer arises, if at all, from the fact of an unlawful expenditure, and not as a consequence of the expenditure's form. . . . The Court's second criterion is similarly unrelated to its standard for the determination of standing. The intensity of a plaintiff's interest in a suit is not measured, even obliquely, by the fact that the constitutional provision under which he claims is, or is not, a "specific limitation" upon Congress' spending powers. . . .

[P]ublic actions, whatever the constitutional provisions on which they are premised, may involve important hazards for the continued effectiveness of the federal judiciary. Although I believe such actions to be within the jurisdiction conferred upon the federal courts by Article III of the Constitution, there surely can be little doubt that they strain the judicial function and press to the limit judicial authority. . . . I do not doubt that there must be "some effectual power in the government to restrain or correct the infractions" of the Constitution's several commands, but neither can I suppose that such power resides only in the federal courts. . . . The powers of the federal judiciary will be adequate for the great burdens placed upon them only if they are employed prudently, with recognition of the strengths as well as the hazards that go with our kind of representative government. [L]itigants have standing to represent the public interest, despite their lack of economic or other personal

---

[8]   I agree that implicit in this question is the belief that the federal courts may decline to accept for adjudication cases or questions that, although otherwise within the perimeter of their constitutional jurisdiction, are appropriately thought to be unsuitable at least for immediate judicial resolution. Compare *Ashwander v. Tennessee Valley Authority*, 297 U.S. 288, 345–348 (1936) (concurring opinion). . . .

interests, if Congress has appropriately authorized such suits. I would adhere to that principle. Any hazards to the proper allocation of authority among the three branches of the Government would be substantially diminished if public actions had been pertinently authorized by Congress and the President.

UNITED STATES V. RICHARDSON
418 U.S. 166 (1974).

CHIEF JUSTICE BURGER delivered the opinion of the Court.

We granted certiorari in this case to determine whether the respondent has standing to bring an action as a federal taxpayer[1] alleging that certain provisions concerning public reporting of expenditures under the Central Intelligence Agency Act . . . violate Art. I, § 9, cl. 7, of the Constitution which provides: "No Money shall be drawn from the Treasury, but in Consequence of Appropriations made by Law; and a regular Statement and Account of the Receipts and Expenditures of all public Money shall be published from time to time."

[T]he respondent asked the federal court to declare unconstitutional that provision of the Central Intelligence Agency Act which permits the Agency to account for its expenditures "solely on the certificate of the Director." The only injury alleged by respondent was that he "cannot obtain a document that sets out the expenditures and receipts" of the CIA but on the contrary was "asked to accept a fraudulent document."

Although [*Flast v. Cohen*] is a starting point in an examination of respondent's claim to prosecute this suit as a taxpayer, that case must be read with reference to its principal predecessor, *Frothingham v. Mellon.* . . . The mere recital of the respondent's claims and an examination of the statute under attack demonstrate how far he falls short of the standing criteria of *Flast* and how neatly he falls within the *Frothingham* holding left undisturbed. Although the status he rests on is that he is a taxpayer, his challenge is not addressed to the taxing or spending power, but to the statutes regulating the CIA. . . . Respondent makes no claim that appropriated funds are being spent in violation of a "specific constitutional limitation upon the . . . taxing and spending power." Rather, he asks the courts to compel the Government to give him information on precisely how the CIA spends its funds. Thus there is no "logical nexus" between the asserted status of taxpayer and the claimed

---

[1] Respondent's complaint alleged that he was "a member of the electorate, and a loyal citizen of the United States." At the same time, he states that he "does not challenge the formulation of the issue contained in the petition for certiorari." . . . The question presented there was: "Whether a federal taxpayer has standing to challenge the provisions of the Central Intelligence Agency Act. . . ."

failure of the Congress to require the Executive to supply a more detailed report of the expenditures of that agency. . . .

The respondent's claim is that without detailed information on CIA expenditures—and hence its activities—he cannot intelligently follow the actions of Congress or the Executive, nor can he properly fulfill his obligations as a member of the electorate in voting for candidates seeking national office. This is surely the kind of a generalized grievance described in both *Frothingham* and *Flast* since the impact on him is plainly undifferentiated and "common to all members of the public." While we can hardly dispute that this respondent has a genuine interest in the use of funds and that his interest may be prompted by his status as a taxpayer, he has not alleged that, as a taxpayer, he is in danger of suffering any particular concrete injury as a result of the operation of this statute. . . .[11]

It can be argued that if respondent is not permitted to litigate this issue, no one can do so. In a very real sense, the absence of any particular individual or class to litigate these claims gives support to the argument that the subject matter is committed to the surveillance of Congress, and ultimately to the political process. . . . Lack of standing within the narrow confines of Art. III jurisdiction does not impair the [respondent's] right to assert his views in the political forum or at the polls. . . . As our society has become more complex, our numbers more vast, our lives more varied, and our resources more strained, citizens increasingly request the intervention of the courts on a greater variety of issues than at any period of our national development. The acceptance of new categories of judicially cognizable injury has not eliminated the basic principle that to invoke judicial power the claimant must have a "personal stake in the outcome;" in short, something more than "generalized grievances."

JUSTICE POWELL, concurring.

I would not overrule *Flast* on its facts, because it is now settled that federal taxpayer standing exists in Establishment Clause cases. I would not, however, perpetuate the doctrinal confusion inherent in the *Flast* two-part "nexus" test. That test is not a reliable indicator of when a federal taxpayer has standing, and it has no sound relationship to the question whether such a plaintiff, with no other interest at stake, should be allowed to bring suit against one of the branches of the Federal Government. In my opinion, it should be abandoned. . . .

---

[11] It is . . . open to serious question whether the Framers of the Constitution ever imagined that general directives to the Congress or the Executive would be subject to enforcement by an individual citizen. . . . The ultimate weapon of enforcement available to the Congress would, of course, be the "power of the purse." Independent of the statute here challenged by respondent, Congress could grant standing to taxpayers or citizens, or both, limited, of course, by the "cases" and "controversies" provisions of [Article III]. . . .

JUSTICE STEWART, with whom JUSTICE MARSHALL joins, dissenting.

Richardson's claim is . . . that the Statement and Account Clause . . . gives him a right to receive, and imposes on the Government a corresponding affirmative duty to supply, a periodic report of the receipts and expenditures "of all public Money." . . . Whether the Statement and Account Clause imposes upon the Government an affirmative duty to supply the information requested and whether that duty runs to every taxpayer or citizen are questions that go to the substantive merits of this litigation. [T]he respondent is in the position of a traditional Hohfeldian plaintiff. He contends that the Statement and Account Clause gives him a right to receive the information and burdens the Government with a correlative duty to supply it. Courts of law exist for the resolution of such right-duty disputes.

VALLEY FORGE CHRISTIAN COLLEGE V. AMERICANS UNITED
454 U.S. 464 (1982).

JUSTICE REHNQUIST delivered the opinion of the Court.

[A]s part of a plan to reduce the number of military installations in the United States, the Secretary of Defense proposed to close [a federal] hospital, and the General Services Administration declared it to be "surplus property." The Department of Health, Education, and Welfare (HEW) eventually assumed responsibility for disposing of portions of the property, and . . . conveyed a 77-acre tract to petitioner, the Valley Forge Christian College. [R]espondents Americans United for Separation of Church and State (Americans United), and four of its employees, learned of the conveyance through a news release. [T]hey brought suit . . . to challenge the conveyance on the ground that it violated the Establishment Clause. In its amended complaint, Americans United described itself as a nonprofit organization composed of 90,000 "taxpayer members." The complaint asserted that each member "would be deprived of the fair and constitutional use of his (her) tax dollar for unconstitutional purposes in violation of his (her) rights under the First Amendment of the United States Constitution." . . .

Unlike the plaintiffs in *Flast v. Cohen*, respondents fail the first prong of the test for taxpayer standing. Their claim is deficient in two respects. First, the source of their complaint is not a congressional action, but a decision by HEW to transfer a parcel of federal property. *Flast* limited taxpayer standing to challenges directed "only [at] exercises of congressional power." Second, and perhaps redundantly, the property transfer about which respondents complain was not an exercise of authority conferred by the Taxing and Spending Clause. . . . The authorizing legislation . . . was an evident exercise of Congress' power under the Property Clause, Art. IV, § 3, cl. 2. . . . Any doubt that once might have existed concerning the rigor with which the *Flast* exception to the *Frothingham* principle ought to be applied should have been erased by . . . *United States v. Richardson.* . . .

In finding that respondents had alleged something more than "the generalized interest of all citizens in constitutional governance," the Court of Appeals [in this case] decided that respondents' claim differed from those in [*Richardson* and *Reservists*], which were predicated, respectively, on the Incompatibility and Accounts Clauses, because "it is at the very least arguable that the Establishment Clause creates in each citizen a 'personal constitutional right' to a government that does not establish religion." The court found it unnecessary to determine whether this "arguable" proposition was correct, since it judged the mere allegation of a legal right sufficient to confer standing.

This reasoning process merely disguises, we think with a rather thin veil, the inconsistency of the court's results with our decisions in [*Richardson* and *Reservists*]. The plaintiffs in those cases plainly asserted a "personal right" to have the Government act in accordance with their views of the Constitution; indeed, we see no barrier to the assertion of such claims with respect to any constitutional provision. But assertion of a right to a particular kind of Government conduct, which the Government has violated by acting differently, cannot alone satisfy the requirements of Art. III without draining those requirements of meaning. . . .

In reaching this conclusion, we do not retreat from our earlier holdings that standing may be predicated on noneconomic injury. We simply cannot see that respondents have alleged an injury of any kind, economic or otherwise, sufficient to confer standing. . . . Their claim that the Government has violated the Establishment Clause does not provide a special license to roam the country in search of governmental wrongdoing and to reveal their discoveries in federal court. The federal courts were simply not constituted as ombudsmen of the general welfare. . . .

Respondents' claim of standing implicitly rests on the presumption that violations of the Establishment Clause typically will not cause injury sufficient to confer standing under the "traditional" view of Art. III. But "[t]he assumption that if respondents have no standing to sue, no one would have standing, is not a reason to find standing." . . . This view would convert standing into a requirement that must be observed only when satisfied. Moreover, we are unwilling to assume that injured parties are nonexistent simply because they have not joined respondents in their suit.

INITIAL NOTES ON TAXPAYER STANDING

1. **Federal Taxpayers.** Do taxpayers really have a personal interest in expenditures from the federal treasury? Justice Sutherland obviously thought not in *Frothingham*. Did Chief Justice Warren offer a convincing basis for distinguishing *Flast* from *Frothingham*? What was that distinction (stated precisely)? Warren made the nature of the Establishment Clause crucial to his analysis. What, then, should we make of the last paragraph of his opinion, in which he suggested that other provisions of the Constitution might also count as "specific limitations" on federal spending and thus invite a similar standing analysis? Do the plaintiffs in Flast actually have an interest in the suit which is distinct from the demand that the government toe the constitutional mark rejected by the Court in *Ex parte Levitt*?

2. **Rights-Based Standing.** Justice Stewart contended that the plaintiffs in *Flast* could rely on the old rights-based conception of standing—there being (in Stewart's view) an individual constitutional right to be free of taxation for religious purposes. Was that argument a complete answer to the question whether the plaintiffs were *factually* injured as taxpayers? Would Stewart have recognized taxpayer standing on the same basis in a case in which plaintiffs attack governmental action as a violation of some feature of the Constitution other than the Establishment Clause? Notice Stewart's dissent in *United States v. Richardson*.

3. **Non-Hohfeldian Plaintiffs.** Justice Harlan refers to the work of Wesley Hohfeld, an early twentieth century legal theorist who (among other things) distinguished between two kinds of litigants—those who assert their legal rights (Hohfeldian plaintiffs, in Justice Harlan's terminology) and those who assert other kinds of interests (Justice Harlan's non-Hohfeldian plaintiffs). Justice Harlan said that the suit in *Flast* could only be understood as a "public action." Harlan acknowledged that non-Hohfeldian plaintiffs can satisfy any constitutional requirements. But how did he define non-Hohfeldians or "private attorneys general" in *Flast*? Plaintiffs who assert no personal legal *rights*? Plaintiffs who lack any personal *interest* apart from ideological concerns? Notice that in the final paragraph of his dissent, Harlan said that plaintiffs who have no "economic or other personal interests" nonetheless have standing if Congress authorizes them to sue. Did he mean that Congress can confer standing on *anyone*, irrespective of whether the individual has any interest that distinguishes him or her from everyone else? On someone whose only interest is the desire to see the law enforced—i.e., the very interest that is *not* ordinarily sufficient for constitutional standing? Can Congress defuse all separation of powers concerns by authorizing suits in federal court and thus, effectively, consenting to an exercise of federal judicial power that would be constitutionally forbidden in the absence of congressional approval?

4. **Arbitrary Distinctions.** Does the Court in *Valley Forge* adequately explain why, in cases such as *Davis v. Passman*, 442 U.S. 228 (1979), the due process clause of the Fifth Amendment confers a right to be

free from sex discrimination while the establishment clause bestows no "personal right" to be free from the intermingling of church and state? The Constitution, since *Marbury*, has been determined to create legally protected interests. Does the particularized harm standard effectively create a "hierarchy" of rights, despite protestations to the contrary? See Gene Nichol, *Rethinking Standing*, 72 CAL.L. REV. 68, 84–87 (1984) and Susan Bandes, *The Idea of a Case*, 42 STAN.L.REV. 227, 230 (1990). The outcome in *Valley Forge* is defended on narrower grounds in Marshall and Flood, *Establishment Clause Standing: The Not Very Revolutionary Decision at Valley Forge*, 11 HOFSTRA L.REV. 63 (1982).

Does it diminish the force and integrity of constitutional law to embrace distinctions as wooden and arbitrary as those separating *Flast* and *Valley Forge*?

HEIN V. FREEDOM FROM RELIGION FOUNDATION
551 U.S. 587 (2007).

JUSTICE ALITO delivered the opinion of the Court.

This is a lawsuit in which it was claimed that conferences held as part of the President's Faith-Based and Community Initiatives program violated the Establishment Clause of the First Amendment because, among other things, President Bush and former Secretary of Education Paige gave speeches that used "religious imagery" and praised the efficacy of faith-based programs in delivering social services. . . .

In light of the size of the federal budget, it is a complete fiction to argue that an unconstitutional federal expenditure causes an individual federal taxpayer any measurable economic harm. And if every federal taxpayer could sue to challenge any Government expenditure, the federal courts would cease to function as courts of law and would be cast in the role of general complaint bureaus. . . .

In *Flast v. Cohen*, . . . we recognized a narrow exception to the general rule against federal taxpayer standing. Under *Flast*, a plaintiff asserting an Establishment Clause claim has standing to challenge a law authorizing the use of federal funds in a way that allegedly violates the Establishment Clause. In the present case, Congress did not specifically authorize the use of federal funds to pay for the conferences or speeches that the plaintiffs challenged. Instead, the conferences and speeches were paid for out of general Executive Branch appropriations. . . .

[T]he President issued an executive order creating the [White House Office of Faith-Based Initiatives]. The purpose of this new office was to ensure that "private and charitable community groups, including religious ones, . . . have the fullest opportunity permitted by law to compete on a level playing field, so long as they achieve valid public purposes" and adhere to "the bedrock principles of pluralism, nondiscrimination, evenhandedness, and neutrality." . . . The office was specifically charged with the task of eliminating unnecessary bureaucratic, legislative, and regulatory barriers that could impede such organizations' effectiveness and ability to compete equally for federal assistance. . . . By separate executive orders, the President also created Executive Department Centers for Faith-Based and Community Initiatives within several federal agencies and departments. . . .

Petitioners, who have been sued in their official capacities, are the directors of the White House Office and various Executive Department Centers. The respondents [members of Freedom From Religion Foundation, an organization "opposed to government endorsement of religion"] brought suit . . . alleging that petitioners violated the Establishment Clause by organizing conferences . . . designed to promote, and had the effect of promoting, religious community groups over secular ones. The only asserted basis for standing was that the individual respondents are federal taxpayers. . . .

No congressional legislation specifically authorized the creation of the White House Office or the Executive Department Centers. Rather, they were "created entirely within the executive branch . . . by Presidential executive order." . . . Nor has Congress enacted any law specifically appropriating money for these entities' activities. Instead, their activities are funded through general Executive Branch appropriations. For example, the Department of Education's Center is funded from money appropriated for the Office of the Secretary of Education, while the Department of Housing and Urban Development's Center is funded through that Department's salaries and expenses account. . . .

[The respondents'] claim is that, having paid lawfully collected taxes into the Federal Treasury at some point, they have a continuing, legally cognizable interest in ensuring that those funds are not used by the Government in a way that violates the Constitution. We have consistently held that this type of interest is too generalized and attenuated to support Article III standing. . . . Because the interests of the taxpayer are, in essence, the interests of the public-at-large, deciding a constitutional claim based solely on taxpayer standing "would be[,] not to decide a judicial controversy, but to assume a position of authority over the governmental acts of another and co-equal department, an authority which plainly we do not possess." . . .

Given that the alleged Establishment Clause violation in *Flast* was funded by a specific congressional appropriation and was undertaken pursuant to an express congressional mandate, the Court concluded that the taxpayer-plaintiffs had established the requisite "logical link between [their taxpayer] status and the type of legislative enactment attacked."

. . . But as this Court later noted, *Flast* [limited taxpayer standing to challenges aimed at Congress' exercise of power under the Taxing and Spending Clause]. *Valley Forge* [*Christian College v. Americans United*]. . . .

The link between congressional action and constitutional violation that supported taxpayer standing in *Flast* is missing here. . . . Respondents . . . can cite no statute whose application they challenge. The best they can do is to point to unspecified, lump-sum "Congressional budget appropriations" for the general use of the Executive Branch—the allocation of which "is a[n] administrative decision traditionally regarded as committed to agency discretion." . . . It cannot be that every legal challenge to a discretionary Executive Branch action implicates the constitutionality of the underlying congressional appropriation. . . .

Respondents argue that it is "arbitrary" to distinguish between money spent pursuant to congressional mandate and expenditures made in the course of executive discretion, because "the injury to taxpayers in both situations is the very injury targeted by the Establishment Clause and *Flast*—the expenditure for the support of religion of funds exacted from taxpayers." . . . But *Flast* focused on congressional action, and we must decline this invitation to extend its holding to encompass discretionary Executive Branch expenditures. *Flast* itself distinguished the "incidental expenditure of tax funds in the administration of an essentially regulatory statute," . . . and we have subsequently rejected the view that taxpayer standing "extends to the Government as a whole, regardless of which branch is at work in a particular [instance]." *Valley Forge*. . . .

It is significant that, in the four decades since its creation, the *Flast* exception has largely been confined to its facts. . . . In effect, we have adopted the position set forth by Justice Powell in his concurrence in *Richardson* and have "limit[ed] the expansion of federal taxpayer and citizen standing in the absence of specific statutory authorization to an outer boundary drawn by the results in *Flast*. . . ."

The rule respondents propose would enlist the federal courts to superintend, at the behest of any federal taxpayer, the speeches, statements, and myriad daily activities of the President, his staff, and other Executive Branch officials. . . . Both the Court of Appeals and respondents implicitly recognize that unqualified federal taxpayer standing to assert Establishment Clause claims would go too far, but neither the Court of Appeals nor respondents has identified a workable limitation.

The Court of Appeals [in an opinion by Judge Posner] conceded only that a taxpayer would lack standing where "the marginal or incremental cost to the taxpaying public of the alleged violation of the establishment clause" is "zero." . . . Applying this rule, the Court of Appeals opined that a taxpayer would not have standing to challenge a President's favorable reference to religion in a State of the Union address because the costs associated with the speech "would be no greater merely because the President had mentioned Moses rather than John Stuart Mill." . . .

[I]f we take the Court of Appeals' test literally—i.e., that any marginal cost greater than zero suffices—taxpayers might well have standing to challenge some (and perhaps many) speeches. As Judge Easterbrook observed: "The total cost of presidential proclamations and speeches by Cabinet officers that touch on religion (Thanksgiving and several other holidays) surely exceeds $500,000 annually; it may cost that much to use Air Force One and send a Secret Service detail to a single speaking engagement." . . . At a minimum, the Court of Appeals' approach (asking whether the marginal cost exceeded zero) would surely create difficult and uncomfortable line-drawing problems. Suppose that it is alleged that a speech writer or other staff member spent extra time doing research for the purpose of including "religious imagery" in a speech. Suppose that a President or a Cabinet officer attends or speaks at a prayer breakfast and that the time spent was time that would have otherwise been spent on secular work.

Respondents take a somewhat different approach, contending that their proposed expansion of *Flast* would be manageable because they would require that a challenged expenditure be "fairly traceable to the conduct alleged to violate the Establishment Clause." . . . Applying this test, they argue, would "scree[n] out . . . challenge[s to] the content of one particular speech." . . .

We find little comfort in this vague and ill-defined test. [T]he "traceability" inquiry, depending on how it is framed, would appear to prove either too little or too much. If the question is whether an allegedly unconstitutional executive action can somehow be traced to taxpayer funds in general, the answer will always be yes: Almost all Executive Branch activities are ultimately funded by some congressional appropriation, whether general or specific, which is in turn financed by tax receipts. If, on the other hand, the question is whether the challenged action can be traced to the contributions of a particular taxpayer-plaintiff, the answer will almost always be no: As we recognized in *Frothingham*, the interest of any individual taxpayer in a particular federal expenditure "is comparatively minute and indeterminable . . . and constantly changing." . . .

Respondents set out a parade of horribles that they claim could occur if *Flast* is not extended to discretionary Executive Branch expenditures. For example, they say, a federal agency could use its discretionary funds to build a house of worship or to hire clergy of one denomination and send them out to spread their faith. Or an agency could use its funds to make bulk purchases of Stars of David, crucifixes, or depictions of the star and crescent for use in its offices or for distribution to the employees or the general public. Of course, none of these things has happened, even though *Flast* has not previously been expanded in the way that respondents urge. In the unlikely event that any of these executive actions did take place, Congress could quickly step in. And respondents make no effort to show that these improbable abuses could not be challenged in federal court by plaintiffs who would possess standing based on grounds other than taxpayer standing.

Over the years, *Flast* has been defended by some and criticized by others. But the present case does not require us to reconsider that precedent. The Court of Appeals did not apply *Flast*; it extended *Flast*. It is a necessary concomitant of the doctrine of stare decisis that a precedent is not always expanded to the limit of its logic. That was the approach that then-Justice Rehnquist took in his opinion for the Court in *Valley Forge*, and it is the approach we take here. We do not extend *Flast*, but we also do not overrule it. We leave *Flast* as we found it. . . .

JUSTICE KENNEDY, concurring.

The Court's decision in *Flast* . . . , and in later cases applying it, must be interpreted as respecting separation-of-powers principles but acknowledging as well that these principles, in some cases, must accommodate the First Amendment's Establishment Clause. . . . In my view the result reached in *Flast* is correct and should not be called into question. For the reasons set forth by Justice Alito, however, *Flast* should not be extended to permit taxpayer standing in the instant matter. . . .

Flast established a "narrow exception" to the rule against taxpayer standing. . . . To find standing in the circumstances of this case would make the narrow exception boundless. The public events and public speeches respondents seek to call in question are part of the open discussion essential to democratic self-government. The Executive Branch should be free, as a general matter, to discover new ideas, to understand pressing public demands, and to find creative responses to address governmental concerns. The exchange of ideas between and among the State and Federal Governments and their manifold, diverse constituencies sustains a free society. Permitting any and all taxpayers to challenge the content of these prototypical executive operations and dialogues would lead to judicial intervention so far exceeding traditional boundaries on the Judiciary that there would arise a real danger of judicial oversight of executive duties. The burden of discovery to ascertain if relief is justified in these potentially innumerable cases would risk altering the free exchange of ideas and information. And were this constant supervision to take place the courts would soon assume the role of speech editors for communications issued by executive officials and event planners for meetings they hold. . . .

It must be remembered that, even where parties have no standing to sue, members of the Legislative and Executive Branches are not excused from making constitutional determinations in the regular course of their duties. Government officials must make a conscious decision to obey the Constitution whether or not their acts can be challenged in a court of law and then must conform their actions to these principled determinations.

JUSTICE SCALIA, with whom JUSTICE THOMAS joins, concurring in the judgment.

If this Court is to decide cases by rule of law rather than show of hands [sic], we must surrender to logic and choose sides: Either *Flast* . . . should be applied to (at a minimum) all challenges to the governmental expenditure of general tax revenues in a manner alleged to violate a constitutional provision specifically limiting the taxing and spending power, or *Flast* should be repudiated. For me, the choice is easy. *Flast* is wholly irreconcilable with the Article III restrictions on federal-court jurisdiction that this Court has repeatedly confirmed are embodied in the doctrine of standing.

We have alternately relied on two entirely distinct conceptions of injury in fact, which for convenience I will call "Wallet Injury" and "Psychic Injury." Wallet Injury is the type of concrete and particularized injury one would expect to be asserted in a taxpayer suit, namely, a claim that the plaintiff's tax liability is higher than it would be, but for the allegedly unlawful government action. The stumbling block for suits challenging government expenditures based on this conventional type of injury is quite predictable. The plaintiff cannot satisfy the traceability and redressability prongs of standing. It is uncertain what the plaintiff's tax bill would have been had the allegedly forbidden expenditure not been made, and it is even more speculative whether the government will, in response to an adverse court decision, lower taxes rather than spend the funds in some other manner.

Psychic Injury, on the other hand, has nothing to do with the plaintiff's tax liability. Instead, the injury consists of the taxpayer's mental displeasure that money extracted from him is being spent in an unlawful manner. This shift in focus eliminates traceability and redressability problems. Psychic Injury is directly traceable to the improper use of taxpayer funds, and it is redressed when the improper use is enjoined, regardless of whether that injunction affects the taxpayer's purse. *Flast* and the cases following its teaching have invoked a peculiarly restricted version of Psychic Injury, permitting taxpayer displeasure over unconstitutional spending to support standing only if the constitutional provision allegedly violated is a specific limitation on the taxing and spending power. Restricted or not, this conceptualizing of injury in fact in purely mental terms conflicts squarely with the familiar proposition that a plaintiff lacks a concrete and particularized injury when his only complaint is the generalized grievance that the law is being violated. . . .

Flast was dismissively and unpersuasively distinguished [in *Valley Forge*]. I cannot fathom why Article III standing should turn on whether the government enables a religious organization to obtain real estate by giving it a check drawn from general tax revenues or instead by buying the property itself and then transferring title. [T]here are only two logical routes available to this Court. We must initially decide whether Psychic Injury is consistent with Article III. If it is, we should apply *Flast* to all challenges to government expenditures in violation of constitutional provisions that specifically limit the taxing and spending power; if it is not, we should overturn *Flast*. . . .

[T]he plurality offers no explanation of why the factual differences between this case and *Flast* are *material*. It virtually admits that express congressional allocation *vel non* has nothing to do with whether the plaintiffs have alleged an injury in fact that is fairly traceable and likely to be redressed. . . . Yet the plurality is also unwilling to acknowledge that the logic of *Flast* (its Psychic Injury rationale) is simply wrong, and *for that reason* should not be extended to other cases. Despite the lack of acknowledgment, however, that is the only plausible explanation for the plurality's indifference to whether the "distinguishing" fact is legally material, and for its determination to limit *Flast* to its ["result"].[3] Why, then, pick a distinguishing fact that may breathe life into *Flast* in future cases, preserving the disreputable disarray of our Establishment Clause standing jurisprudence? Why not hold that only taxpayers raising Establishment Clause challenges to expenditures pursuant to the Elementary and Secondary Education Act of 1965 have standing? That, I suppose, would be too obvious a repudiation of *Flast*, and thus an impediment to the plurality's pose of minimalism. . . .

The logical consequence of respondents' position finds no support in this Court's precedents or our Nation's history. Any taxpayer would be able to sue whenever tax funds were used in alleged violation of the Establishment Clause. So, for example, any taxpayer could challenge the fact that the Marshal of our Court is paid, in part, to call the courtroom to order by proclaiming "God Save the United States and this Honorable

---

[3] This explanation does not suffice with regard to Justice Kennedy, who, unlike the other Members of the plurality, openly and avowedly contends both that *Flast* was correctly decided and that respondents should nevertheless lose this case. . . . He thus has the distinction of being the only Justice who affirms both propositions. I cannot begin to comprehend how the amorphous separation-of-powers concerns that motivate him . . . bear upon whether the express-allocation requirement is grounded in the Article III criteria of injury in fact, traceability, or redressability.

Court." As much as respondents wish to deny that this is what *Flast* logically entails, it blinks reality to conclude otherwise. . . .

Ultimately, the arguments by the parties in this case and the opinions of my colleagues serve only to confirm that *Flast's* adoption of Psychic Injury has to be addressed head-on. Minimalism is an admirable judicial trait, but not when it comes at the cost of meaningless and disingenuous distinctions that hold the sure promise of engendering further meaningless and disingenuous distinctions in the future. The rule of law is ill served by forcing lawyers and judges to make arguments that deaden the soul of the law, which is logic and reason. Either *Flast* was correct, and must be accorded the wide application that it logically dictates, or it was not, and must be abandoned in its entirety. . . .

Just this Term, . . . we held unanimously that suits raising only generalized grievances do not satisfy Article III's requirement that the injury in fact be concrete and particularized. See *Lance* [*v. Coffman*, 549 U.S. 437 (2007)].[5] [We] have noted explicitly that *Flast* failed to recognize the vital separation-of-powers aspect of Article III standing. . . . And once a proper understanding of the relationship of standing to the separation of powers is brought to bear, Psychic Injury, even as limited in *Flast*, is revealed for what it is: a contradiction of the basic propositions that the function of the judicial power "is, solely, to decide on the rights of individuals," *Marbury v. Madison*, . . . and that generalized grievances affecting the public at large have their remedy in the political process.

JUSTICE SOUTER, with whom JUSTICES STEVENS, GINSBURG, and BREYER join, dissenting.

The right of conscience and the expenditure of an identifiable three pence raised by taxes for the support of a religious cause are . . . not to be split off from one another. The three pence implicates the conscience, and the injury from Government expenditures on religion is not accurately classified with the "Psychic Injury" that results whenever a congressional appropriation or executive expenditure raises hackles of disagreement with the policy supported. . . .

Justice Stewart recognized this in his concurring opinion in *Flast*, when he said that "every taxpayer can claim a personal constitutional right not to be taxed for the support of a religious institution," and thus distinguished the case from one in which a taxpayer sought only to air a generalized grievance in federal court. . . . Here, there is no dispute that taxpayer money in identifiable amounts is funding conferences, and these are alleged to have the purpose of promoting religion. . . . The taxpayers

---

[5] It is true that this Court has occasionally in dicta described the prohibition on generalized grievances as merely a prudential bar. But the fountainhead of this dicta, *Warth v. Seldin*, . . . supported its statement only by naked citation of . . . cases squarely rest[ing] on Article III considerations. . . .

therefore seek not to "extend" *Flast*, . . . but merely to apply it. When executive agencies spend identifiable sums of tax money for religious purposes, no less than when Congress authorizes the same thing, taxpayers suffer injury. And once we recognize the injury as sufficient for Article III, there can be no serious question about the other elements of the standing enquiry: the injury is indisputably "traceable" to the spending, and "likely to be redressed by" an injunction prohibiting it. . . .

It would surely violate the Establishment Clause for the Department of Health and Human Services to draw on a general appropriation to build a chapel for weekly church services (no less than if a statute required it), and for good reason: if the Executive could accomplish through the exercise of discretion exactly what Congress cannot do through legislation, Establishment Clause protection would melt away.[1]
. . .

While *Flast* standing to assert the right of conscience is in a class by itself, it would be a mistake to think that case is unique in recognizing standing in a plaintiff without injury to flesh or purse. Cognizable harm takes account of the nature of the interest protected, which is the reason that "the constitutional component of standing doctrine incorporates concepts concededly not susceptible of precise definition," leaving it impossible "to make application of the constitutional standing requirement a mechanical exercise." . . . The question, ultimately, has to be whether the injury alleged is "too abstract, or otherwise not appropriate, to be considered judicially cognizable."[3] . . . This is not to say that any sort of alleged injury will satisfy Article III, but only that intangible harms must be evaluated case by case.[5]

FURTHER NOTES ON TAXPAYER STANDING

1.   Justice Stewart Revisited. The majority opinions in *Valley Forge* and *Hein* plainly rejected Justice Stewart's approach in *Flast* and *Richardson*, don't you think? Is it odd, or at least pretty late, for the dissenters in *Hein* to adopt Stewart's view? Notice that Justice Souter pinned a taxpayer's "right of conscience" to an "injury" caused by a disbursement

---

[1]   The plurality warns that a parade of horribles would result if there were standing to challenge executive action. . . . But even if there is Article III standing in all of the cases posited by the plurality . . . , that does not mean taxpayers will prevail in such suits. If these claims are frivolous on the merits, I fail to see the harm in dismissing them for failure to state a claim instead of for lack of jurisdiction. To the degree the claims are meritorious, fear that there will be many of them does not provide a compelling reason, much less a reason grounded in Article III, to keep them from being heard.

[3]   Although the plurality makes much of the fact that the injury in this case is "generalized," . . . and shared with the "public-at-large," . . . those properties on their own do not strip a would-be plaintiff of standing. See *Federal Election Comm'n v. Akins* [, 524 U.S. 11 (1998)]. . . .

[5]   There will not always be competitors for the funds who would make better plaintiffs (and indeed there appears to be no such competitor here), so after accepting the importance of the injury there is no reason to refuse standing as a prudential matter.

from the federal treasury. Did he mean, then, to insist that taxpayers not only contend that their personal rights are violated when expenditures are made to support religion, but also that they suffer factual, pecuniary injury?

2.   **What Is Left of *Flast*?** The Court has continued its narrow and formalistic interpretation of *Flast*, without overruling it since *Hein*. See, for example, *Arizona Christian School Tuition Organization v. Winn*, 563 U.S. ___, 131 S.Ct. 1436 (2011) where, in a 5–4 decision, the majority ruled that state taxpayers did not have standing under the Establishment Clause to challenge a program in which taxpayers were given dollar-for-dollar tax credits for their contributions to private, non-profit state tuition organizations set up specifically to accept such contributions and then use the donated funds for "scholarships to students attending private schools, including religious schools." Implicitly rejecting intangible, widely shared "psychic" harms as the basis for standing, the *Winn* majority held that though taxpayers might have standing to contest legislative appropriations designed to aid religious enterprises, they had no standing to challenge legislative tax credit programs intended for the same purpose because there is no "extraction and spending" of tax money on aid of religion for the latter program. In *Winn*, the Court seemed to offer legislatures a formula to evade even *Flast*'s narrowest holding. See William Marshall & Gene Nichol, *Not a Winn-Win: Misconstruing Standing and the Establishment Clause*, 2011 SUPREME COURT REVIEW 215. Why not overrule *Flast* and be done with it?

3.   **State and Local Taxpayers.** The Court has applied the standing analysis developed for federal taxpayers to cases in which state taxpayers seek standing to challenge actions that deplete state treasuries. Writing for the Court in *DaimlerChrysler Corp. v. Cuno*, 547 U.S. 332 (2006), Chief Justice Roberts declared that the effect of tax breaks or "tax expenditures" on the tax bills of individual state taxpayers is too speculative to count as personal injury in fact for federal standing purposes. In *Frothingham*, however, the Court distinguished *local* taxpayers in part on the theory that a taxpayer suing municipal authorities is analogous to a stockholder suing a private corporation and also, in part, on the theory that a local taxpayer has a comparatively larger stake in a much smaller pool of municipal funds. In *Cuno*, Chief Justice Roberts appeared to credit that distinction, but did not squarely confirm that municipal taxpayers can secure standing on the basis of their taxpayer status. In light of the Court's treatment of federal and state taxpayers, does it make sense that municipal taxpayers should have standing (on the strength of their taxpayer status alone) to sue municipal defendants in federal court over any action that disburses funds from the local treasury?

D. STANDING AND CONGRESSIONAL AUTHORITY

ASSOCIATION OF DATA PROCESSING SVC. ORG. V. CAMP
397 U.S. 150 (1970).

JUSTICE DOUGLAS delivered the opinion of the Court.

Petitioners sell data processing services to businesses generally. In this suit they seek to challenge a ruling by respondent Comptroller of the Currency that, as an incident to their banking services, national banks . . . may make data processing services available to other banks and to bank customers. . . . The first question is whether the plaintiff alleges that the challenged action has caused him injury in fact, economic or otherwise. There can be no doubt but that petitioners have satisfied this test. . . . The Comptroller was alleged to have caused petitioners injury in fact by his ruling [allowing banks to compete with them for data processing business].

The Court of Appeals viewed the matter differently, stating: "[A] plaintiff may challenge alleged illegal competition when as complainant it pursues: (1) a legal interest by reason of public charter or contract, (2) a legal interest by reason of statutory protection, or (3) a 'public interest' in which Congress has recognized the need for review of administrative action and plaintiff is significantly involved to have standing to represent the [public]."[1]

The "legal interest" test goes to the merits. The question of standing is different. It concerns, apart from the "case" or "controversy" test, the question whether the interest sought to be protected by the complainant is arguably within the zone of interests to be protected or regulated by the statute or constitutional guarantee in question. Thus the Administrative Procedure Act grants standing to a person "aggrieved by agency action within the meaning of a relevant statute." 5 U.S.C. § 702. . . . Certainly he who is "likely to be financially" injured, [*FCC v. Sanders*], may be a reliable private attorney general to litigate the issues of the public interest in the present case.

Apart from Article III jurisdictional questions, problems of standing, as resolved by this Court for its own governance, have involved a "rule of self-restraint." Congress can, of course, resolve the question one way or another, save as the requirements of Article III dictate otherwise. Where statutes are concerned, the trend is toward enlargement of the class of

---

[1]   The first two tests applied by the Court of Appeals required a showing of a "legal interest." But the existence or non-existence of a "legal interest" is a matter quite distinct from the problem of standing. . . . The third test mentioned by the Court of Appeals, which rests on an explicit provision in a regulatory statute conferring standing and is commonly referred to in terms of allowing suits by "private attorneys general," is inapplicable to the present case. See [*FCC v. Sanders*]. . . .

people who may protest administrative action. The whole drive for enlarging the category of aggrieved "persons" is symptomatic of that trend. [Section] 4 of the Bank Service Corporation Act . . . provides: "No bank service corporation may engage in any activity other than the performance of bank services for customers." . . . We [think] that § 4 arguably brings a competitor within the zone of interests protected by it. . . .

Whether anything in the Bank Service Corporation Act or the National Bank Act gives petitioners a "legal interest" that protects them against violations of those Acts, and whether the actions of respondent did in fact violate either of those Acts, are questions which go to the merits and remain to be decided below.

NOTES ON CONGRESSIONAL AUTHORIZATION TO SUE

1. **The Zone of Interest Test.** Justice Douglas explained in *Data Processing* that the standing question turns on whether a litigant's interests (satisfying the "injury" requirement) are "arguably within the zone of interests to be protected or regulated by the statute or constitutional guarantee" sought to be implemented. He linked that question, in turn, to § 702 of the APA, which authorizes standing for persons "aggrieved by agency action within the meaning of a relevant statute." Accordingly, he either interpreted § 702 itself to establish the zone test or, at the least, reworked standing law generally, including § 702, around that test.

a. Having established the zone test, Justice Douglas applied it liberally. It was fairly clear that the Bank Service Corporation Act limited banks to traditional banking business primarily for the protection of depositors, whose interests might be neglected if banks extended their operations into other fields. There was nothing to suggest that the point was to protect the competitive interests of data processing companies. Nevertheless, Douglas concluded that those interests were "arguably" within the zone of interests protected by the Act, and that was sufficient.

b. The Court has continued typically, to apply the zone test generously. See *Clarke v. Securities Indus. Ass'n*, 479 U.S. 388, 399 (1987) (explaining that the test establishes a "presumption" in favor of standing and is not "especially demanding"). Justice Scalia found ranchers' interests to be at least "arguably" within the zone (even though their interests were antithetical to the overall purpose of the Act) in *Bennett v. Spear*, 520 U.S. 154 (1997)—expressly applying the zone of interest test liberally. In *Monsanto v. Geertson Seed Farms*, 561 U.S. 139, 130 S.Ct. 2743 (2010), organic alfalfa farmers complained that an Agriculture Department ruling allowing others to use a biologically engineered seed would compromise their ability to keep their own fields free of engineered genes and, accordingly, their ability to market their crops as "non-genetically engineered." Writing for the Court, Justice Alito acknowledged that the farmers' alleged injuries were primarily economic. They contended that they would have to conduct tests to demonstrate that their produce was not infected and would lose customers who were unconvinced. Yet Alito accepted the district court's conclusion that the farmers' interest in insulating their crops from engineered genes was both commercial and "environmental," such that their interests were arguably within the zone of interests protected by the National Environmental Protection Act—the statute the farmers contended the Department's ruling violated. See also *National Credit Union Admin. v. First Nat'l Bank*, 522 U.S. 479 (1998) (opinion for the Court by Thomas, J.) (identifying a generous zone of interests for purposes of a suit by banks). But in Lexmark Intern, Inc. v. State Control Components, 134 S.Ct. 1377 (2014) the Court suggested an altered tone and rationale for the zone of interest test. In an opinion by Justice Scalia, the Court indicated that, despite prior suggestions to the contrary, the zone of interest standard is not "prudential" but it requires a determination of whether a legislatively conferred cause of action encompasses a particular plaintiff's claim, rooted in traditional norms of statutory analysis. Still, the Court determined that the plaintiff's asserted interests did fall within the zone of interests protected by the Lanham Act.

2.   Congressional Authority to Grant Standing. Section 804(d) of the Fair Housing Act, 42 U.S.C. § 3604, makes it unlawful to "represent to any person because of race, color, religion, sex, handicap, familial status, or national origin that any dwelling is not available . . . for inspection, sale, or rental when such dwelling is in fact so available." Writing for the Court in *Havens Realty Corp. v. Coleman*, 455 U.S. 363 (1982), Justice Brennan read § 804(d) to "confer on all 'persons' a legal right to truthful information about available housing." The defendant, a real estate management firm, thus owed a legal duty to provide accurate information to all persons individually. Brennan then explained that § 804(d) "creates legal rights, the invasion of which creates standing." Accordingly, one of the plaintiffs in *Havens*, an African American who had been misinformed about the availability of space in an apartment complex, had "suffered injury in precisely the form the statute was intended to guard against, and therefore [had] standing to maintain a claim for damages. . . ."

a.   In *Trafficante v. Metropolitan Life Ins. Co.*, 409 U.S. 205 (1972), the tenants of an apartment complex filed complaints with the Secretary of Housing and Urban Development pursuant to sec. 810(a) of the Civil Rights Act of 1968. They asserted that their landlord discriminated against non-whites and that, as a result, the tenants lost social and economic benefits assured by the statute. The Supreme Court held that the tenants had standing under the statutory definition of "person aggrieved". Justice White concurred, expressing the view that "absent in Civil Rights Act of 1968, I would have great difficulty in concluding that petitioners' complaint in this case presented a case or controversy . . . under Article III. But with the statute purporting to give all those who are authorized to complain to the agency the right also to sue in Court, I would sustain the statute insofar as it extends to those in the position of the petitioners in this case." 409 U.S. at 212. *Linda R.S. v. Richard D.*, 410 U.S. 614 617, n.3 (1973) ruled explicitly that "Congress may create a statutory right of entitlement the alleged deprivation of which can confer standing to sue even where the plaintiff would have suffered no judicially cognizable injury in the absence of a statute." *Havens, Trafficante* and *Linda R.S.* moved far toward the conclusion that as long as a plaintiff met the terms of a statutory grant of jurisdiction, Article III poses no effective barrier to access. The *Defenders of Wildlife* decision, below, indicated otherwise.

LUJAN V. DEFENDERS OF WILDLIFE
504 U.S. 555 (1992).

The Court of Appeals found that respondents had standing for an additional reason: because they had suffered a "procedural injury." The so-called "citizen suit" provision of the ESA provides, in pertinent part, that any person may commence [p. 572] a civil suit on his own behalf (A) to enjoin any person, including the United States and any other governmental instrumentality or agency . . . who is alleged to be in violation of any provision of this chapter. 16 U.S.C. § 1540(g). The court held that, because § 7(a)(2) requires interagency consultation, the citizen-suit provision creates a "procedural righ[t]" to consultation in all "persons"—so that anyone can file suit in federal court to challenge the Secretary's (or presumably any other official's) failure to follow the assertedly correct consultative procedure, notwithstanding their inability to allege any discrete injury flowing from that failure. . . .

We have consistently held that a plaintiff raising only a generally available grievance about government—claiming only harm to his and every citizen's interest in proper application of the Constitution and laws, and seeking relief that [p. 574] no more directly and tangibly benefits him than it does the public at large—does not state an Article III case or controversy. For example, in *Fairchild v. Hughes*, 258 U.S. 126, 129–130 (1922), we dismissed a suit challenging the propriety of the process by which the Nineteenth Amendment was ratified. Justice Brandeis wrote for the Court:

> [This is] not a case within the meaning of . . . Article III. . . . Plaintiff has [asserted] only the right, possessed by every citizen, to require that the Government be administered according to law and that the public moneys be not wasted. Obviously this general right does not entitle a private citizen to institute in the federal courts a suit. . . . Ibid.

In *Frothingham v. Mellon*, 262 U.S. 447 (1923), we dismissed for lack of Article III standing a taxpayer suit challenging the propriety of certain federal expenditures. We said: The party who invokes the power [of judicial review] must be able to show not only that the statute is invalid but that he has sustained or is immediately in danger of sustaining some direct injury as the result of its enforcement, and not merely that he suffers in some indefinite way in common with people generally. . . . Here, the parties plaintiff have no such case. . . . [T]heir complaint . . . is merely that officials of the executive department of the government are executing and will execute an act of Congress asserted to be unconstitutional; and this we are asked to prevent. To do so would be not to decide a judicial controversy, but to assume a position of authority over the governmental acts of another and coequal department, an authority which plainly we do not possess. id. at 488–489.

In *Ex parte Levitt*, 302 U.S. 633 (1937), we dismissed a suit contending that Justice Black's appointment to this Court violated the Ineligibility Clause, Art. I, § 6, cl. 2. [p. 575] "It is an established principle," we said, that to entitle a private individual to invoke the judicial power to determine the validity of executive or legislative action, he must show that he has sustained or is immediately in danger of sustaining a direct injury as the result of that action, and it is not sufficient that he has merely a general interest common to all members of the public.

More recent cases are to the same effect. In *United States v. Richardson*, 418 U.S. 166 (1974), we dismissed for lack of standing a taxpayer suit challenging the Government's failure to disclose the expenditures of the Central Intelligence Agency, in alleged violation of the constitutional requirement, Art. I, § 9, cl. 7, that "a regular Statement and Account of the Receipts and Expenditures of all public Money shall be published from time to time." We held that such a suit rested upon an impermissible "generalized grievance," and was inconsistent with "the framework of Article III" because "the impact on [plaintiff] is plainly undifferentiated and common to all members of the public." *Richardson*, supra, at 171, 176–177. And in *Schlesinger v. Reservists Committee to Stop the War*, 418 U.S. 208 (1974), we dismissed for the same reasons a citizen-taxpayer suit contending that it was a violation of the Incompatibility Clause, Art. I, § 6, cl. 2, for Members of Congress to hold commissions in the military Reserves. We said that the challenged action, standing alone, would adversely affect only the generalized interest of all citizens in constitutional governance. . . . We reaffirm Levitt in holding that standing to sue may not be predicated upon an interest of th[is] kind. . . . *Schlesinger*, supra, at 217, 220. Since *Schlesinger*, we have on two occasions held that an injury amounting only to the alleged violation of a right to have the Government act in accordance with law was not judicially cognizable, because [p. 576] assertion of a right to a particular kind of Government conduct, which the Government has violated by acting differently, cannot alone satisfy the requirements of Art. III without draining those requirements of meaning. *Allen*, 468 U.S. at 754;

Valley Forge Christian College v. Americans United for Separation of Church and State, Inc., 454 U.S. 464, 483 (1982).

To be sure, our generalized-grievance cases have typically involved Government violation of procedures assertedly ordained by the Constitution, rather than the Congress. But there is absolutely no basis for making the Article III inquiry turn on the source of the asserted right. . . .

Nothing in this contradicts the principle that "[t]he . . . injury required by Art. III may exist solely by virtue of 'statutes creating legal rights, the invasion of which creates standing.'" *Warth*, 422 U.S. at 500 (quoting *Linda R. S. v. Richard D.*, 410 U.S. 614, 617, n. 3 (1973)). Both of the cases used by *Linda R. S.* as an illustration of that principle involved Congress's elevating to the status of legally cognizable injuries concrete, de facto injuries that were previously inadequate in law (namely, injury to an individual's personal interest in living in a racially integrated community, see *Trafficante v. Metropolitan Life Ins. Co.*, 409 U.S. 205, 208–212 (1972), and injury to a company's interest in marketing its product free from competition, see *Hardin v. Kentucky Utilities Co.*, 390 U.S. 1, 6 (1968)). As we said in Sierra Club, [Statutory] broadening [of] the categories of injury that may be alleged in support of standing is a different matter from abandoning the requirement that the party seeking review must himself have suffered an injury. Whether or not the principle set forth in *Warth* can be extended beyond that distinction, it is clear that in suits against the government, at least, the concrete injury requirement must remain.

We hold that respondents lack standing to bring this action, and that the Court of Appeals erred in denying the summary judgment motion filed by the United States. The opinion of the Court of Appeals is hereby reversed, and the cause remanded for proceedings consistent with this opinion.

It is so ordered.

NOTES ON CONGRESS AND "INJURY"

1. **Statutes, Rights, and Injuries.** Justice Scalia explained in *Defenders of Wildlife* that "nothing in this [opinion] contradicts the principle that the . . . injury required by Art. III may exist solely by virtue of statutes creating legal rights, the invasion of which creates standing." It's easy enough to understand that Congress can enact statutes that establish new personal legal rights. But doesn't the holder of such a right still have to allege independent factual injury to secure standing to enforce his or her statutory right?

2. **The Fair Housing Act Cases.** Justice Scalia said that two earlier precedents, *Trafficante* and *Hardin*, "involved Congress' elevating to the

status of legally cognizable injuries concrete, de facto injuries that were previously inadequate in law. . . ." Previously inadequate for what? The injury in *Trafficante* was loss of the benefits of living in a racially integrated community, and in *Hardin* it was loss of business profits due to competition. Did Justice Scalia mean to say that those injuries, however "concrete" and "de facto" they may have been, were inadequate to supply the "injury in fact" required for standing until Congress enacted legislation giving them legal recognition?

3.   **"Cognizable" and "Non-Cognizable" Injuries?** What did Justice Scalia mean by legislation "elevating" injuries to the "status of legally cognizable injuries"? Is this a place where the adjective "cognizable" does some work—distinguishing factual injuries in general from injuries that suffice for standing? How about this? Judgments about what counts as factual injury are constitutional and reserved for the Court. But not every factual injury the Court recognizes is "cognizable," and the Court itself usually decides which are and which are not. When, however, Congress enacts a statute identifying a factual injury as cognizable, the Court will give effect to that legislative judgment—a judgment not about whether factual injury is required at all, nor about whether an injury is "factual injury" in the necessary sense, but about whether a factual injury warrants judicial attention. If Congress can make choices within the general category of factual injuries (and let's not assume this is what Justice Scalia really means), then, to that extent, does Congress have authority to affect the constitutional injury requirement?

4.   **Justice Kennedy's Dictum.** Concurring in *Defenders of Wildlife*, Justice Kennedy (joined by Justice Souter) said this (apparently in response to Justice Scalia's opinion for the Court):

> As Government programs and policies become more complex and far reaching, we must be sensitive to the articulation of new rights of action that do not have clear analogs in our common-law tradition. Modern litigation has progressed far from the paradigm of Marbury suing Madison to get his commission, . . . or Ogden seeking an injunction to halt Gibbons' steamboat operations. . . . In my view, Congress has the power to define injuries and articulate chains of causation that will give rise to a case or controversy where none existed before, and I do not read the Court's opinion to suggest a contrary view. . . . In exercising this power, however, Congress must at the very least identify the injury it seeks to vindicate and relate the injury to the class of persons entitled to bring suit. The citizen-suit provision of the Endangered Species Act does not meet these minimal requirements, because while the statute purports to confer a right on "any person . . . to enjoin . . . the United States and any other governmental instrumentality or agency . . . who is alleged to be in violation of any provision of this chapter," it does not of its own force establish that there is an injury in "any person" by virtue of any "violation."

The Court's holding that there is an outer limit to the power of Congress to confer rights of action is a direct and necessary consequence of the case and controversy limitations found in Article III. I agree that it would exceed those limitations if, at the behest of Congress and in the absence of any showing of concrete injury, we were to entertain citizen suits to vindicate the public's nonconcrete interest in the proper administration of the laws. While it does not matter how many persons have been injured by the challenged action, the party bringing suit must show that the action injures him in a concrete and personal way . . . An independent judiciary is held to account through its open proceedings and its reasoned judgments. In this process it is essential for the public to know what persons or groups are invoking the judicial power, the reasons that they have brought suit, and whether their claims are vindicated or denied. The concrete injury requirement helps assure that there can be an answer to these questions; and, as the Court's opinion is careful to show, that is part of the constitutional design.

This passage is significant, because it suggests a potentially broad role for Congress. What did Justice Kennedy have in mind when he said that Congress has the power to "define injuries" for standing purposes? Something like what Justice Scalia meant when he said that Congress can "elevate" injuries to something "cognizable" or broaden the "categories of injury"? Something like what Justice Harlan meant in *Flast* when he said that Congress can authorize "public actions" by litigants who have no "economic or other personal interests"?

Justice Kennedy also said that Congress can "articulate chains of causation" for standing purposes. Is that idea easier to digest? Recall that the justices often disagree among themselves over whether the causal chain alleged by a plaintiff is sufficient for standing or too "attenuated." Did Justice Kennedy mean to acknowledge that the "causation" element of constitutional standing entails judgment and that the Court can (and perhaps should) defer to such a judgment made by Congress in the form of a statute authorizing standing? Can *that* idea be squared with the proposition that Congress's power with respect to standing begins and ends with the non-constitutional aspects?

E. THIRD PARTY STANDING

KOWALSKI V. TESMER
543 U.S. 125 (2004).

CHIEF JUSTICE REHNQUIST delivered the opinion of the Court.

In 1994, Michigan amended its Constitution to provide that "an appeal by an accused who pleads guilty or *nolo contendere* shall be by leave of the court" and not as of right. Following this amendment, several

Michigan state judges began to deny appointed appellate counsel to indigents who pleaded guilty, and the Michigan Legislature subsequently codified this practice. Under the statute, which was scheduled to go into effect on April 1, 2000, appointment of appellate counsel for indigents who plead guilty is prohibited, with certain mandatory and permissive exceptions. A challenge to the Michigan practice was filed in the United States District Court for the Eastern District of Michigan. The named plaintiffs included the two attorney respondents and three indigents who were denied appellate counsel after pleading guilty. [T]hey alleged that the Michigan practice and statute denied indigents their federal constitutional rights to due process and equal protection. They sought declaratory and injunctive relief against the practice and the statute. [T]he District Court . . . issued an injunction that bound all Michigan state judges, requiring them not to deny appellate counsel to any indigent who pleaded guilty. [T]he Court of Appeals for the Sixth Circuit held . . . that the attorneys had third-party standing to assert the rights of indigents [and] found that the statute was unconstitutional.

In this case, we do not focus on the constitutional minimum of standing, which flows from Article III's case-or-controversy requ[i]. Instead, we shall assume the attorneys have satisfied Article[I] address the alternative threshold question whether they have st[anding to] raise the rights of others.[2]

We have adhered to the rule that a party "generally must [assert his] own legal rights and interests, and cannot rest his claim to re[lief on the] legal rights or interests of third parties." This rule assumes tha[t the party] with the right has the appropriate incentive to challen[ge (or not challenge) governmental action and to do so with the necessary ze[al and] appropriate presentation. It represents a "healthy concern that if the claim is brought by someone other than one at whom the constitutional protection is aimed," the courts might be "called upon to decide abstract questions of wide public significance even though other governmental institutions may be more competent to address the questions and even though judicial intervention may be unnecessary to protect individual rights."

We have not treated this rule as absolute, however, recognizing that there may be circumstances where it is necessary to grant a third party standing to assert the rights of another. But we have limited this exception by requiring that a party seeking third-party standing make two additional showings. First, we have asked whether the party asserting the right has a "close" relationship with the person who

---

[2]   [T]he attorneys' alleged "injury in fact" flows from their contention that the Michigan system "has reduced the number of cases in which they could be appointed and paid as assigned appellate counsel." . . . This harm, they allege, would be remedied by declaratory and injunctive relief aimed at the system. [W]e assume, without deciding, that these allegations are sufficient.

possesses the right. Second, we have considered whether there is a "hindrance" to the possessor's ability to protect his own interests.

We have been quite forgiving with these criteria in certain circumstances. Beyond these examples—none of which is implicated here—we have not looked favorably upon third-party standing. . . . The attorneys in this case invoke the attorney-client relationship to demonstrate the requisite closeness. Specifically, they rely on a future attorney-client relationship with as yet unascertained Michigan criminal defendants "who will request, but be denied, the appointment of appellate counsel, based on the operation" of the statute. [W]e [have] granted a law firm third-party standing to . . . invoke[e] the rights of an existing client. This existing attorney-client relationship is, of course, quite distinct from the hypothetical attorney-client relationship posited here. . . . The attorneys before us do not have a "close relationship" with their alleged "clients"; indeed, they have no relationship at all.

We next consider whether the attorneys have demonstrated that there is a "hindrance" to the indigents' advancing their own constitutional rights against the Michigan scheme. It is uncontested that an indigent denied appellate counsel has open avenues to argue that denial deprives him of his constitutional rights. He may seek leave to challenge that denial in the Michigan Court of Appeals and, if denied, seek leave in the Michigan Supreme Court. He then may seek a writ of certiorari in this Court. Beyond that, there exists both state and federal collateral review.

The attorneys argue that, without counsel, these avenues are effectively foreclosed to indigents. They claim that unsophisticated, pro se criminal defendants could not satisfy the necessary procedural requirements, and, if they did, they would be unable to coherently advance the substance of their constitutional claim. That hypothesis, however, was disproved in the Michigan courts, see, e.g., *People v. Jackson*, 463 Mich. 949 (2001) (pro se defendant sought leave to appeal denial of appointment of appellate counsel to the Michigan Court of Appeals and the Michigan Supreme Court). While we agree that an attorney would be valuable to a criminal defendant challenging the constitutionality of the scheme, we do not think that the lack of an attorney here is the type of hindrance necessary to allow another to assert the indigent defendants' rights.

We also are unpersuaded by the . . . "hindrance" argument on a more fundamental level. If an attorney is all that the indigents need to perfect their challenge in state court and beyond, one wonders why the attorneys asserting this § 1983 action did not attend state court and assist them. . . . It is a fair inference that the attorneys and the three indigent plaintiffs that filed this § 1983 action did not want to allow the state process to take its course. Rather, they wanted a federal court to short-circuit the State's adjudication of this constitutional question. That is precisely what they got.

The doctrine of *Younger v. Harris*, 401 U.S. 37 (1971), reinforces our federal scheme by preventing a state criminal defendant from asserting ancillary challenges to ongoing state criminal procedures in federal court. In this case, the three indigent criminal defendants who were originally plaintiffs in this § 1983 action were appropriately dismissed under *Younger*. [T]hey had ongoing state criminal proceedings and ample avenues to raise their constitutional challenge in those proceedings. There also was no extraordinary circumstance requiring federal intervention. An unwillingness to allow the *Younger* principle to be thus circumvented is an additional reason to deny the attorneys third-party standing.[3]

We agree with the dissenting opinion in the Court of Appeals that "it would be a short step from the . . . grant of third-party standing in this case to a holding that lawyers generally have third-party standing to bring in court the claims of future unascertained clients."[5]

JUSTICE THOMAS, concurring.

That this case is even remotely close demonstrates that our third-party standing cases have gone far astray. We have granted third-party standing in a number of cases to litigants whose relationships with the directly affected individuals were at best remote. We have held, for instance, that beer vendors have standing to raise the rights of their prospective young male customers, see *Craig v. Boren*, 429 U.S. 190 (1976); that criminal defendants have standing to raise the rights of jurors excluded from service, see *Powers v. Ohio*, 499 U.S. 400 (1991); that sellers of mail-order contraceptives have standing to assert the rights of potential customers, see *Carey v. Population Services Int'l*, 431 U.S. 678 (1977); that distributors of contraceptives to unmarried persons have standing to litigate the rights of the potential recipients, *Eisenstadt v. Baird*, 405 U.S. 438 (1972); and that white sellers of land have standing to litigate the constitutional rights of potential black purchasers, see *Barrows v. Jackson*, 346 U.S. 249 (1953). . . .

It is doubtful whether a party who has no personal constitutional right at stake in a case should ever be allowed to litigate the constitutional rights of others. [T]his Court [once] adhered to the rule

---

[3] The Court of Appeals suggested, however, that adverse Michigan precedent on the merits of the constitutional claim made any resort to the state courts futile and thus justified the attorneys sally into federal court. . . . But forum-shopping of this kind is not a basis for third-party standing. . . .

[5] A medical malpractice attorney could assert an abstract, generalized challenge to tort reform statutes by asserting the rights of some hypothetical malpractice victim (or victims) who might sue. . . . An attorney specializing in Social Security cases could challenge implementation of a new regulation by asserting the rights of some hypothetical claimant (or claimants). And so on.

that "[a] court will not listen to an objection made to the constitutionality of an act by a party whose rights it does not affect and who has therefore no interest in defeating it." *Clark v. Kansas City*, 176 U.S. 114 (1900). . . . This made sense. Litigants who have no personal right at stake may have very different interests from the individuals whose rights they are raising. Moreover, absent a personal right, a litigant has no cause of action (or defense), and thus no right to relief. It may be too late in the day to return to this traditional view. But even assuming it makes sense to grant litigants third-party standing in at least some cases, it is more doubtful still whether third-party standing should sweep as broadly as our cases have held that it does.

JUSTICE GINSBURG, with whom JUSTICES STEVENS and SOUTER join, dissenting.

[A]s I see it, this case turns on the . . . existence of an impediment to the indigent defendants' effective assertion of their own rights through litigation. [O]ne must recognize the incapacities under which these defendants labor and the complexity of the issues their cases may entail. . . . Approximately 70% of indigent defendants represented by appointed counsel plead guilty, and 70% of those convicted are incarcerated. It is likely that many of these indigent defendants, in common with 68% of the state prison population, did not complete high school, and many lack the most basic literacy skills. [A]bout seven out of ten inmates fall in the lowest two out of five levels of literacy—marked by an inability to do such basic tasks as write a brief letter to explain an error on a credit card bill, use a bus schedule, or state in writing an argument made in a lengthy newspaper article. An inmate so handicapped surely does not possess the skill necessary to pursue a competent pro se appeal.[4]

The Court sees a clear path for [the attorney-plaintiffs]: They could have "attend[ed] state court and assist[ed] [indigent defendants]." Had the attorneys taken this course, hundreds, perhaps thousands, of criminal defendants would have gone uncounseled while the attorneys afforded assistance to a few individuals. In order to protect the rights of all indigent defendants, the attorneys sought prospective classwide relief to prevent the statute from taking effect. . . .

The Court concludes that the principle of *Younger v. Harris* . . . "is an additional reason to deny the attorneys third-party standing." Whether a federal court should abstain under *Younger* is, of course, distinct from whether a party has standing to sue. . . . [The attorneys] filed this suit before the Michigan statute took effect. At that time, no state criminal

---

[4] The fact that a handful of pro se defendants has brought claims shows neither that the run-of-the-mine defendant can successfully navigate state procedures nor that he can effectively represent himself on the merits.

proceeding governed by the statute existed with which this suit could interfere.

NOTES ON THE THIRD PARTY RULE

1.   **Rationale.** What is the rationale for the general rule against third-party claims?

a.   In *Warth*, Justice Powell explained this familiar rule as a means of ensuring that federal courts do not decide questions of broad public interest when it is unnecessary to the protection of individual rights. Chief Justice Rehnquist repeated that argument in *Kowalski*. Is there some reason to think that a claim that someone else's personal legal rights have been violated is likely to touch matters of general public concern?

b.   In *Kowalski*, Chief Justice Rehnquist added that prohibiting third-party claims helps to achieve effective advocacy. Is that satisfying? By hypothesis, the plaintiff seeking to advance such a claim satisfies the constitutional prerequisites for standing. The only question, then, is whether the plaintiff should nonetheless be barred from advancing legal claims that belong to someone else. To the extent zealous presentation of the issues is ever in doubt, doesn't the constitutional requirement of factual injury independently ensure it?

c.   Isn't the general rule against third-party claims best understood as in service of individual autonomy—that is, as a means of ensuring that the individuals whose rights are threatened generally determine whether federal litigation is undertaken?

d.   Justice Thomas suggested in *Kowalski* that a plaintiff who cannot allege that the defendant has violated his or her own personal rights has no "interest" in showing that the defendant's action is unlawful. Can that be correct, given that the plaintiff (by hypothesis) suffers injury in fact, caused by the defendant's behavior? Thomas also said that a plaintiff who asserts no personal rights of his own has no "cause of action" and thus "no right to relief." What does that mean? Don't all the modern cases recognizing standing on the basis of factual injury necessarily contemplate that sufficiently injured plaintiffs *can* have a right of action (i.e., an authority to go to court), even though they do not assert violations of their own personal rights, but rather press rights belonging someone else or seek to enforce federal regulatory standards in which no one has a personal right?

2.   **Exceptions.** Despite the general rule against third-party claims, the Supreme Court often allows them on two related grounds. If a would-be plaintiff has a close relationship to the right holder, he or she is likely to be a reliable advocate and the risks that third-party suits ordinarily present are diminished. And if the right holder's ability to sue on his own behalf is "hindered" in some way, there is an additional reason for allowing a suit that would otherwise be turned away. Obviously, the application of these general considerations produced sharp differences of opinion in *Kowalski*. Who do you

think had the better of the argument? Justice Thomas argued that the precedents proved not that the Court should have been more tolerant of the suit in *Kowalski*, but that the Court had already made too many exceptions to the general rule against third-party claims. Is that right? Should we infer from the flexibility the Court has exhibited in the past that the policies underlying the general rule against third-party suits are not so strong as Thomas would have them be? Notice that Justice Thomas himself acknowledged that it may be "too late" actually to revisit so many precedents and adopt a blanket rule against third-party lawsuits.

    3. Potentially Divergent Interests. In *Elk Grove Unified School Dist. v. Newdow*, 542 U.S. 1 (2004), the father of a child in a public elementary school filed suit in federal court, seeking a declaratory judgment that daily recitations of the Pledge of Allegiance at the school violated the Establishment Clause because of the words "under God" in the text. The child's mother intervened and moved to dismiss, claiming that a state court order gave her "the sole right to represent [the daughter's] legal interests" and that the father's suit was not in the child's best interests. The Ninth Circuit Court of Appeals held that, in view of the state court order, the father could not litigate on his daughter's behalf (i.e., the father could not make the child herself the plaintiff in a suit resting on her standing to vindicate her own First Amendment rights), but that the father himself had standing to litigate the Establishment Clause question on the basis of his state law right "as a noncustodial parent . . . to object to unconstitutional government action affecting his child." Writing for the Supreme Court, Justice Stevens acknowledged that the father satisfied the constitutional prerequisites for standing, but concluded that he lacked "prudential standing" to proceed in federal court. The case did not fall neatly under the general rule against third-party standing—nor under the exceptions to the ban on third-party claims. Stevens explained that "the interests of this parent and this child [were] not parallel and, indeed, [were] potentially in conflict." Stevens relied, instead, on an analogy to the "domestic relations exception" to federal diversity jurisdiction. Since the father's personal interests were "entwined inextricably [with] disputed family law rights," it was appropriate for the federal courts to decline jurisdiction. Does *Newdow* suggest that nonconstitutional standing jurisprudence is less a set of discrete doctrines and more a single assertion of discretion to decline the exercise of power?

F. GENERALIZED GRIEVANCE REVISITED

FEDERAL ELECTION COMM'N V. AKINS
524 U.S. 11 (1998).

JUSTICE BREYER delivered the opinion of the Court.

    [T]he Federal Election Campaign Act (FECA) . . . imposes extensive recordkeeping and disclosure requirements upon groups that fall within the Act's definition of a "political committee." . . . This case arises out of an effort by . . . a group of voters . . . to persuade the [Federal Election Commission (FEC)] to treat [the American Israel Public Affairs Committee (AIPAC)] as a "political committee." Respondents filed a complaint with the FEC, stating that AIPAC had made more than $1,000 in qualifying "expenditures" per year, and thereby became a "political committee." They added that AIPAC had violated the FEC provisions requiring "political committee[s]" to register and to make public the information about members, contributions, and expenditures to which we have just referred. They asked the FEC to find that AIPAC had violated the Act, and, among other things, to order AIPAC to make public the information that FECA demands of a "political committee." . . .

The FEC . . . held that AIPAC was not subject to the disclosure requirements. . . . In the FEC's view, the Act's definition of "political committee" includes only those organizations that have as a "major purpose" the nomination or election of candidates. AIPAC . . . was fundamentally an issue-oriented lobbying organization, not a campaign-related organization, and hence AIPAC fell outside the definition of a "political committee." Respondents filed a petition in Federal District Court seeking review of the FEC's determination. . . . The District Court granted summary judgment for the FEC. [The Court of Appeals] reversed, however, on the ground that the FEC's "major purpose" test improperly interpreted the Act's definition of a "political committee." The Solicitor General argues that respondents lack standing to challenge the FEC's decision not to proceed against AIPAC. He claims that they have failed to satisfy the "prudential" standing requirements upon which this Court has insisted. He adds that respondents have not shown that they "suffe[r] injury in fact," that their injury is "fairly traceable" to the FEC's decision, or that a judicial decision in their favor would "redres[s]" the injury. . . .

We do not agree with the [Solicitor General's] "prudential standing" claim. Congress has specifically provided in FECA that "[a]ny person who believes a violation of this Act . . . has occurred, may file a complaint with the Commission." It has added that "[a]ny party aggrieved by an order of the Commission dismissing a complaint filed by such party . . . may file a petition" in district court seeking review of that dismissal. History associates the word "aggrieved" with a congressional intent to cast the standing net broadly—beyond the common-law interests and substantive statutory rights upon which "prudential" standing traditionally rested. [*FCC v. Sanders*]. Cf. Administrative Procedure Act, 5 U.S.C. § 702 (stating that those "suffering legal wrong" or "adversely affected or aggrieved . . . within the meaning of a relevant statute" may seek judicial review of agency action).

Moreover, prudential standing is satisfied when the injury asserted by a plaintiff "arguably [falls] within the zone of interests to be protected or regulated by the statute . . . in question." The injury of which respondents complain—their failure to obtain relevant information—is injury of a kind that FECA seeks to address. We have found nothing in the Act that suggests Congress intended to . . . restrict standing, say, to political parties, candidates, or their committees. Given the language of the statute and the nature of the injury, we conclude that Congress, intending to protect voters such as respondents from suffering the kind of injury here at issue, intended to authorize this kind of suit. Consequently, respondents satisfy "prudential" standing requirements. . . .

Nor do we agree with the FEC or the dissent that Congress lacks the constitutional power to authorize federal courts to adjudicate this lawsuit. . . . The "injury in fact" that respondents have suffered consists of their inability to obtain information—lists of AIPAC donors . . . and campaign-related contributions and expenditures—that, on respondents' view of the law, the statute requires that AIPAC make public. There is no reason to doubt their claim that the information would help them (and others to whom they would communicate it) to evaluate candidates for public office, especially candidates who received assistance from AIPAC, and to evaluate the role that AIPAC's financial assistance might play in a specific election. Respondents' injury consequently seems concrete and particular. Indeed, this Court has previously held that a plaintiff suffers an "injury in fact" when the plaintiff fails to obtain information which must be publicly disclosed pursuant to a statute. *Public Citizen v. Department of Justice*, 491 U.S. 440, 449 (1989).

[The plaintiff in *United States v. Richardson*] claimed that a statute permitting the CIA to keep its expenditures nonpublic violated the Accounts Clause, Art. I, § 9, cl. 7. . . . The Court held that the plaintiff lacked standing because there was "no 'logical nexus' between the [plaintiff's] asserted status of taxpayer and the claimed failure of the Congress to require the Executive to supply a more detailed report of the [CIA's] expenditures." . . . In this case, however, the "logical nexus" inquiry is not relevant. Here, there is no constitutional provision requiring the demonstration of the "nexus" the Court believed must be shown in *Richardson* and *Flast*. Rather, there is a statute which . . . does seek to protect individuals such as respondents from the kind of harm they say they have suffered, i.e., failing to receive particular information about campaign-related activities. The fact that the Court in *Richardson* focused upon taxpayer standing, not voter standing, places that case at still a greater distance from the case before us. We are not suggesting . . . that *Richardson* would have come out differently if only the plaintiff had asserted his standing to sue as a voter, rather than as a taxpayer. Faced with such an assertion, the *Richardson* Court would simply have had to consider whether "the Framers . . . ever imagined that general directives [of the Constitution] . . . would be subject to enforcement by an individual citizen." [*Richardson*], 418 U.S. at 178 n. 11. But since that answer (like the answer to whether there was taxpayer standing in *Richardson*) would have rested in significant part upon the Court's view of the Accounts Clause, it still would not control our answer in this case.

The FEC's strongest argument is its contention that this lawsuit involves only a "generalized grievance." The FEC points out that respondents' asserted harm (their failure to obtain information) is one which is "shared in substantially equal measure by all or a large class of citizens." This Court, the FEC adds, has often said that "generalized grievance[s]" are not the kinds of harms that confer standing. [*Allen v. Wright*; *Valley Forge Christian College v. Americans United*]. Whether styled as a constitutional or prudential limit on standing, the Court has sometimes determined that where large numbers of Americans suffer alike, the political process, rather than the judicial process, may provide the more appropriate remedy for a widely shared grievance.

The kind of judicial language to which the FEC points, however, invariably appears in cases where the harm at issue is not only widely shared, but is also of an abstract and indefinite nature—for example, harm to the "common concern for obedience to law." [See *Allen v. Wright*]. The abstract nature of the harm—for example, injury to the interest in seeing that the law is obeyed—deprives the case of the concrete specificity that characterized those controversies which were "the traditional concern of the courts at Westminster," . . . and which today prevents a plaintiff from obtaining what would, in effect, amount to an advisory opinion.

Often the fact that an interest is abstract and the fact that it is widely shared go hand in hand. But their association is not invariable, and where a harm is concrete, though widely shared, the Court has found "injury in fact." See [*Public Citizen*]. Thus the fact that a political forum may be more readily available where an injury is widely shared (while counseling against, say, interpreting a statute as conferring standing) does not, by itself, automatically disqualify an interest for Article III purposes. Such an interest, where sufficiently concrete, may count as an "injury in fact." This conclusion seems particularly obvious where (to use a hypothetical example) large numbers of individuals suffer the same common-law injury (say, a widespread mass tort), or where large numbers of voters suffer interference with voting rights conferred by law. We conclude that, similarly, the informational injury at issue here, directly related to voting, the most basic of political rights, is sufficiently concrete and specific such that the fact that it is widely shared does not deprive Congress of constitutional power to authorize its vindication in the federal courts.

Respondents have also satisfied the remaining two constitutional standing requirements. The harm asserted is "fairly traceable" to the

FEC's decision about which respondents complain. Of course, . . . it is possible that even had the FEC agreed with respondents' view of the law, it would still have decided in the exercise of its discretion not to require AIPAC to produce the information. But that fact does not destroy Article III "causation," for we cannot know that the FEC would have exercised its prosecutorial discretion in this way. Agencies often have discretion about whether or not to take a particular action. Yet those adversely affected by a discretionary agency decision generally have standing to complain that the agency based its decision upon an improper legal ground.

JUSTICE SCALIA, with whom JUSTICES O'CONNOR and THOMAS join, dissenting.

The provision of law at issue in this case is an extraordinary one, conferring upon a private person the ability to bring an Executive agency into court to compel its enforcement of the law against a third party. Despite its liberality, the Administrative Procedure Act does not allow such suits, since enforcement action is traditionally deemed "committed to agency discretion by law." 5 U.S.C. § 701(a)(2). If provisions such as the present one were commonplace, the role of the Executive Branch in our system of separated and equilibrated powers would be greatly reduced, and that of the Judiciary greatly expanded. Because this provision is so extraordinary, we should be particularly careful not to expand it beyond its fair meaning. In my view the Court's opinion does that. Indeed, it expands the meaning beyond what the Constitution permits.

It is clear that the [FECA] does not intend that all persons filing complaints with the Federal Election Commission have the right to seek judicial review of the rejection of their complaints. This is evident from the fact that the Act permits a complaint to be filed by "[a]ny person who believes a violation of this Act . . . has occurred," but accords a right to judicial relief only to "[a]ny party aggrieved by an order of the Commission dismissing a complaint filed by such party." The interpretation that the Court gives the latter provision deprives it of almost all its limiting force. Any voter can sue to compel the agency to require registration of an entity as a political committee, even though the "aggrievement" consists of nothing more than the deprivation of access to information whose public availability would have been one of the consequences of registration.

[T]he agency action complained of here is not the refusal to make available information in its possession that the Act requires to be disclosed. A person demanding . . . information that the law requires the agency to furnish—one demanding compliance with the Freedom of Information Act, for example—can reasonably be described as being "aggrieved" by the agency's refusal to provide it. What the respondents complain of in this suit, however, is not the refusal to provide information, but the refusal (for an allegedly improper reason) to commence an agency enforcement action against a third person. That refusal itself plainly does not render respondents "aggrieved" within the meaning of the Act, for in that case there would have been no reason for the Act to differentiate between "person" . . . and "party aggrieved." Respondents claim that each of them is elevated to the special status of a "party aggrieved" by the fact that the requested enforcement action (if it was successful) would have had the effect, among others, of placing certain information in the agency's possession, where respondents, along with everyone else in the world, would have had access to it. It seems to me most unlikely that the failure to produce that effect—both a secondary consequence of what respondents immediately seek, and a consequence that affects respondents no more and with no greater particularity than it affects virtually the entire population—would have been meant to set apart each respondent as a "party aggrieved" (as opposed to just a rejected complainant) within the meaning of the statute.

This conclusion is strengthened by the fact that this citizen-suit provision was enacted two years after this Court's decision in *United States v. Richardson*, which . . . gave Congress every reason to believe that a voter's interest in information helpful to his exercise of the franchise was constitutionally inadequate to confer standing. *Richardson* had said that a plaintiff's complaint that the Government was unlawfully depriving him of information he needed to "properly fulfill his obligations as a member of the electorate in voting" was "surely the kind of a generalized grievance" that does not state an Article III case or controversy.

And finally, a narrower reading of "party aggrieved" is supported by the doctrine of constitutional doubt, which counsels us to interpret statutes, if possible, in such fashion as to avoid grave constitutional questions. [I]t is my view that the Court's entertainment of the present suit violates Article III. . . . In *Richardson*, we dismissed for lack of standing a suit whose "aggrievement" was precisely the "aggrievement" respondents assert here: the Government's unlawful refusal to place information within the public domain. The only difference, in fact, is that the aggrievement there was more direct, since the Government already had the information within its possession, whereas here respondents seek enforcement action that will bring information within the Government's possession and then require the information to be made public.

It was alleged in *Richardson* that the Government had denied a right conferred by the Constitution, whereas respondents here assert a right conferred by statute—but of course "there is absolutely no basis for making the Article III inquiry turn on the source of the asserted right." . . . It is true enough that the narrow question presented in *Richardson* was "[w]hether a federal taxpayer has standing." But the *Richardson*

Court did not hold only, as the Court today suggests, that the plaintiff failed to qualify for the exception to the rule of no taxpayer standing established by the "logical nexus" test of *Flast v. Cohen*. The plaintiff's complaint in *Richardson* had also alleged that he was "a member of the electorate," and he asserted injury in that capacity as well. The *Richardson* opinion treated that as fairly included within the taxpayer-standing question. . . .

The Court [says that where a harm is concrete, though widely shared, the Court has found injury in fact]. If that is so—if concrete generalized grievances (like concrete particularized grievances) are OK, and abstract generalized grievances (like abstract particularized grievances) are bad—one must wonder why we ever developed the superfluous distinction between generalized and particularized grievances at all. But of course the Court is wrong to think that generalized grievances have only concerned us when they are abstract.

What is noticeably lacking in the Court's discussion of our generalized-grievance jurisprudence is all reference to two words that have figured in it prominently: "particularized" and "undifferentiated." . . . "Particularized" means that "the injury must affect the plaintiff in a personal and individual way." If the effect is "undifferentiated and common to all members of the public," the plaintiff has a "generalized grievance" that must be pursued by political, rather than judicial, means. These terms explain why it is a gross oversimplification to reduce the concept of a generalized grievance to nothing more than "the fact that [the grievance] is widely shared," thereby enabling the concept to be dismissed as a standing principle by such examples as "large numbers of individuals suffer[ing] the same common-law injury (say, a widespread mass tort), or . . . large numbers of voters suffer[ing] interference with voting rights conferred by law." The exemplified injuries are widely shared, to be sure, but each individual suffers a particularized and differentiated harm. One tort victim suffers a burnt leg, another a burnt arm—or even if both suffer burnt arms they are different arms. One voter suffers the deprivation of his franchise, another the deprivation of hers. With the generalized grievance, on the other hand, the injury or deprivation is not only widely shared but it is undifferentiated. The harm caused to Mr. Richardson by the alleged disregard of the Statement-of-Accounts Clause was precisely the same as the harm caused to everyone else: unavailability of a description of CIA expenditures. Just as the (more indirect) harm caused to Mr. Akins by the allegedly unlawful failure to enforce FECA is precisely the same as the harm caused to everyone else: unavailability of a description of AIPAC's activities.

The Constitution's line of demarcation between the Executive power and the judicial power presupposes a common understanding of the type of interest needed to sustain a "case or controversy" against the Executive in the courts. A system in which the citizenry at large could sue to compel Executive compliance with the law would be a system in which the courts, rather than the President, are given the primary responsibility to "take Care that the Laws be faithfully executed," Art. II, § 3. We do not have such a system because the common understanding of the interest necessary to sustain suit has included the requirement, affirmed in *Richardson*, that the complained-of injury be particularized and differentiated, rather than common to all the electorate. When the Executive can be directed by the courts, at the instance of any voter, to remedy a deprivation that affects the entire electorate in precisely the same way—and particularly when that deprivation (here, the unavailability of information) is one inseverable part of a larger enforcement scheme—there has occurred a shift of political responsibility to a branch designed not to protect the public at large but to protect individual rights. . . . If today's decision is correct, it is within the power of Congress to authorize any interested person to manage (through the courts) the Executive's enforcement of any law that includes a requirement for the filing and public availability of a piece of paper. This is not the system we have had, and is not the system we should desire.

Because this statute should not be interpreted to confer upon the entire electorate the power to invoke judicial direction of prosecutions, and because if it is so interpreted the statute unconstitutionally transfers from the Executive to the courts the responsibility to "take Care that the Laws be faithfully executed," Art. II, § 3, I respectfully dissent.

NOTES ON AKINS, CONGRESS, AND GENERALIZED GRIEVANCE

1. **Implications of *Akins*.** What does *Akins* add to our understanding of congressional power? Did Justice Breyer read the standing provision in FECA to be as generous as the standing provision in the Endangered Species Act, i.e., did he understand that provision to eliminate all the nonconstitutional limits the Court would otherwise engage? If not, why not? Perhaps because the FECA provision confers standing not on "any person," but only on "aggrieved parties"? Is it that the term "aggrieved" is associated historically with a broad net, but not one that captures everyone who satisfies the constitutional prerequisites? Justice Breyer noted, for example, that the same "aggrieved" term appears in § 702 of the Administrative Procedure Act, which, in *Data Processing*, was understood at least to be consistent with the zone test. Did it follow that if the plaintiffs in *Akins* satisfied the zone test, they were home free, i.e., that no other prudential standing requirement was applicable?

2. **Generalized Grievances Revisited.** After the post-*Flast* taxpayer cases, we might have thought that if a plaintiff's only alleged injury is denominated a "generalized grievance," it must follow that the plaintiff lacks the injury in fact the Constitution demands. Justice Breyer acknowledged in *Akins*, however, that the Court had sometimes listed the ban on generalized

grievances among the nonconstitutional limits on standing and thus left the matter ambiguous—at least until *Akins* itself. E.g., *Warth v. Seldin*. Did Breyer resolve the ambiguity? He recognized that the "generalized grievance" label typically identifies interests that are both "widely shared" by large numbers of people and "abstract and indefinite." A taxpayer's interest in expenditures from the federal treasury presumably reflects both those qualities, *Flast* to the contrary notwithstanding. Breyer explained, however, that some generalized grievances are only widely shared, but not abstract and indefinite. When a grievance is only widely shared, the Court on its own may deny standing on prudential grounds and, into the bargain, may be inclined to construe a statute not to permit standing, either. Yet widely shared interests can be sufficiently concrete and personal to satisfy the constitutional "injury in fact" test. Only interests that are abstract and indefinite amount to the generalized concern that the law be obeyed and thus are insufficient for constitutional standing purposes. Accordingly, Congress can validly extend standing to plaintiffs whose injuries are widely shared, though not to anyone who suffers only abstract and indefinite harm. In *Akins*, Justice Breyer concluded that the plaintiffs' interest in obtaining the information they wanted was widely shared but not abstract and indefinite— at least in a context in which the information could be useful in voting. In dissent, Justice Scalia insisted that all generalized grievances are created equal and that, by definition, none can count as injury in fact.

Justice Breyer's treatment of generalized grievances has the practical effect of expanding congressional power touching standing. Consider in this vein another excerpt from Justice Scalia's lecture in 1983:

> If I am correct that the doctrine of standing, as applied to challenges to governmental action, is an essential means of restricting the courts to their assigned role of protecting minority rather than majority interests, several consequences follow. First of all, a consequence of some theoretical interest but relatively small practical effect: it would follow that not *all* "concrete injury" indirectly following from governmental action or inaction would be capable of supporting a congressional conferral of standing. One can conceive of such a concrete injury so widely shared that a congressional specification that the statute at issue was meant to preclude precisely that injury would nevertheless not suffice to mark out a subgroup of the body politic requiring judicial protection. For example, allegedly wrongful governmental action that affects "all who breathe." There is surely no reason to believe that an alleged governmental default of such general impact would not receive fair consideration in the normal political [process].

Are Justice Scalia's concerns about private suits that displace the Executive's prerogative confined to cases in which private litigants press widely shared and/or abstract injuries? Don't the same concerns arise in *any* case in which a private citizen presumes to litigate as a private attorney general? And isn't that why Justice Scalia would prefer to restrict standing to Hohfeldian litigants?

3. Election Law and Generalized Grievances. In *Lance v. Coffman*, 549 U.S. 437 (2007), individual Colorado voters sued in a federal district court, alleging that a provision of the state constitution violated the Elections Clause of the United States Constitution, which specifies that the "Manner of holding Elections for Senators and Representatives, shall be prescribed in each State by the Legislature thereof." Article I, § 4, cl.1. The Supreme Court disposed of the case by *per curiam*. After summarizing a number of standing precedents, among them *Frothingham*, *Richardson*, and *Reservists*, the *per curiam* said this:

> The only injury plaintiffs allege is that the law—specifically the Elections Clause—has not been followed. This injury is precisely the kind of undifferentiated, generalized grievance about the conduct of government that we have refused to countenance in the past. It is quite different from the sorts of injuries alleged by plaintiffs in voting rights cases where we have found standing. See, e.g., *Baker v. Carr*, [369 U.S. 186 (1962)]. Because plaintiffs assert no particularized stake in the litigation, we hold that they lack standing to bring their Elections Clause claim.

It seems pretty clear that the *per curiam* in *Lance* rested on Article III and the ban on generalized grievances. Yet it did not explicitly rehearse the distinction that Justice Breyer drew in *Akins* between generalized grievances that are widely shared (and thus are usually insufficient for standing as a prudential matter) and generalized grievances that are abstract and indefinite (and thus are always insufficient as a constitutional matter). Is that significant? Recall that a general desire to see the law enforced is the paradigm illustration of a generalized grievance of the abstract and indefinite persuasion.

4. *Akins* and *Richardson*. Did Justice Breyer distinguish *Richardson* persuasively? It's true, isn't it, that Chief Justice Burger treated *Richardson* primarily as a taxpayer suit? Justice Breyer acknowledged that the plaintiff in *Richardson* also sued in his capacity as a voter and disclaimed Justice Scalia's suggestion that he meant to say that *Richardson* would have come out differently if the plaintiff had not clouded the standing issue by relying, as well, on his status as a taxpayer. According to Breyer, if Chief Justice Burger had turned his attention to voter standing, he would have had to answer the question he put in footnote 11 of his opinion: whether the "Framers" intended that "general directives to Congress" (apparently including the Statement and Account Clause) "would be subject to enforcement by an individual citizen." Was Breyer's point that the statute the plaintiffs in *Akins* wished to enforce was clearly meant, at least in part, to protect the kind of interest the plaintiffs alleged and that the attendant provision on judicial review plainly contemplated private enforcement suits?

HOLLINGSWORTH V. PERRY

570 U.S. ___, 133 S.Ct. 2652 (2013).

CHIEF JUSTICE ROBERTS delivered the opinion of the Court.

In 2008, the California Supreme Court held that limiting the official designation of marriage to opposite-sex couples violated the equal protection clause of the California Constitution. Later that year, California voters passed the ballot initiative at the center of this dispute, known as Proposition 8. That proposition amended the California Constitution to provide that "[o]nly marriage between a man and a woman is valid or recognized in California." Shortly thereafter, the California Supreme Court rejected a procedural challenge to the amendment, and held that the Proposition was properly enacted under California law.

According to the California Supreme Court, Proposition 8 created a "narrow and limited exception" to the state constitutional rights otherwise guaranteed to same-sex couples. Under California law, same-sex couples have a right to enter into relationships recognized by the State as "domestic partnerships," which carry "the same rights, protections, and benefits, and shall be subject to the same responsibilities, obligations, and duties under law . . . as are granted to and imposed upon spouses." In *In re Marriage Cases*, the California Supreme Court concluded that the California Constitution further guarantees same-sex couples "all of the constitutionally based incidents of marriage," including the right to have that marriage "officially recognized" as such by the State. Proposition 8 left those rights largely undisturbed, reserving only "the official designation of the term 'marriage' for the union of opposite-sex couples as a matter of state constitutional law."

Respondents, two same-sex couples who wish to marry, filed suit in federal court, challenging Proposition 8 under the Due Process and Equal Protection Clauses of the Fourteenth Amendment to the Federal Constitution. The complaint named as defendants California's Governor, attorney general, and various other state and local officials responsible for enforcing California's marriage laws. Those officials refused to defend the law, although they have continued to enforce it throughout this litigation. The District Court allowed petitioners—the official proponents of the initiative to intervene to defend it. After a 12-day bench trial, the District Court declared Proposition 8 unconstitutional, permanently enjoining the California officials named as defendants from enforcing the law, and "directing the official defendants that all persons under their control or supervision" shall not enforce it.

Those officials elected not to appeal the District Court order. When petitioners did, the Ninth Circuit asked them to address "why this appeal should not be dismissed for lack of Article III standing." After briefing and argument, the Ninth Circuit certified a question to the California Supreme Court:

"Whether under Article II, Section 8 of the California Constitution, or otherwise under California law, the official proponents of an initiative measure possess either a particularized interest in the initiative's validity or the authority to assert the State's interest in the initiative's validity, which would enable them to defend the constitutionality of the initiative upon its adoption or appeal a judgment invalidating the initiative, when the public officials charged with that duty refuse to do so."

The California Supreme Court agreed to decide the certified question, and answered in the affirmative. Without addressing whether the proponents have a particularized interest of their own in an initiative's validity, the court concluded that "[i]n a postelection challenge to a voter-approved initiative measure, the official proponents of the initiative are authorized under California law to appear and assert the state's interest in the initiative's validity and to appeal a judgment invalidating the measure when the public officials who ordinarily defend the measure or appeal such a judgment decline to do so."

Relying on that answer, the Ninth Circuit concluded that petitioners had standing under federal law to defend the constitutionality of Proposition 8. California, it reasoned, "'has standing to defend the constitutionality of its [laws],'" and States have the "prerogative, as independent sovereigns, to decide for themselves who may assert their interests." "All a federal court need determine is that the state has suffered a harm sufficient to confer standing and that the party seeking to invoke the jurisdiction of the court is authorized by the state to represent its interest in remedying that harm."

On the merits, the Ninth Circuit affirmed the District Court. The court held the Proposition unconstitutional under the rationale of our decision in *Romer v. Evans*, 517 U.S. 620 (1996). . . . We granted certiorari to review that determination, and directed that the parties also brief and argue "Whether petitioners have standing under Article III, § 2, of the Constitution in this case."

Most standing cases consider whether a plaintiff has satisfied the requirement when filing suit, but Article III demands that an "actual controversy" persist throughout all stages of litigation. That means that standing "must be met by persons seeking appellate review, just as it must be met by persons appearing in courts of first instance." *Arizonans for Official English v. Arizona*, 520 U.S. 43, 64 (1997). We therefore must decide whether petitioners had standing to appeal the District Court's order.

Respondents initiated this case in the District Court against the California officials responsible for enforcing Proposition 8. The parties do not contest that respondents had Article III standing to do so. Each couple expressed a desire to marry and obtain "official sanction" from the State, which was unavailable to them given the declaration in Proposition 8 that "marriage" in California is solely between a man and a woman. After the District Court declared Proposition 8 unconstitutional and enjoined the state officials named as defendants from enforcing it, however, the inquiry under Article III changed. Respondents no longer had any injury to redress—they had won—and the state officials chose not to appeal.

The only individuals who sought to appeal that order were petitioners, who had intervened in the District Court. But the District Court had not ordered them to do or refrain from doing anything. To have standing, a litigant must seek relief for an injury that affects him in a "personal and individual way." He must possess a "direct stake in the outcome" of the case. Here, however, petitioners had no "direct stake" in the outcome of their appeal. Their only interest in having the District Court order reversed was to vindicate the constitutional validity of a generally applicable California law.

We have repeatedly held that such a "generalized grievance," no matter how sincere, is insufficient to confer standing. A litigant "raising only a generally available grievance about government—claiming only harm to his and every citizen's interest in proper application of the Constitution and laws, and seeking relief that no more directly and tangibly benefits him than it does the public at large—does not state an Article III case or controversy."

Petitioners argue that the California Constitution and its election laws give them a " 'unique,' 'special,' and 'distinct' role in the initiative process—one 'involving both authority and responsibilities that differ from other supporters of the measure.' " True enough—but only when it comes to the process of enacting the law. Upon submitting the proposed initiative to the attorney general, petitioners became the official "proponents" of Proposition 8. As such, they were responsible for collecting the signatures required to qualify the measure for the ballot. After those signatures were collected, the proponents alone had the right to file the measure with election officials to put it on the ballot. Petitioners also possessed control over the arguments in favor of the initiative that would appear in California's ballot pamphlets.

But once Proposition 8 was approved by the voters, the measure became "a duly enacted constitutional amendment or statute." Petitioners have no role—special or otherwise—in the enforcement of Proposition 8. They therefore have no "personal stake" in defending its enforcement that is distinguishable from the general interest of every citizen of California. . . . No matter how deeply committed petitioners may be to upholding Proposition 8 or how "zealous [their] advocacy," that is not a "particularized" interest sufficient to create a case or controversy under Article III.

* * *

The dissent eloquently recounts the California Supreme Court's reasons for deciding that state law authorizes petitioners to defend Proposition 8. We do not "disrespect[ ]" or "disparage[ ]" those reasons. Nor do we question California's sovereign right to maintain an initiative process, or the right of initiative proponents to defend their initiatives in California courts, where Article III does not apply. But . . . standing in federal court is a question of federal law, not state law. And no matter its reasons, the fact that a State thinks a private party should have standing to seek relief for a generalized grievance cannot override our settled law to the contrary.

We have never before upheld the standing of a private party to defend the constitutionality of a state statute when state officials have chosen not to. We decline to do so for the first time here.

Because petitioners have not satisfied their burden to demonstrate standing to appeal the judgment of the District Court, the Ninth Circuit was without jurisdiction to consider the appeal. The judgment of the Ninth Circuit is vacated, and the case is remanded with instructions to dismiss the appeal for lack of jurisdiction.

It is so ordered.

JUSTICE KENNEDY, with whom JUSTICE THOMAS, JUSTICE ALITO, and JUSTICE SOTOMAYOR join, dissenting.

There is much irony in the Court's approach to justiciability in this case. A prime purpose of justiciability is to ensure vigorous advocacy, yet the Court insists upon litigation conducted by state officials whose preference is to lose the case. The doctrine is meant to ensure that courts are responsible and constrained in their power, but the Court's opinion today means that a single district court can make a decision with far-reaching effects that cannot be reviewed. And rather than honor the principle that justiciability exists to allow disputes of public policy to be resolved by the political process rather than the courts, see, e.g., *Allen v. Wright*, here the Court refuses to allow a State's authorized representatives to defend the outcome of a democratic election.

* * *

In the end, what the Court fails to grasp or accept is the basic premise of the initiative process. And it is this. The essence of democracy is that the right to make law rests in the people and flows to the government, not the other way around. Freedom resides first in the people without need of a grant from government. The California initiative process embodies these principles and has done so for over a century. "Through the structure of its government, and the character of those who exercise government authority, a State defines itself as sovereign." *Gregory v. Ashcroft*, 501 U.S. 452, 460 (1991). In California and the 26 other States that permit initiatives and popular referendums, the people have exercised their own inherent sovereign right to govern themselves. The Court today frustrates that choice by nullifying . . . a State Supreme Court decision holding that state law authorizes an enacted initiative's proponents to defend the law if and when the State's usual legal advocates decline to do so. The Court's opinion fails to abide by precedent and misapplies basic principles of justiciability. Those errors necessitate this respectful dissent.

NOTES ON HOLLINGSWORTH

1. **Standing and the Initiative Process.** Is the lawsuit in *Hollingsworth* a "generalized grievance" in the same sense that *Levitt*, *Valley Forge* and *United States v. Richardson* are? Does *Hollingsworth* give adequate credence to the nature and purposes of the initiative process? If a state can create legally protected interests through its legislative, common law and even executive processes, why can't it create an enforceable interest personal in defending an initiative?

Does it defy reality to conclude that plaintiffs who have proposed an initiative, collected a massive array of signatures to get it on the ballot, appropriately filed the measure with election officials, crafted the statement in support of the initiative that appears on the ballot, and run a political campaign in favor of its passage, have "no 'personal stake' in defending its enforcement that is distinguishable from the general interest of every citizen of California"? Can we actually doubt that they will bring the fervor and concrete adversity said to be essential to the federal litigation process?

2. **Windsor.** In *United States v. Windsor*, 570 U.S. ___, 133 S.Ct. 2675 (2013), the Supreme Court did reach the merits of an action raising at least some of the issues presented in Hollingsworth—striking down sec. 3 of the federal Defense of Marriage Act. Edith Windsor sought to claim the federal estate tax exemption for surviving spouses, which the IRS denied under the terms of the Defense of Marriage Act. She challenged the statute on federal constitutional grounds. The district court and court of appeals had ruled in favor of Windsor and ordered the United States to repay over $360,000. The United States agreed with Windsor's legal position on the Defense of Marriage Act, but refused to pay her. The Supreme Court said:

> The Government's position—agreeing with Windsor's legal contention but refusing to give it effect—meant that there was a

justiciable controversy between the parties, despite what the claimant would find to be an inconsistency in that stance. [That] the executive may welcome this order to pay the refund if it is accompanied by the constitutional ruling it wants does not eliminate the injury to the national Treasury if payment is made, or to the taxpayer if it is not. [It] would be a different case if the Executive had taken the further step of paying Windsor the refund to which she was entitled under the District Court's ruling.

The Court nonetheless recognized that lack of adverseness was a problem. The House of Representatives, via the Bipartisan Legal Advisory Group (BLAG), had intervened to defend the Defense of Marriage Act. Its participation weighed heavily in resolution of the standing issue:

> While these principles suffice to show that this case presents a justiciable controversy under Article III, the prudential problems inherent in the Executive's unusual position require some further discussion. The Executive's agreement with Windsor's legal argument raises the risk that instead of a real, earnest and vital controversy, the Court faces a friendly, non-adversary, proceeding. [Even] when Article III permits the exercise of federal jurisdiction, prudential considerations demand that the Court insist upon that concrete adverseness which sharpens the presentation of issues upon which the court so largely depends for illumination of difficult constitutional questions.

> [In] the case now before the Court the attorneys for BLAG present a substantial argument for the constitutionality of § 3 of DOMA. BLAG's sharp adversarial presentation of the issues satisfies the prudential concerns that otherwise might counsel against hearing an appeal from a decision with which the principal parties agree. 133 S.Ct. at 2685–88 (internal quotation marks, editorial marks, and citations omitted)

3. Individual Senators and Congressmen. In *Windsor,* the Government's monetary interest satisfied the Article III standing requirements and BLAG's intervention satisfied prudential concerns. Thus, the Court did not need to "decide whether BLAG would have standing to challenge the District Court's ruling and its affirmance in the Court of Appeals on BLAG's own authority." The Supreme Court has shown reluctance to allow standing in cases brought by individual senators and congressmen alleging abridgement of the authorities of the Congress. In *Raines v. Byrd*, 521 U.S. 11 (1997), several members of the 104th Congress, who voted against the passage of the Line item Veto Act, giving power to the president to veto individual tax and spending measures after having signed them into law, sued to challenge the act's constitutionality. In a 7–2 decision, the Court held that individual congressmen lacked Art. III standing to sue— since they failed to show how the allegedly unconstitutional statute resulted in their own personal injury since it applied to the entire institution of

Congress. The congressmen, in the Court's view, asserted a claimed loss of political power rather than a diminution of legally protected interests. Accordingly, there was no case of controversy. After *Windsor*, would the House of Representatives have standing to challenge an executive act on the ground that it violates a federal statute?

4. Evaluating the Court's Performance. Over the past fifty years or so, the growth of public law has meant that, with increasing frequency, issues come up concerning standing to raise claims based on widely shared constitutional and statutory rights and interests. Has the United States Supreme Court done an acceptable job of explaining when it will allow litigation based on intangible and broadly shared legal interests and when it will reject such actions?

V. RIPENESS

NATIONAL PARK HOSPITALITY ASSOCIATION V. DEPARTMENT OF THE INTERIOR

538 U.S. 803 (2003).

JUSTICE THOMAS delivered the opinion of the Court.

Petitioner, a nonprofit trade association that represents concessioners doing business in the national parks, challenges a National Park Service (NPS) regulation [§ 51.3] that purports to render the Contract Disputes Act of 1978 (CDA) inapplicable to concession contracts. The CDA establishes rules governing disputes arising out of certain Government contracts. The statute provides that these disputes first be submitted to an agency's contracting [officer].

Petitioner challenged the validity of § 51.3 in [federal court. The D.C. Circuit agreed with NPS and the Department of the Interior that § 51.3 was valid.] Because petitioner has brought a facial challenge to the regulation and is not litigating any concrete dispute with NPS, we asked the parties to provide supplemental briefing on whether the case is ripe for judicial action.

Ripeness is a justiciability doctrine designed "to prevent the courts, through avoidance of premature adjudication, from entangling themselves in abstract disagreements over administrative policies, and also to protect the agencies from judicial interference until an administrative decision has been formalized and its effects felt in a concrete way by the challenging parties." *Abbott Laboratories v. Gardner*, 387 U.S. 136, 148–149 (1967). The ripeness doctrine is "drawn both from Article III limitations on judicial power and from prudential reasons for refusing to exercise [jurisdiction."]

Determining whether administrative action is ripe for judicial review requires us to evaluate (1) the fitness of the issues for judicial decision and (2) the hardship to the parties of withholding court consideration. [Under] the facts now before us, we conclude this case is not ripe.

We turn first to the hardship inquiry. [NPS] is not empowered to administer the CDA. Rather, the task of applying the CDA rests with agency contracting officers and boards of contract appeals, as well as the Federal Court of Claims, the Court of Appeals for the Federal Circuit, and, ultimately, this [Court.] Consequently, we consider § 51.3 to be nothing more than a "general statemen[t] of policy" designed to inform the public of NPS' views on the proper application of the CDA.

Viewed in this light, § 51.3 does not create "adverse effects of a strictly legal kind," which we have previously required for a showing of hardship. [The regulation] "do[es] not command anyone to do anything or to refrain from doing anything; [it] do[es] not grant, withhold, or modify any formal legal license, power, or authority; [it] do[es] not subject anyone to any civil or criminal liability; [and it] create[s] no legal rights or obligations."

Moreover, § 51.3 does not affect a concessioner's primary conduct. Unlike the regulation at issue in *Abbott Laboratories*, which required drug manufacturers to change the labels, advertisements, and promotional materials they used in marketing prescription drugs on pain of criminal and civil penalties, the regulation here leaves a concessioner free to conduct its business as it sees fit.

[We] have previously found that challenges to regulations similar to § 51.3 were not ripe for lack of a showing of hardship. In *Toilet Goods Assn. [v. Gardner,* 387 U.S. 158 (1967)], for example, the [FDA] issued a regulation requiring producers of color additives to provide FDA employees with access to all manufacturing facilities, processes, and formulae. We concluded the case was not ripe for judicial review because the impact of the regulation could not "be said to be felt immediately by those subject to tin conducting their day-to-day affairs," and "no irremediab[ly] adverse consequences flow[ed] from requiring a later challenge." Indeed, the FDA regulation was more onerous than § 51.3 because failure to comply with it resulted in the suspension of the producer's certification and, consequently, could affect production. Here, by contrast, concessioners suffer no practical harm as a result of § 51.3. All the regulation does is announce the position NPS will take with respect to disputes arising out of concession contracts. [Nothing] in the regulation prevents concessioners from following the procedures set forth in the CDA once a dispute over a concession contract actually [arises].

Petitioner contends that delaying judicial resolution of this issue will result in real harm because the applicability *vel non* of the CDA is one of the factors a concessioner takes into account when preparing its bid for NPS concession contracts. Petitioner's argument appears to be that mere uncertainty as to the validity of a legal rule constitutes a hardship for purposes of the ripeness analysis. We are not persuaded. If we were to follow petitioner's logic, courts would soon be overwhelmed with requests for what essentially would be advisory opinions because most business transactions could be priced more accurately if even a small portion of existing legal uncertainties were resolved. In short, petitioner has failed to demonstrate that deferring judicial review will result in real hardship.

We consider next whether the issue in this case is fit for review. Although the question presented here is 'a purely legal one" and § 51.3 constitutes "final agency action" within the meaning of the [Administrative Procedure Act], we nevertheless believe that further factual development would "significantly advance our ability to deal with the legal issues presented." While the federal respondents generally agree that NPS was correct to conclude that the CDA does not cover concession contracts, they acknowledge that certain types of concession contracts might come under the broad language of the CDA. Similarly, [National Park Hospitality Ass'n and another challenger] present a facial challenge to § 51.3, both rely on specific characteristics of certain types of concession contracts to support their positions. In light of the foregoing, we conclude that judicial resolution of the question presented here should await a concrete dispute about a particular concession [contract].

[JUSTICE STEVENS' opinion concurring in the judgment is omitted.]

JUSTICE BREYER, with whom JUSTICE O'CONNOR joins, dissenting.

[The] challenged Park Service interpretation causes a present injury. If the CDA does not apply to concession contract disagreements, as the Park Service regulation declares, then some of petitioner's members must plan now for higher contract implementation costs. Given the agency's regulation, bidders will likely be forced to pay more to obtain, or to retain, a concession contract than they believe the contract is worth. That is what petitioner argues. [And] several uncontested circumstances indicate that such allegations are likely to prove [true. Justice Breyer then identified features of the contracting process that] make the inapplicability of the CDA more costly to successful [bidders].

Given this threat of immediate concrete harm (primarily in the form of increased bidding costs), this case [is] ripe for judicial review. [The] case now presents a legal issue—the applicability of the CDA to concession contracts—that is fit for judicial determination. That issue is a purely legal one, demanding for its resolution only use of ordinary judicial interpretive techniques. [The] Park Service's interpretation is definite and conclusive, not tentative or likely to change, [and] constitutes "final agency action" within the meaning of the Administrative Procedure [Act].

NOTES ON RIPENESS

1. Ripeness: Article III or Prudential? Justice Thomas was clear that ripeness is in part prudential. Which part is that? The "fitness" part? The "hardship" part? See, generally, Gene Nichol, *Ripeness and the Constitution*, 54 U.CHI.L.REV. 153 (1987). Of course, if a ripeness objection is regarded as nonconstitutional, it can be waived by the interested party. E.g., *Stolt-Nielsen S.A. v. AnimalFeeds Int'l*, 559 U.S. 662, 670 n.2 (2010) (implying that the "hardship" prong is constitutional, and was met in this case). In the same footnote, the Court "express[ed] no view as to whether, in a similar case, a federal court may consider a question of prudential ripeness on its own motion," but then quoted language from *National Park Hospitality Ass'n* to the effect that "even" prudential ripeness "may be considered on a court's own motion).

2. Anticipatory Challenges to Statutes. Review of administrative rule making is not the only context in which the target of a regulation would often like to bring an anticipatory challenge. When the plaintiff brings an anticipatory challenge to the enforcement of criminal or regulatory statute, a similar issue arises. Recent cases treat the prematurity issue in these cases as one of standing, while recognizing that "[t]he doctrines of standing and ripeness 'originate' from the same Article III limitation." See *Susan B. Anthony List v. Driehaus*, 573 U.S. ___, 134 S.Ct. 2334 (2014). See Chapter 6. *National Park* demonstrates that, in suits challenging federal agency action, the Court treats standing and ripeness as distinct, or at least employs a "ripeness" vocabulary. To the extent ripeness is analytically (or even just rhetorically) distinct from standing, the focus of ripeness doctrine is on avoiding premature judicial interference with agency affairs.

3. Ripeness and the Merits. Justice Breyer pointed out that the issue in *National Park* was purely legal and did not depend on the facts of any particular case. Should that have made it easier to conclude that the question was ripe for adjudication immediately? Consider analogous constitutional cases. If a plaintiff challenges the facial validity of a statute, rather than its constitutionality as applied to particular circumstances, isn't any concern about ripeness diminished? There may still be some doubt about whether the statute will be applied to the plaintiff. But if that hurdle is cleared, is anything to be gained by postponing the question of the statute's facial validity until the statute is actually brought to bear in a factual context that, by hypothesis, can have nothing to do with the court's analysis?

CITY OF LOS ANGELES V. LYONS
461 U.S. 95 (1983).

JUSTICE WHITE delivered the opinion of the Court.

Adolph Lyons [filed] a complaint for damages, injunct[ive], and declaratory relief in the United States District Court for the Central District of California. The defendants were the City of Los Angeles and four of its police officers. The complaint alleged that on October 6, 1976, [Lyons] was stopped by the defendant officers for a traffic or vehicle code violation and that although Lyons offered no resistance or threat whatsoever, the officers, without provocation or justification, seized Lyons and applied a "chokehold" [rendering] him unconscious and causing damage to his larynx.

Counts I through IV of the complaint sought damages against the officers and the City. Count V, with which we are principally concerned here, sought a preliminary and permanent injunction against the City barring the use of the control holds. That count alleged that the [C]ity's police officers, "pursuant to the authorization, instruction and encouragement of defendant City of Los Angeles, regularly and routinely apply these chokeholds in innumerable situations where they are not threatened by the use of any deadly force whatsoever," that numerous persons have been injured as the result of the application of the chokeholds, that Lyons and others similarly situated are threatened with irreparable injury in the form of bodily injury and loss of life, and that Lyons "justifiably fears that any contact he has with Los Angeles police officers may result in his being choked and strangled to death without provocation, justification or other legal excuse."

[The district] court concluded that [use of chokeholds] violated Lyons' substantive due process rights under the Fourteenth Amendment. A preliminary injunction was entered enjoining "the use of [chokeholds] under circumstances which do not threaten death or serious bodily injury." An improved training program and regular reporting and record keeping were also ordered.

In *O'Shea v. Littleton*, 414 U.S. 488 (1974), we dealt with a case brought by a class of plaintiffs claiming that they had been subjected to discriminatory enforcement of the criminal law. Among other things, a county magistrate and judge were accused of discriminatory conduct in various respects, such as sentencing members of plaintiff's class more harshly than other defendants. The Court of Appeals reversed the dismissal of the suit by the District Court, ruling that if the allegations were proved, an appropriate injunction could be entered. We reversed for failure of the complaint to allege a case or controversy.

Although it was claimed in [*O'Shea*] that particular members of the plaintiff class had actually suffered from the alleged unconstitutional practices, we observed that "[p]ast exposure to illegal conduct does not in itself show a present case or controversy regarding injunctive relief [if] unaccompanied by any continuing, present adverse effects." Past wrongs were evidence bearing on "whether there is a real and immediate threat of repeated injury." But the prospect of future injury rested "on the likelihood that [plaintiffs] will again be arrested for and charged with violations of the criminal law and will again be subjected to bond proceedings, trial, or sentencing before petitioners." The most that could be said for plaintiffs' standing was "that if [plaintiffs] proceed to violate an unchallenged law and if they are charged, held to answer, and tried in any proceedings before petitioners, they will be subjected to the discriminatory practices that petitioners are alleged to have followed." We could not find a case or controversy in those circumstances: the threat to the plaintiffs was not "sufficiently real and immediate to show an existing controversy simply because they anticipate violating lawful criminal statutes and being tried for their [offenses]." It was to be assumed "that [plaintiffs] will conduct their activities within the law and so avoid prosecution and conviction as well as exposure to the challenged course of conduct said to be followed by petitioners."

We further observed that case or controversy considerations "obviously shade into those determining whether the complaint states a sound basis for equitable relief," and went on to hold that even if the complaint presented an existing case or controversy, an adequate basis for equitable relief against petitioners had not been [demonstrated].

Another relevant decision for present purposes is *Rizzo v. Goode*, 423 U.S. 362 (1976), a case in which plaintiffs alleged widespread illegal and unconstitutional police conduct aimed at minority citizens and against City residents in general. [The] claim of injury rested upon "what one or a small, unnamed minority of policemen might do to them in the future because of that unknown policeman's perception" of departmental procedures. This hypothesis was "even more attenuated than those allegations of future injury found insufficient in *O'Shea* to warrant [the] invocation of federal jurisdiction."

[No] extension of *O'Shea* and *Rizzo* is necessary to hold that respondent Lyons has failed to demonstrate a case or controversy with the City that would justify the equitable relief [sought.] Lyons' standing to seek the injunction requested depended on whether he was likely to suffer future injury from the use of the chokeholds by police officers. That Lyons may have been illegally choked by the police on October 6, 1976, while presumably affording Lyons standing to claim damages against the individual officers and perhaps against the City, does nothing to establish a real and immediate threat that he would again be stopped for a traffic violation, or for any other offense, by an officer or officers who would illegally choke him into unconsciousness without any provocation or resistance on his part. The additional allegation in the complaint that the police in Los Angeles routinely apply chokeholds in situations where they are not threatened by the use of deadly force falls far short of the allegations that would be necessary to establish a case or controversy between these parties.

In order to establish an actual controversy in this case, Lyons would have had not only to allege that he would have another encounter with the police but also to make the incredible assertion either (1) that all police officers in Los Angeles always choke any citizen with whom they happen to have an encounter, whether for the purpose of arrest, issuing a citation or for questioning or (2) that the City ordered or authorized police officers to act in such manner. Although Count V alleged that the City authorized the use of the control holds in situations where deadly force was not threatened, it did not indicate why Lyons might be realistically threatened by police officers who acted within the strictures of the City's policy. If, for example, chokeholds were authorized to be used only to counter resistance to an arrest by a suspect, or to thwart an effort to escape, any future threat to Lyons from the City's policy or from the conduct of police officers would be no more real than the possibility that he would again have an encounter with the police and that either he would illegally resist arrest or detention or the officers would disobey their instructions and again render him unconscious without any provocation.

[The] Court of Appeals viewed *O'Shea* and *Rizzo* as cases in which the plaintiffs sought "massive structural" relief against the local law enforcement systems and therefore that the holdings in those cases were inapposite to cases such as this where the plaintiff, according to the Court of Appeals, seeks to enjoin only an "established," "sanctioned" police practice assertedly violative of constitutional rights. *O'Shea* and *Rizzo*, however, cannot be so easily confined to their facts. If Lyons has made no showing that he is realistically threatened by a repetition of his experience of October, 1976, then he has not met the requirements for seeking an injunction in a federal court, whether the injunction contemplates intrusive structural relief or the cessation of a discrete [practice].

Nor will the injury that Lyons allegedly suffered in 1976 go unrecompensed; for that injury, he has an adequate remedy at law. Contrary to the view of the Court of Appeals, it is not at all "difficult" under our holding "to see how anyone can ever challenge police or similar administrative practices." The legality of the violence to which Lyons claims he was once subjected is at issue in his suit for damages and can be determined there.

JUSTICE MARSHALL, with whom JUSTICES BRENNAN, BLACKMUN, and STEVENS join, dissenting.

The Court today holds that a federal court is without power to enjoin the enforcement of the City's policy, no matter how flagrantly unconstitutional it may be. Since no one can show that he will be choked in the future, no one [has] standing to challenge the continuation of the policy. The City is free to continue the policy indefinitely as long as it is willing to pay damages for the injuries and deaths that result. I dissent from this unprecedented and unwarranted approach to standing.

[Since] 1975 no less than 16 persons have died following the use of a chokehold by an LAPD police officer. Twelve have been Negro males. The evidence submitted to the District Court established that for many years it has been the official policy of the City to permit police officers to employ chokeholds in a variety of situations where they face no threat of violence. In reported "altercations" between LAPD officers and citizens the chokeholds are used more frequently than any other means of physical restraint. Between February 1975 and July 1980, LAPD officers applied chokeholds on at least 975 occasions, which represented more than three-quarters of the reported [altercations].

Since Lyons' claim for damages plainly gives him standing, and since the success of that claim depends upon a demonstration that the City's chokehold policy is unconstitutional, it is beyond dispute that Lyons has properly invoked the District Court's authority to adjudicate the constitutionality of the City's chokehold policy. The dispute concerning the constitutionality of that policy plainly presents a "case or controversy" under Article III. [B]y fragmenting a single claim into multiple claims for particular types of relief and requiring a separate showing of standing for each form of relief, the decision today departs from this Court's traditional conception of standing and of the remedial powers of the federal courts. [By] contrast to this case, *O'Shea* and *Rizzo* involved disputes focusing solely on the threat of future injury which the plaintiffs in those cases alleged they [faced].

As this Court stated in [*Flast v. Cohen*] "the question of standing is related only to whether the dispute sought to be adjudicated will be presented in an adversary context and in a form historically viewed as capable of judicial resolution." [Because] Lyons has a claim for damages against the City, and because he cannot prevail on that claim unless he demonstrates that the City's chokehold policy violates the Constitution, his personal stake in the outcome of the controversy adequately assures an adversary presentation of his challenge to the constitutionality of the policy.[18] Moreover, the resolution of this challenge will be largely dispositive of his requests for declaratory and injunctive relief.

No doubt the requests for injunctive relief may raise additional questions. But these questions involve familiar issues relating to the appropriateness of particular forms of relief, and have never been thought to implicate a litigant's standing to sue. The denial of standing separately

---

[18] It is . . . unnecessary to decide here whether the standing of a plaintiff who alleges past injury that is legally redressable depends on whether he specifically seeks damages. . . .

to seek injunctive relief therefore cannot be justified by the basic concern underlying the Article III standing requirement.[19]

The Court's decision removes an entire class of constitutional violations from the equitable powers of a federal court. It immunizes from prospective equitable relief any policy that authorizes persistent deprivations of constitutional rights as long as no individual can establish with substantial certainty that he will be injured, or injured again, in the future. [I]f the police adopt a policy of "shoot to kill," or a policy of shooting one out of ten suspects, the federal courts will be powerless to enjoin its continuation. The federal judicial power is now limited to levying a toll for such a systematic constitutional violation.

NOTES ON *LYONS*

1.   **Justiciability and Remedies.** A noteworthy aspect of the holding in *Lyons* is that it is not enough for the plaintiff to meet the standing and justiciability requirements in order to maintain his lawsuit. He must meet them separately for each type of relief he seeks. Whether one uses "standing" or "ripeness" to describe the requirement, Lyons has met it in his suit for damages. The Court holds that, even so, he must independently satisfy that requirement for prospective relief. What good reason is there for this rule? Note that there is an alternative means of addressing the distinctive issues that are raised by prospective relief, namely, the body of law on the availability of equitable remedies. One might, for example, distinguish *O'Shea* and *Rizzo* on the ground that the earlier cases were efforts to achieve structural reform of local law enforcement, a task that may be beyond the competence of courts, while the relief requested in *Lyons* is just an injunction limiting the use of chokeholds. The showing of systematic wrongdoing needed to justify such complex remedies seems to have been lacking, or not established to the Court's satisfaction, in *O'Shea* and *Rizzo*. Whether Lyons may have offered enough evidence to show the need for the much narrower regulation on chokeholds is a separate question. By dismissing the complaint, the Court denies Lyons the opportunity to try.

Even if this objection to the Court's reasoning is valid, it is not necessarily decisive. Lyons's suit for prospective relief may fail on account of a distinct justiciability doctrine—that it is moot because he has not shown a sufficient likelihood of recurrence. For a full treatment of the issues raised in this note, see Richard H. Fallon, Jr., *Of Justiciability, Remedies, and Public Law Litigation: Notes on the Jurisprudence of* Lyons, 59 N.Y.U.L.REV. 1 (1984).

---

[19] Whatever may be said for the Court's novel rule that a separate showing of standing must be made for each form of relief requested, the Court is simply wrong in assuming that the scope of the injunction prayed for raises a question of standing. . . . It may well be judicious for the District Court, in the exercise of its discretion, to rest its decision on a theory that would not support the full scope of the injunction that Lyons requests. But this has nothing whatsoever to do with Lyons' standing.

2. *"O'Shea* **Abstention."** The 9th Circuit has taken *O'Shea* in a somewhat different direction. There is a doctrine called *"O'Shea* Abstention," under which courts "should be very reluctant to grant relief that would entail heavy federal interference in such sensitive state activities as administration of the judicial system." *Courthouse News Service v. Planet*, 750 F.3d 776, 789–90 (9th Cir. 2014) (citation and quotation marks omitted). For example, in an earlier case the doctrine was applied to justify dismissal of a case in which the plaintiffs "alleged that the caseloads of court-appointed attorneys representing a putative class of roughly 5,100 foster children in dependency court prevented them from providing constitutionally adequate representation." *E.T. v. Cantil-Sakauye*, 682 F.3d 1121 (9th Cir. 2011). *O'Shea* abstention applied because the plaintiffs there were seeking an "ongoing federal audit" of the dependency court. By contrast, *Courthouse News Service* involved litigation by CNS to require the Ventura County Superior Court clerk to provide immediate access to civil complaints filed with the court. "To determine whether the Ventura County Superior Court is making complaints available on the day they are filed, a federal court would not need to engage in the sort of intensive, context-specific legal inquiry that would be necessary to determine whether counsel's performance was constitutionally adequate." *Id.* at 791.

VI.   MOOTNESS

A. IN GENERAL

CHAFIN V. CHAFIN

568 U.S. ___, 133 S.Ct. 1017 (2013).

ROBERTS, C.J., delivered the opinion for a unanimous Court. GINSBURG, J., filed a concurring opinion, in which SCALIA and BREYER, JJ., joined.

The Hague Convention on the Civil Aspects of International Child Abduction generally requires courts in the United States to order children returned to their countries of habitual residence, if the courts find that the children have been wrongfully removed to or retained in the United States. The question is whether, after a child is returned pursuant to such an order, any appeal of the order is moot.

I

A

The Hague Conference on Private International Law adopted the Hague Convention on the Civil Aspects of International Child Abduction in 1980. In 1988, the United States ratified the treaty and passed implementing legislation, known as the International Child Abduction Remedies Act (ICARA), 102 Stat. 437, 42 U.S.C. § 11601 *et seq.*

The Convention seeks "to secure the prompt return of children wrongfully removed to or retained in any Contracting State" and "to ensure that rights of custody and of access under the law of one Contracting State are effectively respected in the other Contracting States." Art. 1, S. Treaty Doc. No. 99–11, at 7. Article 3 of the Convention provides that the "removal or the retention of a child is to be considered wrongful" when "it is in breach of rights of custody attributed to a person, an institution or any other body, either jointly or alone, under the law of the State in which the child was habitually resident immediately before the removal or retention" and "at the time of removal or retention those rights were actually exercised, either jointly or alone, or would have been so exercised but for the removal or retention." *Ibid.*

Article 12 then states:

"Where a child has been wrongfully removed or retained in terms of Article 3 and, at the date of the commencement of the proceedings before the judicial or administrative authority of the Contracting State where the child is, a period of less than one year has elapsed from the date of the wrongful removal or retention, the authority concerned shall order the return of the child forthwith." *Id.,* at 9.

There are several exceptions to that command. Return is not required if the parent seeking it was not exercising custody rights at the time of removal or had consented to removal, if there is a "grave risk" that return will result in harm, if the child is mature and objects to return, or if return would conflict with fundamental principles of freedom and human rights in the state from which return is requested. Arts. 13, 20, *id.,* at 10, 11. Finally, the Convention directs Contracting States to "designate a Central Authority to discharge the duties which are imposed by the Convention." Art. 6, *id.,* at 8; see also Art. 7, *ibid.*

Congress established procedures for implementing the Convention in ICARA. See 42 U.S.C. § 11601(b)(1). The Act grants federal and state courts concurrent jurisdiction over actions arising under the Convention, § 11603(a), and directs them to "decide the case in accordance with the Convention," § 11603(d). If those courts find children to have been wrongfully removed or retained, the children "are to be promptly returned." § 11601(a)(4). ICARA also provides that courts ordering children returned generally must require defendants to pay various expenses incurred by plaintiffs, including court costs, legal fees, and transportation costs associated with the return of the children. § 11607(b)(3). ICARA instructs the President to designate the U.S. Central Authority, § 11606(a), and the President has designated the Office of Children's Issues in the State Department's Bureau of Consular Affairs, 22 CFR § 94.2 (2012).

Eighty-nine nations are party to the Convention as of this writing. In the 2009 fiscal year, 324 children removed to or retained in other countries were returned to the United States under the Convention, while 154 children removed to or retained in the United States were returned to their countries of habitual residence. Dept. of State, Report on Compliance with the Hague Convention on the Civil Aspects of International Child Abduction 6 (2010).

B

Petitioner Jeffrey Lee Chafin is a citizen of the United States and a sergeant first class in the U.S. Army. While stationed in Germany in 2006, he married respondent Lynne Hales Chafin, a citizen of the United Kingdom. Their daughter E.C. was born the following year.

Later in 2007, Mr. Chafin was deployed to Afghanistan, and Ms. Chafin took E.C. to Scotland. Mr. Chafin was eventually transferred to Huntsville, Alabama, and in February 2010, Ms. Chafin traveled to Alabama with E.C. Soon thereafter, however, Mr. Chafin filed for divorce and for child custody in Alabama state court. Towards the end of the year, Ms. Chafin was arrested for domestic violence, an incident that alerted U.S. Citizenship and Immigration Services to the fact that she had overstayed her visa. She was deported in February 2011, and E.C. remained in Mr. Chafin's care for several more months.

In May 2011, Ms. Chafin initiated this case in the U.S. District Court for the Northern District of Alabama. She filed a petition under the Convention and ICARA seeking an order for E.C.'s return to Scotland. On October 11 and 12, 2011, the District Court held a bench trial. Upon the close of arguments, the court ruled in favor of Ms. Chafin, concluding that E.C.'s country of habitual residence was Scotland and granting the petition for return. Mr. Chafin immediately moved for a stay pending appeal, but the court denied his request. Within hours, Ms. Chafin left the country with E.C., headed for Scotland. By December 2011, she had initiated custody proceedings there. The Scottish court soon granted her interim custody and a preliminary injunction, prohibiting Mr. Chafin from removing E.C. from Scotland. In the meantime, Mr. Chafin had appealed the District Court order to the Court of Appeals for the Eleventh Circuit.

In February 2012, the Eleventh Circuit dismissed Mr. Chafin's appeal as moot in a one-paragraph order, citing *Bekier v. Bekier,* 248 F.3d 1051 (2001). In *Bekier,* the Eleventh Circuit had concluded that an appeal of a Convention return order was moot when the child had been returned to the foreign country, because the court "became powerless" to grant relief. In accordance with *Bekier,* the Court of Appeals remanded this case to the District Court with instructions to dismiss the suit as moot and vacate its order.

On remand, the District Court did so, and also ordered Mr. Chafin to pay Ms. Chafin over $94,000 in court costs, attorney's fees, and travel expenses. Meanwhile, the Alabama state court had dismissed the child custody proceeding initiated by Mr. Chafin for lack of jurisdiction. The Alabama Court of Civil Appeals affirmed, relying in part on the U.S. District Court's finding that the child's habitual residence was not Alabama, but Scotland.

We granted certiorari to review the judgment of the Court of Appeals for the Eleventh Circuit.

II

Article III of the Constitution restricts the power of federal courts to "Cases" and "Controversies." Accordingly, "[t]o invoke the jurisdiction of a federal court, a litigant must have suffered, or be threatened with, an actual injury traceable to the defendant and likely to be redressed by a favorable judicial decision." Federal courts may not "decide questions that cannot affect the rights of litigants in the case before them" or give "opinion[s] advising what the law would be upon a hypothetical state of facts." The "case-or-controversy requirement subsists through all stages of federal judicial proceedings, trial and appellate." "[I]t is not enough that a dispute was very much alive when suit was filed"; the parties must "continue to have a 'personal stake'" in the ultimate disposition of the lawsuit.

There is thus no case or controversy, and a suit becomes moot, "when the issues presented are no longer 'live' or the parties lack a legally cognizable interest in the outcome." But a case "becomes moot only when it is impossible for a court to grant any effectual relief whatever to the prevailing party." "As long as the parties have a concrete interest, however small, in the outcome of the litigation, the case is not moot."

III

This dispute is still very much alive. Mr. Chafin continues to contend that his daughter's country of habitual residence is the United States, while Ms. Chafin maintains that E.C.'s home is in Scotland. Mr. Chafin also argues that even if E.C.'s habitual residence was Scotland, she should not have been returned because the Convention's defenses to return apply. Mr. Chafin seeks custody of E.C., and wants to pursue that relief in the United States, while Ms. Chafin is pursuing that right for herself in Scotland. And Mr. Chafin wants the orders that he pay Ms. Chafin over $94,000 vacated, while Ms. Chafin asserts the money is rightfully owed.

On many levels, the Chafins continue to vigorously contest the question of where their daughter will be raised. This is not a case where a decision would address "a hypothetical state of facts." And there is not the slightest doubt that there continues to exist between the parties "that concrete adverseness which sharpens the presentation of issues." *Camreta v. Greene,* 563 U.S. ___, ___, 131 S.Ct. 2020, 2028 (2011).

A

At this point in the ongoing dispute, Mr. Chafin seeks reversal of the District Court determination that E.C.'s habitual residence was Scotland and, if that determination is reversed, an order that E.C. be returned to the United States (or "re-return," as the parties have put it). In short, Mr. Chafin is asking for typical appellate relief: that the Court of Appeals reverse the District Court and that the District Court undo what it has done. The question is whether such relief would be effectual in this case.

Ms. Chafin argues that this case is moot because the District Court lacks the authority to issue a re-return order either under the Convention or pursuant to its inherent equitable powers. But that argument—which goes to the meaning of the Convention and the legal availability of a certain kind of relief—confuses mootness with the merits. In *Powell v. McCormack,* 395 U.S. 486 (1969), this Court held that a claim for backpay saved the case from mootness, even though the defendants argued that the backpay claim had been brought in the wrong court and therefore could not result in relief. As the Court explained, "this argument . . . confuses mootness with whether [the plaintiff] has established a right to recover . . . , a question which it is inappropriate to treat at this stage of the litigation." Mr. Chafin's claim for re-return—under the Convention itself or according to general equitable principles—cannot be dismissed as so implausible that it is insufficient to preserve jurisdiction, and his prospects of success are therefore not pertinent to the mootness inquiry.

As to the effectiveness of any relief, Ms. Chafin asserts that even if the habitual residence ruling were reversed and the District Court were to issue a re-return order, that relief would be ineffectual because Scotland would simply ignore it. But even if Scotland were to ignore a U.S. re-return order, or decline to assist in enforcing it, this case would not be moot. The U.S. courts continue to have personal jurisdiction over Ms. Chafin, may command her to take action even outside the United States, and may back up any such command with sanctions. No law of physics prevents E.C.'s return from Scotland, and Ms. Chafin might decide to comply with an order against her and return E.C. to the United States, see, *e.g., Larbie v. Larbie,* 690 F.3d 295, 303–304 (C.A.5 2012) (mother who had taken child to United Kingdom complied with Texas court sanctions order and order to return child to United States for trial), cert. pending, No. 12–304. After all, the consequence of compliance presumably would not be relinquishment of custody rights, but simply custody proceedings in a different forum.

Enforcement of the order may be uncertain if Ms. Chafin chooses to defy it, but such uncertainty does not typically render cases moot. Courts often adjudicate disputes where the practical impact of any decision is not assured. For example, courts issue default judgments against defendants who failed to appear or participate in the proceedings and therefore seem less likely to comply. See Fed. Rule Civ. Proc. 55. Similarly, the fact that a defendant is insolvent does not moot a claim for damages. See 13C C. Wright, A. Miller, & E. Cooper, Federal Practice and Procedure § 3533.3, p. 3 (3d ed.2008) (cases not moot "even though the defendant does not seem able to pay any portion of the damages claimed"). Courts also decide cases against foreign nations, whose choices to respect final rulings are not guaranteed. See, *e.g., Republic of Austria v. Altmann,* 541 U.S. 677 (2004) (suit against Austria for return of paintings); *Republic of Argentina v. Weltover, Inc.,* 504 U.S. 607 (1992) (suit against Argentina for repayment of bonds). And we have heard the Government's appeal from the reversal of a conviction, even though the defendants had been deported, reducing the practical impact of any decision; we concluded that the case was not moot because the defendants might "re-enter this country on their own" and encounter the consequences of our ruling. *United States v. Villamonte-Marquez,* 462 U.S. 579, 581, n. 2 (1983).

So too here. A re-return order may not result in the return of E.C. to the United States, just as an order that an insolvent defendant pay $100 million may not make the plaintiff rich. But it cannot be said that the parties here have no "concrete interest" in whether Mr. Chafin secures a re-return order. "[H]owever small" that concrete interest may be due to potential difficulties in enforcement, it is not simply a matter of academic debate, and is enough to save this case from mootness.

B

Mr. Chafin also seeks, if he prevails, vacatur of the District Court's expense orders. The District Court ordered Mr. Chafin to pay Ms. Chafin over $94,000 in court costs, attorney's fees, and travel expenses. That award was predicated on the District Court's earlier judgment allowing Ms. Chafin to return with her daughter to Scotland. Thus, in conjunction with reversal of the judgment, Mr. Chafin desires vacatur of the award. That too is common relief on appeal, and the mootness inquiry comes down to its [effectiveness].

IV

Ms. Chafin is correct to emphasize that both the Hague Convention and ICARA stress the importance of the prompt return of children wrongfully removed or retained. We are also sympathetic to the concern that shuttling children back and forth between parents and across international borders may be detrimental to those children. But courts can achieve the ends of the Convention and ICARA—and protect the well-being of the affected children—through the familiar judicial tools of expediting proceedings and granting stays where appropriate. There is no need to manipulate constitutional doctrine and hold these cases moot. Indeed, doing so may very well undermine the goals of the treaty and harm the children it is meant to protect.

If these cases were to become moot upon return, courts would be more likely to grant stays as a matter of course, to prevent the loss of any right to appeal. See, *e.g., Garrison v. Hudson,* 468 U.S. 1301, 1302, 104 S.Ct. 3496, 82 L.Ed.2d 804 (1984) (Burger, C.J., in chambers) ("When . . . the normal course of appellate review might otherwise cause the case to become moot, issuance of a stay is warranted" (citation and internal quotation marks omitted)); *Nicolson v. Pappalardo,* Civ. No. 10–1125 (C.A.1, Feb. 19, 2010) ("Without necessarily finding a clear probability that appellant will prevail, we grant the stay because . . . a risk exists that the case could effectively be mooted by the child's departure"). In cases in which a stay would not be granted but for the prospect of mootness, a child would lose precious months when she could have been readjusting to life in her country of habitual residence, even though the appeal had little chance of success. Such routine stays due to mootness would be likely but would conflict with the Convention's mandate of prompt return to a child's country of habitual residence.

Routine stays could also increase the number of appeals. Currently, only about 15% of Hague Convention cases are appealed. Hague Conference on Private Int'l Law, N. Lowe, A Statistical Analysis of Applications Made in 2008 Under the Hague Convention of 25 October 1980 on the Civil Aspects of International Child Abduction, Pt. III—National Reports 207 (2011). If losing parents were effectively guaranteed a stay, it seems likely that more would appeal, a scenario that would undermine the goal of prompt return and the best interests of children who should in fact be returned. A mootness holding here might also encourage flight in future Hague Convention cases, as prevailing parents try to flee the jurisdiction to moot the [case].

Courts should apply the four traditional stay factors in considering whether to stay a return order: " '(1) whether the stay applicant has made a strong showing that he is likely to succeed on the merits; (2) whether the applicant will be irreparably injured absent a stay; (3) whether issuance of the stay will substantially injure the other parties interested in the proceeding; and (4) where the public interest lies.' " In every case under the Hague Convention, the well-being of a child is at stake; application of the traditional stay factors ensures that each case will receive the individualized treatment necessary for appropriate consideration of the child's best interests.

Importantly, whether at the district or appellate court level, courts can and should take steps to decide these cases as expeditiously as possible, for the sake of the children who find themselves in such an unfortunate situation. Many courts already do so. See Federal Judicial Center, J. Garbolino, The 1980 Hague Convention on the Civil Aspects of International Child Abduction: A Guide for Judges 116, n. 435 (2012) (listing courts that expedite appeals). Cases in American courts often take over two years from filing to resolution; for a six-year-old such as E. C., that is one-third of her lifetime. Expedition will help minimize the extent to which uncertainty adds to the challenges confronting both parents and child.

* * *

The Hague Convention mandates the prompt return of children to their countries of habitual residence. But such return does not render this case moot; there is a live dispute between the parties over where their child will be raised, and there is a possibility of effectual relief for the prevailing parent. The courts below therefore continue to have jurisdiction to adjudicate the merits of the parties' respective claims.

The judgment of the United States Court of Appeals for the Eleventh Circuit is vacated, and the case is remanded for further proceedings consistent with this opinion.

It is so ordered.

[Justice Ginsburg's concurring opinion is omitted.]

NOTES ON MOOTNESS

1.   **The Nature of Mootness.** The idea behind mootness is that Article III courts cannot (or do not, or at least ordinarily do not) address a legal issue that previously divided the parties when the dispute that generated the issue has become irrelevant to the parties, either because it has been resolved by other means, or because the plaintiff no longer cares, or because the defendant has changed his conduct, or simply because the issue has gone away. This idea sounds other familiar justiciability themes—most obviously the policy against advisory opinions. Yet whether there is really nothing left to fight about is not an all or nothing question; it is often a matter of degree. The issue is not *whether* the dispute is still alive, but *how likely* it is that judicial action will matter. For example, the Court in *Chafin* says that "[n]o law of physics prevents E.C.'s return from Scotland, and Ms. Chafin might decide to comply with an order against her and return E.C. to the United States."

Compare *Camreta v. Greene*, 563 U.S. ___, 131 S.Ct. 2020 (2011). The plaintiff, S. G., was a nine-year-old at the time of the incident giving rise to the litigation. S.G. was interviewed at her school in Deschutes County, Oregon by Camreta and another officer in connection with a child abuse investigation. She sued under § 1983, claiming that the interview was a seizure and that, on account of her status as a minor, the seizure violated her Fourth Amendment rights. By the time the case reached the Supreme Court, it was settled that the officer could successfully assert qualified immunity. The remaining issue was whether he had violated the Fourth Amendment. In the meantime, S.G. had moved to Florida with her family and was approaching her eighteenth birthday. The Court ruled that the case was moot, since "she faces not the slightest possibility of being seized in a school in the Ninth Circuit's jurisdiction as part of a child abuse investigation. [Time] and distance have stymied our ability to consider this petition." 131 S.Ct. at 2034. Is it more likely that Ms. Chafin will return her child to the United States than it is that S.G. will return to Oregon before her eighteenth birthday?

2.   **Mootness and Collateral Consequences.** Even if it is no more likely that Ms. Chafin will return to the United States than there is that S.G. will soon return to Oregon, there are other grounds on which the cases may be distinguished. One is the District Court's expense order. Another, of more systematic importance, is that, in deciding mootness cases, the Court is sensitive to the collateral consequences of its rulings. In this regard, consider the Court's discussion (in part IV) of the Hague Convention and the International Child Abduction Remedies Act (ICARA). Thus, the Court pointed out that "[if] these cases were to become moot upon return, courts would be more likely to grant stays as a matter of course, to prevent the loss of any right to appeal." And the routine granting of stays could interfere with efforts to do what is best for the child, which is the point of the Convention and the statute.

The defendant in *Camreta* (seeking to avoid mootness) suggested that, even if S.G. would never return to Oregon, a ruling on the validity of the search would have other consequences. Camreta argued "that S.G. has a continuing interest in the Ninth Circuit's constitutional ruling because it may help her establish a municipal liability claim against Deschutes County." That claim was no longer pending, but might have been revived. The Court rejected Camreta's reasoning:

> Whatever interest S.G. might have were her municipal liability claim still pending (an issue we need not and do not decide), we do not think S.G.'s *dismissed* claim against a *different* defendant involving a *separate* legal theory can save this case from mootness. 131 S.Ct. at 2034 (emphasis in original)

And yet, on the premise that the suit can be revived, the Ninth Circuit's ruling may be quite useful to S.G. in the municipal liability litigation, at least for its precedential force (or even for preclusive effect, see Chapter 6) on the constitutional merits.

3.   **Voluntary Cessation.** Suppose a city, having been sued on account of some constitutionally dubious practice, simply ceases the practice, tells the court there is no longer any dispute, and moves for a finding of mootness. The

motion will not necessarily be granted, as the court will first need to determine whether the cessation is definitive or merely a tactical maneuver aimed at getting rid of the challenge, after which the city will renew its practice. See *City of Mesquite v. Aladdin's Castle*, 455 U.S. 283 (1982) (applying the rule that "a defendant's voluntary cessation of a challenged practice does not deprive a federal court of its power to determine the legality of the practice." The doctrine is typically applied when the circumstances suggest that the defendant has repealed its challenged ordinance in order to avoid a definitive finding of its unconstitutionality, and may well revive it. E.g., *Northeastern Fla. Chapter of Associated General Contractors v. City of Jacksonville*, 508 U.S. 656 (1993) (since a revised ordinance had already been enacted, the case against mootness was especially strong; "[t]here is no mere risk that Jacksonville will repeat its allegedly wrongful conduct; it has already done so.")

4. Voluntary Cessation and Intellectual Property. Voluntary cessation was the issue in *Already, LLC v. Nike, Inc.*, 568 U.S. ___, 133 S.Ct. 721 (2013). Nike and Already both market athletic shoes. Nike sued Already, claiming that Already's "Soulja Boys" shoe infringed Nike's "Air Force 1" trademark. Already denied the allegations and countersued, claiming that Nike's trademark was invalid. A few months later Nike issued a "Covenant Not to Sue," in which it "promised that Nike would not raise against Already [any] trademark or unfair competition claim based on any of Already's existing footwear designs, or any future designs that constituted a 'colorable imitation' of Already's current products."

Nike then moved to dismiss not only its trademark claims (with prejudice) but also Already's counterclaim "without prejudice on the ground that the covenant had extinguished the case or controversy." Already opposed dismissal of its counterclaim, arguing that there was still a live dispute. In support, it offered, among other things, "affidavits from three potential investors, asserting that they would not consider investing in Already until Nike's trademark was invalidated; and an affidavit from one of Already's executives, stating that Nike had intimidated retailers into refusing to carry Already's shoes."

A unanimous Court sided with Nike. It said that "the question the voluntary cessation doctrine poses" is: "Could the allegedly wrongful behavior reasonably be expected to recur?" Here the covenant was "unconditional and irrevocable. [It] reaches beyond Already to protect Already's distributors and customers. And it covers not just current designs, but any colorable imitations." Already was thus obliged to show that "it engages in or has sufficiently concrete plans to engage in activities not covered by the covenant." When given an opportunity to do that before the District Court, "Already did not assert any intent to design or market a shoe that would expose it to any prospect of infringement liability."

Already argued that "so long as Nike remains free to assert its trademark, investors will be apprehensive about investing in Already; [that]

given Nike's decision to sue in the first place, Nike's trademarks will now hang over Already's operations like a Damoclean sword; and [that] as one of Nike's competitors, it inherently has standing to challenge Nike's intellectual property." But the Court squarely rejected this theory, citing *Lyons* for the proposition that "we have never held that a plaintiff has standing to pursue declaratory relief merely on the basis of being 'once bitten.'"

Justice Kennedy, joined by Justices Thomas, Alito, and Sotomayor, wrote a concurring opinion "to underscore that covenants like the one Nike filed here ought not to be taken as an automatic means for the party who first charged a competitor with trademark infringement suddenly to abandon the suit without incurring the risk of an ensuing adverse adjudication." Thus, "[a]ny demonstrated reluctance by investors, distributors, and retailers to maintain good relations with the alleged infringer might, in an appropriate case, be an indication that the market itself anticipates that a new line of products could be outside the covenant not to sue yet still within a zone of alleged infringement."

5. *Lyons* **and Mootness.** In the course of ruling against Aldoph Lyons's request for prospective relief, the Court also addressed the issue of mootness:

> The Court of Appeals . . . asserted that Lyons "had a live and active claim" against the City "if only for a period of a few seconds" while the stranglehold was being applied to him and that for two reasons the claim had not become moot so as to disentitle Lyons to injunctive relief: First, because under normal rules of equity, a case does not become moot merely because the complained of conduct has ceased; and second, because Lyons' claim is "capable of repetition but evading review" and therefore should be heard.

> We agree that Lyons had a live controversy with the City. Indeed, he still has a claim for damages against the City that appears to meet all Article III requirements. Nevertheless, the issue here is not whether that claim has become moot but whether Lyons meets the preconditions for asserting an injunctive claim in a federal forum. The equitable doctrine that cessation of the challenged conduct does not bar an injunction is of little help in this respect, for Lyons' lack of standing does not rest on the termination of the police practice but on the speculative nature of his claim that he will again experience injury as the result of that practice even if continued.

> The rule that a claim does not become moot where it is capable of repetition, yet evades review, is likewise inapposite. Lyons' claim that he was illegally strangled remains to be litigated in his suit for damages; in no sense does that claim "evade" review. Furthermore, the capable-of-repetition doctrine applies only in exceptional situations, and generally only where the named plaintiff can make a reasonable showing that he will again be subjected to the alleged illegality.

6.　The "Capable of Repetition" Exception. The time required for litigation necessarily results in mootness for many claims arising from short-lived circumstances. Yet in a long line of decisions the Court has recognized that some injuries are by nature *both* transitory *and* likely to arise repeatedly—thus "capable of repetition yet evading review." *Southern Pacific Terminal Co. v. ICC*, 219 U.S. 498, 515 (1911). The famous modern illustration is *Roe v. Wade*, 410 U.S. 113 (1973). By the time the Supreme Court was in a position to determine the validity of the Texas abortion statute, the plaintiff was obviously no longer pregnant and thus no longer suffered the same injury on which she had relied when she filed her complaint. Writing for the Court, Justice Blackmun declared that since "pregnancy often comes more than once to the same woman," the plaintiff's injury was "capable of repetition yet evading review" in the necessary sense, and her challenge to the Texas statute was not moot.

a.　In cases under this heading, the injury must be likely to occur again to the *same person*. It's not enough that a litigant whose own fleeting injury has ended demonstrates that other people, too, are likely to suffer in the same way. *Weinstein v. Bradford*, 423 U.S. 147, 149 (1975). Why should this be true? Surely the "capable of repetition yet evading review" doctrine must count as an exception to mootness jurisprudence generally, tailored to ensure that temporary but recurring harms do not escape judicial attention entirely. In for a penny, in for a pound? Why not let a plaintiff whose own injury is history continue to press a legal claim on behalf of others? Is it that the likelihood that the individual plaintiff will be harmed again establishes the personal stake needed to seek forward-looking relief? If so, is there any daylight between this special mootness doctrine, on the one hand, and the doctrine of standing announced in *Lyons*, on the other?

b.　What would the plaintiff in *Lyons* have had to assert to obtain the benefit of the "capable of repetition yet evading review" rule? Presumably, he would have had to allege sufficient facts to create a genuine likelihood that he would be choked again. Cf. *Kolender v. Lawson*, 461 U.S. 352 (1983) (allowing a plaintiff who had been arrested for vagrancy "approximately" fifteen times to seek an injunction against the enforcement of the same ordinance against him in the future).

B.　CLASS ACTIONS

Another way to avoid mootness is to persuade the federal courts to certify the case as a class action. The key here is that even if the "named plaintiff's" claim becomes moot, others members of the class may have lives claims that will save the case from being dismissed as moot.

UNITED STATES PAROLE COMM'N v. GERAGHTY

445 U.S. 388 (1980).

JUSTICE BLACKMUN delivered the opinion of the Court.

Respondent John M. Geraghty was convicted . . . of conspiracy to commit extortion. . . . [After his application for parole was denied,] Geraghty . . . instituted this civil suit as a class action . . . challenging the [Parole Commission's] guidelines as inconsistent with the [relevant statute] and the Constitution . . . Respondent sought certification of a class of "all federal prisoners who are or will become eligible for release on parole." . . . The District Court subsequently denied Geraghty's request for class certification and granted summary judgment for petitioners on all the claims Geraghty asserted. . . . [Geraghty], individually "and on behalf of a class," appealed to the United States Court of Appeals for the Third Circuit. [B]efore any brief had been filed in the Court of Appeals, Geraghty was mandatorily released from prison. . . .

[M]ootness has two aspects: "when the issues presented are no longer 'live' or the parties lack a legally cognizable interest in the outcome." . . . It is clear that the controversy over the validity of the Parole Release Guidelines is still a "live" one between petitioners and at least some members of the class respondent seeks to represent. . . . We therefore are concerned here with the second aspect of mootness, that is, the parties' interest in the litigation. The Court has referred to this concept as the "personal stake" requirement [, which] relates to the first purpose of the case-or-controversy doctrine—limiting judicial power to disputes capable of judicial resolution. The Court in [*Flast*] stated: "The question whether a particular person is a proper party to maintain the action does not, by its own force, raise separation of powers problems related to improper judicial interference in areas committed to other branches of the Federal Government. . . . Thus, in terms of Article III limitations on federal court jurisdiction, the question of standing is related only to whether the dispute sought to be adjudicated will be presented in an adversary context and in a form historically viewed as capable of judicial resolution. . . ."

On several occasions the Court has considered the application of the "personal stake" requirement in the class-action context. In *Sosna v. Iowa*, 419 U.S. 393 (1975), it held that mootness of the named plaintiff's individual claim after a class has been duly certified does not render the action moot. It reasoned that "even though appellees . . . might not again enforce the Iowa durational residency requirement against [the class representative], it is clear that they will enforce it against those persons in the class that appellant sought to represent and that the District Court certified." . . . The Court stated specifically that an [Article III] case or controversy "may exist . . . between a named defendant and a member of the class represented by the named plaintiff, even though the claim of the named plaintiff has become moot." . . .[6]

Although one might argue that *Sosna* contains at least an implication that the critical factor for [Article III] purposes is the timing of class certification, other cases, applying a "relation back" approach, clearly demonstrate that timing is not crucial. When the claim on the merits is "capable of repetition, yet evading review," the named plaintiff may litigate the class certification issue despite loss of his personal stake in the outcome of the litigation. E.g., *Gerstein v. Pugh*, 420 U.S. 103, 110, n. 11 (1975). The "capable of repetition, yet evading review" doctrine to be sure, was developed outside the class-action context. . . . But it has been applied where the named plaintiff does have a personal stake at the outset of the lawsuit, and where the claim may arise again with respect to that plaintiff; the litigation then may continue notwithstanding the named plaintiff's current lack of a personal stake.

When, however, there is no chance that the named plaintiff's expired claim will reoccur, mootness still can be avoided through certification of a class prior to expiration of the named plaintiff's personal claim. . . . Some claims are so inherently transitory that the trial court will not have even enough time to rule on a motion for class certification before the proposed representative's individual interest expires. . . . *Gerstein* was an action challenging pretrial detention conditions. The Court assumed that the named plaintiffs were no longer in custody awaiting trial at the time the trial court certified a class of pretrial detainees. There was no indication that the particular named plaintiffs might again be subject to pretrial detention. Nonetheless, the case was held not to be moot. . . . The interest of the named plaintiffs in *Gerstein* was precisely the same as that of Geraghty here. [*Gerstein* and other cases] demonstrate the flexible character of the [Article III] mootness doctrine.

Application of the personal-stake requirement to a procedural claim, such as the right to represent a class, is not automatic or readily resolved. A "legally cognizable interest" . . . in the traditional sense rarely ever exists with respect to the class certification claim. The justifications that led to the development of the class action include the protection of the defendant from inconsistent obligations, the protection of the interests of absentees, the provision of a convenient and economical means for disposing of similar lawsuits, and the facilitation of the spreading of litigation costs among numerous litigants with similar claims. . . . Although the named representative receives certain benefits from the

---

[6]   The claim in *Sosna* also fit the traditional category of actions that are deemed not moot despite the litigant's loss of personal stake, that is, those "capable of repetition, yet evading review." . . . In [*Franks v. Bowman Trans. Co.*, 424 U.S. 747 (1976)], however, the Court held that the class-action aspect of mootness doctrine does not depend on the class claim's being so inherently transitory that it meets the "capable of repetition, yet evading review" standard.

class nature of the action, some of which are regarded as desirable and others as less so, these benefits generally are byproducts of the class-action device. In order to achieve the primary benefits of class suits, the Federal Rules of Civil Procedure give the proposed class representative the right to have a class certified if the requirements of the Rules are met. This "right" is more analogous to the private attorney general concept than to the type of interest traditionally thought to satisfy the "personal stake" requirement. . . .

We therefore hold that an action brought on behalf of a class does not become moot upon expiration of the named plaintiff's substantive claim, even though class certification has been denied.[10] The proposed representative retains a "personal stake" in obtaining class certification sufficient to assure that [Article III] values are not undermined. If the appeal results in reversal of the class certification denial, and a class subsequently is properly certified, the merits of the class claim then may be adjudicated pursuant to the holding in *Sosna*.

Our holding is limited to the appeal of the denial of the class certification motion. A named plaintiff whose claim expires may not continue to press the appeal on the merits until a class has been properly certified. If, on appeal, it is determined that class certification properly was denied, the claim on the merits must be dismissed as moot.[11]

Our conclusion that the controversy here is not moot does not automatically establish that the named plaintiff is entitled to continue litigating the interests of the class. "[I]t does shift the focus of examination from the elements of justiciability to the ability of the named representative to 'fairly and adequately protect the interests of the class.' Rule 23(a)." [*Sosna*]. We hold only that a case or controversy still exists. The question of who is to represent the class is a separate issue. . . .

---

[10] We intimate no view as to whether a named plaintiff who settles the individual claim after denial of class certification may, consistent with [Article III], appeal from the adverse ruling on class certification. . . .

[11] The erosion of the strict, formalistic perception of [Article III] was begun well before today's decision. For example, the protestations of the dissent are strikingly reminiscent of Mr. Justice Harlan's dissent in *Flast v. Cohen*. . . . We concede that the prior cases may be said to be somewhat confusing, and that some, perhaps, are irreconcilable with others. Our point is that the strict, formalistic view of [Article III] jurisprudence, while perhaps the starting point of all inquiry, is riddled with exceptions. And, in creating each exception, the Court has looked to practicalities and prudential considerations. . . . Each case must be decided on its own facts. . . . We merely hold that when a District Court erroneously denies a procedural motion, which, if correctly decided, would have prevented the action from becoming moot, an appeal lies from the denial and the corrected ruling "relates back" to the date of the original denial. The judicial process will not become a vehicle for "concerned bystanders," . . . even if one in respondent's position can conceivably be characterized as a bystander, because the issue on the merits will not be addressed until a class with an interest in the outcome has been certified. The "relation back" principle, a traditional equitable doctrine applied to class certification claims in [*Gerstein*], serves logically to distinguish this case from the one brought a day after the prisoner is released. If the named plaintiff has no personal stake in the outcome at the time class certification is denied, relation back of appellate reversal of that denial still would not prevent mootness of the action.

JUSTICE POWELL, with whom THE CHIEF JUSTICE and JUSTICES STEWART and REHNQUIST join, dissenting.

The prudential aspect of standing aptly is described as a doctrine of uncertain contours. But the constitutional minimum has been given definite content. . . .[1] Although noneconomic injuries can confer standing, the Court has rejected all attempts to substitute abstract concern with a subject—or with the rights of third parties—for "the concrete injury required by [Article III]." [*Simon v. EKWRO*].[2]

Prudential considerations not present at the outset may support continuation of an action in which the parties have invested substantial resources and generated a factual record. But an actual case or controversy in the constitutional sense "must be extant at all stages of review." . . . Since the question is one of power, the practical importance of review cannot control. . . . Nor can public interest in the resolution of an issue replace the necessary individual interest in the outcome. . . . Collateral consequences of the original wrong may supply the individual interest in some circumstances. . . . So, too, may the prospect of repeated future injury so inherently transitory that it is unlikely to outlast the normal course of litigation. The essential and irreducible constitutional requirement is simply a nonfrivolous showing of continuing or threatened injury at the hands of the adversary.

[C]ontrary to the Court's view today, . . . the core requirement of a personal stake in the outcome is not "flexible." . . . We have insisted upon the personal stake requirement in mootness and standing cases because it is embedded in the case-or-controversy limitation imposed by the Constitution, "founded in concern about the proper—and properly limited—role of the courts in a democratic society." . . . In this way we have, until today, "prevent[ed] the judicial process from becoming no more than a vehicle for the vindication of the value interests of concerned bystanders." . . .

In short, this is a case in which the putative class representative—respondent here—no longer has the slightest interest in the injuries alleged in his complaint. No member of the class is before the Court; indeed, none has been identified. The case therefore lacks a plaintiff with the minimal personal stake that is a constitutional prerequisite to the jurisdiction of an [Article III] court. In any realistic sense, the only

---

[1]   See, e.g., [*Duke Power* and *Warth v. Seldin*]. Each of these cases rejects the view, once expressed by Mr. Justice Harlan and now apparently espoused by the Court, that the personal stake requirement lacks constitutional significance. [*Flast v. Cohen*]. . . .

[2]   The rule is the same when the question is mootness and a litigant can assert no more than emotional involvement in what remains of the case. . . .

persons before this Court who appear to have an interest are the defendants and a lawyer who no longer has a client.[21]

NOTES ON MOOTNESS AND CLASS ACTIONS

1. The Personal Stake Requirement. In *Geraghty*, Justice Blackmun relied on Chief Justice Warren's opinion in *Flast* for the proposition that a "personal stake in the outcome" is important only to ensure effective advocacy and not to serve the separation of powers values the Court has emphasized in more recent justiciability cases. Wasn't it a little late for that? Isn't it hard to argue with Justice Powell's position that in cases on standing a personal stake equates with injury in fact, which, in turn, is the core prerequisite for an Article III case or controversy?

2. *Sosna.* The named plaintiff in *Sosna v. Iowa* filed a federal class action challenging Iowa's durational residency requirement for obtaining a divorce. The district court certified the class before the named plaintiff had lived in Iowa for the required year. But by the time the case reached the Supreme Court, the named plaintiff was no longer subject to the durational residency requirement. Nor was she herself likely to be subject to that requirement again. Writing for the Court, Justice Rehnquist nonetheless explained that the certified class prevented the suit from becoming moot:

> When the District Court certified the propriety of the class action, the class of unnamed persons described in the certificate [other newly arrived residents of Iowa who wished to divorce] acquired a legal status separate from the interests of the appellant. [E]ven if [state officials] might not again enforce the Iowa durational residency requirement against appellant, it is clear that they will enforce it against those persons in the class that appellant sought to represent and that the District Court certified. In this sense the case before us is one in which state officials will undoubtedly continue to enforce the challenged statute and yet, because of the passage of time, no single challenger will remain subject to its restrictions for the period necessary to see such a lawsuit to its conclusion.

3. *Gerstein.* In *Gerstein v. Pugh*, two detainees at a local jail in Florida filed suit in federal court claiming a constitutional right to a judicial determination of probable cause to hold them for trial. They sought declaratory and injunctive relief on their own behalf and on behalf of the class of similarly situated prisoners. The district court certified the class and issued an order requiring preliminary hearings. The Supreme Court affirmed (in part) on the merits. In footnote 11 of his opinion for the majority, Justice Powell said this:

---

[21] I imply no criticism of counsel in this case. The Court of Appeals agreed with counsel that the certification issue was appealable, and the case was brought to this Court by the United States.

At oral argument counsel informed us that the named respondents have been convicted. Their pretrial detention therefore has ended. This case belongs, however, to that narrow class of cases in which the termination of a class representative's claim does not moot the claims of the unnamed members of the class. See *Sosna v. Iowa*. Pretrial detention is by nature temporary, and it is most unlikely that any given individual could have his constitutional claim decided on appeal before he is either released or convicted. The individual could nonetheless suffer repeated deprivations, and it is certain that other persons similarly situated will be detained under the allegedly unconstitutional procedures. The claim, in short, is one that is distinctly "capable of repetition, yet evading review." At the time the complaint was filed, the named respondents were members of a class of persons detained without a judicial probable cause determination, but the record does not indicate whether any of them were still in custody awaiting trial when the District Court certified the class. Such a showing ordinarily would be required to avoid mootness under *Sosna*. But this case is a suitable exception to that requirement.... The length of pretrial custody cannot be ascertained at the outset, and it may be ended at any time by release on recognizance, dismissal of the charges, or a guilty plea, as well as by acquittal or conviction after trial. It is by no means certain that any given individual, named as plaintiff, would be in pretrial custody long enough for a district judge to certify the class. Moreover, in this case the constant existence of a class of persons suffering the deprivation is certain. The attorney representing the named respondents is a public defender, and we can safely assume that he has other clients with a continuing live interest in the case. . . .

4.   *Franks.* Both *Sosna* and *Gerstein* invoked the "capable of repetition yet evading review" idea, though neither insisted that the named plaintiff must personally be likely to suffer the same kind of injury again in the future. In *Sosna*, the certified class became the complaining party once it was certified; in *Gerstein*, the effective date of certification related back to the time of the complaint. Writing for the Court in *Franks v. Bowman Trans. Co.*, Justice Brennan disclaimed any need for the injuries in class action cases to be both short-lived and recurring—for anyone. Accordingly, prior to *Geraghty*, the Court was already committed to the proposition that class actions do not become moot when a named plaintiff's personal stake in success on the merits is eliminated. If the class has been certified at that time, the interest of the class itself remains sufficient. If the class is certified later, the certification relates back to the time the complaint was filed. In *Geraghty* itself, then, Justice Blackmun arguably took the next logical step of treating an erroneous *failure* to certify a class in the same way.

5.   **The Named Plaintiff's Interest.** Understand that in the absence of a formally certified class, the named plaintiff in *Geraghty* could not rely on

his interest in obtaining a favorable decision on the merits (he had none remaining) but, instead, rested on his procedural interest under F. R. Civ. P. 23 to seek appellate review of the class-certification issue. Was that persuasive? Compare the Court's treatment of standing to advance procedural claims. In any event, the result here is attractive, isn't it, inasmuch as it keeps class action cases in court until there is an authoritative determination of the certification issue, one way or the other?

CHAPTER 5

THE ELEVENTH AMENDMENT AND STATE IMMUNITY FROM SUIT

■ ■ ■

I.   BACKGROUND PRINCIPLES

The first major Supreme Court decision was also the first to be overturned by constitutional amendment. The case, *Chisholm v. Georgia*, 2 U.S. (2 Dall.) 419 (1793), was a contract action brought by the estate of Robert Farquhar, a South Carolina merchant, against Georgia for monies owed for supplies the state purchased from the decedent during the Revolutionary War. The issue in the case was whether the states should be immune from suits brought by private individuals in federal court. It is an issue that, as we shall soon see, continues to confound the Court.

The plaintiff in *Chisholm* sued Georgia directly in the United States Supreme Court, invoking the Court's original jurisdiction. Georgia, however, did not appear in the action, claiming that it was protected from suits brought by individual citizens under the defense of sovereign immunity, a common law doctrine holding that sovereign entities could not be sued without their consent. In a 4–1 decision, the Supreme Court rejected the sovereign immunity claim.

As was the custom of the day, each of the five justices wrote a separate opinion. Chief Justice John Jay and Justice James Wilson directly rejected the state's immunity defense, contending that the notion of sovereign immunity was inconsistent with the constitutional system that vested sovereignty in the people and not in the government. Justice Wilson also went on to argue that susceptibility of states to suits by individuals was intended by the Constitution and that failure to subject the states to suit would make constitutional provisions such as the Contract Clause essentially meaningless. Justices John Rutledge and John Blair wrote more narrowly, contending that the Court's power to hear the case was plainly based on the language of Article III conferring jurisdiction between a State and citizens of another State. All four Justices in the majority also argued that Georgia's contention that states could not be sued in federal court was completely inconsistent with the grant in Article III of federal court jurisdiction over controversies between two or more states. As Chief Justice Jay explained, this jurisdictional grant made "plain then, that a State may be sued, and hence it plainly follows, that suability and state sovereignty are not incompatible."

Justice James Iredell's dissent was narrow. Noting that congressional authorization was necessary for the Court to exercise jurisdiction, Iredell claimed that he could not find a statutory basis to exercise jurisdiction over citizen-state actions in the Judiciary Act of 1789. Nevertheless, Justice Iredell's reading of the Judiciary Act brought him to the heart of the immunity issue. Because he believed that the jurisdictional grants contained in the Judiciary Act must be interpreted in accordance with common law principles, he was obliged to review the Judiciary Act against the common law background that states could not be sued without their consent. On this basis, he concluded that the Judiciary Act did not confer jurisdiction in citizen-state suits. Significantly, however, Justice Iredell reserved judgment on whether states could ever be subject to suits in federal court.

The Court's decision in *Chisholm*, to say the least, was not well received. The states saw the decision as both an assault on their sovereignty and a serious threat to their treasuries that were still in precarious positions as a result of debt burdens stemming from the Revolution. 1 C. Warren, THE SUPREME COURT IN UNITED STATES HISTORY 96–100 (2d 1926). But see CLYDE E. JACOBS, THE ELEVENTH AMENDMENT AND SOVEREIGN IMMUNITY 67–74 (1972) (arguing that the states were relatively solvent by 1794). Accordingly, their reaction to *Chisholm* was angry and immediate. (One of the houses of the Georgia legislature even passed a bill mandating that any federal marshal attempting to enforce the *Chisholm* judgment would "suffer death, without benefit of the clergy, by being hanged.") See JACOBS at 57 (quoting *The Augusta Chronicle*, Nov. 23, 1793). The reaction in Congress was equally vehement and a resolution was immediately introduced to overturn the decision by constitutional amendment. The Eleventh Amendment was quickly drafted, passed by Congress with overwhelming bi-partisan support, and subsequently ratified by the states. It provides that the "[t]he Judicial power of the United States shall not be construed to extend to any suit in law or equity, commenced or prosecuted against one of the United States by Citizens of another State, or by Citizens or Subjects of any Foreign State."

The question of state susceptibility to suit in federal court, however, did not end with the adoption of the Eleventh Amendment. Perhaps because it was passed in haste and its language not fully thought out, the amendment has proved to be inordinately clumsy in addressing numerous immunity issues. The text, for example, mentions only suits brought against states by out-of-state citizens and not suits brought by the states' own citizens. Are states immune from suits brought by in-state citizens as well? And how would the Eleventh Amendment affect constitutional provisions, such as the Contracts Clause, that imposed direct legal constraints against the states? Would Justice Wilson's concern prove true that granting the states immunity would make such constitutional provisions virtually meaningless? Or would the constitutional provisions binding the states be somehow reconciled with the grant of state immunity? These issues, and others, would keep the courts involved in state immunity issues for the next two centuries. They would also lead to the development of a body of law that, for many, can be explained only as inexplicable.

HANS V. LOUISIANA
134 U.S. 1 (1890).

JUSTICE BRADLEY delivered the opinion of the Court

This was an action brought in the Circuit Court of the United States, in December, 1884, against the State of Louisiana by Bernard Hans, a citizen of that State, to recover the amount of certain coupons annexed to bonds of the State, issued under the provisions of an act of the legislature approved January 24, 1874. [Hans' claim was that the state's failure to honor its obligations under the bond agreement violated the Contracts Clause of the United States Constitution, U.S. Const. Art. 1, § 10.]

The question is presented, whether a State can be sued in a Circuit Court of the United States by one of its own citizens upon a suggestion that the case is one that arises under the Constitution or laws of the United States.

In the present case the plaintiff in error contends that he, being a citizen of Louisiana, is not embarrassed by the obstacle of the Eleventh Amendment, inasmuch as that amendment only prohibits suits against a State which are brought by the citizens of another State, or by citizens or subjects of a foreign State. It is true, the amendment does so read: and if there were no other reason or ground for abating his suit, it might be maintainable; and then we should have this anomalous result, that in cases arising under the Constitution or laws of the United States, a State may be sued in the federal courts by its own citizens, though it cannot be sued for a like cause of action by the citizens of other States, or of a foreign state; and may be thus sued in the federal courts, although not allowing itself to be sued in its own courts. If this is the necessary consequence of the language of the Constitution and the law, the result is no less startling and unexpected than was the original decision of this court, that under the language of the Constitution and of the Judiciary Act of 1789, a State was liable to be sued by a citizen of another State, or of a foreign country. That decision was made in the case of *Chisholm v. Georgia*, 2 Dall. 419, and created such a shock of surprise throughout the country that, at the first meeting of Congress thereafter, the Eleventh

Amendment to the Constitution was almost unanimously proposed, and was in due course adopted by the legislatures of the States. This amendment, expressing the will of the ultimate sovereignty of the whole country, superior to all legislatures and all courts, actually reversed the decision of the Supreme Court. It did not in terms prohibit suits by individuals against the States, but declared that the Constitution should not be construed to import any power to authorize the bringing of such suits.

This view of the force and meaning of the amendment is important. It shows that, on this question of the suability of the States by individuals, the highest authority of this country was in accord rather with the minority than with the majority of the court in the decision of the case of *Chisholm v. Georgia*; and this fact lends additional interest to the able opinion of Mr. Justice Iredell on that occasion. The other justices were more swayed by a close observance of the letter of the Constitution, without regard to former experience and usage; and because the letter said that the judicial power shall extend to controversies "between a State and citizens of another State;" and "between a State and foreign states, citizens or subjects," they felt constrained to see in this language a power to enable the individual citizens of one State, or of a foreign state, to sue another State of the Union in the federal courts. Justice Iredell, on the contrary, contended that it was not the intention to create new and unheard of remedies, by subjecting sovereign States to actions at the suit of individuals, (which he conclusively showed was never done before,) but only, by proper legislation, to invest the federal courts with jurisdiction to hear and determine controversies and cases, between the parties designated, that were properly susceptible of litigation in courts. Looking back from our present standpoint at the decision in *Chisholm v. Georgia*, we do not greatly wonder at the effect which it had upon the country. Any such power as that of authorizing the federal judiciary to entertain suits by individuals against the States, had been expressly disclaimed, and even resented, by the great defenders of the Constitution whilst it was on its trial before the American people.

* * *

It seems to us that these views of those great advocates and defenders of the Constitution were most sensible and just; and they apply equally to the present case as to that then under discussion. The letter is appealed to now, as it was then, as a ground for sustaining a suit brought by an individual against a State. The reason against it is as strong in this case as it was in that. It is an attempt to strain the Constitution and the law to a construction never imagined or dreamed of. Can we suppose that, when the Eleventh Amendment was adopted, it was understood to be left open for citizens of a State to sue their own state in the federal courts, whilst the idea of suits by citizens of other states, or of foreign states, was indignantly repelled? Suppose that Congress, when proposing the Eleventh Amendment, had appended to it a proviso that nothing therein contained should prevent a State from being sued by its own citizens in cases arising under the Constitution or laws of the United States: can we imagine that it would have been adopted by the States? The supposition that it would is almost an absurdity on its face.

The suability of a State without its consent was a thing unknown to the law. This has been so often laid down and acknowledged by courts and jurists that it is hardly necessary to be formally asserted. It was fully shown by an exhaustive examination of the old law by Mr. Justice Iredell in his opinion in *Chisholm v. Georgia*; and it has been conceded in every case since, where the question has, in any way been presented, even in the cases which have gone farthest in sustaining suits against the officers or agents of States. *Osborn v. Bank of the United States*, 22 U.S. (9 Wheat.) 738 (1824).

But besides the presumption that no anomalous and unheard-of proceedings or suits were intended to be raised up by the Constitution— anomalous and unheard of when the Constitution was adopted—an additional reason why the jurisdiction claimed for the Circuit Court does not exist, is the language of the act of Congress by which its jurisdiction is conferred. The words are these: "The circuit courts of the United States shall have original cognizance, concurrent with the courts of the several States, of all suits of a civil nature at common law or in equity, . . . arising under the Constitution or laws of the United States, or treaties," etc.— "Concurrent with the courts of the several States." Does not this qualification show that Congress, in legislating to carry the Constitution into effect, did not intend to invest its courts with any new and strange jurisdictions? The state courts have no power to entertain suits by individuals against a State without its consent. Then how does the Circuit Court, having only concurrent jurisdiction, acquire any such power? It is true that the same qualification existed in the Judiciary Act of 1789, which was before the court in *Chisholm v. Georgia*, and the majority of the court did not think that it was sufficient to limit the jurisdiction of the Circuit Court. Justice Iredell thought differently. In view of the manner in which that decision was received by the country, the adoption of the Eleventh Amendment, the light of history and the reason of the thing, we think we are at liberty to prefer Justice Iredell's views in this regard.

To avoid misapprehension it may be proper to add that, although the obligations of a State rest for their performance upon its honor and good faith, and cannot be made the subjects of judicial cognizance unless the State consents to be sued, or comes itself into court; yet where property or rights are enjoyed under a grant or contract made by a State, they cannot wantonly be invaded. Whilst the State cannot be compelled by suit to perform its contracts, any attempt on its part to violate property or rights acquired under its contracts, may be judicially resisted; and any law impairing the obligation of contracts under which such property or rights are held is void and powerless to affect their enjoyment.

It is not necessary that we should enter upon an examination of the reason or expediency of the rule which exempts a sovereign State from prosecution in a court of justice at the suit of individuals. This is fully discussed by writers on public law. It is enough for us to declare its existence. The legislative department of a State represents its polity and its will; and is called upon by the highest demands of natural and political law to preserve justice and judgment, and to hold inviolate the public obligations. Any departure from this rule, except for reasons most cogent, (of which the legislature, and not the courts, is the judge,) never fails in the end to incur the odium of the world, and to bring lasting injury upon the State itself. But to deprive the legislature of the power of judging what the honor and safety of the State may require, even at the expense of a temporary failure to discharge the public debts, would be attended with greater evils than such failure can cause.

The judgment of the circuit court is affirmed.

NOTES ON HANS AND STATE SOVEREIGN IMMUNITY

1. **Sovereign Immunity.** The common law doctrine of sovereign immunity dates back to at least the twelfth century, during which time it was clear that the King could not be sued in his own name. MELVYN R. DURCHSLAG, STATE SOVEREIGN IMMUNITY 3 (2002). Although often said to derive from the proposition that the King can do no wrong, the concept may be better understood, not as a claim to sovereign infallibility, but as standing for the practical proposition that one cannot enforce a right against the state unless the state agrees to such enforcement. As Justice Holmes wrote, "[a] sovereign is exempt from suit, not because of any formal conception or obsolete theory, but on the logical and practical ground that there can be no legal right as against the authority that makes the law on which the right depends." *Kawananakoa v. Polyblank*, 205 U.S. 349, 353 (1907).

2. **Federal Government Immunity.** Although there has been considerable debate as to whether the states should enjoy the protections of sovereign immunity, the immunity of the United States has not been seriously questioned. Thus, in *Cohens v. Virginia*, 19 U.S. (6 Wheat.) 264 (1821), Chief Justice John Marshall wrote, "the universally received opinion is that no suit can be commenced or prosecuted against the United States." *Id.* at 411. The immunity enjoyed by the federal government, moreover, extends to suits brought by the states against the United States, see *Kansas v. United States*, 204 U.S. 331 (1907), although the states are not immune from actions brought by the federal government, *United States v. Mississippi*, 380 U.S. 128 (1965). Are there reasons that support subjecting the states to

suits by individuals while continuing to immunize the federal government from such claims?

Despite the Court's longstanding commitment to protecting the sovereign immunity of the United States, there is at least one notable case where the Court was significantly less than vigorous in its efforts. In *United States v. Lee*, 106 U.S. 196 (1882), the Court was faced with an ejectment action brought by the descendants of Robert E. Lee against two federal officers in a dispute over the ownership of land in Alexandria, Virginia. Rejecting the sovereign immunity defense, the Court construed the action to be one against the federal officials and not one against the United States although obviously the relief in question would be executed against the Federal Government. (Indeed, the Court has since been clear in indicating that similar actions against a state to quiet title trigger a state's immunity defense. *Florida Dept. of State v. Treasure Salvors, Inc.*, 458 U.S. 670 (1982); *Idaho v. Coeur d'Alene Tribe of Idaho*, 521 U.S. 261 (1997).) *Lee* remains significant as an early case in the development of the principle that both federal and state officials may be sued for prospective relief on federal constitutional and statutory grounds. See *Ex parte Young*, infra.

The sovereign immunity of the United States does not mean that it may never be sued. By statute the Government has given up much of its immunity. The Federal Tort Claims Act, 28 U.S.C. § 1346(b), for example, authorizes suits for many ordinary torts committed by officers, and the Tucker Act, 28 U.S.C. §§ 1346(a)(2), 1491(a)(1), gives up immunity for breach of contract claims.

3. **Suits Brought by Sister States.** The Eleventh Amendment does not usually protect states from suits brought by sister states, see, e.g., *Rhode Island v. Massachusetts*, 37 U.S. (12 Pet.) 657 (1838); *Colorado v. New Mexico*, 459 U.S. 176 (1982), and indeed, Article III vests original jurisdiction in such matters in the United States Supreme Court. On the other hand, suits brought by one state against another are barred when the action is one brought by a state for debts owed its citizens. See *New Hampshire v. Louisiana*, 108 U.S. 76 (1883). States are also protected from suits brought by foreign countries. See *Principality of Monaco v. Mississippi*, 292 U.S. 313 (1934).

4. **Local Government Immunity.** In *Lincoln County v. Luning*, 133 U.S. 529 (1890), the Court held that cities, counties, and local agencies do not enjoy the immunity afforded to the states in *Hans*. Notably, *Lincoln County* was decided the same day as *Hans*. Does the Court's distinction between states and local governments make sense given that local government entities are entirely creatures of the state? Are there reasons for treating local government entities differently from states for immunity purposes? *Lincoln County* remains good law even as state immunity in other areas has expanded. See *Mt. Healthy Board of Education v. Doyle*, 429 U.S. 274 (1977). The Court has also indicated that multi-state agencies are not immune from suit unless they are deliberately structured to enjoy the constitutional

protections of the states themselves. *Hess v. Port Authority Trans-Hudson Corp.,* 513 U.S. 30 (1994).

5.   The Eleventh Amendment and the Marshall Court. The Marshall Court did not read the Eleventh Amendment expansively. In *Cohens v. Virginia,* 19 U.S. (6 Wheat.) 264 (1821), for example, Chief Justice Marshall held that the Eleventh Amendment did not bar an appeal to the United States Supreme Court brought by a state court defendant against the state that had originally prosecuted the action in state court. As Marshall explained, such an appeal could "with no propriety, we think, be denominated a suit commenced or prosecuted against the State whose judgment is so far re-examined." Two separate concerns were critical to Marshall's reasoning. First, the appeal did not seek any relief against the state other than to reverse the state court judgment. Second, the availability of appeal to the United States Supreme Court from a state court judgment was necessary to preserve federal law. If such appeals were barred, after all, the erroneous federal law decisions of the state courts could not be overturned.

Marshall also rejected an Eleventh Amendment defense in the important case of *Osborn v. Bank of the United States,* 22 U.S. (9 Wheat.) 738 (1824). In *Osborn,* the Bank of the United States sued state officers to recover monies they had seized from a federal bank office in their execution of an unconstitutional tax. Holding that the action was one against the officers and not the state (even though "the direct interest of the state in the suit, as brought, is admitted"), Marshall found that state immunity was not violated.

The only case in which the Marshall Court upheld an Eleventh Amendment challenge to federal jurisdiction was *Governor of Georgia v. Madrazo,* 26 U.S. (1 Pet.) 110 (1828). The case arose when Georgia seized a number of slaves from Madrazo, purportedly because the slaves had been illegally brought into the country. In response, Madrazo brought an admiralty action against the state's governor seeking both the return of the slaves still remaining in the state's custody and the proceeds from the sales of the slaves that had already been sold. Although *Madrazo,* like *Osborn,* was brought only against a state officer and did not name the state, Marshall nevertheless construed the state to be the real party in interest and, on this basis, found the action barred. *Osborn* was cited but not clearly distinguished. We shall revisit subsequently the question of when suits against state officers should be treated as actions against the state.

6.   The Constitutional Basis of *Hans*. What is the basis of the *Hans* decision? Is *Hans* an Eleventh Amendment case? Is the decision based on common law? Is it based on an assertion that Article III did not authorize individual suits against the states in the first place? Is the Court relying on general non-textual principles of federalism or state sovereignty in reaching its result? Does it make a difference?

7.   Should *Hans* Be Overruled?: The Diversity Theory of the Eleventh Amendment. In *Atascadero State Hospital v. Scanlon,* 473 U.S. 234 (1985), Justice Brennan, writing in dissent, argued that *Hans* should be overruled on the grounds that the Eleventh Amendment was intended to bar only diversity cases and was not intended to prohibit actions against the states based on federal law. This argument has subsequently become known as the "diversity theory" of the Eleventh Amendment. Brennan's dissent raised two major arguments in its support. The first is that since *Chisholm* was a diversity case and the Eleventh Amendment was enacted as a response to *Chisholm*, the provision should be understood primarily in this context. The second is that the states should be deemed to have consented to suit for violations of federal law on the basis of the so-called "plan of the convention," meaning that when they joined the Union they thereby consented to be subject to federal law. The diversity theory has enjoyed significant scholarly support. *See* William Fletcher, *A Historical Interpretation of the Eleventh Amendment: A Narrow Construction of an Affirmative Grant of Jurisdiction Rather than a Prohibition Against Jurisdiction*, 35 STAN L. REV. 1033 (1983); John Gibbons, *The Eleventh Amendment and State Sovereign Immunity: A Reinterpretation*, 83 COLUM. L. REV. 1889 (1983); Akhil Amar, *Of Sovereignty and Federalism,* 96 YALE L. J. 1425 (1987). But see William P. Marshall*, The Diversity Theory of the Eleventh Amendment*, 102 HARV. L. REV. 1372 (1989).

EX PARTE YOUNG
209 U.S. 123 (1908).

[Citizens of Minnesota instituted shareholders' derivative suits in federal court challenging a Minnesota statute establishing maximum railroad rates, claiming that the statute violated their Fourteenth Amendment rights. The plaintiffs also joined the Minnesota Attorney General and sought that he be restrained from seeking to enforce the statute. After the federal court issued a preliminary injunction granting the plaintiffs' requested relief, the Attorney General brought suit in state court for a writ of mandamus against the railroads to compel them to comply with the law. In response to this action, the federal court cited the Attorney General for contempt and ordered him arrested. The Attorney General then made an original application to the United States Supreme Court for leave to file a petition for writs of habeas corpus and certiorari.]

JUSTICE PECKHAM delivered the opinion of the Court.

We have [upon] this record the case of an unconstitutional act of the state legislature and an intention by the Attorney General of the State to endeavor to enforce its provisions, to the injury of the company, in compelling it, at great expense, to defend legal proceedings of a complicated and unusual character, and involving questions of vast importance to all employees and officers of the company, as well as to the company itself. The question that arises is whether there is a remedy that the parties interested may resort to, by going into a Federal court of equity, in a case involving a violation of the Federal Constitution, and obtaining a judicial investigation of the problem, and pending its solution obtain freedom from suits, civil or criminal, by a temporary injunction, and if the question be finally decided favorably to the contention of the company, a permanent injunction restraining all such actions or proceedings.

This inquiry necessitates an examination of the most material and important objection made to the jurisdiction of the Circuit Court, the objection being that the suit is, in effect, one against the State of Minnesota, and that the injunction issued against the Attorney General illegally prohibits state action, either criminal or civil, to enforce obedience to the statutes of the State. This objection is to be considered with reference to the Eleventh and Fourteenth Amendments to the Federal Constitution. The Eleventh Amendment prohibits the commencement or prosecution of any suit against one of the United States by citizens of another State or citizens or subjects of any foreign State. The Fourteenth Amendment provides that no State shall deprive any person of life, liberty or property without due process of law, nor shall it deny to any person within its jurisdiction the equal protection of the laws.

The case before the Circuit Court proceeded upon the theory that the orders and acts heretofore mentioned would, if enforced, violate rights of the complainants protected by the latter Amendment. We think that whatever the rights of complainants may be, they are largely founded upon that Amendment, but a decision of this case does not require an examination or decision of the question whether its adoption in any way altered or limited the effect of the earlier Amendment. We may assume that each exists in full force, and that we must give to the Eleventh Amendment all the effect it naturally would have, without cutting it down or rendering its meaning any more narrow than the language, fairly interpreted, would warrant. It applies to a suit brought against a State by one of its own citizens as well as to a suit brought by a citizen of another State. *Hans v. Louisiana*, 134 U.S. 1. It was adopted after the decision of this court in *Chisholm v. Georgia* (1793), 2 Dall. 419, where it was held that a State might be sued by a citizen of another State. Since that time there have been many cases decided in this court involving the Eleventh Amendment, among them being *Osborn v. Bank of the United States*, which held that the Amendment applied only to those suits in which the State was a party on the record. In the subsequent case of *Governor of Georgia v. Madrazo* (1828), 1 Pet. 110, 122, 123, that holding was somewhat enlarged, and Chief Justice Marshall, delivering the opinion of the court, while citing *Osborn*, supra, said that where the claim was made, as in the case then before the court, against the Governor of Georgia as governor, and the demand was made upon him, not personally, but officially (for moneys in the treasury of the State and for slaves in possession of the state government), the State might be considered as the party on the record, and therefore the suit could not be maintained.

In *Smyth v. Ames*, 169 U.S. 466, it was again held that a suit against individuals, for the purpose of preventing them, as officers of the State, from enforcing, by the commencement of suits or by indictment, an unconstitutional enactment to the injury of the rights of the plaintiff, was not a suit against a State within the meaning of the Amendment. [I]n answer to the objection that the suit was really against the State, it was said: "It is the settled doctrine of this court that a suit against individuals for the purpose of preventing them as officers of a State from enforcing an unconstitutional enactment to the injury of the rights of the plaintiff, is not a suit against the State within the meaning of that Amendment."

The various authorities we have referred to furnish ample justification for the assertion that individuals, who, as officers of the State, are clothed with some duty in regard to the enforcement of the laws of the State, and who threaten and are about to commence proceedings, either of a civil or criminal nature, to enforce against parties affected an unconstitutional act, violating the Federal Constitution, may be enjoined by a Federal court of equity from such action.

It is also argued that the only proceeding which the Attorney General could take to enforce the statute, so far as his office is concerned, was one by mandamus, which would be commenced by the State in its sovereign and governmental character, and that the right to bring such action is a necessary attribute of a sovereign government. It is contended that the complainants do not complain and they care nothing about any action which Mr. Young might take or bring as an ordinary individual, but that he was complained of as an officer, to whose discretion is confided the use of the name of the State of Minnesota so far as litigation is concerned, and that when or how he shall use it is a matter resting in his discretion and cannot be controlled by any court.

The answer to all this is the same as made in every case where an official claims to be acting under the authority of the State. The act to be enforced is alleged to be unconstitutional, and if it be so, the use of the name of the State to enforce an unconstitutional act to the injury of complainants is a proceeding without the authority of and one which does not affect the State in its sovereign or governmental capacity. It is simply an illegal act upon the part of a state official in attempting by the use of the name of the State to enforce a legislative enactment which is void because unconstitutional. If the act which the state Attorney General seeks to enforce be a violation of the Federal Constitution, the officer in proceeding under such enactment comes into conflict with the superior authority of that Constitution, and he is in that case stripped of his official or representative character and is subjected in his person to the consequences of his individual conduct. The State has no power to impart to him any immunity from responsibility to the supreme authority of the United States. It would be an injury to complainant to harass it with a multiplicity of suits or litigation generally in an endeavor to enforce penalties under an unconstitutional enactment, and to prevent it ought to be within the jurisdiction of a court of equity. If the question of unconstitutionality with reference, at least, to the Federal Constitution be first raised in a Federal court that court, as we think is shown by the authorities cited hereafter, has the right to decide it to the exclusion of all other courts.

It is further objected that there is a plain and adequate remedy at law open to the complainants and that a court of equity, therefore, has no jurisdiction in such case. It has been suggested that the proper way to test the constitutionality of the act is to disobey it, at least once, after which the company might obey the act pending subsequent proceedings to test its validity. But in the event of a single violation the prosecutor might not avail himself of the opportunity to make the test, as obedience to the law was thereafter continued, and he might think it unnecessary to start an inquiry. If, however, he should do so while the company was thereafter obeying the law, several years might elapse before there was a final determination of the question, and if it should be determined that the law was invalid the property of the company would have been taken during that time without due process of law, and there would be no possibility of its recovery.

Another obstacle to making the test on the part of the company might be to find an agent or employee who would disobey the law, with a possible fine and imprisonment staring him in the face if the act should be held valid. Take the passenger rate act, for instance: A sale of a single ticket above the price mentioned in that act might subject the ticket agent to a charge of felony, and upon conviction to a fine of five thousand dollars and imprisonment for five years. It is true the company might pay the fine, but the imprisonment the agent would have to suffer personally. It would not be wonderful if, under such circumstances, there would not be a crowd of agents offering to disobey the law. The wonder would be that a single agent should be found ready to take the risk.

We do not say the company could not interpose [the unconstitutionality of the state law as a] defense in an action to recover penalties or upon the trial of an indictment, but the facility of proving it in either case falls so far below that which would obtain in a court of equity that comparison is scarcely possible.

To await proceedings against the company in a state court grounded upon a disobedience of the act, and then, if necessary, obtain a review in this court by writ of error to the highest state court, would place the company in peril of large loss and its agents in great risk of fines and imprisonment if it should be finally determined that the act was valid. This risk the company ought not to be required to take.

All the objections to a remedy at law as being plainly inadequate are obviated by a suit in equity, making all who are directly interested parties to the suit, and enjoining the enforcement of the act until the decision of the court upon the legal question.

Finally it is objected that the necessary result of upholding this suit in the Circuit Court will be to draw to the lower Federal courts a great flood of litigation of this character, where one Federal judge would have it in his power to enjoin proceedings by state officials to enforce the legislative acts of the State, either by criminal or civil actions. To this it may be answered, in the first place, that no injunction ought to be granted unless in a case reasonably free from doubt. We think such rule is, and will be, followed by all the judges of the Federal courts.

And, again, it must be remembered that jurisdiction of this general character has, in fact, been exercised by Federal courts from the time of *Osborn v. United States Bank* up to the present; the only difference in regard to the case of *Osborn* and the case in hand being that in this case the injury complained of is the threatened commencement of suits, civil or criminal, to enforce the act, instead of, as in the *Osborn* case, an actual and direct trespass upon or interference with tangible property. A bill filed to prevent the commencement of suits to enforce an unconstitutional act, under the circumstances already mentioned, is no new invention, as we have already seen. The difference between an actual and direct interference with tangible property and the enjoining of state officers from enforcing an unconstitutional act, is not of a radical nature, and does not extend, in truth, the jurisdiction of the courts over the subject matter. In the case of the interference with property the person enjoined is assuming to act in his capacity as an official of the State, and justification for his interference is claimed by reason of his position as a state official. Such official cannot so justify when acting under an unconstitutional enactment of the legislature. So, where the state official, instead of directly interfering with tangible property, is about to commence suits, which have for their object the enforcement of an act which violates the Federal Constitution, to the great and irreparable injury of the complainants, he is seeking the same justification from the authority of the State as in other cases. The sovereignty of the State is, in reality, no more involved in one case than in the other. The State cannot in either case impart to the official immunity from responsibility to the supreme authority of the United States. See *In re Ayers*, 123 U.S. 507.

This supreme authority, which arises from the specific provisions of the Constitution itself, is nowhere more fully illustrated than in the series of decisions under the Federal *habeas corpus* statute (§ 753, Rev. Stat.), in some of which cases persons in the custody of state officers for alleged crimes against the State have been taken from that custody and discharged by a Federal court or judge, because the imprisonment was adjudged to be in violation of the Federal Constitution. The right to so discharge has not been doubted by this court, and it has never been supposed there was any suit against the State by reason of serving the writ upon one of the officers of the State in whose custody the person was found. In some of the cases the writ has been refused as a matter of discretion, but in others it has been granted, while the power has been fully recognized in all.

It is somewhat difficult to appreciate the distinction which, while admitting that the taking of such a person from the custody of the State by virtue of service of the writ on the state officer in whose custody he is found, is not a suit against the State, and yet service of a writ on the Attorney General to prevent his enforcing an unconstitutional enactment of a state legislature is a suit against the State.

There is nothing in the case before us that ought properly to breed hostility to the customary operation of Federal courts of justice in cases of this character.

The rule to show cause is discharged and the petition for writs of *habeas corpus* and certiorari is dismissed.

JUSTICE HARLAN, dissenting.

[It] would [seem] clear that within the true meaning of the Eleventh Amendment the suit brought in the Federal court was one, in legal effect, against the State—as much so as if the State had been formally named on the record as a party—and therefore it was a suit to which, under the Amendment, so far as the State or its Attorney General was concerned, the judicial power of the United States did not and could not extend. If this proposition be sound it will follow—indeed, it is conceded that if, so far as relief is sought against the Attorney General of Minnesota, this be a suit against the State—then the order of the Federal court enjoining that officer from taking any action, suit, step or proceeding to compel the railway company to obey the Minnesota statute was beyond the jurisdiction of that court and wholly void; in which case, that officer was at liberty to proceed in the discharge of his official duties as defined by the laws of the State, and the order adjudging him to be in contempt for bringing the mandamus proceeding in the state court was a nullity.

The fact that the Federal Circuit Court had, prior to the institution of the mandamus suit in the state court, preliminarily (but not finally) held the statutes of Minnesota and the orders of its Railroad and Warehouse Commission in question to be in violation of the Constitution of the United States, was no reason why that court should have laid violent hands upon the Attorney General of Minnesota and by its orders have deprived the State of the services of its constitutional law officer in its own courts.

This principle, if firmly established, would work a radical change in our governmental system. It would inaugurate a new era in the American judicial system and in the relations of the National and state governments. It would enable the subordinate Federal courts to supervise and control the official action of the States as if they were "dependencies" or provinces. It would place the States of the Union in a condition of inferiority never dreamed of when the Constitution was adopted or when the Eleventh Amendment was made a part of the Supreme Law of the Land. I cannot suppose that the great men who framed the Constitution ever thought the time would come when a subordinate Federal court, having no power to compel a State, in its corporate capacity, to appear before it as a litigant, would yet assume to deprive a State of the right to be represented in its own courts by its regular law officer. That is what the court below did, as to Minnesota, when it adjudged that the appearance of the defendant Young *in the state court*, as the Attorney General of Minnesota, representing his State as its chief law officer, was a contempt of the authority of the Federal court, punishable by fine and imprisonment. Too little consequence has been attached to the fact that the courts of the States are under an obligation equally strong with that resting upon the courts of the Union to respect and enforce the provisions of the Federal Constitution as the Supreme Law of the Land, and to guard rights secured or guaranteed by that instrument. We must assume—a decent respect for the States requires us to assume—that the state courts will enforce every right secured by the Constitution. If they fail to do so, the party complaining has a clear remedy for the protection of his rights; for, he can come by writ of error, in an orderly, judicial way, from the highest court of the State to this tribunal for redress in respect of every right granted or secured by that instrument and denied by the state court.

NOTES ON EX PARTE YOUNG

1. The *Ex parte Young* Fiction. The notion that Attorney General Young should be deemed "stripped" of his authority on grounds that he is a defendant in a suit alleging that a statute that he is empowered to enforce is unconstitutional is of course nonsensical. The plaintiffs were suing Young to prevent him from enforcing a state statute, and if he had no official status, he would have had no authority to enforce the law in the first place. As Justice Harlan exhorted in dissent, the suit was brought against Young "*only* because he was Attorney General of Minnesota." Moreover, if the "stripped" language were taken literally there might not be the requisite state action necessary to support a constitutional claim. Finally, recall that all that is required under *Young* in order to strip the state official of his official authority is that the plaintiff *alleges* that the statute is unconstitutional. Whether the statute actually is unconstitutional is a merits issue that will be decided only after the federal court takes jurisdiction. Nevertheless, the *Ex parte Young* "fiction," as it has subsequently become known, has been defended on policy grounds as being necessary for upholding the Constitution. As one noted scholar has argued, "the doctrine of *Ex parte Young* seems indispensable to the establishment of constitutional government and the rule of law." CHARLES ALAN WRIGHT, LAW OF FEDERAL COURTS 292 (4th ed. 1983). But why is this so? Couldn't the railroads have waited until the state, per Attorney General Young, sued them for violating the state statute?

2. ***Young* in Historical Perspective.** *Ex parte Young* was decided during the *Lochner* era when courts were striking down state social and economic legislation on substantive due process grounds. *Young* was critical to this effort because it provided the procedural mechanism through which the constitutional attacks could be maintained. The *Young* decision itself triggered substantial political fallout both locally and nationally. The House of Representatives, in fact, passed a bill that would have removed from the federal courts the power to enjoin state enforcement actions, but the bill did not pass the Senate.

3. ***Coeur d'Alene* and the Continuing Validity of *Young*.** Although *Young* remains good law, its viability was seriously tested in *Idaho v. Coeur d'Alene Tribe of Idaho*, 521 U.S. 261 (1997). *Coeur d'Alene* involved a suit by the Coeur d'Alene Tribe against the state of Idaho claiming that certain submerged lands belonged to the Tribe and not the state. Relying on *Ex parte Young*, the lower court found that the Eleventh Amendment did not bar the Tribe's claim for injunctive and declaratory relief that would have prevented the state from interfering with the Tribe's ownership rights. In a 5–4 decision, the Court reversed, holding that the state was immune from the forms of injunctive and declaratory relief sought by the plaintiffs. This holding in and of itself was not a major development. The Court had previously ruled that actions against the state to quiet title were barred by state immunity and the relief sought in *Coeur d'Alene*, by prohibiting the state from exercising its rights of ownership, was effectively "the functional equivalent" of such an action. Moreover, the holding was also supported by the fact that state control over submerged lands under navigable waters had historically been considered a particularly integral and fundamental attribute of its sovereignty. As the Court explained, relief against the state that interferes with such an essential sovereign prerogative is "as fully as intrusive as almost any conceivable retroactive levy upon funds in its Treasury." For this reason, the Court's conclusion that *Young* was inapplicable might therefore be seen as a relatively modest decision standing only for some sort of public lands' exception to *Young*'s requirements.

Another part of Justice Kennedy's opinion, however, joined only by Chief Justice Rehnquist, was not so limited. Specifically, Kennedy and Rehnquist argued for what would amount to a general reworking of the *Young* formulation. Under their approach, the availability of prospective relief under *Young* would be decided on a case by case basis analyzing such factors "as whether a state forum is available to hear the dispute, what federal right is at issue, and whether there are special factors that counsel hesitation in the exercise of jurisdiction."

The seven other members of the Court, however, rejected this balancing approach. As Justice O'Connor wrote in her concurrence, "our decisions repeatedly have emphasized that the *Young* doctrine rests on the need to promote the vindication of federal rights. There is no need to call into question the importance of having federal courts interpret federal rights— particularly as a means of serving a federal interest in uniformity—to decide this case." Later the Court reaffirmed its commitment to the broad *Young* principle, for statutory as well as constitutional claims, in *Verizon Md., Inc. v. Public Service Comm'n*, 535 U.S. 635 (2002).

4. ***VOPA* and State Suit Against Itself.** The Court again adhered to *Young* in the highly unusual case of *Virginia Office for Protection and Advocacy v. Stewart* (*VOPA*), 563 U.S. ___, 131 S.Ct. 1632 (2011). In *VOPA*, a state agency charged with protecting and advocating for the rights of the disabled sued the certain state officials charged with operating state mental hospitals in federal court for violations of federal law. The Court of Appeals ruled that the action should be dismissed because it was essentially an "intramural contest" and subjecting states to federal court jurisdiction in these circumstances would encroach "more severely on the dignity and sovereignty of the states than an *Ex parte Young* action brought by a private plaintiff." The Supreme Court, in a 7–2 decision, reversed. According to Justice Scalia's majority opinion, all that was necessary in determining whether the *Ex parte Young* doctrine applied was the "straight-forward inquiry" into whether the complaint alleged an ongoing federal law violation and sought prospective relief. Since both elements were satisfied in the *VOPA* litigation, federal court jurisdiction was appropriate and the fact that the state was both the plaintiff and the defendant was of no matter. As Justice Scalia explained, "there is no warrant in our cases for making the validity of an *Ex parte Young* action turn on the identity of the plaintiff." Chief Justice Roberts, in an opinion joined by Justice Alito, dissented. To Roberts, extending *Young*'s "empty formalism" was not justified in light of the "special sovereignty interests" implicated in an action by one state entity against another.

5. **Historical Postscript.** Although *Ex parte Young* was brought on a petition for *habeas corpus*, Attorney General Edward Young was never incarcerated. Rather he was required to report daily to a United States Marshal, which he proceeded to do while at the same time continuing in his position as Attorney General. Young later ran for Governor claiming that the railroad, liquor, and timber interests in Minnesota would try to defeat him because he had prosecuted the state's laws against them. But although he was well received and had apparently benefitted from his role in the Supreme Court litigation, he did not earn his party's endorsement at its nominating

convention. For a fuller account of the *Young* litigation and its role in the development of constitutional law see RICHARD C. CORTNER, THE IRON HORSE AND THE CONSTITUTION: THE TRANSFORMATION OF THE FOURTEENTH AMENDMENT 176–77, 196–98 (1993).

II.   THE CURRENT CONSTITUTIONAL FRAMEWORK

EDELMAN V. JORDAN
415 U.S. 651 (1974).

JUSTICE REHNQUIST delivered the opinion of the Court.

Respondent John Jordan filed a complaint in the United States District Court for the Northern District of Illinois, individually and as a representative of a class, seeking declaratory and injunctive relief against two former directors of the Illinois Department of Public Aid, the director of the Cook County Department of Public Aid, and the comptroller of Cook County. Respondent alleged that these state officials were administering the federal-state programs of Aid to the Aged, Blind, or Disabled (AABD) in a manner inconsistent with various federal regulations and with the Fourteenth Amendment to the Constitution.

Respondent's complaint charged that the Illinois defendants, operating under those regulations, were improperly authorizing grants to commence only with the month in which an application was approved and not including prior eligibility months for which an applicant was entitled to aid under federal law. The complaint also alleged that the Illinois defendants were not processing the applications within the applicable time requirements of the federal regulations; specifically, respondent alleged that his own application for disability benefits was not acted on by the Illinois Department of Public Aid for almost four months. Such actions of the Illinois officials were alleged to violate federal law and deny the equal protection of the laws. Respondent's prayer requested declaratory and injunctive relief, and specifically requested "a permanent injunction enjoining the defendants to award to the entire class of plaintiffs all AABD benefits wrongfully withheld."

In its judgment of March 15, 1972, the District Court declared § 4004 of the Illinois Manual to be invalid insofar as it was inconsistent with the federal regulations, [and] granted a permanent injunction requiring compliance with the federal time limits for processing and paying AABD applicants. The District Court, in paragraph 5 of its judgment, also ordered the state officials to "release and remit AABD benefits wrongfully withheld to all applicants for AABD in the State of Illinois who applied between July 1, 1968 (the date of the federal regulations) and April 16,

197(1) (the date of the preliminary injunction issued by the District Court) and were determined eligible. . . ."

On appeal to the United States Court of Appeals for the Seventh Circuit, the Illinois officials contended, *inter alia*, that the Eleventh Amendment barred the award of retroactive benefits, that the judgment of inconsistency between the federal regulations and the provisions of the Illinois Categorical Assistance Manual could be given prospective effect only, and that the federal regulations in question were inconsistent with the Social Security Act itself. The Court of Appeals rejected these contentions and affirmed the judgment of the District Court.

[W]e reverse that portion of the Court of Appeals decision which affirmed the District Court's order that retroactive benefits be paid by the Illinois state officials.

While the [Eleventh] Amendment by its terms does not bar suits against a State by its own citizens, this Court has consistently held that an unconsenting State is immune from suits brought in federal courts by her own citizens as well as by citizens of another State. *Hans v. Louisiana; Parden v. Terminal R. Co.* It is also well established that even though a State is not named a party to the action, the suit may nonetheless be barred by the Eleventh Amendment. In *Ford Motor Co. v. Department of Treasury*, 323 U.S. 459 (1945), the Court said:

> "(W)hen the action is in essence one for the recovery of money from the state, the state is the real, substantial party in interest and is entitled to invoke its sovereign immunity from suit even though individual officials are nominal defendants."

Id. at 464. Thus the rule has evolved that a suit by private parties seeking to impose a liability which must be paid from public funds in the state treasury is barred by the Eleventh Amendment.

Petitioner concedes that *Ex parte Young,* supra, is no bar to that part of the District Court's judgment that prospectively enjoined petitioner's predecessors from failing to process applications within the time limits established by the federal regulations. Petitioner argues, however, that *Ex parte Young* does not extend so far as to permit a suit which seeks the award of an accrued monetary liability which must be met from the general revenues of a State, absent consent or waiver by the State of its Eleventh Amendment immunity, and that therefore the award of retroactive benefits by the District Court was improper.

Ex parte Young was a watershed case in which this Court held that the Eleventh Amendment did not bar an action in the federal courts seeking to enjoin the Attorney General of Minnesota from enforcing a statute claimed to violate the Fourteenth Amendment of the United States Constitution. This holding has permitted the Civil War

Amendments to the Constitution to serve as a sword, rather than merely as a shield, for those whom they were designed to protect. But the relief awarded in *Ex parte Young* was prospective only; the Attorney General of Minnesota was enjoined to conform his future conduct of that office to the requirement of the Fourteenth Amendment. Such relief is analogous to that awarded by the District Court in the prospective portion of its order under review in this case.

But the retroactive position of the District Court's order here, which requires the payment of a very substantial amount of money which that court held should have been paid, but was not, stands on quite a different footing. These funds will obviously not be paid out of the pocket of petitioner Edelman.

The Court of Appeals, in upholding the award in this case, held that it was permissible because it was in the form of 'equitable restitution' instead of damages, and therefore capable of being tailored in such a way as to minimize disruptions of the state program of categorical assistance. But we must judge the award actually made in this case, and not one which might have been differently tailored in a different case, and we must judge it in the context of the important constitutional principle embodied in the Eleventh Amendment.

As in most areas of the law, the difference between the type of relief barred by the Eleventh Amendment and that permitted under *Ex parte Young* will not in many instances be that between day and night. The injunction issued in *Ex parte Young* was not totally without effect on the State's revenues, since the state law which the Attorney General was enjoined from enforcing provided substantial monetary penalties against railroads which did not conform to its provisions. Later cases from this Court have authorized equitable relief which has probably had greater impact on state treasuries than did that awarded in *Ex parte Young*. In *Graham v. Richardson*, 403 U.S. 365 (1971), Arizona and Pennsylvania welfare officials were prohibited from denying welfare benefits to otherwise qualified recipients who were aliens. In *Goldberg v. Kelly*, 397 U.S. 254 (1970), New York City welfare officials were enjoined from following New York State procedures which authorized the termination of benefits paid to welfare recipients without prior hearing. But the fiscal consequences to state treasuries in these cases were the necessary result of compliance with decrees which by their terms were prospective in nature. State officials, in order to shape their official conduct to the mandate of the Court's decrees, would more likely have to spend money from the state treasury than if they had been left free to pursue their previous course of conduct. Such an ancillary effect on the state treasury is a permissible and often an inevitable consequence of the principle announced in *Ex parte Young,* supra.

But that portion of the District Court's decree which petitioner challenges on Eleventh Amendment grounds goes much further than any of the cases cited. It requires payment of state funds, not as a necessary consequence of compliance in the future with a substantive federal-question determination, but as a form of compensation to those whose applications were processed on the slower time schedule at a time when petitioner was under no court-imposed obligation to conform to a different standard. While the Court of Appeals described this retroactive award of monetary relief as a form of 'equitable restitution,' it is in practical effect indistinguishable in many aspects from an award of damages against the State. It will to a virtual certainty be paid from state funds, and not from the pockets of the individual state officials who were the defendants in the action. It is measured in terms of a monetary loss resulting from a past breach of a legal duty on the part of the defendant state officials.

Three fairly recent District Court judgments requiring state directors of public aid to make the type of retroactive payment involved here have been summarily affirmed by this Court notwithstanding Eleventh Amendment contentions made by state officers who were appealing from the District Court judgment. *Shapiro v. Thompson*, 394 U.S. 618 (1969), is the only instance in which the Eleventh Amendment objection to such retroactive relief was actually presented to this Court in a case which was orally argued. The three-judge District Court in that case had ordered the retroactive payment of welfare benefits found by that court to have been unlawfully withheld because of residence requirements held violative of equal protection. This Court, while affirming the judgment, did not in its opinion refer to or substantively treat the Eleventh Amendment argument. Nor, of course, did the summary dispositions of the three District Court cases contain any substantive discussion of this or any other issues raised by the parties.

This case, therefore, is the first opportunity the Court has taken to fully explore and treat the Eleventh Amendment aspects of such relief in a written opinion. *Shapiro v. Thompson* and these three summary affirmances obviously are of precedential value in support of the contention that the Eleventh Amendment does not bar the relief awarded by the District Court in this case. Equally obviously, they are not of the same precedential value as would be an opinion of this Court treating the question on the merits. Since we deal with a constitutional question, we are less constrained by the principle of *stare decisis* than we are in other areas of the law. Having now had an opportunity to more fully consider the Eleventh Amendment issue after briefing and argument, we disapprove the Eleventh Amendment holdings of those cases to the extent that they are inconsistent with our holding today.

Respondent [also] urges that since the various Illinois officials sued in the District Court failed to raise the Eleventh Amendment as a defense to the relief sought by respondent, petitioner is therefore barred from raising the Eleventh Amendment defense in the Court of Appeals or in this Court. The Court of Appeals apparently felt the defense was properly presented, and dealt with it on the merits. We approve of this resolution, since it has been well settled since the decision in *Ford Motor Co. v. Department of Treasury,* supra, that the Eleventh Amendment defense sufficiently partakes of the nature of a jurisdictional bar so that it need not be raised in the trial court.

Reversed and remanded.

NOTES ON EDELMAN AND THE RETROSPECTIVE/ PROSPECTIVE DISTINCTION

1. **Suits Against State Officers.** As noted previously, in *Osborn v. Bank of the United States*, 22 U.S. (9 Wheat.) 738 (1824), Chief Justice Marshall held that the Eleventh Amendment was not triggered when the Bank of the United States sued state officers to recover moneys improperly seized. Although Marshall conceded that the suit directly implicated the interests of the state, he found the fact that the case was brought only against state officers to be dispositive. In *Governor of Georgia v. Madrazo*, 26 U.S. (1 Pet.) 110 (1828), Marshall himself later retreated from the broadest implication of *Osborn*, i.e., that state immunity could be avoided merely by the expedience of suing a state officer rather than the state itself, when he ruled that an admiralty action brought in name against the governor seeking both specific and monetary relief resulting from the state's seizing the claimant's slaves should be construed as an action against the state. And by the time of *Young*, the rule was well established that suits against state officers would be deemed to be actions against the state for Eleventh Amendment purposes when the state was deemed to be the real party in interest. See *Ex parte Ayers*, 123 U.S. 443 (1887).

At the same time, as *Osborn* anticipated, state immunity does not bar suits for damages against state officials in their individual capacity. *Scheuer v. Rhodes*, 416 U.S. 232 (1974) (holding that damage suits against a governor are not barred by state immunity). But the question of whether the Eleventh Amendment bars relief depends on more than how the plaintiffs characterize their claim in the complaint. In *Edelman*, for example, the Court, in construing the action as one against the state, appeared to rely heavily on its observation that the defendants would be unlikely to pay the requested relief from their own pockets. But it might equally be true that a standing governor would also not be expected to incur personal financial loss if a plaintiff sued her successfully for actions undertaken while in office. And the Court has also made clear that the fact that a state might otherwise indemnify the state officer is not sufficient to implicate state immunity. The line between permissible suits for damages against state officers and those barred on grounds that the state is the real party in interest, in short, has proved difficult to draw. *See* David Currie, *Sovereign Immunity and Suits Against Government Officers*, 1984 SUP. CT. REV. 149 (1997).

2.   **Consent and Waiver.** Common law principles of sovereign immunity provided that the state could consent to suit if it so desired. And, in fact, both the Federal Government and the states have passed statutes that waive their immunity in many instances, such as for contract claims and certain tort actions. Consistent with this common law approach, the Supreme Court has held that a state can consent to suit in federal court. The Court has consistently held, however, that a state's consent to be sued in federal court must be explicit. Thus, in *Kennecott Copper Corp. v. State Tax Commission*, 327 U.S. 573 (1946), the Court held that a state statute allowing the state to be sued in "any court of competent jurisdiction" was not sufficient to waive the state's immunity from suit in federal court.

The Court has also indicated that a state may waive its immunity by intentionally *invoking* federal jurisdiction for its own purposes. See, e.g., *Gardner v. New Jersey*, 329 U.S. 565 (1947). Thus, in *Lapides v. Board of Regents*, 535 U.S. 613 (2002), the Court held that the state's action in removing a case to federal court constituted a waiver of its federal court immunity. As the *Lapides* Court explained, the state "cannot escape the results of its own voluntary act by invoking the prohibitions of the Eleventh Amendment." Yet, at the same time, the Court has also indicated, in cases such as *Edelman v. Jordan*, supra, that the state would not be deemed to waive its immunity defense if it raised the defense belatedly, including on appeal.

Lapides also made clear that the question of whether a state has waived its immunity in its conduct of litigation is a matter of federal law and not the law of the state. But the fact that a state can waive its immunity in federal court raises a problematic conceptual issue regarding the jurisdictional status of the state immunity defense. Generally, of course, objections to the federal courts' subject matter jurisdiction cannot be waived. Does the fact that state immunity can be waived mean that it is not an aspect of subject matter jurisdiction? If so, then what constitutes the basis of the *Edelman* Court's decision that the defense can be raised belatedly, including on appeal?

3.   **The Rise and Fall of Constructive Consent.** For a time, the Court experimented with a doctrine indicating that states could be deemed to have constructively consented to suit by virtue of their engaging in particular activities. Thus, in *Parden v. Terminal Railway*, 377 U.S. 184 (1964), the Court held that Alabama could be subject to damage suits brought under the Federal Employees' Liability Act (FELA) for its actions in operating an interstate railway. The Court reasoned that since Alabama knew FELA had been enacted at the time it began its railroad operation, it could be deemed to have constructively consented to suit for FELA violations arising out of that operation.

Edelman rejected the conclusion that the state in that case had constructively consented to suit through its participation in a federal welfare program. As Justice Rehnquist explained, "[c]onstructive consent is not a doctrine commonly associated with the surrender of constitutional rights." Nevertheless *Edelman* did not overrule *Parden*. The latter could still be distinguished on grounds that in operating a railroad, the state was acting under its proprietary interests and not in its governmental capacity.

The formal abandonment of the constructive consent doctrine came in two later cases. The first was *Welch v. Texas Department of Highways & Public Transportation,* 483 U.S. 468 (1987), in which a state employee working for a state-owned ferry sued the state under the Jones Act. Although as in *Parden*, the state was acting in its proprietary rather than governmental capacity, the Court nevertheless upheld the state's immunity. Collapsing the question of whether the state constructively waived its immunity with the issue of whether Congress intended to abrogate the state's immunity, the Court held that congressional intent to subject the state to prospectively suit must be expressed in a clear statement before the state's constructive waiver could be found. The Court then overruled *Parden* to the "extent it is inconsistent with the requirement that an abrogation of [the state's] immunity by Congress must be expressed in unmistakably clear language."

The final blow to *Parden* came in *College Savings Bank v. Florida Prepaid Postsecondary Education Expense Board,* 527 U.S. 666 (1999). In that case, the plaintiff-savings bank sued the state under federal law for making false statements about the bank's products in its interstate marketing of the state's own operated tuition prepayment program. The plaintiff's contention that the state should not be immune from such actions was supported by two factors. First, like *Parden* itself, the state's activity in question was not a core state function. Rather, the state was acting, in the words of the plaintiff, as a "market participant," competing with the bank for the same customers. Second, the statute under which the plaintiff sued clearly expressed Congress's intent to subject the state to liability. The Court, however, was unmoved. As it stated:

> *Parden*-style waivers are simply unheard of in the context of *other* constitutionally protected privileges. As we said in *Edelman*, "constructive consent is not a doctrine commonly associated with the surrender of constitutional rights." . . . The classic description of an effective waiver of a constitutional right is the "intentional relinquishment or abandonment of a known right or privilege." . . . We see no reason why the rule should be different with respect to state sovereign immunity.

Thus, the Court concluded, "[w]hatever may remain of our decision in *Parden* is expressly overruled."

4.   Consent, Waiver, and the Spending Clause. Despite the demise of constructive consent, Congress presumably could require the states to explicitly surrender their Eleventh Amendment immunity as a condition for receiving federal funds. See *Sossamon v. Texas*, 563 U.S. ___, 131 S.Ct. 1651,

1663–64 (2011) (Sotamayor, J., dissenting) (citing *College Savings Bank* v. *Florida Prepaid Postsecondary Ed. Expense Bd.*, 527 U.S. 666, 686 (1999) ("Congress may, in the exercise of its spending power, condition its grant of funds to the States upon their taking certain actions that Congress could not require them to take, and . . . acceptance of the funds entails an agreement to the actions"). But the Court has made clear that the states' agreement that it has consented to suits for damages by its receipt of federal funds must be extraordinarily unambiguous. Thus in *Sossamon*, the majority opinion held that the provision of the Religious Land Use and Institutionalized Persons Act of 2000 (RLUIPA) allowing for aggrieved litigants to sue for "appropriate relief against a government," did not contain "the unequivocal expression of state consent that [Court] precedents require" to establish waiver. *Sossamon*, 131 S.Ct. at 1653–54 (majority opinion). As the Court explained, " '[a]ppropriate relief' does not so clearly and unambiguously waive sovereign immunity to private suits for damages that we can 'be certain that the State in fact consents' to such a suit." *Id.* at 1658–59 (citing *College Savings Bank*, 527 U.S. at 680).

    5. The Retrospective/Prospective Distinction. What type of relief is prospective? As the holding in *Edelman*—rejecting the plaintiffs' claims that they should be awarded welfare payments wrongfully withheld as "equitable restitution"—might indicate, the Court's conclusion that the Eleventh Amendment permits prospective relief to be awarded against the state but prohibits retrospective relief can be difficult to apply. Although *Edelman* itself stated that a key factor in deciding whether the relief sought should be considered prospective or retrospective was whether the judgment would be satisfied from state treasuries, the Court also noted that a state may often need to expend significant funds in order to comply with a prospective judgment. Accordingly, the fact that an adverse judgment could cost the state money is not necessarily alone sufficient to trigger the Eleventh Amendment defense. For example, in *Milliken v. Bradley,* 433 U.S. 267 (1977), the Court held that a judgment requiring that the state spend considerable funds in order to achieve compliance with a school desegregation order did not violate the state's immunity protections. Rather, the relief was permissible because it was aimed at bringing the state prospectively into compliance with constitutional requirements. In contrast, however, when the Native American plaintiffs in *Papasan v. Allain,* 478 U.S. 265 (1986), sued the state to replace a trust that it had held for the benefit of the plaintiffs' schools but whose assets the state had improperly lost, the Court barred the claim for relief. Although as in *Milliken*, the relief sought was to be used to aid the plaintiffs' schools, the Court found that replacing the depleted trust should be considered retrospective relief because it was sought to redress a past harm. The Court in *Papasan*, however, did uphold a court order requiring the state to prospectively provide greater funding to the plaintiffs' schools based upon an independent constitutional claim that the state was funding those schools at lower levels than the rest of the state.

6. Ancillary Relief. The prospective/retrospective distinction has also proved nebulous with respect to *Edelman*'s assertion that claims imposing costs "ancillary" to a prospective judgment were permissible even when paid from state treasuries. In *Quern v. Jordan*, 440 U.S. 332 (1979), for example, the Court in a follow-up case to *Edelman* held that ordering the state to incur the costs of providing notice to every member of the plaintiffs' class that the state owed them money was permissible as ancillary to the plaintiffs' winning claim for prospective relief. On the other hand, in *Green v. Mansour*, 474 U.S. 64 (1985), the Court held that a similar notice order alerting members of the plaintiffs' class that they wrongfully may have been denied benefits was impermissible under the Eleventh Amendment because the relief was not tied to any prospective claim alleging an ongoing violation.

7. *Hutto v. Finney* and Attorney's Fees. A particularly important case addressing the definition and availability of ancillary relief is *Hutto v. Finney*, 437 U.S. 678 (1978). In *Hutto*, the Court held that the prevailing plaintiffs in § 1983 cases were not barred from seeking attorneys' fees awards against the states under 42 U.S.C. § 1988 even though these awards would need to be paid from state treasuries. In reaching this conclusion, the Court relied in major part on its conclusion that such relief was merely "ancillary" to the injunctive relief awarded in the case.[1] But are attorneys' fees awards truly ancillary as that term was employed in *Edelman*? As one commentator notes, the type of ancillary effects on state treasuries approved in *Edelman* were those incurred by the state in complying with the prospective judgment. They were not, as in *Hutto*, "an ancillary order to pay money." *See* David Currie, *Sovereign Immunity and Suits Against Government Officers*, 1984 SUP. CT. REV. 149 (1997).

8. *Pennhurst* and Prospective Relief Based on Violations of State Law. The Court created an important exception to its retrospective/prospective relief distinction in *Pennhurst State School and Hospital v. Halderman*, 465 U.S. 89 (1984) (*Pennhurst II*), a class action challenging the conditions at a state institution for the mentally retarded. The *Pennhurst* plaintiffs, basing their claims on a number of federal constitutional and statutory provisions and upon a state statutory provision, sued for prospective relief requiring the defendants to improve the conditions at the facility. The case went to the Supreme Court twice. The first time the Court reversed the appellate court's holding that the plaintiffs were entitled to relief under the federal Developmentally Disabled Assistance and Bill of Rights Act. Concluding that the Act did not create any judicially enforceable rights, the Court remanded the case to the lower court to consider the plaintiffs' other federal and state law claims. *Pennhurst State School and Hospital v. Halderman*, 451 U.S. 1 (1981) (*Pennhurst I*). Accepting this invitation, the lower court ruled that the state had violated state law and the plaintiffs were entitled to injunctive relief on that basis. The Supreme Court,

---

[1] The majority also suggested that the award was permissible because Congress enacted § 1988 pursuant to Section V and therefore abrogated the state's immunity. *See* Section III A, *infra*.

in a 5–4 decision, reversed again, this time on the ground that the Eleventh Amendment barred the federal court from reaching the state law claim. Ignoring precedent to the contrary, the Court held the Eleventh Amendment barred all actions against the state officials based on state law, including state law claims seeking only prospective relief. The Court distinguished *Young* as merely a "fiction" intended to preserve the supremacy of federal law and was therefore inapplicable when the claim against the state officials was based on state law. Moreover, the Court continued, "it is difficult to think of a greater intrusion on state sovereignty than when a federal court instructs state officials on how to conform their conduct to state law." In *VOPA*, above, the Court reiterated the "fiction to preserve the supremacy of federal law" account of *Young*, albeit in a different context, for the sake of applying rather than distinguishing *Young*.

Pennhurst does not easily square with pre-existing Eleventh Amendment jurisprudence. The relief sought by the plaintiffs in *Pennhurst*, after all, was prospective, indicating that the *Edelman* rationale of protecting the states' treasuries from retroactive obligations was not at issue. Moreover, the *Pennhurst* majority's heavy reliance on the need to protect federal law as providing the basis for the decision in *Ex parte Young* might be seen as undercutting the Court's refusal in other cases to allow retrospective relief against the states. If the need to protect federal law is so compelling as to override the state's immunity in suits for prospective relief, shouldn't it be equally sufficiently compelling to override the state's immunity in suits for retrospective relief? If so, what effect does *Pennhurst* have on the reconciliation of *Hans* and *Young* that was at the heart of the *Edelman* decision?

In terms of promoting doctrinal consistency, however, the *Pennhurst* dissenters fare no better. Prior to *Pennhurst*, their claim had been that the Eleventh Amendment was designed only to apply to diversity cases. But the diversity claim makes most sense if one concludes that subjecting the state to the state's own law in federal court is a particularly egregious offense to the state's sovereignty. As such, shouldn't the *Pennhurst* dissenters have been sympathetic to immunizing the state from even prospective relief based on state law as the *Pennhurst* majority ruled?

9.   *Pennhurst* and *Stare Decisis*. In barring prospective actions based on state law, *Pennhurst* overruled a series of cases in which claims based upon state law were allowed to proceed. In response, Justice Stevens, who had previously voted to affirm *Hans* and *Edelman*, switched his position in *Atascadero State Hospital v. Scanlon*, 473 U.S. 234 (1985), decided one year after *Pennhurst*, on the ground that if the *Pennhurst* majority had no respect for *stare decisis* then he need not either. As he wrote:

> [T]he Court has not felt constrained by *stare decisis* in its expansion of the protective mantle of sovereign immunity—having repudiated at least 28 cases in its decision in *Pennhurst State School and Hospital* v. *Halderman*—and additional study has made it

abundantly clear that not only *Edelman*, but *Hans v. Louisiana*, as well, can properly be characterized as egregiously incorrect. I am now persuaded that a fresh examination of the Court's Eleventh Amendment jurisprudence will produce benefits that far outweigh the consequences of further unraveling the doctrine of *stare decisis* in this area of the law.

Id. at 304 (Stevens, J., dissenting) (emphasis in original). Does the fact that the Court rejected *stare decisis* in one case justify its rejection in another?

For an argument that precedent is, across the board, a comparatively weak constraint in federal courts law, see Michael Wells, *The Unimportance of Precedent in the Law of Federal Courts*, 39 DePaul L. Rev. 357 (1990) (arguing that the reliance interest in precedent is low in this area, so that the benefits of fidelity to precedent tend to be weaker than in other areas).

III.   CONGRESSIONAL ABROGATION OF STATE IMMUNITY

A. CONGRESSIONAL ABROGATION UNDER SECTION 5 OF THE FOURTEENTH AMENDMENT

FITZPATRICK V. BITZER
427 U.S. 445 (1976).

JUSTICE REHNQUIST delivered the opinion of the Court.

In the 1972 Amendments to Title VII of the Civil Rights Act of 1964, Congress, acting under § 5 of the Fourteenth Amendment, authorized federal courts to award money damages in favor of a private individual against a state government found to have subjected that person to employment discrimination on the basis of "race, color, religion, sex, or national origin." The principal question presented by these cases is whether, as against the shield of sovereign immunity afforded the State by the Eleventh Amendment, *Edelman v. Jordan*, 415 U.S. 651 (1974), Congress has the power to authorize federal courts to enter such an award against the State as a means of enforcing the substantive guarantees of the Fourteenth Amendment. The Court of Appeals for the Second Circuit held that the effect of our decision in *Edelman* was to foreclose Congress' power. We granted certiorari to resolve this important constitutional question. 423 U.S. 1031 (1975). We reverse.

Petitioners in No. 75–251 sued in the United States District Court for the District of Connecticut on behalf of all present and retired male employees of the State of Connecticut. Their amended complaint asserted, *inter alia,* that certain provisions in the State's statutory retirement benefit plan discriminated against them because of their sex, and therefore contravened Title VII of the 1964 Act, 78 Stat. 253, as amended,

42 U.S.C. § 2000e *et seq.* (1970 ed. and Supp. IV). Title VII, which originally did not include state and local governments, had in the interim been amended to bring the States within its purview.

In *Edelman* this Court held that monetary relief awarded by the District Court to welfare plaintiffs, by reason of wrongful denial of benefits which had occurred previous to the entry of the District Court's determination of their wrongfulness, violated the Eleventh Amendment. Such an award was found to be indistinguishable from a monetary award against the State itself which had been prohibited in *Ford Motor Co. v. Department of Treasury*, 323 U.S. 459, 464 (1945). It was therefore controlled by that case rather than by *Ex parte Young*, which permitted suits against state officials to obtain prospective relief against violations of the Fourteenth Amendment.

All parties in the instant litigation agree with the Court of Appeals that the suit for retroactive benefits by the petitioners is in fact indistinguishable from that sought to be maintained in *Edelman,* since what is sought here is a damages award payable to a private party from the state treasury. [Here,] however, the Eleventh Amendment defense is asserted in the context of legislation passed pursuant to Congress' authority under § 5 of the Fourteenth Amendment. As ratified by the States after the Civil War, that Amendment quite clearly contemplates limitations on their authority. In relevant part, it provides:

> "Section 1 . . . No State shall make or enforce any law which shall abridge the privileges or immunities of citizens of the United States; nor shall any State deprive any person of life, liberty, or property, without due process of law; nor deny to any person within its jurisdiction the equal protection of the laws.

> . . .

> Section 5. The Congress shall have power to enforce, by appropriate legislation, the provisions of this article."

The substantive provisions are by express terms directed at the States. Impressed upon them by those provisions are duties with respect to their treatment of private individuals. Standing behind the imperatives is Congress' power to "enforce" them "by appropriate legislation."

The impact of the Fourteenth Amendment upon the relationship between the Federal Government and the States, and the reach of congressional power under § 5, were examined at length by this Court in *Ex parte Virginia*, 100 U.S. 339 (1880). A state judge had been arrested and indicted under a federal criminal statute prohibiting the exclusion on the basis of race of any citizen from service as a juror in a state court. The judge claimed that the statute was beyond Congress' power to enact under either the Thirteenth or the Fourteenth Amendment. The Court first observed that these Amendments "were intended to be, what they really are, limitations of the power of the States and enlargements of the power of Congress." It then addressed the relationship between the language of § 5 and the substantive provisions of the Fourteenth Amendment:

> The prohibitions of the Fourteenth Amendment are directed to the States, and they are to a degree restrictions of State power. It is these which Congress is empowered to enforce, and to enforce against State action, however put forth, whether that action be executive, legislative, or judicial. Such enforcement is no invasion of State sovereignty. No law can be, which the people of the States have, by the Constitution of the United States, empowered Congress to enact . . . It is said the selection of jurors for her courts and the administration of her laws belong to each State; that they are her rights. This is true in the general. But in exercising her rights, a State cannot disregard the limitations which the Federal Constitution has applied to her power. Her rights do not reach to that extent. Nor can she deny to the general government the right to exercise all its granted powers, though they may interfere with the full enjoyment of rights she would have if those powers had not been thus granted. Indeed, every addition of power to the general government involves a corresponding diminution of the governmental powers of the States. It is carved out of them.

Ex parte Virginia's early recognition of this shift in the federal-state balance has been carried forward by more recent decisions of this Court. See, *e.g., South Carolina v. Katzenbach,* 383 U.S. 301, 308 (1966); *Mitchum v. Foster,* 407 U.S. 225, 238–39 (1972).

There can be no doubt that this line of cases has sanctioned intrusions by Congress, acting under the Civil War Amendments, into the judicial, executive, and legislative spheres of autonomy previously reserved to the States. The legislation considered in each case was grounded on the expansion of Congress' powers—with the corresponding diminution of state sovereignty—found to be intended by the Framers and made part of the Constitution upon the States' ratification of those Amendments, a phenomenon aptly described as a "carv[ing] out" in *Ex Parte Virginia.*

It is true that none of these previous cases presented the question of the relationship between the Eleventh Amendment and the enforcement power granted to Congress under § 5 of the Fourteenth Amendment. But we think that the Eleventh Amendment, and the principle of state sovereignty which it embodies, see *Hans,* are necessarily limited by the enforcement provisions of § 5 of the Fourteenth Amendment. In that section Congress is expressly granted authority to enforce "by appropriate legislation" the substantive provisions of the Fourteenth Amendment, which themselves embody significant limitations on state authority. When Congress acts pursuant to § 5, not only is it exercising legislative authority that is plenary within the terms of the constitutional grant, it is exercising that authority under one section of a constitutional Amendment whose other sections by their own terms embody limitations on state authority. We think that Congress may, in determining what is "appropriate legislation" for the purpose of enforcing the provisions of the Fourteenth Amendment, provide for private suits against States or state officials which are constitutionally impermissible in other contexts.

Reversed.

JUSTICE BRENNAN, concurring in the judgment.

This suit was brought by present and retired employees of the State of Connecticut against the State Treasurer, the State Comptroller, and the Chairman of the State Employees' Retirement Commission. In that circumstance, Connecticut may not invoke the Eleventh Amendment, since that Amendment bars only federal-court suits against States by citizens of other States. Rather, the question is whether Connecticut may avail itself of the nonconstitutional but ancient doctrine of sovereign immunity as a bar to a claim for damages under Title VII. In my view Connecticut may not assert sovereign immunity for the reason I expressed in dissent in *Employees v. Public Health Dept.*, 411 U.S. 279, 298 (1973). The States surrendered that immunity, in Hamilton's words, "in the plan of the Convention" that formed the Union, at least insofar as the States granted Congress specifically enumerated powers. Congressional authority to enact the provisions of Title VII at issue in this case is found in the Commerce Clause, Art. I, § 8, cl. 3, and in § 5 of the Fourteenth Amendment, two of the enumerated powers granted Congress in the Constitution. I remain of the opinion that "because of its surrender, no immunity exists that can be the subject of a congressional declaration or a voluntary waiver."

NOTES ON FITZPATRICK AND CONGRESS'S SECTION 5 POWER

1. *Quern* **and Section 1983.** *Fitzpatrick* was the first case establishing that Congress had the authority to abrogate state immunity. But in relying exclusively on Section 5 of the Fourteenth Amendment, the decision was deliberately narrow. Section 5 grants Congress the authority only to enact legislation to enforce constitutional rights. As such, it is far more constricted than the powers accorded Congress under provisions like the Commerce Clause, which authorizes Congress to legislate on a wide range of social and economic matters. Additionally, the Court was soon to make clear that *Fitzpatrick* would not be broadly applied even in the constitutional rights domain. In *Quern v. Jordan*, 440 U.S. 332 (1979), decided one year after *Fitzpatrick*, the Court held that states were immune from suits brought against them under 42 U.S.C. § 1983 because there was no clear indication that § 1983 was intended to abrogate state sovereign immunity.

   2.   *Hutto* and Section 1988. In *Hutto v. Finney*, 437 U.S. 678 (1978) the Court extended *Fitzpatrick* to allow for attorneys' fees awards to be granted against the states pursuant to 42 U.S.C. § 1988. Its grounds for doing so, however, were ambiguous. On the one hand, the Court appeared to suggest that such awards were permissible because § 1988 was passed pursuant to Section 5. On the other, however, the Court also seemed to base its decision on grounds that attorneys' fees awards were permissible as "ancillary" to the prospective relief awarded in that case. On the general availability of attorneys' fees in § 1983 cases, see Chapter 1, p. 37 supra.

   3.   Section 5 and the "Congruency and Proportionality" Test. Later cases have continued to reinforce the proposition that Congress's power to abrogate state immunity under Section 5 would not be broadly construed. In a series of cases beginning with *City of Boerne v. Flores*, 521 U.S. 507 (1997), the Court has held that for any statute to be sustained as within Congress's Section 5 powers, "there must be a congruence and proportionality between the injury to be prevented or remedied and the means adopted to that end." Applying this test the Court has struck down congressional attempts to subject the states to liability under its Section 5 powers for discrimination against the elderly in the Age Discrimination in Employment Act (ADEA), *Kimel v. Florida Bd. of Regents*, 528 U.S. 62 (2000), and against the disabled in employment under the Americans With Disabilities Act (ADA), *Board of Trustees of the University of Alabama v. Garrett*, 531 U.S. 356 (2001). The Court has upheld Congress's Section 5 powers to hold states liable under the Family and Medical Leave Act, *Nevada Department of Human Resources v. Hibbs*, 538 U.S. 721 (2003), and under the ADA for failing to provide adequate access to "judicial services" for disabled persons, *Tennessee v. Lane*, 541 U.S. 509 (2004), but even those cases appear to demand a considerable showing by Congress before a statute will be sustained. See also *United States v. Georgia*, 546 U.S. 151 (2006) (Title II of the ADA validly abrogates state sovereign immunity insofar as it creates a private cause of action for damages against the States for conduct that actually violates the Fourteenth Amendment).

B. CONGRESSIONAL ABROGATION UNDER THE COMMERCE CLAUSE

Introductory Note

   Fitzpatrick established that Congress had the power to abrogate state immunity when acting pursuant to Section 5 of the Fourteenth Amendment. *Fitzpatrick*, however, did not decide whether state immunity could be abrogated by Congress pursuant to its other powers including, most importantly, the Commerce Clause. Indeed, this question also was left open in *Edelman* and in *Employees of the Department of Public Health and Welfare v. The Department of Health and Welfare*, 411 U.S. 279 (1973), as the Court in both cases suggested that congressional intent to abrogate the state's immunity was not clear from the language of the relevant statutes.

In fact, for over fifteen years, beginning with the *Employees* case, the Court dodged the constitutional issue at stake, each time asserting that the federal statute under which the suit against the state was brought was not sufficiently clear to establish that Congress intended that the state should be liable for violating that particular statute's provisions. As the Court explained it, because of the importance of the constitutional concerns at stake, Congress must express its intention to abrogate state immunity "unmistakably clear in the language of the statute" in order to overcome the state's immunity. *Atascadero State Hospital v. Scanlon,* 473 U.S. 234, 242 (1985). The Court enforced this "clear statement" requirement especially stringently. For example in *Welch v. Texas Department of Highways and Public Transportation,* 483 U.S. 468 (1987), the Court contended that the Jones Act, 46 U.S.C. § 688(a), which provides an action for *any* injured seamen, failed to constitute an "unmistakably clear expression" that it was intended to apply to seamen employed by the state. Similarly, in *Atascadero,* the Court held that § 504 of the Rehabilitation Act of 1973, 29 U.S.C. § 794, which provided that "any recipient of Federal assistance" could bring suit did not contain the unmistakable language necessary to negate the state's immunity, although the obvious target for those remedies would be the state entities administering the program.

Eventually, the Court reached the abrogation issue in the case of *Pennsylvania v. Union Gas*, 491 U.S. 1 (1989). In *Union Gas*, the United States sued the operator of a coal gasification plant to recoup the costs the Federal Government spent in cleaning up an environmental hazard. Union Gas, in turn, filed a third-party claim against Pennsylvania under the Comprehensive Environmental Response, Compensation, and Liability Act ("CERCLA"), 42 U.S.C. § 9601, *et seq.*, claiming that the state was obligated to reimburse the company for its share of the clean-up costs on grounds that the state was also liable for any CERCLA violations because it was both an owner-operator of the hazardous-waste site and because its flood-control efforts had negligently caused or contributed to the environmental damage. In a 5–4 decision, the Court found the language of CERCLA was sufficiently explicit to satisfy the clear statement requirement.[2] The Court then, at long last, reached the

---

[2]   The language of section 107(d)(2) of CERCLA, as set forth in 42 U.S.C. § 9607(d)(2) (1982 ed., Supp. IV), provides: "No State or local government shall be liable under this subchapter for costs or damages as a result of actions taken in response to an emergency created by the release or threatened release of a hazardous substance generated by or from a facility owned by another

constitutional issue, and in a different 5–4 alignment, held that Congress could abrogate state immunity pursuant to its commerce power.[3] Only four Justices, however, could agree on a governing rationale.

Justice Brennan's plurality opinion advanced three separate points. First, he argued that the clear statement cases presumed that Congress had the requisite power to abrogate the state's immunity. After all, if Congress did not have such power why would a clear statement be needed? Second, citing *Fitzpatrick*, he contended that the Commerce Clause, like Section 5, limits state sovereignty. "Like the Fourteenth Amendment, the Commerce Clause with one hand gives power to Congress while, with the other, it takes power away from the States." Third, Justice Brennan argued that congressional power to abrogate state immunity was implicit in the "plan of the convention," meaning that the states, in joining the Union and adopting the Constitution, agreed to be bound by its terms. Accordingly, in giving Congress the authority to regulate commerce under the Constitution, the states agreed to be subject to the laws enacted by Congress pursuant to the commerce power. Thus, to Brennan, "[t]he States held liable under such a congressional enactment are . . . not 'unconsenting'; they gave their consent all at once, in ratifying the Constitution containing the Commerce Clause, rather than on a case-by-case basis."

Whatever its merits, however, Brennan's opinion did not command a majority. Although Justice White stated that he believed Congress had the power to abrogate the state's immunity, he neither joined the plurality opinion nor offered reasons of his own. Rather he cryptically wrote only: "I agree with the conclusion reached by Justice Brennan . . . that Congress has the authority under Article I to abrogate the Eleventh Amendment immunity of the States, although I do not agree with much of his reasoning."

SEMINOLE TRIBE OF FLORIDA V. FLORIDA
517 U.S. 44 (1996).

[An Indian tribe filed suit against the State of Florida to compel negotiations under the Indian Gaming Regulatory Act. The Act, passed by

---

person. This paragraph shall not preclude liability for costs or damages as a result of gross negligence or intentional misconduct by the State or local government." As the Court noted in *Union Gas Co.*, 491 U.S. at 12, "in light of [CERCLA's] very precise language, it would be exceedingly odd to interpret this provision as merely a signal that the United States—rather than private citizens—could sue the States for damages under CERCLA."

[3] Justice Scalia joined the majority in holding that Congress had clearly intended to subject the state to suits under CERCLA, he dissented from the portion of the opinion holding that the Court had the power to abrogate the state's immunity. Justice White, in turn, dissented from the Court's opinion holding that Congress had waived the state's immunity in CERCLA but concurred in the plurality's conclusion that Congress had the power to abrogate the state's immunity if it so chose.

Congress under the Indian Commerce Clause, requires Indian tribes to enter into a valid compact with each state in which they intend to conduct certain gaming activities, 25 U.S.C. § 2710(d)(1)(C), and imposes upon the states a duty to negotiate with the tribes in good faith. Id. at § 2710(d)(3)(A). The Act specifically authorizes a tribe to bring suit in federal court against a State in order to compel performance of that duty. Id. at § 2710(d)(7).]

CHIEF JUSTICE REHNQUIST delivered the opinion of the Court.

[The Court began by examining the statute, finding that Congress intended to abrogate state immunity.]

Having concluded that Congress clearly intended to abrogate the States' sovereign immunity through § 2710(d)(7), we turn now to consider whether the Act was passed "pursuant to a valid exercise of power." *Green v. Mansour,* 474 U.S. 64, 68 (1985). Before we address that question here, however, we think it necessary first to define the scope of our inquiry.

Petitioner suggests that one consideration weighing in favor of finding the power to abrogate here is that the Act authorizes only prospective injunctive relief rather than retroactive monetary relief. But we have often made it clear that the relief sought by a plaintiff suing a State is irrelevant to the question whether the suit is barred by the Eleventh Amendment. See, e.g., *Cory v. White,* 457 U.S. 85, 90 (1982) ("It would be a novel proposition indeed that the Eleventh Amendment does not bar a suit to enjoin the State itself simply because no money judgment is sought"). We think it follows *a fortiori* from this proposition that the type of relief sought is irrelevant to whether Congress has power to abrogate States' immunity. The Eleventh Amendment does not exist solely in order to "preven[t] federal-court judgments that must be paid out of a State's treasury," *Hess v. Port Authority Trans-Hudson Corporation,* 513 U.S. 30, 48 (1994); it also serves to avoid "the indignity of subjecting a State to the coercive process of judicial tribunals at the instance of private parties," *Puerto Rico Aqueduct and Sewer Authority,* 506 U.S. at 146 (internal quotation marks omitted).

Similarly, petitioner argues that the abrogation power is validly exercised here because the Act grants the States a power that they would not otherwise have, viz., some measure of authority over gaming on Indian lands. It is true enough that the Act extends to the States a power withheld from them by the Constitution. Nevertheless, we do not see how that consideration is relevant to the question whether Congress may abrogate state sovereign immunity. The Eleventh Amendment immunity may not be lifted by Congress unilaterally deciding that it will be replaced by grant of some other authority. Cf. *Atascadero State Hospital v. Scanlon,* 473 U.S. 234, 246–47 (1985) ("[T]he mere receipt of federal funds cannot establish that a State has consented to suit in federal court").

Thus our inquiry into whether Congress has the power to abrogate unilaterally the States' immunity from suit is narrowly focused on one question: Was the Act in question passed pursuant to a constitutional provision granting Congress the power to abrogate? See, e.g., *Fitzpatrick v. Bitzer,* 427 U.S. 445, 452–456 (1976). Previously, in conducting that inquiry, we have found authority to abrogate under only two provisions of the Constitution. In *Fitzpatrick,* we recognized that the Fourteenth Amendment, by expanding federal power at the expense of state autonomy, had fundamentally altered the balance of state and federal power struck by the Constitution. *Id.,* at 455. We noted that § 1 of the Fourteenth Amendment contained prohibitions expressly directed at the States and that § 5 of the Amendment expressly provided that "The Congress shall have power to enforce, by appropriate legislation, the provisions of this article." See *id.,* at 453 (internal quotation marks omitted). We held that through the Fourteenth Amendment, federal power extended to intrude upon the province of the Eleventh Amendment and therefore that § 5 of the Fourteenth Amendment allowed Congress to abrogate the immunity from suit guaranteed by that Amendment.

In only one other case has congressional abrogation of the States' Eleventh Amendment immunity been upheld. In *Pennsylvania v. Union Gas Co.,* 491 U.S. 1 (1989), a plurality of the Court found that the Interstate Commerce Clause, Art. I, § 8, cl. 3, granted Congress the power to abrogate state sovereign immunity, stating that the power to regulate interstate commerce would be "incomplete without the authority to render States liable in damages." 491 U.S., at 19–20. Justice White added the fifth vote necessary to the result in that case, but wrote separately in order to express that he "[did] not agree with much of [the plurality's] reasoning." *Id.,* at 57 (opinion concurring in judgment in part and dissenting in part).

Following the rationale of the *Union Gas* plurality, our inquiry is limited to determining whether the Indian Commerce Clause, like the Interstate Commerce Clause, is a grant of authority to the Federal Government at the expense of the States. The answer to that question is obvious. If anything, the Indian Commerce Clause accomplishes a greater transfer of power from the States to the Federal Government than does the Interstate Commerce Clause. This is clear enough from the fact that the States still exercise some authority over interstate trade but have been divested of virtually all authority over Indian commerce and Indian tribes. Under the rationale of *Union Gas,* if the States' partial cession of authority over a particular area includes cession of the immunity from suit, then their virtually total cession of authority over a different area must also include cession of the immunity from suit. See *id.* at 42 (Scalia,

J., joined by Rehnquist, C.J., and O'Connor and Kennedy, JJ., dissenting) ("[I]f the Article I commerce power enables abrogation of state sovereign immunity, so do all the other Article I powers"). We agree with petitioner that the plurality opinion in *Union Gas* allows no principled distinction in favor of the States to be drawn between the Indian Commerce Clause and the Interstate Commerce Clause.

Respondents argue, however, that we need not conclude that the Indian Commerce Clause grants the power to abrogate the States' sovereign immunity. Instead, they contend that if we find the rationale of the *Union Gas* plurality to extend to the Indian Commerce Clause, then "*Union Gas* should be reconsidered and overruled." Brief for Respondents 25. Generally, the principle of *stare decisis,* and the interests that it serves, viz., "the evenhanded, predictable, and consistent development of legal principles, . . . reliance on judicial decisions, and . . . the actual and perceived integrity of the judicial process," *Payne v. Tennessee,* 501 U.S. 808, 827 (1991), counsel strongly against reconsideration of our precedent. Nevertheless, we always have treated *stare decisis* as a "principle of policy," *Helvering v. Hallock,* 309 U.S. 106, 119 (1940), and not as an "inexorable command," *Payne,* 501 U.S. at 828. "[W]hen governing decisions are unworkable or are badly reasoned, 'this Court has never felt constrained to follow precedent.' " *Id.,* at 827. Our willingness to reconsider our earlier decisions has been "particularly true in constitutional cases, because in such cases 'correction through legislative action is practically impossible.' " *Payne,* supra, at 828.

The Court in *Union Gas* reached a result without an expressed rationale agreed upon by a majority of the Court. We have already seen that Justice Brennan's opinion received the support of only three other Justices. Of the other five, Justice White, who provided the fifth vote for the result, wrote separately in order to indicate his disagreement with the plurality's rationale, and four Justices joined together in a dissent that rejected the plurality's rationale. Since it was issued, *Union Gas* has created confusion among the lower courts that have sought to understand and apply the deeply fractured decision.

The plurality's rationale also deviated sharply from our established federalism jurisprudence and essentially eviscerated our decision in *Hans.* It was well established in 1989 when *Union Gas* was decided that the Eleventh Amendment stood for the constitutional principle that state sovereign immunity limited the federal courts' jurisdiction under Article III. The text of the Amendment itself is clear enough on this point: "The Judicial power of the United States shall not be construed to extend to any suit. . . ." And our decisions since *Hans* had been equally clear that the Eleventh Amendment reflects "the fundamental principle of sovereign immunity [that] limits the grant of judicial authority in Art. III," *Pennhurst State School and Hospital v. Halderman,* 465 U.S. 89, 97–98

(1984). As the dissent in *Union Gas* recognized, the plurality's conclusion—that Congress could under Article I expand the scope of the federal courts' jurisdiction under Article III—"contradict[ed] our unvarying approach to Article III as setting forth the *exclusive* catalog of permissible federal-court jurisdiction." *Union Gas,* supra, 491 U.S., at 39.

Never before the decision in *Union Gas* had we suggested that the bounds of Article III could be expanded by Congress operating pursuant to any constitutional provision other than the Fourteenth Amendment. Indeed, it had seemed fundamental that Congress could not expand the jurisdiction of the federal courts beyond the bounds of Article III. *Marbury v. Madison,* 1 Cranch 137 (1803). The plurality's citation of prior decisions for support was based upon what we believe to be a misreading of precedent. The plurality claimed support for its decision from a case holding the unremarkable, and completely unrelated, proposition that the States may waive their sovereign immunity, and cited as precedent propositions that had been merely assumed for the sake of argument in earlier cases.

The plurality's extended reliance upon our decision in *Fitzpatrick v. Bitzer,* 427 U.S. 445 (1976), that Congress could under the Fourteenth Amendment abrogate the States' sovereign immunity was also, we believe, misplaced. *Fitzpatrick* was based upon a rationale wholly inapplicable to the Interstate Commerce Clause, viz., that the Fourteenth Amendment, adopted well after the adoption of the Eleventh Amendment and the ratification of the Constitution, operated to alter the pre-existing balance between state and federal power achieved by Article III and the Eleventh Amendment. *Id.,* at 454. As the dissent in *Union Gas* made clear, *Fitzpatrick* cannot be read to justify "limitation of the principle embodied in the Eleventh Amendment through appeal to antecedent provisions of the Constitution." *Union Gas,* supra, 491 U.S., at 42 (SCALIA, J., dissenting).

In the five years since it was decided, *Union Gas* has proved to be a solitary departure from established law. Reconsidering the decision in *Union Gas,* we conclude that none of the policies underlying *stare decisis* require our continuing adherence to its holding. The decision has, since its issuance, been of questionable precedential value, largely because a majority of the Court expressly disagreed with the rationale of the plurality. See *Nichols v. United States,* 511 U.S. 738 (1994) (the "degree of confusion following a splintered decision . . . is itself a reason for reexamining that decision"). The case involved the interpretation of the Constitution and therefore may be altered only by constitutional amendment or revision by this Court. Finally, both the result in *Union Gas* and the plurality's rationale depart from our established understanding of the Eleventh Amendment and undermine the accepted function of Article III. We feel bound to conclude that *Union Gas* was wrongly decided and that it should be, and now is, overruled.

The dissent makes no effort to defend the decision in *Union Gas*, but nonetheless would find congressional power to abrogate in this case [on other grounds] . . .

The dissent's lengthy analysis of the text of the Eleventh Amendment is directed at a straw man—we long have recognized that blind reliance upon the text of the Eleventh Amendment is " 'to strain the Constitution and the law to a construction never imagined or dreamed of.' " *Monaco, supra*, at 326, quoting Hans, supra, at 15 The text dealt in terms only with the problem presented by the decision in *Chisholm*; in light of the fact that the federal courts did not have federal-question jurisdiction at the time the Amendment was passed (and would not have it until 1875), it seems unlikely that much thought was given to the prospect of federal-question jurisdiction over the States.

In putting forward a new theory of state sovereign immunity, the dissent develops its own vision of the political system created by the Framers, concluding with the statement that "[t]he Framers' principal objectives in rejecting English theories of unitary sovereignty . . . would have been impeded if a new concept of sovereign immunity had taken its place in federal-question cases, and would have been substantially thwarted if that new immunity had been held untouchable by any congressional effort to abrogate it." This sweeping statement ignores the fact that the Nation survived for nearly two centuries without the question of the existence of such power ever being presented to this Court. And Congress itself waited nearly a century before even conferring federal-question jurisdiction on the lower federal courts.

In overruling *Union Gas* today, we reconfirm that the background principle of state sovereign immunity embodied in the Eleventh Amendment is not so ephemeral as to dissipate when the subject of the suit is an area, like the regulation of Indian commerce, that is under the exclusive control of the Federal Government. Even when the Constitution vests in Congress complete law-making authority over a particular area, the Eleventh Amendment prevents congressional authorization of suits by private parties against unconsenting States. The Eleventh Amendment restricts the judicial power under Article III, and Article I cannot be used to circumvent the constitutional limitations placed upon federal jurisdiction. Petitioner's suit against the State of Florida must be dismissed for a lack of jurisdiction.

Petitioner argues that we may exercise jurisdiction over its suit to enforce § 2710(d)(3) against the Governor notwithstanding the jurisdictional bar of the Eleventh Amendment. Petitioner notes that since our decision in *Ex parte Young,* 209 U.S. 123 (1908), we often have found federal jurisdiction over a suit against a state official when that suit seeks only prospective injunctive relief in order to "end a continuing violation of federal law." *Green v. Mansour*, 474 U.S., at 68. The situation presented here, however, is sufficiently different from that giving rise to the traditional *Ex parte Young* action so as to preclude the availability of that doctrine. Here, the "continuing violation of federal law" alleged by petitioner is the Governor's failure to bring the State into compliance with § 2710(d)(3). But the duty to negotiate imposed upon the State by that statutory provision does not stand alone. Rather . . . Congress passed § 2710(d)(3) in conjunction with the carefully crafted and intricate remedial scheme set forth in § 2710(d)(7).

Where Congress has created a remedial scheme for the enforcement of a particular federal right, we have, in suits against federal officers, refused to supplement that scheme with one created by the judiciary. Here, of course, the question is not whether a remedy should be created, but instead is whether the Eleventh Amendment bar should be lifted, as it was in *Ex parte Young,* in order to allow a suit against a state officer. Nevertheless, we think that the same general principle applies: Therefore, where Congress has prescribed a detailed remedial scheme for the enforcement against a State of a statutorily created right, a court should hesitate before casting aside those limitations and permitting an action against a state officer based upon *Ex parte Young.*

Here, Congress intended § 2710(d)(3) to be enforced against the State in an action brought under § 2710(d)(7); the intricate procedures set forth in that provision show that Congress intended therein not only to define, but also to limit significantly, the duty imposed by § 2710(d)(3). For example, where the court finds that the State has failed to negotiate in good faith, the only remedy prescribed is an order directing the State and the Indian tribe to conclude a compact within 60 days. And if the parties disregard the court's order and fail to conclude a compact within the 60-day period, the only sanction is that each party then must submit a proposed compact to a mediator who selects the one which best embodies the terms of the Act. Finally, if the State fails to accept the compact selected by the mediator, the only sanction against it is that the mediator shall notify the Secretary of the Interior who then must prescribe regulations governing class III gaming on the tribal lands at issue. By contrast with this quite modest set of sanctions, an action brought against a state official under *Ex parte Young* would expose that official to the full remedial powers of a federal court, including, presumably, contempt sanctions. If § 2710(d)(3) could be enforced in a suit under *Ex parte Young,* § 2710(d)(7) would have been superfluous; it is difficult to see why an Indian tribe would suffer through the intricate scheme of § 2710(d)(7) when more complete and more immediate relief would be available under *Ex parte Young.*

Here, of course, we have found that Congress does not have authority under the Constitution to make the State suable in federal court under § 2710(d)(7). Nevertheless, the fact that Congress chose to impose upon the State a liability that is significantly more limited than would be the liability imposed upon the state officer under *Ex parte Young* strongly indicates that Congress had no wish to create the latter under § 2710(d)(3). Nor are we free to rewrite the statutory scheme in order to approximate what we think Congress might have wanted had it known that § 2710(d)(7) was beyond its authority. If that effort is to be made, it should be made by Congress, and not by the federal courts. We hold that *Ex parte Young* is inapplicable to petitioner's suit against the Governor of Florida, and therefore that suit is barred by the Eleventh Amendment and must be dismissed for a lack of jurisdiction.

The Eleventh Amendment prohibits Congress from making the State of Florida capable of being sued in federal court. The narrow exception to the Eleventh Amendment provided by the *Ex parte Young* doctrine cannot be used to enforce § 2710(d)(3) because Congress enacted a remedial scheme, § 2710(d)(7), specifically designed for the enforcement of that right. The Eleventh Circuit's dismissal of petitioner's suit is hereby affirmed.

[In a lengthy dissent, Justice Souter made three main points. First, according to Souter, although *Hans* was wrongly decided, it has not proved unworkable, thus it should be treated as a doctrine of federal common law. "For, as so understood, it has formed one of the strands of the federal relationship for over a century now, and the stability of that relationship is itself a value that stare decisis aims to respect." Accordingly as merely a common law defense, it could be overridden by federal legislation. Second, Souter maintained that there is nothing in the history of the Eleventh Amendment that suggests it was meant to preclude suits against states pursuant to federal statutes or to suggest that the plain statement rule did not offer sufficient protection against undue federal encroachments upon traditional state immunity. Third, Souter claimed that because the states consented to the exercise of congressional power in ratifying the Constitution, Congress could subject them to liability.]

ALDEN V. MAINE
527 U.S. 706 (1999).

JUSTICE KENNEDY delivered the opinion of the Court.

In 1992, petitioners, a group of probation officers, filed suit against their employer, the State of Maine, in the United States District Court for the District of Maine. The officers alleged the State had violated the overtime provisions of the Fair Labor Standards Act of 1938 (FLSA), 52

Stat. 1060, as amended, 29 U.S.C. § 201 *et seq.* (1994 ed. and Supp. III), and sought compensation and liquidated damages. While the suit was pending, this Court decided *Seminole Tribe of Fla. v. Florida,* 517 U.S. 44 (1996), which made it clear that Congress lacks power under Article I to abrogate the States' sovereign immunity from suits commenced or prosecuted in the federal courts. Upon consideration of *Seminole Tribe,* the District Court dismissed petitioners' action, and the Court of Appeals affirmed. *Mills v. Maine,* 118 F.3d 37 (C.A.1 1997). Petitioners then filed the same action in state court. The state trial court dismissed the suit on the basis of sovereign immunity, and the Maine Supreme Judicial Court affirmed.

We hold that the powers delegated to Congress under Article I of the United States Constitution do not include the power to subject nonconsenting States to private suits for damages in state courts. We decide as well that the State of Maine has not consented to suits for overtime pay and liquidated damages under the FLSA. On these premises we affirm the judgment sustaining dismissal of the suit.

The Eleventh Amendment makes explicit reference to the States' immunity from suits "commenced or prosecuted against one of the United States by Citizens of another State, or by Citizens or Subjects of any Foreign State." U.S. Const., Amend. 11. We have, as a result, sometimes referred to the States' immunity from suit as "Eleventh Amendment immunity." The phrase is convenient shorthand but something of a misnomer, for the sovereign immunity of the States neither derives from, nor is limited by, the terms of the Eleventh Amendment. Rather, as the Constitution's structure, its history, and the authoritative interpretations by this Court make clear, the States' immunity from suit is a fundamental aspect of the sovereignty which the States enjoyed before the ratification of the Constitution, and which they retain today (either literally or by virtue of their admission into the Union upon an equal footing with the other States) except as altered by the plan of the Convention or certain constitutional Amendments.

Although the Constitution establishes a National Government with broad, often plenary authority over matters within its recognized competence, the founding document "specifically recognizes the States as sovereign entities." *Seminole Tribe of Fla. v. Florida,* supra, at 71, n. 15. Various textual provisions of the Constitution assume the States' continued existence and active participation in the fundamental processes of governance. See *Printz v. United States,* 521 U.S. 898, 919 (1997) (citing Art. III, § 2; Art. IV, §§ 2–4; Art. V). The limited and enumerated powers granted to the Legislative, Executive, and Judicial Branches of the National Government, moreover, underscore the vital role reserved to the States by the constitutional design, see, e.g., Art. I, § 8; Art. II, §§ 2–3; Art. III, § 2. Any doubt regarding the constitutional role of the States as sovereign entities is removed by the Tenth Amendment, which, like the other provisions of the Bill of Rights, was enacted to allay lingering concerns about the extent of the national power. The Amendment confirms the promise implicit in the original document: "The powers not delegated to the United States by the Constitution, nor prohibited by it to the States, are reserved to the States respectively, or to the people." U.S. Const., Amend. 10; see also *Printz,* supra, at 919; *New York v. United States,* 505 U.S. 144, 156–159, 177 (1992).

The federal system established by our Constitution preserves the sovereign status of the States in two ways. First, it reserves to them a substantial portion of the Nation's primary sovereignty, together with the dignity and essential attributes inhering in that status. The States "form distinct and independent portions of the supremacy, no more subject, within their respective spheres, to the general authority than the general authority is subject to them, within its own sphere." The Federalist No. 39, p. 245 (C. Rossiter ed. 1961) (J. Madison).

Second, even as to matters within the competence of the National Government, the constitutional design secures the founding generation's rejection of "the concept of a central government that would act upon and through the States" in favor of "a system in which the State and Federal Governments would exercise concurrent authority over the people—who were, in Hamilton's words, 'the only proper objects of government.'" *Printz,* supra, at 919–920 (quoting The Federalist No. 15, at 109); accord, *New York,* supra, at 166 ("The Framers explicitly chose a Constitution that confers upon Congress the power to regulate individuals, not States"). In this the Founders achieved a deliberate departure from the Articles of Confederation: Experience under the Articles had "exploded on all hands" the "practicality of making laws, with coercive sanctions, for the States as political bodies." 2 Records of the Federal Convention of 1787, p. 9 (M. Farrand ed. 1911) (J. Madison); accord, The Federalist No. 20, at 138 (J. Madison and A. Hamilton); James Iredell: Some Objections to the Constitution Answered, reprinted in 3 Annals of America 249 (1976).

The States thus retain "a residuary and inviolable sovereignty." The Federalist No. 39, at 245. They are not relegated to the role of mere provinces or political corporations, but retain the dignity, though not the full authority, of sovereignty.

In this case we must determine whether Congress has the power, under Article I, to subject nonconsenting States to private suits in their own courts. As the foregoing discussion makes clear, the fact that the Eleventh Amendment by its terms limits only "[t]he Judicial power of the United States" does not resolve the question. To rest on the words of the Amendment alone would be to engage in the type of ahistorical literalism we have rejected in interpreting the scope of the States' sovereign immunity since the discredited decision in *Chisholm. Seminole Tribe,* 517 U.S., at [68.]

Whether Congress has authority under Article I to abrogate a State's immunity from suit in its own courts is . . . a question of first impression. In determining whether there is "compelling evidence" that this derogation of the States' sovereignty is "inherent in the constitutional compact," we continue our discussion of history, practice, precedent, and the structure of the Constitution.

We look first to evidence of the original understanding of the Constitution. Petitioners contend that because the ratification debates and the events surrounding the adoption of the Eleventh Amendment focused on the States' immunity from suit in federal courts, the historical record gives no instruction as to the founding generation's intent to preserve the States' immunity from suit in their own courts.

We believe, however, that the Founders' silence is best explained by the simple fact that no one, not even the Constitution's most ardent opponents, suggested the document might strip the States of the immunity. In light of the overriding concern regarding the States' war-time debts, together with the well-known creativity, foresight, and vivid imagination of the Constitution's opponents, the silence is most instructive. It suggests the sovereign's right to assert immunity from suit in its own courts was a principle so well established that no one conceived it would be altered by the new Constitution.

We have also relied on the States' immunity in their own courts as a premise in our Eleventh Amendment rulings. See *Hans,* 134 U.S., at 10 ("It is true the amendment does so read, and, if there were no other reason or ground for abating his suit, it might be maintainable; and then we should have this anomalous result [that a State may be sued by its own citizen though not by the citizen of another State, and that a State] may be thus sued in the federal courts, although not allowing itself to be sued in its own courts. If this is the necessary consequence of the language of the Constitution and the law, the result is no less startling and unexpected than [*Chisholm*]"); *id.,* at 18 ("The state courts have no power to entertain suits by individuals against a State without its consent. Then how does the Circuit Court, having only concurrent jurisdiction, acquire any such power?").

In particular, the exception to our sovereign immunity doctrine recognized in *Ex parte Young,* 209 U.S. 123 (1908), is based in part on the premise that sovereign immunity bars relief against States and their officers in both state and federal courts, and that certain suits for declaratory or injunctive relief against state officers must therefore be permitted if the Constitution is to remain the supreme law of the land.

Had we not understood the States to retain a constitutional immunity from suit in their own courts, the need for the *Ex parte Young* rule would have been less pressing, and the rule would not have formed so essential a part of our sovereign immunity doctrine. See *Idaho v. Coeur d'Alene Tribe of Idaho,* 521 U.S., at 270–271 (principal opinion).

As it is settled doctrine that neither substantive federal law nor attempted congressional abrogation under Article I bars a State from raising a constitutional defense of sovereign immunity in federal court, our decisions suggesting that the States retain an analogous constitutional immunity from private suits in their own courts support the conclusion that Congress lacks the Article I power to subject the States to private suits in those fora.

Our final consideration is whether a congressional power to subject nonconsenting States to private suits in their own courts is consistent with the structure of the Constitution. We look both to the essential principles of federalism and to the special role of the state courts in the constitutional design.

Although the Constitution grants broad powers to Congress, our federalism requires that Congress treat the States in a manner consistent with their status as residuary sovereigns and joint participants in the governance of the Nation. The founding generation thought it "neither becoming nor convenient that the several States of the Union, invested with that large residuum of sovereignty which had not been delegated to the United States, should be summoned as defendants to answer the complaints of private persons." *In re Ayers,* 123 U.S., at 505. The principle of sovereign immunity preserved by constitutional design "thus accords the States the respect owed them as members of the federation." *Puerto Rico Aqueduct and Sewer Authority,* 506 U.S., at 146; accord, *Coeur d'Alene Tribe,* supra, at 268 (recognizing "the dignity and respect afforded a State, which the immunity is designed to protect").

Petitioners contend that immunity from suit in federal court suffices to preserve the dignity of the States. Private suits against nonconsenting States, however, present "the indignity of subjecting a State to the coercive process of judicial tribunals at the instance of private parties," *In re Ayers,* supra, at 505; accord, *Seminole Tribe,* 517 U.S., at 58, regardless of the forum. Not only must a State defend or default but also it must face the prospect of being thrust, by federal fiat and against its will, into the disfavored status of a debtor, subject to the power of private citizens to levy on its treasury or perhaps even government buildings or property which the State administers on the public's behalf.

In some ways, of course, a congressional power to authorize private suits against nonconsenting States in their own courts would be even more offensive to state sovereignty than a power to authorize the suits in a federal forum. Although the immunity of one sovereign in the courts of another has often depended in part on comity or agreement, the immunity of a sovereign in its own courts has always been understood to be within the sole control of the sovereign itself. A power to press a State's own courts into federal service to coerce the other branches of the State, furthermore, is the power first to turn the State against itself and ultimately to commandeer the entire political machinery of the State against its will and at the behest of individuals. Cf. *Coeur d'Alene Tribe, supra,* at 276. Such plenary federal control of state governmental processes denigrates the separate sovereignty of the States.

It is unquestioned that the Federal Government retains its own immunity from suit not only in state tribunals but also in its own courts. In light of our constitutional system recognizing the essential sovereignty of the States, we are reluctant to conclude that the States are not entitled to a reciprocal privilege.

Underlying constitutional form are considerations of great substance. Private suits against nonconsenting States—especially suits for money damages—may threaten the financial integrity of the States. It is indisputable that, at the time of the founding, many of the States could have been forced into insolvency but for their immunity from private suits for money damages. Even today, an unlimited congressional power to authorize suits in state court to levy upon the treasuries of the States for compensatory damages, attorney's fees, and even punitive damages could create staggering burdens, giving Congress a power and a leverage over the States that is not contemplated by our constitutional design. The potential national power would pose a severe and notorious danger to the States and their resources.

A congressional power to strip the States of their immunity from private suits in their own courts would pose more subtle risks as well. "The principle of immunity from litigation assures the states and the nation from unanticipated intervention in the processes of government." *Great Northern Life Ins. Co. v. Read,* 322 U.S., at 53. When the States' immunity from private suits is disregarded, "the course of their public policy and the administration of their public affairs" may become "subject to and controlled by the mandates of judicial tribunals without their consent, and in favor of individual interests." *In re Ayers,* supra, at 505. While the States have relinquished their immunity from suit in some special contexts—at least as a practical matter, this surrender carries with it substantial costs to the autonomy, the decision making ability, and the sovereign capacity of the States.

A general federal power to authorize private suits for money damages would place unwarranted strain on the States' ability to govern in accordance with the will of their citizens. Today, as at the time of the founding, the allocation of scarce resources among competing needs and interests lies at the heart of the political process. While the judgment creditor of a State may have a legitimate claim for compensation, other important needs and worthwhile ends compete for access to the public fisc. Since all cannot be satisfied in full, it is inevitable that difficult decisions involving the most sensitive and political of judgments must be made. If the principle of representative government is to be preserved to the States, the balance between competing interests must be reached after deliberation by the political process established by the citizens of the State, not by judicial decree mandated by the Federal Government and invoked by the private citizen.

By " 'split[ting] the atom of sovereignty,' " the Founders established " 'two orders of government, each with its own direct relationship, its own privity, its own set of mutual rights and obligations to the people who sustain it and are governed by it.' " *Saenz v. Roe,* 526 U.S. 489, 504, n. 17 (1999). "The Constitution thus contemplates that a State's government will represent and remain accountable to its own citizens." *Printz,* 521 U.S., at 920. When the Federal Government asserts authority over a State's most fundamental political processes, it strikes at the heart of the political accountability so essential to our liberty and republican form of government.

The asserted authority would blur not only the distinct responsibilities of the State and National Governments but also the separate duties of the judicial and political branches of the state governments, displacing "state decisions that 'go to the heart of representative government.' " *Gregory v. Ashcroft,* 501 U.S. 452, 461 (1991). A State is entitled to order the processes of its own governance, assigning to the political branches, rather than the courts, the responsibility for directing the payment of debts. See *id.,* at 460 ("Through the structure of its government, and the character of those who exercise government authority, a State defines itself as a sovereign"). If Congress could displace a State's allocation of governmental power and responsibility, the judicial branch of the State, whose legitimacy derives from fidelity to the law, would be compelled to assume a role not only foreign to its experience but beyond its competence as defined by the very Constitution from which its existence derives.

Congress cannot abrogate the States' sovereign immunity in federal court; were the rule to be different here, the National Government would wield greater power in the state courts than in its own judicial instrumentalities.

In light of history, practice, precedent, and the structure of the Constitution, we hold that the States retain immunity from private suit in their own courts, an immunity beyond the congressional power to abrogate by Article I legislation.

The constitutional privilege of a State to assert its sovereign immunity in its own courts does not confer upon the State a concomitant right to disregard the Constitution or valid federal law. The States and their officers are bound by obligations imposed by the Constitution and by federal statutes that comport with the constitutional design. We are unwilling to assume the States will refuse to honor the Constitution or obey the binding laws of the United States. The good faith of the States thus provides an important assurance that "[t]his Constitution, and the Laws of the United States which shall be made in Pursuance thereof shall be the supreme Law of the Land." U.S. Const., Art. VI.

Sovereign immunity, moreover, does not bar all judicial review of state compliance with the Constitution and valid federal law. Rather, certain limits are implicit in the constitutional principle of state sovereign immunity.

The first of these limits is that sovereign immunity bars suits only in the absence of consent. Many States, on their own initiative, have enacted statutes consenting to a wide variety of suits. The rigors of sovereign immunity are thus "mitigated by a sense of justice which has continually expanded by consent the suability of the sovereign." *Great Northern Life Ins. Co. v. Read,* 322 U.S., at 53. Nor, subject to constitutional limitations, does the Federal Government lack the authority or means to seek the States' voluntary consent to private suits. Cf. *South Dakota v. Dole,* 483 U.S. 203 (1987).

The States have consented, moreover, to some suits pursuant to the plan of the Convention or to subsequent constitutional Amendments. In ratifying the Constitution, the States consented to suits brought by other States or by the Federal Government. A suit which is commenced and prosecuted against a State in the name of the United States by those who are entrusted with the constitutional duty to "take Care that the Laws be faithfully executed," U.S. Const., Art. II, § 3, differs in kind from the suit of an individual: While the Constitution contemplates suits among the members of the federal system as an alternative to extralegal measures, the fear of private suits against nonconsenting States was the central reason given by the Founders who chose to preserve the States' sovereign immunity. Suits brought by the United States itself require the exercise of political responsibility for each suit prosecuted against a State, a control which is absent from a broad delegation to private persons to sue nonconsenting States.

We have held also that in adopting the Fourteenth Amendment, the people required the States to surrender a portion of the sovereignty that had been preserved to them by the original Constitution, so that Congress may authorize private suits against nonconsenting States pursuant to its § 5 enforcement power. *Fitzpatrick v. Bitzer,* 427 U.S. 445 (1976). By imposing explicit limits on the powers of the States and granting Congress the power to enforce them, the Amendment "fundamentally altered the balance of state and federal power struck by the Constitution." *Seminole Tribe,* 517 U.S., at 59. When Congress enacts appropriate legislation to enforce this Amendment, see *City of Boerne v. Flores,* 521 U.S. 507 (1997), federal interests are paramount, and Congress may assert an authority over the States which would be otherwise unauthorized by the Constitution. *Fitzpatrick,* supra, at 456.

The second important limit to the principle of sovereign immunity is that it bars suits against States but not lesser entities. The immunity does not extend to suits prosecuted against a municipal corporation or other governmental entity which is not an arm of the State. Nor does sovereign immunity bar all suits against state officers. Some suits against state officers are barred by the rule that sovereign immunity is not limited to suits which name the State as a party if the suits are, in fact, against the State. See, e.g., *In re Ayers,* 123 U.S., at 505–506; *Idaho v. Coeur d'Alene Tribe of Idaho,* 521 U.S., at 270 ("The real interests served by the Eleventh Amendment are not to be sacrificed to elementary mechanics of captions and pleading"). The rule, however, does not bar certain actions against state officers for injunctive or declaratory relief. Compare *Ex parte Young,* 209 U.S. 123 (1908), and *In re Ayers,* supra, with *Coeur d'Alene Tribe of Idaho,* supra, *Seminole Tribe,* supra, and *Edelman v. Jordan,* 415 U.S. 651 (1974). Even a suit for money damages may be prosecuted against a state officer in his individual capacity for unconstitutional or wrongful conduct fairly attributable to the officer himself, so long as the relief is sought not from the state treasury but from the officer personally. *Scheuer v. Rhodes,* 416 U.S. 232, 237–238 (1974); *Ford Motor Co. v. Department of Treasury of Ind.,* 323 U.S. 459, 462 (1945).

The principle of sovereign immunity as reflected in our jurisprudence strikes the proper balance between the supremacy of federal law and the separate sovereignty of the States. See *Pennhurst State School and Hospital v. Halderman,* 465 U.S., at 105. Established rules provide ample means to correct ongoing violations of law and to vindicate the interests which animate the Supremacy Clause. See *Green v. Mansour,* 474 U.S., at 68. That we have, during the first 210 years of our constitutional history, found it unnecessary to decide the question presented here suggests a federal power to subject nonconsenting States to private suits in their own courts is unnecessary to uphold the Constitution and valid federal statutes as the supreme law.

This case at one level concerns the formal structure of federalism, but in a Constitution as resilient as ours form mirrors substance. Congress has vast power but not all power. When Congress legislates in matters affecting the States, it may not treat these sovereign entities as mere prefectures or corporations. Congress must accord States the esteem due to them as joint participants in a federal system, one beginning with the premise of sovereignty in both the central Government and the separate States. Congress has ample means to ensure compliance with valid federal laws, but it must respect the sovereignty of the States.

The case before us depends upon these principles. The State of Maine has not questioned Congress' power to prescribe substantive rules of federal law to which it must comply. Despite an initial good-faith disagreement about the requirements of the FLSA, it is conceded by all that the State has altered its conduct so that its compliance with federal law cannot now be questioned. The Solicitor General of the United States has appeared before this Court, however, and asserted that the federal interest in compensating the States' employees for alleged past violations of federal law is so compelling that the sovereign State of Maine must be stripped of its immunity and subjected to suit in its own courts by its own employees. Yet, despite specific statutory authorization, see 29 U.S.C. § 216(c), the United States apparently found the same interests insufficient to justify sending even a single attorney to Maine to prosecute this litigation. The difference between a suit by the United States on behalf of the employees and a suit by the employees implicates a rule that the National Government must itself deem the case of sufficient importance to take action against the State; and history, precedent, and the structure of the Constitution make clear that, under the plan of the Convention, the States have consented to suits of the first kind but not of the second. The judgment of the Supreme Judicial Court of Maine is *Affirmed.*

JUSTICE SOUTER, with whom JUSTICE STEVENS, JUSTICE GINSBURG, and JUSTICE BREYER join, dissenting.

In *Seminole Tribe of Fla. v. Florida,* 517 U.S. 44 (1996), a majority of this Court invoked the Eleventh Amendment to declare that the federal judicial power under Article III of the Constitution does not reach a private action against a State, even on a federal question. In the Court's conception, however, the Eleventh Amendment was understood as having been enhanced by a "background principle" of state sovereign immunity (understood as immunity to suit), see *id.,* at 72, that operated beyond its limited codification in the Amendment, dealing solely with federal citizen-state diversity jurisdiction. To the *Seminole Tribe* dissenters, of whom I was one, the Court's enhancement of the Amendment was at odds with constitutional history and at war with the conception of divided sovereignty that is the essence of American federalism.

Today's issue arises naturally in the aftermath of the decision in *Seminole Tribe.* The Court holds that the Constitution bars an individual suit against a State to enforce a federal statutory right under the Fair Labor Standards Act of 1938 (FLSA), 29 U.S.C. § 201 *et seq.* (1994 ed. and Supp. III), when brought in the State's courts over its objection. In thus complementing its earlier decision, the Court of course confronts the fact that the state forum renders the Eleventh Amendment beside the point, and it has responded by discerning a simpler and more straightforward theory of state sovereign immunity than it found in *Seminole Tribe:* a State's sovereign immunity from all individual suits is a "fundamental aspect" of state sovereignty "confirm[ed]" by the Tenth Amendment. Ante, at 2246, 2247. As a consequence, *Seminole Tribe's* contorted reliance on the Eleventh Amendment and its background was presumably unnecessary; the Tenth would have done the work with an economy that the majority in *Seminole Tribe* would have welcomed. Indeed, if the Court's current reasoning is correct, the Eleventh Amendment itself was unnecessary. Whatever Article III may originally have said about the federal judicial power, the embarrassment to the State of Georgia occasioned by attempts in federal court to enforce the State's war debt could easily have been avoided if only the Court that decided *Chisholm v. Georgia,* 2 Dall. 419 (1793), had understood a State's inherent, Tenth Amendment right to be free of any judicial power, whether the court be state or federal, and whether the cause of action arise under state or federal law.

The sequence of the Court's positions prompts a suspicion of error, and skepticism is confirmed by scrutiny of the Court's efforts to justify its holding. There is no evidence that the Tenth Amendment constitutionalized a concept of sovereign immunity as inherent in the notion of statehood, and no evidence that any concept of inherent sovereign immunity was understood historically to apply when the sovereign sued was not the font of the law. Nor does the Court fare any better with its subsidiary lines of reasoning, that the state-court action is barred by the scheme of American federalism, a result supposedly confirmed by a history largely devoid of precursors to the action considered here. The Court's federalism ignores the accepted authority of Congress to bind States under the FLSA and to provide for enforcement of federal rights in state court. The Court's history simply disparages the capacity of the Constitution to order relationships in a Republic that has changed since the founding.

On each point the Court has raised it is mistaken, and I respectfully dissent from its judgment.

NOTES ON ALDEN AND STATE SOVEREIGN
IMMUNITY IN STATE COURT

1.   **The Constitutional Basis of *Alden*.** Like *Hans*, the constitutional basis of *Alden* is unclear. Is it the Eleventh Amendment? Is it the Tenth? Is the Court relying on general non-textual principles of federalism or state sovereignty? Does it make a difference?

2.   ***Alden* and Protecting State Treasuries.** In *Edelman*, as we have discussed, the Court defended state immunity on grounds that it was necessary to protect state treasuries. Yet, if the protection of the state fisc is the interest at stake, the Court's immunity decisions are decidedly under-inclusive. *Alden*, for example, explicitly approved of suits being brought against the states by the federal government, including suits that would seek the exact same monetary relief that the *Alden* plaintiffs themselves were seeking. Other avenues to the state treasury also remain unguarded. As we have seen, private suits for damages may be brought under statutes enacted pursuant to Section 5 of the Fourteenth Amendment, actions that seek affirmative injunctions may end up costing the state more money than retrospective relief, and state officers may be sued individually, and indemnified by the states, without violating immunity strictures. Note, too, *Alden*'s reference to *South Dakota v. Dole*, which held that Congress may condition grants of money to the states on the states' consent to federal regulation. Taking *Dole* as their premise, some lower courts have ruled that Congress may oblige states to consent to private suit as a condition for receiving federal money. See, e.g., *A.W. v. Jersey City Public Schools*, 341 F.3d 234 (3d Cir. 2003) (state gives up immunity by accepting funds under the Rehabilitation Act of 1973).

In light of all this, does the rationale of protecting state treasuries still support the Court's immunity decisions? Is there a better explanation?

3.   **The State Dignity Rationale.** The Court in *Alden* defended state immunity in part as related to protecting the central dignity of the states. Later, in *Federal Maritime Commission v. South Carolina State Ports Authority*, 535 U.S. 743 (2002), the Court echoed this rationale asserting that according the States "the dignity that is consistent with their status as sovereign entities" is the preeminent purpose of sovereign immunity. More recently, in *Virginia Office for Protection and Advocacy v. Stewart* (*VOPA*), 563 U.S. ___, 131 S.Ct. 1632 (2011), the Court per Justice Scalia, in allowing one entity of the state to sue another in federal court, expounded on the dignity rationale as follows:

> Denial of sovereign immunity, to be sure, offends the dignity of a State; but not every offense to the dignity of a State constitutes a denial of sovereign immunity. The specific indignity against which sovereign immunity protects is the insult to a State of being haled into court without its consent. That effectively occurs, our cases reasonably conclude, when (for example) the object of the suit against a state officer is to reach funds in the state treasury or

acquire state lands; it does not occur just because the suit happens to be brought by another state agency. Respondents' asserted dignitary harm is simply unconnected to the sovereign-immunity interest. . . .

Does Justice Scalia's opinion clarify what is meant by the term "dignity" in the Eleventh Amendment immunity context? Is his argument persuasive? Chief Justice Roberts was not convinced. In a dissent joined by Justice Alito, Roberts contended that "[t]he indignity [of the state's being sued in federal court] is compounded when the State is haled into federal court so that a federal judge can decide an internal state dispute." Roberts, therefore, would have dismissed the case. Does Roberts have the better argument? If so, why?

More generally, is protecting state dignity a more persuasive rationale for defending state immunity than protecting state treasuries? Is state dignity even a meaningful legal construct? See generally Peter J. Smith, *States as Nations: Dignity in Cross-Doctrinal Perspective,* 89 Va. L. Rev. 1 (2003) (discussing the possible doctrinal bases for the Court's reliance on dignity in the law of nations and in the common law of sovereign immunity). See also, Daniel A. Farber, *Pledging a New Allegiance: An Essay on Sovereignty and the New Federalism*, 75 Notre Dame L. Rev. 1133, 1136 (2000) (contending that the Court's use of "dignity" is shorthand to emphasize the states' unique role in the federal system).

C. CONGRESSIONAL ABROGATION UNDER THE BANKRUPTCY CLAUSE

CENTRAL VIRGINIA COMMUNITY COLLEGE V. KATZ
546 U.S. 356 (2006).

JUSTICE STEVENS delivered the opinion of the Court.

Petitioners are Virginia institutions of higher education that are considered "arms of the State" entitled to sovereign immunity. See, e.g., *Alden v. Maine*, 527 U.S. 706, 756 (1999) (observing that only arms of the State can assert the State's immunity). Wallace's Bookstores, Inc., did business with petitioners before it filed a petition for relief under chapter 11 of the Bankruptcy Code, 11 U.S.C. § 101 *et seq.* (2000 ed. and Supp. III), in the United States Bankruptcy Court for the Eastern District of Kentucky. Respondent, Bernard Katz, is the court-appointed liquidating supervisor of the bankrupt estate. He has commenced proceedings in the Bankruptcy Court pursuant to §§ 547(b) and 550(a) to avoid and recover alleged preferential transfers to each of the petitioners made by the debtor when it was insolvent. Petitioners' motions to dismiss those proceedings on the basis of sovereign immunity were denied by the Bankruptcy [Court].

Bankruptcy jurisdiction, at its core, is *in rem*. . . . [I]t does not implicate States' sovereignty to nearly the same degree as other kinds of jurisdiction. That was as true in the 18th century as it is today. Then, as now, the jurisdiction of courts adjudicating rights in the bankrupt estate included the power to issue compulsory orders to facilitate the administration and distribution of the res.

It is appropriate to presume that the Framers of the Constitution were familiar with the contemporary legal context when they adopted the Bankruptcy Clause—a provision which, as we explain [below], reflects the States' acquiescence in a grant of congressional power to subordinate to the pressing goal of harmonizing bankruptcy law sovereign immunity defenses that might have been asserted in bankruptcy proceedings. The history of the Bankruptcy Clause, the reasons it was inserted in the Constitution, and the legislation both proposed and enacted under its auspices immediately following ratification of the Constitution demonstrate that it was intended not just as a grant of legislative authority to Congress, but also to authorize limited subordination of state sovereign immunity in the bankruptcy arena. Foremost on the minds of those who adopted the Clause were the intractable problems, not to mention the injustice, created by one State's imprisoning of debtors who had been discharged (from prison and of their debts) in and by another State. As discussed below, to remedy this problem, the very first Congresses considered, and the Sixth Congress enacted, bankruptcy legislation authorizing federal courts to, among other things, issue writs of habeas corpus directed at state officials ordering the release of debtors from state prisons.

We acknowledge that statements in both the majority and the dissenting opinions in *Seminole Tribe of Fla. v. Florida*, 517 U.S. 44 (1996), reflected an assumption that the holding in that case would apply to the Bankruptcy Clause. Careful study and reflection have convinced us, however, that that assumption was erroneous. For the reasons stated by Chief Justice Marshall in *Cohens v. Virginia*, 19 U.S. 264 (1821) we are not bound to follow our dicta in a prior case in which the point now at issue was not fully debated. ("It is a maxim not to be disregarded, that general expressions, in every opinion, are to be taken in connection with the case in which those expressions are used. If they go beyond the case, they may be respected, but ought not to control the judgment in a subsequent suit when the very point is presented for decision").

Insofar as orders ancillary to the bankruptcy courts' *in rem* jurisdiction, like orders directing turnover of preferential transfers, implicate States' sovereign immunity from suit, the States agreed in the plan of the Convention not to assert that immunity. So much is evidenced not only by the history of the Bankruptcy Clause, which shows that the Framers' primary goal was to prevent competing sovereigns' interference with the debtor's discharge . . . but also by legislation considered and enacted in the immediate wake of the Constitution's ratification.

Congress considered proposed legislation establishing uniform federal bankruptcy laws in the first and each succeeding Congress until 1800, when the first Bankruptcy Act was passed. See C. Warren, Bankruptcy in United States History 10 (1935) ("In the very first session of the 1st Congress, during which only the most necessary subjects of legislation were considered, bankruptcy was one of those subjects; and as early as June 1, 1789, a Committee of the House was named to prepare a bankruptcy bill"). The Bankruptcy Act of 1800 was in many respects a copy of the English bankruptcy statute then in force. It was, like the English law, chiefly a measure designed to benefit creditors. Like the English statute, its principal provisions permitted bankruptcy commissioners, on appointment by a federal district court, to arrest the debtor, see § 4, 2 Stat. 22; to "cause the doors of the dwelling-house of [the] bankrupt to be broken," § 4, *id.*, at 23–24; to seize and collect the debtor's assets, § 5, *id.*, at 23; to examine the debtor and any individuals who might have possession of the debtor's property, §§ 14, 18, 19, *id.*, at 25–27; and to issue a "certificate of discharge" once the estate had been distributed, § 36, *id.*, at 31.

The American legislation differed slightly from the English, however. That difference reflects both the uniqueness of a system involving multiple sovereigns and the concerns that lay at the core of the Bankruptcy Clause itself. The English statute gave a judge sitting on a court where the debtor had obtained his discharge the power to order a sheriff, "Bailiff or Officer, Gaoler or Keeper of any Prison" to release the "Bankrupt out of Custody" if he were arrested subsequent to the discharge. 5 Geo. 2, ch. 30, P13 (1732). The American version of this provision was worded differently; it specifically granted federal courts the authority to issue writs of habeas corpus effective to release debtors from state prisons. See § 38, 2 Stat. 32; see also *In re Comstock*, 6 F. Cas. 237 (Vt. 1842) (observing that Bankruptcy Act of 1800, then repealed, would have granted a federal court the power to issue a writ of habeas corpus to release a debtor from state prison if he had been arrested following his bankruptcy discharge).

This grant of habeas power is remarkable not least because it would be another 67 years, after ratification of the Fourteenth Amendment, before the writ would be made generally available to state prisoners. Moreover, the provision of the 1800 Act granting that power was considered and adopted during a period when state sovereign immunity could hardly have been more prominent among the Nation's concerns. *Chisholm v. Georgia*, 2 U.S. 419, the case that had so "shock[ed]" the country in its lack of regard for state sovereign immunity, *Principality of Monaco v. Mississippi*, 292 U.S. 313 (1934) was decided in 1793. The ensuing five years that culminated in adoption of the Eleventh Amendment were rife with discussion of States' sovereignty and their amenability to suit. Yet there appears to be no record of any objection to the bankruptcy legislation or its grant of habeas power to federal courts based on an infringement of sovereign immunity.

This history strongly supports the view that the Bankruptcy Clause of Article I, the source of Congress' authority to effect this intrusion upon state sovereignty, simply did not contravene the norms this Court has understood the Eleventh Amendment to exemplify. Cf. *Blatchford v. Native Village of Noatak*, 501 U.S. 775 (1991) ("We have understood the Eleventh Amendment to stand not so much for what it says, but for the presupposition of our constitutional structure which it confirms . . ."). Petitioners, ignoring this history, contend that nothing in the *words* of the Bankruptcy Clause evinces an intent on the part of the Framers to alter the "background principle" of state sovereign immunity. Specifically, they deny that the word "uniform" in the Clause implies anything about pre-existing immunities or Congress' power to interfere with those immunities. Whatever the merits of petitioners' argument, it misses the point; text aside, the Framers, in adopting the Bankruptcy Clause, plainly intended to give Congress the power to redress the rampant injustice resulting from States' refusal to respect one another's discharge orders. As demonstrated by the First Congress' immediate consideration and the Sixth Congress' enactment of a provision granting federal courts the authority to release debtors from state prisons, the power to enact bankruptcy legislation was understood to carry with it the power to subordinate state sovereignty, albeit within a limited sphere.

The ineluctable conclusion, then, is that States agreed in the plan of the Convention not to assert any sovereign immunity defense they might have had in proceedings brought pursuant to "Laws on the subject of Bankruptcies." . . . The scope of this consent was limited; the jurisdiction exercised in bankruptcy proceedings was chiefly *in rem*—a narrow jurisdiction that does not implicate state sovereignty to nearly the same degree as other kinds of jurisdiction. But while the principal focus of the bankruptcy proceedings is and was always the res, some exercises of bankruptcy courts' powers—issuance of writs of habeas corpus included—unquestionably involved more than mere adjudication of rights in a res. In ratifying the Bankruptcy Clause, the States acquiesced in a subordination of whatever sovereign immunity they might otherwise have asserted in proceedings necessary to effectuate the *in rem* jurisdiction of the bankruptcy courts.

[Previous decisions of this Court] which held that States could not assert sovereign immunity as a defense in adversary proceedings brought to adjudicate the dischargeability of student loans [did not rest] on any statement Congress had made on the subject of state sovereign immunity.

Nor does our decision today. The relevant question is not whether Congress has "abrogated" States' immunity in proceedings to recover preferential transfers. See 11 U.S.C. § 106(a). The question, rather, is whether Congress' determination that States should be amenable to such proceedings is within the scope of its power to enact "Laws on the subject of Bankruptcies." We think it beyond peradventure that it is.

[JUSTICE THOMAS, joined by CHIEF JUSTICE ROBERTS and JUSTICES SCALIA and KENNEDY, dissented.]

Under our Constitution, the States are not subject to suit by private parties for monetary relief absent their consent or a valid congressional abrogation, and it is "settled doctrine" that nothing in Article I of the Constitution establishes those preconditions. *Alden v. Maine*, 527 U.S. 706, 748 (1999). Yet the majority today casts aside these long-established principles to hold that the States are subject to suit by a rather unlikely class of individuals—bankruptcy trustees seeking recovery of preferential transfers for a bankrupt debtor's estate. This conclusion cannot be justified by the text, structure, or history of our Constitution.

The majority does not appear to question the established framework for examining the question of state sovereign immunity under our Constitution. The Framers understood, and this Court reiterated over a century ago in *Hans v. Louisiana*, 134 U.S. 1 (1890), that " 'it is inherent in the nature of sovereignty not to be amenable to the suit of an individual without its consent. This is the general sense and the general practice of mankind; and the exemption, as one of the attributes of sovereignty, is now enjoyed by the government of every state in the Union. *Unless, therefore, there is a surrender of this immunity in the plan of the convention, it will remain with the states. . . .*' " (quoting The Federalist No. 81) ("That a State may not be sued without its consent is a fundamental rule of jurisprudence having so important a bearing upon the construction of the Constitution of the United States that it has become established by repeated decisions of this court that the entire judicial power granted by the Constitution does not embrace authority to entertain a suit brought by private parties against a State without consent given"); *Seminole Tribe of Fla. v. Florida*, 517 U.S. 44 (1996).

These principles were further reinforced early in our Nation's history, when the people swiftly rejected this Court's decision in *Chisholm v. Georgia*, 2 U.S. 419 (1793), by ratifying the Eleventh Amendment less than two years later. Thus, "for over a century [since *Hans*] we have reaffirmed that federal jurisdiction over suits against unconsenting States 'was not contemplated by the Constitution when establishing the judicial power of the United States.' " *Seminole Tribe* (quoting *Hans*).

The majority finds a surrender of the States' immunity from suit in Article I of the Constitution, which authorizes Congress "to establish . . .

uniform Laws on the subject of Bankruptcies throughout the United States." § 8, cl. 4. But nothing in the text of the Bankruptcy Clause suggests an abrogation or limitation of the States' sovereign immunity. Indeed, as this Court has noted on numerous occasions, "the Eleventh Amendment restricts the judicial power under Article III, and Article I cannot be used to circumvent the constitutional limitations placed upon federal jurisdiction." *Seminole Tribe.* "It is settled doctrine that neither substantive federal law nor attempted congressional abrogation under Article I bars a State from raising a constitutional defense of sovereign immunity in federal court." *Alden.* And we have specifically applied this "settled doctrine" to bar abrogation of state sovereign immunity under various clauses within § 8 of Article I. See, *e.g.*, *Seminole Tribe* (the Interstate and Indian Commerce Clauses); *Florida Prepaid Postsecondary Ed. Expense Bd. v. College Savings Bank*, 527 U.S. 627 (1999) (the Patents Clause).

It is difficult to discern an intention to abrogate state sovereign immunity through the Bankruptcy Clause when no such intention has been found in any of the other clauses in Article I. Indeed, our cases are replete with acknowledgments that there is nothing special about the Bankruptcy Clause in this regard. . . . Today's decision thus cannot be reconciled with our established sovereign immunity jurisprudence, which the majority does not purport to [overturn.]

It would be one thing if the majority simply wanted to overrule *Seminole Tribe* altogether. That would be wrong, but at least the terms of our disagreement would be transparent. The majority's action today, by contrast, is difficult to comprehend. Nothing in the text, structure, or history of the Constitution indicates that the Bankruptcy Clause, in contrast to all of the other provisions of Article I, manifests the States' consent to be sued by private citizens.

I respectfully dissent.

NOTES ON KATZ AND ABROGATION UNDER THE BANKRUPTCY POWER

1.   *Katz* **and Abrogation.** The *Katz* majority states that the relevant question in the case is "not whether Congress has 'abrogated' States' immunity in proceedings to recover preferential transfers" but "whether Congress' determination that States should be amenable to such proceedings is within the scope of its power to enact 'Laws on the subject of Bankruptcies.'" Do you understand what the Court means by this distinction? Does it have any practical significance?

2.   **The Bankruptcy Clause, the Commerce Clause, and Section 5 of the Fourteenth Amendment.** Unlike Section 5 of the Fourteenth Amendment (discussed in *Fitzpatrick v. Bitzer*), the Bankruptcy Clause, like

the Commerce Clause, predates the enactment of the Eleventh Amendment. Is this relevant to the Court's analysis? Should it be? What are the implications of *Katz* for congressional efforts to abrogate immunity under other Article I powers, e.g., the war power?

NOTES ON STATE IMMUNITY BEFORE FEDERAL AGENCIES AND IN SISTER STATE COURTS

1. **Immunity Before Federal Agencies.** In *Federal Maritime Commission v. South Carolina State Ports Authority*, 535 U.S. 743 (2002), the Court took *Alden* one step further and held that the states were immune from individual complaints brought before federal administrative agencies. The Court reached this result even though a Commission's order was not self-executing and the party seeking to enforce the order would have to proceed to federal court for enforcement. Although conceding, consistent with *Alden*, that a suit brought by a federal agency to enforce the individual claimant's interest would not be barred by state immunity, the Court nevertheless held that the state could not be coerced to defend itself before the Commission against a proceeding brought by an individual claimant. According to the Court, "[t]he affront to a State's dignity does not lessen when an adjudication takes place in an administrative tribunal as opposed to an Article III Court."

2. **Immunity in Sister State Courts.** In *Nevada v. Hall*, 440 U.S. 410 (1979), California plaintiffs sued the state of Nevada in California state court for damages resulting from an automobile accident with a Nevada state employee who had been driving a state-owned car in California. The California courts, rejecting Nevada's immunity defense, upheld a $1.15 million dollar judgment against the state. The United States Supreme Court affirmed the judgment, holding that the Constitution did not require the California courts to honor the state of Nevada's sovereign immunity. Does the case make sense in light of *Alden* or *South Carolina State Ports Authority*, or *Monaco v. Mississippi*, 292 U.S. 313 (1934) (holding that states are immune from suits by foreign governments)? Does it make sense that states may be immune from damage actions based on federal law but are not immune from actions based upon the law of a sister state? Does anything in the Court's Eleventh Amendment jurisprudence make sense?

CHAPTER 6

THE RELATIONSHIP BETWEEN
THE FEDERAL COURTS AND
THE STATE COURTS

■ ■ ■

I.   INTRODUCTION

The law governing the relationship between the federal courts and the state courts is intricate and complex. This is not surprising. The concurrent jurisdiction shared by the federal and state courts, for example, inevitably triggers complications and friction. When two judicial systems have the jurisdiction to simultaneously decide the same case or issue, and, as often occurs, are *actually* deciding the same case or issue, the likelihood of conflict is manifest and the rules resolving such conflict are unlikely to be easy. Competing policy considerations also serve to make the law in this area more difficult. On the one hand, jurisdictional statutes, such as 28 U.S.C. § 1331 (federal question) and 28 U.S.C. § 1332 (diversity) and substantive provisions, such as 42 U.S.C. § 1983, are premised on the notion that litigants may at times need insulation from potential state court bias or may need access to a presumed greater federal court expertise in order to fairly litigate their claims. On the other hand, traditional notions of judicial comity demand that federal courts respect the states' judicial processes. Further, the fact that state courts are the final arbiters of the state's own law can call for additional federal court deference when the interpretation of state law arises in the federal forum. Finally, federalism concerns complicate the governing law. Respect for state sovereign prerogatives strongly counsels against federal court interference with state enforcement actions and against federal court review of the constitutionality of state statutes. Yet as our previous discussion of 42 U.S.C. § 1983 shows, the federal courts also have a critical role in interposing themselves between the states and the people in order to preserve constitutional guarantees.

The labyrinth of doctrines (and sub-doctrines) that have been generated in response to the difficulties that inhere in the relationship between the federal and state courts is the subject of this chapter. In reviewing these materials, you should consider the following questions and themes: Which doctrines are based on federal statutes and which are judge-made? To what extent (if any) should the federal courts be able to ignore congressional directives in this area and be free to fashion their own rules as to when it is appropriate to exercise the jurisdiction granted to them by Congress? How do the various doctrines interplay with each other? A litigant seeking access to the federal court, for example, may face procedural defenses based upon a number of the doctrines discussed in this chapter. When, and why, will particular doctrinal defenses arise? Which defenses overlap and which (if any) are mutually exclusive? Are the various doctrines presented in this chapter internally consistent or consistent with each other? (Hint: The answer is no.) Which doctrines best reflect the underlying policies involved? Which are ill-advised? Finally, this area of federal courts jurisprudence is marked by its own taxonomy (with many of the doctrines named after leading cases). How well has the Court identified and differentiated the various doctrines involved?

II.   ABSTENTION

A.   PULLMAN ABSTENTION

RAILROAD COMMISSION OF TEXAS V. PULLMAN COMPANY
312 U.S. 496 (1941).

JUSTICE FRANKFURTER delivered the opinion of the Court.

In those sections of Texas where the local passenger traffic is slight, trains carry but one sleeping car. These trains, unlike trains having two or more sleepers, are without a Pullman conductor; the sleeper is in charge of a porter who is subject to the train conductor's control. As is well known, porters on Pullmans are colored and conductors are white. Addressing itself to this situation, the Texas Railroad Commission after due hearing ordered that "no sleeping car shall be operated on any line of railroad in the State of Texas . . . unless such cars are continuously in the charge of an employee . . . having the rank and position of Pullman conductor." Thereupon, the Pullman Company and the railroads affected brought this action in a federal district court to enjoin the Commission's order. Pullman porters were permitted to intervene as complainants, and Pullman conductors entered the litigation in support of the order.

The Pullman Company and the railroads assailed the order as unauthorized by Texas law as well as violative of the Equal Protection, the Due Process and the Commerce Clauses of the Constitution. The intervening porters adopted these objections but mainly objected to the order as a discrimination against Negroes in violation of the Fourteenth Amendment.

The complaint of the Pullman porters undoubtedly tendered a substantial constitutional issue. It is more than substantial. It touches a sensitive area of social policy upon which the federal courts ought not to enter unless no alternative to its adjudication plainly can be avoided if a definitive ruling on state issue would terminate the controversy. It is therefore our duty to turn to a consideration of questions under Texas law.

The Commission found justification for its order in a Texas statute which we quote in the margin.[1] It is common ground that if the order is within the Commission's authority its subject matter must be included in the Commission's power to prevent "unjust discrimination . . . and to prevent any and all other abuses" in the conduct of railroads. Whether arrangements pertaining to the staffs of Pullman cars are covered by the Texas concept of "discrimination" is far from clear. What practices of the railroad may be deemed to be "abuses" subject to the Commission's correction is equally doubtful. Reading the Texas statutes and the Texas decisions as outsiders without special competence in Texas law, we would have little confidence in our independent judgment regarding the application of that law to the present situation. The lower court did deny that the Texas statutes sustained the Commission's assertion of power. And this represents the view of an able and experienced circuit judge of the circuit which includes Texas and two capable district judges trained in Texas law. Had we or they no choice in the matter but to decide what is the law of the state, we should hesitate long before rejecting their forecast of Texas law. But no matter how seasoned the judgment of the district court may be, it cannot escape being a forecast rather than a determination. The last word on the meaning of Article 6445 of the Texas Civil Statutes, and therefore the last word on the statutory authority of the Railroad Commission in this case, belongs neither to us nor the district court but to the supreme court of Texas. In this situation a federal court of equity is asked to decide an issue by making a tentative answer which may be displaced tomorrow by a state adjudication. The reign of law is hardly promoted if an unnecessary ruling of a federal court is thus supplanted by a controlling decision of a state court. The resources of equity are equal to an adjustment that will avoid the waste of tentative decision as well as the friction of a premature constitutional adjudication.

---

[1] Vernon's Ann. Texas Civil Statutes, Article 6445 "Power and authority are hereby conferred upon the Railroad Commission of Texas over all railroads, and suburban, belt and terminal railroads, and over all public wharves, docks, piers, elevators, warehouses, sheds, tracks and other property used in connection therewith in this State, and over all persons, associations and corporations, private or municipal, owning or operating such railroad, wharf, dock, pier, elevator, warehouse, shed, track or other property to fix, and it is hereby made the duty of the said Commission to adopt all necessary rates, charges and regulations, to govern and regulate such railroads, persons, associations and corporations, and to correct the abuses and prevent unjust discrimination in the rates, charges and tolls of such railroads, persons, associations and corporations, and to fix division of rates, charges and regulations between railroads and other utilities and common carriers where a division is proper and correct, and to prevent any and all other abuses in conduct of their business and to do and perform such other duties and details in connection therewith as may be provided by law." [Footnote by the Court.]

An appeal to the chancellor, as we had occasion to recall only the other day, is an appeal to the "exercise of the sound discretion, which guides the determination of courts of equity." The history of equity jurisdiction is the history of regard for public consequences in employing the extraordinary remedy of the injunction. There have been as many and variegated applications of this supple principle as situations that have brought it into play. Few public interests have higher claim upon the discretion of a federal chancellor than the avoidance of needless friction with state policies, whether the policy relates to the enforcement of criminal law, or the administration of a specialized scheme for liquidating embarrassed business enterprises, or the final authority of state court to interpret doubtful regulatory laws of the state. These cases reflect a doctrine of abstention appropriate to our federal system whereby the federal courts, "exercising a wise discretion," restrain their authority because of "scrupulous regard for the rightful independence of the state governments" and for the smooth working of the federal judiciary. This use of equitable powers is a contribution of the courts in furthering the harmonious relation between state and federal authority without the need of rigorous congressional restriction of those powers.

Regard for these important considerations of policy in the administration of federal equity jurisdiction is decisive here. If there was no warrant in state law for the Commission's assumption of authority there is an end of the litigation; the constitutional issue does not arise. The law of Texas appears to furnish easy and ample means for determining the Commission's authority. Article 6453 of the Texas Civil Statutes gives review of such an order in the state courts. Or, if there are difficulties in the way of this procedure of which we have not been apprised, the issue of state law may be settled by appropriate action on the part of the State to enforce obedience to the order. In the absence of any showing that these obvious methods for securing a definitive ruling in the state courts cannot be pursued with full protection of the constitutional claim, the district court should exercise its wise discretion by staying its hands.

We therefore remand the cause to the district court, with directions to retain the bill pending a determination of proceedings, to be brought with reasonable promptness, in the state court in conformity with this opinion.

Reversed.

JUSTICE [OWEN J.] ROBERTS took no part in the consideration or decision of this case.

NOTES ON PULLMAN ABSTENTION

1. **Unclear State Law.** Why should the fact that state law is ambiguous require a federal court to abstain? Federal courts sitting in diversity, after all, are routinely called upon to interpret and apply ambiguous state law. If they can do so in diversity cases, is there any reason why federal courts cannot do the same when their jurisdiction is based upon the existence of a federal question? Is *Pullman* better understood as a doctrine designed to allow the federal courts to avoid deciding constitutional questions unnecessarily than a doctrine designed to clarify ambiguous state law?

2. **Unclear State Constitutional Law.** Abstention is less consistently mandated when the ambiguous state law in question involves a matter of state constitutional law. This is particularly true when the purportedly ambiguous state constitutional provision parallels the federal constitutional guarantee upon which the federal litigant's claim is based, as when, for example, the plaintiff's claim is that a state law violates both federal and state due process requirements. Cf. *Wisconsin v. Constantineau*, 400 U.S. 433 (1971). In contrast, abstention may be required when the challenged statute is based upon an "integrated scheme of related constitutional provisions, statutes, and regulations" and the "scheme as a whole calls for clarifying interpretations by the state courts." *Harris County Commissioners v. Moore*, 420 U.S. 77 (1975). Why the distinction? Would a general policy of abstention for unsettled state constitutional law effectively undermine *Monroe v. Pape*? See Chapter 1.

3. ***Pullman* and *Erie v. Tompkins*.** *Pullman* was decided three years after *Erie v. Tompkins*, 304 U.S. 64 (1938), overruled a one-hundred-year precedent, *Swift v. Tyson*, 41 U.S. (16 Pet.) 1 (1842), and held that federal courts must apply state law in diversity cases. Prior to *Erie*, the federal courts had been applying principles of federal common law as rules of decision in diversity cases but *Erie* held that approach improperly intruded upon state sovereignty. Is *Pullman* consistent, or inconsistent, with the decision in *Erie*?

4. **Abstention and Separation of Powers.** Does *Pullman* abstention violate separation of powers by allowing federal courts to refuse to exercise the jurisdiction granted to them by Congress in 28 U.S.C. § 1331 (the federal question statute)? *See* Martin H. Redish, *Abstention, Separation of Powers, and the Limits of the Judicial Function*, 94 YALE. L.J. 71 (1984). Or is *Pullman* justified by a general notion that courts have considerable discretion to limit their own jurisdiction when they find it appropriate? *See* David Shapiro, *Jurisdiction and Discretion*, 60 N.Y.U. L. REV. 543 (1985). Can *Pullman* also, or alternatively, be justified as a judge-made modification of the equitable *Ex parte Young* cause of action, see Chapter 5, pp. 421–430, on the ground that the federal court's equitable jurisdiction need not be exercised when the state law issue is ambiguous and a constitutional issue

can be avoided? See Michael Wells, *Why Professor Redish Is Wrong About Abstention*, 19 Ga. L. Rev. 1097 (1985).

5. Abstention and Equity. In *Quackenbush v. Allstate Ins. Co.*, 517 U.S. 706 (1996), the Court stated that the abstention doctrines are rooted in "the discretion historically enjoyed by courts of equity." The Court went on to state that this discretion must respect principles of federalism and comity and must be based "on a careful consideration of the federal interests in retaining jurisdiction over the dispute and the competing concern for the independence of state action." Does the decision in *Pullman* appropriately further this balance?

NOTE ON PROCEDURAL ASPECTS OF ABSTENTION

Generally, in a *Pullman* abstention case, the federal court will retain jurisdiction while the state courts determine the state law question to be resolved. The fact that two courts retain jurisdiction over the same matter, however, can be problematic. For example, how will the federal litigant ordered to bring her state claims to the state court be able to protect her federal claims from a preclusive state court decision? The Court attempted to answer this question in *England v. Louisiana State Board of Medical Examiners*, 375 U.S. 411 (1964). Under the procedures outlined in *England*, the litigant can either submit both her federal and state law claims to the state court or reserve her right to return to federal court for resolution of the federal issues. If she elects the latter course, she will then be protected from the *res judicata* effects that would otherwise result from splitting her claims.

But the procedures outlined in *England* are problematic on a number of counts. First, they impose substantial costs. Shuttling back and forth between courts is expensive and time consuming. The decision on the merits in *England* itself, for example, came after nine years of litigation. Second, the *England* procedures place the litigants in an awkward posture before the state court. The party reserving her right to a federal forum must litigate the state issue before the state court while at the same time effectively informing the state court that she does not believe that forum to be adequate to decide the federal issues. Third, whether a party has appropriately reserved her federal claims for federal court can also be a subject of protracted litigation particularly since the *England* decision does not require "explicit reservation" but may instead allow the party to return to federal court unless "it clearly appears that he voluntarily . . . fully litigated his federal claims in state court." Fourth, although the *England* procedures are designed to prevent the effects of claim preclusion with respect to the party's right to litigate her federal claims in federal court, they are ambiguous with respect to the effect of the state decision on issue preclusion (collateral estoppel). Binding adverse factual findings, however, can have substantial effects on the ability of a party to protect her federal claims. Finally, the viability of *England* procedures also depends on the willingness of the state court to hear state claims without having all the issues in a case brought before it for resolution. What happens if a state refuses to go along? The Court answered this last question in *Harris County Commissioners v. Moore*, 420 U.S. 77 (1975), holding that in such circumstances the federal court should dismiss the case "without prejudice so that any remaining federal claim may be raised in a federal forum after the [state] courts have been given the opportunity to address the state-law question in [the] case." Does the resolution in *Harris* adequately protect the right of a party to preserve her claims in the federal forum without *res judicata* effect? Should it?

NOTE ON CERTIFICATION

One alternative to the intricacies of the abstention procedure outlined in *England* is certification. Under the certification process, a federal court may make an inquiry directly to the supreme court of the state when it needs clarification on "a novel or unsettled state law" question. Because the existence of "novel or unsettled state law" is the only condition precedent for certification, the Court has suggested that a federal court may seek certification even in circumstances where it otherwise might not be required to abstain. *Arizonans for Official English v. Arizona*, 520 U.S. 43, 76 (1997). At the same time, however, the Court has also stated that the availability of the certification procedure alone "is not in itself sufficient to render abstention appropriate." *Houston v. Hill*, 482 U.S. 451 (1987).

When certification is requested by a federal court, the state supreme court has the option of answering or refusing to answer the certified question. If the state supreme court refuses, the federal court issues its own interpretation of the meaning of the unsettled law. Guido Calabresi, *Federal and State Courts: Restoring a Workable Balance*, 78 N.Y.U. L. REV. 1293 (2003).

Certification must be authorized by state statute. In 1945, Florida became the first state to pass a certification statute and, since then, most other states have followed suit. Currently, North Carolina is the only state not to have enacted a certification procedure, *see* Eric Eisenberg, Note, *A Divine Comity: Certification (At Last) In North Carolina*, 58 Duke L. J. 69 (2008); but Missouri's statute was held unconstitutional by the Missouri Supreme Court. Grantham v. Missouri Department of Corrections, No. 72576, 1990 WL 602159, at *1 (Mo. July 13, 1990) (*en banc*).

The states' certification procedures vary, however. Several state supreme courts, for example, will only allow certification from the Supreme Court or a Circuit Court of Appeals. 19 WRIGHT & MILLER, FEDERAL PRACTICE & PROCEDURE § 4507 n. 57 (2005).

One commentator has characterized certification as "vastly superior" to *Pullman* abstention, provided that the state law is truly unclear and the question is important enough to defer to the state supreme court. Martha A. Field, *The Abstention Doctrine Today*, 125 U. PA. L. REV. 590, 605 (1977). The Supreme Court has also expounded the virtues of certification stating that certification saves time, energy and resources and helps to build cooperative judicial federalism. *Lehman Brothers v. Schein*, 416 U.S. 386, 390 (1974); see also *Clay v. Sun Insurance Office Ltd.*, 363 U.S. 207 (1960) (praising the Florida legislature's "rare foresight" in enacting the first certification statute), *Bellotti v. Baird,* 428 U.S. 132, 150–51 (1976). Likewise, the certification procedure is popular among some lower court judges as well. For example, Second Circuit Judge Guido Calabresi has written that "whenever there is a question of state law that is even possibly in doubt" the federal court should humbly certify the issue and let the state decide, regardless what the federal judge thinks the state law *ought* to be. Guido Calabresi, supra at 1293.

The support for certification is not universal. Some critics argue that slow responses from already overloaded state supreme courts means that certification does not save time in the long run. Randall T. Shepard, *Is Making State Constitutional Law Through Certified Questions a Good Idea or Bad Idea?*, 38 VAL. U. L. REV. 327, 345 (2004). Further, getting a good response from the state supreme court depends heavily on how the federal court formulates the question. Finally, state supreme courts may have difficulty in interpreting their laws without factual contexts. See M. Bryan Schneider, *"But Answer Came There None:" The Michigan Supreme Court and the Certified Question of State Law*, 41 WAYNE L. REV. 273, 294 (1995). After all, the federal rule against advisory opinions is supported as much by the policy of assuring grounded and concrete judicial decision making as it is in limiting federal judicial power for its own sake. Why should state court resolutions of abstract legal issues fare any better?

B. BURFORD ABSTENTION

BURFORD V. SUN OIL CO.
319 U.S. 315 (1943).

JUSTICE BLACK delivered the opinion of the Court.

In this proceeding brought in a federal district court, the Sun Oil Co. attacked the validity of an order of the Texas Railroad Commission granting the petitioner Burford a permit to drill four wells on a small plot of land in the East Texas oil field. Jurisdiction of the federal court was invoked because of the diversity of citizenship of the parties, and because of the Companies' contention that the order denied them due process of law.

Although a federal equity court does have jurisdiction of a particular proceeding, it may, in its sound discretion, whether its jurisdiction is invoked on the ground of diversity of citizenship or otherwise, "refuse to enforce or protect legal rights, the exercise of which may be prejudicial to the public interest" for it "is in the public interest that federal courts of equity should exercise their discretionary power with proper regard for the rightful independence of state governments in carrying out their domestic policy." While many other questions are argued, we find it necessary to decide only one: Assuming that the federal district court had jurisdiction, should it, as a matter of sound equitable discretion, have declined to exercise that jurisdiction here?

Texas' interests in this matter are more than that very large one of conserving gas and oil, two of our most important natural resources. It must also weigh the impact of the industry on the whole economy of the state and must consider its revenue, much of which is drawn from taxes on the industry and from mineral lands preserved for the benefit of its educational and eleemosynary institutions. To prevent "past, present, and imminent evils" in the production of natural gas, a statute was enacted "for the protection of public and private interests against such evils by prohibiting waste and compelling ratable production." The primary task of attempting adjustment of these diverse interests is delegated to the Railroad Commission which Texas has vested with "broad discretion" in administering the law.

The Commission [has] accepted State oil production quotas and has undertaken to translate the amount to be produced for the State as a whole into a specific amount for each field and for each well. These judgments are made with due regard for the factors of full utilization of the oil supply, market demand, and protection of the individual operators, as well as protection of the public interest. As an essential aspect of the control program, the State also regulates the spacing of wells. The legislature has disavowed a purpose of requiring that "the separately owned properties in any pool (should) be unitized under one management, control or ownership" and the Commission must thus work out the difficult spacing problem with due regard for whatever rights Texas recognizes in the separate owners to a share of the common reservoir. At the same time it must restrain waste, whether by excessive production or by the unwise dissipation of the gas and other geologic factors that cause the oil to flow.

Since 1919 the Commission has attempted to solve this problem by its Rule 37. The rule provides for certain minimum spacing between wells, but also allows exceptions where necessary "to prevent waste or to prevent the confiscation of property." The prevention of confiscation is based on the premises that, insofar as these privileges are compatible with the prevention of waste and the achievement of conservation, each surface owner should be permitted to withdraw the oil under his surface area, and that no one else can fairly be permitted to drain his oil away. Hence the Commission may protect his interest either by adjusting his amount of production upward, or by permitting him to drill additional wells.

Additional wells may be required to prevent waste as has been noticed, where geologic circumstances require immediate drilling. . . . If a substantial amount of oil will be saved by the drilling of a well that otherwise would ultimately be lost, the permit to drill such well may be justified under one of the exceptions provided in Rule 37 to prevent waste.

The delusive simplicity with which these principles of exception to Rule 37 can be stated should not obscure the actual nonlegal complexities involved in their application. While the surface holder may, subject to qualifications noted, be entitled under current Texas law to the oil under his land, there can be no absolute certainty as to how much oil actually is present, and since the waste and confiscation problems are as a matter of physical necessity so closely interrelated, decision of one of the questions necessarily involves recognition of the other. The sheer quantity of exception cases makes their disposition of great public importance. It is estimated that over two-thirds of the wells in the East Texas field exist as exceptions to the rule, and since each exception may provoke a conflict among the interested parties, the volume of litigation arising from the administration of the rule is considerable. The instant case arises from just such an exception. It is not peculiar that the state should be represented here by its Attorney General, for cases like this, involving "confiscation," are not mere isolated disputes between private parties. Aside from the general principles which may evolve from these proceedings, the physical facts are such that an additional permit may affect pressure on a well miles away. The standards applied by the Commission in a given case necessarily affect the entire state conservation system.

To prevent the confusion of multiple review of the same general issues, the legislature provided for concentration of all direct review of the Commission's orders in the State district courts of Travis County. . . . To permit [multiple] state courts to pass upon the Commission's rules and orders, "would lead to intolerable confusion. If all district courts of this state had jurisdiction of such matters, different courts of equal dignity might reach different and conflicting conclusions as to the same rule. Manifestly, the jurisdictional provision under discussion was incorporated in the act for the express purpose of avoiding such confusion." Time and experience, say the Texas courts, have shown the wisdom of this rule. Concentration of judicial supervision of Railroad Commission orders permits the state courts, like the Railroad Commission itself, to acquire a specialized knowledge which is useful in shaping the policy of regulation of the ever-changing demands in this field.

The very "confusion" which the Texas legislature and Supreme Court feared might result from review by many state courts of the Railroad Commission's orders has resulted from the exercise of federal equity jurisdiction. As a practical matter, the federal courts can make small contribution to the well organized system of regulation and review which the Texas statutes provide. Texas courts can give fully as great relief, including temporary restraining orders, as the federal courts. Delay, misunderstanding of local law, and needless federal conflict with the State policy, are the inevitable product of this double system of review. [The Court then offered examples where federal court decisions interpreting state law have disrupted the state processes and required the state authority "to adjust itself to the permutations of the law as seen by the federal courts."]

Insofar as we have discretion to do so, we should leave these problems of Texas law to the State court where each may be handled as "one more item in a continuous series of adjustments." These questions of regulation of the industry by the State administrative agency . . . so clearly involves basic problems of Texas policy that equitable discretion should be exercised to give the Texas courts the first opportunity to consider them. "Few public interests have a higher claim upon the discretion of a federal chancellor and the avoidance of needless friction with state policies. . . . These cases reflect a doctrine of abstention appropriate to our federal system whereby the federal courts, 'exercising a wise discretion,' restrain their authority because of 'scrupulous regard for the rightful independence of the state governments' and for the smooth working of the federal judiciary."

The state provides a unified method for the formation of policy and determination of cases by the Commission and by the state courts. The judicial review of the Commission's decisions in the state courts is expeditious and adequate. Conflicts in the interpretation of state law, dangerous to the success of state policies, are almost certain to result from the intervention of the lower federal courts. On the other hand, if the state procedure is followed from the Commission to the State Supreme Court, ultimate review of the federal questions is fully preserved here. Under such circumstances, a sound respect for the independence of state action requires the federal equity court to stay its hand.

The decision of the Circuit Court of Appeals is reversed and the judgment of the District Court dismissing the complaint is affirmed for the reasons here stated.

It is so ordered.

NOTES ON BURFORD ABSTENTION

1. **The Rationale of *Burford*.** Why did the Court abstain in *Burford*? Is it because the state had set up an elaborate procedure involving both state agency action and state court review to resolve issues regarding drilling rights? Is it because the allocation of drilling rights to a common pool of oil lying underneath the properties of multiple claimants is necessarily interrelated and is best served by one centralized review? Is it because the

allocation of oil drilling rights in Texas involves particularly strong state policies?

2. Subsequent Decisions. Although occasionally raised, *Burford* has not often been followed. Indeed, only in one case, *Alabama Public Service Comm'n v. Southern R. Co.*, 341 U.S. 341 (1951), has the Court authorized abstention on *Burford* grounds. *Alabama Public Service* was a challenge by a railroad to a state agency order refusing to allow it to discontinue an unprofitable intrastate railroad line. As in *Burford*, the state required that reviews of such agency orders be brought in a particular state court. Although the state law in the case was apparently clear, the Court held that "the unified nature of the state regulatory process" and the "predominantly local factor of public need for the service rendered" required abstention. Taken by itself, *Alabama Public Service* might then be read as authorization for *Burford* abstention in a wide range of matters. Later cases, however, have described *Burford* only as an "extraordinary and narrow" exception to the duty of federal courts to adjudicate matters properly within their jurisdiction. *Quackenbush v. Allstate Ins. Co.*, 517 U.S. 706 (1996) (quoting *Colorado River Water Conservation District et al. v. United States,* 424 U.S. 800 (1976)). See *New Orleans Public Service, Inc. v. Council of City of New Orleans* (*NOPSI*), 491 U.S. 350 (1989) (refusing to apply *Burford* abstention to a challenge to a city council order setting the rates for an electric utility).

C. THIBODAUX ABSTENTION

LOUISIANA POWER & LIGHT CO. V. CITY OF THIBODAUX
360 U.S. 25 (1959).

JUSTICE FRANKFURTER delivered the opinion of the Court.

The City of Thibodaux, Louisiana, filed a petition for expropriation in one of the Louisiana District Courts, asserting a taking of the land, buildings, and equipment of petitioner Power and Light Company. Petitioner, a Florida corporation, removed the case to the United States District Court for the Eastern District of Louisiana on the basis of diversity of citizenship. [T]he district judge, on his own motion, ordered that "Further proceedings herein, therefore, will be stayed until the Supreme Court of Louisiana has been afforded an opportunity to interpret Act 111 of 1900, the authority on which the city's expropriation order was based."

[T]he distinction between expropriation proceedings and ordinary diversity cases, though found insufficient to restrict diversity jurisdiction, remains a relevant and important consideration in the appropriate judicial administration of such actions in the federal courts.

We have increasingly recognized the wisdom of staying actions in the federal courts pending the determination by a state court of decisive issues of state law. Thus in *Railroad Comm'n* v. *Pullman Co.*, 312 U.S. 496 (1941) it was said:

> "Had we or they [the lower court judges] no choice in the matter but to decide what is the law of the state, we should hesitate long before rejecting their forecast of Texas law. But no matter how seasoned the judgment of the district court may be, it cannot escape being a forecast rather than a determination."

On the other hand, we have held that the mere difficulty of state law does not justify a federal court's relinquishment of jurisdiction in favor of state court action. *Meredith* v. *Winter Haven*, 320 U.S. 228 (1943). But where the issue touched upon the relationship of City to State, or involved the scope of a previously uninterpreted state statute which, if applicable, was of questionable constitutionality, we have required District Courts, and not merely sanctioned an exercise of their discretionary power, to stay their proceedings pending the submission of the state law question to state determination.

These prior cases have been cases in equity, but they did not apply a technical rule of equity procedure. They reflect a deeper policy derived from our federalism. We have drawn upon the judicial discretion of the chancellor to decline jurisdiction over a part or all of a case brought before him. See *Railroad Comm'n* v. *Pullman Co.*, supra. Although an eminent domain proceeding is deemed for certain purposes of legal classification a "suit at common law," it is of a special and peculiar nature. Mr. Justice Holmes set forth one differentiating characteristic of eminent domain: it is intimately involved with sovereign prerogative. And when, as here, a city's power to condemn is challenged, a further aspect of sovereignty is introduced. A determination of the nature and extent of delegation of the power of eminent domain concerns the apportionment of governmental powers between City and State. The issues normally turn on legislation with much local variation interpreted in local settings. The considerations that prevailed in conventional equity suits for avoiding the hazards of serious disruption by federal courts of state government or needless friction between state and federal authorities are similarly appropriate in a state eminent domain proceeding brought in, or removed to, a federal court.

The special nature of eminent domain justifies a district judge, when his familiarity with the problems of local law so counsels him, to ascertain the meaning of a disputed state statute from the only tribunal empowered to speak definitively—the courts of the State under whose statute eminent domain is sought to be exercised—rather than himself make a dubious and tentative forecast. This course does not constitute abnegation of judicial duty. On the contrary, it is a wise and productive discharge of it. There is only postponement of decision for its best fruition. Eventually the District Court will award compensation if the taking is sustained. If for some reason a declaratory judgment is not promptly sought from the state courts and obtained within a reasonable time, the District Court, having retained complete control of the litigation, will doubtless assert it to decide also the question of the meaning of the state statute. The justification for this power, to be exercised within the indicated limits, lies in regard for the respective competence of the state and federal court systems and for the maintenance of harmonious federal-state relations in a matter close to the political interests of a State.

Reversed.

JUSTICE BRENNAN, with whom THE CHIEF JUSTICE and MR. JUSTICE DOUGLAS join, dissenting.

Until today, the standards for testing this order of the District Court sending the parties to this diversity action to a state court for decision of a state law question might have been said to have been reasonably consistent with the imperative duty of a District Court, imposed by Congress under 28 U.S.C. §§ 1332 and 1441, to render prompt justice in cases between citizens of different States. To order these suitors out of the federal court and into a state court in the circumstances of this case passes beyond disrespect for the diversity jurisdiction to plain disregard of this imperative duty. The doctrine of abstention, in proper perspective, is an extraordinary and narrow exception to this duty, and abdication of the obligation to decide cases can be justified under this doctrine only in the exceptional circumstances where the order to the parties to repair to the state court would clearly serve one of two important countervailing interests: either the avoidance of a premature and perhaps unnecessary decision of a serious federal constitutional question, or the avoidance of the hazard of unsettling some delicate balance in the area of federal-state relationships.

NOTES ON THE SCOPE AND RATIONALE OF THIBODAUX

1. **Abstention in Diversity Cases.** *Thibodaux,* unlike *Pullman,* was a diversity case. Are there reasons to be especially reluctant to allow federal courts to abstain in diversity cases, as opposed to federal question matters? If the state law issue in *Thibodaux* is resolved by the state court, what is left for the federal court to decide? Should the procedures set forth in *England* also apply to *Thibodaux* abstention cases?

2. ***Thibodaux* and Eminent Domain.** The *Thibodaux* Court relied significantly on the proposition that abstention was required because eminent domain proceedings are "intimately involved with sovereign prerogative." Are there other areas besides eminent domain where similar state interests are at stake? Why is eminent domain any more intimately

involved with the state's sovereign prerogatives than any other exercise of the police power?

3. ***Thibodaux* and Unclear State Law.** Although *Thibodaux* has occasionally been explained as requiring abstention in eminent domain cases, the case cannot be so easily categorized. Indeed, in *County of Allegheny v. Frank Mashuda Co.*, 360 U.S. 185 (1959), decided the same day as *Thibodaux*, the Court held that abstention in an eminent domain case was not warranted because the state law in that case was not unclear.

4. **Stays Versus Dismissals.** The Court has subsequently also distinguished *Thibodaux* and *County of Allegheny v. Frank Mashuda, Co.* on grounds that in the former case the federal district court stayed the proceeding while in the latter it dismissed the federal action outright. See *Quackenbush v. Allstate Ins. Co.*, 517 U.S. 706 (1996). Why would this distinction matter?

5. ***Thibodaux* and State Divisions of Powers.** The ambiguous issue in *Thibodaux* left for the state court to resolve concerned the power of a city to initiate eminent domain proceedings under state law. Does the fact that this question involves the division of state power make abstention particularly warranted?

6. ***Thibodaux* and *Burford*.** In at least one case, the Court grouped *Thibodaux* and *Burford* abstention into one category. See *Colorado River Water Conservation District et al. v. United States,* 424 U.S. 800 (1976). Citing both *Thibodaux* and *Burford*, the Court in *Colorado River* described this category as requiring abstention "when there are difficult questions of state law bearing on policy problems of substantial public import whose importance transcends the result in the case then at bar" or when "the exercise of federal review of the question in a case and in similar cases would be disruptive of state efforts to establish a coherent policy with respect to a matter of substantial public concern." See also *New Orleans Public Service, Inc. v. Council of City of New Orleans (NOPSI)*, 491 U.S. 350 (1989) (describing the type of abstention demanded under these criteria as the "*Burford* doctrine"). Did the Court in *Colorado River* mistakenly conflate two doctrines into a single two-part test? Did it ignore the aspect of *Thibodaux* that appears to require the existence of unclear state law?

D. DEFERENCE TO PARALLEL PROCEEDINGS (COLORADO RIVER ABSTENTION)

COLORADO RIVER WATER CONSERVATION DISTRICT ET AL. v. UNITED STATES

424 U.S. 800 (1976).

JUSTICE BRENNAN delivered the opinion of the Court.

The McCarran Amendment, 43 U.S.C. § 666, provides that "consent is hereby given to join the United States as a defendant in any suit (1) for the adjudication of rights to the use of water of a river system or other source, or (2) for the administration of such rights, where it appears that the United States is the owner of or is in the process of acquiring water rights by appropriation under State law, by purchase, by exchange, or otherwise, and the United States is a necessary party to such suit." The questions presented by this case concern the effect of the McCarran Amendment upon the jurisdiction of the federal district courts under 28 U.S.C. § 1345 over suits for determination of water rights brought by the United States as trustee for certain Indian tribes and as owner of various non-Indian Government claims.

It is probable that no problem of the Southwest section of the Nation is more critical than that of scarcity of water. As southwestern populations have grown, conflicting claims to this scarce resource have increased. To meet these claims, several Southwestern States have established elaborate procedures for allocation of water and adjudication of conflicting claims to that resource. In 1969, Colorado enacted its Water Rights Determination and Administration Act in an effort to revamp its legal procedures for determining claims to water within the State.

[T]he Government instituted this suit in the United States District Court for the District of Colorado, invoking the court's jurisdiction under 28 U.S.C. § 1345. The District Court is located in Denver, some 300 miles from Division 7. The suit, against some 1,000 water users, sought declaration of the Government's rights to waters in certain rivers and their tributaries located in Division 7. In the suit, the Government asserted reserved rights on its own behalf and on behalf of certain Indian tribes, as well as rights based on state law. It sought appointment of a water master to administer any waters decreed to the United States. Prior to institution of this suit, the Government had pursued adjudication of non-Indian reserved rights and other water claims based on state law in Water Divisions 4, 5, and 6, and the Government continues to participate fully in those Divisions.

Shortly after the federal suit was commenced, one of the defendants in that suit filed an application in the state court for Division 7, seeking an order directing service of process on the United States in order to make it a party to proceedings in Division 7 for the purposes of adjudicating all of the Government's claims, both state and federal. On January 3, 1973 the United States was served pursuant to authority of the McCarran Amendment. Several defendants and interveners in the federal proceedings then filed a motion in the District Court to dismiss on the ground that under the Amendment, the court was without jurisdiction to determine federal water rights. . . . [T]he District Court, [found] that the doctrine of abstention required deference to the proceedings in Division 7. . . .

B.

Next, we consider whether the District Court's dismissal was appropriate under the doctrine of abstention. We hold that the dismissal cannot be supported under that doctrine in any of its forms.

C.

Although this case falls within none of the abstention categories, there are principles unrelated to considerations of proper constitutional adjudication and regard for federal-state relations which govern in situations involving the contemporaneous exercise of concurrent jurisdictions, either by federal courts or by state and federal courts. These principles rest on considerations of "[wise] judicial administration, giving regard to conservation of judicial resources and comprehensive disposition of litigation." Generally, as between state and federal courts, the rule is that "the pendency of an action in the state court is no bar to proceedings concerning the same matter in the Federal court having jurisdiction. . . ." As between federal district courts, however, though no precise rule has evolved, the general principle is to avoid duplicative litigation. This difference in general approach between state-federal concurrent jurisdiction and wholly federal concurrent jurisdiction stems from the virtually unflagging obligation of the federal courts to exercise the jurisdiction given them. Given this obligation, and the absence of weightier considerations of constitutional adjudication and state-federal relations, the circumstances permitting the dismissal of a federal suit due to the presence of a concurrent state proceeding for reasons of wise judicial administration are considerably more limited than the circumstances appropriate for abstention. The former circumstances, though exceptional, do nevertheless exist.

Turning to the present case, a number of factors clearly counsel against concurrent federal proceedings. The most important of these is the McCarran Amendment itself. The clear federal policy evinced by that legislation is the avoidance of piecemeal adjudication of water rights in a river system. This policy is akin to that underlying the rule requiring that jurisdiction be yielded to the court first acquiring control of property, for the concern in such instances is with avoiding the generation of additional litigation through permitting inconsistent dispositions of property. This concern is heightened with respect to water rights, the relationships among which are highly interdependent. Indeed, we have recognized that actions seeking the allocation of water essentially involve the disposition of property and are best conducted in unified proceedings. The consent to jurisdiction given by the McCarran Amendment bespeaks a policy that recognizes the availability of comprehensive state systems for adjudication of water rights as the means for achieving these goals.

As has already been observed, the Colorado Water Rights Determination and Administration Act established such a system for the adjudication and management of rights to the use of the State's waters. As the Government concedes. . . . The Act established a single continuous proceeding for water rights adjudication which antedated the suit in District Court. That proceeding "reaches all claims, perhaps month by month but inclusively in the totality." Additionally, the responsibility of managing the State's waters, to the end that they be allocated in accordance with adjudicated water rights, is given to the State Engineer.

Beyond the congressional policy expressed by the McCarran Amendment and consistent with furtherance of that policy, we also find significant (a) the apparent absence of any proceedings in the District Court, other than the filing of the complaint, prior to the motion to dismiss (b) the extensive involvement of state water rights occasioned by this suit naming 1,000 defendants, (c) the 300-mile distance between the District Court in Denver and the court in Division 7, and (d) the existing participation by the Government in Division 4, 5, and 6 proceedings. We emphasize, however, that we do not overlook the heavy obligation to exercise jurisdiction. We need not decide, for example, whether, despite the McCarran Amendment, dismissal would be warranted if more extensive proceedings had occurred in the District Court prior to dismissal, if the involvement of state water rights were less extensive than it is here, or if the state proceeding were in some respect inadequate to resolve the federal claims. But the opposing factors here, particularly the policy underlying the McCarran Amendment, justify the District Court's dismissal in this particular case.

[Judgment of appeals court reversed and District Court's dismissal affirmed.]

JUSTICE STEWART, with whom MR. JUSTICE BLACKMUN and MR. JUSTICE STEVENS concur, dissenting.

The Court says that the United States District Court for the District of Colorado clearly had jurisdiction over this lawsuit. I agree. The Court further says that the McCarran Amendment "in no way diminished" the District Court's jurisdiction. I agree. The Court also says that federal courts have a "virtually unflagging obligation . . . to exercise the jurisdiction given them." I agree. And finally, the Court says that nothing in the abstention doctrine "in any of its forms" justified the District Court's dismissal of the Government's complaint. I agree. These views would seem to lead ineluctably to the conclusion that the District Court was wrong in dismissing the complaint. Yet the Court holds that the order of dismissal was "appropriate." With that conclusion I must respectfully disagree.

NOTES ON COLORADO RIVER AND ITS LIMITS

1. **Parallel Litigation.** Generally, there is no prohibition against parallel actions proceeding in both federal and state courts simultaneously. See *Sprint Communications, Inc. v. Jacobs,* 571 U.S. ___, 134 S.Ct. 584 (2013); *Kline v. Burke Constr. Co.,* 260 U.S. 226 (1922). Indeed, because state and federal courts have concurrent jurisdiction over a wide range of matters, the likelihood that duplicative litigation will occur is considerable. Given that duplicative litigation is both costly and inefficient, is *Colorado River* correct in suggesting that federal courts should not normally abstain in deference to ongoing state proceedings?

2. **The *Colorado River* Rationale.** Exactly what are the reasons for abstention in *Colorado River*? Are those reasons consistent with the Court's position that it has a "virtually unflagging obligation" to exercise the jurisdiction given to it? In one particularly creative student note, the author argues *Colorado River* actually limits the range of exercise where the courts can abstain in deference to parallel state proceedings by making clear that such abstention is extraordinary. Michael M. Wilson, Comment, *Federal Court Stays and Dismissals in Deference to Parallel State Court Proceedings: The Impact of* Colorado River, 44 U. CHI. L. REV. 641 (1977). Do you agree with that assessment? For further insightful commentary on the *Colorado River* case and the issues raised by duplicative litigation, *see* Linda S. Mullenix, *A Branch Too Far: Pruning the Abstention Doctrine,* 75 GEO. L. J. 99 (1986); Martin H. Redish, *Intersystemic Redundancy and Federal Court Power: Proposing a Zero Tolerance Solution to the Duplicative Litigation Problem,* 75 NOTRE DAME L. REV. 1347 (2000); and David A. Sonenshein, *Abstention: The Crooked Course of* Colorado River, 59 TUL. L. REV. 651 (1985).

3. **The *Moses H. Cone* Case.** Perhaps signaling that *Colorado River* would be construed narrowly, the Court refused to abstain in *Moses H. Cone Memorial Hospital v. Mercury Constr. Corp.,* 460 U.S. 1 (1983). *Moses Cone* involved a contract dispute between a contractor and a hospital regarding the interpretation of an arbitration provision. After the hospital sued in state court for a declaration, *inter alia,* that the arbitration clause was inapplicable, the contractor sued the hospital in federal court seeking to enforce the arbitration agreement. The district court stayed the federal proceeding but the Court, in an opinion by Justice Brennan, held that the

abstention order constituted an abuse of discretion. The Court ruled that although "the decision whether to defer to the state courts is necessarily left to the discretion of the district court in the first instance," the balance must be "heavily weighted in favor of the exercise of jurisdiction."

4. **Declaratory Judgments.** In *Wilton v. Seven Falls Co.*, 515 U.S. 277 (1995), the Court indicated that the district court's discretion to abstain in light of parallel state proceedings is far broader in declaratory judgment cases than the "exceptional circumstances" test set forth in *Colorado River*. The Court based this conclusion on the broad grant of discretion accorded to the district courts under the Declaratory Judgment Act which provides that a district court "may declare the rights . . . of any interested party." 28 U.S.C. § 2201. As the Court explained, "[s]ince its inception, the Declaratory Judgment Act has been understood to confer on federal courts unique and substantial discretion in deciding whether to declare the rights of litigants . . . The statute's textual commitment to discretion, and the breadth of leeway we have always understood it to suggest, distinguish the declaratory judgment context from other areas of the law in which concepts of discretion surface."

5. **Parallel Proceedings and *Res Judicata*.** The *Colorado River* presumption against deferring to parallel state court proceedings, of course, ends when the state judgment becomes final. The Full Faith and Credit statute, 28 U.S.C. § 1783, provides that federal courts must accord state judgments *res judicata* effect. See Part VI of this chapter, infra.

E. THE DOMESTIC RELATIONS EXCEPTION

ANKENBRANDT V. RICHARDS
504 U.S. 689 (1992).

JUSTICE WHITE delivered the opinion of the Court.

This case presents the issue whether the federal courts have jurisdiction or should abstain in a case involving alleged torts committed by the former husband of petitioner and his female companion against petitioner's children, when the sole basis for federal jurisdiction is the diversity-of-citizenship provision of 28 U. S. C. § 1332.

I.

Petitioner Carol Ankenbrandt, a citizen of Missouri, brought this lawsuit on September 26, 1989, on behalf of her daughters L. R. and S. R. against respondents Jon A. Richards and Debra Kesler, citizens of Louisiana, in the United States District Court for the Eastern District of Louisiana. Alleging federal jurisdiction based on the diversity-of-citizenship provision of § 1332, Ankenbrandt's complaint sought monetary damages for alleged sexual and physical abuse of the children committed by Richards and Kesler. Richards is the divorced father of the children and Kesler his female companion. On December 10, 1990, the District Court granted respondents' motion to dismiss this lawsuit. Citing In re Burrus, 136 U.S. 586, 593–594 (1890), for the proposition that "the whole subject of the domestic relations of husband and wife, parent and child, belongs to the laws of the States and not to the laws of the United States," the court concluded that this case fell within what has become known as the "domestic relations" exception to diversity jurisdiction, and that it lacked jurisdiction over the case.

We granted certiorari limited to the following questions: "(1) Is there a domestic relations exception to federal jurisdiction? (2) If so, does it permit a district court to abstain from exercising diversity jurisdiction over a tort action for damages?" . . .

II.

The domestic relations exception upon which the courts below relied to decline jurisdiction has been invoked often by the lower federal courts. The seeming authority for doing so originally stemmed from the announcement in *Barber v. Barber*, 62 U.S. 582 (1859), that the federal courts have no jurisdiction over suits for divorce or the allowance of alimony.

The statements disclaiming jurisdiction over divorce and alimony decree suits, though technically dicta, formed the basis for excluding "domestic relations" cases from the jurisdiction of the lower federal courts, a jurisdictional limitation those courts have recognized ever since. The *Barber* Court, however, cited no authority and did not discuss the foundation for its announcement. Since that time, the Court has dealt only occasionally with the domestic relations limitation on federal-court jurisdiction, and it has never addressed the basis for such a limitation. Because we are unwilling to cast aside an understood rule that has been recognized for nearly a century and a half, we feel compelled to explain why we will continue to recognize this limitation on federal jurisdiction.

A.

[The Court then analyzed Article III, § 2, of the Constitution, pointing out that none of the terms used to describe jurisdiction—"Cases, in Law and Equity," "Cases," or "Controversies"—include a limitation for domestic relations.]

B.

That Article III, § 2, does not mandate the exclusion of domestic relations cases from federal-court jurisdiction, however, does not mean that such courts necessarily must retain and exercise jurisdiction over such cases. . . . We thus turn our attention to [the diversity of citizenship statute.]

The *Barber* majority itself did not expressly refer to the diversity statute's use of the limitation on "suits of a civil nature at common law or in equity." [The Court then discusses the dissenters' contention in *Barber* that the court of chancery lacked authority to issue divorce and alimony decrees, thus such relief would not fall into the "all suits of civil nature" authorized by the statute.] Because the *Barber* Court did not disagree with this reason for accepting the jurisdictional limitation over the issuance of divorce and alimony decrees, it may be inferred fairly that the jurisdictional limitation recognized by the Court rested on this statutory basis and that the disagreement between the Court and the dissenters thus centered only on the extent of the limitation.

When Congress amended the diversity statute in 1948 to replace the law/equity distinction with the phrase "all civil actions," we presume Congress did so with full cognizance of the Court's nearly century-long interpretation of the prior statutes, which had construed the statutory diversity jurisdiction to contain an exception for certain domestic relations matters.

III.

In the more than 100 years since this Court laid the seeds for the development of the domestic relations exception, the lower federal courts have applied it in a variety of circumstances. Many of these applications go well beyond the circumscribed situations posed by *Barber* and its progeny. *Barber* itself disclaimed federal jurisdiction over a narrow range of domestic relations issues involving the granting of a divorce and a decree of alimony. . . . The *Barber* Court thus did not intend to strip the federal courts of authority to hear cases arising from the domestic relations of persons unless they seek the granting or modification of a divorce or alimony decree. The holding of the case itself sanctioned the exercise of federal jurisdiction over the enforcement of an alimony decree that had been properly obtained in a state court of competent jurisdiction. . . . And from the conclusion that the federal courts lacked jurisdiction to issue divorce and alimony decrees, there was no dissent.

Subsequently, this Court expanded the domestic relations exception to include decrees in child custody cases. In a child custody case brought pursuant to a writ of habeas corpus, for instance, the Court held void a writ issued by a Federal District Court to restore a child to the custody of the father. "As to the right to the control and possession of this child, as it is contested by its father and its grandfather, it is one in regard to which neither the Congress of the United States nor any authority of the United States has any special jurisdiction." *In re Burrus*, 136 U.S. at 594.

Not only is our conclusion rooted in respect for this long-held understanding, it is also supported by sound policy considerations. Issuance of decrees of this type not infrequently involves retention of jurisdiction by the court and deployment of social workers to monitor compliance. As a matter of judicial economy, state courts are more eminently suited to work of this type than are federal courts, which lack the close association with state and local government organizations dedicated to handling issues that arise out of conflicts over divorce, alimony, and child custody decrees. Moreover, as a matter of judicial expertise, it makes far more sense to retain the rule that federal courts lack power to issue these types of decrees because of the special proficiency developed by state tribunals over the past century and a half in handling issues that arise in the granting of such decrees.

By concluding, as we do, that the domestic relations exception encompasses only cases involving the issuance of a divorce, alimony, or child custody decree, we necessarily find that the Court of Appeals erred by affirming the District Court's invocation of this exception. This lawsuit in no way seeks such a decree; rather, it alleges that respondents Richards and Kesler committed torts against L. R. and S. R., Ankenbrandt's children by Richards. Federal subject-matter jurisdiction pursuant to § 1332 thus is proper in this case.

It is so ordered.

JUSTICE BLACKMUN, concurring.

I agree with the Court that the District Court had jurisdiction over petitioner's claims in tort. Moreover, I agree that the federal courts should not entertain claims for divorce, alimony, and child custody. I am unable to agree, however, that the diversity statute contains any "exception" for domestic relations matters. The Court goes to remarkable lengths to craft an exception that is simply not in the statute and is not supported by the case law. In my view, the longstanding, unbroken practice of the federal courts in refusing to hear domestic relations cases is precedent at most for continued discretionary abstention rather than mandatory limits on federal jurisdiction. For these reasons I concur only in the Court's judgment.

[The concurrence of JUSTICE STEVENS, with whom JUSTICE THOMAS joins, is omitted.]

NOTES ON THE DOMESTIC RELATIONS EXCEPTION

1.   **Exception or Abstention?** The refusal of the federal courts to hear domestic relations matters has often been referred to as the domestic relations "exception" to diversity jurisdiction. Is the doctrine truly an exception or, as Justice Blackmun suggests, is it more accurately considered a form of abstention? Does the distinction matter?

2.   **The Probate Law Exception.** The federal courts have also traditionally excepted probate law matters from their jurisdiction. See

Markham v. Allen, 326 U.S. 490 (1946). Like the treatment of the domestic relations exception in *Ankenbrandt*, the probate exception has not been broadly interpreted. As the Court most recently explained in *Marshall v. Marshall*, 547 U.S. 293 (2006):

> the probate exception reserves to state probate courts the probate or annulment of a will and the administration of a decedent's estate; it also precludes federal courts from endeavoring to dispose of property that is in the custody of a state probate court. But it does not bar federal courts from adjudicating matters outside the confines and otherwise within federal jurisdiction.

Thus, for example, the exception does not bar the federal courts from hearing suits brought by creditors, legatees, heirs and other claimants against a decedent's estate as long as the federal lawsuit does not attempt to reach the *res* in custody of the state court. Accordingly, in *Marshall* itself, the Court held that the probate exception did not prevent the federal court from hearing a claim brought by the decedent's widow (Anna Nicole Smith) against the primary beneficiary of her husband's estate alleging that he tortiously interfered with a gift she had expected from her husband. Similarly in *Markham* the Court ruled that a federal court could hear a claim (brought by a federal official appointed to represent the property rights of enemies and their allies during World War II) alleging that a decedent's German legatees and not her United States heirs were entitled to the entire net estate.

3.   The Basis of the Domestic Relations and Probate Exceptions. The foundation of the domestic relations and probate exceptions can be traced, as *Ankenbrandt* suggests, to an understanding of historical practice, most specifically the role of the English chancery courts in hearing domestic and probate matters. See *Marshall v. Marshall*, supra (the domestic relations and probate exceptions "are judicially created doctrines stemming in large measure from misty understandings of English legal history.") Both doctrines, however, are not, according to the Court, "compelled by the text of the Constitution or federal statute," but are supported by the fact that Congress, when it has amended the diversity statute, apparently intended to leave the exceptions undisturbed.

4.   Does the Domestic Relations Exception Make Sense as a Policy Matter? Why should the federal courts refuse to hear domestic relations cases? Is it because domestic relations cases often require continuing supervision and are often the subject matter of specialized family courts? In this sense, is the domestic relations exception parallel to the type of abstention authorized in *Burford*?

Professor Judith Resnik argues that the domestic relations abstention doctrine is based in part on the grounds that federal courts marginalize issues that are important to women. See Judith Resnik, *"Naturally" Without Gender: Women, Jurisdiction, and the Federal Courts*, 66 N.Y.U. L. REV. 1682 (1991). Do you agree?

III.   THE ANTI-INJUNCTION STATUTE

ATLANTIC COAST LINE RAILROAD CO. V. BROTHERHOOD OF LOCOMOTIVE ENGINEERS
398 U.S. 281 (1970).

JUSTICE BLACK delivered the opinion of the Court.

Congress in 1793, shortly after the American Colonies became one united Nation, provided that in federal courts "a writ of injunction [shall not] be granted to stay proceedings in any court of a state." Act of March 2, 1793, 5, 1 Stat. Although certain exceptions to the general prohibition have been added, that statute, directing that state courts shall remain free from interference by federal courts, has remained in effect until this time. Today that amended statute provides:

> A court of the United States may not grant an injunction to stay proceedings in a State court except as expressly authorized by Act of Congress, or where necessary in aid of its jurisdiction, or to protect or effectuate its judgments. 28 U.S.C. § 2283.

Despite the existence of this longstanding prohibition, in this case a federal court did enjoin the petitioner, Atlantic Coast Line Railroad Co. (ACL), from invoking an injunction issued by a Florida state court which prohibited certain picketing by respondent Brotherhood of Locomotive Engineers (BLE). The case arose in the following way.

In 1967, BLE began picketing the Moncrief Yard, a switching yard located near Jacksonville, Florida, and wholly owned and operated by ACL. As soon as this picketing began, ACL went into federal court seeking an injunction. When the federal judge denied the request, ACL immediately went into state court and there succeeded in obtaining an injunction. No further legal action was taken in this dispute until two years later in 1969, after this Court's decision in *Brotherhood of Railroad Trainmen v. Jacksonville Terminal Co.*, 394 U.S. 369 (1969). In that case, the Court considered the validity of a state injunction against picketing by the BLE and other unions at the Jacksonville Terminal, located immediately next to Moncrief Yard. The Court reviewed the factual situation surrounding the Jacksonville Terminal picketing and concluded that the unions had a federally protected right to picket under the Railway Labor Act, 44 Stat. 577, as amended 45 U.S.C. 151, and that right could not be interfered with by state court injunctions. Immediately after a petition for rehearing was denied in that case, the respondent BLE filed a motion in state court to dissolve the Moncrief Yard injunction, arguing that under the *Jacksonville Terminal* decision the injunction was improper. The state judge refused to dissolve the injunction, holding that this Court's *Jacksonville Terminal* decision was not controlling. The union did not elect to appeal that decision directly, but instead went back into federal court and requested an injunction against the enforcement of the state court injunction.

In this Court the union contends that the federal injunction was proper either "to protect or effectuate" the District Court's denial of an injunction in 1967, or as "necessary in aid of" the District Court's jurisdiction. Although the questions are by no means simple and clear, and the decision is difficult, we conclude that the injunction against the state court was not justified under either of these two exceptions to the anti-injunction statute. We therefore hold that the federal injunction in this case was improper.

I

Before analyzing the specific legal arguments advanced in this case, we think it would be helpful to discuss the background and policy that led Congress to pass the anti-injunction statute in 1793. While all the reasons that led Congress to adopt this restriction on federal courts are not wholly clear, it is certainly likely that one reason stemmed from the essentially federal nature of our national government. When this Nation was established by the Constitution, each State surrendered only a part of its sovereign power to the national government. But those powers that were not surrendered were retained by the States and unless a State was restrained by "the supreme Law of the Land" as expressed in the Constitution, laws, or treaties of the United States, it was free to exercise those retained powers as it saw fit. One of the reserved powers was the maintenance of state judicial systems for the decision of legal controversies. Many of the Framers of the Constitution felt that separate federal courts were unnecessary and that the state courts could be entrusted to protect both state and federal rights. Others felt that a complete system of federal courts to take care of federal legal problems should be provided for in the Constitution itself. This dispute resulted in compromise. One "supreme court" was created by the Constitution, and Congress was given the power to create other federal courts. In the first Congress this power was exercised and a system of federal trial and appellate courts with limited jurisdiction was created by the Judiciary Act of 1789.

While the lower federal courts were given certain powers in the 1789 Act, they were not given any power to review directly cases from state courts, and they have not been given such powers since that time. Only the Supreme Court was authorized to review on direct appeal the decisions of state courts. Thus from the beginning we have had in this country two essentially separate legal systems. Each system proceeds independently of the other with ultimate review in this Court of the federal questions raised in either system. Understandably this dual court system was bound to lead to conflicts and frictions. Litigants who foresaw the possibility of more favorable treatment in one or the other system would predictably hasten to invoke the powers of whichever court it was believed would present the best chance of success. Obviously this dual system could not function if state and federal courts were free to fight each other for control of a particular case. Thus, in order to make the dual system work and "to prevent needless friction between state and federal courts," it was necessary to work out lines of demarcation between the two systems. Some of these limits were spelled out in the 1789 Act. Others have been added by later statutes as well as judicial decisions. The 1793 anti-injunction Act was at least in part a response to these pressures.

On its face the present Act is an absolute prohibition against enjoining state court proceedings, unless the injunction falls within one of three specifically defined exceptions. The respondents here have intimated that the Act only establishes a "principle of comity," not a binding rule on the power of the federal courts. The argument implies that in certain circumstances a federal court may enjoin state court proceedings even if that action cannot be justified by any of the three exceptions. We cannot accept any such contention. In 1955 when this Court interpreted this statute, it stated: "This is not a statute conveying a broad general policy for appropriate *ad hoc* application. Legislative policy is here expressed in a clear-cut prohibition qualified only by specifically defined exceptions." Since that time Congress has not seen fit to amend the statute, and we therefore adhere to that position and hold that any injunction against state court proceedings otherwise proper under general equitable principles must be based on one of the specific statutory exceptions to § 2283 if it is to be upheld. Moreover since the statutory prohibition against such injunctions in part rests on the fundamental constitutional independence of the States and their courts, the exceptions should not be enlarged by loose statutory construction. Proceedings in state courts should normally be allowed to continue unimpaired by intervention of the lower federal courts, with relief from error, if any, through the state appellate courts and ultimately this Court.

II

In this case the Florida Circuit Court enjoined the union's intended picketing, and the United States District Court enjoined the railroad "from giving effect to or availing [itself] of the benefits of" that state court [order.] Neither party argues that there is any express congressional authorization for injunctions in this situation and we agree with that conclusion. The respondent union does contend that the injunction was proper either as a means to protect or effectuate the District Court's 1967 order, or in aid of that court's jurisdiction. We do not think that either alleged basis can be supported.

A

The argument based on protecting the 1967 order is not clearly expressed, but in essence it appears to run as follows: In 1967 the railroad sought a temporary restraining order which the union opposed. In the course of deciding that request, the United States District Court determined that the union had a federally protected right to picket Moncrief Yard and that this right could not be interfered with by state courts. When the Florida Circuit Court enjoined the picketing, the United States District court could, in order to protect and effectuate its prior determination, enjoin enforcement of the state court injunction. Although the record on this point is not unambiguously clear, we conclude that no such interpretation of the 1967 order can be [supported.]

The union asserts that [the District Court, in effect, held] that it had a federally protected right to picket and that state law could not be invoked to negate that right. The railroad, on the other hand, argues that the order merely determined that the *federal* court could not enjoin the picketing, in large part because of the general provision in the Norris-LaGuardia Act, 47 Stat. 70, 29 U.S.C. § 101, against issuance by federal courts of injunctions in labor disputes. Based solely on the state of the record when the order was entered, we are inclined to believe that the District Court did not determine whether federal law precluded an injunction based on state law. Not only was the point never argued to the court, but there is no language in the order that necessarily implies any decision on that question. In short we feel that the District Court in 1967 determined that federal law could not be invoked to enjoin the picketing at Moncrief Yard, and that the union did have the right "to engage in self-help" as far as the federal courts were concerned. But that decision is entirely different from a decision that the Railway Labor Act precludes state regulation of the picketing as well, and this latter decision is an essential prerequisite for upholding the 1969 injunction as necessary "to protect or effectuate" the 1967 [order.]

Any lingering doubts we might have as to the proper interpretation of the 1967 order are settled by references to the positions adopted by the parties later in the litigation.

[The Court's discussion of later episodes in the litigation is omitted.]

This record, we think, conclusively shows that neither the parties themselves nor the District Court construed the 1967 order as the union now contends it should be construed. Rather we are convinced that the union in effect tried to get the Federal District Court to decide that the state court judge was wrong in distinguishing the *Jacksonville Terminal* decision. Such an attempt to seek appellate review of a state decision in the Federal District Court cannot be justified as necessary "to protect or effectuate" the 1967 order. The record simply will not support the union's contention on this point.

B

This brings us to the second prong of the union's argument in which it is suggested that even if the 1967 order did not determine the union's right to picket free from state interference, once the decision in the *Jacksonville Terminal* was announced, the District Court was then free to enjoin the state court on the theory that such action was "necessary in aid of [the District Court's] jurisdiction." Again the argument is somewhat unclear, but it appears to go in this way: The District Court had acquired jurisdiction over the labor controversy in 1967 when the railroad filed its complaint, and it determined at that time that it did have jurisdiction. The dispute involved the legality of picketing by the union and the *Jacksonville Terminal* decision clearly indicated that such activity was not only legal, but was protected from state court interference. The state court had interfered with that right, and thus a federal injunction was "necessary in aid of its jurisdiction." For several reasons we cannot accept the contention.

First a federal court does not have inherent power to ignore the limitations of § 2283 and to enjoin state court proceedings merely because those proceedings interfere with a protected federal right or invade an area preempted by federal law, even when the interference is unmistakably clear. This rule applies regardless of whether the federal court itself has jurisdiction over the controversy, or whether it is ousted from jurisdiction for the same reason that the state court is. This conclusion is required because Congress itself set forth the only exceptions to the statute, and those exceptions do not include this situation. Second, if the District Court does have jurisdiction, it is not enough that the requested injunction is related to that jurisdiction, but it must be "necessary in aid of" that jurisdiction. While this language is admittedly broad, we conclude that it implies something similar to the concept of injunctions to "protect or effectuate" judgments. Both exceptions to the general prohibition of § 2283 imply that some federal injunctive relief may be necessary to prevent a state court from so interfering with a federal court's consideration or disposition of a case as to seriously impair the federal court's flexibility and authority to decide that case. Third, no such situation is presented here. Although the federal court did have jurisdiction of the railroad's complaint based on federal law, the state court also had jurisdiction over the complaint based on state law and the union's asserted federal defense as well. While the railroad could probably have based its federal case on the pendant state law claims as well it was free to refrain from doing so and leave the state law questions and the related issue concerning preclusion of state remedies by federal law to the state courts. Conversely, although it could have tendered its federal claims to the state court, it was also free to restrict the state complaint to state grounds alone. In short, the state and federal courts had concurrent jurisdiction in this case, and neither court was free to prevent either party from simultaneously pursuing claims in both courts. Therefore the state court's assumption of jurisdiction over the state law claims and the federal preclusion issue did not hinder the federal court's jurisdiction so as to make an injunction necessary to aid that jurisdiction. Nor was an injunction necessary because the state court may have taken action which the federal court was certain was improper under the *Jacksonville Terminal* decision. Again, lower federal courts possess no power whatever to sit in direct review of state court decisions. If the union was adversely affected by the state court's decision, it was free to seek vindication of its federal right in the Florida appellate courts and ultimately, if necessary, in this Court. Similarly if, because of the Florida Circuit Courts action, the union faced the threat of immediate irreparable injury sufficient to justify an injunction under usual equitable principles, it was undoubtedly free to seek such relief from the Florida appellate courts, and might possibly in certain emergency circumstances seek such relief from this Court as well. Unlike the Federal District Court, this Court does have potential appellate jurisdiction over federal questions raised in state court proceedings, and that broader jurisdiction allows this Court correspondingly broader authority to issue injunctions "necessary in aid of its jurisdiction."

III

This case is by no means an easy one. The arguments in support of the union's contentions are not insubstantial. But whatever doubts we may have are strongly affected by the general prohibition of § 2283. Any doubts as to the propriety of a federal injunction against state court proceedings should be resolved in favor of permitting the state courts to proceed in an orderly fashion to finally determine the controversy. The explicit wording of § 2283 itself implies as much, and the fundamental principle of a dual system of courts leads inevitably to that [conclusion.]

[JUSTICE HARLAN'S concurring opinion and JUSTICE BRENNAN'S dissenting opinion (joined by JUSTICE WHITE) are omitted.]

NOTES ON THE ANTI-INJUNCTION ACT

1. **Background.** Historical evidence suggests that the original version of the Anti-Injunction Act, passed in 1793, was intended only to prohibit a single Supreme Court Justice riding circuit from issuing an injunction and was not enacted as a restriction on the powers of the lower federal courts. See William T. Mayton, *Ersatz Federalism Under the Anti-Injunction Statute*, 78 COLUM. L. REV. 330 (1978). In *Peck v. Jenness*, 48 U.S. (7 How.) 612 (1849), however, the Court construed the Act as applying to all federal courts and this understanding was continued when the Act was amended in 1874.

Nevertheless, the federal courts did not interpret the provision as an absolute bar and proceeded to issue injunctions against state court proceedings in a wide range of cases. Justice Frankfurter's 1941 opinion in *Toucey v. New York Life Insurance Co.*, 314 U.S. 118 (1941), however, signaled a far different approach to the Act's interpretation in holding that exceptions to the statute should be narrowly construed. In 1948, Congress responded to the *Toucey* decision by enacting the current version of the Act, 28 U.S.C. § 2283, setting forth the three categorical exceptions to the anti-injunction provision noted in *Atlantic Coastline*: "A court of the United States may not grant an injunction to stay proceedings in State court except as authorized by Act of Congress, or where necessary in aid of its jurisdiction, or to protect or effectuate its judgments."

    2.   Necessary in Aid of Its Jurisdiction. There are two types of matters that the courts have interpreted as coming within the "necessary in aid of its jurisdiction" exception. The first are cases in which the federal action is brought *in rem* and the injunction is issued to protect the *res*. See *Kline v. Burke Construction*, 260 U.S. 226 (1922). The second is to allow the federal court to enjoin state proceedings in cases where the action has been removed. See *French v. Hay*, 89 U.S. (22 Wall.) 250 (1874). Is *Atlantic Coastline* correct in not interpreting this provision more broadly? Should this exception be triggered when the state court is litigating matters that are within the federal courts' exclusive jurisdiction?

    3.   To Protect or Effectuate Its Judgments (the "Relitigation" Exception). The "to protect or effectuate its judgments" exception has often been referred to as the "relitigation exception" because it is designed to enforce the *res judicata* effects of a federal judgment. Under this provision, the federal prevailing litigant can seek to enjoin a state court action that she believes may undermine the preclusive effects of her federal judgment. The prevailing federal litigant, of course, may also choose to protect her federal judgment by raising the *res judicata* defense in state court. (Why is this latter option not alone sufficient to protect her rights?) But, as the decision in *Parsons Steel, Inc. v. First Alabama Bank*, 474 U.S. 518 (1986), demonstrates, that option can impose some risks. In *Parsons*, the plaintiff sued the defendant in state and federal court. After the defendant prevailed in federal court, the state court rejected the defendant's *res judicata* defense and the action proceeded to judgment in favor of the plaintiff. The defendant then returned to federal court to attempt to enjoin the state court proceeding. The Supreme Court held, however, that the relitigation exception was unavailable because the federal court was required under the Full Faith and Credit Statute (28 U.S.C. § 1738) to give preclusive effect to the *state* court judgment. The injunction remedy, in short, would be available to the prevailing litigant only if the state court had not reached the merits of the *res judicata* claim. Does the result in *Parsons* sensibly further the purported interest underlying the anti-injunction statute in promoting comity between the state and federal courts? Or does it encourage additional friction?

4. The Relitigation Exception and the Same Issue Requirement. Because the relitigation exception is designed to protect the *res judicata* effects of a federal court judgment, it must first be established that *res judicata* would actually bar the state court suit before this exception would apply. This requirement can often pose a formidable obstacle, as the Court recently demonstrated in *Smith v. Bayer Corp.*, 564 U.S. ___, 131 S.Ct. 2368 (2011). In *Bayer* the question before the Court was whether a federal court could enjoin a state court's certification of a class action after the federal court had ruled that the matter was not suitable for class treatment. The Court held that the federal court could not issue the injunction because the standard of whether an action was suitable for class certification under Federal Rule 23 was not necessarily the same as whether it would be suitable for class treatment under the state's class action Rule 23 and therefore the *res judicata* requirement of identity of the issue was not satisfied. See also *Chick Kam Choo v. Exxon*, 486 U.S. 140 (1988) (holding that the a federal court could not enjoin a state court from hearing an action after the federal court dismissed the case on *forum non conveniens* grounds because the state standard for *forum non conveniens* might differ from the federal).

MITCHUM V. FOSTER
407 U.S. 225 (1972).

JUSTICE STEWART delivered the opinion of the Court.

The federal anti-injunction statute provides that a federal court "may not grant an injunction to stay proceedings in a State court except as expressly authorized by Act of Congress, or where necessary in aid of its jurisdiction, or to protect or effectuate its judgments." 28 U.S.C. § 2283. An Act of Congress, 42 U.S.C. § 1983, expressly authorizes a "suit in equity" to redress "the deprivation," under color of state law, "of any rights, privileges, or immunities secured by the Constitution. . . ." The question before us is whether this "Act of Congress" comes within the "expressly authorized" exception of the anti-injunction statute so as to permit a federal court in a § 1983 suit to grant an injunction to stay a proceeding pending in a state court. This question, which has divided the federal courts, has lurked in the background of many of our recent cases, but we have not until today explicitly decided it.

The prosecuting attorney of Bay County, Florida, brought a proceeding in a Florida court to close down the appellant's bookstore as a public nuisance under the claimed authority of Florida law. The state court entered a preliminary order prohibiting continued operation of the bookstore. After further inconclusive proceedings in the state courts, the appellant filed a complaint in the United States District Court for the Northern District of Florida, alleging that the actions of the state judicial and law enforcement officials were depriving him of rights protected by the First and Fourteenth Amendments. Relying upon 42 U. S. C. § 1983, he asked for injunctive and declaratory relief against the state court proceedings, on the ground that Florida laws were being unconstitutionally applied by the state court so as to cause him great and irreparable harm. The district court denied relief

In denying injunctive relief, the District Court relied on this Court's decision in *Atlantic Coast Line R. Co. v. Brotherhood of Locomotive Engineers*, 398 U.S. 281 (1970). The *Atlantic Coast Line* case did not deal with the "expressly authorized" exception of the anti-injunction statute, but the Court's opinion in that case does bring into sharp focus the critical importance of the question now before us. For in that case we expressly rejected the view that the anti-injunction statute merely states a flexible doctrine of comity, and made clear that the statute imposes an absolute ban upon the issuance of a federal injunction against a pending state court proceeding, in the absence of one of the recognized exceptions:

It follows, in the present context, that if § 1983 is not within the "expressly authorized" exception of the anti-injunction statute, then a federal equity court is wholly without power to grant any relief in a § 1983 suit seeking to stay a state court proceeding. In short, if a § 1983 action is not an "expressly authorized" statutory exception, the anti-injunction law absolutely prohibits in such an action all federal equitable intervention in a pending state court proceeding, whether civil or criminal, and regardless of how extraordinary the particular circumstances may be.

The anti-injunction statute goes back almost to the beginnings of our history as a Nation. In 1793, Congress enacted a law providing that no "writ of injunction be granted [by any federal court] to stay proceedings in any court of a state. . . ." Act of March 2, 1793; 1 Stat. 335. The precise origins of the legislation are shrouded in obscurity, but the consistent understanding has been that its basic purpose is to prevent "needless friction between state and federal courts." *Oklahoma Packing Co. v. Gas Co.*, 309 U.S. 4, 9. The law remained unchanged until 1874, when it was amended to permit a federal court to stay state court proceedings that interfered with the administration of a federal bankruptcy proceeding.

Despite the seemingly uncompromising language of the anti-injunction statute prior to 1948, the Court soon recognized that exceptions must be made to its blanket prohibition if the import and purpose of other Acts of Congress were to be given their intended scope. So it was that, in addition to the bankruptcy law exception that Congress explicitly recognized in 1874, the Court through the years found that federal courts were empowered to enjoin state court proceedings, despite the anti-injunction statute, in carrying out the will of Congress under at least six other federal laws. These covered a broad spectrum of congressional action: (1) legislation providing for removal of litigation from state to federal courts, (2) legislation limiting the liability of shipowners, (3 legislation providing for federal interpleader actions, (4) legislation conferring federal jurisdiction over farm mortgages, (5) legislation governing federal habeas corpus proceedings, and (6) legislation providing for control of prices.

In addition to the exceptions to the anti-injunction statute found to be embodied in these various Acts of Congress, the Court recognized other "implied" exceptions to the blanket prohibition of the anti-injunction statute. One was an "*in rem*" exception, allowing a federal court to enjoin a state court proceeding in order to protect its jurisdiction of a *res* over which it had first acquired jurisdiction. Another was a "relitigation" exception, permitting a federal court to enjoin relitigation in a state court of issues already decided in federal litigation. Still a third exception, more recently developed, permits a federal injunction of state court proceedings when the plaintiff in the federal court is the United States itself, or a federal agency asserting "superior federal interests."

In *Toucey v. New York Life Ins. Co.*, 314 U.S. 118, the Court in 1941 issued an opinion casting considerable doubt upon the approach to the anti-injunction statute reflected in its previous decisions. The Court's opinion expressly disavowed the "relitigation" exception to the statute, and emphasized generally the importance of recognizing the statute's basic directive "of 'hands off' by the federal courts in the use of the injunction to stay litigation in a state court." The congressional response to *Toucey* was the enactment in 1948 of the anti-injunction statute in its present form in 28 U. S. C. § 2283, which, as the Reviser's Note makes evident, served not only to overrule the specific holding of *Toucey*, but to restore "the basic law as generally understood and interpreted prior to the *Toucey* decision."

We proceed, then, upon the understanding that in determining whether § 1983 comes within the "expressly authorized" exception of the anti-injunction statute, the criteria to be applied are those reflected in the Court's decisions prior to *Toucey*. A review of those decisions makes reasonably clear what the relevant criteria are. In the first place, it is evident that, in order to qualify under the "expressly authorized" exception of the anti-injunction statute, a federal law need not contain an express reference to that statute. As the Court has said, "no prescribed formula is required; an authorization need not expressly refer to § 2283." *Amalgamated Clothing Workers v. Richman Bros. Co.*, 348 U.S. 511 (1955). Indeed, none of the previously recognized statutory exceptions contains any such reference. Secondly, a federal law need not expressly authorize an injunction of a state court proceeding in order to qualify as an exception. Three of the six previously recognized statutory exceptions contain no such authorization. Thirdly, it is clear that, in order to qualify as an "expressly authorized" exception to the anti-injunction statute, an

Act of Congress must have created a specific and uniquely federal right or remedy, enforceable in a federal court of equity, that could be frustrated if the federal court were not empowered to enjoin a state court proceeding. This is not to say that in order to come within the exception an Act of Congress must, on its face and in every one of its provisions, be totally incompatible with the prohibition of the anti-injunction statute. The test, rather, is whether an Act of Congress, clearly creating a federal right or remedy enforceable in a federal court of equity, could be given its intended scope only by the stay of a state court proceeding.

With these criteria in view, we turn to consideration of 42 U. S. C. § 1983. Section 1983 was originally § 1 of the Civil Rights Act of 1871. 17 Stat. 13. It was "modeled" on § 2 of the Civil Rights Act of 1866, 14 Stat. 27, and was enacted for the express purpose of "enforc[ing] the Provisions of the Fourteenth Amendment." The predecessor of § 1983 was thus an important part of the basic alteration in our federal system wrought in the Reconstruction era through federal legislation and constitutional amendment. As a result of the new structure of law that emerged in the post-Civil War era—and especially of the Fourteenth Amendment, which was its centerpiece—the role of the Federal Government as a guarantor of basic federal rights against state power was clearly established. Section 1983 opened the federal courts to private citizens, offering a uniquely federal remedy against incursions under the claimed authority of state law upon rights secured by the Constitution and laws of the Nation.

It is clear from the legislative debates surrounding passage of § 1983's predecessor that the Act was intended to enforce the provisions of the Fourteenth Amendment "against State action, . . . whether that action be executive, legislative, or *judicial.*" *Ex parte Virginia*, 100 U.S. 339 (1879). Proponents of the legislation noted that state courts were being used to harass and injure individuals, either because the state courts were powerless to stop deprivations or were in league with those who were bent upon abrogation of federally protected rights.

As Representative Lowe stated, the "records of the [state] tribunals are searched in vain for evidence of effective redress [of federally secured rights]. . . . What less than this [the Civil Rights Act of 1871] will afford an adequate remedy? The Federal Government cannot serve a writ of mandamus upon State Executives or upon State courts to compel them to protect the rights, privileges and immunities of citizens. . . . The case has arisen . . . when the Federal Government must resort to its own agencies to carry its own authority into execution. Hence this bill throws open the doors of the United States courts to those whose rights under the Constitution are denied or impaired." Cong. Globe, 42d Cong., 1st Sess., 374–376 (1871). This view was echoed by Senator Osborn: "If the State courts had proven themselves competent to suppress the local disorders, or to maintain law and order, we should not have been called upon to legislate. . . . We are driven by existing facts to provide for the several states in the South what they have been unable to fully provide for themselves; *i. e.*, the full and complete administration of justice in the courts. And the courts with reference to which we legislate must be the United States courts." *Id.* at 653. And Representative Perry concluded: "Sheriffs, having eyes to see, see not; judges, having ears to hear, hear not; witnesses conceal the truth or falsify it; grand and petit juries act as if they might be accomplices. . . . All the apparatus and machinery of civil government, all the processes of justice, skulk away as if government and justice were crimes and feared detection. Among the most dangerous things an injured party can do is to appeal to justice." *Id.* at App. 78.

Those who opposed the Act of 1871 clearly recognized that the proponents were extending federal power in an attempt to remedy the state courts' failure to secure federal rights. The debate was not about whether the predecessor of § 1983 extended to actions of state courts, but whether this innovation was necessary or desirable.

This legislative history makes evident that Congress clearly conceived that it was altering the relationship between the States and the Nation with respect to the protection of federally created rights; it was concerned that state instrumentalities could not protect those rights; it realized that state officers might, in fact, be antipathetic to the vindication of those rights; and it believed that these failings extended to the state courts.

Section 1983 was thus a product of a vast transformation from the concepts of federalism that had prevailed in the late 18th century when the anti-injunction statute was enacted. The very purpose of § 1983 was to interpose the federal courts between the States and the people, as guardians of the people's federal rights—to protect the people from unconstitutional action under color of state law, whether that action be executive, legislative, or judicial. In carrying out that purpose, Congress plainly authorized the federal courts to issue injunctions in § 1983 actions, by expressly authorizing a "suit in equity" as one of the means of redress. And this Court long ago recognized that federal injunctive relief against a state court proceeding can in some circumstances be essential to prevent great, immediate, and irreparable loss of a person's constitutional rights. For these reasons we conclude that, under the criteria established in our previous decisions construing the anti-injunction statute, § 1983 is an Act of Congress that falls within the "expressly authorized" exception of that law.

In so concluding, we do not question or qualify in any way the principles of equity, comity, and federalism that must restrain a federal court when asked to enjoin a state court proceeding. These principles, in the context of state criminal prosecutions, were canvassed at length last

Term in *Younger v. Harris*, 401 U.S. 37 (1971) and its companion cases. They are principles that have been emphasized by this Court many times in the past. Today we decide only that the District Court in this case was in error in holding that, because of the anti-injunction statute, it was absolutely without power in this § 1983 action to enjoin a proceeding pending in a state court under any circumstances whatsoever.

The judgment is reversed and the case is remanded to the District Court for further proceedings consistent with this opinion.

It is so ordered.

[JUSTICE POWELL and JUSTICE REHNQUIST took no part in the consideration or decision of this case.]

[CHIEF JUSTICE BURGER'S concurrence, joined by JUSTICE WHITE and JUSTICE BLACKMUN, is omitted.]

NOTES ON MITCHUM AND THE "EXPRESSLY AUTHORIZED" EXCEPTION

1.   *Mitchum* and Section 1983. *Mitchum* is as much a case about the meaning of 42 U.S.C. § 1983 as it is a case about the Anti-Injunction Act. Do you agree with the Court that Section 1983 implicitly authorizes a federal court to issue an injunction against a state court proceeding? Why?

2.   The "Expressly Authorized" Exception. The fact that *Mitchum* held that the "expressly authorized" exception to the anti-injunction statute could be met without express language might suggest that this provision would not be narrowly interpreted. That has not turned out to be the case. Consider *Vendo Co. v. Lektro-Vend Corp.*, 433 U.S. 623 (1977). *Vendo* was a federal anti-trust action attacking agreements not to compete. During the pendency of the federal action, a state action seeking to enforce those agreements proceeded to judgment and the plaintiff (Vendo) was awarded damages for breach of contract. The federal court enjoined the collection of the state judgment claiming that it was "expressly authorized" under § 16 of the Clayton Act which provides, in pertinent part, that "any person . . . shall be entitled to sue for and have injunctive relief, in any court of the United States having jurisdiction over the parties, against threatened loss or damage by a violation of the antitrust laws . . . when and under the same conditions and principles as injunctive relief against threatened conduct that will cause loss or damage is granted by courts of equity, under the rules governing such proceedings. . . ."

A divided Supreme Court reversed. Justice Rehnquist's opinion for himself and two others stated:

> On its face, the language [of § 16] merely authorizes private injunctive relief for antitrust violations. Not only does the statute not mention § 2283 or the enjoining of state-court proceedings, but the granting of injunctive relief under § 16 is by the terms of that

section limited to "the same conditions and principles" employed by courts of equity, and by "the rules governing such proceedings." In 1793 the predecessor to § 2283 was enacted specifically to limit the general equity powers of a federal court. When § 16 was enacted in 1914 the bar of the Anti-Injunction Act had long constrained the equitable power of federal courts to issue injunctions. Thus, on its face, § 16 is far from an express exception to the Anti-Injunction Act, and may be fairly read as virtually incorporating the prohibitions of the Anti-Injunction Act with restrictive language not found, for example, in 42 U.S.C. § 1983.

Respondents rely, as did the Court of Appeals and the District Court, on the following language from *Mitchum*: "[It] is clear that, in order to qualify as an 'expressly authorized' exception to the anti-injunction statute, an Act of Congress must have created a specific and uniquely federal right or remedy, enforceable in a federal court of equity, that could be frustrated if the federal court were not empowered to enjoin a state court proceeding. This is not to say that in order to come within the exception an Act of Congress must, on its face and in every one of its provisions, be totally incompatible with the prohibition of the anti-injunction statute. The test, rather, is whether an Act of Congress, clearly creating a federal right or remedy enforceable in a federal court of equity, could be given its intended scope only by the stay of a state court proceeding."

But we think it is clear that neither this language from *Mitchum* nor *Mitchum's* ratio decidendi supports the result contended for by respondents. The private action for damages conferred by the Clayton Act is a "uniquely federal right or remedy," in that actions based upon it may be brought only in the federal courts. It thus meets the first part of the test laid down in the language quoted from *Mitchum*.

But that authorization for private actions does not meet the second part of the *Mitchum* test; it is not an "Act of Congress . . . [which] could be given its intended scope only by the stay of a state court proceeding," Crucial to our determination in *Mitchum* that 42 U.S.C. § 1983 fulfilled this requirement—but wholly lacking here— was our recognition that one of the clear congressional concerns underlying the enactment of § 1983 was the possibility that state courts, as well as other branches of state government, might be used as instruments to deny citizens their rights under the Federal Constitution. This determination was based on our review of the legislative history of § 1983; similar review of the legislative history underlying § 16 demonstrates that that section does not meet this aspect of the *Mitchum* test. . . . The relevant history of § 16 simply suggests that in enacting § 16 Congress was interested in extending the right to enjoin antitrust violations to private citizens.

Is the language in § 16 less explicit in authorizing injunctions against suit than is § 1983? Does *Vendo* even ask that question? If the "explicitly authorized" exception is not to be found in the express wording of the statute, how is it to be determined?

NOTE ON THE TAX INJUNCTION ACT

Another major statutory limitation on the power of federal courts to provide injunctive relief is the Tax Injunction Act of 1937 which provides that "[t]he district courts shall not enjoin, suspend or restrain the assessment, levy or collection of any tax under State law where a plain, speedy and efficient remedy may be had in the courts of such State." See 28 U.S.C. § 1341. As explained by the Court, "[t]he statute has its roots in equity practice, in principles of federalism, and in recognition of the imperative need of a State to administer its own fiscal operations." *Rosewell v. LaSalle National Bank*, 450 U.S. 503 (1981).

A key question that arises under the Tax Injunction Act is the meaning of "tax." Should all revenue-raising measures, including fees and special assessments, be construed as a tax under the Act? What if the purpose of the fee or assessment is regulatory rather than fiscal? See generally *Miami Herald Publishing Co. v. City of Hallandale*, 734 F.2d 666 (11th Cir. 1984) (indicating that the applicability of the Tax Injunction Act depends on whether the challenged measure is revenue raising or regulatory). Should a state lottery be considered a tax for Tax Injunction Act purposes because it is designed to raise revenue?

The Court has not given much force to the Act's requirements that the state must provide a "plain, speedy, and efficient remedy" in order to preclude a federal court injunction. In *Rosewell v. LaSalle National Bank*, the state's procedures for seeking the refund of taxes paid under protest took, on average, over two years and successful litigants were not awarded interest for the monies they had wrongfully paid. Even so, the Court found the state remedies to be sufficiently plain, speedy and efficient under the statute.

Even when the Tax Injunction Act does not directly prohibit the federal courts from hearing challenges to state tax laws, general principles of comity may require dismissal of the federal court action. Thus, in *Levin v. Commerce Energy, Inc.*, 560 U.S. 413 (2010), the Court relied on comity in ruling that the federal court should not entertain an action brought by a retail natural gas marketer seeking to enjoin, on due process and commerce clause grounds, the ostensibly favorable tax treatment that the state provided to its public utility competitors. Citing *Younger v Harris*, and other authorities, the *Levin* Court stated:

> The comity doctrine counsels lower federal courts to resist engagement in certain cases falling within their jurisdiction. . . . Comity's constraint has particular force when lower federal courts are asked to pass on the constitutionality of state taxation of commercial activity. For "[i]t is upon taxation that the several

States chiefly rely to obtain the means to carry on their respective governments, and it is of the utmost importance to all of them that the modes adopted to enforce the taxes levied should be interfered with as little as possible. "

But comity principles (apparently) do not mean that all federal court challenges to state tax provisions will be dismissed. In *Hibbs* v. *Winn*, 542 U.S. 88 (2004), decided six years before *Levin*, the Court allowed the plaintiffs to maintain an action in federal court claiming that a state program authorizing tax credits for payments to organizations that disbursed scholarship grants to children attending religious schools violated the Establishment Clause. The *Levin* Court distinguished *Hibbs* on the grounds that the plaintiffs in that case "were outsiders to the tax expenditure, 'third parties' whose own tax liability was not a relevant factor." In *Levin*, on the other hand, "the very premise of respondents' suit is that they are taxed differently from [its competitors."] Persuaded? Do you understand why whether the plaintiffs are "outsiders" to the tax scheme or economic competitors with the entity receiving the purportedly favorable tax treatment should make a difference as to whether comity principles should preclude the federal court from exercising jurisdiction? Four of the Justices in *Levin*, Justices Kennedy, Thomas, Scalia, and Alito, could find no such reason and, in concurring opinions, suggested that after *Levin* the continued viability of *Hibbs* was doubtful.

Comity, rather than the Tax Injunction Act, also provided the basis of the Court's decision in *Fair Assessment in Real Estate Association v. McNary*, 454 U.S. 100 (1981), which held that state taxpayers were barred from bringing a § 1983 claim in federal court, seeking damages for an allegedly unconstitutional administration of a state tax system. According to the *McNary* Court, the taxpayers "must seek protection of their federal rights by state remedies," rather than in federal courts, as long as the state remedies were "plain, adequate, and complete." Taking *McNary* one step further, the Court in *National Private Truck Council v. Oklahoma Tax Commission*, 515 U.S. 582, 588 (1995) held that plaintiffs could not maintain a *state court* action against a state tax provision under § 1983. As stated by the Court, "the background presumption that federal law generally will not interfere with administration of state taxes leads us to conclude that Congress did not authorize injunctive or declaratory relief under § 1983 in state tax cases when there is an adequate [state] remedy at law."

Should federal courts be especially solicitous of state courts and state prerogatives in tax matters? Note the parallels between the Court's concern for the integrity of state taxation programs in the *Levin* and *McNary* line of cases and its concern for the integrity of the state fisc in its Eleventh Amendment jurisprudence. Does the concern for the integrity of state tax programs justify the *Levin* and *McNary* Courts' reliance on judge-made rules rather than on congressional statutes?

NOTE ON THE JOHNSON ACT

A final major federal anti-injunction provision is the Johnson Act which prohibits federal courts from enjoining rate orders of state agencies or regulatory bodies. Codified at 28 U.S.C § 1342, the Act provides:

> The district courts shall not enjoin, suspend or restrain the operation of, or compliance with, any order affecting rates chargeable by a public utility and made by a State administrative agency or a rate-making body of a State political subdivision, where: (1) Jurisdiction is based solely on diversity of citizenship or repugnance of the order to the Federal Constitution; and, (2) The order does not interfere with interstate commerce; and, (3) The order has been made after reasonable notice and hearing; and, (4) A plain, speedy and efficient remedy may be had in the courts of such State.

As one court has explained, "[t]he evil sought to be remedied by the Johnson Act was federal courts' interference with states' own control of their public utility rates." *Tennyson v. Gas Service Co.,* 506 F.2d 1135 (10th Cir. 1974). The Act, however, is limited to proscribing federal court injunctions against rate orders and does not affect orders involving non-rate matters. See *Public Utilities Commission of California v. United States,* 355 U.S. 534 (1958) (holding the Act inapplicable to an action challenging a state statute requiring utilities to submit their rates for approval). The Act, by its terms, also does not prohibit suits to enjoin rate regulations based on the commerce clause although it does prohibit federal court injunctions based on the other constitutional provisions such as the due process clause. Does this distinction make sense? More generally, are there reasons why Congress should single out rate orders from other types of state actions in proscribing federal injunctive relief?

IV.   THE YOUNGER DOCTRINE

A.   *YOUNGER v. HARRIS*

YOUNGER V. HARRIS
401 U.S. 37 (1971).

JUSTICE BLACK delivered the opinion of the Court.

Appellee, John Harris, Jr., was indicted in a California state court, charged with violation of the California Penal Code 11400 and 11401, known as the California Criminal Syndicalism Act, set out below.[1] He

---

[1] "Criminal syndicalism" as used in this article means any doctrine or precept advocating, teaching or aiding and abetting the commission of crime, sabotage (which word is hereby defined as meaning willful and malicious physical damage or injury to physical property), or unlawful acts of force and violence or unlawful methods of terrorism as a means of accomplishing a change in industrial ownership or control, or effecting any political change. [Footnote by the Court.]

then filed a complaint in the Federal District Court, asking that court to enjoin the appellant, Younger, the District Attorney of Los Angeles County, from prosecuting him, and alleging that the prosecution and even the presence of the Act inhibited him in the exercise of his rights of free speech and press, rights guaranteed him by the First and Fourteenth Amendments. Appellees Jim Dan and Diane Hirsch intervened as plaintiffs in the suit, claiming that the prosecution of Harris would inhibit them as members of the Progressive Labor Party from peacefully advocating the program of their party, which was to replace capitalism with socialism and to abolish the profit system of production in this country. Appellee Farrell Broslawsky, an instructor in history at Los Angeles Valley College, also intervened claiming that the prosecution of Harris made him uncertain as whether he could teach about the doctrines of Karl Marx or read from the Communist Manifesto as part of his class work. All claimed that unless the United States court restrained the state prosecution of Harris each would suffer immediate and irreparable injury. A three-judge Federal District Court, held that it had jurisdiction and power to restrain the District Attorney from prosecuting, held that the State's Criminal Syndicalism Act was void for vagueness and over-breadth in violation of the First and Fourteenth Amendments, and accordingly restrained the District Attorney from "further prosecution of the currently pending action against plaintiff Harris for alleged violation of the Act."

We have concluded that the judgment of the District Court, enjoining appellant Younger from prosecuting under these California statutes, must be reversed as a violation of the national policy forbidding federal courts to stay or enjoin pending state court proceedings except under special circumstances. We express no view about the circumstances under which federal courts may act when there is no prosecution pending in state courts at the time the federal proceeding is begun.

I.

Appellee Harris has been indicted, and was actually prosecuted by California for a violation of its Criminal Syndicalism Act at the time this suit was filed. He thus has an acute, live controversy with the State and its prosecutor. But none of the other parties plaintiff in the District Court, Dan, Hirsch, or Broslawsky, has such a controversy. None has been indicted, arrested, or even threatened by the [prosecutor.]

Whatever right Harris, who is being prosecuted under the state syndicalism law may have, Dan, Hirsch, and Broslawsky cannot share it with him. They claim the right to bring this suit solely because, in the language of their complaint, they "feel inhibited." We do not think this allegation, even if true, is sufficient to bring the equitable jurisdiction of the federal courts into play to enjoin a pending state prosecution. A federal lawsuit to stop a prosecution in a state court is a serious matter. And persons having no fears of state prosecution except those that are imaginary or speculative, are not to be accepted as appropriate plaintiffs in such cases. Since Harris is actually being prosecuted under the challenged laws, however, we proceed with him as a proper party.

II.

Since the beginning of this country's history Congress has, subject to few exceptions manifested a desire to permit state courts to try state cases free from interference by federal courts. In 1793 an Act unconditionally provided: "Nor shall a writ of injunction be granted to stay proceedings in any court of a State...." 1 Stat.335, c.22, 5. A comparison of the 1793 Act with 28 U.S.C. 2283, its present-day successor, graphically illustrates how few and minor have been the exceptions granted from the flat, prohibitory language of the old Act. During all this lapse of years from 1793 to 1970 the statutory exceptions to the 1793 congressional enactment have been only three: (1) "except as expressly authorized by Act of Congress"; (2) "where necessary in aid of its jurisdiction"; and (3) "to protect or effectuate its judgments." In addition, a judicial exception to the longstanding policy evidenced by the statute has been made where a person about to be prosecuted in a state court can show that he will, if the proceeding in the state court is not enjoined, suffer irreparable damages. See *Ex parte Young,* 209 U.S. 123 (1908).

The precise reasons for this longstanding public policy against federal court interference with state court proceedings have never been specifically identified but the primary sources of the policy are plain. One is the basic doctrine of equity jurisprudence that courts of equity should not act, and particularly should not act to restrain a criminal prosecution, when the moving party has an adequate remedy at law and will not suffer irreparable injury if denied equitable relief. The doctrine may originally have grown out of circumstances peculiar to the English judicial system and not applicable in this country, but its fundamental purpose of restraining equity jurisdiction within narrow limits is equally important under our Constitution, in order to prevent erosion of the role of the jury and avoid a duplication of legal proceedings and legal sanctions where a single suit would be adequate to protect the rights asserted. This underlying reason for restraining courts of equity from interfering with criminal prosecutions is reinforced by an even more vital consideration, the notion of "comity," that is, a proper respect for state functions, a recognition of the fact that the entire country is made up of a Union of separate state governments, and a continuance of the belief that the National Government will fare best if the States and their institutions are left free to perform their separate functions in their separate ways. This, perhaps for a lack of a better and clearer way to describe it, is referred to by many as "Our Federalism," and one familiar with the profound debates that ushered our Federal Constitution into existence is bound to respect those who remain loyal to the ideals and dreams of "Our Federalism." The concept does not mean blind deference to "States' Rights" any more than it means centralization of control over every important issue in our National Government and its courts. The Framers rejected both these courses. What the concept does represent is a system in which there is sensitivity to the legitimate interest of both the State and National Governments, and in which the National Government, anxious though it may be to vindicate and protect federal rights and federal interests, always endeavors to do so in ways that will not unduly interfere with the legitimate activities of the State. It should never be forgotten that this slogan, "Our Federalism," born in the early struggling days of our Union of States, occupies a highly important place in our Nation's history and its future.

This brief discussion should be enough to suggest some of the reasons why it has been perfectly natural for our cases to repeat time and time again that the normal thing to do when federal courts are asked to enjoin pending proceedings in state courts is not to issue such injunctions.

Ex parte Young and following cases have established the doctrine that when absolutely necessary for protection of constitutional rights courts of the United States have power to enjoin state officers from instituting criminal actions. But this may not be done except under extra ordinary circumstances where the danger or irreparable loss is both great and immediate. Ordinarily, there should be no interference with such officers; primarily, they are charged with the duty of prosecuting offenders against the laws of the State and must decide when and how this is to be done. The accused should first setup and rely upon his defense in the state courts, even though this involves a challenge of the validity of some statute, unless it plainly appears that this course would not afford adequate protection. These principles . . . have been repeatedly followed and reaffirmed in other cases involving threatened prosecutions. See, e.g., *Spielman Motor Sales Co. v. Dodge*, 295 U.S. 89 (1935); *Beal v. Missouri Pac. R. Co.*, 312 U.S. 45 (1941); *Douglas v. City of Jeannette*, 319 U.S. 157 (1943).

In all these cases the Court stressed the importance of showing irreparable injury, the traditional prerequisite to obtaining an injunction. In addition, however, the Court also made clear that in view of the fundamental policy against federal interference with state criminal prosecutions, even irreparable injury is insufficient unless it is "both great and immediate." Certain types of injury, in particular, the cost, anxiety, and inconvenience of having to defend against a single criminal prosecution, could not by themselves be considered "irreparable" in the special legal sense of that term. Instead, the threat to the plaintiff's federally protected rights must be one that cannot be eliminated by his defense against a single criminal prosecution. See, e.g., *Ex parte Young*. Thus, in [*Watson v. Buck*, 313 U.S. 387 (1941)], we stressed:

"Federal injunctions against state criminal statutes, either in their entirety or with respect to their separate and distinct prohibitions, are not to be granted as a matter of course, even if such statutes are unconstitutional. 'No citizen or member of the community is immune from prosecution, in good faith, for his alleged criminal acts. The imminence of such a prosecution even though alleged to be unauthorized and hence unlawful is not alone ground for relief in equity which exerts its extraordinary powers only to prevent irreparable injury to the plaintiff who seeks its [aid.' "]

This is where the law stood when the Court decided *Dombrowski v. Pfister*, 380 U.S. 479 (1965), and held that an injunction against the enforcement of certain state criminal statutes could properly issue under the circumstances presented in that case. In *Dombrowski*, unlike many of the earlier cases denying injunctions, the complaint made substantial allegations that:

"the threats to enforce the statutes against appellants are not made with any expectation of securing valid convictions, but rather are part of a plan to employ arrests, seizures, and threats of prosecution under color of the statutes to harass appellants and discourage them and their supporters from asserting and attempting to vindicate the constitutional rights of Negro citizens of Louisiana."

The appellants in *Dombrowski* had offered to prove that their offices had been raided and all their files and records seized pursuant to search and arrest warrants that were later summarily vacated by a state judge for lack of probable cause. They also offered to prove that despite the state court order quashing the warrants and suppressing the evidence seized, the prosecutor was continuing to threaten to initiate new prosecutions of appellants under the same statutes, was holding public hearings at which photostatic copies of the illegally seized documents were being used, and was threatening to use other copies of the illegally seized documents to obtain grand jury indictments against the appellants on charges of violating that same statutes. These circumstances, as viewed by the Court sufficiently establish the kind of irreparable injury, above and beyond that associated with the defense of a single prosecution brought in good faith, that had always been considered sufficient to justify federal intervention. Indeed, after quoting the Court's statement in *Douglas* concerning the very restricted circumstances under which an injunction could be justified, the Court in *Dombrowski* went on to say:

"But the allegations in this complaint depict a situation in which defense of the State's criminal prosecution will not assure adequate vindication of constitutional rights. They suggest that a substantial loss of or impairment of freedoms of expression will occur if appellants must await the state court's disposition and ultimate review in this Court of any adverse determination. These allegations, if true, clearly show irreparable injury."

And the Court made clear that even under these circumstances the District Court issuing the injunction would have continuing power to lift it at any time and remit the plaintiffs to the state courts if circumstances warranted. Similarly, in *Cameron v. Johnson*, 390 U.S. 611 (1968), a divided Court denied an injunction after finding that the record did not establish the necessary bad faith and harassment; the dissenting Justices themselves stressed the very limited role to be allowed for federal injunctions against state criminal prosecutions and differed with the Court only on the question whether the particular facts of the case were sufficient to show that the prosecution was brought in bad faith.

It is against the background of these principles that we must judge the propriety of an injunction under the circumstances of the present case. Here a proceeding was already pending in the state court, affording Harris an opportunity to raise his constitutional claims. There is no suggestion that this single prosecution against Harris is brought in bad faith or is only one of a series of repeated prosecutions to which he will be subjected. In other words, the injury that Harris faces is solely "that incidental to every criminal proceeding brought lawfully and in good faith," *Douglas,* supra, and therefore under the settled doctrine we have already described he is not entitled to equitable relief "even if such statutes are unconstitutional," *Buck,* supra.

The District Court, however, thought that the *Dombrowski* decision substantially broadened the availability of injunctions against state criminal prosecutions and that under that decision the federal courts may give equitable relief, without regard to any showing of bad faith or harassment, whenever a state statute is found "on its face" to be vague or overly broad, in violation of the First Amendment. We recognize that there are some statements in the *Dombrowski* opinion that would seem to support this argument. But, as we have already seen, such statements were unnecessary to the decision of that case, because the Court found that the plaintiffs had alleged a basis for equitable relief under the long-established standards. In addition, we do not regard the reasons adduced to support this position as sufficient to justify such a substantial departure from the established doctrines regarding the availability of injunctive relief. It is undoubtedly true, as the Court stated in *Dombrowski*, that "[a] criminal prosecution under a statute regulating expression usually involves imponderables and contingencies that themselves may inhibit the full exercise of First Amendment freedoms." But this sort of "chilling effect," as the Court called it, should not by itself justify federal intervention. In the first place, the chilling effect cannot be satisfactorily eliminated by federal injunctive relief. In *Dombrowski* itself the Court stated that the injunction to be issued there could be lifted if the State obtained an "acceptable limiting construction" from the state courts. The Court then made clear that once this was done, prosecutions would then be brought for conduct occurring before the narrowing construction was made, and proper convictions could stand so long as the defendants were not deprived of fair warning. The kind of relief granted in *Dombrowski* thus does not effectively eliminate uncertainty as to the coverage of the state statute and leaves most citizens with virtually the same doubts as before regarding the danger that their conduct might eventually be subjected to criminal sanctions. The chilling effect can, of course, be eliminated by an injunction that would prohibit any prosecution whatever for conduct occurring prior to a satisfactory rewriting of the statute. But the States would then be stripped of all power to prosecute even the socially dangerous and constitutionally unprotected conduct that had been covered by the statute, until a new statute could be passed by the state legislature and approved by the federal courts in potentially lengthy trial and appellate proceedings. Thus, in *Dombrowski* itself the Court carefully reaffirmed the principle that even in the direct prosecution in the State's own courts, a valid narrowing construction can be applied to conduct occurring prior to the date when the narrowing construction was made, in the absence of fair warning problems.

Beyond all this is another, more basic consideration. Procedures for testing the constitutionality of a statute "on its face" in the manner apparently contemplated by *Dombrowski*, and for the enjoining all action to enforce the statute until the State can obtain court approval for a modified version, are fundamentally at odds with the function of the federal courts in our constitutional plan. The power and duty of the judiciary to declare laws unconstitutional is in the final analysis derived from its responsibility for resolving concrete disputes brought before the courts for decision; a statute apparently governing a dispute cannot be applied by judges, consistently with their obligations under the Supremacy Clause, when such an application of the statute would conflict with the Constitution. *Marbury v. Madison,* 1 Cranch 137 (1803). But this vital responsibility, broad as it is, does not amount to an unlimited power to survey the statute books and pass judgment on laws before the courts are called upon to enforce them. Ever since the Constitutional Conventional rejected a proposal for having members of the Supreme Court render advice concerning pending legislation it has been clear that, even when suits of this kind involve a "case or controversy" sufficient to satisfy the requirements of Article III of the Constitution, the task of analyzing a proposed statute, pinpointing its deficiencies, and requiring correction of these deficiencies before the statute is put into effect, is rarely if ever an appropriate task for the judiciary.

For these reasons, fundamental not only to our federal system but also to the basic functions of the Judicial Branch of the National Government under our Constitution, we hold that the *Dombrowski* decision should not be regarded as having upset the settled doctrines that have always confined very narrowly the availability of injunctive relief against state criminal prosecutions. We do not think that opinion stands for the proposition that a federal court can properly enjoin enforcement of a statute solely on the basis of a showing that the statute "on its face" abridges First Amendment rights. There may, of course, be extraordinary circumstances in which the necessary irreparable injury can be shown even in the absence of the usual prerequisites of bad faith and harassment. For example, we [have previously] indicated: "It is of course conceivable that a statute might be flagrantly and patently violative of express constitutional prohibitions in every clause, sentence and paragraph, and in whatever manner and against whomever an effort might be made to apply it."

Other unusual situations calling for federal intervention might also arise, but there is no point in our attempting now to specify what they might be. It is sufficient for purposes of the present case to hold, as we do, that the possible unconstitutionality of a statute "on its face" does not in itself justify an injunction against good-faith attempts to enforce it, and that appellee Harris has failed to make any showing of bad faith, harassment, or any other unusual circumstance that would call for equitable relief. Because our holding rests on the absence of the factors necessary under equitable principles to justify federal intervention, we have no occasion to consider whether 29 U. S. C. § 2283, which prohibits an injunction against state court proceedings "except as expressly authorized by Act of Congress" would in and of itself be controlling under the circumstances of this case.

The judgment of the District Court is reversed, and the case is remanded for further proceedings not inconsistent with this opinion.

Reversed.

JUSTICE STEWART, with whom JUSTICE HARLAN joins, concurring

The questions the Court decides today are important ones. Perhaps as important, however, is recognition of the areas into which today's holdings do not necessarily extend. In all of these cases, the Court deals only with the proper policy to be followed by a federal court when asked to intervene by injunction or declaratory judgment in a criminal prosecution which is contemporaneously pending in a state court.

In basing its decisions on policy grounds, the Court does not reach any questions concerning the independent force of the federal anti-injunction statute, 28 U.S. C. § 2283. Thus we do not decide whether the word "injunction" in § 2283 should be interpreted to include a declaratory judgment, or whether an injunction to stay proceedings in a state court is "expressly authorized" by § 1 of the Civil Rights Act of 1871, now 42 U.S.C. § 1983. And since all these cases involve state criminal prosecutions, we do not deal with the considerations which should govern a federal court when it is asked to intervene in state civil proceedings, where, for various reasons, the balance might be struck differently. Finally, the Court today does not resolve the problems involved when a federal court is asked to give injunctive or declaratory relief from *future* state criminal prosecutions.

The Court confines itself to deciding the policy considerations that in our federal system must prevail when federal courts are asked to interfere with pending state prosecutions. Within this area, we hold that a federal court must not, save in exceptional and extremely limited circumstances, intervene by way of either injunction or declaration in an existing state criminal prosecution. Such circumstances exist only when there is a threat of irreparable injury "both great and immediate." A threat of this nature might be shown if the state criminal statute in question were patently and flagrantly unconstitutional on its face or if there has been bad faith and harassment—official lawlessness—in a statute's enforcement. In such circumstances the reasons of policy for deferring to state adjudication are outweighed by the injury flowing from the very bringing of the state proceedings, by the perversion of the very process that is supposed to provide vindication, and by the need for speedy and effective action to protect federal rights.

[The concurring opinion of JUSTICE BRENNAN, joined by JUSTICE WHITE and JUSTICE MARSHALL, is omitted.]

JUSTICE DOUGLAS, dissenting.

The fact that we are in a period of history when enormous extrajudicial sanctions are imposed on those who assert their First Amendment rights in unpopular causes emphasizes the wisdom of *Dombrowski v. Pfister*. There we recognized that in times of repression, when interests with powerful spokesmen generate symbolic pogroms against nonconformists, the federal judiciary, charged by Congress with special vigilance for protection of civil rights, has special responsibilities to prevent an erosion of the individual's constitutional rights.

Dombrowski represents an exception to the general rule that federal courts should not interfere with state criminal prosecutions. The exception does not arise merely because prosecutions are threatened to which the First Amendment will be the proffered defense. *Dombrowski* governs statutes which are a blunderbuss by themselves or when used en masse—those that have an "overbroad sweep." If the rule were otherwise, the contours of regulation would have to be hammered out case by case—and tested only by those hardy enough to risk criminal prosecution to determine the proper scope of regulation." It was in the context of overbroad state statutes that we spoke of the "chilling effect upon the exercise of First Amendment rights" caused by state prosecutions.

The special circumstances when federal intervention in a state criminal proceeding is permissible are not restricted to bad faith on the part of state officials or the threat of multiple prosecutions. They also exist where for any reason the state statute being enforced is unconstitutional on its face. As Mr. Justice Butler, writing for the Court, said in *Terrace v. Thompson*, 263 U.S. 197, 214:

> "Equity jurisdiction will be exercised to enjoin the threatened enforcement of a state law which contravenes the Federal Constitution wherever it is essential in order effectually to protect property rights and the rights of persons against injuries otherwise irremediable; and in such a case a person, who as an officer of the State is clothed with the duty of enforcing its laws and who threatens and is about to commence proceedings, either civil or criminal, to enforce such a law against parties affected, may be enjoined from such action by a federal court of equity."

Our *Dombrowski* decision was only another facet of the same problem.

The eternal temptation, of course, has been to arrest the speaker rather than to correct the conditions about which he complains. I see no reason why these appellees should be made to walk the treacherous ground of these statutes. They, like other citizens, need the umbrella of the First Amendment as they study, analyze, discuss, and debate the troubles of these days. When criminal prosecutions can be leveled against them because they express unpopular views, the society of dialogue is in danger.

NOTES ON YOUNGER V. HARRIS

1.   **The Role of Equity.** *Younger* may be explained, in part, as an application of traditional rules of equity. Equity generally forbids the granting of an injunction when the plaintiff otherwise has an adequate remedy at law and criminal defendants presumably have such adequate remedies in that they can raise their constitutional claims as defenses to the state criminal proceedings. But is the notion that state courts are adequate arbiters of federal constitutional rights consistent with the decisions in *Monroe v. Pape*, 365 U.S. 167 (1961) and *Mitchum v. Foster*, 407 U.S. 225 (1972) which stressed the purported inadequacy of state courts to protect constitutional guarantees? Is there a reason why state courts may be seen as

providing an adequate remedy at law when adjudicating constitutional defenses in criminal cases, but deemed inadequate in affording plaintiffs, such as those in *Monroe* and *Mitchum*, a sufficient remedy against the state? See Chapter 1, supra.

2. **The Adequacy of the State Proceedings.** The Court's suggestion that state proceedings provide a sufficiently adequate remedy at law to preclude the federal courts from exercising equitable jurisdiction, however, has its limits. In *Gibson v. Berryhill*, 411 U.S. 564 (1973), for example, the Court held that *Younger* would not prevent a federal court from enjoining a state administrative proceeding found to be biased. Moreover, as *Gibson* also explained, because "*Younger v. Harris* contemplates the outright dismissal of the federal suit, and the presentation of all claims, both state and federal, to the state courts . . . [it] naturally presupposes the opportunity to raise and have timely decided by a competent state tribunal the federal issues involved." Thus, *Younger* will not apply in circumstances where the federal issue cannot be raised in the state proceeding. See *Gerstein v. Pugh*, 420 U.S. 103 (1975) (allowing the federal court to issue an injunction requiring the state to hold preliminary hearings for pretrial incarceration because the issue "could not be raised in defense of the criminal prosecution.")

Gibson's "biased tribunal" principle does not oblige the federal plaintiff to show a subjective bias on the part of an adjudicator. *Structural* bias is sufficient. In that case, Alabama required that optometrists maintain independent practices. The federal plaintiffs were optometrists who worked at a chain store. In the state administrative proceeding before the Alabama Board of Optometry, they were charged with "unprofessional conduct" and threatened with revocation of their licenses. All of the members of the Board maintained independent practices. The Court approved the District Court's conclusion "that the pecuniary interest of the members of the Board of Optometry had sufficient substance to disqualify them in this case."

3. **Antecedent Cases.** In *Douglas v. City of Jeannette,* 319 U.S. 157, 167 (1943), the Jehovah's Witnesses in Jeannette, Pennsylvania, instituted a campaign to visit the homes of each of the city's 16,000 inhabitants and distribute religious leaflets. After a large number of complaints from residents due to visits on the Palm Sunday of 1939, the local police arrested twenty-one Jehovah's Witnesses. The police charged them with violating a city ordinance which prohibited solicitation or canvassing without a license. The Witnesses then brought suit in federal court to enjoin the prosecution. Although the Court ruled that it had federal question jurisdiction, it dismissed the action on grounds that the case did not comport with its equity jurisdiction. The Court found that Congress had adopted a policy of generally leaving to the state courts the trial of criminal cases arising under state laws and, as courts of equity, federal courts should refuse to interfere in threatened proceedings in state courts except in cases when the federal court can prevent clear, imminent, and irreparable injury to the plaintiff.

In *Dombrowski v. Pfister*, 380 U.S. 479 (1965), a group of civil rights workers from Louisiana sought an injunction to restrain state officials from prosecuting or threatening to prosecute them for violating the Louisiana Subversive Activities and Communist Control Law. Louisiana state and local police had arrested the workers, raided their offices and seized records. Although a state court judge quashed the arrest warrants, discharged the workers, and suppressed the evidence seized in the police raid, Louisiana officials continued to threaten the civil rights workers and the group was later indicted even after the federal complaint was filed. This complaint alleged that the Louisiana statute facially violated the First and Fourteenth Amendments because it was vague and overbroad. The Court held that abstention was not appropriate. The Court reasoned that in this situation the petitioners' defense to the state's criminal prosecution would not assure adequate vindication of constitutional rights and that if the allegations were true, the petitioners could suffer irreparable injury to their freedoms of expression while waiting for the state court's disposition and appeal. Further, the Court was concerned about the chilling effect upon the exercise of First Amendment rights that may arise from the fact of prosecution alone, regardless of the outcome of the case.

Younger made it clear that it considered *Douglas* the rule and *Dombrowski* a limited exception. For an excellent analysis of *Douglas*, *Dombrowski*, and the other pre-*Younger* cases, see Douglas Laycock, *Federal Interference with State Prosecutions, The Cases* Dombrowski *Forgot*, 46 U. CHI. L. REV. 636 (1979).

4. *Younger* and the Anti-Injunction Act. The *Younger* opinion stated that it did not reach the question of whether issuing the injunction might also be prohibited under the anti-injunction statute. One year later, however, in *Mitchum v. Foster*, 407 U.S. 225 (1972), the Court ruled that *Younger* implicitly held that § 1983 was an expressly authorized exception to the anti-injunction statute. According to *Mitchum*:

> While the Court in *Younger* and its companion cases expressly disavowed deciding the question now before us—whether § 1983 comes within the "expressly authorized" exception of the anti-injunction statute—it is evident that our decisions in those cases cannot be disregarded in deciding this question. In the first place, if § 1983 is not within the statutory exception, then the anti-injunction statute would have absolutely barred the injunction issued in *Younger*, as the appellant in that case argued, and there would have been no occasion whatever for the Court to decide that case upon the "policy" ground of "Our Federalism." Secondly, if § 1983 is not within the "expressly authorized" exception of the anti-injunction statute, then we must overrule *Younger* and its companion cases insofar as they recognized the permissibility of injunctive relief against pending criminal prosecutions in certain limited and exceptional circumstances. For, under the doctrine of *Atlantic Coast Line*, the anti-injunction statute would, in a § 1983

case, then be an "absolute prohibition" against federal equity intervention in a pending state criminal *or* civil proceeding—under any circumstances whatever.

Is this passage from *Mitchum* a fair reading of the *Younger* decision? Do you understand why the *Younger* Court based its decision on principles of equity, comity, and federalism rather than on the Anti-Injunction Act? Does it make any practical difference?

5. *Younger* **and State Criminal Law Administration.** As a practical matter, a contrary ruling in *Younger* could have had devastating effects on the state criminal justice system. If, in every state prosecution, a criminal defendant had the recourse of running to the federal courthouse to enjoin the state proceeding, the time and resource constraints imposed on state prosecutors (and federal courts) would have been considerable. Consider, for example, the havoc that might occur if state criminal defendants were able to enjoin prosecutions every time they were able to raise Fourth Amendment objections to the admissibility of the state's evidence against them.

Justice Douglas's dissent in *Younger* argues that first amendment cases are exceptional and state defendants raising First Amendment defenses to purportedly overbroad criminal statutes should have access to the federal courts in order to prevent the chilling effects on free speech that would otherwise be generated by state criminal prosecutions of expressive activity. Is Justice Douglas's opinion persuasive? Should the *Younger* doctrine exempt suits for injunctions based upon the First Amendment?

6. **The Immediate Impact of** *Younger.* The Court's decision in *Younger* was accompanied by an exclamation point. Along with *Younger*, the Court decided four companion cases all reinforcing *Younger*'s central proposition that federal courts should not interfere with state criminal prosecutions. In addition, the Court summarily remanded thirty other cases from its docket for reconsideration in light of the *Younger* decision.

7. *Younger* **and Justiciability.** Note the relationship between the *Younger* doctrine and questions of standing. If the federal plaintiffs, such as Harris's co-parties, have not been adequately threatened with state criminal charges, their federal action will be dismissed for lack of standing. If, on the other hand, they have been criminally charged, such as Harris himself, their federal suit will be dismissed on *Younger* grounds. Are there any circumstances in which the federal plaintiff will face enough of a threat of criminal action to warrant standing but not yet be subject to actual proceedings so as to implicate *Younger*? See *Steffel v. Thompson*, and the notes on anticipatory challenges following *Steffel*, below.

B. YOUNGER'S PROGENY

The blackletter holding of *Younger v. Harris* is that a federal court may not enjoin an ongoing state criminal proceeding absent extraordinary circumstances. Cases since *Younger*, however, have expanded this rule well beyond the specific holding of the decision itself. In fact, virtually every aspect of the *Younger* holding has raised its own set of issues. Are *Younger*'s prohibitions limited to suits for injunctive relief or do they also apply to other requests for relief? Are they applicable only when the state proceedings are ongoing or do they apply in other circumstances as well? Are they confined to state criminal cases or do they also apply to civil matters? Do they limit the ability of the federal courts to enjoin state administrative proceedings as well as state judicial actions? Do they affect litigation between private parties or are they only pertinent when the state is somehow a party to the state proceeding? The remainder of this section addresses each of these issues.

1.   The Meaning of "Enjoin"

STEFFEL V. THOMPSON
415 U.S. 452 (1974).

JUSTICE BRENNAN delivered the opinion of the Court.

The parties stipulated to the relevant facts: On October 8, 1970, while petitioner and other individuals were distributing handbills protesting American involvement in Vietnam on an exterior sidewalk of the North DeKalb Shopping Center, shopping center employees asked them to stop handbilling and leave. They declined to do so, and police officers were summoned. The officers told them that they would be arrested if they did not stop handbilling. The group then left to avoid arrest. Two days later petitioner and a companion returned to the shopping center and again began handbilling. The manager of the center called the police, and petitioner and his companion were once again told that failure to stop their handbilling would result in their arrests. Petitioner left to avoid arrest. His companion stayed, however, continued handbilling, and was arrested and subsequently arraigned on a charge of criminal trespass in violation of § 26–1503. Petitioner alleged in his complaint that, although he desired to return to the shopping center to distribute handbills, he had not done so because of his concern that he, too, would be arrested for violation of § 26–1503; the parties stipulated that, if petitioner returned and refused upon request to stop handbilling, a warrant would be sworn out and he might be arrested and charged with a violation of the Georgia statute.

Unlike three of the appellees in *Younger* v. *Harris,* 401 U.S. 37 (1971), petitioner has alleged threats of prosecution that cannot be characterized as "imaginary or speculative." He has been twice warned to stop handbilling that he claims is constitutionally protected and has been told by the police that if he again handbills at the shopping center and disobeys a warning to stop he will likely be prosecuted. The prosecution of petitioner's handbilling companion is ample demonstration that petitioner's concern with arrest has not been "chimerical." In these circumstances, it is not necessary that petitioner first expose himself to actual arrest or prosecution to be entitled to challenge a statute that he claims deters the exercise of his constitutional rights.

We now turn to the question of whether the District Court and the Court of Appeals correctly found petitioner's request for declaratory relief inappropriate.

Sensitive to principles of equity, comity, and federalism, we recognized in *Younger v. Harris* that federal courts should ordinarily refrain from enjoining ongoing state criminal prosecutions. We were cognizant that a pending state proceeding, in all but unusual cases, would provide the federal plaintiff with the necessary vehicle for vindicating his constitutional rights, and, in that circumstance, the restraining of an ongoing prosecution would entail an unseemly failure to give effect to the principle that state courts have the solemn responsibility, equally with the federal courts "to guard, enforce, and protect every right granted or secured by the Constitution of the United States. . . ." In *Samuels* v. *Mackell,* 401 U.S. 66 (1971), the Court also found that the same principles ordinarily would be flouted by issuance of a federal declaratory judgment when a state proceeding was pending, since the intrusive effect of declaratory relief "will result in precisely the same interference with and disruption of state proceedings that the long-standing policy limiting injunctions was designed to avoid." We therefore held in *Samuels* that, "in cases where the state criminal prosecution was begun prior to the federal suit, the same equitable principles relevant to the propriety of an injunction must be taken into consideration by federal district courts in determining whether to issue a declaratory judgment. . . ."

Neither *Younger* nor *Samuels,* however, decided the question whether federal intervention might be permissible in the absence of a pending state prosecution.

These reservations anticipated the Court's recognition that the relevant principles of equity, comity, and federalism "have little force in the absence of a pending state proceeding." When no state criminal proceeding is pending at the time the federal complaint is filed, federal intervention does not result in duplicative legal proceedings or disruption of the state criminal justice system; nor can federal intervention, in that circumstance, be interpreted as reflecting negatively upon the state court's ability to enforce constitutional principles. In addition, while a pending state prosecution provides the federal plaintiff with a concrete opportunity to vindicate his constitutional rights, a refusal on the part of the federal courts to intervene when no state proceeding is pending may place the hapless plaintiff between the Scylla of intentionally flouting state law and the Charybdis of forgoing what he believes to be constitutionally protected activity in order to avoid becoming enmeshed in a criminal proceeding.

A "storm of controversy" raged in the wake of *Ex parte Young*, focusing principally on the power of a single federal judge to grant *ex parte* interlocutory injunctions against the enforcement of state statutes. From a State's viewpoint the granting of injunctive relief—even by these courts of special dignity—"rather clumsily" crippled state enforcement of its statutes pending further review. Furthermore, plaintiffs were dissatisfied with this method of testing the constitutionality of state statutes, since it placed upon them the burden of demonstrating the traditional prerequisites to equitable relief—most importantly, irreparable injury.

To dispel these difficulties, Congress in 1934 enacted the Declaratory Judgment Act, 28 U. S. C. §§ 2201–2202.

"It was this history that formed the backdrop to our decision in *Zwickler* v. *Koota*, 389 U.S. 241 (1967), where a state criminal statute was attacked on grounds of unconstitutional overbreadth and no state prosecution was pending against the federal plaintiff. There, we found error in a three-judge district court's considering, as a single question, the propriety of granting injunctive and declaratory relief. Although we noted that injunctive relief might well be unavailable under principles of equity jurisprudence canvassed in *Douglas* v. *City of Jeannette*, 319 U.S. 157 (1943), we held that a federal district court has the duty to decide the appropriateness and the merits of the declaratory request irrespective of its conclusion as to the propriety of the issuance of the injunction."

The "different considerations" entering into a decision whether to grant declaratory relief have their origins in the preceding historical summary. First, as Congress recognized in 1934, a declaratory judgment will have a less intrusive effect on the administration of state criminal laws. As was observed in *Perez* v. *Ledesma*, 401 U.S. 82 (1971) (separate opinion of Brennan, J.):

"Of course, a favorable declaratory judgment may nevertheless be valuable to the plaintiff though it cannot make even an unconstitutional statute disappear. A state statute may be declared unconstitutional *in toto*—that is, incapable of having constitutional applications; or it may be declared unconstitutionally vague or overbroad—that is, incapable of being constitutionally applied to the full extent of its purport. In either case, a federal declaration of unconstitutionality reflects the opinion of the federal court that the statute cannot be fully enforced. If a declaration of total unconstitutionality is affirmed by this Court, it follows that this Court stands ready to reverse any conviction under the statute. If a declaration of partial unconstitutionality is affirmed by this Court, the implication is that this Court will overturn particular applications of the statute, but that if the statute is narrowly construed by the state courts it will not be incapable of constitutional applications. Accordingly, the declaration does not necessarily bar prosecutions under the statute, as a broad injunction would. Thus, where the highest court of a State has had an opportunity to give a statute regulating expression a narrowing or clarifying construction but has failed to do so, and later a federal court declares the statute unconstitutionally vague or overbroad, it may well be open to a state prosecutor, after the federal court decision, to bring a prosecution under the statute if he reasonably believes that the defendant's conduct is not constitutionally protected and that the state courts may give the statute a construction so as to yield a constitutionally valid conviction. Even where a declaration of unconstitutionality is not reviewed by this Court, the declaration may still be able to cut down the deterrent effect of an unconstitutional state statute. The persuasive force of the court's opinion and judgment may lead state prosecutors, courts, and legislators to reconsider their respective responsibilities toward the statute. Enforcement policies or judicial construction may be changed, or the legislature may repeal the statute and start anew. Finally, the federal court judgment may have some res judicata effect, though this point is not free from difficulty and the governing rules remain to be developed with a view to the proper workings of a federal system. What is clear, however, is that even though a declaratory judgment has 'the force and effect of a final judgment,' 28 U. S. C. § 2201, it is a much milder form of relief than an injunction. Though it may be persuasive, it is not ultimately coercive; noncompliance with it may be inappropriate, but is not contempt."

Second, engrafting upon the Declaratory Judgment Act a requirement that all of the traditional equitable prerequisites to the issuance of an injunction be satisfied before the issuance of a declaratory judgment is considered would defy Congress' intent to make declaratory relief available in cases where an injunction would be inappropriate.

Were the law to be that a plaintiff could not obtain a declaratory judgment that a local ordinance was unconstitutional when no state prosecution is pending unless he could allege and prove circumstances justifying a federal injunction of an existing state prosecution, the

Federal Declaratory Judgment Act would have been *pro tanto* repealed. *Wulp* v. *Corcoran*, 454 F.2d 826, 832 (1st Cir. 1972).

Thus, the Court of Appeals was in error when it ruled that a failure to demonstrate irreparable injury—a traditional prerequisite to injunctive relief, having no equivalent in the law of declaratory judgments, precluded the granting of declaratory relief.

The only occasions where this Court has disregarded these "different considerations" and found that a preclusion of injunctive relief inevitably led to a denial of declaratory relief have been cases in which principles of federalism militated altogether against federal intervention in a class of adjudications. In the instant case, principles of federalism not only do not preclude federal intervention, they compel it. Requiring the federal courts totally to step aside when no state criminal prosecution is pending against the federal plaintiff would turn federalism on its head. When federal claims are premised on 42 U. S. C. § 1983 and 28 U. S. C. § 1343(3)—as they are here—we have not required exhaustion of state judicial or administrative remedies, recognizing the paramount role Congress has assigned to the federal courts to protect constitutional rights. But exhaustion of state remedies is precisely what would be required if both federal injunctive and declaratory relief were unavailable in a case where no state prosecution had been commenced.

We therefore hold that, regardless of whether injunctive relief may be appropriate, federal declaratory relief is not precluded when no state prosecution is pending and a federal plaintiff demonstrates a genuine threat of enforcement of a disputed state criminal statute, whether an attack is made on the constitutionality of the statute on its face or as applied. The judgment of the Court of Appeals is reversed, and the case is remanded for further proceedings consistent with this opinion.

It is so ordered.

JUSTICE STEWART, with whom the CHIEF JUSTICE joins, concurring.

While joining the opinion of the Court, I add a word by way of emphasis. Our decision today must not be understood as authorizing the invocation of federal declaratory judgment jurisdiction by a person who thinks a state criminal law is unconstitutional, even if he genuinely feels 'chilled' in his freedom of action by the law's existence, and even if he honestly entertains the subjective belief that he may now or in the future be prosecuted under it. As the Court stated in *Younger* v. *Harris*, "[t]he power and duty of the judiciary to declare laws unconstitutional is in the final analysis derived from its responsibility for resolving concrete disputes brought the courts for decision. . . ."

The petitioner in this case has succeeded in objectively showing that the threat of imminent arrest, corroborated by the actual arrest of his companion, has created an actual concrete controversy between himself and the agents of the State. He has, therefore, demonstrated a genuine threat of enforcement of a disputed state criminal [statute.] Cases where such a 'genuine threat' can be demonstrated will, I think, be exceedingly rare.

[The concurring opinion of JUSTICE WHITE is omitted.]

JUSTICE REHNQUIST, with whom THE CHIEF JUSTICE joins, concurring.

If the declaratory judgment remains, as I think the Declaratory Judgment Act intended, a simple declaration of rights without more, it will not be used merely as a dramatic tactical maneuver on the part of any state defendant seeking extended delays. Nor will it force state officials to try cases time after time, first in the federal courts and then in the state courts. I do not believe Congress desired such unnecessary results, and I do not think that today's decision should be read to sanction them. Rather the Act, and the decision, stand for the sensible proposition that both a potential state defendant, threatened with prosecution but not charged, and the State itself, confronted by a possible violation of its criminal laws, may benefit from a procedure which provides for a declaration of rights without activation of the criminal process. If the federal court finds that the threatened prosecution would depend upon a statute it judges unconstitutional, the State may decide to forgo prosecution of similar conduct in the future, believing the judgment persuasive. Should the state prosecutors not find the decision persuasive enough to justify forbearance, the successful federal plaintiff will at least be able to bolster his allegations of unconstitutionality in the state trial with a decision of the federal district court in the immediate locality. The state courts may find the reasoning convincing even though the prosecutors did not. Finally, of course, the state legislature may decide, on the basis of the federal decision, that the statute would be better amended or repealed. Other more intrusive forms of relief should not be routinely available.

NOTES ON STEFFEL AND DECLARATORY, INJUNCTIVE, AND DAMAGE ACTIONS

1. **Samuels v. Mackell.** In *Samuels v. Mackell*, 401 U.S. 66 (1971), a companion case to *Younger*, the Court held that the prohibition against federal court interference with ongoing state criminal proceedings would also apply to suits for declaratory relief claiming that an ongoing prosecution was unconstitutional. As the *Samuels* Court reasoned:

> [O]rdinarily a declaratory judgment will result in precisely the same interference with and disruption of state proceedings that the long-standing policy limiting injunctions was designed to avoid. This is

true for at least two reasons. In the first place, the Declaratory Judgment Act provides that after a declaratory judgment is issued the district court may enforce it by granting "[f]urther necessary or proper relief" 28 U.S.C. [§] 2202, and therefore a declaratory judgment issued while state proceedings are pending might serve as the basis for a subsequent injunction against those proceedings to "protect or effectuate" the declaratory judgment, 28 U.S.C. [§] 2283, and thus result in a clearly improper interference with the state proceedings. Secondly, even if the declaratory judgment is not used as a basis for actually issuing an injunction, the declaratory relief alone has virtually the same practical impact as a formal injunction would.

Does *Steffel* undercut *Samuels* in its discussion of how declaratory relief is less invasive of state interests than is an injunction? Or are the two cases distinguishable solely on grounds that in *Samuels* there was an ongoing prosecution while in *Steffel* no state proceeding was pending? If so, what is the purpose of the *Steffel* Court's extended discussion of the particular nature of declaratory relief?

   2.   The Rehnquist Concurrence in *Steffel*. Justice Rehnquist's concurrence is notable in that it suggests that a declaratory order should have no binding effect on a subsequent state prosecution, other than perhaps to persuade the state authorities to forbear prosecution or to convince the state court of the merits of the defendant's position. But if the effects of the remedy are this academic, does a federal court issuing an order of declaratory relief violate Article III limitations on advisory opinions? In this respect, it is notable that in a non-excerpted part of his concurrence, Justice Rehnquist argued that failure to comply with a declaratory order should not be deemed as evidence of prosecutorial bad faith thereby bringing the state action within *Younger*'s extraordinary circumstances exception.

   3.   Permanent Injunctions. Does *Younger* prohibit suits for injunctive relief against state prosecutions even when there are, as yet, no ongoing proceedings? Traditional equitable principles would not bar such suits because, in the absence of the state prosecution, there is no remedy at law. Does *Steffel*'s heavy reliance on the purported distinction between the injunction and declaratory relief remedies in terms of their relative intrusiveness on state prerogatives suggest that permanent injunctive relief is impermissible? In *Wooley v. Maynard*, 430 U.S. 705 (1977), the Court shed some light on this subject in sustaining a request for a permanent injunction against future prosecutions, *Younger* notwithstanding. But the *Wooley* Court also appeared to hedge its bets by obliquely suggesting that the case might also come within *Younger*'s exception for extraordinary circumstances. (The federal plaintiff in *Wooley* had been previously prosecuted three times for the same violation that he sought to enjoin.) Should *Younger* be deemed to bar injunctions against future prosecutions? What effect might such a ruling have on cases such as *Ex parte Young*?

4. Preliminary Injunctions. In *Doran v. Salem Inn*, 422 U.S. 922 (1975), the Court held that *Younger* did not bar the issuance of a preliminary injunction in support of a claim for declaratory relief in the absence of an ongoing state proceeding. The Court stated, "[a]t the conclusion of a successful federal challenge to a state statute or local ordinance, a district court can generally protect the interests of a federal plaintiff by entering a declaratory judgment, and therefore the stronger injunctive medicine will be unnecessary. But prior to final judgment there is no established declaratory remedy comparable to a preliminary injunction; unless preliminary relief is available upon a proper showing, plaintiffs in some situations may suffer unnecessary and substantial irreparable harm." Are preliminary injunctions in support of suits for declaratory relief less invasive than permanent injunctions? Is *Doran* just further evidence that *Steffel* was all about the absence of an ongoing state proceeding rather than the distinction between declaratory and injunctive relief?

5. Parallel Suits for Damages. In *Deakins v. Monaghan*, 484 U.S. 193 (1988), the Court, without directly resolving the issue, indicated that *Younger* principles required that federal actions for damages be stayed when there are ongoing state court proceedings addressing the same constitutional issues. Suits for damages are, of course, legal actions and traditional equitable principles generally have no role in determining whether a legal action should proceed. Does *Deakins* suggest that *Younger* is less about equity than comity and federalism? Or will a federal court act consistently with its role in legal actions if it merely stays the damage action rather than dismisses it outright? *See Quackenbush v. Allstate Ins. Co.*, 517 U.S. 706 (1996) (indicating that a federal court not sitting in equity may stay, but should not dismiss, a legal action properly within its jurisdiction). If the federal damage action is stayed and the state defendant loses his constitutional defenses, should principles of *res judicata* bar him from relitigating those claims in federal court as part of his suit for damages? See Part VI, infra.

NOTES ON STEFFEL AND ANTICIPATORY CHALLENGES

1. *Steffel* and Anticipatory Challenges. A plaintiff such as Steffel, who challenges a provision prior to its enforcement against him, will necessarily have to demonstrate that the threat of injury is sufficient to justify the federal court's granting equitable relief as well as overcoming justiciability defenses such as ripeness or standing. See Chapter 4, supra. In *Younger*, for example, the Court dismissed Harris's co-plaintiffs from the federal action on grounds that they had not been sufficiently threatened with prosecution to meet equitable and justiciability requirements. In *Steffel*, on the other hand, the Court found that the threat of prosecution adequately satisfied equitable and justiciability concerns; and, to be sure, the facts in *Steffel* appear to support such a holding, given that Steffel himself had been directly threatened with prosecution and his companion was actually arrested when she, unlike Steffel, refused to stop handbilling after receiving the police warnings.

Justice Stewart's concurrence in *Steffel* contends that cases in which a plaintiff who has not yet been prosecuted will be able to meet justiciability requisites will be "exceedingly rare," but later cases indicate that the ability to maintain an anticipatory challenge to an allegedly unconstitutional provision prior to prosecution may be somewhat easier than either Stewart's *Steffel* concurrence or *Younger* would otherwise suggest. In *Babbitt v. United Farm Workers National Union*, 442 U.S. 289 (1979), for example, the Court allowed an anticipatory challenge to a state statute based only upon the thin reed that the plaintiff's alleged fear of prosecution under the statute was "not imaginary or wholly speculative."

    2.   *Susan B. Anthony List v. Driehaus*. Most recently, in *Susan B. Anthony List v. Driehaus*, 573 U.S. ___, 134 S.Ct. 2334 (2014), the Court allowed the plaintiffs to maintain an anticipatory challenge against the enforcement of state election laws barring false statements concerning a candidate or a voting record of a candidate although the election cycle in which those statements would be made had not yet started and a specific candidate that could be the target of the purportedly false statements had not yet emerged. The plaintiff in the case, the Susan B. Anthony List (SBA), had been the respondent in an action brought before the Ohio Elections Commission by then-Congressman Stephen Driehaus alleging that the SBA had violated the Ohio statute during the 2010 elections by claiming that Driehaus had voted for "taxpayer funded abortion." (The SBA based this claim on Driehaus's vote for the Affordable Care Act.) The Elections Commission issued a finding of probable cause in response to this complaint and, independently, an advertising company refused to rent a billboard to display SBA's message after Driehaus threatened legal action before the Commission. The SBA sued in federal court seeking to enjoin the state proceeding before it proceeded to a full hearing but the federal court stayed the action under *Younger* and the parties agreed to delay the Commission's hearing on the merits until after the election. Driehaus, however, ended up losing the election and, after he subsequently withdrew his complaint with SBA's consent, the federal court lifted its stay.

SBA then amended its complaint and its action was consolidated with a similar lawsuit brought by the Coalition Opposed to Additional Spending and Taxes (COAST). The amended complaint alleged "that SBA's speech about Driehaus had been chilled; that SBA 'intends to engage in substantially similar activity in the future;' and that it 'face[d] the prospect of its speech and associational rights again being chilled and burdened,' because '[a]ny complainant can hale [it] before the [Commission], forcing it to expend time and resources defending itself." The District Court dismissed the case for lack of ripeness and the 6th Circuit affirmed the dismissal, relying primarily on three separate considerations. First, it concluded that SBA's prior harms— the probable cause finding and the billboard rejection—did not show an "imminent threat of *future* prosecution," particularly where "the Commission never found that SBA . . . violated Ohio's false-statement law.' Second, the court asserted that it was speculative whether any person would file a complaint with the Commission in the future, in part, because Driehaus was unlikely to be a candidate in the next election having taken an overseas assignment with the Peace Corps. Third, the court noted that SBA had not alleged that 'it plans to lie or recklessly disregard the veracity of its speech' in the future, but rather maintains that the statements were true.

The Supreme Court reversed and in a unanimous opinion by Justice Thomas, the Court explained its decision as follows:

> One recurring issue in our cases is determining when the threatened enforcement of a law creates an Article III injury. When an individual is subject to such a threat, an actual arrest, prosecution, or other enforcement action is not a prerequisite to challenging the law. . . . Instead, we have permitted pre-enforcement review under circumstances that render the threatened enforcement sufficiently imminent. Specifically, we have held that a plaintiff satisfies the injury-in-fact requirement where he alleges 'an intention to engage in a course of conduct arguably affected with a constitutional interest, but proscribed by a statute, and there exists a credible threat of prosecution thereunder.' *Babbitt* v. *Farm Workers,* 442 U.S. 289, 298 (1979). Here, SBA and COAST contend that the threat of enforcement of the false statement statute amounts to an Article III injury in fact. We agree.
>
> First, petitioners have alleged 'an intention to engage in a course of conduct arguably affected with a constitutional interest.' Both petitioners have pleaded specific statements they intend to make in future election cycles. SBA has already stated that representatives who voted for the ACA supported 'taxpayer-funded abortion,' and it has alleged an 'inten[t] to engage in substantially similar activity in the future.'
>
> Next, petitioners' intended future conduct is 'arguably . . . proscribed by [the] statute' they wish to challenge. The Ohio false statement law sweeps broadly and covers the subject matter of petitioners' intended speech. . . . And, a Commission panel here already found probable cause to believe that SBA violated the statute when it stated that Driehaus had supported 'taxpayer-funded abortion'—the same sort of statement petitioners plan to disseminate in the future. Under these circumstances, we have no difficulty concluding that petitioners' intended speech is 'arguably proscribed' by the law. Respondents incorrectly rely on *Golden* v. *Zwickler,* 394 U.S. 103 (1969). In that case, the plaintiff had previously distributed anonymous leaflets criticizing a particular Congressman who had since left office. The Court dismissed the plaintiff's challenge to the electoral leafletting ban as nonjusticiable because his '*sole concern* was literature relating to the Congressman

and his record,' and 'it was most unlikely that the Congressman would again be a candidate.' Under those circumstances, any threat of future prosecution was 'wholly conjectural.'

Here, by contrast, petitioners' speech focuses on the broader issue of support for the ACA, not on the voting record of a single candidate. Because petitioners' alleged future speech is not directed exclusively at Driehaus, it does not matter whether he 'may run for office again.'

Respondents, echoing the Sixth Circuit, [also] contend that SBA's fears of enforcement are misplaced because SBA has not said it 'plans to lie or recklessly disregard the veracity of its speech.' . . . The Sixth Circuit misses the point. SBA's insistence that the allegations in its press release were true did not prevent the Commission panel from finding probable cause to believe that SBA had violated the law the first time around. And, there is every reason to think that similar speech in the future will result in similar proceedings, notwithstanding SBA's belief in the truth of its allegations. Nothing in this Court's decisions requires a plaintiff who wishes to challenge the constitutionality of a law to confess that he will in fact violate that law.

Finally, the threat of future enforcement of the false statement statute is substantial. Most obviously, there is a history of past enforcement here: SBA was the subject of a complaint in a recent election cycle. We have observed that past enforcement against the same conduct is good evidence that the threat of enforcement is not 'chimerical.' Here, the threat is even more substantial given that the Commission panel actually found probable cause to believe that SBA's speech violated the false statement statute.

The *Driehaus* Court then went on to address whether the threat of an administrative enforcement action (as opposed to a state criminal prosecution) would be sufficient to satisfy Article III requirements but on this point the Court offered no clear rule:

We take the threatened Commission proceedings into account because administrative action, like arrest or prosecution, may give rise to harm sufficient to justify preenforcement review. The burdens that Commission proceedings can impose on electoral speech are of particular concern here. As the Ohio Attorney General himself notes, the 'practical effect' of the Ohio false statement scheme is 'to permit a private complainant . . . to gain a campaign advantage without ever having to prove the falsity of a statement.' '[C]omplainants may time their submissions to achieve maximum disruption of their political opponents while calculating that an ultimate decision on the merits will be deferred until after the relevant election.' Moreover, the target of a false statement complaint may be forced to divert significant time and resources to hire legal counsel and respond to discovery requests in the crucial days leading up to an election. And where, as here, a Commission panel issues a preelection probable-cause finding, 'such a determination itself may be viewed [by the electorate] as a sanction by the State.'

Although the threat of Commission proceedings is a substantial one, we need not decide whether that threat standing alone gives rise to an Article III injury. The burdensome Commission proceedings here are backed by the additional threat of criminal prosecution. We conclude that the combination of those two threats suffices to create an Article III injury under the circumstances of this case.

3. Summary. The Seventh Circuit, in an opinion by Judge Easterbrook, has taken the position that in order to justify the granting of an injunction, the threat of enforcement has only to be "actual" rather than "imminent." See *520 South Michigan Ave. Associates v. Devine*, 433 F.3d 961, 962–64 (7th Cir. 2006). Does *Driehaus* affirm the 7th Circuit's approach or is the case more properly understood as being confined to its unique circumstances and the fact that during a political campaign, a finding of probable cause by a state enforcement agency can be as politically harmful as any final determination of wrongdoing?

2. The Meaning of "Ongoing"

DORAN v. SALEM INN, INC.
422 U.S. 922 (1975).

JUSTICE REHNQUIST delivered the opinion of the Court.

Appellant is a town attorney in Nassau County, N.Y., who, along with other local law enforcement officials, was preliminarily enjoined by the United States District Court for the Eastern District of New York from enforcing a local ordinance of the town of North Hempstead. In addition to defending the ordinance on the merits, he contends that the complaint should have been dismissed on the authority of *Younger v. Harris* and its companion cases.

Appellees are three corporations which operate bars at various locations within the town. Prior to enactment of the ordinance in question, each provided topless dancing as entertainment for its customers. On July 17, 1973, the town enacted Local Law No. 1–1973, an ordinance making it unlawful for bar owners and others to permit waitresses, barmaids, and entertainers to appear in their establishments with breasts uncovered or so thinly draped as to appear uncovered. Appellees complied with the ordinance by clothing their dancers in bikini tops, but on August 9, 1973, brought this action in the District Court under 42 U.S.C. § 1983. They alleged that the ordinance violated their rights under the First and Fourteenth Amendments to the United States Constitution.

On August 10, the day after the appellees' complaint was filed, and their application for a temporary restraining order denied, one of them, M & L Restaurant, Inc., resumed its briefly suspended presentation of topless dancing. On that day, and each of the three succeeding days, M & L and its topless dancers were served with criminal summonses based on violation of the ordinance. The other two appellees, Salem Inn, Inc., and Tim-Rob Bar, Inc., did not resume the presentation of topless entertainment in their bars until after the District Court issued its preliminary [injunction.]

Turning to the *Younger* issues raised by petitioner, we are faced with the necessity of determining whether the holdings of *Younger, Steffel v. Thompson,* 415 U.S. 452 (1974), and *Samuels v. Mackell,* 401 U.S. 66 (1971), must give way before such interests in efficient judicial administration as were relied upon by the Court of Appeals. We think that the interest of avoiding conflicting outcomes in the litigation of similar issues, while entitled to substantial deference in a unitary system, must of necessity be subordinated to the claims of federalism in this particular area of the law. The classic example is the petitioner in *Steffel* and his companion. Both were warned that failure to cease pamphleteering would result in their arrest, but while the petitioner in *Steffel* ceased and brought an action in the federal court, his companion did not cease and was prosecuted on a charge of criminal trespass in the state court. The same may be said of the interest in conservation of judicial manpower. As worthy a value as this is in a unitary system, the very existence of one system of federal courts and 50 systems of state courts, all charged with the responsibility for interpreting the United States Constitution, suggests that on occasion there will be duplicating and overlapping adjudication of cases which are sufficiently similar in content, time, and location to justify being heard before a single judge had they arisen within a unitary system.

We do not agree with the Court of Appeals, therefore, that all three plaintiffs should automatically be thrown into the same hopper for *Younger* purposes, and should thereby each be entitled to injunctive relief. We cannot accept that view, any more than we can accept petitioner's equally Procrustean view that because M & L would have been barred from injunctive relief had it been the sole plaintiff, Salem and Tim-Rob should likewise be barred not only from injunctive relief but from declaratory relief as well. While there plainly may be some circumstances in which legally distinct parties are so closely related that they should all be subject to the *Younger* considerations which govern any one of them, this is not such a case—while respondents are represented by common counsel, and have similar business activities and problems, they are apparently unrelated in terms of ownership, control, and management. We thus think that each of the respondents should be placed in the position required by our cases as if that respondent stood alone.

Respondent M & L could have pursued the course taken by the other respondents after the denial of their request for a temporary restraining order. Had it done so, it would not have subjected itself to prosecution for violation of the ordinance in the state court. When the criminal summonses issued against M & L on the days immediately following the filing of the federal complaint, the federal litigation was in an embryonic stage and no contested matter had been decided. In this posture, M & L's prayer for injunction is squarely governed by *Younger*. We likewise believe that for the same reasons *Samuels v. Mackell* bars M & L from obtaining declaratory relief, absent a showing of *Younger's* special circumstances, even though the state prosecution was commenced the day following the filing of the federal complaint. Having violated the ordinance, rather than awaiting the normal development of its federal lawsuit, M & L cannot now be heard to complain that its constitutional contentions are being resolved in a state court. Thus M & L's prayers for both injunctive and declaratory relief are subject to *Younger's* restrictions.

The rule with regard to the coplaintiffs, Salem and Tim-Rob, is equally clear, insofar as they seek declaratory relief. Salem and Tim-Rob were not subject to state criminal prosecution at any time prior to the issuance of a preliminary injunction by the District Court. Under *Steffel* they thus could at least have obtained a declaratory judgment upon an ordinary showing of entitlement to that relief. The District Court, however, did not grant declaratory relief to Salem and Tim-Rob, but instead granted them preliminary injunctive relief. Whether injunctions of future criminal prosecutions are governed by *Younger* standards is a question which we reserved in both *Steffel* and *Younger*. We now hold that on the facts of this case the issuance of a preliminary injunction is not subject to the restrictions of *Younger*. The principle underlying *Younger* and *Samuels* is that state courts are fully competent to adjudicate constitutional claims, and therefore a federal court should, in all but the most exceptional circumstances, refuse to interfere with an ongoing state criminal proceeding. In the absence of such a proceeding, however, as we recognized in *Steffel,* a plaintiff may challenge the constitutionality of the state statute in federal court, assuming he can satisfy the requirements for federal jurisdiction. No state proceedings were pending against either Salem or Tim-Rob at the time the District Court issued its preliminary injunction. Nor was there any question that they satisfied the requirements for federal jurisdiction. As we have already stated, they were assuredly entitled to declaratory relief, and since we have previously recognized that "[o]rdinarily . . . the practical effect of [injunctive and declaratory] relief will be virtually identical," *Samuels,* 401 U.S., at 73, we think that Salem and Tim-Rob were entitled to have their claims for preliminary injunctive relief considered without regard to *Younger*'s restrictions. At the conclusion of a successful federal challenge to a state statute or local ordinance, a district court can generally protect the interests of a federal plaintiff by entering a declaratory judgment, and therefore the stronger injunctive medicine will be unnecessary. But prior to final judgment there is no established declaratory remedy comparable to a preliminary injunction; unless preliminary relief is available upon a proper showing, plaintiffs in some situations may suffer unnecessary and substantial irreparable harm. Moreover, neither declaratory nor injunctive relief can directly interfere with enforcement of contested statutes or ordinances except with respect to the particular federal plaintiffs, and the State is free to prosecute others who may violate the statute.

NOTES ON DORAN V. SALEM INN AND INTERIM RELIEF

1.   The Timing of the State Court Action. The first issue addressed in *Doran* regarding the meaning of "ongoing" concerns whether the state criminal proceeding had to already be commenced at the time the federal court action was initiated in order to implicate *Younger*. *Doran* answered this question in the negative. Although the state prosecution against the M & L restaurant was brought after the federal suit was filed, M & L was prohibited from maintaining its federal suit because of the existence of the state proceeding.

The Court reached a similar conclusion regarding the timing of the state prosecution in *Hicks v. Miranda*, 422 U.S. 332 (1975). In *Hicks*, theater owners sued local officials in federal court under 42 U.S.C. § 1983 for injunctive and declaratory relief against the enforcement of a state obscenity law and for return of copies of films that had been seized by those officials as part of an obscenity prosecution that had been brought against two employees of the theater. One day after the officials were served with the federal complaint (but six weeks after the complaint was originally filed, during which time a motion for a temporary restraining order was heard, and denied, by the district court), the state officials amended the state criminal action to include the theater owners as defendants. On review, the Supreme Court held that, despite the fact that at the time the federal suit was filed there were no ongoing proceedings against the theater owners, dismissal under *Younger* was warranted. As the Court stated:

> Neither *Steffel v. Thompson* nor any other case in this Court has held that for *Younger v. Harris* to apply, the state criminal proceedings must be pending on the day the federal case is filed. Indeed, the issue has been left open; and we now hold that where state criminal proceedings are begun against the federal plaintiffs

after the federal complaint is filed but before any proceedings of substance on the merits have taken place in the federal court, the principles of *Younger v. Harris* should apply in full force. . . . Unless we are to trivialize the principles of *Younger v. Harris*, the federal complaint should have been dismissed on the appellants' motion absent satisfactory proof of those extraordinary circumstances calling into play one of the limited exceptions to the rule of *Younger v. Harris* and related cases.

Justice Stewart, joined by three other Justices, dissented on grounds that the *Hicks* decision creates an incentive for state officials to file criminal proceedings in order to oust the federal court of its jurisdiction. To Stewart, "the Court's new rule creates a reality which few state prosecutors can be expected to ignore. It is an open invitation to state officials to institute state proceedings in order to defeat federal jurisdiction. One need not impugn the motives of state officials to suppose that they would rather prosecute a criminal suit in state court than defend a civil case in a federal forum. Today's opinion virtually instructs state officials to answer federal complaints with state indictments."

Do you agree with the *Hicks* majority that failing to dismiss the action would have trivialized *Younger* principles? In traditional equity jurisprudence, the fact that a legal remedy later becomes available does not oust an equity court's jurisdiction. Should *Doran* and *Hicks* have adhered to the traditional equity rule?

   2.   Ongoing Actions Against Third Parties. *Doran* also addressed whether an ongoing criminal proceeding against one party can be sufficient to prevent another party from moving to obtain federal court relief enjoining similar prosecutions. In *Doran* itself, the Court held that the two bars not being prosecuted had the right to maintain their action in federal court while the action against the third bar was ongoing even though the three bars in the case were engaging in similar activities, were attacking the same ordinance, and were represented by the same attorney. Does this aspect of the *Doran* decision comport with the policies advanced in *Younger*? Would not a final judgment in favor of the federal plaintiffs have a substantial effect on the ongoing prosecution against the state court defendant?

   Although not finding the relationship between the three bars pertinent in that case, *Doran* left open the possibility that in certain circumstances, a state prosecution against a related party could militate in favor of invoking *Younger*. In this context, again consider *Hicks v. Miranda*, 422 U.S. 332 (1975). In *Hicks*, as noted above, the state officials had already instituted proceedings against the theater employees for showing obscene films and had seized the films that were in the possession of the theater by the time the theater owners commenced their suit in federal court. On this basis, the *Hicks* Court characterized the federal plaintiffs as having "a substantial stake" in the state criminal proceedings and having their interests "intertwined" with the interests of their employees (the state criminal defendants). Accordingly, after also observing that the theater owners and their employees had the same lawyers, the *Hicks* Court concluded that *Younger*'s comity principles would apply "where the interference [with the state court proceeding] is sought by some, such as appellees, not parties to the state case." Is *Hicks* consistent with *Doran* in its treatment of pending actions against third parties? Which decision best furthers the policy interests of *Younger*? Of federal court jurisdiction and § 1983? Interestingly, although *Doran* and *Hicks* were decided within the same week, the two opinions do not cite or reference each other.

   3.   Failure to Appeal. In *Huffman v. Pursue, Ltd.*, 420 U.S. 592 (1975), the state brought a civil nuisance action in state court against the defendant seeking to enjoin the defendant's operation of a movie house for showing allegedly obscene films. After the state prevailed, the defendant chose to forego his state appeal and to proceed instead in federal court where he sought to enjoin the execution of the state court decree. The Court held *Younger* applicable reasoning that the defendant "may not avoid the standards of *Younger* by simply failing to comply with the procedures of perfecting its appeal [in the state courts]." Do you agree that failing to pursue appellate remedies constitutes an impermissible end run around *Younger*?

   In contrast to *Huffman*, consider the Court's decision in *Wooley v. Maynard*, 430 U.S. 705 (1977). *Wooley* involved a Jehovah's Witness, George Maynard, who was prosecuted three times for violating a New Hampshire law prohibiting the defacing of license plates. Each time, Maynard pled guilty and did not appeal. Maynard then brought suit in federal court against the state claiming that the law was unconstitutional under the First Amendment because it forced him to display on his license plate the state motto, "Live Free or Die," which he alleged conflicted with his freedom of conscience. The Court held *Younger* inapplicable on grounds that Maynard's action was designed to prevent future prosecutions. From the perspective of the policies announced in *Younger*, is there a meaningful difference between enjoining the state from enforcing a continuing state judicial remedy against a defendant forbidding her from engaging in certain activity (*Huffman*) and enjoining the state from bringing a subsequent prosecution against a defendant continuing to engage in prohibited conduct after previous prosecutions against him had been successful? Would the state in *Wooley* have been better off if it sought to enjoin Maynard for defacing his license plates rather than successively (and successfully) prosecuting him for violating the law?

3. The Meaning of "Criminal"

HUFFMAN V. PURSUE, LTD.
420 U.S. 592 (1975).

JUSTICE REHNQUIST delivered the opinion of the Court.

[Ohio officials brought a civil nuisance action in state court against a theater operator for exhibiting obscene films and the state court ordered that the theater be closed for one year and the personal property used in the theater operation be seized and sold. The theater operator then sued the state officials in federal court under 42 U.S.C. § 1983 seeking injunctive relief and declaratory judgment that the statute was unconstitutional and unenforceable.]

This case requires that we decide whether our decision in *Younger v. Harris*, 401 U.S. 37 (1971), bars a federal district court from intervening in a state civil proceeding such as this, when the proceeding is based on a state statute believed by the district court to be unconstitutional. . . .

The seriousness of federal judicial interference with state civil functions has long been recognized by this Court. We have consistently required that when federal courts are confronted with requests for such relief, they should abide by standards of restraint that go well beyond those of private equity jurisprudence. For example, *Massachusetts State Grange v. Benton,* 272 U.S. 525 (1926), involved an effort to enjoin the operation of a state daylight savings act. Writing for the Court, Justice Holmes . . . emphasized a rule that "should be very strictly observed," that no injunction ought to issue against officers of a State clothed with authority to enforce the law in question, unless in a case reasonably free from doubt and when necessary to prevent great and irreparable injury.

Although Justice Holmes was confronted with a bill seeking an injunction against state executive officers, rather than against state judicial proceedings, we think that the relevant considerations of federalism are of no less weight in the latter setting. If anything, they counsel more heavily toward federal restraint, since interference with a state judicial proceeding prevents the state not only from effectuating its substantive policies, but also from continuing to perform the separate function of providing a forum competent to vindicate any constitutional objections interposed against those policies. Such interference also results in duplicative legal proceedings, and can readily be interpreted "as reflecting negatively upon the state court's ability to enforce constitutional principles." Cf. *Steffel v. Thompson.*

The component of *Younger* which rests upon the threat to our federal system is thus applicable to a civil proceeding such as this quite as much as it is to a criminal proceeding. *Younger,* however, also rests upon the traditional reluctance of courts of equity, even within a unitary system, to interfere with a criminal prosecution. Strictly speaking, this element of *Younger* is not available to mandate federal restraint in civil cases. But whatever may be the weight attached to this factor in civil litigation involving private parties, we deal here with a state proceeding which in important respects is more akin to a criminal prosecution than are most civil cases. The State is a party to the Court of Common Pleas proceeding, and the proceeding is both in aid of and closely related to criminal statutes which prohibit the dissemination of obscene materials. Thus, an offense to the State's interest in the nuisance litigation is likely to be every bit as great as it would be were this a criminal proceeding. Similarly, while in this case the District Court's injunction has not directly disrupted Ohio's criminal justice system, it has disrupted that State's efforts to protect the very interests which underlie its criminal laws and to obtain compliance with precisely the standards which are embodied in its criminal laws.

In spite of the critical similarities between a criminal prosecution and Ohio nuisance proceedings, appellee nonetheless urges that there is also a critical difference between the two which should cause us to limit *Younger* to criminal proceedings. This difference, says appellee, is that whereas a state-court criminal defendant may, after exhaustion of his state remedies, present his constitutional claims to the federal courts through habeas corpus, no analogous remedy is available to one, like appellee, whose constitutional rights may have been infringed in a state proceeding which cannot result in custodial detention or other criminal sanction.

A civil litigant may, of course, seek review in this Court of any federal claim properly asserted in and rejected by state courts. . . . But quite apart from appellee's right to [to later seek review in the Supreme Court] had it remained in state court, we conclude that it should not be permitted the luxury of federal litigation of issues presented by ongoing state proceedings, a luxury which, as we have already explained, is quite costly in terms of the interests which *Younger* seeks to protect. Appellee's argument, that because there may be no civil counterpart to federal habeas it should have contemporaneous access to a federal forum for its federal claim, apparently depends on the unarticulated major premise that every litigant who asserts a federal claim is entitled to have it decided on the merits by a federal, rather than a state, court. We need not consider the validity of this premise in order to reject the result which appellee seeks. Even assuming, arguendo, that litigants are entitled to a federal forum for the resolution of all federal issues, that entitlement is most appropriately asserted by a state litigant when he seeks to relitigate a federal issue adversely determined in completed state court proceedings. We do not understand why the federal forum must be available prior to completion of the state proceedings in which the federal issue arises, and the considerations canvassed in *Younger* militate against such a result.

[The Court vacated the order of the District Court granting the injunction.]

NOTES ON HUFFMAN V. PURSUE, LTD., YOUNGER, AND CIVIL LITIGATION

1. "In Aid of and Closely Related to Criminal Statutes." *Huffman* based its decision in part on the rationale that the civil nuisance statute at issue was "in aid of and closely related to criminal statutes." Civil proceedings presumably, however, do not provide a defendant with as many procedural protections as do criminal prosecutions. Should that matter in deciding whether or not a federal court should exercise jurisdiction under *Younger*? Is it pertinent that a civil defendant will not have the remedy of habeas corpus available if she is successfully prosecuted?

2. *Trainor v. Hernandez.* *Huffman* was extended in *Trainor v. Hernandez*, 431 U.S. 434 (1977), to forbid a federal court from interfering with a civil fraud action brought by the state to recover welfare payments that were purportedly wrongfully obtained. The federal plaintiffs sought to enjoin the state proceedings on grounds that the state statute under which they were sued violated their due process rights because it allowed their property to be attached without a prior hearing. The Court found that *Younger* principles required that the federal suit be dismissed because the state was a party to the proceedings and the suit was brought to "vindicate important state policies." Does *Trainor* stand for the proposition that any action brought by the state triggers *Younger*? Would *Younger* forbid a federal court to enjoin a contract action brought by the state in state court to collect an outstanding debt? Compare *Moore v. Sims*, 442 U.S. 415 (1979) (holding *Younger* bars federal court interference with custody proceedings brought by the state to protect children from allegedly abusive parents) with *New Orleans Public Service, Inc. v. Council of City of New Orleans* (*NOPSI*), 491 U.S. 350 (1989) (holding *Younger* does not bar federal court interference with a state court review of a local government rate making procedure).

3. Private Civil Litigation. The federal plaintiffs in *Trainor* argued that *Huffman* was distinguishable because, unlike the civil nuisance action at issue in *Huffman*, the statute utilized by the government in *Trainor* was available to private parties. The Court, however, was unimpressed with this argument, noting that the state was the party instituting the state action. In later cases, however, the Court indicated that *Younger* could apply even to purely private civil actions. Those cases are discussed below.

4. *Huffman* and *Mitchum*. *Huffman*, like *Mitchum v. Foster*, 407 U.S. 225 (1972), involved a § 1983 lawsuit brought to enjoin a state nuisance action against an establishment allegedly dispensing adult materials. Does the holding in *Huffman* mean that plaintiffs such as those in *Mitchum,* who were able to overcome the Anti-Injunction Act hurdle against federal court relief in that case, will nevertheless lose their claims on *Younger* grounds?

Mitchum, you may recall, however, held that the policies underlying § 1983 were so substantial that they required a determination that § 1983 was an expressly authorized exception to the anti-injunction act. As the *Mitchum* Court stated: "The very purpose of § 1983 was to interpose the federal courts between the States and the people, as guardians of the people's federal rights—to protect the people from unconstitutional action under color of state law, whether that action be executive, legislative, or judicial. . . . And this Court long ago recognized that federal injunctive relief against a state court proceeding can in some circumstances be essential to prevent great, immediate, and irreparable loss of a person's constitutional rights." Yet if the policy of interposing the federal courts between the States and the people is so substantial that it requires an exception to a congressional statute prohibiting federal injunctions against state proceedings, why does that policy not equally apply to require an exception to a judge-made rule (*Younger*) that also proscribes federal court injunctions against suit?

4.   The Meaning of "Proceedings"

OHIO CIVIL RIGHTS COMMISSION V. DAYTON CHRISTIAN SCHOOLS, INC.
477 U.S. 619 (1986).

JUSTICE REHNQUIST delivered the opinion of the Court.

Appellee Dayton Christian Schools, Inc. (Dayton), and various individuals brought an action in the United States District Court for the Southern District of Ohio under 42 U. S. C. § 1983, seeking to enjoin a pending state administrative proceeding brought against Dayton by appellant Ohio Civil Rights Commission (Commission). Dayton asserted that the Free Exercise and Establishment Clauses of the First Amendment prohibited the Commission from exercising jurisdiction over it or from punishing it for engaging in employment discrimination. The District Court refused to issue the injunction on grounds that any conflict between the First Amendment and the administrative proceedings was not yet ripe, and that in any case the proposed action of the Commission violated neither the Free Exercise Clause nor the Establishment Clause of the First Amendment, as made applicable to the States by the Fourteenth Amendment. The Court of Appeals for the Sixth Circuit reversed, holding that the exercise of jurisdiction and the enforcement of the statute would impermissibly burden appellees' rights under the Free Exercise Clause and would result in excessive entanglement under the Establishment Clause. We postponed the question of jurisdiction pending consideration of the merits. We now conclude that we have jurisdiction, and we reverse, holding that the District Court should have abstained under our cases beginning with *Younger*.

Dayton is a private nonprofit corporation that provides education at both the elementary and secondary school levels. It was formed by two local churches, the Patterson Park Brethren Church and the Christian Tabernacle, and it is regarded as a "nondenominational" extension of the Christian education ministries of these two churches. Dayton's corporate charter establishes a board of directors (board) to lead the corporation in both spiritual and temporal matters. The charter also includes a section entitled "Statement of Faith," which serves to restrict membership on the board and the educational staff to persons who subscribe to a particular set of religious beliefs. The Statement of Faith requires each board or staff member to be a born-again Christian and to reaffirm his or her belief annually in the Bible, the Trinity, the nature and mission of Jesus Christ, the doctrine of original sin, the role of the Holy Ghost, the resurrection and judgment of the dead, the need for Christian unity, and the divine creation of human beings.

The board has elaborated these requirements to include a belief in the internal resolution of disputes through the "Biblical chain of command." The core of this doctrine, rooted in passages from the New Testament, is that one Christian should not take another Christian into courts of the State. Teachers are expected to present any grievance they may have to their immediate supervisor, and to acquiesce in the final authority of the board, rather than to pursue a remedy in civil court. The board has sought to ensure compliance with this internal dispute resolution doctrine by making it a contractual condition of employment.

Linda Hoskinson was employed as a teacher at Dayton during the 1978–1979 school year. She subscribed to the Statement of Faith and expressly agreed to resolve disputes internally through the Biblical chain of command. In January 1979, she informed her principal, James Rakestraw, that she was pregnant. After consulting with his superiors, Rakestraw informed Hoskinson that her employment contract would not be renewed at the end of the school year because of Dayton's religious doctrine that mothers should stay home with their preschool age children. Instead of appealing this decision internally, Hoskinson contacted an attorney who sent a letter to Dayton's superintendent, Claude Schindler, threatening litigation based on state and federal sex discrimination laws if Dayton did not agree to rehire Hoskinson for the coming school year.

Upon receipt of this letter, Schindler informed Hoskinson that she was suspended immediately for challenging the nonrenewal decision in a manner inconsistent with the internal dispute resolution doctrine. The board reviewed this decision and decided to terminate Hoskinson. It stated that the sole reason for her termination was her violation of the internal dispute resolution doctrine, and it rescinded the earlier nonrenewal decision because it said that she had not received adequate prior notice of the doctrine concerning a mother's duty to stay home with her young children.

Hoskinson filed a complaint with appellant Ohio Civil Rights Commission (Commission), alleging that Dayton's nonrenewal decision constituted sex discrimination, in violation of Ohio Rev. Code Ann. § 4112.02(A) (Supp. 1985), and that its termination decision penalized her for asserting her rights, in violation of Ohio Rev. Code Ann. § 4112.02(I) (Supp. 1985). The Commission notified Dayton that it was conducting a preliminary investigation into the matter, and repeatedly urged Dayton to consider private settlement, warning that failure to do so could result in a formal adjudication of the matter.

The Commission eventually determined that there was probable cause to believe that Dayton had discriminated against Hoskinson based on her sex and had retaliated against her for attempting to assert her rights in violation of §§ 4112(A) and (I). Pursuant to Ohio Rev. Code Ann. § 4112.05(B) (Supp. 1985), it sent Dayton a proposed Conciliation Agreement and Consent Order that would have required Dayton to reinstate Hoskinson with backpay, and would have prohibited Dayton from taking retaliatory action against any employee for participating in the preliminary investigation. The Commission warned Dayton that failure to accede to this proposal or an acceptable counteroffer would result in formal administrative proceedings being initiated against it. When Dayton failed to respond, the Commission initiated administrative proceedings against it by filing a complaint. Dayton answered the complaint by asserting that the First Amendment prevented the Commission from exercising jurisdiction over it since its actions had been taken pursuant to sincerely held religious beliefs.

While these administrative proceedings were pending, Dayton filed this action against the Commission in the United States District Court for the Southern District of Ohio under 42 U. S. C. § 1983, seeking a permanent injunction against the state proceedings on the ground that any investigation of Dayton's hiring process or any imposition of sanctions for Dayton's nonrenewal or termination decisions would violate the Religion Clauses of the First Amendment.

We conclude that the District Court should have abstained from adjudicating this case under *Younger* and later cases.

In *Younger*, we held that a federal court should not enjoin a pending state criminal proceeding except in the very unusual situation that an injunction is necessary to prevent great and immediate irreparable injury. We justified our decision both on equitable principles, and on the "more vital consideration" of the proper respect for the fundamental role of States in our federal system. Because of our concerns for comity and federalism, we thought that it was "perfectly natural for our cases to repeat time and time again that the *normal* thing to do when federal courts are asked to enjoin pending proceedings in state courts is not to issue such injunctions." *Id.* at 45.

We have since recognized that our concern for comity and federalism is equally applicable to certain other pending state proceedings. We have applied the *Younger* principle to civil proceedings in which important state interests are involved. We have also applied it to state administrative proceedings in which important state interests are vindicated, so long as in the course of those proceedings the federal plaintiff would have a full and fair opportunity to litigate his constitutional claim. We stated in *Gibson v. Berryhill*, 411 U.S. 564 (1973), that "administrative proceedings looking toward the revocation of a license to practice medicine may in proper circumstances command the respect due court proceedings." Similarly, we have held that federal courts should refrain from enjoining lawyer disciplinary proceedings initiated by state ethics committees if the proceedings are within the appellate jurisdiction of the appropriate State Supreme Court. *Middlesex County Ethics Committee v. Garden State Bar Assn.*, 457 U.S. 423 (1982). Because we found that the administrative proceedings in *Middlesex* were "judicial in nature" from the outset, it was not essential to the decision that they had progressed to state-court review by the time we heard the federal injunction case.

We think the principles enunciated in these cases govern the present one. We have no doubt that the elimination of prohibited sex discrimination is a sufficiently important state interest to bring the present case within the ambit of the cited authorities. We also have no reason to doubt that Dayton will receive an adequate opportunity to raise its constitutional claims. Dayton contends that the mere exercise of jurisdiction over it by the state administrative body violates its First Amendment rights. But we have repeatedly rejected the argument that a constitutional attack on state procedures themselves "automatically vitiates the adequacy of those procedures for purposes of the *Younger-Huffman* line of cases." Even religious schools cannot claim to be wholly free from some state regulation. *Wisconsin v. Yoder*, 406 U.S. 205, 213 (1972). We therefore think that however Dayton's constitutional claim should be decided on the merits, the Commission violates no constitutional rights by merely investigating the circumstances of Hoskinson's discharge in this case, if only to ascertain whether the ascribed religious-based reason was in fact the reason for the discharge.

Dayton also contends that the administrative proceedings do not afford the opportunity to level constitutional challenges against the potential sanctions for the alleged sex discrimination. But even if Ohio law is such that the Commission may not consider the constitutionality of the statute under which it operates, it would seem an unusual doctrine, and one not supported by the cited case, to say that the Commission could not construe its own statutory mandate in the light of federal constitutional principles. In any event, it is sufficient under *Middlesex,* that constitutional claims may be raised in state-court judicial review of the administrative proceeding. Section 4112.06 of Ohio Rev. Code Ann. (1980) provides that any "respondent claiming to be aggrieved by a final order of the commission . . . may obtain judicial review thereof." Dayton cites us to no Ohio authority indicating that this provision does not authorize judicial review of claims that agency action violates the United States Constitution.

The judgment of the Court of Appeals is therefore reversed, and the case remanded for further proceedings consistent with this opinion.

NOTES ON *DAYTON CHRISTIAN SCHOOLS* AND *ADMINISTRATIVE PROCEEDINGS*

1. ***Younger, Middlesex,* and State Administrative Proceedings.** *Dayton* thus far has been limited to administrative enforcement proceedings initiated by the state. But should *Younger* extend to administrative proceedings at all? And if so, what types of administrative proceedings should require federal court deference? In *Middlesex County Ethics Committee v. Garden State Bar Assn.,* 457 U.S. 423 (1982) the Court applied *Younger* to prohibit federal court interference with a state ethic's committee disciplinary proceedings and, in so holding, relied on three factors as justifying abstention: 1) the importance of the state interest "in maintaining and assuring the professional conduct of the attorneys it licenses"; 2) the fact that the state proceeding provided an adequate opportunity to raise the federal challenges; and 3) the fact the proceedings were ongoing. Compare *Hawaii Housing Authority v. Midkiff,* 467 U.S. 229 (1984) (holding *Younger* inapplicable because ongoing administrative proceedings were not "part of, and are not themselves, a judicial proceeding"). More recently, in *Sprint Communications, Inc. v. Jacobs,* 571 U.S. ___, 134 S.Ct. 584 (2013), the Court held that the three factors announced in *Middlesex* were not alone sufficient to justify abstention and *Middlesex* as resting on the premise that the state ethics committee process was "akin to a criminal proceeding." Does that rationale explain *Dayton?* The *Sprint* case is set forth below in Section 7.

2. ***Patsy v. Florida Board of Regents.*** In contrast to *Dayton Christian Schools,* consider *Patsy v. Florida Board of Regents,* 457 U.S. 496 (1982). In *Patsy,* the Court held that a discrimination plaintiff did not have to first exhaust state administrative procedures against her employer before bringing a federal court action under 42 U.S.C. § 1983. As the Court explained, citing *Mitchum v. Foster,* 407 U.S. 225 (1972), an exhaustion requirement would be inconsistent with the purposes of § 1983 which included interposing the federal courts between the states and the people.

The Court then rejected the argument that an exhaustion requirement should be imposed to "further the goal of comity and improve federal-state relationships by postponing federal review." According to *Patsy*, "[p]olicy considerations alone cannot justify judicially imposed exhaustion requirements unless exhaustion is consistent with congressional intent." Is *Patsy* consistent with *Dayton Christian School*? Is its conclusion that policy considerations such as comity and the improvement of federal-state relations cannot justify judicially imposed restraints on federal court power consistent with *Younger*? Is *Patsy* consistent with any of the abstention cases?

5. The Meaning of "State"

PENNZOIL CO. V. TEXACO, INC.
481 U.S. 1 (1987).

JUSTICE POWELL delivered the opinion of the Court.

The principal issue in this case is whether a federal district court lawfully may enjoin a plaintiff who has prevailed in a trial in state court from executing the judgment in its favor pending appeal of that judgment to a state appellate court.

Getty Oil Co. and appellant Pennzoil Co. negotiated an agreement under which Pennzoil was to purchase about three-sevenths of Getty's outstanding shares for $110 a share. Appellee Texaco Inc. eventually purchased the shares for $128 a share. On February 8, 1984, Pennzoil filed a complaint against Texaco in the Harris County District Court, a state court located in Houston, Texas, the site of Pennzoil's corporate headquarters. The complaint alleged that Texaco tortiously had induced Getty to breach a contract to sell its shares to Pennzoil; Pennzoil sought actual damages of $7.53 billion and punitive damages in the same amount. On November 19, 1985, a jury returned a verdict in favor of Pennzoil, finding actual damages of $7.53 billion and punitive damages of $3 billion. The parties anticipated that the judgment, including prejudgment interest, would exceed $11 billion.

[Texaco wanted to appeal the judgment but Texas law required that in order to do so, Texaco would have had to post a bond which in this case would amount to more than $13 billion. It was clear that Texaco could not afford to post such a bond.] Texaco did not argue to the trial court that the judgment, or execution of the judgment, conflicted with federal law. Rather, on December 10, 1985—before the Texas court entered judgment, Texaco filed this action in the United States District Court for the Southern District of New York in White Plains, New York, the site of Texaco's corporate headquarters. Texaco alleged that the Texas proceedings violated rights secured to Texaco by the Constitution and various federal statutes. [In particular, Texaco argued that the application of the appellate bond requirement would deprive it of property without due process of law.]

The courts below should have abstained under the principles of federalism enunciated in *Younger v. Harris*, 401 U.S. 37 (1971). Both the District Court and the Court of Appeals failed to recognize the significant interests harmed by their unprecedented intrusion into the Texas judicial system. Similarly, neither of those courts applied the appropriate standard in determining whether adequate relief was available in the Texas courts. The first ground for the *Younger* decision was "the basic doctrine of equity jurisprudence that courts of equity should not act, and particularly should not act to restrain a criminal prosecution, when the moving party has an adequate remedy at law." The Court also offered a second explanation for its decision:

> This underlying reason . . . is reinforced by an even more vital consideration, the notion of 'comity,' that is, a proper respect for state functions, a recognition of the fact that the entire country is made up of a Union of separate state governments, and a continuance of the belief that the National Government will fare best if the States and their institutions are left free to perform their separate functions in their separate ways. . . . The concept does not mean blind deference to 'States' Rights' any more than it means centralization of control over every important issue in our National Government and its courts. The Framers rejected both these courses. What the concept does represent is a system in which there is sensitivity to the legitimate interests of both State and National Governments, and in which the National Government, anxious though it may be to vindicate and protect federal rights and federal interests, always endeavors to do so in ways that will not unduly interfere with the legitimate activities of the States.

This concern mandates application of *Younger* abstention not only when the pending state proceedings are criminal, but also when certain civil proceedings are pending, if the State's interests in the proceeding are so important that exercise of the federal judicial power would disregard the comity between the States and the National Government. E.g., *Huffman v. Pursue, Ltd.*, 420 U.S. 592, 603–605 (1975).

Another important reason for abstention is to avoid unwarranted determination of federal constitutional questions. When federal courts interpret state statutes in a way that raises federal constitutional questions, "a constitutional determination is predicated on a reading of the statute that is not binding on state courts and may be discredited at any time—thus essentially rendering the federal-court decision advisory and the litigation underlying it meaningless." This concern has special significance in this case. Because Texaco chose not to present to the Texas courts the constitutional claims asserted in this case, it is impossible to be certain that the governing Texas statutes and procedural rules actually raise these claims. Moreover, the Texas Constitution contains an "open courts" provision, Art. I, 13, that appears to address Texaco's claims more specifically than the Due Process Clause of the Fourteenth Amendment. Thus, when this case was filed in federal court, it was entirely possible that the Texas courts would have resolved this case on state statutory or constitutional grounds, without reaching the federal constitutional questions Texaco raises in this case. As we have noted, *Younger* abstention in situations like this "offers the opportunity for narrowing constructions that might obviate the constitutional problem and intelligently mediate federal constitutional concerns and state interests."

Texaco's principal argument against *Younger* abstention is that exercise of the District Court's power did not implicate a "vital" or "important" state interest. This argument reflects a misreading of our precedents. This Court repeatedly has recognized that the States have important interests in administering certain aspects of their judicial systems. In *Juidice v. Vail*, 430 U.S. 327 (1977), we held that a federal court should have abstained from adjudicating a challenge to a State's contempt process. The Court's reasoning in that case informs our decision today:

A State's interest in the contempt process, through which it vindicates the regular operation of its judicial system, so long as that system itself affords the opportunity to pursue federal claims within it, is surely an important interest. Perhaps it is not quite as important as is the State's interest in the enforcement of its criminal laws, *Younger, supra,* or even its interest in the maintenance of a quasi-criminal proceeding such as was involved in *Huffman,* supra. But we think it is of sufficiently great import to require application of the principles of those cases. *Id.,* at 335.

Our comments on why the contempt power was sufficiently important to justify abstention also are illuminating: "Contempt in these cases, serves, of course, to vindicate and preserve the private interests of competing litigants, . . . but its purpose is by no means spent upon purely private concerns. It stands in aid of the authority of the judicial system, so that its orders and judgments are not rendered nugatory." *Id.,* at 336, n. 12 (citations omitted).

The reasoning of *Juidice* controls here. That case rests on the importance to the States of enforcing the orders and judgments of their courts. There is little difference between the State's interest in forcing persons to transfer property in response to a court's judgment and in forcing persons to respond to the court's process on pain of contempt. Both

Juidice and this case involve challenges to the processes by which the State compels compliance with the judgments of its courts. Not only would federal injunctions in such cases interfere with the execution of state judgments, but they would do so on grounds that challenge the very process by which those judgments were obtained. So long as those challenges relate to pending state proceedings, proper respect for the ability of state courts to resolve federal questions presented in state-court litigation mandates that the federal court stay its hand.

The judgment of the Court of Appeals is reversed. The case is remanded to the District Court with instructions to vacate its order and dismiss the complaint.

NOTES ON YOUNGER, PENNZOIL, AND PRIVATE LITIGATION

1.   *Juidice v. Vail.* *Pennzoil* was not the first case to apply *Younger* principles to cases involving private parties. *Juidice v. Vail*, 430 U.S. 327 (1977), involved a New York statutory debt collection procedure in which private creditors who won judgments could subpoena debtors to divulge information relevant to the satisfaction of the judgment. The state courts were then empowered to hold any debtors who failed to comply in contempt. Vail, who had been arrested and jailed pursuant to this procedure, joined with other judgment debtors and brought suit in federal court challenging the constitutionality of the statutory contempt proceedings under 42 U.S.C. § 1983. The named defendants in the case were the state judges who had issued contempt orders. Finding that the contempt process "lies at the core of the administration of a State's judicial system," the court held that the federal action was barred under *Younger*.

2.   **The State Interest.** Justice Brennan's dissent in *Pennzoil* characterized the state's interest as "negligible." Do you understand what the state's interest was in *Pennzoil*? The state of Texas itself did not participate in any of the proceedings in the case and did not even file an amicus brief. Should that be considered relevant to the question of whether or not there exist state interests of significant importance to trigger *Younger* concerns?

3.   *Younger* **and Private Civil Litigation.** Taken to its logical conclusion, *Pennzoil* might be thought to extend *Younger* to all private civil litigation. After all, if the state has an interest in its administration of justice, that rationale would presumably apply in all cases. More recent cases, however, have held that *Pennzoil* does not reach this far and is instead limited to "civil proceedings involving certain orders uniquely in furtherance of the state courts' ability to perform their judicial functions." *See Sprint Communications, Inc. v. Jacobs*, 571 U.S. ___, 134 S.Ct. 584 (2014); *see also New Orleans Public Service, Inc. v. Council of City of New Orleans (NOPSI)*, 491 U.S. 350, 368 (1989) ("it has never been suggested that *Younger* requires abstention in deference to a state judicial proceeding reviewing legislative or executive action").

Can you identify what constitutes an order in a civil case that "is uniquely in furtherance of the state courts' ability to perform their judicial functions"? Why was the bond requirement at issue in Pennzoil itself such an order?

6. The Meaning of "Extraordinary Circumstances"

Surprisingly, the one aspect of *Younger* that has not generated much Court elaboration is the meaning of extraordinary circumstances. In *Gibson v. Berryhill*, 411 U.S. 564 (1973) the Court held that *Younger* would not apply when the state proceeding was biased, but it is unclear whether the holding in that case was based on *Younger*'s "extraordinary circumstances" exception or, more likely upon the traditional equitable principle that courts of equity could maintain jurisdiction when there was not an adequate remedy at law. There was some discussion in *Wooley v. Maynard*, 430 U.S. 705 (1977) (discussed above) that suggests the Court believed the fact that the federal plaintiff in that case had been prosecuted three times for defacing his license plate might be construed as the type of harassing state action appropriate to come within *Younger*'s extraordinary circumstances exception. But *Wooley* hardly seems like an appropriate candidate. After all, in *Wooley* the federal plaintiff/state defendant had pled guilty three times in state court without raising his constitutional objections and it is difficult to imagine why the state's repeated prosecutions of a person who continues to engage in prohibited conduct and pleads guilty for his actions constitutes bad faith on the part of the state.

What types of matters should meet the "extraordinary circumstances" requirement? Should it be sufficient if the state action is brought in bad faith? Cf. *Dombrowski v. Pfister*, 380 U.S. 479 (1965). If the challenged law is flagrantly unconstitutional? Cf. *Watson v. Buck*, 313 U.S. 387 (1941). Would not the state's judicial processes be able to cure such defects in either case? Given *Younger*'s implicit conclusion that states are fully and fairly able to litigate constitutional claims, are there any instances in which the "extraordinary circumstances" exception should be deemed warranted?

7. The Limits of Younger

SPRINT COMMUNICATIONS, INC. V. JACOBS
571 U.S. ___, 134 S.Ct. 584 (2014).

JUSTICE GINSBURG delivered the opinion of the Court.

This case involves two proceedings, one pending in state court, the other in federal court. Each seeks review of an Iowa Utilities Board (IUB or Board) order. And each presents the question whether Windstream

Iowa Communications, Inc. (Windstream), a local telecommunications carrier, may impose on Sprint Communications, Inc. (Sprint), intrastate access charges for telephone calls transported via the Internet.... Invoking *Younger v. Harris*, the U.S. District Court for the Southern District of Iowa abstained from adjudicating Sprint's complaint in deference to the parallel state-court proceeding, and the Court of Appeals for the Eighth Circuit affirmed. We reverse the judgment of the Court of Appeals.

I

Sprint, a national telecommunications service provider, has long paid intercarrier access fees to the Iowa communications company Windstream (formerly Iowa Telecom) for certain long distance calls placed by Sprint customers to Windstream's in-state customers. In 2009, however, Sprint decided to withhold payment for a subset of those calls, classified as Voice over Internet Protocol (VoIP), after concluding that the Telecommunications Act of 1996 preempted intrastate regulation of VoIP traffic. In response, Windstream threatened to block all calls to and from Sprint customers.

Sprint filed a complaint against Windstream with the IUB asking the Board to enjoin Windstream from discontinuing service to Sprint. In Sprint's view, Iowa law entitled it to withhold payment while it contested the access charges and prohibited Windstream from carrying out its disconnection threat. In answer to Sprint's complaint, Windstream retracted its threat to discontinue serving Sprint, and Sprint moved, successfully, to withdraw its complaint. Because the conflict between Sprint and Windstream over VoIP calls was "likely to recur," however, the IUB decided to continue the proceedings to resolve the underlying legal question, i.e., whether VoIP calls are subject to intrastate regulation. The question retained by the IUB, Sprint argued, was governed by federal law, and was not within the IUB's adjudicative jurisdiction. The IUB disagreed, ruling that the intrastate fees applied to VoIP calls.

Seeking to overturn the Board's ruling, Sprint commenced two lawsuits. First, Sprint sued the members of the IUB (respondents here) in their official capacities in the United States District Court for the Southern District of Iowa. In its federal-court complaint, Sprint sought a declaration that the Telecommunications Act of 1996 preempted the IUB's decision; as relief, Sprint requested an injunction against enforcement of the IUB's order. Second, Sprint petitioned for review of the IUB's order in Iowa state court. The state petition reiterated the preemption argument Sprint made in its federal-court complaint; in addition, Sprint asserted state law and procedural due process claims. Because Eighth Circuit precedent effectively required a plaintiff to exhaust state remedies before proceeding to federal court, Sprint urges that it filed the state suit as a protective measure. Failing to do so, Sprint explains, risked losing the opportunity to obtain any review, federal or state, should the federal court decide to abstain after the expiration of the Iowa statute of limitations.

As Sprint anticipated, the IUB filed a motion asking the Federal District Court to abstain in light of the state suit, citing *Younger v. Harris.* [The District Court granted the motion and the Eighth Circuit affirmed]. We granted certiorari to decide whether, consistent with our delineation of cases encompassed by the *Younger* doctrine, abstention was appropriate here.

II

A

Federal courts, it was early and famously said, have "no more right to decline the exercise of jurisdiction which is given, than to usurp that which is not given." *Cohens v. Virginia*, 6 Wheat. 264, 404 (1821). Jurisdiction existing, this Court has cautioned, a federal court's "obligation" to hear and decide a case is "virtually unflagging." *Colorado River Water Conservation Dist. v. United States*, 424 U.S. 800, 817 (1976). Parallel state-court proceedings do not detract from that obligation.

In *Younger*, we recognized a "far-from-novel" exception to this general rule. *New Orleans Public Service, Inc. v. Council of City of New Orleans*, 491 U.S. 350, 364 (1989) (*NOPSI*). The plaintiff in *Younger* sought federal-court adjudication of the constitutionality of the California Criminal Syndicalism Act. Requesting an injunction against the Act's enforcement, the federal-court plaintiff was at the time the defendant in a pending state criminal prosecution under the Act. In those circumstances, we said, the federal court should decline to enjoin the prosecution, absent bad faith, harassment, or a patently invalid state statute. Abstention was in order, we explained, under "the basic doctrine of equity jurisprudence that courts of equity should not act . . . to restrain a criminal prosecution, when the moving party has an adequate remedy at law and will not suffer irreparably injury if denied equitable relief." "[R]estraining equity jurisdiction within narrow limits," the Court observed, would "prevent erosion of the role of the jury and avoid a duplication of legal proceedings and legal sanctions." We explained as well that this doctrine was "reinforced" by the notion of " 'comity,' that is, a proper respect for state functions."

We have since applied *Younger* to bar federal relief in certain civil actions. *Huffman v. Pursue, Ltd.* 420 U.S. 592 (1975) is the pathmarking decision. There, Ohio officials brought a civil action in state court to abate the showing of obscene movies in Pursue's theater. Because the State was a party and the proceeding was "in aid of and closely related to [the

State's] criminal statutes," the Court held *Younger* abstention appropriate.

More recently, in *NOPSI*, the Court had occasion to review and restate our *Younger* jurisprudence. *NOPSI* addressed and rejected an argument that a federal court should refuse to exercise jurisdiction to review a state council's ratemaking decision. "[O]nly exceptional circumstances," we reaffirmed, "justify a federal court's refusal to decide a case in deference to the States." Those "exceptional circumstances" exist, the Court determined after surveying prior decisions, in three types of proceedings. First, *Younger* precluded federal intrusion into ongoing state criminal prosecutions. Second, certain "civil enforcement proceedings" warranted abstention. *Huffman.* Finally, federal courts refrained from interfering with pending "civil proceedings involving certain orders uniquely in furtherance of the state courts' ability to perform their judicial functions." *Juidice v. Vail* and *Pennzoil Co. v. Texaco Inc.* We have not applied *Younger* outside these three "exceptional" categories, and today hold, in accord with *NOPSI*, that they define *Younger's* scope.

B

The IUB does not assert that the Iowa state court's review of the Board decision, considered alone, implicates *Younger*. Rather, the initial administrative proceeding justifies staying any action in federal court, the IUB contends, until the state review process has concluded. We will assume without deciding, as the Court did in *NOPSI*, that an administrative adjudication and the subsequent state court's review of it count as a "unitary process" for *Younger* purposes. The question remains, however, whether the initial IUB proceeding is of the "sort . . . entitled to *Younger* treatment."

The IUB proceeding, we conclude, does not fall within any of the three exceptional categories described in *NOPSI* and therefore does not trigger *Younger* abstention. The first and third categories plainly do not accommodate the IUB's proceeding. That proceeding was civil, not criminal in character, and it did not touch on a state court's ability to perform its judicial function.

Nor does the IUB's order rank as an act of civil enforcement of the kind to which Younger has been extended. Our decisions applying *Younger* to instances of civil enforcement have generally concerned state proceedings "akin to a criminal prosecution" in "important respects." Such enforcement actions are characteristically initiated to sanction the federal plaintiff, i.e., the party challenging the state action, for some wrongful act. In cases of this genre, a state actor is routinely a party to the state proceeding and often initiates the action . Investigations are commonly involved, often culminating in the filing of a formal complaint or charges.

The IUB proceeding does not resemble the state enforcement actions this Court has found appropriate for *Younger* abstention. It is not "akin to a criminal prosecution." Nor was it initiated by "the State in its sovereign capacity." A private corporation, Sprint, initiated the action. No state authority conducted an investigation into Sprint's activities, and no state actor lodged a formal complaint against Sprint.

In its brief, the IUB emphasizes Sprint's decision to withdraw the complaint that commenced proceedings before the Board. At that point, the IUB argues, Sprint was no longer a willing participant, and the proceedings became, essentially, a civil enforcement action. The IUB's adjudicative authority, however, was invoked to settle a civil dispute between two private parties, not to sanction Sprint for commission of a wrongful act. Although Sprint withdrew its complaint, administrative efficiency, not misconduct by Sprint, prompted the IUB to answer the underlying federal question. By determining the intercarrier compensation regime applicable to VoIP calls, the IUB sought to avoid renewed litigation of the parties' dispute. Because the underlying legal question remained unsettled, the Board observed, the controversy was "likely to recur." Nothing here suggests that the IUB proceeding was "more akin to a criminal prosecution than are most civil cases."

In holding that abstention was the proper course, the Eighth Circuit relied heavily on this Court's decision in *Middlesex*. *Younger* abstention was warranted, the Court of Appeals read *Middlesex* to say, whenever three conditions are met: There is (1) "an ongoing state judicial proceeding, which (2) implicates important state interests, and (3) provide[s] an adequate opportunity to raise [federal] challenges." Before this Court, the IUB has endorsed the Eighth Circuit's approach.

The Court of Appeals and the IUB attribute to this Court's decision in *Middlesex* extraordinary breadth. We invoked *Younger* in *Middlesex* to bar a federal court from entertaining a lawyer's challenge to a New Jersey state ethics committee's pending investigation of the lawyer. Unlike the IUB proceeding here, the state ethics committee's hearing in *Middlesex* was indeed "akin to a criminal proceeding." As we noted, an investigation and formal complaint preceded the hearing, an agency of the State's Supreme Court initiated the hearing, and the purpose of the hearing was to determine whether the lawyer should be disciplined for his failure to meet the State's standards of professional conduct. The three *Middlesex* conditions recited above were not dispositive; they were, instead, additional factors appropriately considered by the federal court before invoking *Younger*.

Divorced from their quasi-criminal context, the three *Middlesex* conditions would extend *Younger* to virtually all parallel state and federal proceedings, at least where a party could identify a plausibly important state interest.. That result is irreconcilable with our dominant instruction that, even in the presence of parallel state proceedings, abstention from the exercise of federal jurisdiction is the "exception, not the rule." In short, to guide other federal courts, we today clarify and affirm that Younger extends to the three "exceptional circumstances" identified in NOPSI, but no further.

NOTES ON SPRINT

1. **New Orleans Public Service, Inc. v. Council of City of New Orleans (NOPSI).** Justice Ginsburg's opinion in *Sprint* relies heavily on language from the Court's decision in *New Orleans Public Service, Inc. v. Council of City of New Orleans (NOPSI)*. *NOPSI*, involved a federal court challenge by a regulated utility against the New Orleans City Council for its denial of the utility's request for a rate increase. The question before the Court was whether the district court should have abstained in light of the fact that there were ongoing state proceedings that also questioned the legality of the Council's order. Writing for the Court, Justice Scalia determined that abstention was not appropriate because the Council's rate-making decision was essentially a completed legislative act and *Younger* had never been held to require abstention in deference to a parallel state proceeding challenging final legislative action. The state utility board proceedings in *Sprint*, on the other hand, were not legislative but were rather adjudicative in that they endeavored to resolve a dispute between Sprint Communications and Windstream. Should the *Sprint* Court have found *NOPSI* controlling? Did they?

2. **Does *Sprint* Signal the End of *Younger* Expansion?** One of the more interesting aspects of the *Sprint* decision is its heavy and repeated emphasis on *Younger* abstention as being an exception to the normal rule that a federal court has an "unflagging" obligation to hear cases that are otherwise properly brought before it. The opinion in fact ends with Justice Ginsburg's strong admonition that *Younger* is limited only to three "exceptional circumstances" and goes no further—those circumstances being 1) state criminal prosecutions, 2) civil enforcement proceedings, and 3) civil proceedings involving certain orders uniquely in furtherance of the state courts' ability to perform their judicial functions.

Does *Sprint's* narrow reading of *Younger* signal that the Court in future cases is likely to be less concerned with federalism and comity issues than it was in cases like *Huffman, Middlesex,* and *Dayton Christian Schools*? Is it significant in this respect that the decision in *Sprint* was unanimous?

V.   THE ROOKER-FELDMAN DOCTRINE

EXXON MOBIL CORP. V. SAUDI BASIC INDUSTRIES CORP.
544 U.S. 280 (2005).

JUSTICE GINSBURG delivered the opinion of the Court.

This case concerns what has come to be known as the *Rooker-Feldman* doctrine, applied by this Court only twice, first in *Rooker* v. *Fidelity Trust Co.*, 263 U.S. 413 (1923), then, 60 years later, in *District of Columbia Court of Appeals* v. *Feldman*, 460 U.S. 462 (1983). Variously interpreted in the lower courts, the doctrine has sometimes been construed to extend far beyond the contours of the *Rooker* and *Feldman* cases, overriding Congress' conferral of federal-court jurisdiction concurrent with jurisdiction exercised by state courts, and superseding the ordinary application of preclusion law pursuant to 28 U.S.C. § 1738.

Rooker was a suit commenced in Federal District Court to have a judgment of a state court, adverse to the federal court plaintiffs, "declared null and void." In *Feldman*, parties unsuccessful in the District of Columbia Court of Appeals (the District's highest court) commenced a federal-court action against the very court that had rejected their applications. Holding the federal suits impermissible, we emphasized that appellate jurisdiction to reverse or modify a state-court judgment is lodged, initially by § 25 of the Judiciary Act of 1789, 1 Stat. 85, and now by 28 U.S.C. § 1257 exclusively in this Court. Federal district courts, we noted, are empowered to exercise original, not appellate, jurisdiction. Plaintiffs in *Rooker* and *Feldman* had litigated and lost in state court. Their federal complaints, we observed, essentially invited federal courts of first instance to review and reverse unfavorable state-court judgments. We declared such suits out of bounds, *i.e.*, properly dismissed for want of subject-matter jurisdiction.

The *Rooker-Feldman* doctrine, we hold today, is confined to cases of the kind from which the doctrine acquired its name: cases brought by state-court losers complaining of injuries caused by state-court judgments rendered before the district court proceedings commenced and inviting district court review and rejection of those judgments. *Rooker-Feldman* does not otherwise override or supplant preclusion doctrine or augment the circumscribed doctrines that allow federal courts to stay or dismiss proceedings in deference to state-court actions.

II.

In 1980, two subsidiaries of petitioner Exxon Mobil Corporation (then the separate companies Exxon Corp. and Mobil Corp.) formed joint ventures with respondent Saudi Basic Industries Corp. (SABIC) to produce polyethylene in Saudi Arabia. Two decades later, the parties began to dispute royalties that SABIC had charged the joint ventures for sublicenses to a polyethylene manufacturing method.

SABIC preemptively sued the two ExxonMobil subsidiaries in Delaware Superior Court in July 2000 seeking a declaratory judgment that the royalty charges were proper under the joint venture agreements. About two weeks later, ExxonMobil and its subsidiaries countersued SABIC in the United States District Court for the District of New Jersey, alleging that SABIC overcharged the joint ventures for the sublicenses. ExxonMobil invoked subject-matter jurisdiction in the New Jersey action under 28 U.S.C. § 1330 which authorizes district courts to adjudicate actions against foreign states.

In January 2002, the ExxonMobil subsidiaries answered SABIC's state-court complaint, asserting as counterclaims the same claims ExxonMobil had made in the federal suit in New Jersey. The state suit went to trial in March 2003, and the jury returned a verdict of over $400 million in favor of the ExxonMobil subsidiaries. SABIC appealed the judgment entered on the verdict to the Delaware Supreme Court.

Before the state-court trial, SABIC moved to dismiss the federal suit, alleging, *inter alia*, immunity under the Foreign Sovereign Immunities Act of 1976. The Federal District Court denied SABIC's motion to dismiss. SABIC took an interlocutory appeal, and the Court of Appeals heard argument in December 2003, over eight months after the state-court jury verdict.

The Court of Appeals, on its own motion, raised the question whether "subject matter jurisdiction over this case fails under the *Rooker-Feldman* doctrine because ExxonMobil's claims have already been litigated in state court." The court did not question the District Court's possession of subject-matter jurisdiction at the outset of the suit, but held that federal jurisdiction terminated when the Delaware Superior Court entered judgment on the jury verdict. The court rejected ExxonMobil's argument that *Rooker-Feldman* could not apply because ExxonMobil filed its federal complaint well before the state-court judgment. The only relevant consideration, the court stated, "is whether the state judgment precedes a federal judgment on the same claims." If *Rooker-Feldman* did not apply to federal actions filed prior to a state-court judgment, the Court of Appeals worried, "we would be encouraging parties to maintain federal actions as 'insurance policies' while their state court claims were pending." Once ExxonMobil's claims had been litigated to a judgment in state court, the Court of Appeals held, *Rooker-Feldman* "preclude[d] [the] federal district court from proceeding."

ExxonMobil, at that point prevailing in Delaware, was not seeking to overturn the state-court judgment. Nevertheless, the Court of Appeals hypothesized that, if SABIC won on appeal in Delaware, ExxonMobil would be endeavoring in the federal action to "invalidate" the state-court judgment, "the very situation," the court concluded, "contemplated by *Rooker-Feldman*'s 'inextricably intertwined' bar."

III

Rooker and *Feldman* exhibit the limited circumstances in which this Court's appellate jurisdiction over state-court judgments, 28 U.S.C. § 1257 precludes a United States district court from exercising subject-matter jurisdiction in an action it would otherwise be empowered to adjudicate under a congressional grant of authority, *e.g.*, § 1330 (suits against foreign states), § 1331 (federal question), and § 1332 (diversity). In both cases, the losing party in state court filed suit in federal court after the state proceedings ended, complaining of an injury caused by the state-court judgment and seeking review and rejection of that judgment. Plaintiffs in both cases, alleging federal-question jurisdiction, called upon the District Court to overturn an injurious state-court judgment. Because § 1257, as long interpreted, vests authority to review a state court's judgment solely in this Court, the District Courts in *Rooker* and *Feldman* lacked subject matter jurisdiction.

When there is parallel state and federal litigation, *Rooker-Feldman* is not triggered simply by the entry of judgment in state court. This Court has repeatedly held that "the pendency of an action in the state court is no bar to proceedings concerning the same matter in the Federal court having jurisdiction." *McClellan* v. *Carland*, 217 U.S. 268 (1910); accord *Doran* v. *Salem Inn, Inc.*, 422 U.S. 922 (1975); *Atlantic Coast Line R. Co., v. Locomotive Engineers*, 398 U.S. 281 (1970). Comity or abstention doctrines may, in various circumstances, permit or require the federal court to stay or dismiss the federal action in favor of the state-court litigation. See, e.g., *Colorado River Water Conservation Dist.* v. *United States*, 424 U.S. 800 (1976); *Younger* v. *Harris*, 401 U.S. 37 (1971); *Burford* v. *Sun Oil Co.*, 319 U.S. 315 (1943); *Railroad Comm'n of Tex.* v. *Pullman Co.*, 312 U.S. 496 (1941). But neither *Rooker* nor *Feldman* supports the notion that properly invoked concurrent jurisdiction vanishes if a state court reaches judgment on the same or related question while the case remains *sub judice* in a federal court.

Disposition of the federal action, once the state-court adjudication is complete, would be governed by preclusion law. The Full Faith and Credit Act, 28 U.S.C. § 1738, originally enacted in 1790, requires the federal court to "give the same preclusive effect to a state-court judgment as another court of that State would give." *Parsons Steel, Inc.* v. *First Alabama Bank*, 474 U.S. 518 (1986). [Preclusion,] of course, is not a jurisdictional matter. See Fed. Rule Civ. Proc. 8(c) (listing res judicata as an affirmative defense). In parallel litigation, a federal court may be bound to recognize the claim- and issue-preclusive effects of a state-court judgment, but federal jurisdiction over an action does not terminate automatically on the entry of judgment in the state court.

Nor does § 1257 stop a district court from exercising subject-matter jurisdiction simply because a party attempts to litigate in federal court a matter previously litigated in state court. If a federal plaintiff "present[s] some independent claim, albeit one that denies a legal conclusion that a state court has reached in a case to which he was a party ... then there is jurisdiction and state law determines whether the defendant prevails under principles of preclusion."

ExxonMobil plainly has not repaired to federal court to undo the Delaware judgment in its favor. Rather, it appears ExxonMobil filed suit in Federal District Court (only two weeks after SABIC filed in Delaware and well before any judgment in state court) to protect itself in the event it lost in state court on grounds (such as the state statute of limitations) that might not preclude relief in the federal venue. *Rooker-Feldman* did not prevent the District Court from exercising jurisdiction when ExxonMobil filed the federal action, and it did not emerge to vanquish jurisdiction after ExxonMobil prevailed in the Delaware courts.

For the reasons stated, the judgment of the Court of Appeals for the Third Circuit is reversed, and the case is remanded for further proceedings consistent with this opinion.

It is so ordered.

NOTES ON ROOKER-FELDMAN IN THE AFTERMATH OF EXXON

1. ***Rooker-Feldman*** **and** ***Res Judicata.*** Do you understand the difference between a federal court dismissal based on *res judicata* (which is discussed in Part VI below) and one based on the application of *Rooker-Feldman*? Is there any practical difference in result? *Exxon* explains that *Rooker-Feldman* is jurisdictional while *res judicata* is not. What is the significance of that distinction?

2. ***Lance v. Dennis.*** One year after *Exxon*, the Court revisited *Rooker-Feldman* in *Lance v. Dennis*, 546 U.S. 459 (2006). *Lance* addressed the issue of whether *Rooker-Feldman* barred the district court from hearing a claim brought by a plaintiff in privity with the party who had lost an action in state court. The Court, in a *per curiam* opinion, held that *Rooker-Feldman* did not apply. Emphasizing the "narrowness" of the doctrine, the Court held that its application "was confined to 'cases brought by state-court losers complaining of injuries caused by state-court judgments rendered before the district court proceedings commenced and inviting district court review and rejection of those judgments.'" (quoting *Exxon.*) As the Court explained, "*Rooker-Feldman* is not simply preclusion by another name," and "simply because, for purposes of preclusion law, [a non-party] could be considered in privity with a

party to the [state court] judgment" was not sufficient to implicate the doctrine.

3. *Rooker-Feldman* and Judicial Economy. The appellate court argued in *Exxon* that its application of *Rooker-Feldman* would discourage litigants from maintaining federal suits as insurance policies against unfavorable results. Why did the Court not find that argument persuasive? Would such a strategy actually work in any event given the obligation of the federal court to accord *res judicata* effects to the final judgments of state courts? Are there circumstances where *res judicata* might not apply?

4. *Rooker-Feldman* and Comity. How does the *Rooker-Feldman* doctrine interrelate with the other doctrines discussed in this chapter? Does it sufficiently protect the interests of the federal courts? Of the state courts? Does it appropriately foster principles of comity?

VI.   PRECLUSION

ALLEN V. MCCURRY
449 U.S. 90 (1980).

JUSTICE STEWART delivered the opinion of the Court.

In April 1977, several undercover police officers, following an informant's tip that [respondent, Willie] McCurry was dealing in heroin, went to his house in St. Louis, Mo., to attempt a purchase. Two officers, petitioners Allen and Jacobsmeyer, knocked on the front door, while the other officers hid nearby. When McCurry opened the door, the two officers asked to buy some heroin "caps." McCurry went back into the house and returned soon thereafter, firing a pistol at and seriously wounding Allen and Jacobsmeyer. After a gun battle with the other officers and their reinforcements, McCurry retreated into the house; he emerged again when the police demanded that he surrender. Several officers then entered the house without a warrant, purportedly to search for other persons inside. One of the officers seized drugs and other contraband that lay in plain view, as well as additional contraband he found in dresser drawers and in auto tires on the porch.

McCurry was charged with possession of heroin and assault with intent to kill. At the pretrial suppression hearing, the trial judge excluded the evidence seized from the dresser drawers and tires, but denied suppression of the evidence found in plain view. McCurry was convicted of both the heroin and assault offenses.

McCurry subsequently filed the present 1983 action for $1 million in damages against petitioners Allen and Jacobsmeyer, other unnamed individual police officers, and the city of St. Louis and its police department. The complaint alleged a conspiracy to violate McCurry's

Fourth Amendment rights, an unconstitutional search and seizure of his house, and an assault on him by unknown police officers after he had been arrested and handcuffed. The petitioners moved for summary judgment. The District Court apparently understood the gist of the complaint to be the allegedly unconstitutional search and seizure and granted summary judgment, holding that collateral estoppel prevented McCurry from relitigating the search-and-seizure question already decided against him in the state courts.

The Court of Appeals reversed the judgment and remanded the case for trial. The appellate court said it was not holding that collateral estoppel was generally inapplicable in a 1983 suit raising issues determined against the federal plaintiff in a state criminal trial. But noting that *Stone v. Powell*, 428 U.S. 465 (1976), barred McCurry from federal habeas corpus relief, and invoking "the special role of the federal courts in protecting civil rights," the court concluded that the 1983 suit was McCurry's only route to a federal forum for his constitutional claim and directed the trial court to allow him to proceed to trial unencumbered by collateral estoppel.

II

The federal courts have traditionally adhered to the related doctrines of res judicata and collateral estoppel. Under res judicata, a final judgment on the merits of an action precludes the parties or their privies from relitigating issues that were or could have been raised in that action. Under collateral estoppel, once a court has decided an issue of fact or law necessary to its judgment, that decision may preclude relitigation of the issue in a suit on a different cause of action involving a party to the first case. As this Court and other courts have often recognized, res judicata and collateral estoppel relieve parties of the cost and vexation of multiple lawsuits, conserve judicial resources, and, by preventing inconsistent decisions, encourage reliance on adjudication.

In recent years, this Court has reaffirmed the benefits of collateral estoppel in particular, finding the policies underlying it to apply in contexts not formerly recognized at common law. Thus, the Court has eliminated the requirement of mutuality in applying collateral estoppel to bar relitigation of issues decided earlier in federal-court suits, and has allowed a litigant who was not a party to a federal case to use collateral estoppel "offensively" in a new federal suit against the party who lost on the decided issue in the first case. But one general limitation the Court has repeatedly recognized is that the concept of collateral estoppel cannot apply when the party against whom the earlier decision is asserted did not have a "full and fair opportunity" to litigate that issue in the earlier case.

The federal courts generally have also consistently accorded preclusive effect to issues decided by state courts. Thus, res judicata and collateral estoppel not only reduce unnecessary litigation and foster reliance on adjudication, but also promote the comity between state and federal courts that has been recognized as a bulwark of the federal system. *See Younger v. Harris*, 401 U.S. 37 (1971).

Indeed, though the federal courts may look to the common law or to the policies supporting res judicata and collateral estoppel in assessing the preclusive effect of decisions of other federal courts, Congress has specifically required all federal courts to give preclusive effect to state-court judgments whenever the courts of the State from which the judgments emerged would do so:

> "[Judicial] proceedings [of any court of any State] shall have the same full faith and credit in every court within the United States and its Territories and Possessions as they have by law or usage in the courts of such State. 28 U.S.C. 1738."

It is against this background that we examine the relationship of 1983 and collateral estoppel, and the decision of the Court of Appeals in this case.

III

Because the requirement of mutuality of estoppel was still alive in the federal courts until well into this century, the drafters of the 1871 Civil Rights Act, of which 1983 is a part, may have had less reason to concern themselves with rules of preclusion than a modern Congress would. Nevertheless, in 1871 res judicata and collateral estoppel could certainly have applied in federal suits following state-court litigation between the same parties or their privies, and nothing in the language of 1983 remotely expresses any congressional intent to contravene the common-law rules of preclusion or to repeal the express statutory requirements of the predecessor of 28 U.S.C. § 1738. Section 1983 creates a new federal cause of action. It says nothing about the preclusive effect of state-court judgments.

Moreover, the legislative history of 1983 does not in any clear way suggest that Congress intended to repeal or restrict the traditional doctrines of preclusion. The main goal of the Act was to override the corrupting influence of the Ku Klux Klan and its sympathizers on the governments and law enforcement agencies of the Southern States, *see Monroe v. Pape*, 365 U.S. 167 (1961), and of course the debates show that one strong motive behind its enactment was grave congressional concern that the state courts had been deficient in protecting federal rights, *Mitchum v. Foster*, 407 U.S. 225 (1972), *Monroe v. Pape*. But in the context of the legislative history as a whole, this congressional concern lends only the most equivocal support to any argument that, in cases where the state courts have recognized the constitutional claims asserted and provided fair procedures for determining them, Congress intended to override 1738 or the common-law rules of collateral estoppel and res judicata. Since repeals by implication are disfavored, much clearer support than this would be required to hold that 1738 and the traditional rules of preclusion are not applicable to 1983 suits.

As the Court has understood the history of the legislation, Congress realized that in enacting 1983 it was altering the balance of judicial power between the state and federal courts. *See Mitchum v. Foste*r. But in doing so, Congress was adding to the jurisdiction of the federal courts, not subtracting from that of the state courts. *See Monroe v. Pape,* ("The federal remedy is supplementary to the state remedy . . ."). The debates contain several references to the concurrent jurisdiction of the state courts over federal questions, and numerous suggestions that the state courts would retain their established jurisdiction so that they could, when the then current political passions abated, demonstrate a new sensitivity to federal rights.

To the extent that it did intend to change the balance of power over federal questions between the state and federal courts, the 42d Congress was acting in a way thoroughly consistent with the doctrines of preclusion. In reviewing the legislative history of 1983 in *Monroe v. Pape,* the Court inferred that Congress had intended a federal remedy in three circumstances: where state substantive law was facially unconstitutional, where state procedural law was inadequate to allow full litigation of a constitutional claim, and where state procedural law, though adequate in theory, was inadequate in practice. In short, the federal courts could step in where the state courts were unable or unwilling to protect federal rights. This understanding of 1983 might well support an exception to res judicata and collateral estoppel where state law did not provide fair procedures for the litigation of constitutional claims, or where a state court failed to even acknowledge the existence of the constitutional principle on which a litigant based his claim. Such an exception, however, would be essentially the same as the important general limit on rules of preclusion that already exists: Collateral estoppel does not apply where the party against whom an earlier court decision is asserted did not have a full and fair opportunity to litigate the claim or issue decided by the first court. But the Court's view of 1983 in *Monroe* lends no strength to any argument that Congress intended to allow relitigation of federal issues decided after a full and fair hearing in a state court simply because the state court's decision may have been erroneous.

The Court of Appeals . . . concluded that since *Stone v. Powell* had removed McCurry's right to a hearing of his Fourth Amendment claim in federal habeas corpus, collateral estoppel should not deprive him of a federal judicial hearing of that claim in a 1983 suit.

Stone v. Powell does not provide a logical doctrinal source for the court's ruling. This Court in *Stone* assessed the costs and benefits of the judge-made exclusionary rule within the boundaries of the federal courts' statutory power to issue writs of habeas corpus, and decided that the incremental deterrent effect that the issuance of the writ in Fourth Amendment cases might have on police conduct did not justify the cost the writ imposed upon the fair administration of criminal justice. The *Stone* decision concerns only the prudent exercise of federal-court jurisdiction under 28 U.S.C. § 2254. It has no bearing on 1983 suits or on the question of the preclusive effect of state-court judgments.

The actual basis of the Court of Appeals' holding appears to be a generally framed principle that every person asserting a federal right is entitled to one unencumbered opportunity to litigate that right in a federal district court, regardless of the legal posture in which the federal claim arises. But the authority for this principle is difficult to discern. It cannot lie in the Constitution, which makes no such guarantee, but leaves the scope of the jurisdiction of the federal district courts to the wisdom of Congress. And no such authority is to be found in § 1983 itself. For reasons already discussed at length, nothing in the language or legislative history of § 1983 proves any congressional intent to deny binding effect to a state-court judgment or decision when the state court, acting within its proper jurisdiction, has given the parties a full and fair opportunity to litigate federal claims, and thereby has shown itself willing and able to protect federal rights. And nothing in the legislative history of § 1983 reveals any purpose to afford less deference to judgments in state criminal proceedings than to those in state civil proceedings. There is, in short, no reason to believe that Congress intended to provide a person claiming a federal right an unrestricted opportunity to relitigate an issue already decided in state court simply because the issue arose in a state proceeding in which he would rather not have been engaged at all.

Through § 1983, the 42d Congress intended to afford an opportunity for legal and equitable relief in a federal court for certain types of injuries. It is difficult to believe that the drafters of that Act considered it a substitute for a federal writ of habeas corpus, the purpose of which is not to redress civil injury, but to release the applicant from unlawful physical confinement, particularly in light of the extremely narrow scope of federal habeas relief for state prisoners in 1871.

The only other conceivable basis for finding a universal right to litigate a federal claim in a federal district court is hardly a legal basis at all, but rather a general distrust of the capacity of the state courts to render correct decisions on constitutional issues. It is ironic that *Stone v. Powell* provided the occasion for the expression of such an attitude in the present litigation, in view of this Court's emphatic reaffirmation in that case of the constitutional obligation of the state courts to uphold federal law, and its expression of confidence in their ability to do so.

The Court of Appeals erred in holding that McCurry's inability to obtain federal habeas corpus relief upon his Fourth Amendment claim renders the doctrine of collateral estoppel inapplicable to his § 1983 suit. Accordingly, the judgment is reversed, and the case is remanded to the Court of Appeals for proceedings consistent with this opinion.

JUSTICE BLACKMUN, with whom JUSTICE BRENNAN and JUSTICE MARSHALL join, dissenting.

The legal principles with which the Court is concerned in this civil case obviously far transcend the ugly facts of respondent's criminal convictions in the courts of Missouri for heroin possession and assault.

The Court today holds that notions of collateral estoppel apply with full force to this suit brought under 42 U.S.C. § 1983. In my view, the Court, in so ruling, ignores the clear import of the legislative history of that statute and disregards the important federal policies that underlie its enforcement. It also shows itself insensitive both to the significant differences between the 1983 remedy and the exclusionary rule, and to the pressures upon a criminal defendant that make a free choice of forum illusory. I do not doubt that principles of preclusion are to be given such effect as is appropriate in a 1983 action. In many cases, the denial of res judicata or collateral estoppel effect would serve no purpose and would harm relations between federal and state tribunals. Nonetheless, the Court's analysis in this particular case is unacceptable to me. It works injustice on this 1983 plaintiff, and it makes more difficult the consistent protection of constitutional rights, a consideration that was at the core of the enacters' intent. Accordingly, I dissent.

NOTES ON PRECLUSION AND FEDERALISM

1. *Allen* and *Mitchum*. The Court in *Allen* stated that there was no indication that Congress, in enacting § 1983, intended to repeal or restrict traditional doctrines of preclusion. Was there any greater indication that Congress, in enacting § 1983, was intending to carve out an expressly authorized exception to the Anti-Injunction Act? See *Mitchum v. Foster*, 407 U.S. 225 (1972). Which exception is likely to create more friction between the federal and state courts—one in which the federal court is authorized to enjoin an ongoing state court proceeding or one in which the federal court is empowered to reject the collateral estoppel effects of a state court judgment? Does it matter?

2. *Allen* and *England*. Justice Blackmun's dissent in *Allen* relied heavily on *England v. Medical Examiners*, 375 U.S. 411 (1964), the case that held that a federal plaintiff, required by the abstention doctrine to submit her constitutional claims first to a state court, could preserve her federal claims

for resolution in federal court without risking the preclusive effects of a state court judgment. For the purposes of preserving her right to have her federal claim heard in federal court, is the federal plaintiff in *England,* who originally filed her action in federal court, in the same situation as the federal plaintiff in *Allen,* who originally was a state court defendant? Is one more entitled than the other to have her federal claim heard in federal court without the preclusive effects of an adverse state court judgment?

3.   **Section 1983 and the Abandonment of Mutuality of Estoppel.** As *Allen* acknowledged, the abandonment of the doctrine of mutuality of estoppel means that the preclusive effects of judgments are now far broader than they were when Congress enacted § 1983. On this basis, the Court conceded that the Congress that enacted § 1983 would have had less reason to concern themselves with issues of preclusion than would a modern Congress. Nevertheless, the Court maintained that these changes in preclusion law should not affect whether the current rules of collateral estoppel should apply to federal court damage actions brought pursuant to § 1983. Do you agree with the Court's logic?

4.   **Determining the Preclusive Effects of State Judgments.** Under the Full Faith and Credit Statute, the preclusive effect of a final judgment is generally determined by the law of the rendering court (absent statutory authority to the contrary). See 28 U.S.C. § 1738 (judicial proceedings "shall have the same full faith and credit in every court within the United States and its Territories and Possessions as they have by law or usage in the courts of such State, Territory or Possession from which they are taken.") Accordingly, federal courts must "accept the [preclusion] rules chosen by the state from which the judgment is taken." *Kremer v. Chemical Construction Corporation,* 456 U.S. 461 (1982).

5.   **State Administrative Decisions.** *Kremer v. Chemical Construction Corporation,* 456 U.S. 461 (1982), noted above, involved a state judicial decision that reviewed a state administrative agency ruling. In *University of Tennessee v. Elliott,* 478 U.S. 788 (1986), an employee of the University first took his complaint of race discrimination before a state agency. The agency found certain key facts against him. He then brought suit in federal court under § 1983 and Title VII. On the § 1983 claim the Court held that federal courts generally should accord preclusive effects to unreviewed determinations of fact by state agencies. Although recognizing that § 1738 itself did not demand this result (because it applies only to judicial proceedings and not agency actions), the Court nevertheless reached this outcome relying on its authority to fashion "common law rules of preclusion." As the Court explained, "giving preclusive effect to administrative factfinding serves the value underlying general principles of collateral estoppel: enforcing repose [a value] which encompasses both the parties' interest in avoiding the cost and vexation of repetitive litigation and the public's interest in conserving judicial resources." In addition, "[h]aving federal courts give preclusive effect to the factfinding of state administrative tribunals also serves the value of federalism."

Interestingly, although the *Elliott* Court held that preclusion principles applied to the federal plaintiff's § 1983 claim, it allowed his Title VII claim to proceed without *res judicata* effect on the grounds that preclusion would be inconsistent with Title VII's mandate that claimants are entitled to a trial de novo following agency action.

6. Claim Preclusion. *Allen* addressed only issues of collateral estoppel (issue preclusion) and did not reach the issue of whether state court judgments could also impose claim preclusion effects on state court defendants. The claim preclusion issue was raised and resolved in favor of finding preclusive effects in *Migra v. Warren City School District Board of Education*, 465 U.S. 75 (1984). A schoolteacher was fired and brought suit for breach of contract in state court. She could have, but did not, raise a First Amendment claim in that case. She won the suit and then brought a § 1983 suit in federal court, asserting that she was dismissed in retaliation for her exercise of First Amendment rights. As the *Migra* Court stated:

> The Court in *Allen* left open the possibility . . . that the preclusive effect of a state-court judgment might be different as to a federal issue that a 1983 litigant could have raised but did not raise in the earlier state-court proceeding. That is the central issue to be resolved in the present case. Petitioner did not litigate her 1983 claim in state court, and she asserts that the state-court judgment should not preclude her suit in federal court simply because her federal claim could have been litigated in the state-court proceeding. Thus, petitioner urges this Court to interpret the interplay of 1738 and 1983 in such a way as to accord state-court judgments preclusive effect in 1983 suits only as to issues actually litigated in state court.

> It is difficult to see how the policy concerns underlying 1983 would justify a distinction between the issue preclusive and claim preclusive effects of state-court judgments. The argument that state-court judgments should have less preclusive effect in § 1983 suits than in other federal suits is based on Congress' expressed concern over the adequacy of state courts as protectors of federal rights. *See,* e. g., *Mitchum v. Foster*, 407 U.S. 225 (1972). *Allen* recognized that the enactment of 1983 was motivated partially out of such concern, but *Allen* nevertheless held that 1983 did not open the way to relitigation of an issue that had been determined in a state criminal proceeding. Any distrust of state courts that would justify a limitation on the preclusive effect of state judgments in 1983 suits would presumably apply equally to issues that actually were decided in a state court as well as to those that could have been. If 1983 created an exception to the general preclusive effect accorded to state-court judgments, such an exception would seem to require similar treatment of both issue preclusion and claim preclusion. Having rejected in *Allen* the view that state-court judgments have no issue preclusive effect in 1983 suits, we must

reject the view that 1983 prevents the judgment in petitioner's state-court proceeding from creating a claim preclusion bar in this case.

Is there a reason to distinguish between claim preclusion and issue preclusion in this context? How, after *Migra*, could a state court defendant preserve his federal claims for a later federal court proceeding without having them barred by *res judicata*?

7. The Preclusive Effects of Guilty Pleas. In *Haring v. Prosise*, 462 U.S. 306 (1983), a Virginia criminal defendant who pled guilty to a drug charge subsequently brought a § 1983 action in federal court challenging the constitutionality of the search leading to his arrest. A unanimous Court, based on its reading of the Virginia preclusion law, held that the guilty plea would not bar the § 1983 claim. The *Haring* Court also rejected the government officers' assertion that the Court should adopt a rule finding guilty pleas to be preclusive of later § 1983 actions regardless of the applicable state's preclusion law. In so holding, the Court appeared to raise the possibility that guilty pleas should not be deemed preclusive on later § 1983 actions even if a state's preclusion law would hold otherwise. According to the Court:

> Adoption of petitioners' rule of preclusion would threaten important interests in preserving federal courts as an available forum for the vindication of constitutional rights. *See England v. Medical Examiners*, 375 U.S. 411 (1964). Under petitioners' rule, whether or not a state judgment would be accorded preclusive effect by state courts, a federal court would be barred from entertaining a 1983 claim. The rule would require "an otherwise unwilling party to try [Fourth Amendment] questions to the hilt" and prevail in state court "in order to [preserve] the mere possibility" of later bringing a 1983 claim in federal court. Defendants who have pleaded guilty and who wish to bring a 1983 claim would be forced to bring that claim in state court, if at all. Not only have petitioners failed to advance any compelling justification for a rule confining the litigation of constitutional claims to a state forum, but such a rule would be wholly contrary to one of the central concerns which motivated the enactment of 1983, namely, the "grave congressional concern that the state courts had been deficient in protecting federal rights." *Allen v. McCurry*, 449 U.S. 90 (1980), citing *Mitchum v. Foster*, 407 U.S. 225 (1972), and *Monroe v. Pape*, 365 U.S. 167 (1961). See *Patsy v. Florida Board of Regents*, 457 U.S. 496 (1982).

8. *Res Judicata* and the Exclusive Jurisdiction of the Federal Courts. A particularly difficult issue arises concerning the potential *res judicata* effects of a state court judgment over matters in which the federal courts have exclusive jurisdiction. The issue was raised in *Marrese v. American Academy of Orthopaedic Surgeons*, 470 U.S. 373 (1985). In *Marrese* the plaintiffs originally sued in Illinois state court claiming the denial of their applications to join the defendant organization violated their common law rights under state law. After the state court dismissed the action for failure to state a claim, the plaintiffs brought a federal antitrust action against the defendant in federal court. Although recognizing that the federal court's jurisdiction over federal antitrust claims was exclusive, the Court held, on review, that the case should be remanded for a determination of whether Illinois preclusion law would bar the federal claim. According to *Marrese*, the fact that an allegedly precluded claim "is within the exclusive jurisdiction of the federal courts does not necessarily make § 1738 inapplicable." See also *Matsushita Electric Industrial Co. v. Epstein*, 516 U.S. 367 (1996) (holding that a federal court must give full faith and credit to a state court judgment approving a class action settlement that included the release of federal claims within the exclusive jurisdiction of the federal courts). Do *Marrese* and *Matsushita* fully resolve the question of whether state court judgments may have preclusive effects on claims within the exclusive jurisdiction of the federal courts or does that issue still remain open?

9. ***Res Judicata* and Takings Cases.** The application of *res judicata* can have a particularly powerful effect in limiting access to the federal courts in takings cases. Because the rule in takings cases is that a claim does not become ripe until after the property owner is denied just compensation under a state procedure, see *Williamson County Regional Planning Commission v. Hamilton Bank of Johnson City*, 473 U.S. 172 (1985), the takings plaintiff necessarily has to first litigate the takings issue in state court. In *San Remo Hotel, L.P. v. San Francisco*, 545 U.S. 323 (2005), the Court held that *res judicata* would apply to takings issues even though it meant that the takings plaintiffs would effectively be precluded from bringing their takings claims to federal court through the combination of *Williamson*'s ripeness and the Full Faith and Credit Statute's *res judicata* requirements. As the Court held, "[t]he relevant question . . . is not whether the plaintiff has been afforded access to a federal forum; rather, the question is whether the state court actually decided an issue of fact or law that was necessary to its judgment."

10. The Habeas Corpus/Section 1983 Intersection: *Heck v. Humphrey*. Persons convicted of state crimes, and who wish to challenge their convictions on constitutional grounds, are ordinarily obliged to do so through appeal and, if an appeal is unavailing, through the habeas corpus process examined in Chapter 9. As *Allen v. McCurry* illustrates, some litigants try to take a different route, suing under § 1983, and one obstacle they encounter is the doctrine of issue preclusion that thwarted the plaintiff in that case. In *Heck v. Humphrey*, 512 U.S. 477 (1994), the Court set up another barrier to such suits, holding that "in order to recover damages for allegedly unconstitutional conviction or imprisonment, or for other harm caused by actions whose unlawfulness would render a conviction or sentence invalid, a § 1983 plaintiff must prove that the conviction or sentence has been reversed on direct appeal, expunged by executive order, declared invalid by a state tribunal authorized to make such determination, or called into question by a federal court's issuance of a writ of habeas corpus." Whether a prisoner may sue under § 1983 turns on "whether a judgment in favor of the plaintiff would necessarily imply the invalidity of his conviction or sentence." *Id.* at 486–87.

Some of the complexities of the *Heck* doctrine are illustrated by *Ballard v. Burton*, 444 F.3d 391 (5th Cir. 2006). The plaintiff, Stephen Ballard, was shot during a confrontation with law enforcement officers, arrested, and pled guilty to "simple assault on a law enforcement officer, Deputy Leroy Boling." He then sued another officer, Brian Burton, under § 1983, charging that Burton used excessive force in violation of his Fourth Amendment rights. The court ruled that:

> To prevail on his § 1983 claim for damages due to Burton's use of excessive force, Ballard must prove, inter alia, that Burton's use of deadly force was objectively unreasonable in the circumstances. Therefore, the dispositive question in determining whether *Heck* applies to preclude Ballard's § 1983 claim is as follows: would a finding that Burton's use of force was objectively unreasonable necessarily call into question the validity of Ballard's conviction for simple assault upon Boling?

Distinguishing earlier Fifth Circuit cases that had dismissed § 1983 claims under *Heck* when the § 1983 plaintiff had been convicted of aggravated assault, a crime that "required proof that the § 1983 plaintiff had caused serious bodily injury," the court held:

> Those decisions turned on the fact that, because serious bodily injury to the defendant was an element of the § 1983 plaintiff's conviction, it was impossible for the [§ 1983] defendant to have used excessive force because the statute authorized use of deadly force to Defend Against the bodily injury that the § 1983 plaintiff had inflicted upon him.

> By contrast Ballard's conviction was for assault, by physical menace, on an officer who is not a defendant in his § 1983 claim. Ballard's conviction did not require proof that he caused bodily injury, serious or otherwise. Not a single element of Ballard's simple assault conviction would be undermined if Ballard were to prevail in his excessive force claim against Burton.

Turning to the merits of the § 1983 claim, the court held that Burton did not use excessive force.

CONCLUDING NOTE

According to the majority opinion in *Allen v. McCurry*, the Court of Appeals erred in apparently assuming that there existed "a generally framed principle that every person asserting a federal right is entitled to one unencumbered opportunity to litigate that right in a federal district court, regardless of the legal posture in which the federal claim arises." To the *Allen* Court, "the authority for this principle is difficult to discern. It cannot lie in the Constitution, which makes no such guarantee, but leaves the scope of the jurisdiction of the federal district courts to the wisdom of Congress."

Consider, however, the cumulative effects of the cases and doctrines discussed in this chapter in combination with the Court's rules on justiciability and habeas corpus. A federal litigant challenging the constitutionality of state action will first have her case dismissed if she is unable to establish a threat of injury necessary to establish standing. If she brings her claim after the state has begun prosecution against her, her action will be dismissed under *Younger* or *Huffman* (if the state action against her is civil). If she waits until after the state proceeding has ended, she will face potential dismissal based upon *res judicata*. If she then attempts to bring a habeas action, she will face dismissal because of *Stone v. Powell* (if it's a Fourth Amendment claim) or because of a number of other habeas defenses (see Chapter 9) or she will have no collateral recourse available to her at all if the initial state proceeding against her was civil. Does such a system afford a litigant sufficient access to the federal courts to litigate her federal claims? Does it accord with the purposes of § 1983 as interpreted in cases such as *Monroe*, *Mitchum*, and *Patsy*?

CHAPTER 7

FEDERAL LAW IN THE STATE COURTS

■ ■ ■

This chapter examines the relations between the state courts and federal law. These materials focus on litigation brought in state court in order to obtain relief on a federal cause of action. Part I addresses the authority of state courts to adjudicate federal causes of action, while Part II considers the narrower issue of whether state courts may grant relief against federal officers. Part III takes up the power of state courts to decline to hear federal causes of action. Part IV discusses the extent to which state courts may apply state law in adjudicating federal causes of action.

Do not be misled by the emphasis we place on state court adjudication of federal causes of action. Raising a federal *defense* is by far the more important avenue by which federal law is litigated in state court. State courts routinely adjudicate federal defenses, mainly when a litigant raises a federal law objection to the application of state law. In criminal cases, for example, the defendant may raise defenses based on the Fourth, Fifth, Sixth, Eighth and Fourteenth Amendments. Similarly, a state tort suit for libel may turn on the defendant's First Amendment challenge to the application of state defamation law. But the practical importance of federal defenses in state court is not accompanied by a complex doctrine. Few jurisdictional issues arise with regard to raising federal defenses in state court. By contrast, the litigation of federal causes of action in state court raises a number of jurisdictional issues.

In No. 82 of *The Federalist* Alexander Hamilton discussed the role of state courts in adjudicating federal questions. His framework is relevant to many of the issues discussed here, and has significantly influenced Supreme Court decisions:

> I hold that state courts will be divested of no part of their primitive jurisdiction further than may relate to an appeal; and I am even of opinion that in every case in which they were not expressly excluded by the future acts of the national legislature, they will of course take cognizance of the causes to which those acts may give birth. This I infer from the nature of judiciary power, and from the general genius of the system. The judiciary power of every government looks beyond its own local or municipal laws, and in civil cases lays hold of all subjects of litigation between parties within its jurisdiction, though the

577

causes of dispute are relative to the laws of the most distant part of the globe. Those of Japan, not less of New York, may furnish the objects of legal discussion to our courts. When in addition to this we consider the State governments and the national governments, as they truly are, in the light of kindred systems, and as parts of ONE WHOLE, the inference seems to be conclusive that the State courts would have a concurrent jurisdiction in all cases arising under the laws of the Union where it was not expressly prohibited.

I.   STATE COURT AUTHORITY TO ADJUDICATE FEDERAL CAUSES OF ACTION

A.   EXCLUSIVE FEDERAL JURISDICTION

TAFFLIN V. LEVITT
493 U.S. 455 (1990).

JUSTICE O'CONNOR delivered the opinion of the Court.

This case requires us to decide whether state courts have concurrent jurisdiction over civil actions brought under the Racketeer Influenced and Corrupt Organizations Act (RICO).

I

The underlying litigation arises from the failure of Old Court Savings & Loan, Inc. (Old Court), a Maryland savings and loan association, and the attendant collapse of the Maryland Savings-Share Insurance Corp. (MSSIC), a state-chartered nonprofit corporation created to insure accounts in Maryland savings and loan associations that were not federally insured. Petitioners are nonresidents of Maryland who hold unpaid certificates of deposit issued by Old Court. Respondents are the former officers and directors of Old Court, the former officers and directors of MSSIC, the law firm of Old Court and MSSIC, the accounting firm of Old Court, and the State of Maryland Deposit Insurance Fund Corp., the state-created successor to MSSIC. Petitioners allege various state law causes of action as well as claims under the Securities Exchange Act of 1934 (Exchange Act) and RICO.

The District Court granted respondents' motions to dismiss, concluding that petitioners had failed to state a claim under the Exchange Act and that, because state courts have concurrent jurisdiction over civil RICO claims, federal abstention was appropriate for the other causes of action because they had been raised in pending litigation in state court. The Court of Appeals for the Fourth Circuit affirmed. The Court of Appeals agreed with the District Court that the Old Court certificates of deposit were not "securities" within the meaning of the Exchange Act, and that petitioners' Exchange Act claims were therefore properly dismissed. The Court of Appeals further held [that] "a RICO action could be instituted in a state court and that Maryland's 'comprehensive scheme for the rehabilitation and liquidation of insolvent state-chartered savings and loan associations,' provided a proper basis for the district court to abstain under the authority of *Burford v. Sun Oil Co.*"

To resolve a conflict among the federal appellate courts and state supreme courts, we granted certiorari limited to the question whether state courts have concurrent jurisdiction over civil RICO claims. We hold that they do and accordingly affirm the judgment of the Court of Appeals.

II

We begin with the axiom that, under our federal system, the States possess sovereignty concurrent with that of the Federal Government, subject only to limitations imposed by the Supremacy Clause. Under this system of dual sovereignty, we have consistently held that state courts have inherent authority, and are thus presumptively competent, to adjudicate claims arising under the laws of the United States. See, e.g., *Claflin v. Houseman*, 93 U.S. 130, 136–137 (1876); *Charles Dowd Box Co. v. Courtney*, 368 U.S. 502, 507–08 (1962); *Gulf Offshore Co. v. Mobil Oil Corp.*, 453 U.S. 473, 477–478 (1981). As we noted in *Claflin*, "if exclusive jurisdiction be neither express nor implied, the State courts have concurrent jurisdiction whenever, by their own constitution, they are competent to take it." 93 U.S. at 136; see also *Dowd Box*, supra, 368 U.S. at 507–508 ("We start with the premise that nothing in the concept of our federal system prevents state courts from enforcing rights created by federal law. Concurrent jurisdiction has been a common phenomenon in our judicial history, and exclusive federal court jurisdiction over cases arising under federal law has been the exception rather than the rule"). See generally 1 J. Kent, Commentaries on American Law *400; The Federalist No. 82 (A. Hamilton); F. Frankfurter & J. Landis, The Business of the Supreme Court 5–12 (1927); H. Friendly, Federal Jurisdiction: A General View 8–11 (1973). This deeply rooted presumption in favor of concurrent state court jurisdiction is, of course, rebutted if Congress affirmatively ousts the state courts of jurisdiction over a particular federal claim. See, e.g., *Claflin*, supra, 93 U.S. at 137 ("Congress may, if it see[s] fit, give to the Federal courts exclusive jurisdiction"). As we stated in *Gulf Offshore*:

> In considering the propriety of state-court jurisdiction over any particular federal claim, the Court begins with the presumption that state courts enjoy concurrent jurisdiction. Congress, however, may confine jurisdiction to the federal courts either explicitly or implicitly. Thus, the presumption of concurrent jurisdiction can be rebutted by an explicit statutory directive, by unmistakable implication from legislative history, or by a clear incompatibility between state-court jurisdiction and federal interests.

[These] principles, which have "remained unmodified through the years," *Dowd Box*, supra, 368 U.S. at 508, provide the analytical framework for resolving this case.

III

The precise question presented, therefore, is whether state courts have been divested of jurisdiction to hear civil RICO claims "by an explicit statutory directive, by unmistakable implication from legislative history, or by a clear incompatibility between state-court jurisdiction and federal interests." *Gulf Offshore*, supra, 453 U.S. at 478. Because we find none of these factors present with respect to civil claims arising under RICO, we hold that state courts retain their presumptive authority to adjudicate such claims.

At the outset, petitioners concede that there is nothing in the language of RICO—much less an "explicit statutory directive"—to suggest that Congress has, by affirmative enactment, divested the state courts of jurisdiction to hear civil RICO claims. The statutory provision authorizing civil RICO claims provides in full:

> Any person injured in his business or property by reason of a violation of section 1962 of this chapter *may* sue therefor in any appropriate United States district court and shall recover threefold the damages he sustains and the cost of the suit, including a reasonable attorney's fee. 18 U.S.C. § 1964(c) (emphasis added).

This grant of federal jurisdiction is plainly permissive, not mandatory, for "[t]he statute does not state nor even suggest that such jurisdiction shall be exclusive. It provides that suits of the kind described 'may' be brought in the federal district courts, not that they must be." *Dowd Box*, supra, 368 U.S., at 506. Indeed, "[i]t is black letter law . . . that the mere grant of jurisdiction to a federal court does not operate to oust a state court from concurrent jurisdiction over the cause of action." *Gulf Offshore*, supra, 453 U.S., at 479.

Petitioners thus rely solely on the second and third factors suggested in *Gulf Offshore*, arguing that exclusive federal jurisdiction over civil RICO actions is established "by unmistakable implication from legislative history, or by a clear incompatibility between state-court jurisdiction and federal interests," 453 U.S., at 478.

Our review of the legislative history, however, reveals no evidence that Congress even considered the question of concurrent state court jurisdiction over RICO claims, much less any suggestion that Congress affirmatively intended to confer exclusive jurisdiction over such claims on the federal [courts]. Petitioners nonetheless insist that if Congress had considered the issue, it would have granted federal courts exclusive jurisdiction over civil RICO claims. This argument, however, is misplaced, for even if we could reliably discern what Congress' intent might have been had it considered the question, we are not at liberty to so speculate; the fact that Congress did not even consider the issue readily disposes of any argument that Congress unmistakably intended to divest state courts of concurrent jurisdiction.

Sensing this void in the legislative history, petitioners rely, in the alternative, on our decisions in *Sedima, S.P.R.L. v. Imrex Co.*, 473 U.S. 479 (1985), and *Agency Holding Corp. v. Malley-Duff & Assocs.*, 483 U.S. 143 (1987), in which we noted that Congress modeled § 1964(c) after § 4 of the Clayton Act. Petitioners assert that, because we have interpreted § 4 of the Clayton Act to confer exclusive jurisdiction on the federal courts, see, e.g., *General Investment Co. v. Lake Shore & M.S.R. Co.*, 260 U.S. 261, 286–288 (1922), and because Congress may be presumed to have been aware of and incorporated those interpretations when it used similar language in RICO, cf. *Cannon v. University of Chicago*, 441 U.S. 677, 694–699 (1979), Congress intended, by implication, to grant exclusive federal jurisdiction over claims arising under § 1964(c).

This argument is also flawed. To rebut the presumption of concurrent jurisdiction, the question is not whether any intent at all may be divined from legislative silence on the issue, but whether Congress in its deliberations may be said to have affirmatively or unmistakably intended jurisdiction to be exclusively federal. In the instant case, the lack of any indication in RICO's legislative history that Congress either considered or assumed that the importing of remedial language from the Clayton Act into RICO had any jurisdictional implications is dispositive. The mere borrowing of statutory language does not imply that Congress also intended to incorporate all of the baggage that may be attached to the borrowed language. Indeed, to the extent we impute to Congress knowledge of our Clayton Act precedents, it makes no less sense to impute to Congress knowledge of *Claflin* and *Dowd Box*, under which Congress, had it sought to confer exclusive jurisdiction over civil RICO claims, would have had every incentive to do so [expressly].

Petitioners finally urge that state court jurisdiction over civil RICO claims would be clearly incompatible with federal interests. We noted in *Gulf Offshore* that factors indicating clear incompatibility "include the desirability of uniform interpretation, the expertise of federal judges in federal law, and the assumed greater hospitality of federal courts to peculiarly federal claims." 453 U.S., at 483–484. Petitioners' primary contention is that concurrent jurisdiction is clearly incompatible with the federal interest in uniform interpretation of federal criminal laws, see 18 U.S.C. § 3231,[2] because state courts would be required to construe the federal crimes that constitute predicate acts defined as "racketeering

---

[2] Title 18 U.S.C. § 3231 provides in full: The district courts of the United States shall have original jurisdiction, exclusive of the courts of the States, of all offenses against the laws of the United States. Nothing in this title shall be held to take away or impair the jurisdiction of the courts of the several States under the laws thereof.

activity," see 18 U.S.C. §§ 1961(1)(B), (C), and (D). Petitioners predict that if state courts are permitted to interpret federal criminal statutes, they will create a body of precedent relating to those statutes and that the federal courts will consequently lose control over the orderly and uniform development of federal criminal law.

We perceive no "clear incompatibility" between state court jurisdiction over civil RICO actions and federal interests. As a preliminary matter, concurrent jurisdiction over § 1964(c) suits is clearly not incompatible with § 3231 itself, for civil RICO claims are not "offenses against the laws of the United States," § 3231, and do not result in the imposition of criminal sanctions—uniform or otherwise. More to the point, however, our decision today creates no significant danger of inconsistent application of federal criminal law. Although petitioners' concern with the need for uniformity and consistency of federal criminal law is well taken, federal courts, pursuant to § 3231, would retain full authority and responsibility for the interpretation and application of federal criminal law, for they would not be bound by state court interpretations of the federal offenses constituting RICO's predicate acts. State courts adjudicating civil RICO claims will, in addition, be guided by federal court interpretations of the relevant federal criminal statutes, just as federal courts sitting in diversity are guided by state court interpretations of state law. State court judgments misinterpreting federal criminal law would, of course, also be subject to direct review by this [Court].

Moreover, contrary to petitioners' fears, we have full faith in the ability of state courts to handle the complexities of civil RICO actions, particularly since many RICO cases involve asserted violations of state law, such as state fraud claims, over which state courts presumably have greater [expertise].

Petitioners further note, as evidence of incompatibility, that RICO's procedural mechanisms include extended venue and service-of-process provisions that are applicable only in federal court, see 18 U.S.C. § 1965. We think it sufficient, however, to observe that we have previously found concurrent state court jurisdiction even where federal law provided for special procedural mechanisms similar to those found in RICO. See, e.g., *Dowd Box*, supra (finding concurrent jurisdiction over Labor Management Relations Act § 301(a) suits, despite federal enforcement and venue provisions); *Maine v. Thiboutot*, 448 U.S. 1, 3, n. 1 (1980) (finding concurrent jurisdiction over 42 U.S.C. § 1983 suits, despite federal procedural provisions in § 1988); cf. *Hathorn v. Lovorn*, 457 U.S. 255, 269 (1982) (finding concurrent jurisdiction over disputes regarding the applicability of § 5 of the Voting Rights Act of 1965, despite provision for a three-judge panel). Although congressional specification of procedural mechanisms applicable only in federal court may tend to suggest that Congress intended exclusive federal jurisdiction, it does not by itself suffice to create a "clear incompatibility" with federal interests.

Finally, we note that, far from disabling or frustrating federal interests, "[p]ermitting state courts to entertain federal causes of action facilitates the enforcement of federal rights." *Gulf Offshore*, 453 U.S., at 478, n. 4. Thus, to the extent that Congress intended RICO to serve broad remedial [purposes], concurrent state court jurisdiction over civil RICO claims will advance rather than jeopardize federal policies underlying the statute.

For all of the above reasons, we hold that state courts have concurrent jurisdiction to consider civil claims arising under RICO. Nothing in the language, structure, legislative history, or underlying policies of RICO suggests that Congress intended otherwise. The judgment of the Court of Appeals is accordingly

Affirmed.

JUSTICE WHITE, concurring.

[RICO] is an unusual federal criminal statute. It borrows heavily from state law; racketeering activity is defined in terms of numerous offenses chargeable under state law, as well as various federal offenses. To the extent that there is any danger under RICO of nonuniform construction of criminal statutes, it is quite likely that the damage will result from federal misunderstanding of the content of state law—a problem, to be sure, but not one to be solved by exclusive federal jurisdiction. Many of the federal offenses named as racketeering activity under RICO have close, though perhaps not exact, state-law analogues, . . . and it is unlikely that the state courts will be incompetent to construe those federal statutes. Nor does incorrect state-court construction of those statutes present as significant a threat to federal interests as that posed by improper interpretation of the federal antitrust laws, which could have a disastrous effect on interstate commerce, a particular concern of the Federal Government.

Racketeering activity as defined by RICO includes other federal offenses without state-law analogues, but given the history as written until now of civil RICO litigation, I doubt that state-court construction of these offenses will be greatly disruptive of important federal [interests].

JUSTICE SCALIA, with whom JUSTICE KENNEDY joins, concurring.

I join the opinion of the Court, addressing the issues before us on the basis argued by the parties, which has included acceptance of the dictum in *Gulf Offshore Co. v. Mobil Oil Corp.*, 453 U.S. 473, 478 (1981), that " 'the presumption of concurrent jurisdiction can be rebutted by an explicit statutory directive, by unmistakable implication from legislative history, or by a clear incompatibility between state-court jurisdiction and federal interests.' " Such dicta, when repeatedly used as the point of departure for analysis, have a regrettable tendency to acquire the practical status of legal rules. I write separately, before this one has become too entrenched, to note my view that in one respect it is not a correct statement of the law, and in another respect it may not be. State courts have jurisdiction over federal causes of action not because it is "conferred" upon them by the Congress; nor even because their inherent powers permit them to entertain transitory causes of action arising under the laws of foreign sovereigns, but because "[t]he laws of the United States are laws in the several States, and just as much binding on the citizens and courts thereof as the State laws are. . . . The two together form one system of jurisprudence, which constitutes the law of the land for the State; and the courts of the two jurisdictions are not foreign to each other. . . ." *Claflin v. Houseman*, 93 U.S. 130, 136–137 (1876).

It therefore takes an affirmative act of power under the Supremacy Clause to oust the States of jurisdiction—an exercise of what one of our earliest cases referred to as "the power of congress to *withdraw*" federal claims from state-court jurisdiction. *Houston v. Moore*, 5 Wheat. 1, 26 (1820) (emphasis added). As an original proposition, it would be eminently arguable that depriving state courts of their sovereign authority to adjudicate the law of the land must be done, if not with the utmost clarity, cf. *Atascadero State Hospital v. Scanlon*, 473 U.S. 234, 243 (1985) (state sovereign immunity can be eliminated only by "clear statement"), at least expressly. That was the view of Alexander Hamilton:

> When . . . we consider the State governments and the national governments, as they truly are, in the light of kindred systems, and as parts of ONE WHOLE, the inference seems to be conclusive that the State courts would have a concurrent jurisdiction in all cases arising under the laws of the Union, where it was not expressly prohibited. The Federalist No. 82, p. 132 (E. Bourne ed. 1947).

[Although] as early as *Claflin*, see 93 U.S., at 137, and as late as *Gulf Offshore*, we have said that the exclusion of concurrent state jurisdiction could be achieved by implication, the only cases in which to my knowledge we have acted upon such a principle are those relating to the Sherman Act and the Clayton Act—where the full extent of our analysis was the less than compelling statement that provisions giving the right to sue in United States District Court "show that [the right] is to be exercised *only* in a 'court of the United States.'" *General Investment Co. v. Lake Shore & Michigan Southern R. Co.*, 260 U.S. 261, 287 (1922) (emphasis added). In the standard fields of exclusive federal jurisdiction, the governing statutes specifically recite that suit may be brought "only" in federal court, Investment Company Act of 1940, 15 U.S.C. § 80a–35(b)(5); that the jurisdiction of the federal courts shall be "exclusive," Securities Exchange Act of 1934, 15 U.S.C. § 78aa; Natural Gas Act of 1938, 15 U.S.C. § 717u; Employee Retirement Income Security Act of 1974, 29 U.S.C. § 1132(e)(1); or indeed even that the jurisdiction of the federal courts shall be "exclusive of the courts of the States," 18 U.S.C. § 3231 (criminal cases); 28 U.S.C. §§ 1333 (admiralty, maritime, and prize cases),

1334 (bankruptcy cases), 1338 (patent, plant variety protection, and copyright cases), 1351 (actions against consuls or vice consuls of foreign states), 1355 (actions for recovery or enforcement of fine, penalty, or forfeiture incurred under Act of Congress), 1356 (seizures on land or water not within admiralty and maritime jurisdiction).

Assuming, however, that exclusion by implication is possible, surely what is required is implication in the text of the statute, and not merely, as the second part of the *Gulf Offshore* dictum would permit, through "unmistakable implication from legislative history." 453 U.S., at 478. Although *Charles Dowd Box Co. v. Courtney*, 368 U.S. 502 (1962), after concluding that the statute "does not state nor even suggest that [federal] jurisdiction shall be exclusive," id., at 506, proceeded quite unnecessarily to examine the legislative history, it did so to reinforce rather than contradict the conclusion it had already reached. We have never found state jurisdiction excluded by "unmistakable implication" from legislative history. [It] is simply wrong in principle to assert that Congress can effect this affirmative legislative act by simply talking about it with unmistakable clarity. What is needed to oust the States of jurisdiction is congressional *action* (i.e., a provision of law), not merely congressional discussion.

It is perhaps also true that implied preclusion can be established by the fact that a statute expressly mentions only federal courts, plus the fact that state-court jurisdiction would plainly disrupt the statutory scheme. That is conceivably what was meant by the third part of the *Gulf Offshore* dictum, "clear incompatibility between state-court jurisdiction and federal interests." 453 U.S., at 478. If the phrase is interpreted more broadly than that, however—if it is taken to assert some power on the part of this Court to exclude state-court jurisdiction when systemic federal interests make it undesirable—it has absolutely no foundation in our [precedent].

In sum: As the Court holds, the RICO cause of action meets none of the three tests for exclusion of state-court jurisdiction recited in *Gulf Offshore*. Since that is so, the proposition that meeting any one of the tests would have sufficed is dictum here, as it was there. In my view meeting the second test is assuredly not enough, and meeting the third may not be.

NOTES ON EXCLUSIVE FEDERAL JURISDICTION

1. Relating "Exclusive Federal Jurisdiction" to Other Issues. The question of whether federal jurisdiction is exclusive may arise when a plaintiff seeks to litigate in state court and the defendant objects. *Tafflin* illustrates that the issue may arise in other contexts as well. This case was litigated in federal court from the beginning. Why, then, did the question of exclusive federal jurisdiction over RICO claims arise at all? Note the link between that issue and the *Burford* abstention issue. Was the district court correct in choosing to abstain? *Burford* is discussed in Chapter 6. Another example is *Yellow Freight System v. Donnelly*, 494 U.S. 820 (1990). The plaintiff commenced the litigation, a Title VII case, in state court, but then failed to meet a statutory deadline for exhausting administrative remedies. The plaintiff then refiled the case in federal court and the defendant sought to dismiss based on the failure to meet the deadline. The plaintiff argued that the failure made no difference, because federal jurisdiction was exclusive and the state proceedings were irrelevant. See the following note for the Court's treatment of the "exclusive federal jurisdiction" issue.

2.   Justice Scalia Triumphant? Shortly after *Tafflin*, the Court ruled unanimously in *Yellow Freight System v. Donnelly*, supra, that state courts have concurrent jurisdiction over civil actions brought under Title VII of the Civil Rights Act of 1964. Justice Stevens's opinion for the Court reasoned, 494 U.S. at 823, that:

> Title VII contains no language that expressly confines jurisdiction to federal courts or ousts state courts of their presumptive jurisdiction. The omission of any such provision is strong, and arguably sufficient, evidence that Congress had no such intent.

As for legislative history, "passages in the legislative history indicating that many participants in the complex process that finally produced the law fully expected that all Title VII cases would be tried in federal court" were to no avail. "[T]he legislative history of the Act affirmatively describes the jurisdiction of the federal courts, but is completely silent on any role of the state courts over Title VII claims." *Id.* at 824–25. The Court also dismissed an argument based on the statute's reference to procedures available in the federal court, noting that it had "rejected a similar argument based on statutory references to procedures applicable to federal courts in *Tafflin*." *Id.* at 826.

The starting point for resolving the "exclusive federal jurisdiction" issue in connection with any particular statute is that the decision is for Congress to make. *Tafflin* and *Yellow Freight* seem to rest on the premise that, in determining whether Congress has made federal jurisdiction exclusive, the Court should require especially strong evidence of congressional intent. Note that in *Tafflin* Justice Scalia cites an Eleventh Amendment case, *Atascadero State Hospital v. Scanlon*, in this regard. Given that there are grounds for requiring explicit evidence of Congress's intent to abrogate state sovereign immunity, is Justice Scalia on solid ground in drawing an analogy between that context and exclusive federal jurisdiction?

Does *Yellow Freight* in effect abandon the three-part *Gulf Shore* test and adopt the position staked out by Justice Scalia in *Tafflin*? For an affirmative answer to that question, see Michael Solimine, *Rethinking Exclusive Federal Jurisdiction*, 52 U. PITT. L. REV. 383 (1991). On the other hand, keep in mind that in earlier cases, e.g., those finding exclusive federal jurisdiction over antitrust cases, the Court was far more willing to rely on other factors besides the text of the statute. Is this an area in which, for the sake of predictability, stability, and fairness, it is important for the Court to remain faithful to one approach?

3. Federal Defenses. Suppose that *A* contracts to sell widgets to *B* at a certain price. *A* performs and *B* refuses to pay the bill. *A* sues in state court for breach of contract; *B* seeks to defend on the ground that *A* conspired with other sellers to fix prices in violation of the federal antitrust laws. *A* argues that, on account of exclusive federal jurisdiction over antitrust claims, the state court may not hear this defense. Who wins? The blackletter rule is that the court may adjudicate *B*'s antitrust issue. The Court holds that exclusive federal jurisdiction does not preclude state courts from hearing federal defenses. See Solimine, supra, at 426. Would the contrary view violate the defendant's right to due process of law?

What result if, in response to *A*'s breach of contract suit, *B* sought to bring a *counterclaim*, seeking damages for *A*'s violation of the antitrust laws? See *Holmes Group, Inc. v. Vornado Air Circulation Systems,* 535 U.S. 826 (2002), discussed in Chapter 3, Section I C.

B. REMOVAL

Concurrent state court jurisdiction *permits* state courts to adjudicate federal causes of action, but it does not oblige litigants to remain in state court. Even if the plaintiff prefers state court, the defendant may remove the case to federal court under 28 U.S.C. § 1441(a):

> Except as otherwise expressly provided by Act of Congress, any civil action brought in a State court of which the district courts of the United States have original jurisdiction, may be removed by the defendant or the defendants, to the [United States] district [court].

Recall the doctrine governing the jurisdiction of the lower federal courts (and in particular the "well-pleaded complaint rule") which is described in Chapter 3. Given the limits on federal question jurisdiction resulting from the Court's construction of 28 U.S.C. § 1331 and other "arising under" statutes, the practical import of § 1441 is that a case can be removed if the *plaintiff* could have proceeded in federal court originally, but not on the basis of a federal *defense*.

Another statute, 28 U.S.C. § 1442, authorizes federal officers and certain other persons to remove in a broader range of circumstances:

> A civil action or criminal prosecution commenced in a State court against any officer (or any person acting under that officer) of the United [States], sued in an official or individual capacity for any act under color of such office [may be removed by the defendant to United States District Court].

The following two cases address the scope of this statute.

1.   Suits Against Federal Officers

MESA V. CALIFORNIA

489 U.S. 121 (1989).

JUSTICE O'CONNOR delivered the opinion of the Court.

We decide today whether United States Postal Service employees may, pursuant to 28 U.S.C. § 1442(a)(1), remove to Federal District Court state criminal prosecutions brought against them for traffic violations committed while on duty.

I

In the summer of 1985 petitioners Kathryn Mesa and Shabbir Ebrahim were employed as mailtruck drivers by the United States Postal Service in Santa Clara County, California. In unrelated incidents, the State of California issued criminal complaints against petitioners, charging Mesa with misdemeanor-manslaughter and driving outside a laned roadway after her mail truck collided with and killed a bicyclist, and charging Ebrahim with speeding and failure to yield after his mailtruck collided with a police car. Mesa and Ebrahim were arraigned in the San Jose Municipal Court of Santa Clara County on September 16 and October 2, 1985, respectively. The Municipal Court set a pretrial conference in Mesa's case for November 4, 1985, and set trial for Ebrahim on November 7, 1985.

On September 24 and October 4, 1985, the United States Attorney for the Northern District of California filed petitions in the United States District Court for the Northern District of California for removal to that court of the criminal complaints brought against Ebrahim and Mesa. The petitions alleged that the complaints should properly be removed to the Federal District Court pursuant to 28 U.S.C. § 1442(a)(1) because Mesa and Ebrahim were federal employees at the time of the incidents and because "the state charges arose from an accident involving defendant which occurred while defendant was on duty and acting in the course and scope of her employment with the Postal Service." The District Court granted the United States Government's petitions for removal and denied California's motions for remand. [The 9th Circuit reversed.] We now affirm.

II

[The] United States and California agree that Mesa and Ebrahim, in their capacity as employees of the United States Postal Service, were "person[s] acting under" an "officer of the United States or any agency thereof" within the meaning of § 1442(a)(1). Their disagreement concerns whether the California criminal prosecutions brought against Mesa and Ebrahim were "for act[s] under color of such office" within the meaning of that subsection. The United States, largely adopting the view taken by the Court of Appeals for the Third Circuit in *Pennsylvania v. Newcomer*, 618 F.2d 246 (1980), would read "under color of office" to permit removal "whenever a federal official is prosecuted for the manner in which he has performed his federal duties. . . ." California, following the Court of Appeals below, would have us read the same phrase to impose a requirement that some federal defense be alleged by the federal officer seeking removal.

On numerous occasions in the last 121 years we have had the opportunity to examine § 1442(a) or one of its long line of statutory forebears. In *Willingham v. Morgan*, 395 U.S. 402, 405 (1969), we traced the "long history" of the federal officer removal statute from its origin in the Act of February 4, 1815 as a congressional response to New England's opposition to the War of 1812, through its expansion in response to South Carolina's 1833 threats of nullification, and its further expansion in the Civil War era as the need to enforce revenue laws became acute, to enactment of the Judicial Code of 1948 when the removal statute took its present form encompassing all federal officers. "The purpose of all these enactments," we concluded, "is not hard to discern. [The] Federal Government 'can act only through its officers and agents, and they must act within the States. If, when thus acting, and within the scope of their authority, those officers can be arrested and brought to trial in a State court, for an alleged offense against the law of the State, yet warranted by the Federal authority they possess, and if the general government is powerless to interfere at once for their protection,—if their protection must be left to the action of the State court,—the operations of the general government may at any time be arrested at the will of one of its members.' " *Id*. 395 U.S. at 406.

Tennessee v. Davis, 100 U.S. 257 (1880), involved a state murder prosecution brought against a revenue collector who claimed that, while he was in the act of seizing an illegal distillery under the authority of the federal revenue laws, "he was assaulted and fired upon by a number of armed men, and that in defence of his life he returned the fire," killing one of the assailants. Davis sought to remove the prosecution to federal court and Tennessee challenged the constitutionality of the removal statute. Justice Strong framed the question presented thus:

> Has the Constitution conferred upon Congress the power to authorize the removal, from a State court to a Federal court, of an indictment against a revenue officer for an alleged crime against the State, and to order its removal before trial, *when it appears that a Federal question or a claim to a Federal right is raised in the case, and must be decided therein*? 100 U.S., at 262 (emphasis added).

Justice Strong's emphasis on the presence of a federal defense unifies the entire opinion. He thought it impossible that the Constitution should so weaken the Federal Government as to prevent it from protecting itself against unfriendly state legislation which "may affix penalties to acts done under the immediate direction of the national government, and in obedience to its laws [or] may deny the authority conferred by those laws." *Id.*, at 263.

[The] successful legal defense of "self-defense" depends on the truth of two distinct elements: that the act committed was, in a legal sense, an act of self-defense, and that the act was justified, that is, warranted under the circumstances. In Davis' case, the truth of the first element depended on a question of federal law: was it Davis' duty under federal law to seize the distillery? If Davis had merely been a thief attempting to steal his assailants' property, returning their fire would simply not have been an act of self-defense, pretermitting any question of justification. Proof that Davis was not a thief depended on the federal revenue laws and provided the necessary predicate for removal. Accordingly, as Justice Strong's conclusion in *Davis* makes clear, we upheld the constitutionality of the federal officer removal statute precisely because the statute predicated removal on the presence of a federal defense: "It ought, therefore, to be considered as settled that the constitutional powers of Congress to authorize the removal of criminal cases for alleged offences against State laws from State courts to the circuit courts of the United States, *when there arises a Federal question in them*, is as ample as its power to authorize the removal of a civil case." 100 U.S., at 271 (emphasis added).

[The Court then discussed other precedents. In particular, it distinguished *Maryland v. Soper*, 270 U.S. 9 (1926), a state murder prosecution brought against federal alcohol agents during the prohibition era. There the Court had "suggested that careful pleading, demonstrating the close connection between the state prosecution and the federal officer's performance of his duty, might adequately replace the specific averment of a federal defense. We are not today presented with such a pleading."]

In sum, an unbroken line of this Court's decisions extending back nearly a century and a quarter have understood all the various incarnations of the federal officer removal statute to require the averment of a federal defense.

[In the remainder of the opinion the Court rejected an argument advanced by the Government that the text of the statute allows removal here. The Court observed that "[t]he Government's view, which would eliminate the federal defense requirement, raises serious doubt whether, in enacting § 1442(a), Congress would not have expanded the jurisdiction of the federal courts beyond the bounds established by the Constitution." For discussion of this aspect of the case, see Chapter 10.]

JUSTICE BRENNAN, with whom JUSTICE MARSHALL joins, concurring.

While I concur in the judgment and opinion of the Court, I write separately to emphasize a point that might otherwise be overlooked. In most routine traffic-accident cases like those presented here, no significant federal interest is served by removal; it is, accordingly, difficult to believe that Congress would have intended the statute to reach so far. It is not at all inconceivable, however, that Congress' concern about local hostility to federal authority could come into play in some circumstances where the federal officer is unable to present any "federal defense." The days of widespread resistance by state and local governmental authorities to Acts of Congress and to decisions of this Court in the areas of school desegregation and voting rights are not so distant that we should be oblivious to the possibility of harassment of federal agents by local law enforcement authorities. Such harassment could well take the form of unjustified prosecution for traffic or other offenses, to which the federal officer would have no immunity or other federal defense. The removal statute, it would seem to me, might well have been intended to apply in such unfortunate and exceptional circumstances.

The Court today rightly refrains from deciding whether removal in such a situation is possible, since that is not the case before us. But the Court leaves open the possibility that where a federal officer is prosecuted because of local hostility to his function, "careful pleading, demonstrating the close connection between the state prosecution and the federal officer's performance of his duty, might adequately replace the specific averment of a federal defense." With the understanding that today's decision does not foreclose the possibility of removal in such circumstances even in the absence of a federal defense, I join the Court's opinion.

2. Suits Against "Any Person Acting Under That Officer"

WATSON V. PHILIP MORRIS
551 U.S. 142 (2007).

JUSTICE BREYER delivered the opinion of the Court.

The federal officer removal statute permits a defendant to remove to federal court a state-court action brought against the

"United States or any agency thereof or any officer (*or any person acting under that officer*) of the United States or of any agency thereof, sued in an official or individual capacity for any act under color of such office. . . ." 28 U.S.C. § 1442(a)(1) (emphasis added).

The question before us is whether the fact that a federal regulatory agency directs, supervises, and monitors a company's activities in considerable detail brings that company within the scope of the italicized language ("*acting under*" an "*officer*" of the United States) and thereby permits removal. We hold that it does not.

I

Lisa Watson and Loretta Lawson, the petitioners, filed a civil lawsuit in Arkansas state court claiming that the Philip Morris Companies, the respondents, violated state laws prohibiting unfair and deceptive business practices. The complaint focuses upon advertisements and packaging that describe certain Philip Morris brand cigarettes (Marlboro and Cambridge Lights) as "light," a term indicating lower tar and nicotine levels than those present in other cigarettes. More specifically, the complaint refers to the design and performance of Philip Morris cigarettes that are tested in accordance with the Cambridge Filter Method, a method that "the tobacco industry [uses] to 'measure' tar and nicotine levels in cigarettes." The complaint charges that Philip Morris "manipulat[ed] the design" of its cigarettes, and "employ[ed] techniques that" would cause its cigarettes "to register lower levels of tar and nicotine on [the Cambridge Filter Method] than would be delivered to the consumers of the product." The complaint adds that the Philip Morris cigarettes delivered "greater amounts of tar and nicotine when smoked under actual conditions" than the adjective "light" as used in its advertising indicates. In view of these and other related practices, the complaint concludes that Philip Morris' behavior was "deceptive and misleading" under Arkansas law.

Philip Morris, referring to the federal officer removal statute, removed the case to Federal District Court. That court, in turn, held that the statute authorized the removal. The court wrote that the complaint attacked Philip Morris' use of the *Government's* method of testing cigarettes. For this reason (and others), it held that the petitioners had sued Philip Morris for "act[s]" taken "under" the Federal Trade Commission, a federal agency (staffed by federal "officer[s]").

The District Court certified the question for interlocutory review. And the United States Court of Appeals for the Eighth Circuit affirmed. Like the District Court, it emphasized the FTC's detailed supervision of the cigarette testing process. It also cited lower court cases permitting removal by heavily supervised Government contractors. The Eighth Circuit concluded that Philip Morris was "acting under" federal "officer[s]," namely the FTC, with respect to the challenged conduct.

We granted certiorari. And we now reverse the Eighth Circuit's determination.

II

The federal statute permits removal only if Philip Morris, in carrying out the "act[s]" that are the subject of the petitioners' complaint, was "acting under" any "agency" or "officer" of "the United States." 28 U.S.C. § 1442(a)(1). The words "acting under" are broad, and this Court has made clear that the statute must be "liberally construed." *Colorado v. Symes*, 286 U.S. 510, 517 (1932); see *Arizona v. Manypenny*, 451 U.S. 232, 242 (1981); *Willingham v. Morgan*, 395 U.S. 402, 406–407 (1969). But broad language is not limitless. And a liberal construction nonetheless can find limits in a text's language, context, history, and purposes.

Beginning with history, we note that Congress enacted the original federal officer removal statute near the end of the War of 1812, a war that was not popular in New England. Indeed, shipowners from that region filed many state-court claims against federal customs officials charged with enforcing a trade embargo with England. See Wiecek, The Reconstruction of Federal Judicial Power, 1863–1875, 13 Am. J. Legal Hist. 333, 337 (1969). Congress responded with a provision that permitted federal customs officers and *"any other person aiding or assisting"* those officers to remove a case filed against them "in any state court" to federal court. Customs Act of 1815, ch. 31, § 8, 3 Stat. 198 (emphasis added). This initial removal statute was "[o]bviously . . . an attempt to protect federal officers from interference by hostile state courts." *Willingham*, 395 U.S., at 405.

In the early 1830's, South Carolina passed a Nullification Act declaring federal tariff laws unconstitutional and authorizing prosecution of the federal agents who collected the tariffs. Congress then enacted a new statute that permitted "any officer of the United States, *or other person*" to remove to federal court a lawsuit filed against the officer "for or on account of any act done under the revenue laws of the United States." Act of Mar. 2, 1833, ch. 57, § 3, 4 Stat. 633 (emphasis added). As Senator Daniel Webster explained at the time, where state courts might prove hostile to federal law, and hence to those who enforced that law, the removal statute would "give a chance to the [federal] officer to defend himself where the authority of the law was recognized."

Soon after the Civil War, Congress enacted yet another officer removal statute, permitting removal of a suit against any revenue officer "on account of any act done under color of his office" by the revenue officer and *"any person acting under or by authority of any such officer."* Act of July 13, 1866, ch. 184, § 67, 14 Stat. 171 (emphasis added). Elsewhere the statute restricted these latter persons to those engaged in acts "for the collection of taxes." § 67, *id.,* at 172.

In 1948, Congress again revised the statute, dropping its limitation to the revenue context. And it included the rewritten statute within its 1948 recodification. See Act of June 25, 1948, ch. 646, § 1442(a), 62 Stat. 938, 28 U.S.C. § 1442(a). It is this version of the statute that [is] now before us. While Congress expanded the statute's coverage to include all federal officers, it nowhere indicated any intent to change the scope of words, such as "acting under," that described the triggering relationship between a private entity and a federal officer.

Turning to precedent, we point to three cases, all involving illegal liquor, which help to illustrate the need for, and the workings of, the pre-1948 removal statutes. In 1878, a federal revenue officer, James Davis, raided an illegal distillery in Tennessee; was ambushed by several armed men; returned the ambushers' gunfire; and shot one of his attackers dead. See *Tennessee v. Davis*, 100 U.S. 257, 261 (1880). Tennessee indicted Davis for murder. The Court held that the statute permitted Davis to remove the case to federal court, reasoning that the Federal Government "can act only through its officers and agents, and they must act within the States." Removal, the Court found, would help to prevent hostile States from "paralyz[ing]" the Federal Government and its initiatives.

About the same time, a U.S. Army corporal (also called Davis, Lemuel Davis) along with several other soldiers helped a federal revenue officer try to arrest a distiller for violating the internal-revenue laws. The soldiers surrounded the house; the distiller escaped through a hole in a side wall; Corporal Davis shot the suspect; and South Carolina indicted Davis for murder. Davis removed the case, and this Court upheld the removal. The Court acknowledged that, although Davis was not a revenue officer, he was a person "who lawfully assist[ed]" a revenue officer "in the performance of his official duty." *Davis v. South Carolina*, 107 U.S. 597, 600 (1883).

In the 1920's, Maryland charged a group of prohibition agents and a private person acting as their driver with a murder committed during a distillery raid. See *Maryland v. Soper*, 270 U.S. 9 (1926). The prohibition agents and their driver sought to remove the state murder trial to federal court. This Court ultimately rejected their removal efforts for reasons not relevant here. But in doing so it pointed out that the private person acting "as a chauffeur and helper to the four officers under their orders and . . . direction" had "the same right to the benefit of" the removal provision as did the federal agents.

Apart from demonstrating the dangers associated with working in the illegal alcohol business, these three cases—*Tennessee v. Davis*, *Davis v. South Carolina*, and *Maryland v. Soper*—illustrate that the removal statute's "basic" purpose is to protect the Federal Government from the interference with its "operations" that would ensue were a State able, for example, to "arres[t]" and bring "to trial in a State cour[t] for an alleged offense against the law of the State," "officers and agents" of the Federal Government "acting . . . within the scope of their authority."

Where a private person acts as an assistant to a federal official in helping that official to enforce federal law, some of these same considerations may apply. Regardless, in *Davis v. South Carolina* the Court wrote that the removal statute applies to private persons "who lawfully assist" the federal officer "in the performance of his official duty." . . . And in *City of Greenwood v. Peacock*, 384 U.S. 808, 824 (1966), in interpreting a related removal provision, the Court repeated that the statute authorized removal by private parties "only" if they were "authorized to act with or for [federal officers or agents] in affirmatively executing duties under . . . federal law." All the Court's relevant post-1948 federal officer removal cases that we have found reflect or are consistent with this Court's pre-1948 views.

III

With this history and precedent in mind, we return to the statute's language. The relevant relationship is that of a private person "*acting under*" a federal "officer" or "agency." 28 U.S.C. § 1442(a)(1) (emphasis added). In this context, the word "under" must refer to what has been described as a relationship that involves "acting in a certain capacity, considered in relation to one holding a superior position or office." 18 Oxford English Dictionary 948 (2d ed.1989). That relationship typically involves "subjection, guidance, or control." Webster's New International Dictionary 2765 (2d ed.1953). See also Funk & Wagnalls New Standard Dictionary of the English Language 2604 (1942) (defining "under" as meaning "[s]ubordinate or subservient to," "[s]ubject to guidance, tutorship, or direction of"); 18 Oxford English Dictionary, *supra,* at 949 ("[s]ubject to the instruction, direction, or guidance of"). In addition, precedent and statutory purpose make clear that the private person's "acting under" must involve an effort to *assist,* or to help *carry out,* the duties or tasks of the federal superior.

In our view, the help or assistance necessary to bring a private person within the scope of the statute does *not* include simply *complying* with the law. We recognize that sometimes an English speaker might say that one who complies with the law "helps" or "assists" governmental law enforcement. Taxpayers who fill out complex federal tax forms, airline passengers who obey federal regulations prohibiting smoking, for that matter well-behaved federal prisoners, all "help" or "assist" federal law enforcement authorities in some sense of those words. But that is not the sense of "help" or "assist" that can bring a private action within the scope of this statute. That is in part a matter of language. One would usually describe the behavior of the taxpayers, airline passengers, and prisoners we have described as *compliance* with the law (or *acquiescence* to an order), not as "acting under" a federal official who is giving an order or enforcing the law. It is also in part a matter of the history and the precedent we have discussed.

Finally, it is a matter of statutory purpose. When a company subject to a regulatory order (even a highly complex order) complies with the order, it does not ordinarily create a significant risk of state-court "prejudice." Nor is a state-court lawsuit brought against such a company likely to disable federal officials from taking necessary action designed to enforce federal law. Nor is such a lawsuit likely to deny a federal forum to an individual entitled to assert a federal claim of immunity.

The upshot is that a highly regulated firm cannot find a statutory basis for removal in the fact of federal regulation alone. A private firm's compliance (or noncompliance) with federal laws, rules, and regulations does not by itself fall within the scope of the statutory phrase "acting under" a federal "official." And that is so even if the regulation is highly detailed and even if the private firm's activities are highly supervised and monitored. A contrary determination would expand the scope of the statute considerably, potentially bringing within its scope state-court actions filed against private firms in many highly regulated industries. See, *e.g.,* Federal Insecticide, Fungicide, and Rodenticide Act, 7 U.S.C. § 136a (2000 ed. and Supp. IV) (mandating disclosure of testing results in the context of pesticide registration). Neither language, nor history, nor purpose lead us to believe that Congress intended any such expansion.

IV

Philip Morris advances two important arguments to the contrary. First, it points out that lower courts have held that Government contractors fall within the terms of the federal officer removal statute, at least when the relationship between the contractor and the Government is an unusually close one involving detailed regulation, monitoring, or supervision. See, *e.g., Winters v. Diamond Shamrock Chemical Co.,* 149 F.3d 387 (5th Cir. 1998). And it asks why, if close supervision is sufficient to turn a private contractor into a private firm "acting under" a Government "agency" or "officer," does it not do the same when a company is subjected to intense regulation.

The answer to this question lies in the fact that the private contractor in such cases is helping the Government to produce an item that it needs. The assistance that private contractors provide federal officers goes beyond simple compliance with the law and helps officers fulfill other basic governmental tasks. In the context of *Winters* for example, Dow Chemical fulfilled the terms of a contractual agreement by providing the Government with a product that it used to help conduct a war. Moreover, at least arguably, Dow performed a job that, in the absence of a contract with a private firm, the Government itself would have had to perform.

These circumstances distinguish *Winters* from this case. For present purposes that distinction is sufficient. And we need not further examine here (a case where private contracting is not at issue) whether and when particular circumstances may enable private contractors to invoke the statute.

Second, Philip Morris argues that its activities at issue here did not consist simply of compliance with regulatory laws, rules, and orders. It contends that the FTC, after initially testing cigarettes for tar and nicotine, "*delegated authority*" for that task to an industry-financed testing laboratory in 1987. And Philip Morris asserts that (along with other cigarette companies) it was acting pursuant to that delegation. It adds that ever since this initial "delegation" the FTC has "extensive[ly] ... supervis[ed]" and "closely monitored" the manner in which the laboratory tests cigarettes. Philip Morris concludes that, given all these circumstances, just as Dow was "acting under" officers of the Department of Defense when it manufactured Agent Orange, see *Winters, supra,* at 399, so Philip Morris is "acting under" officers of the FTC when it conducts cigarette testing.

For argument's sake we shall overlook the fact that the petitioners appear to challenge the way in which Philip Morris "designed" its *cigarettes,* not the way in which it (or the industry laboratory) conducted cigarette testing. We also shall assume the following testing-related facts that Philip Morris sets forth in its brief:

(1) In the 1950's, the FTC ordered tobacco companies to stop advertising the amount of tar and nicotine contained in their cigarettes.

(2) In 1966, the FTC altered course. It permitted cigarette companies to advertise "tar and nicotine yields" provided that the company had substantiated its statement through use of the Cambridge Filter Method, a testing method developed by Dr. Clyde Ogg, a Department of Agriculture employee.

(3) The Cambridge Filter Method uses "a smoking machine that takes a 35 milliliter puff of two seconds' duration on a cigarette every 60 seconds until the cigarette is smoked to a specified butt length." It then measures the amount of tar and nicotine that is delivered. That data, in turn, determine whether a cigarette may be labeled as "light." This method, Dr. Ogg has testified, "will not tell a smoker how much tar and nicotine he will get from any given cigarette," but it "will indicate" whether a smoker "will get more from one than from another cigarette if there is a significant difference between the two and if he smokes the two in the same manner."

(4) In 1967, the FTC began to use its own laboratory to perform these tests. And the Cambridge Filter Method began to be referred to as "the 'FTC Method.' "

(5) The FTC published the testing results periodically and sent the results annually to Congress.

(6) Due to cost considerations, the FTC stopped testing cigarettes for tar and nicotine in 1987. Simultaneously, the tobacco industry assumed responsibility for cigarette testing, running the tests according to FTC specifications and permitting the FTC to monitor the process closely.

(7) The FTC continues to publish the testing results and to send them to Congress.

(8) The tobacco industry has followed the FTC's requirement that cigarette manufacturers disclose (and make claims about) tar and nicotine content based exclusively on the results of this testing.

Assuming this timeline, Philip Morris' argument nonetheless contains a fatal flaw—a flaw of omission. Although Philip Morris uses the word "delegation" or variations many times throughout its brief, we have found no evidence of any delegation of legal authority from the FTC to the industry association to undertake testing on the Government agency's behalf. Nor is there evidence of any contract, any payment, any employer/employee relationship, or any principal/agent arrangement.

We have examined all of the documents to which Philip Morris and certain supporting *amici* refer. Some of those documents refer to cigarette testing specifications, others refer to the FTC's inspection and supervision of the industry laboratory's testing, and still others refer to the FTC's prohibition of statements in cigarette advertising. But none of these documents establish [sic] the type of formal delegation that might authorize Philip Morris to remove the case.

Several former FTC officials, for example, filed an *amicus* brief in which they state that "[i]n 198[7] the FTC delegated testing responsibility to the private Tobacco Industry Testing Lab (the 'TITL')." Brief for Former Commissioners and Senior Staff of the FTC 11. But in support of this proposition the brief cites a single source, a letter from the cigarette manufacturers' lawyer to an FTC official. That letter states:

> [M]ajor United States cigarette manufacturers, who are responsible for the TITL's operations and on whose behalf we are writing, do not believe that Commission oversight is needed. . . . Nevertheless, as an accommodation and in the spirit of cooperation, the manufacturers are prepared to permit Commission employees to monitor the TITL testing program. . . .

Nothing in this letter refers to a delegation of authority. And neither Congress nor federal agencies normally delegate legal authority to private entities without saying that they are doing so.

Without evidence of some such special relationship, Philip Morris' analogy to Government contracting breaks down. We are left with the FTC's detailed rules about advertising, specifications for testing, requirements about reporting results, and the like. This sounds to us like regulation, not delegation. If there is a difference between this kind of regulation and, say, that of Food and Drug Administration regulation of prescription drug marketing and advertising (which also involve [sic] testing requirements), that difference is one of degree, not kind.

As we have pointed out, however, differences in the degree of regulatory detail or supervision cannot by themselves transform Philip Morris' regulatory *compliance* into the kind of assistance that might bring the FTC within the scope of the statutory phrase *"acting under"* a federal "officer." And, though we find considerable regulatory detail and supervision, we can find nothing that warrants treating the FTC/Philip Morris relationship as distinct from the usual regulator/regulated relationship. This relationship, as we have explained, cannot be construed as bringing Philip Morris within the terms of the statute.

For these reasons, the judgment of the Eighth Circuit is reversed, and the case is remanded for further proceedings consistent with this opinion.

It is so ordered.

NOTE ON THE *"ACTING UNDER"* CLAUSE

In *Bennett v. MIS Corp.*, 607 F.3d 1076 (6th Cir. 2010), federal air traffic controllers brought state law tort suits against a mold removal company that, according to their complaint, had done a faulty job of removing mold at their workplace, a facility operated by the United States. MIS defended based on its contract with the federal government, claiming that any shortcomings could be traced to compliance with its obligations under the contract. MIS sought removal under the "acting under" clause. Should the motion have been granted? The court said that removal was appropriate:

> In its removal motion, MIS claimed that "its work was performed at the direction of, and in accordance with, [ ] detailed mold abatement specifications established by the FAA" and that "[t]he FAA provided detailed [instructions] pertaining to the materials that MIS was required to use and the manner in which MIS was to perform the [mold] remedial activities." In support of its removal, MIS attached its FAA contracts. The FAA contracts included precise specifications. For example, during the January 2005 remediation, the FAA mandated that MIS follow explicit parameters for site containment and waste disposal:
>
> > The Contractor must establish a work area perimeter around the area containing the visible mold on the DTW-ATCT fourth and ninth floors. The area where mold is present is to be isolated utilizing a minimum of 6-mil plastic sheeting. Negative pressure is to be supplied to the enclosure with the use of negative air scrubber machines equipped with HEPA (high-efficiency particulate air) filtration.
> >
> > * * *
>
> The mold contaminated drywall and mold spore-containing waste is to be double bagged in labeled 6-mil polyethylene bags. Each bag shall be adequately sealed. The exterior bag is to be

HEPA vacuumed in the equipment room of the Decon chamber prior to exiting to work area. Finally, the bags are transported to and then disposed of in a landfill approved for the disposal of mold and mold-spore containing waste by the State of Michigan.

Federal officers closely monitored MIS's work. Specifically, each contract designated a federal officer who "direct[ly]" supervised each remediation. These on-site federal officers (hereinafter "FAA contracting officers") were prohibited from modifying or deviating from the FAA's specifications without first obtaining the "signature of the [Lead] Contractor Officer," Judy Ryckman, also an FAA officer. Furthermore, FAA contracting officers had the authority to "require" MIS to "dismiss from work those [MIS] employees which [they] deem[ed] incompetent, insubordinate, unsuitable, or otherwise objectionable." The FAA also controlled the working hours of MIS employees, who were "escorted by FAA personnel at all times[,]" and were prohibited from entering the work site without prior FAA approval.

Unlike the cigarette manufacturer in *Watson,* MIS's assistance went beyond "simple compliance with the law." MIS helped FAA officers carry out their task of ridding a federal employee occupied building of an allegedly hazardous contaminant—"a job that, in the absence of a contract with [MIS] [or another private mold remediation firm] the [FAA] itself would have had to perform." Under these facts, we conclude that the contractual "relationship between [MIS] and [the FAA] [was] an unusually close one[,] involving detailed regulation, monitoring, [and] supervision." For these reasons, we conclude that MIS has satisfied § 1442(a)(1)'s "acting under" requirement.

Next, MIS must show that it performed the actions for which it is being sued "under color of [federal] office." "To satisfy [this] requirement, [MIS] must show a nexus, a 'causal connection' between the charged conduct and [the] asserted official authority." In other words, the removing party must show that it is being sued because of the acts it performed at the direction of the federal officer. The Supreme Court has indicated that "[t]he hurdle erected by this requirement is quite low."

Here, MIS's mold remediation work, which was performed at the direction of FAA officers under contract, was also the alleged cause of plaintiffs' personal injuries. This establishes the nexus required by § 1442(a)(1). Furthermore, even if plaintiffs were able to demonstrate that the alleged cross-contamination occurred because of an act not contemplated by MIS's contracts with the FAA, it is sufficient for our purposes that MIS's execution of the FAA contracts gave rise to the alleged cross-contamination. "Indeed, whether the challenged act was outside the scope of [MIS's] official duties, or whether it was specifically directed by the [FAA], is one for the federal—not state—courts to answer."

II. STATE COURT POWER TO GRANT RELIEF AGAINST FEDERAL OFFICERS

TARBLE'S CASE

80 U.S. (13 Wall.) 397 (1872).

This was a proceeding on habeas corpus for the discharge of one Edward Tarble, held in the custody of a recruiting officer of the United States as an enlisted soldier, on the alleged ground that he was a minor, under the age of eighteen years at the time of his enlistment, and that he enlisted without the consent of his father.

The writ was issued on the 10th of August, 1869, by a court commissioner of Dane County, Wisconsin, an officer authorized by the laws of that State to issue the writ of habeas corpus upon the petition of parties imprisoned or restrained of their liberty, or of persons on their behalf. It was issued in this case upon the petition of the father of Tarble, in which he alleged that his son, who had enlisted under the name of Frank Brown, was confined and restrained of his liberty by Lieutenant Stone, of the United States army, in the city of Madison, in that State and county; that the cause of his confinement and restraint was that he had, on the 20th of the preceding July, enlisted, and been mustered into the military service of the United States; that he was under the age of eighteen years at the time of such enlistment; that the same was made without the knowledge, consent, or approval of the petitioner; and was, therefore, as the petitioner was advised and believed, illegal; and that the petitioner was lawfully entitled to the custody, care, and services of his son.

[The state court ordered that Tarble be released from the army, and the Wisconsin Supreme Court affirmed.]

JUSTICE FIELD, after stating the case, delivered the opinion of the Court, as follows:

The important question is presented by this case, whether a State court commissioner has jurisdiction, upon habeas corpus, to inquire into the validity of the enlistment of soldiers into the military service of the United States, and to discharge them from such service when, in his judgment, their enlistment has not been made in conformity with the laws of the United States. The question presented may be more generally stated thus: Whether any judicial officer of a State has jurisdiction to issue a writ of habeas corpus, or to continue proceedings under the writ when issued, for the discharge of a person held under the authority, or claim and color of the authority, of the United States, by an officer of that [government].

The decision of this court in the two cases which grew out of the arrest of Booth, that of *Ableman v. Booth*, and that of *The United States v. Booth*, disposes alike of the claim of jurisdiction by a State court, or by a State judge, to interfere with the authority of the United States, whether that authority be exercised by a Federal officer or be exercised by a Federal tribunal. In the first of these cases Booth had been arrested and committed to the custody of a marshal of the United States by a commissioner appointed by the District Court of the United States, upon a charge of having aided and abetted the escape of a fugitive slave. Whilst thus in custody a justice of the Supreme Court of Wisconsin issued a writ of habeas corpus directed to the marshal, requiring him to produce the body of Booth with the cause of his imprisonment. [The state courts ordered Booth's release from federal custody]. The decision proceeded upon the ground that the act of Congress respecting fugitive slaves was unconstitutional and void.

In the second case, Booth had been indicted for the offence with which he was charged before the commissioner, and from which the State judge had discharged him, and had been tried and convicted in the District Court of the United States for the District of Wisconsin, and been sentenced to pay a fine of $1000, and to be imprisoned for one month. [Booth filed another habeas petition in state court. The state court] adjudged the imprisonment of Booth to be illegal, and ordered him to be discharged from custody, and he was accordingly set at liberty.

[The Supreme Court reviewed both cases] and the decision of both was announced in the same opinion. In that opinion the Chief Justice details the facts of the two cases at length, and comments upon the character of the jurisdiction asserted by the State judge and the State [court]. And in answer to this assumption of judicial power by the judges and by the Supreme Court of Wisconsin thus made, the Chief Justice said as follows: If they "possess the jurisdiction they claim, they must derive it either from the United States or the State. It certainly has not been conferred on them by the United States; and it is equally clear it was not in the power of the State to confer it, even if it had attempted to do so; for no State can authorize one of its judges or courts to exercise judicial power, by habeas corpus or otherwise, within the jurisdiction of another and independent government. And although the State of Wisconsin is sovereign within its territorial limits to a certain extent, yet that sovereignty is limited and restricted by the Constitution of the United States. And the powers of the General government and of the State, although both exist and are exercised within the same territorial limits, are yet separate and distinct sovereignties, acting separately and independently of each other, within their respective spheres. And the sphere of action appropriated to the United States, is as far beyond the reach of the judicial process issued by a State judge or a State court, as if the line of division was traced by landmarks and monuments visible to the eye. And the State of Wisconsin had no more power to authorize these proceedings of its judges and courts, than it would have had if the prisoner had been confined in Michigan, or in any other State of the Union, for an offence against the laws of the State in which he was imprisoned."

It is in the consideration of this distinct and independent character of the government of the United States, from that of the government of the several States, that the solution of the question presented in this case, and in similar cases, must be found. There are within the territorial limits of each State two governments, restricted in their spheres of action, but independent of each other, and supreme within their respective spheres. Each has its separate departments; each has its distinct laws, and each has its own tribunals for their enforcement. Neither government can intrude within the jurisdiction, or authorize any interference therein by its judicial officers with the action of the other. The two governments in each State stand in their respective spheres of action in the same independent relation to each other, except in one particular, that they would if their authority embraced distinct territories. That particular consists in the supremacy of the authority of the United States when any conflict arises between the two governments. The Constitution and the laws passed in pursuance of it, are declared by the Constitution itself to be the supreme law of the land, and the judges of every State are bound thereby, "anything in the constitution or laws of any State to the contrary notwithstanding."

[Such] being the distinct and independent character of the two governments, within their respective spheres of action, it follows that neither can intrude with its judicial process into the domain of the other, except so far as such intrusion may be necessary on the part of the National government to preserve its rightful supremacy in cases of conflict of authority. In their laws, and mode of enforcement, neither is responsible to the other. How their respective laws shall be enacted; how they shall be carried into execution; and in what tribunals, or by what officers; and how much discretion, or whether any at all shall be vested in their officers, are matters subject to their own control, and in the regulation of which neither can interfere with the other.

Now, among the powers assigned to the National government, is the power "to raise and support armies," and the power "to provide for the government and regulation of the land and naval forces." The execution of these powers falls within the line of its duties; and its control over the subject is plenary and exclusive. [No] interference with the execution of this power of the National government in the formation, organization, and government of its armies by any State officials could be permitted without greatly impairing the efficiency, if it did not utterly destroy, this branch of the public service. Probably in every county and city in the several States there are one or more officers authorized by law to issue writs of habeas corpus on behalf of persons alleged to be illegally restrained of their liberty; and if soldiers could be taken from the army of the United States, and the validity of their enlistment inquired into by any one of these officers, such proceeding could be taken by all of them, and no movement could be made by the National troops without their commanders being subjected to constant annoyance and embarrassment from this source. The experience of the late rebellion has shown us that, in times of great popular excitement, there may be found in every State large numbers ready and anxious to embarrass the operations of the government, and easily persuaded to believe every step taken for the enforcement of its authority illegal and void. Power to issue writs of habeas corpus for the discharge of soldiers in the military service, in the hands of parties thus disposed, might be used, and often would be used, to the great detriment of the public service. In many exigencies the measures of the National government might in this way be entirely bereft of their efficacy and value. An appeal in such cases to this court, to correct the erroneous action of these officers, would afford no adequate remedy. Proceedings on habeas corpus are summary, and the delay incident to bringing the decision of a State officer, through the highest tribunal of the State, to this court for review, would necessarily occupy years, and in the meantime, where the soldier was discharged, the mischief would be accomplished. It is manifest that the powers of the National government could not be exercised with energy and efficiency at all times, if its acts could be interfered with and controlled for any period by officers or tribunals of another sovereignty.

It is true similar embarrassment might sometimes be occasioned, though in a less degree, by the exercise of the authority to issue the writ possessed by judicial officers of the United States, but the ability to provide a speedy remedy for any inconvenience following from this source would always exist with the National legislature.

[This] limitation upon the power of State tribunals and State officers furnishes no just ground to apprehend that the liberty of the citizen will thereby be endangered. The United States are as much interested in protecting the citizen from illegal restraint under their authority, as the several States are to protect him from the like restraint under their authority, and are no more likely to tolerate any oppression. Their courts and judicial officers are clothed with the power to issue the writ of habeas corpus in all cases, where a party is illegally restrained of his liberty by an officer of the United States, whether such illegality consist in the character of the process, the authority of the officer, or the invalidity of the law under which he is held. And there is no just reason to believe that they will exhibit any hesitation to exert their power, when it is properly invoked. Certainly there can be no ground for supposing that their action will be less prompt and effective in such cases than would be that of State tribunals and State officers.

It follows, from the views we have expressed, that the court commissioner of Dane County was without jurisdiction to issue the writ of habeas corpus for the discharge of the prisoner in this [case].

THE CHIEF JUSTICE, dissenting.

I cannot concur in the opinion just read. I have no doubt of the right of a State court to inquire into the jurisdiction of a Federal court upon habeas corpus, and to discharge when satisfied that the petitioner for the writ is restrained of liberty by the sentence of a court without jurisdiction. If it errs in deciding the question of jurisdiction, the error must be corrected in the mode prescribed by the 25th section of the Judiciary Act; not by denial of the right to make inquiry.

I have still less doubt, if possible, that a writ of habeas corpus may issue from a State court to inquire into the validity of imprisonment or detention, without the sentence of any court whatever, by an officer of the United States. The State court may err; and if it does, the error may be corrected here. The mode has been prescribed and should be followed.

To deny the right of State courts to issue the writ, or, what amounts to the same thing, to concede the right to issue and to deny the right to adjudicate, is to deny the right to protect the citizen by habeas corpus against arbitrary imprisonment in a large class of cases; and, I am thoroughly persuaded, was never within the contemplation of the Convention which framed, or the people who adopted, the Constitution. That instrument expressly declares that "the privilege of the writ of habeas corpus shall not be suspended, unless when, in case of rebellion or invasion, the public safety may require it."

NOTES ON STATE COURT AUTHORITY OVER FEDERAL OFFICERS

1. **Executive and Judicial Detentions.** The Court relies on *Ableman v. Booth* and *United States v. Booth*, in which the Court held that state courts may not order the release of persons held in federal custody as a result of judicial process. In *Tarble* the soldier was being held by army officers, without access to any judicial process to determine the legality of the detention. By lumping the two situations together, the Court implicitly denies that there is a significant difference between them. Do you agree?

2. ***Tarble*'s Pedigree.** The Court ruled that the state courts may not order the release of persons held in federal custody. But what is the *source* of that principle? Did the Court hold that the *Constitution* limits state court authority? Alternatively, does the decision rest on a construction of the federal habeas corpus statute? Or is *Tarble* best understood as neither a statutory nor a constitutional decision, but rather a federal common law rule?

A problem with the "statutory construction" theory of the case is that the Court never adverts to the habeas statute, nor to any other statute. One would surely need to repudiate the interpretive principle set forth in *Tafflin* in order to read *Tarble* in this way. "Federal common law" (as that doctrine is currently understood) is an implausible historical explanation, simply because *Tarble's Case* was decided long before the advent of federal common law. Before *Erie*, federal courts could follow their own understanding of "general law" in a wide range of cases, but they did not assert the power to make federal law.

The reasoning of the opinion suggests that the Court meant to make a constitutional rule. If so, can it be reconciled with *Tafflin, Federalist No. 82*, and the general principle that state courts have concurrent jurisdiction over federal claims unless Congress chooses to make federal jurisdiction exclusive? Can the specific problem of state court interference with federal officers be distinguished from the general issue of state court jurisdiction? Is there reason to doubt the ability or willingness of Congress to step in to protect federal interests against the dangers that worried the Court in *Tarble*? Recall the discussion, supra, of federal officer removal, 28 U.S.C. § 1442.

Critics of *Tarble* are unconvinced by the constitutional argument. Acknowledging the anachronism, could one plausibly defend the case today as a kind of federal common law, setting up a presumption that Congress may override if it chooses? Would *Tafflin* stand in the way of this reading of *Tarble*?

3.   Other Types of Relief Against Federal Officers. *McClung v. Silliman*, 19 U.S. (6 Wheat.) 598 (1821), barred state courts from issuing a writ of mandamus against a federal officer. On the other hand, a number of nineteenth-century cases permit state courts to award damages against federal officers. Whether state courts may issue injunctions against federal officers seems to be an open question. See R. FALLON ET AL., HART & WECHSLER'S THE FEDERAL COURTS AND THE FEDERAL SYSTEM 407 (6th ed. 2009). The larger point here is that most of the cases are very old, pre-dating the modern federal officer removal provision in § 1442. Today, any case that raises an issue as to state court authority will probably be one in which the federal officer has a colorable federal defense, and will likely be removed by the federal officer.

4.   State Court Interference with Federal Court Jurisdiction. *Donovan v. City of Dallas*, 377 U.S. 408 (1964), involved a controversy over building a new runway at the Dallas airport. Opponents of the runway sued in state court and lost. Undeterred, the anti-runway group then sued in federal court seeking similar relief. The city returned to the state court and requested an injunction forbidding the anti-runway plaintiffs from proceeding in federal court. The Texas Supreme Court agreed. The United States Supreme Court reversed:

> It may be that a full hearing in an appropriate court would justify a finding that the state-court judgment in favor of Dallas in the first suit barred the issues raised in the second suit. [But] plaintiffs in the second suit chose to file that case in the federal court. They had a right to do this, a right which is theirs by reason of congressional enactments. [And] whether or not a plea of *res judicata* in the second suit would be good is a question for the federal court to decide. While Congress has seen fit to authorize courts of the United States to restrain state-court proceedings in some special

circumstances, [citing the Anti-Injunction Act, 28 U.S.C. § 2283], it has in no way relaxed the old and well-established judicially declared rule that state courts are completely without power to restrain federal-court proceedings in *in personam* actions like the one here.

[An] exception has been made in cases where a court has custody of property, that is, proceedings *in rem* or *quasi in rem*. In such cases this Court has said that the state or federal court having custody of such property has exclusive jurisdiction to proceed.

5. State Courts as Courts of Last Resort. The Court in *Tarble* relied on the premise that federal court would be available for the habeas petition. Situations in which Congress has foreclosed access to federal court raise a different set of problems, which are addressed in Chapters 9 and 10. Suppose that

[a] Congress attempts to foreclose access to both federal and state courts for a given claim; [b] the court concludes that some court must be available; and [c] Congress has not specified whether, in the event its general foreclosure is struck down, the available forum should be federal or state.

In such a case, should the court demand that the federal courts be available, or should the default position be that the state courts remain open, while Congress shuts the federal courts? For one view, see Henry M. Hart, *The Power of Congress to Limit the Jurisdiction of the Federal Courts: An Exercise in Dialectic*, 66 HARV. L. REV. 1362, 1401 (1953) (favoring the state courts). Would Hart's default rule apply to prisoners held at Guantanamo Bay, in Cuba? See Chapters 9 and 10 for discussion of that issue.

III. STATE COURT AUTHORITY TO REJECT JURISDICTION OVER FEDERAL CLAIMS

HAYWOOD V. DROWN
556 U.S. 729 (2009).

JUSTICE STEVENS delivered the opinion of the Court.

In our federal system of government, state as well as federal courts have jurisdiction over suits brought pursuant to 42 U.S.C. § 1983, the statute that creates a remedy for violations of federal rights committed by persons acting under color of state law. While that rule is generally applicable to New York's supreme courts—the State's trial courts of general jurisdiction, New York Correction Law § 24 divests those courts of jurisdiction over § 1983 suits that seek money damages from correction officers. New York thus prohibits the trial courts that generally exercise jurisdiction over § 1983 suits brought against other state officials from hearing virtually all such suits brought against state correction officers.

The question presented is whether that exceptional treatment of a limited category of § 1983 claims is consistent with the Supremacy Clause of the United States Constitution.

I

Petitioner, an inmate in New York's Attica Correctional Facility, commenced two § 1983 actions against several correction employees alleging that they violated his civil rights in connection with three prisoner disciplinary proceedings and an altercation. Proceeding *pro se,* petitioner filed his claims in State Supreme Court and sought punitive damages and attorney's fees. The trial court dismissed the actions on the ground that, under N.Y. Correct. Law Ann. § 24 (West 1987) (hereinafter Correction Law § 24), it lacked jurisdiction to entertain any suit arising under state or federal law seeking money damages from correction officers for actions taken in the scope of their employment. The intermediate appellate court summarily affirmed the trial court.

The New York Court of Appeals, by a 4-to-3 vote, also affirmed the dismissal of petitioner's damages action. The Court of Appeals rejected petitioner's argument that Correction Law § 24's jurisdictional limitation interfered with § 1983 and therefore ran afoul of the Supremacy Clause of the United States Constitution. The majority reasoned that, because Correction Law § 24 treats state and federal damages actions against correction officers equally (that is, neither can be brought in New York courts), the statute should be properly characterized as a "neutral state rule regarding the administration of the courts" and therefore a "valid excuse" for the State's refusal to entertain the federal cause of action. 9 N.Y.3d 481, 487, 851 N.Y.S.2d 84, 881 N.E.2d 180, 183, 184 (2007) (quoting *Howlett v. Rose,* 496 U.S. 356, 369, 372, 110 S.Ct. 2430, 110 L.Ed.2d 332 (1990) (internal quotation marks omitted)). The majority understood our Supremacy Clause precedents to set forth the general rule that so long as a State does not refuse to hear a federal claim for the "sole reason that the cause of action arises under federal law," its withdrawal of jurisdiction will be deemed constitutional. 9 N.Y.3d, at 488, 851 N.Y.S.2d 84, 881 N.E.2d, at 184. So read, discrimination *vel non* is the focal point of Supremacy Clause analysis.

In dissent, Judge Jones argued that Correction Law § 24 is not a neutral rule of judicial administration. Noting that the State's trial courts handle all other § 1983 damages actions, he concluded that the State had created courts of competent jurisdiction to entertain § 1983 suits. In his view, "once a state opens its courts to hear section 1983 actions, it may not selectively exclude section 1983 actions by denominating state policies as jurisdictional."

Recognizing the importance of the question decided by the New York Court of Appeals, we granted certiorari. We now reverse.

II

Motivated by the belief that damages suits filed by prisoners against state correction officers were by and large frivolous and vexatious, New York passed Correction Law § 24. The statute employs a two-step process to strip its courts of jurisdiction over such damages claims and to replace those claims with the State's preferred alternative. The provision states in full:

"1. No civil action shall be brought in any court of the state, except by the attorney general on behalf of the state, against any officer or employee of the department, in his personal capacity, for damages arising out of any act done or the failure to perform any act within the scope of employment and in the discharge of the duties by such officer or employee.

"2. Any claim for damages arising out of any act done or the failure to perform any act within the scope of employment and in the discharge of the duties of any officer or employee of the department shall be brought and maintained in the court of claims as a claim against the state."

Thus, under this scheme, a prisoner seeking damages from a correction officer will have his claim dismissed for want of jurisdiction and will be left, instead, to pursue a claim for damages against an entirely different party (the State) in the Court of Claims—a court of limited jurisdiction. [A plaintiff seeking damages against the State in that court cannot use § 1983 as a vehicle for redress because a State is not a "person" under § 1983. See *Will v. Michigan Dept. of State Police,* 491 U.S. 58, 66 (1989).]

For prisoners seeking redress, pursuing the Court of Claims alternative comes with strict conditions. In addition to facing a different defendant, plaintiffs in that Court are not provided with the same relief, or the same procedural protections, made available in § 1983 actions brought in state courts of general jurisdiction. Specifically, under New York law, plaintiffs in the Court of Claims must comply with a 90-day notice requirement, are not entitled to a jury trial, have no right to attorney's fees, and may not seek punitive damages or injunctive relief.

We must decide whether Correction Law § 24, as applied to § 1983 claims, violates the Supremacy Clause.

III

This Court has long made clear that federal law is as much the law of the several States as are the laws passed by their legislatures. Federal and state law "together form one system of jurisprudence, which constitutes the law of the land for the State; and the courts of the two jurisdictions are not foreign to each other, nor to be treated by each other as such, but as courts of the same country, having jurisdiction partly different and partly concurrent." *Claflin v. Houseman,* 93 U.S. 130, 136–137 (1876); see *Minneapolis & St. Louis R. Co. v. Bombolis,* 241 U.S. 211, 222 (1916); The Federalist No. 82, p. 132 (E. Bourne ed. 1947) (A.Hamilton) ("[T]he inference seems to be conclusive, that the State courts would have a concurrent jurisdiction in all cases arising under the laws of the Union, where it was not expressly prohibited"). Although § 1983, a Reconstruction-era statute, was passed "to interpose the federal courts between the States and the people, as guardians of the people's federal rights," *Mitchum v. Foster,* 407 U.S. 225, 242 (1972), state courts as well as federal courts are entrusted with providing a forum for the vindication of federal rights violated by state or local officials acting under color of state law. See *Patsy v. Board of Regents of Fla.,* 457 U.S. 496, 506–507 (1982) (canvassing the legislative debates of the 1871 Congress and noting that "many legislators interpreted [§ 1983] to provide dual or concurrent forums in the state and federal system, enabling the plaintiff to choose the forum in which to seek relief"); *Maine v. Thiboutot,* 448 U.S. 1, 3, n. 1 (1980).

So strong is the presumption of concurrency that it is defeated only in two narrowly defined circumstances: first, when Congress expressly ousts state courts of jurisdiction, and second, "[w]hen a state court refuses jurisdiction because of a neutral state rule regarding the administration of the courts." Focusing on the latter circumstance, we have emphasized that only a neutral jurisdictional rule will be deemed a "valid excuse" for departing from the default assumption that "state courts have inherent authority, and are thus presumptively competent, to adjudicate claims arising under the laws of the United States." *Tafflin v. Levitt,* 493 U.S. 455, 458 (1990).

In determining whether a state law qualifies as a neutral rule of judicial administration, our cases have established that a State cannot employ a jurisdictional rule "to dissociate [itself] from federal law because of disagreement with its content or a refusal to recognize the superior authority of its source." In other words, although States retain substantial leeway to establish the contours of their judicial systems, they lack authority to nullify a federal right or cause of action they believe is inconsistent with their local policies. "The suggestion that [an] act of Congress is not in harmony with the policy of the State, and therefore that the courts of the State are free to decline jurisdiction, is quite inadmissible, because it presupposes what in legal contemplation does not exist."

It is principally on this basis that Correction Law § 24 violates the Supremacy Clause. In passing Correction Law § 24, New York made the judgment that correction officers should not be burdened with suits for damages arising out of conduct performed in the scope of their employment. Because it regards these suits as too numerous or too frivolous (or both), the State's longstanding policy has been to shield this narrow class of defendants from liability when sued for damages. The

State's policy, whatever its merits, is contrary to Congress' judgment that *all* persons who violate federal rights while acting under color of state law shall be held liable for damages. As we have unanimously recognized, "[a] State may not . . . relieve congestion in its courts by declaring a whole category of federal claims to be frivolous. Until it has been proved that the claim has no merit, that judgment is not up to the States to make." *Howlett [v. Rose],* 496 U.S., [356] at 380. [That] New York strongly favors a rule shielding correction officers from personal damages liability and substituting the State as the party responsible for compensating individual victims is irrelevant. The State cannot condition its enforcement of federal law on the demand that those individuals whose conduct federal law seeks to regulate must nevertheless escape liability.

IV

While our cases have uniformly applied the principle that a State cannot simply refuse to entertain a federal claim based on a policy disagreement, we have yet to confront a statute like New York's that registers its dissent by divesting its courts of jurisdiction over a disfavored federal claim in addition to an identical state claim. The New York Court of Appeals' holding was based on the misunderstanding that this equal treatment of federal and state claims rendered Correction Law § 24 constitutional. 9 N.Y.3d, at 489, 851 N.Y.S.2d 84, 881 N.E.2d, at 185 ("Put simply, because Correction Law § 24 does not treat section 1983 claims differently than it treats related state law causes of action, the Supremacy Clause is not offended"). To the extent our cases have created this misperception, we now make clear that equality of treatment does not ensure that a state law will be deemed a neutral rule of judicial administration and therefore a valid excuse for refusing to entertain a federal cause of action.

Respondents correctly observe that, in the handful of cases in which this Court has found a valid excuse, the state rule at issue treated state and federal claims equally. In *Douglas v. New York, N.H. & H.R. Co.,* 279 U.S. 377 (1929), we upheld a state law that granted state courts discretion to decline jurisdiction over state and federal claims alike when neither party was a resident of the State. Later, in *Herb v. Pitcairn,* 324 U.S. 117 (1945), a city court dismissed an action brought under the Federal Employers' Liability Act (FELA), for want of jurisdiction because the cause of action arose outside the court's territorial jurisdiction. We upheld the dismissal on the ground that the State's venue laws were not being applied in a way that discriminated against the federal claim. In a third case, *Missouri ex rel. Southern R. Co. v. Mayfield,* 340 U.S. 1 (1950), we held that a State's application of the *forum non conveniens* doctrine to bar adjudication of a FELA case brought by nonresidents was constitutionally sound as long as the policy was enforced impartially. And our most recent decision finding a valid excuse, *Johnson v. Fankell,* 520 U.S. 911 (1997), rested largely on the fact that Idaho's rule limiting interlocutory jurisdiction did not discriminate against § 1983 actions.

Although the absence of discrimination is necessary to our finding a state law neutral, it is not sufficient. A jurisdictional rule cannot be used as a device to undermine federal law, no matter how evenhanded it may appear. As we made clear in *Howlett,* "[t]he fact that a rule is denominated jurisdictional does not provide a court an excuse to avoid the obligation to enforce federal law if the rule does not reflect the concerns of power over the person and competence over the subject matter that jurisdictional rules are designed to protect." 496 U.S., at 381. Ensuring equality of treatment is thus the beginning, not the end, of the Supremacy Clause analysis.

In addition to giving too much weight to equality of treatment, respondents mistakenly treat this case as implicating the "great latitude [States enjoy] to establish the structure and jurisdiction of their own courts." *[Howlett].* Although Correction Law § 24 denies state courts authority to entertain damages actions against correction officers, this case does not require us to decide whether Congress may compel a State to offer a forum, otherwise unavailable under state law, to hear suits brought pursuant to § 1983. The State of New York has made this inquiry unnecessary by creating courts of general jurisdiction that routinely sit to hear analogous § 1983 actions. New York's constitution vests the state supreme courts with general original jurisdiction, and the "inviolate authority to hear and resolve all causes in law and equity." *Pollicina v. Misericordia Hospital Medical Center,* 82 N.Y.2d 332, 339, 604 N.Y.S.2d 879, 624 N.E.2d 974, 977 (1993). For instance, if petitioner had attempted to sue a police officer for damages under § 1983, the suit would be properly adjudicated by a state supreme court. Similarly, if petitioner had sought declaratory or injunctive relief against a correction officer, that suit would be heard in a state supreme court. It is only a particular species of suits—those seeking damages relief against correction officers—that the State deems inappropriate for its trial courts.

We therefore hold that, having made the decision to create courts of general jurisdiction that regularly sit to entertain analogous suits, New York is not at liberty to shut the courthouse door to federal claims that it considers at odds with its local policy. A State's authority to organize its courts, while considerable, remains subject to the strictures of the Constitution. We have never treated a State's invocation of "jurisdiction" as a trump that ends the Supremacy Clause inquiry, and we decline to do so in this case. Because New York's supreme courts generally have personal jurisdiction over the parties in § 1983 suits brought by prisoners against correction officers and because they hear the lion's share of all other § 1983 actions, we find little concerning "power over the person and competence over the subject matter" in Correction Law § 24. [*Howlett v. Rose*] (conducting a similar analysis and concluding that the Florida courts of general jurisdiction were "fully competent to provide the remedies [§ 1983] requires").

Accordingly, the dissent's fear that "no state jurisdictional rule will be upheld as constitutional" is entirely unfounded. Our holding addresses only the unique scheme adopted by the State of New York—a law designed to shield a particular class of defendants (correction officers) from a particular type of liability (damages) brought by a particular class of plaintiffs (prisoners). Based on the belief that damages suits against correction officers are frivolous and vexatious, see *supra,* at 2112—2113, n. 3, Correction Law § 24 is effectively an immunity statute cloaked in jurisdictional garb. Finding this scheme unconstitutional merely confirms that the Supremacy Clause cannot be evaded by formalism.

V

The judgment of the New York Court of Appeals is reversed, and the case is remanded to that court for further proceedings not inconsistent with this opinion.

JUSTICE THOMAS, with whom THE CHIEF JUSTICE, JUSTICE SCALIA, and JUSTICE ALITO join as to Part III, dissenting.

The Court holds that New York Correction Law Annotated § 24, which divests New York's state courts of subject-matter jurisdiction over suits seeking money damages from correction officers, violates the Supremacy Clause of the Constitution, Art. VI, cl. 2, because it requires the dismissal of federal actions brought in state court under 42 U.S.C. § 1983. I disagree. Because neither the Constitution nor our precedent requires New York to open its courts to § 1983 federal actions, I respectfully dissent.

I

Although the majority decides this case on the basis of the Supremacy Clause, see *ante,* at 2113–2118, the proper starting point is Article III of the Constitution. Article III, § 1, provides that "[t]he judicial Power of the United States, shall be vested in one supreme Court, and in such inferior Courts as the Congress may from time to time ordain and establish." The history of the drafting and ratification of this Article establishes that it leaves untouched the States' plenary authority to decide whether their local courts will have subject-matter jurisdiction over federal causes of action.

The text of Article III reflects the Framers' agreement that the National Government needed a Supreme Court. There was sharp disagreement at the Philadelphia Convention, however, over the need for lower federal courts. [Justice Thomas recounted the debates over this issue. Those debates resulted in the "Madisonian Compromise," under which the creation of lower federal courts was left up to Congress to decide].

This so-called Madisonian Compromise bridged the divide "between those who thought that the establishment of lower federal courts should be constitutionally mandatory and those who thought there should be no federal courts at all except for a Supreme Court with, *inter alia,* appellate jurisdiction to review state court judgments." R. Fallon, D. Meltzer, & D. Shapiro, Hart and Wechsler's The Federal Courts and the Federal System 348 (4th ed.1996). In so doing, the compromise left to the wisdom of Congress the creation of lower federal courts: "So far as the inferior Federal Courts were concerned, it was entirely discretionary with Congress to what extent it would vest Federal judicial power in them. It could grant to them as much or as little as it chose of those classes of jurisdiction, enumerated in Article III as belonging to the judicial power of the United States. It could, if it chose, leave to the State Courts all or any of these classes." Warren, Federal Criminal Laws and the State Courts, 38 Harv. L.Rev. 545, 547 (1925) (footnote omitted).

The assumption that state courts would continue to exercise concurrent jurisdiction over federal claims was essential to this compromise. See The Federalist No. 82, pp. 130, 132 (E. Bourne ed. 1947) (A.Hamilton) ("[T]he inference seems to be conclusive, that the State courts would have a concurrent jurisdiction in all cases arising under the laws of the Union, where it was not expressly prohibited").

The Constitution's implicit preservation of state authority to entertain federal claims, however, did not impose a duty on state courts to do so. [There] was at least one proposal to expressly require state courts to take original jurisdiction over federal claims (subject to appeal in federal court) that was introduced in an attempt to forestall the creation of lower federal courts. But in light of the failure of this proposal—which was offered before the adoption of the Madisonian Compromise—the assertions by its supporters that state courts would ordinarily entertain federal causes of action cannot reasonably be viewed as an assurance that the States would never alter the subject-matter jurisdiction of their courts. The Framers' decision to empower Congress to create federal courts that could either supplement or displace state-court review of federal claims, as well as the exclusion of any affirmative command requiring the States to consider federal claims in the text of Article III, confirm this [understanding].

The earliest decisions addressing this question, written by then-serving and future Supreme Court Justices, confirm that state courts remain "tribunals over which the government of the Union has no adequate control, and which may be closed to any claim asserted under a law of the United States." *Osborn v. Bank of United States,* 9 Wheat. 738, 821 (1824). [In] short, there was "a very clear intimation given by the judges of the Supreme Court, that the state courts were not bound in consequence of any act of congress, to assume and exercise jurisdiction in such cases. It was merely permitted to them to do so as far, as was compatible with their state obligations." Kent 375; see also *id.,* at 377 (explaining that the Constitution "permits state courts which are competent for the purpose, and have an inherent jurisdiction adequate to the case, to entertain suits in the given cases"). Under our federal system, therefore, the States have unfettered authority to determine whether their local courts may entertain a federal cause of action. Once a State exercises its sovereign prerogative to deprive its courts of subject-matter jurisdiction over a federal cause of action, it is the end of the matter as far as the Constitution is concerned.

The present case can be resolved under this principle alone. New York Correction Law Annotated § 24, ¶ 1 (West 1987) (N.Y.CLA) provides that "[n]o civil action shall be brought in any court of the state, except by the attorney general on behalf of the state, against any officer or employee of the department, in his personal capacity, for damages arising out of any act done or the failure to perform any act within the scope of the employment and in the discharge of the duties by such officer or employee." The majority and petitioner agree that this statute erects a jurisdictional bar that prevents the state courts from entertaining petitioner's claim for damages under § 1983. Because New York's decision to withdraw jurisdiction over § 1983 damages actions—or indeed, over any claims—does not offend the Constitution, the judgment below should be affirmed.

II

The Court has evaded Article III's limitations by finding that the Supremacy Clause constrains the States' authority to define the subject-matter jurisdiction of their own courts. In particular, the Court has held that "the Federal Constitution prohibits state courts of general jurisdiction from refusing" to entertain a federal claim "solely because the suit is brought under a federal law" as a "state may not discriminate against rights arising under federal laws." *McKnett v. St. Louis & San Francisco R. Co.*, 292 U.S. 230, 233–234 (1934). There is no textual or historical support for the Court's incorporation of this antidiscrimination principle into the Supremacy Clause.

A

1

The Supremacy Clause provides that "[t]his Constitution, and the Laws of the United States which shall be made in Pursuance thereof . . . shall be the supreme Law of the Land; and the Judges in every State shall be bound thereby, any Thing in the Constitution or Laws of any State to the Contrary notwithstanding." Art. VI, cl. 2. Under this provision, "[t]he laws of the United States are laws in the several States, and just as much binding on the citizens and courts thereof as the State laws are. . . . The two together form one system of jurisprudence, which constitutes the law of the land for the State." Thus, a valid federal law is substantively superior to a state law; "if a state measure conflicts with a federal requirement, the state provision must give way." As a textual matter, however, the Supremacy Clause does not address whether a state court must entertain a federal cause of action; it provides only a rule of decision that the state court must follow if it adjudicates the claim. See R. Berger, Congress v. The Supreme Court 245 (1969) (The Supremacy Clause only " 'enacts what the law shall be'. . . . [I]t defines the governing 'supreme law,' and *if* a State court *has* jurisdiction, it commands that that law shall govern").

The Supremacy Clause's path to adoption at the Convention confirms this focus. [Justice Thomas discussed the Convention's consideration of the Supremacy Clause.] This historical record makes clear that the Supremacy Clause's exclusive function is to disable state laws that are substantively inconsistent with federal law—not to require state courts to hear federal claims over which the courts lack [jurisdiction]. The Supremacy Clause's exclusive focus on substantive state law is also evident from the context in which it was revived. First, the Clause was [adopted] as part of the [debate] over Madison's proposal to grant Congress the power to "negative" the laws of the States. By then, the Framers had already adopted Article III, thereby ending the fight over state-court jurisdiction. The question before the Convention thus was not which courts (state or federal) were best suited to adjudicate federal claims, but which branch of government (Congress or the courts) would be most effective in vindicating the substantive superiority of federal law. The Supremacy Clause was directly responsive to that question.

Second, the timing of the Clause's adoption suggests that the Framers viewed it as achieving the same end as Madison's congressional "negative" proposal. Although Madison believed that Congress could most effectively countermand inconsistent state laws, the Framers decided that the Judiciary could adequately perform that function. There is no evidence that the Framers envisioned the Supremacy Clause as having a substantively broader sweep than the proposal it replaced. And, there can be no question that Madison's congressional "negative" proposal was entirely unconcerned with the dispute over whether state courts should be required to exercise jurisdiction over federal claims. Indeed, Madison's proposal did not require the States to become enmeshed in any federal business at all; it merely provided that state laws could be directly nullified if Congress found them to be inconsistent with the Constitution or laws of the United States. The role of the Supremacy Clause is no different. It does not require state courts to entertain federal causes of action. Rather, it only requires that in reaching the merits of such claims, state courts must decide the legal question in favor of the "law of the Land." Art. VI, cl. 2.

For this reason, Representative Fisher Ames explained during the debate over the First Judiciary Act that "[t]he law of the United States is a rule to [state-court judges], but no authority for them. It controlled their decisions, but could not enlarge their powers." 1 Annals of Congress 808 (1789) (reprint 2003). And because the Constitution requires from state judges only an oath of "Allegiance and not an Oath of Office," the federal government "[c]annot compel them to act—or to become our Officers."

Notes of William Patterson from Speech on Judiciary Act (June 23, 1789), in 9 Documentary History of the First Federal Congress 1789–1791, p. 477 (K. Bowling & H. Veit eds.1988); 1 Annals of Congress 805 (remarks of Rep. Sedgwick, Debate of Aug. 29, 1789) (arguing that inferior federal courts should be established because state courts "might refuse or neglect to attend to the national business"); 10 *id.*, at 892 (remarks of Rep. Harper) (explaining that Congress "cannot enforce on the State courts, as a matter of duty, a performance of the acts we confide to them" but arguing that there was "no cause to complain" "until they refuse to exercise" the jurisdiction granted over federal claims).

The supremacy of federal law, therefore, is not impugned by a State's decision to strip its local courts of subject-matter jurisdiction to hear certain federal claims. Subject-matter jurisdiction determines only whether a court has the power to entertain a particular claim—a condition precedent to reaching the merits of a legal dispute. Although the line between subject-matter jurisdiction over a claim and the merits of that claim can at times prove difficult to draw, the distinction is crucial in the Supremacy Clause context. If the state court does not reach the merits of the dispute for lack of statutory or constitutional jurisdiction, the preeminence of federal law remains undiminished.

Accordingly, the superiority of federal law as a substantive matter does not trigger an obligation on States to keep their courts jurisdictionally neutral with respect to federal and state-law claims. "The federal law in any field within which Congress is empowered to legislate is the supreme law of the land in the sense that it may supplant state legislation in that field, but not in the sense that it may supplant the existing rules of litigation in state courts. Congress has full power to provide its own courts for litigating federal rights. The state courts belong to the States." *Brown v. Gerdes,* 321 U.S. 178, 193 (1944) (Frankfurter, J., concurring).

2

The Court was originally faithful to this conception of federal supremacy. In *Claflin,* the Court concluded that because the federal statute under consideration did not deprive the state court of jurisdiction, the state court was competent to resolve the claim. See 93 U.S., at 136–137 ("[R]ights, whether legal or equitable, acquired under the laws of the United States, may be prosecuted in the United States courts, or in the State courts, competent to decide rights of the like character and class; subject, however, to this qualification, that where a right arises under a law of the United States, Congress may, if it see[s] fit, give to the Federal courts exclusive jurisdiction"). But the Court was careful to also explain that the Constitution did not impose an obligation on the States to accept jurisdiction over such claims. See *id.*, at 137 (explaining that there "is no reason why the State courts should not be open for the prosecution of rights growing out of the laws of the United States, to which their jurisdiction is competent, and not denied"). The Constitution instead left the States with the choice—but not the obligation—to entertain federal actions. See *id.*, at 139 ("[W]here no direction is given [from Congress] on the subject, it was assumed, in our early judicial history, that the State courts retained their usual jurisdiction concurrently with the Federal Courts invested with jurisdiction in like cases").

[Justice Thomas discussed other early cases, including *Douglas*, and then turned to *McKnett*.]

3

It was not until five years after *Douglas* that the Court used the Supremacy Clause to strike down a state jurisdictional statute for its failure to permit state-court adjudication of federal claims. See *McKnett,* 292 U.S. 230. The Court started by correctly noting "that a state court whose ordinary jurisdiction as prescribed by local laws is appropriate to the occasion, may not refuse to entertain suits under [FELA]." Yet, even though the Alabama court *lacked* such jurisdiction over the relevant federal claim pursuant to a state statute, the *McKnett* Court held that the state court had improperly dismissed the federal claim. According to the Court, "[w]hile Congress has not attempted to compel states to provide courts for the enforcement of [FELA], the Federal Constitution prohibits state courts of general jurisdiction from refusing to do so solely because the suit is brought under a federal law. The denial of jurisdiction by the Alabama court is based solely upon the source of law sought to be enforced. The plaintiff is cast out because he is suing to enforce a federal act. A state may not discriminate against rights arising under federal laws."

For all the reasons identified above, *McKnett* cannot be reconciled with the decisions of this Court that preceded it. Unlike [*Mondou v. New York, New Haven & H. R.Co.*, 223 U.S. 1 (1912), where the Connecticut Supreme Court had declined to enforce the FELA on the ground that the FELA conflicted with Connecticut policy, the] Alabama Supreme Court did not indulge its own bias against adjudication of federal claims in state court by refusing to hear a federal claim over which it had subject-matter jurisdiction. Rather, like the New York court decision affirmed in *Douglas,* the Alabama court's dismissal merely respected a jurisdictional barrier to adjudication of the federal claim imposed by state law. The fact that Alabama courts were competent to hear similar state-law claims should have been immaterial. Alabama had exercised its sovereign right to establish the subject-matter jurisdiction of its courts. Under *Claflin* and its progeny, that legislative judgment should have been upheld.

Despite *McKnett*'s infidelity to the Constitution and more than a century of Supreme Court jurisprudence, the Court's later decisions have repeated *McKnett*'s declaration that state jurisdictional statutes must be policed for antifederal discrimination. See, *e.g., Testa v. Katt,* 330 U.S. 386, 394 (1947) ("It is conceded that this same type of claim arising under

Rhode Island law would be enforced by that State's courts. . . . Under these circumstances the State courts are not free to refuse enforcement of petitioners' claim"); *Howlett v. Rose,* 496 U.S. 356, 375 (1990) ("[W]hether the question is framed in pre-emption terms, as petitioner would have it, or in the obligation to assume jurisdiction over a 'federal' cause of action, . . . the Florida court's refusal to entertain one discrete category of § 1983 claims [i.e., those brought against local governments, ed.], when the court entertains similar state-law actions against state defendants, violates the Supremacy Clause"). The outcome in these cases, however, can be reconciled with first principles notwithstanding the Court's stated reliance on *McKnett*'s flawed interpretation of the Supremacy Clause.

In *Testa,* the Court struck down the Rhode Island Supreme Court's refusal to entertain a claim under the federal Emergency Price Control Act. There was no dispute that "the Rhode Island courts [had] jurisdiction adequate and appropriate under established local law to adjudicate this [action."] In *Howlett,* the Court likewise correctly struck down a Florida Supreme Court decision affirming the dismissal of a § 1983 suit on state-law sovereign immunity grounds. The Florida court had interpreted the State's statutory "waiver of sovereign immunity" not to extend to federal claims brought in state court. According to the state court, absent a statutory waiver, Florida's pre-existing common-law sovereign immunity rule provided a "blanket immunity on [state] governmental entities from federal civil rights actions under § 1983" brought in Florida courts. Based on this rule, the Florida Supreme Court affirmed the dismissal with prejudice of the § 1983 suit against the state officials. No antidiscrimination rule was required to strike down the Florida Supreme Court's decision. Even though several Florida courts had concluded that the defense of sovereign immunity was jurisdictional, [state] courts cannot evade their obligation to enforce federal law by simply characterizing a statute or common-law rule as "jurisdictional"; the state law must in fact operate in a jurisdictional manner. No matter where the line between subject-matter jurisdiction and the merits is drawn, Florida's "common law immunity" rule crossed it. First, because the Florida Supreme Court had dismissed the § 1983 lawsuit with prejudice, its decision was on the merits. Second, Florida's sovereign immunity rule violated the Supremacy Clause, operating as a state-law defense to a federal law.

[Contrary] to *McKnett,* the Constitution does not require state courts to give equal billing to state and federal claims. To read the Supremacy Clause to include an anti-discrimination principle undermines the compromise that shaped Article III and contradicts the original understanding of Constitution. There is no justification for preserving such a principle. But even if the Court chooses to adhere to the antidiscrimination rule as part of the Supremacy Clause inquiry, the rule's infidelity to the text, structure, and history of the Constitution counsels against extending the principle any further than our precedent requires.

B

Although the Supremacy Clause does not, on its own force, pre-empt state jurisdictional statutes of any kind, it may still pre-empt state law once Congress has acted. Federal law must prevail when Congress validly enacts a statute that expressly supersedes state law, or when the state law conflicts with a federal statute. [In this section, Justice Thomas argued that the New York statute "does not fall prey to either category of preemption."]

III

Even accepting the entirety of the Court's precedent in this area of the law, however, I still could not join the majority's resolution of this case as it mischaracterizes and broadens this Court's decisions. The majority concedes not only that NYCLA § 24 is jurisdictional, but that the statute is neutral with respect to federal and state claims. Nevertheless, it concludes that the statute violates the Supremacy Clause because it finds that "equality of treatment does not ensure that a state law will be deemed a neutral rule of judicial administration and therefore a valid excuse for refusing to entertain a federal cause of action." This conclusion is incorrect in light of Court precedent for several reasons.

A

The majority mischaracterizes this Court's precedent when it asserts that jurisdictional neutrality is "the beginning, not the end, of the Supremacy Clause [analysis]." Here, it is conceded that New York has deprived its courts of subject-matter jurisdiction over a particular class of claims on terms that treat federal and state actions equally. That is all this Court's precedent requires.

The majority's assertion that jurisdictional neutrality is not the touchstone because "[a] jurisdictional rule cannot be used as a device to undermine federal law, no matter how even-handed it may appear," reflects a misunderstanding of the law. A jurisdictional statute simply deprives the relevant court of the power to decide the case [altogether]. Such a statute necessarily operates without prejudice to the adjudication of the matter in a competent forum. Jurisdictional statutes therefore by definition are incapable of undermining federal law. NYCLA § 24 no more undermines § 1983 than the amount-in-controversy requirement for federal diversity jurisdiction undermines state law. See 28 U.S.C. § 1332. The relevant law (state or federal) remains fully operative in both circumstances. The sole consequence of the jurisdictional barrier is that the law cannot be enforced in one particular judicial forum.

As a result, the majority's focus on New York's reasons for enacting this jurisdictional statute is entirely misplaced. The States "remain independent and autonomous within their proper sphere of authority."

Printz v. United States, 521 U.S. 898, 928 (1997). New York has the organic authority, therefore, to tailor the jurisdiction of state courts to meet its policy [goals]. It may be true that it was "Congress' judgment that *all* persons who violate federal rights while acting under color of state law shall be held liable for damages." But Congress has not enforced that judgment by statutorily requiring the States to open their courts to *all* § 1983 claims. And this Court has "never held that state courts must entertain § 1983 suits." *National Private Truck Council, Inc. v. Oklahoma Tax Comm'n,* 515 U.S. 582, 587, n. 4 (1995). Our decisions have held only that the States cannot use jurisdictional statutes to discriminate against federal claims. Because NYCLA § 24 does not violate this command, any policy-driven reasons for depriving jurisdiction over a "federal claim in addition to an identical state claim," are irrelevant for purposes of the Supremacy Clause.

This Court's decision in *Howlett* is not to the contrary. Despite the majority's assertion, *Howlett* does not stand for the proposition "that a State cannot employ a jurisdictional rule to dissociate itself from federal law because of disagreement with its content or a refusal to recognize the superior authority of its source." As an initial matter, the majority lifts the above quotation—which was merely part of a passage explaining that a "State may not discriminate against federal causes of action,"—entirely out of context. *Howlett*'s reiteration of *McKnett*'s neutrality command, which is all the selected quotation reflects, offers no refuge to the majority in light of its concession that NYCLA § 24 affords "equal treatment" to "federal and state claims."

Howlett instead stands for the unremarkable proposition that States may not add immunity defenses to § 1983. A state law is not jurisdictional just because the legislature has "denominated" it as such. As the majority observes, the State's "invocation of 'jurisdiction'" cannot "trump" the "Supremacy Clause inquiry." The majority, therefore, is correct that a state court's decision "to nullify a federal right or cause of action [that it] believe[s] is inconsistent with [its] local policies" cannot evade the Supremacy Clause by hiding behind a jurisdictional label, because "the Supremacy Clause cannot be evaded by formalism." Rather, a state statute must in fact *operate* jurisdictionally: It must deprive the court of the power to hear the claim and it must not preclude relitigation of the action in a proper forum. *Howlett* proved the point by striking down a state-law immunity rule that bore the jurisdictional label but operated as a defense on the merits and provided for the dismissal of the state court action with prejudice.

But the majority's axiomatic refrain about jurisdictional labels is entirely unresponsive to the issue before the Court—*i.e.,* whether NYCLA § 24 operates jurisdictionally. Unlike the Florida immunity rule in *Howlett,* NYCLA § 24 is not a defense to a federal claim and the dismissal it authorizes is without prejudice. [For] this reason, NYCLA § 24 is not merely "denominated" as jurisdictional—it actually is jurisdictional. The

New York courts, therefore, have not declared a "category" of § 1983 claims to be " 'frivolous' " or to have " 'no merit' " in order to " 'relieve congestion' " in the state-court system [as in *Howlett*]. These courts have simply recognized that they lack the power to adjudicate this category of claims regardless of their [merit].

The majority's principal response is that NYCLA § 24 "is effectively an immunity statute cloaked in jurisdictional garb." But this curious rejoinder resurrects an argument that the majority abandons earlier in its own opinion. The majority needs to choose. Either it should definitively commit to making the impossible case that a statute denying state courts the power to entertain a claim without prejudice to its reassertion in federal court is an immunity defense in disguise, or it should clearly explain why some other aspect of *Howlett* controls the outcome of this case. This Court has required Congress to speak clearly when it intends to "upset the usual constitutional balance of federal and state powers." It should require no less of itself.

At bottom, the majority's warning that upholding New York's law "would permit a State to withhold a forum for the adjudication of any federal cause of action with which it disagreed as long as the policy took the form of a jurisdictional rule" is without any basis in fact. This Court's jurisdictional neutrality command already guards against antifederal discrimination. A decision upholding NYCLA § 24, which fully adheres to that rule, would not "circumvent our prior decisions." It simply would adhere to them.

B

The majority also incorrectly concludes that NYCLA § 24 is not a neutral jurisdictional statute because it applies to a "narrow class of defendants," and because New York courts "hear the lion's share of all other § 1983 actions." A statute's jurisdictional status does not turn on its narrowness or on its breadth. Rather, [a] statute's jurisdictional status turns on the grounds on which the state-law dismissal rests and the consequences that follow from such rulings. No matter how narrow the majority perceives NYCLA § 24 to be, it easily qualifies as jurisdictional under this established standard. Accordingly, it is immaterial that New York has chosen to allow its courts of general jurisdiction to entertain § 1983 actions against certain categories of defendants but not others (such as correction officers), or to entertain § 1983 actions against particular defendants for only certain types of [relief].

Under [the majority's] reasoning, if a State grants its trial courts jurisdiction to hear § 1983 claims for damages against *any* state official, the State's decision to deny those courts the power to entertain some narrower species of § 1983 claims—even on jurisdictionally neutral terms—*a fortiori* violates the Supremacy Clause. The majority's assurance that its holding is applicable only to New York's "unique scheme" thus rings hollow. The majority is forcing States into an all-or-nothing choice that neither the Constitution nor this Court's decisions require. Indeed, the majority's novel approach breaks the promise that the States still enjoy " 'great latitude . . . to establish the structure and jurisdiction of their own courts.' " It cannot be that New York has forsaken the right to withdraw a particular class of claims from its courts' purview simply because it has created courts of general jurisdiction that would otherwise have the power to hear suits for damages against correction officers. The Supremacy Clause does not fossilize the jurisdiction of state courts in their original form. Under this Court's precedent, States remain free to alter the structure of their judicial system even if that means certain federal causes of action will no longer be heard in state court, so long as States do so on nondiscriminatory terms. [Today's] decision thus represents a dramatic and unwarranted expansion of this Court's precedent.

IV

[By] imposing on state courts a duty to accept subject-matter jurisdiction over federal § 1983 actions, the Court has stretched the Supremacy Clause beyond all reasonable bounds and upended a compromise struck by the Framers in Article III of the Constitution. Furthermore, by declaring unconstitutional even those laws that divest state courts of jurisdiction over federal claims on a non-discriminatory basis, the majority has silently overturned this Court's unbroken line of decisions upholding state statutes that are materially indistinguishable from the New York law under review. And it has transformed a single exception to the rule of state judicial autonomy into a virtually ironclad obligation to entertain federal business. I respectfully dissent.

NOTES ON THE AUTHORITY OF STATE COURTS TO REFUSE TO ADJUDICATE FEDERAL CLAIMS

1.   Article III, the Supremacy Clause, and the State Courts. The Supreme Court's doctrine, illustrated by *Haywood* and the cases cited there, requires a state court to adjudicate federal claims unless the state court articulates a "valid excuse." Based on the Court's discussion of prior cases, what guidelines govern whether a particular reason is a valid excuse?

A key premise of the Court's ruling in *Haywood* is "the principle that a State cannot simply refuse to entertain a federal claim based on a policy disagreement." Justice Thomas argues that "the majority's focus on New York's reasons for enacting this jurisdictional statute is entirely misplaced." What are Justice Thomas's grounds for rejecting the majority's premise? Does his understanding of Article III and of the Supremacy Clause differ from that of the majority? Why might the Chief Justice and Justices Scalia and Alito have chosen to join only Part III of his opinion?

Suppose a State has no quarrel with federal law, but would simply prefer to deploy its scarce judicial resources in other ways rather than enforcing federal law. Does the supremacy of federal law necessarily entail an obligation on state courts to adjudicate federal causes of action? Is this so even where a State has deprived its courts of subject-matter jurisdiction over a particular class of claims on terms that treat federal and state actions equally?

2.   A Role for Congress? Would the argument for requiring state courts to hear federal cases be stronger if it were grounded in Congress's intent? See Terrence Sandalow, Henry v. Mississippi *and the Adequate State Ground Doctrine: Proposals for a Revised Doctrine,* 1965 SUP. CT. REV. 187, 206–07, for an argument along these lines. Besides avoiding the awkward leap of logic from the "supremacy" premise to an obligation on state courts, putting the focus on Congress would strengthen the role of democratic decision making and allow for distinctions to be drawn among the broad array of federal statutes.

Professor Sandalow seems to think that state courts should not be obliged to hear federal causes of action absent "a declaration by Congress." Why not simply employ conventional methods of statutory interpretation? In this regard, note that *Mondou, McKnett, Mayfield,* and *Douglas* were all Federal Employers Liability Act cases. That statute sets up a federal law tort cause of action on behalf of railroad workers. Though the Court did not rely on legislative intent, an exploration of the background of the statute may have revealed that Congress intended that state courts be available to litigants, because of the volume of litigation, because state courts are familiar with the governing tort principles, and because state courts would often be more convenient to plaintiffs. Similar arguments may have been available in *Testa,* as the price control legislation generated a heavy volume of litigation. As for *Haywood* and *Howlett,* does the background of § 1983, discussed in Chapter 1, suggest that Congress intended to oblige state courts to hear these cases?

Are there constitutional limits on how far Congress may go in regulating state court jurisdiction? The scope of congressional power remains unsettled on some points, "including whether Congress may give state courts jurisdiction of federal criminal actions, or require that plaintiffs bring state law actions only in particular jurisdictions." Anthony J. Bellia, Jr., *Congressional Power and State Court Jurisdiction,* 94 GEO. L. J. 949, 1012 (2006). On what ground might federal criminal prosecutions be distinguished from federal civil litigation?

3.   State Sovereign Immunity. In *Howlett v. Rose,* a case discussed by both the majority and the dissent in *Haywood,* the state courts tried, without success, to assert sovereign immunity as a justification for refusing to adjudicate certain § 1983 cases. Distinguish between the doctrine of sovereign immunity as a matter of *state* law and the federal law sovereign immunity discussed in Chapter 5. States are presumably free, as a matter of state law, to define "sovereign immunity" as they please. But the issue in *Howlett v. Rose* was whether a defendant may defend against a federal claim on grounds of sovereign immunity. On that issue, the state's law of sovereign immunity is not controlling.

The *federal* law of state sovereign immunity sometimes overrides the principle that a state court may not refuse to adjudicate a federal cause of action. *Alden v. Maine*, 527 U.S. 706 (1999) (state avoided monetary liability for claim under the Fair Labor Standards Act). See Chapter 5.

Why did the sovereign immunity argument fail in *Howlett*? The Court said that municipal corporations (like the defendant school district in that case) are not "arms of the state" and therefore do not share its federal law sovereign immunity. The Court's answer is fully in line with its general approach to determining what entities are entitled to assert federal law sovereign immunity. For example, the Court has unanimously rejected the notion that political subdivisions may assert a "residual immunity" predating ratification of the Constitution. *Northern Insurance Co. v. Chatham County, Georgia*, 547 U.S. 189 (2006).

IV.   APPLYING STATE LAW IN ADJUDICATING FEDERAL CAUSES OF ACTION

FELDER V. CASEY
487 U.S. 131 (1988).

JUSTICE BRENNAN delivered the opinion of the Court.

A Wisconsin statute provides that before suit may be brought in state court against a state or local governmental entity or officer, the plaintiff must notify the governmental defendant of the circumstances giving rise to the claim, the amount of the claim, and his or her intent to hold the named defendant liable. The statute further requires that, in order to afford the defendant an opportunity to consider the requested relief, the claimant must refrain from filing suit for 120 days after providing such notice. Failure to comply with these requirements constitutes grounds for dismissal of the action. In the present case, the Supreme Court of Wisconsin held that this notice-of-claim statute applies to federal civil rights actions brought in state court under 42 U.S.C. § 1983. Because we conclude that these requirements are pre-empted as inconsistent with federal law, we reverse.

I

[Felder brought a § 1983 suit in state court, charging that police officers violated his constitutional rights in connection with his arrest for disorderly conduct.] The officers moved to dismiss the suit based on petitioner's failure to comply with the State's notice-of-claim statute. That statute provides that no action may be brought or maintained against any state governmental subdivision, agency, or officer unless the claimant either provides written notice of the claim within 120 days of the alleged injury, or demonstrates that the relevant subdivision, agency, or officer had actual notice of the claim and was not prejudiced by the lack of written notice. The statute further provides that the party seeking redress must also submit an itemized statement of the relief sought to the governmental subdivision or agency, which then has 120 days to grant or disallow the requested relief. Finally, claimants must bring suit within six months of receiving notice that their claim has been disallowed.

[The officers sought dismissal on account of Felder's failure to satisfy the requirements of the notice of claim statute. The Wisconsin Supreme Court upheld the application of the statute and ordered dismissal of the § 1983 suit.] Passing on the question for the first time, the court reasoned that while Congress may establish the procedural framework under which claims are heard in federal courts, States retain the authority under the Constitution to prescribe the rules and procedures that govern actions in their own tribunals. Accordingly, a party who chooses to vindicate a congressionally created right in state court must abide by the State's procedures. Requiring compliance with the notice-of-claim statute, the court determined, does not frustrate the remedial and deterrent purposes of the federal civil rights laws because the statute neither limits the amount a plaintiff may recover for violation of his or her civil rights, nor precludes the possibility of such recovery altogether. Rather, the court reasoned, the notice requirement advances the State's legitimate interests in protecting against stale or fraudulent claims, facilitating prompt settlement of valid claims, and identifying and correcting inappropriate conduct by governmental employees and officials. Turning to the question of compliance in this case, the court concluded that the complaints lodged with the local police by petitioner's neighbors and the letter submitted to the police chief by the local alderman failed to satisfy the statute's actual notice standard, because these communications neither recited the facts giving rise to the alleged injuries nor revealed petitioner's intent to hold the defendants responsible for those injuries.

We granted certiorari, and now reverse.

II

No one disputes the general and unassailable proposition relied upon by the Wisconsin Supreme Court below that States may establish the rules of procedure governing litigation in their own courts. By the same token, however, where state courts entertain a federally created cause of action, the "federal right cannot be defeated by the forms of local practice." *Brown v. Western R. Co. of Alabama*, 338 U.S. 294, 296 (1949). The question before us today, therefore, is essentially one of pre-emption: is the application of the State's notice-of-claim provision to § 1983 actions brought in state courts consistent with the goals of the federal civil rights laws, or does the enforcement of such a requirement instead " 'stan[d] as an obstacle to the accomplishment and execution of the full purposes and objectives of Congress' "? *Perez v. Campbell*, 402 U.S. 637, 649 (1971).

Under the Supremacy Clause of the Federal Constitution, "[t]he relative importance to the State of its own law is not material when there is a conflict with a valid federal law," for "any state law, however clearly within a State's acknowledged power, which interferes with or is contrary to federal law, must yield." *Free v. Bland*, 369 U.S. 663, 666 (1962). Because the notice-of-claim statute at issue here conflicts in both its purpose and effects with the remedial objectives of § 1983, and because its enforcement in such actions will frequently and predictably produce different outcomes in § 1983 litigation based solely on whether the claim is asserted in state or federal court, we conclude that the state law is pre-empted when the § 1983 action is brought in a state court.

A

Section 1983 creates a species of liability in favor of persons deprived of their federal civil rights by those wielding state authority. As we have repeatedly emphasized, "the central objective of the Reconstruction-Era civil rights statutes ... is to ensure that individuals whose federal constitutional or statutory rights are abridged may recover damages or secure injunctive relief." *Burnett v. Grattan*, 468 U.S. 42, 55 (1984). Thus, § 1983 provides "a uniquely federal remedy against incursions ... upon rights secured by the Constitution and laws of the Nation," *Mitchum v. Foster*, 407 U.S. 225, 239 (1972), and is to be accorded "a sweep as broad as its language." *United States v. Price*, 383 U.S. 787, 801 (1966).

Any assessment of the applicability of a state law to federal civil rights litigation, therefore, must be made in light of the purpose and nature of the federal right. This is so whether the question of state-law applicability arises in § 1983 litigation brought in state courts, which possess concurrent jurisdiction over such actions, see *Patsy v. Board of Regents of Florida*, 457 U.S. 496, 506–507 (1982), or in federal-court litigation, where, because the federal civil rights laws fail to provide certain rules of decision thought essential to the orderly adjudication of rights, courts are occasionally called upon to borrow state law. See 42 U.S.C. § 1988. Accordingly, we have held that a state law that immunizes government conduct otherwise subject to suit under § 1983 is preempted, even where the federal civil rights litigation takes place in state court, because the application of the state immunity law would thwart the congressional remedy, see *Martinez v. California*, 444 U.S. 277, 284 (1980), which of course already provides certain immunities for state officials. Similarly, in actions brought in federal courts, we have disapproved the adoption of state statutes of limitation that provide only a truncated period of time within which to file suit, because such statutes inadequately accommodate the complexities of federal civil rights litigation and are thus inconsistent with Congress' compensatory aims. And we have directed the lower federal courts in § 1983 cases to borrow the state-law limitations period for personal injury claims because it is "most unlikely that the period of limitations applicable to such claims ever was, or ever would be, fixed [by the forum State] in a way that would discriminate against federal claims, or be inconsistent with federal law in any respect." *Wilson v. Garcia*, 471 U.S. 261, 279 (1985).

Although we have never passed on the question, the lower federal courts have all, with but one exception, concluded that notice-of-claim provisions are inapplicable to § 1983 actions brought in federal court. These courts have reasoned that, unlike the lack of statutes of limitations in the federal civil rights laws, the absence of any notice-of-claim provision is not a deficiency requiring the importation of such statutes into the federal civil rights scheme. Because statutes of limitation are among the universally familiar aspects of litigation considered indispensable to any scheme of justice, it is entirely reasonable to assume that Congress did not intend to create a right enforceable in perpetuity. Notice-of-claim provisions, by contrast, are neither universally familiar nor in any sense indispensable prerequisites to litigation, and there is thus no reason to suppose that Congress intended federal courts to apply such rules, which "significantly inhibit the ability to bring federal actions."

While we fully agree with this near-unanimous conclusion of the federal courts, that judgment is not dispositive here, where the question is not one of adoption but of pre-emption. Nevertheless, this determination that notice-of-claim statutes are inapplicable to federal-court § 1983 litigation informs our analysis in two crucial respects. First, it demonstrates that the application of the notice requirement burdens the exercise of the federal right by forcing civil rights victims who seek redress in state courts to comply with a requirement that is entirely absent from civil rights litigation in federal courts. This burden, as we explain below, is inconsistent in both design and effect with the compensatory aims of the federal civil rights laws. Second, it reveals that the enforcement of such statutes in § 1983 actions brought in state court will frequently and predictably produce different outcomes in federal civil rights litigation based solely on whether that litigation takes place in state or federal court. States may not apply such an outcome-determinative law when entertaining substantive federal rights in their courts.

B

As we noted above, the central purpose of the Reconstruction-Era laws is to provide compensatory relief to those deprived of their federal rights by state actors. Section 1983 accomplishes this goal by creating a form of liability that, by its very nature, runs only against a specific class of defendants: government bodies and their officials. Wisconsin's notice-of-claim statute undermines this "uniquely federal remedy," in several interrelated ways. First, it conditions the right of recovery that Congress has authorized, and does so for a reason manifestly inconsistent with the purposes of the federal statute: to minimize governmental liability. Nor is this condition a neutral and uniformly applicable rule of procedure;

rather, it is a substantive burden imposed only upon those who seek redress for injuries resulting from the use or misuse of governmental authority. Second, the notice provision discriminates against the federal right. While the State affords the victim of an intentional tort two years to recognize the compensable nature of his or her injury, the civil rights victim is given only four months to appreciate that he or she has been deprived of a federal constitutional or statutory right. Finally, the notice provision operates, in part, as an exhaustion requirement, in that it forces claimants to seek satisfaction in the first instance from the governmental defendant. We think it plain that Congress never intended that those injured by governmental wrongdoers could be required, as a condition of recovery, to submit their claims to the government responsible for their injuries.

(1)

Wisconsin's notice-of-claim statute is part of a broader legislative scheme governing the rights of citizens to sue the State's subdivisions. The statute, both in its earliest and current forms, provides a circumscribed waiver of local governmental immunity that limits the amount recoverable in suits against local governments and imposes the notice requirements at issue [here]. Such statutes "are enacted primarily for the benefit of governmental defendants," and enable those defendants to "investigate early, prepare a stronger case, and perhaps reach an early settlement." Moreover, where the defendant is unable to obtain a satisfactory settlement, the Wisconsin statute forces claimants to bring suit within a relatively short period after the local governing body disallows the claim, in order to "assure prompt initiation of litigation." To be sure, the notice requirement serves the additional purpose of notifying the proper public officials of dangerous physical conditions or inappropriate and unlawful governmental conduct, which allows for prompt corrective measures. This interest, however, is clearly not the predominant objective of the statute. Indeed, the Wisconsin Supreme Court has emphasized that the requisite notice must spell out both the amount of damages the claimant seeks and his or her intent to hold the governing body responsible for those damages precisely because these requirements further the State's interest in minimizing liability and the expenses associated with it. In sum, as respondents explain, the State has chosen to expose its subdivisions to large liability and defense costs, and, in light of that choice, has made the concomitant decision to impose conditions that "assis[t] municipalities in controlling those costs." Brief for Respondents 12. The decision to subject state subdivisions to liability for violations of federal rights, however, was a choice that Congress, not the Wisconsin Legislature, made, and it is a decision that the State has no authority to override. Thus, however understandable or laudable the State's interest in controlling liability expenses might otherwise be, it is patently incompatible with the compensatory goals of the federal legislation, as are the means the State has chosen to effectuate [it].

This burdening of a federal right, moreover, is not the natural or permissible consequence of an otherwise neutral, uniformly applicable state rule. Although it is true that the notice-of-claim statute does not discriminate between state and federal causes of action against local governments, the fact remains that the law's protection extends only to governmental defendants and thus conditions the right to bring suit against the very persons and entities Congress intended to subject to liability. We therefore cannot accept the suggestion that this requirement is simply part of "the vast body of procedural rules, rooted in policies unrelated to the definition of any particular substantive cause of action, that forms no essential part of 'the cause of action' as applied to any given plaintiff." Brief for International City Management Association et al. as Amici Curiae 22 (Brief for Amici Curiae). On the contrary, the notice-of-claim provision is imposed only upon a specific class of plaintiffs—those who sue governmental defendants—and, as we have seen, is firmly rooted in policies very much related to, and to a large extent directly contrary to, the substantive cause of action provided those plaintiffs. This defendant-specific focus of the notice requirement serves to distinguish it, rather starkly, from rules uniformly applicable to all suits, such as rules governing service of process or substitution of parties, which respondents cite as examples of procedural requirements that penalize noncompliance through dismissal. That state courts will hear the entire § 1983 cause of action once a plaintiff complies with the notice-of-claim statute, therefore, in no way alters the fact that the statute discriminates against the precise type of claim Congress has created.

(2)

While respondents and amici suggest that prompt investigation of claims inures to the benefit of claimants and local governments alike, by providing both with an accurate factual picture of the incident, such statutes "are enacted primarily for the benefit of governmental defendants," and are intended to afford such defendants an opportunity to prepare a stronger case. Sound notions of public administration may support the prompt notice requirement, but those policies necessarily clash with the remedial purposes of the federal civil rights laws. In *Wilson*, we held that, for purposes of choosing a limitations period for § 1983 actions, federal courts must apply the state statute of limitations governing personal injury claims because it is highly unlikely that States would ever fix the limitations period applicable to such claims in a manner that would discriminate against the federal right. Here, the notice-of-claim provision most emphatically does discriminate in a manner detrimental to the federal right: only those persons who wish to sue governmental defendants are required to provide notice within such an abbreviated time period. Many civil rights victims, however, will fail to appreciate the compensable nature of their injuries within the 4-month window provided by the notice-of-claim provision, and will thus be barred from asserting their federal right to recovery in state court unless they can show that the defendant had actual notice of the injury, the circumstances giving rise to it, and the claimant's intent to hold the defendant responsible—a showing which, as the facts of this case vividly demonstrate, is not easily made in Wisconsin.

(3)

Finally, the notice provision imposes an exhaustion requirement on persons who choose to assert their federal right in state courts, inasmuch as the § 1983 plaintiff must provide the requisite notice of injury within 120 days of the civil rights violation, then wait an additional 120 days while the governmental defendant investigates the claim and attempts to settle it. In *Patsy v. Board of Regents of Florida*, 457 U.S. 496 (1982), we held that plaintiffs need not exhaust state administrative remedies before instituting § 1983 suits in federal court. The Wisconsin Supreme Court, however, deemed that decision inapplicable to this state-court suit on the theory that States retain the authority to prescribe the rules and procedures governing suits in their courts. As we have just explained, however, that authority does not extend so far as to permit States to place conditions on the vindication of a federal right. Moreover, as we noted in *Patsy*, Congress enacted § 1983 in response to the widespread deprivations of civil rights in the Southern States and the inability or unwillingness of authorities in those States to protect those rights or punish wrongdoers. Although it is true that the principal remedy Congress chose to provide injured persons was immediate access to federal courts, it did not leave the protection of such rights exclusively in the hands of the federal judiciary, and instead conferred concurrent jurisdiction on state courts as well. Given the evil at which the federal civil rights legislation was aimed, there is simply no reason to suppose that Congress meant "to provide these individuals immediate access to the federal courts notwithstanding any provision of state law to the contrary," yet contemplated that those who sought to vindicate their federal rights in state courts could be required to seek redress in the first instance from the very state officials whose hostility to those rights precipitated their [injuries].

C

Respondents and their supporting amici urge that we approve the application of the notice-of-claim statute to § 1983 actions brought in state court as a matter of equitable federalism. [Litigants] who choose to bring their civil rights actions in state courts presumably do so in order to obtain the benefit of certain procedural advantages in those courts, or to draw their juries from urban populations. Having availed themselves of these benefits, civil rights litigants must comply as well with those state rules they find less to their liking.

However equitable this bitter-with-the-sweet argument may appear in the abstract, it has no place under our Supremacy Clause analysis. [As] we have seen, enforcement of the notice-of-claim statute in § 1983 actions brought in state court so interferes with and frustrates the substantive right Congress created that, under the Supremacy Clause, it must yield to the federal interest. This interference, however, is not the only consequence of the statute that renders its application in § 1983 cases invalid. In a State that demands compliance with such a statute before a § 1983 action may be brought or maintained in its courts, the outcome of federal civil rights litigation will frequently and predictably depend on whether it is brought in state or federal court. Thus, the very notions of federalism upon which respondents rely dictate that the State's outcome-determinative law must give way when a party asserts a federal right in state court.

Under *Erie R. Co. v. Tompkins*, when a federal court exercises diversity or pendent jurisdiction over state-law claims, "the outcome of the litigation in the federal court should be substantially the same, so far as legal rules determine the outcome of a litigation, as it would be if tried in a State court." *Guaranty Trust Co. v. York*, 326 U.S. 99, 109 (1945). Accordingly, federal courts entertaining state-law claims against Wisconsin municipalities are obligated to apply the notice-of-claim provision. Just as federal courts are constitutionally obligated to apply state law to state claims, see *Erie*, supra, so too the Supremacy Clause imposes on state courts a constitutional duty "to proceed in such manner that all the substantial rights of the parties under controlling federal law [are] protected." *Garrett v. Moore-McCormack, Co.*, 317 U.S. 239, 245 (1942).

Civil rights victims often do not appreciate the constitutional nature of their injuries, and thus will fail to file a notice of injury or claim within the requisite time period, which in Wisconsin is a mere four months. Unless such claimants can prove that the governmental defendant had actual notice of the claim, which, as we have already noted, is by no means a simple task in Wisconsin, and unless they also file an itemized claim for damages, they must bring their § 1983 suits in federal court or not at all. Wisconsin, however, may not alter the outcome of federal claims it chooses to entertain in its courts by demanding compliance with outcome-determinative rules that are inapplicable when such claims are brought in federal court, for " '[w]hatever spring the State may set for those who are endeavoring to assert rights that the State confers, the assertion of federal rights, when plainly and reasonably made, is not to be defeated under the name of local practice.' " *Brown v. Western R. Co. of Alabama*, supra, 338 U.S., at 298–299. The state notice-of-claim statute is more than a mere rule of procedure: as we discussed above, the statute is a substantive condition on the right to sue governmental officials and entities, and the federal courts have therefore correctly recognized that the notice statute governs the adjudication of state-law claims in diversity actions. In *Guaranty Trust*, supra, we held that, in order to give effect to a State's statute of limitations, a federal court could not hear a state-law action that a state court would deem time barred. Conversely, a state court may not decline to hear an otherwise properly presented federal claim because that claim would be barred under a state law requiring timely filing of notice. State courts simply are not free to vindicate the substantive interests underlying a state rule of decision at the expense of the federal right.

Finally, in *Wilson*, we characterized § 1983 suits as claims for personal injuries because such an approach ensured that the same limitations period would govern all § 1983 actions brought in any given State, and thus comported with Congress' desire that the federal civil rights laws be given a uniform application within each State. A law that predictably alters the outcome of § 1983 claims depending solely on whether they are brought in state or federal court within the same State is obviously inconsistent with this federal interest in intrastate uniformity.

III

In enacting § 1983, Congress entitled those deprived of their civil rights to recover full compensation from the governmental officials responsible for those deprivations. A state law that conditions that right of recovery upon compliance with a rule designed to minimize governmental liability, and that directs injured persons to seek redress in the first instance from the very targets of the federal legislation, is inconsistent in both purpose and effect with the remedial objectives of the federal civil rights law. Principles of federalism, as well as the Supremacy Clause, dictate that such a state law must give way to vindication of the federal right when that right is asserted in state court.

Accordingly, the judgment of the Supreme Court of Wisconsin is reversed, and the case is remanded for further proceedings not inconsistent with this opinion.

JUSTICE WHITE, concurring.

[The] application of the Wisconsin notice-of-claim statute to bar petitioner's § 1983 suit—which is "in reality, 'an action for injury to personal rights'" [undermines] the purposes of *Wilson v. Garcia* to promote "[t]he federal interests in uniformity, certainty, and the minimization of unnecessary litigation," and assure that state procedural rules do not "discriminate against the federal civil rights remedy." I therefore agree that in view of the adverse impact of Wisconsin's notice-of-claim statute on the federal policies articulated in *Wilson v. Garcia*, the Supremacy Clause proscribes the statute's application to § 1983 suits brought in Wisconsin state courts.

JUSTICE O'CONNOR, with whom THE CHIEF JUSTICE joins, dissenting.

"A state statute cannot be considered 'inconsistent' with federal law merely because the statute causes the plaintiff to lose the litigation." *Robertson v. Wegmann*, 436 U.S. 584, 593 (1978). Disregarding this self-evident principle, the Court today holds that Wisconsin's notice of claim statute is pre-empted by federal law as to actions under 42 U.S.C. § 1983 filed in state court. This holding is not supported by the statute whose pre-emptive force it purports to invoke, or by our [precedents].

Wisconsin's notice of claim statute [serves] at least two important purposes apart from providing municipal defendants with a special affirmative defense in litigation. First, the statute helps ensure that public officials will receive prompt notice of wrongful conditions or practices, and thus enables them to take prompt corrective action. Second, it enables officials to investigate claims in a timely fashion, thereby making it easier to ascertain the facts accurately and to settle meritorious claims without litigation. These important aspects of the Wisconsin statute bring benefits to governments and claimants alike, and it should come as no surprise that 37 other States have apparently adopted similar notice of claim requirements. Without some compellingly clear indication that Congress has forbidden the States to apply such statutes in their own courts, there is no reason to conclude that they are "pre-empted" by federal law. Allusions to such vague concepts as "the compensatory aims of the federal civil rights laws," which are all that the Court actually relies on, do not provide an adequate substitute for the statutory analysis that we customarily require of ourselves before we reach out to find statutory pre-emption of legitimate procedures used by the States in their own courts. Section 1983, it is worth recalling, creates no substantive law. It merely provides one vehicle by which certain provisions of the Constitution and other federal laws may be judicially enforced. Its purpose, as we have repeatedly said, " 'was to interpose the federal courts between the States and the people, as guardians of the people's federal rights. . . .' " [Congress] has never given the slightest indication that § 1983 was meant to replace state procedural rules with those that apply in the federal courts. The majority does not, because it cannot, cite any evidence to the [contrary.]

Unable to find support for its position in § 1983 itself, or in its legislative history, the majority suggests that the Wisconsin statute somehow "discriminates against the federal right." The Wisconsin statute, however, applies to all actions against municipal defendants, whether brought under state or federal law. The majority is therefore compelled to adopt a new theory of discrimination, under which the challenged statute is said to "conditio[n] the right to bring suit against the very persons and entities [viz., local governments and officials] Congress intended to subject to liability." This theory, however, is untenable. First, the statute erects no barrier at all to a plaintiff's right to bring a § 1983 suit against anyone. Every plaintiff has the option of proceeding in federal court, and the Wisconsin statute has not the slightest effect on that right. Second, if a plaintiff chooses to proceed in the Wisconsin state courts, those courts stand ready to hear the entire federal cause of action, as the majority concedes. Thus, the Wisconsin statute "discriminates" only against a right that Congress has never created: the right of a plaintiff to have the benefit of selected federal court procedures after the plaintiff has rejected the federal forum and chosen a state forum instead. The majority's "discrimination" theory is just another version of its unsupported conclusion that Congress intended to force the state courts to adopt procedural rules from the federal [courts].

The Court also suggests that there is some parallel between this case and cases that are tried in federal court under the doctrine of *Erie R. Co. v. Tompkins*. [The] Court opines today that state courts hearing federal suits are obliged to mirror federal procedures to the same extent that federal courts are obliged to mirror state procedures in diversity suits. This suggestion seems to be based on a sort of upside-down theory of federalism, which the Court attributes to Congress on the basis of no evidence at all. Nor are the implications of this "reverse-*Erie*" theory quite clear. If the Court means the theory to be taken seriously, it should follow that defendants, as well as plaintiffs, are entitled to the benefit of all federal court procedural rules that are "outcome determinative." If, however, the Court means to create a rule that benefits only plaintiffs, then the discussion of *Erie* principles is simply an unsuccessful effort to find some analogy, no matter how attenuated, to today's unprecedented holding.

"Borrowing" cases under 42 U.S.C. § 1988, which the Court cites several times, have little more to do with today's decision than does *Erie*. Under that statute and those cases, we are sometimes called upon to fill in gaps in federal law by choosing a state procedural rule for application in § 1983 actions brought in federal court. The congressionally imposed necessity of *supplementing* federal law with state procedural rules might well caution us against *supplanting* state procedural rules with federal gaps, but it certainly offers no support for what the Court does [today].

As I noted at the outset, the majority correctly characterizes the issue before us as one of statutory pre-emption. In order to arrive at the result it has chosen, however, the Court is forced to search for "inconsistencies" between Wisconsin's notice of claim statute and some ill-defined federal policy that Congress has never articulated, implied, or suggested, let alone enacted. Nor is there any difficulty in explaining the absence of congressional attention to the problem that the Court wrongly imagines it is solving. A plaintiff who chooses to bring a § 1983 action in state court necessarily rejects the federal courts that Congress has provided. Virtually the only conceivable reason for doing so is to benefit from procedural advantages available exclusively in state court. Having voted with their feet for state procedural systems, such plaintiffs would hardly be in a position to ask Congress for a new type of forum that combines the advantages that Congress gave them in the federal system with those that Congress did not give them, and which are only available in state [courts].

NOTES ON THE ROLE OF STATE LAW IN STATE COURT ADJUDICATION OF FEDERAL CLAIMS

1. **Borrowing State Law Under § 1988.** Be careful to distinguish, as the Court does, between the *Felder* issue (whether a given state procedural rule should be applied in state court § 1983 suits) and the issue of whether a federal court should borrow a state statute for some purpose. 42 U.S.C. § 1988 directs federal courts in civil rights cases to apply state law to fill in gaps, "so far as the same is not inconsistent with the Constitution and laws of the United States." As a practical matter, the Court directs federal courts to borrow state law to deal with issues that are ordinarily addressed by statute, like the statute of limitations issue in *Wilson v. Garcia,* or the circumstances in which a tort suit survives the death of the victim, see *Robertson v. Wegmann,* 436 U.S. 584 (1978). As Justice O'Connor points out in her *Felder* dissent, no issue of federal preemption of state law comes up in such a case. Displacing the state law notice-of-claim requirement in state court litigation involves a greater intrusion on state prerogatives and, consequently, requires greater justification. Nonetheless, the Court thought the general rejection of state notice-of-claim statutes in federal court § 1983 litigation was relevant to the preemption issue. Why?

2. **Factors That Matter in Deciding Whether Federal Law Displaces the State Rule.** The first principle to keep in mind in dealing with the preemption issue is that state law will be displaced if it squarely conflicts with federal law, like a rule granting absolute immunity to conduct which is actionable under federal law. That was the problem in *Martinez v. California.* The notice of claim provision in *Felder* does not directly obstruct federal law, but it does put a hurdle in the way of achieving the goals of § 1983. Besides the goals of the federal statute, one factor that mattered in *Felder* was whether (or the extent to which) the rule determines the outcome. The Court thought that the notice-of-claim rule would decide cases often enough to be worrisome. In support of this emphasis on outcome, Justice Brennan cited the *Erie* doctrine and continued:

> Just as federal courts are constitutionally obligated to apply state law to state claims, see *Erie*, supra, so too the Supremacy Clause imposes on state courts a constitutional duty "to proceed in such manner that all the substantial rights of the parties under controlling federal law [are] protected."

The dissent responded: "This suggestion seems to be based on a sort of upside-down theory of federalism, which the Court attributes to Congress on the basis of no evidence at all."

Is the *Erie* doctrine, which places constitutional limits on the power of the federal courts to make common law, sufficiently similar to the preemption issue in *Felder* to warrant the Court's analogy? Is the dissent right that, in the event one endorses the analogy, federal rules that favor defendants would also preempt state law? See note 3 infra.

Another factor in *Felder* was that the "predominant objective" of the notice-of-claim provision was "to further the State's interest in minimizing liability," a policy that is at odds with the compensatory goal of § 1983. Suppose, however, the state rule puts obstacles in the plaintiff's way, yet the rule is aimed at "neutral" policies having nothing to do with hindering plaintiffs. For example, the Federal Rules allow broader discovery than many state systems. Should the state rules have to give way in state court § 1983 cases because they could stand in the way of the plaintiff's success. In *Denari v. Superior Court*, 215 Cal.App.3d 1488, 264 Cal.Rptr. 261 (1989), the court applied an evidentiary privilege under state law to deny a discovery request for the names of persons arrested and booked at a county jail, made by a § 1983 plaintiff seeking potential witnesses.

The court thought that this case differed from *Felder*:

> The recognition of the right to privacy of all citizens of the state, along with the concomitant protection of such right in the context of civil discovery, is certainly not antagonistic to the remedial objectives of section 1983; the effect of such right does not necessarily conflict with the objectives of the civil rights tort. [Unlike] the [notice of claim statute at issue in *Felder*] our qualified protection of a privacy right does not play a conclusive role in defining the outcome of the cause of action. [This] is not to say that in a particular case the results might not differ depending upon the forum, only that the rule itself is not outcome determinative with respect to litigation in general. [Finally,] the *Felder* Court considered whether the rule was a "neutral and uniformly applicable rule of procedure." Here, of course, the limits on discovery pursuant to the right of privacy apply in both civil and criminal cases and are equally applicable to both parties. 215 Cal.App. 3d at 1499, 1501–02.

Does the court successfully distinguish *Felder*? What result if a state rule forbids discovery of official documents? Should state court pleading rules be overridden, if they require more specific pleading of facts than the federal rules? State law limits on class actions? See Burt Neuborne, *Toward Procedural Parity in Constitutional Litigation*, 22 WM. & MARY L. REV. 725 (1981).

3. State Court Rules that Disfavor Defendants. In *Mitchell v. Forsyth*, 472 U.S. 511 (1985), the Court ruled that a § 1983 defendant in federal court has a right to an interlocutory appeal of a district judge's denial of official immunity. *Johnson v. Fankell*, 520 U.S. 911 (1997), was a § 1983 case litigated in an Idaho state court. The trial judge denied official immunity and the state courts declined to allow an interlocutory appeal, despite *Mitchell*. The Supreme Court affirmed, ruling that state courts are not required to follow *Mitchell*. They may apply their own rules on interlocutory appeals:

Petitioners [contend] that, to the extent that Idaho Appellate Rule 11(a)(1) does not allow an interlocutory appeal, it is pre-empted by § 1983. Relying heavily on *Felder*, petitioners first assert that pre-emption is necessary to avoid "different outcomes in § 1983 litigation based solely on whether the claim is asserted in state or federal court." Second, they argue that the state procedure "impermissibly burden[s]" the federal immunity from suit because it does not adequately protect their right to prevail on the immunity question in advance of trial.

For two reasons, petitioners have a heavy burden of persuasion in making this argument. First, our normal presumption against pre-emption is buttressed by the fact that the Idaho Supreme Court's dismissal of the appeal rested squarely on a neutral state Rule regarding the administration of the state courts. A second barrier to petitioners' argument arises from the nature of the interest protected by the defense of qualified immunity. Petitioners' argument for pre-emption is bottomed on their claims that the Idaho rules are interfering with their federal rights. While it is true that the defense has its source in a federal statute (§ 1983), the ultimate purpose of qualified immunity is to protect the State and its officials from overenforcement of federal rights. The Idaho Supreme Court's application of the State's procedural rules in this context is thus less an interference with federal interests than a judgment about how best to balance the competing state interests of limiting interlocutory appeals and providing state officials with immediate review of the merits of their defense.

Petitioners' arguments for pre-emption are not strong enough to overcome these considerable hurdles. Contrary to petitioners' assertions, Idaho's decision not to provide appellate review for the vast majority of interlocutory orders—including denials of qualified immunity in § 1983 cases—is not "outcome determinative" in the sense that we used that term when we held that Wisconsin's notice-of-claim statute could not be applied to defeat a federal civil rights action brought in state courts under § 1983. The failure to comply with the Wisconsin statute in *Felder* resulted in a judgment dismissing a complaint that would not have been dismissed—at least not without a judicial determination of the merits of the claim—if the case had been filed in a federal court. One of the primary grounds for our decision was that, because the notice-of-claim requirement would "frequently and predictably produce different outcomes" depending on whether § 1983 claims were brought in state or federal court, it was inconsistent with the federal interest in uniformity. Petitioners' reliance on *Felder* is misplaced because "outcome," as we used the term there, referred to the ultimate disposition of the case.

If petitioners' claim to qualified immunity is meritorious, there is no suggestion that the application of the Idaho rules of procedure will produce a final result different from what a federal ruling would produce. Petitioners were able to argue their immunity from suit claim to the trial court, just as they would to a federal court. And the claim will be reviewable by the Idaho Supreme Court after the trial court enters a final judgment, thus providing petitioners with a further chance to urge their immunity. Consequently, the postponement of the appeal until after final judgment will not affect the ultimate outcome of the case.

Petitioners' second argument for pre-emption of the state procedural Rule is that the Rule does not adequately protect their right to prevail in advance of trial. In evaluating this contention, it is important to focus on the precise source and scope of the federal right at issue. The right to have the trial court rule on the merits of the qualified immunity defense presumably has its source in § 1983, but the right to immediate appellate review of that ruling in a federal case has its source in § 1291. The former right is fully protected by Idaho. The latter right, however, is a federal procedural right that simply does not apply in a nonfederal forum.

[When] preemption of state law is at issue, we must respect the "principles [that] are fundamental to a system of federalism in which the state courts share responsibility for the application and enforcement of federal law." *Howlett*, 496 U.S., at 372–373. This respect is at its apex when we confront a claim that federal law requires a State to undertake something as fundamental as restructuring the operation of its courts. We therefore cannot agree with petitioners that § 1983's recognition of the defense of qualified immunity pre-empts a State's consistent application of its neutral procedural rules, even when those rules deny an interlocutory appeal in this context.

Is the Court's reasoning faithful to *Mitchell*'s characterization of immunity as "an entitlement not to stand trial or face the other burdens of litigation," and not simply a defense against liability?

The foregoing materials focus on state court § 1983 suits. The issue of whether a state court must follow federal rules in adjudicating federal causes of action comes up in other contexts as well. In particular, tort suits brought against railroads by their employees under the Federal Employers' Liability Act are often litigated in state courts. The following case illustrates the choice of law problem in that context.

DICE V. AKRON, CANTON & YOUNGSTOWN R.R.

342 U.S. 359 (1952).

Opinion of the Court by MR. JUSTICE BLACK, announced by MR. JUSTICE DOUGLAS.

Petitioner, a railroad fireman, was seriously injured when an engine in which he was riding jumped the track. Alleging that his injuries were due to respondent's negligence, he brought this action for damages under the Federal Employers' Liability Act in an Ohio court of common pleas. Respondent's defenses were (1) a denial of negligence and (2) a written document signed by petitioner purporting to release respondent in full for $924.63. Petitioner admitted that he had signed several receipts for payments made him in connection with his injuries but denied that he had made a full and complete settlement of all his claims. He alleged that the purported release was void because he had signed it relying on respondent's deliberately false statement that the document was nothing more than a mere receipt for back wages. After both parties had introduced considerable evidence the jury found in favor of petitioner and awarded him a $25,000 verdict. The trial judge later entered judgment notwithstanding the verdict. In doing so he reappraised the evidence as to fraud, found that petitioner had been "guilty of supine negligence" in failing to read the release, and accordingly held that the facts did not "sustain either in law or equity the allegations of fraud by clear, unequivocal and convincing evidence." This judgment notwithstanding the verdict was reversed by the Court of Appeals of Summit County, Ohio, on the ground that under federal law, which controlled, the jury's verdict must stand because there was ample evidence to support its finding of fraud. The Ohio Supreme Court, one judge dissenting, reversed the Court of Appeals' judgment and sustained the trial court's action, holding that: (1) Ohio, not federal, law governed; (2) under that law petitioner, a man of ordinary intelligence who could read, was bound by the release even though he had been induced to sign it by the deliberately false statement that it was only a receipt for back wages; and (3) under controlling Ohio law factual issues as to fraud in the execution of this release were properly decided by the judge rather than by the jury. We granted certiorari because the decision of the Supreme Court of Ohio appeared to deviate from previous decisions of this Court that federal law governs cases arising under the Federal Employers' Liability Act.

First. We agree with the Court of Appeals of Summit County, Ohio, and the dissenting judge in the Ohio Supreme Court and hold that validity of releases under the Federal Employers' Liability Act raises a federal question to be determined by federal rather than state law. Congress in § 1 of the Act granted petitioner a right to recover against his employer for damages negligently inflicted. State laws are not controlling in determining what the incidents of this federal right shall be. Manifestly the federal rights affording relief to injured railroad employees under a federally declared standard could be defeated if states were permitted to have the final say as to what defenses could and could not be properly interposed to suits under the Act. Moreover, only if federal law controls can the federal Act be given that uniform application throughout the country essential to effectuate its purposes. Releases and other devices designed to liquidate or defeat injured employees' claims play an important part in the federal Act's administration. Their validity is but one of the many interrelated questions that must constantly be determined in these cases according to a uniform federal law.

Second. In effect the Supreme Court of Ohio held that an employee trusts his employer at his peril, and that the negligence of an innocent worker is sufficient to enable his employer to benefit by its deliberate fraud. Application of so harsh a rule to defeat a railroad employee's claim is wholly incongruous with the general policy of the Act to give railroad employees a right to recover just compensation for injuries negligently inflicted by their employers. And this Ohio rule is out of harmony with modern judicial and legislative practice to relieve injured persons from the effect of releases fraudulently obtained. We hold that the correct federal rule is that announced by the Court of Appeals of Summit County, Ohio, and the dissenting judge in the Ohio Supreme Court—a release of rights under the Act is void when the employee is induced to sign it by the deliberately false and material statements of the railroad's authorized representatives made to deceive the employee as to the contents of the release. The trial court's charge to the jury correctly stated this rule of law.

Third. Ohio provides and has here accorded petitioner the usual jury trial of factual issues relating to negligence. But Ohio treats factual questions of fraudulent releases differently. It permits the judge trying a negligence case to resolve all factual questions of fraud "other than fraud in the factum." The factual issue of fraud is thus split into fragments, some to be determined by the judge, others by the jury.

It is contended that since a state may consistently with the Federal Constitution provide for trial of cases under the Act by a nonunanimous verdict, *Minneapolis & St. Louis R. Co. v. Bombolis*, 241 U.S. 211, Ohio may lawfully eliminate trial by jury as to one phase of fraud while allowing jury trial as to all other issues raised. The *Bombolis* case might be more in point had Ohio abolished trial by jury in all negligence cases including those arising under the federal Act. But Ohio has not done this. It has provided jury trials for cases arising under the federal Act but seeks to single out one phase of the question of fraudulent releases for determination by a judge rather than by a jury. Compare *Testa v. Katt*, 330 U.S. 386.

We have previously held that "The right to trial by jury is 'a basic and fundamental feature of our system of federal jurisprudence'" and that it is "part and parcel of the remedy afforded railroad workers under the Employers' Liability Act." *Bailey v. Central Vermont R. Inc.*, 319 U.S. 350, 354. We also recognized in that case that to deprive railroad workers of the benefit of a jury trial where there is evidence to support negligence 'is to take away a goodly portion of the relief which Congress has afforded them.' It follows that the right to trial by jury is too substantial a part of the rights accorded by the Act to permit it to be classified as a mere 'local rule of procedure' for denial in the manner that Ohio has here used." *Brown v. Western R. Co.*, 338 U.S. 294.

The trial judge and the Ohio Supreme Court erred in holding that petitioner's rights were to be determined by Ohio law and in taking away petitioner's verdict when the issues of fraud had been submitted to the jury on conflicting evidence and determined in petitioner's favor. The judgment of the Court of Appeals of Summit County, Ohio, was correct and should not have been reversed by the Supreme Court of Ohio. The cause is reversed and remanded to the Supreme Court of Ohio for further action not inconsistent with this opinion.

Reversed and remanded with directions.

MR. JUSTICE FRANKFURTER, whom MR. JUSTICE REED, MR. JUSTICE JACKSON and MR. JUSTICE BURTON join, concurring for reversal but dissenting from the Court's opinion.

Ohio, as do many other States, maintains the old division between law and equity as to the mode of trying issues, even though the same judge administers both. The Ohio Supreme Court has told us what, on one issue, is the division of functions in all negligence actions brought in the Ohio courts: "Where it is claimed that a release was induced by fraud (other than fraud in the factum) or by mistake, it is * * * necessary, before seeking to enforce a cause of action which such release purports to bar, that equitable relief from the release be secured." 155 Ohio St. 185, 186, 98 N.E.2d 301, 304. Thus, in all cases in Ohio, the judge is the trier of fact on this issue of fraud, rather than the jury. It is contended that the Federal Employers' Liability Act requires that Ohio courts send the fraud issue to a jury in the cases founded on that Act. To require Ohio to try a particular issue before a different fact-finder in negligence actions brought under the Employers' Liability Act from the fact-finder on the identical issue in every other negligence case disregards the settled distribution of judicial power between Federal and State courts where Congress authorizes concurrent enforcement of federally-created rights.

It has been settled ever since *Mondou* that no State which gives its courts jurisdiction over common law actions for negligence may deny access to its courts for a negligence action founded on the Federal Employers' Liability Act. Nor may a State discriminate disadvantageously against actions for negligence under the Federal Act as compared with local causes of action in negligence. *McKnett, Mayfield*.

Conversely, however, simply because there is concurrent jurisdiction in Federal and State courts over actions under the Employers' Liability Act, a State is under no duty to treat actions arising under that Act differently from the way it adjudicates local actions for negligence, so far as the mechanics of litigation, the forms in which law is administered, are concerned. This surely covers the distribution of functions as between judge and jury in the determination of the issues in a negligence case.

In 1916 the Court decided without dissent that States in entertaining actions under the Federal Employers' Liability Act need not provide a jury system other than that established for local negligence actions. States are not compelled to provide the jury required of Federal courts by the Seventh Amendment. *Minneapolis & St. L.R. Co. v. Bombolis.* In the thirty-six years since this early decision after the enactment of the Federal Employers' Liability Act, 35 Stat. 65 (1908), the *Bombolis* case has often been cited by this Court but never questioned. Until today its significance has been to leave to States the choice of the fact-finding tribunal in all negligence actions, including those arising under the Federal [Act].

Although a State must entertain negligence suits brought under the Federal Employers' Liability Act if it entertains ordinary actions for negligence, it need conduct them only in the way in which it conducts the run of negligence litigation. The *Bombolis* case directly establishes that the Employers' Liability Act does not impose the jury requirements of the Seventh Amendment on the States pro tanto for Employers' Liability litigation. If its reasoning means anything, the *Bombolis* decision means that, if a State chooses not to have a jury at all, but to leave questions of fact in all negligence actions to a court, certainly the Employers' Liability Act does not require a State to have juries for negligence actions brought under the Federal Act in its courts. Or, if a State chooses to retain the old double system of courts, common law and equity—as did a good many States until the other day, and as four States still do—surely there is nothing in the Employers' Liability Act that requires traditional distribution of authority for disposing of legal issues as between common law and chancery courts to go by the board. And, if States are free to make a distribution of functions between equity and common law courts, it surely makes no rational difference whether a State chooses to provide that the same judge preside on both the common law and the chancery sides in a single litigation, instead of in separate rooms in the same building. So long as all negligence suits in a State are treated in the same way, by the same mode of disposing equitable, non-jury, and common law, jury issues, the State does not discriminate against Employers' Liability suits nor does it make any inroad upon substance.

Ohio and her sister States with a similar division of functions between law and equity are not trying to evade their duty under the Federal Employers' Liability Act; nor are they trying to make it more difficult for railroad workers to recover, than for those suing under local law. The States merely exercise a preference in adhering to historic ways of dealing with a claim of fraud; they prefer the traditional way of making unavailable through equity an otherwise valid defense. The State judges and local lawyers who must administer the Federal Employers' Liability Act in State courts are trained in the ways of local practice; it multiplies the difficulties and confuses the administration of justice to require, on purely theoretical grounds, a hybrid of State and Federal practice in the State courts as to a single class of cases. Nothing in the Employers' Liability Act or in the judicial enforcement of the Act for over forty years forces such judicial hybridization upon the States. The fact that Congress authorized actions under the Federal Employers' Liability Act to be brought in State as well as in Federal courts seems a strange basis for the inference that Congress overrode State procedural arrangements controlling all other negligence suits in a State, by imposing upon State courts to which plaintiffs choose to go the rules prevailing in the Federal courts regarding juries. Such an inference is admissible, so it seems to me, only on the theory that Congress included as part of the right created by the Employers' Liability Act an assumed likelihood that trying all issues to juries is more favorable to plaintiffs. At least, if a plaintiff's right to have all issues decided by a jury rather than the court is "part and parcel of the remedy afforded railroad workers under the Employers Liability Act," the *Bombolis* case should be overruled explicitly instead of left as a derelict bound to occasion collisions on the waters of the law. We have put the questions squarely because they seem to be precisely what will be roused in the minds of lawyers properly pressing their clients' interests and in the minds of trial and appellate judges called upon to apply this Court's opinion. It is one thing not to borrow trouble from the morrow. It is another thing to create trouble for the morrow.

Even though the method of trying the equitable issue of fraud which the State applies in all other negligence cases governs Employers' Liability cases, two questions remain for decision: Should the validity of the release be tested by a Federal or a State standard? And if by a Federal one, did the Ohio courts in the present case correctly administer the standard? If the States afford courts for enforcing the Federal Act, they must enforce the substance of the right given by Congress. They cannot depreciate the legislative currency issued by Congress—either expressly or by local methods of enforcement that accomplish the same result. *Davis v. Wechsler*, 263 U.S. 22, 24. In order to prevent diminution of railroad workers' nationally-uniform right to recover, the standard for the validity of a release of contested liability must be [Federal]. The admitted fact that the injured worker signed the release is material in tending to show the release to be valid, but presumptions must not be drawn from that fact so as to hobble the plaintiff's showing that it would be unjust to allow a formally good defense to prevail.

The judgment of the Ohio Supreme Court must be reversed for it applied the State rule as to validity of [releases]. Moreover, we cannot say with confidence that the Ohio trial judge applied the Federal standard correctly. He duly recognized that "the Federal law controls as to the validity of a release pleaded and proved in bar of the action, and the burden of showing that the alleged fraud vitiates the contract or compromise or release rests upon the party attacking the release." And he made an extended analysis of the relevant circumstances of the release, concluding, however, that there was no "clear, unequivocal and convincing evidence" of fraud. Since these elusive words fail to assure us that the trial judge followed the Federal test and did not require some larger quantum of proof, we would return the case for further proceedings on the sole question of fraud in the release.

NOTE ON CONFLICTS BETWEEN STATE RULES AND FEDERAL POLICY

It is folly to think that there is a bright line between situations in which the state rule does and does not interfere too much with federal policy. There is a spectrum of "interferences" with *Martinez* at one extreme, and administrative rules regarding, say, the composition of the jury pool at the other. *Felder*, *Johnson*, and *Dice* are all somewhere in the middle. Is *Dice* a stronger case for preemption than *Felder*? In this regard, is it relevant that § 1983 protects *constitutional* rights? Do the opinions in *Dice* and *Felder* suggest that the Court has altered its general approach to the preemption issue over the years? If so, how? Notice, for example, that the *Dice* Court did not rely on the *Erie* analogy. Should it have done so?

Besides the goals of the federal statute and the impact of the state rule on outcome, judicial stances on general issues of federalism versus nationalism will probably play a role in the close cases. In *Dice*, Justice Frankfurter, an ardent champion of the state courts, was not persuaded that the state's rule on judicial fact finding should be preempted. Why did he distinguish, as Justice Douglas did not, between the jury trial issue and the issue of whether the validity of a release should be governed by federal or state law?

CHAPTER 8

SUPREME COURT REVIEW OF
STATE JUDGMENTS

■ ■ ■

The United States Supreme Court reviews the work of both federal and state courts and has the last word in resolving federal questions. No one questions the legitimacy of Supreme Court review of state court judgments that turn on federal law. But state courts are the ultimate authorities on matters of state law. If a state court case concerns solely state law questions, the Supreme Court may not review it. The hard issues regarding the scope of Supreme Court review arise in "mixed" cases from the state courts, by which we mean cases that involve *both* state and federal law. Because federal law often governs some of the issues raised by a dispute, without wholly displacing state law, there are in practice many such cases.

Most of the relevant constitutional text is found in Article III. Section 1 provides that "[t]he judicial power of the United States, shall be vested in one supreme Court, and in such inferior courts as Congress may from time to time ordain and establish." Under Section 2, "[t]he judicial power shall extend to all Cases [arising] under this Constitution, the Laws of the United States," and to other matters. On most topics, "the supreme Court shall have appellate jurisdiction, both as to Law and Fact, with such Exceptions, and under such Regulations, as the Congress shall make." And keep in mind the Supremacy Clause of Article VI: "This Constitution, and the Laws of the United States which shall be made in Pursuance thereof [shall] be the Supreme Law of the Land; and the Judges in every State shall be bound thereby, any Thing in the Constitution or Laws of any State to the Contrary notwithstanding."

Article III's reference to "Exceptions" and "Regulations" grants Congress some measure of control over the Supreme Court's jurisdiction. The scope of this congressional power is taken up in Chapter 10. For now, it suffices to note that Congress has often accorded the Supreme Court something less than the full scope of the jurisdiction allowable under Article III. Section 25 of the Judiciary Act of 1789 authorized Supreme Court review, but limited it to the federal questions raised by state decisions that ruled *against* claims of federal right. A 1914 statute extended review to judgments *upholding* the federal claim. Before 1988, the jurisdictional statutes obliged the Supreme Court to hear some cases, (i.e., the jurisdiction was by "appeal") while granting the Court discretion to decide whether to take other cases (i.e., "by writ of certiorari"). In practice, this meant that many cases were technically decided on their merits (because they reached the Supreme Court on "appeal") even though the Court gave them scant attention and prepared no opinion. That year Congress largely eliminated the mandatory jurisdiction, leaving the Court free to decide for itself what cases to hear.

Special circumstances aside, the general statute on Supreme Court review of state judgments is 28 U.S.C. § 1257(a):

> Final judgments or decrees rendered by the highest court of a State in which a decision could be had, may be reviewed by the Supreme Court by writ of certiorari where the validity of a treaty or statute of the United States is drawn in question or where the validity of a statute of any State is drawn in question on the ground of its being repugnant to the Constitution, treaties, or laws of the United States, or where any title, right, privilege, or immunity is specially set up or claimed under the Constitution or the treaties or statutes of, or any commission held or authority exercised under, the United States.

The basic rule embodied in this language is that the Supreme Court may, at its discretion, review any state judgment that turns on a matter of federal law. The big issue—an issue of both statutory construction and constitutional principle—is determining what the term "drawn in question" means.

In this chapter we focus on the questions raised by Supreme Court review of *state* court decisions. There are few constraints on the Court's power to review rulings by the lower federal courts. It may, for example, take cases from those courts that involve only state law questions, though it rarely chooses to do so in the post-*Erie* jurisdictional regime. Review is generally by certiorari, i.e., at the Court's discretion. The most important limit on review concerns whether or not a given order is "final." See Part V, infra. Except where Congress specially provides otherwise, the statute governing review of federal court rulings is 28 U.S.C. § 1254. The main exception is that the Court is obliged to hear certain challenges to reapportionment of legislative districts. Sometimes exceptional circumstances lead Congress to require the Court to take a particular case. For example, the McCain-Feingold campaign finance legislation contained a provision that Supreme Court review of challenges to the statute would be by way of appeal, and thus mandatory. Pub. L. 107–155, Title IV, § 403, Mar. 27, 2002, 116 Stat. 113. See *McConnell v. Federal Election Comm'n*, 540 U.S. 93 (2003).

I.   ESTABLISHING THE CONSTITUTIONAL VALIDITY OF SUPREME COURT REVIEW OF STATE JUDGMENTS

The proposition that the Supreme Court may review the judgments of state courts may seem obvious from the language of Article III and the Supremacy Clause of Article VI. The legislative history of Article III leads to the same conclusion. The debates at the 1787 Constitutional Convention over the content of Article III include fierce arguments over the need for lower federal courts, but indicate broad agreement on the need for a national Supreme Court to finally decide issues of federal law. The members of the First Congress evidently thought Supreme Court review of state judgments raised no constitutional problem. Even so, partisans of states' rights in the early Republic challenged the practice.

In 1813 the Supreme Court took a case involving title to a vast tract of land in northern Virginia. One of the parties, named Martin, was a British subject whose claim came from a devise to him by Lord Fairfax, who had earlier obtained the property under a grant from the British Crown. The other party, "Hunter's Lessee," asserted a claim that derived from a land grant by the state of Virginia, after Virginia had taken the land away from Martin. The core substantive issue was whether a federal law, the 1783 peace treaty with Great Britain, protected Martin's rights against later efforts by Virginia to control the property. Virginia maintained that it had obtained the property before 1783, by a statute that escheated property held by enemy aliens, so that the treaty had no bearing on the case. A difficulty for Virginia's position was that Lord Fairfax, though a British subject, had remained neutral during the Revolution.

After years of intermittent litigation, the Virginia Supreme Court of Appeals (as the highest court in Virginia was called at that time) ruled in favor of Hunter's Lessee. Martin appealed and the U.S. Supreme Court overturned the Virginia Court's decision in *Fairfax's Devisee v. Hunter's Lessee*, 11 U.S. (7 Cranch) 603 (1813). The Virginia Court then declined to obey the mandate, declaring "that the appellate power of the supreme court of the United States does not extend to this court, under a sound construction of the constitution of the United States; that so much of the 25th section of the act of congress to establish the judicial courts of the United States, as extends the appellate jurisdiction of the supreme court to this court, is not in pursuance of the constitution of the United States."

Staking out the ground on which the Virginia judges stood, Judge Cabell maintained that the Article III directives were not aimed at giving the United States Supreme Court the authority to settle the controverted issues:

It must have been foreseen that controversies would sometimes arise as to the boundaries of the two jurisdictions. Yet the constitution has provided no umpire, has erected no tribunal by which they shall be settled. [Before] one Court can dictate to another, the judgment it shall pronounce, it must bear, to that other, the relation of an appellate Court. The term appellate, however, necessarily includes the idea of superiority. But one Court cannot be correctly said to be superior to another, unless both of them belong to the same sovereignty. [The] Courts of the United States, therefore, belonging to one sovereignty, cannot be appellate Courts in relation to the State Courts, which belong to a different sovereignty.

When the case came again to the Supreme Court the issue was no longer the title problem resolved in 1813. It was the constitutional validity of Supreme Court review of state judgments. In the following excerpts from the Court's opinion, Justice Story sets forth the justifications for upholding the constitutionality of Supreme Court review.

MARTIN V. HUNTER'S LESSEE
14 U.S. (1 Wheat.) 304 (1816).

STORY, J., delivered the opinion of the Court.

[The] questions involved in this judgment are of great importance and delicacy. Perhaps it is not too much to affirm, that, upon their right decision, rest some of the most solid principles which have hitherto been supposed to sustain and protect the constitution itself. [The] constitution of the United States was ordained and established, not by the states in their sovereign capacities, but emphatically, as the preamble of the constitution declares, by "the people of the United States." There can be no doubt that it was competent to the people to invest the general government with all the powers which they might deem proper and necessary; to extend or restrain these powers according to their own good pleasure, and to give them a paramount and supreme authority. As little doubt can there be, that the people had a right to prohibit to the states the exercise of any powers which were, in their judgment, incompatible with the objects of the general compact; to make the powers of the state governments, in given cases, subordinate to those of the nation, or to reserve to themselves those sovereign authorities which they might not choose to delegate to either. The constitution was not, therefore, necessarily carved out of existing state sovereignties, nor a surrender of powers already existing in state institutions, for the powers of the states depend upon their own constitutions; and the people of every state had the right to modify and restrain them, according to their own views of policy or principle. On the other hand, it is perfectly clear that the sovereign powers vested in the state governments, by their respective constitutions, remained unaltered and unimpaired, except so far as they were granted to the government of the United States.

[The] government, then, of the United States, can claim no powers which are not granted to it by the constitution, and the powers actually granted, must be such as are expressly given, or given by necessary implication. On the other hand, this instrument, like every other grant, is to have a reasonable construction, according to the import of its terms; and where a power is expressly given in general terms, it is not to be restrained to particular cases, unless that construction grow out of the context expressly, or by necessary implication.

The words are to be taken in their natural and obvious sense, and not in a sense unreasonably restricted or enlarged. [The] third article of the constitution is that which must principally attract our attention. [Justice Story quoted Article III, sections 1 and 2.] Such is the language of the article creating and defining the judicial power of the United States. It is the voice of the whole American people solemnly declared, in establishing one great department of that government which was, in many respects, national, and in all, supreme. It is a part of the very same instrument which was to act not merely upon individuals, but upon states; and to deprive them altogether of the exercise of some powers of sovereignty, and to restrain and regulate them in the exercise of others.

[Appellate] jurisdiction is given by the constitution to the supreme court in all cases where it has not original jurisdiction; subject, however, to such exceptions and regulations as congress may prescribe. It is, therefore, capable of embracing every case enumerated in the constitution, which is not exclusively to be decided by way of original jurisdiction. But the exercise of appellate jurisdiction is far from being limited by the terms of the constitution to the supreme court. There can be no doubt that congress may create a succession of inferior tribunals, in each of which it may vest appellate as well as original jurisdiction. The judicial power is delegated by the constitution in the most general terms, and may, therefore, be exercised by congress under every variety of form, of appellate or original jurisdiction. And as there is nothing in the constitution which restrains or limits this power, it must, therefore, in all other cases, subsist in the utmost latitude of which, in its own nature, it is susceptible.

As, then, by the terms of the constitution, the appellate jurisdiction is not limited as to the supreme court, and as to this court it may be exercised in all other cases than those of which it has original cognizance, what is there to restrain its exercise over state tribunals in the enumerated cases? The appellate power is not limited by the terms of the third article to any particular courts. The words are, "the judicial power (which includes appellate power) shall extend to all cases," & c., and "in all other cases before mentioned the supreme court shall have appellate jurisdiction." It is the case, then, and not the court, that gives the jurisdiction. If the judicial power extends to the case, it will be in vain to search in the letter of the constitution for any qualification as to the tribunal where it depends. It is incumbent, then, upon those who assert such a qualification to show its existence by necessary implication. If the text be clear and distinct, no restriction upon its plain and obvious import ought to be admitted, unless the inference be irresistible.

If the constitution meant to limit the appellate jurisdiction to cases pending in the courts of the United States, it would necessarily follow that the jurisdiction of these courts would, in all the cases enumerated in the constitution, be exclusive of state tribunals. How otherwise could the jurisdiction extend to all cases arising under the constitution, laws, and treaties of the United States, or to all cases of admiralty and maritime jurisdiction? [But] it is plain that the framers of the constitution did contemplate that cases within the judicial cognizance of the United States not only might but would arise in the state courts, in the exercise of their ordinary jurisdiction. With this view the sixth article declares, that "this constitution, and the laws of the United States which shall be made in pursuance thereof, and all treaties made, or which shall be made, under the authority of the United States, shall be the supreme law of the land, and the judges in every state shall be bound thereby, any thing in the constitution or laws of any state to the contrary notwithstanding." It is obvious that this obligation is imperative upon the state judges in their official, and not merely in their private, capacities. From the very nature of their judicial duties they would be called upon to pronounce the law applicable to the case in judgment. They were not to decide merely according to the laws or constitution of the state, but according to the constitution, laws and treaties of the United States—"the supreme law of the land."

[It] must, therefore, be conceded that the constitution not only contemplated, but meant to provide for cases within the scope of the judicial power of the United States, which might yet depend before state tribunals. It was foreseen that in the exercise of their ordinary jurisdiction, state courts would incidentally take cognizance of cases arising under the constitution, the laws, and treaties of the United States. Yet to all these cases the judicial power, by the very terms of the constitution, is to extend. It cannot extend by original jurisdiction if that was already rightfully and exclusively attached in the state courts, which (as has been already shown) may occur; it must, therefore, extend by appellate jurisdiction, or not at all. It would seem to follow that the appellate power of the United States must, in such cases, extend to state tribunals; and if in such cases, there is no reason why it should not equally attach upon all others within the purview of the constitution.

It has been argued that such an appellate jurisdiction over state courts is inconsistent with the genius of our governments, and the spirit of the constitution. That the latter was never designed to act upon state sovereignties, but only upon the people, and that if the power exists, it will materially impair the sovereignty of the states, and the independence of their courts. We cannot yield to the force of this reasoning; it assumes principles which we cannot admit, and draws conclusions to which we do not yield our assent.

It is a mistake that the constitution was not designed to operate upon states, in their corporate capacities. It is crowded with provisions which restrain or annul the sovereignty of the states in some of the highest branches of their prerogatives. The tenth section of the first article contains a long list of disabilities and prohibitions imposed upon the states. Surely, when such essential portions of state sovereignty are taken away, or prohibited to be exercised, it cannot be correctly asserted that the constitution does not act upon the states. The language of the constitution is also imperative upon the states as to the performance of many duties. It is imperative upon the state legislatures to make laws prescribing the time, places, and manner of holding elections for senators and representatives, and for electors of president and vice-president. And in these, as well as some other cases, congress have a right to revise, amend, or supercede the laws which may be passed by state legislatures. When, therefore, the states are stripped of some of the highest attributes of sovereignty, and the same are given to the United States; when the legislatures of the states are, in some respects, under the control of congress, and in every case are, under the constitution, bound by the paramount authority of the United States; it is certainly difficult to support the argument that the appellate power over the decisions of state courts is contrary to the genius of our institutions. The courts of the United States can, without question, revise the proceedings of the executive and legislative authorities of the states, and if they are found to be contrary to the constitution, may declare them to be of no legal validity. Surely the exercise of the same right over judicial tribunals is not a higher or more dangerous act of sovereign power.

Nor can such a right be deemed to impair the independence of state judges. It is assuming the very ground in controversy to assert that they possess an absolute independence of the United States. In respect to the powers granted to the United States, they are not independent; they are expressly bound to obedience by the letter of the constitution; and if they should unintentionally transcend their authority, or misconstrue the constitution, there is no more reason for giving their judgments an absolute and irresistible force, than for giving it to the acts of the other co-ordinate departments of state sovereignty.

The argument urged from the possibility of the abuse of the revising power, is equally unsatisfactory. It is always a doubtful course, to argue against the use or existence of a power, from the possibility of its abuse. It is still more difficult, by such an argument, to ingraft upon a general power a restriction which is not to be found in the terms in which it is given. From the very nature of things, the absolute right of decision, in the last resort, must rest somewhere—wherever it may be vested it is susceptible of abuse. In all questions of jurisdiction the inferior, or appellate court, must pronounce the final judgment; and common sense, as well as legal reasoning, has conferred it upon the latter.

[It] is further argued, that no great public mischief can result from a construction which shall limit the appellate power of the United States to cases in their own courts: first, because state judges are bound by an oath to support the constitution of the United States, and must be presumed to be men of learning and integrity; and, secondly, because congress must have an unquestionable right to remove all cases within the scope of the judicial power from the state courts to the courts of the United States, at any time before final judgment, though not after final judgment. As to the first reason—admitting that the judges of the state courts are, and always will be, of as much learning, integrity, and wisdom, as those of the courts of the United States, (which we very cheerfully admit,) it does not aid the argument. It is manifest that the constitution has proceeded upon a theory of its own, and given or withheld powers according to the judgment of the American people, by whom it was adopted. We can only construe its powers, and cannot inquire into the policy or principles which induced the grant of them. The constitution has presumed (whether rightly or wrongly we do not inquire) that state attachments, state prejudices, state jealousies, and state interests, might sometimes obstruct, or control, or be supposed to obstruct or control, the regular administration of justice. Hence, in controversies between states; between citizens of different states; between citizens claiming grants under different states; between a state and its citizens, or foreigners, and between citizens and foreigners, it enables the parties, under the authority of congress, to have the controversies heard, tried, and determined before the national tribunals. No other reason than that which has been stated can be assigned, why some, at least, of those cases should not have been left to the cognizance of the state courts. In respect to the other enumerated cases—the cases arising under the constitution, laws, and treaties of the United States, cases affecting ambassadors and other public ministers, and cases of admiralty and maritime jurisdiction—reasons of a higher and more extensive nature, touching the safety, peace, and sovereignty of the nation, might well justify a grant of exclusive jurisdiction.

This is not all. A motive of another kind, perfectly compatible with the most sincere respect for state tribunals, might induce the grant of appellate power over their decisions. That motive is the importance, and even necessity of uniformity of decisions throughout the whole United States, upon all subjects within the purview of the constitution. Judges of equal learning and integrity, in different states, might differently interpret a statute, or a treaty of the United States, or even the constitution itself: If there were no revising authority to control these jarring and discordant judgments, and harmonize them into uniformity, the laws, the treaties, and the constitution of the United States would be different in different states, and might, perhaps, never have precisely the same construction, obligation, or efficacy, in any two states. The public mischiefs that would attend such a state of things would be truly deplorable; and it cannot be believed that they could have escaped the enlightened convention which formed the constitution. What, indeed, might then have been only prophecy, has now become fact; and the appellate jurisdiction must continue to be the only adequate remedy for such evils.

[On] the whole, the court are of opinion, that the appellate power of the United States does extend to cases pending in the state courts; and that the 25th section of the judiciary act, which authorizes the exercise of this jurisdiction in the specified cases, by a writ of error, is supported by the letter and spirit of the constitution. We find no clause in that instrument which limits this power; and we dare not interpose a limitation where the people have not been disposed to create one.

Strong as this conclusion stands upon the general language of the constitution, it may still derive support from other sources. It is an historical fact, that this exposition of the constitution, extending its appellate power to state courts, was, previous to its adoption, uniformly and publicly avowed by its friends, and admitted by its enemies, as the basis of their respective reasonings, both in and out of the state conventions. It is an historical fact, that at the time when the judiciary act was submitted to the deliberations of the first congress, composed, as it was, not only of men of great learning and ability, but of men who had acted a principal part in framing, supporting, or opposing that constitution, the same exposition was explicitly declared and admitted by the friends and by the opponents of that system. It is an historical fact, that the supreme court of the United States have, from time to time, sustained this appellate jurisdiction in a great variety of cases, brought from the tribunals of many of the most important states in the union, and that no state tribunal has ever breathed a judicial doubt on the subject, or declined to obey the mandate of the supreme court, until the present occasion. This weight of contemporaneous exposition by all parties, this acquiescence of enlightened state courts, and these judicial decisions of the supreme court through so long a period, do, as we think, place the doctrine upon a foundation of authority which cannot be shaken, without delivering over the subject to perpetual and irremediable doubts.

[JUSTICE JOHNSON's concurring opinion is omitted.]

NOTE ON THE POWER OF CONGRESS TO AUTHORIZE SUPREME COURT REVIEW

In addition to the reasons excerpted above, Justice Story pointed out that the plaintiff generally decides on the forum. Yet both defendants and plaintiffs ought to have the same right of access to federal court:

> The judicial power [was] not to be exercised exclusively for the benefit of parties who might be plaintiffs and would elect the national forum, but also for the protection of defendants who might be entitled to try their rights, or assert their privileges, before the same forum. Yet, if the construction contended for be correct, it will follow, that as the plaintiff may always elect the state court, the defendant may be deprived of all the security which the Constitution intended in aid of his rights.

In 1816 the Supreme Court may have had sufficient resources to decide every significant case within its jurisdiction. Today the Court is asked to rule on over 10,000 cases a year, of which it chooses fewer than 100 for full consideration. Does Justice Story's "right of access to federal court" reasoning still have force?

Martin's defense of Supreme Court review of state judgments is a linchpin of Federal Courts law. The case also represents one of the early battles between states' rights and national power that culminated in the Civil War. The Virginia Supreme Court of Appeals' refusal here to follow the U.S. Supreme Court's earlier mandate, and its assertion that one sovereign cannot dictate to another, foreshadowed later conflicts between state claims to independence and assertions of national authority.

II.   THE SCOPE OF SUPREME COURT REVIEW

In *Martin*, Justice Story was concerned with justifying Supreme Court review of state court judgments. Understandably, he paid little attention to identifying the ambit of the Court's power. Later cases have focused on the range of cases and issues that the Court may review. Either by finding that Article III restricts its authority or by construing the jurisdictional statutes, the Court in the years since *Martin* has imposed significant limits on the scope of its review of state judgments. Three basic rules govern Supreme Court review. First, the Court ordinarily will review only the federal issues raised by a state court judgment, and not the state issues. Second, the Court will not even review the federal issues if the judgment rests on an "adequate state ground." Third, the Court *will* review state judgments that ostensibly turn on state grounds in order to determine whether the state ground is "independent" of federal law. If it is not, the Court will examine the federal ground.

A. LIMITING REVIEW TO FEDERAL ISSUES

Martin upheld Section 25 of the Judiciary Act of 1789 against constitutional objections. That statute authorized Supreme Court review of state judgments, but confined review to "questions of validity or construction of the [United States] constitution, treaties, statutes, commissions, or authorities in dispute." In 1867, Congress eliminated this language, thereby giving rise to the contention that the Court should review state as well as federal issues. *Murdock* addressed that argument.

MURDOCK V. CITY OF MEMPHIS
87 U.S. (20 Wall.) 590 (1875).

[In 1844 Murdock's ancestors had conveyed land to the city for use as a United States naval depot, providing that the land would revert to their heirs in the event the land was not "appropriated by the United States for that purpose." The same year, the city conveyed the land to the United States, and the United States made various improvements with that end in view. Ten years later, the United States abandoned the project and Congress transferred the land back to the city. Murdock claimed that the land reverted to him under the terms of the original conveyance; and the Act of Congress transferring the land back to the city should be construed as a directive to the city to hold it in a constructive trust for his benefit. The first of these is a state law issue and the latter a federal matter. Murdock lost on both questions in the state courts and sought Supreme Court review. He argued that under the 1867 amendment to section 25 the Court had the authority to review both of them.]

MR. JUSTICE MILLER delivered the opinion of the Court.

[Murdock's] argument may be thus stated: 1. That the Constitution declares that the judicial power of the United States shall extend to cases of a character which includes the questions described in the section, and that by the word case, is to be understood all of the case in which such a question arises. 2. That by the fair construction of the act of 1789 in regard to removing those cases to this court, the power and the duty of re-examining the whole case would have been devolved on the court, but for the restriction of the clause omitted in the act of 1867; and that the same language is used in the latter act regulating the removal, but omitting the restrictive clause. And, 3. That by re-enacting the statute in the same terms as to the removal of cases from the State courts, without the restrictive clause, Congress is to be understood as conferring the power which the clause prohibited.

We will consider the last proposition first.

What were the precise motives which induced the omission of this clause it is impossible to ascertain with any degree of satisfaction. In a legislative body like Congress, it is reasonable to suppose that among those who considered this matter at all, there were varying reasons for consenting to the change. No doubt there were those who, believing that the Constitution gave no right to the Federal judiciary to go beyond the line marked by the omitted clause, thought its presence or absence immaterial; and in a revision of the statute it was wise to leave it out, because its presence implied that such a power was within the competency of Congress to bestow. There were also, no doubt, those who believed that the section standing without that clause did not confer the power which it prohibited, and that it was, therefore, better omitted. It may also have been within the thought of a few that all that is now claimed would follow the repeal of the clause. But if Congress, or the framers of the bill, had a clear purpose to enact affirmatively that the court should consider the class of errors which that clause forbid, nothing hindered that they should say so in positive terms; and in reversing the policy of the government from its foundation in one of the most important subjects on which that body could act, it is reasonably to be expected that Congress would use plain, unmistakable language in giving expression to such intention.

There is, therefore, no sufficient reason for holding that Congress, by repealing or omitting this restrictive clause, intended to enact affirmatively the thing which that clause had prohibited.

We are thus brought to the examination of the section as it was passed by the Congress of 1867, and as it now stands, as part of the revised statutes of the United States.

[The] most important part of the statute [declares] that it is only upon the existence of certain questions in the case that this court can entertain jurisdiction at all. Nor is the mere existence of such a question in the case sufficient to give jurisdiction—the question must have been *decided* in the State court. Nor is it sufficient that such a question was raised and was decided. It must have been decided in a certain way, that is, against the right set up under the Constitution, laws, treaties, or authority of the United States. The Federal question may have been erroneously decided. It may be quite apparent to this court that a wrong construction has been given to the Federal law, but if the right claimed under it by plaintiff in error has been conceded to him, this court cannot entertain jurisdiction of the case, so very careful is the statute, both of 1789 and of 1867, to narrow, to limit, and define the jurisdiction which this court exercises over the judgments of the State courts. Is it consistent with this extreme caution to suppose that Congress intended, when those cases came here, that this court should not only examine those questions, but all others found in the record?—questions of common law, of State statutes, of controverted facts, and conflicting evidence. Or is it the more reasonable inference that Congress intended that the case should be brought here that *those questions* might be decided and *finally* decided by the court established by the Constitution of the Union, and the court which has always been supposed to be not only the most appropriate but the only proper tribunal for their final decision? No such reason nor any necessity exists for the decision by this court of other questions in those cases. The jurisdiction has been exercised for nearly a century without serious inconvenience to the due administration of justice. The State courts are the appropriate tribunals, as this court has repeatedly held, for the decision of questions arising under their local law, whether statutory or otherwise. And it is not lightly to be presumed that Congress acted upon a principle which implies a distrust of their integrity or of their ability to construe those laws correctly.

Let us look for a moment into the effect of the proposition contended for upon the cases as they come up for consideration in the conference-room. If it is found that no such question is raised or decided in the court below, then all will concede that it must be dismissed for want of jurisdiction. But if it is found that the Federal question was raised and was decided against the plaintiff in error, then the first duty of the court obviously is to determine whether it was correctly decided by the State court. Let us suppose that we find that the court below was right in its decision on that question. What, then, are we to do? Was it the intention of Congress to say that while you can only bring the case here on account of this question, yet when it is here, though it may turn out that the plaintiff in error was wrong on that question, and the judgment of the court below was right, though he has wrongfully dragged the defendant into this court by the allegation of an error which did not exist, and without which the case could not rightfully be here, he can still insist on an inquiry into all the other matters which were litigated in the case? This is neither reasonable nor just.

In such case both the nature of the jurisdiction conferred and the nature and fitness of things demand that, no error being found in the matter which authorized the re-examination, the judgment of the State court should be affirmed, and the case remitted to that court for its further enforcement.

The whole argument we are combating, however, goes upon the assumption that when it is found that the record shows that one of the questions mentioned has been decided against the claim of the plaintiff in error, this court has jurisdiction, and that jurisdiction extends to the whole case. If it extends to the whole case then the court must re-examine the whole case, and if it re-examines it must decide the whole case. It is difficult to escape the logic of the argument if the first premise be conceded. But it is here the error lies. We are of opinion that upon a fair construction of the whole language of the section the jurisdiction conferred is limited to the decision of the questions mentioned in the statute, and, as a necessary consequence of this, to the exercise of such powers as may be necessary to cause the judgment in that decision to be respected.

[The] twenty-fifth section of the act of 1789 has been the subject of innumerable decisions, some of which are to be found in almost every volume of the reports from that year down to the present. These form a system of appellate jurisprudence relating to the exercise of the appellate power of this court over the courts of the States. That system has been based upon the fundamental principle that this jurisdiction was limited to the correction of errors relating solely to Federal law. And though it may be argued with some plausibility that the reason of this is to be found in the restrictive clause of the act of 1789, which is omitted in the act of 1867, yet an examination of the cases will show that it rested quite as much on the conviction of this court that without that clause and on general principles the jurisdiction extended no further. It requires a very bold reach of thought, and a readiness to impute to Congress a radical and hazardous change of a policy vital in its essential nature to the independence of the State courts, to believe that that body contemplated, or intended, what is claimed, by the mere omission of a clause in the substituted statute, which may well be held to have been superfluous, or nearly so, in the old one.

Another consideration, not without weight in seeking after the intention of Congress, is found in the fact that where that body has clearly shown an intention to bring the whole of a case which arises under the constitutional provision as to its subject-matter under the jurisdiction of a Federal court, it has conferred its cognizance on Federal courts of original jurisdiction and not on the Supreme Court.

[It] is not difficult to discover what the purpose of Congress in the passage of this law was. In a vast number of cases the rights of the people of the Union, as they are administered in the courts of the States, must depend upon the construction which those courts gave to the Constitution, treaties, and laws of the United States. The highest courts of the States were sufficiently numerous, even in 1789, to cause it to be feared that, with the purest motives, this construction given in different courts would be various and conflicting. It was desirable, however, that whatever conflict of opinion might exist in those courts on other subjects, the rights which depended on the Federal laws should be the same everywhere, and that their construction should be uniform. This could only be done by conferring upon the Supreme Court of the United States—the appellate tribunal established by the Constitution—the right to decide these questions finally and in a manner which would be conclusive on all other courts, State or National. This was the first purpose of the statute, and it does not require that, in a case involving a variety of questions, any other should be decided than those described in the act.

Secondly. It was no doubt the purpose of Congress to secure to every litigant whose rights depended on any question of Federal law that that question should be decided for him by the highest Federal tribunal if he desired it, when the decisions of the State courts were against him on that question. That rights of this character, guaranteed to him by the Constitution and laws of the Union, should not be left to the exclusive and final control of the State courts.

There may be some plausibility in the argument that these rights cannot be protected in all cases unless the Supreme Court has final control of the whole case. But the experience of eighty-five years of the administration of the law under the opposite theory would seem to be a satisfactory answer to the argument. It is not to be presumed that the State courts, where the rule is clearly laid down to them on the Federal question, and its influence on the case fully seen, will disregard or overlook it, and this is all that the rights of the party claiming under it require. Besides, by the very terms of this statute, when the Supreme Court is of opinion that the question of Federal law is of such relative importance to the whole case that it should control the final judgment, that court is authorized to render such judgment and enforce it by its own process. It cannot, therefore, be maintained that it is in any case necessary for the security of the rights claimed under the Constitution, laws, or treaties of the United States that the Supreme Court should examine and decide other questions not of a Federal character.

And we are of opinion that the act of 1867 does not confer such a jurisdiction.

This renders unnecessary a decision of the question whether, if Congress had conferred such authority, the act would have been constitutional. It will be time enough for this court to inquire into the existence of such a power when that body has attempted to exercise it in language which makes such an intention so clear as to require [it.]

[The Court addressed the federal issue and concluded that the 1854 Act of Congress did not establish any federal rights on Murdock's behalf.]

[JUSTICE BRADLEY'S dissenting opinion is omitted.]

NOTE ON MURDOCK

It is quite possible that the *Murdock* Court misapprehended the 1867 Congress's intent in amending Section 25. For a general discussion, see William M. Wiecek, Murdock v. Memphis: *Section 25 of the 1789 Judiciary Act and Judicial Federalism*, in ORIGINS OF THE FEDERAL JUDICIARY: ESSAYS ON THE JUDICIARY ACT OF 1789, at 223 (Maeva Marcus, ed., 1992). The post-Civil War Reconstruction was underway, white Southerners remained recalcitrant, and Congress—under the control of Radical Republicans—may well have sought to subject to greater scrutiny the decisions of state courts they distrusted. On the other hand, the greater scrutiny would, of course, have applied to state courts in the North as well. Suppose Congress in fact desires to make the kind of fundamental change that Murdock argued for in the relation between the state courts and the Supreme Court. What do you think of the Court's argument that Congress should be explicit and direct, rather than attempting to do so indirectly by omitting language from the existing statute?

Murdock is often characterized as "the *Erie* of Supreme Court review." Do you see why? Given *Murdock*, why did we have to wait another sixty-three years for *Erie*? Or are there not only similarities but also differences between the issues addressed in the two cases, such that *Erie* is a harder case?

B. "ADEQUATE" STATE SUBSTANTIVE GROUNDS

1. Adequate State Substantive Grounds Will Foreclose Supreme Court Review

In a section of the *Murdock* opinion that we have omitted, the Court ruled that it would resolve the federal issue in cases brought from state court, even if overturning the state court on the federal issue would not change the outcome of the case. In later years the Court took a different approach, refusing to review a case if the judgment rested on an "adequate state ground." An adequate state ground is one that disposes of the case by itself, no matter how the federal issues are resolved. For present purposes, we focus on state *substantive* grounds. Procedural grounds are examined in Part IV, below. For reasons that will become apparent, clarity will be served by treating the two separately.

Suppose a state law makes it a crime to sell alcohol to a minor. Al sells alcohol to a minor, in the good faith belief that the purchaser is an adult. Nonetheless, Al, after confessing to the police in an interview conducted without *Miranda* warnings, is convicted in state court. The state's highest court then reverses the conviction on two grounds: [i] it construes the state law as requiring that the state prove that the seller had no good faith belief that the purchaser was an adult, and finds lack of such proof here; and [ii] it holds that the interview was a custodial interrogation, and that the absence of *Miranda* warnings means that, as a matter of federal constitutional law, evidence gained from it cannot be used to convict Al. Should the state try to obtain Supreme Court review, it would be told that the Court will not even review the federal law *Miranda* ruling, because the state court's construction of the state law furnishes an adequate state ground supporting the judgment that Al must go free. By contrast, suppose the state court had ruled otherwise on both [i] and [ii], thereby affirming the conviction. Now a different outcome on the federal issue would result in overturning the conviction, and the state ground is not adequate to support the judgment. Accordingly, the Supreme Court may review the case.

The following illustrative case is a bit trickier than the foregoing hypothetical, but the principle is the same.

FOX FILM CORP. V. MULLER
296 U.S. 207 (1935).

MR. JUSTICE SUTHERLAND delivered the opinion of the Court.

This is an action brought in a Minnesota state court of first instance by the Film Corporation against Muller, to recover damages for an alleged breach of two contracts by which Muller was licensed to exhibit certain moving-picture films belonging to the corporation. Muller answered, setting up the invalidity of the contracts under the Sherman Anti-trust Act. It was and is agreed that these contracts are substantially the same as the one involved in *United States v. Paramount Famous Lasky Corp.*, 34 F.2d 984, aff'd 282 U.S. 30; that petitioner was one of the defendants in that action; and that the "arbitration clause," paragraph 18 of each of the contracts sued upon, is the same as that held in that case to be invalid. In view of the disposition which we are to make of this writ, it is not necessary to set forth the terms of the arbitration clause or the other provisions of the contract.

The court of first instance held that each contract sued upon violated the Sherman Anti-trust Act, and dismissed the action. In a supplemental opinion that court put its decision upon the grounds, first, that the arbitration plan is so connected with the remainder of the contract that the entire contract is tainted, and, second, that the contract violates the Sherman Anti-trust law. The state supreme court affirmed.

[In] its opinion, the state supreme court, after a statement of the case, said: "The question presented on this appeal is whether the arbitration clause is severable from the contract, leaving the remainder of the contract enforceable, or not severable, permeating and tainting the whole contract with illegality and making it void." That court then proceeded to refer to and discuss a number of decisions of state and federal courts, some of which took the view that the arbitration clause was severable, and others that it was not severable, from the remainder of the contract. After reviewing the opinion and decree of the federal district court in the *Paramount* case, the lower court reached the conclusion that the holding of the federal court was that the entire contract was illegal; and upon that view and upon what it conceived to be the weight of authority, held the arbitration plan was inseparable from the other provisions of the contract. Whether this conclusion was right or wrong we need not determine. It is enough that it is, at least, not without fair support.

Respondent contends that the question of severability was alone decided and that no federal question was determined by the lower court. This contention petitioner challenges, and asserts that a federal question was involved and decided. We do not attempt to settle the dispute; but, assuming for present purposes only that petitioner's view is the correct one, the case is controlled by the settled rule that where the judgment of a state court rests upon two grounds, one of which is federal and the other non-federal in character, our jurisdiction fails if the non-federal ground is independent of the federal ground and adequate to support the judgment. This rule had become firmly fixed at least as early as *Klinger v. Missouri*, 13 Wall. 257, 263, and has been reiterated in a long line of cases since that time [citing cases].

Whether the provisions of a contract are non-severable, so that if one be held invalid the others must fall with it, is clearly a question of general and not of federal law. The invalidity of the arbitration clause which the present contracts embody is conceded. [The] question, therefore, was foreclosed; and was not the subject of controversy in the state courts. In that situation, the primary question to be determined by the court below was whether the concededly invalid clause was separable from the other provisions of the contract. The ruling of the state supreme court that it was not, is sufficient to conclude the case without regard to the determination, if, in fact, any was made, in respect of the federal question. It follows that the non-federal ground is adequate to sustain the judgment.

The rule [to] the effect that our jurisdiction attaches where the non-federal ground is so interwoven with the other as not to be an independent matter, does not apply. The construction put upon the contracts did not constitute a preliminary step which simply had the effect of bringing forward for determination the federal question, but was a decision which automatically took the federal question out of the case if otherwise it would be there. The non-federal question in respect of the construction of the contracts, and the federal question in respect of their validity under the Anti-trust Act, were clearly independent of one another. The case, in effect, was disposed of before the federal question said to be involved was reached. A decision of that question then became unnecessary; and whether it was decided or not, our want of jurisdiction is clear.

NOTES ON THE "ADEQUATE STATE GROUND" DOCTRINE

1.   The Policy Issue. The basic argument in favor of the adequate state ground doctrine is that the Supreme Court's ruling on the federal issue would have no impact on the outcome and is therefore an unnecessary exercise of judicial power, a kind of advisory opinion:

> This Court from the time of its foundation has adhered to the principle that it will not review judgments of state courts that rest on adequate and independent state grounds. The reason is so obvious that it has rarely been thought to warrant statement. It is found in the partitioning of power between the state and federal judicial systems and in the limitations of our own jurisdiction. Our only power over state judgments is to correct them to the extent that they incorrectly adjudge federal rights. And our power is to correct wrong judgments, not to revise opinions. We are not permitted to render an advisory opinion, and if the same judgment would be rendered by the state court after we corrected its views of federal laws, our review could amount to nothing more than an advisory opinion.

Herb v. Pitcairn, 324 U.S. 117, 125–26 (1945).

Critics of the rule respond that the state court may nonetheless have made an error on a matter of federal law, that other actors may be misled, and that the value of correcting misunderstandings of federal law outweighs the concern about rendering unnecessary rulings. They argue that the Court's reluctance to issue advisory opinions is not a constitutional prohibition but a policy that can and should be overridden in order to obtain these benefits. See Richard Matasar & Gregory Bruch, *Procedural Common Law, Federal Jurisdictional Policy, and Abandonment of the Adequate and Independent State Grounds Doctrine*, 86 COLUM. L REV. 1291 (1986).

2.   *Fairfax's Devisee* Revisited. In the land title litigation leading up to *Martin v. Hunter's Lessee*, the Supreme Court resolved a state law question, namely, whether Virginia had taken title to the land before the 1783 peace treaty. In doing so, the Court seems to have disregarded the Judiciary Act of 1789, which limited Supreme Court review to "questions of validity or construction of the [United States] constitution, treaties, statutes, commissions, or authorities in dispute." Viewed in retrospect, *Fairfax's Devisee* also seems at odds with the adequate state ground doctrine, as the Virginia Court's holding on the state law issue would support its judgment in favor of Hunter no matter what the impact of the 1783 treaty may be on titles still held by British subjects at that time.

A possible (though quite controversial) explanation for the Court's approach, advanced in 2 WILLIAM W. CROSSKEY, POLITICS AND THE

CONSTITUTION IN THE HISTORY OF THE UNITED STATES 785–817 (1953), is that the framers of the Constitution considered the common law to be federal, not state, law. Note that accepting Crosskey's view would cast doubt on the holding of *Erie Railroad Company v. Tompkins*, 304 U.S. 64 (1938), that "[t]here is no federal general common law." For his part, Crosskey thought that *Erie* was "one of the most grossly unconstitutional governmental acts in the nation's entire history." 2 CROSSKEY, supra, at 916.

Another explanation is that the Court in *Fairfax's Devisee* perceived, without fully articulating its insight, that federal review of state law issues is sometimes necessary in order to vindicate federal rights, in situations in which federal law (the 1783 treaty) protects an "antecedent" state-created right (the land title). According to this reading of the case, the Virginia court, in an effort to evade that protection, had distorted state law by finding that Virginia had taken Lord Fairfax's land before the 1783 treaty, even though a fair reading of the Virginia statute and its common law background would lead to the opposite conclusion. That theme is illustrated by *Indiana* ex rel. *Anderson v. Brand*, below.

3. The Principle of Institutional Settlement. Aspects of the *Martin* litigation can be used to illustrate a basic feature of judicial federalism, so basic that it is often simply taken for granted. For the sake of making this point, let us stipulate that the Virginia Court correctly decided the land title issue and that the Supreme Court in *Fairfax's Devisee* violated § 25 of the Judiciary Act when it reviewed that ruling. On those premises, was the Virginia Court justified in declining to enforce the Supreme Court's mandate in *Fairfax's Devisee*? Justice Story's opinion in *Martin* does not address that question directly. But Story's implicit premise, and the Supreme Court's practice throughout our history, is that the Supreme Court has the final say, right or wrong. Defying the U.S. Supreme Court's mandate, however mistaken the Court may have been in *Fairfax's Devisee* in its resolution of the merits, is not an acceptable option. This is an application of "the principle of institutional settlement," which "requires that a decision which is the due result of duly established procedures be accepted whether it is right or wrong—at least for the time being." That principle "is itself an ethical concept, resting on the recognition that defiance of institutional settlements touches or may touch the very foundations of civil order, and that without civil order, morality and justice in anybody's view of them are impossible." HENRY M. HART, JR. & ALBERT M. SACKS, THE LEGAL PROCESS: BASIC PROBLEMS IN THE MAKING AND APPLICATION OF LAW 109 (William N. Eskridge, Jr. and Philip P. Frickey eds. 1994).

2. Determining Whether State Substantive Grounds Are Adequate

When the state substantive ground in a case is wholly separate from the federal ground, as in our "selling alcohol to a minor" hypothetical, the adequate state ground doctrine is easy to apply. The Court has no reason to examine the state court's reasoning on the state law matter, because there is no federal interest in the way it is resolved. But one class of cases requires special attention. Sometimes the state ground and the federal ground are linked in the following way: As in *Fairfax's Devisee,* the point of the claimed federal right is to protect the right created by state law. In such a case there is a federal interest in the ruling on the state law issue in the case, and the state court's decision, even on the state issue, will not be accepted without question.

INDIANA EX REL. ANDERSON V. BRAND
303 U.S. 95 (1938).

MR. JUSTICE ROBERTS delivered the opinion of the Court.

The petitioner sought [to] compel the respondent to continue her in employment as a public school teacher. Her complaint alleged that as a duly licensed teacher she entered into a contract in September, 1924, to teach in the township schools and, pursuant to successive contracts, taught continuously to and including the school year 1932–1933; that her contracts for the school years 1931–1932 and 1932–1933 contained this clause: "It is further agreed by the contracting parties that all of the provisions of the Teachers' Tenure Law, approved March 8, 1927, shall be in full force and effect in this contract"; and that by force of that Act she had a contract, indefinite in duration, which could be cancelled by the respondent only in the manner and for the causes specified in the Act. She charged that in July, 1933, the respondent notified her he proposed to cancel her contract for cause; that, after a hearing, he adhered to his decision and the County Superintendent affirmed his action; that, despite what occurred in July, 1933, the petitioner was permitted to teach during the school year 1933–1934 and the respondent was presently threatening to terminate her employment at the end of that year. The complaint alleged the termination of her employment would be a breach of her contract with the school corporation. The respondent [defended on the ground that] the Teachers' Tenure Law had been repealed in respect of teachers in township schools by a 1933 Indiana statute. [The Indiana Supreme Court agreed, reasoning that] the repeal did not deprive the petitioner of a vested property right and did not impair her contract within the meaning of the Constitution.

The court below holds that in Indiana teachers' contracts are made for but one year; that there is no contractual right to be continued as a teacher from year to year; that the law grants a privilege to one who has taught five years and signed a new contract to continue in employment under given conditions; that the statute is directed merely to the exercise of their powers by the school authorities and the policy therein expressed may be altered at the will of the legislature; that in enacting laws for the government of public schools the legislature exercises a function of sovereignty and the power to control public policy in respect of their management and operation cannot be contracted away by one legislature so as to create a permanent public policy unchangeable by succeeding legislatures. In the alternative the court declares that if the relationship be considered as controlled by the rules of private contract the provision for reemployment from year to year is unenforceable for want of mutuality.

As in most cases brought to this court under the contract clause of the Constitution, the question is as to the existence and nature of the contract and not as to the construction of the law which is supposed to impair it. The principal function of a legislative body is not to make contracts but to make laws which declare the policy of the state and are subject to repeal when a subsequent legislature shall determine to alter that policy. Nevertheless, it is established that a legislative enactment may contain provisions which, when accepted as the basis of action by individuals, become contracts between them and the State or its subdivisions within the protection of Art. I, § 10. If the people's representatives deem it in the public interest they may adopt a policy of contracting in respect of public business for a term longer than the life of the current session of the legislature. This the petitioner claims has been done with respect to permanent teachers. The Supreme Court has decided, however, that it is the state's policy not to bind school corporations by contract for more than one year.

On such a question, one primarily of state law, we accord respectful consideration and great weight to the views of the State's highest court but, in order that the constitutional mandate may not become a dead letter, we are bound to decide for ourselves whether a contract was made, what are its terms and conditions, and whether the State has, by later legislation, impaired its obligation. This involves an appraisal of the statutes of the State and the decisions of its courts.

The courts of Indiana have long recognized that the employment of school teachers was contractual and have afforded relief in actions upon teachers' contracts [citing cases]. An Act adopted in 1899 required all contracts between teachers and school corporations to be in writing, signed by the parties to be charged, and to be made a matter of public record. A statute of 1921 enacted that every such contract should be in writing and should state the date of the beginning of the school term, the number of months therein, the amount of the salary for the term, and the number of payments to be made during the school year.

In 1927 the State adopted the Teachers' Tenure Act under which the present controversy arises. [By] this Act it was provided that a teacher who has served under contract for five or more successive years, and thereafter enters into a contract for further service with the school corporation, shall become a permanent teacher and the contract, upon the expiration of its stated term, shall be deemed to continue in effect for an indefinite period, shall be known as an indefinite contract, and shall remain in force unless succeeded by a new contract or cancelled as provided in the Act. The corporation may cancel the contract, after notice and hearing, for incompetency, insubordination, neglect of duty, immorality, justifiable decrease in the number of teaching positions, or other good or just cause, but not for political or personal reasons. The teacher may not cancel the contract during the school term nor for a period of thirty days previous to the beginning of any term (unless by mutual agreement) and may cancel only upon five days' notice.

By an amendatory Act of 1933 township school corporations were omitted from the provisions of the Act of 1927. The court below construed this Act as repealing the Act of 1927 so far as township schools and teachers are concerned and as leaving the respondent free to terminate the petitioner's employment. But we are of opinion that the petitioner had a valid contract with the respondent, the obligation of which would be impaired by the termination of her employment.

Where the claim is that the State's policy embodied in a statute is to bind its instrumentalities by contract, the cardinal inquiry is as to the terms of the statute supposed to create such a contract. The State long prior to the adoption of the Act of 1927 required the execution of written contracts between teachers and school corporations, specified certain subjects with which such contracts must deal, and required that they be made a matter of public record. These were annual contracts, covering a single school term. The Act of 1927 announced a new policy that a teacher who had served for five years under successive contracts, upon the execution of another was to become a permanent teacher and the last contract was to be indefinite as to duration and terminable by either party only upon compliance with the conditions set out in the statute. The policy which induced the legislation evidently was that the teacher should have protection against the exercise of the right, which would otherwise inhere in the employer, of terminating the employment at the end of any school term without assigned reasons and solely at the employer's pleasure. The state courts in earlier cases so declared [citing cases].

The title of the Act is couched in terms of contract. It speaks of the making and cancelling of indefinite contracts. In the body the word "contract" appears ten times in § 1, defining the relationship; eleven times in § 2, relating to the termination of the employment by the employer, and four times in § 4, stating the conditions of termination by the teacher.

The tenor of the Act indicates that the word "contract" was not used inadvertently or in other than its usual legal meaning. By § 6 it is expressly provided that the Act is a supplement to that of March 7, 1921, requiring teachers' employment contracts to be in writing. By § 1 it is provided that the written contract of a permanent teacher "shall be deemed to continue in effect for an indefinite period and shall be known as an indefinite contract." Such an indefinite contract is to remain in force unless succeeded by a new contract signed by both parties or cancelled as provided in § 2. No more apt language could be employed to define a contractual relationship. By § 2 it is enacted that such indefinite contracts may be cancelled by the school corporation only in the manner specified. The admissible grounds of cancellation, and the method by which the existence of such grounds shall be ascertained and made a matter of record, are carefully set out. Section 4 permits cancellation by the teacher only at certain times consistent with the convenient administration of the school system and imposes a sanction for violation of its requirements. Examination of the entire Act convinces us that the teacher was by it assured of the possession of a binding and enforceable contract against school districts.

Until its decision in the present case the Supreme Court of the State had uniformly held that the teacher's right to continued employment by virtue of the indefinite contract created pursuant to the Act was contractual.

In *School City of Elwood v. State ex rel. Griffin*, 203 Ind. 626; 180 N. E. 471, it was said:

> The position of a teacher in the public schools is not a public office, but an employment by contract between the teacher and the school corporation. The relation remains contractual after the teacher has, under the provisions of a teachers' tenure law, become a permanent teacher—but the terms and conditions of the contract are thereafter governed primarily by the statute.

[The Court quoted three other cases to similar effect.]

We think the decision in this case runs counter to the policy evinced by the Act of 1927, to its explicit mandate and to earlier decisions construing its [provisions]. *Dodge v. Board of Education*, 302 U.S. 74, on which the respondent relies is distinguishable, because the statute there involved did not purport to bind the respondent by contract to the payment of retirement annuities, and similar legislation in respect of other municipal employees had been consistently construed by the courts as not creating contracts.

The respondent urges that every contract is subject to the police power and that in repealing the Teachers' Tenure Act the legislature validly exercised that reserved power of the state. The sufficient answer is found in the statute. By § 2 of the Act of 1927 power is given to the school corporation to cancel a teacher's indefinite contract for incompetency, insubordination (which is to be deemed to mean wilful refusal to obey the school laws of the state or reasonable rules prescribed by the employer), neglect of duty, immorality, justifiable decrease in the number of teaching positions or other good and just cause. The permissible reasons for cancellation cover every conceivable basis for such action growing out of a deficient performance of the obligations undertaken by the teacher, and diminution of the school requirements. Although the causes specified constitute in themselves just and reasonable grounds for the termination of any ordinary contract of employment, to preclude the assumption that any other valid ground was excluded by the enumeration, the legislature added that the relation might be terminated for any other good and just cause. Thus in the declaration of the state's policy, ample reservations in aid of the efficient administration of the school system were made. The express prohibitions are that the contract shall not be cancelled for political or personal reasons. We do not think the asserted change of policy evidenced by the repeal of the statute is that school boards may be at liberty to cancel a teacher's contract for political or personal reasons. We do not understand the respondent so to contend. The most that can be said for his position is that, by the repeal, township school corporations were again put upon the basis of annual contracts, renewable at the pleasure of the board. It is significant that the Act of 1933 left the system of permanent teachers and indefinite contracts untouched as respects school corporations in cities and towns of the state. It is not contended, nor can it be thought, that the legislature of 1933 determined that it was against public policy for school districts in cities and towns to terminate the employment of teachers of five or more years' experience for political or personal reasons and to permit cancellation, for the same reasons, in townships.

Our decisions recognize that every contract is made subject to the implied condition that its fulfillment may be frustrated by a proper exercise of the police power but we have repeatedly said that, in order to have this effect, the exercise of the power must be for an end which is in fact public and the means adopted must be reasonably adapted to that end, and the Supreme Court of Indiana has taken the same view in respect of legislation impairing the obligation of the contract of a state instrumentality. The causes of cancellation provided in the Act of 1927 and the retention of the system of indefinite contracts in all municipalities except townships by the Act of 1933 are persuasive that the repeal of the earlier Act by the latter was not an exercise of the police power for the attainment of ends to which its exercise may properly be directed.

[Besides arguing that the 1933 statute justified the dismissal, the defendant had argued that Anderson had been fired for "cause," after proper notice and hearing, so that the dismissal was valid even if she had tenure. The Supreme Court remanded, explaining that:]

As the court below has not passed upon one of the grounds of demurrer which appears to involve no federal question, and may present a defense still open to the respondent, we reverse the judgment and remand the cause for further proceedings not inconsistent with this opinion.

MR. JUSTICE CARDOZO took no part in the consideration or decision of this case.

MR. JUSTICE BLACK, dissenting.

[Justice Black disputed the majority's reading of the Indiana case law. He argued that "the Indiana Supreme Court has consistently held, even before its decision in this case, that the right of teachers, under the 1927 Act, to serve until removed for cause, was *not given by contract, but by statute.*" (emphasis in original.)]

NOTES ON "ANTECEDENT" STATE GROUNDS

1.   The Scope of Review After the *Anderson* Remand. At the end of its opinion the Court remands for consideration of the question of whether Anderson was dismissed for cause, characterizing this as a ground "which appears to involve no federal question." Suppose it turns out that, at the hearing preceding the termination, the school district presented no evidence of incompetence, misconduct or other "cause," yet Anderson was fired anyway. Would she have a basis in federal law for challenging the dismissal?

2.   Federal Protection of State-Created Rights: The Standard of Review. Cases like *Anderson* have been labeled "antecedent" state rights cases, because "the federal rightholder must prevail on both state and federal grounds in order to obtain relief." R. FALLON, ET AL., HART & WECHSLER'S THE FEDERAL COURTS AND THE FEDERAL SYSTEM 462 (6th ed. 2009).

In *Anderson* the Court says that "in order that the constitutional mandate not become a dead letter, we must decide for ourselves whether a contract was made, what are its terms and conditions, and whether the state has, by later legislation, impaired its obligation." Does this mean that the Court will make its own *de novo* evaluation of state law? The Court also said that it would accord "respectful consideration and great weight to the views of the state's highest court." Other decisions also suggest that the Court will give some deference to state court determinations in cases of this type, requiring only that they have "fair support" in the state law materials. See *Fox Film*, supra. One argument for the "fair support" test is that both state and federal interests are at stake in these cases. An independent review of state law by the Supreme Court may give too little weight to the state's interest in the development of state law. On the other hand, the "fair support" test requires the Justices to make a rather subtle distinction between "error" and "inadequate support." In a case where the Justices think the state was wrong on a matter of state law, and that the error compromised a federal right, the "fair support" norm calls upon them, nonetheless, to decide whether the state ground had fair support, and to defer in the event they find it.

For the view that the cases in fact support "two competing standards of review: independent judgment and deference (fair support) review," see Henry Paul Monaghan, *Supreme Court Review of State-Court Determinations of State Law in Constitutional Cases*, 103 COLUM. L. REV. 1919, 1957 (2003). Recognizing that there are arguments in favor of each, and that "fair support" works well as "the operative working-day premise of Supreme Court practice," *id.* at 1989, Monaghan favors "independent judgment" as the basic principle when an important federal issue is at stake in the litigation. *Id.* at 1989–90.

3. The Modern Approach to Federal Protection of State-Created Rights: "Property," "Due Process," and Section 1983. There is no better case than *Anderson* to illustrate the "federal protection of state-created rights" fact pattern in Supreme Court review. But in fact *Anderson* is an anachronism. Today, someone in Anderson's position would sue on a different theory and in a different forum. The Fourteenth Amendment forbids states from depriving persons of "property" without due process of law. "Property," within the meaning of the clause, consists not only of land, chattels, and intangibles. In addition to this "old" property, there is a category sometimes called "new" property. In 1972 the Supreme Court held that some government employees have "property" interests in their jobs. See *Board of Regents v. Roth*, 408 U.S. 564 (1972); *Perry v. Sindermann*, 408 U.S. 593 (1972). Whether a given employee holds such an interest depends upon whether he can establish "the existence of rules and understandings [that] may justify his legitimate claim of entitlement to continued employment absent sufficient 'cause.' " *Sindermann*, supra.

Anderson held just this kind of post. If she were fired today, she would bring a § 1983 suit, charging that her dismissal deprived her of property without due process of law. The key issue in the case would be whether the hearing satisfied the requirements of procedural due process. Though these cases can be brought in state court, see Chapter 7, most plaintiffs prefer federal court. The federal courts examine state law and decide for themselves whether, in the circumstances of the case, state law creates a property interest. See SHELDON NAHMOD, ET AL., CONSTITUTIONAL TORTS 111–14 (3rd ed. 2010). The doctrine extends not just to jobs but to other interests created by state law. See, e.g., *Goss v. Lopez*, 419 U.S. 565 (1975) (state laws recognizing a right to public education have the effect of creating a property right). Given the existence of a property interest, the issue of what due process requires is a purely federal question. See *Cleveland Board of Education v. Loudermill*, 470 U.S. 532, 538–41 (1985).

Consider the following problem: The Supreme Court said in *Roth* and *Sindermann* that state law and practices may create Fourteenth Amendment "property." Suppose that, in a given case, there is a dispute over whether the particular set of state laws and practices have created "property." Is this a matter of state law or federal law? Federal courts in these cases implicitly treat this as a federal question, simply because they never look to state authorities in resolving it. But it does not necessarily follow that they are right. On account of the availability of the federal § 1983 cause of action, state courts today rarely have the opportunity to address the issue of whether state law has created a property interest, so they rarely have the chance to disagree with what a federal court has said on the matter. But suppose we construct a hypothetical case that squarely presents the issue of whether federal or state law governs: The § 1983 case is litigated in state court and the state court decides that a given set of legal arrangements does not create "property" within the meaning of the Fourteenth Amendment. The case then goes to the United States Supreme Court. Has the state court thereby decided a *state law* issue, which the Supreme Court, following *Anderson*, may review only under a deferential "fair support" test? Or is the question whether state law creates property a *federal* question?

In cases addressing the content of the term "property" in the Takings Clause of the Fifth Amendment, the Court has taken the latter view, rejecting the notion that state law controls the issue. See *Phillips v. Washington Legal Foundation*, 524 U.S. 156 (1998); *Webb's Fabulous Pharmacies v. Beckwith*, 449 U.S. 155 (1980). In *Phillips* and *Webb's Fabulous Pharmacies*, the interest income from money held in escrow accounts for the plaintiffs' benefit had been used for other purposes. The Court treated the issue as one of federal law. It held that, notwithstanding state law to the contrary, the interest income on the plaintiffs' money was the plaintiffs' property. Do these rulings on the content of "old" property mean that federal law also governs the "new" property issue of whether there is, in a given set of circumstances, a legitimate claim of entitlement to continued employment?

C. THE REQUIREMENT THAT STATE GROUNDS BE "INDEPENDENT" OF FEDERAL LAW

Sometimes the state court relies on federal law even when it might have chosen state grounds. In that event, Supreme Court review is available. See, e.g., *Oregon v. Guzek*, 546 U.S. 517, 520–23 (2006). In other cases, the bearing of federal law on the state court's holding may be unclear. Federal law, especially federal constitutional law, constrains state authority in many ways. In order to avoid conflicts with federal law, state courts may well pay attention to federal law in deciding state issues. On Supreme Court review, the question arises whether the state court's ruling on state law is independent of federal law.

STATE TAX COMMISSION V. VAN COTT
306 U.S. 511 (1939).

MR. JUSTICE BLACK delivered the opinion of the Court.

The State of Utah's income tax law, effective in 1935, exempts all "amounts received as compensation, salaries or wages from the United States . . . for services rendered in connection with the exercise of *an essential governmental function*." (Italics supplied.) In his return of income taxes to the State for 1935 under this law, respondent claimed "as deduction" and "as exempt" salaries paid him as attorney for the Reconstruction Finance Corporation and the Regional Agricultural Credit Corporation, both federal agencies. The exemptions were denied by the Tax Commission of Utah, but the Utah Supreme Court reversed. Before the Commission and in the Supreme Court of Utah, respondent asserted, first, that his salaries were exempt by the terms of the state statute itself, and, second, that they could not be taxed by the State without violating an immunity granted by the Federal Constitution. In holding respondent's income not taxable, the Supreme Court of Utah said: "We shall have to be content to follow, as we think we must, the doctrine of [*Rogers v. Graves*, 299 U.S. 401 (1937)], until such time as a different rule is laid down by the courts, the Congress, or the people through amendment to the Constitution." The *Graves* case applied the doctrine that the Federal Constitution prohibits the application of state income taxes to salaries derived from federal instrumentalities. We granted certiorari, in the present case, because of the importance of the principle of constitutional immunity from state taxation which the Utah court apparently thought controlled its judgment.

Respondent contends that the Utah Supreme Court's decision "was based squarely upon the construction of the Utah taxing statute which was held to omit respondent's salaries as a subject of taxation, and therefore that decision did not and could not reach the federal question and should not be reviewed." But that decision cannot be said to rest squarely upon a construction of the state statute. The Utah court stated that the question before it was whether respondent's salaries from the agencies in question were "taxable income for the purpose of the state income tax law," and that the answer depended upon whether these agencies exercised "essential governmental functions." But the opinion as a whole shows that the court felt constrained to conclude as it did because of the Federal Constitution and this Court's prior adjudications of constitutional immunity. Otherwise, it is difficult to explain the court's declaration that respondent could not be taxed under the "doctrine of the *Graves* case *until such time as a different rule is laid down by the courts, the Congress or the people through amendment to the Constitution*." (Italics supplied.) If the court were only incidentally referring to decisions of this Court in determining the meaning of the state law, and had concluded therefrom that the statute was itself intended to grant exemption to respondent, this Court would have no jurisdiction to review that question. But, if the state court did in fact intend alternatively to base its decision upon the state statute and upon an immunity it thought granted by the Constitution as interpreted by this Court, these two grounds are so interwoven that we are unable to conclude that the judgment rests upon an independent interpretation of the state law. Whatever exemptions the Supreme Court of Utah may find in the terms of this statute, its opinion in the present case only indicates that "it thought the Federal Constitution [as construed by this Court] required" it to hold respondent not taxable.

After careful review of this Court's decisions on the question of intergovernmental immunity, the state court concluded that the Reconstruction Finance Corporation and the Regional Agricultural Credit Corporation were "instrumentalities" performing "essential governmental duties" and that state taxation of respondent's salaries violated the Federal Constitution as interpreted by the *Graves* case. Anticipating that this Court might reexamine that interpretation and apply a "different test," the state court said that "until such is done the States are bound by the decision of the Supreme Court in . . . *Rogers v. Graves,* supra."

We have now re-examined and overruled the doctrine of *Rogers* v. *Graves* in *Graves v. O'Keefe,* [306 U.S. 466 (1939).] Salaries of employees or officials of the Federal Government or its instrumentalities are no longer immune, under the Federal Constitution, from taxation by the States. Whether the Utah income tax, by its terms, exempts respondent, can now be decided by the state's highest court apart from any question of constitutional immunity, and without the necessity, so far as the federal constitution is concerned, of attempting to divide functions of government into those which are essential and those which are non-essential.

We have frequently held that in the exercise of our appellate jurisdiction we have power not only to correct error in the judgment under review but to make such disposition of the case as justice requires. And in determining what justice does require, the Court is bound to consider any change, either in fact or in law, which has supervened since the judgment was entered. We may recognize such a change, which may affect the result, by setting aside the judgment and remanding the case so that the state court may be free to act. We have said that to do this is not to review, in any proper sense of the term, the decision of the state court upon a non-federal question, but only to deal appropriately with a matter arising since its judgment and having a bearing upon the right disposition of the case.

Applying this principle, we vacate the judgment of the Supreme Court of Utah and remand the cause to that court for further proceedings.

NOTES ON THE "INDEPENDENCE" OF STATE GROUNDS

1. ***Van Cott* on Remand.** What options are available to the Utah court? May it affirm its earlier ruling? In fact, the court did just that. See 96 P.2d 740 (Utah 1939). Does it follow, in hindsight, that the Supreme Court erred in deciding the federal issue?

2. **The Policy Behind Supreme Court Review.** When a state court rejects a federal claim of right, the justification for Supreme Court review is the need to assure that federal rights are vindicated. Justice Story argued along those lines in *Martin*. In cases like *Van Cott,* review is based on the possibility that the state court has given federal policy *more* weight than it deserves. What is the rationale for Supreme Court review in such a case? Why should the Court be concerned with seeing to it that state courts do not *mistakenly* believe federal law restricts state authority? Absent Supreme Court review, is there any way for state legislatures and courts to know what aims the states are permitted to pursue?

Consider the following argument advanced by Justice Stevens. He wrote in a case featuring an "ambiguous" state court opinion, *Michigan v. Long,* see below, but his point applies to any case in which the state court has ruled in favor of the federal claimant, relying on the Federal Constitution. Justice Stevens agreed that cases like *Van Cott* were within the Court's jurisdiction, yet he argued against selecting them from among the thousands the Court is asked to review each term:

> [My view is] that a policy of judicial restraint—one that allows other decisional bodies to have the last word in legal interpretation until it is truly necessary for this Court to intervene—enables this Court to make its most effective contribution to our federal system of government. The nature of the case before us hardly compels a departure from tradition. These are not cases in which an American citizen has been deprived of a right secured by the United States Constitution or a federal statute. Rather, they are cases in which a state court has upheld a citizen's assertion of a right, finding the citizen to be protected under both federal and state law. The complaining party is an officer of the state itself, who asks us to rule that the state court interpreted federal rights too broadly and "overprotected" the citizen.

> Such cases should not be of inherent concern to this Court. The reason may be illuminated by assuming that the events underlying this case had arisen in another country, perhaps the Republic of Finland. If the Finnish police had arrested a Finnish citizen for possession of marijuana, and the Finnish courts had turned him loose, no American would have standing to object. If instead they had arrested an American citizen and acquitted him, we might have been concerned about the arrest but we surely could not have complained about the acquittal, even if the Finnish court had based its decision on its understanding of the United States Constitution.

That would be true even if we had a treaty with Finland requiring it to respect the rights of American citizens under the United States Constitution. We would only be motivated to intervene if an American citizen were unfairly arrested, tried, and convicted by the foreign tribunal.

In this case the State of Michigan has arrested one of its citizens and the Michigan Supreme Court has decided to turn him loose. The respondent is a United States citizen as well as a Michigan citizen, but since there is no claim that he has been mistreated by the State of Michigan, the final outcome of the state processes offended no federal interest whatever. Michigan simply provided greater protection to one of its citizens than some other state might provide or, indeed, than this Court might require throughout the country.

I believe that in reviewing the decisions of state courts, the primary role of this Court is to make sure that persons who seek to vindicate federal rights have been fairly heard. The Court offers only one reason for asserting authority over cases such as the one presented today: "an important need for uniformity in federal law [that] goes unsatisfied when we fail to review an opinion that rests primarily upon federal grounds and where the independence of an alleged state ground is not apparent from the four corners of the opinion." Of course, the supposed need to "review an opinion" clashes directly with our oft-repeated reminder that "our power is to correct wrong judgments, not to revise opinions." *Herb v. Pitcairn*. The clash is not merely one of form: the "need for uniformity in federal law" is truly an ungovernable engine. That same need is no less present when it is perfectly clear that a state ground is both independent and adequate. In fact, it is equally present if a state prosecutor announces that he believes a certain policy of nonenforcement is commanded by federal law. Yet we have never claimed jurisdiction to correct such errors, no matter how egregious they may be, and no matter how much they may thwart the desires of the state electorate. We do not sit to expound our understanding of the Constitution to interested listeners in the legal community; we sit to resolve disputes. If it is not apparent that our views would affect the outcome of a particular case, we cannot presume to interfere.

3.   Can Michigan be Distinguished from Finland? Does Justice Stevens draw an apt analogy between Michigan and Finland? How would he meet the argument that, if his view prevails, Michigan lawmakers would find themselves unable to reform Michigan law on account of the Michigan courts' misunderstanding of federal law?

4.   Degrees of Dependence. When a state court thinks that federal law *requires* a certain outcome, it is clear that the content of state law is being made to depend on the court's understanding of federal law. But some cases present closer questions as to whether a state judgment is dependent on federal law:

a. Suppose a state court rules 4–3 on some issue, with two of the judges in the majority reasoning solely from state law premises, and the other two relying on federal law. Is the decision independent of federal law? See *United Air Lines v. Mahin*, 410 U.S. 623 (1973) (not independent). What if only one of the four state judges in the majority relied on state law?

b. May the Supreme Court review a state court judgment in a case where the state court justifies its ruling on state law, not by claiming that federal law compels that result, but by pointing out that a different result would raise doubts as to whether state law meets federal requirements? Suppose that the state court divides 4-3 and only one of the four judges in the majority reasons in this way?

Given that there is a spectrum running from "independence" to "dependence," what considerations should the Court take into account in deciding where to draw the line between cases it can and cannot review?

5. Gratuitous Incorporation. Distinguish the "dependence" issue illustrated by *Van Cott* and *Mahin* from the question that arises when a state, under no compulsion to follow a federal rule, nonetheless borrows federal law for some purpose. For example, a federal statute, the Food, Drug and Cosmetic Act (FDCA), requires that a prescription drug label include adequate warnings of the drug's danger. The tort law of Connecticut (and every other state) recognizes a cause of action for damages caused by an inadequate warning. In administering this cause of action, Connecticut (so far as we know) is not obliged to follow the federal test for adequacy of a warning. Nonetheless, it has chosen to borrow the federal standard of adequacy, allowing plaintiffs to establish a rebuttable presumption of breach of duty by showing a violation of the federal standard. The Supreme Court has said that it has the power to review state court determinations of what the FDCA requires. *Merrell Dow Pharmaceuticals Inc. v. Thompson*, 478 U.S. 804, 816 & n.14 (1986).

What is the federal interest in reviewing state court rulings in such a case? The Court cited "concerns about the uniformity of interpretation." Yet the Court seemed to assume that the state could, if it chose, ignore the federal standards altogether in adjudicating state tort cases. How is the state's decision to use federal standards any different from a state court decision to borrow the law of another state? In the event Connecticut borrowed a Vermont rule, no one would suggest that the Vermont Supreme Court could review Connecticut judgments. Is it relevant that, whether or not Connecticut decides to borrow the federal test for tort purposes, the federal law *does* apply to Merrell Dow's labeling? By contrast, would Supreme Court review be appropriate in a case where a state borrows a "seaworthiness" test from federal admiralty law and uses it to determine tort liability in a wholly different context—e.g., boat accidents in a pond in an amusement park—to which the federal law does not apply? See Ronald Greene, *Hybrid State Law in the Federal Courts,* 83 HARV. L. REV. 289, 309 (1969) (arguing that the "touchstone [is] whether the federal law is itself operative in the circumstances of the case—whether Supreme Court jurisdiction could effect the coordination of two coextensive and possible conflicting obligations").

6. Georgia Evidence Code. In 2011, Georgia adopted a new code of evidence. Section 1 of the new statute states:

> It is the intent of the General Assembly in enacting this Act to adopt the Federal Rules of Evidence, as interpreted by the Supreme Court of the United States and the United States circuit courts of appeal as of January 1, 2013, to the extent that such interpretation is consistent with the Constitution of Georgia. Where conflicts were found to exist among the decisions of the various circuit courts of appeal interpreting the federal rules of evidence, the General Assembly considered the decisions of the 11th Circuit Court of Appeals. It is the intent of the General Assembly to revise, modernize, and reenact the general laws of this state relating to evidence while adopting, in large measure, the Federal Rules of Evidence. The General Assembly is cognizant that there are many issues regarding evidence that are not covered by the Federal Rules of Evidence and in those situations the former provisions of Title 24 have been retained. Unless displaced by the particular provisions of this Act, the General Assembly intends that the substantive law of evidence in Georgia as it existed on December 31, 2012, be retained.

Suppose the Georgia Supreme Court resolves an evidence issue, e.g., involving attorney-client privilege. In justifying its holding, it relies on a 2012 ruling by the 11th Circuit that addresses a similar issue under the Federal Rules of Evidence. May the losing party in the Georgia Supreme Court obtain review by the U.S. Supreme Court?

III. AMBIGUOUS STATE COURT OPINIONS

Closely linked to the "independence" issue is the problem of ambiguous state court opinions. In *Van Cott,* the Utah court quite plainly relied on its understanding of federal law. Conversely, a state court may make it clear that its ruling is based on state law, despite the possible availability of a federal ground. But some state opinions cite both federal and state authority, especially in situations where provisions of the state and federal constitutions address similar issues, and perhaps even use the same language. How should the Supreme Court proceed when the state court opinion is ambiguous?

MICHIGAN V. LONG
463 U.S. 1032 (1983).

JUSTICE O'CONNOR delivered the opinion of the Court.

[In] the present case, respondent David Long was convicted for possession of marijuana found by police in the passenger compartment and trunk of the automobile that he was driving. The police searched the passenger compartment because they had reason to believe that the vehicle contained weapons potentially dangerous to the officers. We hold that the protective search of the passenger compartment was reasonable under the principles articulated in [*Terry v. Ohio*, 392 U.S. 1 (1968)]. We also examine Long's argument that the decision below rests upon an adequate and independent state ground, and we decide in favor of our jurisdiction.

* * *

II

Before reaching the merits, we must consider Long's argument that we are without jurisdiction to decide this case because the decision below rests on an adequate and independent state ground. The court below referred twice to the state constitution in its opinion, but otherwise relied exclusively on federal law.[3] Long argues that the Michigan courts have provided greater protection from searches and seizures under the state constitution than is afforded under the Fourth Amendment, and the references to the state constitution therefore establish an adequate and independent ground for the decision below.

Although we have announced a number of principles in order to help us determine whether various forms of references to state law constitute adequate and independent state grounds, we openly admit that we have thus far not developed a satisfying and consistent approach for resolving this vexing issue. In some instances, we have taken the strict view that if the ground of decision was at all unclear, we would dismiss the case. See, e.g., *Lynch v. New York*, 293 U.S. 52 (1934). In other instances, we have vacated, see, e.g., *Minnesota v. National Tea Co.*, 309 U.S. 551 (1940), or continued a case, see e.g., *Herb v. Pitcairn*, 324 U.S. 117 (1945), in order to obtain clarification about the nature of a state court decision. In more recent cases, we have ourselves examined state law to determine whether state courts have used federal law to guide their application of state law or to provide the actual basis for the decision that was reached. See *Texas v. Brown*, 460 U.S. 730, 732–33 n.1 (1983) (plurality opinion). In *Oregon*

---

[3] On the first occasion, the court merely cited in a footnote both the state and federal constitutions. On the second occasion, at the conclusion of the opinion, the court stated: "We hold, therefore, that the deputies' search of the vehicle was proscribed by the Fourth Amendment to the United States Constitution and art. 1, § 11 of the Michigan Constitution."

v. Kennedy, 456 U.S. 667, 670–671 (1982), we rejected an invitation to remand to the state court for clarification even when the decision rested in part on a case from the state court, because we determined that the state case itself rested upon federal grounds. We added that "[e]ven if the case admitted of more doubt as to whether federal and state grounds for decision were intermixed, the fact that the state court relied to the extent it did on federal grounds requires us to reach the merits." *Id.*, at 671.

This ad hoc method of dealing with cases that involve possible adequate and independent state grounds is antithetical to the doctrinal consistency that is required when sensitive issues of federal-state relations are involved. Moreover, none of the various methods of disposition that we have employed thus far recommends itself as the preferred method that we should apply to the exclusion of others, and we therefore determine that it is appropriate to reexamine our treatment of this jurisdictional issue in order to achieve the consistency that is necessary.

The process of examining state law is unsatisfactory because it requires us to interpret state laws with which we are generally unfamiliar, and which often, as in this case, have not been discussed at length by the parties. Vacation and continuance for clarification have also been unsatisfactory both because of the delay and decrease in efficiency of judicial administration, and, more important, because these methods of disposition place significant burdens on state courts to demonstrate the presence or absence of our jurisdiction. Finally, outright dismissal of cases is clearly not a panacea because it cannot be doubted that there is an important need for uniformity in federal law, and that this need goes unsatisfied when we fail to review an opinion that rests primarily upon federal grounds and where the independence of an alleged state ground is not apparent from the four corners of the [opinion].

Respect for the independence of state courts, as well as avoidance of rendering advisory opinions, have been the cornerstones of this Court's refusal to decide cases where there is an adequate and independent state ground. It is precisely because of this respect for state courts, and this desire to avoid advisory opinions, that we do not wish to continue to decide issues of state law that go beyond the opinion that we review, or to require state courts to reconsider cases to clarify the grounds of their decisions. Accordingly, when, as in this case, a state court decision fairly appears to rest primarily on federal law, or to be interwoven with the federal law, and when the adequacy and independence of any possible state law ground is not clear from the face of the opinion, we will accept as the most reasonable explanation that the state court decided the case the way it did because it believed that federal law required it to do so. If a state court chooses merely to rely on federal precedents as it would on the precedents of all other jurisdictions, then it need only make clear by a plain statement in its judgment or opinion that the federal cases are being used only for the purpose of guidance, and do not themselves compel the result that the court has reached. In this way, both justice and judicial administration will be greatly improved. If the state court decision indicates clearly and expressly that it is alternatively based on bona fide separate, adequate, and independent grounds, we, of course, will not undertake to review the decision.

This approach obviates in most instances the need to examine state law in order to decide the nature of the state court decision, and will at the same time avoid the danger of our rendering advisory opinions.[6] It also avoids the unsatisfactory and intrusive practice of requiring state courts to clarify their decisions to the satisfaction of this Court. We believe that such an approach will provide state judges with a clearer opportunity to develop state jurisprudence unimpeded by federal interference, and yet will preserve the integrity of federal law. "It is fundamental that state courts be left free and unfettered by us in interpreting their state constitutions. But it is equally important that ambiguous or obscure adjudications by state courts do not stand as barriers to a determination by this Court of the validity under the federal constitution of state action." *National Tea Co.*, supra, 309 U.S., at 557.

The principle that we will not review judgments of state courts that rest on adequate and independent state grounds is based, in part, on "the limitations of our own jurisdiction." *Herb v. Pitcairn*, 324 U.S. 117, 125 (1945). The jurisdictional concern is that we not "render an advisory opinion, and if the same judgment would be rendered by the state court after we corrected its views of federal laws, our review could amount to nothing more than an advisory opinion." *Id.*, at 126. Our requirement of a "plain statement" that a decision rests upon adequate and independent state grounds does not in any way authorize the rendering of advisory opinions. Rather, in determining, as we must, whether we have jurisdiction to review a case that is alleged to rest on adequate and independent state grounds, we merely assume that there are no such grounds when it is not clear from the opinion itself that the state court relied upon an adequate and independent state ground and when it fairly appears that the state court rested its decision primarily on federal law.

[Our] review of the decision below under this framework leaves us unconvinced that it rests upon an independent state ground. Apart from its two citations to the state constitution, the court below relied exclusively on its understanding of *Terry* and other federal cases. Not a single state case was cited to support the state court's holding that the search of the passenger compartment was unconstitutional. Indeed, the court declared that the search in this case was unconstitutional because

---

[6] There may be certain circumstances in which clarification is necessary or desirable, and we will not be foreclosed from taking the appropriate action.

"[t]he Court of Appeals erroneously applied the principles of *Terry v. Ohio* . . . to the search of the interior of the vehicle in this case." 413 Mich., at 471, 320 N.W.2d, at 869. The references to the state constitution in no way indicate that the decision below rested on grounds in any way independent from the state court's interpretation of federal law. Even if we accept that the Michigan constitution has been interpreted to provide independent protection for certain rights also secured under the Fourth Amendment, it fairly appears in this case that the Michigan Supreme Court rested its decision primarily on federal law.

Rather than dismissing the case, or requiring that the state court reconsider its decision on our behalf solely because of a mere possibility that an adequate and independent ground supports the judgment, we find that we have jurisdiction in the absence of a plain statement that the decision below rested on an adequate and independent state ground. It appears to us that the state court "felt compelled by what it understood to be federal constitutional considerations to construe . . . its own law in the manner it did." *Zacchini v. Scripps-Howard Broadcasting Co.*, 433 U.S. 562, 568 (1977).

[In Parts III and IV of the opinion, the Court rejected Long's Fourth Amendment objection to the search and addressed other issues.]

JUSTICE BLACKMUN, concurring in part and concurring in the judgment.

I join Parts I, III, IV, and V of the Court's opinion. While I am satisfied that the Court has jurisdiction in this particular case, I do not join the Court, in Part II of its opinion, in fashioning a new presumption of jurisdiction over cases coming here from state courts. Although I agree with the Court that uniformity in federal criminal law is desirable, I see little efficiency and an increased danger of advisory opinions in the Court's new approach.

JUSTICE BRENNAN, with whom JUSTICE MARSHALL joins, dissenting.

[Justice Brennan dissented on the 4th Amendment issue. He agreed that the Michigan judgment rested on federal grounds, but did not endorse the Court's presumption.]

JUSTICE STEVENS, dissenting.

[The point of Justice Stevens' dissent was that the Court should be mainly concerned with reviewing state cases that wrongly deny federal rights, and not cases like this one, in which "the complaining party is an officer of the state itself, who asks us to rule that the state court interpreted federal rights too broadly and 'overprotected' the citizen." For excerpts from his dissent, see note 2 after *Van Cott*, above.]

NOTE ON THE AFTERMATH OF LONG

For the most part, the Court has adhered to *Long*, though later cases have sometimes reverted to one or another of the approaches the *Long* Court said it was abandoning. See R. FALLON, ET AL., supra, at 477–78. For an illustration of the general practice under *Long*, see *Florida v. Powell*, 559 U.S. 50 (2009), in which the Court held that, because a state supreme court decision did not "indicate clearly and expressly that it is . . . based on bona fide separate, adequate, and independent state grounds," the U.S. Supreme Court had jurisdiction to review the federal claim.

IV.   PROCEDURAL STATE GROUNDS

In the foregoing cases, the state law rules have been *substantive* grounds for the outcomes of cases. In *Van Cott*, for example, the ultimate ruling by the state court was that, under Utah law, employees of the United States have a substantive right not to pay certain state taxes. In *Fox Film*, lack of severability of the invalid clause under state contract law was a substantive justification for refusing to enforce the contract. We now turn to state *procedural* grounds. State civil and criminal procedure prescribe the ways issues should be litigated in the state courts. For example, a "contemporaneous objection" rule requires that objections to the introduction of evidence be made at the time the adversary proposes to introduce the evidence. Procedural rules such as this are typically enforced by imposing a severe sanction on the litigant who disobeys them—he forfeits the right to litigate the substantive issue. Suppose a litigant violates a state procedural rule and thereby is foreclosed from raising a federal issue in the state courts. As a result, he loses in the state courts even though, by hypothesis, he has a good federal claim. On review by the Supreme Court, the forfeiture imposed by the state courts as a sanction for failure to obey a state procedural rule will ordinarily be an adequate state ground to support the judgment.

As with substantive grounds, determining the adequacy of state procedural grounds requires that the Court focus on the competing interests at stake. A useful comparison and contrast can be drawn between procedural and substantive grounds. Procedural grounds often differ from the bulk of substantive ones with regard to the impact of the adequate state ground rule on the outcome of a case. Typically, cases in which the state *substantive* ground is adequate to support the judgment are ones in which the winner is the party asserting a federal claim. This is so because most cases in which the state substantive ground goes against the federal claimant are ones in which that party may nonetheless prevail on the federal ground.

By contrast, state procedural grounds generally have precisely the opposite impact on the outcome of the litigation. Usually the litigant stymied by a state procedural ground is someone seeking to raise a federal defense against a state criminal or civil enforcement action directed at him. If the state procedural ground is adequate to support the judgment, this litigant with a federal claim will lose the case even though he may have a sound federal claim. If, as is often the case, this litigant is a state criminal defendant, he may be convicted and imprisoned without ever getting a hearing on a federal constitutional defense, just because of the procedural default. The Court will, in certain cases, approach state procedural grounds with a more skeptical eye, sometimes finding them inadequate even though they are constitutionally unexceptionable.

JAMES V. KENTUCKY
466 U.S. 341 (1984).

JUSTICE WHITE delivered the opinion of the Court.

In *Carter v. Kentucky*, 450 U.S. 288 (1981), we held that a trial judge must, if requested to do so, instruct the jury not to draw an adverse inference from the defendant's failure to take the stand. In this case, the Kentucky Supreme Court found that the trial judge was relieved of that obligation because defense counsel requested an "admonition" rather than an "instruction."

I

Petitioner Michael James was indicted for receipt of stolen property, burglary, and rape. James had been convicted of two prior felonies—forgery and murder—and the prosecution warned that were James to take the stand it would use the forgery conviction to impeach his testimony. During voir dire, defense counsel asked the prospective jurors how they would feel were James not to testify. After a brief exchange between counsel and one member of the venire, the trial judge interrupted, stating: "They have just said they would try the case solely upon the law and the evidence. That excludes any other consideration." With that, voir dire came to a close. James did not testify at trial.

At the close of testimony, counsel and the judge had an off-the-record discussion about instructions. When they returned on the record, James' lawyer noted that he objected to several of the instructions being given, and that he "requests that an admonition be given to the jury that no emphasis be given to the defendant's failure to testify which was overruled." The judge then instructed the jury, which returned a verdict of guilty on all counts. At a subsequent persistent felony offender proceeding, the jury sentenced James to life imprisonment in light of his two previous convictions. On appeal, James argued that the trial judge's refusal to tell the jury not to draw an adverse inference from his failure to testify violated *Carter v. Kentucky*. The Kentucky Supreme Court conceded that Carter requires the trial judge, upon request, to instruct the jury not to draw an adverse inference. The court noted, however, that James had requested an admonition rather than an instruction, and there is a "vast difference" between the two under state law. He "was entitled to the instruction, but did not ask for it. The trial court properly denied the request for an admonition." We granted certiorari to determine whether petitioner's asserted procedural default adequately supports the result below. We now reverse.

II

In *Carter* we held that, in order fully to effectuate the right to remain silent, a trial judge must instruct the jury not to draw an adverse inference from the defendant's failure to testify if requested to do so. James argues that the essence of the holding in *Carter* is that the judge must afford some form of guidance to the jury, and that the admonition he sought was the "functional equivalent" of the instruction required by *Carter*. The State responds that the trial judge was under no obligation to provide an admonition when under Kentucky practice James should have sought an instruction. An examination of the state-law background is necessary to understand these arguments.

A

Kentucky distinguishes between "instructions" and "admonitions." The former tend to be statements of black-letter law, the latter cautionary statements regarding the jury's conduct. Thus, "admonitions" include statements to the jury requiring it to disregard certain testimony, to consider particular evidence for purposes of evaluating credibility only, and to consider evidence as to one codefendant only. The State Rules of Criminal Procedure provide that at each adjournment the jury is to be "admonished" not to discuss the case.

Instructions, on the other hand, set forth the legal rules governing the outcome of a case. They "state what the jury must believe from the evidence . . . in order to return a verdict in favor of the party who bears the burden of proof." *Webster v. Commonwealth*, 508 S.W.2d 33, 36 (1974). The judge reads the instructions to the jury at the end of the trial, and provides it a written copy. Ky. Rule Crim. Proc. 9.54(1). After *Carter*, Kentucky amended its Criminal Rules to provide that, if the defendant so requests, the instructions must state that he is not compelled to testify and that the jury shall not draw an adverse inference from his election not to. Rule 9.54(3). The substantive distinction between admonitions and instructions is not always clear or closely hewn to. Kentucky's highest court has recognized that the content of admonitions and instructions can overlap. In a number of cases, for example, it has referred to a trial court's failure either to instruct or to admonish the jury on a particular point, indicating that either was a possibility. E.g., *Caldwell v. Commonwealth*, 503 S.W.2d 485, 493–494 (1972) ("instructions" did not contain a particular "admonition," but the "failure to admonish or instruct" was harmless). See also *Bennett v. Horton*, 592 S.W.2d 460, 464 (1979) ("instructions" included the "admonition" that the jury could make a certain setoff against the award); *Carson v. Commonwealth*, 382 S.W.2d 85, 95 (1964) ("The fourth instruction was the usual reasonable doubt admonition"). The court has acknowledged that "sometimes matters more appropriately the subject of admonition are included with or as a part of the instructions." *Webster v. Commonwealth*, supra, at 36.

In pre-*Carter* cases holding that a defendant had no right to have the jury told not to draw an adverse inference, Kentucky's highest court did not distinguish admonitions from instructions. See, e.g., *Luttrell v. Commonwealth*, 554 S.W.2d 75, 79–80 (1977) ("instruction"). [A] statement to the jury not to draw an adverse inference from the defendant's failure to testify would seem to fall more neatly into the admonition category than the instruction category. Cautioning the jury against considering testimony not given differs little from cautioning it not to consider testimony that was.[5] However, the Kentucky Criminal Rules treat it as an instruction.

One procedural difference between admonitions and instructions is that the former are normally oral, while the latter, though given orally, are also provided to the jury in writing. However, this distinction is not strictly adhered to. As the cases cited above indicate, "admonitions" frequently appear in the written instructions. Conversely, instructions may be given only orally if the defendant waives the writing requirement. The State contends, though without citing any authority, that the instructions must be all in writing or all oral, and that it would have been reversible error for the trial judge to have given this "instruction" orally. Yet the Kentucky Court of Appeals has held, for example, that there was no error where the trial court, after reading the written instructions, told the jury orally that its verdict must be unanimous, a statement normally considered an "instruction." *Freeman v. Commonwealth*, 425 S.W.2d 575, 579 (1968). And in several cases the Court of Appeals has found no error where the trial court gave oral explanations of its written instructions. [citing cases]. Finally, given Kentucky's strict contemporaneous-objection rule, see Ky. Rule Crim. Proc. 9.54(2), it would be odd if it were reversible error for the trial court to have given a *Carter* instruction orally at the defendant's request. See also *Weichhand v. Garlinger*, 447 S.W.2d 606, 610 (Ky. App. 1969) (harmless error to give oral admonition where written instruction was requested and appropriate).

---

[5]   Indeed, such a statement is substantively indistinguishable from an "admonition" given in this very case. When James was brought into court for the persistent-felony-offender hearing, he was in handcuffs. After requesting and being denied a mistrial, his attorney asked: "Can we at least have an admonition to the jury, your Honor?" The judge obliged, telling the jury it was "admonished not to consider the fact that the defendant was brought into the courtroom shackled and handcuffed. That should have nothing to do, no bearing at all, on your decision in this case."

B

There can be no dispute that, for federal constitutional purposes, James adequately invoked his substantive right to jury guidance. The question is whether counsel's passing reference to an "admonition" is a fatal procedural default under Kentucky law adequate to support the result below and to prevent us from considering petitioner's constitutional claim. In light of the state-law background described above, we hold that it is not. Kentucky's distinction between admonitions and instructions is not the sort of firmly established and regularly followed state practice that can prevent implementation of federal constitutional rights. *Carter* holds that if asked to do so the trial court must tell the jury not to draw the impermissible inference. To insist on a particular label for this statement would "force resort to an arid ritual of meaningless form," *Staub v. City of Baxley*, 355 U.S. 313, 320 (1958), and would further no perceivable state interest, *Henry v. Mississippi*, 379 U.S. 443, 448–449 (1965). "Admonition" is a term that both we and the State Supreme Court have used in this context and which is reasonable under state law and normal usage. As Justice Holmes wrote 60 years ago: "Whatever springs the State may set for those who are endeavoring to assert rights that the State confers, the assertion of federal rights, when plainly and reasonably made, is not to be defeated under the name of local practice." *Davis v. Wechsler*, 263 U.S. 22 (1923).

C

The State argues that this is more than a case of failure to use the required magic word, however. It considers James' request for an admonition to have been a deliberate strategy. He sought an oral statement only in order to put "less emphasis on this particular subject, not before the jury, not in writing to be read over and over, but to have been commented upon and passed by." James, now represented by his third attorney, seems to concede that the first attorney did seek an oral admonition. He does not argue that the trial court had to include the requested statement in the instructions, though he suggests that it could have done so, and that he would have been happy with either a written or an oral statement.

We would readily agree that the State is free to require that all instructions be in writing; and to categorize a no-adverse-inference statement as an instruction. The Constitution obliges the trial judge to tell the jury, in an effective manner, not to draw the inference if the defendant so requests; but it does not afford the defendant the right to dictate, inconsistent with state practice, how the jury is to be told. In *Lakeside v. Oregon*, 435 U.S. 333 (1978), we held that the judge may give a no-adverse-inference instruction over the defendant's objection. Given that, the State may surely give a written instruction over the defendant's request that it be oral only. And if that is so, the State can require that if the instruction is to be given, it be done in writing. For reasons similar to those set out in *Lakeside*, we do not think that a State would impermissibly infringe the defendant's right not to testify by requiring that if the jury is to be alerted to it, it be alerted in writing.

This is not a case, however, of a defendant attempting to circumvent such a firm state procedural rule. For one thing, as the discussion in Part II-A, supra, indicates, the oral/written distinction is not as solid as the State would have us believe. Admonitions can be written and instructions oral, and the Kentucky Supreme Court has itself used the term "admonition" in referring to instructions that "admonish." In addition, our own examination of the admittedly incomplete record reveals little to support the State's view of petitioner's request. The single passing reference to an "admonition" is far too slender a reed on which to rest the conclusion that petitioner insisted on an oral statement and nothing but.

Apart from this one use of the term, there is absolutely nothing in the record to indicate any such insistence. Indeed, other indications are to the contrary. Before going off the record, defense counsel stated that he had "a matter in regards to the *instructions*." Tr. of Hearing (Jan. 19, 1982), p. 3 (emphasis added). Returning to the record, he noted that he "object[ed] to several of the instructions being given to the jury" and that his request for "an admonition" to the jury regarding the defendant's failure to testify had been overruled. The court below inferred from these two statements that counsel had sought an oral statement apart from the instructions. Yet the statements could also be a shift from an objection to what was being said to the jury ("the instructions being given"), to an objection to what was not ("requests an admonition . . . which was overruled"). It is also possible that counsel sought both a written and an oral statement and was denied on both counts.

Where it is inescapable that the defendant sought to invoke the substance of his federal right, the asserted state-law defect in form must be more evident than it is here. In the circumstances of this case, we cannot find that petitioner's constitutional rights were respected or that the result below rests on independent and adequate state grounds.

III

Respondent argues that even if there was error, it was harmless. It made the same argument below, but the Kentucky Supreme Court did not reach it in light of its conclusion that no error had been committed. We have not determined whether *Carter* error can be harmless, and we do not do so now. Even if an evaluation of harmlessness is called for, it is best made in state court before it is made here. The case is remanded for further proceedings not inconsistent with this opinion.

JUSTICE MARSHALL took no part in the decision of this case.

JUSTICE REHNQUIST dissents for the reasons stated in his dissenting opinion in *Carter v. Kentucky*, 450 U.S. 288, 307–310 (1981).

NOTES ON STATE PROCEDURAL GROUNDS

1. **Testing the Adequacy of State Procedural Grounds.** The key circumstance behind the Court's finding of inadequacy in *James* seems to be that, under scrutiny, Kentucky's "rule" collapses. Thus, "Kentucky's distinction between admonitions and instructions is not the sort of firmly established and regularly followed state practice that can prevent implementation of federal constitutional rights." *James* relied on *Staub v. City of Baxley*, where the Court emphasized the pointlessness of applying the rule as a ground for finding inadequacy. The City of Baxley prosecuted Staub, a labor organizer, for "soliciting members for an organization without a permit & license," as required by a local ordinance. The ordinance consisted of eight sections detailing the requirements. Staub raised a First Amendment defense, asserting that the ordinance as a whole was invalid. A state procedural rule required that she specify the section she wished to challenge, and the state courts declined to hear her defense on the ground that she had failed to comply with this rule. The Court found the state ground inadequate:

> The several sections of the ordinance are interdependent in their application to one in [Staub's] position and constitute but one complete act for the licensing and taxing of her described activities. For that reason, no doubt, she challenged the constitutionality of the whole ordinance, and in her objections used language challenging the constitutional effect of all its sections. She did challenge all sections of the ordinance, though not by number. To require her, in these circumstances, to count off, one by one, the several sections of the ordinance would be to force resort to an arid ritual of meaningless form.

355 U.S. at 320.

In *Lee v. Kemna*, 534 U.S. 362 (2002), the Court focused on the lack of proportion between the heavy burden imposed by the rule and the goal that it served. Lee was on trial for murder in Missouri. His lawyer planned to call witnesses to show that he was in California at the time, and so informed the jury in his opening statement. The witnesses traveled from California under subpoena, showed up on the morning of the trial, and were sequestered. But they left the courthouse before they were called. Surprised by this development, the lawyer explained the situation to the judge and orally asked for a continuance until the next day. The judge refused, citing a personal commitment of his own. Neither the judge nor the prosecutor raised any objection to the form in which the request was made.

Lee was convicted. He sought to challenge the conviction in the Missouri courts on the ground that his right to due process was violated by the refusal of the continuance. The Missouri Court of Appeals never reached the constitutional issue, relying instead on a state law ground. Missouri Supreme Court Rule 24.09 requires that continuance motions be in writing and accompanied by an affidavit; Rule 24.10 specifies the showing one must make in order to obtain a continuance due to absence of a witness. The oral request here did not comply.

Finding the state procedural ground inadequate, the Supreme Court reversed. The case fell within "the general principle that an objection which is ample and timely to bring the alleged federal error to the attention of the trial court and enable it to take appropriate corrective action is sufficient to serve legitimate state interests, and therefore sufficient to preserve the claim for review here." The Court continued:

> Three considerations, in combination, lead us to conclude that this case falls within the small category of cases in which asserted state grounds are inadequate to block adjudication of a federal claim. First, when the trial judge denied Lee's motion, he stated a reason that could not have been countered by a perfect motion for continuance. The judge said he could not carry the trial over until the next day because he had to be with his daughter in the hospital; the judge further informed counsel that another scheduled trial prevented him from concluding Lee's case on the following business day. Second, no published Missouri decision directs flawless compliance with Rules 24.09 and 24.20 in the unique circumstances this case presents—the sudden, unanticipated, and at the time unexplained disappearance of critical subpoenaed witnesses on what became the trial's last day. Lee's predicament, from all that appears, was one Missouri courts had not confronted before. Third, and most important, given "the realities of trial," Lee substantially complied with Missouri's key rule. In sum, we are drawn to the conclusion reached by [a dissenting judge]: "[Any] seasoned trial lawyer would agree that insistence on a written continuance application, supported by an affidavit, in the midst of trial upon the discovery that subpoenaed witnesses are suddenly absent, would be so bizarre as to inject an Alice-in-Wonderland quality into the proceedings."

534 U.S. at 381–83.

More recently the Supreme Court has ruled that a state procedural rule is not necessarily inadequate because it is discretionary rather than mandatory. In *Beard v. Kindler*, 558 U.S. 53 (2009), a defendant convicted of capital murder, with a jury recommendation of the death penalty, escaped and fled to Canada while his postverdict motions were pending before the state convicting court. Pennsylvania applied an apparently discretionary "fugitive forfeiture rule" to bar subsequent review of Kindler's unaddressed federal postverdict claims. Writing for the Court, Chief Justice Roberts said:

We have framed the adequacy inquiry by asking whether the state rule in question was "firmly established and regularly followed." (quoting *James v. Kentucky*, 466 U.S. 341, 348 (1984)). [We] hold that a discretionary state procedural rule can serve as an adequate ground to bar federal [review.] Nothing inherent in such a rule renders it inadequate for purposes of the adequate state ground doctrine. To the contrary, a discretionary rule can be "firmly established" and "regularly followed"—even if the appropriate exercise of discretion may permit consideration of a federal claim in some cases but not others. [A] contrary holding would pose an unnecessary dilemma for the States: States could preserve flexibility for granting courts discretion to excuse procedural errors, but only at the cost of undermining the finality of state court judgments. Or States could preserve the finality of their judgments by withholding such discretion, but only at the cost of precluding any flexibility in applying the rules.

The *Beard* majority rejected any conclusion that discretionary procedural rules are "automatically" inadequate. But the justices refused to speak more broadly since "the procedural default at issue—escape from prison—is hardly a typical . . . default, making [the] case an unsuitable vehicle for . . . broad guidance on the adequate state ground doctrine."

    2. State Waiver of Procedural Default. When a litigant fails to raise or preserve a federal claim in accordance with state procedure, but the state appellate courts adjudicate it anyway, the state may not, on Supreme Court review, assert the procedural default as an adequate state ground supporting the judgment. The state courts' decision to reach the merits is taken as a waiver of the state's interest in imposing a sanction for violation of its procedural rules. See, e.g., *Orr v. Orr*, 440 U.S. 268, 274–75 (1979).

    3. Distinguishing "Inadequate" State Grounds from Unconstitutional State Procedures. In order to appreciate the analytical significance of cases like *James*, *Staub*, and *Lee*, it is important to separate the "inadequacy" problem they illustrate from the more conventional problem presented by cases in which the state's procedures violate the litigant's constitutional right to due process of law, for example, by imposing unforeseeable requirements after it is too late to meet them. See, e.g., *Reich v. Collins*, 513 U.S. 106, 112–13 (1994); *Brinkerhoff-Faris Trust & Savings Co. v. Hill*, 281 U.S. 673 (1930). By contrast, rulings like *James*, *Staub*, and *Lee* do not rest on the premise that the state procedure is unconstitutional, either on its face or as applied to the case at hand. Accordingly, the Court's refusal to honor the state ground cannot be based on its power to override unconstitutional state laws and practices. Scholars have suggested that the inadequate state ground doctrine is "a form of 'federal common law' that places limits, beyond those demanded by the Due Process Clause, on the freedom of states to refuse to entertain federal claims because not presented in compliance with state procedural rules." R. FALLON, ET AL., supra, at 517.

4. Direct Review and Habeas Corpus. Our focus in this chapter is on direct review by the Supreme Court of state court judgments. State court judgments of conviction in criminal cases also may be reviewed by federal district courts (and ultimately by the Supreme Court) by way of a habeas corpus petition. Habeas is treated in detail in Chapter 9. For now, two points should be noted. First, the inadequate state procedural ground doctrine, illustrated by *James, Staub,* and *Lee,* also applies in habeas corpus cases. Second, in principle, a habeas court may ignore even an "adequate" state ground, provided the prisoner can show "cause" for the procedural default, and "prejudice" resulting from the state court's failure to address his federal claim.

Both points can be illustrated by the facts of *Lee v. Kemna.* That case was, as it happens, a habeas case. We have used it in this chapter because the Court addressed the "adequacy" of the state ground, and the standards for resolving this question do not vary depending on whether it comes to the Court on direct review or on habeas. After the Missouri appellate court denied relief, Lee had obtained affidavits from his missing witnesses, in which they explained that they left the courthouse because "a court officer told them their testimony would not be needed that day." 534 U.S. at 373 & n. 6. At least one of the affidavits raised the possibility of prosecutorial misconduct. Even if there were an adequate state ground precluding direct review of the conviction, a showing of prosecutorial misconduct would establish "cause" for the procedural default, thereby authorizing a federal district court to grant habeas relief.

5. The Federal Law Requirement That Litigants Raise Their Federal Claims in the State Courts. Suppose a litigant never raises a federal claim in state court at all, but seeks to do so in the Supreme Court. Quite apart from the adequate state ground doctrine, there is in such a case a *federal* ground for denying access to Supreme Court review. See, e.g., *Cardinale v. Louisiana,* 394 U.S. 437, 438–39 (1969):

> This Court has consistently refused to decide federal constitutional issues raised here for the first time on review of state court [decisions]. In addition to the question of jurisdiction arising under the statute controlling our power to review final judgments of state courts, 28 U.S.C. § 1257, there are sound reasons for this. Questions not raised below are those on which the record is very likely to be inadequate, since it certainly was not compiled with those questions in mind. And in a federal system it is important that state courts be given the first opportunity to consider the applicability of state statutes in light of constitutional challenge, since the statutes may be construed in a way which saves their constitutionality. Or the issue may be blocked by an adequate state ground. Even though States are not free to avoid constitutional issues on inadequate state grounds, they should be given the first opportunity to consider them.

While this requirement may seem obvious, issues arise as to [a] whether a litigant made it sufficiently clear in the lower courts that he meant to raise a *federal* issue (e.g., where the state and federal constitutions both address the matter at hand and the litigant seems to rely on state authority in the lower courts); and [b] whether a given contention made for the first time at the Supreme Court level is a new *claim* or merely a new *argument* in support of a claim litigated below.

See, e.g., *Yee v. City of Escondido*, 503 U.S. 519 (1992). In the state courts the Yees had challenged a rent control ordinance on the ground that it was a physical taking of their property without just compensation, in violation of the Takings Clause. In the Supreme Court, they raised two additional grounds: that the ordinance constituted "a denial of substantive due process and a regulatory taking." The Court ruled that the substantive due process theory was a different claim: "Because petitioners did not raise their substantive due process claim below, and because the state courts did not address it, we will not consider it here."

By contrast, the "regulatory taking" theory was merely a new argument in support of the takings claim they had advanced all along:

> Petitioners' arguments that the ordinance constitutes a taking in two different ways, by physical occupation and by regulation, are not separate *claims*. They are, rather, separate *arguments* in support of a single claim—that the ordinance effects an unconstitutional taking. Having raised a taking claim in the state courts, therefore, petitioners could have formulated any argument they liked in support of that claim here.

503 U.S. at 534–35 (emphasis in original).

V.   THE FINAL JUDGMENT RULE

COX BROADCASTING CORP. V. COHN
420 U.S. 469 (1975).

MR. JUSTICE WHITE delivered the opinion of the Court.

The issue before us in this case is whether, consistently with the First and Fourteenth Amendments, a State may extend a cause of action for damages for invasion of privacy caused by the publication of the name of a deceased rape victim which was publicly revealed in connection with the prosecution of the crime.

I

In August 1971, appellee's 17-year-old daughter was the victim of a rape and did not survive the incident. Six youths were soon indicted for murder and rape. Although there was substantial press coverage of the crime and of subsequent developments, the identity of the victim was not disclosed pending trial, perhaps because of Ga.Code Ann. § 26–9901 (1972), which makes it a misdemeanor to publish or broadcast the name or identity of a rape victim. In April 1972, some eight months later, the six defendants appeared in court. Five pleaded guilty to rape or attempted rape, the charge of murder having been dropped. The guilty pleas were accepted by the court, and the trial of the defendant pleading not guilty was set for a later date. In the course of the proceedings that day, appellant Wasell, a reporter covering the incident for his employer, learned the name of the victim from an examination of the indictments which were made available for his inspection in the courtroom. That the name of the victim appears in the indictments and that the indictments were public records available for inspection are not disputed. Later that day, Wassell broadcast over the facilities of station WSB-TV, a television station owned by appellant Cox Broadcasting Corp., a news report concerning the court proceedings. The report named the victim of the crime and was repeated the following day.

In May 1972, appellee brought an action for money damages against appellants, relying on § 26–9901 and claiming that his right to privacy had been invaded by the television broadcasts giving the name of his deceased daughter. Appellants admitted the broadcasts but claimed that they were privileged under both state law and the First and Fourteenth Amendments. The trial court, rejecting appellants' constitutional claims and holding that the Georgia statute gave a civil remedy to those injured by its violation, granted summary judgment to appellee as to liability, with the determination of damages to await trial by jury.

On appeal, the Georgia Supreme Court, in its initial opinion, held that the trial court had erred in construing § 26–9901 to extend a civil cause of action for invasion of privacy and thus found it unnecessary to consider the constitutionality of the statute. The court went on to rule, however, that the complaint stated a cause of action "for the invasion of the appellee's right of privacy, or for the tort of public disclosure"—a "common law tort exist(ing) in this jurisdiction without the help of the statute that the trial judge in this case relied on." Although the privacy invaded was not that of the deceased victim, the father was held to have stated a claim for invasion of his own privacy by reason of the publication of his daughter's name. The court explained, however, that liability did not follow as a matter of law and that summary judgment was improper; whether the public disclosure of the name actually invaded appellee's "zone of privacy," and if so, to what extent, were issues to be determined by the trier of fact. Also, "in formulating such an issue for determination by the fact-finder, it is reasonable to require the appellee to prove that the appellants invaded his privacy with wilful or negligent disregard for the fact that reasonable men would find the invasion highly offensive." The Georgia Supreme Court did agree with the trial court, however, that the

First and Fourteenth Amendments did not, as a matter of law, require judgment for appellants. The court concurred with the statement in *Briscoe v. Reader's Digest Assn., Inc.*, 4 Cal.3d 529, 541, 93 Cal.Rptr. 866, 874, 483 P.2d 34, 42 (1971), that "the rights guaranteed by the First Amendment do not require total abrogation of the right to privacy. The goals sought by each may be achieved with a minimum of intrusion upon the other."

Upon motion for rehearing the Georgia court countered the argument that the victim's name was a matter of public interest and could be published with impunity by relying on § 26–9901 as an authoritative declaration of state policy that the name of a rape victim was not a matter of public concern. This time the court felt compelled to determine the constitutionality of the statute and sustained it as a "legitimate limitation on the right of freedom of expression contained in the First [Amendment]".

II

[Among the issues addressed by the Supreme Court was "whether the decision from which this appeal has been taken is a '[f]inal judgment or decree'" within § 1257.]

Since 1789, Congress has granted this Court appellate jurisdiction with respect to state litigation only after the highest state court in which judgment could be had has rendered a "[f]inal judgment or decree." Title 28 U.S.C. § 1257 retains this limitation on our power to review cases coming from state courts. The Court has noted that "[c]onsiderations of English usage as well as those of judicial policy" would justify an interpretation of the final-judgment rule to preclude review "where anything further remains to be determined by a State court, no matter how dissociated from the only federal issue that has finally been adjudicated by the highest court of the State." *Radio Station WOW, Inc. v. Johnson*, 326 U.S. 120, 124 (1945). But the Court there observed that the rule had not been administered in such a mechanical fashion and that there were circumstances in which there has been "a departure from this requirement of finality for federal appellate jurisdiction." *Ibid.*

These circumstances were said to be "very few," *ibid.*; but as the cases have unfolded, [there] are now at least four categories of [cases] in which the Court has treated the decision on the federal issue as a final judgment for the purposes of 28 U.S.C. § 1257 and has taken jurisdiction without awaiting the completion of the additional proceedings anticipated in the lower state courts. In most, if not all, of the cases in these categories, these additional proceedings would not require the decision of other federal questions that might also require review by the Court at a later date,[6] and immediate rather than delayed review would be the best way to avoid "the mischief of economic waste and of delayed justice," *Radio Station WOW*, supra, at 124, as well as precipitate interference with state litigation.[7] In the cases in the first two categories considered below, the federal issue would not be mooted or otherwise affected by the proceedings yet to be had because those proceedings have little substance, their outcome is certain, or they are wholly unrelated to the federal question. In the other two categories, however, the federal issue would be mooted if the petitioner or appellant seeking to bring the action here prevailed on the merits in the later state-court proceedings, but there is nevertheless sufficient justification for immediate review of the federal question finally determined in the state courts. In the first category are those cases in which there are further proceedings—even entire trials—yet to occur in the state courts but where for one reason or another the federal issue is conclusive or the outcome of further proceedings preordained. In these circumstances, because the case is for all practical purposes concluded, the judgment of the state court on the federal issue is deemed final. In *Mills v. Alabama*, 384 U.S. 214 (1966), for example, a demurrer to a criminal complaint was sustained on federal constitutional grounds by a state trial court. The State Supreme Court reversed, remanding for jury trial. This Court took jurisdiction on the reasoning that the appellant had no defense other than his federal claim and could not prevail at trial on the facts or any nonfederal ground. To dismiss the appeal "would not only be an inexcusable delay of the benefits Congress intended to grant by providing for appeal to this Court, but it would also result in a completely unnecessary waste of time and energy in judicial systems already troubled by delays due to congested dockets." *Id.*, at 217–218.

---

[6]   Eminent domain proceedings are of the type that may involve an interlocutory decision as to a federal question with another federal question to be decided later. "For in those cases the federal constitutional question embraces not only a taking but a taking on payment of just compensation. A state judgment is not final unless it covers both aspects of that integral problem.' *North Dakota State Board of Pharmacy v. Snyder's Drug Stores, Inc.*, 414 U.S. 156, 163 (1973).

[7]   *Gillespie v. United States Steel Corp.*, 379 U.S. 148 (1964), arose in the federal courts and involved the requirement of 28 U.S.C. § 1291 that judgments of district courts be final if they are to be appealed to the courts of appeals. In the course of deciding that the judgment of the District Court in the case had been final, the Court indicated its approach to finality requirements: "And our cases long have recognized that whether a ruling is 'final' within the meaning of § 1291 is frequently so close a question that decision of that issue either way can be supported with equally forceful arguments, and that it is impossible to devise a formula to resolve all marginal cases coming within what might well be called the 'twi-light zone' of finality. Because of this difficulty this Court has held that the requirement of finality is to be given a 'practical rather than a technical construction." *Cohen v. Beneficial Industrial Loan Corp.* (337 U.S. 541, 546). *Dickinson v. Petroleum Conversion Corp.*, 338 U.S. 507, 511, pointed out that in deciding the question of finality the most important competing considerations are "the inconvenience and costs of piecemeal review on the one hand and the danger of denying justice by delay on the other." 379 U.S., at 152–53.

Second, there are cases such as *Radio Station WOW*, supra, and *Brady v. Maryland*, 373 U.S. 83 (1963), in which the federal issue, finally decided by the highest court in the State, will survive and require decision regardless of the outcome of future state-court proceedings. In Radio Station WOW, the Nebraska Supreme Court directed the transfer of the properties of a federally licensed radio station and ordered an accounting, rejecting the claim that the transfer order would interfere with the federal license. The federal issue was held reviewable here despite the pending accounting on the "presupposition . . . that the federal questions that could come here have been adjudicated by the State court, and that the accounting which remains to be taken could not remotely give rise to a federal question . . . that may later come here. . . ." 326 U.S., at 127. The judgment rejecting the federal claim and directing the transfer was deemed "dissociated from a provision for an accounting even though that is decreed in the same order." *Id.*, at 126. Nothing that could happen in the course of the accounting, short of settlement of the case, would foreclose or make unnecessary decision on the federal question. Older cases in the Court had reached the same result on similar facts. In [one of these] the Court, in an opinion by Mr. Chief Justice Taney, stated that the Court had not understood the final-judgment rule 'in this strict and technical sense, but has given (it) a more liberal, and, as we think, a more reasonable construction, and one more consonant to the intention of the legislature."

In the third category are those situations where the federal claim has been finally decided, with further proceedings on the merits in the state courts to come, but in which later review of the federal issue cannot be had, whatever the ultimate outcome of the case. Thus, in these cases, if the party seeking interim review ultimately prevails on the merits, the federal issue will be mooted; if he were to lose on the merits, however, the governing state law would not permit him again to present his federal claims for review. The Court has taken jurisdiction in these circumstances prior to completion of the case in the state courts. *California v. Stewart*, 384 U.S. 436 (1966) (decided with *Miranda v. Arizona*), epitomizes this category. There the state court reversed a conviction on federal constitutional grounds and remanded for a new trial. Although the State might have prevailed at trial, we granted its petition for certiorari and affirmed, explaining that the state judgment was 'final' since an acquittal of the defendant at trial would preclude, under state law, an appeal by the State.

A recent decision in this category is *North Dakota State Board of Pharmacy v. Snyder's Drug Stores, Inc.*, 414 U.S. 156 (1973), in which the Pharmacy Board rejected an application for a pharmacy operating permit relying on a state statute specifying ownership requirements which the applicant did not meet. The State Supreme Court held the statute unconstitutional and remanded the matter to the Board for further consideration of the application, freed from the constraints of the ownership statute. The Board brought the case here, claiming that the statute was constitutionally acceptable under modern cases. After reviewing the various circumstances under which the finality requirement has been deemed satisfied despite the fact that litigation had not terminated in the state courts, we entertained the case over claims that we had no jurisdiction. The federal issue would not survive the remand, whatever the result of the state administrative proceedings. The Board might deny the license on state-law grounds, thus foreclosing the federal issue, and the Court also ascertained that under state law the Board could not bring the federal issue here in the event the applicant satisfied the requirements of state law except for the invalidated ownership statute. Under these circumstances, the issue was ripe for review.[10]

Lastly, there are those situations where the federal issue has been finally decided in the state courts with further proceedings pending in which the party seeking review here might prevail on the merits on nonfederal grounds, thus rendering unnecessary review of the federal issue by this Court, and where reversal of the state court on the federal issue would be preclusive of any further litigation on the relevant cause of action rather than merely controlling the nature and character of, or determining the admissibility of evidence in, the state proceedings still to come. In these circumstances, if a refusal immediately to review the state court decision might seriously erode federal policy, the Court has entertained and decided the federal issue, which itself has been finally determined by the state courts for purposes of the state litigation.

In *Construction Laborers v. Curry*, 371 U.S. 542 (1963), the state courts temporarily enjoined labor union picketing over claims that the National Labor Relations Board had exclusive jurisdiction of the controversy. The Court took jurisdiction for two independent reasons. First, the power of the state court to proceed in the face of the preemption claim was deemed an issue separable from the merits and ripe for review in this Court, particularly "when postponing review would seriously erode the national labor policy requiring the subject matter of respondents' cause to be heard by the . . . Board, not by the state courts.' Id., at 550. Second, the Court was convinced that in any event the union had no defense to the entry of a permanent injunction other than the preemption

---

[10] *Cohen v. Beneficial Industrial Loan Corp.*, 337 U.S. 541 (1949), was a diversity action in the federal courts in the course of which there arose the question of the validity of a state statute requiring plaintiffs in stockholder suits to post security for costs as a prerequisite to bringing the action. The District Court held the state law inapplicable, the Court of Appeals reversed, and this Court, after granting certiorari, held that the issue of security for costs was separable from and independent of the merits and that if review were to be postponed until the termination of the litigation, "it will be too late effectively to review the present order and the rights conferred by the statute, if it is applicable, will have been lost, probably irreparably." *Id.*, at 546.

claim that had already been ruled on in the state courts. Hence the case was for all practical purposes concluded in the state tribunals.

In *Mercantile National Bank v. Langdeau*, 371 U.S. 555 (1963), two national banks were sued, along with others, in the courts of Travis County, Tex. The claim asserted was conspiracy to defraud an insurance company. The banks as a preliminary matter asserted that a special federal venue statute immunized them from suit in Travis County and that they could properly be sued only in another county. Although trial was still to be had and the banks might well prevail on the merits, the Court, relying on Curry, entertained the issue as a "separate and independent matter, anterior to the merits and not enmeshed in the factual and legal issues comprising the plaintiff's cause of action.' Id., at 558. Moreover, it would serve the policy of the federal statute 'to determine now in which state court appellants may be tried rather than to subject them . . . to long and complex litigation which may all be for naught if consideration of the preliminary question of venue is postponed until the conclusion of the proceedings.' *Ibid.*

Miami Herald Publishing Co. v. Tornillo, 418 U.S. 241 (1974), is the latest case in this category. There a candidate for public office sued a newspaper for refusing, allegedly contrary to a state statute, to carry his reply to the paper's editorial critical of his qualifications. The trial court held the act unconstitutional, denying both injunctive relief and damages. The State Supreme Court reversed, sustaining the statute against the challenge based upon the First and Fourteenth Amendments and remanding the case for a trial and appropriate relief, including damages. The newspaper brought the case here. We sustained our jurisdiction, relying on the principles elaborated in the North Dakota case and observing:

> Whichever way we were to decide on the merits, it would be intolerable to leave unanswered, under these circumstances, an important question of freedom of the press under the First Amendment; an uneasy and unsettled constitutional posture of § 104.38 could only further harm the operation of a free press. 418 U.S., at 247 n. 6.

In light of the prior cases, we conclude that we have jurisdiction to review the judgment of the Georgia Supreme Court rejecting the challenge under the First and Fourteenth Amendments to the state law authorizing damage suits against the press for publishing the name of a rape victim whose identity is revealed in the course of a public prosecution. The Georgia Supreme Court's judgment is plainly final on the federal issue and is not subject to further review in the state courts. Appellants will be liable for damages if the elements of the state cause of action are proved. They may prevail at trial on nonfederal grounds, it is true, but if the Georgia court erroneously upheld the statute, there should be no trial at all. Moreover, even if appellants prevailed at trial and made unnecessary further consideration of the constitutional question, there would remain in effect the unreviewed decision of the State Supreme Court that a civil action for publishing the name of a rape victim disclosed in a public judicial proceeding may go forward despite the First and Fourteenth Amendments. Delaying final decision of the First Amendment claim until after trial will "leave unanswered . . . an important question of freedom of the press under the First Amendment," "an uneasy and unsettled constitutional posture [that] could only further harm the operation of a free press." *Tornillo*, supra, 418 U.S., at 247 n. 6. On the other hand, if we now hold that the First and Fourteenth Amendments bar civil liability for broadcasting the victim's name, this litigation ends. Given these factors—that the litigation could be terminated by our decision on the merits[13] and that a failure to decide the question now will leave the press in Georgia operating in the shadow of the civil and criminal sanctions of a rule of law and a statute the constitutionality of which is in serious doubt—we find that reaching the merits is consistent with the pragmatic approach that we have followed in the past in determining finality.

[The Court went on to hold that, in the circumstances of this case, "the protection of freedom of the press provided by the First and Fourteenth Amendments bars [Georgia] from making appellants' broadcast the basis of civil liability."]

MR. JUSTICE REHNQUIST, dissenting.

[Over] the years, [this] Court has steadily discovered new exceptions to the finality requirement, such that they can hardly any longer be described as "very few." [Although] the Court's opinion today does accord detailed consideration to this problem, I do not believe that the reasons it expresses can support its result.

I

The Court has taken what it terms a "pragmatic" approach to the finality problem presented in this case. In so doing, it has relied heavily on *Gillespie v. United States Steel Corp.*, 379 U.S. 148 (1964). As the

---

[13] Mr. Justice Rehnquist is correct in saying that this factor involves consideration of the merits in determining jurisdiction. But it does so only to the extent of determining that the issue is substantial and only in the context that if the state court's final decision on the federal issue is incorrect, federal law forecloses further proceedings in the state court. That the petitioner who protests against the state court's decision on the federal question might prevail on the merits on nonfederal grounds in the course of further proceedings anticipated in the state court and hence obviate later review of the federal issue here is not preclusive of our jurisdiction. *Curry, Langdeau, North Dakota State Board of Pharmacy, California v. Stewart*, 384 U.S. 436 (1966) (decided with *Miranda v. Arizona*), and *Miami Herald Publishing Co. v. Tornillo*, make this clear. In those cases, the federal issue having been decided, arguably wrongly, and being determinative of the litigation if decided the other way, the finality rule was [satisfied.]

Court acknowledges, *Gillespie* involved 28 U.S.C. § 1291, which restricts the appellate jurisdiction of the federal courts of appeals to "final decisions of the district courts." Although acknowledging this distinction, the Court accords it no importance and adopts *Gillespie*'s approach without any consideration of whether the finality requirement for this Court's jurisdiction over a "judgment or decree" of a state court is grounded on more serious concerns than is the limitation of court of appeals jurisdiction to final "decisions" of the district courts. I believe that the underlying concerns are different, and that the difference counsels a more restrictive approach when § 1257 finality is at issue.

According to *Gillespie*, the finality requirement is imposed as a matter of minimizing "the inconvenience and costs of piecemeal review'. This proposition is undoubtedly sound so long as one is considering the administration of the federal court system. Were judicial efficiency the only interest at stake there would be less inclination to challenge the Court's resolution in this case, although, as discussed below, I have serious reservations that the standards the Court has formulated are effective for achieving even this single goal. The case before us, however, is an appeal from a state court, and this fact introduces additional interests which must be accommodated in fashioning any exception to the literal application of the finality requirement. I consider § 1257 finality to be but one of a number of congressional provisions reflecting concern that uncontrolled federal judicial interference with state administrative and judicial functions would have untoward consequences for our federal system.[4] This is by no means a novel view of the § 1257 finality requirement. In *Radio Station WOW*, Mr. Justice Frankfurter's opinion for the Court explained the finality requirement as follows:

> [This] prerequisite to review derives added force when the jurisdiction of this Court is invoked to upset the decision of a State court. Here we are in the realm of potential conflict between the courts of two different governments. And so, ever since 1789, Congress has granted this Court the power to intervene in State litigation only after "the highest court of a State in which a decision in the suit could be had" has rendered a "final judgment or decree." *This requirement is not one of those technicalities to be easily scorned. It is an important factor in the smooth working of our federal system.* (Emphasis added.)

[We] have in recent years emphasized and re-emphasized the importance of comity and federalism in dealing with a related problem,

---

[4]   See, e.g., 28 U.S.C. § 1341 (limitation on power of district courts to enjoin state taxing systems); 28 U.S.C. § 1739 (requiring that state judicial proceedings be accorded full faith and credit in federal courts); 28 U.S.C. §§ 2253–2254 (prescribing various restrictions on federal habeas corpus for state prisoners); 28 U.S.C. § 2281 (three-judge district court requirement); 28 U.S.C. § 2283 (restricting power of federal courts to enjoin state-court proceedings).

that of district court interference with ongoing state judicial proceedings. See *Younger v. Harris*, 401 U.S. 37 (1971). Because these concerns are important, and because they provide "added force" to § 1257's finality requirement, I believe that the Court has erred by simply importing the approach of cases in which the only concern is efficient judicial administration.

II

But quite apart from the considerations of federalism which counsel against an expansive reading of our jurisdiction under § 1257, the Court's holding today enunciates a virtually formless exception to the finality requirement, one which differs in kind from those previously carved out. [While] the totality of [the exceptions recognized in prior cases] certainly indicates that the Court has been willing to impart to the language "final judgment or decree" a great deal of flexibility, each of them is arguably consistent with the intent of Congress in enacting § 1257, if not with the language it used, and each of them is relatively workable in practice.

To those established exceptions is now added one so formless that it cannot be paraphrased, but instead must be quoted:

> Given these factors—that the litigation could be terminated by our decision on the merits and that a failure to decide the question now will leave the press in Georgia operating in the shadow of the civil and criminal sanctions of a rule of law and a statute the constitutionality of which is in serious doubt—we find that reaching the merits is consistent with the pragmatic approach that we have followed in the past in determining finality.

There are a number of difficulties with this test. One of them is the Court's willingness to look to the merits. It is not clear from the Court's opinion, however, exactly now great a look at the merits we are to take. On the one hand, the Court emphasizes that if we reverse the Supreme Court of Georgia the litigation will end, and it refers to cases in which the federal issue has been decided "arguably wrongly." On the other hand, it claims to look to the merits "only to the extent of determining that the issue is substantial." If the latter is all the Court means, then the inquiry is no more extensive than is involved when we determine whether a case is appropriate for plenary consideration; but if no more is meant, our decision is just as likely to be a costly intermediate step in the litigation as it is to be the concluding event. If, on the other hand, the Court really intends its doctrine to reach only so far as cases in which our decision in all probability will terminate the litigation, then the Court is reversing the traditional sequence of judicial decisionmaking. Heretofore, it has generally been thought that a court first assumed jurisdiction of a case, and then went on to decide the merits of the questions it presented. But henceforth in determining our own jurisdiction we may be obliged to determine whether or not we agree with the merits of the decision of the highest court of a State.

Yet another difficulty with the Court's formulation is the problem of transposing to any other case the requirement that "failure to decide the question now will leave the press in Georgia operating in the shadow of the civil and criminal sanctions of a rule of law and a statute the constitutionality of which is in serious doubt." Assuming that we are to make this determination of "serious doubt" at the time we note probable jurisdiction of such an appeal, is it enough that the highest court of the State has ruled against any federal constitutional claim? If that is the case, then because § 1257 by other language imposes that requirement, we will have completely read out of the statute the limitation of our jurisdiction to a "final judgment or decree." Perhaps the Court's new standard for finality is limited to cases in which a First Amendment freedom is at issue. The language used by Congress, however, certainly provides no basis for preferring the First Amendment, as incorporated by the Fourteenth Amendment, to the various other Amendments which are likewise "incorporated," or indeed for preferring any of the "incorporated" Amendments over the due process and equal protection provisions which are embodied literally in the Fourteenth Amendment.

Another problem is that in applying the second prong of its test, the Court has not engaged in any independent inquiry as to the consequences of permitting the decision of the Supreme Court of Georgia to remain undisturbed pending final state-court resolution of the case. This suggests that in order to invoke the benefit of today's rule, the "shadow" in which an appellant must stand need be neither deep nor wide. In this case nothing more is at issue than the right to report the name of the victim of a rape. No hindrance of any sort has been imposed on reporting the fact of a rape or the circumstances surrounding it. Yet the Court unquestioningly places this issue on a par with the core First Amendment interest involved in *Miami Herald Publishing Co. v. Tornillo*, that of protecting the press in its role of providing uninhibited political discourse.

But the greatest difficulty with the test enunciated today is that it totally abandons the principle that constitutional issues are too important to be decided save when absolutely necessary, and are to be avoided if there are grounds for decision of lesser dimension. The long line of cases which established this rule makes clear that it is a principle primarily designed, not to benefit the lower courts, or state-federal relations, but rather to safeguard this Court's own process of constitutional [adjudication].

In this case there has yet to be an adjudication of liability against appellants, and unlike the appellant in *Mills v. Alabama*, they do not concede that they have no nonfederal defenses. Nonetheless, the Court rules on their constitutional defense. Far from eschewing a constitutional holding in advance of the necessity for one, the Court construes § 1257 so that it may virtually rush out and meet the prospective constitutional litigant as he approaches our doors.

III

This Court is obliged to make preliminary determinations of its jurisdiction at the time it votes to note probable jurisdiction. At that stage of the proceedings, prior to briefing on the merits or oral argument, such determinations must of necessity be based on relatively cursory acquaintance with the record of the proceedings below. The need for an understandable and workable application of a jurisdictional provision such as § 1257 is therefore far greater than for a similar interpretation of statutes dealing with substantive law. We, of course, retain the authority to dismiss a case for want of a final judgment after having studied briefs on the merits and having heard oral argument, but I can recall not a single instance of such a disposition during the last three Terms of the Court. While in theory this may be explained by saying that during these Terms we have never accorded plenary consideration to a § 1257 case which was not a "final judgment or decree," I would guess it just as accurate to say that after the Court has studied briefs and heard oral argument, it has an understandable tendency to proceed to a decision on the merits in preference to dismissing for want of jurisdiction. It is thus especially disturbing that the rule of this case, unlike the more workable and straightforward exceptions which the Court has previously formulated, will seriously compound the already difficult task of accurately determining, at a preliminary stage, whether an appeal from a state-court judgment is a "final judgment or [decree]". I would dismiss for want of jurisdiction.

NOTES ON APPEALABILITY

1. **The Final Judgment "Rule."** In *Cox* the Court points out that the Judiciary Act of 1789 limited Supreme Court review to the "final judgment or decree" of a state court. Early in its history the Court adhered to a literal reading of the term. Over time, however, the Court has abandoned a strict reading of the term "final," developing the four categories of disputes it will review, even though the state courts are not yet finished with the case. The fourth category is particularly flexible, allowing review when "reversal of the state court on the federal issue would be preclusive of any further litigation on the relevant cause of action" and "a refusal immediately to review the state-court decision might seriously erode federal policy." And some findings of appealability may not fall within any of the categories.

A rule is "an abstract or general statement of what the law permits or requires of classes of persons in classes of circumstances." STEVEN J. BURTON,

AN INTRODUCTION TO LEGAL REASONING 13 (1985). Given the many circumstances that bear on whether the Court will review a state judgment, it seems somewhat misleading to characterize the doctrine as the application of a rule. There remains, however, the normative issue addressed by Justice Rehnquist's dissent. Should the Court be faulted for making the kind of pragmatic judgments reflected in the four categories? In answering this question, keep in mind that rule-based decision making has both costs and benefits. It helps to achieve predictability, stability, and consistency across the range of cases to which the rule is applied, all of which are worthwhile goals. On the other hand, the whole point of a rule is to exclude the decision maker from taking into account the array of factors (like the reasoning behind the *Cox* categories) that bear on achieving the best outcome of the particular case at hand. An argument in favor of the Court's approach is that the goals served by rules are not especially compelling in this context. Predictability, stability, and consistency matter greatly in bodies of law that bear on "primary activity," i.e., the conduct of daily activity. The reason is that people, businesses, and governments need to know how courts will treat a given transaction in order to decide whether to engage in it. Arguably, these goals are not so important in the context of appealability, a legal issue that has little bearing on primary activity. If this is so, then the value of looking at a number of factors so as to adapt the appealability ruling to the particulars of the case at hand may be relatively stronger. For a general discussion of the value of rules versus standards in Federal Courts law, see Michael Wells, *Positivism and Antipositivism in Federal Courts Law*, 29 GA. L. REV. 655 (1995).

   2.   The Policy of "Constitutional Avoidance." According to Justice Rehnquist, the "greatest difficulty" with the Court's fourth category is "that it totally abandons the principle that constitutional issues are too important to be decided save when absolutely necessary, and are to be avoided if there are grounds for decision of lesser dimension." The general point is that judicial review, though necessary, is (arguably) anti-democratic and therefore ought to be cabined.

   a.   The policy of avoiding constitutional issues lies behind a number of doctrines examined in this book, including [i] *Pullman* abstention, see Chapter 6, which directs federal courts to order the parties to ask state courts for resolution of state law issues if doing so may avert the need to decide a constitutional issue; [ii] some limits on "standing" to sue, as well as the "mootness" and "ripeness" doctrines, discussed in Chapter 5; and [iii] the adequate state ground doctrine, see Section II, supra. One question raised by Justice Rehnquist's objection to *Cox* is whether the Court's disposition of that case represents a departure from a well-established avoidance policy or, alternatively, signals a general movement away from the avoidance policy on the part of the modern Court. Consider this question as you study other doctrines bearing on the avoidance policy.

   b.   Whether or not the avoidance policy is in *general* decline, there seems to be a tension between that policy and the Court's approach to the adjudication of free speech issues. The First Amendment "overbreadth" doctrine permits federal courts to adjudicate a challenge to the facial validity of a statute, brought by a person whose conduct could validly be prohibited, if the statute covers a substantial amount of protected speech as well. By the same token, using the fourth *Cox* category, the Court has taken a liberal approach to appealability of First Amendment issues. See, e.g., *Fort Wayne Books, Inc. v. Indiana*, 489 U.S. 46 (1989). There Indiana had brought a criminal racketeering case against Fort Wayne Books, charging it with distributing obscenity. The Indiana trial court found the statute impermissibly vague as applied to obscenity and dismissed the charges. The state appealed and the Indiana appellate court reversed, rejecting the vagueness challenge and reinstating the charges. The Supreme Court found that the case fit into the fourth *Cox* category, because Fort Wayne Books "could well prevail on nonfederal grounds at a subsequent trial, and reversal [would] bar further prosecution on the [charges] at issue here," and because "[r]esolution of this important issue of the possible limits the First amendment places on state and federal efforts to control organized crime should not remain in doubt." *Id.* at 55–56.

3.   Federalism and Appealability. Justice Rehnquist points out that the Court draws no distinction between the standards governing appealability within the federal court system and the appealability of a state judgement in the Supreme Court. He argues, to the contrary, that § 1257 finality should be viewed as "one of a number of congressional provisions reflecting concern that uncontrolled federal judicial interference with state administrative and judicial functions would have untoward consequences for our federal system." The examples he cites (in his footnote 4) relate to the powers of *lower* federal courts. Recall that Article III specifies "one Supreme court" to finally resolve issues of federal law, and that, at least since *Martin v. Hunter's Lessee*, the legitimacy and utility of this role have rarely been questioned. Do the institutional differences between the Supreme Court and the lower federal courts weaken the force of Justice Rehnquist's federalism argument?

4.   State and Federal Appealability Rules. States are ordinarily free to adopt whatever rules they like for appealability *within* the state court system, so long as their rules comply with federal norms. For example, in *Mitchell v. Forsyth*, 472 U.S. 511 (1985), a federal court case, and official who had been sued for damages for a constitutional violation raised an official immunity defense. He lost before the federal district court and sought to bring an interlocutory appeal. The Court allowed an immediate appeal in this context, so long as the outcome turned on a question of law, because "qualified immunity is in fact an entitlement not to stand trial under certain circumstances." By contrast, *Johnson v. Fankell*, 520 U.S. 911 (1997), was a state court § 1983 case presenting the same issue. The Court ruled that federal law does not oblige the state courts to allow an interlocutory appeal of denial of immunity. It distinguished *Mitchell* on the ground that the source of the right to appeal in the federal courts is the federal statute governing appeals from federal district courts to federal circuit courts, 28 U.S.C. § 1291.

5.   The Collateral Order Doctrine and Constitutional Litigation in the Federal Courts. More recently, the Court narrowly construed the *Mitchell* doctrine even within the federal court system. In *Will v. Hallock*, 546 U.S. 345 (2006), federal government agents had searched the plaintiffs' house and seized their computers. The government never brought criminal charges, but "[w]hen the computer equipment was returned, several of the disk drives were damaged, all of the stored data (including trade secrets and account files) were lost, and the Hallocks were forced out of business." The Hallocks then brought two suits, one against the United States under the Federal Tort Claims Act, "alleging negligence by the customs agents in executing the search," and another against the agents under the *Bivens* doctrine, alleging that the agents' conduct deprived them of property without due process of law. The District Court dismissed the FTCA suit, "holding that the agents' activities occurred in the course of detaining goods and thus fell within an exception to the Act's waiver of sovereign immunity."

The agents then sought dismissal of the *Bivens* case, citing a provision of the FTCA under which a judgment in an FTCA suit "shall constitute a complete bar to any action by the claimant, by reason of the same subject matter, against the employee of the government whose act or omission gave rise to the claim." 28 U.S.C. § 2676. The District Court rejected this argument, "holding that dismissal of the action against the Government under the Tort Claims Act was solely on a procedural ground, and thus failed to raise the judgment bar."

The issue before the Supreme Court was whether the agents could immediately appeal this ruling. A unanimous Court held that they could not. Distinguishing *Mitchell v. Forsyth* and other cases where immediate appeals were allowed, it said that

> In each case, some particular value of a high order was marshaled in support of the interest in avoiding trial: honoring the separation of powers, preserving the efficiency of government and the initiative of its officials, respecting a State's dignitary interests, and mitigating the government's advantage over the individual. That is, it is not mere avoidance of a trial, but avoidance of a trial that would imperil a substantial public interest, that counts when asking whether an order is effectively unreviewable if review is to be left until later.

> Does the claim of the customs agents in this case serve such a weighty public objective that the judgment bar should be treated as an immunity demanding the protection of a collateral order appeal? One can argue, of course, that if the *Bivens* action goes to trial the efficiency of Government will be compromised and the officials burdened and distracted, as in the qualified immunity case. [But] the cases are different. Qualified immunity is not the law simply to

save trouble for the Government and its employees; it is recognized because the burden of trial is unjustified in the face of a colorable claim that the law on point was not clear when the official took action, and the action was reasonable in light of the law as it was. The nub of immunity is the need to induce officials to show reasonable initiative when the relevant law is not "clearly established;" a quick resolution of a qualified immunity claim is essential.

There is, however, no such public interest at stake simply because the judgment bar is said to be applicable. It is not the preservation of initiative but the avoidance of litigation for its own sake that supports the judgment bar, and if simply abbreviating litigation troublesome to Government employees were important enough for [interlocutory appeal,] collateral order appeal would be a matter of right whenever the government lost a motion to dismiss under the Tort Claims Act, or a federal officer lost one on a *Bivens* action, or a state official was in that position in a case under § 1983 or *Ex Parte Young*.

The Court then analogized the judgment bar to *res judicata*, which "has not been thought to protect values so great that only immediate appeal can effectively vindicate them." For an illustration from the daily work of the lower courts in § 1983 litigation, see *Goodman v. Harris County*, 443 F.3d 464 (5th Cir. 2006) (in a § 1983 suit by the mother of someone shot and killed by a deputy constable, the court ruled that an order requiring the deputy to undergo mental examination was not appealable under the collateral order doctrine).

CHAPTER 9

HABEAS CORPUS

■ ■ ■

Habeas corpus is a distinctive remedy governed by a set of special rules. Filing a habeas corpus petition enables a person held in custody to challenge the validity of the confinement. The prisoner sues the jailor and demands that he or she justify the detention to the satisfaction of a judge. Habeas is a very old procedure, established in England centuries ago, brought to America by British colonists, and then incorporated into American law, including the Constitution. Thus, the Suspension Clause, Art. I, § 9, cl. 2, provides that "The Privilege of the Writ of Habeas Corpus shall not be suspended, unless when in Cases of Rebellion or Invasion the public Safety may require it." While habeas corpus may be available in both state and federal courts, we are not at all concerned with state court habeas except to the extent its availability bears on access to federal habeas. Recall, however, the nineteenth-century ruling in *Tarble's Case* (Chapter 7) that state courts may not grant habeas relief against a federal officer. If *Tarble* is still viable, there is no state court habeas for persons held in federal custody.

This chapter focuses on the rules governing access to habeas corpus in federal court, and mainly on access to federal habeas for state prisoners held after criminal conviction. Three major federal statutes should be noted. Section 14 of the Judiciary Act of 1789 authorized federal courts to hear habeas petitions brought by persons held in federal custody. In 1867 Congress extended federal habeas corpus to persons held in state custody. Although the statute remained largely unchanged over the next 129 years, Supreme Court decisions first expanded access to habeas for state convicts and then, beginning in the 1970s, contracted it. The most recent statutory revisions include the Antiterrorism and Effective Death Penalty Act of 1996 (AEDPA), 110 Stat. 1214, which codifies some of the Court's restrictions and imposes others, and the Military Commissions Act of 2006, which was struck down in *Boumediene*, below. The habeas statutes are cpdified at 28 U.S.C. § 2241 et seq.

In studying habeas, bear in mind two basic distinctions. First, we focus on whether a given detainee may obtain a ruling from a federal judge on the validity of the confinement. We are only occasionally (and as the need arises) concerned with the substantive law to be applied by the judge in making that ruling. Second, the chapter is organized in two parts. Part I deals with executive detentions, i.e., those in which the incarceration itself has been effected by the police, or (of more current importance) the military, or other officers of the executive branch, with no judicial involvement. Part II addresses the issues that arise when the habeas petitioner is a prisoner confined pursuant to a criminal conviction and challenges the validity of the process that led to the conviction. Our attention will be on cases in which the habeas petitioner was convicted in state court and seeks relief from a federal judge. Part II is far longer than Part I because the latter type of case has generated more litigation and more Supreme Court doctrine than the former.

I.   EXECUTIVE DETENTIONS

Seventeenth-century British kings sometimes locked people up with no judicial process, a practice that gave rise to strong objections from both Parliament and the common law courts. This aggressive use of royal power contributed to the downfall of the monarchy as it used to be. More important for our purposes, the objections ultimately led to broader access to habeas corpus to challenge such detentions. Some of the history is recounted in *Boumediene v. Bush*, 553 U.S. 723 (2008). In modern times, it is well-settled that the police may not simply arrest persons, confine them, and avoid judicial inquiry into the grounds for the detention. As a matter of due process, a hearing must be held soon after the arrest to determine whether there is probable cause for the confinement and whether, even if the arrest can be justified, the prisoner should be released pending trial. In the day-to-day administration of the criminal law, almost no one held in pretrial detention files a habeas corpus petition, simply because other means are available to oversee police and prosecutors who neglect constitutional requirements.

Yet the availability of habeas to challenge confinement raises a distinct constitutional problem: May Congress foreclose access to the courts, or is congressional power limited by the Suspension Clause? For a long time this question remained unanswered, because Congress had not tried to bar habeas, or at least had not done so with sufficient clarity to squarely present the issue. Before 2001 questions bearing on access to habeas corpus to challenge executive detention typically came up in only one context—when immigration authorities sought to detain and deport an alien without obtaining a judicial order authorizing the expulsion. In *INS v. St. Cyr*, 533 U.S. 289 (2001), the Supreme Court interpreted the relevant statute as requiring a judicial hearing before deportation, despite language in the statute that seemed to suggest otherwise. The Court explained that "a serious Suspension Clause issue would be presented if we were to accept the INS's submission that the 1996 statutes have withdrawn [the power to issue a writ of habeas corpus] from federal judges and provided no adequate substitute for its exercise. [The] necessity of resolving such a serious and difficult constitutional issue—and the desirability of avoiding that necessity—simply reinforce the reasons for requiring a clear and unambiguous statement of congressional intent."

Ultimately, in *Boumediene*, below, the Court ruled on the constitutional issue of whether Congress could cut off access to the courts to challenge executive detentions. The Court held that there are indeed constitutional limits on Congress's power. In order to fully understand *Boumediene*, it is helpful to keep in mind the developments that gave rise to that case. (It will also be helpful to learn several acronyms along the way.) In response to the September 11, 2001 attacks Congress passed a joint resolution authorizing the President to use "all necessary and appropriate force against those nations, organizations, or persons he determines planned, authorized, committed, or aided the terrorist attacks . . . or harbored such organizations or persons." Authorization for Use of Military Force, Pub. L. 107–40 (2001) (AUMF). The United States sent military forces to Afghanistan and other places, captured a number of people, and confined many of them at the U.S. base in Guantanamo, Cuba. In *Hamdi v. Rumsfeld*, 542 U.S. 507 (2004), a majority of the Justices recognized that detention of individuals who fought against the United States in Afghanistan is authorized by the AUMF. In *Rasul v. Bush*, 542 U.S. 466 (2004), the Court held that, under the federal habeas statute, 28 U.S.C. § 2241, an alien held outside the United States could seek habeas relief in a federal court. Another Supreme Court case, *Hamdan v. Rumsfeld*, 548 U.S. 557 (2006), held that, absent congressional authorization, the President could not set up military commissions to prosecute persons accused of collaboration in terrorist attacks. (*Hamdan* is discussed in Chapter 10.)

After *Hamdi* the government established Combattant Status Review Tribunals (CSRTs) to determine whether persons detained at Guantanamo were "enemy combattants." (The CSRT procedure was examined and found constitutionally suspect in *Boumediene*.) In response to *Rasul* the Congress enacted the Detainee Treatment Act of 2005 (DTA), 119 Stat. 2739, which provided that "no court, justice, or judge shall have jurisdiction to hear or consider . . . an application for a writ of habeas corpus filed by or on behalf of an alien detained by the Department of Defense at Guantanamo Bay, Cuba." 119 Stat. 2742. The DTA also provided that the D.C. Circuit Court of Appeals would have exclusive jurisdiction to review decisions of the CSRTs. Later, in response to *Hamdan*, Congress enacted the Military Commissions Act (MCA), which not only provided authorization for military commissions, but also reiterated the DTA provision purporting to preclude access to habeas corpus for "an alien detained by the United States who has been determined by the United States to have been properly detained as an enemy combatant or is awaiting such determination." 28 U.S.C. § 2241(e) (Supp. 2007).

The habeas petitioners in *Boumediene* were aliens held at Guantanamo. When they sought access to habeas in federal court, the government asked for dismissal on the ground that this provision of the MCA deprived the court of jurisdiction. Their only recourse, the government argued, was D.C. Circuit review of CSRT decisions under the DTA provision noted above.

* * *

BOUMEDIENE V. BUSH
553 U.S. 723 (2008).

JUSTICE KENNEDY delivered the opinion of the Court.

Petitioners are aliens designated as enemy combatants and detained at the United States Naval Station at Guantanamo Bay, Cuba. [They] present a question not resolved by our earlier cases relating to the detention of aliens at Guantanamo: whether they have the constitutional privilege of habeas corpus, a privilege not to be withdrawn except in conformance with the Suspension Clause, Art. I, § 9, cl.2. We hold these petitioners do have the habeas corpus privilege. Congress has enacted a statute, the Detainee Treatment Act of 2005 (DTA), [that] provides certain procedures for review of the detainees' status. We hold that those procedures are not an adequate and effective substitute for habeas corpus. Therefore § 7 of the Military Commissions Act of 2006 (MCA), 28 U.S.C.A. § 2241(e), [operates] as an unconstitutional suspension of the writ. We do not address whether the President has authority to detain these petitioners nor do we hold that the writ must issue. These and other questions regarding the legality of the detention are to be resolved in the first instance by the District Court.

I

After [*Hamdi v. Rumsfeld*], the Deputy Secretary of Defense established Combatant Status Review Tribunals (CSRTs) to determine whether individuals detained at Guantanamo were "enemy combatants," as the Department defines that term. [A] later memorandum established procedures to implement the CSRTs. [The] Government maintains these procedures were designed to comply with the due process requirements identified by the plurality in *Hamdi*. Some of these [petitioners] were apprehended on the battlefield in Afghanistan, others in places as far away from there as Bosnia and Gambia. All are foreign nationals, but none is a citizen of a nation now at war with the United States. Each denies he is a member of the al Qaeda terrorist network that carried out the September 11 attacks or of the Taliban regime that provided sanctuary for al Qaeda. Each petitioner appeared before a separate CSRT; was determined to be an enemy combatant; and has sought a writ of habeas corpus in the United States District Court for the District of Columbia.

The constitutional issue presented in the instant cases was not reached in [*Rasul v. Bush*]. After *Rasul*, [Congress] passed the DTA, [which purports to withdraw habeas jurisdiction of petitions filed by aliens detained at Guantanamo and to give the Court of Appeals for the District of Columbia Circuit "exclusive" jurisdiction to review decisions by CSRTs.] In [*Hamdan v. Rumsfeld*], the Court held this provision did not apply to cases (like petitioners') pending when the DTA was enacted. Congress responded by passing the MCA, [which] again amended § 2241. The text of the statutory amendment is discussed below. [The] Court of Appeals concluded that MCA § 7 must be read to strip from it, and all federal courts, jurisdiction to consider petitioners' habeas corpus applications, [that] petitioners are not entitled to the privilege of the writ or the protections of the Suspension Clause, [and] as a result, that it was unnecessary to consider whether Congress provided an adequate and effective substitute for habeas corpus in the DTA.

II

As a threshold matter, we must decide whether MCA § 7 denies the federal courts jurisdiction to hear habeas corpus actions pending at the time of its enactment. We hold the statute does deny that jurisdiction, so that, if the statute is valid, petitioners' cases must be dismissed. [There] is little doubt that the effective date provision [§ 7(b)] applies to habeas corpus actions. Those actions, by definition, are cases "which relate to [detention."]

III

In deciding the constitutional questions now presented we must determine whether petitioners are barred from seeking the writ or invoking the protections of the Suspension Clause either because of their status, i.e., petitioners' designation by the Executive Branch as enemy combatants, or their physical location, i.e., their presence at Guantanamo Bay. The Government contends that noncitizens designated as enemy combatants and detained in territory located outside our Nation's borders have no constitutional rights and no privilege of habeas corpus. Petitioners contend they do have cognizable constitutional rights and that Congress, in seeking to eliminate recourse to habeas corpus as a means to assert those rights, acted in violation of the Suspension Clause.

We begin with a brief account of the history and origins of the writ. Our account proceeds from two propositions. First, protection for the privilege of habeas corpus was one of the few safeguards of liberty specified in a Constitution that, at the outset, had no Bill of Rights. In the system conceived by the Framers the writ had a centrality that must inform proper interpretation of the Suspension Clause. Second, to the extent there were settled precedents or legal commentaries in 1789 regarding the extraterritorial scope of the writ or its application to enemy aliens, those authorities can be instructive for the present cases.

A

The Framers viewed freedom from unlawful restraint as a fundamental precept of liberty, and they understood the writ of habeas corpus as a vital instrument to secure that freedom. Experience taught, however, that the common-law writ all too often had been insufficient to guard against the abuse of monarchial power. That history counseled the necessity for specific language in the Constitution to secure the writ and ensure its place in our legal system. Magna Carta decreed that no man would be imprisoned contrary to the law of the [land]. Important as the principle was, the Barons at Runnymede prescribed no specific legal process to enforce it. [Yet] gradually the writ of habeas corpus became the means by which the promise of Magna Carta was fulfilled.

[The Court's discussion of the English history of habeas corpus is omitted.]

This history was known to the Framers. It no doubt confirmed their view that pendular swings to and away from individual liberty were endemic to undivided, uncontrolled power. The Framers' inherent distrust of governmental power was the driving force behind the constitutional plan that allocated powers among three independent branches. This design serves not only to make Government accountable but also to secure individual liberty. [Because] the Constitution's separation-of-powers structure, like the substantive guarantees of the Fifth and Fourteenth Amendments, protects persons as well as citizens, foreign nationals who have the privilege of litigating in our courts can seek to enforce separation-of-powers [principles].

Surviving accounts of the ratification debates provide additional evidence that the Framers deemed the writ to be an essential mechanism in the separation-of-powers scheme. In a critical exchange with Patrick Henry at the Virginia ratifying convention Edmund Randolph referred to the Suspension Clause as an "exception" to the "power given to Congress to regulate courts." [A] resolution passed by the New York ratifying convention made clear its understanding that the Clause not only protects against arbitrary suspensions of the writ but also guarantees an affirmative right to judicial inquiry into the causes of detention. [Alexander] Hamilton likewise explained that by providing the detainee a judicial forum to challenge detention, the writ preserves limited [government].

[T]he Suspension Clause [protects] the rights of the detained by a means consistent with the essential design of the Constitution. It ensures that, except during periods of formal suspension, the Judiciary will have a time-tested device, the writ, to maintain the "delicate balance of governance" that is itself the surest safeguard of liberty. See *Hamdi* (plurality opinion). The Clause protects the rights of the detained by affirming the duty and authority of the Judiciary to call the jailer to account. [The] separation-of-powers doctrine, and the history that influenced its design, therefore must inform the reach and purpose of the Suspension Clause.

B

The broad historical narrative of the writ and its function is central to our analysis, but we seek guidance as well from founding-era authorities addressing the specific question before us: whether foreign nationals, apprehended and detained in distant countries during a time of serious threats to our Nation's security, may assert the privilege of the writ and seek its protection. The Court has been careful not to foreclose the possibility that the protections of the Suspension Clause have expanded along with post-1789 developments that define the present scope of the writ. [But] the analysis may begin with precedents as of 1789, for the Court has said [in *INS v. St. Cyr*] that "at the absolute minimum" the Clause protects the writ as it existed when the Constitution was drafted and ratified.

[The Court's discussion of founding era authorities is omitted.]

IV

Drawing from its position that at common law the writ ran only to territories over which the Crown was sovereign, the Government says the Suspension Clause affords petitioners no rights because the United States does not claim sovereignty over the place of detention. [W]e accept the Government's position that Cuba, and not the United States, retains *de jure* sovereignty over Guantanamo Bay. As we did in *Rasul,* however, we take notice of the obvious and uncontested fact that the United States, by virtue of its complete jurisdiction and control over the base, maintains *de facto* sovereignty over this [territory].

A

The Court has discussed the issue of the Constitution's extraterritorial application on many occasions. These decisions undermine the Government's argument that, at least as applied to noncitizens, the Constitution necessarily stops where *de jure* sovereignty ends.

[Much of the Court's discussion of the extraterritorial application of the Constitution throughout U.S. history is omitted. The Court relied mainly on *Reid v. Covert*, 351 U.S. 487 (1956) and *Johnson v. Eisentrager*, 339 U.S. 763 (1950).]

[In] *Reid* [the] petitioners [were] spouses of American servicemen, [who] lived on American military bases in England and Japan. They were charged with crimes committed in those countries and tried before military courts, consistent with executive agreements the United States had entered into with the British and Japanese governments. Because the petitioners were not themselves military personnel, they argued they were entitled to trial by jury. [That] the petitioners in *Reid* were American citizens was a key factor in the case and was central to the plurality's conclusion that the Fifth and Sixth Amendments apply to American civilians tried outside the United States. But practical considerations, related not to the petitioners' citizenship but to the place of their confinement and trial, were relevant to each Member of the *Reid* majority. And to Justices Harlan and Frankfurter (whose votes were necessary to the Court's disposition) those considerations were the decisive factors in the case. [The "practical considerations" included the feasibility of jury trial in the circumstances of these cases.]

Practical considerations weighed heavily as well in *Johnson v. Eisentrager*, where the Court addressed whether habeas corpus jurisdiction extended to enemy aliens who had been convicted of violating the laws of war. The prisoners were detained at Landsberg Prison in Germany during the Allied Powers' postwar occupation. The Court stressed the difficulties of ordering the Government to produce the prisoners in a habeas corpus proceeding. It "would require allocation of shipping space, guarding personnel, billeting and rations" and would damage the prestige of military commanders at a sensitive time. [In] considering these factors the Court sought to balance the constraints of military occupation with constitutional necessities. [True,] the Court in *Eisentrager* denied access to the writ, and it noted the prisoners "at no relevant time were within any territory over which the United States is sovereign, and [that] the scenes of their offense, their capture, their trial and their punishment were all beyond the territorial jurisdiction of any court of the United States." [The] Government seizes upon this language as proof positive that the *Eisentrager* Court adopted a formalistic, sovereignty-based test for determining the reach of the Suspension Clause. [We] reject this reading for three reasons.

First, we do not accept the idea that the above-quoted passage from *Eisentrager* is the only authoritative language in the opinion and that all the rest is dicta. The Court's further determinations, based on practical considerations, were integral to Part II of its opinion and came before the decision announced its holding. Second, because the United States lacked both *de jure* sovereignty and plenary control over Landsberg Prison, it is far from clear that the *Eisentrager* Court used the term sovereignty only in the narrow technical sense and not to connote the degree of control the military asserted over the facility. [Third,] if the Government's reading of *Eisentrager* were correct, the opinion would have marked not only a change in, but a complete repudiation of [the] functional approach to questions of extraterritoriality.

[The reference here is to a functional approach the Court had discerned not only in *Reid* bit also in cases from the early twentieth century, called the *Insular Cases*. The Court's discussion of those cases is omitted.]

A constricted reading of *Eisentrager* overlooks what we see as a common thread uniting the *Insular Cases, Eisentrager,* and *Reid:* the idea that questions of extraterritoriality turn on objective factors and practical concerns, not formalism.

B

The Government's formal sovereignty-based test raises troubling separation-of-powers concerns as well. The political history of Guantanamo illustrates the deficiencies of this approach. [T]he Government's view is that the Constitution had no effect there, at least as to noncitizens, because the United States disclaimed sovereignty in the formal sense of the term. The necessary implication of the argument is that by surrendering formal sovereignty over any unincorporated territory to a third party, while at the same time entering into a lease that grants total control over the territory back to the United States, it would be possible for the political branches to govern without legal constraint. Our basic charter cannot be contracted away like this. The Constitution grants Congress and the President the power to acquire, dispose of, and govern territory, not the power to decide when and where its terms apply. Even when the United States acts outside its borders, its powers are not "absolute and unlimited" but are subject "to such restrictions as are expressed in the Constitution." [Abstaining] from questions involving formal sovereignty and territorial governance is one thing. To hold the political branches have the power to switch the Constitution on or off at will is quite another. The former position reflects this Court's recognition that certain matters requiring political judgments are best left to the political branches. The latter would permit a striking anomaly in our tripartite system of government, leading to a regime in which Congress and the President, not this Court, say "what the law is." [*Marbury v. Madison.*] These concerns have particular bearing upon the Suspension Clause question in the cases now before us, for the writ of habeas corpus is itself an indispensable mechanism for monitoring the separation of powers. The test for determining the scope of this provision must not be subject to manipulation by those whose power it is designed to restrain.

C

[The] outlines of a framework for determining the reach of the Suspension Clause are suggested by the factors the Court relied upon in *Eisentrager*. In addition to the practical concerns discussed above, the *Eisentrager* Court found relevant that each petitioner: "(a) is an enemy alien; (b) has never been or resided in the United States; (c) was captured outside of our territory and there held in military custody as a prisoner of war; (d) was tried and convicted by a Military Commission sitting outside the United States; (e) for offenses against laws of war committed outside the United States; (f) and is at all times imprisoned outside the United States." Based on this language from *Eisentrager,* and the reasoning in our other extraterritoriality opinions, we conclude that at least three factors are relevant in determining the reach of the Suspension Clause: (1) the citizenship and status of the detainee and the adequacy of the process through which that status determination was made; (2) the nature of the sites where apprehension and then detention took place; and (3) the practical obstacles inherent in resolving the prisoner's entitlement to the writ.

Applying this framework, we note at the onset that the status of these detainees is a matter of dispute. The petitioners, like those in *Eisentrager,* are not American citizens. But the petitioners in *Eisentrager* did not contest, it seems, the Court's assertion that they were "enemy alien[s]." In the instant cases, by contrast, the detainees deny they are enemy combatants. They have been afforded some process in CSRT proceedings to determine their status; but, unlike in *Eisentrager,* there has been no trial by military commission for violations of the laws of war. The difference is not trivial. The records from the *Eisentrager* trials suggest that, well before the petitioners brought their case to this Court, there had been a rigorous adversarial process to test the legality of their detention. The *Eisentrager* petitioners were charged by a bill of particulars that made detailed factual allegations against them. To rebut the accusations, they were entitled to representation by counsel, allowed to introduce evidence on their own behalf, and permitted to cross-examine the prosecution's witnesses.

In comparison the procedural protections afforded to the detainees in the CSRT hearings are far more limited, and, we conclude, fall well short of the procedures and adversarial mechanisms that would eliminate the need for habeas corpus review. Although the detainee is assigned a "Personal Representative" to assist him during CSRT proceedings, the Secretary of the Navy's memorandum makes clear that person is not the detainee's lawyer or even his "advocate." The detainee is allowed to present "reasonably available" evidence, but his ability to rebut the Government's evidence against him is limited by the circumstances of his confinement and his lack of counsel at this stage. And although the detainee can seek review of his status determination in the Court of Appeals, that review process cannot cure all defects in the earlier proceedings.

As to the second factor relevant to this analysis, the detainees here are similarly situated to the *Eisentrager* petitioners in that the sites of their apprehension and detention are technically outside the sovereign territory of the United States. As noted earlier, this is a factor that weighs against finding they have rights under the Suspension Clause.

But there are critical differences between Landsberg Prison, circa 1950, and the United States Naval Station at Guantanamo Bay in 2008. Unlike its present control over the naval station, the United States' control over the prison in Germany was neither absolute nor indefinite. [Guantanamo] Bay, on the other hand, is no transient possession. In every practical sense Guantanamo is not abroad; it is within the constant jurisdiction of the United States.

As to the third factor, we recognize, as the Court did in *Eisentrager,* that there are costs to holding the Suspension Clause applicable in a case of military detention abroad. Habeas corpus proceedings may require expenditure of funds by the Government and may divert the attention of military personnel from other pressing tasks. While we are sensitive to these concerns, we do not find them dispositive. Compliance with any judicial process requires some incremental expenditure of resources. Yet civilian courts and the Armed Forces have functioned alongside each other at various points in our history. The Government presents no credible arguments that the military mission at Guantanamo would be compromised if habeas corpus courts had jurisdiction to hear the detainees' claims. And in light of the plenary control the United States asserts over the base, none are apparent to us.

The situation in *Eisentrager* was far different, given the historical context and nature of the military's mission in post-War Germany. [The Court contrasted the relatively insecure political and social environment of post-War Germany with the situation at Guantanamo Bay, where the U.S. exercises firm control.]

It is true that before today the Court has never held that noncitizens detained by our Government in territory over which another country maintains *de jure* sovereignty have any rights under our Constitution. But the cases before us lack any precise historical parallel. They involve individuals detained by executive order for the duration of a conflict that, if measured from September 11, 2001, to the present, is already among the longest wars in American history. The detainees, moreover, are held in a territory that, while technically not part of the United States, is under the complete and total control of our Government. Under these circumstances the lack of a precedent on point is no barrier to our holding.

We hold that Art. I, § 9, cl.2 of the Constitution has full effect at Guantanamo Bay. If the privilege of habeas corpus is to be denied to the detainees now before us, Congress must act in accordance with the requirements of the Suspension Clause. [This] Court may not impose a *de facto* suspension by abstaining from these controversies. [The] MCA does not purport to be a formal suspension of the writ; and the Government, in its submissions to us, has not argued that it is. Petitioners, therefore, are entitled to the privilege of habeas corpus to challenge the legality of their detention.

V

In light of this holding the question becomes whether the statute stripping jurisdiction to issue the writ avoids the Suspension Clause mandate because Congress has provided adequate substitute procedures for habeas corpus. The Government submits there has been compliance with the Suspension Clause because the DTA review process in the Court of Appeals provides an adequate substitute. Congress has granted that court jurisdiction to consider: "(i) whether the status determination of the [CSRT] was consistent with the standards and procedures specified by the Secretary of Defense . . . and (ii) to the extent the Constitution and laws of the United States are applicable, whether the use of such standards and procedures to make the determination is consistent with the Constitution and laws of the United States."

[Although the Court of Appeals had not addressed the "adequate substitute" issue, the Court decided that "the cost of further delay substantially outweigh any benefits of remanding to the Court of Appeals to consider the issue it did not address in these cases."]

A

Our case law does not contain extensive discussion of standards defining suspension of the writ or of circumstances under which suspension has occurred. [Unlike earlier cases,] here we confront statutes, the DTA and the MCA, that were intended to circumscribe habeas review. Congress' purpose is evident not only from the unequivocal nature of MCA § 7's jurisdiction-stripping language ("No court, justice, or judge shall have jurisdiction to hear or consider an application for a writ of habeas corpus . . .") but also from a comparison of the DTA to [prior statutes. When] Congress has intended to replace traditional habeas corpus with habeas-like substitutes [it] has granted to the courts broad remedial powers to secure the historic office of the writ. [In] contrast, the DTA's jurisdictional grant is quite limited. The Court of Appeals has jurisdiction not to inquire into the legality of the detention generally but only to assess whether the SCRT complied with the "standards and procedures specified by the Secretary of Defense" and whether those standards and procedures are lawful. [Unlike earlier cases] moreover, there has been no effort to preserve habeas corpus review as an avenue of last resort.

[The] differences between the DTA and the habeas statute that would govern in MCA § 7's absence, 28 U.S.C. § 2241, are likewise telling. Congress confirmed the authority of "any justice" or "circuit judge" to issue the writ. That statute accommodates the necessity for fact-finding that will arise in some cases by allowing the appellate judge to transfer the case to a district court of competent jurisdiction, whose institutional capacity for fact-finding is superior to his or her own. [See 28 U.S.C. § 2241 (b).] By granting the Court of Appeals "exclusive" jurisdiction over petitioners' cases [in the DTA], Congress has foreclosed that [option].

[The] legislative history confirms what the plain text strongly suggests: In passing the DTA Congress did not intend to create a process that differs from traditional habeas corpus in name only. It intended to create a more limited [procedure].

[The Court's discussion of legislative history is omitted.]

B

[We] do not endeavor to offer a comprehensive summary of the requisites for an adequate substitute for habeas corpus. We do consider it uncontroversial, however, that the privilege of habeas corpus entitles the prisoner to a meaningful opportunity to demonstrate that he is being held pursuant to "the erroneous application or interpretation" of relevant law. [*INS v. St. Cyr.*] And the habeas court must have the power to order the conditional release of an individual unlawfully detained—though release need not be the exclusive remedy and is not the appropriate one in every case in which the writ is granted. [These] are the easily identified attributes of any constitutionally adequate habeas corpus proceeding. But, depending on the circumstances, more may be required.

Indeed, common-law habeas corpus was, above all, an adaptable remedy. Its precise application and scope changed depending upon the circumstances. [The] idea that the necessary scope of habeas review in part depends upon the rigor of any earlier proceedings accords with our test for procedural adequacy in the due process context. See *Mathews v. Eldridge*, 424 U.S. 319, 335 (1976) (noting that the Due Process Clause requires an assessment of, *inter alia*, "the risk of an erroneous deprivation of [a liberty interest;] and the probable value, if any, of additional or substitute procedural safeguards"). This principle has an established foundation in habeas corpus jurisprudence as [well].

Where a person is detained by executive order, rather than, say, after being tried and convicted in a court, the need for collateral review is most pressing. A criminal conviction in the usual course occurs after a judicial hearing before a tribunal disinterested in the outcome and committed to procedures designed to ensure its own independence. These dynamics are not inherent in executive detention orders or executive review procedures. In this context the need for habeas corpus is more urgent. The intended duration of the detention and the reasons for it bear upon the precise scope of the inquiry. Habeas corpus proceedings need not resemble a criminal trial, even when the detention is by executive order. But the writ must be effective. The habeas court must have sufficient authority to conduct a meaningful review of both the cause for detention and the Executive's power to detain.

To determine the necessary scope of habeas corpus review, therefore, we must assess the CSRT process, the mechanism through which petitioners' designation as enemy combatants became [final].

Petitioners identify what they see as myriad deficiencies in the CSRTs. The most relevant for our purposes are the constraints upon the detainee's ability to rebut the factual basis for the Government's assertion that he is an enemy combatant. [At] the CSRT stage the detainee has limited means to find or present evidence to challenge the Government's case against him. He does not have the assistance of counsel and may not be aware of the most critical allegations that the Government relied upon to order his detention. [A detainee can access only "unclassified" information.] The detainee can confront witnesses that testify during the CSRT proceedings. But given that there are in effect no limits on the admission of hearsay evidence—the only requirement is that the tribunal deem the evidence "relevant and helpful"—the detainee's opportunity to question witnesses is likely to be more theoretical than [real].

Although we make no judgment as to whether the CSRTs, as currently constituted, satisfy due process standards, we agree with petitioners that, even when all the parties involved in this process act with diligence and in good faith, there is considerable risk of error in the tribunal's findings of fact. This is a risk inherent in any process that [is] "closed and accusatorial." And given that the consequence of error may be detention of persons for the duration of hostilities that may last a generation or more, this is a risk too significant to ignore.

For the writ of habeas corpus, or its substitute, to function as an effective and proper remedy in this context, the court that conducts the habeas proceeding must have the means to correct errors that occurred during the CSRT proceedings. This includes some authority to assess the sufficiency of the Government's evidence against the detainee. It also must have the authority to admit and consider relevant exculpatory evidence that was not introduced during the earlier proceeding. Federal habeas petitioners long have had the means to supplement the record on review, even in the post-conviction habeas setting. Here that opportunity is constitutionally [required].

The extent of the showing required of the Government in these cases is a matter to be determined. We need not explore it further at this stage. We do hold that when the judicial power to issue habeas corpus is properly invoked the judicial officer must have adequate authority to make a determination in light of the relevant law and facts and to formulate and issue appropriate orders for relief, including, if necessary, an order directing the prisoner's release.

We now consider whether the DTA allows the Court of Appeals to conduct a proceeding meeting these [standards]. The DTA does not explicitly empower the Court of Appeals to order to applicant in a DTA review proceeding released should the court find that the standards and procedures used at his CSRT hearing were insufficient to justify detention. This is troubling. Yet, for present purposes, we can assume congressional silence permits a constitutionally required remedy. In that case it would be possible to hold that a remedy of release is impliedly provided for. The DTA might be read, furthermore, to allow the petitioners to assert most, if not all, of the legal claims they seek to advance, including their most basic claim: that the President has no authority under the AUMF to detain them [indefinitely].

The absence of a release remedy and specific language allowing AUMF challenges are not the only constitutional infirmities from which the statute potentially suffers, however. The more difficult question is whether the DTA permits the Court of Appeals to make requisite findings of fact. [The Court's discussion of the statutory provisions is omitted.]

Assuming the DTA can be construed to allow the Court of Appeals to review or correct the CSRT's factual determinations, as opposed to merely certifying that the tribunal applied the correct standard of proof, we see no way to construe the statute to allow what is also constitutionally required in this context: an opportunity for the detainee to present relevant exculpatory evidence that was not made part of the record in the earlier [proceedings].

By foreclosing consideration of evidence not presented or reasonably available to the detainee at the CSRT proceedings, the DTA disadvantages the detainee by limiting the scope of collateral review to a record that may not be accurate or complete. In other contexts, *e.g.,* in post-trial habeas cases where the prisoner already has had a full and fair opportunity to develop the factual predicate of his claims, similar limitations on the scope of habeas review may be appropriate. See *Michael Williams v. Taylor*, 529 U.S. 420 (2000). In this context, however, where the underlying detention proceedings lack the necessary adversarial character, the detainee cannot be held responsible for all deficiencies in the [record].

We do not imply DTA review would be a constitutionally sufficient replacement for habeas corpus but for these limitations on the detainee's ability to present exculpatory evidence. For even if it were possible, as a textual matter, to read into the statute each of the necessary procedures we have identified, we could not overlook the cumulative effect of our doing so. To hold that the detainees at Guantanamo may, under the DTA, challenge the President's legal authority to detain them, contest the CSRT's findings of fact, supplement the record on review with exculpatory evidence, and request an order of release would come close to reinstating the § 2241 habeas corpus process Congress sought to deny them. The language of the statute, read in light of Congress' reasons for enacting it, cannot bear this interpretation. Petitioners have met their burden of establishing that the DTA review process is, on its face, an inadequate substitute for habeas corpus.

Although we do not hold that an adequate substitute must duplicate § 2241 in all respects, it suffices that the Government has not established that the detainees' access to the statutory review provisions at issue is an adequate substitute for the writ of habeas corpus. MCA § 7 thus effects an unconstitutional suspension of the writ. In view of our holding we need not discuss the reach of the writ with respect to claims of unlawful conditions of treatment or confinement.

VI

A

[Our] decision today holds only that the petitioners before us are entitled to seek the writ; that the DTA review procedures are an inadequate substitute for habeas corpus; and that the petitioners in these cases need not exhaust the review procedures in the Court of Appeals before proceeding with their habeas actions in the District Court. The only law we identify as unconstitutional is MCA § 7, 28 U.S.C.A. § 2241(e). Accordingly, both the DTA and the CSRT process remain [intact].

B

Although we hold that the DTA is not an adequate and effective substitute for habeas, it does not follow that a habeas corpus court may disregard the dangers the detention in these cases was intended to prevent. [The] Suspension Clause does not resist innovation in the field of habeas corpus. Certain accommodations can be made to reduce the burden habeas corpus proceedings will place on the military without impermissibly diluting the protections of the [writ]. Channeling future cases to one district court would no doubt reduce administrative burdens on the Government. [We also recognize] that the Government has a legitimate interest in protecting sources and methods of intelligence gathering; and we expect that the District Court will use its discretion to accommodate this interest to the greatest extent possible.

[It] bears repeating that our opinion does not address the content of the law that governs petitioners' detention. That is a matter yet to be determined. We hold that petitioners may invoke the fundamental procedural protections of habeas corpus. The laws and Constitution are designed to survive, and remain in force, in extraordinary times. Liberty and security can be reconciled; and in our system they are reconciled within the framework of the law. The Framers decided that habeas corpus, a right of first importance, must be a part of that framework, a part of that law.

The determination by the Court of Appeals that the Suspension Clause and its protections are inapplicable to petitioners was in error. The judgment of the Court of Appeals is reversed. The cases are remanded to the Court of Appeals with instructions that it remand the cases to the District Court for proceedings consistent with this opinion.

It is so ordered.

JUSTICE SOUTER, with whom JUSTICES GINSBURG and BREYER join, concurring.

[I] add this afterword only to emphasize two things one might overlook after reading the dissents. [Justice] Scalia is [correct] that here, for the first time, this Court holds there is (he says "confers") constitutional habeas jurisdiction over aliens imprisoned by the military outside an area of *de jure* national sovereignty. But no one who reads the Court's opinion in *Rasul* could seriously doubt that the jurisdictional question must be answered the same way in purely constitutional cases, given the Court's reliance on the historical background of habeas generally in answering the statutory question.

[A] second fact insufficiently appreciated by the dissents is the length of the disputed imprisonments, some of the prisoners represented here today having been locked up for six years. Hence the hollow ring when the dissenters suggest that the Court is somehow precipitating the judiciary into reviewing claims that the military (subject to appeal to the Court of Appeals for the District of Columbia Circuit) could handle within some reasonable period of time. [After] six years of sustained executive detentions in Guantanamo, subject to habeas jurisdiction but without any actual habeas scrutiny, today's decision is no judicial victory, but an act of perseverance in trying to make habeas review, and the obligation of the courts to provide it, mean something of value both to prisoners and to the Nation.

CHIEF JUSTICE ROBERTS, with whom JUSTICES SCALIA, THOMAS, and ALITO join, dissenting.

Today the Court strikes down as inadequate the most generous set of procedural protections ever afforded aliens detained by this country as enemy combatants. The political branches crafted these procedures amidst an ongoing military conflict, after much careful investigation and thorough debate. The Court rejects them today out of hand, without bothering to say what due process rights the detainees possess, without explaining how the statute fails to vindicate those rights, and before a single petitioner has even attempted to avail himself of the law's operation. And to what effect? The majority merely replaces a review system designed by the people's representatives with a set of shapeless procedures to be defined by federal courts at some future date. One cannot help but think, after surveying the modest practical results of the majority's ambitious opinion, that this decision is not really about the detainees at all, but about control of federal policy regarding enemy combatants.

[How] the detainees' claims will be decided now that the DTA is gone is anybody's guess. But the habeas process the Court mandates will most likely end up looking a lot like the DTA system it replaces, as the district court judges shaping it will have to reconcile review of the prisoners' detention with the undoubted need to protect the American people from the terrorist threat—precisely the challenge Congress undertook in drafting the DTA. All that today's opinion has done is shift responsibility for those sensitive foreign policy and national security decisions from the elected branches to the Federal [Judiciary].

JUSTICE SCALIA, with whom THE CHIEF JUSTICE and JUSTICES THOMAS and ALITO join, dissenting.

Today, for the first time in our Nation's history, the Court confers a constitutional right to habeas corpus on alien enemies detained abroad by our military forces in the course of an ongoing war. [The] writ of habeas corpus does not, and never has, run in favor of aliens abroad; the Suspension Clause thus has no application, and the Court's intervention in this military matter is entirely *ultra vires*.

I shall devote most of what will be a lengthy opinion to the legal errors contained in the opinion of the Court. Contrary to my usual practice, however, I think it appropriate to begin with a description of the disastrous consequences of what the Court has done today.

I

America is at war with radical Islamists. The enemy began by killing Americans and American allies abroad: 241 at the Marine barracks in Lebanon, 19 at the Khobar Towers in Dhahran, 224 at our embassies in Dar es Salaam and Nairobi, and 17 on the USS Cole in Yemen. On September 11, 2001, the enemy brought the battle to American soil, killing 2,749 at the Twin Towers in New York City, 184 at the Pentagon in Washington, D. C., and 40 in Pennsylvania. It has threatened further attacks against our homeland; one need only walk about buttressed and barricaded Washington, or board a plane anywhere in the country, to know that the threat is a serious one. Our Armed Forces are now in the field against the enemy, in Afghanistan and Iraq. Last week, 13 of our countrymen in arms were killed.

The game of bait-and-switch that today's opinion plays upon the Nation's Commander in Chief will make the war harder on us. It will almost certainly cause more Americans to be killed. That consequence would be tolerable if necessary to preserve a time-honored legal principle vital to our constitutional Republic. But it is this Court's blatant *abandonment* of such a principle that produces the decision today. The President relied on our settled precedent in [*Eisentrager*], when he established the prison at Guantanamo Bay for enemy aliens. [Had] the law been otherwise, the military surely would not have transported prisoners there, but would have kept them in Afghanistan, transferred them to another of our foreign military bases, or turned them over to allies for detention. Those other facilities might well have been worse for the detainees themselves.

In the long term, then, the Court's decision today accomplishes little, except perhaps to reduce the well-being of enemy combatants that the

Court ostensibly seeks to protect. In the short term, however, the decision is devastating. At least 30 of those prisoners hitherto released from Guantanamo Bay have returned to the battlefield. [Others] have succeeded in carrying on their atrocities against innocent civilians. In one case, a detainee released from Guantanamo Bay masterminded the kidnapping of two Chinese dam workers, one of whom was later shot to death when used as a human shield against Pakistani commandoes. Another former detainee promptly resumed his post as a senior Taliban commander and murdered a United Nations engineer and three Afghan soldiers. Still another murdered an Afghan judge. It was reported only last month that a released detainee carried out a suicide bombing against Iraqi soldiers in Mosul, Iraq.

These, mind you, were detainees whom *the military* had concluded were not enemy combatants. Their return to the kill illustrates the incredible difficulty of assessing who is and who is not an enemy combatant in a foreign theater of operations where the environment does not lend itself to rigorous evidence collection. Astoundingly, the Court today raises the bar, requiring military officials to appear before civilian courts and defend their decisions under procedural and evidentiary rules that go beyond what Congress has [specified].

II

A

[The] writ as preserved in the Constitution could not possibly extend farther than the common law provided when that Clause was written. The Court admits that it cannot determine whether the writ historically extended to aliens held abroad, and it concedes (necessarily) that Guantanamo Bay lies outside the sovereign territory of the United States. Together, these two concessions establish that it is (in the Court's view) perfectly ambiguous whether the common-law writ would have provided a remedy for these petitioners. If that is so, the Court has no basis to strike down the Military Commissions Act, and must leave undisturbed the considered judgment of the coequal branches.

How, then, does the Court weave a clear constitutional prohibition out of pure interpretive equipoise? The Court resorts to "fundamental separation-of-powers principles" to interpret the Suspension [Clause]. That approach distorts the nature of the separation of powers and its role in the constitutional structure. The "fundamental separation-of-powers principles" that the Constitution embodies are to be derived not from some judicially imagined matrix, but from the sum total of the individual separation-of-powers provisions that the Constitution sets forth. Only by considering them one-by-one does the full shape of the *Constitution's* separation-of-powers principles emerge. It is nonsensical to interpret those provisions themselves in light of some general "separation-of-powers principles" dreamed up by the Court. Rather, they must be interpreted to mean what they were understood to mean when the people ratified them. And if the understood scope of the writ of habeas corpus was "designed to restrain" (as the Court says) the actions of the Executive, the understood *limits* upon that scope were (as the Court seems not to grasp) just as much "designed to restrain" the incursions of the Third Branch. "Manipulation" of the territorial reach of the writ by the Judiciary poses just as much a threat to the proper separation of powers as "manipulation" by the Executive. As I will show below, manipulation is what is afoot here. The understood limits upon the writ deny our jurisdiction over the habeas petitions brought by these enemy aliens, and entrust the President with the crucial wartime determinations about their status and continued confinement.

B

The Court purports to derive from our precedents a "functional" test for the extraterritorial reach of the writ, which shows that the Military Commissions Act unconstitutionally restricts the scope of habeas. That is remarkable because the most pertinent of those precedents, [*Eisentrager*], conclusively establishes the opposite. [*Eisentrager* held]—*held* beyond any doubt—that the Constitution does not ensure habeas for aliens held by the United States in areas over which our Government is not [sovereign].

The Court also relies on the "[p]ractical considerations" that influenced our decision in *Reid v. Covert*. But all the Justices in the majority except Justice Frankfurter limited their analysis to the rights of *citizens* abroad. [To] say that "practical considerations" determine the precise content of the constitutional protections American citizens enjoy when they are abroad is quite different from saying that "practical considerations" determine whether aliens abroad enjoy any constitutional protections whatever, including habeas. In other words, merely because citizenship is not a *sufficient* factor to extend constitutional rights abroad does not mean that it is not a *necessary* [one].

After transforming the *a fortiori* elements discussed above into a "functional" test, the Court is still left with the difficulty that most of those elements exist here as well with regard to all the detainees. To make the application of the newly crafted "functional" test produce a different result in the present cases, the Court must [distinguish *Eisentrager* on the ground that the] Germans had been tried by a military commission for violations of the laws of war, [while] the present petitioners, by contrast, have been tried by a Combatant Status Review Tribunal (CSRT) whose procedural protections, according to the Court's *ipse dixit,* "fall well short of the procedures and adversarial mechanisms that would eliminate the need for habeas corpus review." But no one looking for "functional" equivalents would put *Eisentrager* and the present cases in the same category, much less place the present cases in a preferred category. The difference between them cries out for lesser procedures in the present cases. The prisoners in *Eisentrager* were *prosecuted* for crimes after the cessation of hostilities; the prisoners here are enemy combatants *detained* during an ongoing [conflict].

The category of prisoner comparable to these detainees are not the *Eisentrager* criminal defendants, but the more than 400,000 prisoners of war detained in the United States alone during World War II. Not a single one was accorded the right to have his detention validated by a habeas corpus action in federal court-and that despite the fact that they were present on U.S. soil. The Court's analysis produces a crazy result: Whereas those convicted and sentenced to death for war crimes are without judicial remedy, all enemy combatants detained during a war, at least insofar as they are confined in an area away from the battlefield over which the United States exercises "absolute and indefinite" control, may seek a writ of habeas corpus in federal court. And, as an even more bizarre implication from the Court's reasoning, those prisoners whom the military plans to try by full-dress Commission at a future date may file habeas petitions and secure release before their trials take [place].

C

What drives today's decision is neither the meaning of the Suspension Clause, nor the principles of our precedents, but rather an inflated notion of judicial supremacy. The Court says that if the extraterritorial applicability of the Suspension Clause turned on formal notions of sovereignty, "it would be possible for the political branches to govern without legal constraint" in areas beyond the sovereign territory of the United States. That cannot be, the Court says, because it is the duty of this Court to say what the law is. It would be difficult to imagine a more question-begging analysis. [Our] power "to say what the law is" is circumscribed by the limits of our statutorily and constitutionally conferred jurisdiction. And that is precisely the question in these cases: whether the Constitution confers habeas jurisdiction on federal courts to decide petitioners' claims. It is both irrational and arrogant to say that the answer must be yes, because otherwise we would not be [supreme].

III

Putting aside the conclusive precedent of *Eisentrager,* it is clear that the original understanding of the Suspension Clause was that habeas corpus was not available to aliens abroad. [The] nature of the writ of habeas corpus that cannot be suspended must be defined by the common-law writ that was available at the time of the founding. [Justice Scalia's historical analysis is omitted.] In sum, *all* available historical evidence points to the conclusion that the writ would not have been available at common law for aliens captured and held outside the sovereign territory of the Crown. Despite three opening briefs, three reply briefs, and support from a legion of *amici,* petitioners have failed to identify a single case in the history of Anglo-American law that supports their claim to jurisdiction. The Court finds it significant that there is no recorded case *denying* jurisdiction to such prisoners either. But a case standing for the remarkable proposition that the writ could issue to a foreign land would surely have been reported, whereas a case denying such a writ for lack of jurisdiction would likely not. At a minimum, the absence of a reported case either way leaves unrefuted the voluminous commentary stating that habeas was confined to the dominions of the Crown.

What history teaches is confirmed by the nature of the limitations that the Constitution places upon suspension of the common-law writ. It can be suspended only "in Cases of Rebellion or Invasion." The latter case (invasion) is plainly limited to the territory of the United States; and while it is conceivable that a rebellion could be mounted by American citizens abroad, surely the overwhelming majority of its occurrences would be domestic. If the extraterritorial scope of habeas turned on flexible, "functional" considerations, as the Court holds, why would the Constitution limit its suspension almost entirely to instances of domestic crisis? Surely there is an even greater justification for suspension in foreign lands where the United States might hold prisoners of war during an ongoing conflict. And correspondingly, there is less threat to liberty when the Government suspends the writ's (supposed) application in foreign lands, where even on the most extreme view prisoners are entitled to fewer constitutional rights. It makes no sense, therefore, for the Constitution generally to forbid suspension of the writ abroad if indeed the writ has application [there].

NOTES ON BOUMEDIENE, EXECUTIVE DETENTION, AND THE SUSPENSION CLAUSE

1. Habeas Corpus and the Constitution. *Boumediene* rejects the notion that habeas corpus for executive detentions is a matter of legislative grace. The constitutional issue had to be faced, because Congress had explicitly precluded habeas for these petitioners. Unlike *St. Cyr*, in which the Court had construed the statute so as to avoid the constitutional question of whether Congress could foreclose habeas for executive detentions, the majority could find no other plausible interpretation of the statute. The Court's point in striking down MCA § 7 is not that habeas *must* be available no matter what. The Suspension Clause authorizes Congress to cut off habeas "when in cases of rebellion or invasion the public safety may require it." But the MCA could not be understood as a suspension. It simply blocked access to habeas for inmates at Guantanamo. The constitutional holding is that Congress could not do this unless it provided an adequate substitute. The CSRTs did not provide such a substitute (see note 4 below). Both the separation of powers and the right to access to habeas that is implicit in the Suspension Clause figure in the Court's reasoning. Thus, "[t]he Clause protects the rights of the detained. [It] ensures that, except during periods of formal suspension, the Judiciary will have a time-tested device, the writ, to maintain the delicate balance of government that is itself the surest safeguard of liberty." Justice Scalia takes issue with the Court's treatment of the separation of powers. On what grounds? Who has the better of the argument?

Notice that the Court addressed two distinct issues. One is whether there is a constitutional right to access to habeas embedded in the Suspension Clause. Upon holding that there is such a right, the second is whether aliens held outside territory over which the United States is formally sovereign hold that right. The dissents do not take issue with the Court's affirmative answer to the first question, though they do not explicitly endorse it either. As for the Court's affirmative answer to the second question, the biggest hurdle for the majority seems to be *Eisentrager*, in which Germans held in an American prison in Germany were denied access to habeas in U.S. courts. Justice Scalia asserts that *Eisentrager* controls *Boumediene*. How does Justice Kennedy distinguish the earlier case?

Besides Guantanamo, the United States holds persons it characterizes as enemy combatants at the Bagram Theater Internment Facility in Afghanistan. Does it follow from *Boumeidene* that inmates at Bagram also have access to habeas? In *Al Maqaleh v. Gates*, 605 F.3d 84 (D.C.Cir. 2010), the D.C. Circuit said no. One of the factors identified by the Supreme Court in *Boumediene*, the "adequacy of process" afforded to the detainees, weighed in favor of habeas, since the procedural protections at Bagram were weaker than those at Guantanamo. Nonetheless, the D.C. Circuit distinguished *Boumediene*, partly on the ground that the case for *de facto* sovereignty is weaker there. For example, unlike Guantanamo, "[i]n Bagram . . . there is no indication of any intent to occupy the base with permanence." Bagram more closely resembled Landsberg (the prison at issue in *Eisentrager*). In addition, the *Boumediene* factor of "practical obstacles inherent in resolving the prisoner's entitlement to the writ" weighed "overwhelmingly" against habeas, because Bagram "remains a theater of war." The court did not rule definitively, but left the door open for further litigation.

2. Congressional Control of Federal Jurisdiction. *Boumediene* is significant not only for its recognition of a constitutional guarantee that had remained uncertain before *Boumediene*, but also for carving out an exception to the general rule that Congress, acting under its Article III power over the creation of lower federal courts, has broad power to limit the jurisdiction of those courts. For discussion of this aspect of the case, see Chapter 10.

3. The Suspension Clause. Congress has suspended the writ on four occasions, once during the Civil War, once in the South after that war, in the Philippines in 1905 (shortly after acquiring those islands from Spain in the Spanish-American War), and in Hawaii (then a territory) during World War II. The suspension during the Civil War is especially noteworthy because it involved litigation over which branch of government may suspend the writ. Early in the war, President Lincoln had purported to suspend the writ without congressional action. Ruling on a habeas petition Chief Justice Taney ruled that only Congress had that power. *Ex parte Merryman*, 17 Fed. Cas. 144 (1861). Congress then suspended the writ, ratifying Lincoln's action.

Congress's suspension gave rise to *Ex parte Milligan*, 71 U.S. 2 (1866), in which the Court ordered the prisoner released, but did not challenge Congress's power to suspend. Rather, it ruled that his custody was not covered by the suspension Congress had approved. So it appears that the power to suspend is Congress's alone. In this regard, note that the Suspension Clause appears in Article I, which is concerned with legislative powers, not Article II, which deals with the executive.

Many issues regarding the Suspension Clause remain undecided (and were not presented by *Boumediene*.) For example, suppose Congress, in response to the holding in *Boumediene*, were to enact a statute "suspending" the writ. Could the statute be challenged on the ground that there is no "rebellion" or "invasion," or that, if there is, the "public safety" does not "require" suspension? Are these questions nonjusticiable, such that Congress's judgment cannot be challenged? If so, may Congress simply declare as a naked pretext that the nation faces a rebellion or invasion and suspend the writ? What answers are suggested by *Boumediene*'s recognition that "the writ of habeas corpus is itself an indispensable mechanism for monitoring the separation of powers. The test for determining the scope of this provision must not be subject to manipulation by those whose power it is designed to restrain."

4. Unanswered Questions Regarding Guantanamo Detainees. *Boumediene* also leaves unanswered a number of questions that may well arise in habeas suits brought by detainees. In his dissent, Chief Justice Roberts argues that the CSRTs satisfy due process and hence meet the requirements for an adequate substitute for habeas. Why does the Court disagree? One problem the Court identifies is the hurdles to introducing exculpatory evidence as grounds for a constitutional objection to the CSRTs. The majority also said that the DTA would be constitutionally suspect unless it is read as authorizing the Court of Appeals to order the prisoner's release and to make "requisite findings of fact." In addition, it must be read to allow challenges to the President's authority under the AUMF to detain the petitioners indefinitely. The Court left the door open to finding other constitutional objections, warning that DTA review may not "be a constitutionally sufficient replacement for habeas corpus but for these limitations on the detainee's ability to present exculpatory evidence." The basic problem is that failure to comply with standard § 2241 procedure will raise a vast array of procedural issues (e.g., to what extent are the ordinary rules of evidence applicable?; to what extent may the government limit confidential contact between lawyers and clients?; to what extent to the ordinary rules on speedy trials, double jeopardy, and the Fourth Amendment apply?). Extensive litigation may be needed in order to resolve these issues.

A more basic question remains open: Stipulating that the procedure governing the habeas case (or an adequate substitute) meets constitutional requirements, just what showing on the merits must be made by a detainee in order to obtain release? Or, depending on which side ultimately is determined to have the burden of proof, what showing must the government make in order to justify continued detention? The broader challenge is to delineate the set of circumstances, besides criminal conviction, that justify depriving someone of physical liberty. For very rough analogies, see *Kansas v. Hendricks*, 521 U.S. 346 (1997) (persons convicted of sexually violent offenses may, on a proper showing of dangerousness, be involuntarily confined *after* completion of their sentences); *O'Connor v. Donaldson*, 422 U.S. 563 (1975) (persons may be involuntarily committed to mental hospitals and kept there only on a showing that they are dangerous to themselves or others).

In *Boumediene* the Court does not reach this issue. Thus, the "opinion does not address the content of the law that governs petitioners' detention. That is a matter yet to be determined." Suppose, for example, the government has concluded that the petitioner is an "enemy combatant" and, in support of that characterization, can show that the petitioner more likely than not aided terrorists affiliated with al Qaeda by providing them with food and shelter, and did so in reckless disregard of the affiliation. Would that showing be sufficient, as a matter of constitutional law, to justify indefinite detention pending the end of hostilities between the United States and al Qaeda? If a detainee's recklessness would be sufficient to justify detention, what about negligence? How does one determine the date at which there is an end of hostilities between the United States and al Qaeda? In determining the end of hostilities, what if al Qaeda disintegrates but elements of it morph into some other entity, called, e.g., "the Islamic State," with similar aims and some of the same leaders?

5. ***Boumediene* and the Distinction Between Executive and Judicial Detentions.** In defense of its ruling that the CSRT procedure is an inadequate substitute for habeas, the Court stressed that this case involves an executive detention: "When a person is detained by executive order, rather than, say, after being tried and convicted in a court, the need for collateral review is most pressing. A criminal conviction in the usual course occurs after a judicial hearing before a tribunal disinterested in the outcome and committed to procedures designed to ensure its own independence. These dynamics are not inherent in executive detention orders or executive review procedures. In this context, the need for habeas corpus is more urgent."

The remainder of this chapter examines the less urgent context—habeas corpus for judicially ordered detentions, typically after a criminal trial. But custody pursuant to a criminal conviction may nonetheless be unjust. And the national security concerns that complicate the cases of Guantanamo detainees are not present. Granting that the ordinary prisoner's interest in access to habeas is not as strong as that of a military detainee, what grounds are there for denying him an opportunity to challenge the validity of confinement?

Broadly speaking, there are two. One is the value of finality in criminal law—by which we mean the need for confidence in the judgments reached by courts, for a sense of repose once a dispute is fully litigated and decided, and for economy in the deployment of judicial resources. A distinctive feature of habeas corpus is that the standard rules of issue preclusion do not apply here. Yet we will see that the underlying value of finality has considerable force.

The other value is federalism. The federal habeas statute permits state prisoners to challenge their convictions in federal district court. Respect for the independence of state courts and confidence in their judgments counsels against access to habeas. The overarching policy debate, across a range of particular issues, is how we should balance federalism and finality against the interest of the habeas petitioner in obtaining federal review of the validity of his custody.

II.   JUDICIALLY AUTHORIZED DETENTIONS

Part II deals with access to federal habeas by state prisoners. Federal habeas for state prisoners is called "collateral" review (as distinguished from "appellate" review) because the petitioner, after unsuccessfully appealing his state court conviction within the state system, starts a new proceeding in federal district court seeking review of the process leading to the substantive validity of his confinement or sentence. Federal habeas for state prisoners first became widely available under a statute enacted in 1867. At that time the petitioner could challenge the jurisdiction of the court that committed him to prison, but little else. Although the statute remained largely unchanged between 1867 and 1996, the Supreme Court took an active role in shaping habeas law. First, the issues cognizable in habeas cases steadily expanded, culminating in *Brown v. Allen*, 344 U.S. 443 (1953). In *Brown* the Court ruled that petitioner could obtain reexamination by the federal habeas court of any federal constitutional issue he had properly raised and preserved in the state system in compliance with valid state procedural requirements. But the Court also placed an obligation on the state prisoner. Early in this development the Court ruled that, as a condition of access to federal court, the petitioner must first exhaust state remedies. *Ex parte Royall*, 117 U.S. 241 (1886) (now codified in 28 U.S.C. § 2254 (b)–(c).

In the 1960s the Court loosened some restrictions on habeas. Ten years after *Brown*, in *Fay v. Noia*, 372 U.S. 391 (1963), the Court ruled that even "procedural default," i.e., failure to raise or preserve constitutional objections in the state courts, would not bar access to habeas, unless default amounted to a "deliberate bypass" of the state courts. In the past, habeas had been available only for persons actually confined. *Jones v. Cunningham*, 371 U.S. 236 (1963), held that a petitioner free on parole could satisfy the "custody" requirement for habeas because parole "imposes conditions that significantly confine and restrain his freedom." Habeas petitioners may seek federal court hearings on issues of fact. *Townsend v. Sain*, 372 U.S. 293 (1963) identified several circumstances when hearings should be held and accorded federal district-wide discretion to conduct hearings in other cases. Federal habeas became a generally available extra layer of review of state criminal convictions.

Beginning in the 1970s, the Court contracted access to habeas corpus. In *Stone v. Powell*, 428 U.S. 465 (1976), it excluded Fourth Amendment claims (so long as the petitioner had had a full and fair opportunity to litigate them in the criminal trial) partly on the ground that a Fourth Amendment violation does not affect the basic justice of the incarceration, as it has nothing to do with guilt or innocence. *Wainwright v. Sykes* (see Section A) rejected *Noia*'s deliberate bypass test in favor of a requirement that the petitioner show "cause" for the default and "prejudice" resulting from inability to raise the constitutional issue now. *Teague v. Lane* (see Section B) directed habeas courts to dismiss petitions which depended on "new law", and later cases defined "new law" broadly. In the Antiterrorism and Effective Death Penalty Act of 1996, Congress imposed other constraints, including a one-year statute of limitations, a ban on filing more than one habeas petition, and high hurdles to evidentiary hearings. (See Section B.) The new limits on habeas are not absolute. There are exceptions, typically for cases in which the habeas petitioner can make a showing of "actual innocence." Section C includes a case that illustrates that theme. Overall, however, contemporary habeas corpus litigation is not only complex but also hard for the petitioner to win, even if he has a lawyer.

Prisoners have many and varied complaints about their situation. A threshold issue for habeas jurisdiction is whether a given prisoner suit is properly brought under the habeas statute or under § 1983, the cause of action discussed in Chapter 1. In *Preiser v. Rodriguez*, 411 U.S. 475 (1983) the Court distinguished between complaints that go to the validity of the confinement or its duration, and those that concern the conditions of confinement. The former are properly brought under the habeas statute and are subject to the rules described in this chapter. The latter are properly brought under § 1983. Thus, a prisoner charging that the guards have abused him in violation of his Eighth Amendment right against cruel and unusual punishment must bring a § 1983 suit. A prisoner seeking release on the ground that his conviction or sentence was constitutionally invalid must sue under the habeas statute.

In principle, an important difference between the two types of litigation is that, before bringing the federal habeas suit, the prisoner must exhaust state remedies, e.g., by appealing his conviction through the state system, or, in some cases, pursuing state habeas corpus or other collateral remedies. Recall that under *Monroe v. Pape*, 365 U.S. 167 (1961), there is usually no exhaustion requirement before filing a § 1983 suit in federal court. However, in the Prison Litigation Reform Act of

1995, 42 U.S.C. § 1997e(a), Congress carved out an exception for suits brought by prisoners challenging the conditions of their confinement, requiring them to exhaust administrative remedies. See *Porter v. Nussle*, 534 U.S. 516 (2002) (ruling that the exhaustion requirement "applies to all prisoners seeking redress for prison circumstances or occurrences").

The habeas/§ 1983 divide sometimes gives rise to fine distinctions. The prisoners in *Preiser* had been deprived of "good-conduct-time credits as a result of disciplinary proceedings and sought to get them back through a § 1983 suit. The Court held that habeas was the appropriate remedy. By contrast, in *Wilkinson v. Dotson*, 544 U.S. 74 (2005), prisoners sought to challenge administrative decisions that they were ineligible or unsuitable to be considered for parole. The Court permitted them to sue under § 1983, explaining that success for them would not necessarily affect the length of their sentences but merely ease their access to early release. Does the unavailability of § 1983 to Guantanamo detainees (who are held under color of federal, not state, law) mean that they may challenge the conditions of their confinement in habeas corpus suits? For an affirmative answer, see *Aamer v. Obama*, 742 F.3d 1023 (D.C. Cir. 2014).

Note two limits on the scope of Part II. First, these materials concern federal habeas corpus for state prisoners in suits brought under 28 U.S.C. § 2254 and related statutes. Federal prisoners may seek post-conviction relief under a different statute, 28 U.S.C. § 2255. For the most part the two remedies are governed by similar rules, and the Supreme Court cites cases decided under one statute in addressing issues that arise under the other. Differences between the two include: (1) Federal prisoners must seek relief from the judge who presided over the trial and sentenced the prisoner. (2) Federal prisoners may assert not only constitutional claims but some federal statutory objections as well.

Second, our focus here is on *federal* post-conviction review of criminal convictions. Every state provides for collateral review (in addition to direct appellate review) of criminal convictions in the state court system. Except insofar as state post-conviction review has a bearing on federal review, we ignore the state court regime.

A. PROCEDURAL DEFAULT IN STATE COURT

WAINWRIGHT V. SKYES
433 U.S. 72 (1977).

MR. JUSTICE REHNQUIST delivered the opinion of the Court.

We granted certiorari to consider the availability of federal habeas corpus to review a state convict's claim that testimony was admitted at his trial in violation of his rights under *Miranda v. Arizona*, a claim which the Florida courts have previously refused to consider on the merits because of noncompliance with a state contemporaneous-objection rule. Petitioner Wainwright, on behalf of the State of Florida, here challenges a decision of the Court of Appeals for the Fifth Circuit ordering a hearing in state court on the merits of respondent's contention.

Respondent Sykes was convicted of third-degree murder after a jury trial in the Circuit Court of DeSoto County. He testified at trial that on the evening of January 8, 1972, he told his wife to summon the police because he had just shot Willie Gilbert. Other evidence indicated that when the police arrived at respondent's trailer home, they found Gilbert dead of a shotgun wound, lying a few feet from the front porch. Shortly after their arrival, respondent came from across the road and volunteered that he had shot Gilbert, and a few minutes later respondent's wife approached the police and told them the same thing. Sykes was immediately arrested and taken to the police station.

Once there, it is conceded that he was read his *Miranda* rights, and that he declined to seek the aid of counsel and indicated a desire to talk. He then made a statement, which was admitted into evidence at trial through the testimony of the two officers who heard it, to the effect that he had shot Gilbert from the front porch of his trailer home. There were several references during the trial to respondent's consumption of alcohol during the preceding day and to his apparent state of intoxication, facts which were acknowledged by the officers who arrived at the scene. At no time during the trial, however, was the admissibility of any of respondent's statements challenged by his counsel on the ground that respondent had not understood the *Miranda* warnings. Nor did the trial judge question their admissibility on his own motion or hold a fact-finding hearing bearing on that issue.

Respondent appealed his conviction, but apparently did not challenge the admissibility of the inculpatory statements. He later filed in the trial court a motion to vacate the conviction and, in the State District Court of Appeals and Supreme Court, petitions for habeas corpus. These filings, apparently for the first time, challenged the statements made to police on grounds of involuntariness. In all of these efforts respondent was unsuccessful.

Having failed in the Florida courts, respondent initiated the present action under 28 U.S.C. § 2254, asserting the inadmissibility of his statements by reason of his lack of understanding of the *Miranda* warnings. The United States District Court for the Middle District of Florida ruled that *Jackson v. Denno*, 378 U.S. 368 (1964), requires a hearing in a state criminal trial prior to the admission of an inculpatory out-of-court statement by the defendant. It held further that respondent had not lost his right to assert such a claim by failing to object at trial or on direct appeal, since only "exceptional circumstances" of "strategic decisions at trial" can create such a bar to raising federal constitutional claims in a federal habeas action. The court stayed issuance of the writ to allow the state court to hold a hearing on the "voluntariness" of the statements.

Petitioner warden appealed this decision to the United States Court of Appeals for the Fifth Circuit. That court first considered the nature of the right to exclusion of statements made without a knowing waiver of the right to counsel and the right not to incriminate oneself. It noted that *Jackson v. Denno*, supra, guarantees a right to a hearing on whether a defendant has knowingly waived his rights as described to him in the *Miranda* warnings, and stated that under Florida law "(t)he burden is on the State to secure (a) prima facie determination of voluntariness, not upon the defendant to demand it."

The court then directed its attention to the effect on respondent's right of Florida Rule Crim.Proc. 3.190(i), which it described as "a contemporaneous objection rule" applying to motions to suppress a defendant's inculpatory statements. It focused on this Court's decisions in *Henry v. Mississippi*, 379 U.S. 443 (1965); *Davis v. United States*, 411 U.S. 233 (1973); and *Fay v. Noia*, 372 U.S. 391 (1963), and concluded that the failure to comply with the rule requiring objection at the trial would only bar review of the suppression claim where the right to object was deliberately bypassed for reasons relating to trial [tactics].

The simple legal question before the Court calls for a construction of the language of 28 U.S.C. § 2254(a), which provides that the federal courts shall entertain an application for a writ of habeas corpus "in behalf of a person in custody pursuant to the judgment of a state court only on the ground that he is in custody in violation of the Constitution or laws or treaties of the United States." But, to put it mildly, we do not write on a clean slate in construing this statutory provision. Its earliest counterpart, applicable only to prisoners detained by federal authority, is found in the Judiciary Act of 1789. Construing that statute for the Court in *Ex parte Watkins*, 3 Pet. 193, 202, 7 L.Ed. 650 (1830), Mr. Chief Justice Marshall said:

> "An imprisonment under a judgment cannot be unlawful, unless that judgment be an absolute nullity; and it is not a nullity if the Court has general jurisdiction of the subject, although it should be erroneous."

In 1867, Congress expanded the statutory language so as to make the writ available to one held in state as well as federal custody. For more than a century since the 1867 amendment, this Court has grappled with the relationship between the classical common-law writ of habeas corpus and the remedy provided in 28 U.S.C. § 2254. Sharp division within the

Court has been manifested on more than one aspect of the perplexing problems which have been litigated in this connection. Where the habeas petitioner challenges a final judgment of conviction rendered by a state court, this Court has been called upon to decide no fewer than four different questions, all to a degree interrelated with one another: (1) What types of federal claims may a federal habeas court properly consider? (2) Where a federal claim is cognizable by a federal habeas court, to what extent must that court defer to a resolution of the claim in prior state proceedings? (3) To what extent must the petitioner who seeks federal habeas exhaust state remedies before resorting to the federal court? (4) In what instances will an adequate and independent state ground bar consideration of otherwise cognizable federal issues on federal habeas review?

Each of these four issues has spawned its share of litigation. With respect to the first, the rule laid down in *Ex parte Watkins*, supra, was gradually changed by judicial decisions expanding the availability of habeas relief beyond attacks focused narrowly on the jurisdiction of the sentencing court. See *Ex parte Wells*, 18 How. 307 (1856); *Ex parte Lange*, 18 Wall. 163 (1874). *Ex parte Siebold*, 100 U.S. 371 (1880), authorized use of the writ to challenge a conviction under a federal statute where the statute was claimed to violate the United States Constitution. *Frank v. Mangum*, 237 U.S. 309 (1915), and *Moore v. Dempsey*, 261 U.S. 86 (1923), though in large part inconsistent with one another, together broadened the concept of jurisdiction to allow review of a claim of "mob domination" of what was in all other respects a trial in a court of competent jurisdiction.

In *Johnson v. Zerbst*, 304 U.S. 458, 463 (1938), an indigent federal prisoner's claim that he was denied the right to counsel at his trial was held to state a contention going to the "power and authority" of the trial court, which might be reviewed on habeas. Finally, in *Waley v. Johnston*, 316 U.S. 101 (1942), the Court openly discarded the concept of jurisdiction by then more a fiction than anything else as a touchstone of the availability of federal habeas review, and acknowledged that such review is available for claims of "disregard of the constitutional rights of the accused, and where the writ is the only effective means of preserving his rights." In *Brown v. Allen*, 344 U.S. 443 (1953), it was made explicit that a state prisoner's challenge to the trial court's resolution of dispositive federal issues is always fair game on federal habeas. Only last Term in *Stone v. Powell*, 428 U.S. 465 (1976), the Court removed from the purview of a federal habeas court challenges resting on the Fourth Amendment, where there has been a full and fair opportunity to raise them in the state court.

The degree of deference to be given to a state court's resolution of a federal-law issue was elaborately canvassed in the Court's opinion in

Brown v. Allen, supra. Speaking for the Court, Mr. Justice Reed stated: "(Such) state adjudication carries the weight that federal practice gives to the conclusion of a court of last resort of another jurisdiction on federal constitutional issues. It is not res judicata." The duty of the federal habeas court to hold a fact-finding hearing in specific situations, notwithstanding the prior resolution of the issues in state court, was thoroughly explored in this Court's later decision in *Townsend v. Sain*, 372 U.S. 293 (1963).

[The] exhaustion-of-state-remedies requirement was first articulated by this Court in the case of *Ex parte Royall*, 117 U.S. 241 (1886). There, a state defendant sought habeas in advance of trial on a claim that he had been indicted under an unconstitutional statute. The writ was dismissed by the District Court, and this Court affirmed, stating that while there was power in the federal courts to entertain such petitions, as a matter of comity they should usually stay their hand pending consideration of the issue in the normal course of the state trial. This rule has [been] incorporated into the language of § 2254.

[There] is no need to consider here in greater detail these first three areas of controversy attendant to federal habeas review of state convictions. Only the fourth area the adequacy of state grounds to bar federal habeas review is presented in this case. The foregoing discussion of the other three is pertinent here only as it illustrates this Court's historic willingness to overturn or modify its earlier views of the scope of the writ, even where the statutory language authorizing judicial action has remained unchanged.

As to the role of adequate and independent state grounds, it is a well-established principle of federalism that a state decision resting on an adequate foundation of state substantive law is immune from review in the federal courts. *Fox Film Corp. v. Muller*, 296 U.S. 207 (1935); *Murdock v. Memphis*, 20 Wall. 590 (1875). The application of this principle in the context of a federal habeas proceeding has therefore excluded from consideration any questions of state substantive law, and thus effectively barred federal habeas review where questions of that sort are either the only ones raised by a petitioner or are in themselves dispositive of his case. The area of controversy which has developed has concerned the reviewability of federal claims which the state court has declined to pass on because not presented in the manner prescribed by its procedural rules. The adequacy of such an independent state procedural ground to prevent federal habeas review of the underlying federal issue has been treated very differently than where the state-law ground is [substantive].

In *Brown*, supra, petitioner Daniels' lawyer had failed to mail the appeal papers to the State Supreme Court on the last day provided by law for filing, and hand delivered them one day after that date. Citing the state rule requiring timely filing, the Supreme Court of North Carolina refused to hear the appeal. This Court [held] that federal habeas was not available to review a constitutional claim which could not have been reviewed on direct appeal here because it rested on an independent and adequate state procedural ground.

In *Fay v. Noia*, supra, respondent Noia sought federal habeas to review a claim that his state-court conviction had resulted from the introduction of a coerced confession in violation of the Fifth Amendment to the United States Constitution. While the convictions of his two codefendants were reversed on that ground in collateral proceedings following their appeals, Noia did not appeal and the New York courts ruled that his subsequent coram nobis action was barred on account of that failure. This Court held that petitioner was nonetheless entitled to raise the claim in federal habeas, and thereby overruled its decision 10 years earlier in *Brown v. Allen*, supra:

> "(T)he doctrine under which state procedural defaults are held to constitute an adequate and independent state law ground barring direct Supreme Court review is not to be extended to limit the power granted the federal courts under the federal habeas statute."

As a matter of comity but not of federal power, the Court acknowledged "a limited discretion in the federal judge to deny relief [to] an applicant who had deliberately by-passed the orderly procedure of the state courts and in so doing has forfeited his state court remedies." In so stating, the Court made clear that the waiver must be knowing and [actual]. Noting petitioner's "grisly choice" between acceptance of his life sentence and pursuit of an appeal which might culminate in a sentence of death, the Court concluded that there had been no deliberate bypass of the right to have the federal issues reviewed through a state appeal.

A decade later we decided *Davis v. United States*, supra, in which a federal prisoner's application under 28 U.S.C. § 2255 sought for the first time to challenge the makeup of the grand jury which indicted him. The Government contended that he was barred by the requirement of Fed. Rule Crim. Proc. 12(b)(2) providing that such challenges must be raised "by motion before trial." The Rule further provides that failure to so object constitutes a waiver of the objection, but that "the court for cause shown may grant relief from the waiver." We noted that the Rule [governs] by its terms the manner in which the claims of defects in the institution of criminal proceedings may be waived, and held that this standard contained in the Rule, rather than the *Fay v. Noia* concept of waiver, should pertain in federal habeas as on direct review. [W]e concluded that review of the claim should be barred on habeas, as on direct appeal, absent a showing of cause for the noncompliance and some showing of actual prejudice resulting from the alleged constitutional violation.

Last Term, in *Francis v. Henderson*, supra, the rule of *Davis* was applied to the parallel case of a state procedural requirement that challenges to grand jury composition be raised before trial. The Court noted that there was power in the federal courts to entertain an application in such a case, but rested its holding on "considerations of comity and concerns for the orderly administration of criminal justice . . ." While there was no counterpart provision of the state rule which allowed an exception upon some showing of cause, the Court concluded that the standard derived from the Federal Rule should nonetheless be applied in that context since "(t)here is no reason to . . . give greater preclusive effect to procedural defaults by federal defendants than to similar defaults by state defendants." As applied to the federal petitions of state convicts, the *Davis* cause-and-prejudice standard was thus incorporated directly into the body of law governing the availability of federal habeas corpus review.

To the extent that the dicta of *Fay v. Noia* may be thought to have laid down an all-inclusive rule rendering state contemporaneous-objection rules ineffective to bar review of underlying federal claims in federal habeas proceedings absent a "knowing waiver" or a "deliberate bypass" of the right to so object its effect was limited by *Francis*, which applied a different rule and barred a habeas challenge to the makeup of a grand jury. Petitioner Wainwright in this case urges that we further confine its effect by applying the principle enunciated in *Francis* to a claimed error in the admission of a defendant's confession.

[Sykes'] failure to timely object to its admission amounted to an independent and adequate state procedural ground which would have prevented direct review here. We thus come to the crux of this case. Shall the rule of *Francis v. Henderson*, supra, barring federal habeas review absent a showing of "cause" and "prejudice" attendant to a state procedural waiver, be applied to a waived objection to the admission of a confession at trial? We answer that question in the affirmative.

As earlier noted in the opinion, since *Brown v. Allen*, 344 U.S. 443 (1953), it has been the rule that the federal habeas petitioner who claims he is detained pursuant to a final judgment of a state court in violation of the United States Constitution is entitled to have the federal habeas court make its own independent determination of his federal claim, without being bound by the determination on the merits of that claim reached in the state proceedings. This rule of *Brown v. Allen* is in no way changed by our holding today. Rather, we deal only with contentions of federal law which were not resolved on the merits in the state proceeding due to respondent's failure to raise them there as required by state procedure. We leave open for resolution in future decisions the precise definition of the "cause"-and-"prejudice" standard, and note here only that it is narrower than the standard set forth in dicta in *Fay v. Noia*, 372 U.S. 391 (1963), which would make federal habeas review generally available to state convicts absent a knowing and deliberate waiver of the federal constitutional contention. It is the sweeping language of *Fay v. Noia*, going far beyond the facts of the case eliciting it, which we today reject.

The reasons for our rejection of it are several. The contemporaneous-objection rule itself is by no means peculiar to Florida, and deserves greater respect than *Fay* gives it, both for the fact that it is employed by a coordinate jurisdiction within the federal system and for the many interests which it serves in its own right. A contemporaneous objection enables the record to be made with respect to the constitutional claim when the recollections of witnesses are freshest, not years later in a federal habeas proceeding. It enables the judge who observed the demeanor of those witnesses to make the factual determinations necessary for properly deciding the federal constitutional question. While the 1966 amendment to § 2254 requires deference to be given to such determinations made by state courts, the determinations themselves are less apt to be made in the first instance if there is no contemporaneous objection to the admission of the evidence on federal constitutional grounds.

A contemporaneous-objection rule may lead to the exclusion of the evidence objected to, thereby making a major contribution to finality in criminal litigation. Without the evidence claimed to be vulnerable on federal constitutional grounds, the jury may acquit the defendant, and that will be the end of the case; or it may nonetheless convict the defendant, and he will have one less federal constitutional claim to assert in his federal habeas petition. If the state trial judge admits the evidence in question after a full hearing, the federal habeas court pursuant to the 1966 amendment to § 2254 will gain significant guidance from the state ruling in this regard. [The amendment directed federal habeas courts to ordinarily presume that state court findings of fact were correct.] Subtler considerations as well militate in favor of honoring a state contemporaneous-objection rule. An objection on the spot may force the prosecution to take a hard look at its hole card, and even if the prosecutor thinks that the state trial judge will admit the evidence he must contemplate the possibility of reversal by the state appellate courts or the ultimate issuance of a federal writ of habeas corpus based on the impropriety of the state court's rejection of the federal constitutional claim.

We think that the rule of *Fay v. Noia*, broadly stated, may encourage "sandbagging" on the part of defense lawyers, who may take their chances on a verdict of not guilty in a state trial court with the intent to raise their constitutional claims in a federal habeas court if their initial gamble does not pay off. The refusal of federal habeas courts to honor contemporaneous-objection rules may also make state courts themselves less stringent in their enforcement. Under the rule of *Fay v. Noia*, state appellate courts know that a federal constitutional issue raised for the first time in the proceeding before them may well be decided in any event by a federal habeas tribunal. Thus, their choice is between addressing the issue notwithstanding the petitioner's failure to timely object, or else face the prospect that the federal habeas court will decide the question without the benefit of their views.

The failure of the federal habeas courts generally to require compliance with a contemporaneous-objection rule tends to detract from the perception of the trial of a criminal case in state court as a decisive and portentous event. A defendant has been accused of a serious crime, and this is the time and place set for him to be tried by a jury of his peers and found either guilty or not guilty by that jury. To the greatest extent possible all issues which bear on this charge should be determined in this proceeding: the accused is in the court-room, the jury is in the box, the judge is on the bench, and the witnesses, having been subpoenaed and duly sworn, await their turn to testify. Society's resources have been concentrated at that time and place in order to decide, within the limits of human fallibility, the question of guilt or innocence of one of its citizens. Any procedural rule which encourages the result that those proceedings be as free of error as possible is thoroughly desirable, and the contemporaneous-objection rule surely falls within this classification.

We believe the adoption of the *Francis* rule in this situation will have the salutary effect of making the state trial on the merits the "main event," so to speak, rather than a "tryout on the road" for what will later be the determinative federal habeas hearing. There is nothing in the Constitution or in the language of § 2254 which requires that the state trial on the issue of guilt or innocence be devoted largely to the testimony of fact witnesses directed to the elements of the state crime, while only later will there occur in a federal habeas hearing a full airing of the federal constitutional claims which were not raised in the state proceedings. If a criminal defendant thinks that an action of the state trial court is about to deprive him of a federal constitutional right there is every reason for his following state procedure in making known his objection.

The "cause"-and-"prejudice" [test] will afford an adequate guarantee, we think, that the [preclusion] rule will not prevent a federal habeas court from adjudicating for the first time the federal constitutional claim of a defendant who in the absence of such an adjudication will be the victim of a miscarriage of justice. Whatever precise content may be given those terms by later cases, we feel confident in holding without further elaboration that they do not exist here. Respondent has advanced no explanation whatever for his failure to object at trial, and, as the proceeding unfolded, the trial judge is certainly not to be faulted for failing to question the admission of the confession himself. The other evidence of guilt presented at trial, moreover, was substantial to a degree that would negate any possibility of actual prejudice resulting to the respondent from the admission of his inculpatory statement.

We accordingly conclude that the judgment of the Court of Appeals for the Fifth Circuit must be reversed, and the cause remanded to the United States District Court for the Middle District of Florida with instructions to dismiss respondent's petition for a writ of habeas corpus.

It is so ordered.

[CHIEF JUSTICE BURGER's concurring opinion, JUSTICE STEVENS' concurring opinion, and JUSTICE WHITE's opinion concurring in the judgment are omitted.]

MR. JUSTICE BRENNAN, with whom MR. JUSTICE MARSHALL joins, dissenting. [What follows are excerpts from the lengthy dissenting opinion.]

[If] the standard adopted today is later construed to require that the simple mistakes of attorneys are to be treated as binding forfeitures, it would serve to subordinate the fundamental rights contained in our constitutional charter to inadvertent defaults of rules promulgated by state agencies, and would essentially leave it to the States, through the enactment of procedure and the certification of the competence of local attorneys, to determine whether a habeas applicant will be permitted the access to the federal forum that is guaranteed him by Congress. [But] federal review is not the full measure of Sykes' interest, for there is another of even greater immediacy: assuring that his constitutional claims can be addressed to *some* court. For the obvious consequence of barring Sykes from the federal courthouse is to insulate Florida's alleged constitutional violation from any and all judicial review because of a lawyer's mistake.

[Any] realistic system of federal habeas corpus jurisdiction must be premised on the reality that the ordinary procedural default is born of the inadvertence, negligence, inexperience, or incompetence of trial [counsel]. I persist in the belief that the interests of Sykes and the State of Florida are best rationalized by adherence to [the deliberate bypass] test, and by declining to react to inadvertent defaults through the creation of an "airtight system of forfeitures." [Punishing] a lawyer's unintentional errors by closing the federal courthouse door to his client is both a senseless and misdirected method of deterring the slighting of state rules. It is senseless because unplanned and unintentional action of any kind generally is not subject to deterrence; and, to the extent that it is hoped that a threatened sanction addressed to the defense will induce greater care and caution on the part of trial lawyers, thereby forestalling negligent conduct or error, the potential loss of all valuable state remedies would be sufficient to this end. And it is a misdirected sanction because even if the penalization of incompetence or carelessness will encourage more thorough legal training and trial preparation, the habeas applicant, as opposed to his lawyer, hardly is the proper recipient of such a penalty. Especially with fundamental constitutional rights at stake, no fictional relationship of principal-agent or the like can justify holding the criminal defendant accountable for the naked errors of his attorney. This is especially true when so many indigent defendants are without any realistic choice in selecting who ultimately represents them at trial. Indeed, if responsibility for error must be apportioned between the parties, it is the State, through its attorney's admissions and certification policies, that is more fairly held to blame for the fact that practicing lawyers too often are ill-prepared or ill-equipped to act carefully and knowledgeably when faced with decisions governed by state procedural [requirements].

In short, I believe that the demands of our criminal justice system warrant visiting the mistakes of a trial attorney on the head of a habeas corpus applicant only when we are convinced that the lawyer actually exercised his expertise and judgment in his client's service, and with his client's knowing and intelligent participation where possible. This, of course, is the precise system of habeas review established by *Fay v. Noia.*

NOTES ON PROCEDURAL DEFAULT

1. Habeas Corpus and the Inadequate State Procedural Ground Doctrine. Recall *Lee v. Kemna*, a habeas case discussed in Chapter 8. One of the points made in that case is that a state procedural ground which is "inadequate" to foreclose Supreme Court review of a state judgment will also be inadequate to foreclose access to habeas corpus. Another point made in *Lee*, and in *Sykes* as well, is that even if a state ground is adequate to foreclose Supreme Court review of a state criminal conviction, the prisoner may have access to habeas corpus in federal district court. *Sykes* and the doctrine discussed in these notes concern the rules governing habeas in such cases. Thus, *Sykes* states the general principle that currently governs this topic: Even if the state procedural ground for declining to consider the criminal defendant's constitutional claim is adequate to support the judgment on Supreme Court review, the situation may be different in habeas corpus. When the (now convicted) prisoner brings a habeas corpus petition he may obtain review in federal district court by showing "cause" for the procedural default and "prejudice" resulting from the state court's failure to consider the constitutional claim.

In current practice, the habeas petitioner is not much better off than the applicant for Supreme Court review. But why should there be any difference at all? The answer is that habeas is conceptually distinct from direct review. It is a separate proceeding, not inextricably tied to the proceedings in the state court. Justice Holmes made this point in a frequently quoted passage in his dissent in *Frank v. Mangum*, 237 U.S. 309 (1915) ("[H]abeas corpus cuts through all forms and goes to the very tissue of the structure. It comes in from the outside, not in subordination to the proceedings, and although every form may have been preserved, opens the inquiry whether they have been more than an empty shell.") Conceiving of habeas in this way provides a foundation for ignoring state procedural rules. Thus, in *Fay v. Noia* Justice Brennan's opinion for the Court starts from Holmes's premise and ultimately holds that only a "deliberate bypass" of state processes by the petitioner will foreclose habeas. In principle habeas would be far more often available under that test than under *Sykes*' "cause" and "prejudice" test.

2. **The Scope of *Sykes*.** In *Sykes* the Court limited its holding, and its discussion of policy issues, to the narrow issue of procedural default in the context of a state rule requiring contemporaneous objection to the admission of evidence. Later it adopted "cause" and "prejudice" as the general test for the whole range of procedural default. The Court explicitly overruled *Fay v. Noia* and said that the *Sykes* test generally governs state court procedural defaults in *Coleman v. Thompson*, 501 U.S. 722, 749 (1991). According to *Coleman*, "*Fay* was based on a conception of federal/state relations that undervalued the importance of state procedural rules. [We] now recognize the important interest in finality served by state procedural rules, and the significant harm to the States that results from the failure of federal courts to respect them." 501 U.S. at 750.

But there is one exception: "[I]n an extraordinary case, where a constitutional violation has probably resulted in the conviction of one who is actually innocent, a federal habeas court may grant the writ even in the absence of a showing of cause for the procedural default." *Murray v. Carrier*, 477 U.S. 478 (1986). The prisoner can meet this test if he can show that "it is more likely than not that no reasonable juror would have convicted." *House v. Bell*, 547 U.S. 518 (2006). In *House* the petitioner was able to produce considerable new evidence that he did not commit the crime. Few other habeas petitioners have met this test.

3. **"Cause" and "Prejudice."** In *Sykes* the Court did not address the content of "cause" and "prejudice." The latter term has received little elaboration in the cases. For one formulation, see *United States v. Frady*, 456 U.S. 152 (1982). A federal prisoner challenged a jury instruction that had been used at his trial. The Court ruled that prejudice could be shown only if he proved that "the ailing instruction by itself so infected the entire trial that the resulting conviction violate[d] due process." But in other cases the Court has said that "prejudice" is satisfied if, but for the error, there would be a "reasonable probability of a different result." E.g., *Banks v. Dredke*, 540 U.S. 668, 699 (2004).

As for "cause," a key case is *Murray v. Carrier*, supra, in which the Court ruled that attorney error is not "cause" for procedural default. Writing for the Court, Justice O'Connor explained that the federalism and finality costs of habeas review "do not disappear when the default stems from counsel's ignorance or inadvertence rather than from a deliberate decision" to withhold a claim. Rather, the petitioner can establish cause by showing that "some objective factor external to the defense impeded counsel's efforts to comply with the State's procedural rule."

Reed v. Ross, 468 U.S. 1 (1984), held that the novelty of a constitutional claim, and thus the seeming futility of raising it, can qualify as "cause" for not advancing it in the state criminal trial. But there are two problems with attempting to show novelty. First, the Court sometimes requires considerable imagination and enterprise on the part of the lawyer at the criminal trial. Defense counsel must exploit any basis they have to advance novel theories and have no cause for withholding a claim even if existing precedents make the effort futile anywhere short of the Supreme Court. See *Engle v. Isaac*, 456 U.S. 107 (1982). Second, several years after *Reed* the Court undermined the "novelty" holding of that case, turning "novelty" against the habeas petitioner rather than in his favor. In *Teague v. Lane*, 489 U.S. 288 (1989), it ruled that constitutional claims resting on "new law" are presumptively unavailable to the habeas petitioner. The *Teague* doctrine is examined in Section B, below. For now the point is that the novelty of a constitutional claim is rarely helpful to the habeas petitioner. Novelty may excuse procedural default but also trigger dismissal on *Teague* grounds.

Besides novelty, *Murray* said that the "objective factor external to the defense" test would be met "if state authorities interfered with counsel's ability to comply with a rule, making compliance 'impracticable.'" This test can be met if the prosecutor conceals crucial evidence from the defense, see *Amadeo v. Zant*, 486 U.S. 214 (1988), or leads the defense lawyer to believe that there is nothing to disclose, thereby dissuading him from asking. *Strickler v. Greene*, 527 U.S. 263 (1999). Recall *Lee v. Kemna*, supra. Would the "interference" test be met if a police officer or a court employee had told the defendant's witnesses they could leave? Or must the "interference" be traced to the prosecutor in order to justify a finding of "cause"?

Murray also said that "cause" could be established if counsel's failure to follow a procedural rule was so fundamentally incompetent and prejudicial as to constitute ineffective assistance of counsel, in violation of the defendant's Sixth Amendment right to counsel. As a practical matter "ineffective assistance" is the most important way to show "cause."

4. Ineffective Assistance of Counsel. Since an "ineffective assistance" claim enables the habeas petitioner to avoid the procedural default bar to habeas relief, many habeas petitions raise ineffective assistance. But this is hardly a complete solution to the prisoner's effort to obtain federal review of the constitutional issues raised by his conviction. In order to win an ineffective assistance case, the petitioner must show not merely [a] that the underlying claims the lawyer should have but did not raise are meritorious, but also [b] that the lawyer's performance amounts to a Sixth Amendment violation of "ineffective assistance." Establishing ineffective assistance, in turn, requires more than a showing that the defense lawyer erred. Assistance is ineffective (in the Sixth Amendment sense) only if the lawyer's representation "fell below an objective standard of reasonableness." *Strickland v. Washington,* 466 U.S. 668 (1984). In practice, "ineffective assistance claims rarely succeed on the merits." R. FALLON ET AL., HART & WECHSLER'S THE FEDERAL COURT'S AND THE FEDERAL SYSTEM 1285–86 (6th ed. 2009).

"Ineffective assistance at trial" claims typically must be made *after* the trial, either on direct appellate review or in state court collateral review of the conviction. To what extent is the convict constitutionally entitled to effective assistance of counsel at this stage, i.e., in obtaining review of his trial counsel's performance? In answering this question, it is first necessary to distinguish between [a] direct appellate review and [b] state post-conviction collateral review. [a] There is a constitutional right to appointed counsel in an appeal as of right. *Douglas v. California*, 372 U.S. 353 (1963). When the "ineffective assistance at trial" claim is raised on appellate review, the appellant is entitled to "effective assistance on appeal." *Martinez v. Ryan*, 566 U.S. ___, 132 S.Ct. 1309, 1317 (2012). [b] But "ineffective assistance at trial" claims are typically raised in *state court* post-conviction proceedings (rather than on appellate review of the conviction). In these proceedings, there is, presumptively, no Sixth Amendment right to appointed counsel, *Coleman v. Thompson*, 501 U.S. 722 (1991), and therefore, presumptively, no Sixth Amendment right to effective assistance.

But there is an exception to the rule of *Coleman v. Thompson*: Lack of counsel, or ineffective assistance of counsel, in the post-conviction proceeding may be "cause" for failing to raise an "ineffective assistance at trial" claim, when state procedural law formally or practically requires that the "ineffective assistance at trial" claim be raised in a state court post-conviction proceeding. *Martinez*, supra; *Trevino v. Thaler*, 569 U.S. ___, 133 S.Ct. 1911 (2013). *Martinez* and *Trevino*, both involved ineffective assistance *at trial*. Is there, under the reasoning of those cases, a Sixth Amendment right to appointed counsel in post-conviction collateral review proceedings brought to challenge the effectiveness of the convict's counsel *on direct appeal*?

5. Waiver by the State. When state courts ignore the procedural default and decide the federal claim, the federal court may also reach the merits. E.g., *Cone v. Bell*, 556 U.S. 449 (2009); *County Court of Ulster County v. Allen*, 442 U.S. 140, 149 (1979). Distinguish the situation in which the state courts did not address the federal issue, but the state's lawyer fails to raise the procedural default as a defense in the habeas proceeding. *Trest v. Cain*, 522 U.S. 87 (1997), holds that procedural default is ordinarily a defense the state must raise, not a jurisdictional bar to habeas. On the other hand, the Court has acknowledged, without repudiating, the practice of lower courts of sometimes raising procedural default defenses the state's lawyer has not brought up. *Day v. McDonough,* 547 U.S. 198, 206 (1996).

6.   Procedural Default and the Exhaustion Requirement. A person convicted of a crime in state court, and placed in "custody" as a consequence, is not permitted to bring a habeas corpus petition in federal court immediately afterward. He must first exhaust state remedies. 28 U.S.C. §§ 2254 (b) (c). Ordinarily this means that he must appeal his conviction through the state system. But it is not enough that he appeal. He must seek review of the constitutional issues he later raises on habeas. See, e.g., *Baldwin v. Reese,* 541 U.S. 27 (2004) (holding that the habeas petitioner had not "fairly presented" his federal claims to state appellate court, as required by 28 U.S.C. § 2254(b)(1)). Once the state Supreme Court has either rejected the constitutional claims, or ignored them, or refused to consider them, the prisoner may file a habeas petition in federal court. See, e.g., *Smith v. Digmon,* 434 U.S. 332 (1978) (*per curiam*) (state court ignored the federal issue). Suppose the habeas petitioner, raises several claims, some of which he has exhausted and others not. In *Rose v. Lundy,* 455 U.S. 509 (1982), the Court adopted a "total exhaustion" rule, which requires dismissal of such a petition. That is, none of the claims in a given habeas petition will be considered unless all of the claims in the petition have been exhausted. Sometimes, the state's appellate process is not available to the petitioner, e.g., because he learns of the claim after the time for appeal has passed. Then he must exhaust by seeking post-conviction review in the state law habeas regime.

Suppose the prisoner fails to pursue state remedies within the state's time limits, brings a habeas case, and claims that his failure to exhaust is no bar, because the habeas statute only requires exhaustion of "remedies available in the courts of the State", 28 U.S.C. § 2254(b)(1)(A). In that event, the failure to exhaust is a procedural default and will ordinarily only be excused for "cause" and "prejudice." See, e.g., *Coleman v. Thompson,* 501 U.S. 722, 744–51 (1991).

B.   ISSUES COGNIZABLE IN HABEAS CASES

Brown v. Allen, 344 U.S. 443 (1953), authorized access to federal habeas corpus for the whole range of constitutional defenses to criminal convictions. In 1953, the universe of possible challenges was not especially large. That universe expanded quite a lot over the course of the next fifteen years, as the Warren Court identified an array of Fourth, Fifth, and Sixth Amendment rights, thereby broadening the scope of constitutional criminal procedure. The Court also made most of those rights available to state prisoners for the first time, by "incorporating" most of the Bill of Rights into the Fourteenth Amendment. See, e.g., *Duncan v. Louisiana,* 391 U.S. 145 (1968). Combined with the "deliberate bypass" regime of *Fay v. Noia,* the broad cognizability of constitutional issues on habeas corpus meant, in effect, that most state prisoners could in the ordinary course obtain federal district court review of their convictions.

As with procedural default, the Court in the 1970s began to restrict the issues cognizable on habeas corpus. *Stone v. Powell*, 428 U.S. 465 (1976), held that a Fourth Amendment claim may not be raised by a habeas petitioner so long as he had been given a full and fair opportunity to litigate it in the state criminal proceeding. The "basic justice" of the conviction, the Court noted, was not at issue. *Stone* might have signaled a general principle that only claims that go to guilt or innocence may be litigated in habeas, but it produced no progeny. See, e.g., *Rose v. Mitchell*, 443 U.S. 545 (1979), in which the Court declined to extend *Stone* to cover a claim that grand jury selection procedures discriminated on the basis of race, a claim that did not assert a close link between the discrimination and the conduct of the trial or the basic justice of the conviction. The possibility that *Stone* would be extended to other non-guilt-related claims was effectively buried by *Withrow v. Williams*, 507 U.S. 680 (1993) (declining to apply the *Stone* principle to *Miranda* violations).

1. Retroactivity and "New Law"

A decade after *Stone*, the Court imposed a different, and far more consequential, constraint on access to habeas. Suppose a court—in any kind of litigation, habeas or otherwise—issues a ruling that changes the law. An issue may arise as to whether the ruling should be applied prospectively only, or "retroactively," to actions taken under the old rule and perhaps in reliance upon it. Exactly what counts as "prospective," and what counts as "retroactive" is itself an issue in this area of law, but one we need not comprehensively address for present purposes. For now, the key point is that the Warren Court had dealt with retroactivity on a case-by-case basis, without distinguishing between direct review and habeas corpus. *Stovall v. Denno*, 388 U.S. 293, 297 (1967) identified factors bearing on whether to make a new ruling retroactive. These included "(a) the purpose to be served by the new standards, (b) the extent of reliance by law enforcement authorities on the old standards, and (c) the effect on the administration of justice of a retroactive application of the new standards." A good illustration is *Linkletter v. Walker*, 381 U.S. 618 (1965), a case decided before *Stovall* had firmly established this three-factor approach, but fully consistent with it. The issue was whether to give retroactive effect to the holding in *Mapp v. Ohio*, 367 U.S. 643 (1961) (applying the Fourth Amendment exclusionary rule to the states). The Court ruled against retroactivity. Applying the exclusionary rule retroactively would not serve the deterrent purpose of the rule, would upset reliance on the old regime, and may result in many guilty inmates going free, to the detriment of the administration of justice. By contrast, the holding in *Gideon v. Wainwright*, 372 U.S. 335

(1963), requiring appointed counsel for indigent defendants, was given full retroactive effect.

Justice Harlan criticized this case-by-case approach. He argued for a distinction between habeas and direct review. On direct review, the Court's rulings should be fully retroactive. But habeas is a supplementary remedy, "a necessary additional incentive for trial and appellate courts throughout the land to conduct their proceedings in a matter consistent with established constitutional standards." *Desist v. United States*, 394 U.S. 244 (1969) (Harlan, J., dissenting)

In the 1980s, the Supreme Court adopted Justice Harlan's distinction between direct review and habeas. In *Griffith v. Kentucky*, 479 U.S. 314 (1987) the Court held that new rules should be fully retroactive on direct appellate review. Thus, any litigant whose case is not yet final can take advantage of the new rule, even if the new rule upsets prior law. Of course, the new rule does not reopen old disputes. It is not available to litigants who lost under the old rule, would win under the new one, but have no recourse to appeal because they have exhausted all of their appeals and certiorari has been denied, or because the time limit for filing an appeal has expired.

The question then arises: How should the retroactivity issue be handled in habeas corpus? In order to appreciate the significance of this issue in the habeas context, it is important to keep in mind a distinctive feature of habeas: In most types of litigation, the parties must cope with statutes of limitations and doctrines of issue and claim preclusion, all of which limit their ability to litigate or relitigate earlier disputes. As a result, the *Griffith* rule has limited practical impact. Habeas is different. Collateral estoppel and *res judicata* do not apply. Traditionally (and up until 1996) the habeas petitioner faced no definite statute of limitations, nor was he absolutely barred from filing more than one habeas petition. In cases of late or repetitive filing, the pre-1996 barrier was an amorphous doctrine called "abuse of the writ." For an illustration of its application, see *McCleskey v. Zant,* 499 U.S. 467 (1991). For these reasons, the resolution of his case was rarely "final" in any definitive sense as long as he remained in prison. Applying the *Griffith* rule in habeas would generate massive litigation by prisoners who now could raise issues hitherto unavailable to them, and would probably result in victories for a significant number of them.

Teague v. Lane addressed the retroactivity issue in the habeas context.

TEAGUE V. LANE

489 U.S. 288 (1989).

JUSTICE O'CONNOR announced the judgment of the Court and delivered the opinion of the Court with respect to Parts I, II, and III, and an opinion with respect to Parts IV and V, in which THE CHIEF JUSTICE, JUSTICE SCALIA, and JUSTICE KENNEDY join.

In *Taylor v. Louisiana,* 419 U.S. 522 (1975), this Court held that the Sixth Amendment required that the jury venire be drawn from a fair cross section of the community. The Court stated, however, that "in holding that petit juries must be drawn from a source fairly representative of the community we impose no requirement that petit juries actually chosen must mirror the community and reflect the various distinctive groups in the population. Defendants are not entitled to a jury of any particular composition." The principal question presented in this case is whether the Sixth Amendment's fair cross section requirement should now be extended to the petit jury. Because we adopt Justice Harlan's approach to retroactivity for cases on collateral review, we leave the resolution of that question for another day.

I

Petitioner, a black man, was convicted by an all-white Illinois jury of three counts of attempted murder, two counts of armed robbery, and one count of aggravated battery. During jury selection for petitioner's trial, the prosecutor used all 10 of his peremptory challenges to exclude blacks. Petitioner's counsel used one of his 10 peremptory challenges to exclude a black woman who was married to a police officer. After the prosecutor had struck six blacks, petitioner's counsel moved for a mistrial. The trial court denied the motion. When the prosecutor struck four more blacks, petitioner's counsel again moved for a mistrial, arguing that petitioner was "entitled to a jury of his peers." The prosecutor defended the challenges by stating that he was trying to achieve a balance of men and women on the jury. The trial court denied the motion, reasoning that the jury "appear[ed] to be a fair [one]."

On appeal, petitioner argued that the prosecutor's use of peremptory challenges denied him the right to be tried by a jury that was representative of the community. The Illinois Appellate Court rejected petitioner's fair cross section claim. The Illinois Supreme Court denied leave to appeal, and we denied certiorari.

Petitioner then filed a petition for a writ of habeas corpus in the United States District Court for the Northern District of Illinois. [Both the District Court and the Seventh Circuit ultimately ruled against him.]

[In Parts II and III of the opinion, the Court ruled against Teague on issues that do not concern us.]

IV

Petitioner's third and final contention is that the Sixth Amendment's fair cross section requirement applies to the petit jury. As we noted at the outset, *Taylor* expressly stated that the fair cross section requirement does not apply to the petit jury. Petitioner nevertheless contends that the *ratio decidendi* of *Taylor* cannot be limited to the jury venire, and he urges adoption of a new rule. Because we hold that the rule urged by petitioner should not be applied retroactively to cases on collateral review, we decline to address petitioner's contention.

A

In the past, the Court has, without discussion, often applied a new constitutional rule of criminal procedure to the defendant in the case announcing the new rule, and has confronted the question of retroactivity later when a different defendant sought the benefit of that rule. In several cases, however, the Court has addressed the retroactivity question in the very case announcing the new rule. These two lines of cases do not have a unifying theme, and we think it is time to clarify how the question of retroactivity should be resolved for cases on collateral [review].

In our view, the question "whether a decision [announcing a new rule should] be given prospective or retroactive effect should be faced at the time of [that] decision." Mishkin, Foreword: the High Court, the Great Writ, and the Due Process of Time and Law, 79 Harv.L.Rev. 56, 64 (1965). Retroactivity is properly treated as a threshold question, for, once a new rule is applied to the defendant in the case announcing the rule, evenhanded justice requires that it be applied retroactively to all who are similarly situated. Thus, before deciding whether the fair cross section requirement should be extended to the petit jury, we should ask whether such a rule would be applied retroactively to the case at [issue].

It is admittedly often difficult to determine when a case announces a new rule, and we do not attempt to define the spectrum of what may or may not constitute a new rule for retroactivity purposes. In general, however, a case announces a new rule when it breaks new ground or imposes a new obligation on the States or the Federal Government. To put it differently, a case announces a new rule if the result was not *dictated* by precedent existing at the time the defendant's conviction became final.

Not all new rules have been uniformly treated for retroactivity purposes. Nearly a quarter of a century ago, in *Linkletter,* the Court attempted to set some standards by which to determine the retroactivity of new rules. The question in *Linkletter* was whether *Mapp v. Ohio,* which made the exclusionary rule applicable to the States, should be applied retroactively to cases on collateral review. The Court determined that the retroactivity of *Mapp* should be determined by examining the purpose of the exclusionary rule, the reliance of the States on prior law, and the effect on the administration of justice of a retroactive application of the exclusionary rule. Using that standard, the Court held that *Mapp* would only apply to trials commencing after that case was decided.

The *Linkletter* retroactivity standard has not led to consistent results. Instead, it has been used to limit application of certain new rules to cases on direct review, other new rules only to the defendants in the cases announcing such rules, and still other new rules to cases in which trials have not yet commenced. See *Desist v. United States,* 394 U.S. 244, 256–257 (1969) (Harlan, J., dissenting) (citing examples).

[Dissatisfied] with the *Linkletter* standard, Justice Harlan advocated a different approach to retroactivity. He argued that new rules should always be applied retroactively to cases on direct review, but that generally they should not be applied retroactively to criminal cases on collateral review. See *Mackey v. United States,* 401 U.S. 667, 675 (1971) (opinion concurring in judgments in part and dissenting in part); *Desist,* 394 U.S., at 256 (dissenting opinion).

B

Justice Harlan believed that new rules generally should not be applied retroactively to cases on collateral review. He argued that retroactivity for cases on collateral review could "be responsibly [determined] only by focusing, in the first instance, on the nature, function, and scope of the adjudicatory process in which such cases arise. The relevant frame of reference, in other words, is not the purpose of the new rule whose benefit the [defendant] seeks, but instead the purposes for which the writ of habeas corpus is made available." *Mackey,* 401 U.S., at 682. With regard to the nature of habeas corpus, Justice Harlan wrote:

> Habeas corpus always has been a *collateral* remedy, providing an avenue for upsetting judgments that have become otherwise final. It is not designed as a substitute for direct review. The interest in leaving concluded litigation in a state of repose, that is, reducing the controversy to a final judgment not subject to further judicial revision, may quite legitimately be found by those responsible for defining the scope of the writ to outweigh in some, many, or most instances the competing interest in readjudicating convictions according to all legal standards in effect when a habeas petition is filed."

Given the "broad scope of constitutional issues cognizable on habeas," Justice Harlan argued that it is "sounder, in adjudicating habeas petitions, generally to apply the law prevailing at the time a conviction became final than it is to seek to dispose of [habeas] cases on the basis of intervening changes in constitutional interpretation." As he had explained in *Desist,* "the threat of habeas serves as a necessary additional incentive for trial and appellate courts throughout the land to conduct their proceedings in a manner consistent with established constitutional standards. In order to perform this deterrence function, . . . the habeas court need only apply the constitutional standards that prevailed at the time the original proceedings took place."

Justice Harlan identified only two exceptions to his general rule of nonretroactivity for cases on collateral review. First, a new rule should be applied retroactively if it places "certain kinds of primary, private individual conduct beyond the power of the criminal law-making authority to proscribe." *Mackey,* 401 U.S., at 692. Second, a new rule should be applied retroactively if it requires the observance of "those procedures that . . . are 'implicit in the concept of ordered liberty.' " *Id.,* at 693.

[We] agree with Justice Harlan's description of the function of habeas corpus. "[T]he Court never has defined the scope of the writ simply by reference to a perceived need to assure that an individual accused of crime is afforded a trial free of constitutional error." *Kuhlmann v. Wilson,* 477 U.S. 436, 447 (1986) (plurality opinion). Rather, we have recognized that interests of comity and finality must also be considered in determining the proper scope of habeas review. Thus, if a defendant fails to comply with state procedural rules and is barred from litigating a particular constitutional claim in state court, the claim can be considered on federal habeas only if the defendant shows cause for the default and actual prejudice resulting therefrom. See *Wainwright v. Sykes,* 433 U.S., at 87–91.

[This] Court has not "always followed an unwavering line in its conclusions as to the availability of the Great Writ. Our development of the law of federal habeas corpus has been attended, seemingly, with some backing and filling." *Fay v. Noia,* 372 U.S. 391, 411–412 (1963). Nevertheless, it has long been established that a final civil judgment entered under a given rule of law may withstand subsequent judicial change in that rule. In *Chicot County Drainage District v. Baxter State Bank,* 308 U.S. 371 (1940), the Court held that a judgment based on a jurisdictional statute later found to be unconstitutional could have res judicata effect. The Court based its decision in large part on finality concerns. "The actual existence of a statute, prior to such a determination [of unconstitutionality], is an operative fact and may have consequences which cannot justly be ignored. The past cannot always be erased by a new judicial declaration . . . Questions of . . . prior determinations deemed to have finality and acted upon accordingly . . . demand examination." Accord, *Rooker v. Fidelity Trust Co.,* 263 U.S. 413, 415 (1923) ("Unless and until . . . reversed or modified" on appeal, an erroneous constitutional decision is "an effective and conclusive adjudication"); *Thompson v.*

Tolmie, 2 Pet. 157, 169 (1829) (errors or mistakes of court with competent jurisdiction "cannot be corrected or examined when brought up collaterally").

These underlying considerations of finality find significant and compelling parallels in the criminal context. Application of constitutional rules not in existence at the time a conviction became final seriously undermines the principle of finality which is essential to the operation of our criminal justice system. Without finality, the criminal law is deprived of much of its deterrent effect. The fact that life and liberty are at stake in criminal prosecutions "shows only that 'conventional notions of finality' should not have *as much* place in criminal as in civil litigation, not that they should have *none.*" Friendly, Is Innocence Irrelevant? Collateral Attacks on Criminal Judgments, 38 U.Chi.L.Rev. 142, 150 (1970). "[I]f a criminal judgment is ever to be final, the notion of legality must at some point include the assignment of final competence to determine legality." Bator, Finality in Criminal Law and Federal Habeas Corpus for State Prisoners, 76 Harv.L.Rev. 441, 450–451 (1963) (emphasis omitted). See also *Mackey,* 401 U.S., at 691, 91 S.Ct., at 1179 (Harlan, J., concurring in judgments in part and dissenting in part) ("No one, not criminal defendants, not the judicial system, not society as a whole is benefited by a judgment providing that a man shall tentatively go to jail today, but tomorrow and every day thereafter his continued incarceration shall be subject to fresh litigation").

[The] "costs imposed upon the State[s] by retroactive application of new rules of constitutional law on habeas corpus ... generally far outweigh the benefits of this application." In many ways the application of new rules to cases on collateral review may be more intrusive than the enjoining of criminal prosecutions, cf. *Younger v. Harris,* 401 U.S. 37, 43–54 (1971), for it *continually* forces the States to marshal resources in order to keep in prison defendants whose trials and appeals conformed to then-existing constitutional standards. Furthermore, as we recognized in *Engle v. Isaac,* "[s]tate courts are understandably frustrated when they faithfully apply existing constitutional law only to have a federal court discover, during a [habeas] proceeding, new constitutional commands."

We find these criticisms to be persuasive, and we now adopt Justice Harlan's view of retroactivity for cases on collateral review. Unless they fall within an exception to the general rule, new constitutional rules of criminal procedure will not be applicable to those cases which have become final before the new rules are announced.

V

Petitioner's conviction became final in 1983. As a result, the rule petitioner urges would not be applicable to this case, which is on collateral review, unless it would fall within an exception.

The first exception suggested by Justice Harlan—that a new rule should be applied retroactively if it places "certain kinds of primary, private individual conduct beyond the power of the criminal law-making authority to proscribe"—is not relevant here. Application of the fair cross section requirement to the petit jury would not accord constitutional protection to any primary activity whatsoever.

The second exception suggested by Justice Harlan—that a new rule should be applied retroactively if it requires the observance of "those procedures that . . . are 'implicit in the concept of ordered liberty,' "—we apply with a modification. The language used by Justice Harlan in *Mackey* leaves no doubt that he meant the second exception to be reserved for watershed rules of criminal procedure:

> Typically, it should be the case that any conviction free from federal constitutional error at the time it became final, will be found, upon reflection, to have been fundamentally fair and conducted under those procedures essential to the substance of a full hearing. However, in some situations it might be that time and growth in social capacity, as well as judicial perceptions of what we can rightly demand of the adjudicatory process, will properly alter our understanding of the *bedrock procedural elements* that must be found to vitiate the fairness of a particular conviction. For example, such, in my view, is the case with the right to counsel at trial now held a necessary condition precedent to any conviction for a serious crime." (emphasis added).

In *Desist,* Justice Harlan had reasoned that one of the two principal functions of habeas corpus was "to assure that no man has been incarcerated under a procedure which creates an impermissibly large risk that the innocent will be convicted," and concluded "from this that all 'new' constitutional rules which significantly improve the pre-existing fact-finding procedures are to be retroactively applied on [habeas].

We believe it desirable to combine the accuracy element of the *Desist* version of the second exception with the *Mackey* requirement that the procedure at issue must implicate the fundamental fairness of the [trial]. Finally, we believe that [the] scope of the second exception [should be limited] to those new procedures without which the likelihood of an accurate conviction is seriously diminished.

Because we operate from the premise that such procedures would be so central to an accurate determination of innocence or guilt, we believe it unlikely that many such components of basic due process have yet to [emerge]. [A]doption of the rule petitioner urges would be a far cry from the kind of absolute prerequisite to fundamental fairness that is "implicit in the concept of ordered liberty." [As] we stated in *Daniel v. Louisiana,* 420 U.S. 31, 32 (1975), [the] fair cross section requirement "[does] not rest on the premise that every criminal trial, or any particular trial, [is] necessarily unfair because it [is] not conducted in accordance with what we determined to be the requirements of the Sixth Amendment." Because the absence of a fair cross section on the jury venire does not undermine the fundamental fairness that must underlie a conviction or seriously diminish the likelihood of obtaining an accurate conviction, we conclude that a rule requiring that petit juries be composed of a fair cross section of the community would not be a "bedrock procedural element" that would be retroactively applied under the second exception we have articulated.

Were we to recognize the new rule urged by petitioner in this case, we would have to give petitioner the benefit of that new rule even though it would not be applied retroactively to others similarly [situated]. If there were no other way to avoid rendering advisory opinions, we might well agree that the inequitable treatment described above is "an insignificant cost for adherence to sound principles of decision-making." *Stovall v. Denno*, 388 U.S., at 301. But there is a more principled way of dealing with the problem. We can simply refuse to announce a new rule in a given case unless the rule would be applied retroactively to the defendant in the case and to all others similarly situated. [We] think this approach is a sound one. Not only does it eliminate any problems of rendering advisory opinions, it also avoids the inequity resulting from the uneven application of new rules to similarly situated defendants. We therefore hold that, implicit in the retroactivity approach we adopt today, is the principle that habeas corpus cannot be used as a vehicle to create new constitutional rules of criminal procedure unless those rules would be applied retroactively to *all* defendants on collateral review through one of the two exceptions we have articulated. Because a decision extending the fair cross section requirement to the petit jury would not be applied retroactively to cases on collateral review under the approach we adopt today, we do not address petitioner's claim.

For the reasons set forth above, the judgment of the Court of Appeals is affirmed.

It is so ordered.

[JUSTICE WHITE's opinion concurring in part and concurring in the judgment, JUSTICE BLACKMUN's opinion concurring in part and concurring in the judgment, and JUSTICE STEVENS' opinion, concurring in part and concurring in the judgment. Are omitted.]

JUSTICE BRENNAN, with whom JUSTICE MARSHALL joins, dissenting.

[The] plurality turns its back on established case law and would erect a formidable new barrier to relief. Any time a federal habeas petitioner's claim, if successful, would result in the announcement of a new rule of law, the plurality says, it may only be adjudicated if that rule would "plac[e] 'certain kinds of primary, private individual conduct beyond the

rooted in the command of Article III of the Constitution that we resolve issues solely in concrete cases or controversies, and in the possible effect upon the incentive of counsel to advance contentions requiring a change in the law, militate against denying Wade and Gilbert the benefit of today's decisions. Inequity arguably results from according the benefit of a new rule to the parties in the case in which it is announced but not to other litigants similarly situated in the trial or appellate process who have raised the same issue. But we regard the fact that the parties involved are chance beneficiaries as an insignificant cost for adherence to sound principles of decision-making.

I see no reason to abandon these views. Perfectly even-handed treatment of habeas petitioners can by no means justify the plurality's *sua sponte* renunciation of the ample benefits of adjudicating novel constitutional claims on habeas corpus that do not bear substantially on guilt or [innocence].

I dissent.

NOTES ON TEAGUE AND RETROACTIVITY IN HABEAS

1. A Fifth Vote for *Teague*. Justice O'Connor wrote for a plurality of four in *Teague*. A few months later Justice White endorsed her approach in *Penry v. Lynaugh*, 492 U.S. 302 (1989), making it the Court's rule.

2. "New Law." The impact of *Teague* depends on how courts apply the "new law" test. If state courts are expected to enforce not only the blackletter of Supreme Court opinions but also the implications of the Court's reasoning, then only a few decisions would be considered "new law." In that event, *Teague* would have few consequences for access to habeas. In his dissent, Justice Brennan expressed his concern that "new law" would be defined differently, so as to encompass a considerable number of potential rulings. Soon after *Teague*, the Court confirmed that fear. The key case is *Butler v. McKellar* 494 U.S. 407 (1990), which involved a custodial interrogation. *Edwards v. Arizona*, 451 U.S. 477 (1981), had held that once the suspect had requested a lawyer the police could not question him without making counsel available. Butler had been arrested on suspicion of crime *A*, and had requested counsel. The police then questioned him (a bit later, and without providing counsel) about crime *B*. Butler was convicted of crime B with the aid of information he provided in this interrogation. He filed a habeas petition, seeking release based on the *Edwards* principle. The Court applied *Teague*, denying his petition on the ground that he was trying to rely on a new rule. It so held even though the Court itself, in between Butler's interrogation and his habeas petition, had extended *Edwards* to *Butler's* fact pattern, in *Arizona v. Roberson*, 486 U.S. 675 (1988). Although *Roberson* had relied heavily on *Edwards*, it was a "new rule." The Court explained:

[T]he fact that a court says that its decision is within the "logical compass" of an earlier decision, or indeed that it is "controlled" by a prior decision, is not conclusive for purposes of deciding whether the current decision is a "new rule" under *Teague*. Courts frequently view their decisions as being "controlled" or "governed" by prior opinions even when aware of reasonable contrary conclusions reached by other courts. In *Roberson*, for instance, the Court found *Edwards* controlling but acknowledged a significant difference of opinion on the part of several lower courts that had considered the question previously. [It] would not have been an illogical or even a grudging application of *Edwards* to decide that it did not extend to the facts of *Roberson*.

A few years later the verb "dictate" entered the Court's lexicon. See *Lambrix v. Singletary*, 520 U.S. 518, 538 (1997) (opinion for the Court by Scalia, J.) (a result is "dictated" only if "*no other* interpretation was reasonable" at the time) (emphasis in original).

Teague's "new law" doctrine resembles the "clearly established law" test for officials' qualified immunity from damages, discussed in Chapter 1. Are the two doctrines grounded in similar policy considerations? Would it be appropriate to treat the two as aspects of a single general doctrine and use precedents from one context in resolving issues that arise in the other? Those questions aside, the finality and federalism policies advanced by Justice O'Connor in *Teague* certainly deserve weight in determining the scope of habeas. Does their strength depend on how "new law" is defined? Would the settled expectations of state courts and the value of repose be unduly upset by a ruling that *Roberson* was simply an application of *Edwards*, and not "new law"?

3. The Exception for Constitutionally Protected Primary Conduct and Other Changes in Substantive Law. Besides turning *Teague* from a plurality opinion into a rule, *Penry,* supra, is significant for another, and quite distinct, reason. The Court ruled that *Teague*'s exception for substantive constitutional limits on the imposition of criminal sanctions includes substantive limits on imposition of the death penalty. Thus, the Court addressed the petitioner's claim that executing someone with the mental capacity of a seven-year old would violate the Eighth Amendment. (It ruled against him, but later overruled that holding in *Atkins v. Virginia*, 536 U.S. 304 (2002).)

Schriro v. Summerlin, 542 U.S. 348, 351–52 & n.4 (2004), exempted *all* changes in substantive law from *Teague*, on the theory that they almost always entail the risk of an erroneous conviction or sentence. As an example, the Court cited *Bousley v. United States*, 523 U.S. 614 (1998). Bousley had pleaded guilty to the federal crime, defined in 18 U.S.C. § 924 (c)(1), of "using" a firearm in connection with a separate drug offense. Later the Court ruled that § 924(c)(1) requires the government to show "active employment of the firearm," not mere possession. *Bailey v. United States*, 516 U.S. 137

(1995). The Court allowed Bousley to challenge his conviction on the ground that he had merely possessed but not actually employed the firearm. Note that *Bousley* does not involve habeas corpus for state prisoners, but post-conviction review for federal prisoners, under 28 U.S.C. § 2255. On this and many other issues, the doctrine governing the two contexts is the same.

Suppose Al is convicted in 2015 of possessing child pornography, under a statute that makes no exception for material of serious literary, artistic, political, or scientific value. In 2016, the Court holds, in *B v. C*, that statutes lacking such a provision violate the First Amendment. Stipulate that *B v. C* is a new rule, and stipulate that the material Al possessed has serious value. In 2017 Al files a habeas petition. May Al obtain release under this exception? Would the outcome be the same if the material Al possessed did *not* have serious value? With regard to this last question, is the First Amendment overbreadth doctrine helpful to Al?

4. The Exception for New Watershed Rules of Criminal Procedure. In the years since *Teague*, the Court has never found a claim that falls into the second exception, for "new procedures without which the likelihood of an accurate conviction is seriously diminished." For example, in 1990 the Court held (in a direct appellate review case) that a jury instruction is unconstitutional if there is a reasonable likelihood that the jury understood the instruction to allow conviction without proof beyond a reasonable doubt. *Cage v. Louisiana*, 498 U.S. 39 (1990) Turning to habeas, the question is whether that holding falls within the second exception. In *Tyler v. Cain*, 533 U.S. 656 (2001), a divided Court declined an opportunity to rule that it did, although the five-member majority also avoided a direct holding that it did not, by finding that the issue was not properly before the Court. In *Whorton v. Bockting*, 549 U.S. 406 (2007), the Court unanimously declared that only a "watershed" rule would meet the test. This would not only require that the rule is "necessary to prevent an impermissibly large risk of an inaccurate conviction." It must also "alter our understanding of the bedrock procedural elements essential to the fairness of a proceeding." Does the constitutional shortcoming in *Tyler* meet this test?

5. *Teague* in the State Courts. In addition to ordinary appellate review through the state court system, every state provides a post-conviction collateral remedy for examination of criminal convictions. The following situation may arise: At the criminal trial and on appellate review of the conviction, the defendant loses on a constitutional claim. He applies for certiorari and is denied Supreme Court review, or he allows the conviction to become final without applying for certiorari. After his conviction has become final, the Supreme Court adopts the constitutional rule he had unsuccessfully argued for in the state system.

On the premise that this rule is "new law," and is not within one of the exceptions discussed above in notes 3 and 4, *Teague* bars federal habeas corpus. But the prisoner sidesteps *Teague*. He seeks relief in a *state* court post-conviction relief proceeding. The issue presented in *Danforth v.*

Minnesota, 552 U.S. 264 (2008), was whether the state court is required to dismiss the case on the ground that the prisoner is seeking to obtain release based on new law. The Court ruled that the state court may grant relief despite *Teague*. Writing for the Court, Justice Stevens noted that *Teague* "was an exercise of this Court's power to interpret the federal habeas statute." Moreover,

> [*Teague*] justified the general rule of nonretroactivity in part by reference to comity and respect for the finality of state convictions. [If] anything, considerations of comity militate in favor of allowing state courts to grant habeas relief to a broader class of individuals than is required by *Teague*. And while finality is, of course, implicated in the context of state as well as federal habeas, finality of state convictions is a *state* interest, not a federal one. It is a matter that States should be free to evaluate, and weigh the importance of, when prisoners held in state custody are seeking a remedy for a violation of federal rights by their lower courts.

Some of the policies advanced in *Teague*—notably "concerns over uniformity and the inequity inherent in the *Linkletter* approach"—would favor holding state courts to *Teague*, as Chief Justice Roberts argued in dissent. The Court struck a different balance:

> This interest in uniformity, however, does not outweigh the general principle that States are independent sovereigns with plenary authority to make and enforce their own laws as long as they do not infringe on federal constitutional guarantees.

2.   AEDPA and Issues Adjudicated by the State Court

Between 1867 and 1996 Congress tinkered with the habeas statute from time to time, but did not comprehensively revise it. The Antiterrorism and Effective Death Penalty Act of 1996 (AEDPA) revised the statute in several ways. AEDPA does not speak to executive detentions, see Part I, nor to the procedural default issue treated in Part II A. But one of its sections does bear on the issues cognizable on habeas corpus. A provision codified at 28 U.S.C. § 2254(d) provides:

> (d) An application for a writ of habeas corpus on behalf of a person in custody pursuant to the judgment of a State court shall not be granted with respect to any claim that was adjudicated on the merits in State court proceedings unless the adjudication of the claim—
>
>> (1) resulted in a decision that was contrary to, or involved an unreasonable application of, clearly established Federal law, as determined by the Supreme Court of the United States; or

(2) resulted in a decision that was based on an unreasonable determination of the facts in light of the evidence presented in the state court proceeding.

The Court has addressed the meaning of the phrase "contrary to, or involved an unreasonable application of, clearly established Federal law, as determined by the Supreme Court" in several cases. *White v. Woodall* is notable for the clarity of its exposition of the issues raised by this phrase, in both the majority and dissenting opinions.

WHITE V. WOODALL

572 U.S. ___, 134 S.Ct. 1697 (2014).

JUSTICE SCALIA delivered the opinion of the Court.

Respondent brutally raped, slashed with a box cutter, and drowned a 16-year-old high-school student. After pleading guilty to murder, rape, and kidnaping, he was sentenced to death. The Kentucky Supreme Court affirmed the sentence, and we denied certiorari. Ten years later, the Court of Appeals for the Sixth Circuit granted respondent's petition for a writ of habeas corpus on his Fifth Amendment claim. In so doing, it disregarded the limitations of 28 U.S.C. § 2254(d)—a provision of law that some federal judges find too confining, but that all federal judges must obey. We reverse.

I

[Faced] with overwhelming evidence of his guilt, respondent pleaded guilty to capital murder. He also pleaded guilty to capital kidnaping and first-degree rape, the statutory aggravating circumstance for the murder. At the ensuing penalty-phase trial, respondent called character witnesses but declined to testify himself. Defense counsel asked the trial judge to instruct the jury that "[a] defendant is not compelled to testify and the fact that the defendant did not testify should not prejudice him in any way." The trial judge denied the request, and the Kentucky Supreme Court affirmed that denial. While recognizing that the Fifth Amendment requires a no-adverse-inference instruction to protect a nontestifying defendant at the guilt phase, see *Carter v. Kentucky,* 450 U.S. 288 (1981), the court held that *Carter* and our subsequent cases did not require such an instruction here. We denied respondent's petition for a writ of certiorari from that direct appeal.

In 2006, respondent filed this petition for habeas corpus in Federal District Court. The District Court granted relief, holding, as relevant here, that the trial court's refusal to issue a no-adverse-inference instruction at the penalty phase violated respondent's Fifth Amendment privilege against self-incrimination. The Court of Appeals affirmed and ordered Kentucky to either resentence respondent within 180 days or release him. Judge Cook dissented.

We granted certiorari.

II

A

Section 2254(d) of Title 28 provides that "[a]n application for a writ of habeas corpus on behalf of a person in custody pursuant to the judgment of a State court shall not be granted with respect to any claim that was adjudicated on the merits in State court proceedings unless the adjudication of the claim . . . resulted in a decision that was contrary to, or involved an unreasonable application of, clearly established Federal law, as determined by the Supreme Court of the United States." "This standard," we recently reminded the Sixth Circuit, "is 'difficult to meet.' " *Metrish v. Lancaster,* 569 U.S. ___, ___ (2013). " '[C]learly established Federal law' " for purposes of § 2254(d)(1) includes only " 'the holdings, as opposed to the dicta, of this Court's decisions.' " And an "unreasonable application of" those holdings must be " 'objectively unreasonable,' " not merely wrong; even "clear error" will not suffice. Rather, "[a]s a condition for obtaining habeas corpus from a federal court, a state prisoner must show that the state court's ruling on the claim being presented in federal court was so lacking in justification that there was an error well understood and comprehended in existing law beyond any possibility for fairminded disagreement."

Both the Kentucky Supreme Court and the Court of Appeals identified as the relevant precedents in this area our decisions in *Carter, Estelle v. Smith,* 451 U.S. 454 (1981), and *Mitchell v. United States,* 526 U.S. 314 (1999). *Carter* held that a no-adverse-inference instruction is required at the *guilt* phase. *Estelle* concerned the introduction at the penalty phase of the results of an involuntary, un-Mirandized pretrial psychiatric examination. And *Mitchell* disapproved a trial judge's drawing of an adverse inference from the defendant's silence at sentencing "with regard to factual determinations respecting the circumstances and details of the crime."

It is clear that the Kentucky Supreme Court's conclusion is not "contrary to" the actual holding of any of these cases. 28 U.S.C. § 2254(d)(1). The Court of Appeals held, however, that the "Kentucky Supreme Court's denial of this constitutional claim was an unreasonable application of" those cases. In its view, "reading *Carter, Estelle,* and *Mitchell* together, the only reasonable conclusion is that" a no-adverse-inference instruction was required at the penalty phase.[2]

---

2   The Court of Appeals also based its conclusion that respondent "was entitled to receive a no adverse inference instruction" on one of its own cases, *Finney v. Rothgerber,* 751 F.2d 858,

We need not decide here, and express no view on, whether the conclusion that a no-adverse-inference instruction was required would be correct in a case not reviewed through the lens of § 2254(d)(1). For we are satisfied that the issue was, at a minimum, not "beyond any possibility for fairminded disagreement."

We have, it is true, held that the privilege against self-incrimination applies to the penalty phase. See *Estelle, supra; Mitchell, supra,* at 328–329. But it is not uncommon for a constitutional rule to apply somewhat differently at the penalty phase than it does at the guilt phase. We have "never directly held that *Carter* applies at a sentencing phase where the Fifth Amendment interests of the defendant are different."

Indeed, *Mitchell* itself leaves open the possibility that some inferences might permissibly be drawn from a defendant's penalty-phase silence. In that case, the District Judge had actually *drawn* from the defendant's silence an adverse inference about the drug quantity attributable to the defendant. We held that this ran afoul of the defendant's "right to remain silent at sentencing." But we framed our holding narrowly, in terms implying that it was limited to inferences pertaining to the facts of the crime: "We decline to adopt an exception for the sentencing phase of a criminal case *with regard to factual determinations respecting the circumstances and details of the crime.*" *Mitchell,* 526 U.S., at 328 (emphasis added). "The Government retains," we said, "*the burden of proving facts relevant to the crime* . . . and cannot enlist the defendant in this process at the expense of the self-incrimination privilege." *Id.,* at 330 (emphasis added). And *Mitchell* included an express reservation of direct relevance here: "Whether silence bears upon the determination of a lack of remorse, or upon acceptance of responsibility for purposes of the downward adjustment provided in § 3E1.1 of the United States Sentencing Guidelines (1998), is a separate question. It is not before us, and we express no view on it."[3]

863–864 (C.A.6 1985). 685 F.3d, at 579 (internal quotation marks omitted). That was improper. As we cautioned the Sixth Circuit two Terms ago, a lower court may not "consul[t] its own precedents, rather than those of this Court, in assessing" a habeas claim governed by § 2254. *Parker v. Matthews,* 567 U.S. ___, ___ (2012) (*per curiam*).

[3] The Courts of Appeals have recognized that *Mitchell* left this unresolved; their diverging approaches to the question illustrate the possibility of fairminded disagreement. Compare *United States v. Caro,* 597 F.3d 608, 629–630 (C.A.4 2010) (direct appeal) (noting that *Mitchell* "reserved the question of whether silence bears upon lack of remorse," but reasoning that " *Estelle* and *Mitchell* together suggest that the Fifth Amendment may well prohibit considering a defendant's silence regarding the nonstatutory aggravating factor of lack of remorse"), with *Burr v. Pollard,* 546 F.3d 828, 832 (C.A.7 2008) (habeas) (while the right to remain silent persists at sentencing, "silence can be consistent not only with exercising one's constitutional right, but also with a lack of remorse," which "is properly considered at sentencing" (citing *Mitchell,* 526 U.S., at 326–327); *Lee v. Crouse,* 451 F.3d 598, 605, n. 3 (C.A.10 2006) (habeas) ("[T]he circuit courts have readily confined *Mitchell* to its stated holding, and have allowed sentencing courts to rely on, or draw inferences from, a defendant's exercise of his Fifth Amendment rights for purposes other than determining the facts of the offense of conviction").

Indeed, the Sixth Circuit itself has previously recognized that *Mitchell* "explicitly limited its holding regarding inferences drawn from a defendant's silence to facts about the substantive offense and did not address other inferences that may be drawn from a defendant's silence." *United States v. Kennedy,* 499 F.3d 547, 552 (2007) (direct appeal). *Kennedy* upheld under *Mitchell* a sentencing judge's consideration of the defendant's refusal to complete a court-ordered psychosexual examination.

Mitchell's reservation is relevant here for two reasons. First, if *Mitchell* suggests that *some* actual inferences might be permissible at the penalty phase, it certainly cannot be read to require a *blanket* no-adverse-inference instruction at every penalty-phase trial. And it was a blanket instruction that was requested and denied in this case; respondent's requested instruction would have informed the jury that "[a] defendant is not compelled to testify and the fact that the defendant did not testify should not prejudice him *in any way*." (emphasis added). Counsel for respondent conceded at oral argument that remorse was at issue during the penalty-phase trial, yet the proposed instruction would have precluded the jury from considering respondent's silence as indicative of his lack of remorse. Indeed, the trial judge declined to give the no-adverse-inference instruction precisely because he was "aware of no case law that precludes the jury from considering the defendant's lack of expression of remorse . . . in sentencing." This alone suffices to establish that the Kentucky Supreme Court's conclusion was not "objectively unreasonable."

Second, regardless of the scope of respondent's proposed instruction, any inferences that could have been drawn from respondent's silence would arguably fall within the class of inferences as to which *Mitchell* leaves the door open. Respondent pleaded guilty to all of the charges he faced, including the applicable aggravating circumstances. Thus, Kentucky could not have shifted to respondent its "burden of proving facts relevant to the crime," 526 U.S., at 330: Respondent's own admissions had already established every relevant fact on which Kentucky bore the burden of proof. There are reasonable arguments that the logic of *Mitchell* does not apply to such cases. See, *e.g., United States v. Ronquillo,* 508 F.3d 744, 749 (C.A.5 2007) (" *Mitchell* is inapplicable to the sentencing decision in this case because 'the facts of the offense' were based entirely on Ronquillo's admissions, not on any adverse inference. . . . Ronquillo, unlike the defendant in *Mitchell,* admitted all the predicate facts of his offenses").

The dissent insists that *Mitchell* is irrelevant because it merely declined to create an exception to the "normal rule," supposedly established by *Estelle,* "that a defendant is entitled to a requested no-adverse-inference instruction" at sentencing. That argument disregards perfectly reasonable interpretations of *Estelle* and *Mitchell* and hence contravenes § 2254(d)'s deferential standard of review. *Estelle* did not involve an adverse inference based on the defendant's silence or a corresponding jury instruction. Thus, whatever *Estelle* said about the Fifth Amendment, its holding[4]—the only aspect of the decision relevant here—does not "requir[e]" the categorical rule the dissent ascribes to it. Likewise, fairminded jurists could conclude that *Mitchell*'s reservation regarding remorse and acceptance of responsibility would have served no meaningful purpose if *Estelle* had created an across-the-board rule against adverse inferences; we are, after all, hardly in the habit of reserving "separate question[s]," *Mitchell, supra,* at 330, that have already been definitively answered. In these circumstances, where the "precise contours" of the right remain "unclear," state courts enjoy "broad discretion" in their adjudication of a prisoner's claims.

B

In arguing for a contrary result, respondent leans heavily on the notion that a state-court " 'determination may be set aside . . . if, under clearly established federal law, the state court was unreasonable in refusing to extend the governing legal principle to a context in which the principle should have controlled.' " Brief for Respondent 21 (quoting *Ramdass v. Angelone,* 530 U.S. 156, 166 (2000) (plurality opinion)). The Court of Appeals and District Court relied on the same proposition in sustaining respondent's Fifth Amendment claim.

The unreasonable-refusal-to-extend concept originated in a Fourth Circuit opinion we discussed at length in [*Terry Williams v. Taylor*], 529 U.S. 362 (2000) our first in-depth analysis of the Antiterrorism and Effective Death Penalty Act of 1996 (AEDPA). See 529 U.S., at 407–409 (citing *Green v. French,* 143 F.3d 865, 869–870 (C.A.4 1998)). We described the Fourth Circuit's interpretation of § 2254(d)(1)'s "unreasonable application" clause as "generally correct," and approved its conclusion that "a state-court decision involves an unreasonable application of this Court's precedent if the state court identifies the correct governing legal rule . . . but unreasonably applies it to the facts of the particular state prisoner's case," (citing *Green, supra,* at 869–870). But we took no position on the Fourth Circuit's further conclusion that a

---

4   The dissent says *Estelle* "held that 'so far as the protection of the Fifth Amendment is concerned,' it could 'discern no basis to distinguish between the guilt and penalty phases of a defendant's 'capital murder trial.' " Of course, it did not "hold" that. Rather, it held that the defendant's Fifth Amendment "rights were abridged by the State's introduction of" a pretrial psychiatric evaluation that was administered without the preliminary warning required by *Miranda v. Arizona,* 384 U.S. 436 (1966). In any event, even *Estelle*'s dictum did not assume an entitlement to a blanket no-adverse-inference instruction. The quoted language is reasonably read as referring to the *availability* of the Fifth Amendment privilege at sentencing rather than the precise *scope* of that privilege when applied in the sentencing context. Indeed, it appears in a passage responding to the State's argument that the defendant "was not entitled to the protection of the Fifth Amendment" in the first place.

state court commits AEDPA error if it "unreasonably refuse[s] to extend a legal principle to a new context where it should apply," (citing *Green, supra,* at 869–870). We chose not "to decide how such 'extension of legal principle' cases should be treated under § 2254(d)(1)" because the Fourth Circuit's proposed rule for resolving them presented several "problems of precision."

Two months later, a plurality paraphrased and applied the unreasonable-refusal-to-extend concept in *Ramdass.* See 530 U.S., at 166–170. It did not, however, grant the habeas petitioner relief on that basis, finding that there was no unreasonable refusal to extend. Moreover, Justice O'Connor, whose vote was necessary to form a majority, cited *Williams* and made no mention of the unreasonable-refusal-to-extend concept in her separate opinion concurring in the judgment. *Ramdass* therefore did not alter the interpretation of § 2254(d)(1) set forth in *Williams.* Aside from one opinion *criticizing* the unreasonable-refusal-to-extend doctrine, see *Yarborough v. Alvarado,* 541 U.S. 652, 666 (2004), we have not revisited the issue since *Williams* and *Ramdass.* During that same 14-year stretch, however, we have repeatedly restated our "hold[ing]" in *Williams, supra,* at 409, that a state-court decision is an unreasonable application of our clearly established precedent if it correctly identifies the governing legal rule but applies that rule unreasonably to the facts of a particular prisoner's case.

Thus, this Court has never adopted the unreasonable-refusal-to-extend rule on which respondent relies. It has not been so much as endorsed in a majority opinion, let alone relied on as a basis for granting habeas relief. To the extent the unreasonable-refusal-to-extend rule differs from the one embraced in *Williams* and reiterated many times since, we reject it. Section 2254(d)(1) provides a remedy for instances in which a state court unreasonably *applies* this Court's precedent; it does not require state courts to *extend* that precedent or license federal courts to treat the failure to do so as error. See Scheidegger, Habeas Corpus, Relitigation, and the Legislative Power, 98 Colum. L.Rev. 888, 949 (1998). Thus, "if a habeas court must extend a rationale before it can apply to the facts at hand," then by definition the rationale was not "clearly established at the time of the state-court decision." *Yarborough,* 541 U.S., at 666. AEDPA's carefully constructed framework "would be undermined if habeas courts introduced rules not clearly established under the guise of extensions to existing law."

This is not to say that § 2254(d)(1) requires an " 'identical factual pattern before a legal rule must be applied.' " To the contrary, state courts must reasonably apply the rules "squarely established" by this Court's holdings to the facts of each case. "[T]he difference between applying a rule and extending it is not always clear," but "[c]ertain principles are fundamental enough that when new factual permutations arise, the necessity to apply the earlier rule will be beyond doubt." *Yarborough, supra,* at 666. The critical point is that relief is available under § 2254(d)(1)'s unreasonable-application clause if, and only if, it is so obvious that a clearly established rule applies to a given set of facts that there could be no "fairminded disagreement" on the question.

Perhaps the logical next step from *Carter, Estelle,* and *Mitchell* would be to hold that the Fifth Amendment requires a penalty-phase no-adverse-inference instruction in a case like this one; perhaps not. Either way, we have not yet taken that step, and there are reasonable arguments on both sides—which is all Kentucky needs to prevail in this AEDPA case. The appropriate time to consider the question as a matter of first impression would be on direct review, not in a habeas case governed by § 2254(d)(1).

* * *

Because the Kentucky Supreme Court's rejection of respondent's Fifth Amendment claim was not objectively unreasonable, the Sixth Circuit erred in granting the writ. We therefore need not reach its further holding that the trial court's putative error was not harmless. The judgment of the Court of Appeals is reversed, and the case is remanded for further proceedings consistent with this opinion.

It is so ordered.

JUSTICE BREYER, with whom JUSTICE GINSBURG and JUSTICE SOTOMAYOR join, dissenting.

During the penalty phase of his capital murder trial, respondent Robert Woodall asked the court to instruct the jury not to draw any adverse inferences from his failure to testify. The court refused, and the Kentucky Supreme Court agreed that no instruction was warranted. The question before us is whether the Kentucky courts unreasonably applied clearly established Supreme Court law in concluding that the Fifth Amendment did not entitle Woodall to a no-adverse-inference instruction. See 28 U.S.C. § 2254(d)(1). In my view, the answer is yes.

I

[*Carter*] and [*Estelle*] clearly establish that a criminal defendant is entitled to a requested no-adverse-inference instruction in the penalty phase of a capital trial. First consider *Carter.* The Court held that a trial judge "has the constitutional obligation, upon proper request," to give a requested no-adverse-inference instruction in order "to minimize the danger that the jury will give evidentiary weight to a defendant's failure to testify." This is because when "the jury is left to roam at large with only its untutored instincts to guide it," it may "draw from the defendant's silence broad inferences of guilt." A trial court's refusal to give a requested no-adverse-inference instruction thus "exacts an impermissible toll on the full and free exercise of the [Fifth Amendment] privilege."

Now consider *Estelle*. The Court held that "so far as the protection of the Fifth Amendment privilege is concerned," it could "discern no basis to distinguish between the guilt and penalty phases" of a defendant's "capital murder trial." The State had introduced at the penalty phase the defendant's compelled statements to a psychiatrist, in order to show the defendant's future dangerousness. Defending the admission of those statements, the State argued that the defendant "was not entitled to the protection of the Fifth Amendment because [his statements were] used only to determine punishment after conviction, not to establish guilt." This Court rejected the State's argument on the ground that the Fifth Amendment applies equally to the penalty phase and the guilt phase of a capital trial.

What is unclear about the resulting law? If the Court holds in Case A that the First Amendment prohibits Congress from discriminating based on viewpoint, and then holds in Case B that the Fourteenth Amendment incorporates the First Amendment as to the States, then it is clear that the First Amendment prohibits the States from discriminating based on viewpoint. By the same logic, because the Court held in *Carter* that the Fifth Amendment requires a trial judge to give a requested no-adverse-inference instruction during the guilt phase of a trial, and held in *Estelle* that there is no basis for distinguishing between the guilt and punishment phases of a capital trial for purposes of the Fifth Amendment, it is clear that the Fifth Amendment requires a judge to provide a requested no-adverse-inference instruction during the penalty phase of a capital trial.

II

The Court avoids this logic by reading *Estelle* too narrowly. First, it contends that *Estelle*'s holding that the Fifth Amendment applies equally to the guilt and penalty phases was mere dictum. But this rule was essential to the resolution of the case, so it is binding precedent, not dictum.

Second, apparently in the alternative, the majority acknowledges that *Estelle* "held that the privilege against self-incrimination *applies* to the penalty phase," but it concludes that *Estelle* said nothing about the *content* of the privilege in the penalty phase (emphasis added). This interpretation of *Estelle* ignores its rationale. The reason that *Estelle* concluded that the Fifth Amendment applies to the penalty phase of a capital trial is that the Court saw "no basis to distinguish between the guilt and penalty phases of [a defendant's] capital murder trial so far as the protection of the Fifth Amendment privilege is concerned." And as there is no basis to distinguish between the two contexts for Fifth

Amendment purposes, there is no basis for varying either the application or the content of the Fifth Amendment privilege in the two contexts.

The majority also reads our decision in [*Mitchell*] to change the legal landscape where it expressly declined to do so. In *Mitchell,* the Court considered whether to create an exception to the "normal rule in a criminal case . . . that no negative inference from the defendant's failure to testify is permitted." We refused: "We decline to adopt an exception for the sentencing phase of a criminal case with regard to factual determinations respecting the circumstances and details of the crime." *Mitchell* thus reiterated what *Carter* and *Estelle* had already established. The "normal rule" is that Fifth Amendment protections apply during trial and sentencing. Because the Court refused "to adopt an *exception*" to this default rule, (emphasis added), the law before and after *Mitchell* remained the same.

The majority seizes upon the limited nature of *Mitchell*'s holding, concluding that by refusing to adopt an exception to the normal rule for *certain* "factual determinations," *Mitchell* suggested that inferences about *other* matters might be permissible at the penalty phase. The majority seems to believe that *Mitchell* somehow casts doubt upon whether *Estelle*'s Fifth Amendment rule applies to matters unrelated to the "circumstances and details of the crime," such as remorse, or as to which the State does not bear the burden of proof.

As an initial matter, *Mitchell* would have had to overrule—or at least substantially limit—*Estelle* to create an exception for matters unrelated to the circumstances and details of the crime or for matters on which the defendant bears the burden of proof. Sentencing proceedings, particularly capital sentencing proceedings, often focus on factual matters that do not directly concern facts of the crime. Was the defendant subject to flagrant abuse in his growing-up years? Is he suffering from a severe physical or mental impairment? Was he supportive of his family? Is he remorseful? *Estelle* itself involved compelled statements introduced to establish the defendant's future dangerousness—another fact often unrelated to the circumstances or details of a defendant's crime. In addition, States typically place the burden to prove mitigating factors at the penalty phase on the defendant. A reasonable jurist would not believe that *Mitchell,* by refusing to create an exception to *Estelle,* intended to undermine the very case it reaffirmed.

Mitchell held, simply and only, that the normal rule of *Estelle* applied in the circumstances of the particular case before the Court. That holding does not destabilize settled law beyond its reach. We frequently resist reaching beyond the facts of a case before us, and we often say so. That does not mean that we throw cases involving all other factual circumstances into a shadow-land of legal doubt.

The majority also places undue weight on dictum in *Mitchell* reserving judgment as to whether to create additional exceptions to the normal rule of *Estelle* and *Carter*. We noted: "Whether silence bears upon the determination of a lack of remorse, or upon acceptance of responsibility for purposes of the downward adjustment provided in § 3E1.1 of the United States Sentencing Guidelines (1998), is a separate question. It is not before us, and we express no view on it." 526 U.S., at 330, 119 S.Ct. 1307. This dictum, says the majority, suggests that some inferences, including about remorse (which was at issue in Woodall's case), may be permissible.

When the Court merely reserves a question that is "not before us" for a future case, we do not cast doubt on legal principles that are already clearly established. The Court often identifies questions that it is *not* answering in order to clarify the question it *is* answering. In so doing—that is, in "express[ing] no view" on questions that are not squarely before us—we do not create a state of uncertainty as to those questions. And in respect to *Mitchell,* where the Court reserved the question whether to create an exception to the normal rule, this is doubly true. The normal rule that a defendant is entitled to a requested no-adverse-inference instruction at the penalty phase as well as the guilt phase remained clearly established after *Mitchell.*

III

In holding that the Kentucky courts did not unreasonably apply clearly established law, the majority declares that if a court must "extend" the rationale of a case in order to apply it, the rationale is not clearly established. I read this to mean simply that if there may be "fairminded disagreement" about whether a rationale applies to a certain set of facts, a state court will not unreasonably apply the law by failing to apply that rationale, and I agree. I do not understand the majority to suggest that reading two legal principles together would necessarily "extend" the law, which would be a proposition entirely inconsistent with our case law. As long as fairminded jurists would conclude that two (or more) legal rules considered together would dictate a particular outcome, a state court unreasonably applies the law when it holds otherwise.

That is the error the Kentucky Supreme Court committed here. Failing to consider together the legal principles established by *Carter* and *Estelle,* the state court confined those cases to their facts. It held that *Carter* did not apply because Woodall had already pleaded guilty—that is, because Woodall requested a no-adverse-inference instruction at the penalty phase rather than the guilt phase of his trial. And it concluded that *Estelle* did not apply because *Estelle* was not a "jury instruction case." The Kentucky Supreme Court unreasonably failed to recognize that together *Carter* and *Estelle* compel a requested no-adverse-inference instruction at the penalty phase of a capital trial. And reading *Mitchell* to rein in the law in contemplation of never-before-recognized exceptions to this normal rule would be an unreasonable *retraction* of clearly established law, not a proper failure to "extend" it. Because the Sixth Circuit correctly applied clearly established law in granting Woodall's habeas petition, I would affirm.

With respect I dissent from the Court's contrary conclusion.

NOTES ON § 2254(d)

1. ***Teague* and AEDPA.** Keep in mind several points regarding the relation between *Teague* and § 2254(d)(1). First, the statute applies only to "any claim that was adjudicated on the merits in State court proceedings." See, e.g., *Cone v. Bell*, 556 U.S. 449 (2009) ("Because the Tennessee courts did not reach the merits of Cone's *Brady* claim, federal habeas review is not subject to the deferential standard that applies under AEDPA.") *Teague* is not limited in this way. "A threshold question in every habeas [case] is whether the Court is obliged to apply the *Teague* rule to the defendant's claim." *Caspari v. Bohlen*, 510 U.S. 383, 389 (1994). Post-AEDPA, the Court reiterated this point in *Horn v. Banks*, 536 U.S. 266, 271 (2002) (*per curiam*). As for cases in which the state court *does* adjudicate the merits of the federal issue, the Court ruled in *Horn* that "the AEDPA and *Teague* inquiries are distinct. [Thus], in addition to performing any analysis required by AEDPA, a federal court considering a habeas petition must conduct a threshold *Teague* analysis when the issue is properly raised by the state."

Second, under *Teague*, circuit court precedents are relevant to the "new law" issue. By contrast, § 2254(d)(1) explicitly restricts the source of clearly established law to the Supreme Court's jurisprudence. Notice that, despite the language of the statute, the 6th Circuit in *White* cited one of its precedents, only to be scolded by the Supreme Court in a footnote. The practical importance of this feature of the statute is that no matter how firmly established a circuit court precedent or a state court precedent may be, it cannot be a source of "clearly established law" for purposes of § 2254(d)(1). See *Renico v. Lett*, 559 U.S. 766 (2010). On the other hand, it does appear that one may cite disagreement among lower courts as evidence that disagreement is reasonable, so that law is not "clearly established." See the Court's footnote 3. Is that footnote consistent with the statute?

Third, as a practical matter both *Teague* and § 2254(d)(1) present significant obstacles to the habeas petitioner. As a matter of fact, a large number of constitutional norms are embodied in (more or less flexible) "standards" rather than bright-line rules. It is often hard to make a successful argument that the petitioner should win, just because the application of a standard calls for the exercise of judgment, and the exercise of judgment is often fatal to the petitioner's argument (under *Teague*) that the outcome he seeks is "dictated" by the settled rule, and his argument (under § 2254(d)(1) as illustrated by *White*) that he state court decision "was contrary to, or involved an unreasonable application of clearly established Federal law." For another example (and one that reflects a problem that comes up in many cases) see *Renico v. Lett*, 559 U.S. 766 (2010). The constitutional issue was whether the judge at the petitioner's first criminal trial had improperly declared a mistrial. (If so, retrial would violate the Double Jeopardy Clause.) The Court reiterated that § 2254(d)(1) "creates a substantially higher threshold for obtaining relief than *de novo* review." Thus,

> [T]he question before us . . . is not whether the trial judge should have declared a mistrial. It is not even whether it was an abuse of discretion for her to have done so—the applicable standard on direct review. The question under AEDPA is instead whether the determination of the Michigan Supreme Court that there was no abuse of discretion was "an unreasonable application of . . . clearly established Federal [law]. The legal standard applied by the Michigan Supreme court in this case was whether there was an abuse of the "broad discretion" reserved to the trial [judge]. Because AEDPA authorizes federal courts to grant relief only when state courts act *unreasonably*, it follows that the more general the rule at issue—and thus the greater the potential for reasoned disagreement among fair-minded judges—the more leeway [state] courts have in reaching outcomes in case-by-case determinations.

Few petitioners win in this regime. On the other hand, the terms "new law," "clearly established," and "unreasonable" are defined in large part by their application. A differently constituted Court could in effect redefine their content merely by applying them differently without making any change in the formal law.

2.   *Teague*'s Exceptions. Unlike *Teague*, AEDPA § 2254(d) does not by its terms make exceptions for watershed rules of criminal procedure or claims that the conviction is substantively invalid. Does it follow that Congress has eliminated these exceptions? The answer is almost certainly that the exceptions survive. Other provisions of AEDPA impose procedural restrictions on access to habeas, including a one-year statute of limitations and restrictions on filing successive petitions. These provisions of AEDPA seem to contemplate that the exceptions remain in place. For example, 28 U.S.C. § 2244 (b)(2) states that "[a] claim presented in a second or successive habeas corpus application under section 2254 that was not presented in a prior application shall be dismissed unless—(A) the applicant shows that the claim relies on a new rule of constitutional law, made retroactive to cases on collateral review by the Supreme Court, that was previously [unavailable]."

Similarly, 28 U.S.C. § 2244(d)(1) provides that "[a] 1-year period of limitation shall apply to an application for a writ of habeas corpus by a person in custody pursuant to the judgment of a State court. The limitation period shall run from the latest of—

(A) the date on which the judgment became final by the conclusion of direct review or the expiration of the time for seeking such review;

(B) the date on which the impediment to filing an application created by State action in violation of the Constitution or laws of the United States is removed, if the applicant was prevented from filing by such State action;

(C) the date on which the constitutional right asserted was initially recognized by the Supreme Court, if the right has been newly recognized by the Supreme Court and made retroactively applicable to cases on collateral review; or

(D) the date on which the factual predicate of the claim or claims presented could have been discovered through the exercise of due diligence.

In *Felker v. Turpin*, 518 U.S. 651 (1996), these provisions were upheld against a charge that they violated the Suspension Clause. The new statutory limits codified (and expanded) the judicially developed "abuse of the writ" doctrine, a "complex and evolving body of equitable principles." A unanimous Court ruled that the new rules were "well within the compass of this evolutionary process." 518 U.S. at 664.

   3.   2254(d)(2). The second paragraph of § 2254(d) involves a highly particularized inquiry, i.e., into whether the state court proceeding "resulted in a decision that was based on an unreasonable determination of the facts." Perhaps for that reason, it has received far less attention from the Supreme Court than (d)(1), the provision at issue in *White*. For an illustrative case, see *Miller-El v. Dretke*, 545 U.S. 231 (2005) (overturning a state court's findings of fact on whether the prosecutor's use of preemptory challenges to prospective jurors were impermissibly motivated by race).

   Suppose a habeas petitioner has a good claim under (d)(2), but must also rely on an extension of current constitutional doctrine in order to win (and therefore cannot meet the hurdle of (d)(1).) Does the "or" between the two clauses signify that each is a separate "gateway" to habeas, such that he is entitled to relief even if he cannot meet the (d)(1) standard applied in *White*?

C. ACTUAL INNOCENCE

   Petitioners who can credibly claim "actual innocence" have easier access to habeas than others. In a variety of contexts, the Court creates exceptions for them to the hurdles faced by other prisoners. One of these is *Teague*'s exception for conduct that cannot validly be punished as a matter of substantive constitutional law. Distinguish *Teague* from situations in which the conduct charged by the state may validly be punished, but the habeas petitioner asserts that he did not commit the crime. The latter fact pattern is the focus of this section.

McQUIGGIN V. PERKINS

569 U.S. ___, 133 S.Ct. 1924 (2013).

JUSTICE GINSBURG delivered the opinion of the Court.

This case concerns the "actual innocence" gateway to federal habeas review applied in *Schlup v. Delo,* 513 U.S. 298 (1995), and further explained in *House v. Bell,* 547 U.S. 518 (2006). In those cases, a convincing showing of actual innocence enabled habeas petitioners to overcome a procedural bar to consideration of the merits of their constitutional claims. Here, the question arises in the context of 28 U.S.C. § 2244(d)(1), the statute of limitations on federal habeas petitions prescribed in the Antiterrorism and Effective Death Penalty Act of 1996. Specifically, if the petitioner does not file her federal habeas petition, at the latest, within one year of "the date on which the factual predicate of the claim or claims presented could have been discovered through the exercise of due diligence," § 2244(d)(1)(D), can the time bar be overcome by a convincing showing that she committed no crime? We hold that actual innocence, if proved, serves as a gateway through which a petitioner may pass whether the impediment is a procedural bar, as it was in *Schlup* and *House,* or, as in this case, expiration of the statute of limitations. We caution, however, that tenable actual-innocence gateway pleas are rare: "[A] petitioner does not meet the threshold requirement unless he persuades the district court that, in light of the new evidence, no juror, acting reasonably, would have voted to find him guilty beyond a reasonable doubt." And in making an assessment of the kind *Schlup* envisioned, "the timing of the [petition]" is a factor bearing on the "reliability of th[e] evidence" purporting to show actual [innocence].

I

A

[Rodney Henderson was murdered on March 4, 1993. Perkins was convicted of the murder in October, 1993. His conviction became final in 1997.]

B

Under the Antiterrorism and Effective Death Penalty Act of 1996 (AEDPA), a state prisoner ordinarily has one year to file a federal petition for habeas corpus, starting from "the date on which the judgment became final by the conclusion of direct review or the expiration of the time for seeking such review." 28 U.S.C. § 2244(d)(1)(A). If the petition alleges newly discovered evidence, however, the filing deadline is one year from "the date on which the factual predicate of the claim or claims presented could have been discovered through the exercise of due diligence." § 2244(d)(1)(D).

Perkins filed his federal habeas corpus petition on June 13, 2008, more than 11 years after his conviction became final. He alleged, *inter alia,* ineffective assistance on the part of his trial attorney, depriving him of his Sixth Amendment right to competent counsel. To overcome AEDPA's time limitations, Perkins asserted newly discovered evidence of actual innocence. He relied on three affidavits, each pointing to [another man, named Jones] as Henderson's murderer.

The first affidavit, dated January 30, 1997, was submitted by Perkins' sister, Ronda Hudson. Hudson stated that she had heard from a third party, Louis Ford, that Jones bragged about stabbing Henderson and had taken his clothes to the cleaners after the murder. The second affidavit, dated March 16, 1999, was subscribed to by Demond Louis, [who] stated that, on the night of the murder, Jones confessed to him that he had just killed Henderson. Louis also described the clothes Jones wore that night, bloodstained orange shoes and orange pants, and a colorful shirt. The next day, Louis added, he accompanied Jones, first to a dumpster where Jones disposed of the bloodstained shoes, and then to the cleaners. Finally, Perkins presented the July 16, 2002 affidavit of Linda Fleming, an employee at Pro-Clean Cleaners in 1993. She stated that, on or about March 4, 1993, a man matching Jones's description entered the shop and asked her whether bloodstains could be removed from the pants and a shirt he brought in. The pants were orange, she recalled, and heavily stained with blood, as was the multicolored shirt left for cleaning along with the pants. [The] Sixth Circuit held that Perkins' gateway actual-innocence allegations allowed him to present his ineffective-assistance-of-counsel claim as if it were filed on [time.]

We granted certiorari to resolve a Circuit conflict on whether AEDPA's statute of limitations can be overcome by a showing of actual [innocence].

II

A

[1] In *Holland v. Florida,* 560 U.S. ___, 130 S.Ct. 2549 (2010), this Court addressed the circumstances in which a federal habeas petitioner could invoke the doctrine of "equitable tolling." *Holland* held that "a [habeas] petitioner is entitled to equitable tolling only if he shows (1) that he has been pursuing his rights diligently, and (2) that some extraordinary circumstance stood in his way and prevented timely filing." As the courts below comprehended, Perkins does not qualify for equitable tolling. In possession of all three affidavits by July 2002, he waited nearly six years to seek federal postconviction relief. "Such a delay falls far short of demonstrating the . . . diligence" required to entitle a petitioner to equitable tolling.

Perkins, however, asserts not an excuse for filing after the statute of limitations has run. Instead, he maintains that a plea of actual innocence can overcome AEDPA's one-year statute of limitations. He thus seeks an equitable *exception* to § 2244(d)(1), not an extension of the time statutorily prescribed.

Decisions of this Court support Perkins' view of the significance of a convincing actual-innocence claim. We have not resolved whether a prisoner may be entitled to habeas relief based on a freestanding claim of actual innocence. *Herrera v. Collins,* 506 U.S. 390, 404–405 (1993). We have recognized, however, that a prisoner "otherwise subject to defenses of abusive or successive use of the writ [of habeas corpus] may have his federal constitutional claim considered on the merits if he makes a proper showing of actual innocence." In other words, a credible showing of actual innocence may allow a prisoner to pursue his constitutional claims (here, ineffective assistance of counsel) on the merits notwithstanding the existence of a procedural bar to relief. "This rule, or fundamental miscarriage of justice exception, is grounded in the 'equitable discretion' of habeas courts to see that federal constitutional errors do not result in the incarceration of innocent persons." *Herrera,* 506 U.S., at 404.

We have applied the miscarriage of justice exception to overcome various procedural defaults. These include "successive" petitions asserting previously rejected claims, *Kuhlmann v. Wilson,* 477 U.S. 436, 454 (1986) (plurality opinion), "abusive" petitions asserting in a second petition claims that could have been raised in a first petition, failure to develop facts in state court, and failure to observe state procedural rules, including filing deadlines.

The miscarriage of justice exception, our decisions bear out, survived AEDPA's passage. In *Calderon v. Thompson,* 523 U.S. 538 (1998), we applied the exception to hold that a federal court may, consistent with AEDPA, recall its mandate in order to revisit the merits of a decision. ("The miscarriage of justice standard is altogether consistent . . . with AEDPA's central concern that the merits of concluded criminal proceedings not be revisited in the absence of a strong showing of actual innocence"). In *Bousley v. United States,* 523 U.S. 614, 622 (1998), we held, in the context of § 2255, that actual innocence may overcome a prisoner's failure to raise a constitutional objection on direct review. Most recently, in *House,* we reiterated that a prisoner's proof of actual innocence may provide a gateway for federal habeas review of a procedurally defaulted claim of constitutional error.

These decisions "see[k] to balance the societal interests in finality, comity, and conservation of scarce judicial resources with the individual interest in justice that arises in the extraordinary case." *Schlup,* 513 U.S., at 324. Sensitivity to the injustice of incarcerating an innocent individual should not abate when the impediment is AEDPA's statute of [limitations].

A federal court may invoke the miscarriage of justice exception to justify consideration of claims defaulted in state court under state timeliness rules. The State's reading of AEDPA's time prescription would thus accord greater force to a federal deadline than to a similarly designed state deadline. It would be passing strange to interpret a statute seeking to promote federalism and comity as requiring stricter enforcement of federal procedural rules than procedural rules established and enforced by the *States*.

B

The State ties to § 2244(d)'s text its insistence that AEDPA's statute of limitations precludes courts from considering late-filed actual-innocence gateway claims. "Section 2244(d)(1)(D)," the State contends, "forecloses any argument that a habeas petitioner has unlimited time to present new evidence in support of a constitutional claim." That is so, the State maintains, because AEDPA prescribes a comprehensive system for determining when its one-year limitations period begins to run. "Included within that system," the State observes, "is a specific trigger for the precise circumstance presented here: a constitutional claim based on new evidence." Section 2244(d)(1)(D) runs the clock from "the date on which the factual predicate of the claim . . . could have been discovered through the exercise of due diligence." In light of that provision, the State urges, "there is no need for the courts to act in equity to provide additional time for persons who allege actual innocence as a gateway to their claims of constitutional error." Perkins' request for an equitable exception to the statute of limitations, the State charges, would "rende[r] superfluous this carefully scripted scheme."

The State's argument in this regard bears blinders. AEDPA's time limitations apply to the typical case in which no allegation of actual innocence is made. The miscarriage of justice exception, we underscore, applies to a severely confined category: cases in which new evidence shows "it is more likely than not that no reasonable juror would have convicted [the petitioner]." Section 2244(d)(1)(D) is both modestly more stringent (because it requires diligence) and dramatically less stringent (because it requires no showing of innocence). Many petitions that could not pass through the actual-innocence gateway will be timely or not measured by § 2244(d)(1)(D)'s triggering provision. That provision, in short, will hardly be rendered superfluous by recognition of the miscarriage of justice exception.

The State further relies on provisions of AEDPA other than § 2244(d)(1)(D), namely, §§ 2244(b)(2)(B) and 2254(e)(2), to urge that Congress knew how to incorporate the miscarriage of justice exception when it was so minded. Section 2244(b)(2)(B), the State observes, provides that a petitioner whose first federal habeas petition has already been adjudicated when new evidence comes to light may file a second-or-successive petition when, and only when, the facts underlying the new claim would "establish by clear and convincing evidence that, but for constitutional error, no reasonable factfinder would have found the applicant guilty of the underlying offense." § 2244(b)(2)(B)(ii). And § 2254(e)(2), which generally bars evidentiary hearings in federal habeas proceedings initiated by state prisoners, includes an exception for prisoners who present new evidence of their innocence. See §§ 2254(e)(2)(A)(ii), (B) (permitting evidentiary hearings in federal court if "the facts underlying the claim would be sufficient to establish by clear and convincing evidence that but for constitutional error, no reasonable factfinder would have found the applicant guilty of the underlying offense").

But Congress did not simply incorporate the miscarriage of justice exception into §§ 2244(b)(2)(B) and 2254(e)(2). Rather, Congress constrained the application of the exception. Prior to AEDPA's enactment, a court could grant relief on a second-or-successive petition, then known as an "abusive" petition, if the petitioner could show that "a fundamental miscarriage of justice would result from a failure to entertain the claim." Section 2244(b)(2)(B) limits the exception to cases in which "the factual predicate for the claim could not have been discovered previously through the exercise of due diligence," and the petitioner can establish that no reasonable factfinder "would have found [her] guilty of the underlying offense" by "clear and convincing evidence." Congress thus required second-or-successive habeas petitioners attempting to benefit from the miscarriage of justice exception to meet a higher level of proof ("clear and convincing evidence") and to satisfy a diligence requirement that did not exist prior to AEDPA's passage.

Likewise, petitioners asserting actual innocence pre-AEDPA could obtain evidentiary hearings in federal court even if they failed to develop facts in state court. Under AEDPA, a petitioner seeking an evidentiary hearing must show diligence and, in addition, establish her actual innocence by clear and convincing evidence. §§ 2254(e)(2)(A)(ii), (B).

Sections 2244(b)(2)(B) and 2254(e)(2) thus reflect Congress' will to *modify* the miscarriage of justice exception with respect to second-or-successive petitions and the holding of evidentiary hearings in federal court. These provisions do not demonstrate Congress' intent to preclude courts from applying the exception, unmodified, to "the type of petition at issue here"—an untimely first federal habeas petition alleging a gateway actual-innocence claim The more rational inference to draw from Congress' incorporation of a modified version of the miscarriage of justice exception in §§ 2244(b)(2)(B) and 2254(e)(2) is simply this: In a case not governed by those provisions, *i.e.,* a first petition for federal habeas relief, the miscarriage of justice exception survived AEDPA's passage intact and unrestricted.

Our reading of the statute is supported by the Court's opinion in *Holland.* "[E]quitable principles have traditionally governed the substantive law of habeas corpus," *Holland* reminded, and affirmed that "we will not construe a statute to displace courts' traditional equitable authority absent the clearest command." The text of § 2244(d)(1) contains no clear command countering the courts' equitable authority to invoke the miscarriage of justice exception to overcome expiration of the statute of limitations governing a first federal habeas petition. As we observed in *Holland,*

> "AEDPA seeks to eliminate delays in the federal habeas review process. But AEDPA seeks to do so without undermining basic habeas corpus principles and while seeking to harmonize the new statute with prior law. . . . When Congress codified new rules governing this previously judicially managed area of law, it did so without losing sight of the fact that the writ of habeas corpus plays a vital role in protecting constitutional rights."

III

Having rejected the State's argument that § 2244(d)(1)(D) precludes a court from entertaining an untimely first federal habeas petition raising a convincing claim of actual innocence, we turn to the State's further objection to the Sixth Circuit's opinion. Even if a habeas petitioner asserting a credible claim of actual innocence may overcome AEDPA's statute of limitations, the State argues, the Court of Appeals erred in finding that no threshold diligence requirement at all applies to Perkins' petition.

While formally distinct from its argument that § 2244(d)(1)(D)'s text forecloses a late-filed claim alleging actual innocence, the State's contention makes scant sense. Section 2244(d)(1)(D) requires a habeas petitioner to file a claim within one year of the time in which new evidence "could have been discovered through the exercise of due diligence." It would be bizarre to hold that a habeas petitioner who asserts a convincing claim of actual innocence may overcome the statutory time bar § 2244(d)(1)(D) erects, yet simultaneously encounter a court-fashioned diligence barrier to pursuit of her [petition].

While we reject the State's argument that habeas petitioners who assert convincing actual-innocence claims must prove diligence to cross a federal court's threshold, we hold that the Sixth Circuit erred to the extent that it eliminated timing as a factor relevant in evaluating the reliability of a petitioner's proof of innocence. To invoke the miscarriage of justice exception to AEDPA's statute of limitations, we repeat, a petitioner "must show that it is more likely than not that no reasonable juror would have convicted him in the light of the new evidence." Unexplained delay in presenting new evidence bears on the determination whether the petitioner has made the requisite [showing].

Considering a petitioner's diligence, not discretely, but as part of the assessment whether actual innocence has been convincingly shown, attends to the State's concern that it will be prejudiced by a prisoner's untoward delay in proffering new evidence. The State fears that a prisoner might "lie in wait and use stale evidence to collaterally attack his conviction . . . when an elderly witness has died and cannot appear at a hearing to rebut new evidence." The timing of such a petition, however, should seriously undermine the credibility of the actual-innocence claim. Moreover, the deceased witness' prior testimony, which would have been subject to cross-examination, could be introduced in the event of a new [trial]. And frivolous petitions should occasion instant dismissal. See 28 U.S.C. § 2254 Rule 4. Focusing on the merits of a petitioner's actual-innocence claim and taking account of delay in that context, rather than treating timeliness as a threshold inquiry, is tuned to the rationale underlying the miscarriage of justice exception—*i.e.,* ensuring "that federal constitutional errors do not result in the incarceration of innocent persons." *Herrera,* 506 U.S., at 404.

IV

We now return to the case at hand. The District Court proceeded properly in first determining that Perkins' claim was filed well beyond AEDPA's limitations period and that equitable tolling was unavailable to Perkins because he could demonstrate neither exceptional circumstances nor diligence. The District Court then found that Perkins' alleged newly discovered evidence, *i.e.,* the information contained in the three affidavits, was "substantially available to [Perkins] at trial." Moreover, the proffered evidence, even if "new," was hardly adequate to show that, had it been presented at trial, no reasonable juror would have convicted Perkins.

The Sixth Circuit granted a certificate of appealability limited to the question whether reasonable diligence is a precondition to reliance on actual innocence as a gateway to adjudication of a federal habeas petition on the merits. We have explained that untimeliness, although not an unyielding ground for dismissal of a petition, does bear on the credibility of evidence proffered to show actual innocence. On remand, the District Court's appraisal of Perkins' petition as insufficient to meet *Schlup*'s actual-innocence standard should be dispositive, absent cause, which we do not currently see, for the Sixth Circuit to upset that evaluation. We stress once again that the *Schlup* standard is demanding. The gateway should open only when a petition presents "evidence of innocence so strong that a court cannot have confidence in the outcome of the trial unless the court is also satisfied that the trial was free of nonharmless constitutional error."

* * *

For the reasons stated, the judgment of the Sixth Circuit is vacated, and the case is remanded for further proceedings consistent with this opinion.

It is so ordered.

JUSTICE SCALIA, with whom THE CHIEF JUSTICE and JUSTICE THOMAS join, and with whom JUSTICE ALITO joins as to Parts I, II, and III, dissenting.

The Antiterrorism and Effective Death Penalty Act of 1996 (AEDPA) provides that a "1-year period of limitation shall apply" to a state prisoner's application for a writ of habeas corpus in federal court. 28 U.S.C. § 2244(d)(1). The gaping hole in today's opinion for the Court is its failure to answer the crucial question upon which all else depends: What is the source of the Court's power to fashion what it concedes is an "exception" to this clear statutory command?

That question is unanswered because there is no answer. This Court has no such power, and not one of the cases cited by the opinion says otherwise. The Constitution vests legislative power only in Congress, which never enacted the exception the Court creates today. That inconvenient truth resolves this case.

I

A

"Actual innocence" has, until today, been an exception only to judge-made, prudential barriers to habeas relief, or as a means of channeling judges' statutorily conferred discretion not to apply a procedural bar. Never before have we applied the exception to circumvent a categorical *statutory* bar to relief. We have not done so because we have no power to do so. Where Congress has erected a constitutionally valid barrier to habeas relief, a court *cannot* decline to give it effect. Before AEDPA, the Supreme Court had developed an array of doctrines, see, *e.g., Wainwright v. Sykes,* 433 U.S. 72, 87 (1977) (procedural default); *McCleskey v. Zant,* 499 U.S. 467, 489 (1991) (abuse of the writ), to limit the habeas practice that it had radically expanded in the early or mid-20th century to include review of the merits of conviction and not merely jurisdiction of the convicting court. For example, the doctrine of procedural default holds that a state prisoner's default [is] not a statutory or jurisdictional command; rather, it is a "prudential" rule "grounded in 'considerations of comity and concerns for the orderly administration of criminal justice.'"

And what courts have created, courts can modify. One judge-made exception to procedural default allows a petitioner to proceed where he can demonstrate "cause" for the default and "prejudice." As relevant here, we have also expressed a willingness to excuse a petitioner's default, even absent a showing of cause, "where a constitutional violation has probably resulted in the conviction of one who is actually innocent." *Murray v. Carrier,* 477 U.S. 478, 496 (1986); see *Schlup v. Delo,* 513 U.S. 298, 326–327 (1995); *House v. Bell,* 547 U.S. 518, 536–537 (2006).

There is nothing inherently inappropriate (as opposed to merely unwise) about judge-created exceptions to judge-made barriers to [relief]. Where a petitioner would, but for a judge-made doctrine like procedural default, have a good habeas claim, it offends no command of Congress's for a federal court to consider the petition. But that free-and-easy approach has no place where a statutory bar to habeas relief is at issue. "[T]he power to award the writ by any of the courts of the United States, must be given by written law," *Ex parte Bollman,* 4 Cranch 75, 94, 2 L.Ed. 554 (1807) (Marshall, C.J.), and "judgments about the proper scope of the writ are 'normally for Congress to make,'" *Felker v. Turpin,* 518 U.S. 651, 664 (1996). One would have thought it too obvious to mention that this Court is duty bound to enforce AEDPA, not amend it.

B

Because we have no "equitable" power to discard statutory barriers to habeas relief, we cannot simply extend judge-made exceptions to judge-made barriers into the statutory realm. The Court's insupportable leap from judge-made procedural bars to *all* procedural bars, including *statutory* bars, does all the work in its opinion—and there is not a whit of precedential support for [it]. Not one of the cases on which the Court relies today supports the extraordinary premise that courts can create out of whole cloth an exception to a statutory bar to relief.

The opinion for the Court also trots out post-AEDPA cases to prove the irrelevant point that "[t]he miscarriage of justice exception . . . survived AEDPA's passage." What it ignores, yet again, is that after AEDPA's passage, as before, the exception applied only to *nonstatutory* obstacles to relief. *Bousley v. United States* and *House v. Bell* were applications of the judge-made doctrine of procedural [default.] *Calderon v. Thompson,* 523 U.S. 538 (1998), a non-AEDPA case, involved the courts of appeals' "inherent power to recall their mandates, subject to review for an abuse of discretion;" it stands only for the proposition that the miscarriage-of-justice exception is an appropriate "'means of channeling'" that discretion.

The Court's opinion, in its way, acknowledges the dearth of precedential support for its holding. "Prior to AEDPA," it concedes, "this Court had not ruled that a credible claim of actual innocence could supersede a federal statute of limitations." Its explanation for this lack of precedent is that before AEDPA, "petitions for federal habeas relief were not governed by any statute of limitations." That is true but utterly unprobative. There are many statutory bars to relief other than statutes of limitations, and we had never (and before today, have never) created an actual-innocence exception to *any* of them. The reason why is obvious: Judicially amending a validly enacted statute in this way is a flagrant breach of the separation of powers.

II

The Court has no qualms about transgressing such a basic principle. It does not even attempt to cloak its act of judicial legislation in the pretense that it is merely construing the statute; indeed, it freely admits that its opinion recognizes an "exception" that the statute does not contain. And it dismisses, with a series of transparent non sequiturs, Michigan's overwhelming textual argument that the statute provides no such exception and envisions none.

The key textual point is that two provisions of § 2244, working in tandem, provide a comprehensive path to relief for an innocent prisoner who has newly discovered evidence that supports his constitutional claim. Section 2244(d)(1)(D) gives him a fresh year in which to file, starting on "the date on which the factual predicate of the claim or claims presented could have been discovered through the exercise of due diligence," while § 2244(b)(2)(B) lifts the bar on second or successive petitions. Congress clearly anticipated the scenario of a habeas petitioner with a credible innocence claim and addressed it by crafting an exception (and an exception, by the way, more restrictive than the one that pleases the Court today). One cannot assume that Congress left room for other, judge-made applications of the actual-innocence exception, any more than one would add another gear to a Swiss watch on the theory that the watchmaker surely would have included it if he had thought of it. In both cases, the intricate craftsmanship tells us that the designer arranged things just as he wanted them.

The Court's feeble rejoinder is that its (judicially invented) version of the "actual innocence" exception applies only to a "severely confined category" of cases. Since cases qualifying for the actual-innocence exception will be rare, it explains, the statutory path for innocent petitioners will not "be rendered superfluous." That is no answer at all. That the Court's exception would not *entirely* frustrate Congress's design does not weaken the force of the State's argument that Congress addressed the issue comprehensively and chose to exclude dilatory prisoners like respondent. By the Court's logic, a statute banning littering could simply be deemed to contain an exception for cigarette butts; after all, the statute as thus amended would still cover *something*. That is not how a court respectful of the separation of powers should interpret statutes.

Even more bizarre is the Court's concern that applying AEDPA's statute of limitations without recognizing an atextual actual-innocence exception would "accord greater force to a federal deadline than to a similarly designed state deadline." The Court terms that outcome "passing strange," but it is not strange at all. Only *federal* statutes of limitations bind federal habeas courts with the force of law; a state statute of limitations is given effect on federal habeas review only by virtue of the *judge-made* doctrine of procedural default. With its eye firmly fixed on something it likes—a shiny new exception to a statute unloved in the best circles—the Court overlooks this basic distinction, which would not trouble a second-year law student armed with a copy of Hart & Wechsler. The Court simply ignores basic legal principles where they pose an obstacle to its policy-driven, free-form improvisation.

The Court's statutory-construction blooper reel does not end there. Congress's express inclusion of innocence-based exceptions in two neighboring provisions of the Act confirms, one would think, that there is no actual-innocence exception to § 2244(d)(1). Section 2244(b)(2)(B), as already noted, lifts the bar on claims presented in second or successive petitions where "the factual predicate for the claim could not have been discovered previously through . . . due diligence" and "the facts underlying the claim . . . would be sufficient to establish by clear and convincing evidence that, but for constitutional error, no reasonable factfinder would have found" the petitioner guilty. Section 2254(e)(2) permits a district court to hold an evidentiary hearing where a diligent state prisoner's claim relies on new facts that "would be sufficient to establish by clear and convincing evidence that but for constitutional error, no reasonable factfinder would have found" him guilty. Ordinarily, we would draw from the express enumeration of these two actual-innocence exceptions the inference that no others were intended.

The Court's twisting path to the contrary conclusion is not easy to follow, but I will try. In the Court's view, the key fact here is that these two provisions of AEDPA codified what had previously been judge-made barriers to relief and applied to them a stricter actual-innocence standard than the courts had been applying. See *ante,* at 1933–1934. From this, the Court reasons that Congress made a conscious choice not also to apply the more restrictive actual-innocence standard to the statute of limitations. Ergo, the Court concludes, we are free to apply the more lenient version of the actual-innocence exception. That clever account ignores the background against which Congress legislated. *Of course* Congress did not "constrain" application of the actual-innocence exception to the statute of limitations. It felt no need to do so, because it had no reason whatsoever to suspect that *any* version of the exception would *apply* to the statute of limitations. The collective efforts of respondent and the majority have turned up not a single instance where this Court has applied the actual-innocence exception to *any* statutory barrier to habeas relief, much less to a statute of limitations. See Part I-B, *supra*. What has been said of equitable tolling applies in spades to non-tolling judicial inventions: "Congress cannot intend to incorporate, by silence, various forms of equitable tolling that were not generally recognized in the common law at the time of enactment." The only conceivable relevance of §§ 2244(b)(2)(B) and 2254(e)(2) is (1) as we have said, that no other actual-innocence exception was intended, and (2) that *if* Congress had anticipated that this Court would amend § 2244(d)(1) to add an actual-innocence exception (which it surely did not), it would have desired the more stringent formulation and not the expansive formulation applied today, which it specifically rejected for those other provisions.

III

Three years ago, in *Holland v. Florida,* 560 U.S. ___ (2010), we held that AEDPA's statute of limitations is subject to equitable tolling. That holding offers no support for importing a novel actual-innocence exception. Equitable tolling—extending the deadline for a filing because of an event or circumstance that deprives the filer, through no fault of his own, of the full period accorded by the statute—seeks to vindicate what might be considered the genuine intent of the statute. By contrast, suspending the statute because of a separate policy that the court believes should trump it ("actual innocence") is a blatant overruling. Moreover, the doctrine of equitable tolling is centuries old, and dates from a time when the separation of the legislative and judicial powers was [incomplete].

American courts later adoption of the English equitable-tolling practice need not be regarded as a violation of the separation of powers, but can be seen as a reasonable assumption of genuine legislative intent. Colonial legislatures would have assumed that equitable tolling would attend any statute of limitations they adopted. In any case, equitable tolling surely represents such a reasonable assumption today. "It is hornbook law that limitations periods are customarily subject to equitable tolling, unless tolling would be inconsistent with the text of the relevant statute. Congress must be presumed to draft limitations periods in light of this background principle." Congress, being well aware of the longstanding background presumption of equitable tolling, "may provide otherwise if it wishes to do so." The majority and dissenting opinions in *Holland* disputed whether that presumption had been overcome, but all agreed that the presumption existed and was a legitimate tool for construing statutes of limitations.

Here, by contrast, the Court has ambushed Congress with an utterly unprecedented (and thus unforeseeable) maneuver. Congressional silence, "while permitting an inference that Congress intended to apply *ordinary* background" principles, "cannot show that it intended to apply an unusual modification of those rules." Because there is no plausible basis for inferring that Congress intended or could have anticipated this exception, its adoption here amounts to a pure judicial override of the statute Congress enacted. "It is wrong for us to reshape" AEDPA "on the very lathe of judge-made habeas jurisprudence it was designed to repair." *Stewart v. Martinez-Villareal,* 523 U.S. 637, 647 (1998) (SCALIA, J., dissenting).

* * *

"It would be marvelously inspiring to be able to boast that we have a criminal-justice system in which a claim of 'actual innocence' will always be heard, no matter how late it is brought forward, and no matter how much the failure to bring it forward at the proper time is the defendant's own fault." *Bousley,* 523 U.S., at 635 (SCALIA, J., dissenting). I suspect it is this vision of perfect justice through abundant procedure that impels the Court today. Of course, "we do not have such a system, and no society unwilling to devote unlimited resources to repetitive criminal litigation ever could." Until today, a district court could dismiss an untimely petition without delving into the underlying facts. From now on, each time an untimely petitioner claims innocence—and how many prisoners asking to be let out of jail do not?—the district court will be obligated to expend limited judicial resources wading into the murky merits of the petitioner's innocence claim. The Court notes "that tenable actual-innocence gateway pleas are rare." That discouraging reality, intended as reassurance, is in truth "the condemnation of the procedure which has encouraged frivolous cases." *Brown,* 344 U.S., at 537 (Jackson, J., concurring in result).

It has now been 60 years since *Brown v. Allen,* in which we struck the Faustian bargain that traded the simple elegance of the common-law writ of habeas corpus for federal-court power to probe the substantive merits of state-court convictions. Even after AEDPA's pass through the Augean stables, no one in a position to observe the functioning of our byzantine federal-habeas system can believe it an efficient device for separating the truly deserving from the multitude of prisoners pressing false claims. "[F]loods of stale, frivolous and repetitious petitions inundate the docket of the lower courts and swell our own. . . . It must prejudice the occasional meritorious applicant to be buried in a flood of worthless ones." *Id.,* at 536–537.

The "inundation" that Justice Jackson lamented in 1953 "consisted of 541" federal habeas petitions filed by state prisoners. By 1969, that number had grown to 7,359. In the year ending on September 30, 2012, 15,929 such petitions were filed. Today's decision piles yet more dead weight onto a postconviction habeas system already creaking at its rusted joints.

I respectfully dissent.

NOTES ON "ACTUAL INNOCENCE"

1. **The Court's Response to Justice Scalia.** The majority responded to Justice Scalia's dissent in a footnote, which appears just before Part III of the opinion:

> [The] dissent stridently insists that federal (although not state) statutes of limitations allow no exceptions not contained in the text. Well, not quite so, the dissent ultimately acknowledges. Even AEDPA's statute of limitations, the dissent admits, is subject to equitable tolling. But that is because equitable tolling "can be seen as a reasonable assumption of genuine legislative intent." Why is it not an equally reasonable assumption that Congress would want a limitations period to yield when what is at stake is a State's incarceration of an individual for a crime, it has become clear, no reasonable person would find he committed? For all its bluster, the dissent agrees with the Court on a crucial point: Congress legislates against the backdrop of existing law. At the time of AEDPA's enactment, multiple decisions of this Court applied the miscarriage of justice exception to overcome various threshold barriers to relief. It is hardly "unprecedented," therefore, to conclude that "Congress intended or could have anticipated [a miscarriage of justice] exception" when it enacted AEDPA.

Which side has the better of this argument?

2. ***Herrera v. Collins*: Can "Actual Innocence" Be a *Ground* for Release in Habeas?** *McQuiggen* allows a (sufficiently well-founded) claim of actual innocence to override the statute of limitations. *House* held that a showing of actual innocence could excuse procedural default. In these cases the petitioners sought access to habeas in order to raise constitutional defenses to their criminal convictions or sentences, such as the ineffective assistance claim in *McQuiggen*. The role of "actual innocence" is to provide a "gateway" to habeas in the face of procedural obstacles The issue in *Herrera v. Collins,* 506 U.S. 390 (1993), was of a different nature: The habeas petitioner sought relief *on the ground that* he was actually innocent, without claiming any constitutional infirmities in the process that led to his conviction. Herrera had been convicted of murder and sentenced to death. Separate and distinct from claiming irregularities in the criminal process leading to his conviction and sentence, he argued that he was actually innocent, and offered affidavits in support of that claim. Executing him, he maintained, would violate his Eighth Amendment right against cruel and

unusual punishment and his Fourteenth Amendment right against deprivation of life without due process of law.

The Court denied Herrera's claim, but it did not resolve the issue of whether a claim of actual innocence could be raised in habeas corpus. Writing for the Court, Chief Justice Rehnquist noted that "[c]laims of actual innocence based on newly discovered evidence have never been held to state a ground for habeas relief absent an independent constitutional violation occurring in the underlying state criminal proceeding." Adverting to the doctrine applied in *McQuiggin*, he pointed out that "federal habeas cases have treated claims of 'actual innocence' not as an independent constitutional claim, but as a basis upon which a habeas petitioner may have an independent constitutional claim considered on the merits, even though his habeas petition would otherwise be regarded as successive or abusive." Nonetheless, the majority declined to set forth a rule that such claims could not be brought. Rather, "assum[ing], for the sake of argument in deciding this case that in a capital case a truly persuasive demonstration of 'actual innocence' made after trial would render the execution of a defendant unconstitutional," the Court ruled that Herrera had not made a strong enough showing.

Justice O'Connor, joined by Justice Kennedy, wrote a concurring opinion that stated:

> Resolving the issue is neither necessary nor advisable in this case. The question is a sensitive and, to say the least, troubling one. It implicates not just the life of a single individual, but also the state's powerful and legitimate interest in punishing the guilty, and the nature of state-federal relations.

Justice Scalia, joined by Justice Thomas, wrote in a concurring opinion:

> I would have preferred to decide that question, particularly since, as the Court's discussion shows, it is perfectly clear what the answer is: There is no basis in text, tradition, or even in contemporary practice (if that were enough), for finding in the Constitution a right to demand judicial consideration of newly discovered evidence brought forward after conviction.

Concurring in the judgment, Justice White took the Court's assumption as his premise and undertook to specify the showing a habeas petitioner would have to make:

> To be entitled to relief, however, petitioner would at the very least be required to show that based on proffered newly discovered evidence and the entire record before the jury that convicted him, "no rational trier of fact could [find] proof of guilt beyond a reasonable doubt."

Justice Blackmun, joined by Justices Stevens and Souter, dissented. They squarely disagreed with Justices Scalia and Thomas on access to habeas, and with Justice White on the appropriate standard for relief:

> Nothing could be more contrary to contemporary standards of decency or more shocking to the conscience that to execute a person who is actually innocent. [I] would hold that, to obtain relief on a claim of actual innocence, the petitioner must show that he probably is innocent.

3. Does Death Make a Difference? *Herrera* was a capital case. Assuming that he makes an adequate showing of actual innocence (under whatever standard may be adopted), should it make a difference whether the habeas petitioner has been sentenced to death? One way to think about this question is to ask whether the finality and federalism policies behind restrictions on habeas are too weak to overcome the argument for access to habeas for actual innocence claims in the death context, yet strong enough to prevail in other contexts.

4. Does Habeas Corpus for Judicially Authorized Detentions Have a Statutory Pedigree? *Boumediene* holds that habeas or an adequate substitute is constitutionally required for executive detentions. Is the same true of habeas for judicially authorized detentions? Section 14 of the Judiciary Act of 1789 authorized federal courts to grant writs of habeas corpus. In *Ex parte Bollman* 8 U.S. (4 Cranch) 75 (1807), the Supreme Court applied the statute to order the release (for lack of jurisdiction) of two persons held in the District of Columbia but charged with crimes committed elsewhere. Chief Justice Marshall asserted that "the power to award the writ by any of the courts of the United States must be given by written law," held that Section 14 so gave it, and held that the statute was constitutional. Thus, *Bollman* seems to imply that federal habeas corpus would not exist without the congressional authorization provided by Section 14. Is this holding or dicta in *Bollman*? If it is a holding (and Marshall does stress the point at the outset of the opinion) is *Bollman* consistent with the Suspension Clause, U.S. Const. article I, § 9? The point here is that the Suspension Clause pre-dates Section 14 and seems to suppose the existence of habeas as a default rule, subject to suspension by Congress "when in cases of rebellion or invasion the public safety may require it." If *Bollman* is right, does it follow that the Suspension Clause is a constitutional guarantee of access to *state* habeas? If that is so, is *Tarble's Case*, see Chapter 7, rightly decided? Suppose there is a constitutional right under the Suspension Clause to habeas for judicially authorized detentions: Does that right cover only the issues cognizable in habeas in 1787 (arguably just jurisdictional issues) or does it include a right to litigate the whole panoply of constitutional claims recognized since 1787?

5. The Role of Equity. Both the *McQuiggin* Court and Justice Scalia's dissent cite *Holland v. Florida*, 130 U.S. 2549 (2010). *Holland* was not an "actual innocence" case, but it does allow a petitioner to seek relief despite failure to meet § 2254(d)'s one-year statute of limitations. In *Holland* the prisoner offered to show that he had diligently pursued his efforts to obtain habeas review but that his lawyer had repeatedly neglected his responsibilities. He sought an *extension* of the time period. The Court held that "§ 2254(d) is subject to equitable tolling in appropriate cases," and remanded for a determination of whether "the facts of this case . . . constitute extraordinary circumstances sufficient to warrant equitable relief." By contrast, in *McQuiggin* the petitioner had no excuse for failing to meet § 2254(d). He argued, and the Court agreed, that a sufficient showing of "actual innocence" would justify an *exception* to § 2254(d).

A feature that *Holland* and *McQuiggin* have in common is reliance on the general principle that equitable adjustments can be made to the statutory requirement. This theme runs through much of habeas corpus doctrine. Thus, there is a requirement that state remedies be exhausted, but the rule does not require repeated efforts to obtain state court relief, see, e.g., *Castille v. Peoples*, 489 U.S. 346, 350 (1989), nor does it apply if no state remedy is available, *Engle v. Isaac*, 456 U.S. 107,125 n.28 (1982). The Court has also recognized equitable exceptions ("cause" and "prejudice") to the procedural default rule, see, e.g., *Trevino v. Thaler*, 133 S.Ct. 1911 (2013). The AEDPA contains a roughly similar, though rather demanding, statutory exception to the rule barring successive petitions, see 28 U.S.C. § 2244(b)(2)(B)(i)(ii) (1996).

These exceptions provide support for the proposition that "[e]quity runs through the law of habeas corpus." Erica Hashimoto, *Reclaiming the Equitable Heritage of Habeas*, 108 NW. U. L. REV. 139 (2013). Professor Hashimoto goes on to note that the *Teague v. Lane* retroactivity doctrine is a conspicuous exception to the general principle, and to call for "three individualized equitable exceptions to the now-absolute retroactivity bar that take account of applicants' conduct in pursuing claims, the merits of the claim and the stakes involved, and the unavailability of alternative remedies." Professor Hashimoto's argument draws an analogy between the exceptions to procedural default, successive petitions and statute of limitations, on the one hand, and retroactivity on the other. Yet the latter doctrine, unlike the others, is in no way based on the conduct of either the litigant or his lawyer. Does this difference undermine the analogy?

CHAPTER 10

CONGRESS'S AUTHORITY OVER
FEDERAL JURISDICTION

■ ■ ■

The framers of the U.S. Constitution sought to prevent too great an accumulation of power in any one organ of government. They divided the powers of the national government among the executive, the legislative, and the judicial branches. The very structure of the document reflects this principle of separation of powers. Article I deals with legislative power and Article II with the executive. We are concerned here with Article III, which sets forth the basic constitutional principles governing the judicial power of the national government. The dual aims of Article III are to shield the federal courts from undue interference by the other branches while at the same time guarding against abuses of the judicial power. With those ends in mind, Section 1 directs the creation of a "supreme Court" but authorizes Congress to determine whether to set up lower federal courts. In order to assure the independence of federal judges, Section 1 guarantees them life tenure during "good behavior," and forbids diminishing their salaries. Section 2 specifies the outer boundaries of federal jurisdiction and grants Congress the power to make "Exceptions and Regulations" to the Supreme Court's appellate jurisdiction.

These provisions raise three broad questions. Section I of this chapter considers the scope of Congress's power to *bestow* federal jurisdiction. Section II addresses the more complex issue of how far Congress may go in *restricting* federal jurisdiction. Section III deals with judicial independence.

The legislative history of Article III has a bearing on all three topics. One of the hardest problems at the 1787 Constitutional Convention was how to resolve the conflict between the perceived need for a strong national government and the fear that creating such a government would intrude too far into state prerogatives. "Federalists" emphasized nationalizing authority while "Anti-Federalists" pressed for traditions of state autonomy. This debate arose in connection with a range of issues. Our topic in this chapter is its impact on Article III and the judicial power.

The two sides agreed on the need for one national court, thus the provision in Article III for "one supreme Court." They agreed that, whatever the scope of their powers, federal judges ought to be independent of the other branches, thus the tenure and salary protections. They also agreed that, unlike the state courts, the federal courts should *not* be courts of general jurisdiction. The scope of their jurisdiction should be limited by the Constitution to matters in which, for one reason or another, there was a significant federal interest. With that aim in mind, Section 2 lists the permissible scope of federal jurisdiction, extending it to cases "arising under" federal law, matters involving admiralty, foreign governments and nationals, suits between citizens of different states, and suits between states.

While there were areas of agreement, the delegates differed sharply on the need for a system of lower federal courts. Federalists favored a strong federal judicial branch while Anti-Federalists argued that the state courts were fully capable of handling most federal issues. James Madison devised a solution. Under the "Madisonian Compromise" the issue of whether to create "inferior" federal courts would be left up to Congress. In this way the states, through representatives elected by the people and senators elected (at that time) by state legislatures, would determine the extent of federal judicial power. For present purposes, the main issue raised by the Madisonian Compromise concerns the *scope* of Congress's power. Since, under the Compromise, Congress has power over federal jurisdiction, we are concerned with how far Congress may go—in one direction or the other.

I.   THE OUTER BOUNDARIES OF FEDERAL JURISDICTION

Article III authorizes Congress to grant federal courts jurisdiction over cases "arising under this Constitution, the Laws of the United States, and Treaties made, or which shall be made, under their authority." The general jurisdictional statute, 28 U.S.C. § 1331, and statutes modeled on it, extend federal jurisdiction to "all civil actions arising under the Constitution, laws, or treaties of the United States." From the similarity between these provisions one might infer that the constitutional rules are identical to the statutory rules. But this is not so. The statute was enacted in 1875, and there is reason to believe that it was meant to reach the full constitutional limits of Article III. But whatever the framers of § 1331 may have had in mind, the Court accords the statute a far narrower scope than Article III. As described in Chapter 3, § 1331 typically reaches only cases in which federal law creates the cause of action, and always requires that the federal issue appear on the face of a well-pleaded complaint. By contrast, Article III permits Congress to extend federal jurisdiction to any case in which there is a federal "ingredient."

Are there good policy reasons for the Court's divergent treatment of these statutory and constitutional issues? Consider the following argument: The general point of the constitutional provision listing the types of cases and controversies federal courts may adjudicate is to maintain a big role for the state courts in our system. Article III pursues this goal by guaranteeing that federal courts do not become courts of general jurisdiction. But inflexible constitutional rules arguably put too many fetters on Congress. Therefore, it can be prudent to craft a doctrine that allows Congress broad authority. By contrast, the purpose of the general federal question statute is to determine the everyday business of the federal courts. A narrower doctrine, namely the standard examined in Chapter 3, is appropriate to that end.

Does this argument give adequate weight to the states' interest in curbing the power of the federal courts? Does the argument imply that there should be virtually no limits on Congress's power, and that states should address any complaints to Congress, not the courts? If not, what are the appropriate limits on Congress's power to expand federal jurisdiction?

A. FEDERAL QUESTIONS

We will see that in some respects the scope of congressional power over federal jurisdiction remains unclear. But there is at least one blackletter rule: Congress may authorize federal courts to adjudicate any case that raises a federal question, whether the federal question is presented on the face of the complaint, in a defense, or otherwise. One corollary of this rule is that Congress may authorize the Supreme Court to review any state judgment raising a federal issue. A second corollary is that Congress may authorize removal of a case from state to federal court, if that case raises a federal issue.

The authority for the first corollary is *Martin v. Hunter's Lessee*, a case we treated in detail in Chapter 8. The second corollary was established in the following case. James Davis, a tax collector for the United States, was indicted for murder in state court in Tennessee. Invoking a federal statute, he sought to remove the case from state to federal court, and the state objected.

TENNESSEE V. DAVIS
100 U.S. (10 Otto) 257 (1880).

MR. JUSTICE STRONG delivered the opinion of the court.

The first of the questions certified is one of great importance, bringing as it does into consideration the relation of the general government to the government of the States, and bringing also into view not merely the construction of an act of Congress, but its constitutionality. [The] defendant's petition for removal [represented] that what he did was done under and by right of his office, to wit, as deputy collector of internal revenue; that it was his duty to seize illicit distilleries and the apparatus that is used for the illicit and unlawful distillation of spirits; and that while so attempting to enforce the revenue laws of the United States, as deputy collector as aforesaid, he was assaulted and fired upon by a number of armed men, and that in defence of his life he returned the [fire]. The language of the [removal] statute (so far as it is necessary at present to refer to it) is as follows: "When any civil suit or criminal prosecution is commenced in any court of a State against any officer appointed under, or acting by authority of, any revenue law of the United States, now or hereafter enacted, or against any person acting by or under authority of any such officer, on account of any act done under color of his office or of any such law, or on account of any right, title, or authority claimed by such officer or other person under any such law," the case may be removed into the Federal court. [Revised Statutes § 643.]

That the act of Congress does provide for the removal of criminal prosecutions for offences against the State laws, when there arises in them the claim of the Federal right or authority, is too plain to admit of [denial].

We come, then, to the inquiry, most discussed during the argument, whether sect. 643 is a constitutional exercise of the power vested in [Congress]. By the last clause of the eighth section of the first article of the Constitution, Congress is invested with power to make all laws necessary and proper for carrying into execution not only all the powers previously specified, but also all other powers vested by the Constitution in the government of the United States, or in any department or officer thereof. Among these is the judicial power of the government. That is declared by the second section of the third article to "extend to all cases in law and equity arising under the Constitution, the laws of the United States, and treaties made or which shall be made under their authority." This provision embraces alike civil and criminal cases arising under the Constitution and laws. *Cohens v. Virginia*, 6 Wheat. 264. Both are equally within the domain of the judicial powers of the United States, and there is nothing in the grant to justify an assertion that whatever power may be exerted over a civil case may not be exerted as fully over a criminal one. And a case arising under the Constitution and laws of the United States may as well arise in a criminal prosecution as in a civil suit. What constitutes a case thus arising was early defined in [*Cohens*]. It is not merely one where a party comes into court to demand something conferred upon him by the Constitution or by a law or treaty. A case consists of the right of one party as well as the other, and may truly be said to arise under the Constitution or a law or a treaty of the United States whenever its correct decision depends upon the construction of either. Cases arising under the laws of the United States are such as grow out of the legislation of Congress, whether they constitute the right or privilege, or claim or protection, or defence of the party, in whole or in part, by whom they are asserted. It was said in *Osborn v. The Bank of the United States* (9 Wheat. 738), "When a question to which the judicial power of the Union is extended by the Constitution forms an ingredient of the original cause, it is in the power of Congress to give the circuit courts jurisdiction of that cause, although other questions of fact or of law may be involved in it." And a case arises under the laws of the United States, when it arises out of the implication of the [law].

The constitutional right of Congress to authorize the removal before trial of civil cases arising under the laws of the United States has long since passed beyond doubt. It was exercised almost contemporaneously with the adoption of the Constitution, and the power has been in constant use ever since. The Judiciary Act of Sept. 24, 1789, was passed by the first Congress, many members of which had assisted in framing the Constitution; and though some doubts were soon after suggested whether cases could be removed from State courts before trial, those doubts soon disappeared. Whether removal from a State to a Federal court is an exercise of appellate jurisdiction, as laid down in Story's Commentaries on the Constitution, sect. 1745, or an indirect mode of exercising original jurisdiction, as intimated in *Railway Company v. Whitton* (13 Wall. 270), we need not now inquire. Be it one or the other, it was ruled in the case last cited to be constitutional. But if there is power in Congress to direct a removal before trial of a civil case arising under the Constitution or laws of the United States, and direct its removal because such a case has arisen, it is impossible to see why the same power may not order the removal of a criminal prosecution, when a similar case has arisen in it. The judicial power is declared to extend to all cases of the character described, making no distinction between civil and criminal, and the reasons for conferring upon the courts of the national government superior jurisdiction over cases involving authority and rights under the laws of the United States are equally applicable to both.

[Such] a jurisdiction is necessary for the preservation of the acknowledged powers of the government. It is essential, also, to a uniform and consistent administration of national laws. It is required for the preservation of that supremacy which the Constitution gives to the general government by declaring that the Constitution and laws of the United States made in pursuance thereof, and the treaties made or which shall be made under the authority of the United States, shall be the supreme laws of the land, and the judges in every State shall be bound thereby, any thing in the constitution or laws of any State to the contrary notwithstanding. The founders of the Constitution could never have intended to leave to the possibly varying decisions of the State courts what the laws of the government it established are, what rights they confer, and what protection shall be extended to those who execute them. If they did, where is the supremacy over those questions vested in the government by the Constitution? If, whenever and wherever a case arises under the Constitution and laws or treaties of the United States, the national government cannot take control of it, whether it be civil or criminal, in any stage of its progress, its judicial power is, at least, temporarily silenced, instead of being at all times supreme. In criminal as well as in civil proceedings in State courts, cases under the Constitution and laws of the United States might have been expected to arise, as, in fact, they do. Indeed, the powers of the general government and the lawfulness of authority exercised or claimed under it, are quite as frequently in question in criminal cases in State courts as they are in civil cases, in proportion to their number.

The argument so much pressed upon us, that it is an invasion of the sovereignty of a State to withdraw from its courts into the courts of the general government the trial of prosecutions for alleged offences against the criminal laws of a State, even though the defense presents a case arising out of an act of Congress, ignores entirely the dual character of our government. It assumes that the States are completely and in all respects sovereign. But when the national government was formed, some of the attributes of State sovereignty were partially, and others wholly, surrendered and vested in the United States. Over the subjects thus surrendered the sovereignty of the States ceased to extend. Before the adoption of the Constitution, each State had complete and exclusive authority to administer by its courts all the law, civil and criminal, which existed within its borders. Its judicial power extended over every legal question that could arise. But when the Constitution was adopted, a portion of that judicial power became vested in the new government created, and so far as thus vested it was withdrawn from the sovereignty of the [State].

The subject has more than once been before this court, and it has been fully considered. In *Martin v. Hunter* it was admitted in argument [that] there might be a removal before judgment, though it was contended there could not be after; but the contention was overruled, and it was declared that Congress might authorize a removal either before or after judgment; that the time, the process, and the manner must be subject to its absolute legislative control. In that case, also, it was said that the remedy of the removal of suits would be utterly inadequate to the purposes of the Constitution, if it could act only upon the parties, and not upon the State courts. Judge Story, who delivered the opinion, adding: "In respect to criminal prosecutions, the difficulty seems admitted to be insurmountable, and, in respect to civil suits, there would in many cases be rights without corresponding remedies." . . . "In respect to criminal prosecutions there would at once be an end of all control, and the State decisions would be paramount to the Constitution." The expression that the difficulty in the way of the removal of criminal prosecutions seems admitted to be insurmountable has been laid hold of here, in argument, as a declaration of the court that criminal prosecutions cannot be removed. It is a very shortsighted and unwarranted inference. What the court said was, that the remedy in such cases seems to be insurmountable, *if it could not act upon State courts as well as parties*; and it was ruled that it does thus act. The expression must be read in its connection. In *Martin v. Hunter* the removal was by writ of error after final judgment in the State court; which certainly seems more an invasion of State jurisdiction than a removal before trial. The case was followed by *Cohens v. Virginia*, a criminal case, in which the defendant set up against a criminal prosecution an authority under an act of Congress. There it was decided that cases might be removed in which a State was a party. This also was a writ of error after a final judgment; but it, as well as the former case, recognized the right of Congress to authorize removals either before or after trial, and neither case made any distinction between civil and criminal [proceedings].

It follows that the first question certified to us from the Circuit Court of Tennessee must be answered in the [affirmative].

MR. JUSTICE CLIFFORD, with whom concurred MR. JUSTICE FIELD, dissenting.

[The lengthy dissenting opinion concluded:]

Large concessions were made by the States to the United States, but they never ceded to the national government their police powers or the power to define and punish offences against their authority, as admitted by all courts and all commentators upon the Constitution, which leads me to the following conclusions: 1. That the section of the Revised Statutes in question does not authorize the removal of a State indictment for an offence against the laws of the State from the State court where it is pending into the Circuit Court of the United States for trial. 2. That if it does purport to confer that authority, it is unconstitutional and void. 3. That the answer to each of the three questions certified here from the Circuit Court should be in the negative.

B. THE "INGREDIENT" TEST

Congress's power to expand federal jurisdiction is not limited to cases in which federal issues arise. As the Court pointed out in *Tennessee v. Davis*, it may authorize federal jurisdiction over cases even though the federal element remains in the background, as an "ingredient" of the case. The leading case is *Osborn*, below. The facts of the case did not require the Court to resolve any hard issue concerning the extent of congressional power to grant federal jurisdiction. In the course of a dispute with the Bank, Ohio officials had broken into the Bank and taken $100,000 for state taxes the state claimed it was owed. The Bank sued to recover the money, relying on its federal immunity from state taxation. While the federal question is evident in *Osborn*, the case is noteworthy because the Court addressed the broader issue of whether the Bank could sue in federal court on causes of action arising under state law. That issue was directly presented by a companion case, *Bank of the United States v. Planters' Bank of Georgia*, 22 U.S. (9 Wheat.) 904 (1824), where the Bank sued to collect on negotiable notes issued by the Planters' Bank. The questions litigated in *Planters' Bank* were matters of state law, yet the

Bank of the United States claimed federal jurisdiction. It relied on the federal statute that incorporated the Bank, which authorized it to "sue and be sued" in both federal and state courts.

OSBORN V. BANK OF THE UNITED STATES

22 U.S. (9 Wheat.) 738 (1824).

[We] will now consider the constitutionality of the clause in the act of incorporation, which authorizes the Bank to sue in the federal Courts.

In support of this clause, it is said, that the legislative, executive, and judicial powers, of every well constructed government, are co-extensive with each other; that is, they are potentially co-extensive. The executive department may constitutionally execute every law which the Legislature may constitutionally make, and the judicial department may receive from the Legislature the power of construing every such law. All governments which are not extremely defective in their organization, must possess, within themselves, the means of expounding, as well as enforcing, their own laws. If we examine the Constitution of the United States, we find that its framers kept this great political principle in view. The 2d article vests the whole executive power in the President; and the 3d article declares, "that the judicial power shall extend to all cases in law and equity arising under this constitution, the laws of the United States, and treaties made, or which shall be made, under their authority."

This clause enables the judicial department to receive jurisdiction to the full extent of the constitution, laws, and treaties of the United States, when any question respecting them shall assume such a form that the judicial power is capable of acting on it. That power is capable of acting only when the subject is submitted to it by a party who asserts his rights in the form prescribed by law. It then becomes a case, and the constitution declares, that the judicial power shall extend to all cases arising under the Constitution, laws, and treaties of the United States.

The suit of *The Bank of the United States v. Osborn* and others, is a case, and the question is, whether it arises under a law of the United States? The appellants contend, that it does not, because several questions may arise in it, which depend on the general principles of the law, not on any act of Congress.

If this were sufficient to withdraw a case from the jurisdiction of the federal Courts, almost every case, although involving the construction of a law, would be withdrawn; and a clause in the constitution, relating to a subject of vital importance to the government, and expressed in the most comprehensive terms, would be construed to mean almost nothing. There is scarcely any case, every part of which depends on the Constitution, laws, or treaties of the United States. The questions, whether the fact alleged as the foundation of the action, be real or fictitious; whether the conduct of the plaintiff has been such as to entitle him to maintain his action; whether his right is barred; whether he has received satisfaction, or has in any manner released his claims, are questions, some or all of which may occur in almost every case; and if their existence be sufficient to arrest the jurisdiction of the Court, words which seem intended to be as extensive as the Constitution, laws, and treaties of the Union, which seem designed to give the Courts of the government the construction of all its acts, so far as they affect the rights of individuals, would be reduced to almost [nothing].

We ask, then, if it can be sufficient to exclude this jurisdiction, that the case involves questions depending on general principles? A cause may depend on several questions of fact and law. Some of these may depend on the construction of a law of the United States; others on principles unconnected with that law. If it be a sufficient foundation for jurisdiction, that the title or right set up by the party, may be defeated by one construction of the constitution or law of the United States, and sustained by the opposite construction, provided the facts necessary to support the action be made out, then all the other questions must be decided as incidental to this, which gives that jurisdiction. Those other questions cannot arrest the proceedings. Under this construction, the judicial power of the Union extends effectively and beneficially to that most important class of cases, which depend on the character of the cause. On the opposite construction, the judicial power never can be extended to a whole case, as expressed by the constitution, but to those parts of cases only which present the particular question involving the construction of the constitution or the law. We say it never can be extended to the whole case, because, if the circumstance that other points are involved in it, shall disable Congress from authorizing the Courts of the Union to take jurisdiction of the original cause, it equally disables Congress from authorizing those Courts to take jurisdiction of the whole cause, on an appeal, and thus will be restricted to a single question in that cause; and words obviously intended to secure to those who claim rights under the constitution, laws, or treaties of the United States, a trial in the federal Courts, will be restricted to the insecure remedy of an appeal upon an insulated point, after it has received that shape which may be given to it by another tribunal, into which he is forced against his will.

We think, then, that when a question to which the judicial power of the Union is extended by the Constitution, forms an ingredient of the original cause, it is in the power of Congress to give the Circuit Courts jurisdiction of that cause, although other questions of fact or of law may be involved in it. The case of the Bank is, we think, a very strong case of this description. The charter of incorporation not only creates it, but gives it every faculty which it possesses. The power to acquire rights of any description, to transact business of any description, to make contracts of any description, to sue on those contracts, is given and measured by its charter, and that charter is a law of the United States. This being can acquire no right, make no contract, bring no suit, which is not authorized by a law of the United States. It is not only itself the mere creature of a law, but all its actions and all its rights are dependant on the same law. Can a being, thus constituted, have a case which does not arise literally, as well as substantially, under the law?

Take the case of a contract, which is put as the strongest against the Bank. When a Bank sues, the first question which presents itself, and which lies at the foundation of the cause, is, has this legal entity a right to sue? Has it a right to come, not into this Court particularly, but into any Court? This depends on a law of the United States. The next question is, has this being a right to make this particular contract? If this question be decided in the negative, the cause is determined against the plaintiff; and this question, too, depends entirely on a law of the United States. These are important questions, and they exist in every possible case. The right to sue, if decided once, is decided for ever; but the power of Congress was exercised antecedently to the first decision on that right, and if it was constitutional then, it cannot cease to be so, because the particular question is decided. It may be revived at the will of the party, and most probably would be renewed, were the tribunal to be changed. But the question respecting the right to make a particular contract, or to acquire a particular property, or to sue on account of a particular injury, belongs to every particular case, and may be renewed in every case. The question forms an original ingredient in every cause. Whether it be in fact relied on or not, in the defence, it is still a part of the cause, and may be relied on. The right of the plaintiff to sue, cannot depend on the defence which the defendant may choose to set up. His right to sue is anterior to that defense, and must depend on the state of things when the action is brought. The questions which the case involves, then, must determine its character, whether those questions be made in the cause or not.

It is said, that a clear distinction exists between the party and the cause; that the party may originate under a law with which the cause has no connection; and that Congress may, with the same propriety, give a naturalized citizen, who is the mere creature of a law, a right to sue in the Courts of the United States, as give that right to the Bank.

This distinction is not denied; and, if the act of Congress was a simple act of incorporation, and contained nothing more, it might be entitled to great consideration. But the act does not stop with incorporating the Bank. It proceeds to bestow upon the being it has made, all the faculties and capacities which that being possesses. Every act of the Bank grows out of this law, and is tested by it. To use the language of the Constitution, every act of the Bank arises out of this law. A naturalized citizen is indeed made a citizen under an act of Congress, but the act does not proceed to give, to regulate, or to prescribe his capacities. He becomes a member of the society, possessing all the rights of a native citizen, and standing, in the view of the Constitution, on the footing of a native. The Constitution does not authorize Congress to enlarge or abridge those rights. The simple power of the national Legislature, is to prescribe a uniform rule of naturalization, and the exercise of this power exhausts it, so far as respects the individual. The Constitution then takes him up, and, among other rights, extends to him the capacity of suing in the Courts of the United States, precisely under the same circumstances under which a native might sue. He is distinguishable in nothing from a native citizen, except so far as the Constitution makes the distinction. The law makes none.

There is, then, no resemblance between the act incorporating the Bank, and the general naturalization law.

Upon the best consideration we have been able to bestow on this subject, we are of opinion, that the clause in the act of incorporation, enabling the Bank to sue in the Courts of the United States, is consistent with the Constitution, and to be obeyed in all Courts.

NOTE ON THE CONTINUING VITALITY OF OSBORN

In *American National Red Cross v. S.G.*, 505 U.S. 247 (1992), recipients of blood transfusions brought state law tort suits against the Red Cross. One issue presented was whether the suit could be removed to federal court under a similar "sue and be sued" clause in the federal statute chartering the Red Cross. The Court interpreted the statute to allow federal jurisdiction. See Chapter 3. It then upheld the statute against constitutional challenge:

> Our holding leaves the jurisdiction of the federal courts well within Article III's limits. As long ago as *Osborn*, this Court held that Article III's "arising under" jurisdiction is broad enough to authorize Congress to confer federal-court jurisdiction over actions involving federally chartered corporations. We would be loath to repudiate such a longstanding and settled rule, on which Congress has surely been entitled to rely, and this case gives us no reason to contemplate overruling it.

Is *ANRC* explicable solely as a matter of following precedent? Or is there some good reason of constitutional principle to read the Article III "arising under" clause so broadly? Does the "ingredient" test of *Osborn* accord due weight to the "Anti-Federalist" side of the compromise at the Convention? Could a persuasive (if anachronistic) argument be made that the Bank's rights and obligations should be governed by federal common law, thereby sidestepping the jurisdictional issue altogether?

C. PROTECTIVE JURISDICTION

Osborn may be defended on a theory that Chief Justice Marshall never articulated in the opinion. The Bank of the United States was an unpopular institution in much of the country and the justices may well have thought that the state courts would not treat it fairly, even in resolving cases like *Planters' Bank* that turned solely on state law. Justice Johnson dissented in *Osborn*, but he acknowledged this problem:

I have very little doubt, that the public mind will be easily reconciled to the decision of the Court here rendered: for, whether necessary or unnecessary, originally, a state of things has now grown up, in some of the states, which renders all the protection necessary, that the general government can give to this bank. The policy of the decision is obvious, that is, if the Bank is to be sustained; and few will bestow upon its legal correctness, the reflection, that it is necessary to test it by the constitution and laws, under which it is rendered.

Though Justice Johnson dissented, "protective jurisdiction" may be defended on the pragmatic grounds he identified but rejected. It would provide a rationale for extending federal jurisdiction over cases that turn entirely on state law where it is necessary to do so in order to safeguard national interests. Is protective jurisdiction a more persuasive rationale than the reasoning set forth in *Osborn* for extending federal jurisdiction to cases in which federal issues are not litigated? Does the application of this principle turn on whether there is a federal "ingredient" in the case? Can the holding in *ANRC*, be justified under a protective jurisdiction rationale?

The notion of protective jurisdiction has arisen in a variety of contexts since *Osborn*. The Court has neither forthrightly endorsed nor repudiated the theory. The Court's ambivalence is illustrated by its reasoning in *Mesa v. California*, 489 U.S. 121 (1989), a case we examined in Chapter 7 in connection with the statutes on removal of cases from state to federal court. The defendants were postal service employees charged with traffic violations in state court. They unsuccessfully argued that the federal officer removal statute, 28 U.S.C. § 1442, should be read as allowing federal officers to remove even in cases where they assert no federal defense. They argued that such a reading would be constitutional under the protective jurisdiction thesis.

The Court said that eliminating the federal defense requirement would raise "serious doubts," *id.* at 136, as to the constitutionality of § 1442. Addressing the protective jurisdiction rationale, it said:

> We have, in the past, not found the need to adopt a theory of "protective jurisdiction" to support Art. III "arising under" jurisdiction and we do not see any need for doing so here because we do not recognize any federal interests that are not protected by limiting removal to situations in which a federal defense is alleged. In these prosecutions, no state court hostility or interference has even been [alleged]. *Id.* at 137–38.

Earlier in the opinion, however, the Court suggested that "careful pleading, demonstrating the close connection between the state prosecution and the federal officer's performance of his duty, might adequately replace the specific averment of a federal defense." *Id.* at 132. Justice Brennan highlighted this point in his concurrence. *Id.* at 140.

The most extensive discussion of protective jurisdiction in a Supreme Court case is Justice Frankfurter's dissenting opinion in *Textile Workers Union v. Lincoln Mills*, 353 U.S. 448 (1957). The Labor Management Relations Act of 1947 provided that suits for breach of contract between labor unions and employers could be brought in federal court. Lincoln Mills and the Textile Workers Union made an agreement under which the employer agreed to arbitration of disputes. When Lincoln Mills refused to arbitrate, the union sued. The Court held that the statute authorized the federal courts to make a body of federal common law on labor contracts. Justice Frankfurter took the view that the contract was governed by state law and therefore dissented from that holding. He continued:

> Since I do not agree with the Court's conclusion that federal substantive law is to govern in actions under § 301, I am forced to consider [the] constitutionality of a grant of jurisdiction to federal courts over contracts that came into being entirely by virtue of state substantive law, a jurisdiction not based on diversity of citizenship, yet one in which a federal court would, as in diversity cases, act in effect merely as another court of the State in which it sits. The scope of allowable federal judicial power that this grant must satisfy is constitutionally described as "Cases, in Law and Equity, arising under this Constitution, the Laws of the United States, and Treaties made, or which shall be made, under their Authority.' Art. III, § 2. While interpretive decisions are legion under general statutory grants of jurisdiction strikingly similar to this constitutional wording, it is generally recognized that the full constitutional power has not been exhausted by these statutes. Almost without exception, decisions under the general statutory grants have tested jurisdiction in terms of the presence, as an integral part of plaintiff's cause of action, of an issue calling for interpretation or application of federal [law]. The litigation-provoking problem has been the degree to which federal law must be in the forefront of the case and not collateral, peripheral or remote.

> In a few exceptional cases, arising under special jurisdictional grants, the criteria by which the prominence of the federal question is measured against constitutional requirements have been found satisfied under circumstances suggesting a variant theory of the nature of these requirements. The first, and the leading case in the field, is *Osborn v. Bank of United States*.

> There, Chief Justice Marshall sustained federal jurisdiction in a situation—hypothetical in the case before him but presented by the companion case of *Bank of United States v. Planters' Bank*—involving suit by a federally incorporated bank upon a contract. Despite the assumption that the cause of action and the interpretation of the contract would be governed by state law, the case was found to "arise under the laws of the United States"

because the propriety and scope of a federally granted authority to enter into contracts and to litigate might well be challenged. This reasoning was subsequently applied to sustain jurisdiction in actions against federally chartered railroad corporations. *Pacific Railroad Removal Cases (Union Pac. Ry. Co. v. Myers)*, 115 U.S. 1. The traditional interpretation of this series of cases is that federal jurisdiction under the "arising" clause of the Constitution, though limited to cases involving potential federal questions, has such flexibility that Congress may confer it whenever there exists in the background some federal proposition that might be challenged, despite the remoteness of the likelihood of actual presentation of such a federal question. The views expressed in *Osborn* and the *Pacific Railroad Removal Cases* were severely restricted in construing general grants of jurisdiction. But the Court later sustained this jurisdictional section of the Bankruptcy Act of 1898: The United States district courts shall have jurisdiction of all controversies at law and in equity, as distinguished from proceedings in bankruptcy, between trustees as such and adverse claimants concerning the property acquired or claimed by the trustees, in the same manner and to the same extent only as though bankruptcy proceedings had not been instituted and such controversies had been between the bankrupts and such adverse claimants. Under this provision the trustee could pursue in a federal court a private cause of action arising under and wholly governed by state law. *Schumacher v. Beeler*, 293 U.S. 367; *Williams v. Austrian*, 331 U.S. 642. To be sure, the cases did not discuss the basis of jurisdiction. It has been suggested that they merely represent an extension of the approach of the *Osborn* case; the trustee's right to sue might be challenged on obviously federal grounds—absence of bankruptcy or irregularity of the trustee's appointment or of the bankruptcy proceedings. So viewed, this type of litigation implicates a potential federal [question].

With this background, many theories have been proposed to sustain the constitutional validity of § 301. [One theory is called "protective jurisdiction."] The suggestion is that in any case for which Congress has the constitutional power to prescribe federal rules of decision and thus confer "true" federal question jurisdiction, it may, without so doing, enact a jurisdictional statute, which will provide a federal forum for the application of state statute and decisional law. Analysis of the "protective jurisdiction" theory might also be attempted in terms of the language of Article III—construing "laws" to include jurisdictional statutes where Congress could have legislated substantively in a field. This is but another way of saying that because Congress could have legislated substantively and thereby could give rise to litigation under a statute of the United

States, it can provide a federal forum for state-created rights although it chose not to adopt state law as federal law or to originate federal rights. Surely the truly technical restrictions of Article III are not met or respected by a beguiling phrase that the greater power here must necessarily include the lesser. In the compromise of federal and state interests leading to distribution of jealously guarded judicial power in a federal system, it is obvious that very different considerations apply to cases involving questions of federal law and those turning solely on state law. It may be that the ambiguity of the phrase "arising under the laws of the United States' leaves room for more than traditional theory could accommodate. But, under the theory of "protective jurisdiction," the "arising under" jurisdiction of the federal courts would be vastly extended. For example, every contract or tort arising out of a contract affecting commerce might be a potential cause of action in the federal courts, even though only state law was involved in the decision of the case. At least in *Osborn* and the bankruptcy cases, a substantive federal law was present somewhere in the background. But this theory rests on the supposition that Congress could enact substantive federal law to govern the particular case. It was not held in those cases, nor is it clear, that federal law could be held to govern the transactions of all persons who subsequently become bankrupt, or of all suits of a Bank of the United States.

"Protective jurisdiction," once the label is discarded, cannot be justified under any view of the allowable scope to be given to Article III. "Protective jurisdiction" is a misused label for the statute we are here considering. That rubric is properly descriptive of safeguarding some of the indisputable, staple business of the federal courts. It is a radiation of an existing jurisdiction. "Protective jurisdiction" cannot generate an independent source for adjudication outside of the Article III sanctions and what Congress has defined. The theory must have as its sole justification a belief in the inadequacy of state tribunals in determining state law. The Constitution reflects such a belief in the specific situation within which the Diversity Clause was confined. The intention to remedy such supposed defects was exhausted in this provision of Article III. That this "protective" theory was not adopted by Chief Justice Marshall at a time when conditions might have presented more substantial justification strongly suggests its lack of constitutional merit. Moreover, Congress in its consideration of § 301 nowhere suggested dissatisfaction with the ability of state courts to administer state law properly. Its concern was to provide access to the federal courts for easier enforcement of state-created rights.

[Justice Frankfurter then considered and rejected a narrower version of protective jurisdiction, under which the doctrine would apply only where Congress has articulated federal policy and enacted legislation in the field.] I believe that we should not extend the precedents of *Osborn* and the *Pacific Railroad Removal Cases* to this case even though there be some elements of analytical similarity. *Osborn*, the foundation for the *Removal Cases*, appears to have been based on premises that [today] are subject to criticism. The basic premise was that every case in which a federal question might arise must be capable of being commenced in the federal courts, and when so commenced it might, because jurisdiction must be judged at the outset, be concluded there despite the fact that the federal question was never raised. Marshall's holding was undoubtedly influenced by his fear that the bank might suffer hostile treatment in the state courts that could not be remedied by an appeal on an isolated federal question. There is nothing in Article III that affirmatively supports the view that original jurisdiction over cases involving federal questions must extend to every case in which there is the potentiality of appellate jurisdiction. We also have become familiar with removal procedures that could be adapted to alleviate any remaining fears by providing for removal to a federal court whenever a federal question was raised. In view of these developments, we would not be justified in perpetuating a principle that permits assertion of original federal jurisdiction on the remote possibility of presentation of a federal [question].

Analysis of the bankruptcy power also reveals a superficial analogy to § 301. The trustee enforces a cause of action acquired under state law by the bankrupt. Federal law merely provides for the appointment of the trustee, vests the cause of action in him, and confers jurisdiction on the federal courts. Section 301 similarly takes the rights and liabilities which under state law are vested distributively in the individual members of a union and vests them in the union for purposes of actions in federal courts, wherein the unions are authorized to sue and be sued as an entity. While the authority of the trustee depends on the existence of a bankrupt and on the propriety of the proceedings leading to the trustee's appointment, both of which depend on federal law, there are similar federal propositions that may be essential to an action under § 301. Thus, the validity of the contract may in any case be challenged on the ground that the labor organization negotiating it was not the representative of the employees concerned, a question that has been held to be federal, or on the ground that subsequent change in the representative status of the union has affected the continued validity of the [agreement]. Consequently, were the bankruptcy cases to be viewed as dependent solely on the background existence of federal questions, there would be little analytical basis for distinguishing actions under § 301. But the bankruptcy decisions may be justified by the scope of the bankruptcy power, which may be deemed to sweep within its scope interests analytically outside the "federal question" category, but sufficiently related to the main purpose of bankruptcy to call for comprehensive [treatment].

If there is in the phrase "arising under the laws of the United States" leeway for expansion of our concepts of jurisdiction, the history of Article III suggests that the area is not great and that it will require the presence of some substantial federal interest, one of greater weight and dignity than questionable doubt concerning the effectiveness of state procedure. The bankruptcy cases might possibly be viewed as such an expansion. But even so, not merely convenient judicial administration but the whole purpose of the congressional legislative program—conservation and equitable distribution of the bankrupt's estate in carrying out the constitutional power over bankruptcy—required the availability of federal jurisdiction to avoid expense and delay. Nothing pertaining to § 301 suggests vesting the federal courts with sweeping power under the Commerce Clause comparable to that vested in the federal courts under the bankruptcy power.

NOTES ON PROTECTIVE JURISDICTION

1.   **Federal Common Law and Protective Jurisdiction.** One of Justice Frankfurter's premises is that, in the event Congress decided that some national goal required federal intervention, the appropriate response was for Congress to displace state law with federal law. Is this always an adequate answer to the need for federal jurisdiction? Suppose there are topics on which Congress cannot act, because they are too small to warrant its attention or too controversial to be resolved with dispatch. Federal common law is another alternative. Does the growth of federal common law obviate the need for protective jurisdiction? Are there issues on which the federal interest is not sufficiently compelling to warrant making federal common law, yet the federal interest is strong enough to justify protective jurisdiction?

2.   **Public Liability for Nuclear Incidents.** Consider whether the following jurisdictional provision is constitutional under the principles described in this chapter:

> With respect to any public liability action arising out of or resulting from a nuclear incident, the United States district court in the district where the nuclear incident takes place, or in the case of a nuclear incident taking place outside the United States, the United States District Court for the District of Columbia, shall have

original jurisdiction without regard to the citizenship of any party or the amount in controversy. 42 U.S.C. § 2210(2).

The term "public liability action," as used in § 2210 of this title, means any suit asserting public liability. A public liability action shall be deemed to be an action arising under section 2210 of this title, and the substantive rules of decision in such action shall be derived from the law of the State in which the nuclear incident involved occurs, unless such law is inconsistent with the provisions of such section. 42 U.S.C. § 2014(hh).

3.   Supreme Court Review for the "Adequacy" of State Grounds. *Indiana ex rel. Anderson v. Brand*, Chapter 8, supra, involved Supreme Court review of cases in which federal law protected state-created rights. The specific issue in that case was whether the state had made a contract with the plaintiff, thus giving rise to federal protection under the Contracts Clause of the Constitution. The Court ruled that it would review state court decisions against putative right-holders to assure that the rulings had fair support in state law. Applying this principle to *Anderson*, it determined that the state had made a contract with the plaintiff, despite the state court's ruling to the contrary. Is this a kind of "protective jurisdiction"?

4.   The *Tidewater* Problem. Our focus here has been Congress's power to extend federal question jurisdiction to cases in which no federal question is actually litigated. In *National Mutual Insurance Co. v. Tidewater Transfer Co.*, 337 U.S. 582 (1949), the issue was the scope of Congress's power to extend diversity jurisdiction to cases in which there is no diversity of citizenship. A federal statute—now codified in 28 U.S.C. § 1332 (e)—gave the district courts jurisdiction over suits between citizens of the District of Columbia and citizens of the states. Invoking this jurisdictional provision, a D. C. citizen sued a Maryland citizen, raising only issues of Maryland law. The Court upheld the statute against a challenge that the jurisdictional grant violated Article III, but there was no majority opinion as to the rationale. By 7–2, the Court ruled that the District of Columbia is not a state. Nonetheless, the two dissenters from that holding voted to uphold jurisdiction. Beginning from their premise that the District of Columbia is a state, they reasoned that no Article III problem arises. Of more importance for our purposes, three justices took the position that Congress may, under its Article I powers, authorize the federal courts to adjudicate cases that do not fall within Article III, so long as federal jurisdiction is "limited to controversies of a judicial nature." This, too, was a dissenting position, losing by 6–3. Nonetheless, three plus two makes five votes for upholding the statute, and the upshot of *Tidewater* is that the diversity jurisdiction applies to D.C. citizens.

II. RESTRICTING FEDERAL (AND STATE) JURISDICTION

This Section takes up the following topics:

- Article III, Section 1 provides that "[t]he judicial power shall be vested in one supreme Court, and in such inferior Courts as Congress may from time to time ordain and establish."

To what extent does this provision allow Congress to deny jurisdiction to federal courts once it has created them?

- Article III, Section 2 provides that:

> In all Cases affecting ambassadors, other public Ministers and Consuls, and those in which a State shall be a Party, the supreme Court shall have original Jurisdiction. In all the other Cases before mentioned, the supreme Court shall have appellate Jurisdiction, both as to Law and Fact, with such Exceptions, and under such Regulations as the Congress shall make.

To what extent does this provision allow Congress to deprive the Supreme Court of jurisdiction?

- We have seen in Chapter 7 that Congress may cut off state court jurisdiction in favor of exclusive federal jurisdiction over federal causes of action. To what extent can Congress combine that power with its power over federal jurisdiction, so as to foreclose access to *all* courts?

- In what circumstances may Congress displace judges protected by Article III's tenure and salary guarantees by employing non-Article III federal adjudicators to handle matters that otherwise would go the Article III federal courts?

A. THE LOWER FEDERAL COURTS

SHELDON V. SILL

49 U.S. (8 How.) 441 (1850).

JUSTICE GRIER delivered the opinion of the Court.

The only question which it will be necessary to notice in this case is, whether the Circuit Court had jurisdiction. Sill, the complainant below, a citizen of New York, filed his bill in the Circuit Court of the United States for Michigan, against Sheldon, claiming to recover the amount of a bond and mortgage, which had been assigned to him by Hastings, the President of the Bank of Michigan.

Sheldon, in his answer, among other things, pleaded that "the bond and mortgage in controversy, having been originally given by a citizen of Michigan to another citizen of the same state, and the complainant being assignee of them, the Circuit Court had no jurisdiction."

The eleventh section of the Judiciary Act, which defines the jurisdiction of the Circuit Courts, restrains them from taking "cognizance of any suit to recover the contents of any promissory note or other chose in action, in favor of an assignee, unless a suit might have been prosecuted in such court to recover the contents, if no assignment had been made, except in cases of foreign bills of exchange."

The third article of the Constitution declares that "the judicial power of the United States shall be vested in one Supreme Court, and such inferior courts as the Congress may, from time to time, ordain and establish." The second section of the same article enumerates the cases and controversies of which the judicial power shall have cognizance, and, among others, it specifies "controversies between citizens of different states."

It has been alleged, that this restriction of the Judiciary Act, with regard to assignees of choses in action, is in conflict with this provision of the Constitution, and therefore void.

It must be admitted, that if the Constitution had ordained and established the inferior courts, and distributed to them their respective powers, they could not be restricted or divested by Congress. But as it has made no such distribution, one of two consequences must result—either that each inferior court created by Congress must exercise all the judicial powers not given to the Supreme Court, or that Congress, having the power to establish the courts, must define their respective jurisdictions. The first of these inferences has never been asserted, and could not be defended with any show of reason, and if not, the latter would seem to follow as a necessary consequence. And it would seem to follow, also, that, having a right to prescribe, Congress may withhold from any court of its creation jurisdiction of any of the enumerated controversies. Courts created by statute can have no jurisdiction but such as the statute confers. No one of them can assert a just claim to jurisdiction exclusively conferred on another, or withheld from all.

The Constitution has defined the limits of the judicial power of the United States, but has not prescribed how much of it shall be exercised by the Circuit Court; consequently, the statute which does prescribe the limits of their jurisdiction, cannot be in conflict with the Constitution, unless it confers powers not enumerated therein.

Such has been the doctrine held by this court since its first establishment. To enumerate all the cases in which it has been either directly advanced or tacitly assumed would be tedious and unnecessary.

In the case of *Turner v. Bank of North America*, 4 Dall., 10, it was contended, as in this case, that, as it was a controversy between citizens of different states, the Constitution gave the plaintiff a right to sue in the Circuit Court, notwithstanding he was an assignee within the restriction of the eleventh section of the Judiciary Act. But the court said—"The political truth is, that the disposal of the judicial power (except in a few specified instances) belongs to Congress; and Congress is not bound to enlarge the jurisdiction of the Federal courts to every subject, in every form which the Constitution might warrant." This decision was made in 1799; since that time, the same doctrine has been frequently asserted by this court, as may be seen in *McIntire v. Wood*, 7 Cranch, 506; *Kendall v. United States*, 12 Pet., 616; *Cary v. Curtis*, 3 How., 245.

The only remaining inquiry is, whether the complainant in this case is the assignee of a "chose in action," within the meaning of the [statute]. The complainant in this case is the purchaser and assignee of a sum of money, a debt, a chose in action, not of a tract of land. He seeks to recover by this action a debt assigned to him. He is therefore the "assignee of a chose in action," within the letter and spirit of the act of Congress under consideration, and cannot support this action in the Circuit Court of the United States, where his assignor could not.

The judgment of the Circuit Court must therefore be reversed, for want of jurisdiction.

NOTES ON CONGRESSIONAL POWER OVER LOWER FEDERAL COURT JURISDICTION

1. Does the Power to "Ordain and Establish" Inferior Federal Courts Imply Plenary Power over Their Jurisdiction? Congress's power over the creation of lower federal courts is set forth in the text of Article III. The Court in *Sheldon* seems to reason in a straightforward fashion that the power to create these courts necessarily entails power over their jurisdiction. No later case squarely challenges this expansive account of congressional power, and the prudent lawyer would no doubt presumptively treat Congress's power as absolute. Yet we do not know whether the broad reading of *Sheldon* would withstand modern scrutiny, for the scope of *Sheldon* has rarely been put to the test. Most, if not all, of Congress's limits on federal jurisdiction can be defended without resort to the broad reading of *Sheldon*. As a result, the question of whether Article III contains limits on congressional power remains open to debate.

Sheldon itself can be rationalized on the narrower principle that Congress may make exceptions that are consistent with the *purposes* of Article III. In the general effort at the Convention to accommodate both state and federal interests, the framers of Article III began from the premise that state law cases should ordinarily remain in state courts. The point of diversity jurisdiction was to protect out-of-staters from potentially hostile state courts by carving out a neutral federal forum. Yet some litigants may prefer federal courts for reasons of their own, having nothing to do with the framers' delicate balance between state and federal power. Though A, the holder of a note, and B, its maker, are both residents of Michigan, A may seek to "manufacture" diversity jurisdiction by a fictitious assignment of the note to C, a New Yorker. Congressional action to forbid this tactic would be entirely in keeping with the purpose of Article III. In order to uphold the outcome of *Sheldon*, one need not go so far as to hold that Congress may make whatever exceptions it pleases to the jurisdiction of federal courts, whether or not the exception is compatible with Article III's aims.

There are harder cases than *Sheldon*. Consider the Tax Injunction Act, 28 U.S.C. § 1341, enacted in 1937. This statute provides that "[t]he district courts shall not enjoin, suspend or restrain the assessment, levy or collection of any tax under State law where a plain, speedy and efficient remedy may be had in the courts of such State." The Johnson Act, 28 U.S.C. § 1342, enacted in 1934, imposes a somewhat similar constraint on federal jurisdiction over suits challenging state utility rate orders. Notice the context in which these statutes were enacted: The federal courts, in the era of "economic substantive due process," had often overturned state tax statutes and utility rate rulings on the ground that they deprived railroads and utilities of their property without due process of law. When the Democrats swept into power in the 1932 election, they enacted these statutes. Congress's evident purpose was to see to it that due process challenges to state tax and utility rate regulation would take place in fora that would be less sympathetic to the plaintiffs' constitutional claims, and correspondingly more likely to rule in favor of the state. See Paul M. Bator, *Congressional Power Over the Jurisdiction of the Federal Courts*, 27 VILL. L. REV. 1030, 1037 (1982). The Supreme Court seems never to have questioned the constitutionality of either the Tax Injunction Act or the Johnson Act. Should it have done so?

Keep in mind that economic substantive due process was one of several doctrines under which the Court, usually by a narrow majority, invalidated New Deal legislation in the 1930s. The Court eventually abandoned strict scrutiny of economic and social legislation, see, e.g., *West Coast Hotel Co. v. Parrish*, 300 U.S. 379 (1937), and the whole theory of economic due process rapidly lost favor in the federal courts. See KATHLEEN M. SULLIVAN & NOAH FELDMAN, CONSTITUTIONAL LAW 481–88 (18th ed. 2013). Does this episode help explain why the constitutionality of the Tax Injunction Act and the Johnson Act never became a hot issue?

2. **"External" Constraints on Congress's Power.** It is useful to distinguish between two kinds of limits on congressional power over federal district court jurisdiction: (a) those that are "internal" to Article III, which are discussed in note 1, and (b) those that are "external" to Article III. Everyone would agree in principle that other constitutional provisions, such as free speech, due process, equal protection, and so on, may constrain Congress's power over federal jurisdiction, just as those provisions constrain other exercises of legislative power. The hard question here is whether a plausible case can be made that a jurisdictional statute actually offends any other clause of the Constitution. The proper analysis of this issue depends on exactly what the jurisdictional statute does. There are four possibilities: (i) it directs federal cases to state courts instead of federal courts; (ii) it divides up the issues in a federal case among two or more federal courts; (iii) it forbids *any* court from deciding the case; (iv) it authorizes a non-Article III federal

tribunal to hear the case, at least in the first instance. This note deals with (i). Note 3 takes up (ii), section B discusses (iii), and section D addresses (iv).

With regard to (i), a whole array of jurisdictional doctrines would have to be jettisoned in order to support the broad proposition that anyone with a federal issue has a constitutional right to litigate it in federal court. These include, among others, the "face of the complaint" rule for federal question jurisdiction, the *Younger* (and most of the other) abstention doctrines, limits on habeas corpus, and the application of principles of collateral estoppel in section 1983 litigation. The issue has been raised mainly in a narrower set of cases, as an objection to proposals (rarely enacted) to forbid federal jurisdiction over some class of cases based on the constitutional rights raised. For example, bills have been introduced that would bar federal jurisdiction over school prayer or abortion cases. Some commentators have suggested that, in the event such a bill were enacted, it should be struck down on the ground that Congress may not selectively target certain constitutional claims in this way. But their argument seems unlikely to prevail. The problem with bringing an "external" challenge to a statute that merely channels cases to state rather than federal courts is that there is no authority whatsoever for the proposition that foreclosing access to lower federal courts, in favor of the state courts, would offend due process, equal protection, free speech, or any other constitutional directive. The Court has repeatedly asserted that no one has a constitutional right to litigate federal claims in a federal forum. See, e.g., *Allen v. McCurry*, Chapter 5, supra. See also *Palmore v. United States*, 411 U.S. 389 (1973) (upholding the local criminal jurisdiction of non-Article III federal tribunals in Washington, D. C.). Is the addition of a "targeting" motive a sufficient ground to invalidate jurisdictional rules that, absent that motive, would be valid? Does the (presumed) validity of the Tax Injunction Act and the Johnson Act stand in the way of the notion that targeting is inappropriate?

3. **Congress's Power to Divide the Federal Issues in a Case Among Two or More Courts.** The best example of this problem is the litigation over World War II price control legislation. The Emergency Price Control Act of 1942 was a massive regulatory effort, affecting the prices of goods and services throughout the nation. An agency called the "Price Administrator" set prices under the statute's norms. Congress sought to enhance the efficacy of enforcement of the legislation by limiting (without wholly foreclosing) opportunities to raise objections to the administration of the scheme. One (and *only* one) Article III court, called the "Emergency Court of Appeals," would have jurisdiction to enjoin enforcement of the Price Administrator's decrees, subject to Supreme Court review. *Lockerty v. Phillips*, 319 U.S. 182 (1943), upheld this limit on the jurisdiction of other federal courts, relying on the broad reading of congressional power that dates back to *Sheldon*.

The *Lockerty* plaintiffs raised another objection to the enforcement scheme. No court, not even the Emergency Court of Appeals, was given jurisdiction to issue interim relief. Ordinarily a litigant can obtain a preliminary injunction against enforcement of the rule he challenges, provided he can show (a) that he will likely prevail on the ultimate merits, and (b) that he will suffer irreparable harm absent relief during the pendency of the litigation. The Supreme Court avoided answering the question whether the unavailability of interim relief to persons challenging decisions of the Price Administrator would ever violate the Due Process Clause. How should that issue be resolved?

Violations of the Price Administrator's regulations were enforced by criminal prosecutions. Yet the statute channeled challenges to the regulations to the Emergency Court of Appeals, thereby prohibiting enforcement courts from considering constitutional objections to the regulations. (The validity of the statute itself could be challenged in the enforcement court.) In *Yakus v. United States*, 321 U.S. 414 (1944), the Court upheld the constitutionality of this arrangement against attacks based on due process, the right to jury trial, and separation of powers.

Could Congress, on the authority of *Yakus,* routinely forbid all constitutional challenges to a criminal statute in enforcement courts by setting up a special court analogous to the Emergency Court of Appeals, and giving it exclusive jurisdiction over challenges not only to regulations but to the statute itself? Though the Court has never renounced *Yakus*, it has pointed out that "the decision in that case was motivated by the exigencies of wartime, dealt with the propriety of regulations rather than the legitimacy of an adjudicative procedure, and, most significantly, turned on the fact that adequate judicial review of the validity of the regulation was available in another forum. Under different circumstances, the propriety of using an administrative ruling in such a way remains open to question." *United States v. Mendoza-Lopez*, 481 U.S. 828, 838 n. 15 (1987).

Though the Court in *Mendoza-Lopez* commented on *Yakus*, *Mendoza-Lopez* actually dealt with a somewhat different problem. That case raised the question of whether an earlier administrative ruling could be used as the basis for a criminal prosecution without allowing the defendant an opportunity to challenge the validity of the earlier ruling. An alien had, at an earlier time, been deported pursuant to an administrative hearing. He then returned to the United States and was prosecuted for the crime of re-entry following deportation. In the criminal prosecution for re-entry, he sought to challenge the validity of the earlier deportation on the ground that the deportation hearing violated his due process rights. Yet he had not sought judicial review of the deportation order. The government reasoned that, under *Yakus*, the administrative determination could not be challenged in this criminal prosecution. The Court declined to rule on the merits of this argument. It instead distinguished *Yakus*, holding that "at a minimum, the result of an administrative proceeding may not be used as a conclusive element of a criminal offense where the judicial review that legitimated such a practice in the first instance has effectively been denied." In *Yakus* no one disputed the availability of the Emergency Court of Appeals for challenges to the regulations. Here, the Court ruled, Mendoza-Lopez had not been given a fair opportunity to seek judicial review of the earlier deportation order. Accordingly, due process required that he be allowed to challenge it in the prosecution for re-entry.

In his dissent, Chief Justice Rehnquist, joined by Justices White and O'Connor, argued that there was no problem with the deportation proceeding. Justice Scalia dissented on a broader ground, asserting that basing a criminal prosecution on an unreviewable administrative decision would not violate due process.

B. FORECLOSING ACCESS TO ALL COURTS

A key premise of all of the foregoing cases is that *some* court is available to the litigant, whether it be the state courts or, in the price control statute, the federal "Emergency Court of Appeals." Now consider the case in which Congress deprives *all* courts, state and federal, of jurisdiction over a given issue. The practical effect of such a rule, were the Court to uphold it, would be to take away the litigant's substantive rights, as she would have no forum in which to vindicate them. The question, then, is quite different from the ones addressed above. It is not the scope of Congress's power to allocate jurisdiction among courts. It is, rather, Congress's power to define substantive rights. In principle, the answer is straightforward: Congress may deprive all courts of jurisdiction over a given issue so long as the right asserted by the plaintiff is not a constitutional right. See *Battaglia v. General Motors Corp.*, 169 F.2d 254 (2d Cir. 1948). Just as Congress may extinguish non-constitutional rights by repealing the statutes or displacing the common law doctrines that created them, it may (if, for whatever reason, it prefers an indirect route) accomplish the same end by depriving all courts of jurisdiction to hear the claims. By the same token, Congress may not override *constitutional* rights by enacting statutes that abolish them. Nor may it accomplish that goal indirectly by enacting jurisdictional statutes that deprive all courts of jurisdiction to rule on constitutional claims. For example, Congress could not evade the First Amendment by enacting a "jurisdictional" statute that deprived courts of jurisdiction to hear free speech defenses to criminal prosecutions (though *Yakus* suggests that Congress may in certain circumstances require that the free speech defense be raised in one forum while enforcement of the criminal law takes place in another).

So long as the issue arises in connection with the use of the Constitution as a defensive shield against criminal prosecution or civil liability, the application of this principle is uncontroversial. But the relations between constitutional rights and "offensive" constitutional remedies are complex. *Battaglia* does not stand for the proposition that Congress may not restrict access to the courts for offensive constitutional remedies. A more precise way of putting the *Battaglia* principle is that "limits on Congress's power to preclude judicial remedies for constitutional rights violations also function as limits on Congress's power to eliminate the judicial jurisdiction that would be necessary for courts to award constitutionally necessary remedies." Richard H. Fallon, Jr., *Jurisdiction-Stripping Reconsidered*, 96 VA. L. REV. 1043, 1104 (2010). As for just how far Congress may go in curbing access to the courts, the Supreme Court has provided few definitive answers. But it is clear that the circumstances in which the litigant seeks a remedy may make a difference. For a careful discussion of various contexts in which this question arises, see Fallon, *Jurisdiction-Stripping Reconsidered, supra*, at 1104–15. Here are three variations on the theme:

Boumediene. The case for access to the courts is especially strong when persons are imprisoned by the executive without any prior judicial process. This was the issue in *Boumediene v. Bush*, 553 U.S. 723 (2008) (discussed at greater length in Chapter 9). In the Military Commissions Act of 2006 (MCA) and the Detainee Treatment Act of 2005 (DTA) Congress had foreclosed access to habeas corpus for persons captured in Afghanistan and held by the military at Guantanamo Bay. Detainees successfully argued that they were entitled to access to the courts to challenge the legality of their confinement. *Boumediene* held that Congress had provided no adequate substitute for habeas, and that the jurisdiction-stripping provisions of the Military Commissions Act violated the Suspension Clause of Article I of the Constitution.

Boumediene demonstrated, first, that it is possible for the Congress to speak with sufficient clarity to accomplish, if constitutional, an elimination of federal jurisdiction over constitutional claims—at least in the context of habeas corpus review. Justice Kennedy's opinion for the majority concluded:

> We acknowledge [the] litigation history that prompted Congress to pass the MCA. If the ongoing dialogue between and among the branches of Government is to be respected, we cannot ignore that the MCA was a direct response to *Hamdan*'s holding that the DTA's jurisdiction-stripping provision had no application to pending cases. The Court of Appeals was correct to take note of the legislative history when construing the statute [and] we agree with its conclusion that the MCA deprives the federal courts of jurisdiction to entertain the habeas corpus actions now before us.

Still, the majority held that "Article I, sec. 9, cl. 2 of the Constitution has full effect at Guantanamo Bay." So, "if the privilege of habeas corpus is to be denied to the detainees now before us, Congress must act in accordance with the requirements of the Suspension Clause." In passing the DTA, "Congress did not intend to create a process that differs from traditional habeas corpus in name only." It "intended to create a more limited procedure."

> For the writ of habeas corpus, or its substitute, to function as an effective and proper remedy in this context, the court that conducts the habeas proceeding must have the means to correct

errors that occurred during the [detainee] proceedings. This includes some authority to assess the sufficiency of the Government's evidence against the detainee. It also must have the authority to admit and consider relevant exculpatory evidence that was not introduced during the earlier proceeding. Federal habeas petitioners long have had the means to supplement the record on review, even in the postconviction habeas setting. [Here] that opportunity is constitutionally required. [We] hold that when the judicial power to issue habeas corpus properly is invoked the judicial officer must have adequate authority to make a determination in light of the relevant law and facts and to formulate and issue appropriate orders for relief, including, if necessary, an order directing the prisoner's release.

In rejecting the government's claim that the Detainee Treatment Act provided an adequate substitute for habeas corpus, the Supreme Court also noted that the limited review available in Court of Appeals under the DTA was constitutionally problematic. The "DTA review proceeding falls short of being a constitutionally adequate substitute, for the detainee still would have no opportunity to present evidence discovered after the Combat Status Review Tribunals proceedings concluded." The "role of an Article III court in the exercise of its habeas corpus function cannot be circumscribed in this manner." Accordingly, "there is no jurisdictional bar to the District Court entertaining petitioners' (habeas corpus) claims."

Do you think that *Boumediene*'s rejection of the jurisdiction-stripping provisions of the Military Commissions Act, as contrary to the demands of the Suspension Clause, has applicability beyond the singular context of federal habeas corpus? Is it potentially inconsistent with the traditional understanding that Congress is not required to create inferior federal courts? Does it present enhanced separation of powers constraints upon the ability of Congress to limit the jurisdiction of the federal courts? Is the Suspension Clause a restriction upon Congress's jurisdiction-controlling authority notably distinct from other limitations on legislative power like the due process clause or the First Amendment?

St. Cyr. Suppose the issue is not whether a person can be confined indefinitely by the military without judicial process, but whether the executive branch of government can detain or deport an alien without judicial process. In *Immigration and Naturalization Service v. St. Cyr*, 533 U.S. 289 (2001) (see Chapter 9) the Court avoided ruling on the validity of such a regime by narrowly construing the governing statute, the Antiterrorism and Effective Death Penalty Act of 1996. In interpreting the AEDPA the *St. Cyr* majority invoked "the strong presumption in favor of judicial review of administrative" action, and required that Congress employ especially plain language in order to overcome that presumption.

What if the statute were amended to unambiguously foreclose access to habeas, thereby forcing the Court to confront the constitutional issue? Does it follow from *Boumediene* that aliens are constitutionally entitled to similar access to the courts in connection with deportation? Just how the constitutional issue would be resolved if the Court faced it squarely remains uncertain, for immigration is a special context. See Richard H. Fallon, Jr., *Applying the Suspension Clause to Immigration Cases*, 98 COLUM. L. REV. 1068, 1069–70 (1998). Fallon notes that "for over a century the Supreme Court has held that Congress enjoys 'plenary' power to establish substantive immigration policies" and that "[a]s a result, under current doctrine aliens have few if any judicially recognized substantive constitutional rights in matters involving immigration and deportation."

Webster. A third example of this theme, from a context that does not involve physical liberty, is *Webster v. Doe*, 486 U.S. 592 (1988). A former CIA employee sought to sue the Director of the agency, charging that his dismissal violated his constitutional rights. The government argued that Congress had precluded judicial review, but the Court read the statute as applying only to *non-constitutional* claims, leaving the courts open to hear complaints of constitutional violations. The text of the statute made no such distinction.

It is not necessarily appropriate to lump *St. Cyr* and *Webster v. Doe* together as manifestations of a single problem, for the rights of the detainee and those of the former employee may differ. The *content* of the constitutional rights people hold in government employment may not be as extensive as the rights they hold in physical liberty. A holding that judicial process must be available for challenges to detention or deportation does not necessarily imply that it must be available for employment issues. See Richard H. Fallon, Jr., *Some Confusions About Due Process, Judicial Review, and Constitutional Remedies*, 93 COLUM. L. REV. 309, 366–72 (1993).

C. CONGRESS'S POWER OVER THE SUPREME COURT'S JURISDICTION

Whatever the framers' differences on other matters related to the federal courts, they agreed that there should be "one supreme Court," and so provided in Article III, Section 1. There are many good reasons why even a (moderate) champion of states' rights would favor the creation of such a court. A viable body of federal law could hardly be created and maintained if adjudication of federal issues were left up to the state courts with no ultimate federal tribunal to protect national interests and resolve conflicts among lower courts. Absent such a court, disputes among states could not otherwise be resolved by adjudication. No means would be available for protecting out-of-staters against potential state court prejudice.

Yet the framers also seem to have believed that Congress should have some measure of control over the Supreme Court's jurisdiction. The first paragraph of Article III, Section 2, lists the permissible scope of federal jurisdiction, including cases arising under federal law and cases involving citizens from different states, among others. The second paragraph provides:

> In all Cases affecting Ambassadors, other public Ministers and Consuls, and those in which a State shall be a Party, the supreme Court shall have original Jurisdiction. In all the other Cases before mentioned, the supreme Court shall have appellate jurisdiction, both as to Law and Fact, with such Exceptions, and under such Regulations as the Congress shall make.

How far may Congress go in limiting Supreme Court jurisdiction under this "Exceptions and Regulations" power? A great deal of academic ink has been spilled over this question. Some read the passage literally and assert that Congress's power is limitless. Some maintain that the "Exceptions and Regulations" power relates only to review of issues of fact. Others point out that the comma after "Exceptions" tends to suggest that the rest of the sentence after "Fact" bears on both "Law" and "Fact." Henry Hart favored a more holistic approach to the Constitution. He argued that one of the main goals of the document was to set up a system of checks and balances among the branches of government. A literal reading of "Exceptions and Regulations" would effectively nullify the checking function of the judicial branch, as Congress could take away jurisdiction from lower federal courts under the *Sheldon* reading of Article I, and deprive the Supreme Court of jurisdiction under this clause. Hart maintained that Congress could not go so far as to impede the "essential role" of the Supreme Court. See Henry M. Hart, Jr., *The Power of Congress to Limit the Jurisdiction of Federal Courts: An Exercise in Dialectic*, 66 HARV. L. REV. 1362, 1364–65 (1953). Other scholars have debated the scope of the Court's "essential role." See, e.g., Ratner, *Congressional Power Over the Appellate Jurisdiction of the Supreme Court*, 109 U.PA.L.REV. 157, 201–02 (1960) ("maintaining the uniformity and supremacy of federal law").

Professor Herbert Wechsler took a rather different view of the scope of congressional power over the Supreme Court's jurisdiction:

> There is, to be sure, a school of thought that argues that "exceptions" has a narrow meaning, not including cases that have constitutional dimension; or that the supremacy clause or the due process clause of the Fifth Amendment would be violated by an alteration of the jurisdiction motivated by hostility to the decisions of the Court. I see no basis for this view and think it antithetical to the plan of the Constitution for the courts—which was quite simply that the Congress would decide from time to time how far the federal judicial institution should be used

within the limits of the federal judicial power; or, stated differently, how far judicial jurisdiction should be left to the state courts, bound as they are by the Constitution as the "supreme Law of the Land . . . any Thing in the Constitution or Laws of any State to the Contrary notwithstanding." Federal courts, including the Supreme Court, do not pass on constitutional questions because there is a special function vested in them to enforce the Constitution or police the other agencies of government. They do so rather for the reason that they must decide a litigated issue that is otherwise within their jurisdiction and in doing so must give effect to the supreme law of the land. That, at least, is what *Marbury v. Madison* was all about.

Herbert Wechsler, *The Courts and the Constitution*, 65 COLUM. L. REV. 1001, 1005–06 (1965).

Can the Supreme Court serve as an effective check on abuses by the other branches of government under Professor Wechsler's view of the Exceptions Clause? Does the argument he advances help to legitimate the Court's constitutional decisions, by stressing that the Court's jurisdiction is subject to control by the majoritarian branches of government?

————————

Scholarly commentary on the Exceptions Clause is highly theoretical in nature. It has mainly been generated in response to bills introduced by legislators who disapprove of Supreme Court decisions on controversial and highly visible topics like school prayer or abortion. Since no statute of this kind has ever been enacted, none of the academic theories regarding the Exceptions and Regulations Clause has ever been tested in a modern case (though they frequently receive attention in the hypothetical cases that appear on law school exams).

The point here is not that Congress has always authorized Supreme Court jurisdiction over the whole range of cases within the federal judicial power. On the contrary, the first Congress, in the Judiciary Act of 1789, restricted Supreme Court review of state judgments raising federal questions. It provided for review only when the state judgment went *against* the party asserting a federal right, but not when the state court ruled in his favor. The Court never hinted at any constitutional problem with this limit on the scope of its jurisdiction, and Congress did not repeal it until 1914. Is this limit compatible with Professor Hart's "essential role" principle?

The most direct and explicit congressional limit on Supreme Court jurisdiction validated by the high court is the subject of the following case.

EX PARTE MCCARDLE

74 U.S. (7 Wall.) 506 (1868).

[Congress] on the 5th February, 1867, by "an act to amend an act to establish the judicial courts of the United States, approved September 24, 1789," provided that the several courts of the United States, and the several justices and judges of such courts, within their respective jurisdiction, in addition to the authority already conferred by law, should have power to grant writs of habeas corpus in all cases where any person may be restrained of his or her liberty in violation of the Constitution, or of any treaty or law of the United States. And that, from the final decision of any judge, justice, or court inferior to the Circuit Court, appeal might be taken to the Circuit Court of the United States for the district in which the cause was heard, and from the judgment of the said Circuit Court to the Supreme Court of the United States.

This statute being in force, one McCardle, alleging unlawful restraint by military force, preferred a petition in the court below, for the writ of habeas corpus. The writ was issued, and a return was made by the military commander, admitting the restraint, but denying that it was unlawful.

It appeared that the petitioner was not in the military service of the United States, but was held in custody by military authority for trial before a military commission, upon charges founded upon the publication of articles alleged to be incendiary and libellous, in a newspaper of which he was editor. The custody was alleged to be under the authority of certain acts of Congress.

Upon the hearing, the petitioner was remanded to the military custody; but, upon his prayer, an appeal was allowed him to this [court]. The appeal was taken under the above-mentioned act of February 5, 1867.

A motion to dismiss this appeal was made at the last term, and, after argument, was [denied]. Subsequently, on the 2d, 3d, 4th, and 9th of March, the case was argued very thoroughly and ably upon the merits, and was taken under advisement. While it was thus held, and before conference in regard to the decision proper to be made, an act was passed by Congress, returned with objections by the President, and, on the 27th March, repassed by the constitutional majority, the second section of which was as follows:

> And be it further enacted, That so much of the act approved February 5, 1867, entitled "An act to amend an act to establish the judicial courts of the United States, approved September 24, 1789," as authorized an appeal from the judgment of the Circuit Court to the Supreme Court of the United States, or the exercise of any such jurisdiction by said Supreme Court, on appeals

which have been, or may hereafter be taken, be, and the same is hereby repealed.

The attention of the court was directed to this statute at the last term, but counsel having expressed a desire to be heard in argument upon its effect, and the Chief Justice being detained from his place here, by his duties in the Court of Impeachment, the cause was continued under advisement. Argument was now heard upon the effect of the repealing [act].

THE CHIEF JUSTICE delivered the opinion of the Court.

The first question necessarily is that of jurisdiction; for, if the act of March, 1868, takes away the jurisdiction defined by the act of February, 1867, it is useless, if not improper, to enter into any discussion of other questions. It is quite true, as was argued by the counsel for the petitioner, that the appellate jurisdiction of this court is not derived from acts of Congress. It is, strictly speaking, conferred by the Constitution. But it is conferred "with such exceptions and under such regulations as Congress shall make." It is unnecessary to consider whether, if Congress had made no exceptions and no regulations, this court might not have exercised general appellate jurisdiction under rules prescribed by itself. For among the earliest acts of the first Congress, at its first session, was the act of September 24th, 1789, to establish the judicial courts of the United States. That act provided for the organization of this court, and prescribed regulations for the exercise of its jurisdiction.

The source of that jurisdiction, and the limitations of it by the Constitution and by statute, have been on several occasions subjects of consideration here. In the case of *Durousseau v. United States* particularly, the whole matter was carefully examined, and the court held, that while "the appellate powers of this court are not given by the judicial act, but are given by the Constitution," they are, nevertheless, "limited and regulated by that act, and by such other acts as have been passed on the subject." The court said, further, that the judicial act was an exercise of the power given by the Constitution to Congress "of making exceptions to the appellate jurisdiction of the Supreme Court." "They have described affirmatively," said the court, "its jurisdiction, and this affirmative description has been understood to imply a negation of the exercise of such appellate power as is not comprehended within it." The principle that the affirmation of appellate jurisdiction implies the negation of all such jurisdiction not affirmed having been thus established, it was an almost necessary consequence that acts of Congress, providing for the exercise of jurisdiction, should come to be spoken of as acts granting jurisdiction, and not as acts making exceptions to the constitutional grant of it.

The exception to appellate jurisdiction in the case before us, however, is not an inference from the affirmation of other appellate jurisdiction. It is made in terms. The provision of the act of 1867, affirming the appellate jurisdiction of this court in cases of habeas corpus is expressly repealed. It is hardly possible to imagine a plainer instance of positive exception.

We are not at liberty to inquire into the motives of the legislature. We can only examine into its power under the Constitution; and the power to make exceptions to the appellate jurisdiction of this court is given by express words.

What, then, is the effect of the repealing act upon the case before us? We cannot doubt as to this. Without jurisdiction the court cannot proceed at all in any cause. Jurisdiction is power to declare the law, and when it ceases to exist, the only function remaining to the court is that of announcing the fact and dismissing the cause. And this is not less clear upon authority than upon [principle].

It is quite clear, therefore, that this court cannot proceed to pronounce judgment in this case, for it has no longer jurisdiction of the appeal; and judicial duty is not less fitly performed by declining ungranted jurisdiction than in exercising firmly that which the Constitution and the laws confer.

Counsel seem to have supposed, if effect be given to the repealing act in question, that the whole appellate power of the court, in cases of habeas corpus, is denied. But this is an error. The act of 1868 does not except from that jurisdiction any cases but appeals from Circuit Courts under the act of 1867. It does not affect the jurisdiction which was previously exercised.

The appeal of the petitioner in this case must be dismissed for want of jurisdiction.

NOTE ON MCCARDLE AND THE 1868 STATUTE

Does *McCardle* identify any limits on Congress's power over the Supreme Court's jurisdiction? Does it follow that Congress's power is unqualified? The argument for a negative answer to that question begins with the next-to-last sentence of the opinion. Apart from the 1867 statute upon which McCardle relied for access to the Supreme Court via habeas, there existed an older avenue, under Section 14 of the Judiciary Act of 1789, by which persons held in federal custody could petition the Supreme Court for habeas corpus. Under the terms of the March 27, 1868 statute (reprinted in the statement of facts preceding the Chief Justice's opinion), Congress repealed only the jurisdiction it had granted in the 1867 statute.

The Court's statement that the 1868 statute "does not affect the jurisdiction which was previously exercised" provides grounds for an argument that Supreme Court jurisdiction over habeas remains intact, so long as the litigant proceeds under Section 14 of the Judiciary Act of 1789. A year later, the Court addressed the issue in another case involving military detention.

The words of the repealing section are, "that so much of the act approved February 5th, 1867, as authorizes an appeal from the judgment of the Circuit Court to the Supreme Court of the United States, or the exercise of any such jurisdiction by said Supreme Court on appeals which have been, or may be hereafter taken, be, and the same is hereby repealed."

These words are not of doubtful interpretation. They repeal only so much of the act of 1867 as authorized appeals, or the exercise of appellate jurisdiction by this court. They affected only appeals and appellate jurisdiction authorized by that act. They do not purport to touch the appellate jurisdiction conferred by the Constitution, or to except from it any cases not excepted by the act of 1789. They reach no act except the act of 1867.

It has been suggested, however, that the act of 1789, so far as it provided for the issuing of writs of habeas corpus by this court, was already repealed by the act of 1867. We have already observed that there are no repealing words in the act of 1867. If it repealed the act of 1789, it did so by implication, and any implication which would give to it this effect upon the act of 1789, would give it the same effect upon the acts of 1833 and 1842. If one was repealed, all were repealed.

Repeals by implication are not favored. They are seldom admitted except on the ground of repugnancy; and never, we think, when the former act can stand together with the new act. It is true that exercise of appellate jurisdiction, under the act of 1789, was less convenient than under the act of 1867, but the provision of a new and more convenient mode of its exercise does not necessarily take away the old; and that this effect was not intended is indicated by the fact that the authority conferred by the new act is expressly declared to be "in addition" to the authority conferred by the former acts. Addition is not substitution.

The appeal given by the act of 1867 extended, indeed, to cases within the former acts; and the act, by its grant of additional authority, so enlarged the jurisdiction by habeas corpus that it seems, as was observed in the McCardle case, "impossible to widen" it. But this effect does not take from the act its character of an additional grant of jurisdiction, and make it operate as a repeal of jurisdiction theretofore allowed.

Our conclusion is, that none of the acts prior to 1867, authorizing this court to exercise appellate jurisdiction by means of the writ of habeas corpus, were repealed by the act of that year, and that the repealing section of the act of 1868 is limited in terms, and must be limited in effect to the appellate jurisdiction authorized by the act of 1867.

We could come to no other conclusion without holding that the whole appellate jurisdiction of this court, in cases of habeas corpus, conferred by the Constitution, recognized by law, and exercised from the foundation of the government hitherto, has been taken away, without the expression of such intent, and by mere implication, through the operation of the acts of 1867 and 1868.

The suggestion made at the bar, that the provision of the act of 1789, relating to the jurisdiction of this court by habeas corpus, if repealed by the effect of the act of 1867, was revived by the repeal of the repealing act, has not escaped our consideration. We are inclined to think that such would be the effect of the act of 1868, but having come to the conclusion that the act of 1789 was not repealed by the act of 1867, it is not necessary to express an opinion on that point.

The argument having been confined, by direction of the court, to the question of jurisdiction, this opinion is limited to that question. The jurisdiction of the court to issue the writ prayed for is affirmed.

NOTE ON THE POST-CIVIL WAR CASES

Does *Yerger* repudiate the "broad congressional power" reading of *McCardle*? Does it, at least, help to drive home the point that the "broad congressional power" principle reflected in *McCardle* is, strictly speaking, dicta? Does it furnish support for Professor Hart's view that the language of the "Exceptions and Regulations" Clause should be read in the context of the general structural principle of separation of powers? If the answer to any of these questions is "yes", why did the Court not produce a less deferential opinion in *McCardle*? Note that Chief Justice Chase wrote both opinions.

In one post-Civil War case, the Court struck down a statute that attempted to limit the Supreme Court's jurisdiction. *Ex parte Klein*, 80 U.S. (13 Wall.) 128 (1871). But the opinion is murky and no assessment of it can be ventured with confidence. Congress had attempted to prescribe the effect of a presidential pardon, and had tried to achieve this aim by cutting off the Supreme Court's jurisdiction to examine the issue. The substantive holding of the case appears to be that the statute "infring[ed] the constitutional power of the Executive." *Id.* at 147. Viewed in this way, *Klein* would be the Supreme Court analogue of the "external constraints" principle concerning Congress's power over lower federal court jurisdiction. That is, constitutional provisions external to Article III limit Congress's power in connection with jurisdictional statutes not only for lower federal courts, but also for the Supreme Court.

D. LEGISLATIVE COURTS

Article III, Section 1, provides:

The judicial power of the United States, shall be vested in one supreme Court, and in such inferior Courts as the Congress may from time to time ordain and establish. The Judges, both of the supreme and inferior Courts, shall hold their Offices during good Behaviour, and shall, at stated Times, receive for their Services a Compensation, which shall not be diminished during their Continuance in Office.

The point of the "tenure" and "salary" guarantees in the second sentence is to assure the judges' independence from the other branches, shielding them somewhat from executive and legislative pressure to rule one way rather than another. And so it is that federal judges can only be dismissed for serious misconduct; nor can Congress cut their pay, though it is not obliged to follow through on promises to increase their salaries, see *United States v. Will*, 449 U.S. 200 (1980). Article III seems to envision that *all* of the federal judicial power will be held by judges who are protected in this way.

Nonetheless, Congress has for a long time created other tribunals that adjudicate questions about the content of federal (and, occasionally, state) law. The practice began in the early Republic. From the beginning, it was broadly understood that military justice was a separate field. Other, less easily distinguished, exceptions soon appeared. Congress authorized non-Article III courts to administer justice in federally controlled territories in the years before they became states. The Court approved of these "legislative courts" in *American Insurance Co. v. Canter*, 26 U.S (1 Pet.) 511 (1828). In the late nineteenth century, and increasingly in the twentieth, Congress found that it could not effectively regulate a wide array of matters by legislation alone. It created administrative agencies and authorized them to interpret and enforce federal norms by adjudicating disputes involving private entities. Neither the "administrative law judges" that hear these disputes nor the commissioners that oversee their work are protected by the tenure and salary provisions of Article III.

There may be good practical reasons, chiefly based on the need for flexibility, for avoiding rigid application of the tenure and salary rules to this body of federal adjudicators. At the same time, Article III independence would be threatened if there were no constraints on Congress's power to allocate the adjudication of federal law issues to non-Article III tribunals that it controls. The broad issue facing the Supreme Court in this area is how to resolve the conflict between these competing values.

NORTHERN PIPELINE CONSTRUCTION CO. V. MARATHON PIPE LINE CO.

458 U.S. 50 (1982).

[The issue here was the validity of a provision of the Bankruptcy Act of 1978 that permitted non-Article III bankruptcy judges to adjudicate state law issues that arise in the course of federal bankruptcy proceedings, such as a breach of contract suit brought by the bankrupt against someone else.]

JUSTICE BRENNAN announced the judgment of the Court and delivered an opinion, in which JUSTICE MARSHALL, JUSTICE BLACKMUN, and JUSTICE STEVENS joined.

[Basic] to the constitutional structure established by the Framers was their recognition that "[t]he accumulation of all powers, legislative, executive, and judiciary, in the same hands, whether of one, a few, or many, and whether hereditary, self-appointed, or elective, may justly be pronounced the very definition of tyranny." The Federalist No. 47 (J. Madison). To ensure against such tyranny, the Framers provided that the Federal Government would consist of three distinct Branches, each to exercise one of the governmental powers recognized by the Framers as inherently distinct. "The Framers regarded the checks and balances that they had built into the tripartite Federal Government as a self-executing safeguard against the encroachment or aggrandizement of one branch at the expense of the other." *Buckley v. Valeo*, 424 U.S. 1, 122 (1976) (per curiam).

The Federal Judiciary was therefore designed by the Framers to stand independent of the Executive and Legislature—to maintain the checks and balances of the constitutional structure, and also to guarantee that the process of adjudication itself remained [impartial].

As an inseparable element of the constitutional system of checks and balances, and as a guarantee of judicial impartiality, Art. III both defines the power and protects the independence of the Judicial [Branch]. The inexorable command of this provision is clear and definite: The judicial power of the United States must be exercised by courts having the attributes prescribed in Art. [III]. The "good Behaviour" Clause guarantees that Art. III judges shall enjoy life tenure, subject only to removal by impeachment. The Compensation Clause guarantees Art. III judges a fixed and irreducible compensation for their services. Both of these provisions were incorporated into the Constitution to ensure the independence of the Judiciary from the control of the Executive and Legislative Branches of government.[10] In sum, our Constitution unambiguously enunciates a fundamental principle—that the "judicial Power of the United States" must be reposed in an independent Judiciary. It commands that the independence of the Judiciary be jealously guarded, and it provides clear institutional protections for that independence.

It is undisputed that the bankruptcy judges whose offices were created by the Bankruptcy Act of 1978 do not enjoy the protections constitutionally afforded to Art. III judges. [Appellants] suggest two grounds for upholding the Act's conferral of broad adjudicative powers

---

[10] These provisions serve other institutional values as well. The independence from political forces that they guarantee helps to promote public confidence in judicial determinations. See The Federalist No. 78 (A. Hamilton). The security that they provide to members of the Judicial Branch helps to attract well-qualified persons to the federal bench. Ibid. The guarantee of life tenure insulates the individual judge from improper influences not only by other branches but by colleagues as well, and thus promotes judicial individualism.

upon judges unprotected by Art. III. First, it is urged that "pursuant to its enumerated Article I powers, Congress may establish legislative courts that have jurisdiction to decide cases to which the Article III judicial power of the United States extends." Referring to our precedents upholding the validity of "legislative courts," appellants suggest that "the plenary grants of power in Article I permit Congress to establish non-Article III tribunals in specialized areas having particularized needs and warranting distinctive treatment," such as the area of bankruptcy law. Second, appellants contend that even if the Constitution does require that this bankruptcy-related action be adjudicated in an Art. III court, the Act in fact satisfies that requirement. "Bankruptcy jurisdiction was vested in the district court" of the judicial district in which the bankruptcy court is located, "and the exercise of that jurisdiction by the adjunct bankruptcy court was made subject to appeal as of right to an Article III court." Analogizing the role of the bankruptcy court to that of a special master, appellants urge us to conclude that this "adjunct" system established by Congress satisfies the requirements of Art. III. We consider these arguments in turn.

Congress did not constitute the bankruptcy courts as legislative courts. Appellants contend, however, that the bankruptcy courts could have been so constituted, and that as a result the "adjunct" system in fact chosen by Congress does not impermissibly encroach upon the judicial power. In advancing this argument, appellants rely upon cases in which we have identified certain matters that "congress may or may not bring within the cognizance of [Art. III courts], as it may deem proper." *Murray's Lessee v. Hoboken Land & Improvement Co.*, 18 How. 272, 284 (1856). But when properly understood, these precedents represent no broad departure from the constitutional command that the judicial power of the United States must be vested in Art. III courts.[15] Rather, they reduce to three narrow situations not subject to that command, each recognizing a circumstance in which the grant of power to the Legislative and Executive Branches was historically and constitutionally so exceptional that the congressional assertion of a power to create legislative courts was consistent with, rather than threatening to, the constitutional mandate of separation of powers. These precedents simply acknowledge that the literal command of Art. III, assigning the judicial power of the United States to courts insulated from Legislative or Executive interference, must be interpreted in light of the historical

---

[15] Justice White's dissent finds particular significance in the fact that Congress could have assigned all bankruptcy matters to the state courts. But, of course, virtually all matters that might be heard in Art. III courts could also be left by Congress to state courts. This fact is simply irrelevant to the question before us. Congress has no control over state-court judges; accordingly the principle of separation of powers is not threatened by leaving the adjudication of federal disputes to such judges. The Framers chose to leave to Congress the precise role to be played by the lower federal courts in the administration of justice. But the Framers did not leave it to Congress to define the character of those courts—they were to be independent of the political branches and presided over by judges with guaranteed salary and life tenure.

context in which the Constitution was written, and of the structural imperatives of the Constitution as a whole.

Appellants first rely upon a series of cases in which this Court has *exception 1* upheld the creation by Congress of non-Art. III "territorial courts." This exception from the general prescription of Art. III dates from the earliest days of the Republic, when it was perceived that the Framers intended that as to certain geographical areas, in which no State operated as sovereign, Congress was to exercise the general powers of government. For example, in *American Ins. Co. v. Canter*, the Court observed that Art. IV bestowed upon Congress alone a complete power of government over territories not within the States that constituted the United States. [The] Court followed the same reasoning when it reviewed Congress' creation of non-Art. III courts in the District of [Columbia].

Appellants next advert to a second class of cases—those in which this Court has sustained the exercise by Congress and the Executive of the *2* power to establish and administer courts-martial. The situation in these cases strongly resembles the situation with respect to territorial courts: It too involves a constitutional grant of power that has been historically understood as giving the political Branches of Government extraordinary control over the precise subject matter at issue. Article I, § 8, cls. 13, 14, confer upon Congress the power "[t]o provide and maintain a Navy," and "[t]o make Rules for the Government and Regulation of the land and naval Forces." The Fifth Amendment, which requires a presentment or indictment of a grand jury before a person may be held to answer for a capital or otherwise infamous crime, contains an express exception for "cases arising in the land or naval forces." And Art. II, § 2, cl. 1, provides that "The President shall be Commander in Chief of the Army and Navy of the United States, and of the Militia of the several States, when called into the actual Service of the United States."

Finally, appellants rely on a third group of cases, in which this Court has upheld the constitutionality of legislative courts and administrative *3* agencies created by Congress to adjudicate cases involving "public rights." The "public rights" doctrine was first set forth in *Murray's Lessee v. Hoboken Land & Improvement Co.*:

> "[W]e do not consider congress can either withdraw from judicial cognizance any matter which, from its nature, is the subject of a suit at the common law, or in equity, or admiralty; nor, on the other hand, can it bring under the judicial power a matter which, from its nature, is not a subject for judicial determination. At the same time there are matters, *involving public rights,* which may be presented in such form that the judicial power is capable of acting on them, and which are susceptible of judicial determination, but which congress may or may not bring within the cognizance of the courts of the United States, as it may deem proper." (emphasis added.)

This doctrine may be explained in part by reference to the traditional principle of sovereign immunity, which recognizes that the Government may attach conditions to its consent to be sued. But the public-rights doctrine also draws upon the principle of separation of powers, and a historical understanding that certain prerogatives were reserved to the political Branches of Government. The doctrine extends only to matters arising "between the Government and persons subject to its authority in connection with the performance of the constitutional functions of the executive or legislative departments," *Crowell v. Benson*, 285 U.S. 22, 50 (1932), and only to matters that historically could have been determined exclusively by those departments. The understanding of these cases is that the Framers expected that Congress would be free to commit such matters completely to nonjudicial executive determination, and that as a result there can be no constitutional objection to Congress' employing the less drastic expedient of committing their determination to a legislative court or an administrative agency.

The public-rights doctrine is grounded in a historically recognized distinction between matters that could be conclusively determined by the Executive and Legislative Branches and matters that are "inherently . . . judicial." For example, the Court in *Murray's Lessee* looked to the law of England and the States at the time the Constitution was adopted, in order to determine whether the issue presented was customarily cognizable in the courts. Concluding that the matter had not traditionally been one for judicial determination, the Court perceived no bar to Congress' establishment of summary procedures, outside of Art. III courts, to collect a debt due to the Government from one of its customs agents.[20] On the same premise, the Court in *Ex parte Bakelite Corp.* held that the Court of Customs Appeals had been properly constituted by Congress as a legislative court:

> The full province of the court under the act creating it is that of determining matters arising between the Government and others in the executive administration and application of the customs laws. . . . The appeals include nothing which inherently or necessarily requires judicial determination, but only matters the determination of *which may be, and at times has been, committed exclusively to executive officers.* (emphasis added.)

The distinction between public rights and private rights has not been definitively explained in our precedents. Nor is it necessary to do so in the present case, for it suffices to observe that a matter of public rights must at a minimum arise "between the government and others." In contrast, "the liability of one individual to another under the law as defined," is a

---

[20] Doubtless it could be argued that the need for independent judicial determination is greatest in cases arising between the Government and an individual. But the rationale for the public-rights line of cases lies not in political theory, but rather in Congress' and this Court's understanding of what power was reserved to the Judiciary by the Constitution as a matter of historical fact.

matter of private rights. Our precedents clearly establish that only controversies in the former category may be removed from Art. III courts and delegated to legislative courts or administrative agencies for their determination.[24] Private-rights disputes, on the other hand, lie at the core of the historically recognized judicial power.

In sum, this Court has identified three situations in which Art. III does not bar the creation of legislative courts. In each of these situations, the Court has recognized certain exceptional powers bestowed upon Congress by the Constitution or by historical consensus. Only in the face of such an exceptional grant of power has the Court declined to hold the authority of Congress subject to the general prescriptions of Art. III.

We discern no such exceptional grant of power applicable in the cases before us. The courts created by the Bankruptcy Act of 1978 do not lie exclusively outside the States of the Federal Union, like those in the District of Columbia and the Territories. Nor do the bankruptcy courts bear any resemblance to courts-martial, which are founded upon the Constitution's grant of plenary authority over the Nation's military forces to the Legislative and Executive Branches. Finally, the substantive legal rights at issue in the present action cannot be deemed "public rights." Appellants argue that a discharge in bankruptcy is indeed a "public right," similar to such congressionally created benefits as "radio station licenses, pilot licenses, or certificates for common carriers" granted by administrative agencies. But the restructuring of debtor-creditor relations, which is at the core of the federal bankruptcy power, must be distinguished from the adjudication of state-created private rights, such as the right to recover contract damages that is at issue in this case. The former may well be a "public right," but the latter obviously is not. Appellant Northern's right to recover contract damages to augment its estate is "one of private right, that is, of the liability of one individual to another under the law as defined." *Crowell v. Benson.*

Recognizing that the present cases may not fall within the scope of any of our prior cases permitting the establishment of legislative courts, appellants argue that we should recognize an additional situation beyond the command of Art. III, sufficiently broad to sustain the Act. Appellants contend that Congress' constitutional authority to establish "uniform Laws on the subject of Bankruptcies throughout the United States," Art. I, § 8, cl. 4, carries with it an inherent power to establish legislative courts capable of adjudicating "bankruptcy-related" [controversies].

The flaw in appellants' analysis is that it provides no limiting principle. It thus threatens to supplant completely our system of adjudication in independent Art. III tribunals and replace it with a system of "specialized" legislative courts. True, appellants argue that under their analysis Congress could create legislative courts pursuant

---

[24] Of course, the public-rights doctrine does not extend to any criminal matters, although the Government is a proper party.

only to some "specific" Art. I power, and "only when there is a particularized need for distinctive treatment." They therefore assert that their analysis would not permit Congress to replace the independent Art. III Judiciary through a "wholesale assignment of federal judicial business to legislative courts." But these "limitations" are wholly illusory. For example, Art. I, § 8, empowers Congress to enact laws, inter alia, regulating interstate commerce and punishing certain crimes. Art. I, § 8, cls. 3, 6. On appellants' reasoning Congress could provide for the adjudication of these and "related" matters by judges and courts within Congress' exclusive control. The potential for encroachment upon powers reserved to the Judicial Branch through the device of "specialized" legislative courts is dramatically evidenced in the jurisdiction granted to the courts created by the Act before us. The broad range of questions that can be brought into a bankruptcy court because they are "related to cases under title 11," 28 U.S.C. § 1471(b), is the clearest proof that even when Congress acts through a "specialized" court, and pursuant to only one of its many Art. I powers, appellants' analysis fails to provide any real protection against the erosion of Art. III jurisdiction by the unilateral action of the political Branches. In short, to accept appellants' reasoning, would require that we replace the principles delineated in our precedents, rooted in history and the Constitution, with a rule of broad legislative discretion that could effectively eviscerate the constitutional guarantee of an independent Judicial Branch of the Federal [Government].

In sum, Art. III bars Congress from establishing legislative courts to exercise jurisdiction over all matters related to those arising under the bankruptcy laws. The establishment of such courts does not fall within any of the historically recognized situations in which the general principle of independent adjudication commanded by Art. III does not apply. Nor can we discern any persuasive reason, in logic, history, or the Constitution, why the bankruptcy courts here established lie beyond the reach of Art. III.

IV

Appellants advance a second argument for upholding the constitutionality of the Act: that "viewed within the entire judicial framework set up by Congress," the bankruptcy court is merely an "adjunct" to the district court, and that the delegation of certain adjudicative functions to the bankruptcy court is accordingly consistent with the principle that the judicial power of the United States must be vested in Art. III courts. As support for their argument, appellants rely principally upon *Crowell v. Benson* and *United States v. Raddatz*, 447 U.S. 667 (1980), cases in which we approved the use of administrative agencies and magistrates as adjuncts to Art. III courts. The question to which we turn, therefore, is whether the Act has retained "the essential attributes of the judicial power," *Crowell v. Benson*, supra, 285 U.S., at 51, in Art. III tribunals.

The use of administrative agencies as adjuncts was first upheld in *Crowell v. Benson*, supra. The congressional scheme challenged in *Crowell* empowered an administrative agency, the United States Employees' Compensation Commission, to make initial factual determinations pursuant to a federal statute requiring employers to compensate their employees for work-related injuries occurring upon the navigable waters of the United States. The Court began its analysis by noting that the federal statute administered by the Compensation Commission provided for compensation of injured employees "irrespective of fault," and that the statute also prescribed a fixed and mandatory schedule of compensation. The agency was thus left with the limited role of determining "questions of fact as to the circumstances, nature, extent and consequences of the injuries sustained by the employee for which compensation is to be made." The agency did not possess the power to enforce any of its compensation orders: On the contrary, every compensation order was appealable to the appropriate federal district court, which had the sole power to enforce it or set it aside, depending upon whether the court determined it to be "in accordance with law" and supported by evidence in the record. The Court found that in view of these limitations upon the Compensation Commission's functions and powers, its determinations were "closely analogous to findings of the amount of damages that are made, according to familiar practice, by commissioners or assessors." Observing that "there is no requirement that, in order to maintain the essential attributes of the judicial power, all determinations of fact in constitutional courts shall be made by judges," the Court held that Art. III imposed no bar to the scheme enacted by Congress.

Crowell involved the adjudication of congressionally created rights. But this Court has sustained the use of adjunct fact finders even in the adjudication of constitutional rights—so long as those adjuncts were subject to sufficient control by an Art. III district court. In *United States v. Raddatz*, supra, the Court upheld [the] Federal Magistrates Act, which permitted district court judges to refer certain pretrial motions, including suppression motions based on alleged violations of constitutional rights, to a magistrate for initial determination. The Court observed that the magistrate's proposed findings and recommendations were subject to de novo review by the district court, which was free to rehear the evidence or to call for additional evidence. Moreover, it was noted that the magistrate considered motions only upon reference from the district court, and that the magistrates were appointed, and subject to removal, by the district court. In short, the ultimate decision making authority respecting all pretrial motions clearly remained with the district court. Under these circumstances, the Court held that the Act did not violate the constraints of Art. III.

Together these cases establish two principles that aid us in determining the extent to which Congress may constitutionally vest traditionally judicial functions in non-Art. III officers. First, it is clear that when Congress creates a substantive federal right, it possesses substantial discretion to prescribe the manner in which that right may be adjudicated—including the assignment to an adjunct of some functions historically performed by judges. Thus *Crowell* recognized that Art. III does not require "all determinations of fact [to] be made by judges;" with respect to congressionally created rights, some factual determinations may be made by a specialized fact finding tribunal designed by Congress, without constitutional bar. Second, the functions of the adjunct must be limited in such a way that "the essential attributes" of judicial power are retained in the Art. III court. Thus in upholding the adjunct scheme challenged in *Crowell*, the Court emphasized that "the reservation of full authority to the court to deal with matters of law provides for the appropriate exercise of the judicial function in this class of cases." And in refusing to invalidate the Magistrates Act at issue in *Raddatz,* the Court stressed that under the congressional scheme "[t]he authority—and the responsibility—to make an informed, final determination . . . remains with the judge;" the statute's delegation of power was therefore permissible, since "the ultimate decision is made by the district court."

These two principles assist us in evaluating the "adjunct" scheme presented in these cases. Appellants assume that Congress' power to create "adjuncts" to consider all cases related to those arising under Title 11 is as great as it was in the circumstances of *Crowell*. But while *Crowell* certainly endorsed the proposition that Congress possesses broad discretion to assign factfinding functions to an adjunct created to aid in the adjudication of congressionally created statutory rights, *Crowell* does not support the further proposition necessary to appellants' argument— that Congress possesses the same degree of discretion in assigning traditionally judicial power to adjuncts engaged in the adjudication of rights not created by Congress. Indeed, the validity of this proposition was expressly denied in *Crowell*, when the Court rejected "the untenable assumption that the constitutional courts may be deprived in all cases of the determination of facts upon evidence even though a *constitutional* right may be involved." 285 U.S., at 60–61. (emphasis added), and stated that "the essential independence of the exercise of the judicial power of the United States in the enforcement of *constitutional* rights requires that the Federal court should determine . . . an issue [of agency jurisdiction] upon its own record and the facts elicited before it." (emphasis added.)

Appellants' proposition was also implicitly rejected in *Raddatz*. Congress' assignment of adjunct functions under the Federal Magistrates Act was substantially narrower than under the statute challenged in *Crowell*. Yet the Court's scrutiny of the adjunct scheme in *Raddatz*— which played a role in the adjudication of constitutional rights—was far stricter than it had been in *Crowell*. Critical to the Court's decision to uphold the Magistrates Act was the fact that the ultimate decision was made by the district court.

Although *Crowell* and *Raddatz* do not explicitly distinguish between rights created by Congress and other rights, such a distinction underlies in part *Crowell*'s and *Raddatz*' recognition of a critical difference between rights created by federal statute and rights recognized by the Constitution. Moreover, such a distinction seems to us to be necessary in light of the delicate accommodations required by the principle of separation of powers reflected in Art. III. The constitutional system of checks and balances is designed to guard against "encroachment or aggrandizement" by Congress at the expense of the other branches of government. *Buckley v. Valeo*, 424 U.S., at 122. But when Congress creates a statutory right, it clearly has the discretion, in defining that right, to create presumptions, or assign burdens of proof, or prescribe remedies; it may also provide that persons seeking to vindicate that right must do so before particularized tribunals created to perform the specialized adjudicative tasks related to that right. Such provisions do, in a sense, affect the exercise of judicial power, but they are also incidental to Congress' power to define the right that it has created. No comparable justification exists, however, when the right being adjudicated is not of congressional creation. In such a situation, substantial inroads into functions that have traditionally been performed by the Judiciary cannot be characterized merely as incidental extensions of Congress' power to define rights that it has created. Rather, such inroads suggest unwarranted encroachments upon the judicial power of the United States, which our Constitution reserves for Art. III courts.

We hold that the Bankruptcy Act of 1978 carries the possibility of such an unwarranted encroachment. Many of the rights subject to adjudication by the Act's bankruptcy courts, like the rights implicated in *Raddatz*, are not of Congress' creation. Indeed, the cases before us, which center upon appellant Northern's claim for damages for breach of contract and misrepresentation, involve a right created by state law, a right independent of and antecedent to the reorganization petition that conferred jurisdiction upon the Bankruptcy Court. Accordingly, Congress' authority to control the manner in which that right is adjudicated, through assignment of historically judicial functions to a non-Art. III "adjunct," plainly must be deemed at a minimum. Yet it is equally plain that Congress has vested the "adjunct" bankruptcy judges with powers over Northern's state-created right that far exceed the powers that it has vested in administrative agencies that adjudicate only rights of Congress' own creation.

Unlike the administrative scheme that we reviewed in *Crowell*, the Act vests all "essential attributes" of the judicial power of the United States in the "adjunct" bankruptcy court. First, the agency in *Crowell* made only specialized, narrowly confined factual determinations regarding a particularized area of law. In contrast, the subject-matter jurisdiction of the bankruptcy courts encompasses not only traditional matters of bankruptcy, but also "all civil proceedings arising under title

11 or arising in or *related to* cases under title 11." Second, while the agency in *Crowell* engaged in statutorily channeled factfinding functions, the bankruptcy courts exercise "*all* of the jurisdiction" conferred by the Act on the district courts (emphasis added). Third, the agency in *Crowell* possessed only a limited power to issue compensation orders pursuant to specialized procedures, and its orders could be enforced only by order of the district court. By contrast, the bankruptcy courts exercise all ordinary powers of district courts, including the power to preside over jury trials, the power to issue declaratory judgments, the power to issue writs of habeas corpus, and the power to issue any order, process, or judgment appropriate for the enforcement of the provisions of Title 11. Fourth, while orders issued by the agency in *Crowell* were to be set aside if "not supported by the evidence," the judgments of the bankruptcy courts are apparently subject to review only under the more deferential "clearly erroneous" standard. Finally, the agency in *Crowell* was required by law to seek enforcement of its compensation orders in the district court. In contrast, the bankruptcy courts issue final judgments, which are binding and enforceable even in the absence of an appeal. In short, the "adjunct" bankruptcy courts created by the Act exercise jurisdiction behind the facade of a grant to the district courts, and are exercising powers far greater than those lodged in the adjuncts approved in either *Crowell* or *Raddatz*.

We conclude that 28 U.S.C. § 1471 (1976 ed., Supp. IV), as added by § 241(a) of the Bankruptcy Act of 1978, has impermissibly removed most, if not all, of "the essential attributes of the judicial power" from the Art. III district court, and has vested those attributes in a non-Art. III adjunct. Such a grant of jurisdiction cannot be sustained as an exercise of Congress' power to create adjuncts to Art. III courts.

V

[We] must now determine whether our holding should be applied retroactively to the effective date of the Act. Our decision in *Chevron Oil Co. v. Huson*, 404 U.S. 97 (1971), sets forth the three considerations recognized by our precedents as properly bearing upon the issue of retroactivity. They are, first, whether the holding in question "decid[ed] an issue of first impression whose resolution was not clearly foreshadowed" by earlier cases; second, "whether retrospective operation will further or retard [the] operation" of the holding in question; and third, whether retroactive application "could produce substantial inequitable results" in individual cases, ibid. In the present cases, all of these considerations militate against the retroactive application of our holding today. It is plain that Congress' broad grant of judicial power to non-Art. III bankruptcy judges presents an unprecedented question of interpretation of Art. III. It is equally plain that retroactive application would not further the operation of our holding, and would surely visit substantial injustice and hardship upon those litigants who relied upon the Act's vesting of jurisdiction in the bankruptcy courts. We hold, therefore, that our decision today shall apply only prospectively.

The judgment of the District Court is affirmed. However, we stay our judgment until October 4, 1982. This limited stay will afford Congress an opportunity to reconstitute the bankruptcy courts or to adopt other valid means of adjudication, without impairing the interim administration of the bankruptcy laws.

JUSTICE REHNQUIST, with whom JUSTICE O'CONNOR joins, concurring in the judgment.

[From] the record before us, the lawsuit in which Marathon was named defendant seeks damages for breach of contract, misrepresentation, and other counts which are the stuff of the traditional actions at common law tried by the courts at Westminster in 1789. There is apparently no federal rule of decision provided for any of the issues in the lawsuit; the claims of Northern arise entirely under state law. No method of adjudication is hinted, other than the traditional common-law mode of judge and jury. The lawsuit is before the Bankruptcy Court only because the plaintiff has previously filed a petition for reorganization in that court.

The cases dealing with the authority of Congress to create courts other than by use of its power under Art. III do not admit of easy [synthesis]. I need not decide whether these cases in fact support a general proposition and three tidy exceptions, as the plurality believes, or whether instead they are but landmarks on a judicial "darkling plain" where ignorant armies have clashed by night, as Justice White apparently believes them to be. None of the cases has gone so far as to sanction the type of adjudication to which Marathon will be subjected against its will under the provisions of the 1978 Act. To whatever extent different powers granted under that Act might be sustained under the "public rights" [doctrine] I am satisfied that the adjudication of Northern's lawsuit cannot be so sustained.

I am likewise of the opinion that the extent of review by Art. III courts provided on appeal from a decision of the bankruptcy court in a case such as Northern's does not save the grant of authority to the latter under the rule espoused in *Crowell v. Benson*. All matters of fact and law in whatever domains of the law to which the parties' dispute may lead are to be resolved by the bankruptcy court in the first instance, with only traditional appellate review by Art. III courts apparently contemplated. Acting in this manner the bankruptcy court is not an "adjunct" of either the district court or the court of appeals.

I would, therefore, hold so much of the Bankruptcy Act of 1978 as enables a Bankruptcy Court to entertain and decide Northern's lawsuit over Marathon's objection to be violative of Art. III of the United States Constitution. Because I agree with the plurality that this grant of authority is not readily severable from the remaining grant of authority to bankruptcy courts under § 1471, I concur in the judgment. I also agree with the discussion in Part V of the plurality opinion respecting retroactivity and the staying of the judgment of this Court.

[CHIEF JUSTICE BURGER'S dissenting opinion and JUSTICE WHITE'S dissenting opinion are omitted.]

NOTE ON CFTC v. SCHOR

Four years after *Northern Pipeline*, the Court took another stab at the problem of non-Article III federal adjudicators. A federal statute, the Commodity Exchange Act (CEA), regulates the commodities market. Under the CEA, an agency called the Commodity Futures Trading Commission (CFTC), a non-Article III body, adjudicates disputes between traders and commodities brokers. When a trader claims that a broker has violated federal law, the trader may either file suit in federal court or bring a claim for reparations before the CFTC. The CEA provides that, in the event a disappointed trader takes his claim to the CFTC, the agency may also adjudicate state law counterclaims brought by the broker, such as a claim that the trader owes the broker the amount of a debit balance in the trader's account.

Schor, a trader, sued his broker before the CFTC for violation of the CEA. The broker counterclaimed against Schor, claiming state law breach of contract. Schor lost and then sued in federal court, claiming that the CFTC's jurisdiction over state law contract claims violated Article III.

In *Commodity Futures Trading Commission v. Schor,* 478 U.S. 833 (1986), in an opinion written by Justice O'Connor, joined by Justice Rehnquist and the *Northern Pipeline* dissenters, the Court upheld this scheme. (Justice Brennan, joined by Justice Marshall, dissented, in an opinion that echoed his plurality opinion in *Northern Pipeline*.) Writing for the Court, Justice O'Connor said that the litigant's interest in an impartial decision maker was not strong in this case, because Schor had voluntarily taken his case to the CFTC, though he could have chosen federal court instead. As for the Article III separation of powers concern, the Court said:

> To the extent that this structural principle is implicated in a given case, the parties cannot by consent cure the constitutional difficulty for the same reason that the parties by consent cannot confer on federal courts subject-matter jurisdiction beyond the limitations imposed by Article III, § 2. When these Article III limitations are at issue, notions of consent and waiver cannot be dispositive because the limitations serve institutional interests that the parties cannot be expected to protect.

> In determining the extent to which a given congressional decision to authorize the adjudication of Article III business in a non-Article III tribunal impermissibly threatens the institutional integrity of the

Judicial Branch, the Court has declined to adopt formalistic and unbending rules. Although such rules might lend a greater degree of coherence to this area of the law, they might also unduly constrict Congress' ability to take needed and innovative action pursuant to its Article I powers. Thus, in reviewing Article III challenges, we have weighed a number of factors, none of which has been deemed determinative, with an eye to the practical effect that the congressional action will have on the constitutionally assigned role of the federal judiciary. Among the factors upon which we have focused are the extent to which the "essential attributes of judicial power" are reserved to Article III courts, and, conversely, the extent to which the non-Article III forum exercises the range of jurisdiction and powers normally vested only in Article III courts, the origins and importance of the right to be adjudicated, and the concerns that drove Congress to depart from the requirements of Article III.

Factors

An examination of the relative allocation of powers between the CFTC and Article III courts in light of the considerations given prominence in our precedents demonstrates that the congressional scheme does not impermissibly intrude on the province of the judiciary. The CFTC's adjudicatory powers depart from the traditional agency model in just one respect: the CFTC's jurisdiction over common law counterclaims. While wholesale importation of concepts of pendent or ancillary jurisdiction into the agency context may create greater constitutional difficulties, we decline to endorse an absolute prohibition on such jurisdiction out of fear of where some hypothetical "slippery slope" may deposit [us].

In the instant cases, [there] is little practical reason to find that this single deviation from the agency model is fatal to the congressional scheme. Aside from its authorization of counterclaim jurisdiction, the CEA leaves far more of the "essential attributes of judicial power" to Article III courts than did that portion of the Bankruptcy Act found unconstitutional in *Northern Pipeline*. The CEA scheme in fact hews closely to the agency model approved by the Court in *Crowell v. Benson*.

The CFTC, like the agency in *Crowell*, deals only with a "particularized area of law," whereas the jurisdiction of the bankruptcy courts found unconstitutional in *Northern Pipeline* extended to broadly "all civil proceedings arising under title 11 or arising in or *related to* cases under title 11." (emphasis added). CFTC orders, like those of the agency in *Crowell*, but unlike those of the bankruptcy courts under the 1978 Act, are enforceable only by order of the district court. CFTC orders are also reviewed under the same "weight of the evidence" standard sustained in *Crowell*, rather than the more deferential standard found lacking in *Northern Pipeline*. The legal rulings of the CFTC, like the legal determinations of the agency in *Crowell*, are subject to de novo review. Finally, the CFTC, unlike the bankruptcy courts under the 1978 Act, does not exercise "all ordinary powers of district courts," and thus may not, for instance, preside over jury trials or issue writs of habeas corpus.

Of course, the nature of the claim has significance in our Article III analysis quite apart from the method prescribed for its adjudication. The counterclaim asserted in this litigation is a "private" right for which state law provides the rule of decision. It is therefore a claim of the kind assumed to be at the "core" of matters normally reserved to Article III courts. Yet this conclusion does not end our inquiry; just as this Court has rejected any attempt to make determinative for Article III purposes the distinction between public rights and private rights, there is no reason inherent in separation of powers principles to accord the state law character of a claim talismanic power in Article III inquiries.

[The] state law character of a claim is significant for purposes of determining the effect that an initial adjudication of those claims by a non-Article III tribunal will have on the separation of powers for the simple reason that private, common law rights were historically the types of matters subject to resolution by Article III courts. The risk that Congress may improperly have encroached on the federal judiciary is obviously magnified when Congress "withdraw[s] from judicial cognizance any matter which, from its nature, is the subject of a suit at the common law, or in equity, or admiralty" and which therefore has traditionally been tried in Article III courts, and allocates the decision of those matters to a non-Article III forum of its own creation. Accordingly, where private, common law rights are at stake, our examination of the congressional attempt to control the manner in which those rights are adjudicated has been searching. In this litigation, however, "[l]ooking beyond form to the substance of what" Congress has done, we are persuaded that the congressional authorization of limited CFTC jurisdiction over a narrow class of common law claims as an incident to the CFTC's primary, and unchallenged, adjudicative function does not create a substantial threat to the separation of powers.

It is clear that Congress has not attempted to "withdraw from judicial cognizance" the determination of Conti's right to the sum represented by the debit balance in Schor's account. Congress gave the CFTC the authority to adjudicate such matters, but the decision to invoke this forum is left entirely to the parties and the power of the federal judiciary to take jurisdiction of these matters is unaffected. In such circumstances, separation of powers concerns are diminished, for it seems self-evident that just as Congress may encourage parties to settle a dispute out of court or resort to arbitration without impermissible incursions on the separation of powers, Congress may make available a quasi-judicial mechanism through which willing parties may, at their option, elect to resolve their differences. This is not to say, of course, that if Congress created a phalanx of non-Article III tribunals equipped to handle the entire business of the Article III courts without any Article III supervision or control and without evidence of valid and specific legislative necessities, the fact that the parties had the election to proceed in their forum of choice would necessarily save the scheme from constitutional attack. But this case obviously bears no resemblance to such a scenario, given the degree of judicial control saved to the federal courts, as well as the congressional purpose behind the jurisdictional delegation, the demonstrated need for the delegation, and the limited nature of the delegation.

When Congress authorized the CFTC to adjudicate counterclaims, its primary focus was on making effective a specific and limited federal regulatory scheme, not on allocating jurisdiction among federal tribunals. Congress intended to create an inexpensive and expeditious alternative forum through which customers could enforce the provisions of the CEA against professional brokers. Its decision to endow the CFTC with jurisdiction over such reparations claims is readily understandable given the perception that the CFTC was relatively immune from political pressures, see H.R. Rep. No. 93–975, pp. 44, 70, and the obvious expertise that the Commission possesses in applying the CEA and its own regulations. This reparations scheme itself is of unquestioned constitutional validity. It was only to ensure the effectiveness of this scheme that Congress authorized the CFTC to assert jurisdiction over common law counterclaims. Indeed, as was explained above, absent the CFTC's exercise of that authority, the purposes of the reparations procedure would have been confounded.

It also bears emphasis that the CFTC's assertion of counterclaim jurisdiction is limited to that which is necessary to make the reparations procedure workable. [The] CFTC adjudication of common law counterclaims is incidental to, and completely dependent upon, adjudication of reparations claims created by federal law, and in actual fact is limited to claims arising out of the same transaction or occurrence as the reparations claim.

In such circumstances, the magnitude of any intrusion on the Judicial Branch can only be termed *de minimis*. Conversely, were we to hold that the Legislative Branch may not permit such limited cognizance of common law counterclaims at the election of the parties, it is clear that we would "defeat the obvious purpose of the legislation to furnish a prompt, continuous, expert and inexpensive method for dealing with a class of questions of fact which are peculiarly suited to examination and determination by an administrative agency specially assigned to that task." *Crowell.* We do not think Article III compels this degree of [prophylaxis].

STERN V. MARSHALL

564 U.S. ___, 131 S.Ct. 2594 (2011).

[When J. Howard Marshall died, his son Pierce and his wife Vickie (Pierce's stepmother) fought over his estate. Meanwhile, Vickie declared bankruptcy. Pierce Marshall filed a claim in Federal Bankruptcy Court against the bankruptcy estate of Vickie Marshall. His claim asserted that Vickie Marshall had . . . accused him of trying to prevent her from obtaining money that his father had wanted her to have; that her accusations violated state defamation law; and that she consequently owed Pierce Marshall damages. Vickie Marshall filed a compulsory counterclaim in which she asserted that Pierce Marshall had unlawfully interfered with her husband's efforts to grant her an *inter vivos* gift and that he consequently owed her damages. The Bankruptcy Court adjudicated the claim and the counterclaim. In doing so, the court followed statutory procedures applicable to "core" bankruptcy proceedings. See 28 U.S.C. § 157(b). And ultimately the Bankruptcy Court entered judgment in favor of Vickie Marshall. The question before us is whether the Bankruptcy Court possessed jurisdiction to adjudicate Vickie Marshall's counterclaim].[1]

CHIEF JUSTICE ROBERTS delivered the opinion of the Court.

With certain exceptions not relevant here, the district courts of the United States have "original and exclusive jurisdiction of all cases under title [11.]" District courts may refer any or all such proceedings to the bankruptcy judges of their district, [which] is how the Bankruptcy Court in this case came to preside over Vickie's bankruptcy proceedings. [Since] Congress enacted the Bankruptcy Amendments and Federal Judgeship Act of 1984 (the 1984 Act), bankruptcy judges for each district have been appointed to 14-year terms by the courts of appeals for the circuits in which their district is [located.]

Bankruptcy judges may hear and enter final judgments in "all core proceedings arising under title [11.]" Vickie's counterclaim against Pierce for tortious interference is a "core proceeding" under the plain text of § 157(b)(2)(C). That provision specifies that core proceedings include "counterclaims by the estate against persons filing claims against the estate." [We] agree with Vickie that § 157(b)(2)(C) permits the bankruptcy court to enter a final judgment on her tortious interference [counterclaim.]

Although [§ 157(b)(2)(C)] permits the Bankruptcy Court to enter final judgment on Vickie's counterclaim, Article III of the Constitution does [not.]

---

[1]   Editors' footnote: This statement is taken from Justice Breyer's dissent. The editors have added a few details for the sake of clarity and have screened out details that are not pertinent here.

In [*Northern Pipeline*], we considered whether bankruptcy judges serving under the Bankruptcy Act of 1978—appointed by the President and confirmed by the Senate, but lacking the tenure and salary guarantees of Article III—could "constitutionally be vested with jurisdiction to decide [a] state-law contract claim" against an entity that was not otherwise part of the bankruptcy proceedings. [The] Court concluded that assignment of such state law claims for resolution by those judges "violates Art. III of the Constitution."

[The] plurality in *Northern Pipeline* recognized that there was a category of cases involving "public rights" that Congress could constitutionally assign to "legislative" courts for resolution. [A] full majority of the Court, while not agreeing on the scope of the exception, concluded that the doctrine did not encompass adjudication of the state law claim at issue in that case. [A] full majority [also] rejected the debtor's argument that the bankruptcy court's exercise of jurisdiction was constitutional because the bankruptcy judge was acting merely as an adjunct of the district court or court of appeals. [After] our decision in *Northern Pipeline*, Congress revised the statutes governing bankruptcy jurisdiction and bankruptcy judges. In the 1984 Act, Congress provided that the judges of the new bankruptcy courts would be appointed by the courts of appeals for the circuits in which their districts are located. [And,] as we have explained, Congress permitted the newly constituted bankruptcy courts to enter final judgments only in "core" [proceedings.]

With respect to such "core" matters, however, the bankruptcy courts under the 1984 Act exercise the same powers they wielded under the Bankruptcy Act of 1978. [As] in *Northern Pipeline*, for example, the newly constituted bankruptcy courts are charged [with] resolving "[a]ll matters of fact and law in whatever domains of the law to which" a counterclaim may lead. [As] in *Northern Pipeline*, the new courts in core proceedings "issue final judgments, which are binding and enforceable even in the absence of an appeal." [And,] as in *Northern Pipeline*, the district courts review the judgments of the bankruptcy courts in core proceedings only under the usual limited appellate [standards.]

Vickie's counterclaim cannot be deemed a matter of "public right" that can be decided outside the Judicial Branch. [Although] our discussion of the public rights exception since [*Northern Pipeline*] has not been entirely consistent, and the exception has been the subject of some debate, this case does not fall within any of the various formulations of the concept that appear in this Court's [opinions.]

[*Murray's Lessee*] involved the Treasury Department's sale of property belonging to a customs collector who had failed to transfer payments to the Federal Government that he had collected on its behalf. [The] plaintiff, who claimed title to the same land through a different transfer, objected that the Treasury Department's [sale] of the property was void, because it was a judicial act that could not be assigned to the

Executive under Article III. [The] challenge in *Murray's Lessee* to the Treasury Department's sale of the collector's land [fell] within the "public rights" category of cases, because it could only be brought if the Federal Government chose to allow it by waiving sovereign immunity. [The] point of *Murray's Lessee* was simply that Congress may set the terms of adjudicating a suit when the suit could not otherwise proceed at [all.]

Subsequent decisions from this Court contrasted cases within the reach of the public rights exception. [*Crowell v. Benson*][6] Shortly after *Northern Pipeline*, the Court rejected the limitation of the public rights exception to actions involving the Government as a party. The Court has continued, however, to limit the exception to cases in which the claim at issue derives from a federal regulatory scheme, or in which resolution of the claim by an expert government agency is deemed essential to a limited regulatory objective within the agency's authority. In other words, it is still the case that what makes a right "public" rather than private is that the right is integrally related to particular federal government [action.]

Our decision in [*Thomas v. Union Carbide*], for example, involved a data-sharing arrangement between companies under a federal statute providing that disputes about compensation between the companies would be decided by binding arbitration. [This] Court held that the scheme did not violate Article III, explaining that "[a]ny right to compensation [results] from [the statute] and does not depend on or replace a right to such compensation under state law."

[*Commodity Futures Trading Comm'n v. Schor*] concerned a statutory scheme that created a procedure for customers injured by a broker's violation of the federal commodities law to seek reparations from the broker before the [CFTC]. A customer filed such a claim to recover a debit balance in his account, while the broker filed a lawsuit in Federal District Court to recover the same amount as lawfully due from the customer. The broker later submitted its claim to the CFTC, but after that agency ruled against the customer, the customer argued that agency jurisdiction over the broker's counterclaim violated Article III. [This] Court disagreed, but only after observing that (1) the claim and the counterclaim concerned a "single dispute"—the same account balance; (2) the CFTC's assertion of authority involved only "a narrow class of common law claims" in a " 'particularized area of law;' " (3) the area of law

---

[6] Although the Court in *Crowell* . . . decide[d] that the facts of the private dispute before it could be determined by a non-Article III tribunal in the first instance, subject to judicial review, the Court did so only after observing that the administrative adjudicator had only limited authority to make specialized, narrowly confined factual determinations regarding a particularized area of law and to issue orders that could be enforced only by action of the District Court. . . . In other words, the agency in *Crowell* functioned as a true "adjunct" of the District Court. . . . [The] dissent . . . recognizes . . . that *Crowell* by its terms addresses the determination of *facts* outside Article III. . . . *Crowell* may well have additional significance in the context of expert administrative agencies that oversee particular substantive federal regimes, but we have no occasion to and do not address those issues today. . . .

in question was governed by "a specific and limited federal regulatory scheme" as to which the agency had "obvious expertise;" (4) the parties had freely elected to resolve their differences before the CFTC; and (5) CFTC orders were "enforceable only by order of the district court." [Most] significantly, given that the customer's reparations claim before the agency and the broker's counterclaim were competing claims to the same amount, the Court repeatedly emphasized that it was "necessary" to allow the agency to exercise jurisdiction over the broker's claim, or else "the reparations procedure would have been confounded."

[In *Granfinanciera v. Nordberg*, 492 U.S. 33 (1989)], we rejected a bankruptcy trustee's argument that a fraudulent conveyance action filed on behalf of a bankruptcy estate against a noncreditor in a bankruptcy proceeding fell within the "public rights" exception. We explained that, "[i]f a statutory right is not closely intertwined with a federal regulatory program Congress has power to enact, and if that right neither belongs to nor exists against the Federal Government, then it must be adjudicated by an Article III court." [We] reasoned that fraudulent conveyance suits were "quintessentially suits at common law that more nearly resemble state law contract claims brought by a bankrupt corporation to augment the bankruptcy estate than they do creditors' hierarchically ordered claims to a pro rata share of the bankruptcy res." [As] a consequence, we concluded that fraudulent conveyance actions were "more accurately characterized as a private rather than a public right as we have used those terms in our Article III decisions."[7]

[Vickie's] counterclaim—like the fraudulent conveyance claim at issue in *Granfinanciera*—does not fall within any of the varied formulations of the public rights exception in this Court's cases. It is not a matter that can be pursued only by grace of the other branches, [or] one that "historically could have been determined exclusively by" those branches. [The] claim is instead one under state common law between two private parties. It does not "depend[ ] on the will of [congress.]" Congress has nothing to do with it.

In addition, Vickie's claimed right to relief does not flow from a federal statutory scheme, as in *Thomas*. [It] is not "completely dependent upon" adjudication of a claim created by federal law, as in *Schor*. [And] in contrast to the objecting party in *Schor*, [Pierce] did not truly consent to resolution of Vickie's claim in the bankruptcy court proceedings. He had nowhere else to go if he wished to recover from Vickie's estate.[8]

---

[7] We noted that we did not mean to "suggest that the restructuring of debtor-creditor relations is in fact a public right." [Our] conclusion was that, "even if one accepts this thesis," Congress could not constitutionally assign resolution of the fraudulent conveyance action to a non-Article III court. [Because] neither party asks us to reconsider the public rights framework for bankruptcy, we follow the same approach here.

[8] Contrary to the claims of the dissent, [Pierce] did not have another forum in which to pursue his claim to recover from Vickie's prebankruptcy assets, rather than take his chances with whatever funds might remain after the Title 11 proceedings. Creditors who possess claims that do not satisfy the requirements for nondischargeability [have] no choice but to file their

[Furthermore,] the asserted authority to decide Vickie's claim is not limited to a "particularized area of the law," as in *Crowell, Thomas,* and *Schor.* [We] deal here not with an agency but with a court, with substantive jurisdiction reaching any area of the *corpus juris.* [This] is not a situation in which Congress devised an "expert and inexpensive method for dealing with a class of questions of fact which are particularly suited to examination and determination by an administrative agency specially assigned to that task." [The] "experts" in the federal system at resolving common law counterclaims such as Vickie's are the Article III courts, and it is with those courts that her claim must stay. [We] recognize that there may be instances in which the distinction between public and private rights—at least as framed by some of our recent cases—fails to provide concrete guidance as to whether, for example, a particular agency can adjudicate legal issues under a substantive regulatory scheme. Given the extent to which this case is so markedly distinct from the agency cases discussing the public rights exception in the context of such a regime, however, we do not in this opinion express any view on how the doctrine might apply in that different [context.]

Vickie [argues] that the Bankruptcy Court's final judgment was constitutional because bankruptcy courts under the 1984 Act are properly deemed "adjuncts" of the district [courts.] We rejected a similar argument in *Northern Pipeline,* [and] our reasoning there holds true today. [The] new bankruptcy courts, like the old, do not "ma[k]e only specialized, narrowly confined factual determinations regarding a particularized area of law" or engage in "statutorily channeled factfinding functions." [Instead,] bankruptcy courts under the 1984 Act resolve "[a]ll matters of fact and law in whatever domains of the law to which" the parties' counterclaims might [lead.]

In addition, whereas the adjunct agency in [*Crowell*] "possessed only a limited power to issue compensation orders [that] could be enforced only by order of the district court," [a] bankruptcy court resolving a counterclaim [has] the power to enter "appropriate orders and judgments"—including final judgments—subject to review only if a party chooses to appeal. [It] is thus no less the case here than it was in *Northern Pipeline* that "[t]he authority—and the responsibility—to make an informed, final determination [remains] with" the bankruptcy judge, not the district court. [Given] that authority, a bankruptcy court can no more be deemed a mere "adjunct" of the district court than a district court can be deemed such an "adjunct" of the court of appeals. We certainly cannot accept the dissent's notion that judges who have the power to enter final, binding orders are the "functional[ ]" equivalent of "law clerks[ ] and the Judiciary's administrative officials." [And] even were we wrong in this regard, that would only confirm that such judges should not be in the business of entering final judgments in the first place.

---

claims in bankruptcy proceedings if they want to pursue the claims at all. That is why [the] notion of "consent" does not apply in bankruptcy proceedings as it might in other contexts.

It does not affect our analysis that, as Vickie notes, bankruptcy judges under the current Act are appointed by the Article III courts, rather than the President. [If]—as we have concluded—the bankruptcy court itself exercises "the essential attributes of judicial power [that] are reserved to Article III courts," [it] does not matter who appointed the bankruptcy judge or authorized the judge to render final judgments in such [proceedings.]

D

Finally, Vickie and her *amici* predict as a practical matter that restrictions on a bankruptcy court's ability to hear and finally resolve compulsory counterclaims will create significant delays and impose additional costs on the bankruptcy [process.] It goes without saying that "the fact that a given law or procedure is efficient, convenient, and useful in facilitating functions of government, standing alone, will not save it if it is contrary to the Constitution." [In] addition, we are not convinced that the practical consequences of such limitations on the authority of bankruptcy courts to enter final judgments are as significant as Vickie and the dissent suggest. [The] framework Congress adopted in the 1984 Act already contemplates that certain state law matters in bankruptcy cases will be resolved by judges other than those of the bankruptcy courts. Section 1334(c)(2), for example, requires that bankruptcy courts abstain from hearing specified non-core, state law claims that "can be timely adjudicated[ ] in a State forum of appropriate jurisdiction." [The] current bankruptcy system also requires the district court to review *de novo* and enter final judgment on any matters that are "related to" the bankruptcy proceedings [and] permits the district court to withdraw from the bankruptcy court any referred case, proceeding, or part thereof.

[If] our decision today does not change all that much, then why the fuss? Is there really a threat to the separation of powers where Congress has conferred the judicial power outside Article III only over certain counterclaims in bankruptcy? The short but emphatic answer is yes. A statute may no more lawfully chip away at the authority of the Judicial Branch than it may eliminate it entirely. [We] cannot compromise the integrity of the system of separated powers and the role of the Judiciary in that system, even with respect to challenges that may seem innocuous at first [blush.]

JUSTICE SCALIA, concurring.

I agree with the Court's interpretation of our Article III precedents, and I accordingly join its opinion. I adhere to my view, however, that—our contrary precedents notwithstanding—"a matter of public [rights] must at a minimum arise between the government and others[.]" The sheer surfeit of factors that the Court was required to consider in this case should arouse the suspicion that something is seriously amiss with our jurisprudence in this [area.] Apart from their sheer numerosity, the more fundamental flaw in the many tests suggested by our jurisprudence is that they have nothing to do with the text or tradition of Article III. [The] multifactors relied upon today seem to have entered our jurisprudence almost [randomly.] Leaving aside certain adjudications by federal administrative agencies, which are governed (for better or worse) by our landmark decision in [*Crowell*], in my view an Article III judge is required in *all* federal adjudications, unless there is a firmly established historical practice to the contrary. For that reason—and not because of some intuitive balancing of benefits and harms—I agree that Article III judges are not required in the context of territorial courts, courts-martial, or true "public rights" [cases.] Perhaps historical practice permits non-Article III judges to process claims against the bankruptcy [estate;] the subject has not been briefed, and so I state no position on the matter. But Vickie points to no historical practice that authorizes a non-Article III judge to adjudicate a counterclaim of the sort at issue here.

JUSTICE BREYER, with whom JUSTICES GINSBURG, SOTOMAYOR, and KAGAN join, dissenting.

I agree with the Court that the bankruptcy [statute] authorizes a bankruptcy court to adjudicate the counterclaim. But I do not agree with the majority about the statute's [constitutionality.]

In *Murray's Lessee*, the Court [wrote]:

> "[W]e do not consider congress can either withdraw from judicial cognizance any matter which, from its nature, is the subject of a suit at the common law, or in equity, or admiralty; nor, on the other hand, can it bring under the judicial power a matter which, from its nature, is not a subject for judicial determination. At the same time there are matters, involving public rights, which may be presented in such form that the judicial power is capable of acting on them, and which are susceptible of judicial determination, but which congress may or may not bring within the cognizance of the courts of the United States, as it may deem proper."

[The] majority reads the first part of the statement's first sentence as authoritatively defining the boundaries of Article III. [I] would read the statement in a less absolute way. For one thing, the statement is in effect dictum. For another, it is the remainder of the statement, announcing a distinction between "public rights" and "private rights," that has had the more lasting impact. Later Courts have seized on that distinction when *upholding* non-Article III adjudication, not when striking it down. [The] one exception is *Northern Pipeline*, where the Court struck down the Bankruptcy Act of 1978. But in that case there was no majority. And a plurality, not a majority, read the statement roughly in the way the Court does today.

[I] believe the majority places insufficient weight on *Crowell*, a seminal case that clarified the scope of the dictum in *Murray's Lessee*. In that case, the Court considered whether Congress could grant to an Article I administrative agency the power to adjudicate an employee's workers' compensation claim against his employer. The Court assumed that an Article III court would review the agency's decision *de novo* in respect to questions of law but it would conduct a less searching review (looking to see only if the agency's award was "supported by evidence in the record") in respect to questions of fact. [The] Court pointed out that the case involved a dispute between private persons (a matter of "private rights") and (with one exception not relevant here) it upheld Congress' delegation of primary factfinding authority to the [agency.]

Crowell has been hailed as "the greatest of the cases validating administrative adjudication." [Yet,] in a footnote, the majority distinguishes *Crowell* as a case in which the Court upheld the delegation of adjudicatory authority to an administrative agency simply because the agency's power to make the "specialized, narrowly confined factual determinations" at issue arising in a "particularized area of law," made the agency a "true 'adjunct' of the District Court." [Were] *Crowell's* holding as narrow as the majority suggests, one could question the validity of Congress' delegation of authority to adjudicate disputes among private parties to other agencies such as the National Labor Relations Board, the Commodity Futures Trading Commission, the Surface Transportation Board, and the Department of Housing and Urban Development, thereby resurrecting important legal questions previously thought to have been decided.

[The] majority, in my view, overemphasizes the precedential effect of the plurality opinion in *Northern Pipeline*. [Three] years later, the Court held that *Northern Pipeline* "establishes only that Congress may not vest in a non-Article III court the power to adjudicate, render final judgment, and issue binding orders in a traditional contract action arising under state law, without consent of the litigants, and subject only to ordinary appellate review." [*Thomas v. Union Carbide*].

Rather than leaning so heavily on the approach taken by the plurality in *Northern Pipeline*, I would look to this Court's more recent Article III cases[,] *Thomas* and *Schor*—cases that commanded a clear majority. In both cases the Court took a more pragmatic approach to the constitutional question. It sought to determine whether, in the particular instance, the challenged delegation of adjudicatory authority posed a genuine and serious threat that one branch of Government sought to aggrandize its own constitutionally delegated authority by encroaching upon a field of authority that the Constitution assigns exclusively to another branch.

[In] *Thomas*, the Court stated that "*practical attention to substance rather than doctrinaire reliance on formal categories should inform application of Article III.*" [It] indicated that Article III's requirements could not be "determined" by "the identity of the parties alone," [or] by the "private rights"/"public rights" distinction[.]

Most recently, in *Schor*, the Court [expressly] "declined to adopt formalistic and unbending rules." [Rather,] it "weighed a number of factors, none of which has been deemed determinative, with an eye to the practical effect that the congressional action will have on the constitutionally assigned role of the federal judiciary." [Applying] *Schor's* approach here, I conclude that the delegation of adjudicatory authority before us is [constitutional.]

First, I concede that *the nature of the claim to be adjudicated* argues against my conclusion. Vickie Marshall's counterclaim—a kind of tort suit—resembles "a suit at the common law." [Although] not determinative of the question, [a] delegation of authority to a non-Article III judge to adjudicate a claim of that kind poses a heightened risk of encroachment on the Federal Judiciary[.] At the same time the significance of this factor is mitigated here by the fact that bankruptcy courts often decide claims that similarly resemble various common-law actions. Suppose, for example, that ownership of 40 acres of land in the bankruptcy debtor's possession is disputed by a creditor. If that creditor brings a claim in the bankruptcy court, resolution of that dispute requires the bankruptcy court to apply the same state property law that would govern in a state court proceeding. This kind of dispute arises with regularity in bankruptcy proceedings.

Of course, in this instance the state-law question is embedded in a debtor's counterclaim, not a creditor's claim. But the counterclaim is "compulsory." It "arises out of the transaction or occurrence that is the subject matter of the opposing party's claim." [Thus,] resolution of the counterclaim will often turn on facts identical to, or at least related to, those at issue in a creditor's claim that is undisputedly proper for the bankruptcy court to decide.

Second, *the nature of the non-Article III tribunal* argues in favor of constitutionality. That is because the tribunal is made up of judges who enjoy considerable protection from improper political influence. Unlike the 1978 Act which provided for the appointment of bankruptcy judges by the President with the advice and consent of the Senate, [current] law provides that the federal courts of appeals appoint federal bankruptcy [judges.] Bankruptcy judges are removable by the circuit judicial council (made up of federal court of appeals and district court judges) and only for [cause.] Their salaries are pegged to those of federal district court judges, [and] the cost of their courthouses and other work-related expenses are paid by the Judiciary. [Thus,] although Congress technically exercised its Article I power when it created bankruptcy courts, functionally, bankruptcy judges can be compared to magistrate judges, law clerks, and the Judiciary's administrative officials, whose lack of Article III tenure and compensation protections do not endanger the independence of the Judicial Branch.

Third, *the control exercised by Article III judges over bankruptcy proceedings* argues in favor of constitutionality. Article III judges control and supervise the bankruptcy court's determinations—at least to the same degree that Article III judges supervised the agency's determinations in *Crowell*, if not more so. Any party may appeal those determinations to the federal district court, where the federal judge will review all determinations of fact for clear error and will review all determinations of law *de* [*novo.*]

Moreover, in one important respect Article III judges maintain greater control over the bankruptcy court proceedings at issue here than they did over the relevant proceedings in any of the previous cases in which this Court has upheld a delegation of adjudicatory power. The District Court here may "withdraw, in whole or in part, any case or proceeding referred [to the Bankruptcy Court] on its own motion or on timely motion of any party, for cause shown."

[Fourth,] the fact that *the parties have consented* to Bankruptcy Court jurisdiction argues in favor of constitutionality, and strongly so. Pierce Marshall, the counterclaim defendant, is not a stranger to the litigation, forced to appear in Bankruptcy Court against his [will.] Rather, he appeared voluntarily in Bankruptcy Court as one of Vickie Marshall's creditors, seeking a favorable resolution of his claim against Vickie Marshall to the detriment of her other creditors. He need not have filed a claim, perhaps not even at the cost of bringing it in the future, for he says his claim is "nondischargeable," in which case he could have litigated it in a state or federal court after distribution. [Thus,] Pierce Marshall likely had "an alternative forum to the bankruptcy court in which to pursue [his [claim]."

The Court has held, in a highly analogous context, that this type of consent argues strongly in favor of using ordinary bankruptcy court proceedings. In *Granfinanciera*, the Court held that when a bankruptcy trustee seeks to void a transfer of assets from the debtor to an individual on the ground that the transfer to that individual constitutes an unlawful "preference," the question of whether the individual has a right to a jury trial "depends upon whether the creditor has submitted a claim against the estate." [The] jury trial question and the Article III question are highly analogous. [Even] when private rights are at issue, non-Article III adjudication may be appropriate when both parties [consent.]

Fifth, *the nature and importance of the legislative purpose served* by the grant of adjudicatory authority to bankruptcy tribunals argues strongly in favor of constitutionality. Congress' delegation of adjudicatory powers over counterclaims asserted against bankruptcy claimants constitutes an important means of securing a constitutionally authorized end. Article I, § 8, of the Constitution explicitly grants Congress the

"Power To . . . establish . . . uniform Laws on the subject of Bankruptcies throughout the United States."

[Congress] established the first Bankruptcy Act in 1800. [From] the beginning, the "core" of federal bankruptcy proceedings has been "the restructuring of debtor-creditor relations." [And,] to be effective, a single tribunal must have broad authority to restructure those relations, "having jurisdiction of the parties to controversies brought before them," "decid[ing] all matters in dispute," and "decree[ing] complete [relief."]

Considering these factors together, I conclude that, as in *Schor*, "the magnitude of any intrusion on the Judicial Branch can only be termed *de minimis*." [I] would similarly find the statute before us constitutional.

NOTES ON LEGISLATIVE COURTS

1. **From *Northern Pipeline* to *Schor* to *Stern*.** The *Northern Pipeline* plurality seems to take a categorical approach to the problem of reconciling Article III values with the exigencies that give rise to non-Article III federal adjudication. *CFTC v. Schor* adopts a balancing approach, at least once the litigant's interest in an impartial adjudicator is satisfied or waived. Indeed, the lineup of the justices in the two cases confirms the Court's internal division on the question of how to frame the doctrine. *Stern* adopts *Northern Pipeline* as its template, yet the Court does not denigrate *Schor*. Instead, it seems to put *Schor in the* "public rights" category by distinguishing it from Vickie Marshall's claim. Thus, the issue in *Schor* differs from the one Vickie Marshall seeks to raise because "Vickie's claimed right to relief [is] not 'completely dependent upon' adjudication of a claim created by federal law, as in *Schor,*" where the broker's state law issue arose as a counterclaim to Schor's federal law claim. In *Stern* the Court practically admits that the line between "public" and "private" rights is not well-defined: "We recognize that there may be instances in which the distinction between public and private rights—at least as framed by some of our recent cases— fails to provide concrete guidance as to whether, for example, a particular agency can adjudicate legal issues under a substantive regulatory scheme." Even when legislative courts adjudicate "public rights," separation of powers issues may arise. See *Kuretski v. Commissioner of Internal Revenue*, 755 F.3d 929 (D.C.Cir. 2014) (upholding the statute which authorizes the President to remove judges of the Tax Court for cause, 26 U.S.C. § 7443(f), against a separation of powers challenge.

2. ***De Novo* Review.** The Court was sharply divided in *Northern Pipeline*, *Schor*, and *Stern*. But some of the reasoning in Chief Justice Roberts's majority opinion in *Stern* suggested that the bankruptcy courts' jurisdiction over the counterclaim in that case would pass constitutional muster if the district judge exercised *de novo* review of decisions of the bankruptcy judge. In addition, the issue of what matters the bankruptcy judges may adjudicate is one of great practical importance in the administration of bankruptcy law. A system in which bankruptcy judges

could adjudicate some but not all state law issues would be hard to manage. See, e.g., *In re Frazin*, 732 F.3d 313 (5th Cir. 2013) (distinguishing between two state law issues and holding that the bankruptcy court could resolve one but not the other). Thus, the Article III issues that beset bankruptcy jurisdiction returned to the Court, in *Executive Benefits Insurance Agency v. Arkison*, 573 U.S. ___, 134 S.Ct. 2165 (2014). The Court unanimously held, in an opinion by Justice Thomas, that "when, under *Stern*'s reasoning, the Constitution does not permit a bankruptcy court to enter final judgment on a bankruptcy-related claim, the relevant statute nevertheless permits a bankruptcy court to issue proposed findings of fact and conclusions of law to be reviewed de novo by the district court." The main focus of the opinion is on rebutting objections (based on provisions of the Bankruptcy Act) to that approach. Does the Court's solution to the problem of bankruptcy court jurisdiction adequately address the Article III values Justice Brennan identified in a footnote in his opinion in *Northern Pipeline*?

3. **Probation Officers.** "Adjuncts" figure prominently in the Court's approach to Article III issues. What functions may properly be delegated to an adjunct? That issue was addressed in a quotidian context in *United States v. Nash*, 438 F.3d 1302 (11th Cir. 2006), a criminal case. Nash was convicted of theft of government property and sentenced to eight months imprisonment and two years of release under the supervision of a probation officer. The conditions of the probation included participating in mental health counseling, "as deemed necessary by the Probation Officer." While upholding other conditions of the probation, the court struck down this one. It distinguished between sentences that required defendants to participate in mental health programs approved by the probation officer, and the condition at issue here, which left it up to the probation officer to decide *whether* the defendant must enroll in a program.

> Article III courts may not delegate the ultimate responsibility of judicial functions to probation officers. [Under the condition here] whether Nash "shall" participate in mental health counseling turns on the judgment of the probation officer, not the court. [The] district court has delegated to the probation officer the ultimate responsibility of whether Nash must participate in mental health counseling instead of the ministerial function of how, when, and where the defendant must participate. *Id.* at 1305–06.

4. **An Elite Federal Judiciary.** The Article III objection to schemes like the ones that gave rise to *Northern Pipeline* and *Schor* is simply that the judges lack tenure and salary protection. Why not cure the problem that gives rise to the doctrinal complications addressed in these cases by obliging Congress to award those protections to all federal adjudicators? Is it important to limit the number of federal adjudicators with Article III status? Would a general tenure and salary rule imply that all federal adjudicators receive the *same* salary and other perquisites? Would federal judges be demoralized if that status were granted to administrative law judges and United States Magistrate Judges as well? Would they, as a result, perform

less well? Would lawyers decline to accept federal judgeships? Is maintaining the prestige of the federal bench a sufficiently strong value to warrant compromising Article III's concern with judicial independence? For a skeptical view of the "elitism" argument, see Michael Wells, Against an Elite Federal Judiciary, 1991 B. Y. U. L. Rev. 923.

Apart from the value of an elite federal judiciary, once bankruptcy judges and other federal adjudicators were granted life tenure, they could not be dismissed simply because the need for their services has diminished. Does the value of flexibility in federal workforce justify departures from the textual command of Article III? Consider whether the "flexibility" argument takes adequate account of (a) the ever-expanding role of government, and the consequent unlikelihood that the volume of administrative adjudication will ever actually diminish; (b) the fact that specialized adjudicators like bankruptcy judges and administrative law judges at the CFTC in fact will decide many state law claims outside any area of specialization, thereby diminishing the force of the charge that they are specialized; (c) the civil service protections accorded administrative law judges and other federal employees make it hard to dismiss them in any event, even if they do not have life tenure during good behavior.

The "anti-elitism" argument favors a general award of tenure and salary protection to federal adjudicators. One objection is that it would be unwise to grant those protections to certain adjudicators. For example, adjudicatory decisions by administrative law judges working at the Federal Communications Commission are reviewable by the five Commissioners, who are appointed by the President for fixed terms and carry out both adjudicatory and (more overt) policymaking tasks. No doubt the current working arrangements of such administrative agencies serve worthy purposes, and could not continue under a blanket tenure and salary rule. Could this objection be overcome by treating tenure and salary as a strong *presumption*, but one which could be overcome on a sufficient showing?

The notion of a presumption raises issues of its own: Suppose the administrative law judges who work at the FCC enjoyed tenure and salary protection, but their decisions could still be overturned by the non-Article III commissioners. Would this arrangement be compatible with the longstanding principle that decisions by Article III judges should not be subject to executive revision? See *Hayburn's Case*, 2 U.S. 408 (1792) (rejecting a scheme under which judges were to determine eligibility of veterans for Revolutionary War pensions, subject to review by the Secretary of War). For a modern iteration of the principle, see *Plaut v. Spendthrift Farm*, 514 U.S. 211, 218 (1995). See Chapter 4, supra.

5. Limits on Presidential Power. Military justice is one of the areas in which, according to the plurality in *Northern Pipeline*, "Article III does not bar the creation of legislative courts." Drawing support from Congress's Article I power to maintain armed forces and the President's Article II power as commander in chief, the "Court has sustained the exercise by Congress and the Executive of the power to establish and administer courts-martial." A separate question is whether the President is empowered to constitute military tribunals *without* congressional approval. In *Hamdan v. Rumsfeld*, 548 U.S. 557 (2006), the Court addressed this issue. Dividing 5–3, (with Chief Justice Roberts—author of the D.C. Circuit ruling under review—not participating) the Court curbed executive power.

President Bush had set up a system of military commissions, independent of the congressionally authorized court martial system, to prosecute persons accused of participation in al Qaeda's violent attacks against the United States. The power to choose members of the commissions was delegated by the Secretary of Defense to an "Appointing Authority for Military Commissions." The President argued that Congress had granted him the power to employ the commissions, but the Court ruled that neither of the statutes he cited "expands the President's power to convene military commissions."

Turning to the President's power to try persons before such commissions in the absence of specific congressional authorization, Justice Stevens's opinion for the Court recognized that the "exigencies of war" may give "rise to a need for military commissions." But the majority found fault with the President's assertion of broad executive power:

> Exigency alone [will] not justify the establishment and use of penal tribunals not contemplated by Article I, § 8 and Article III, § 1 of the Constitution unless some other part of that document authorizes a response to a felt need. And that authority, if it exists, can derive only from the powers granted jointly to the President and Congress in time of war. [Whether] the President may constitutionally convene military commissions without the sanction of Congress in cases of controlling necessity is a question this Court has not answered definitively, and need not answer [today].

> Together, the [Uniform Code of Military Justice and other relevant statutes] at most acknowledge a general Presidential authority to convene military commissions in circumstances where justified under the Constitution and laws, including the law of war. Absent a more specific Congressional authorization, the task of this Court is [to] decide whether Hamdan's military commission is so [justified.]

> The UCMJ conditions the President's use of military commissions on compliance not only with the American common law of war, but also with the rest of the UCMJ itself, insofar as applicable, and with the rules and precepts of the law of nations, including the four Geneva Conventions signed in 1949. The procedures that the Government has decreed will govern Hamdan's trial by commission violate these laws.

The Court identified several features of the commissions' procedures that depart from the UCMJ, including, among others:

The accused and his civilian counsel may be excluded from, and precluded from ever learning what evidence was presented during, any part of the proceeding that either the Appointing Authority or the presiding officer decides to "close." [Not] only is testimonial hearsay and evidence obtained through coercion fully admissible, but neither live testimony nor witnesses' written statements need be sworn. Moreover, the accused and his civilian counsel may be denied access to evidence in the form of "protected information" [so] long as the presiding officer concludes that the evidence is "probative" [and] that its admission without the accused's knowledge would not "result in the denial of a full and fair trial." Finally, a presiding officer's determination that evidence "would not have any probative value to a reasonable person" may be overridden by a majority of the other commission members.

Responding to the Government's argument that it would be impracticable to apply the UCMJ rules, the Court noted that the President had not made an official determination to that effect, and continued:

Nothing in the record before us demonstrates that it would be impracticable to apply court-martial rules in this case. There is no suggestion, for example, of any logistical difficulty in securing properly sworn and authenticated evidence or in applying the usual principles of relevance and admissibility. [Without] for one moment underestimating [the] danger [posed by international terrorism], it is not evident to us why it should require, in the case of Hamdan's trial, any variance from the rules that govern courts-martial.

In a concurring opinion joined by three others, Justice Breyer stressed the role of Congress:

The Court's decision ultimately rests upon a single ground: Congress has not issued the Executive a "blank check." Indeed, Congress has denied the President the legislative authority to create military commissions of the kind at issue here. Nothing prevents the President from returning to Congress to seek the authority he believes necessary.

Where, as here, no emergency prevents consultation with Congress, judicial insistence upon that consultation does not weaken our Nation's ability to deal with danger. To the contrary, that insistence strengthens the Nation's ability to determine—through democratic means—how best to do so. The Constitution places its faith in these democratic means. Our Court today simply does the same.

INDEX

References are to Pages
